Fortin's Children's Rights and the

FOURTH EDITION

The notion that children constitute an important group of rights-holders has gained increasing acceptance both domestically and internationally. Nevertheless, this rhetorical commitment to children's rights is not necessarily realised in practice. Now in its fourth edition, *Fortin's Children's Rights and the Developing Law* explores the extent to which law and policy in England promotes or undermines the rights of children. Fully revised and updated, this textbook uses current research on child development and welfare to reflect on the extent to which the law fulfils children's rights in a wide range of areas, including medical law, education and child poverty. These developments are measured against domestic law and the UK's international obligations under, for example, the United Nations Convention on the Rights of the Child.

Rachel E. Taylor is Fellow and Tutor in Law at Exeter College, Oxford and Associate Professor in Law at Oxford University. She writes widely on issues relating to children and family law.

Law in Context

Series editors

Professor Kenneth Armstrong
University of Cambridge
Professor Maksymilian Del Mar
Queen Mary, University of London
Professor Sally Sheldon
University of Bristol and University of Technology, Sydney

Editorial advisory board

Professor Bronwen Morgan
University of New South Wales
Emeritus Professor William Twining
University College London

Since 1970, the Law in Context series has been at the forefront of a movement to broaden the study of law. The series is a vehicle for the publication of innovative monographs and texts that treat law and legal phenomena critically in their cultural, social, political, technological, environmental and economic contexts. A contextual approach involves treating legal subjects broadly, using materials from other humanities and social sciences, and from any other discipline that helps to explain the operation in practice of the particular legal field or legal phenomena under investigation. It is intended that this orientation is at once more stimulating and more revealing than the bare exposition of legal rules. The series includes original research monographs, coursebooks and textbooks that foreground contextual approaches and methods. The series includes and welcomes books on the study of law in all its contexts, including domestic legal systems, European and international law, transnational and global legal processes, and comparative law.

Books in the Series

Acosta: *The National versus the Foreigner in South America: 200 Years of Migration and Citizenship Law*
Alaattinoğlu: *Grievance Formation, Rights and Remedies*
Ali: *Modern Challenges to Islamic Law*
Alyagon Darr: *Plausible Crime Stories: The Legal History of Sexual Offences in Mandate Palestine*
Anderson, Schum & Twining: *Analysis of Evidence, 2nd Edition*
Ashworth: *Sentencing and Criminal Justice, 6th Edition*
Barton & Douglas: *Law and Parenthood*
Baxi, McCrudden & Paliwala: *Law's Ethical, Global and Theoretical Contexts: Essays in Honour of William Twining*
Beecher-Monas: *Evaluating Scientific Evidence: An Interdisciplinary Framework for Intellectual Due Process*

Roberts & Palmer: *Dispute Processes: ADR and the Primary Forms of Decision-Making, 2nd Edition*

Rowbottom: *Democracy Distorted: Wealth, Influence and Democratic Politics*

Sauter: *Public Services in EU Law*

Scott & Black: *Cranston's Consumers and the Law*

Seneviratne: *Ombudsmen: Public Services and Administrative Justice*

Seppänen: *Ideological Conflict and the Rule of Law in Contemporary China: Useful Paradoxes*

Siems: *Comparative Law, 3rd Edition*

Stapleton: *Product Liability*

Stewart: *Gender, Law and Justice in a Global Market*

Tamanaha: *Law as a Means to an End: Threat to the Rule of Law*

Tuori: *Properties of Law: Modern Law and After*

Turpin & Tomkins: *British Government and the Constitution: Text and Materials, 7th Edition*

Twining: *General Jurisprudence: Understanding Law from a Global Perspective*

Twining: *Globalisation and Legal Theory*

Twining: *Human Rights, Southern Voices: Francis Deng, Abdullahi An-Na'im, Yash Ghai and Upendra Baxi*

Twining: *Jurist in Context: A Memoir.*

Twining: *Karl Llewellyn and the Realist Movement, 2nd Edition*

Twining: *Rethinking Evidence: Exploratory Essays, 2nd Edition*

Twining & Miers: *How to Do Things with Rules, 5th Edition*

Wan: *Film and Constitutional Controversy: Visualizing Hong Kong Identity in the Age of 'One Country, Two Systems'*

Ward: *A Critical Introduction to European Law, 3rd Edition*

Ward: *Law, Text, Terror*

Ward: *Shakespeare and Legal Imagination*

Watt: *The Making Sense of Politics, Media, and Law: Rhetorical Performance as Invention, Creation, Production*

Wells & Quick: *Lacey, Wells and Quick: Reconstructing Criminal Law: Text and Materials, 4th Edition*

Woodhead: *Caring for Cultural Heritage: An Integrated Approach to Legal and Ethical Initiatives in the United Kingdom*

Young: *Turpin and Tomkins' British Government and the Constitution: Text and Materials, 8th Edition*

Zander: *Cases and Materials on the English Legal System, 10th Edition*

Zander: *The Law-Making Process, 6th Edition*

International Journal of Law in Context: A Global Forum for Interdisciplinary Legal Studies

The *International Journal of Law in Context* is the companion journal to the Law in Context book series and provides a forum for interdisciplinary legal studies and offers intellectual space for ground-breaking critical research. It publishes contextual work about law and its relationship with other disciplines, including but not limited to science, literature, humanities, philosophy, sociology, psychology, ethics, history and geography. More information about the journal and how to submit an article can be found at http://journals.cambridge.org/ijc.

Fortin's Children's Rights and the Developing Law

Fourth Edition

RACHEL E. TAYLOR

University of Oxford

CAMBRIDGE
UNIVERSITY PRESS

CAMBRIDGE
UNIVERSITY PRESS

Shaftesbury Road, Cambridge CB2 8EA, United Kingdom

One Liberty Plaza, 20th Floor, New York, NY 10006, USA

477 Williamstown Road, Port Melbourne, VIC 3207, Australia

314–321, 3rd Floor, Plot 3, Splendor Forum, Jasola District Centre,
New Delhi – 110025, India

103 Penang Road, #05–06/07, Visioncrest Commercial, Singapore 238467

Cambridge University Press is part of Cambridge University Press & Assessment,
a department of the University of Cambridge.

We share the University's mission to contribute to society through the pursuit of
education, learning and research at the highest international levels of excellence.

www.cambridge.org
Information on this title: www.cambridge.org/highereducation/isbn/9781108426961

DOI: 10.1017/9781108680158

First published 1998
Second edition 2003
Third edition 2009
Fourth edition 2024

Printed in the United Kingdom by CPI Group Ltd, Croydon CR0 4YY

A catalogue record for this publication is available from the British Library.

Library of Congress Cataloging-in-Publication Data
Names: Fortin, Jane, author. | Taylor, R. (Rachel) (Professor of Law), author.
Title: Fortin's Children's rights and the developing law
Other titles: Children's rights and the developing law | Children's rights and the
developing law
Description: Fourth edition / Rachel E. Taylor, University of Oxford. | Cambridge, United
Kingdom ; New York, NY : Cambridge University Press, 2024. | Series: Lic law in context |
Includes bibliographical references and index.
Identifiers: LCCN 2023026040 | ISBN 9781108426961 (hardback) | ISBN 9781108446938
(paperback) | ISBN 9781108680158 (ebook)
Subjects: LCSH: Children's rights – Great Britain. | Children – Legal status, laws, etc. – Great
Britain. | Parent and child (Law) – Great Britain.
Classification: LCC KD735 .F67 2024 | DDC 346.420135–dc21
LC record available at https://lccn.loc.gov/2023026040

ISBN 978-1-108-42696-1 Hardback
ISBN 978-1-108-44693-8 Paperback

Contents

Table of Cases

Table of Statutes

Table of Statutory Instruments

Table of International Instruments

1

Theoretical Perspectives

(1) Introduction

Children's lives are underpinned by an incoherent hotchpotch of legal principles and government policies. A rights-based approach can bring greater consistency and child focus. In particular, such an approach can address the problem experienced by children, alongside other minority groups, of being the focus of various specialised branches of law and policy, all with their own distinctive character, with no coherence or similarity in objectives. By placing the differing aspects of childhood in a framework of rights, rather than, for example, in a medical- or educational-based context, the boundaries between the various disciplines start becoming irrelevant, with a far more coherent outcome being possible.

There appears now to be more sympathy with a desire to promote children's rights in more realistic and practical ways. The UK's ratification, in 1991, of the UN Convention on the Rights of the Child (CRC) and the incorporation of the European Convention for the Protection of Human Rights and Fundamental Freedoms (1950) (ECHR) by the Human Rights Act (HRA) 1998, into domestic law, have undoubtedly played their part in achieving this. Children's rights are now routinely cited by the judiciary, not merely in disputes over children's upbringing, but also in such diverse areas as immigration,[1] social security[2] and planning.[3] At the same time, children's rights have been given a more prominent role in policy-making, both in England, where the Children's Commissioner is now charged with 'promoting and protecting the rights of children',[4] and in the devolved administrations in Wales and Scotland, where ministers have specific legal duties to consider children's rights.[5] Alongside

---

[1] E.g. *ZH (Tanzania) v. Secretary of State for the Home Department* [2011] UKSC 4, [2011] 2 AC 166.

[2] E.g. *R (SG) v. Secretary of State for Work and Pensions* [2015] UKSC 16, [2015] 1 WLR 1449.

[3] E.g. *Stevens v. Secretary of State for Communities and Local Government* [2013] EWHC 792 (Admin).

[4] Children Act 2004, s. 2(1), inserted by Children and Families Act 2014, s. 107. In contrast, the legislation originally required the commissioner to raise 'awareness of the views and interests of children in England'. Discussed further in Chapter 3.

[5] The Rights of Children and Young Persons (Wales) Measure 2011; Children and Young People (Scotland) Act 2014, s. 1. Discussed further in Chapter 3.

these national changes, international and regional organisations, including the European Union and Council of Europe, are increasingly adopting strategies to promote and protect children's rights.[6] Children's rights are now firmly established on the national and international stage.

As children are now undoubtedly recognised as holding legal and human rights, it may seem arcane and unnecessary to engage in theoretical debate as to the foundations and existence of such rights. Rights can be recognised and enforced within a legal system without consensus as to whether they also exist as moral or theoretical rights.[7] It might be argued that time is better spent on defining and protecting those legal and human rights, rather than on the academic question of their theoretical basis. Nevertheless, it would be foolish to ignore the theoretical debates and real concerns that many retain over the wisdom of utilising the concept of rights to increase children's well-being. Indeed, although writers have often approached this field of thought from a variety of viewpoints, they have all identified common areas of concern, principally surrounding how to identify children's rights, how to balance one set of rights against another in the event of a conflict between them, and how to mediate between children's rights and those of adults. Practitioners are wrong to assume that such a voluminous body of theoretical inquiry should be confined to the realm of intellectual speculation. If made more accessible, it might usefully inform their own attempts to apply legal principles to individual children in a way which promotes those children's moral and legal rights more effectively. Better still, when it can be demonstrated that existing legal principles clearly reflect such theoretical ideals, the law gains a greater intellectual validity. Conversely, if there is no recognised theoretical basis for children's rights, they become open to manipulation, as John Tobin aptly explains:

> A right for which there is no recognised conceptual foundation quickly risks becoming an empty rhetorical vessel into which subjective preferences or political agendas may be poured.[8]

This chapter sets out to identify these recurring themes and provide a brief exploration of the theoretical debates over children's rights. In doing so, it seeks to provide a foundation for the detailed consideration of children's specific rights contained in later chapters.

(2) Rights Awareness and Rights Scepticism

(A) Children's Liberation

The ideas of the American 'children's liberationists' generated a wealth of valuable debate about the extent to which society should encourage children to develop their powers of self-determination. In the 1960s and early 1970s, the American civil rights movement had encouraged a far more sympathetic

---

[6] Discussed in Chapter 2.   [7] D. Archard (2014) ch. 4.   [8] J. Tobin (2013).

attitude to the treatment of all minority groups, including children. In the long run, however, the early American children's liberationists probably did the concept of children's rights a disservice, in so far as they conveyed the misleading impression that it is almost wholly concerned with giving children adult freedoms. It was Foster and Freed, writing in the 1970s, who claimed that adults exploited their power over children and that children's inferior status should be radically reassessed.[9] They gathered inspiration from a series of decisions reached by the United States Supreme Court.[10] Most notable of these was the landmark decision of *Re Gault*, in which the court ruled that 'neither the Fourteenth Amendment nor the Bill of Rights is for adults alone'[11] and that, as 'persons', children were entitled to claim the same procedural safeguards as those offered to adults by the United States Constitution.

Holt and Farson, the most well-known of the children's liberationists, adopting the view of Ariès[12] that childhood is a relatively recent Western social 'invention', argued that it was a form of oppressive and unwarranted discrimination to exclude children from the adult world. They maintained that since children's ability for self-determination was greatly underestimated, there was little reason to exclude them from the freedoms granted by the state to adults. Thus, Holt argued that children of any age should have, among other things, the right to vote, to work for money, to own and sell property, to travel, to be paid a guaranteed minimum state income, to direct their own education, to use drugs and to control their own private sexual lives.[13] The fact that children might be too young to wish to exercise any of these rights was merely part of their freedom of choice; they could exercise them, when and if they chose, in precisely the same way as adults do. The publicity these radical views attracted led to the movement for children's rights becoming inextricably associated with giving adult rights to children[14] and being treated with considerable scepticism.[15]

To modern readers, the claims of writers like Holt and Farson for children to enjoy adult freedoms might seem not only unrealistic, but also reckless. Indeed, the views of the children's liberationists were, from the first, extremely controversial. Much of the criticism, both in the 1970s[16] and after,[17] has focused on a variety of relatively practical issues. Two main topics have been recurrent themes. The first is that there are obvious dangers in ignoring

---

[9] H. Foster and D. Freed (1972).

[10] E.g. *Tinker* v. *Des Moines Independent Community School District* 393 US 503 (1969); *Goss* v. *Lopez* 419 US 565 (1975).

[11] 387 US 1, at 13 (1967).

[12] P. Ariès (1962). The strength of his view has been undermined by later historical research. See e.g. L. Pollock (1983).

[13] J. Holt (1974) p. 18. Farson's list of rights was very similar to that set out by Holt: R. Farson (1974). See also the list of rights proposed by H. Foster and D. Freed (1972) p. 347.

[14] The work of the children's liberationists is described by D. Archard (2014) Pt II.

[15] E.g. B. Hafen (1976).   [16] Inter alia, M. Wald (1979); B. Hafen (1976).

[17] Inter alia, L. Fox Harding (1997) ch. 5; see also D Archard (2014) chs 5 and 6.

children's physical and mental development by giving them the same rights and responsibilities as fully mature adults. The second is the danger of interfering with the relationship between children and parents, including the potential damage to the family unit as a whole.

Many writers have voiced considerable concern over the liberationists' failure to accord sufficient attention to the physical and mental differences between childhood and adulthood. Indeed, this is the most obvious weakness of the liberationists' ideas. They appeared to ignore the evidence on developmental growth through childhood, which establishes clearly that children are different from adults in development, behaviour, knowledge and skills, and in their dependence on adults, most often their parents. Research evidence now reinforces the view that the liberationists' ideas were based on an unrealistic perception of children's capacities.[18] It is obviously impossible to set a single age when all children can be deemed competent to reach any particular type of decision. It seems clear, however, that the relatively long process of development of children's cognitive processes makes the *majority* of children unfit to take complete responsibility for their own lives by being granted adult freedoms before they reach mid-adolescence.[19] Moreover, as Fox Harding cogently points out, a failure to regulate childhood would lead to more exploitation of children, rather than less.[20]

The need to protect children from being forced into adulthood before they are sufficiently mature is also a common theme of those opposing calls for recognition of children's autonomy rights. Campbell points to the constant stress on children's adult-like competence to make rational decisions for themselves, which in his view is tantamount to claims to redraw the boundaries between childhood and adulthood. He urges that the current needs of the child *here and now* should not be sacrificed to those of the future child. Children have a right to be children and not adults.[21] The frequency with which these arguments and counter-arguments are raised reinforces the notion that the same child may need both care for one purpose and autonomy or self-determination for another.[22]

The later proponents of the children's liberation school, such as Franklin,[23] though less radical than the early writers, continue to promote their central premise – that even quite young children are capable of competent thought and of making informed choices, and some are far more competent to make decisions than many adults. Indeed, adults, like children, make mistakes; they too may be ignorant and lack education and experience. There is also the not unreasonable criticism that until quite young children are trusted with more decision-making, they are denied the opportunity of gaining experience in doing so and, more importantly, of developing any decision-making skills. It is certainly difficult to defend some of the more arbitrary and inconsistent age

---

[18] Discussed in Chapter 9.   [19] L. Fox Harding (1997) pp. 128–37.   [20] Ibid. p. 134.
[21] T. Campbell (1992) p. 20.   [22] M. Minow (1986) p. 14.   [23] B. Franklin (2002) pp. 22–8.

limits determining children's competence to take part in various activities.[24] Such arguments came to the fore once again in the debate over lowering the minimum age for voting. Those advocating reform criticised the laws prohibiting intelligent 17-year-olds from voting, while allowing incompetent adults to exercise such rights.[25]

The answer to the criticism of arbitrary age limits is, of course, that all lines are essentially arbitrary and that they must be drawn somewhere.[26] Nevertheless, at the very least, the views of the liberationists justified a more critical examination of the law's treatment of children. The majority of the House of Lords in *Gillick v. West Norfolk and Wisbech Area Health Authority*[27] obviously sympathised with the notion of adopting a more nuanced approach to assessing children's legal competence. Lord Scarman commented:

> If the law should impose on the process of 'growing up' fixed limits where nature knows only a continuous process, the price would be artificiality and a lack of realism in an area where the law must be sensitive to human development and social change.[28]

Freeman wisely suggests that while the special treatment of children can be justified on the basis of the child's incapacity or immaturity, at the same time they should be brought 'to a capacity where they are able to take full responsibility as free, rational agents for their own system of ends'.[29]

An alternative account of children's development focuses not on capacity for adult-like decisions, but on developing the capabilities needed to obtain freedom to achieve well-being over the child's lifetime.[30] Rosalind Dixon and Martha Nussbaum have been particularly influential in applying the capabilities approach to children's rights.[31] This approach starts from a position of valuing the full human dignity of each individual and identifying the central capabilities essential to achieving the ability to pursue and enjoy well-being. These capabilities, such as health, bodily integrity and practical reason, must all reach a minimum threshold in order for a person to exercise agency over their own life and achieve well-being.[32] While the capabilities approach is not primarily concerned with children,[33] when applied to children's rights it can illuminate the importance of recognising children's entitlement to develop their capabilities. Given that childhood is a particularly fruitful time for developing many of the capabilities, which will themselves be a fertile means of promoting further capabilities, there are good reasons for giving priority for those interests, such as education, in childhood. The capabilities approach is a helpful way of valuing children's agency, but doing so in a way that

---

[24] Discussed further in Chapter 10.   [25] Ibid.   [26] D. Archard (2001) p. 47.
[27] [1986] AC 112.   [28] Ibid. at 186.   [29] M. Freeman (1983) p. 57.   [30] N. Peleg (2013).
[31] R. Dixon and M. Nussbaum (2012).
[32] Ibid. p. 558; these capabilities are derived from Martha Nussbaum's work and are not utilised by all theorists adopting the capabilities approach.
[33] Indeed, some theorists would not apply the approach to children; for discussion, see N. Peleg (2013) p. 534.

concentrates on achieving the essential preconditions for effective agency, rather than cognitive capacity alone.[34]

(B) Children's Rights and the Parental Role

A constant theme of those questioning the notion of children as rights-holders concerns their relationship with their parents. These doubts are often rooted in the assumption that the concept of children's rights revolves solely around children's autonomy, as strongly suggested by the children's liberationists. Such an assumption is false; children have a whole range of rights and many, such as the right to care and protection, have little to do with making decisions or challenging parental authority. This is especially true of those welfare rights that lay claim to the resources of the state, such as the right to education, which enable children to develop their capabilities. Acknowledging these may be much more important, particularly to young children, than any claimed right to autonomy. Nevertheless, children soon move out of dependence and into a developmental stage where their capacity for taking responsibility for their lives also needs encouraging. There is a persuasive argument that teenagers should be provided with far greater opportunities for developing their decision-making capacities and their sense of responsibility, not only for their own sake, but also for the sake of the communities in which they live. Children are expected to emerge from minority immediately ready to take their place as newly minted citizens. In truth, childhood is short and it is unrealistic to argue that children who are protected throughout from responsibility and from participation in import-ant decisions regarding their upbringing will become confident young people and responsible citizens.[35]

Schools undoubtedly play an important part in producing confident young people, but most writers agree that the parent's role is infinitely more import-ant. While in Victorian times it might have suited society well to promote the idea that children should be seen and not heard and that parents could treat their children with some disdain, today such ideas have lost their appeal. 'Good' parents should help their children develop 'the ability to conceive, evaluate alternatives, and act on a life plan – to pursue, in other words, a self-given system of ends that has at least rough internal consistency'.[36] However mature, they will be unable to make a successful transition to adulthood unless they are given opportunities for practising their decision-making skills and are provided with 'a dry run' at adulthood.[37] Indeed, contemporary society may

---

[34] Nussbaum and Dixon would justify denying children choices that they have not yet achieved the capabilities to exercise, e.g., voting, on the basis that removing such a choice is a reflection of actual differences in capabilities and not a means of denying respect to the child's equal dignity. R. Dixon and M. Nussbaum (2012) pp. 564–5.

[35] M. de Winter (1997) p. 26.   [36] P. Brown (1982) pp. 210–12.

[37] Jane Fortin expresses gratitude to John Gardner for his 'dry run' idea.

have contrived a situation whereby its children can only thrive if they are able to take on more responsibility for their own lives at an earlier age than before and in more complex situations. As Gardner has said: 'We have remade childhood experience in a way which requires an earlier engagement with adult concerns, and hence an earlier submission to ideals of adulthood such as autonomy.'[38] Is it reasonable to make such demands of parents? Requiring them to promote their children's capacity for autonomy may result in a diminution of their own confidence and ability to bring up their children according to their family beliefs and values. A recurring concern is that by promoting the rights of children, law and policy will undermine the status and authority of parents.

Anxieties such as these drove Victoria Gillick and Sue Axon to seek legal confirmation of their right to bring their daughters up as they thought fit.[39] These concerns are well expressed by O'Brien Steinfels:

> There is a deep contradiction between the political theory underlying our law with its impulse to protect individuals by an appeal to rights, and the biological and psychological requirements for successfully rearing children to participate as adults in such a polity. In effect, one of the most perplexing questions raised by these changes is whether the efforts to extend rights of citizens to minors will not inhibit and undermine the kind of parental authority and family autonomy necessary to foster the qualities and virtues adult citizens must possess and be able to exercise in our society.[40]

Many of the children's liberationists were sceptical of parents' capacity to adopt a more liberal family regime. Indeed, Holt saw childhood as an oppressed state and parents as the chief oppressors. Rather than the family being a protective haven, it was the place where, at best, parents might exploit their children and treat them as a mixture of expensive nuisance, slave and 'Ideal Cute Child';[41] at worst, a place where parents could abuse their children in private. Holt undoubtedly had a distorted view of the parent–child relationship in the majority of modern homes. He failed to recognise that, although parents may once have treated their children like chattels, this is no longer the case. Furthermore, although a minority of parents abuse their children, most parents are, in reality, the adults who know and love their children best and are therefore rightly cast by the state in the caring role and in a position to exercise powers over their children.

Admittedly, the privacy of family life does allow a minority of parents to undermine their children's self-confidence and capacity for self-determination. Does it follow that the government should intervene to promote a 'better'

---

[38] J. Gardner, unpublished communications with Jane Fortin.
[39] *Gillick* v. *West Norfolk and Wisbech Area Health Authority* [1986] AC 112; *R (Axon)* v. *Secretary of State for Health and the Family Planning Association* [2006] EWHC 37 (Admin), [2006] 2 FLR 206; discussed further in Chapters 9 and 11.
[40] M. O'Brien Steinfels (1982) p. 232.   [41] J. Holt (1974) p. 126.

relationship between all parents and children? The more radical children's liberationists certainly considered parents quite incapable of giving children greater freedom without being forced to do so. Nevertheless, the prospect of government interference with the parental role has traditionally provoked strong hostility. Fox Harding notes that nineteenth-century laws restricting child labour and introducing compulsory education were opposed on grounds that they constituted an unacceptable interference with family responsibility and parental rights.[42] Today, anxieties about family privacy are often linked with the fear that if children's capacity for autonomy were promoted by the state, this would involve a much closer monitoring of the way parents bring up their children, with the consequent undermining of their authority. Goldstein, Freud and Solnit, the most famous proponents of a 'laissez-faire approach', argued strongly that privacy is essential to family life and that state interference detracts from its value to its members.[43] Guggenheim adopts a not dissimilar approach, proposing a 'parental rights doctrine' which, he asserts:

> guarantees children at least that the important decisions in their lives will be made by those who are most likely to know them best and to care the most for them. There may be no assurances that, in any given case, parents will make the best choice for their children . . . But the alternative of unleashing state oversight is also unable to promise any of these things.[44]

He continues:

> Children do not need rights within the family. What they need are rules that work. Keeping families free from state oversight will do more for children than encouraging litigation and judicial intervention.[45]

Such views are diametrically opposed to those of the children's liberationists, but as extreme. Although a degree of family privacy is obviously desirable, a hands-off presumption endangers the concept of children's rights by fostering the view that parental behaviour towards their children should largely be outside the scope of the law. The family may be likened to a state within a state; interference by the public state within family affairs is a grave matter, comparable to interference by one state with the internal affairs of another.[46] The consequence of such an approach is that children are doubly dependent. Not only are they themselves excluded from a rights-bearing status, but they are also within the sphere of the private family, with parents standing between them and the state.[47]

---

[42] L. Fox Harding (1997) p. 35.
[43] J. Goldstein *et al.* (1973), (1980). For a more detailed assessment of their views and those of their critics, see J. Fortin (2003) pp. 8–9.
[44] M. Guggenheim (2005) p. 46.   [45] Ibid. p. 249.   [46] J. Bigelow *et al.* (1988) p. 185.
[47] M. Minow (1986) p. 18. Discussed further in Chapter 4.

(C) The Dangers of 'Rights Talk'

The view that rights claims can protect the minority of children who need protection against their parents seems irrefutable. Nevertheless, 'rights talk' has, on a more general basis, a variety of opponents. Wellman urges far greater restraint over employing the language of rights. As he points out, asserting the existence of unreal moral rights discredits the genuine ones and even produces public scepticism over the very existence of such a concept.[48] Similarly, Freeman has observed: 'Many references to children's rights turn out on inspection to be aspirations for the accomplishment of particular social or moral goals.'[49] As discussed below, this comment is particularly apposite to some aspects of international human rights law. A failure to distinguish between real and illusory rights undoubtedly plays into the hands of the media, who are only too keen to lampoon the concept of children having rights. The cartoons depicting small children consulting their solicitors over trivial grievances provoke derision. Furthermore, the language of rights sometimes becomes a shield, used to mask claims made by adults on behalf of children, which might not otherwise escape critical analysis.[50]

The language of rights should not be used loosely. But from a slightly different perspective, another group of commentators are united in their view that rights themselves are a destructive concept. They argue that a rights-based society is 'a cold, hollow one, drained of the sentiments of mutual care and love', where individuals assert their rights *against* each other.[51] Sir John Laws asserts the view that rights are not a moral but a legal construct,[52] and that while the language of rights is a necessary ingredient in any developed system of law,[53] interpersonal morality is not a function of law and not governed by a framework of moral rights, but of duties.[54] Indeed, when discussing the then impending introduction of the HRA 1998, he pointed out the limitations of the concept of rights:

> ... the idea of a rights-based society represents an immature stage in the development of a free and just society ... nothing is more important, if we are truly dedicated to freedom and justice, than to see the shortcomings of this fragile pedestal. A society whose values are defined by reference to individual rights is by that very fact already impoverished. Its culture says nothing about individual duty – nothing about virtue. We speak of respect for other people's rights. But, crudely at least, this comes more and more to mean only that we should accept that what someone wants to do, he should be allowed to do. Self-discipline, self-restraint, to say nothing of self-sacrifice, are at best regarded as optional extras and at worst (and the worst is too often the reality) as old-fashioned ideas worth nothing but a scoff and a gibe.[55]

---

[48] C. Wellman (1999) pp. 3, 176–81.   [49] M. Freeman (1983) p. 37.
[50] E.g. the 'right' of children to know their biological parents, considered in Chapter 6.
[51] D. Archard (2014) p. 100.   [52] J. Laws (1998) p. 255.   [53] J. Laws (2003) p. 273.
[54] Ibid. pp. 265–8.   [55] J. Laws (1998) p. 255.

Many authors consider that children's worlds are genuinely different from those of adults, due to their vulnerability and their dependence on their parents and other carers.[56] As noted above, O'Brien Steinfels argues that loving family relationships can be damaged by assertions which not only promote individualism, but also inhibit and undermine parental authority and family autonomy.[57] Some feminist theorists also argue that a rights approach focuses on the wrong things, downplaying the relationships which underlie the reality of daily life.[58] Their ideas on women's experience of family life throw light on the way that rights theories relating to children are similarly influenced by children's dependence.[59]

Nevertheless, as Archard points out, such views would lead to the dubious proposition that even if children are to be deemed rights-holders, they should not be permitted to enforce them against their parents, for fear of undermining their relationship of love and affection. This argument is difficult to maintain: the fact that relationships are often underpinned by a safety net of rights does not mean that the participants conceive of their relationships primarily in terms of rights and duties.[60] Furthermore, this type of criticism implies that family relationships can *either* be based on mutual affection *or* the existence of rights and duties, but not both. Archard refutes this as being far from the truth. For a child to have rights against its parents does not prevent the parent from acting through love rather than merely from duty. But love can fail and even actions motivated by sincere love can cause harm if their aim is misplaced.[61] Recourse to rights may well be second-best to actions founded in love and care, but this is not a reason not to have rights.[62] The position is summed up well by Waldron:

> the structure of rights is not constitutive of social life, but is instead to be understood as a position of fallback and security in case other constitutive elements of a social relationship ever come apart.[63]

Articulating children's interests in terms of rights may indeed lead to the behaviour of their caretakers being submitted to far more intensive examination than before, however well-intentioned such behaviour is. This, in turn, may risk undermining the relationships through which their needs are usually met. Nevertheless, as Minow asserts, children would not be better off if schools and families were removed from the purview of public scrutiny permitted by rights claims. She suggests that if rights need asserting, conflict has occurred

---

[56] Although Jonathan Herring argues that such arguments underestimate the vulnerabilities of adults and that in fact vulnerability is experienced by everyone, rather than representing a division between the world of adults and that of children: J. Herring (2012).

[57] M. O'Brien Steinfels (1982) p. 240.   [58] E. Kiss (1997); V. Held (2006) ch. 1.

[59] H. Lim and J. Roche (2000) esp. pp. 235–41.   [60] H. Brighouse and A. Swift (2014) pp. 17–22.

[61] This can be seen, e.g., in the tragic cases of parents who seek medical treatment to sustain the lives of their seriously ill children, even to the point at which the continued treatment is causing harm: discussed further in Chapter 7.

[62] D. Archard (2014) pp. 101–2.   [63] J. Waldron (1993) p. 374.

already, and the process of enforcing the right often gives it expression and provides a method of resolution.[64] The validity of Minow's approach is borne out by the case law, particularly that involving children who apply to court for legal authority to reside with an adult other than their parents.[65] It seems quite unrealistic to argue that without the prospect of court proceedings, the child and parents would become reconciled. While mediation might avoid the polarising effect of litigation, the damage to the relationships between child and parents probably pre-dates the litigation. In summary, many authors conclude that it is better to be a rights-holder than to 'depend on the kindness and favors of others'.[66]

(3) Do Children Have Any Rights and, If So, Which Ones?

Moral philosophers have devoted much theoretical thought to the nature of rights and, in the context of children's rights, whether children can be rights-holders at all. Practitioners and policy-makers are more likely to worry about protecting the rights children have, or should have, under the HRA 1998 and international human rights law. As discussed in the following chapter, under these provisions children are entitled to almost all of the rights guaranteed for adults,[67] but also possess rights that are not extended to adults.[68] Naturally, the extent to which children benefit from these rights will ultimately depend on the courts' interpretation of these provisions. Furthermore, a conceptual analysis of moral rights provides no final answers on how the law should be interpreted. Nevertheless, a clearer understanding of rights theory will help practitioners and policy-makers to shape the law in a way that promotes children's interests. Further, rights acquire much of their protective force from their authority and influence in legislation, policy-making and in society. If the rights that are extended to children lack a sound theoretical foundation, this moral authority is undermined and their effectiveness diminished.

(A) Children as Rights-Holders

An acceptance of the existence of the rights of the individual underlies most liberal political theories. Indeed, while there have been endless theoretical debates over the part to be played by the concept of rights in the social order and over how rights are to be defined, the premise central to rights theories is that moral rights do exist.[69] First though, no assessment of children's rights

---

[64] M. Minow (1987) pp. 1890–1.
[65] Under the Children Act (CA) 1989, s. 8, discussed in Chapter 10.
[66] B. Bandman (1973) p. 236.
[67] A good example of a right that is not extended to children is ECHR, Art. 12, which guarantees the right to marry to 'men and women of marriageable age'.
[68] E.g. the right to have their best interests treated as a primary consideration in all actions concerning them: CRC, Art. 3.
[69] J. Waldron (1984) provides a usefully brief but seminal consideration of general rights theories.

would be complete without a brief reference to the philosophical and jurisprudential controversies over whether children can justifiably be described as
rights-holders at all.[70] The main doubt over this issue stems from disagreements over the nature of rights themselves – which in turn are linked with
a related controversy over the relevance of choice or freedom. This disagreement over the place of freedom within a theoretically convincing account of
rights is not unique to the context of children's rights: despite the longevity of
the debate, there is still no dominant consensus as to the theoretical basis for
rights, whether for adults or children. Nonetheless, the debate has particular
resonance in relation to children's rights as, for at least a significant portion of
their childhood, children are not in a position to make informed choices about
many of the interests that are most fundamental to their well-being. There is an
important theoretical position that is based on the view that a person cannot be
described as a rights-holder unless he or she is able to exercise a choice over the
exercise of that right. The 'choice' or 'will'[71] theory of rights invests the
importance of choice with such significance that it alone is capable of grounding all rights. Since the existence of a right is therefore dependent on the rights-
holder's interest in choosing and since the majority of children lack the
competence to make many choices, proponents argue they cannot be described
as having any rights. Thus, Hart considers the term 'rights' inappropriate for
application to babies, or indeed to animals.[72] The assertion that children who
are too young and incompetent to claim rights therefore have no rights is an
unattractive conclusion, but follows logically from the central premise of the
will theory. It is an unattractive conclusion because it negates the intuitive view
that children must have rights because it would be wrong to deny such
a proposition. If the foundation of rights is indeed choice, then the exclusion
of young children from their remit may be unpalatable, but inevitable. On the
other hand, for those who found their understanding of rights on the basis of
alternative accounts such as dignity[73] or as a means of redressing
powerlessness,[74] the exclusion of children from the ambit of rights is
a reason to doubt the ability of the theory to explain what it means to possess
a right.

---

[70] M. Freeman (1983) ch. 2 provides an exhaustive theoretical discussion of the concept of
children's rights.

[71] Alternatively sometimes described as the 'power' or 'claim' theory of rights. For proponents,
see, inter alia, H.L.A. Hart (1984) and J. Feinberg (1980a).

[72] H.L.A. Hart (1984) p. 82. In Hart's view, the fact that it is considered *wrong* to ill-treat babies or
animals does not justify utilising the expression 'rights' when describing such situations.
One way around this problem is, as Hart does, to appoint a proxy who will exercise choice on
behalf of the incompetent rights-holder until such time as they acquire competence to make their
own choices. For example, parents may be seen as proxies for their children during minority.
D. Archard (2014) pp. 59–60 notes the difficulties with this approach, not least the difficulty for
the proxy in discharging the duty to determine the choices that the child would make if
competent, rather than merely adopting the proxy's view of what would be best for the rights-
holder. This point is discussed further below.

[73] Discussed by J. Tobin (2013) pp. 405–7.   [74] K. Federle (2017).

Theorists such as MacCormick,[75] Raz[76] and Campbell[77] provide a competing view that the concept of rights need not be confined only to those who can lay claim to or waive them. They present an interest theory of rights which posits that a person has a right where his or her *interests* are protected in certain ways 'by the imposition of (legal or moral) normative constraints on the acts and activities of other people with respect to the object of one's interests'.[78] Children, like adults, have interests which require protecting in such a way and the use of this model avoids denying them moral and legal rights until they have acquired the capacity to reach reasoned decisions. Such a rights model fully accommodates the view that children are no less precious because of their lack of adult capacities.[79] MacCormick forcefully sets out the value of applying such a model to children:

> To argue, on the other hand [when countering the choice or will theory of rights], that each and every child is a being whose needs and capacities command our respect, so that denial to any child of the wherewithal to meet his or her needs and to develop his or her capacities would be wrong in itself (at least in so far as it is physically possible to provide the wherewithal), and would be wrong regardless of the ulterior disadvantages or advantages to anyone else – so to argue, would be to put a case which is intelligible as a justification of the opinion that children have such rights.[80]

MacCormick proceeds to criticise the proponents of the choice theory of rights for putting the cart before the horse in their insistence on there being a means of remedying a child's right, through the enforcement of someone else's correlative duty, before they can accept the existence of the right itself.[81] He considers this to be an obsession with the existence of remedies, *ubi remedium ibi ius*, rather than with rights themselves. By contrast, he maintains that it is *because* children have the right, for example, to care and nurture, that the imposition of legal provisions requiring others to provide that care and nurture is justified. In other words, the existence of the right presupposes the remedy, *ubi ius, ibi remedium*.

Before gratefully accepting these assurances that children are respectable rights-holders, brief attention should be paid to the theoretical concerns revolving around the difficulties involved in enforcing children's rights. In the first place, children are often dependent on those very adults who are acting in breach of their rights, most commonly their parents, and, secondly, they may be too young to take steps to enforce their rights. O'Neill, who considers that adopting a rights-based approach for children suffers from many

---

[75] N. MacCormick (1982) ch. 8. MacCormick (pp. 154–6) clearly sets out the basis for the two competing views on the importance of choice.

[76] J. Raz (1986) esp. pp. 165–92.   [77] T. Campbell (1992) pp. 1–23.

[78] N. MacCormick (1982) p. 154. See also J. Raz (1984), (1986) esp. pp. 165–92.

[79] T. Campbell (1992) p. 5.   [80] N. MacCormick (1982) p. 160.

[81] The choice model of rights is underpinned by Hohfeld's classification involving the existence of duties in others, correlative to the rights asserted. See W. Hohfeld (1919).

theoretical problems, including that of enforcement, would prefer to couch children's rights in terms of the obligations owed to them by others. Although the 'rhetoric of rights' has relevance for oppressed adults, she considers that an appeal to rights has little chance of empowering children. If they are too young they will be unable to respond to such an appeal, and if they are old enough to respond, they are well on their way to adulthood and freedom from dependence. Indeed, as she points out, the fundamental difference between children and groups of oppressed adults is that children emerge from their powerless state. This leads her to conclude that the main remedy for children's powerlessness 'is to grow up'.[82]

Fortunately, not everyone agrees with O'Neill's diagnosis or remedy, which might, to children, appear to be a counsel of despair. According to MacCormick, neither problem prevents rights vesting in children. Indeed, in his view, children may have moral rights *prior* to any correlative duties vesting in anyone to fulfil them or indeed without it being clear who is obliged to fulfil the right. He cites, by way of example, the child's right to be educated to the limit of his or her abilities. Although such a right exists, it may be unclear whose is the power to enforce it and whose is the duty to provide it. He nevertheless concedes the purely practical difficulty which attaches to the enforcement of children's rights.[83]

Ultimately, agreement over a universally acceptable theory of rights for dependent children may always prove elusive.[84] Some feminist theorists consider that the interest theory of rights disadvantages children, in so far as it recognises their need for protection and care, as opposed to recognising their competency and autonomy.[85] This surely misinterprets the interest theory of rights, which accommodates the view that children acquire freedom of action like adults, as they become the best judge of what is for their own good.[86] In other words, children have an interest *in* choice, as they develop an ability to reach choices.[87] Such issues are discussed below. Meanwhile, MacCormick's description of a moral right as 'a good of such importance that it would be wrong to deny it to or withhold it from any member of C (a given class)'[88] has an arresting simplicity that many non-theorists may find attractive. Without underestimating the difficulties implicit in its generality, it provides a scheme of thought which promotes a compelling and flexible assessment of the

---

[82] O. O'Neill (1992) pp. 38–9. For an account of rights as a remedy to powerlessness, see K. Federle (2017).

[83] N. MacCormick (1982) pp. 162–6.

[84] Some maintain that the theorists are striving to describe with the term 'rights' what are in truth totally different concepts. See J. Harris (1980) p. 86.

[85] K. Federle (1994) p. 353.   [86] N. MacCormick (1982) p. 165.

[87] Discussed below. S. Brennan (2002) pp. 63–4 considers that children progress from having their interests protected by rights to having their choices protected as they become better able to judge for themselves what is in their interests.

[88] N. MacCormick (1982) p. 160.

concept of children's rights. Its drawback is that it provides little guidance over defining what interests may become translated into moral rights.

(B) What Rights Do Children Have?

There are two questions that follow on from the adoption of MacCormick's interest model of rights. What interests can be translated into moral rights and what moral rights might be translated into legal rights? The second question is slightly easier to answer than the first. Most commentators accept that moral rights are translated into legal rights[89] if there is some recognition of their importance by the rest of society and consequently the imposition of correlative legal duties on others regarding the fulfilment of those rights.[90] The law thereby makes it unlawful to withhold a particular moral right from any one of a class of individuals. Meanwhile, unhappily, there appear to be no clear answers to the first question. Indeed, proponents of the interest theory of rights often tend to refer to children's interests rather than their rights, because of their uncertainty over whether there is sufficient unanimity over the wrongness of denying any particular good for it to be translated into a moral right. Eekelaar's words reflect this dilemma:

> whether these interests can also be said to be 'rights' depends on the extent to which it is generally believed that children have them and that they should be protected by law. If such beliefs were part of 'official' ideology it might make sense to say that children had those rights. It is not claimed that such an ideology actually exists. But it could be put forward as a challenge. Should not our community behave towards its children as if they had rights? If so, are these not the rights which they should have?[91]

Perhaps inevitably, a common criticism of the interest theory is that it is far too broad; the interests relevant to the justification of rights are without clear demarcation.[92] Adoption of MacCormick's description of a moral right as 'a good of such importance that it would be wrong to deny it to or withhold it from any member of C (a given class)' inevitably leads to uncertainty over the

---

[89] D. Lyons (1984) pp. 113–17 discusses Bentham's rejection of the concept of moral rights being an essential ingredient of legal rights. The extent to which Bentham's arguments undermine the concept of natural law is considered at length by J. Finnis in his seminal work (1980).

[90] E.g. J. Raz (1984) pp. 13–14 proposes that 'a law creates a right if it is based on and expresses the view that someone has an interest which is sufficient ground for holding another to be subject to a duty ... His right is a legal right if it is recognized by law, that is if the law holds his interest to be sufficient ground to hold another to be subject to a duty'. But it does not follow that moral rights once asserted should always be followed by endorsement as legal rights. J. Eekelaar (2004) p. 187 suggests that such an assumption is a dangerous one.

[91] J. Eekelaar (1991) p. 103. He subsequently suggests that the concept of rights is bound up with promoting a person's well-being, as opposed to his interests. See J. Eekelaar (2004) pp. 182–4.

[92] E.g. O. O'Neill (1992), who criticises the whole concept of children having 'fundamental rights', considering that far more would be achieved by way of improving children's lives if a theoretical framework of obligations were adopted.

'wrongness' of denying the importance of many potential interests. MacCormick acknowledges this and merely responds, a little unhelpfully, that 'rights belong to the class of essentially contested concepts'.[93] Campbell, who uses a description of moral rights not dissimilar to that adopted by MacCormick,[94] claims neither that all children's interests give rise to rights nor underestimates the difficulty of identifying and classifying the full range of the sometimes conflicting interests protected by rights. Indeed, he admits that it may be a weakness of the interest theory of rights that 'it leaves us with a very open ended basis for determining which interests are to serve as the ground of rights'.[95] Nevertheless, the extent of children's rights cannot be left in the realms of philosophical debate. An appreciation of this problem has led to various attempts to provide a more practical framework for children's rights, not by attempting to list them, but by classifying them into identifying groups.

In a seminal article, Eekelaar explores the type of children's interests that might deserve recognition and protection.[96] He reviews what benefits children 'might plausibly claim for themselves' and produces a threefold classification.[97] In doing so, he adopts a 'hypothetical retrospective judgement' approach: he makes an 'imaginative leap' to 'guess what a child might retrospectively have wanted once it reaches a position of maturity'.[98] Although Eekelaar subsequently reformulates this method of discerning what interests children might claim,[99] the classification he adopts remains of considerable value. In his view, children's interests fall into three groups: basic, developmental and autonomy interests.[100] Their 'basic' interests arise from children's claims regarding their immediate physical, emotional and intellectual care and well-being. Children's 'developmental' interests revolve round their claims on the wider community to maximise their potential. All children should have an equal opportunity to maximise the resources available to them during their childhood. A child's autonomy interests relate to 'the freedom to choose his own lifestyle and to enter social relations according to his own inclinations uncontrolled by the authority of the adult world, whether parents or institutions'.[101] In the event of a child's autonomy interest conflicting with his developmental or basic interest, Eekelaar suggests that the latter interests should prevail. As discussed below, this suggestion has obvious and far-reaching implications if applied to practical situations involving adolescents refusing to accept life-saving medical treatment.[102] He justifies this view by asserting that few adults

---

[93] N. MacCormick (1982) p. 160.

[94] T. Campbell (1992) p. 9: 'Moral rights may be regarded as those interests which are thought to be of such significance to the life of the human individual that they ought to be given priority in the organization of societal existence wherever possible.'

[95] Ibid. p. 16; see also pp. 6–7.

[96] J. Eekelaar (1986) pp. 166ff. He adopts an interest theory of moral rights similar to that set out by J. Raz (1984).

[97] J. Eekelaar (1986) p. 169.   [98] Ibid. p. 170.   [99] Discussed below.

[100] J. Eekelaar (1986) pp. 170–1.   [101] Ibid. p. 171.

[102] Discussed below and further in Chapter 11.

would retrospectively approve of the exercise of their autonomy interest being allowed to prejudice their life-chances in adulthood.

Many other classifications of children's rights have been formulated. Freeman proposes four categories: welfare rights, protective rights, those grounded in social justice and those based on children's claims to more freedom from control and more autonomy over their lives.[103] This is similar to another fourfold classification of rights proposed by Wald, described as: 'Rights Against the World', 'Protection from Inadequate Care', 'Rights to an Adult Legal Status' and 'Rights Versus Parents'.[104] Campbell suggests a fourfold classification according to the minor's status as person, child, juvenile and future adult.[105] Arguably, Bevan's scheme, which simply divides children's rights into two broad categories: protective and self-assertive,[106] has a more pragmatic relevance. It reflects the fundamental conflict currently underlying the whole of child law as it is developing in practice – that is, the conflict between the need to fulfil children's rights to protection and to promote their capacity for self-determination. Children's 'protective rights' arise from their innate dependence and vulnerability and an obvious need for nurture, love and care, both physical and psychological. These rights must include the right to protection from ill-treatment and the right to state intervention in order to achieve such protection. Bevan's term 'assertive rights' is usefully broad enough to include their claims to adult human rights, such as the right to bodily integrity and to freedom of expression and thought, conscience and religion, and to certain 'decision-making rights'. Many theorists draw similar distinctions between liberty rights, such as free speech, which are concerned with the exercise of free choice, and welfare rights, such as protection of health, which involve safeguarding interests that are fundamental to well-being.[107] While some theorists would deny that children can ever possess rights, it is the question of liberty, or self-assertive, rights that attracts the sharpest debate.

While many theorists currently accept that children can be rights-holders, there remains no clear test providing guidance over what rights they have or should have. Eekelaar's threefold classification, basic, developmental and autonomy interests, is posed in terms of the '*interests*' children have, rather than the rights that they have. His uncertainty over whether they can be correctly described as rights is emphasised by his words quoted above. But, as these words suggest, perhaps strict theoretical justifications for the existence of moral rights do not matter so much as believing that children have rights. More pragmatically, as noted below when discussing the rights protected by international conventions, the language or 'rhetoric' of rights is a politically useful tool to ensure the achievement of certain goals for children.

---

[103] M. Freeman (1983) p. 40.   [104] M. Wald (1979) pp. 260ff.   [105] T. Campbell (1992) p. 22.
[106] H. Bevan (1989) p. 11.
[107] D. Archard (2014) pp. 86–92 assesses the debate. See R. Dixon and M. Nussbaum (2012) for similar distinction between agency and welfare rights.

(C) International Human Rights and Children's Moral Rights

When considering whether children have rights, one may look to international human rights law and the international consensus that has coalesced around the CRC's affirmation of children as rights-holders. This consensus tends to give the rights defined therein credibility as respectable moral rights. Nevertheless, a variety of writers are sceptical about the 'rights talk' adopted in such documents. The fact that the CRC contains a long list of substantive rights does not necessarily legitimise the belief that children enjoy all the rights it contains.[108] Indeed, one might argue that some of the rights contained in the CRC are written in aspirational language and are not rights at all, but merely claims based on ideals regarding children's needs in a perfect world. These provisions describe how children should be treated and what they should be granted, were governments to take their rights seriously.[109] The fact that there is widespread agreement that children do have human rights does not automatically entail acceptance that these rights are moral rights, although the remarkable consensus formed around the CRC requires serious consideration by those who would seek to show that the Convention does not reflect children's moral rights.

These human rights principles and their application to children's legal rights are considered throughout this book, but it is worth outlining the theoretical issues that that law raises. Children benefit from being recognised as distinct rights-holders under the CRC and also as holding rights under various general human rights treaties such as the ECHR.[110] This raises the theoretical questions of whether children possess the same rights as adults and also whether they hold additional rights that are distinct from those held by adults.[111] The vast majority of rights contained in general human rights treaties, such as the ECHR, are guaranteed to 'everyone' and, like adults, children are entitled to claim the protection of these articles. The extension of welfare and protection rights, such as the right to life, to children is uncontentious to the extent that

---

[108] See further discussion of the strengths and weaknesses of the CRC in Chapter 2.

[109] O. O'Neill (1992) p. 37; J. Feinberg (1980a) p. 153. Although see A. Nolan (2014) for a defence of children's socio-economic rights as enforceable rights.

[110] For discussion of the extent to which children are recognised in international human rights law, see further Chapter 2.

[111] Lucinda Ferguson draws a distinction between 'rights for children', which concern children as holders of fundamental human rights, and 'children's rights', by which she means 'both rights targeted specifically at children and rights in relation to which the identity of the right-holder, who happens to be a child is critical': L. Ferguson (2013) pp. 178 and 179–82. This can be a helpful distinction in considering the theoretical questions that are raised in this section and can assist in providing analytical clarity on those questions. It can, however, be a difficult distinction to draw in practice as the fact that the rights-holder is a child, or at a particular stage of childhood, is often 'critical to the scope and content of the right'. For example, the fact that young children are often subject to significant restraint on their freedom is crucial to determining the scope of their right to liberty: see discussion in Chapter 9. For these reasons, this book uses the term 'children's rights' to include all rights that children possess, whether distinct from adult rights or shared with them.

moral justification for recognising such rights tends to apply equally to children and adults.[112] As discussed below, a greater dilemma arises when considering liberty rights and the claims of older children who value personal freedom and can demonstrate greater decision-making competence than that of younger children. The converse question, raised by the CRC, is whether children are morally entitled to rights that adults do not possess. To some extent, the existence of a separate convention for children is not concerned with excluding adults from rights granted to children, but instead fills the gap left by general human rights treaties that are often silent on their application to important aspects of children's lives.[113] To the extent that children's rights are seen as a detailed outworking of human rights principles for children, they are relatively straightforward to justify. Far more contentious is the notion that children are entitled to additional rights, including the apparent priority given to children's interests by the best interests principle that forms a core right and principle in the CRC and is reflected in children's law throughout the world.[114] Despite the voluminous literature on the moral basis for children's rights, the disjunct between theory and practice can be seen in the fact that the CRC does not demonstrate fidelity to any single theoretical position. It is perhaps inevitable that a convention that has attracted near universal support and which was born of contentious negotiation would be incompletely theorised.[115] The moral authority of the CRC comes, primarily, from that global agreement. Nonetheless, the Convention contains a core of theoretical agreement which has been developed by the ongoing work of the Committee on the Rights of the Child and which is explored further in the following chapter.

(D) Children's Rights and the Role of Paternalism

(i) Children's 'Autonomy' and the Role of Paternalism

Claims that children have a right to autonomy are derived from liberal political philosophies which emphasise the need to promote as fully as possible an individual's freedom to make rational autonomous decisions. It is argued that children, as human beings, should, like adults, also be free to lead their own lives according to their own conception of a good or worthwhile life, provided that this does not illegitimately restrict the liberty of others to do the same.[116]

---

[112] Although there may be contentious questions as to whether certain rights should be interpreted in a different way for children. See e.g. the way in which the right to protection from inhuman and degrading punishment in ECHR, Art. 3 has been interpreted to apply to corporal punishment; discussed further in Chapter 4.

[113] E.g. the fundamental importance of birth registration to children's identity and protection: CRC, Art. 7.

[114] See esp. UNCRC, Art. 3, discussed in Chapter 2. The principle's application in domestic law is considered in Chapter 3.

[115] J. Tobin (2013) presents a thoughtful theoretical analysis of the CRC, primarily from the perspective of social interest theory.

[116] R. Lindley (1989) p. 75.

The early children's liberationists saw the child's right to autonomy as of overriding importance. Farson made his views on this clear:

> the issue of self-determination is at the heart of children's liberation. It is in fact, the only issue, a definition of the entire concept. The acceptance of the child's right to self-determination is fundamental to all the rights to which children are entitled.[117]

As these words suggest, the children's liberationists deplored any paternalistic restrictions on children's freedom. In their view, it was a mistake to assume that children lacked the competence for it. These extreme views gathered little support. The growing scientific research literature on children's neurological development and capacity for decision-making gives good reason to reject these extreme claims.[118] The neurological skills necessary for decision-making develop during childhood and adolescence, while structural changes in the brain that affect the way that decisions are made continue into early adulthood. The fact that competence is acquired over time and will vary according to the child and the decision in question raises difficult issues, particularly in adolescence, as to how competence should be attributed.[119] Nonetheless, this research literature supports the view that it is right to reject the extreme position of the early child liberationists. Few philosophers today consider that children have the competence for complete autonomy and some see paternalism as having an important role to play in restricting their powers of self-determination.

John Stuart Mill gave a classic exposition of the concept of an adult's right to autonomy[120] and other philosophers have constantly reassessed it.[121] Despite the importance Mill attached to autonomy, he considered it self-evident that children are too immature to be autonomous. Since they lacked the capacity for autonomy, for them there was an obvious need for paternalism:

> It is, perhaps, hardly necessary to say that this doctrine is meant to apply only to human beings in the maturity of their faculties. We are not speaking of children, or of young persons below the age which the law may fix as that of manhood or womanhood. Those who are still in a state to require being taken care of by others, must be protected against their own actions as well as against external injury.[122]

Mill considered that adults should make choices on behalf of children who are not yet capable of rational autonomy. They have not yet developed the cognitive capacity to make intelligent decisions in the light of relevant information and their judgement is prone to be 'wild and variable' under the influence of 'emotional inconstancy'.[123]

---

[117] R. Farson (1974) p. 27.   [118] Discussed further in Chapter 9.
[119] Discussed further in Chapter 9.   [120] J.S. Mill (1859).
[121] E.g. J. Rawls (1971) pp. 90–5 and 130–6. See also J. Raz (1986) pp. 245–50.
[122] J.S. Mill (1859) p. 73.
[123] Archard discussing Mill's approach in D. Archard (2014) pp. 71–2.

A variety of writers have subsequently discussed the concept of paternalism, in the context of children's decision-making powers.[124] Many point to the danger of adopting a rights theory which accepts that children have a right to make choices, when, in fact, they may lack the ability to make good choices.[125] The varying theoretical models of rights appear to place a different weight on the importance of children's autonomy. Adoption of the choice or will theory of rights leads to particular emphasis being placed on a child's capacity for rational choice, an obvious prerequisite of autonomy.[126] As Brennan points out, while a child's capacity to plan and choose develops gradually, the choice theory seems to 'commit us to the view that, prior to this acquisition of choosing skills, children have no rights'.[127] But after that they apparently have complete autonomy, an equally problematic notion. Indeed, MacCormick attacks the choice theory of rights for presuming that children's rights carry the option of waiver or enforcement by the children themselves or on their behalf. He argues that while such a theory can be appropriate for adults, who may be the best judge of what is good for them, it is not appropriate for children while they are not.[128]

Brennan considers that neither the interest nor choice theory of rights adequately accommodates the problem of young children developing competence and prefers a 'gradualist account of children's rights', which, she argues, includes protections for both interests and choices.[129] Under such an account, as 'children acquire the ability to choose, their rights will change from protecting interests primarily to protecting primarily choices'.[130] The interest theory of rights itself can accommodate such a proposition, since children may indeed gradually acquire rights to self-determination based on their interest *in* choice, without having a right to complete autonomy.[131] As Campbell points out, during the transitional period between childhood and 'full-blown adulthood', a child's capacity for different sorts of adult activity emerges at different points of his or her development: 'As a juvenile the child has considerable autonomy interests and many of the rights of the child may be seen as recognizing this fact.'[132] Further, even very young children may be able to express views on a decision even if they are not able to weigh the full consequences of the options available.[133] Children may therefore be recognised as having an

---

[124] Freeman discusses the paternalistic ideas of Hobbes, Locke and Mill relating to the dependence of children in M. Freeman (1983) pp. 52–4. See also D. Archard (2014) ch. 1 for a discussion of Locke's approach to childhood.

[125] E.g. L. Purdy (1992) opposes the concept of children having *equal* rights to those of adults, because of her view that children's choosing can go wrong; discussed by S. Brennan (2002) p. 60. See also H. Brighouse (2002) pp. 39–51, who argues that unlike adults, children lack the competence and rationality to exercise 'agency rights' involving the exercise of choice.

[126] T. Campbell (1992) p. 20.   [127] S. Brennan (2002) p. 62.

[128] N. MacCormick (1982) p. 166.   [129] S. Brennan (2002) p. 62.   [130] Ibid. p. 66.

[131] Jane Fortin expressed gratitude to J. Gardner for his lucid explanation of this point.

[132] T. Campbell (1992) p. 19.   [133] Discussed in Chapter 9.

interest in contributing to a decision before the point at which they acquire the right to make the decision itself.[134]

Feinberg similarly distinguishes between a child's right to 'an open future' and an adult's right to get what he or she wants now. Whereas an adult's right to autonomy now takes precedence over his or her probable future good, respect for a child's future autonomy as an adult often means preventing free choice now.[135] Many authors take as an example the child's right to education, a right unaffected by his or her choices. A young child may not wish to go to school and may adversely affect his or her own potential development by refusing to do so. MacCormick explains his position persuasively:

> Children are not always or even usually the best judges of what is good for them, so much so that even the rights that are most important to their long-term well-being, such as the right to discipline or to a safe environment, they regularly perceive as being the reverse of rights or advantages.[136]

But by utilising an interest model of rights, he is:

> at once glad and regretful to discover that it is possible for me to acknowledge that my children have rights, without being thereby committed to the outrageous permissiveness to which my natural indolence inclines me.[137]

As this discussion demonstrates, when considering theoretical accounts of children's rights, many theorists see little need to accord children choice rights before they gain the capacity to reach wise choices. Such views provide a morally coherent justification for adopting a degree of paternalism within an interpretation of children's rights,[138] but they fill some authors with dismay. As discussed more fully below, Eekelaar considers that it is quite wrong to assert that an individual's interests can be determined and asserted by someone else.[139] Furthermore, these explanations do not sufficiently clarify *when* interventions to restrict children's choices could be fully justified. This question assumes an obvious relevance when attempts are made to incorporate theoretical analyses of children's rights into legal principles. At this point, the HRA 1998 also produces a number of dilemmas, the most important being whether children can claim Convention rights in precisely the same way as adults or whether such rights can be interpreted paternalistically. As discussed below, a growing emphasis on adults' right to autonomy under the ECHR is inevitably influencing ideas about adolescents' decision-making rights.[140]

---

[134] This is recognised by the important place of the right to be heard contained in CRC, Art. 12, discussed further in Chapter 2.

[135] J. Feinberg (1980b) pp. 126–7.   [136] N. MacCormick (1982) p. 166.   [137] Ibid.

[138] T. Campbell (1992) p. 15.   [139] J. Eekelaar (2004) p. 183.

[140] A good example of this tension can be seen re. the law on deprivation of liberty, discussed in Chapter 9.

(ii) Welfare and Rights – Restraining Paternalism?

As the above discussion has demonstrated, few theorists now consider that children have a broad right to self-determination, at least before they reach the more contentious period of mature adolescence considered further below. While children are unable to exercise self-determination, many theorists see little need to rule out paternalistic interventions to restrict their actions; indeed, they consider them justified by reference to the rights of those constrained.[141] The principle that decisions concerning children should be made to their best interests is a ubiquitous feature of child law,[142] but as Eekelaar notes, welfare decisions have their dark side:[143] the determination of a child's best interests can operate as a means of protecting adult interests or upholding existing social structures. The question then arises as to how a rights-based approach should approach decision-making for children who are not competent to make those decisions. In particular, this requires consideration of the relationship between a child's best interests and their rights.

If a child is not yet able to make their own decisions, those decisions will have to be made for them; parents are those most obviously fitted to exercise this role in relation to most children. Society recognises the importance of the parental role by imposing legal and moral duties on those who brought the children into the world, on the basis that they are the most likely to have their interests at heart.[144] How then should parents, and the courts in the event of a dispute, discharge this role if they are to uphold their child's rights? Parents may well consider that their role is simply one of making the decisions that they consider to be in their child's best interests. MacCormick, in his words quoted above, seems to assume that his paternalism, as a parent, will be 'good' for his children. Indeed, there is the view that paternalism, rather than being seen as 'an odious tyranny',[145] is essential to the relationship of parent and child and that an abandonment of parental authority would be 'an act of immorality, as well as a failure in nurturing'.[146] Many writers are, however, sceptical of the idea that a paternalistic determination of a child's interests can really be considered as promoting their rights. The prospect of unrestricted paternalism being applied to override children's choices leaves many writers with a sense of unease, particularly because powers of coercion are largely vested in parents and sometimes the judiciary. Furthermore, the ability to exercise paternalism may be exploited by those in a position of power over

---

[141] Some theorists may also extend aspects of this proposition to those who can reach their own decisions, including adults. Hart was well known for his view that society may prevent people doing themselves physical harm. See H.L.A. Hart (1963).

[142] E.g. Children Act 1989, s. 1(1); CRC, Art. 3. These two contexts vary both on the way in which children's interests are accommodated within decision-making and the circumstances in which the principle applies: discussed further in Chapter 3.

[143] J. Eekelaar (2017) pp. 56–60.

[144] G. Dworkin (1982) p. 204: these are the reasons for society selecting parents as proxies for their children when reaching decisions, e.g., decisions on healthcare.

[145] D. Archard (2014) p. 13.   [146] W. Gaylin (1982) pp. 30–1.

children and exercised in a manner that does not promote the child's interests. Eekelaar goes further than this when considering ideas about children's welfare, in the context of children's rights. He rejects what he describes as the 'welfarist' stance that a child may be described as having a 'right' to have performed for him or her what someone else considers to be in accordance with that child's welfare:[147]

> Although it might logically be held that B has the right that A should promote B's welfare in accordance with A's conception of that welfare, such a right is really no right at all. A person who surrenders to another the power to determine where his own welfare lies has in a real sense abdicated his personal autonomy.[148]

He subsequently suggests that although 'it is not necessarily wrong to force an outcome on people which they do not want, it is wrong to do this under the guise of protecting their rights'.[149]

An influential approach to this problem is to regard the decision-making rights of children who are not yet competent as rights held in trust[150] and exercised on behalf of the child by proxies until they acquire the competence to make that decision themselves. This approach is distinguished from simple paternalism in that the proxy decision-maker is obliged to make decisions through the lens of the future adult that the child will become. This future adult might reasonably be assumed to wish to have obtained the competencies necessary to live a worthwhile and autonomous life, or one might argue, as Feinberg famously puts it, children have a right to an 'open future'.[151] On this basis, it may be argued that children can be compelled to act in order to secure their future rights: 'present compulsion is a precondition for subsequent choice'.[152] So, for example, a reluctant child may be compelled to attend school as 'going to school is necessary for maturation into a rational autonomous individual'.[153] There are, however, a number of problems with the proxy approach. The future adult is, of course, a fiction and in constructing that fiction it is difficult for the decision-maker to avoid projecting their own view of a worthwhile life onto that of the future adult. Further, as Lucinda Ferguson points out, the future adult will be shaped by the experiences of their childhood:[154] the choices that the proxy makes may result in any number of adult selves, all of whom may approve, or perhaps disapprove, of the various decisions by which they came into being. If this is the case, then the proxy approach is no guide to decision-making and may be no more than a disguised imposition of the proxy's interpretation of the child's best interests. Finally, the approach is only justified to the extent that it is considered justifiable to

---

[147] J. Eekelaar (1994a) p. 301. See also J. Eekelaar (2004) p. 183.   [148] J. Eekelaar (1994a) p. 301.
[149] J. Eekelaar (2004) p. 183.   [150] J. Feinberg (1980b).   [151] J. Feinberg (1980b).
[152] D. Archard (2014) p. 75. This is presented as part of Archard's 'caretaker thesis', one of a number of approaches to children's rights.
[153] Ibid.   [154] L. Ferguson (2013) p. 194.

privilege the decisions of the future adult over that of the current child. While it may be possible to justify paternalistic coercion to ensure that children fulfil their potential for future choices, it should not unduly restrict their capacities for decision-making in the present.

One way of addressing some of these concerns is to seek to incorporate the child's own developing views into the determination of his or her best interests. In many of his papers, Eekelaar discusses his concern that when the courts reach decisions that are said to conform with the 'welfare' or 'best interests' principle, this formula is sufficiently indeterminate to take little account of the child's true views. Indeed, he fears that adults, and particularly the judiciary, subject children to 'coercive paternalism' and, in so doing, may ignore their interest in making choices in their lives.[155] Maintaining his concern to ensure that children's interest in choice should not be overlooked, he develops a sophisticated approach to promoting children's own views. He proposes a method of decision-making in the place of the best interests test, described as the concept of 'dynamic self-determinism' in which the child influences the decisions taken to bring them to 'the threshold of adulthood with the maximum opportunities to form and pursue life-goals which reflect as closely as possible an autonomous choice'.[156] Eekelaar explains this approach as follows:

> The duty of a child's carers is to establish the most propitious environment in which the child will be able in due course to make a decision that is in accord with the personality growing within him or her. It is dynamic because it allows for revision of outcomes in accordance with the child's developing personality, and involves self-determinism because of the scope given to the child to influence the outcome.[157]

Eekelaar's dynamic self-determinism provides an influential means of having regard to the current child while also safeguarding their future adulthood. Nonetheless, there is an important criticism that such approaches to children's rights value children as 'becomings' rather than 'beings': that by valuing children against the comparator of the ideal autonomous adult, we lose sight of the value of childhood itself and the unique interests that come with it.[158] This is particularly important for those writers who argue that there are 'goods of childhood', such as play, that have intrinsic value during childhood, regardless of whether they also have an instrumental value in contributing to a good adulthood.[159]

A practical example of the way in which the assumed future adult can be privileged over the current child through the language of rights can be seen in *Re W (Contact: Joining Child as Party)*.[160] Dame Elizabeth Butler-Sloss P disapproved of the way in which the trial judge had accepted the independent

---

[155] See particularly, J. Eekelaar (1986), (1992), (1994b).   [156] J. Eekelaar (1994b) p. 53.
[157] J. Eekelaar (2017) p. 55.   [158] B. Arneil (2002).   [159] S. Brennan (2014).
[160] [2001] EWCA Civ 1830, [2003] 1 FLR 681.

social worker's view that the 7-year-old boy needed the finality of knowing that there would be no more litigation about contact with his father. She said:

> The child has a right to a relationship with his father even if he does not want it. The child's welfare demands that efforts should be made to make it possible that it can be.[161]

This assertion is in tune with the views of the theorists discussed above, that a child may well have a right to an outcome which keeps his options open, rather than complying with his own short-term wishes. Nevertheless, such an approach has attracted criticism:

> This particularly legal construction of the concept of the child's right has the effect of transforming the child's right into a responsibility or even duty to see his father, since such a conception of rights fails to endow the child with the equivalent right *not* to have such contact. It also clearly demonstrates not only the readiness of courts to set aside children's wishes and feelings but also the power of the language of welfare to deny children's agency.[162]

Such a conclusion is not an inevitable outcome of a rights-based approach to decision-making for children: indeed, while the Court of Appeal uses the language of rights, it might be criticised for failing to engage with the meaning of those rights or their relationship with welfare. The vision of children's rights set out in the CRC is not in conflict with children's best interests, but treats those interests as a fundamental principle for the interpretation of children's rights. Similarly, children's best interests must be understood through the lens of the child's full range of rights within the Convention. These rights include the child's right to be heard under Article 12 of the CRC.[163] So, as John Tobin explains, the determination of a child's best interests is intimately connected to her rights and must take into account: '(a) the wishes of a child; (b) the relevance of any other rights under the CRC; (c) the particular circumstances of the child as informed by the views of any persons caring for, or working with, the child; and (d) any available empirical evidence that may be of relevance'.[164] While the ECHR does not accommodate children's needs particularly effectively, adopting a similar approach will enable the courts to recognise children's rights while taking account of children's inability to reach wise choices. Importantly, there is no necessary conflict between these rights and children's best interests. As Jane Fortin has noted:

> The rights contained in the European Convention are formulations, albeit sometimes in awkward phraseology, of aspects of the good life, not the bad and should be interpreted in a way that enhances a person's life. Admittedly, a person may suffer a deficit in well-being if his or her rights are displaced by those of another, but no concept of rights can prevent such an occurrence nor can the courts always balance the rights of one person against another in an ideal

---

[161] Ibid. at [16].   [162] A. James *et al.* (2004) p. 201 (emphasis in the original).
[163] Discussed further in Chapters 2 and 12.   [164] J. Tobin (2012).

fashion. Developing this notion, and adopting an interest theory of rights as a basis for the proposition that children are rights holders, it follows that a child's welfare cannot be inconsistent with his rights.[165]

The assumption that rights and welfare are discrete matters and that appeals to children's rights may produce a potentially damaging outcome for the child produces deep confusion in the case law. Such an approach is not supported by the works of the theorists and, indeed, appears to be a contradiction in terms.[166]

(iii) Adolescents and Paternalism

The claims of the children's liberationists that children should be autonomous and free of paternalistic restraints become most cogent when applied to mature adolescents. Freeman points out that 'no one can seriously believe that there is a real distinction ... between someone of 18 years and a day and someone of 17 years and 364 days'.[167] Although the argument that childhood is purely a social construct[168] is difficult to justify in relation to young children, it becomes compelling at the point at which adolescence is divided from adulthood.[169] The suggestion that adolescence, as a new stage after infancy and before adulthood, artificially prolongs the inferior status of childhood is rather more plausible. It can be argued that the requirement that children are in education or training to age 18, together with legislation banning children from full-time employment, artificially postpones the time when adolescents can start engaging in activities carrying fuller responsibility.[170] At the same time, many young adults remain dependent on their parents after their 18th birthday and important structural changes in the brain continue into early adulthood.[171]

As commented earlier, adoption of MacCormick's description of a moral right as 'a good of such importance that it would be wrong to deny it to or withhold it from any member of C (a given class)' inevitably leads to controversy over the 'wrongness' of denying the importance of certain interests to certain groups. It is unlikely that there could ever be agreement over the wrongness of denying complete autonomy to all mature adolescents. Nevertheless, many adults would approve of their having a degree of personal autonomy, by acknowledging their right to reach certain major decisions for themselves. Inevitably though, there would be disagreement over which decisions such adolescents should and should not have a right to determine. Gerald Dworkin considers that: 'Our self-esteem and sense of worth are bound up with the right to determine what shall be done to and with our bodies and minds.'[172] While not underestimating the younger child's right to dignity and

---

[165] J. Fortin (2006) p. 311. Jane Fortin expresses gratitude to Kenneth Campbell for his time discussing this area of thought.
[166] J. Fortin (2006) pp. 310–11.   [167] M. Freeman (1992) p. 35.   [168] See P. Ariès (1962).
[169] Discussed further in Chapter 9.   [170] Discussed further in Chapter 10.
[171] For further discussion, see Chapter 9.   [172] G. Dworkin (1982) p. 203.

self-respect, these words are particularly apposite when applied to adolescents. As Archard comments:

> While it is easy to represent an infant as evidently not an adult, lacking all but the most basic, and unimportant, characteristics of the mature human being, it is correspondingly harder to do so for a late adolescent. What is true of the six-month-old baby by contrast with an adult is false of a sixteen-year-old adolescent. To the extent that this is true it is problematic to deny to the adolescent that standing which is denied to all children in virtue of their not being adults.[173]

In a landmark decision reached in the late 1980s, the House of Lords accepted that adolescents need formal acknowledgment of their right to reach decisions for themselves over a variety of matters, particularly regarding their own bodily integrity. The *Gillick* decision marked an acceptance that adolescents were capable of giving valid consent on a variety of matters long before they reach legal maturity.[174] More recently, the courts have confirmed that the notions of autonomy developed by the House of Lords are reinforced by the values underlying many Convention rights. The HRA 1998 is clearly able to provide adolescents with extra protection against attempts to restrict their personal freedom.[175]

But what if adolescents foreclose on their future opportunities by reaching decisions which adults consider unwise or even dangerous? They may truant from school, take up smoking or drinking and, more dramatically, take risks with their health by refusing life-saving medical treatment. Although adolescents are individuals nearing adulthood and respect for their views is arguably more important to their own self-respect than it is to a toddler, many theorists are reluctant to allow them the freedom to make life-threatening mistakes. Many theorists seem prepared to grant more autonomy generally to adolescents, while still supporting a paternalistic role for the state in protecting them against foolish, self-destructive choices. This is variously described as a form of 'justified paternalism',[176] or 'liberal paternalism'.[177] Freeman considers that protection against a teenager reaching decisions which threaten death or serious physical or mental harm to him or her can be justified, and suggests the following formula:

> The question we should ask ourselves is: what sorts of action or conduct would we wish, as children, to be shielded against on the assumption that we would want to mature to a rationally autonomous adulthood and be capable of deciding on our own system of ends as free and rational beings?[178]

---

[173] D. Archard (2001) p. 47.

[174] *Gillick* v. *West Norfolk and Wisbech Area Health Authority* [1986] AC 112. Discussed in more detail in Chapters 9 and 11.

[175] E.g. *Re Roddy (A Child) (Identification: Restriction on Publication)* [2003] EWHC 2927 (Fam), [2004] 2 FLR 949; *R (Axon)* v. *Secretary of State for Health and the Family Planning Association* [2006] EWHC 37 (Admin), [2006] 2 FLR 206; *Mabon* v. *Mabon* [2005] EWCA Civ 634, [2005] 2 FLR 1011; *Re S (Child as Parent: Adoption: Consent)* [2017] EWHC 2729 (Fam), [2018] 2 WLR 1029.

[176] R. Macklin (1982) pp. 293–4.   [177] M. Freeman (1983) p. 57.   [178] Ibid.

Similarly, Eekelaar's concept of 'dynamic self-determinism' also avoids the position whereby even 'competent'[179] adolescents are given complete powers of self-determination if their decisions are contrary to their self-interests, in terms of their physical and mental well-being.[180] More recently, he acknowledged that there are major constraints on a child's competence[181] and that: 'Self determination under a mistake is a cruel illusion. This possibility permits certain restraints on children's freedom to be imposed in order to further the[ir] basic and developmental interests.'[182] Nevertheless, the balance is a sensitive one. Paternalistic restrictions should not deny adolescents all opportunity to take risks, for as Freeman states: 'We cannot treat persons as equals without also respecting their capacity to take risks and make mistakes.'[183] Moreover, a 'dry run' at adulthood loses all credibility if it contains no risks. Such questions have a practical relevance, as was made clear in two cases decided by the Court of Appeal soon after the *Gillick* decision.[184] Although controversial, the outcome achieved by the judiciary in these and later decisions, which was to force the adolescents involved to undergo life-saving treatment, might be justified by appeal to the model of rights outlined above.[185] To date, the courts have upheld this approach, despite the Strasbourg jurisprudence developing notions of adult autonomy and the fact that teenagers themselves, fast approaching adulthood, are increasingly recognised as having valuable autonomy interests.[186] These cases remain contentious. The question of how far mature adolescents are to be protected from autocratic and arbitrary adult restrictions on their potential for autonomy and whether this can and should be accommodated alongside protection for their long-term welfare remains open. The substantial body of theoretical debate on the precise limits of autonomy and paternalism may be informative if the courts come under pressure to review their position.[187]

(4) Children and the State

Human rights are, first and foremost, obligations on the state to respect, protect and fulfil the rights that are guaranteed. It is notable that the theoretical literature in relation to children's rights pays relatively scant attention to the

---

[179] Eekelaar devotes some discussion to the significance of this term in J. Eekelaar (1994b) pp. 54–7. A child's legal competence to reach decisions is discussed in Chapter 9.

[180] J. Eekelaar (1994b) esp. p. 57.

[181] J. Eekelaar (2017) p. 54, i.e. insufficient comprehension of the 'workings of the world', instability in the child's appreciation of his or her own medium-term life-goals, and the presence of excessive or improper pressure.

[182] Ibid.   [183] M. Freeman (1992) p. 38. But now see M. Freeman (2005) pp. 212–13.

[184] *Re R (A Minor) (Wardship: Consent to Treatment)* [1992] Fam 11; *Re W (A Minor) (Medical Treatment: Courts' Jurisdiction)* [1993] Fam 64.

[185] This case law is discussed further in Chapters 9 and 11.

[186] See esp. *Re X (A Child) (No. 2)* [2021] EWHC 65 (Fam), [2021] 4 WLR 11, discussed in Chapters 9 and 11.

[187] Discussed further in Chapter 9 and in J. Fortin (2006) pp. 314–26.

relationship between children and the state,[188] preferring instead to focus on the parent–child relationship and the child's developing competence. This is no doubt because children's upbringing is primarily situated as the responsibility of parents, with the state playing a supplementary and supporting role.[189] For this reason, theoretical discussion of the role of the state has tended to concern the question of when the state may legitimately intrude within the 'private' sphere of the family and imposing limits on the exercise of state power to do so.

To restrict discussion of the relationship between children and the state to the question of the limits of intervention in the family is to neglect an important and growing dimension of children's rights law. Children are citizens whose interests may be deeply affected by state action or inaction, just as those of adults may be.[190] The position of children as citizens is precarious, given their lack of rights to political participation. Further, children are often dependent on state action to further their interests; as Baroness Hale has explained, 'children often need a great deal of state interference if they are to survive, let alone thrive'.[191] This is most obvious for those children who are in state care or detention, but all children rely on the state for the provision or regulation of services such as education, health and policing to live a healthy and safe life and to develop the competencies necessary for future well-being. Government policies in areas such as welfare or immigration can have a serious impact on children's lives and future prospects. While the interests of children may be addressed through their parents' democratic rights, this is often insufficient. Not all children have stable adult carers and not all parents have the will or resources to represent their children's interests effectively. Even when they do, the characterisation of those interests by the parent may be misguided, selfish or at odds with the child's own perception of their interests. The fact that state decisions and policies are usually directed at adults places children in a particularly vulnerable position in the democratic process, and a great deal more work is needed to understand children's citizenship and to ensure that their rights are properly considered in state decision-making.[192]

(5) Conclusion

The literature on children's rights theory is complex as the subject sits at the intersection of a large number of contested concepts, including: the jurisprudential definition of rights; the nature and definition of childhood; the relationship between moral, legal and human rights; the meaning and relevance of competence; and the place of the state in family life. The myriad views on each of these areas means that it is unlikely that any single conception of children's

---

[188] See A. Nolan (2014) for a valuable exception.
[189] As is clear from CRC, Arts 5 and 18. See discussion of the parental role in Chapter 4.
[190] Discussed further in Chapter 13. See esp. A. Nolan (2014).   [191] B. Hale (2006) p. 351.
[192] Discussed further in Chapter 13.

rights will establish widespread consensus. It is perhaps for this reason that children's rights are often said to be under theorised.[193] This is not intended as a counsel of despair.[194] The considerable wealth of scholarship discussed above reflects a common assumption that children's rights are of immense importance, but that attempts to satisfy them require considerable care. As explored throughout this book, the concerns expressed by the theorists often resurface in the conflicts involving children that practitioners tussle with on a day-to-day basis. The following two chapters will consider the foundational principles of children's rights law in both international and domestic law. The remaining parts of the book are grouped around three themes: children's rights in the family; children's autonomy and role in decision-making; and children and the state. These themes are not intended as watertight categories, but as a means of grouping together issues that raise similar theoretical questions. These theoretical accounts considered in this chapter do not provide a straightforward answer to such questions, but may provide a sound intellectual basis for preferring one course of action to another. Reflection on this theoretical literature can also help to shape a more considered approach to children in the law; without a clearer understanding of rights theory, there is a risk that children's challenges will be dealt with on an ad hoc basis and in a confused and inconsistent manner.

Bibliography

Archard, D. (2001) 'Philosophical Perspectives on Childhood' in Fionda, J. (ed.) *Legal Concepts of Childhood*, Hart Publishing.
(2014) *Children: Rights and Childhood*, 3rd edn, Routledge.
Ariès, P. (1962) *Centuries of Childhood*, Jonathan Cape.
Arneil, B. (2002) 'Becoming versus Being: A Critical Analysis of the Child in Liberal Theory' in Archard, D. and Macleod, C. (eds) *The Moral and Political Status of Children*, Oxford University Press.
Bandman, B. (1973) 'Do Children Have Any Natural Rights? A Look at Rights and Claims in Legal, Moral and Educational Discourse'. Proceedings of the 29th Annual Meeting of the Philosophy of Education Society.
Bevan, H. (1989) *Child Law*, Butterworths.
Bigelow, J., Campbell, J., Dodds, S., Pargetter, R., Prior, E. and Young, R. (1988) 'Parental Autonomy' 5 *Journal of Applied Philosophy* 183.
Brennan, S. (2002) 'Children's Choices or Children's Interests: Which Do Their Rights Protect?' in Archard, D. and Macleod, M. (eds) *The Moral and Political Status of Children*, Oxford University Press.
(2014) 'The Goods of Childhood and Children's Rights' in Baylis, F. and McLeod, C. (eds) *Family-Making: Contemporary Ethical Challenges*, Oxford University Press.
Brighouse, H. (2002) 'What Rights (If Any) Do Children Have?' in Archard, D. and Macleod, M. (eds) *The Moral and Political Status of Children*, Oxford University Press.
Brighouse, H. and Swift, A. (2014) *Family Values: The Ethics of Parent–Child Relationships*, Princeton University Press.

---

[193] See e.g. R. Dixon and M. Nussbaum (2012); N. Peleg (2013).
[194] K. Hanson and N. Peleg (2020).

Brown, P. (1982) 'Human Independence and Parental Proxy' in Gaylin, W. and Macklin, R. (eds) *Who Speaks for the Child: The Problems of Proxy Consent*, Plenum Press.

Campbell, T. (1992) 'The Rights of the Minor' in Alston, P., Parker, S. and Seymour, J. (eds) *Children, Rights and the Law*, Clarendon Press.

Dixon, R. and Nussbaum, M. (2012) 'Children's Rights and a Capabilities Approach: The Question of Special Priority' 97 *Cornell Law Review* 549.

Dworkin, G. (1982) 'Consent, Representation and Proxy Consent' in Gaylin, W. and Macklin, R. (eds) *Who Speaks for the Child: The Problems of Proxy Consent*, Plenum Press.

Eekelaar, J. (1986) 'The Emergence of Children's Rights' 6 *Oxford Journal of Legal Studies* 161.

(1991) *Regulating Divorce*, Clarendon Press.

(1992) 'The Importance of Thinking that Children Have Rights' in Alston, P., Parker, S. and Seymour, J. (eds) *Children, Rights and the Law*, Clarendon Press.

(1994a) 'Families and Children: From Welfarism to Rights' in McCrudden, C. and Chambers, G. (eds) *Individual Rights and Law in Britain*, Clarendon Press.

(1994b) 'The Interests of the Child and the Child's Wishes: The Role of Dynamic Self-Determinism' 8 *International Journal of Law and the Family* 42.

(2004) 'Personal Rights and Human Rights' in Lødrup, P. and Modvar, E. (eds) *Family Life and Human Rights*, Gyldendal.

(2017) *Family Law and Personal Life*, 2nd edn, Oxford University Press.

Farson, R. (1974) *Birthrights*, Collier Macmillan.

Federle, K. (1994) 'Rights Flow Downhill' 2 *International Journal of Children's Rights* 343.

(2017) 'Do Rights Still Flow Downhill?' 25 *International Journal of Children's Rights* 273.

Feinberg, J. (1980a) *Rights, Justice and the Bounds of Liberty*, Princeton University Press.

(1980b) 'The Child's Right to an Open Future' in Aiken, W. and LaFollette, H. (eds) *Whose Child?*, Littlefield, Adams & Co.

Ferguson, L. (2013) 'Not Merely Rights for Children But Children's Rights' 21 *International Journal of Children's Rights* 177.

Finnis, J. (1980) *Natural Law and Natural Rights*, Clarendon Press.

Fortin, J. (2003) *Children's Rights and the Developing Law*, LexisNexis Butterworths.

(2006) 'Accommodating Children's Rights in a Post Human Rights Act Era' 69 *Modern Law Review* 299.

Foster, H. and Freed, D. (1972) 'A Bill of Rights for Children' 6 *Family Law Quarterly* 343.

Fox Harding, L. (1997) *Perspectives in Child Care Policy*, Longman.

Franklin, B. (ed.) (2002) *The New Handbook of Children's Rights: Comparative Policy and Practice*, Routledge.

Freeman, M. (1983) *The Rights and Wrongs of Children*, Frances Pinter.

(1992) 'The Limits of Children's Rights' in Freeman, M. and Veerman, P. (eds) *The Ideologies of Children's Rights*, Martinus Nijhoff Publishers.

(2005) 'Rethinking *Gillick*' 13 *International Journal of Children's Rights* 201.

Gaylin, W. (1982) 'Who Speaks for the Child?' in Gaylin, W. and Macklin, R. (eds) *Who Speaks for the Child: The Problems of Proxy Consent*, Plenum Press.

Goldstein, J., Freud, A. and Solnit, A. (1973) *Beyond the Best Interests of the Child*, New York Free Press.

(1980) *Before the Best Interests of the Child*, Burnett Books Ltd.

Guggenheim, M. (2005) *What's Wrong with Children's Rights?*, Harvard University Press.

Hafen, B. (1976) 'Children's Liberation and the New Egalitarianism: Some Reservations about Abandoning Youth to their "Rights"' *Brigham Young University Law Review* 605.

Hale, B. (2006) 'Understanding Children's Rights: Theory and Practice' 44 *Family Court Review* 350.

Hanson, K. and Peleg, N. (2020) 'Waiting for Children's Rights Theory' 28 *International Journal of Children's Rights* 15.

Harris, J. (1980) *Legal Philosophies*, Butterworths.

Hart, H.L.A. (1963) *Law, Liberty and Morality*, Oxford University Press.

(1984) 'Are There Any Natural Rights?' reproduced in Waldron, J. *Theories of Rights*, Oxford University Press.

Held, V. (2006) *The Ethics of Care*, Oxford University Press.

Herring, J. (2012) 'Vulnerability, Children and the Law' in Freeman, M. (ed.) *Law and Childhood Studies*, Oxford University Press.

Hohfeld, W. (1919) *Fundamental Legal Conceptions as Applied in Judicial Reasoning*, Yale University Press.

Holt, J. (1974) *Escape from Childhood: The Needs and Rights of Childhood*, E.P. Dutton and Co. Inc.

James, A., James, A. and McNamee, S. (2004) 'Turn Down the Volume? – Not Hearing Children in Family Proceedings' 16 *Child and Family Law Quarterly* 189.

Kiss, E. (1997) 'Alchemy or Fool's Gold? Assessing Feminist Doubts about Rights' in Shanley, M. and Narayan, U. (eds) *Reconstructing Political Theory*, Polity Press.

Laws, J. (1998) 'The Limitations of Human Rights' *Public Law* 254.

(2003) 'Beyond Rights' 23 *Oxford Journal of Legal Studies* 265.

Lim, H. and Roche, J. (2000) 'Feminism and Children's Rights' in Bridgeman, J. and Monk, D. (eds) *Feminist Perspectives on Child Law*, Cavendish.

Lindley, R. (1989) 'Teenagers and Other Children' in Scarre, G. (ed.) *Children, Parents and Politics*, Cambridge University Press.

Lyons, D. (1984) 'Utility and Rights' in Waldron, J. (ed.) *Theories of Rights*, Oxford University Press.

MacCormick, N. (1982) *Legal Right and Social Democracy: Essays in Legal and Political Philosophy*, Clarendon Press.

Macklin, R. (1982) 'Return to the Best Interests of the Child' in Gaylin, W. and Macklin, R. (eds) *Who Speaks for the Child: The Problems of Proxy Consent*, Plenum Press.

Mill, J.S. (1859) 'On Liberty' in Acton, H. (ed.) (1972) *Utilitarianism, Liberty, Representative Government*, Dent.

Minow, M. (1986) 'Rights for the Next Generation: A Feminist Approach to Children's Rights' 9 *Harvard Women's Law Journal* 1.

(1987) 'Interpreting Rights: An Essay for Robert Cover' 96 *Yale Law Journal* 1860.

Nolan, A. (2014) *Children's Socio-Economic Rights, Democracy and the Courts*, Hart Publishing.

O'Brien Steinfels, M. (1982) 'Children's Rights, Parental Rights, Family Privacy, and Family Autonomy' in Gaylin, W. and Macklin, R. (eds) *Who Speaks for the Child: The Problems of Proxy Consent*, Plenum Press.

O'Neill, O. (1992) 'Children's Rights and Children's Lives' in Alston, P., Parker, S. and Seymour, J. (eds) *Children, Rights and the Law*, Clarendon Press.

Peleg, N. (2013) 'Reconceptualising the Child's Right to Development: Children and the Capability Approach' 21 *International Journal of Children's Rights* 523.

Pollock, L. (1983) *Forgotten Children: Parent–Child Relations from 1500–1900*, Cambridge University Press.

Purdy, L. (1992) *In Their Best Interest? The Case against Equal Rights for Children*, Cornell University Press.

Rawls, J. (1971) *A Theory of Justice*, Oxford University Press.

Raz, J. (1984) 'Legal Rights' 4 *Oxford Journal of Legal Studies* 1.

(1986) *The Morality of Freedom*, Clarendon Press.

Tobin, J. (2012) 'Courts and the Construction of Childhood: A New Way of Thinking' in Freeman, M. (ed.) *Law and Childhood Studies*, Oxford University Press.

(2013) 'Justifying Children's Rights' 21 *International Journal of Children's Rights* 395.

Wald, M. (1979) 'Children's Rights: A Framework for Analysis' 12 *University of California Davis Law Review* 255.

Waldron, J. (ed.) (1984) *Theories of Rights*, Oxford University Press.

(1993) *Liberal Rights: Collected Papers 1891–1991*, Cambridge University Press.

Wellman, C. (1999) *The Proliferation of Rights: Moral Progress or Empty Rhetoric?*, Westview Press.

de Winter, M. (1997) *Children as Fellow Citizens: Participation and Commitment*, Radcliffe Medical Press Ltd.

2

International Children's Rights

(1) Introduction

A large body of international and regional human rights law exists today which informs the way that domestic law promotes children's rights in the UK.[1] The translation of ideas about children's rights into principles of English law was undoubtedly accelerated by the British government ratifying a series of international instruments prepared by the General Assembly of the United Nations and by the Council of Europe. An event of outstanding importance was the ratification by the UK of the UN Convention on the Rights of the Child (CRC) in 1991. This long and ambitious list of children's rights constitutes a painstaking attempt to define children's needs and aspirations and to commit ratifying states to their accomplishment. Although not part of English law as such, it currently exerts an increasingly powerful influence on the developing law and is often used as an international template against which to measure domestic standards.

Unlike the CRC, the European Convention on Human Rights and Fundamental Freedoms (ECHR) was not designed specifically to protect children as a group. But they, as human beings, are entitled to claim its protection and it has a direct influence on the way in which children's rights are protected in this country. Although little distinct consideration was given to children in the drafting of the ECHR, the European Court of Human Rights (ECtHR) has made increasing use of the CRC to interpret the ECHR in a way that is effective and relevant for children. Whether this approach is able to address some of the shortcomings of the ECHR for children remains an open question. While the influence of the ECHR in English law comes primarily through its incorporation into domestic law in the Human Rights Act (HRA) 1998,[2] no chapter devoted to an assessment of children's rights from an

---

[1] This chapter is concerned with those aspects of international law that are of particular relevance to protection of children's rights in the UK. It does not consider other aspects of international and regional law affecting children, such as the African Charter on the Rights and Welfare of the Child.

[2] Discussed in Chapter 3.

international perspective would be complete without a discussion of the ECHR's singular significance.

The following chapter focuses on these two Conventions and the manner in which they have been interpreted, as they are of particular importance to understanding the way in which children's rights have been interpreted and implemented in domestic law. The contrast between the CRC's exclusive focus on the position of children and the ECHR's general application illuminates the theoretical debates on the extent to which children's rights can be seen as separable from human rights. These two Conventions are by no means the only international and regional instruments to provide influential sources of children's rights. The chapter briefly considers a variety of other sources which provide insight on international expectations regarding the treatment of children in various areas of activity. Of particular note is the European Union's comparatively recent attention to children's rights.[3] The rapidly developing EU law on children's rights, coupled with the principle of supremacy of EU law over domestic law, offered the potential to become an important source of protection for children in the UK, a potential now cut short by the UK's withdrawal from the EU.

(2) Rights Theories and International Human Rights

The jurisprudential doubts underlying the existence and scope of children's rights[4] did not inhibit the efforts of those seeking to promote children's protection in an international context. Indeed, had it not been for the driving force of international human rights lawyers, ideas and theories about children's rights might have remained in the realms of intellectual speculation. At first sight, the academics and legal practitioners concerned with the field of international human rights appear to be interested in entirely different concepts from the pure rights theories which concern the moral philosophers and jurists. These differences are perhaps more apparent than real and are exacerbated by the different language they employ. It was not until the aftermath of the Second World War that the term 'human rights' crept into common parlance as a way of describing the moral rights considered fundamental to civilised existence.[5] The draftsmen of the post-war international treaties adopted the new term in preference to the well-known phrase 'rights of man' favoured by natural law theorists. Thus, the United Nations in its founding charter of 1945 stated that one of its primary purposes was to promote and encourage 'respect for human rights and for fundamental freedoms for all without distinction as to race, sex, language, or religion'. Only 3 years later, in 1948, the Universal Declaration of Human Rights, adopted by the UN General

---

[3] Stalford (2012).   [4] Discussed in Chapter 1.
[5] C. Wellman (1999) esp. pp. 13–21: the historical development of the concept of natural rights and their later translation into 'human rights', as set out in a series of international treaties.

Assembly, contained a general statement guaranteeing 'the inherent dignity and . . . equal and inalienable rights of all members of the human family'.[6]

It was the civil and political rights selected for protection by the post-war treaties that were most clearly based on the ideas of the earlier natural law philosophers. They were derived from those inalienable rights of man that seventeenth-century theorists, like Hugo Grotius and John Locke, considered to be fundamental to human nature. Locke argued that, according to the laws of nature, each human being is entitled to the inalienable moral right to life, liberty and property.[7] These ideas had grounded the eighteenth-century bills of rights emanating from America and France – the American Declaration of Independence of 1776 and the French Declaration of the Rights of Man and of the Citizen of 1789. Although interest in natural rights theories waned during the nineteenth century, it revived in the 1940s in response to the manner in which totalitarian regimes, such as that of Nazi Germany, had been able to commit atrocities on a horrifying scale. As Feldman observes:

> the idea at the root of human rights thinking is that there are certain rights which are so fundamental to society's well-being and to people's chance of leading a fulfilling life that governments are obligated to respect them, and the international order has to protect them.[8]

The ECHR 1950 and the International Covenant on Civil and Political Rights (ICCPR) 1966 were both primarily concerned with fundamental liberties. The 'first generation human rights' they listed sought to protect the individual from oppressive interference by a nation state. Their provisions typically guarantee freedom from torture, from conviction without a fair trial, of expression and the right to peaceful assembly. By contrast, documents such as the Universal Declaration of Human Rights 1948[9] and the International Covenant on Economic, Social and Cultural Rights (ICESCR) 1966, which contain a list of 'second generation rights', reflect a more developed theory of indivisible human rights.[10] These seek to ensure that the first generation of 'negative' liberties are complemented by requiring states to take positive action to promote the welfare of individual human beings. In an approach later echoed in the CRC, the ICESCR reflects the view that it is not enough for human rights documents to identify certain liberties essential to individual autonomy, such

---

[6] K. Marshall and P. Parvis (2004) pp. 103–6 and pp. 129–31. See also pp. 114–16 for a useful analysis of the term 'inalienable', as used in many human rights documents.

[7] C. Wellman (1999) esp. pp. 13–21. See also K. Marshall and P. Parvis (2004) pp. 95–103.

[8] D. Feldman (2002) pp. 34–5.

[9] Esp. Arts 22–9; cf. Arts 1–21, which embrace the traditional civil and political rights.

[10] C. Wellman (1999) pp. 29–30 discusses the emergence of third generation human rights – the 'solidarity rights' or the rights of normally vulnerable groups to protection, *as a group*, rather than as individuals. E.g., inter alia, the Convention on the Prevention of the Crime of Genocide 1948, which was motivated by the German attempts to destroy the Jewish race throughout Europe; the Convention on the Elimination of All Forms of Discrimination against Women 1979.

as freedom of speech and assembly.[11] These rights may be of no value to those too poor or ill to benefit from them, whose time is taken up surviving from day to day.[12] Consequently, the Covenant obliges states to take a more active role. They are required to make resources available for certain additional social welfare rights; for example, by guaranteeing the right to an adequate standard of living[13] and to the highest attainable standard of physical and mental health,[14] thereby enabling people to take advantage of their innate freedoms. Some international lawyers are sceptical of acknowledging social welfare rights as having the force of international law, primarily due to the difficulties of enforcing them, particularly in view of the divergent resources available to different states.[15] Nevertheless, these rights are recognised in a variety of international documents, including the CRC, and are increasingly treated as justiciable both in national and international legal systems.[16]

The notion that children are, as human beings, entitled to human rights was gradually accepted in an international and domestic context. Indeed, during the second half of the twentieth century, it became widely acknowledged that children's human rights were theoretically no different from those of adults – they too were entitled to certain fundamental moral rights carrying the force of international law. This perception underpins the CRC. That document not only contains the civil and political rights derived from the inalienable 'rights of man', but also the second generation social welfare rights guaranteed by documents like the ICESCR. The concept of children's rights thereby acquired an important international dimension which is difficult for government and public agencies to ignore.

(3) Children and the Wider UN Human Rights Framework

The atrocities perpetrated before and during the Second World War led to a firm resolve to strengthen international unity. A determination to prevent such appalling events occurring again was accompanied by the promulgation of a large number of human rights instruments setting out those rights deemed essential to civilised life. Attempts to strengthen international unity included establishing the United Nations, whose charter came into force in 1945. This post-war activity was intended to strengthen human rights generally. Although children implicitly benefited from it, they received no special protection as a group. The Charter of the United Nations simply seeks to promote and encourage the human rights and fundamental freedoms 'for all without

---

[11] This approach was also evident in the Universal Declaration of Human Rights, Arts 22–9.
[12] D. Feldman (2002) pp. 12–14.   [13] ICESCR, Art. 11.   [14] ICESCR, Art. 12.
[15] See Nolan (2014) pp. 21–38 for a defence of socio-economic rights against these points.
[16] The adoption of a communications procedure for ICESCR is of particular note: Optional Protocol of the International Covenant on Economic, Social and Cultural Rights, UN Doc. A/RES/63/117 (entered into force 5 May 2013).

distinction as to race, sex, language or religion'.[17] While it certainly does not exclude children from its ambit, it contains no specific reference to them. Similarly, the Universal Declaration of Human Rights adopted in 1948 contains references to children,[18] guarantees the 'equal and inalienable rights of all members of the human family'[19] and recognises the family as 'the natural and fundamental group unit of society', entitled to the protection of society and the state.[20] It does not, however, attempt to provide for a range of rights more suitable for children with needs of their own.

The twin covenants adopted by the General Assembly of the United Nations in 1966, the ICCPR and the ICESCR, do give some specific protection to children's needs. The ICCPR protects children's rights to name, nationality and birth registration, alongside the right to measures of protection, without discrimination, as 'are required by his status as a minor'.[21] The ICESCR protects children from 'economic and social exploitation', including harmful work.[22] The UN Committee on Human Rights has confirmed that children benefit from all of the civil rights contained in the ICCPR and not merely those that refer specifically to children's rights.[23] Nonetheless, outside of these specific rights, the Covenants give no guidance as to how the rights are to be implemented so as to be practically effective for children. In particular, the Covenants each recognise extensive rights for parents, especially in determining their children's education, without reference to the rights and interests of children.[24]

The foundational human rights framework includes children within its remit, but makes no attempt to deal with the broad spectrum of children's needs or to make them their main focus of attention. By contrast, the CRC achieves both aims outstandingly well, providing a child-focused understanding of many of the rights contained in these foundational instruments. Following the CRC's pioneering role in establishing children's rights as a distinct facet of human rights, a wide variety of UN human rights instruments now exist which refer to children's rights in various different contexts.[25]

(4) Establishing Children's International Human Rights

Although the special vulnerability of children as a group had been recognised much earlier than the international human rights activity generated by the Second World War, little progress was made towards producing an instrument

---

[17] Art. 55(c).
[18] Art. 25(2) refers to motherhood and childhood both requiring special care and assistance; see also Art. 26, which concerns educational rights.
[19] Preamble.   [20] Art. 16(3).
[21] Art. 24. Art. 10 also gives specific protection to juvenile offenders.   [22] Art. 10(3).
[23] Committee on Human Rights (1989) esp. para. 2.
[24] ICCPR, Art. 18(4); ICESCR, Art. 10(3).
[25] R. Hodgkin and P. Newell (2007) Appendix 4; MacDonald (2011) ch. 2. E.g. Convention on the Rights of Persons with Disabilities, Art. 7.

which had binding force, covering the full scope of their needs and recognising them as independent rights-holders. The first important international document devoted entirely to protecting the rights of children was adopted by the Fifth Assembly of the League of Nations in 1924. This was the Declaration of the Rights of the Child, known as the Declaration of Geneva.[26] It contained only five basic principles, all of which were couched in forthright terms. Thus, the first commenced with the words: 'The child must be given the means requisite for its normal development, both materially and spiritually.' The second went on to state that: 'The child that is hungry must be fed; the child that is sick must be nursed.' The third was even more to the point, stating merely that: 'The child must be the first to receive relief in times of distress.' The fourth stated that: 'The child must be put in a position to earn a livelihood, and must be protected against every form of exploitation.' While the fifth considered that: 'The child must be brought up in the consciousness that its talents must be devoted to the service of fellow men.' The Declaration was an important step in recognising the interests of individual children as a legitimate object of international protection and as such was an important step in paving the way for future recognition of children's rights. Nonetheless, despite its title, it remained a document concerned with a particular perception of children's welfare, rather than their independent rights. Further, the brief text of the Declaration was written in aspirational terms with no legally binding force. The Declaration itself referred to the duties of 'men and women of all nations' rather than those of the state. The League of Nations, in adopting the Declaration, merely invited the member states to be 'guided by its principles in the work of child welfare'. The Declaration of Geneva was undoubtedly a foundation and inspiration for future recognition of children's rights in international law, but did not itself create a binding set of rights.

A more substantial statement of children's interests followed in the Declaration of the Rights of the Child adopted in 1959 by the UN General Assembly.[27] This longer document contained ten principles, but again, it had the limited status of a declaration. It did not attempt to claim that the 'rights' listed constituted legal obligations. Instead, states were merely required to take note of the principles contained therein, on the basis that they were universally accepted as being applicable to all children. While the 1959 Declaration is significant for its clear statement of the child's status as a rights-holder, it remains focused on children's protection and welfare. As Freeman notes, the Declaration has 'no recognition of a child's agency, the importance of a child's views, nor any appreciation of the concept of empowerment'.[28]

Some of the principles set out in the 1959 Declaration now appear idealistic, others simply vague and outdated. Nevertheless, as Alston and Tobin point out, the document is significant for the way it emphasises children's emotional

---

[26] D. Hodgson (1992) pp. 260–1. See also P. Alston and J. Tobin (2005) p. 4.
[27] P. Alston and J. Tobin (2005) pp. 5–6.   [28] Freeman (2014) p. 4.

well-being.[29] Principle 6 refers to a child's need for 'love and understanding', and to grow up in an atmosphere of 'affection and of moral and material security'. Other parts, however, reflect outmoded stereotyped ideas about the roles to be played by mothers and fathers in the lives of their children. Principle 6 asserts that a 'child of tender years shall not, save in exceptional circumstances, be separated from his mother'. As Thorpe LJ emphasised, when trenchantly rejecting a mother's claim that Principle 6 strengthened her application for a residence order:

> The relevance and value of the UN 1959 Declaration is most doubtful. In terms of relevant social policy it could be said to be almost antiquated since it is now nearly 40 years old and in terms of social development and in terms of understanding of child development and welfare that is an exceedingly long time.[30]

The real importance of the 1959 Declaration lies in the fact that it embodies the first serious attempt to describe in a reasonably detailed manner what constitutes children's overriding claims and entitlements. While not overlooking its weaknesses, some of the ideas it contains are surprisingly modern and reappear in an elaborated form in the CRC, introduced 30 years later in 1989. For example, the references to the child's right to name and nationality; to treatment without discrimination; to socioeconomic rights, such as housing, medical care and food; to rights to education and protection from exploitation, neglect and cruelty, all found their way into the 1989 Convention.

To a modern eye, the greatest weakness of the 1959 document was its failure to list any of the first generation human rights, the freedoms from state oppression. Indeed, barring the reference to name and nationality, there is no mention of children's civil and political rights.[31] The CRC was born out of calls for a more systematic approach to protecting children's rights. By the 1970s, growing concern over the violations of children's rights throughout the world led finally to a move to establish an international document guaranteeing children's rights through the imposition of legal obligations.[32] In 1976, the UN General Assembly, fulfilling a request from the executive board of UNICEF, declared 1979 the International Year of the Child and urged governments to commemorate the year by making special contributions to improving the well-being of children. As its contribution to the year, the Polish government, in 1978, submitted to the UN Commission on Human Rights a draft for a new CRC. It was virtually identical in format to the 1959 Declaration and it was hoped that it could be adopted by the United Nations the following year, as a legally binding international document. Such an optimistic timescale proved unrealistic. Although there was general agreement that a document of this nature should be created, it was considered that there was little point in

---

[29] P. Alston and J. Tobin (2005) p. 5.

[30] *Re A (children: 1959 UN Declaration)* [1998] 1 FLR 354, at 358. The father successfully appealed their 3.5-year-old son being the subject of a residence order in the mother's favour.

[31] P. Alston and J. Tobin (2005) p. 5.   [32] Ibid. pp. 6–7; D. Hodgson (1992) pp. 275–6.

repeating the mistakes of the 1959 Declaration. Governments would continue to ignore their obligations to children unless the provisions were sufficiently specific and realistic. Nearly 10 years were to elapse before a final draft of the CRC was completed in 1988 and submitted to the Commission on Human Rights for approval in 1989. It was finally adopted by the General Assembly in November 1989, entering into force in 1990. It was ratified by the UK in 1991 and came into force in the UK in January 1992. The CRC, together with its later optional protocols,[33] firmly embeds children's rights within the international human rights framework. In doing so, it addresses many of the weaknesses of the earlier Declarations – creating binding legal standards that centre the child as an active participant and subject, rather than merely the object, of international human rights law.

(5) The Convention on the Rights of the Child

(A) A Broad Spectrum of Rights

The Preamble to the CRC makes plain the size of the task taken on by its draftsmen and the conflicting ideals that required accommodation within a document commanding international respect. While recognising the importance of the family as 'the fundamental group of society' and the child's need to 'grow up in a family environment' with love and understanding, it also asserts that 'a child should be fully prepared to live an individual life in society, and brought up in the spirit of the ideals proclaimed in the UN Charter, and in particular in the spirit of peace, dignity, tolerance, freedom, equality and solidarity'.[34] Despite the enormity of these challenges, the decade of drafting produced a document which, if fully complied with, would indeed achieve many of these aims.

The rights listed cover the broad spectrum of children's needs and aspirations. Its fifty-four articles, some forty of which are concerned with substantive rights, cover civil, political, economic and social issues. In contrast to earlier international human rights treaties, notably the ICCPR and the ICESCR, the CRC contains both sets of rights in one single document. The Convention applies to 'every human being below the age of eighteen years'[35] and by including all the traditional civil and political rights, such as freedom of expression,[36] religion,[37] association and assembly,[38] it departs radically from the earlier international documents which primarily aimed to address

---

[33] Optional Protocol to the Convention on the Rights of the Child on the Sale of Children, Child Prostitution and Child Pornography, UN Doc. A/RES/54/263 (entered into force 18 January 2002); Optional Protocol to the Convention on the Rights of the Child on the Involvement of Children in Armed Conflict, UN Doc. A/RES/54/263 (entered into force 12 February 2002); Optional Protocol to the Convention on the Rights of the Child on a Communications Procedure, UN Doc. A/RES/66/138 (entered into force 14 April 2014).

[34] Preamble to the CRC, para. 7.   [35] Unless the age of majority is attained earlier; see Art. 1.

[36] Art. 13.   [37] Art. 14.   [38] Art. 15.

children's immaturity and need for care. By including children's social and economic rights, the Convention also emphasises that states must not only protect children and safeguard their fundamental freedoms, but also devote resources to ensuring that they realise their potential for maturing into a healthy and happy adulthood. Indeed, although the wording of Article 4 reflects 'a realistic acceptance that lack of resources – financial and other resources – can hamper the full implementation of economic, social and cultural rights in some States ... States need to be able to demonstrate that they have implemented "to the maximum extent of their available resources"'.[39]

The CRC's provisions demonstrate a strange mixture of idealism and practical realism. Some, like Article 28 on education, descend into the detailed aspects of schooling, such as ensuring regular attendance and 'the reduction of drop-out rates'.[40] Others, like Article 12, assuring respect for the child's views, maintain a more philosophical approach to their capacity for autonomy. When interpreting some of the more opaque provisions, valuable assistance can be derived from the research which has analysed the 'Concluding Observations'[41] and 'General Comments' of the Committee on the Rights of the Child (the 'Committee'). This throws light on the Committee's view of the Convention's intentions and its application to some of the difficult questions of implementation.

(B) The 'General Principles'

Although the Committee has stressed that the articles of the Convention are interrelated and should be considered together, it has itself elevated Articles 2,[42] 3,[43] 6[44] and 12[45] to the status of 'general principles'.[46] The general principles approach has attracted some criticism, both in the legitimacy of the process by which they were chosen and the justification for the choice made. In contrast to the UN Convention on the Rights of Persons with Disabilities, which explicitly sets out its general principles,[47] the general principles of the CRC are not identified within the text of the Convention and did not gain their legitimacy by a process of negotiation and state agreement. Instead, the Committee itself identified the principles, initially as an aspect of its reporting guidelines[48] and subsequently through its Concluding Observations and General Comments. The rather opaque process by which the principles were identified and developed raises further questions as to whether the chosen articles best represent the overarching principles of the

---

[39] Committee on the Rights of the Child (2003) para. 7.   [40] Art. 28(1)(e).
[41] Discussed below.   [42] The right to protection from discrimination.
[43] The child's best interests.   [44] The right to life, survival and development.
[45] The right to respect for the child's views and the right to be heard.
[46] Committee on the Rights of the Child (2003) para. 12.   [47] In Art. 3.
[48] Committee on the Rights of the Child (1991).

Convention.[49] There is, for example, a good case for recognising the evolving capacity of the child in Article 5 as a general principle.[50] Despite these criticisms, the 'general principles' have been widely accepted and are now a well-established means of understanding and implementing the Convention.

Theoretically, none of these four principles is more important than any other; nevertheless, Article 3, requiring a commitment to the child's best interests, underpins all the other provisions. It should be noted, however, that unlike the Children Act (CA) 1989, section 1, which provides that the child's best interests are paramount,[51] Article 3(1) only provides that 'the best interests of the child shall be *a* primary consideration'.[52] The difference between these approaches can be explained by the breadth of application of Article 3, which is framed to include *all* actions concerning children; this covers not only actions that directly affect children, but also those that indirectly do so and as such could apply to almost any administrative or legislative act.[53] Given this broad application, the delegates were concerned that there might be other competing interests, for example, those of justice and society, at times making paramountcy inappropriate.[54] In contrast, the Convention recognises children's interests as paramount in cases of adoption where no such competing concerns apply.[55] Despite the 'best interests' formula not adopting the paramountcy criterion, the Committee on the Rights of the Child is keen not to allow it to be downplayed.[56] The Committee's detailed General Comment on Article 3 defines the best interests of the child as a threefold concept: a substantive right of children to have their best interests assessed and treated as a primary consideration; an interpretive tool to resolve ambiguity in legal provisions; and a procedural rule to ensure that children's interests are fully considered in decisions that concern them.[57] If properly implemented, Article 3 has the potential to have a transformative effect, embedding the interests of children within all levels of state decision-making. As the Committee recognises, the term 'best interests' is notoriously difficult to define and can be easily manipulated to sideline children's rights in the name of their best interests.[58] To protect against this very real concern, the process by which best interests are determined is of particular importance and requires careful attention to the Convention as a whole.

Article 12 is often singled out as being one of the most important in the Convention, both in its own right and in the interpretation and

---

[49] K. Hanson and L. Lundy (2017).   [50] J. Tobin (2011).

[51] See also Principle 2 of the 1959 Declaration of the Rights of the Child, which made the child's interests paramount.

[52] Emphasis added.   [53] Committee on the Rights of the Child (2013) para. 6.

[54] D. McGoldrick (1991) pp. 135–7; U. Kilkelly and L. Lundy (2006) p. 337.

[55] Art. 21; see also Art. 9(1) and (3), which treat children's best interests as the defining test in determining the separation of children from their parents, and Art. 18(1), which defines children's interests as the 'basic concern' of those with parental responsibility.

[56] R. Hodgkin and P. Newell (2007) pp. 39–48.

[57] Committee on the Rights of the Child (2013) para. 6.   [58] Ibid. para. 34.

implementation of the other rights protected by the CRC.[59] It assures to children capable of forming their own views 'the right to express those views freely in all matters affecting (them), the views of the child being given due weight in accordance with the age and maturity of the child'.[60] Article 12(2) further provides children with the procedural right to be heard in any judicial or administrative proceedings affecting them – this latter provision being crucially important to children who are the subject of parental disputes.[61] The right does not only apply to questions of children's upbringing, but applies to a wide range of situations in which individual or groups of children are affected.[62] The Committee has observed that the obligation to *assure* the right to be heard is of 'special strength', leaving no leeway to state parties as to whether or not to comply.[63] The Article has, however, been criticised for appearing to link children's right to be heard to their capacity.[64] It applies only to those capable of forming views and assigns weight to those views according to the child's age and maturity, which may be taken to imply that the views of younger children will be of limited weight. Nonetheless, even extremely young children may have strong views on their circumstances, regardless of whether they are able to articulate those views in adult terms.[65] It is not clear that the views of young children should necessarily carry less weight than those who are older: the right to express a view is not the same as a right to decide the matter in hand. The Committee's General Comment on Article 12 goes some way to addressing these criticisms. It stresses that states should start from the position that children have the capacity to form their own views. It further recognises that children who are too young, or otherwise unable, to express their views verbally can communicate non-verbally. This goes some way to ensuring that all children have a right to be heard in matters concerning them.[66]

The remaining 'general principles' were already well established within the wider human rights framework at the time the CRC was drafted. Article 2, which protects the right to enjoy the rights contained in the CRC free of discrimination, reflects the principle of equality that is well established in international human rights law.[67] The right should be interpreted in line with the extensive wider human rights law on the subject. The 'inherent right to life', protected by Article 6, is also one of the most important and widely recognised human rights.[68] The CRC extends this right further by obliging states to 'ensure to the maximum extent possible the survival and development of the child'. The right to development includes a wide range of

---

[59] Committee on the Rights of the Child (2009) para. 2.   [60] Art. 12(1).
[61] Discussed further in Chapter 12.
[62] Committee on the Rights of the Child (2009) paras 86–88.   [63] Ibid. para. 19.
[64] A. Daly (2018), discussed further in Chapter 12.   [65] M. Henaghan (2017).
[66] Committee on the Rights of the Child (2009) paras 20–21.
[67] E.g. ICCPR, Art. 2; ICESCR, Art. 2. The CRC also adds ethnic origin and disability to the prohibited grounds of discrimination.
[68] ICCPR, Art. 6(1).

facets, including physical, mental, spiritual, moral, psychological and social development.[69] The question of what constitutes healthy development in this broad sense raises complex questions of social and scientific understandings of childhood. These issues go to the heart of many of the most difficult issues in implementing children's rights and it is surprising that the Committee has paid relatively little attention to resolving them, despite the prominent role of Article 6 as a general principle.[70]

(C) Classifying the Convention Rights

Important though they are, the four general principles cannot stand alone. They are underpinned by a broad array of substantive rights, together comprising a bewildering hotchpotch of provisions, some overlapping considerably in their aims.[71] The contents of the Convention have been classified in a variety of ways, none of which avoids overlap or criticism.[72] While no classification should be used rigidly or in a way that undermines the interdependent and indivisible nature of the rights contained in the Convention, they do have utility in creating a framework for explaining what might otherwise seem an impenetrable set of rights. Although not immune from these concerns, LeBlanc's classification,[73] by including 'membership rights', emphasises the way in which the Convention addresses children's need for community. According to his arrangement, the rights are classified into 'survival rights', 'membership rights', 'protection rights' and 'empowerment rights'.[74]

The survival rights include not only the right to life itself, but also the right to all those rights which sustain life and promote the child's development. For example, the Convention recognises rights to: a standard of living adequate for the child's physical, mental, spiritual, moral and social development;[75] social security benefits;[76] and the highest attainable standard of health.[77] It is clear that many of these rights impose positive obligations on the state that require considerable resources to be fully implemented. Membership of the Convention includes states where resources are scarce; Article 4 recognises this, stating that in protecting economic, social and cultural rights, states should take 'measures to the maximum extent of their available resources'.

Membership rights include those which treat the child as a member of his or her community and family. The Convention recognises the importance to children of the family unit and preservation of relationships within the family,[78] as well as placing particular weight on the responsibilities of parents

---

[69] Committee on the Rights of the Child (2003) para. 12.   [70] N. Peleg (2017).
[71] K. Marshall and P. Parvis (2004) pp. 12–20.
[72] Most prominently, the '3Ps' categorises rights as concerning protection, provision and participation. For criticism of this approach, see A. Quennerstedt (2010).
[73] Adapted from that proposed by J. Donnelly and R. Howard (1988).
[74] L. LeBlanc (1995) Pt Two.   [75] Art. 27(1).   [76] Art. 26.   [77] Art. 24.   [78] Arts 9 and 10.

to their children.[79] Children's participation in the wider community is also protected; the Convention recognises that for children to be part of a community, they must have a name and nationality[80] and the right to preserve their identity.[81] This latter right was introduced by the Argentinian representatives to prevent children being allowed to 'disappear' as they had during the rule of the Argentinian Junta. These rights are particularly important for children in times of conflict. The rights of children born into minority groups to follow their own culture, language and religion is protected, including the right to enjoy those rights with other members of the group.[82] Further, there is also recognition of the need to take positive measures to ensure that children with disabilities are able to fully participate within the community.[83]

Protection rights guard the child against abuses of power by individuals and the state. The Convention protects children from a wide range of abuse, exploitation and mistreatment. This includes: sexual exploitation and abuse;[84] economic exploitation and hazardous employment;[85] torture and cruel, inhuman or degrading treatment;[86] parental abuse;[87] and drug abuse.[88] There is specific protection for child refugees[89] and children involved in armed conflict.[90] The need to take measures to assist children who have been victims of abuse, neglect and ill-treatment is also recognised.[91]

Finally, empowerment rights secure a respect for children as effective members of the communities in which they live, through protecting their freedom of thought and conscience and encouraging their capacity for self-determination. It is the protection of these rights that is perhaps the most remarkable, given that many of the delegates involved in the drafting sessions were from traditional countries whose conceptions of the role of children in families and the wider community were relatively narrow. The Convention recognises that children are active and creative and may need encouragement to shape their own lives. As such, they must be assisted to develop their independence and ability to take responsibility for their future. In particular, by extending the traditional civil and political rights to children, the Convention indicates that all children, irrespective of age, have the same dignity and worth as adults.[92] In particular, they require the liberties essential to notions of adult autonomy if they are to develop their own capacity for

---

[79] Arts 5 and 18.   [80] Art. 7.   [81] Art. 8.   [82] Art. 30.   [83] Art. 23.

[84] Art. 34; see also Optional Protocol to the Convention on the Rights of the Child on the Sale of Children, Child Prostitution and Child Pornography, UN Doc. A/RES/54/263 (entered into force 18 January 2002).

[85] Art. 32.   [86] Art. 37.   [87] Art. 19.   [88] Art. 33.   [89] Art. 22.

[90] Art. 38; see also Optional Protocol to the Convention on the Rights of the Child on the Involvement of Children in Armed Conflict, UN Doc. A/RES/54/263 (entered into force 12 February 2002).

[91] Art. 39.

[92] The second paragraph of the Preamble to the Convention reminds states that the UN Charter reaffirmed faith in 'fundamental human rights and in the dignity and worth of the human person'.

autonomy and play an active part in society. Article 13 recognises children's right to freedom of expression, including the right to seek, receive and impart information and ideas, as already guaranteed by the more general human rights documents.[93] The Convention also recognises that in order to form and express their own views, children need access to information and material from a variety of sources.[94] Even more fundamental, they are entitled to respect and dignity as they mature to adulthood. States must secure their rights to freedom of thought, conscience and religion,[95] to privacy[96] and a freedom to meet and mix with others and share views.[97] Crucially, children cannot develop their views and critical thought without a right to education. This too is fully recognised, with detailed provisions regarding the practical aspects of providing schooling,[98] and additionally setting out the more philosophical aims of education, including the need to promote a respect for the child's parents and his or her cultural identity.[99]

(D) Internal Inconsistencies

The aims of the Convention, as set out in the Preamble, are ambitious. In particular, it emphasises the need to promote children's capacity for autonomy, while simultaneously supporting the traditional role of the family in society and the authority of parents over their children. Some might argue that these aims are irreconcilable. Certainly, the wording of the Preamble, and some of the other articles, contain internal inconsistencies that reflect the many disagreements during the drafting sessions. Conflicting views were expressed by delegates from countries deeply opposed to giving children freedom from parental direction and religious teaching and by those from countries like the US, who, influenced by their own constitutional history, strongly favoured the concept of children enjoying similar civil and political rights to adults.[100] Some delegates also feared that providing families with protection from state interference would provide parents with arbitrary control over their children, thereby inhibiting children from being able to develop their own views.

The compromises resulting from attempts to balance these differing approaches to the family are reflected in tensions in the Convention and within many of the articles. For this reason, the Convention is often said to be incompletely theorised:[101] many of the most important controversies

---

[93] E.g. the Universal Declaration of Human Rights. R. Hodgkin and P. Newell (2007) p. 177.
[94] Art. 17.   [95] Art. 14(1).   [96] Art. 16.   [97] Art. 15.   [98] Art. 28(1)(a)–(e).
[99] Art. 29.   [100] L. LeBlanc (1995) ch. 1 and pp. 112–17.
[101] J. Tobin (2013) acknowledges this criticism, but defends the CRC from a conclusion that this means it lacks moral authority or is incoherent and arbitrary. He does so on the basis of social interest theory and especially on the moral consensus that emerged from the drafting process that led to the CRC. It may be inevitable that any international agreement that attracts such widespread support as the CRC will not be capable of being understood on the basis of a single theoretical model.

concerning theoretical conceptions of children's rights are left unresolved by the text of the Convention. For example, while the Convention represents broad agreement that childhood is a time that requires special consideration, there is no consensus as to when childhood starts or ends. Similarly, there is an ambiguity as to the limits of parental powers and responsibilities and how these relate to the child's own needs and developing capacity. Thus, while Article 3(2) requires states to ensure the child 'such protection and care as is necessary for his or her well-being', they must do so 'taking into account the rights and duties of his or her parents'. Similarly, Article 5, which respects the parents' right to direct and guide their children, requires that this is done in a manner consistent with the 'evolving capacities of the child', but gives no further guidance as to how that tension is to be resolved.[102] Further, there is an ambiguity as to how far the Convention is concerned primarily with the child's development into a future adult and how far it is concerned with the child in the present:[103] or as Janusz Korczak put it, whether the child's 'right to the present' is sacrificed to their future.[104]

A particularly good example of disagreement and compromise can be found in the treatment of the right to freedom of religion. It is notable that Article 14 does not, unlike its counterpart in the ICCPR, specifically set out a correlative right to 'have or adopt a religion or belief of his choice'.[105] Indeed, an earlier draft, based on the ICCPR, which specifically included that freedom of choice, had been rejected during the drafting process.[106] Further, Article 14(2) stresses the parental right 'to provide direction to the child in the exercise of his or her right in a manner consistent with the evolving capacities of the child'. This could imply that the CRC merely gives children the right to *practise* their own religion, rather than the freedom to 'choose' it, thereby maintaining the parental right to impose a 'choice' of religion on their children. This would be problematic as children are also rights-holders under the ICCPR, the function of the CRC should be to ensure that children's human rights are protected in a practically relevant form, not to limit children's existing human rights. Nevertheless, it is better to regard the right to religion as that of the child, with parents only able to provide direction which is consistent with the child's own developing competence under Article 5, and with the child's own rights under Articles 12 and 13.[107] Nonetheless, the ambiguity in the wording has allowed states to enter substantially different interpretive declarations and reservations, giving entirely contrary meanings of the right. Belgium and the Netherlands have made declarations indicating their intention to interpret it in

---

[102] Although the Committee has given some guidance on this balance in its General Comments, taking the view that 'the more a child knows and understands, the more his or her parents will have to transform direction and guidance into reminders and gradually to an exchange on an equal footing': Committee on the Rights of the Child (2016b) para. 18.

[103] N. Peleg (2012). See Chapter 1 for discussion of the theoretical aspects of this question.

[104] Discussed in M. Freeman (2020) ch. 1. See Chapter 9 for further discussion of children's development. For critical comment of this aspect of the CRC, see A. Barnes (2012).

[105] ICCPR, Art. 18(1).   [106] G. Van Bueren (1995) p. 156.   [107] R. Taylor (2017).

accordance with the provisions of Article 18 of the ICCPR, to give the child the right to choose their religion once capable of doing so.[108] In contrast, a large number of Islamic states have entered reservations on the basis that the freedom of a child to choose their religion runs counter to national law[109] or the provisions of Shari'a law.[110] Further, both Poland and the Holy See have stated that the provision should not be interpreted so as to undermine the authority of parents. These state responses to Article 14 demonstrate how apparent consensus on the face of the Convention can mask very real differences in interpretation and practice.

It would be foolish to deny the existence of compromises and internal inconsistencies within the Convention. Indeed, as in many domestic legal systems, including our own, it reflects an obvious ambivalence over the need to promote children's capacity for self-determination, while at the same time maintaining the traditional rights of parents to provide direction, support and discipline.[111] Like many other international conventions, it contains little very practical or specific advice. Indeed, as King rightly says, it 'contains a wide range of rather vague political and economic rights and duties which require further precision and transformation at the national level if they are to become amenable to lawful/unlawful decisions'.[112] But for all its faults, the Convention remains a remarkable document, which provides a wide-ranging set of standards against which ratifying states may measure the extent to which they fulfil children's rights.

(E) Enforcement and Implementation

Whether states are held to the standards set out in the Convention depends on the strength of its enforcement proceedings in international law and the extent to which it is implemented in national law. It is often the implementation of children's rights in domestic law, policy and practice that is best equipped to translate international children's rights from aspiration into reality. An increasing number of states have chosen to fulfil their obligations by incorporating the Convention, or aspects of it, into domestic law. National legislation most frequently incorporates the provisions on children's best interests and the voice of the child, although these are sometimes limited to a relatively narrow band of 'children's' issues such as family disputes.[113] Legislation can be an important step in safeguarding children's rights in practice, but it is not in itself sufficient to do so. To be effective, implementation requires non-legal measures, including: training and awareness; monitoring; data-collection; budgeting; and planning.[114] While these measures of implementation do not require direct incorporation of the CRC into domestic law, there is evidence

---

[108] Ibid.; R. Hodgkin and P. Newell (2007).   [109] E.g. Malaysia and Algeria.
[110] E.g. the United Arab Emirates and Iraq.   [111] J. Fortin (2002) p. 19.
[112] M. King (1994) p. 395.   [113] L. Lundy et al. (2014).
[114] Committee on the Rights of the Child (2003).

that incorporation can be an effective means of raising awareness of children's rights and creating momentum for more effective implantation of children's rights in policy and practice.[115] There is also an increasing tendency for national courts and regional bodies to use the CRC as an interpretive tool and as of persuasive influence, even in those states that have not chosen to incorporate the Convention into domestic law.[116]

At the international level, a fundamental weakness of the Convention has been that it has had no direct method of formal enforcement available to individual rights-holders. This changed on 14 April 2014, the date on which Optional Protocol 3, establishing an individual communication procedure, came into force. That procedure has the potential to strengthen enforcement of the CRC, although whether it will do so in practice remains to be seen. At present, only a minority of state parties to the CRC have ratified the optional protocol.[117] The UK has neither signed nor ratified the optional protocol. This means that, at present, for the vast majority of children protected by the Convention, international enforcement depends on periodic state reports.

The body with responsibility for 'examining the progress made by States Parties in achieving the realisation of the obligations' under the Convention is the Committee on the Rights of the Child, established under the auspices of the UN General Assembly.[118] The Committee sits in Geneva and consists of eighteen experts elected from within the ranks of state parties who have ratified the Convention. The Committee wields considerable influence in its interpretation of the Convention. Its Concluding Observations, which have gradually become more detailed and complex, are read with considerable interest by human rights experts throughout the world. It has also followed the model of the Human Rights Committee responsible for monitoring the ICCPR, by producing a series of 'General Comments' explaining how the Committee interprets many of the articles of the CRC and addressing particular areas of implementation. This guidance is available for use by governments to inform their policies regarding implementation. Although neither the Concluding Observations nor the General Comments are strictly legally binding, they have considerable authority and this growing body of jurisprudence is of great utility to practitioners and researchers in developing understanding of the Convention.[119] The Committee is also responsible for deciding cases brought under the complaints procedure and these decisions will no doubt add to the developing jurisprudence surrounding the Convention. In doing so, the Committee has the opportunity to remedy many of the ambiguities and inconsistencies that have been identified within the Convention.

---

[115] L. Lundy *et al.* (2014).   [116] T. Liefaard and J. Doek (2015).

[117] At the time of writing, forty-eight countries had ratified the Optional Protocol out of the 196 parties to the CRC itself.

[118] Art. 43 sets out the reporting mechanism and establishes the Committee on the Rights of the Child. See R. Hodgkin and P. Newell (2007) pp. 639–41.

[119] E.g. C. Price Cohen and S. Kilbourne (1998); R. Hodgkin and P. Newell (2007).

(i) The Reporting Mechanism

As most state parties, including the UK, have not yet ratified Optional Protocol 3, the reporting mechanism remains the primary means by which the Committee has oversight of the implementation of the Convention.[120] Two years after ratification, each government is expected to send an initial report to the Committee, detailing the progress it has made in fulfilling its obligations and any difficulties experienced in doing so. Thereafter, it is normally required to submit periodic reports at five-year intervals,[121] although in practice this timetable is often not adhered to, not least because the Committee has struggled to manage the workload generated by such a large number of state parties.[122] After receiving a report, the Committee will obtain additional information on the government's record on implementation from other UN organisations and domestic non-governmental organisations (NGOs) by inviting them to comment on the report itself. In the Committee's final report, its 'Concluding Observations', the Committee may identify and criticise areas of non-compliance and make suggestions for remedy.

The reporting process is intended to be constructive, reflecting the positive steps that the state has taken, as well as identifying failures. The Committee also makes recommendations as to how the state can achieve greater compliance in the future. It was hoped that the need to produce periodic reports, and the knowledge that they would be subjected to detailed consideration by the Committee, would encourage states to implement its provisions effectively. Certainly, the publication of the Committee's detailed observations on these reports produces media attention and a heightened public awareness of the principles contained in the Convention, as well as the extent to which governments are implementing its obligations. There is some evidence that the reporting process can have an important role in raising awareness and respect for children's rights and that this has, in many states, led to improved implementation, including incorporation into domestic law.[123]

The reporting mechanism relies on governments to subject their implementation programme to an objective and critical analysis before compiling their reports. Reports must indicate to the Committee 'factors and difficulties, if any, affecting the degree of fulfilment' of their obligations under the Convention.[124] Nevertheless, the absence of any supervision or coercion over this can lead to reports painting an over-optimistic and complacent picture of governmental achievements. This weakness in the reporting procedure has led to many countries providing reports indicating little or no difficulty with implementing some of their more onerous obligations.[125] The UK's own performance has been no exception. The government's reports have often been highly selective

---

[120] C. Price Cohen and S. Kilbourne (1998) pp. 640–2.   [121] Art. 44(1)(b).
[122] T. Buck (2014) pp. 98–106.   [123] L. Lundy et al. (2014) pp. 325–6.   [124] Art. 44(2).
[125] L. Scherer and S. Hart (2001) pp. 84–5: an analysis of the initial reports of forty-nine countries (regarding compliance with Arts 28 and 29) found that most failed to specify any difficulties relating to education.

and unbalanced in their coverage of the Convention's requirements. A good example of this can be seen in the UK's 5th Periodic Report in 2014, which failed to give any detailed analysis of the impact of government spending cuts on children or any evidence for the assertion that the CRC had been a 'key point in reference' in determining public expenditure.[126] In contrast, the Committee expressed 'serious concern' at the impact of these decisions on child poverty,[127] while the JCHR found that the impact of austerity on children, particularly disadvantaged children, had been greater than for many other groups.[128]

A further weakness of state party reporting is that the vagueness and internal inconsistencies within the Convention can be exploited to allow governments to avoid critical analysis. Again, the UK government has been no exception, at times even distorting the aims of current legislation to justify spurious claims of compliance with the Convention's provisions. For example, in its second report, the government made the astonishing claim that changes made to the law on youth offending, notably the abolition of the presumption of *doli incapax* for accused children between the ages of 10 and 14,[129] would promote children's rights, on the basis that it would:

> ensure that, if a child has begun to offend, he or she is entitled to the earliest possible intervention to address that offending behaviour and eliminate its causes. The changes will also have the result of putting all juveniles on the same footing as far as courts are concerned, and will contribute to the *right* of children appearing there to develop responsibility for themselves.[130]

The Committee was plainly not deceived by such disingenuous claims and emphasised its 'serious concern' that the 'law has worsened since the consideration of the initial report' with the age of criminal responsibility being retained at 10 and the *doli incapax* presumption being abolished.[131]

Failure to participate in critical self-analysis can undermine the value of the reporting mechanism, although the involvement of NGOs, National Human Rights Institutions and children's groups can go some way to mitigating these weaknesses. The CRC is remarkable for the extent to which such groups have been involved in drafting and implementing the Convention, including playing a vital role in providing information and analysis to the Committee in the reporting process[132] and exposing weaknesses in government reports. This collaborative approach to reporting goes some way to addressing the weaknesses caused by the Committee's limited capacity and the limitations of self-reporting.

[126] HM Government (2014) para. 10.
[127] Committee on the Rights of the Child (2016a) paras 70–71.
[128] JCHR (2015) paras 86–101.   [129] Crime and Disorder Act 1998, s. 36.
[130] DH (1999) para. 10.30.1 (emphasis added); see also HM Government (2007) p. 160, para. 54.
[131] Committee on the Rights of the Child (2002) para. 59. See also Committee on the Rights of the Child (2008) para. 78.
[132] Committee on the Rights of the Child (2003) para. 59; T. Buck (2014) p. 100.

(ii) Optional Protocol 3: Individual Communications

Optional Protocol 3 creates three new forms of enforcement for the CRC: individual communication; an inquiry procedure; and inter-state communication. The inquiry procedure obliges the Committee to conduct an inquiry upon receipt of 'reliable information indicating grave or systematic violations' of the CRC.[133] State parties may opt out of this procedure when signing or ratifying the Protocol.[134] In contrast, the inter-state communication procedure allows states to opt in to allow the Committee to receive communications from one state party alleging that another party is not fulfilling its obligations under the CRC and its protocols.[135] It is, however, the individual communications procedure that forms the primary means of implementation and which brings the CRC into line with the other core UN human rights treaties, all of which now possess individual complaints mechanisms. In this context, the Protocol is undoubtedly of great symbolic significance, recognising children's rights as enforceable in the same way as those of the rights of adults. Whether it will also be of practical importance remains to be seen.

Children face significant hurdles in bringing effective complaints to courts and other institutions. Lack of information, funding, legal standing and access to advice can seriously impede the ability of children to bring their own complaints, while complaints brought on behalf of children raise the difficulty of ensuring that those who claim to speak for children actually do so.[136] While these problems are not unique to children, they require child-sensitive solutions if the communications procedure is to give a realistic means of addressing violations of children's rights. The Protocol makes surprisingly little reference to the difficulties faced by children, primarily modelling itself on the procedures used in other human rights treaties. There are a number of notable problems for children on the face of the procedure. In particular, complaints that have not yet exhausted domestic remedies will, ordinarily, be inadmissible, as will those not submitted within a year of the exhaustion of domestic remedies.[137] The difficulties that children face in accessing domestic remedies are well-known, particularly if the domestic legal system does not regard them as having capacity to litigate, and it is surprising that there is no consideration of these problems within the text of the Protocol.[138] A further problem is the question of complaints brought on behalf of children.

---

[133] Optional Protocol 3, Art. 13(1).

[134] At the time of writing, one of the forty-eight parties to Optional Protocol 3, Monaco, has exercised this opt-out.

[135] Optional Protocol 3, Art. 12. At the time of writing, twelve of the forty-eight parties had opted in to this procedure.

[136] See Chapter 12 for discussion of these problems in the domestic context.

[137] Optional Protocol 3, Art. 7.

[138] S. Egan (2014) pp. 214–15. The Committee has shown itself to be aware of these difficulties and willing to look closely at whether domestic litigation is accessible to the child litigants: see esp. the decision adopted in *Sacchi and others* v. *Argentina and others* (Communication No. 104/2019) on 22 September 2021, CRC/C/88/D/104/2019.

A persistent difficulty with children's rights litigation is the ease with which children's rights can be dominated by the interests of those acting 'on behalf' of the child.[139] Although the child's consent is required before a complaint can be lodged on their behalf,[140] there is little attention to how to ensure that the child's consent is genuine and informed, or how to ensure that the child's complaint is not subsumed into the interests of adults, particularly where those adults are the child's parents.[141] The Protocol does identify the best interests of the child and the need to have regard to the rights and views of the child as general principles to guide the Committee in its application. Creative application of these principles may allow the Committee to create a child-focused system, although it is only with experience that this can be tested.

If these difficulties can be overcome, the Protocol has the potential to play an important role in developing understanding and implementation of the Convention. To achieve this will require sufficient resources, particularly given the problems that the Committee has faced in managing the workload generated by the reporting requirement. At the time of writing, the Committee had adopted decisions in thirty-nine cases and already had seventy-seven applications pending before it,[142] suggesting that adequate resourcing is required before the Committee is able to fulfil the potential of the Protocol. The need to avoid delay is particularly important for children, who may fail to receive an effective remedy during their childhood if they have to endure lengthy waits having already exhausted domestic procedures. Deciding these cases will also require the Committee to address some of the gaps and inconsistencies within the CRC. For example, many of the pending cases concern questions of migration, which are largely unaddressed within the text of the CRC. In deciding these applications, the Committee has the potential to revitalise the Convention and give guidance to national courts and institutions. A good example of such a case is the decisions in *Sacchi and others* v. *Argentina and others*,[143] in which the Committee heard a set of joined claims by sixteen children against five nations. The authors of the complaint claimed that the state parties had caused, perpetuated and failed to take effective action on climate change, thereby violating their rights under Articles 6, 24 and 30 of the CRC. Although the complaints were found inadmissible for failure to exhaust domestic remedies, the Committee made a number of findings in favour of the child authors and committed to drafting a new General Comment concerning children's rights and the environment, on which the authors would be invited to comment. Although unsuccessful, the complaints show the potential for the

---

[139] Discussed in Chapter 12.   [140] Optional Protocol 3, Art. 5.
[141] R. Smith (2014) pp. 189–90.
[142] Information on applications decided by and pending before the Committee is available from its website: www.ohchr.org/EN/HRBodies/CRC/Pages/CRCIndex.aspx.
[143] The Committee adopted similar decisions in relation to each state party. See e.g. the decision adopted on 22 September 2021 in *Sacchi and others* v. *Argentina and others* (Communication No. 104/2019), CRC/C/88/D/104/2019.

optional protocol to be used in a dynamic process through which the Committee can give detailed interpretation of the application of the CRC in areas not originally contemplated when the Convention was drafted.

(F) Success or Failure?

The CRC has, in many ways, been a remarkable success. It has been ratified by every country in the world, bar the US;[144] a record unmatched by any other international convention. This near universal consensus gives the Convention considerable moral authority and establishes beyond doubt the position of children as rights-holders in international law. This is a considerable achievement, particularly given the complexity and sensitivity of its subject matter and the divergence of social, religious, political and developmental conditions in the state parties. The CRC's success is not merely one of rhetoric. The CRC has been enormously influential – indeed, to many, it is the touchstone for children's rights throughout the world. It constitutes the most comprehensive list of human rights created for a specific group. It is increasingly referred to by regional courts, notably the Inter-American Court of Human Rights and the ECtHR, in applying regional human rights law to children.[145] Similarly, the European Union is embedding the CRC within its legislation,[146] and has included the core principles of children's best interests and the right to be heard within the Charter of Fundamental Rights.[147] Many domestic courts, when dealing with children's cases, are now quite commonly drawing attention to its provisions and using them as an interpretive guide even in those jurisdictions where the CRC has not been incorporated into domestic law.[148]

Despite this near-universal acclaim, the Convention is not without its critics, although some are based on an incorrect interpretation of its provisions and of its underlying aims. The reluctance of the US to ratify the CRC is partly based on a fear that it will undermine parents' authority over their children through 'its sweeping and unprecedented creation of autonomy rights for children [which] may, in the long run, threaten children's well being'.[149] This criticism neglects the central place that the CRC gives to the family as 'the fundamental group of society' and the protection given to both the responsibilities of parents and the protection of the relationships between parents and children.[150] Indeed, as Michael Freeman points out, if anything, the CRC is over-protective of parents' rights.[151] From a different perspective, others argue that by encouraging children's independence, the Convention is attempting to impose on non-industrialised countries the ideas and values of the richer

---

[144] The US is a signatory to the Convention, but has not ratified it.
[145] T. Liefaard and J. Doek (2015). See further discussion of the ECtHR's use of the CRC below.
[146] H. Stalford (2012) esp. pp. 32–6.   [147] Art. 24.
[148] T. Liefaard and J. Doek (2015). See Chapter 3 for further discussion of the use of the CRC in the English courts.
[149] R. Wilkins (2004) p. 998.   [150] E.g. Arts 5 and 9(1).   [151] Freeman (2014) p. 6.

Western states.[152] There are also those who consider that while the ruling elites in many non-Western countries enthusiastically endorse the Western human rights ideals implicit in the CRC, the local populations have very different cultural norms.[153] The compromises and ambiguities within the texts, together with large numbers of reservations and interpretive declarations made on ratification, suggest that the impression of near-universal consensus created by the number of state parties may be illusory in practice, particularly in those areas of controversy such as freedom of religion.

Whether the CRC is successful in the future will depend in part on addressing these ambiguities in meaning and interpreting the ageing Convention to maintain its continued relevance.[154] The Convention omits many subjects which would certainly have been covered had it been drafted today; its age means that in the text of the Convention no attention is given to children's rights in the digital world, nor to developments in reproduction, while little mention is made of environmental harm. Further, the Convention has little to say on the specific problems faced by different groups of children – for example, those facing children on the basis of sexuality, gender or indigenous status, or as migrants. Critics writing from an intersectional perspective argue that by treating children as a homogenous group, the CRC neglects the divergent experiences of children with very different experiences and identities.[155] The age of the Convention also means that it presents an image of childhood which may need to be reassessed in the light of developments in neurobiological science.[156] The Committee is increasingly using General Comments to address some of these gaps and ambiguities;[157] the individual communications procedure and increased reference to the CRC in regional and domestic courts also offers the opportunity for interpretation and clarity. A further problem for implementation is the jurisprudential doubt about the true status of some of the 'rights' listed in the Convention.[158] It has been argued that although acceptable as moral claims, many of the 'rights' listed by the Convention are too vague to be translated into enforceable international or domestic law.[159] Indeed, Wellman argues that by asserting so many 'legal rights' on behalf of children, the Convention contributes to the process of rights 'devaluation'.[160] Many of the rights listed are written in aspirational language, stating what *should* happen if governments were to take children's needs seriously. Indeed, as noted above, Article 4 clearly acknowledges that the resource implications of such provisions may rule out their immediate or

---

[152] S. Timimi (2006) p. 38. See Tobin (2013) for a response to this criticism.

[153] S. Harris-Short (2003).   [154] P. Veerman (2010).   [155] K. Hanson and N. Peleg (2020).

[156] Discussed further in Chapter 9.

[157] E.g. the Committee has produced a General Comment on children's rights in the digital environment: Committee on the Rights of the Child (2021).

[158] Discussed in Chapter 1.

[159] E.g. Arts 23, 24 and 27. Although cases such as the complaint in *Sacchi and others* v. *Argentina and others* (Communication No. 104/2019) (discussed above) demonstrate the potential that such rights have for enforcement in practice.

[160] C. Wellman (1999) esp. ch. 7.

even long-term fulfilment. Its use of the future tense, when enlarging on states' obligations under these articles, emphasises this realism.[161] Where rights are expressed in aspirational, declaratory language, it can be difficult to determine whether they are justiciable and so legally enforceable.[162] This lack of clarity can undermine the CRC's usefulness as a practical monitoring tool.[163] Nevertheless, many authors consider that the 'rhetoric of rights' is justified,[164] expressing the conviction that these aspirations ought to be recognised by states here and now as potential rights and that they provide guides to present policies.[165] Eekelaar is surely right to argue that the symbolism of the CRC is its most successful achievement. In his view, 'to recognize people as having rights from the moment of their birth continuously into adulthood could turn out, politically, to be the most radical step of all'.[166] This recognition of children as rights-holders applies not only to the rights protected by the CRC itself, but also to the full range of national, regional and international human rights that protect all people. The challenge remains to turn this recognition of children as rights-holders into practical reality. In meeting this challenge, as Michael Freeman observes, the CRC 'should be seen as a beginning rather than the final word on children's rights'.[167]

(6) The European Convention on Human Rights

(A) The Post-War Background

On 2 October 2000, the HRA 1998 incorporated the ECHR into the domestic law of the UK. The importance of this change can only be fully appreciated if it is placed within the Convention's own historical context. The ECHR was a product of the late 1940s, a period when there was considerable enthusiasm for the concept of a united Europe – an enthusiasm provoked by the destructive havoc wreaked on European countries by the Second World War. The Statute on the Council of Europe, signed in 1949, provided for a Committee of Ministers and a Parliamentary Assembly. The Council of Europe soon initiated and became involved in many cultural, economic and scientific activities and in 1961 adopted the European Social Charter with a view to protecting economic and social rights.[168] Possibly its greatest achievement in the human rights field, however, was to adopt the ECHR, signed in 1950.

---

[161] See also Art. 24(4), which directs states, regarding children's health rights, to 'promote and encourage international cooperation *with a view to achieving progressively* the full realization of the right recognized in the present article' (emphasis added).

[162] A. MacDonald (2011) pp. 88–93. See also A. Nolan (2014) for consideration of litigating children's socio-economic rights.

[163] U. Kilkelly and L. Lundy (2006) pp. 335–8.   [164] Discussed in Chapter 1.

[165] J. Feinberg (1980) p. 153; M. Minow (1987) p. 1887.   [166] J. Eekelaar (1992) p. 234.

[167] M. Freeman (2016) p. 388.

[168] In 1996, the Charter was revised to create the Revised European Social Charter; this recognises a number of specific rights for children, most notable the right to protection (Art. 7) and the right to social, legal and economic protection (Art. 17).

The ECHR reflected a revived interest, in the late 1940s, in the natural rights theories of an earlier generation of political philosophers.[169] Strongly influenced by the Universal Declaration of Human Rights 1948,[170] the intention was to guarantee certain inalienable freedoms, namely those first generation civil and political rights considered essential to life in a civilised society. Consequently, the Convention's aims are relatively limited. Its main focus is to prevent governments from interfering with certain fundamental but negative liberties, rather than obliging them to promote, in positive ways, people's civil, economic, social and cultural rights.[171] Overarching those listed is Article 14, which has no independent existence,[172] but which governs the interpretation of all the other rights, ensuring that they are all secured 'without discrimination on any ground such as sex, race, colour, language, religion, political or other opinion, national or social origin, association with a national minority, property, birth or other status'.

The ECHR quickly became immensely influential, largely because it was the first international instrument of its kind to provide a mechanism for its own interpretation and enforcement. The Commission and Court of Human Rights were established to receive and examine complaints about infringements of the Convention by state parties, thereby providing an authoritative interpretation of its terms.[173] This special feature undoubtedly enhanced the Convention's reputation for being one of the world's foremost human rights instruments. The original complicated procedure[174] was simplified in 1998,[175] with the part-time Commission and court being replaced by a single full-time court, which has thereafter decided both on the admissibility and merits of each case. In the event of the court finding a violation of the Convention, it can order adequate reparation,[176] but in practice its most important function is often to bring it to the attention of the state in question, together with the need for a change in its domestic law.

---

[169] Discussed above.   [170] Arts 1–21.

[171] Protocol 1, Art. 2 is a notable exception, in so far as it protects a social welfare right, the right to education.

[172] An infringement of Art. 14 cannot be complained about discretely, it must instead be linked with one of the other articles. A freestanding prohibition on discrimination is contained in Protocol 12 to the ECHR. The UK has not signed or ratified Protocol 12 and it does not form part of the rights protected by the HRA 1998.

[173] The ECtHR was established in 1959.

[174] Whereby the European Commission on Human Rights (EComHR) investigated and filtered out manifestly ill-founded applications before referring well-founded cases to the ECtHR for adjudication.

[175] The current system was implemented by Protocol 11 to the ECHR, which came into force on 1 November 1998.

[176] Unless a friendly settlement is reached between the two parties.

(B) The European Convention on Human Rights and Its Interpretation – Strengths and Weaknesses for Children

(i) Offsetting the Convention's Narrow Focus

The text of the ECHR was drafted at a point where the concept of children's rights in international law was at an embryonic stage, predating even the, relatively limited, 1959 UN Declaration of the Rights of the Child.[177] In consequence, the list of rights set out in the ECHR looks relatively unprepossessing so far as children are concerned. Indeed, as Alston and Tobin observe, 'it contains not a single provision which is specifically addressed to children'.[178] A fundamental problem is that its very limited scope prevents its addressing the wide variety of children's needs. With the exception of Protocol 1, Article 2 (A2P1) of the ECHR, which protects the right to education, the Convention is principally concerned with civil and political rights – the basic freedoms deemed essential to individual autonomy and to privacy from state interference, such as freedom from torture and the right to a fair trial. Unlike the CRC, which guarantees both children's basic civil and political freedoms and their social, economic and cultural rights, the ECHR primarily seeks to protect individuals from state interference with their lives. Civil and political rights of this kind are usually relatively unimportant to those children who are brought up in the protected environment of their own homes. This probably explains why there have been relatively few applications taken to the ECtHR testing the scope of children's right to enjoy some of the more traditional political and civil rights.[179]

Some of the more obvious weaknesses of the Convention have, however, been addressed by the ECtHR interpreting its provisions in a surprisingly purposeful way. An imaginative interpretation of its awkwardly worded provisions has produced unexpectedly effective protection for children. Many parents might balk at the suggestion that using physical punishment could, in some circumstances, be described as a form of 'torture' or even as 'inhuman or degrading treatment'. Nevertheless, Article 3 has been pressed into service to protect children from severe forms of physical punishment.[180] Equally, it is unlikely that the draftsmen of the Convention ever considered the need to prevent parental child abuse. But through a combination of Articles 2, 3 and 8, the Convention now imposes an obligation on child welfare authorities to protect children from abusive treatment.[181]

An increasingly broad interpretation of the concept of respect for a person's private and family life, as protected by Article 8, has probably borne the most

---

[177] See discussion above.   [178] P. Alston and J. Tobin (2005) p. 16.

[179] J. Fortin (2004) pp. 254–6.

[180] *A v. United Kingdom (Human Rights: Punishment of Child)* [1998] 2 FLR 959; discussed further in Chapter 4.

[181] *Z v. United Kingdom* [2001] 2 FLR 612, esp. at [73]–[75]. While Art. 2 protects children from life-threatening abuse, Art. 3 protects them from abusive treatment amounting to inhuman or degrading treatment and Art. 8 protects them from infringements of their physical integrity.

fruit, so far as children are concerned. The concept of family life itself has been interpreted flexibly, so that it protects the relationships between children and unmarried, as well as married, parents,[182] and their relationships with other members of de facto family groupings.[183] The protection Article 8 offers family life is not only substantive, but procedural as well. Thus, any form of decision-making, judicial or administrative, which might infringe it is within its scope.[184] The right to respect for private life has also been widely interpreted. It has secured for children the right to obtain information about themselves held by any public agencies which enables them to know and understand their childhood and early development.[185] It also recognises their need to have uncertainty over their personal identity (arising from ignorance of their parents' identity) eliminated without unnecessary delay.[186] Its interpretation to include respect for private sexual life has ensured equality of the age of consent regardless of the young person's sexuality.[187]

Arguably, the full protection that Article 8 could offer children, through the concept of respect for their private life, has not yet been fully realised. The ECtHR's recent jurisprudence exploring this aspect of the article's protection has been in the context of adults' claims. But, as Munby J has pointed out, it also has considerable potential for protecting children in a variety of ways.[188] Since respect for a person's private life includes psychological integrity, its protection should enable children not only to live their own personal lives as they choose, but also to establish relationships with others. According to the case law, Article 8 protects their right to develop their own personalities free from interference,[189] and with their mental stability fully preserved.[190] Indeed, Munby J suggests 'that a child's Article 8 rights may be engaged if he is being brought up in surroundings that isolate him socially or confine or stultify him emotionally'.[191] The ECtHR's affirmation that the notion of personal autonomy is an important principle underlying the interpretation of Article 8[192] also has an obvious relevance for adolescents, particularly in the context of unwanted medical treatment.[193]

---

[182] *Marckx* v. *Belgium* (1979) 2 EHRR 330.

[183] E.g. inter alia: *X, Y and Z* v. *United Kingdom* [1997] 2 FLR 892 (transsexual parent); *Marckx* v. *Belgium* (1979) 2 EHRR 330 (grandparent); *Boyle* v. *United Kingdom* (1994) 19 EHRR 179 (uncle).

[184] *McMichael* v. *United Kingdom* (1995) 20 EHRR 205; *W* v. *United Kingdom* (1988) 10 EHRR 29; *Venema* v. *Netherlands* [2003] 1 FLR 552; *B* v. *United Kingdom* (1998) 10 EHRR 87.

[185] *Gaskin* v. *United Kingdom* (1989) 12 EHRR 36; J. Fortin (1999) pp. 362–3.

[186] *Mikulic* v. *Croatia* [2002] 1 FCR 720.

[187] *Sutherland* v. *United Kingdom* (1997) 24 EHRR CD 22 led to the introduction of the Sexual Offences (Amendment) Act 2000, which lowered the age of consent to homosexual activity from 18 years to 16 years.

[188] J. Munby (2004) pp. 341–2; and in *Re Roddy (A Child) (Identification: Restriction on Publication)* [2003] EWHC 2927 (Fam), [2004] 2 FLR 949, at [29]–[30].

[189] *Niemitz* v. *Germany* (1993) 16 EHRR 97, at [29]; *Botta* v. *Italy* (1998) 26 EHRR 97, at [32].

[190] *Bensaid* v. *United Kingdom* (2001) 33 EHRR 1, at [47].   [191] J. Munby (2004) p. 341.

[192] *Pretty* v. *United Kingdom* [2002] 2 FLR 45, at [61].   [193] Discussed further in Chapter 9.

Three particular aspects of Strasbourg's interpretive approach have been especially important in reading the text of the ECHR to include children: reference to international instruments; the imposition of positive obligations; and use of best interests. Although the approach of the ECtHR is sometimes inconsistent, each of these has had a significant impact in creating far more effective protection for children's rights than the limited text of the Convention would suggest and the contribution of each of these aspects will be considered in turn.

(ii) International Law as an Interpretive Tool

The ECtHR has increasingly looked to international obligations in its interpretation and application of a wide range of Convention rights. This approach is captured in the Grand Chamber decision of *Neulinger and Shuruk v. Switzerland*, in which the court observed that:

> The Convention cannot be interpreted in a vacuum but must be interpreted in harmony with the general principles of international law. Account should be taken, as indicated in art.31(3)(c) of the Vienna Convention on the Law of Treaties of 1969, of 'any relevant rules of international law applicable in the relations between the parties', and in particular the rules concerning the international protection of human rights.[194]

The ECtHR's use of international law is not merely limited to resolving uncertainty; the court takes into account evolving norms of international law to ensure that the ECHR remains practical, effective and harmonious.[195] The ECtHR has drawn on international law as an interpretive tool even in cases in which the state in question has not ratified the relevant instrument.[196] This has been explained on the basis that the court is not enforcing the obligation itself, but interpreting the ECHR to be consistent with the prevailing international standards.

Most importantly for children, there has been a marked increase in the ECtHR's reference to the CRC in interpreting the provisions of the ECHR for children.[197] Arguably, even in those cases that do not refer to the CRC directly, its provisions have been influential in setting norms in the Strasbourg approach to children's cases, particularly in relation to the CRC, Article 3 best interests

---

[194] *Neulinger and Shuruk v. Switzerland* (2012) 54 EHRR 31, at [131]. As discussed below, the actual use of international law in *Neulinger* has been controversial, in that the court's use of children's best interests could be read so as to undermine the principle of summary return in the Hague Convention on the Civil Aspects of Child Abduction.

[195] *Demir v. Turkey* (2008) 48 EHRR 1272, esp. at [66]–[68].

[196] *NTS v. Georgia* [2017] 1 FLR 898, at [76]: the European Convention on the Exercise of Children's Rights had not been ratified by Georgia but was a 'useful tool for the interpretation of relevant principles'.

[197] A. Jacobsen (2016) provides a statistical analysis of the use of the CRC in ECHR judgments in the 10 years from 2005–14, noting a sharp increase in references after 2010. Examples include: *X v. Latvia* (2014) 59 EHRR 3, at [37]; *Neulinger and Shuruk v. Switzerland* (2012) 54 EHRR 31, at [48]; *X v. Austria* (2013) 57 EHRR 405, at [48].

principle and the Article 12 right to be heard.[198] The influence of international law extends beyond the CRC to other instruments protecting the rights of children, such as the European Convention on the Adoption of Children[199] and the UN Standard Minimum Rules for the Administration of Juvenile Justice (the 'Beijing Rules').[200] This approach offers considerable scope for the ECtHR to interpret the ECHR dynamically to remedy some of the lacunae left by the failure to consider children in the drafting of the original text. In some cases, the court limits itself to a brief and formal survey of the relevant international instruments at the start of the case, but makes no further reference to those provisions,[201] making it difficult to assess whether the international law has made a discernible impact to the interpretation and application of the ECHR. In others, the use of international law has clearly had a material effect on the reasoning of the court and achieved considerable practical protection for children's rights. For example, in *Tlapak* v. *Germany*,[202] a case concerning corporal punishment, the ECtHR engaged in detailed analysis of the requirements of the CRC, including its interpretation in the CRC Committee's General Comments, as well as drawing on the European Social Charter. The CRC Committee's robust interpretation of the CRC as prohibiting all forms of violence against children was influential in the ECtHR's finding that that the treatment of the children fell within the scope of Article 3 of the ECHR[203] despite its earlier case law suggesting that a higher degree of physical or mental suffering was required.[204]

Cases such as *Tlapak* demonstrate the potential of the ECtHR to utilise international law to transform the limited text of the ECHR and to offer greater protection for children. There are, however, considerable limitations to the extent to which the court can incorporate international law on children's rights into its reading of the ECHR. Most importantly, the narrow range of rights protected by the ECHR imposes clear constraints on the reach of the interpretive approach. Many of the rights protected by the CRC, particularly those concerning social and economic rights, have no corresponding provision under the ECHR through which they might operate to inform its interpretation. The use of interpretation is influential within its sphere, but cannot operate as an indirect route to incorporation of the CRC as a whole into the ECHR.

---

[198] U. Kilkelly (2014).

[199] *Pini and Bertani; Manera and Atripaldi* v. *Romania* [2005] 2 FLR 596, at [100] and [139], the case also references the CRC and the Hague Convention on Protection of Children and Co-operation in Respect of Intercountry Adoption.

[200] *T* v. *United Kingdom* (2000) 20 EHRR 121, at [41] and [71]–[75]. The case also refers to the CRC and to the Committee's Concluding Observations on the UK's compliance with the CRC.

[201] A. Jacobsen (2016) p. 554; e.g. *Sahin* v. *Germany; Sommerfeld v Germany* [2002] 1 FLR 119, [2003] 2 FLR 671.

[202] [2018] ECHR 262, discussed further in Chapter 4.

[203] Ibid. at [86] and in finding that the decision of the national authorities to remove the children pursued a legitimate aim at [79].

[204] Ibid. at [90]. Although, as discussed further in Chapter 4, the ECtHR would only go so far as to say that it would be commendable if member states prohibit in law all forms of corporal punishment of children rather than finding a prohibition on corporal punishment in ECHR, Art. 3.

(iii) Positive Obligations

As can be seen, the Strasbourg jurisprudence has forcefully extended the protection available to children beyond the limitations in its original drafting. The Convention's ability to promote children's rights has also been greatly strengthened through the notion of positive obligations attaching to many of its provisions.[205] Thus, the view has been taken by the ECtHR that certain parts of the Convention not only compel states to abstain from interfering with the rights they protect, they also require them to take active steps to secure these rights effectively. Thus, it is not enough for states to refrain from the intentional and unlawful killing of a child under Article 2, they must also take appropriate steps to safeguard his or her life.[206] Local authorities must therefore protect children effectively from abusive parental behaviour, in order to fulfil their positive obligations under Article 3 to protect children against inhuman or degrading treatment. They must not stand back and allow abuse that they are aware of to continue, they must intervene to prevent its continuation.[207] Similarly, rather than merely refraining from interfering with a child's private life under Article 8, a state must take appropriate steps to ensure that laws are in place to make such a right practical and effective,[208] including those safeguarding his or her right to physical integrity.[209] The positive obligations attaching to Article 8 are particularly relevant in cases involving parents who, having successfully obtained orders in the domestic courts aimed at reuniting them with their children, find it impossible to enforce such orders, due to the recalcitrance of the children's carers. In such cases, the ECtHR has repeatedly stressed that although not absolute,[210] the state has a positive obligation to take all necessary steps as can reasonably be demanded in the circumstances of the case to facilitate such a reunion, and as swiftly as possible.[211]

It is through employing the concept of positive obligations that Strasbourg has achieved a truly dramatic extension of its jurisdiction; going beyond 'vertical application', whereby individuals are only protected from public agencies, to include a 'horizontal approach', protecting rights in the realm of private relationships. The development of positive obligations with horizontal application has particularly far-ranging implications for children, whose rights and interests are often hidden behind the veil of family privacy,[212]

---

[205] U. Kilkelly (2010).   [206] *Osman* v. *United Kingdom* [1999] 1 FLR 193, at [115].

[207] *Z* v. *United Kingdom* [2001] 2 FLR 612, at [73]–[74]; *Mayeka* v. *Belgium* [2006] 3 FCR 367, at [53].

[208] *Marckx* v. *Belgium* (1979) 2 EHRR 330, at [31]; the Convention is intended to guarantee rights which are not merely 'theoretical and illusory', but 'practical and effective'.

[209] E.g. *X and Y* v. *Netherlands* (1985) 8 EHRR 235.

[210] E.g. if the child strongly opposes such a reunion, as in *Hokkanen* v. *Finland* (1995) 19 EHRR 139.

[211] E.g. *Ignaccolo-Zenide* v. *Romania* (2001) 31 EHRR 7, at [94]–[96] and [102]; discussed further in Chapter 6.

[212] See discussion in Chapter 4.

rather than directly threatened by interference from the state. By requiring states to establish laws ensuring that private individuals behave towards one another in a way which does not infringe their rights under the articles in question, the ECHR can pierce this veil of family privacy and offer effective protection for children in the home and from other individuals. For example, the ECtHR has ruled that Article 3 does not merely require public authorities like schools to refrain from punishing children in a way which infringes their right to freedom from inhuman or degrading treatment.[213] States must also ensure that children are protected from such behaviour in the privacy of their own homes, even when it is administered by their parents under the guise of physical punishment.[214] Similarly, while Article 8 clearly protects individuals against arbitrary interference by public authorities, states are also under a positive obligation to adopt measures to ensure that private individuals respect one another's private and family life and bodily integrity. So, for example, the state is required to have effective systems to prosecute sexual abuse[215] and to protect children from abuse and neglect.[216] In this way, the ECtHR has recognised that state intervention to protect children from harm in the 'private' sphere is essential to protecting their rights in practice.

(iv) No 'Welfare or Best Interests' Formula

The absence of a formula referring to the child's best interests in the text of the ECHR is a stark reminder of the failure to consider children in the drafting of the Convention. One of the most important interpretive achievements of the ECtHR has been the integration of best interests into the application of the Convention. This is, in part, a reflection of the increased use of international law at Strasbourg; as the court observed in *Neulinger and Shuruk v. Switzerland*:

> there is currently a broad consensus – including in international law – in support of the idea that in all decisions concerning children, their best interests must be paramount.[217]

The best interests principle in the CRC applies to *all* actions concerning children and is relevant to the interpretation of all CRC rights; the Strasbourg court has also recognised its application to a range of ECHR rights.[218] Nonetheless, most of the ECHR cases concerning children's best interests have, like *Neulinger* itself, concentrated on the right to family

---

[213] Successful challenges taken to the ECtHR based on Art. 3 led to legislation abolishing the use of physical punishment in all schools; discussed further in Chapter 4.

[214] *A v. United Kingdom (Human Rights: Punishment of Child)* [1998] 2 FLR 959.

[215] *X and Y v. Netherlands* (1985) 8 EHRR 235.   [216] *Z v. United Kingdom* [2001] 2 FLR 612.

[217] *Neulinger and Shuruk v. Switzerland* (2012) 54 EHRR 31, at [135]; the use of the word 'paramount' is discussed further below.

[218] E.g. *SL v. Croatia* (13712/11), 7 May 2015 (best interests applied in relation to property rights under ECHR, Protocol 1, Art. 1); *X v. Austria* (2013) 57 EHRR 405 (best interests applied in a case concerning discrimination under ECHR, Art. 14).

life under Article 8. These cases normally involve a conflict between the rights of several family members; the question for the ECtHR is usually whether the state has fulfilled its positive obligation to achieve a 'fair balance' between those rights. Within these parameters, the court goes as far as it can to give children's interests a special weighting. Thus, it maintains that while a fair balance must be struck between the interests of the child, those of the parent and the public interest,[219] 'crucial'[220] or 'particular'[221] importance is attached:

> to the best interests of the child, which, depending on their nature and serious-ness, may override those of the parent. In particular ... the parent cannot be entitled under article 8 of the Convention to have such measures taken as would harm the child's health and development.[222]

In this way, the ECtHR has compensated for the absence of any best interests formula within the Convention itself.

One issue of controversy is whether the ECtHR treats children's interests as *paramount*, so determining the issue in question,[223] or merely as *a primary* consideration that may be balanced against other considerations, as is the case under Article 3 of the CRC. While the ECtHR has referred to children's rights as being 'paramount' in a number of cases,[224] it seems unlikely that it intends the term to have the same technical meaning as in domestic law. Certainly, the court appears to use the term 'paramount' interchangeably with 'primary', 'crucial' or 'particular' in the case law, even mixing the terms within the same case without seeming to attach any significance to the change in language.[225] It seems clear that the term 'paramount' is not intended to displace the need to find a 'fair balance' between differing rights. This can be seen in *Yousef* v. *Netherlands*, the first case to use the term 'paramount', in which the court also refers to the 'balancing of interests'.[226] Indeed, the ECtHR commonly reverts to the standard and far more familiar formula:

> a fair balance must be struck between the interests of the child and those of the parent and that, in striking such a balance, particular importance must be

---

[219] *Olsson* v. *Sweden (No. 2)* (1992) 17 EHRR 134, at [90].

[220] *Johansen* v. *Denmark* (1996) 23 EHRR 33, at [64].   [221] Ibid. at [78].   [222] Ibid.

[223] As is the case in domestic law in decisions determining a child's upbringing: Children Act 1989, s. 1.

[224] *Yousef* v. *Netherlands* [2003] 1 FLR 210, at [73]; *Kearns* v. *France* [2008] 1 FLR 888, at [79]; *Neulinger and Shuruk* v. *Switzerland* (2012) 54 EHRR 31, at [135]; *YC* v. *United Kingdom* (2012) 55 EHRR 33, at [134].

[225] *Neulinger and Shuruk* v. *Switzerland* (2012) 54 EHRR 31, at [134]–[135]. See also *YC* v. *United Kingdom* (2012) 55 EHRR 33, at [134], in which the court uses the term 'paramount', but cites *Johansen* v. *Denmark* (1996) 23 EHRR 33, which uses 'particular' as authority for this proposition.

[226] [2003] 1 FLR 210, at [73]. See also *Kearns* v. *France* [2008] 1 FLR 888, at [79]: 'In striking a balance between these different interests, the child's best interests should be paramount.'

attached to the best interests of the child which, depending on their nature and seriousness, may override those of the parent.[227]

Despite the confusion of language, the ECtHR's position appears to be tolerably clear: the court will balance the different rights and interests, but give the child's interests primary importance within the balancing exercise. Children's interests do not displace adult rights from entering the balancing process in the first place, but will frequently prevail over those rights as a *result* of the balancing exercise.[228] It is, however, not inevitable that they will do so.[229] This is made clear by the Grand Chamber decision in *Strand Lobben* v. *Norway*,[230] in which Norway was found to have violated the Article 8 rights of a birth mother in placing her child for adoption. In particular, the Grand Chamber was critical of Norway for failing to perform a 'genuine balancing exercise between the interests of the child and his biological family'.[231] As the dissenting judges in this case observed, this highlights a core difference between the ECHR, which is rooted in the protection of the rights of everyone, and the CRC which is 'focused on strengthening and protecting children as holders of distinct individual rights'.[232]

The ECtHR has repeatedly stressed that in balancing rights in children's cases its task is not to substitute its decision-making for that of the domestic courts.[233] The ECtHR has also stressed that countries have a wide margin of appreciation when assessing the justification for the infringement.[234] The ECtHR must consider whether the domestic court has balanced the parties' rights against each other appropriately and, in so doing, whether the measures taken were relevant and sufficient for the purposes of Article 8(2).[235] But the ECtHR is aware that such a decision will have been influenced largely by the domestic court's assessment of how to promote the child's best interests and that that decision will have been reached with the court having had the benefit of seeing the adults concerned and receiving welfare reports.[236] In other words, it does not normally second guess the domestic court's decision over whether it was necessary to infringe an

---

[227] S. Choudhry (2003) pp. 130–1. Inter alia: *Hoppe* v. *Germany* [2003] 1 FLR 384, at [49]; *Görgülü* v. *Germany* [2004] 1 FLR 894, at [43]; *Süss* v. *Germany* [2006] 1 FLR 522, at [88].

[228] E.g. *Neulinger and Shuruk* v. *Switzerland* (2012) 54 EHRR 31, at [134], is clear that, despite the interests of the child being described as paramount, the parent's interests in contact with the child remained a factor in the balance.

[229] Despite some suggestion to the contrary in cases such as *R* v. *United Kingdom* (2012) 54 EHRR 2, at [77], where it was stated that the interests of the parents 'must inevitably give way to that of the child' when making a freeing order in adoption proceedings. Nonetheless, in the same paragraph, the court refers to the need for balancing and concludes that the process gave sufficient respect to the rights of all concerned.

[230] [2020] 1 FLR 297.   [231] Ibid. at [220].

[232] Ibid., dissenting opinion, at [9]. CRC, Art. 21 obliges states to ensure that the best interests of the child are paramount in adoption decisions.

[233] *Sahin* v.*Germany; Sommerfeld v Germany* [2002] 1 FLR 119, [2003] 2 FLR 671.

[234] Ibid. at [65].

[235] Inter alia: *Hokkanen* v. *Finland* (1995) 19 EHRR 139, at [55]; *Sahin* v. *Germany; Sommerfeld v Germany* [2002] 1 FLR 119, [2003] 2 FLR 671, at [64].

[236] E.g. *Sahin* v. *Germany; Sommerfeld v Germany* [2002] 1 FLR 119, [2003] 2 FLR 671, at [64].

applicant's rights in the first place or the balance achieved by the domestic court between the parents' interests and those of the child. In public law cases, it only rarely criticises the reasons for a child being taken into state care; similarly, in private law cases, it only rarely criticises the reasons for making an order in favour of one parent, as opposed to the other. Some decisions attract more intense scrutiny. In particular, the ECtHR tends to apply a narrower margin of appreciation when considering whether the state has made sufficient efforts to ensure the child is reintegrated into his or her family after being removed into care, or to avoid a non-resident parent remaining out of contact with his child.[237] Nonetheless, in most cases, the ECtHR will not carry out the balancing exercise afresh, but will scrutinise carefully *how* the domestic decision was reached – whether the decision-making process, seen as a whole, provided the applicant with the requisite protection of his or her interests.[238] In some cases, the distinction between review of the process and review of the decision itself can seem rather fine, as the scrutiny of process employed is sufficiently intense to effectively become a rebalancing by the ECtHR itself. This was arguably the case in the Grand Chamber decision in *Jeunesse* v. *Netherlands*, which concerned a decision to deport the mother of three children.[239] The court accepted that domestic courts had considered the interests of the children in general terms, but found that such a case required more detailed assessment of the evidence and detailed implications of removal for the children.[240] Failure to consider the children's interests properly led directly to a finding that insufficient weight had been given to the children's interests and that there had been a breach of Article 8, despite the wide margin of appreciation usually given in immigration cases. Similarly, in a number of abduction cases, the court has found a breach of Article 8 where there has been insufficient in-depth[241] or 'effective'[242] consideration of the interests of the child by the domestic courts. In these cases, the intense scrutiny of the domestic process effectively permits the court to draw its own balance on the weight to be given to the rights themselves.

The ECtHR's use of the best interest principle has undoubtedly succeeded in giving children's interests greater prominence and effective protection than the limited text of the ECHR would suggest. An unfortunate consequence of this approach, when combined with the fact that cases involving children tend to be brought by adults rather than the children themselves, is that evidence

---

[237] Inter alia: *Johansen* v. *Norway* (1996) 23 EHRR 33, at [64]; *K and T* v. *Finland* [2001] 2 FLR 707, at [155] and [178]; *Sahin* v. *Germany; Sommerfeld v Germany* [2002] 1 FLR 119, [2003] 2 FLR 671, at [63]; *Elsholz* v. *Germany* [2000] 2 FLR 486, at [49]; *K.B.* v. *Croatia*, App. No. 36216/13, unreported, Judgment of 14 March 2017. Discussed further in Chapter 6.

[238] Inter alia: *W* v. *United Kingdom* (1988) 10 EHRR 29, at [64]; *Haase* v. *Germany* [2004] 2 FLR 39, at [97]; *Elsholz* v. *Germany* [2000] 2 FLR 486, at [52].

[239] (2015) 60 EHRR 17.   [240] Ibid. at [120].

[241] *Neulinger and Shuruk* v. *Switzerland* (2012) 54 EHRR 31.

[242] *X* v. *Latvia* (2014) 59 EHRR 3. The court's approach in these cases has received criticism on the basis that it risks undermining the summary return principle in the Hague Convention on the Civil Aspects of International Child Abduction: see A. Jacobsen (2016).

regarding children tends to be treated by the ECtHR as 'best interests' material, used to counterbalance parents' claims regarding their own rights. Excepting those cases where applications are made on behalf of children themselves, such evidence is therefore not examined to see whether it concerns the child's own rights. In consequence, children's *rights* are sidelined by a paternalistic assessment of their best *interests*.[243] This risk might be mitigated if the ECtHR were to follow the guidance of the CRC Committee that 'an adult's judgment of a child's best interests cannot override the obligation to respect all the child's rights under the Convention' and that assessing children's best interests requires full consideration of their rights.[244]

(v) Articulating Children's Claims?

(a) Differing Approaches

As discussed above, the ECtHR has played an important part in developing the protection available to children under the ECHR. Furthermore, it is increasingly willing to be guided by the principles set out by the CRC, with regular references to its provisions in its decisions. The value of this jurisprudence for children is, however, hampered by the fact that the court often fails to articulate children's claims at all. Applications to the ECtHR which might focus on children's rights will almost inevitably be brought on their behalf by adults, quite simply because most children are too young to cope with the procedural complications of making claims themselves. The adults bringing such applications are usually parents and their claims largely centre on their own rights, rather than those of their children. Thus, in public law cases, parents object to attempts to interfere with what they see as their right to bring up their children, free of state interference. In private law cases, they will often argue that their right to enjoy their children's company under Article 8 has been unnecessarily infringed through the domestic courts favouring the other parent. In both of these cases, the court has rarely articulated the children's rights separately from those of the parents.

A much smaller group of cases involves applications brought by adults, on children's behalf, who are genuinely objecting to the way in which the state has interfered with the children's own rights. There is a stark contrast in the manner in which the two types of challenges are dealt with. Indeed, it is arguable that the ECtHR has played a poor part in championing children's rights, as opposed to those of their parents. Nonetheless, a series of recent cases has shown an increased awareness of the need to articulate the rights of children separately, at least in those cases in which the child is a party.

---

[243] Fortin (2014) pp. 58–9.   [244] Committee on the Rights of the Child (2013) paras 4 and 5.

(b) State Interference

In the context of child protection law, the focus will usually be on the parents' right to family life under Article 8, the wording of which appears to suggest that as long as families are protected from undue state interference, the regulation of family life can be safely left to its adult members.[245] The early case law established a rigidly formal manner of processing such cases.[246] When considering a parent's claim that his or her rights under Article 8 had been infringed, the ECtHR made little attempt to assess the evidence in terms of the child's own rights under the Convention. Evidence suggesting that the child might have suffered considerable harm at the hands of his or her parents was dealt with only within a discussion of whether the infringement of the parents' rights under Article 8(1) of the Convention can be justified under Article 8(2), as being a 'necessary' infringement, with the discussion being couched in terms of the child's best interests.[247] There was therefore no analysis of the infringement of the child's own rights, say under Articles 3 and 8. Although, as considered above, as the ECtHR has developed its jurisprudence on children's interests to give greater weight to them in the balancing exercise, the neglect of their rights continues.[248] The consistent theme in these cases is that adults have rights, while children have interests, albeit 'best' interests.

When reviewing the 'necessity' of the state's intervention (within the terms of Article 8(2)), and asserting the state's wide margin of appreciation when considering the need for state intervention, the ECtHR adopts a viewpoint which starts from the rights of the adult applicants – the parents.[249] As Woolf points out, the child's best interests are sidelined, with the court concentrating on whether the authorities have acted proportionately when interfering with the parents' right to family life.[250] This was certainly the view of Judge Bonello in *EP* v. *Italy*,[251] who passionately opposed the majority decision of the ECtHR, concluding that the Italian authorities had failed to take necessary steps to reunite a mother and her 7-year-old daughter.[252] He pointed to the well-based concerns that the way the mother had constantly sought medical attention for her daughter was pathological and argued:

> The core question, in my view, should have been: did this unfortunate child have a right to a normal family and a happy home once her mother became unable to provide her with those basic minima? Saying, as the majority did, that the child's adoption was wrong is tantamount to saying that this particularly wretched child, did not, for reasons undisclosed, deserve a normal family life.[253]

---

[245] J. Fortin (1999) p. 357.   [246] E.g. *Olsson* v. *Sweden (No. 2)* (1992) 17 EHRR 134.

[247] E.g. *K and T* v. *Finland* [2001] 2 FLR 707, at [154]–[155].

[248] C. Fenton-Glynn (2020) pp. 304–8 charts the developments in ECtHR jurisprudence on child protection.

[249] M. Woolf (2003) pp. 211–12.   [250] Ibid. p. 220.   [251] (2001) 31 EHRR 17.

[252] Judge Bonello's dissent, at [4]–[6].   [253] Ibid. at [13].

Similarly, the court's criticism of state authorities for using emergency powers over-precipitously to protect very young children may, to child-care practitioners, appear to stem from an unduly adult-orientated position. While it is understandable for the ECtHR to stress that removing very young babies from their mothers soon after birth can only be justified by extraordinarily compelling reasons,[254] child welfare authorities are confronted by an obvious dilemma if they doubt a mother's ability to care for her baby.[255] Babies are particularly vulnerable to abuse. While the ECtHR criticises them for unacceptably intervening, they would have been blamed by the public had they not intervened and the child had been harmed.[256] In none of this case law is there any specific mention of the child's own Convention rights which might have counter-balanced those of the parent.

(c) Parental Disputes

When it comes to dealing with disputes between private individuals over children, the ECtHR takes an equally formalistic and adult-centred approach. While children are the focus of such complaints, these applications are brought by adults unhappy about the way in which their right to enjoy their children's company under Article 8 has been infringed through the domestic courts favouring the other parent. Admittedly, the ECtHR considers whether the disputed order can be justified under Article 8(2), by reference to protecting the 'rights and freedoms of others', including the rights of the children concerned. But again, it usually does so without articulating their specific Convention rights, merely assessing the evidence relating to their best interests. Such an approach may lead to a relatively superficial assessment of the child's own position in any given case. Thus, in cases like *Hoffmann* v. *Austria*[257] and *Yousef* v. *Netherlands*,[258] the complexities of the children's own position are hardly referred to. In the first, there is no discussion of the children's own religious rights and, in the second, no mention of the child's own right to retain a relationship

---

[254] *K and T* v. *Finland* [2001] 2 FLR 707, at [168]; *Haase* v. *Germany* [2004] 2 FLR 39, at [102].

[255] E.g. in *K and T* v. *Finland* [2001] 2 FLR 707, the mother was a paranoid schizophrenic with a poor parenting record regarding her older child.

[256] *K and T* v. *Finland*, ibid., per dissenting judges, Judge Palm, joined by Judge Gaukur Jörundsson (see esp. at 752) and Judge Bonello (see esp. at 755). The latter complained that those who had wanted to place the baby beyond reach of harm were now themselves 'branded violators of human rights' (at 756).

[257] (1993) 17 EHRR 293: per ECtHR (five votes to four), by denying the Jehovah's Witness mother custody on the grounds of her religion, the Austrian courts had violated her rights under Art. 8, in conjunction with Art. 14. See also *Palau-Martinez* v. *France* [2004] 2 FLR 810; cf. *Ismailova* v. *Russia* [2008] 1 FLR 533.

[258] [2003] 1 FLR 210: an unmarried father unsuccessfully challenged the Dutch courts' refusal to allow him to recognise or take over the care of his 5-year-old child who was being cared for by her maternal grandparents after her mother's death.

with her father or, indeed, any discussion of her relationship with her maternal grandparents. In *Yousef*, the ECtHR gave the following guidance:

> The court reiterates that in judicial decisions where the rights under Art 8 of parents and those of a child are at stake, the child's rights must be the paramount consideration. If any balancing of interests is necessary, the interests of the child must prevail.[259]

By using the word 'rights' in relation to the child, the court appeared to acknowledge that the child did have rights of her own, but this concept was not developed. Indeed, the use of the word 'interests' was swiftly reverted to – the word employed throughout the remainder of the discussion devoted to the child's own position.

The ECtHR adopts a similarly myopic approach to children's own Convention rights when considering the claims of parents whom states fail to assist adequately with enforcing orders aimed at reuniting them with their children. There is often the additional complication that time has elapsed, and the child him or herself, perhaps due to indoctrination by the residential parent or carer, now refuses contact with the applicant parent.[260] In all of these cases, the ECtHR constantly stresses that:

> Whilst national authorities must do their utmost to facilitate such co-operation [leading to reunion], any obligation to apply coercion in this area must be limited since the ... rights and freedoms of all concerned must be taken into account ... and more particularly the best interests of the child and his or her rights under Art 8 of the Convention.[261]

Nevertheless, this rather vague reference to the child's rights is normally followed by a discussion of the strength of evidence acceding to the child's wishes on the matter, all in the context of finding an outcome which safeguards the child's best interests.[262] Again, there is no systematic analysis of what Convention rights a child might have in circumstances of this kind.

(d) Children's Own Applications

The ECtHR is most likely to explore the full scope of children's own rights within the Convention's framework when the applications are brought on behalf[263] of children themselves. Their rights are then specifically articulated.

---

[259] Ibid. at [73].

[260] E.g. *Hansen* v. *Turkey* [2004] 1 FLR 142; *Wdowiak* v. *Poland* [2017] ECHR 133.

[261] *Kosmopoulou* v. *Greece* [2004] 1 FLR 800, at [45].

[262] E.g. *Süss* v. *Germany* [2006] 1 FLR 522, at [90].

[263] ECHR, Art. 34 requires that claims are brought by those claiming to be a 'victim' of the alleged violation. Claims may be brought by authorised representatives of the victim or, if there is a risk that the alleged violations would not otherwise be heard and the victim denied effective protection of their rights, the court may allow a victim to be represented without their authorisation. Children have been represented by parents and by legal advisors on the basis of this exception: *Lambert and others* v. *France* (Grand Chamber) (2016) 62 EHRR 2, at [89]–[95], sets out the relevant rules and authority. The problem of children's rights being

Thus, the ECtHR has explored the scope of Article 3 when addressing the claims of children objecting to being physically punished in school[264] or at home.[265] Furthermore, while, as noted above, there is a large body of Strasbourg jurisprudence considering parents' complaints over the way in which their children have been removed into state care, a tiny number of applications is also brought on behalf of abused children themselves. These have produced decisions exploring the scope of Articles 2, 3 and 8 of the Convention, all of which offer abused children important forms of protection.[266] Equally well known are the important principles that have emerged from applications brought by young people objecting to being restrained in secure units of various kinds[267] and by young offenders objecting to their methods of trial.[268]

In some cases, because parent and child are both actively involved in a family dispute, it appears almost coincidental who takes a case to Strasbourg. But an application may assume an entirely different set of perspectives when it is the child's application and not that of the parent. Thus, in *Mikulic v. Croatia*,[269] instead of focusing on the lack of effective procedures enabling an unmarried mother to establish the paternity of her child's father and obtain financial support for her child, the ECtHR explored her daughter's own right to respect for her private life within Article 8.[270] It concluded that states should have in place a procedure striking a fair balance between the need of a child to have eliminated without unnecessary delay any uncertainty over his or her personal identity (arising from ignorance of a parent's identity) and those of the alleged father not to be forced into DNA testing.[271]

Unfortunately, even when dealing with individual child applicants, the ECtHR's record is not entirely consistent. In particular, in situations where the parent and child are both applicants, the court has often failed to consider the child's rights separately from those of their parents; it is frequently the case that cases are primarily resolved through consideration of the parents' right, even in circumstances in which it is the child who is most closely affected by the circumstances in question. Thus, in *Valsamis v. Greece*,[272] the ECtHR saw no reason to subject a 12-year-old girl's claim to religious freedom under

---

represented by parents whose interests may conflict with those of the children is considered further below.

[264] E.g. *Tyrer v. United Kingdom* (1979–80) 2 EHRR 1; *Campbell and Cosans v. United Kingdom* (1982) 4 EHRR 293. In the latter case, the parents, who claimed an infringement of the child's Art. 3 rights, fell back on a claim based on their own rights under A2P1 of the ECHR. As discussed in Chapter 4, it was this parental claim that determined the outcome.

[265] *A v. United Kingdom* (1998) 27 EHRR 611.

[266] E.g. *Z v. United Kingdom* [2001] 2 FLR 612; *TP and KM v. United Kingdom* [2001] 2 FLR 549; *E v. United Kingdom* [2002] 3 FCR 700.

[267] E.g. *Bouamar v. Belgium* (1988) 11 EHRR 1; *Koniarska v. United Kingdom*, App. No. 33670/96, 12 October 2000, unreported.

[268] *V and T v. United Kingdom* (1999) 30 EHRR 121; *SC v. United Kingdom* (2004) 40 EHRR 10.

[269] [2002] 1 FCR 720.　　[270] Ibid. at [53]–[55].　　[271] Ibid. at [64]–[66].

[272] (1996) 24 EHRR 294; discussed further in Chapter 8.

Article 9 to a separate examination, once it had considered and rejected her parents' claim that their own religious rights had been infringed, despite the fact that it was the daughter who had been disciplined and who would have been required to take part in activities against her beliefs. Similarly, in *Lautsi v. Italy*,[273] the Grand Chamber devoted extensive attention to the question of whether the mother's rights to respect for her convictions had been breached by the presence of crucifixes in her children's classroom. It was, however, content to dismiss the children's own claims with nothing more than a brief reference to the discussion of the mother's rights, with no consideration to the fact that the right claimed was different and that the children had been directly affected by the situation.[274] There are, however, some later cases in which the court has been willing to recognise the distinct rights of children. *Mennesson v. France*[275] concerned the failure of the state to recognise the legal parent–child relationship following the birth of twins through an international surrogacy arrangement. The court found that there was no breach of the rights of the children or the parents to *family* life, as they had been able to live together as a family with relatively minor inconvenience. There was, however, a breach of the children's right to *private* life as the legal relationship with the parents constituted a core aspect of their identity. At present, such cases are relatively sparse,[276] but do give some grounds for optimism that the court will be able to recognise the distinct position of children, even in cases in which their parents complain of the same conduct.

A far more difficult situation arises in cases in which there is an apparent conflict between a child's rights and those of his or her parent. The ECtHR has found it difficult to disentangle the child's rights in such conflicts. Most notoriously, in *Nielsen v. Denmark*,[277] the court found that a mother's decision to have her son placed in the closed psychiatric ward for five-and-a-half months, against his wishes, despite the fact that he was not mentally ill, was a proper use of her parental rights under Article 8 and that as a result the boy had not been deprived of his liberty contrary to Article 5. The *Nielsen* decision reinforces those who view the Convention as ill-equipped to help courts find an appropriate balance between parents' powers and children's rights.[278] A particular problem then arises if parents whose interests may conflict with

---

[273] (2012) 54 EHRR 3; discussed further in Chapter 8.

[274] *Lautsi v. Italy* (2012) 54 EHRR 3, at [78]. The children's claims concerned their right to education under the first sentence of ECHR, Protocol 1, Art. 2, whereas the mother's concerned her right for that education to respect her convictions under the second sentence of the same provision.

[275] *Mennesson v. France*, App. No. 65192/11, Judgment of 26 June 2014. Discussed in Chapter 5.

[276] A further good example can be seen in *Grzelak v. Poland*, App. No. 7710/02 (2010), in which the court gave its primary attention to the right of the child, before that of the parents, in a case in which the state had refused to make appropriate arrangements for the teaching of a child who had been removed from religious education classes due to his parents' agnostic beliefs.

[277] (1988) 11 EHRR 175.

[278] J. Fortin (2002) p. 22; see Chapters 9 and 10 for further discussion of *Nielsen* and its subsequent interpretation.

those of their child seek to bring a case to Strasbourg on their behalf. Again, the ECtHR has recently shown itself to be more alert to the separate position of children whose parents seek to speak for them. In *Gard v. United Kingdom (Admissibility)*,[279] the court considered an application by parents and their terminally ill baby, objecting to the domestic courts' authorisation of the withdrawal of life-sustaining treatment. The court emphasised that parents have no automatic right to bring claims on behalf of their children, although it could be permitted where there was a risk that the child would otherwise be deprived of effective protection of their rights and where there was no conflict of interests between them. In this case, while the parents were undoubtedly sincere in their representation of their view of their son's rights, the domestic courts had repeatedly found that the parents' plans for his treatment would not be in his best interests. Given this conflict and the fact that he had been represented by an independent guardian throughout the domestic process, the parents were unlikely to be permitted to bring a case on his behalf.[280] The court also refused to allow a case to be brought on behalf of a child in the very different case of *Paradiso v. Italy*.[281] In this case, the child had purportedly been born through a surrogacy agreement, although there was no biological connection to the applicants. The child had been removed from the care of the applicants, who were subject to criminal proceedings in relation to the circumstances surrounding the birth. Given the clear conflict of interest between the child and the intended parents, they were not permitted to bring his rights before the court. Similarly, non-custodial parents[282] and grandparents[283] raising disputes concerning custody and contact have been prevented from representing the rights of the children involved.[284] These cases show a greater awareness by the court of the potential for children's rights to be used in a way that bolsters the interests of adults rather than those of the child themselves.

Although the ECtHR's awareness of the potential conflict of interests between children and parents who seek to act on their behalf is welcome, there remains the significant problem that it is rare for children to be able to bring a case to the

---

[279] (2017) 2 FLR 773.

[280] Ibid. at [59]–[70]; the court did not finally decide on this point as it considered that the case was inadmissible in any event as the claims were manifestly ill-founded.

[281] (2017) 65 EHRR 22, the decision was reversed on a number of points by the Grand Chamber at (2017) 65 EHRR 2. The child's rights were not pursued before the Grand Chamber, which agreed with the initial decision on this point.

[282] E.g. *K.B. v. Croatia*, App. No. 36216/13, unreported, Judgment of 14 March 2017, at [107]–[110].

[283] *Kruškić v. Croatia*, App. No. 10140/13, unreported, Judgment of 25 November 2014, at [99]–[103].

[284] Although the court has emphasised that it does not take a technical approach to such cases and in some cases will allow the child's rights to be presented by an adult who is not responsible for the child under domestic law. E.g. in *A.K. and L v. Croatia* (37956/11) unreported, Judgment of 8 January 2013, at [46]–[50], the child's birth mother was able to raise the child's rights in a case concerning adoption, despite the fact that under national law the adoption had deprived the birth mother of all parental rights and responsibilities.

court without assistance. In a small number of cases, the ECtHR has accepted the standing of wider family members[285] or NGOs[286] to bring cases on children's behalf in which there is a sufficiently close connection to the child and a likelihood that a case would not otherwise be brought. The ECtHR has also taken the unusual step of requesting independent legal representation for a child in a case in which it was clear that there was a significant conflict of interest between the child and the mother, who was also an applicant before the court.[287] The issue of standing and representation of children before the ECtHR is fraught with the potential for conflict of interest. It does, however, require further development to ensure that the ECHR is able to offer protection to children in practice.[288] Without such developments, cases concerning children will either not be brought or will continue to be presented as disputes between adults and the state, with children seldom separately represented, even though it is the child who is often most closely affected by the decision.

(7) The Council of Europe and Children's Rights

As noted above, perhaps the greatest achievement of the Council of Europe was to adopt the ECHR. This had no specific remit to protect children's rights; had it been designed with this purpose in mind, it could have done so far more efficiently. Nevertheless, the Council of Europe has developed its activity on children's rights, including an ambitious *Strategy for the Rights of the Child*.[289] This work is overseen by the Steering Committee for the Rights of the Child, whose terms of reference require it to 'mainstream' children's rights throughout the Council of Europe's work. In doing so, the Committee is to provide expertise on a full range of international children's rights, including the CRC. The Strategy and the work of the Committee go far beyond the limited provision of the rights in the ECHR itself and encompass developing areas of law such as children's rights in a digital environment and the impact of austerity. If implemented effectively, the Strategy has the potential to make an important contribution to the realisation of a wide range of children's rights in practice.

The current Strategy builds on a long history of engagement with children's rights. Much of this has been conducted through Resolutions and Recommendations of the Parliamentary Assembly[290] and of the Committee

---

[285] *NTS* v. *Georgia* [2017] 1 FLR 898.

[286] *LR* v. *North Macedonia*, App. No. 38067/15, unreported, Judgment of 23 January 2020, at [46]–[54].

[287] *A and B* v. *Croatia*, App. No. 7144/15, unreported, Judgment of 20 June 2019. See also the concurring opinion of Judge Wojtyczek in this case and his partially dissenting judgment in *LR* v. *North Macedonia* (ibid.) for further discussion on this point.

[288] Discussed by C. Fenton-Glynn (2019).

[289] Council of Europe (2016). The Council of Europe's ongoing work on children's rights is documented at: www.coe.int/en/web/children/home.

[290] E.g., inter alia: Recommendation 1065 (1987) on the Traffic in Children and Other Forms of Child Exploitation; Recommendation 1071 (1988) Providing Institutional Care for Infants and

of Ministers.[291] While these instruments only have persuasive influence, many reflect a clear and refreshingly forthright approach to the concept of children's rights. Some of these recommendations have achieved concrete results, in so far as they have led to the preparation of binding international instruments whose specific aim is to harmonise the laws of European member states in order to promote children's interests more effectively.[292] Many, as far back as the European Convention on the Legal Status of Children Born Out of Wedlock, have achieved improvements in domestic law. It was the combination of the *Marckx* decision[293] and the UK's ratification of this Convention in 1981 which led the English Law Commission to recommend the widespread reform of the English law relating to children born to unmarried parents.[294] Further influential legal standards include the European Convention on the Exercise of Children's Rights, designed to supplement the CRC by assisting children to exercise their substantive rights set out in the Convention. It recognises that the most practical means for children to claim and enforce their rights is through legal proceedings. The European Convention on the Exercise of Children's Rights therefore confines itself to creating and strengthening procedural rights to be exercised by children when becoming involved in family proceedings.[295] The European Convention on the Protection of Children against Sexual Exploitation and Sexual Abuse[296] has also been influential in requiring criminalisation of defined acts of sexual abuse and in setting

Children; Recommendation 1286 (1996) on a European Strategy for Children; Recommendation 1336 (1997) on Combating Child Labour Exploitation; Recommendation 1666 (2004) on a Europe-wide Ban on Corporal Punishment of Children; Resolution 1468; Recommendation 1723 (2005) on Forced Marriage and Child Marriages; Resolution 1995 (2014) on Ending Child Poverty in Europe; Resolution 2010 (2014) Child-friendly Juvenile Justice: From Rhetoric to Reality; Resolution 2049 (2015) on Social Services in Europe: Legislation and Practice of the Removal of Children from Their Families in Council of Europe Member States.

[291] E.g., inter alia: Recommendation 16 (2001) on the Protection from Sexual Exploitation of Children and Young Adults; Recommendation 20 (2003) on New Ways of Dealing with Juvenile Justice and the Role of Juvenile Justice; Recommendation 5 (2005) on the Rights of Children Living in Residential Institutions; Recommendation 12 (2006) on Empowering Children in the New Information and Communications Environment; Recommendation 7 (2018) on Guidelines for Member States to Respect, Protect and Fulfil the Rights of the Child in the Digital Environment.

[292] Inter alia: the European Convention on the Legal Status of Children Born Out of Wedlock 1975; the European Convention on Recognition and Enforcement of Decisions Concerning Custody of Children and on Restoration of Custody of Children 1980; the European Convention on the Exercise of Children's Rights 1996; the European Convention for the Protection of Human Rights and Dignity of the Human Being with Regard to the Application of Biology and Medicine 1997; the European Convention on Contact Concerning Children 2003; the European Convention on the Protection of Children from Sexual Exploitation and Sexual Abuse 2007; the European Convention on the Adoption of Children (Revised) 2008.

[293] *Marckx* v. *Belgium* (1979) 2 EHRR 330.

[294] Law Commission (1982) paras 4.11–4.12, followed by the Family Law Reform Act 1987.

[295] Council of Europe (1997) p. 18. The Convention has not yet been signed or ratified by the UK.

[296] Finally ratified by the UK in 2018, some 10 years after it was signed. The Convention is widely known as the Lanzarote Convention.

out the standards for effective action. The Convention includes a requirement to criminalise sexual abuse committed abroad in a concerted effort to protect children from 'sex tourism'. A monitoring procedure and information sharing are good examples of the way in which international cooperation on children's rights can be coordinated through the Council of Europe.

Although these developments have been of some significance, calls have been made from time to time for the Council to adopt a specialist treaty dealing with children's rights.[297] Its failure to do so may stem from the view that a European Charter on the Rights of the Child could do little more than reproduce a list similar to that provided by the CRC. Nevertheless, Alston and Tobin argue that the ECHR's weaknesses so far as children are concerned justify the Council pressing ahead with a specialist convention of its own. An alternative would be for it to adopt a protocol to the ECHR, ensuring the addition of various rights contained in the CRC which are not already adequately covered.[298] At present, the approach of the Council of Europe's strategy is to focus on priority areas, such as digital rights and protection from violence, rather than on creating a general set of rights similar to the CRC. Arguably, it is through such detailed regional implementation of the rights already protected in CRC and beyond that the Council of Europe can be most effective.

(8) The European Union and Children's Rights

For much of its history, the European Union has not been directly concerned with children's rights, which may have seemed remote from its primary concern of advancing political and economic cooperation. Recent changes mean that this is no longer the case: the EU is increasingly engaging with children's rights and has demonstrated potential to offer effective protection for children within its areas of competence.[299] At a constitutional level, this change has been implemented by the Treaty of Lisbon, in force from 2009, which added 'protection of the rights of the child' to the aims of the EU.[300] The Treaty of Lisbon also enhanced the legal status of fundamental rights, including children's rights within the EU; in particular, it raised the legal status of the EU's Charter of Fundamental Rights to that of the EU Treaties,[301] so producing legally binding effects. The Charter of Fundamental Rights, introduced in 2000, is an important source of rights for children within the EU areas of competence, not least because it gives express recognition to the distinct rights

---

[297] P. Alston and J. Tobin (2005) p. 17.   [298] Ibid.
[299] H. Stalford (2012) chs 1–2 provide a very helpful analysis of the development of the EU's role in relation to children's rights and the advantages and limitations of its involvement.
[300] Treaty of the European Union, Art. 3(3). Art. 3(5) also includes protection for the rights of the child as an objective in the EU's relations with the wider world.
[301] Treaty of the European Union, Art. 6.

of children.[302] Admittedly, Article 24 on 'the rights of the child' is something of a hodgepodge of existing rights concerning best interests, protection for parental relationships and expressing their views.[303] While in itself this might be seen as creating a rather 'uneasy compromise',[304] the very fact that children's rights are singled out for attention is itself an important step. The EU has also increasingly looked to the CRC and ECHR in informing its interpretation of children's rights, particularly through the EU Agenda for the Rights of the Child, which states that 'standards and principles of the UNCRC must continue to guide EU policies and actions that have an impact on the rights of the child'.[305] The EU is increasingly engaging with the CRC in legislation and policy, so bringing a fuller understanding of children's rights to the EU, while giving more effective implementation to the CRC.[306]

The reach of the EU's ability to implement children's rights is limited by its legal competence; the fact that children's rights are recognised within the Lisbon Treaty does not extend that competence to include all areas that might be affected by children's rights, but merely requires their consideration within the existing areas of EU competence. Within these parameters, the EU has effective legislation and policy of importance to children in areas such as child trafficking and sexual exploitation.[307] EU law is of particular relevance to children in cross-border families; EU-wide cooperation in areas such as parental responsibility and child abduction[308] provides effective reciprocal enforcement of judgments in disputes that range across national boundaries. Further, children's position as EU citizens has also achieved greater

---

[302] Art. 24 (Rights of the Child) and Art. 32 (Prohibition of Child Labour and Protection of Young People at Work). Arts 7 (Right to Respect for Private and Family Life) and 14 (Right to Education) also have particular importance for children, although they are not mentioned specifically.

[303] Charter of Fundamental Rights, Art. 24 states:

> (1) Children shall have the right to such protection and care as is necessary for their well-being. They may express their views freely. Such views shall be taken into consideration on matters which concern them in accordance with their age and maturity. (2) In all actions relating to children, whether taken by public authorities or private institutions, the child's best interests must be a primary consideration. (3) Every child shall have the right to maintain on a regular basis a personal relationship and direct contact with both his or her parents, unless that is contrary to his or her interests.

> It is noticeable that the protection for children's views is considerably weaker than CRC, Art. 12, which expresses this as a 'right'.

[304] C. McGlynn (2006) p. 70.

[305] Commission, 'An EU Agenda for the Rights of the Child' (Communication) COM (2011) 60; see further H. Stalford (2012) ch. 2.

[306] H. Stalford and E. Drywood (2011).

[307] E.g. Directive 2011/36/EU of the European Parliament and of the Council of 5 April 2011 on preventing and combating trafficking in human beings and protecting its victims; Directive 2011/92/EU of the European Parliament and of the Council of 13 December 2011 on combating the sexual abuse and sexual exploitation of children and child pornography.

[308] Brussels IIa: Council Regulation No. 2201/2003 concerning jurisdiction and the recognition and enforcement of judgments in matrimonial matters and the matters of parental responsibility. Replaced by Council Regulation No. 2019/1111 from 1 August 2022.

recognition and protection by the European Court of Justice, with cases such as *Zambrano v. Office National de l'Emploi*[309] protecting the rights of EU citizen children in cases involving the threatened deportation of their non-citizen parents. The value of the EU to children's rights is not in creating new, abstract rights, but in its potential to create the legal and policy structures to ensure that children's existing rights are justiciable entitlements within its areas of competence.

An unfortunate consequence of the UK's decision to leave the EU is that children have been deprived of this developing law and the EU legal structures that provide protection in areas such as child trafficking and abduction. Following the UK's withdrawal, the EU Charter of Fundamental Rights ceased to have any force in domestic law.[310] Although the UK will remain committed to the children's rights contained in the Charter, given their derivation from the CRC, the primacy of EU law over domestic law and the central place of the Charter within EU law had combined to create an extremely effective means of protecting those rights. It is unlikely that the Charter will be replaced by any domestic legislation expanding fundamental rights; instead, the implementation of the CRC will depend on its weaker enforcement mechanisms and the extent to which it can be 'read in' to the ECHR. As a result, children have been deprived of an effective means of protecting their rights in practice.

(9) Conclusion

The contribution made by international human rights law to promoting the rights of children has been of inestimable importance. Ratification of the CRC by nearly all countries throughout the world means that it has become an international treaty of major significance that is widely recognised as setting the benchmark for children's rights. The near-universal acceptance of the CRC has ensured that there is widespread awareness of and commitment to children's rights in international and regional law. While the weaknesses surrounding its enforcement remain, the optional protocol offers a new means of implementation. More important in practice has been the way in which the CRC has been used to inform law and policy nationally and internationally. The value of using the CRC can be seen in the way in which the ECtHR has taken the ECHR, a relatively unpromising text for children, and through creative interpretation has managed to make a remarkably effective set of protections for children. Despite this progress, limitations remain, especially given that the practical obstacles to children's claims means that their interests are usually litigated through the rights of adults rather than as rights claims for the children themselves. Effective protection of children's rights does not depend solely, or even primarily, on litigation, but also on the integration of

---

[309] (Case C-34/09) [2011] INLR 481, discussed by J. Fortin (2014).
[310] European Union (Withdrawal) Act 2018, s. 5(4).

those rights into policy and law. The greater prominence of children's rights on the international stage is reflected by the way in which both the Council of Europe and the EU have created new agendas on children's rights and integrated them into legislation, policy and cross-border cooperation. While these initiatives are still at a relatively early stage, the cross-fertilisation of ideas and cooperation between the CRC, Council of Europe and EU has provided an increasingly effective framework for children's rights at both international and regional levels.

Bibliography

NB: Some of these publications can be obtained on the relevant organisation's website.

Alston, P. and Tobin, J. (2005) *Laying the Foundations for Children's Rights*, UNICEF.
Barnes, A. (2012) 'CRC's Performance of the Child as Developing' in Freeman, M. (ed.)*Law and Childhood Studies*, Oxford University Press.
Buck, T. (2014) *International Child Law*, 3rd edn, Routledge.
Choudhry, S. (2003) 'The Adoption and Children Act 2002, the Welfare Principle and the Human Rights Act 1998 – a Missed Opportunity' 15 *Child and Family Law Quarterly* 119.
Committee on Human Rights (1989) *General Comment No. 17 on the Rights of the Child (Art. 24)*, HRI/GEN/Rev.8, Centre for Human Rights, Geneva.
Committee on the Rights of the Child (1991) *General Guidelines Regarding the Form and Content of Initial Reports to Be Submitted by States Parties under Article 44, Paragraph 1 (a), of the Convention*, CRC/C/5, Centre for Human Rights, Geneva.
(2002) *Concluding Observations of the Committee on the Rights of the Child: United Kingdom of Great Britain and Northern Ireland*, CRC/C/15/Add 188 2002, Centre for Human Rights, Geneva.
(2003) *General Comment No. 5 on the Measures of Implementation of the Convention on the Rights of the Child (Arts 4, 42 and 44, Para. 6)*, CRC/GC/2003/5, Centre for Human Rights, Geneva.
(2008) *Concluding Observations of the Committee on the Rights of the Child: United Kingdom of Great Britain and Northern Ireland*, CRC/C/GBR/CO/4, Centre for Human Rights, Geneva.
(2009) *General Comment No. 12 on the Right of the Child to be Heard*, CRC/C/GC/12, Centre for Human Rights, Geneva.
(2013) *General Comment No. 14 on the Right of the Child to Have His or Her Best Interests Taken as a Primary Consideration (Art. 3, Para. 1)*, CRC/C/GC/14, Centre for Human Rights, Geneva.
(2016a) *Concluding Observations of the Committee on the Rights of the Child: United Kingdom of Great Britain and Northern Ireland*, CRC/C/GBR/CO/5, Centre for Human Rights, Geneva.
(2016b) *General Comment No. 20 on the Implementation of the Rights of the Child During Adolescence*, CRC/C/GC/20, Centre for Human Rights, Geneva.
(2021) *General Comment No. 25 on Children's Rights in relation to the Digital Environment*, CRC/C/GC/25, Centre for Human Rights, Geneva.
Council of Europe (1997) *European Convention on the Exercise of Children's Rights and Explanatory Report*, Council of Europe Publishing.
(2016) *Council of Europe Strategy for the Rights of the Child 2016–2021*, Council of Europe Publishing.
Daly, A. (2018) *Children, Autonomy and the Courts: Beyond the Right to be Heard*, Brill Nijhoff.
Department of Health (DH) (1999) *United Nations Convention on the Rights of the Child: Second Report to the UN Committee by the United Kingdom 1999*, The Stationery Office.
Donnelly, J. and Howard, R. (1988) 'Assessing National Human Rights Performance: A Theoretical Framework' 10 *Human Rights Quarterly* 214.
Eekelaar, J. (1992) 'The Importance of Thinking that Children Have Rights' in Alston, P., Parker, S. and Seymour, J. (eds.) *Children, Rights and the Law*, Clarendon Press.

Egan, S. (2014) 'The New Complaints Mechanism for the Convention on the Rights of the Child' 22 *International Journal of Children's Rights* 205.

Feinberg, J. (1980) *Rights, Justice and the Bounds of Liberty*, Princeton University Press.

Feldman, D. (2002) *Civil Liberties and Human Rights in England and Wales*, Oxford University Press.

Fenton-Glynn, C. (2019) 'Children, Parents and the European Court of Human Rights' 6 *European Human Rights Law Review* 643.

(2020) *Children and the European Court of Human Rights*, Oxford University Press.

Fortin, J. (1999) 'Rights Brought Home for Children' 62 *Modern Law Review* 350.

(2002) 'Children's Rights and the Impact of Two International Conventions: The UNCRC and the ECHR' in The Rt Hon. Thorpe, L.J. and Cowton, C. (eds) *Delight and Dole: The Children Act 10 Years on*, Jordan Publishing Ltd.

(2004) 'Children's Rights: Are the Courts Now Taking Them More Seriously?' 15 *King's College Law Journal* 253.

(2014) 'Children's Rights – Flattering to Deceive?' 26 *Child and Family Law Quarterly* 51.

Freeman, M. (2014) *The Future of Children's Rights*, Brill Nijhoff.

(2016) 'Children's Rights as Human Rights' in Ovortrup, J., Corsaro, W. and Honig, M. (eds) *The Palgrave Handbook of Childhood Studies*, Springer.

(2020) *A Magna Carta for Children?: Rethinking Children's Rights*, Cambridge University Press.

Hanson, K. and Lundy, L. (2017) 'Does Exactly What It Says on the Tin? A Critical Analysis and Alternative Conceptualisation of the So-Called "General Principles" of the Convention on the Rights of the Child' 25 *International Journal of Children's Rights* 285.

Hanson, K. and Peleg, N. (2020) 'Waiting for Children's Rights Theory' 28 *International Journal of Children's Rights* 15.

Harris-Short, S. (2003) 'International Human Rights Law: Imperialist, Inept and Ineffective? Cultural Relativism and the UN Convention on the Rights of the Child' 25 *Human Rights Quarterly* 130.

Henaghan, M, (2017) 'Article 12 of the UN Convention on the Rights of Children' 25 *International Journal of Children's Rights* 537.

HM Government (2007) *The Consolidated 3rd and 4th Periodic Report to UN Committee on the Rights of the Child*, DCSF.

(2014) *The 5th Periodic Report to the UN Committee on the Rights of the Child*, CRC/C/GBR/5, Centre for Human Rights, Geneva.

Hodgkin, R. and Newell, P. (eds) (2007) *Implementation Handbook for the Convention on the Rights of the Child*, UNICEF.

Hodgson, D. (1992) 'The Historical Development and "Internationalisation" of the Children's Rights Movement' 6 *Australian Journal of Family Law* 25.

Jacobsen, A.F. (2016) 'Children's Rights in the European Court of Human Rights – An Emerging Power Structure' 24 *International Journal of Children's Rights* 548.

Joint Committee on Human Rights (JCHR) (2015) *The UK's Compliance with the UN Convention on the Rights of the Child, Eighth Report of Session 2014–15*, HL Paper 144, HC 1016, The Stationery Office.

Kilkelly, U. (2010) 'Protecting Children's Rights under the ECHR: The Role of Positive Obligations' 61 *Northern Ireland Law Quarterly* 245.

(2014) 'The CRC in litigation under the ECHR' in Liefaard, T. and Doek, J. (eds) *Litigating the Rights of the Child*, Springer.

Kilkelly, U. and Lundy, L. (2006) 'Children's Rights in Action: Using the UN Convention on the Rights of the Child as an Auditing Tool' 18 *Child and Family Law Quarterly* 331.

King, M. (1994) 'Children's Rights as Communication: Reflections on Autopoietic Theory and the United Nations Convention' 57 *Modern Law Review* 385.

Law Commission (1982) *Family Law Report on Illegitimacy*, Law Com No. 118, Her Majesty's Stationery Office.

LeBlanc, L. (1995) *The Convention on the Rights of the Child: United Nations Lawmaking on Human Rights*, University of Nebraska Press.

Liefaard, T. and Doek, J. (eds) (2015) *Litigating the Rights of the Child: The UN Convention on the Rights of the Child in Domestic and International Jurisprudence*, Springer.

Lundy, L., Kilkelly, U. and Byrne, B. (2014) 'Incorporation of the United Nations Convention on the Rights of the Child in Law: A Comparative Review' in Freeman, M. (ed.) *The Future of Children's Rights*, Brill Nijhoff.

MacDonald, A. (2011) *The Rights of the Child: Law and Practice*, Family Law.

McGlynn, C. (2006) *Families and the European Union: Law, Politics and Pluralism*, Cambridge University Press.

McGoldrick, D. (1991) 'The United Nations Convention on the Rights of the Child' 5 *International Journal of Law and the Family* 132.

Marshall, K. and Parvis, P. (2004) *Honouring Children*, Saint Andrew Press.

Minow, M. (1987) 'Interpreting Rights: An Essay for Robert Cover' 96 *Yale Law Journal* 1860.

Munby, J. (2004) 'Making Sure the Child Is Heard' 34 *Family Law* 338.

Nolan, A. (2014) *Children's Socio-Economic Rights, Democracy and the Courts*, Hart Publishing.

Peleg, N. (2012) 'Time to Grow Up: The UN Committee on the Rights of the Child's Jurisprudence of the Right to Development' in Freeman, M. (ed.) *Law and Childhood Studies*, Oxford University Press.

(2017) 'Developing the Right to Development' 25 *International Journal of Children's Rights* 280.

Price Cohen, C. and Kilbourne, S. (1998) 'Jurisprudence of the Committee on the Rights of the Child: A Guide for Research and Analysis' 19 *Michigan Journal of International Law* 633.

Quennerstedt, A. (2010) 'Children, But Not Really Humans? Critical Reflections on the Hampering Effect of the 3 "Ps"' 8 *International Journal of Children's Rights* 619.

Scherer, L. and Hart, S. (2001) 'Reporting on the Status of Education to the Committee on the Rights of the Child' in Hart, S., Price Cohen, C., Farrell Erickson, M. and Flekkøy, M. (eds) *Children's Rights in Education*, Jessica Kingsley Publishers.

Smith, R. (2014) 'The Third Optional Protocol to the UN Convention on the Rights of the Child? Challenges Arising from Transforming Rhetoric into Reality' in Freeman, M. (ed.) *The Future of Children's Rights*, Brill Nijhoff.

Stalford, H. (2012) *Children and the European Union: Rights, Welfare and Accountability*, Hart Publishing.

Stalford, H. and Drywood, E. (2011) 'The Use of the UNCRC in EU Law and Policy-Making' in Invernizzi, A. and Williams, J. (eds) *The Human Rights of Children: From Vision to Implementation*, Routledge.

Taylor, R. (2017) 'The Child's Right to Religion in International Law' in Strahn, A., Parker, S. and Ridgely, S. (eds) *Bloomsbury Reader in Religion and Childhood*, Bloomsbury.

Timimi, S. (2006) 'Children's Mental Health: The Role of Culture, Markets and Prescribed Drugs' 13 *Public Policy Research* 35.

Tobin, J. (2011) 'Understanding a Human Rights Based Approach to Matters Involving Children: Conceptual Foundations and Strategic Considerations' in Invernizzi, A. and Williams, J. (eds) *The Human Rights of Children: From Vision to Implementation*, Routledge.

(2013) 'Justifying Children's Rights' 21 *International Journal of Children's Rights* 395.

Van Bueren, G. (1995) *The International Law on the Rights of the Child*, Martinus Nijhoff Publishers.

Veerman, P. (2010) 'The Ageing of the UN Convention on the Rights of the Child' 18 *International Journal of Children's Rights* 585.

Wellman, C. (1999) *The Proliferation of Rights: Moral Progress or Empty Rhetoric?*, Westview Press.

Wilkins, R. (2004) 'International Law, Social Change and the Family' in Lødrup, P. and Modvar, E. (eds) *Family Life and Human Rights*, Gyldendal.

Woolf, M. (2003) 'Coming of Age? – The Principle of "The Best Interests of the Child"' *European Human Rights Law Review* 205.

3

Children's Rights in Domestic Law

(1) Introduction

The previous chapters have considered the theoretical basis of children's rights and the firm acceptance within international law that children possess fundamental rights. To be of real benefit to children, these rights must be translated from the theoretical and international realm and become practically enforceable rights within the domestic sphere. There are some formidable obstacles facing the creation of a truly child-centred domestic system for protecting children's rights. The fact that the UN Convention on the Rights of the Child (CRC) has not been incorporated into domestic law leaves those seeking to enforce children rights primarily reliant on the adult-focused Human Rights Act 1998 (HRA). Although the HRA can offer significant protection for children, it is by no means a panacea. The European Convention on Human Rights and Fundamental Freedoms (ECHR), on which the HRA is based, was not written with children in mind and its text does not resolve many of the difficulties in providing rights that are relevant and effective for children. The heart of the problem for children's rights in domestic law is that those international rights that are designed for children are not directly enforceable, while those rights that are directly enforceable have not been written for children. Children also lack accessible means of enforcing their rights in court, while their exclusion from much of the political process creates barriers to challenging policies affecting them.

Nonetheless, there are reasons for cautious optimism. The domestic courts have been increasingly willing to follow the European Court of Human Rights in drawing on the CRC and other international instruments in interpreting rights to be more effective for children. This approach has created some real advances in protecting children, particularly in requiring state agencies to take children's best interests seriously. Further, while there is an understandable tendency for lawyers to focus on judicial decisions in assessing the effectiveness of children's rights, the most effective protection for children's rights will be found if legislation and policy is created and implemented with a clear commitment to those rights. Although progress in the political sphere has been slow, there is an increased awareness of children's rights in Parliament and pressure to create formal assessment of the impact of legislation on children as part of the legislative process. Political progress still falls some way off the position in the devolved administrations in Scotland and Wales, which have shown real progress in creating obligations and procedures for incorporating children's rights within government and policy-making. Finally, the role of the Children's Commissioner has become increasingly effective and rights-focused. While it is still all too easy for children's rights to be ignored, the mechanisms are gradually being put in place to create a more effective and systematic means of protection.

(2) Applying Children's Rights in Domestic Law

(A) International Law and Domestic Law

As the UK is a dualist state, obligations accepted in international law are not binding in domestic law unless incorporated by legislation.[1] This fundamental constitutional rule poses a significant hurdle for those wishing to rely on the many unincorporated obligations that protect children's rights. The fact that there has been a clear breach of international obligations does not in itself entail consequences in domestic law. A good example of this problem can be seen in the Supreme Court decision of *R (SG)* v. *Secretary of State for Work and Pensions*.[2] The case involved a challenge to the 'benefit cap', which limited the amount payable in benefits to non-working households in any one year. The burden of the cap fell particularly heavily on lone-parent households and was likely to deprive affected families of income needed to meet their children's basic needs for adequate food, clothing, warmth and housing.[3] For a majority of the Supreme Court,[4] this was a clear failure to treat children's interests as a primary consideration and a violation of Article 3(1) of the CRC. Nonetheless, there was no route by which this failure to comply with international law was a violation of domestic law[5] and so the challenge failed. The case illustrates the sobering reality that even the most well-established children's rights will often fail to be practically enforceable in domestic law.

Despite the formidable barrier illustrated by *SG*, there are a number of routes by which unincorporated instruments such as the CRC have had an increasing influence in domestic law.[6] Where there are ambiguities in legislation, there is a well-established presumption that Parliament intends to

---

[1] See *R (SC)* v. *Work and Pensions Secretary* [2021] UKSC 26, [2021] 3 WLR 428, at [75]–[78].
[2] [2015] UKSC 16, [2015] 1 WLR 1449.   [3] Ibid. at [226]–[227] (Baroness Hale).
[4] Ibid., Baroness Hale at [225], Lord Kerr at [268], Lord Carnwath at [128].
[5] By a different majority: Lord Carnwath, Lord Reed and Lord Hughes. See further discussion in Chapter 13.
[6] See A. MacDonald (2011) ch. 3 for detailed analysis of the application on international instruments in domestic law. See also Lord Kerr in *SG* at [235]–[257] for an ambitious argument that CRC, Art. 3 is directly enforceable in English law, although he recognises that this argument is not likely to find favour in the courts of this country at present.

legislate in a manner that does not violate the UK's international obligations.[7] This rule has been used in relation to the CRC, for example in construing the statutory power then possessed by the Home Secretary to set the minimum tariff to be served by children convicted of murder, to take into account Articles 3 and 40 of the CRC.[8] This case also demonstrates the way in which those same principles can be used to guide the limits of administrative discretion. A further route for can be found in the principle that any development of the common law should be in harmony with the UK's international obligations.[9] In this way, the CRC has been used, for example, in developing the duty of confidentiality owed to competent minors seeking advice on sexual health.[10] Despite not being directly incorporated into domestic law, the CRC and similar instruments can have an important impact on the interpretation of statute and development of the common law.[11] It is, however, the Human Rights Act 1998 which offers the most potential as a secure means of protecting children's rights in domestic law.

(B) The Human Rights Act 1998

Although there are routes by which unincorporated international obligations may be relied upon, it is the incorporation of the ECHR[12] into domestic law through the HRA that provides the most effective means of litigating rights. The clear imposition of duties on courts and public authorities, together with the enhanced remedies that it offers, creates a far more secure basis for litigating children's rights than the limited means available for unincorporated instruments described above. In particular, the requirement that legislation 'must be read' 'as far as it is possible to do so' to be compatible with the protected rights[13] gives a much more powerful tool to the courts to produce rights-compliant reading of legislation than the limited role of unincorporated rights in resolving ambiguous provisions. If a rights-compliant reading is not possible, the availability of declarations of incompatibility duty fails offers a limited additional safeguard.[14] For example, the failure of domestic legislation to recognise the relationship between a child and single father, following a surrogacy agreement entered into abroad, has been held to be incompatible

---

[7] *Garland* v. *British Rail* [1983] 2 AC 751, 771 A–C (Lord Diplock).

[8] *R* v. *Secretary of State for the Home Department, ex p Venables and Thompson* [1997] 3 WLR 23, at 49F and H.

[9] *A* v. *Secretary of State for the Home Department (No. 2)* [2005] UKHL 71, [2006] 2 AC 221, at [27] (Lord Bingham).

[10] *R (Axon)* v. *Secretary of State for Health* [2006] EWHC 37 (Admin), [2006] 2 FLR 206, at [64] (Silber J).

[11] E.g. *Re CS (A Child)* [2019] EWHC 634 (Fam), [2019] 1 WLR 4286, at [38], interpreting Family Procedure Rules in assessing child's competence to instruct solicitor. S. Gilmore (2017) surveys the use of the CRC in domestic family law cases.

[12] Those rights set out in HRA 1998, Sch. 1. [13] HRA 1998, s. 3. [14] HRA 1998, s. 4.

with the rights of both the father and the child.[15] A further important provision is the requirement that all public authorities act compatibly with the protected rights,[16] a duty that is of particular importance to children in education or in state care. The court itself, as a 'public authority', is bound to act compatibly with protected rights in adapting the principles of the common law and in exercising discretion. For all of these reasons, the HRA offers the promise of a far more effective means of securing rights than those directly available in respect of the unincorporated, child-centred rights instruments, most notably the CRC.

Whether the HRA has been able to realise this potential to secure enhanced rights for children in practice is a more difficult question to answer and one that is reflected on throughout this book. There is no doubt that the HRA applies to children just as it does to adults: almost all of the incorporated rights[17] are written in inclusive terms and apply irrespective of age. There are, however, considerable difficulties for children seeking to enforce those rights. A fundamental problem is that children rarely possess the knowledge and means to access courts to enforce their rights or to be heard in adult-focused litigation.[18] Even if these practical problems are overcome, the HRA remains hampered by the limitations of the ECHR: an adult-focused convention with no specific consideration of the interests and needs of children.[19]

(C) Interpreting the Human Rights Act for Children

The ECHR was not written with children in mind: it contains no explicit reference to children's development, their welfare or the relationship between their rights and the responsibilities of their adult carers. The most promising line of cases to address this problem adopts a dynamic reading of the ECHR through the lens of child-focused human rights instruments, such as the CRC. As we have seen,[20] the European Court of Human Rights (ECtHR) has used this approach to overcome some of the limitations of the text of the ECHR. In a series of judgments, domestic courts have followed this Strasbourg jurisprudence to significantly improve the practical protection of children's rights. This approach is, however, not a panacea for those seeking to implement international children's rights in domestic law and falls far short of incorporation. Further, recent judgments of the Supreme Court have signalled a more restrictive approach to the use of international material in applying the ECHR and imposed substantial hurdles in the path of litigants who seek to do so.

---

[15] *Re X (Surrogate Father: Parental Order) (No. 2)* [2016] EWHC 1191 (Fam), [2017] Fam 25. See discussion in Chapter 5.
[16] HRA 1998, s. 6.
[17] Art. 12, the right to marry, only applies to men and women of marriageable age.
[18] See further discussion in Chapter 12.   [19] See further discussion in Chapter 2.
[20] Chapter 2.

The Supreme Court decision in *ZH (Tanzania)* v. *Secretary of State for the Home Department*,[21] which first brought the importance of the use of the CRC in applying the ECHR to prominence, provides a good illustration of the potential benefits of doing so. The case concerned a decision to deport a mother following a number of failed applications for asylum. If she were removed, her two children would inevitably have to accompany her as there were no suitable alternative arrangements for their care. The children, aged 12 and 9, were British citizens. The mother's deportation would in effect require them to leave the only home they had ever known and deprive them of their rights to be educated and brought up within the country of their citizenship. The decision to deport clearly interfered with the rights of the children, as well as the mother, under Article 8 of the ECHR. In applying that right, Lady Hale considered that:

> ... it is clear from the recent jurisprudence that the Strasbourg court will expect national authorities to apply article 3.1 of UNCRC and treat the best interests of a child as 'a primary consideration'.[22]

Applying that approach, it was disproportionate on the facts of this case to deport the mother in circumstances that would deprive the children of their ability to enjoy their rights as citizens.

The decision in *ZH (Tanzania)* formed the foundation for a series of decisions advancing children's rights in a wide range of areas of public decision-making, including: extradition;[23] planning;[24] benefits;[25] and prisoners' leave.[26] This use of Article 3 of the CRC in public law has had a particularly important impact in making children's rights visible in adult-focused public decisions.[27] The use of the international children's rights in applying the HRA is not limited to this context and has been used in a range of different aspects of children's cases.[28] Together, these cases opened a pathway to a more child-focused interpretation of the HRA. They do not, however, amount to an incorporation of international children's rights into domestic law. A child will only be able to use this approach to remedy a violation of international law if they can identify a relevant right under the HRA. This problem was evident in the *R (SG)* v. *Secretary of State for Work and Pensions*[29] case concerning the benefit cap. While the majority of members of the Supreme Court considered that the Secretary of State had failed to comply with the

---

[21] [2011] UKSC 4, [2011] 2 AC 166.   [22] Ibid. at [25].

[23] *H(H)* v. *Deputy Prosecutor of the Italian Republic* [2012] UKSC 25, [2013] 1 AC 338.

[24] *Stevens* v. *Secretary of State for Communities and Local Government* [2013] EWHC 792 (Admin).

[25] *Mathieson* v. *Secretary of State for Work and Pensions* [2015] UKSC 47, [2015] 1 WLR 3250.

[26] *R (MP)* v. *Secretary of State for Justice* [2012] EWHC 214 (Admin), esp. at [170].

[27] Considered further in Chapter 13 and R. Taylor (2016).

[28] E.g. the use of CRC, Art. 12 in relation to children's participation in family proceedings, discussed in Chapter 12.

[29] [2015] UKSC 16, [2015] 1 WLR 1449, discussed above and in Chapter 13.

international obligations imposed by Article 3 of the CRC, that failure was not relevant to the challenge in hand, which concerned sex discrimination against the claimant parents. Further, as the basis for the use of international law is found in Strasbourg jurisprudence, a court is much more likely to be receptive if a claimant can point to an established line of ECtHR cases in which the relevant international right has been used to interpret the right in question. Finally, while Lady Hale's judgment in *ZH (Tanzania)*[30] spoke of Strasbourg expecting national authorities to *apply* Article 3 of the CRC, later judgments have given a more limited role to international law. For example, *Mathieson v. Secretary of State for Work and Pensions*[31] considered whether the decision 'harmonised' with the child's rights under international law, rather than applying that law directly. These limitations have come to the fore in recent jurisprudence of the Supreme Court.

Two cases handed down by the Supreme Court on the same day in 2021 appear to signal a marked change in tone to the use of international children's rights in applying the HRA. In *R (SC) v. Work and Pensions Secretary*,[32] the parties had agreed that one of the questions to be asked in assessing whether a restriction of benefits to two children was justified under Article 14 of the ECHR, was whether there had been a breach of Article 3 of the CRC. Lord Reed regarded this approach as mistaken. Strasbourg did not treat international treaties as if they were incorporated into the ECHR and did not purport to determine whether states were in breach of those obligations.[33] Accordingly, Lord Reed was clear that Strasbourg jurisprudence did not require the courts to assess compliance with the CRC or to treat the Convention as if it formed a part of domestic law. Any domestic authority that appeared to suggest otherwise was either obiter or formed part of a dissenting judgment.[34] This did not mean that the CRC was irrelevant; Strasbourg jurisprudence had treated children's interests as a relevant factor in assessing justification under Article 14. Domestic courts should not, however, assess whether there had been a breach of the CRC itself. The decision in *R (SC)* appears to represent a marked change in tone from earlier judgments and places far less weight on the CRC than that in the earlier cases. The second decision, *R (AB) v. Secretary of State for the Home Department*,[35] also adopts a restrictive approach to the use of international law. The case concerned a 15-year-old who had been held in conditions that were said to amount to solitary confinement while detained at Feltham Young Offenders' Institution. The appellant sought to argue that these conditions constituted inhuman and degrading treatment contrary to Article 3 of the ECHR. In doing so he relied on Article 37 of the CRC, General Comments and country reports produced by the UN Committee on the Rights of the Child, and a number of further sources of international law. Lord Reed,

---

[30] [2011] UKSC 4, [2011] 2 AC 166, at [25].   [31] [2015] UKSC 47, [2015] 1 WLR 3250, at [44].
[32] [2021] UKSC 26, [2021] 3 WLR 428. This case is considered in more detail in Chapter 13.
[33] Ibid. at [72]–[86].   [34] Ibid. at [86]–[96].   [35] [2021] UKSC 28, [2021] 3 WLR 494.

again giving the sole judgment, found that it was for the ECtHR to determine which of these instruments were relevant to interpreting the ECHR and to what extent. It was not for domestic courts to use international law to develop the meaning of those rights beyond that given by Strasbourg.[36]

Taken together, these recent judgments appear to place firm limits on the extent to which children's international rights can be used in applying the HRA.[37] In doing so, they jeopardise the progress that has been made in creating domestic protection for children's rights in practice. Future litigants would be well-advised to pay close attention to the use that the ECtHR has made of international law if they wish to advance claims for children under the HRA. Strasbourg jurisprudence has made increasing use of international law in its judgments and if this trend continues the more restrictive approach of the Supreme Court will still permit those developments to apply in domestic law.

(D) Welfare and the Human Rights Act

Much of domestic law concerning children is phrased in terms of their welfare, or best interests, rather than their rights. Most importantly, section 1(1) of the Children Act 1989 sets out the welfare principle, which makes the child's welfare the court's paramount consideration in determining any question concerning their upbringing. It is this principle that applies to parental disputes about children's living arrangements or upbringing[38] and which determines whether children who have suffered, or are at risk of, significant harm will be taken into care.[39] Similarly, a modified welfare principle, requiring consideration of the child's lifelong welfare, applies in allocating parenthood in adoption and surrogacy cases.[40] Courts using the inherent jurisdiction to decide disputes between parents and medical professionals will do so according to the child's best interests.[41] Duties placed on certain public authorities such as local authorities, NHS trusts and immigration officers require them to have regard to children's welfare.[42] Indeed, almost every chapter in this book touches on the question of how the law approaches children's welfare. Given the importance of welfare to the law concerning children, the relationship between a child's welfare and rights is crucial to understanding how children's rights operate in domestic law.

---

[36] Ibid. esp. at [61]. Lord Reed also stressed that the work of the UN Committee was not regarded as authoritative in international law and should not be treated as such: ibid. at [64].

[37] Arguably, these cases have no bearing on the use of CRC, Art. 3 to interpret the obligations under the Children Act 2004, s. 11(2) and Borders, Citizenship and Immigration Act 2009, s. 55, both of which were drafted with the intention of fulfilling the obligations under CRC, Art. 3. Discussed further in Chapter 13.

[38] Chapter 6. [39] Chapter 15. [40] Adoption and Children Act 2002, s. 1(2). [41] Chapter 7.

[42] Children Act 2004, s. 11(2); Borders, Citizenship and Immigration Act 2009, s. 55. Discussed further in Chapter 13.

Children's rights and welfare are sometimes portrayed as being in direct opposition to each other, with the question being which of the two competing approaches should prevail.[43] This question is misconceived for two reasons. First, welfare and rights are not co-extensive: while welfare is used as a domestic legal test in a wide range of areas, it applies far more narrowly than rights do. Welfare tends to be used as a test for judicial resolution of disputes that directly concern children, but without the medium of rights it has little purchase beyond the court room. Rights apply much more broadly; in particular, they are effective because they are a source of duties including the positive obligations that they impose on the state.[44] For example, the UK's positive duty to protect children from inhuman and degrading punishment has been used successfully to challenge the law on corporal punishment in a way that would not have been possible without rights.[45] The question is not, therefore, whether we should choose a rights-based or welfare-based approach to children: it is how the two interact when they *both* apply to a decision. Second, the picture of a stark division between rights and welfare mischaracterises the relationship between them; it implies that matters pertaining to the child's welfare are outside and often opposed to matters relating to the child's rights. In reality, a child's rights will usually closely align with their welfare. This is no mere accident: the best theoretical understanding of children's rights views rights as a means of protecting interests required for human flourishing.[46] Rights should therefore be interpreted in a way which enhances children's lives, not harms them.[47] This understanding of rights is reflected in Article 3 of the CRC, which grants children a *right* to have their best interests treated as a primary consideration in decisions concerning them.[48] It is through the medium of rights that best interests have been given a more prominent role in public decision-making. Rights and welfare tend to have a mutually reinforcing relationship: rights are an effective way of enforcing and understanding best interests, while best interests can be an important guide to interpreting rights.

Despite the close relationship between rights and welfare, there are circumstances in which they can be in tension with each other. Two particular concerns merit close consideration. The first is that a focus on welfare can lead to a complacent attitude to children's rights, in which it is assumed that a welfare analysis will *inevitably* fulfil requirements of children's rights without the need for explicit consideration of those rights. Although welfare will often point to the same outcome as rights, this is not always so, particularly in circumstances in which the child's wish to exercise her autonomy rights conflicts with the court's assessment of her welfare. The second, particular to

---

[43] J. Herring (2017) p. 475.   [44] Discussed in Chapter 2.

[45] *A v. United Kingdom (Human Rights: Punishment of a Child)* [1998] 2 FLR 959. Although the law in this area is still unsatisfactory; see Chapter 4.

[46] Chapter 1.   [47] J. Fortin (2006) p. 311.

[48] Committee on the Rights of the Child (2013). Discussed in Chapter 2.

the paramountcy principle, is that a focus on welfare can neglect the rights of adults that may also be engaged by the decision being made, as well as those of children. It is these two concerns that have been the foundation of arguments that the application of welfare, particularly the paramountcy principle found in section 1(1) of the Children Act 1989, is inconsistent with the HRA.

(i) Welfare and Children's Rights

The courts have a somewhat patchy record of recognising that children's rights are engaged in welfare disputes, often preferring to bypass mention of rights to focus solely on welfare.[49] This is a mistake: recognition of the close relationship between children's rights and welfare does not mean that children's rights should be regarded as irrelevant to a court considering the child's welfare or best interests. Rights are important both in enhancing the welfare analysis and in treating children as rights-holders, rather than objects of the courts' assessment of their best interests.

The first reason that rights are important is that a child-focused understanding of rights can inform the application of welfare. A good example of this is the way in which the child's right to be heard, including the protection of that right in Article 12 of the CRC, has been regarded as an integral part of the welfare assessment.[50] Consideration of rights can be particularly important in novel situations or in complex situations in which the child may have conflicting rights. For example, in *Re T (Paternity: Ordering Blood Tests)*,[51] recognition of the competing rights of a child to knowledge of his genetic origins and to a stable family life informed the court's understanding of his welfare. Recognition of rights can enhance the welfare analysis in this way by emphasising considerations that are important to a child's flourishing.

A second reason for recognising rights in applying welfare is because rights can represent entitlements and a more secure basis for securing that entitlement, even if welfare would reach the same result. Jane Fortin gives a good example of this point in contrasting the way in which the UK Supreme Court and the European Court of Justice have approached the problem of citizen children whose parents are threatened with deportation. The Supreme Court's protection for children in this position comes through an assessment of their best interests, whereas the European Court of Justice recognises the citizen child as entitled to a right to reside.[52] This is an important point: the specific rights of children give a more certain basis than 'best interests' and require that children's rights are recognised as protected entitlements rather than merely as an important consideration in decision-making. While this case is concerned with EU law, the same point might be made with regard to a child's human rights under the HRA.

---

[49] Fortin (2006).
[50] E.g. *Re S (Child) (Abduction)* [2014] EWCA Civ 1557. See Chapter 12 for further discussion.
[51] [2001] 2 FLR 1190; discussed in Chapter 5.   [52] Fortin (2011).

Finally, although in most cases rights and welfare will reach the same result, where they do not, careful consideration should be given to the question of whether there are proportionate reasons to justify interference with the child's rights. This is particularly important in respect of the autonomy rights of older children. Welfare and autonomy are not necessarily in conflict with each other: it is very much in a child's best interests to acquire the capacity to make decisions and to learn from making mistakes.[53] Recognition of a child's right to autonomy does not give the child a trump card: proportionate interference to protect her interests can be justified under the qualified rights protected by the HRA. Proportionality, however, requires careful reasoning and not a paternalistic assumption that the court's assessment of welfare necessarily outweighs the child's own determination of her interests. The courts have often failed to consider rights that appear to conflict with their own determination of a child's welfare. For example, in F v. F,[54] a 15-year-old vegan objected to having the MMR vaccine, in part because it contained animal products. The court decided that it would be in her best interests to receive the vaccine, dismissing her contrary views on the basis that adopting such a fixed stance demonstrated a lack of maturity. As Jonathan Herring points out, many people hold strong moral principles that they believe to be absolute.[55] Nonconsensual vaccination against the considered objections of a mature minor appears to be a considerable interference with her bodily autonomy protected by Article 8 of the ECHR, but astoundingly the judgment gives no recognition of these rights or her right to 'due weight' to be given to her views under Article 12 of the CRC. Had this been done, there is a good argument that the result may have been very different: there may be good reasons to respect a decision to take a small medical risk in order to uphold a strong moral principle. F v. F is a good example of the way in which the courts have been willing to interfere with children's rights in the name of welfare, without giving consideration as to whether that can be justified.

(ii) Welfare and the Rights of Others

Just as the rights of children may be deeply affected by a welfare decision, so might the interests of parents and other family members. Many of the decisions to which the welfare principle applies will have fundamental consequences for the lives of parents. Decisions as to whether a child should be permitted to relocate with one parent, or whether no contact should be ordered, or whether the child should be adopted, will all have potentially devastating consequences for a parent. Most frequently, the parent's right to family life, under Article 8 of the ECHR, will be affected by these decisions, but other rights may also be impacted. The orthodox approach to the welfare principle in section 1(1) of the Children Act 1989 regards the welfare of the

---

[53] See discussion in Chapter 9.
[54] [2013] EWHC 2683 (Fam). Considered further in Chapter 9.   [55] J. Herring (2016) p. 51.

child as the decisive consideration for the court, with the rights of parents and others receiving no independent weight. This is potentially problematic because, as we saw in Chapter 2, while children's interests will often justify interference with parents' rights under the ECHR, this is not *inevitably* the case.[56] This raises the prospect that a decision made using the orthodox welfare principle may result in a violation of the rights of another family member.

A good example of this problem can be seen in the first instance decision, later reversed on appeal, in *Re A (Children) (Contact: Ultra-Orthodox Judaism: Transgender Parent).*[57] In this case, five children were being brought up in an ultra-orthodox Jewish community, receiving all of their education at ultra-orthodox schools. The parents' marriage had come to an end because the children's father[58] had left the community to live as a transgender woman. The children remained within the community with their mother. The mother was deeply opposed to the children having direct contact with the trans parent, on the basis that the community was likely to react with hostility to any such contact and that this risked the children being excluded from their community. The court reluctantly agreed with this assessment and considered it to be in the children's best interests for no direct contact with the trans parent to be ordered, despite the contact itself being beneficial to the children. This difficult but entirely orthodox application of the welfare principle demonstrates the problem: the trans parent's Article 8 and Article 14 ECHR rights receive no detailed consideration and the order of the court appears to 'reward' the discriminatory stance of the community.[59]

One way of avoiding this problem is to emphasise, as Jonathan Herring does, the connection between the welfare of children and the rights and interests of other family members.[60] On this relationship-based view of welfare, the child has an interest in being brought up in healthy relationships in which all members of the family are valued and their rights respected. In *Re A*, that might be applied by a finding that it was in these children's interests for the trans parent to be treated with respect and without discrimination. There is certainly truth in the observation that children's welfare can never be detached from their relationships and the well-being of those closest to them. Nonetheless, relationship-based welfare cannot fully accommodate the rights

---

[56] See esp. *Strand Lobben* v. *Norway* [2020] 1 FLR 297, discussed in Chapter 2.

[57] [2017] EWFC 4, [2017] 4 WLR 201.

[58] The term used by the court, cf. *Carpenter* v. *Secretary of State for Justice* [2015] EWHC 464 (Admin).

[59] The Court of Appeal reversed the decision on a number of grounds, including that the judge had 'lost sight' of the paramountcy principle: *Re A (Children) (Contact: Ultra-Orthodox Judaism: Transgender Parent)* [2017] EWCA Civ 2164, [2018] 4 WLR 60. As John Eekelaar observes, it is difficult to follow this aspect of the Court of Appeal's reasoning as the points made in support appear to have little relevance to the children's welfare. As Eekelaar argues, 'in contrast, far from losing sight of the paramountcy principle, the judge's decision was directly based on uncontradicted evidence about the effect of direct contact on the children's welfare': J. Eekelaar (2018).

[60] Herring (1999).

of parents. Children's relationships can be a source of their well-being, but they can also be a source of harm; those cases that come before the courts are disproportionately likely to include the latter. One of the greatest problems that children face in court is that their interests are often articulated by adults and open to manipulation to reflect those adults' interests. A decision that it is good for children to put others first risks distorting the interests of children, especially if they are presented by the parent whose own interests are at stake.

The Court of Appeal similarly sought to integrate respect for human rights with the welfare principle by finding that in assessing welfare the judge should act as a 'judicial reasonable parent', valuing tolerance, broad-mindedness, equality and human rights.[61] It found that the judge had failed to adopt this approach to welfare and so remitted the case back to be reheard on this basis. The difficulty with this approach is that it obscures the very real conflict of rights that can arise in the family. In particular, there is a question of whether the child's welfare must sometimes yield to the need to protect parents from the discriminatory actions of others, or to promote the values espoused by the 'judicial reasonable parent'. This point is highlighted by the Court of Appeal's view that such a judge would consider removing the children from being 'lovingly cared for by their mother' and placing them into public care to facilitate contact.[62] The very real conflict between the parent's rights and the welfare of the children was sadly apparent in the final conclusion to the case.[63] Once remitted back to the Family Court, it proved impossible to devise a plan that did not have a 'catastrophic' impact on the children's lives. The children had been traumatised by what had happened and the application was withdrawn, so relieving the court of the dilemma posed by the Court of Appeal.

(iii) Can the Welfare Principle Be Reconciled with the Human Rights Act?

It is clear from the cases discussed above that there are circumstances in which the court's evaluation of the child's welfare may be in conflict with the rights of the child or others. In these circumstances, ECtHR case law shows that the child's welfare may be sufficiently important to justify interfering with protected rights,[64] but it is not *inevitably* the case that any benefit to the child's welfare will always outweigh interference with a right. The case of *Re A* is a particularly good example. A decision that there would be no direct contact between the children and the trans parent would be an interference with their right to family life under Article 8 that was almost akin to adoption.[65] The case law on adoption places a heavy burden on the court to show sufficiently

---

[61] *Re A (Children) (Contact: Ultra-Orthodox Judaism: Transgender Parent)* [2017] EWCA Civ 2164, [2018] 4 WLR 60, esp. at [60] and [77].

[62] Ibid. at [71] and [77].

[63] *Re A (Children) (Contact: Ultra-Orthodox Judaism: Transgender Parent)* [2020] EWFC 3.

[64] Chapter 2.

[65] *Re A (Children) (Contact: Ultra-Orthodox Judaism: Transgender Parent)* [2017] EWFC 4, [2018] 4 WLR 60, at [166(15)].

exceptional reasons for finding that the child's welfare requires severance of the existing family relationships. Further, the hostility to contact was directly connected to the father's transgender identity and any such difference in treatment would be difficult to justify under Article 14 of the ECHR.[66] The eventual 'catastrophic' consequences of contact for the children may well have been sufficient to justify even this severe outcome, but that judgment is a difficult one that requires careful attention to all of the relevant rights.

For these reasons, as the HRA came into force, there was considerable speculation that the welfare principle would require modification to meet the demands to recognise the rights of children and adults within the reasoning process. In particular, it was argued that courts applying the welfare principle should engage in a 'parallel analysis' in which all of the rights engaged – whether of the child or others – should be explicitly identified, assessed through proportionality and weighed against one another to ensure that any interference was justified.[67] That modification has not occurred; instead, the courts have proved very resistant to any claim that the HRA requires the court routinely to engage in detailed analysis of the rights at stake, rather than resolving disputes through the question of the child's welfare. The tone of the judicial response was set by the influential judgment of Lord Nicholls of Birkenhead in *Re B*, decided not long after the HRA had come into force.[68] He stated firmly that the balancing exercise required by the ECHR does not differ in substance from that undertaken by the courts when deciding whether a particular order is in the child's best interests.[69] On this view, despite the differing phraseology, rights-based reasoning and welfare reasoning would lead to the same result and it was this result, not the reasoning process that led to it, that was of importance. This approach was maintained by the judiciary,[70] despite attracting considerable academic criticism.[71] In particular, as Sonia Harris-Short argued,[72] it appeared to be based on an assumption that by carrying out a welfare analysis, the courts would automatically fulfil the ECHR proportionality requirements and that therefore the courts need not make reference to the Convention. The difficulty with this assumption was, as Jonathan Herring pointed out, that there is a significant difference between starting from the premise that a parent's rights must not be infringed *unless* the court can fulfil the detailed requirements of proportionality and starting from

---

[66] *Re A (Children) (Contact: Ultra-Orthodox Judaism: Transgender Parent)* [2017] EWCA Civ 2164, [2018] 4 WLR 60, esp. at [99]–[100] and [115].

[67] H. Fenwick (2004) p. 917; S. Choudhry and H. Fenwick (2005) pp. 481–4.

[68] *Re B (A Child) (Adoption by One Natural Parent)* [2001] UKHL 70, [2002] 1 All ER 641.

[69] Ibid. at [31].

[70] *Payne* v. *Payne* [2001] EWCA Civ 166, [2001] 1 FLR 1052, per Thorpe LJ, at [38]–[39]; *Re H (Contact Order) (No. 2)* [2002] 1 FLR 22, per Wall J, at [59].

[71] See, inter alia: S. Harris-Short (2002) pp. 336–8; S. Choudhry (2003) pp. 128–36; D. Bonner *et al.* (2003) pp. 575–84; J. Fortin (2004) pp. 267–9; S. Choudhry and H. Fenwick (2005) pp. 462–9.

[72] S. Harris-Short (2002) pp. 336–8.

the premise that the outcome of the dispute must be determined by the child's best interests, and *then* considering the rights of the parties involved. Judicial reluctance to engage with these criticisms means that there appeared to be something of a standoff between the dominant academic opinion, that rights needed to be explicitly considered and weighed, and the judicial view, that the traditional approach to the welfare principle was consistent with the HRA.

Despite the gulf between these approaches, there now appears to be a narrowing of the gap between them. This has partly come about as there is now greater clarity on the way in which the judiciary are expected to reason under the HRA and ECHR. Recent cases from outside of child law have developed the courts' understanding of what exactly is required by the HRA. The Supreme Court has made it clear that the courts should first look to domestic law, much of which embodies the values protected by the HRA, rather than first looking rather to the rights themselves.[73] It is only when domestic law gives insufficient protection to rights that the court should reach for the HRA and use it to develop that law. Domestic law, interpreted through the HRA if necessary, is therefore the prime means by which rights are protected, with direct engagement with rights only playing a secondary role. Baroness Hale, one of the architects of the Children Act 1989, has emphasised that the Act was drafted with the requirements of the ECHR and the developing jurisprudence on proportionality in mind.[74] Given that background, it should be expected that many cases applying the welfare principle will also respect ECHR rights, without the need for overt analysis of those rights. This view is reinforced by recent jurisprudence of the ECtHR, notably *YC* v. *United Kingdom*,[75] in which the court found that there had been no violation of the Convention, despite the fact that there had been no explicit reference to it in placing a child for adoption.[76] Further, the court found that the welfare checklist in the domestic legislation[77] broadly reflected the considerations required to show that interference was necessary under Article 8(2).[78] Taken together, these developments seem to indicate that the HRA does not require the courts to explicitly conduct a proportionality assessment as a matter of course; instead, the courts should apply the welfare principle, but interpret it to be consistent with rights where possible.

In parallel with these developments, the courts have also become increasingly alert to the fact that there are circumstances in which application of the welfare principle *does* fail to protect the rights of children and parents and emphasised the importance of interpreting and applying the legislation to comply with the Convention. The Supreme Court decision in *Re B*[79] has played

---

[73] E.g. *Osborn* v. *The Parole Board* [2013] UKSC 31, at [55]–[57].
[74] *Re B (A Child)* [2013] UKSC 33, [2013] 1 WLR 1911, at [194].   [75] [2012] 2 FLR 332.
[76] Ibid. at [147].
[77] Here the Adoption and Children Act 2002, s. 1(4), setting out a similar range of factors to Children Act 1989, s. 1(3).
[78] *YC* v. *United Kingdom* [2012] 2 FLR 332, at [135].
[79] [2013] UKSC 33, [2013] 1 WLR 1911.

a decisive role in setting this approach. This was a child protection case in which a care order had been made with a plan for adoption, primarily based on the likelihood of future harm. The order therefore represented a serious interference with the Article 8 rights of the parents and the child. Under ECtHR case law, such a serious interference with Article 8 could only be justified in exceptional circumstances, on the basis of overriding requirements of the child's welfare.[80] The Supreme Court held that the welfare principle had to be construed and applied to comply with this ECtHR case law as far as was possible.[81] This meant that the care order would only be lawful if the interference with the Article 8 rights was proportionate within the meaning of Article 8(2). To ensure that this was so, the court should analyse those rights and ensure that the interference was proportionate to the risk of harm to the child, given the seriousness of the rights involved in this case.[82] Taking these developments together, the position that is emerging is that application of the welfare principle will usually be compatible with the HRA, but the courts should be alert to the fact that it could be applied in ways that *do* disproportionately infringe Convention rights. The welfare principle does not absolve the court of its responsibility to ensure that it acts compatibly with Convention rights. In cases where infringement may be likely, the rights should be considered and weighed by the court, not because there is a universal procedural requirement to do so, but in order to avoid making an order that is incompatible with the ECHR in practice.

The developing law demonstrates how the interaction between welfare and rights can work, but does not fully resolve the problem. It is no accident that this approach has been developed in the context of public law cases such as *Re B*. In these cases, the potential for interference with the rights of all involved, including the child, tends to be extreme and the Strasbourg case law is complex and detailed. Importantly, Strasbourg has also given a dominant role to welfare in public law cases; this means that it is far less of a challenge to reconcile rights and welfare. The problem that now faces the courts is how far this approach applies to private law cases. It is quite clear that private law orders can also have a profound impact on rights, particularly when they may lead to a similar severance of family relationships as public law cases. As Lord Justice McFarlane has observed:

> ... the impact of Art 8 is by no means confined to public law orders. There will be a range of private law children orders which engage Art 8 and which must now be approached on appeal in the manner established by the majority of the Supreme Court in *Re B*. It is not necessary for the purposes of this judgment to establish where the outer limit of this 'range' may be, and I expressly do not

---

[80] Ibid. at [34], [77], [130] and [195]–[198].
[81] Ibid. esp. at [73]–[78] (also considering the CRC).
[82] Ibid. at [32]–[34], [75]–[76] and [199].

intend to do so, but an order refusing all direct contact between parent and child must plainly be on the *Re B* side of the boundary.[83]

There are then three challenges that remain. The first is defining this 'outer limit' of the requirement to adopt the *Re B* approach in private law cases. It has been applied in cases where there will be a serious impact on the parent–child relationship, including relocation cases that are likely to sever that relationship,[84] or orders for refusing direct contact. Further, the Court of Appeal in *Re A (Children) (Contact: Ultra-Orthodox Judaism: Transgender Parent)* emphasised the court's duty to act compatibly with the parent's right under Article 14 of the ECHR.[85] How far the requirement applies beyond such circumstances is not clear. The Court of Appeal has stressed that in 'many if not most' private law cases, there is no need for a separate proportionality evaluation.[86] This lack of clarity means that the courts seem to be able to avoid difficult questions of rights in private cases, even if the interference with rights is serious. Second, there is a question of what the *Re B* approach means in private law cases and how the courts are to assess proportionality in cases between private parties. For example, the Court of Appeal, considering relocation in *Re C*, rejected the proposal that they should separately conduct a welfare exercise and then a proportionality exercise as a cross-check with Black LJ, noting that:

> If the cross-check produced the same result as the welfare analysis, it would be unproblematic but not very useful except as reassurance. If it produced a different result, that result could only have an impact on the outcome of the case if the provisions of section 1 of the 1989 Act were to be ignored. I am afraid that there also seems to me to be a real danger of the parties and the court getting so tangled up in the strands of the two separate exercises that they lose sight of what really matters for the child.[87]

This demonstrates the fundamental problem identified above, that there are circumstances in which welfare and rights can lead to different answers. The Court of Appeal's solution to this problem was to consider the proportionality of interfering with the parents' rights as part of the welfare analysis. This takes us to the final, and possibly most important, challenge in the developing law. There is a danger that greater integration of the HRA and welfare will simply

---

[83] *Re A (A Child)* [2013] EWCA Civ 1104, [2014] 1 FLR 1185, at [43].

[84] *Re F* [2015] EWCA Civ 882, [2017] 1 FLR 979, at [31]–[33]. See also *WS v. KL* [2020] EWHC 2548 (Fam).

[85] I.e. the right to enjoy Convention rights without discrimination: [2017] EWCA Civ 2164, [2018] 4 WLR 60, at [99]–[115]. Exactly how this duty applied in this case is unclear, given that the allegedly discriminatory behaviour was that of members of the community who were not party to the case: J. Eekelaar (2018).

[86] *Re F* [2015] EWCA Civ 882, [2017] 1 FLR 979, at [32]. See also *Re Y (Children) (Removal from Jurisdiction) (Interests of Non-Subject Child)* [2014] EWCA Civ 1287, [2015] 1 FLR 1350, at [40]–[43], although the court's views are difficult to reconcile with those in *Re A (Children) (Contact: Ultra-Orthodox Judaism: Transgender Parent)*, ibid. at [100].

[87] *Re C (A child)* [2015] EWCA Civ 1305, at [61].

result in the interests of parents distorting the welfare assessment to the detriment of children.[88] The recent cases that emphasise the need for a rights-compliant approach to welfare have tended to focus on the parents' Article 8 right to a relationship with the child, briefly mentioning the child's reciprocal right. Given the rather inconsistent approach that the Strasbourg court has taken to children's rights, there is a danger that bringing rights into the welfare analysis will focus on those of parents and so diminish the standing of children's rights and interests. Avoiding this will require greater attention to the rights of children themselves, including rights beyond the child's Article 8 right to family relationships. For example, the right to bodily autonomy of the vegan 15-year-old in *F* v. *F* could have been integrated into the welfare analysis in a similar manner to the approach described here. While some might fear that this would lead to harm to the child, this is not the case. Such rights are not absolute and the close relationship between rights and welfare means that reflecting on a child's rights is often a good way of ensuring that there has been a full understanding of her welfare.

(3) Children's Rights in Legislation and Policy

For children's rights to be truly effective, it is not enough to look to the judicial remedies available when rights are violated; those rights must be embedded in legislation, policy-making and policy implementation.[89] The importance of this point is recognised in Article 4 of the CRC, which states: 'States Parties shall undertake all appropriate legislative, administrative, and other measures for the implementation of the rights recognized in the present Convention.' Just as children face difficulties in being heard in judicial processes, so their lack of enfranchisement and their limited opportunity for participation in political processes leaves their rights in a precarious position in the public sphere.[90] The democratic rights of parents may be able to address this problem for some groups of children, but this is often inadequate. Many of the most vulnerable children lack stable adult care or have families whose own position means that they are unable to engage in the democratic process. In still more cases, the interests of children may be at risk precisely because of the decisions of their parents. For all of these reasons, children find themselves vulnerable to majoritarian neglect:[91] their interests are often not closely enough aligned with those of the electorate for majoritarian politics to adequately respond to those interests without enhanced procedural protection to correct this democratic deficit. Although there is some tentative evidence that on occasion children's rights are being taken more seriously by the UK government and in Parliament, there is still no systematic or serious attempt to embed children's rights in legislative and administrative processes. This conclusion stands in

---

[88] J. Fortin (2006) p. 309.   [89] Discussed further in Chapter 13.   [90] A. Nolan (2011) ch. 2.
[91] J. King (2012) pp. 181–5.

stark contrast to the far more effective approaches taken by the devolved nations in Scotland and Wales.

One of the main recommendations of the UN Committee on the Rights of the Child in their 2016 Concluding Observations on the UK's compliance with the CRC was that the UK should:

> (a) Introduce a statutory obligation at the national and devolved levels to systematically conduct a child rights impact assessment when developing laws and policies affecting children, including in international development cooperation;
>
> (b) Publish the results of such assessments and demonstrate how they have been taken into consideration in the proposed laws and policies.[92]

The government has accepted that 'more needs to be done to ensure that the impact of legislation, policy and delivery of services on children's rights is assessed more routinely and analytically', particularly in those departments that are not focused on children.[93] This is not the first time that the government has expressed commitment to improve consideration of children's rights in policy and legislation,[94] but to date it has resisted any statutory obligation to do so.

(A) Children's Rights and Legislation

Parliament is sovereign and able to act inconsistently with rights if it chooses; nonetheless, the HRA has had a notable impact on the way in which human rights are considered in the legislative process.[95] The requirement that the minister presenting the bill makes a statement as to whether the bill is compatible with Convention rights has been a catalyst for greater parliamentary engagement,[96] particularly through the work of the Joint Committee on Human Rights (JCHR). While children, as rights-holders under the HRA, do benefit from this greater scrutiny, engagement with wider children's rights is much more inconsistent. Whether children's rights are considered in the legislative process seems very much to depend on the political will of the department in question.[97] The Cabinet Office's 'Guide to Making Legislation' merely states that:

> *It would be helpful* to Parliament and the Joint Committee on Human Rights (JCHR) if explanatory notes included a summary of the anticipated effects of legislation on children and on the compatibility of draft legislation with the UNCRC.[98]

There is no sense of obligation or commitment to children's rights in this statement; instead, consideration of the effect on children is phrased as an

---

[92] Committee on the Rights of the Child (2016) para. 10.   [93] JCHR (2016) para. 25.
[94] HC Deb col 7WS, 6 December 2010.   [95] M. Hunt *et al.* (2015).   [96] M. Hunt (2010).
[97] JCHR (2015) esp. para. 24.   [98] Cabinet Office (2017) para. 12.29 (emphasis added).

optional courtesy to Parliament and the JCHR. Assessment of children's rights is only mentioned in the context of the explanatory notes to the bill; there is no suggestion that a separate impact assessment is required. Further, there are no rules or guidance as to how any assessment is to take place or the standards against which the legislation is to be assessed. The Cabinet Office prefaces this statement by noting that 'the Government and the UN committee may at times disagree on what compliance with certain articles entails', suggesting that even the meaning of the rights themselves is open for redefinition when assessing the compatibility of the legislation. Legislative scrutiny of children's rights suffers from these twin weaknesses: there are no circumstances in which it is mandatory and there are no agreed standards by which assessment should take place.

Despite these weaknesses, there has been some increased willingness to assess draft legislation for compliance with children's rights. Children's rights impact assessments (CRIA) have been produced for draft legislation, including: the Education Bill in 2011; the Children and Families Bill in 2013; the Modern Slavery Bill in 2014; the Welfare Reform and Work Bill in 2015; and the Children and Social Work Bill 2016. The majority of these bills have directly concerned children and most have been sponsored by the Department for Education.[99] A valuable aspect of the CRIA system is in alerting departments to the children's rights implications of bills that are not overtly concerned with children. Children's lives can be profoundly affected by rules that are ostensibly concerned with their parents – for example, changes in welfare payments, access to housing or immigration. Similarly, legislation that affects wider society can have a differential impact on children – for example, legislation affecting air pollution. For these reasons, all legislation benefits from CRIA, perhaps *especially* where the impact on children is not immediately apparent.

Given these concerns, it is worrying that there has been little willingness to conduct CRIA in departments that are not primarily concerned with children. There are a small number of such examples. For example, the Welfare Reform and Work Bill 2015, which reduced the benefit cap, was the subject of review for compliance with children's rights,[100] in contrast to earlier welfare reform legislation.[101] Unfortunately, that assessment is also a good example of just how limited a CRIA can be without any template for assessment or understanding of the rights against which the legislation is assessed. The assessment amounted to little more than two paragraphs asserting that the government's objectives in the bill would encourage people into work and in this way would benefit children generally. There was no consideration of the needs of the

---

[99] The Department of Education has also created an assessment template for CRIA to ensure a more systematic approach to assessing the impact on children's rights: *Hansard*, HC, vol. 662, col. 447, 24 June 2019 (N. Zahawi).

[100] Department for Work and Pensions (2015) paras 76 and 77.

[101] JCHR (2011) esp. para. 1.35.

children who would actually be affected by the reduction in the benefit cap or of their specific and protected rights. This itself is staggering given that the majority of the Supreme Court had in *SG*, discussed above, concluded that the benefit cap had been imposed in a manner that was in violation of Article 3 of the CRC. Instead, the assessment demonstrated the same erroneous assumption, criticised by Lady Hale in *SG*,[102] that the requirements of the CRC can be satisfied by considering children's interests generally, rather than the rights of affected individual children, including their right to adequate food, warmth and housing.[103] A CRIA produced with such limited engagement with the distinctive rights of the children most directly affected is of no real value in legislative scrutiny.

Some of the CRIA that have been produced show a far more serious attempt to assess the impact on children's rights. For example, the Department of Education's CRIA on the Children and Social Work Bill 2016 involved far more detailed assessment of specific CRC rights and consultation with both children and the Children's Commissioner. Even this does not meet the detailed requirements that would have applied had the legislation been before the Welsh Assembly rather than the Westminster Parliament. Wales has, since 2011, adopted a requirement on ministers to have due regard to the CRC in exercising all of their functions, including preparing draft legislation.[104] The CRIA process in Wales is the subject of detailed guidance[105] and has widely been credited with improving outcomes for children in Wales.[106] A similar, more rigorous approach at Westminster, using children's rights as standards against which legislation could be assessed, could have real benefits for children.

Despite the rather slow progress in adopting CRIA, Parliament as a whole has shown greater awareness of, and willingness to engage with, children's rights. The JCHR, in particular, has paid close attention to children's rights, both in scrutinising legislation and holding the government to account for their record on children's rights.[107] Similarly, debates on the floor of both Houses have shown increasing attention to children's rights, in part informed by the JCHR.[108] Real progress could be made for children if this commitment is harnessed to create effective, systematic assessment of children's rights. Key

---

[102] *R (SG)* v. *Secretary of State for Work and Pensions* [2015] UKSC 16, [2015] 1 WLR 1449, at [226].

[103] Despite these shortcomings, the legislation survived later challenge, in part because the relevant issues were raised in Parliament: *R (DA)* v. *Secretary of State for Work and Pensions* [2019] UKSC 21, [2019] 1 WLR 3289, esp. at [79]–[87]; *R (SC)* v. *Work and Pensions Secretary* [2021] UKSC 26, [2021] 3 WLR 428, esp. at [163]–[166]. Discussed further in Chapter 13.

[104] The Rights of Children and Young Persons (Wales) Measure 2011. See J. Williams (2013) esp. ch. 4.

[105] Welsh Government (2014).   [106] S. Hoffman (2015).   [107] E.g. JCHR (2011), (2015).

[108] E.g. debates concerning the Children and Social Work Bill (2016), Children and Families Bill (2013) and Immigration Bill (2015).

to that progress is access to high-quality understanding of children's rights to avoid the selective and malleable approach evident to date.

(B) Children's Rights and Policy

The same problems that prevent detailed consideration of children's rights in legislation also affect their treatment in the creation and implementation of policy more broadly. Inconsistent commitment to children's rights and a limited understanding of their requirements hamper the realisation of children's rights across public administration, just as they do in legislation. A promising way of ensuring that children's rights are given proper consideration in public administration is to introduce a specific legislative obligation to do just that. For rights protected by the HRA, there is a clear, enforceable legal obligation on all public authorities to act compatibly with the protected rights.[109] This can be a powerful means of redress for children in respect of those rights that are protected by the HRA. There is, however, no equivalent duty in respect of the CRC in England. Instead, limited duties to 'have regard to the need to safeguard and promote the welfare of children' are imposed on specific public authorities.[110] Useful as these duties can be, they fall short of a commitment to children's rights, instead focusing on welfare and merely requiring 'regard' to be had to that welfare, rather than for rights compliance to be secured. Further, they are limited in their application to named public authorities, rather than applying to all public authorities, including ministers.

In the absence of a legal obligation, whether or not children's rights are taken seriously in drafting policy is largely a matter of the political commitment of the minister in question. Prior to 2015, the Ministerial Code set out an overarching duty on ministers to 'comply with the law, including international law and treaty obligations',[111] which, while not legally binding, at least set a clear conventional expectation that ministers would consider and comply with that law in exercising their functions. Following the 2015 election, the reference to international law and treaty obligations was removed, creating an impression that compliance with international law was no longer a priority in setting standards expected of ministers.[112] The government's statement to

---

[109] HRA 1998, s. 6.

[110] Children Act 2004, s. 11(2); Borders, Citizenship and Immigration Act 2009, s. 55. Discussed further in Chapter 13. See e.g. *R (Project for the Registration of British Citizens)* v. *Home Secretary, Speaker Intervening* [2021] EWCA Civ 193, [2021] 1 WLR 3049: in which failure to conduct a review of the impact on children led to a declaration that the duty under s. 55 had not been fulfilled. The decision concerned the imposition of a mandatory fee of over £1,000 on children applying for citizenship, an amount that was unaffordable for many children and their families.

[111] Cabinet Office (2010).

[112] *R (Gulf Centre for Human Rights)* v. *Prime Minister* [2018] EWCA Civ 1855: an application for permission to apply for judicial review of the decision to amend the Code failed on the basis that the change was not one of substance, as ministers remained under an obligation to act in accordance with law.

Parliament in response to the concluding observations of the UN Committee on the Rights of the Child, in 2016, also suggested that ministerial consideration of the CRC was a matter of choice rather than expectation. That statement made clear that ministers were 'encouraged' to consider the recommendations and to treat these and the CRC itself as a 'helpful and important guide' to making sure that policies consider children.[113] The clear message given is that consideration of children's rights in policy is a matter of choice rather than commitment.

This voluntary approach at Westminster is very different from the approach required in the devolved administrations in Wales and Scotland. As discussed above, Welsh ministers have a duty 'when exercising any of their functions' to 'have due regard to the requirements of' the CRC and its protocols.[114] In Scotland, a more limited duty is imposed, requiring ministers to 'keep under consideration whether there are any steps which they could take which would or might secure better or further effect in Scotland of the UNCRC requirements, and if they consider it appropriate to do so, take any of the steps identified by that consideration'.[115] Early research into the effectiveness of these duties has identified real and measurable impact on changes that improve the lives of children – for example, in addressing family homelessness in Wales and raising the age of criminal responsibility in Scotland.[116] Scotland has committed to further implementation of the CRC into domestic law.[117] So far, the Westminster government has proved resistant to any such obligation, preferring to rely on voluntary commitments.

During the passage of the Children and Social Work Bill in 2016, an attempt was made to add a specific legislative obligation to protect CRC rights in England. This obligation, proposed by the JCHR, would have applied to all public authorities in the same way as the HRA. The new duty would have required those authorities to have 'due regard' to the CRC in the 'exercise of its functions relating to safeguarding and the welfare of children'.[118] The obligation would have been weaker than the equivalent HRA obligations, both in that it would not have applied to all functions, just those relating to children, and also in that the requirement was merely to have 'due regard' to the CRC rather than to act compatibly with it. The 'due regard' requirement is used in the public-sector equality duty[119] and reflects that used in the CRC Welsh

---

[113] *Hansard*, HC, vol. 615, HCWS 194, 17 October 2016 (Edward Timpson).

[114] The Rights of Children and Young Persons (Wales) Measure 2011.

[115] Children and Young People (Scotland) Act 2014, s. 1.

[116] Equality and Human Rights Commission (2016); S. Hoffman (2015).

[117] An attempt to incorporate much of the CRC into Scottish law was contained in the UN Convention on the Rights of the Child (Incorporation) (Scotland) Bill. This Bill was found to be outside of the legislative competence of the Scottish Parliament, although the judgment did not preclude legislation to incorporate the CRC into Scottish law in a different form: *Re Attorney-General's Reference, United Nations Convention on the Rights of the Child (Incorporation) (Scotland) Bill* [2021] UKSC 42, [2021] 1 WLR 5106.

[118] JCHR (2016) paras 18–30.   [119] Equality Act 2010, s. 149(1).

measure. While not as stringent as a requirement to comply with the rights in question, it does require that the decision-maker approaches the duty 'in substance, with rigour and with an open mind' rather than merely adopting a 'tick box' approach.[120] There are strong arguments in favour of introducing such a duty given the positive impact that it has had in Wales and the patchy commitment to children's rights in England. The government resisted the amendment, accepting that more needs to be done to embed the CRC in policy and practice, but suggesting that that could be better achieved by training and process than by the introduction of the duty.[121]

The government's recognition that children's rights require greater protection in legislation and policy is welcome. At present, there are pockets of good practice, but protection is too often hampered by an inconsistent approach to considering the CRC and by a lack of in-depth understanding of what children's rights require. Whether these problems can be dealt with without mandatory duties remains to be seen. The importance of recognising children's rights in Parliament and government is now more widely accepted as vital to creating an effective system of protection and that in itself is important progress.

(4) The Children's Commissioner

An increasingly important aspect of domestic protection of children's rights is the role of the Children's Commissioners.[122] The provisions of the CRC require states to establish specialised institutional arrangements to promote and protect children's rights.[123] The Committee on the Rights of the Child regards the creation of independent human rights institutions, with responsibility for children's rights, as vital to proper implementation of the CRC, and has issued detailed recommendations on their powers.[124] These are, inter alia: to undertake investigations into violations of children's rights, on complaint or on their own initiative; to prepare and publicise opinions and recommendations regarding children's rights; to review and report on the government's implementation and monitoring of such rights; and to promote public understanding and awareness of children's rights.[125]

The first Children's Ombudsman, Målfrid Flekkøy, was appointed in Norway in 1981,[126] with many other countries soon following suit.[127] Nevertheless, it was not until 2005[128] that English children finally acquired

---

[120] *R (Brown)* v. *Secretary of State for Work and Pensions* [2008] EWHC 3158, at [92].
[121] HL Deb 23 November 2016 vol 776 c1960 (Lord Nash).
[122] O. Rees and J. Williams (2016).   [123] Arts 4 and 42.
[124] Committee on the Rights of the Child (2002b). See also the 'Paris Principles': Office of the High Commissioner for Human Rights (1993).
[125] Committee on the Rights of the Child (2002b) para. 19 lists twenty recommended activities.
[126] M. Flekkøy (1991).   [127] P. Alston and J. Tobin (2005) pp. 40–51.
[128] Children Act 2004, Pt 1.

a Children's Commissioner, some time after their peers in Wales,[129] Northern Ireland[130] and Scotland.[131] This omission was particularly significant as the Children's Commissioner for England currently has responsibility for those matters which are not devolved to the nations. The initial position of the Children's Commissioner for England was extremely weak and reflected an ambivalent commitment to children's rights on the part of the UK government. In contrast to the commissioners for the devolved nations,[132] the role of the commissioner for England lacked any grounding in children's rights of the CRC. Instead, the function of the role was limited to promoting '*awareness* of the views and interests of children in England',[133] with a remit focused on promoting a version of well-being based on government policy[134] rather than implementation of independent legal rights. This stunted remit was coupled with very limited powers and an absence of real independence from government.[135] An independent review of the first 5 years of the role found its overall impact to be 'disappointing' – a finding that was perhaps inevitable given the narrow vision of the role displayed in the legislation.[136]

Despite this unpromising start, the role has now received a significant overhaul, with a decisive shift towards a rights-based approach. The commissioner's primary role is now 'promoting and protecting the rights of children in England',[137] with a requirement to have regard to the CRC in interpreting those rights,[138] and to monitor the implementation of the CRC in England.[139] The legislation also creates greater freedom from government constraint. While the initial legislation gave the Secretary of State for Education considerable influence to direct the commissioner's inquiries, these provisions have now been removed.[140] There remain some questions as to whether the role is sufficiently independent from government to enable the commissioner to take a robust and critical approach to policy. In particular, the appointment of the commissioner remains in the hands of government and the office of the commissioner remains a non-departmental body, sponsored by the Department for Education and deriving its funding from government. Nonetheless, recent experience gives tentative cause for optimism. The appointments of Anne Longfield in 2014 and Rachel De Souza in 2020 involved Parliamentary pre-appointment hearings before the Education Select Committee once they had

---

[129] Care Standards Act 2000, Pt V and Children's Commissioner for Wales Act 2001.

[130] Commissioner for Children and Young People (Northern Ireland) Order 2003 (SI 2003/439 (NI11)).

[131] Commissioner for Children and Young People (Scotland) Act 2003.

[132] J. Williams (2005) pp. 40–8. She notes (at pp. 40–1) that the Welsh Children's Commissioner only subsequently, by regulations, became obliged to pay regard to the CRC.

[133] Children Act 2004, s. 2(1) (as enacted) (emphasis added).

[134] CA 2004, s. 2(3) (as enacted).   [135] Committee on the Rights of the Child (2002a) para. 17.

[136] J. Dunford (2010).

[137] Children Act 2004, s. 2(1), inserted by Children and Families Act 2014, s. 107.

[138] Ibid. s. 2A, inserted by Children and Families Act 2014, s. 107.

[139] Ibid. s. 2(3)(i), inserted by Children and Families Act 2014, s. 107.

[140] Ibid. ss 3(3) and 4(1) (as enacted), repealed by Children and Families Act 2014, s. 139.

been identified as the preferred candidate for the role. This limited role for Parliament is bolstered by the fact that the commissioner now sends annual reports directly to Parliament[141] and is specifically empowered to bring any matter to Parliament's attention.[142] There is a good case, supported by the Children's Commissioners themselves, for complete transfer of appointment and oversight of the commissioner for England from government to Parliament, as is the case in Scotland, to create complete institutional independence.[143]

While some questions on ensuring institutional independence remain, the commissioner has proved well able to act in a manner that is openly critical of government. A good example of willingness to challenge key government policy can be seen in the extensive criticism of the impact of austerity policies on children's rights. This has included producing CRIA of budget decisions,[144] and welfare reform legislation,[145] along with joint representations to the Committee on the Rights of the Child as part of the UK's periodic review.[146] Reports have also been produced into a wide range of areas, including: sexual abuse; provision for care leavers; the impact of the Covid-19 pandemic; children's rights in the digital world; and the impact of the UK's exit from the EU. Many of these interventions have received extensive media coverage and attention in Parliament. The Children's Commissioner for England has also intervened in judicial review proceedings – for example, challenging government limitations to availability of legal aid[147] – and her involvement has been invited by the judiciary in addressing wider problems facing children before the courts.[148] In these ways, successive commissioners have used their expanded remit to raise awareness of children's rights and experiences both in public and in Parliament, and have an increasingly important role in public decision-making.[149]

Given the difficulties that children face in accessing courts[150] and the UK's refusal to accept the CRC communications procedure,[151] there are limited practical options available to children or groups of children whose rights have been violated. One way of addressing the difficulties is for the Children's

---

[141] Ibid. s. 8(3)(b), amended by Children and Families Act 2014, s. 113.

[142] Ibid. s. 2(3)(e), inserted by Children and Families Act 2014, s. 107.

[143] Children's Commissioners (2015) p. 5; a similar point applies to Wales and Northern Ireland.

[144] Office of the Children's Commissioner (2013).

[145] Office of the Children's Commissioner (2012).

[146] Children's Commissioners (2015), (2020).

[147] *R (on the application of Public Law Project)* v. *Lord Chancellor* [2016] UKSC 39.

[148] E.g. *Re S (Child in Care) (Unregistered Placement)* [2020] EWHC 1012 (Fam), [2020] 2 FLR 605, esp. at [28]: engagement with the Children's Commissioner in addressing the specific problems facing the vulnerable child in this case and the wider shortage of adequate placements for older children in care.

[149] E.g. in *R (on the application of Article 39)* v. *Secretary of State for Education* [2020] EWCA Civ 1577, the Secretary of State acted unlawfully by failing to consult the Children's Commissioner before introducing regulations amending duties to look after children during the Covid-19 pandemic.

[150] See Chapter 12.   [151] See Chapter 2.

Commissioners to have power to investigate children's individual complaints and petitions and ensure that they are remedied. Indeed, the Committee on the Rights of the Child considers such a power to be essential for *all* national human rights institutions, alongside the ability to support children taking cases to court.[152] Målfrid Flekkøy's list of those functions considered to be fundamental to an ombudsman's work places 'responding to complaints and/or violations' as a 'core function', enabling children 'to overcome a faceless, inhuman bureaucracy by having their grievances identified and pursued by a personal advocate'.[153] The Children's Commissioners in Wales and Northern Ireland[154] have the power to investigate individual complaints – a power also extended to the commissioner in Scotland in 2014.[155] The role of the commissioner in England in respect of individuals is much more limited, with a power to provide advice and assistance to those children living away from home or in social care.[156] Important as this provision is, it still leaves other children in England without accessible forms of redress for rights violations that are available in the other nations of the UK. The introduction of a power to investigate individual complaints would, of course, need to be properly resourced to avoid detraction from the commissioner's other functions.[157] That power is essential if the commissioner's role is to fully comply with international standards and to create an effective system for protection of children's rights.[158]

The reform of the role of Children's Commissioner for England demonstrates a stronger commitment to children's rights within government and real progress towards an effective system for protection of children's rights. The Children's Commissioner has produced high-quality reports and raised this awareness of children's rights both in public and in Parliament. Whether this activity translates into actual impact on government decision-making is more difficult to assess.[159] Certainly, greater guarantees of independence from government and the creation of an individual complaints procedure would do much to further improve the role of the commissioner.

(5) Conclusions: Looking to the Future

This chapter started by noting the fundamental problem that those international rights that are designed for children are not directly enforceable in domestic law, while those rights that are directly enforceable have not been written for children. To create a human rights system that works for children, both of these problems need to be addressed. While still at an early stage, there have been important recent steps towards creating a domestic system that

---

[152] Committee on the Rights of the Child (2002b) paras 13–14.   [153] M. Flekkøy (1991) p. 159.
[154] J. Williams (2005).   [155] Children and Young People (Scotland) Act 2014, ss 5–6.
[156] Children Act 2004, s. 2D, inserted by Children and Families Act 2014, s. 108.
[157] O. Rees (2010).   [158] Committee on the Rights of the Child (2016) para. 15.
[159] O. Rees and J. Williams (2016).

works for children. Although the CRC is not directly enforceable in domestic law, it has come to greater prominence both in the judicial and political spheres. The willingness of the judiciary to view children's HRA rights through the CRC lens has helped to interpret rights in a manner relevant to children and founded important duties on public authorities to take children seriously. These benefits should not be overstated – they remain reliant on the HRA as a conduit for translation into domestic law – but have had a powerful impact in the areas in which they apply. At the same time, there has been greater political will to take children's rights seriously and a strengthening of the role of Children's Commissioner. Again, these benefits should also not be overstated: there has been a strong resistance to mandatory duties on government and serious commitment to children's rights often depends on the political will within the responsible department. The far more serious commitment to children's rights in Scotland and, especially, Wales, demonstrates the way in which children's rights can be given more robust protection within the political sphere. For the UK to be fully compliant with its international obligations to protect children's rights, similar measures to systematically embed those rights at Westminster are required. The most effective means of protecting children's rights is in creating laws and policies that take them seriously, rather than relying on individual remedies through the courts.

A further area that needs consideration is the relationship between children's rights and their welfare. There has often been a greater willingness to engage with children's welfare than the full range of their rights. It has been the best interests principle in Article 3 of the CRC that has been particularly influential in developing the HRA. Similarly, the courts have been reluctant to consider the wider rights of children when applying the welfare principle. Children's welfare should be considered as harmonising with their rights rather than in isolation from them. Considering children's welfare without having regard to their rights neglects the complexity of children's needs and entitlements.

The future of the HRA within the UK is currently uncertain. Scepticism about the interpretation and enforcement of rights in the HRA has led to proposals for its reform and replacement with a UK Bill of Rights.[160] There is a strong case for using the opportunity of a new Bill of Rights to incorporate the Convention into domestic law, as has been done by many other ratifying countries and has been urged on the government here by the Committee on the Rights of the Child.[161] The Commission on a Bill of Rights, reporting in 2012, found strong support for including children's rights within any new Bill.[162] The JCHR has also said that it would 'ideally' like to see the CRC incorporated into domestic law, although in 'practical terms' has focused on integrating the CRC into legislation and policy as discussed above.[163] This is, of course, an aim that is entirely consistent with incorporation into domestic law, which would create clearer, enforceable

---

[160] MoJ (2021).   [161] Committee on the Rights of the Child (2002a) paras 8–9.
[162] Commission on a Bill of Rights (2012) para. 38.   [163] JCHR (2015) para. 34.

obligations to comply with the CRC, in place of the easily avoided voluntary measures currently in place. Whether or not a Bill of Rights is introduced in the UK, there are now powerful arguments favouring incorporation of the CRC. It would give children enforceable rights, focused on their own needs and development, with the potential to effect real change. Unfortunately, the current direction of rights reform seems more likely to lead to a curtailment of children's rights rather than an expansion.[164] Current proposals for a Bill of Rights would retain the current rights derived from the ECHR, but replace the framework by which those rights are protected. These proposals would be a double blow for children: not only would the opportunity to incorporate specific rights for children be missed, but the watered-down protection for those rights is likely to have a disproportionate impact on children.[165] The progress made in protecting children's rights currently appears precarious in the face of a renewed climate of rights scepticism.

Bibliography

Alston, P. and Tobin, J. (2005) *Laying the Foundations for Children's Rights*, UNICEF.

Bonner, D., Fenwick, H. and Harris-Short, S. (2003) 'Judicial Approaches to the Human Rights Act' 52 *International and Comparative Law Quarterly* 549.

Cabinet Office (2010) *Ministerial Code*, Cabinet Office.

  (2017) *Guide to Making Legislation*, Cabinet Office.

Children's Commissioners (2015) *Report of the UK's Children's Commissioners*, Children's Commissioners.

  (2020) *Report of the Children's Commissioners of the United Kingdom of Great Britain and Northern Ireland to the United Nations Committee on the Rights of the Child*, Children's Commissioners.

Choudhry, S. (2003) 'The Adoption and Children Act 2002, the Welfare Principle and the Human Rights Act 1998 – a Missed Opportunity' 15 *Child and Family Law Quarterly* 119.

Choudhry, S. and Fenwick, H. (2005) 'Taking the Rights of Parents and Children Seriously: Confronting the Welfare Principle under the Human Rights Act' 25 *Oxford Journal of Legal Studies* 453.

Commission on a Bill of Rights (2012) *A UK Bill of Rights: The Choice Before Us*, Vol. 1.

Committee on the Rights of the Child (2002a) *Concluding Observations of the Committee on the Rights of the Child: United Kingdom of Great Britain and Northern Ireland*, CRC/C/15/Add 188 2002, Centre for Human Rights, Geneva.

  (2002b) *General Comment No. 2 on the Role of Independent National Human Rights Institutions in the Promotion and Protection of the Rights of the Child*, CRC/GC/2002/2, Centre for Human Rights, Geneva.

  (2013) *General Comment No. 14 on the Right of the Child to Have His or Her Best Interests Taken as a Primary Consideration (Art. 3, Para. 1)*, CRC/C/GC/14, Centre for Human Rights, Geneva.

  (2016) *Concluding Observations of the Committee on the Rights of the Child: United Kingdom of Great Britain and Northern Ireland*, CRC/C/GBR/CO/5, Centre for Human Rights, Geneva.

Department for Work and Pensions (2015) *Memorandum to the Joint Committee on Human Rights: The Welfare Reform and Work Bill 2015*.

---

[164] MoJ (2021), discussed further in Chapter 17.

[165] Particularly the proposals to limit recognition of positive obligations, require greater deference to public bodies and restrict the courts' approach to interpretation of the text of the Convention: discussed further in Chapter 17.

Dunford, J. (2010) *Review of the Office of Children's Commissioner (England)*, The Stationery Office.

Eekelaar, J. (2018) 'Welfare and Discrimination: Re M' *Family Law* 393.

Equality and Human Rights Commission (2016) *EHRC Briefing on the Impact of Statutory Children's Rights Duties in Scotland and Wales*, written evidence for the JCHR CHSW0002.

Fenwick, H. (2004) 'Clashing Rights, the Welfare of the Child and the Human Rights Act' 67 *Modern Law Review* 889.

Flekkøy, M. (1991) *A Voice for Children: Speaking Out as their Ombudsman*, Jessica Kingsley Publishers.

Fortin, J. (2004) 'Children's Rights: Are the Courts Now Taking Them More Seriously?' 15 *King's College Law Journal* 253.

(2006) 'Accommodating Children's Rights in a Post Human Rights Act Era' 69 *Modern Law Review* 299.

(2011) 'Are Children's Interests Really Best? ZH (Tanzania) (FC) v. Secretary of State for the Home Department' 74 *Modern Law Review* 932.

Gilmore, S. (2017) 'Use of the UNCRC in Family Law Cases in England and Wales' 25 *International Journal of Children's Rights* 500.

Harris-Short, S. (2002) 'Re B (Adoption: Natural Parent) Putting the Child at the Heart of Adoption?' 14 *Child and Family Law Quarterly* 325.

Herring, J. (1999) 'The Human Rights Act and the Welfare Principle in Family Law: Conflicting or Complementary?' 11 *Child and Family Law Quarterly* 223.

(2016) *Vulnerable Adults and the Law*, Oxford University Press.

(2017) *Family Law*, 8th edn, Pearson.

Hoffman, S. (2015) *Evaluation of the Welsh Government's Child Rights Impact Assessment Procedure under the Children's Rights Scheme pursuant to the Rights of Children and Young Persons (Wales) Measure 2011*, Wales Observatory on Human Rights of Children and Young People.

Hunt, M. (2010) 'The impact of the Human Rights Act on the Legislature: A Diminution of Democracy or a New Voice for Parliament?' 6 *European Human Rights Law Review* 601.

Hunt, M., Hooper, H. and Yowell, P. (2015) *Parliaments and Human Rights: Redressing the Democratic Deficit*, Hart Publishing.

Joint Committee on Human Rights (JCHR) (2011) *21st Report Legislative Scrutiny – Welfare Reform Bill*, HC 1704.

(2015) *The UK's Compliance with the UN Convention on the Rights of the Child*, HC 1016.

(2016) *Legislative Scrutiny: Children and Social Work Bill*, HC 739.

King, J. (2012) *Judging Social Rights*, Cambridge University Press.

MacDonald, A. (2011) *The Rights of the Child: Law and Practice*, Family Law.

Ministry of Justice (MoJ) (2021) *Human Rights Act Reform: A Modern Bill of Rights, CP 588*, Her Majesty's Stationery Office.

Nolan, A. (2011) *Children's Socio-Economic Rights, Democracy and the Courts*, Hart Publishing.

Office of the Children's Commissioner (2012) *A Child's Rights Impact Assessment of the Welfare Reform Bill*, www.childrenscommissioner.gov.uk/resource/.

(2013) *A Child's Rights Impact Assessment of Budget Decisions*, www.childrenscommissioner.gov.uk/resource/.

Office of the High Commissioner for Human Rights (1993) *Principles Relating to the Status and Functioning of National Institutions (The Paris Principles)*, United Nations.

Rees, O. (2010) 'Dealing with Individual Cases: An Essential Role for National Human Rights Institutions for Children?' 18 *International Journal of Children's Rights* 417.

Rees, O. and Williams, J. (2016) 'Framing Asymmetry: Devolution and the United Kingdom's Four Children's Commissioners' 24 *International Journal of Children's Rights* 408.

Taylor, R. (2016) 'Putting Children First? Children's Interests as a Primary Consideration in Public Law' 28 *Child and Family Law Quarterly* 45.

Welsh Government (2014) *Children's Rights Scheme*.

Williams, J. (2005) 'Effective Government Structures for Children?: The UK's Four Children's Commissioners' 17 *Child and Family Law Quarterly* 37.

(ed.) (2013) *United Nations Convention on the Rights of the Child in Wales*, University of Wales.

4

Children's Rights within the Family
Parental Rights and Responsibilities

(1) Introduction

Most children live within families; it is the family that can be both the greatest source of protection for children, but also the gravest threat to their safety and development. While parents[1] are usually best placed to protect and promote their children's interests, the privacy of family life can also allow parents to tyrannise, abuse and neglect their children. Indeed, the dependence of young children makes an imbalance in power between them and their parents inevitable. The question of how far the law should intervene in family life to protect children and secure their rights is controversial. Social policy and political debate are often strongly influenced by common assumptions about family privacy and parental autonomy that discourage interference with family life and instead promote the authority of parents.

The following chapters consider the complex question of the relationship between family life and children's rights. Chapter 5 addresses the child's right to identity, both an identity that is rooted in family relationships and the right to forge an identity that rejects that presented by the family. Chapter 6 considers the child's right to family life and the relevance of children's rights to disputes between adults as to who will care for the child. Chapters 7 and 8 return to the question of parents' rights and responsibilities, considering whether the rights of parents protect or challenge children's rights in health and in education. A theme of these chapters is the extent to which the assumption that the family should be free from legal regulation underlies current law governing the relationship between children and their parents. Many areas considered in these chapters demonstrate well the law's reluctance to intervene in order to promote children's rights, instead relying on parental authority and on 'private ordering' within the family. This chapter starts by laying the groundwork for these later chapters by considering the place of rights within the family. It starts by addressing the objections to conceiving of family life in terms of rights, particularly children's rights. It then turns to look

---

[1] This chapter uses the term 'parents' to include those, such as legal guardians, with legal responsibility for the child's upbringing. The question of how 'parents' are identified and when they might be displaced by carers is considered in Chapter 6.

at the nature of parental rights and responsibilities and their relationship to children's rights. Finally, it assesses the legal principles governing parents' right to control and discipline their children as they think fit – one of the best examples of the way in which the current law protects parental authority at the expense of children's rights.

(2) Objections to Rights within the Family

The Preamble to the UN Convention on the Rights of the Child (CRC) places the family at the heart of its conception of children's rights:

> Convinced that the family, as the fundamental group of society and the natural environment for the growth and well-being of all its members and particularly children, should be afforded the necessary protection and assistance so that it can fully assume its responsibilities within the community.
>
> Recognizing that the child, for the full and harmonious development of his or her personality, should grow up in a family environment, in an atmosphere of happiness, love and understanding.

Recognition of the family as the 'fundamental' and 'natural' unit of society echoes throughout international and regional human rights documents.[2] This starting point should reassure those who object that children's rights are inappropriate for, and incompatible with, family life. These objections come in very different forms, but tend to start from the position that viewing a child as an independent rights-holder improperly separates her interests from those of her family members and neglects the interconnected importance of family relationships. Any understanding of children's rights constructed in this way would indeed fail children, but this is not the vision of children's rights protected by the CRC. Instead, the CRC's vision of rights is deeply relational: understanding the child, not as an isolated, autonomous individual, but as intimately connected to family, community and culture.[3]

An influential objection to the place of children's rights within the family, particularly within the US, is the argument that recognising the rights of children undermines the right of parents to raise their children as they see fit. Perhaps the best-known proponent of this view, Martin Guggenheim, views children's rights as a means of state intrusion into the family, which 'empowers state officials to meddle in family affairs and base their decisions on their own values'.[4] For Guggenheim, this is an illegitimate interference in parental autonomy, which he finds better served by a parental rights doctrine that allows parents to act as they see fit, subject to a minimum standard of fitness.

---

[2] Universal Declaration of Human Rights, Art. 16(3); International Covenant on Civil and Political Rights, Art. 23(1); International Covenant on Economic, Social and Cultural Rights, Art. 10(1); African Charter on the Rights and Welfare of the Child, Art. 18(1); American Convention on Human Rights, Art. 17(1); Arab Charter on Human Rights (revised), Art. 33(1).
[3] J. Tobin (2013) pp. 423–6.   [4] M. Guggenheim (2005) p. 38.

While he acknowledges that this doctrine allows some parents to act towards their children in a manner that is disagreeable, unacceptable and not in their best interests,[5] he considers that children are no better served by an increased power of state intervention. Although expressed as an argument against children's rights, in reality this is an objection to discretionary state intervention in parental decision-making, whether that is based on children's rights or otherwise. For example, a legal system that did not recognise children's rights but allowed intervention based purely on state paternalism towards children would also attract the same criticism.[6] It is not only children's rights that can found legal limits on parental autonomy: any legal system that seeks to advance the welfare of children, or to recognise societal interests in their upbringing, will at some point place limits on the ability of parents to raise their children as they see fit and will often grant considerable discretion in employing those limits. In so far as it is a criticism directed at children's rights, the parental rights critique understates the central role of parents within most models of children's rights. In particular, the CRC's conception of children's rights is not antagonistic to parental decision-making, but instead situates respect for parents' rights and responsibilities as a central obligation of state parties. The CRC's commitment to the importance of the family flows from its Preamble and through the legal obligations that it recognises. Article 18 of the CRC clearly states that parents 'have the primary responsibility for the upbringing and development of the child',[7] and this fundamental principle is similarly recognised in Article 5, which obliges states to respect the responsibilities, rights and duties of parents.[8] The emphasis on the role of parents can also be seen in further rights within the CRC. For example, the state's duties to respect children's freedom of thought, conscience and religion and to protect the child's well-being include obligations to take account of the rights and duties of parents in so doing.[9] The Convention further protects the relationship between parents and children by constraining the circumstances in which the state can interfere in that relationship and placing positive duties to facilitate reunification.[10] While the CRC no doubt allows greater interference with parental autonomy than many defenders of the parental rights doctrine would find acceptable, it presents an understanding of children's rights in which the central role of parents in the lives of their children is recognised and protected. Indeed, there is a stronger argument, explored below, that the CRC gives too much protection to the role of parents and too little attention to the tensions that can arise between children's interests and the parental role.

---

[5] Ibid. p. 46.

[6] Indeed, much of Guggenheim's critique is concerned with the application of the 'best interests' test rather than with analysis of children's rights as protected in international law, e.g., ibid. pp. 36–41. For a detailed analysis of Guggenheim's argument, see M. Freeman (2006).

[7] See also Art. 27.

[8] See E. Sutherland (2020) for discussion of the drafting and interpretation of Art. 5.

[9] Arts 3(2) and 14(2).   [10] Arts 7, 9 and 10.

The deeply relational concept of rights within the CRC should also reassure those who object to children's rights within the family for very different reasons. There is an important body of literature that conceives of rights as based on an atomistic and individualised view of children that is incompatible with the interdependent relationships of love and care that characterise family life.[11] On this view, rights create an impoverished view of children's lives, conceiving of family members as self-interested individuals, whose relationships can be reduced to claims against one another. Any understanding of children's rights constructed in this way could indeed be criticised for failing to reflect the reality of many children's lives and neglecting the value of family relationships that are mutually interdependent relationships of sacrifice, love and care. It is clearly the case that the language of children's rights has sometimes been employed in a way that disconnects children from their relationships and harms children by failing to recognise the interconnectedness of family members.[12] Nonetheless, these cases represent a failure of understanding of the relational vision of children's rights embedded within the CRC.[13] Where rights are constructed in a way that reflects this reality, they can be a powerful tool for protecting relationships. This can be seen, for example, in the application of Article 8 of the ECHR to recognise the mutually supportive relationships of parents and children and to use this to challenge government action that impedes that relationship – for example, through the deportation of a parent.[14] Given the powerful role that rights can have in legal reasoning and in access to remedies, there are good reasons for those who value relational approaches to children's interests to develop an understanding of children's rights that recognises and protects the importance of their relationships.

It is, however, important to recognise that interconnected relationships can also be a source of harm; particularly to children, who have little choice in entering or exiting their family relationships. It is often precisely those children whose family relationships represent a threat to their interests who are most in need of the protection that comes from rights. Relationships can be harmful to children, not only when parents are cruel or negligent, but also when they are blinded by the deepest love. Take, for example, a parent who wishes to put a terminally ill child through painful and futile treatment because the loss of the child is one they cannot contemplate.[15] The recognition of children as separate from their parents, with interests that may sometimes conflict with

---

[11] There is insufficient space here to consider the different strands within this complex and wide-ranging literature. A good summary of the central arguments can be found in S. Choudhry and J. Herring (2010) ch. 3.

[12] E.g. the assertion of a child's right to contact to support contact with a family member who has perpetrated domestic abuse against their primary carer: see Chapter 6.

[13] See S. Choudhry and J. Herring (2010) for a relational approach to rights within the family.

[14] E.g. *ZH (Tanzania)* v. *Secretary of State for the Home Department* [2011] UKSC 4, [2011] 2 AC 166.

[15] See e.g. the litigation concerning Charlie Gard, discussed further below.

those of their parents, is crucial for protecting the rights of children whose relationships pose a risk to them. Rights within the family are perhaps best seen, as David Archard suggests, as an insurance policy:[16] while one might hope never to have to have recourse to them, rights act as a safety net to protect the child when caring relationships fail to do so. The existence of rights as a safety net does not mean that families ought to conceive of their own relationships primarily in terms of rights and duties.[17] A family in which parents acted purely out of a sense of legal duty, rather than from love and intimacy, would be unlikely to be a healthy environment for their children; although a parent contemplating how best to bring up her children may sometimes find it helpful to reflect on their rights as a guide to her decision-making.[18] Ultimately, however, rights are valuable, not because they purport to explain the entirety of family relationships, but because they protect vital interests when those relationships fail or are threatened.

(3) Family Privacy and the Role of the Law

The CRC's emphasis on the family as the 'fundamental' and 'natural' environment for children to thrive is also reflected in domestic and ECHR law. Article 8 of the ECHR protects 'family life', a term which 'encompasses a broad range of parental rights and responsibilities with regard to the care and upbringing of minor children', including the protection of parental authority within the family.[19] In so doing, it requires the state to respect family privacy, including parental authority, unless there are proportionate reasons for intervening under Article 8(2). These principles are also found in Baroness Hale's well-known summary of the position in English law in *Williamson*:

> Children have the right to be properly cared for and brought up so that they can fulfil their potential and play their part in society. Their parents have both the primary responsibility and the primary right to do this. The state steps in to regulate the exercise of that responsibility in the interests of children and society as a whole. But 'the child is not the child of the state' and it is important in a free society that parents should be allowed a large measure of autonomy in the way in which they discharge their parental responsibilities.[20]

Given that children, at least when they are young, are dependent on others to meet their needs, there are many good reasons for giving parents a zone of discretion in the way in which they exercise their responsibilities. Children have an interest in being able to trust that important decisions about their lives will be made by those adults who have an intimate and caring relationship with

---

[16] D. Archard (2014) p. 102.   [17] H. Brighouse and A. Swift (2014) pp. 17–22.

[18] H. Brighouse and A. Swift (2014) p. 20.

[19] *Nielsen* v. *Denmark* (1989) 11 EHRR 175, at [61]; see *The Christian Institute and others* v. *The Lord Advocate* [2016] UKSC 51, [2016] HRLR 19, at [71].

[20] *R (on the application of Williamson and others)* v. *Secretary of State for Education and Employment and others* [2005] UKHL 15, [2005] 2 All ER 1, at [72]; further discussed below.

them and who are able to respond to the child as an individual.[21] If parents are to make decisions that respond to their child's individual needs and interests, they will need sufficient discretion and choice to be able to do so – for example, in choosing education provision that best suits their particular child. More pragmatically, care for children places heavy demands on the time and resources of most parents. The reality for many parents is that they may have to compromise in some of the decisions that they make for their children in order to meet the competing interests of other family members and to balance the demands on their resources. Parents often need the flexibility to meet their children's needs within the confines of these competing demands, in order to meet their responsibilities in practice. A further reason for giving parents a large measure of autonomy in meeting their parental responsibilities is that reasonable people will frequently disagree on what is 'best' for children and predicting the future impact of a decision on a child can be speculative. As Baroness Hale's observation demonstrates, in a free society, the state should be cautious in imposing a particular view as to what is best for children without good reason and clear evidence to support that view. This discretion is particularly important as care for children will often intimately involve the parents' own personal values and convictions. A law which required parents to act against their own conscience – for example, by requiring a vegetarian parent to feed their child meat – could be a disproportionate interference in the parents' own private life. For all of these reasons, the law tends to give parents considerable discretion in choosing how to discharge their responsibility towards their children.

There are, however, dangers in situating primary responsibility for children in the protected private sphere. As Minow states, the approach of the law often:

> rests on a sharp distinction between public and private responsibilities for children. Using this public/private distinction, the framework assigns childcare responsibilities to parents, and thereby avoids public responsibility for children. Public power becomes relevant only in exceptional circumstances, when parents default. The government is not supposed to 'intervene' in the private realm of the family, where children's needs and interests are managed by their parents.[22]

By treating responsibility for children as a private matter for the family, states can avoid fulfilling their own obligations to provide for children's needs. For example, by framing responses to child poverty as a matter of parental responsibility, rather than addressing the external causes of poverty and public responsibility to children in poverty.[23] The ECHR does little to address this.

---

[21] In some circumstances, failure to involve a parent in important decisions may amount to a breach of the child's own rights: *Glass v. United Kingdom* [2004] 1 FLR 1019.

[22] M. Minow (1986) p. 7.

[23] E.g. DWP (2011), which explains the reduced role of the state in enforcing child maintenance on the basis that '[i]t is right that families are empowered to take responsibility for the welfare of their children', p. 4. See further Chapter 13.

As Baroness Hale has also pointed out, while the ECHR is mainly about securing freedom *from* state interference, 'children often need a great deal of state interference if they are to survive, let alone thrive'.[24] The more developed understanding of children's rights in the CRC is, however, clear that responsibility for children is collaborative.[25] Article 18 of the CRC may recognise parents as having primary responsibility for children, but it also obliges the state to 'render appropriate assistance to parents and legal guardians' and 'ensure the development of institutions, facilities and services for the care of children'. Similarly, while parents have the primary responsibility to provide the 'conditions of living necessary for the child's development', Article 27 also obliges states to 'take appropriate measures to assist parents and others responsible for the child to implement this right', including the obligation to 'in case of need provide material assistance and support programmes'. The vision of children's rights in the CRC sees responsibility towards children as collective: parents are to be supported by the state and wider community, rather than sheltered behind an impermeable private sphere.

A sharp distinction between public and private responsibilities for children also places children in a vulnerable position within the private sphere. For many children, the most important aspects of their lives are determined behind the veil of family privacy, where parents have the dominant role. Where parents exercise that role well, placing the individual child at the heart of their decisions, the private family sphere can be a place where children thrive. Where parents are not willing or able to do so, the separation of children's lives into the private space of parental authority can act as a shield that inhibits protection of children's rights and interests. Whether children's rights within the family amount to more than mere rhetoric for these children will depend on the nature and limits of that parental authority.

(4) The Nature and Scope of Parental Authority

Parental authority is not now, if it ever was, absolute. Although just over a century ago fathers had extensive authority over their children, the nineteenth-century case law supporting such a principle is now 'remaindered to the history books'.[26] In the twentieth century, legislation and case law firmly embedded the principle that the child's welfare is paramount in judicial decisions concerning their upbringing.[27] Further, the term 'parental responsibility' replaced 'parental rights' as the foundation of the legal relationship between parents and children. This change in language was of enormous

---

[24] B. Hale (2006) p. 351.   [25] J. Tobin (2013) p. 425.

[26] Per Lord Scarman in *Gillick* v. *West Norfolk and Wisbech Area Health Authority* [1986] AC 112, at 183, when commenting on the decision in *Re Agar Ellis, Agar Ellis* v. *Lascelles* (1883) 24 Ch D 317. See also Lord Denning's criticisms of the same case in *Hewer* v. *Bryant* [1970] 1 QB 357, at 369.

[27] E.g. *J* v. *C* [1970] AC 668.

symbolic significance: children are no longer regarded as the possession of their parents, but as their parents' responsibility.

Recognition of the child as an individual, with independent interests, was an essential precondition to establishing their position as rights-holders. The drafters of the CRC rejected the proprietary model of parenthood in favour of one based on responsibility. This is particularly clear in Article 18 of the CRC, which recognises that the primary responsibility for children lies with their parents and directs that 'the best interests of the child will be their basic concern'. Similarly, Article 5, which requires states to respect 'the rights, responsibilities and duties of parents', is very specific as to the nature of the parental role that it protects.[28] Parents are expected to give 'appropriate direction and guidance in the exercise by the child of the rights' in the CRC, 'in a manner consistent with the evolving capacities of the child'. In this way, the CRC clearly positions the parental role as one of responsibility to the developing child. It is the child's rights and interests that demarcate the legitimate scope of the parental role within the Convention.

Domestic law is also underpinned by the understanding that parental authority exists for the benefit of the child, and not for the adult exercising it. This principle was clearly reflected in the decision of the House of Lords in *Gillick*.[29] The case was famously concerned with the question of parental authority over 'mature minors', an issue of complexity and importance that is given detailed attention later in this book.[30] For present purposes, it is enough to note that the majority judgments were based on a firm understanding that parental authority was derived from duties towards children and that those duties defined the scope of that authority. This point was succinctly expressed by Lord Fraser:

> parental rights to control a child do not exist for the benefit of the parent. They exist for the benefit of the child and they are justified only in so far as they enable the parent to perform his duties towards the child, and towards other children in the family.[31]

The point was reinforced by Lord Scarman:

> The principle of the law, as I shall endeavour to show, is that parental rights are derived from parental duty and exist only so long as they are needed for the protection of the person and property of the child.[32]

Lord Templeman, while dissenting on the facts, took a similar view of the basic principle:

---

[28] See E. Sutherland (2020) for discussion of the potential tensions that this entails.
[29] *Gillick* v. *West Norfolk and Wisbech Area Health Authority* [1986] AC 112.
[30] See Chapters 9 and 11.
[31] *Gillick* v. *West Norfolk and Wisbech Area Health Authority* [1986] AC 112, at 170.
[32] Ibid. at 184.

> Parental power must be exercised in the best interests of the infant and the court may intervene in the interests of the infant at the behest of the parent or at the behest of a third party.[33]

Gillick was soon followed by the Children Act (CA) 1989, the most comprehensive piece of domestic legislation relating specifically to children. The Law Commission report that preceded the Act explicitly endorsed the *Gillick* approach to parents' rights. It took the view that since parents' rights are derived from their duties and exist to secure the welfare of their children, they were better described as 'responsibilities'.[34] As a result, the CA 1989 introduced the concept of 'parental responsibility' into domestic law, embedding the change of emphasis from parental rights to responsibilities.[35]

Although the importance of these changes should not be underestimated, the introduction of parental responsibility did not erase the concept of parental rights. The rights and authority of parents are preserved within the very definition of parental responsibility as 'all the rights, duties, powers, responsibilities and authority which by law a parent of a child has in relation to the child and his property'.[36] This is perhaps unsurprising: parents require legal authority to enable them to discharge their extensive responsibilities effectively. For example, in exercising their duty to ensure that the child receives a suitable education,[37] parents may need the legal authority to apply for a school place[38] or obtain information on the school's record.[39] Similarly, parents need the authority to consent to their child's medical treatment[40] in order to fulfil their responsibility for their child's health. In this way, parents have rights, in the sense of legal authority, which would be ineffective and unnecessary for those who do not have duties towards the child. Nonetheless, these rights can be broad and open to potentially draconian use. For example, parents will often need to restrain the freedom that their children enjoy in order to keep them safe; the extent of parental authority to do so means that parents can authorise limits on their children which might amount to a deprivation of liberty if imposed outside of the parent–child relationship.[41] Further, while some parental rights are an inevitable corollary of parental responsibility, the law grants parents far broader legal rights than those required by their duties towards their children. For example, the law permits parents to consent to the circumcision of their male child, regardless of whether there are any medical or health reasons to do so. In this context, the parents' cultural, religious or conventional reasons can justify what would otherwise amount to significant harm to the child.[42] Parents are also given legal authority or exemption from penalty in circumstances that may be in

---

[33] Ibid. at 200.   [34] Law Commission (1988) para. 2.4.   [35] CA 1989, s. 3.
[36] CA 1989, s. 3(1).   [37] See further Chapter 8.
[38] School Standards and Framework Act 1998, s. 86.
[39] The Education (Pupil Information) (England) Regulations 2005.   [40] See further Chapter 7.
[41] See further Chapter 9.
[42] *B and G (Children) (No. 2)* [2015] EWFC 3, [2015] 1 FLR 905, at [68]–[73].

direct conflict with their children's rights. This conflict is particularly clear in relation to corporal punishment, discussed further below, where parents are given an exemption from the criminal law on common assault despite widespread international recognition that such assault violates the rights of children. The existence of these parental rights is difficult to reconcile with the principle that the parental role is *solely* defined by welfare and responsibility to children.

(5) The Limits of Parental Responsibility in Practice

There is further ambiguity as to the nature and limits of parental responsibility within the CA 1989. As John Eekelaar has observed, parental responsibility 'can represent two ideas: one, that parents must behave dutifully towards their children; the other, that responsibility for child care belongs to parents, not the state'.[43] Both of these meanings can be found in domestic law, including the CA 1989, and the fault line between them is at the heart of many of the most difficult questions for children's rights within the family. To put the problem another way, in what circumstances does the veil of family privacy prevent inquiry as to whether parental responsibility is being properly used to further the rights and interests of the child?

The fault line between these two meanings of parental responsibility means that, although it is often said that parental responsibility is controlled by the welfare of the child, it is far from clear that this is the case in practice.[44] While any court deciding a matter of the child's upbringing is to treat the child's welfare as the paramount concern,[45] there is no domestic equivalent to Article 18 of the CRC, directing *parents* to consider the child's best interests.[46] A further barrier to the role of welfare is found in the sharp division that the legislation draws between the public realm and the privacy of family life. The pivot on which this division turns is found in the significant harm test, the threshold that must be passed before the court can consider whether it would be in the child's welfare for a compulsory child protection order to be made.[47] This test represents a candid acceptance that some children will be left with parents who are *not* acting in their best interests, indeed, with parents who are causing them harm, provided that that harm is not 'significant'. Mr Justice Hedley's oft-quoted observations in *Re L* make this clear:

---

[43] J. Eekelaar (1991).   [44] S. Gilmore (2009).   [45] CA 1989, s. 1(1).

[46] It might be said that any provision obliging parents to have regard to their child's interests in exercising their parental responsibility would be futile, as it would be almost entirely unenforceable. Nonetheless, legislation on the parental role has been used to send 'messages' to parents and attempt to create social norms, e.g., in the insertion of the presumption of parental involvement in CA 1989, s. 1(2A) and (2B), discussed further in Chapter 6.

[47] CA 1989, s. 31; a similar test in CA 1989, s. 100(4) applies to an application by a local authority to invoke the court's inherent jurisdiction.

society must be willing to tolerate very diverse standards of parenting, including the eccentric, the barely adequate and the inconsistent. It follows too that children will inevitably have both very different experiences of parenting and very unequal consequences flowing from it. It means that some children will experience disadvantage and harm, while others flourish in atmospheres of loving security and emotional stability. These are the consequences of our fallible humanity and it is not the provenance of the state to spare children all the consequences of defective parenting. In any event, it simply could not be done.[48]

In this way, the significant harm test[49] demarcates an extensive private sphere in which parents are shielded from compulsory child protection intervention.

Within this private sphere, in practice parents are largely free to act as they wish so long as they are in agreement and do not contravene the general standards of law.[50] Although the CA 1989 contains detailed provisions about the duties owed by local authorities to children they look after,[51] it fails to set out a basic list of parental responsibilities or obligations towards their children.[52] Further, it does not direct them as to how to discharge their responsibility – for example, by encouraging more consultation between parents and children,[53] or by requiring that they act in the best interests of their children. This means that in practice parents may pay scant regard to the fact that they are only legally entitled to act towards their children in accordance with the welfare principle and can be challenged, even overridden, if they fail to do so.[54] Although the average parent will usually seek to bring up his or her children with the best of intentions, the essential subjectivity of the 'welfare' or 'best interests' test[55] does little to persuade repressive parents to adjust their parenting style to promote their children's rights more effectively.

If parents disagree on the child's upbringing and take that disagreement as far as a court room, the welfare standard will be applied to resolve that dispute.[56] The law is, however, structured in a way that places hurdles in the way of court scrutiny of parental decision-making. Indeed, the CA 1989 reinforced the privatisation of family life by withdrawing the law from areas where it formerly had had some influence,[57] and adopting what has been described as a 'hands-off approach' on the basis of scepticism as to the value

---

[48] *Re L (Care: Threshold Criteria)* [2007] 1 FLR 2050, at [50].   [49] Chapter 15.

[50] The impact of the views of a competent minor who objects to the decisions of their parents is considered further in Chapter 9.

[51] CA 1989, ss 22–4 and the regulations made thereunder.

[52] In contrast to the approach in Scotland: Children (Scotland) Act 1995, ss 1 and 2.

[53] Discussed in Chapter 12.

[54] Per Lord Scarman in *Gillick* v. *West Norfolk and Wisbech Area Health Authority* [1986] AC 112, at 184.

[55] See Chapter 3.   [56] CA 1989, ss 1(1) and 8.

[57] E.g. the CA 1989, Sch. 12, para. 31 scaled down the courts' role in the arrangements made by divorcing parents for their children's future upbringing under the Matrimonial Causes Act 1973, s. 41. Even this minimal oversight was later removed by Children and Families Act 2014, s. 17.

of legal intervention in the family.[58] Subsequent legislative amendment has reinforced the role of 'private ordering': seeking to withdraw the law still further from the private family sphere by encouraging parties to resolve disputes without resort to the courts and imposing severe limitations on access to legal aid in private family cases.[59] If parents are in agreement with each other, then it is still less likely that their decisions will be challenged before a court. Third parties can only use the CA 1989 to challenge the, otherwise lawful, exercise of parental responsibility if they have the leave of the court to do so,[60] a test designed to protect the family from unwarranted interference.[61] While the court retains its own protective jurisdiction to act to safeguard the welfare of the child under both the CA 1989[62] and the inherent jurisdiction,[63] this is dependent on the child's plight being brought to the attention of the court. As a result, in practice, parents in agreement with each other are generally free to act in a way that would not be regarded as being in their children's best interests if challenged in court.[64] Although there are good reasons to avoid extensive judicial intervention in family life, the combination of permissive legislation, protected parental authority and limited court intervention effectively carves out a space in which parents who do not act in their children's best interests are protected from interference, provided that they do not cause them significant harm or breach the general law. In this space, children's interests are vulnerable, but the law operates on an assumption that responsible parents will automatically protect their children's interests, an assumption that is not always fulfilled in practice.

Despite the practical hurdles to challenging parents, the law remains clear that the parental role is one of responsibility to children and is both founded on, and limited by, the welfare principle. A number of high-profile cases have sought to challenge this position and to elevate to a legal principle the observation that parents are often free to act as they wish unless they cause significant harm. This challenge came to particular prominence in the case of Charlie Gard,[65] concerning a seriously ill baby whose parents wished to take him

---

[58] B. Hoggett (1994) p. 10.

[59] See esp. Legal Aid, Sentencing and Punishment of Offenders Act 2012 and Children and Families Act 2014, discussed in J. Eekelaar (2015).

[60] CA 1989, s. 10, limited categories of non-parents, who have acted in a quasi-parental role, are also entitled to apply without leave.

[61] Lord Chancellor, Lord Mackay of Clashfern, *Hansard*, HL Deb on the Children Bill, col. 491, 6 December 1988.

[62] CA 1989, s. 10(1)(b).

[63] Practice Direction 12D: Inherent Jurisdiction (Including Wardship) Proceedings.

[64] E.g. *Re G (Children)* [2012] EWCA Civ 1233, [2012] 3 FCR 524. Discussed further in Chapter 8, a parental dispute in which the Court of Appeal took the view that children would generally be best served by an education that offers them equality of opportunity, aspiration and future choice within the secular world, as these are the values that a reasonable parent would wish to encourage, but that no intervention would have been appropriate had the parents jointly chosen to educate their children at the schools in question.

[65] *Great Ormond Street Hospital for Children v. Yates* [2017] EWHC 1909 (Fam), [2017] 4 WLR 131 (Family Division) and [2017] EWCA Civ 410, [2018] 4 WLR 5 (Court of Appeal). The

abroad to pursue speculative medical treatment. His medical team at Great Ormond Street Hospital (GOSH) considered that the proposed treatment had no prospect of success, but had the potential to cause Charlie pain and distress and as such would not be in his best interests. Instead, GOSH sought permission from the court to withdraw life-sustaining treatment. The parents argued that the decision to take Charlie abroad to the care of a new medical team was an exercise of their parental rights and separable from GOSH's own duties to Charlie. As such, they argued, the court had no jurisdiction to hear a challenge to the decision of united parents unless that decision caused Charlie significant harm.[66] This challenge effectively sought to elevate the principle that responsibility for children is primarily that of parents, to a jurisdictional rule that would prevent parental decisions from being questioned unless they themselves brought the question to court, or risked causing significant harm. Had this challenge succeeded, it would have fundamentally undermined the principle, recognised in *Gillick*, that parental authority exists for the benefit of children and that the court may intervene to protect the child's interests. The Court of Appeal, Supreme Court and European Court of Human Rights were united in rejecting the parents' challenge and reaffirming the foundational rule that the exercise of parental responsibility should be assessed on the principle of the child's best interests, which forms the basis and legal limit of the parental role.

The *Gard* litigation reinforces the principle that the upbringing of children is a collaborative exercise in which parents take the leading role, but do not possess sole authority. This is important, both for those children whose cases do come before the court and for the message that it sends more widely. Nonetheless, for parents who avoid the judiciary's ambit, the reality remains that the law will often do little to restrain or guide their decisions. This is clearly demonstrated in the law on corporal punishment considered in section (6), below.

(6) Corporal Punishment

(A) Introduction

The law on corporal punishment provides a particularly good example of the way in which children's rights can be concealed behind the veil of family privacy. The extent to which parents should be allowed to discipline and punish their children as they think fit produces deeply polarised views over

Supreme Court gave a reasoned judgment, refusing permission to appeal on 8 June 2017. *Gard* v. *United Kingdom (Admissibility)* [2017] 2 FLR 773 (ECtHR). This litigation and similar cases are discussed in Chapter 7.

[66] In the event, the Court of Appeal considered that the parents' decision was likely to cause Charlie significant harm, although no such finding was sought, or made, at the initial hearing: *Great Ormond Street Hospital for Children* v. *Yates* [2017] EWCA Civ 410, [2018] 4 WLR 5, at [114].

whether the use of physical punishment on children can be justified on practical and ethical grounds, and more generally, over the extent to which the state should interfere with parents' family privacy and autonomy. There is undoubtedly a parental responsibility to bring children up in a safe environment and to teach them to moderate their behaviour appropriately. The law expects parents to impose a degree of discipline on the household and parents may be found to be in breach of their duty to care adequately for them if they fail to control them sufficiently to prevent accidents in the home occurring. A parent or foster parent failing to maintain a standard of care which can be expected from a reasonably careful and prudent parent may be liable in tort to a child who suffers an injury as a result. There are also dangers in imposing too many restrictions on children, who will be unable to develop the confidence to make decisions of their own if parents provide them with little opportunity to do so, by imposing on them an over-strict atmosphere of control and discipline. This leaves parents with a difficult balance to draw. In *Surtees* v. *Kingston-upon-Thames Borough Council; Surtees* v. *Hughes*, the Court of Appeal warned that the courts should be cautious and avoid imposing 'an impossibly high standard' in the light of the demands of family life.[67] Indeed:

> We should be slow to characterise as negligent the care which ordinary loving and careful mothers are able to give to individual children, given the rough-and-tumble of home life.[68]

Despite this call for flexibility, parents must impose some discipline to maintain a safe level of control on the household. The approach of domestic law is to view parental use of corporal punishment as a legitimate means by which parents may choose to discharge this duty, albeit one that is limited by the broad and rather vague boundaries of the criminal law. Within these boundaries, the law takes the 'hands-off' approach that underlies so many of the legal principles applied to children within the family. It is this approach to family life which has consistently prevented any legislative attempt to adequately regulate the way in which parents discipline their children.

There is, however, an increasing consensus, both in international law and in the domestic law of many states, that children are entitled to equal protection from physical assault, regardless of whether that is carried out by a parent under the guise of reasonable discipline. Most notably, the Committee on the Rights of the Child has interpreted the CRC to include an obligation on all states 'to move quickly to prohibit and eliminate all corporal punishment'.[69] Within the UK itself, deeply divergent views are evident. While both Scotland and Wales have prohibited corporal punishment in the home,[70] the

---

[67] [1991] 2 FLR 559, per Stocker LJ, at 571.   [68] Ibid., per Browne-Wilkinson VC, at 583–4.

[69] Committee on the Rights of the Child (2006).

[70] Children (Equal Protection from Assault) (Scotland) Act 2019; Children (Abolition of Defence of Reasonable Punishment) (Wales) Act 2020.

government has resisted calls for similar changes in the law in England. The story of the campaign for reform of the law on corporal punishment is a good case study for the strengths and weaknesses of children's rights. On the one hand, children's rights litigation has had a direct and tangible impact on that law, acting as the catalyst both for the ban on corporal punishment in all schools,[71] and the restriction of the defence of reasonable chastisement as it applies to parents.[72] Given the deep resistance to limiting the power of parents in this area, it is undoubtedly the case that this is an area in which litigating children's rights has been crucial for changing the law to protect children. Nonetheless, it is also the case that the Westminster government has acted in a way that disregards and minimises the obligations imposed by the CRC, an approach made possible because the CRC has not been incorporated into domestic law. The obligations of the ECHR, which does have direct domestic application, are much more limited and uncertain than those of the CRC. Again, this is a good example of the way in which a law designed for adults pays little attention to the specific rights and needs of children. While domestic law has been amended following adverse ECHR judgments, in England, the response to date has been to adapt the law to the minimum extent possible. The approach of domestic law to corporal punishment, whether in litigation, statute or government policy, is almost entirely concerned with determining the legitimate limits of parental discretion, rather than implementing the rights of children. This leaves the law on corporal punishment with two central defects: first, it is increasingly clear that the law is inconsistent with the emerging consensus on children's rights; and, second, in reforming the law to the minimum extent possible, it has been left in a hopelessly confusing state.

(B) Children's Rights to Protection from Corporal Punishment in International Law

The CRC does not explicitly address the question of corporal punishment within its text, nor do the *travaux préparatoires* for the Convention record any discussion of that topic during the drafting sessions. Despite this, the CRC is certainly not silent on the question of children's protection from physical harm. Article 19(1) includes the obligation to take all appropriate measures 'to protect the child from all forms of physical or mental violence, injury or abuse . . . while in the care of parent(s), legal guardian(s) or any other person who has the care of the child'. Article 37(a) states that 'No child shall be subjected to torture or other cruel, inhuman or degrading treatment or

---

[71] *Campbell and Cosans* v. *United Kingdom* (1982) 4 EHRR 293; *Costello-Roberts* v. *United Kingdom* (1993) 19 EHRR 112. Although, as discussed further below, these cases might be criticised as focusing on the rights of parents rather than those of the children themselves.

[72] *A* v. *United Kingdom (Human Rights: Punishment of Child)* [1998] 2 FLR 959.

punishment.'[73] The UK government has argued that the prohibition on violence against children does not amount to a prohibition on all forms of physical punishment, stating in the 5th Periodic Report to the Committee on the Rights of the Child:

> The UK Government does not condone any violence towards children and has clear laws to deal with it. Our view is that a mild smack does not constitute violence and that parents should not be criminalised for giving a mild smack.[74]

This somewhat disingenuous view that 'mild' hitting does not constitute violence[75] is clearly inconsistent with the Committee's long-standing interpretation of the CRC's obligations. The Committee issued a General Comment in 2006, which made a detailed assessment of the way in which the CRC protects children against *all* forms of physical punishment. As it explains, the articles referred to above unambiguously rule out all forms of violence against children.[76] To the extent that there is any doubt caused by the absence of explicit reference to corporal punishment in the text of the CRC, the Committee urges that the Convention must be regarded as a living instrument whose interpretation develops over time.[77] The Committee further locates the rights of children within their broader human rights framework and the right of children to equal respect for human dignity, stating emphatically that:

> it is clear that the practice directly conflicts with the equal and inalienable rights of children to respect for their human dignity and physical integrity ... The Committee emphasizes that eliminating violent and humiliating punishment of children, through law reform and other necessary measures, is an immediate and unqualified obligation of States parties.[78]

As a result, the Committee is clear that there is an obligation on states to prohibit and eliminate all forms of 'punishment in which physical force is used and intended to cause some degree of pain or discomfort, *however light*.'[79] The UK government's contention that a 'mild smack' does not constitute violence is clearly inconsistent with the Committee's interpretation of the CRC. The Committee also emphasises that the use of such punishment cannot be justified on the basis of the best interests of the child or on the Article 5 requirement

---

[73] CRC, Art. 28(2) also addresses the question of discipline in schools: 'States Parties shall take all appropriate measures to ensure that school discipline is administered in a manner consistent with the child's human dignity and in conformity with the present Convention.'

[74] HM Government (2014) para. 11.

[75] As Lord Nicholls observed in *R (on the application of Williamson and others)* v. *Secretary of State for Education and Employment and others* [2005] UKHL 15, [2005] 2 All ER 1, at [49], 'corporal punishment involves deliberately inflicting physical violence'.

[76] Committee on the Rights of the Child (2006) para. 18.

[77] Ibid. para. 20. This conclusion is reinforced by Committee on the Rights of the Child (2011) esp. para. 24.

[78] Ibid. paras 21–22. See also UN General Assembly (2006) para. 98, calling on all states to prohibit the corporal punishment of children in all settings.

[79] Committee on the Rights of the Child (2006) paras 2 and 5 (emphasis added).

that states respect the rights and responsibilities of parents to provide direction and guidance to their children, as each of these provisions should be interpreted in light of the CRC as a whole. The Committee recognises that parental responsibility includes giving guidance to children and providing discipline, but rejects any notion that corporal punishment is a legitimate form of providing such discipline.[80] Instead, the state has an obligation to promote positive and non-violent forms of fulfilling this responsibility.[81]

For all of these reasons, the Committee has consistently rejected the UK's defence of the current law, and recommended that it:

> Prohibit as a matter of priority all corporal punishment in the family, including through the repeal of all legal defences, such as 'reasonable chastisement', and
>
> Strengthen its efforts to promote positive and non-violent forms of discipline and respect for children's equal right to human dignity and physical integrity, with a view to eliminating the general acceptance of the use of corporal punishment in child-rearing.[82]

The CRC's clear and unequivocal affirmation of the right of children to protection from all forms of physical punishment is part of a wider body of international law. The General Comment is firmly based on the understanding that children are equal subjects of international law and of the protection of human dignity and physical integrity guaranteed in the Universal Declaration of Human Rights and the International Covenants on Civil and Political Rights and on Economic, Social and Cultural Rights.[83] The UN Committee on Economic, Social and Cultural Rights has interpreted that Covenant to prohibit all forms of physical punishment of children, while the European Committee of Social Rights has drawn the same conclusion from Article 17 of the European Social Charter.[84] The international monitoring bodies of human rights conventions have echoed the conclusions of the Committee on the Rights of the Child and have repeatedly drawn attention to the UK's failure to abide by their terms so far as the punishment of children is concerned.[85]

It is unquestionably the case that the UK's stance on corporal punishment in England is inconsistent with its international obligations under a wide range of instruments, as interpreted by the international human rights bodies. This is reflected in an increasing number of states that have prohibited all forms of corporal punishment in their domestic law. At the time of writing, sixty-three states globally had a complete prohibition on corporal punishment, including

---

[80] Ibid. paras 13 and 14.   [81] Ibid. paras 38–39.

[82] Committee on the Rights of the Child (2016) para. 40. Similar recommendations were made in the Committee's Concluding Observations in 1995, 2002 and 2008.

[83] Committee on the Rights of the Child (2006) para. 16.

[84] Committee of Ministers of the Council of Europe (2015).

[85] Committee on Economic, Social and Cultural Rights (2002) para. 36, (2009) para. 24; Committee against Torture (2013) para. 29; Human Rights Committee (2015) para. 20; Committee on the Elimination of Discrimination against Women (2008) paras 33–34, (2013) paras 34–35.

thirty-four of the forty-seven signatories to the European Convention on Human Rights and Fundamental Freedoms.[86] The law in England is increasingly out of step with the emerging European consensus and with developments in international law. Nonetheless, domestic law is not directly affected by these provisions: while they may carry weight in political argument and judicial interpretation, they are not directly enforceable. Unfortunately, the position in the ECHR, which is directly enforceable through the Human Rights Act 1998 (HRA), is much more equivocal than the international consensus discussed above and has developed at a slower rate. The position in the ECHR has, nonetheless, had a pivotal role in developing domestic law and is best explored through an explanation of the how domestic law has reached its current position.

(C) Physical Punishment in Domestic Law: The Historical Background

The common law recognised a broad, but not unlimited, right of parents and those in *loco parentis* to inflict 'moderate and reasonable' corporal punishment on their children. The seminal case of *R* v. *Hopley* stated the limits of the law to be that:

> If it be administered for the gratification of passion or of rage, or if it be immoderate and excessive in its nature or degree, or if it be protracted beyond the child's powers of endurance, or with an instrument unfitted for the purpose and calculated to produce danger to life or limb; in all such cases the punishment is excessive, the violence is unlawful, and if evil consequences to life or limb ensue, then the person inflicting it is answerable to the law, and if death ensues it will be manslaughter.[87]

In *Hopley* itself, a schoolmaster was convicted of manslaughter after his teenaged pupil died following a particularly savage beating. Although Hopley was acting in *loco parentis*, with the specific authorisation of the child's father, his actions were far in excess of the limits of the law's recognition of 'reasonable and moderate' punishment. Children had long complained of the brutal use of physical punishment in schools,[88] but it was not until the late twentieth century and the intervention of the European Court of Human Rights that its use was banned. In *Campbell and Cosans* v. *United Kingdom*,[89] the ECtHR found a violation of the rights of the parents to ensure that their children's education was in conformity with the parents' philosophical convictions against corporal punishment.[90] This case was an important catalyst in the statutory abolition of such punishment in state-funded schools 4 years later.[91] It took another decision of the ECtHR, *Costello-Roberts* v. *United Kingdom*,[92]

---

[86] The Global Initiative to End All Corporal Punishment of Children monitors developments in international and national law: www.endcorporalpunishment.org.
[87] (1860) 2 F & F 202, at 206.
[88] See the remarkable *Children's Petition* to Parliament of 1669.   [89] (1982) 4 EHRR 293.
[90] ECHR, Protocol 1, Art. 2.   [91] Education Act (No. 2) 1986, s. 47.
[92] (1993) 19 EHRR 112.

for the ban to be extended to independent schools.[93] Similar prohibitions on its use in children's homes,[94] foster care[95] and early years education[96] mean that children are free from the threat of physical punishment in most institutional settings. There is, however, not yet a complete ban on its use outside of the home. In particular, there have been widespread reports of physical punishment in religious out-of-school settings, which at present remain unregulated.

While progress towards banning physical punishment in education owes much to the decisions of the ECtHR, it is notable that that case law was not based on a right of children to be educated in an environment free from physical punishment. The leading case of *Campbell and Cosans* was concerned with children who had been suspended from school due to their parents' refusal to allow them to be educated in an environment in which corporal punishment might be administered. The children had not suffered any form of physical punishment themselves and the court found that they had no right under the ECHR to be educated in an environment where they were free from its threat. The parents, however, did have a right under Article 2 of Protocol 1 of the ECHR, to ensure that their children were educated in an environment that respected their convictions against corporal punishment and the failure of the state to provide such an education was a violation of those rights. As one of the children had been suspended from school for a whole year, his right to education had also been violated in this case. It is important to note, however, that this violation arose because the state had not been able to offer an education that complied with his parents' rights, and not because the child had a freestanding right to an education in an environment free from physical punishment. As a result, protection for the child's right to education derived from the parents' right to educate their children in line with their philosophical convictions and so depended on the good fortune of a child to have a parent with such convictions.[97] It was in response to this violation of *parental* rights that physical punishment was prohibited in state schools. In contrast, the case of *Costello-Roberts* was brought solely on the basis of the rights of the child and not those of his parents. The case concerned a 7-year-old boy who had been beaten with a slipper by his head teacher at an independent school. The ECtHR found that the punishment inflicted was of insufficient severity to engage his rights under Article 3 or 8,[98] a decision which, the dissenting judges noted, did

---

[93] Education Act 1996, ss 548–9, as amended by the School Standards and Framework Act 1998, s. 131, makes the use of physical punishment in schools unlawful not only for civil purposes, but also for criminal purposes, unless there was an immediate danger of personal injury or an immediate danger to the property (s. 548(5)).

[94] Children's Homes Regulations 2001 (SI 2001/3967) reg. 17(5)(a). See now Children's Homes (England) Regulations 2015 (SI 2015/541) reg. 19(2)(a).

[95] Fostering Services Regulations 2002 (SI 2002/57) reg. 13(2)(a). See now Fostering Services (England) Regulations 2011 (SI 2011/581) reg. 13(2)(a).

[96] The Day Care and Child Minding (National Standards) (England) Regulations 2003 (SI 2003/1996), reg. 5.

[97] (1982) 4 EHRR 293, at [39]–[41].   [98] (1993) 19 EHRR 112, at [32] and [36].

little to take account of the impact of institutionalised punishment on a lonely and insecure young child who had only recently started at the boarding school. While punishment of sufficient severity may breach their rights,[99] children had no right under the ECHR to freedom from *all* forms of physical punishment. The court nonetheless found that the state was responsible for ensuring that schools did not impose punishment of a severity to violate the Article 3 or 8 rights of children, regardless of whether the school in question were state-funded or independent. In response, the ban on corporal punishment in schools was extended to independent schools.

The advent of the HRA 1998 initially did little to strengthen the position of children; instead, it was the vehicle for an attempt by parents to overturn the prohibition on the use of corporal punishment in independent schools. In *R (on the application of Williamson and others)* v. *Secretary of State for Education and Employment and others*[100] (*Williamson*), a group of fundamentalist Christian parents unsuccessfully argued that the teachers' inability to use physical punishment in the private school to which they sent their children violated their own right to freedom of religion under Article 9 of the ECHR. Despite finding that the statutory ban had indeed interfered with the parents' rights under Article 9, the House of Lords held that the interference could be justified[101] to protect the rights and freedoms of *others*. These 'others' included children generally: Parliament was entitled to take the view that it was appropriate to enforce a blanket ban to protect the interests of children *as a class*.[102] In contrast, the rights and interests of the specific children involved received very little mention. By the time it reached the House of Lords, the litigation had been pursued with hardly any reference to the children who were the focus of their parents' beliefs that a strict Christian faith demanded the administration of corporal punishment for indiscipline. It was only Baroness Hale who gave consideration to the interests of these children's individual rights or to the rights of children under the CRC to be free from corporal punishment. As Baroness Hale noted:

> My Lords, this is, and always has been, a case about children, their rights and the rights of their parents and teachers. Yet there has been no one here or in the courts below to speak on behalf of the children . . . The battle has been fought on ground selected by the adults.[103]

The legality of the legislation barring the use of physical punishment in schools was thereby confirmed, but again the litigation was primarily concerned with the legitimacy of state interference in the freedoms of parents, rather than the

---

[99] As was the case in *Tyrer* v. *United Kingdom* (1979–80) 2 EHRR 1, concerning a sentence of birching handed down by the juvenile court.
[100] [2005] UKHL 15, [2005] 2 All ER 1; discussed by B. Hale (2006).
[101] I.e. under ECHR, Art. 9(2).
[102] [2005] UKHL 15, [2005] 2 All ER 1, at [49]–[51] (Lord Nicholls) and [80] Baroness Hale.
[103] [2005] UKHL 15, [2005] 2 All ER 1, at [71].

rights of children. The case is also a good example of the way in which parents may single-mindedly pursue their own rights within the 'private' sphere, while arguing that they are promoting their children's best interests, without reference to the voice or rights of those children.

The cases discussed above all concern the use of physical punishment in institutionalised settings; restrictions on its use within the 'private' sphere of the home are much more limited. The defence of 'reasonable and moderate' chastisement, confirmed in *Hopley*, remained available to a wide range of criminal offences,[104] despite considerable efforts to scrap it while the CA 1989 was progressing through Parliament. A further opportunity for amending the law appeared when the government was required to respond to the landmark decision of the ECtHR in *A* v. *United Kingdom (Human Rights: Punishment of Child)*.[105] In this case, a jury had acquitted a stepfather of assault occasioning actual bodily harm, despite his having treated his 9-year-old stepson with sufficient severity to infringe the boy's rights under Article 3 of the ECHR.[106] The court held that the UK government had a positive obligation to provide children with practical and effective state protection against treatment or punishment contrary to Article 3. This it had manifestly failed to do; the government had expressly conceded that domestic law currently failed to protect children adequately from violations of their Article 3 rights and that it would require amending. Reform of the law throughout the UK then appeared inevitable.

Despite the apparent victory for children's rights in *A*, the response of the government was slow and limited. In 2000, the government duly established a 'consultation' exercise over how best to reform the law, but prejudged its outcome by declaring that outlawing all physical punishment would be a 'heavy-handed intrusion into family life'.[107] Such laws would, it said, 'victimise parents unfairly and compromise public confidence in the legal system'.[108] The government's reluctance to change the law was influenced by the results of an opinion poll indicating that the majority of parents considered that smacking children was acceptable and that the law should allow them to do so. In the event, the government reneged on its commitment to amend English law to take account of the ECtHR's decision in *A* v. *United Kingdom*. It argued that reforms had been rendered unnecessary[109] because, by implementing the HRA 1998, the law already provided children with sufficient protection from infringements of their Convention rights. In reaching such a conclusion, it was influenced by the decision of the Court of Appeal in *R* v. *H (Assault of*

---

[104] The defence was also preserved in the Children and Young Persons Act 1933, s. 1(7) (now repealed).

[105] [1998] 2 FLR 959.

[106] He had beaten the boy with a garden cane on several occasions, thereby bruising his buttocks, thighs and calves. The jury accepted his defence that the boy's punishment amounted to 'reasonable chastisement' under CYPA 1933, s. 1(7) and *R* v. *Hopley* (1860) 2 F & F 202.

[107] DH (2000) para. 2.4.　　[108] Ibid. para. 2.14.　　[109] DH (2001) para. 76.

a Child: Reasonable Chastisement),[110] which, as discussed below, had adapted the direction to a jury in order to prevent the defence being used to justify actions that breached the child's right under Article 3 of the ECHR.

Many doubted the government's confidence that the law had been brought into line with the requirements of the ECHR, or the CRC. Nevertheless, no further moves occurred until the passage of the CA 2004 provided yet another opportunity for law reform. At this point, section 58, introduced by Liberal Democrat peer, Lord Lester of Herne Hill, produced a compromise between abolishing entirely the defence of reasonable chastisement and providing children with extra legal protection against unacceptable physical violence in the home. It is this section which forms the basis of the current law and, while undoubtedly an improvement on the previous position, has caused considerable confusion.

(D) The Current Law

A child attempting to ascertain whether his or her parents are behaving lawfully in adopting a particular form of punishment will find that there are few clear answers. Parents will be equally puzzled. The government itself, having reviewed the current state of the law, produced the following sophism:

> The current legal position is clear and appropriate, but can be difficult to understand. It is neither correct nor incorrect to say that 'smacking is legal'.[111]

The terms of section 58 of the CA 2004, which governs this area of the law, cause considerable confusion. Section 58 starts by stating that, for a list of specified offences, 'battery of a child cannot be justified on the ground that it constituted reasonable punishment'. Surprisingly, it fails to state clearly whether or not the law maintains the defence for any purposes. One might assume its demise, given the specific repeal of its statutory embodiment.[112] But section 58 merely prohibits such a defence being used by a parent prosecuted for having used punishment amounting to a serious assault[113] or to child cruelty.[114] Implicit, but not stated,[115] is that the defence of 'reasonable punishment'[116] still avails a parent who has punished his child with less severity, meriting only a charge of common assault, as opposed to those offences specifically listed in section 58. Little wonder that this legislation,

---

[110] [2001] EWCA Crim 1024, [2001] 2 FLR 431.   [111] DfES (2007) para. 42.

[112] CYPA 1933, s. 1(7), which confirmed the right of any person with lawful control or charge of a child or young person to punish him, was repealed by CA 2004, s. 58(5).

[113] CA 2004, s. 58(2)(a) and (b): an assault occasioning either grievous bodily harm or actual bodily harm.

[114] CA 2004, s. 58(2)(c).

[115] CA 2004, s. 58(1): 'In relation to any offence specified in subs. (2), battery of a child cannot be justified on the ground that it constituted reasonable punishment.'

[116] The term 'punishment' was substituted for 'chastisement' – presumably because the latter term was considered anachronistic.

which fails to clarify what level or type of punishment the law allows parents to adopt, is not widely understood.

The crucial first question in deciding whether the defence will be available in a particular case is the offence that is charged. If a parent is charged with common assault, the defence of reasonable punishment remains available, whereas if the charge is more serious, such as assault occasioning actual bodily harm (ABH), it will not be. The dividing line between these offences is hopelessly unclear, depending primarily on the nature of the injuries sustained, meaning that the extent to which children are protected from the defence will depend to a significant degree on the discretion of the Crown Prosecution Service (CPS). The CPS's Charging Standard on Offences Against the Person advises that unless the injury is 'transient and trifling' and amounts to 'no more than temporary reddening of the skin', then the charge should be ABH, for which the defence does not apply.[117] This approach, also found in the current Prosecution Guidance on Child Abuse,[118] limits the number of cases in which the defence will apply, but does little to guide parents confused about the law. It seems unlikely that a parent will plan the force with which he or she can hit a child, to calculate if the intended smack or blow will produce a reddening of the skin or other injury, and if so, how long it will last for. It also appears that on this approach the parents of a child who bruises easily may face prosecution without a defence, but not if there is no lasting mark, despite the same degree of force having been used. To add to this confusion, the advice only considers physical injury to the child and makes no reference to psychological harm in cases in which the reasonable punishment defence might be used or how psychological harm might be assessed in relation to children, despite directing that it should be considered in deciding whether to bring a charge of ABH in general cases. Given the inconsistency and vague language in the guidance for prosecutors, it is unsurprising that the government's review of the operation of the defence found that neither practitioners nor parents understand what the law allows and does not allow.[119]

If a parent is charged with common assault, both he or she and any jury may find themselves unclear over the exact point at which physical punishment is too severe to be deemed 'reasonable punishment', thereby negating the defence entirely. When interpreting the common law, courts must consider the demands of the HRA 1998. Thus, judges and juries considering whether punishment is 'reasonable' and within the common law defence must also take into account the considerations underpinning a child's right to protection from torture or inhuman or degrading treatment or punishment under Article

---

[117] Last revised on 6 January 2020. The references to 'transient and trifling' and 'temporary reddening of the skin' were removed from the Charging Standard in 2011 and replaced by general references to the seriousness of the injury, with no explanation as to how that seriousness should be judged in the case of a child. The references to 'transient and trifling' and 'temporary reddening of the skin' were reinstated in 2018.
[118] Last updated on 5 November 2021.   [119] DfES (2007) paras 48–9 and 56.

3 of the ECHR. According to the Court of Appeal in *R* v. *H (Assault of a Child: Reasonable Chastisement)*,[120] the defence will be available only if the punishment was reasonable, taking account of the following criteria: the nature and context of the defendant's behaviour; its duration; its physical and mental consequences for the child; the child's age and personal characteristics;[121] and the reasons given by the defendant for administering the punishment.[122] This direction superimposed on the common law defence makes the law so confusing that it is extremely difficult for anyone to decide on the lawfulness of using physical punishment.

The confusing state of the law creates uncertainty and inhibits protection of children from physical violence. A parent earnestly trying to stay within the law in using physical punishment will find it difficult to ascertain how to do so. Children are given the message that violence from adults against children is tolerated, with no clear way of explaining when such treatment becomes impermissible physical abuse. Further, as the government itself acknowledges, practitioners working with children consider that it 'leaves the door open not just to mild smacking but to more severe punishment that would in fact not be covered by the reasonable punishment defence'.[123] Such severe physical punishment may amount to 'significant harm' and so meet the threshold for intervention in the care system, but even in cases where it does so, parents can be seen justifying their actions on the basis of their right to use physical punishment.[124] It is clear that the message that physical punishment is permissible creates difficulties for practitioners in challenging its use and encouraging positive, non-violent, parenting techniques. Consequently, children have been left insufficiently protected by a convoluted set of legal principles.

Despite the confusing nature of the current law, the government is committed to retaining it in its present form. In 2007, it reviewed the practical operation of section 58 2 years after its implementation. Its result was predictable – to make no further changes:

> But we do not believe that the state should intervene in family life unnecessarily – unless there are clear reasons to intervene, parents should be able to bring up their children as they think fit.[125]

---

[120] [2001] EWCA Crim 1024, [2001] 2 FLR 431, per Rose LJ, at [31].

[121] Factors all contained in the guidance provided by the ECtHR in *Costello-Roberts* v. *United Kingdom* [1994] 1 FCR 65, at [30], and repeated in *A* v. *United Kingdom (Human Rights: Punishment of Child)* [1998] 2 FLR 959, at [20].

[122] Northern Ireland Office of Law Reform (2001) pp. 40–1, described this last requirement, added by Rose LJ in *R* v. *H* [2001] EWCA Crim 1024, [2001] 2 FLR 431, as an impermissible 'gloss' placed on the ECtHR's own guidance, which does not make reference to the reasons for the punishment. See also S. Choudhry and J. Herring (2010) p. 211.

[123] DfES (2007) para. 49.

[124] E.g. *Bristol City Council* v. *M*, Case No: DX14C00126, unreported; *Re LK* [2015] EWCA Civ 830. In the latter case, the Recorder initially appeared to find it difficult to assess whether the repeated use of an implement to hit a 5-year-old boy was within the definition of 'reasonable punishment'.

[125] DfES (2007) para. 55.

The government's definition of 'clear reasons' did not apparently include the need to redress the gross imbalance between parents' rights and children's rights or the law's extreme complexity. Successive governments have maintained this stance as evident in submissions to human rights monitoring bodies,[126] prioritising parental discretion in the face of an increasingly clear international obligation to protect the rights of children to freedom from physical punishment.

(E) The Case for Further Reform

Perhaps the strongest argument in favour of finally banning the use of physical punishment entirely is that social attitudes and understanding have changed radically over the last century. Whereas in Victorian society the physical punishment of adult and child criminal offenders was routine and domestic violence in the home was condoned, society today considers both unacceptable. It is now difficult to justify the law protecting adults from assaulting one another, while allowing adults to assault their smaller and more vulnerable offspring. 'Children are the only people in the United Kingdom whose right to physical integrity – to protection from all forms of inter-personal violence – is not yet supported by the law and social attitudes.'[127] Furthermore, as Baroness Hale of Richmond has indicated, there is a growing body of international and professional opinion opposing its use.[128] Research shows that physical punishment is less effective than other forms of discipline and is associated with increased aggression and anti-social behaviour in children. It also demonstrates that physical punishment is associated with anxiety and depression in childhood and with long-term negative psychological effects, including substance abuse and domestic violence among adults who had been physically punished as children.[129] When parents use physical punishment as a form of discipline, they indicate to their children that violent and aggressive behaviour is an acceptable method of dealing with stressful situations, thereby reinforcing violent behaviour in society. Worryingly, there is also a serious risk that physical punishment escalates into physical abuse and maltreatment. A comprehensive review of research on the subject found that the research evidence supported 'the notion that physical punishment and physical abuse are part of a continuum of violence, differing only by severity or degree'.[130]

Underlying the debate over physical punishment is some uncertainty over the role that the law should be playing. Arguably, the law should 'send out a clear message about what behaviour is unacceptable in families, or what we, as a society, feel about violence'.[131] As the experience of other European

---

[126] E.g. HM Government (2014) para. 11.
[127] Commission on Children and Violence (1995) p. 15.
[128] *Williamson* [2005] UKHL 15, [2005] 2 All ER 1, at [85].
[129] For a detailed review of the empirical evidence, see A. Heilman *et al.* (2015).
[130] Ibid. pp. 34–9.   [131] Northern Ireland Office of Law Reform (2001) p. 42.

countries, notably Sweden,[132] demonstrates, the law can promote attitudinal changes in society. Indeed, prohibiting physical punishment may well produce a different approach to discipline.[133] By contrast, the UK government's inconsistent attitude towards promoting attitudinal change[134] has produced a confused and incoherent body of legal principles regarding punishment. On the one hand, it has clearly indicated its disapproval of the use of physical punishment by practitioners working with children, but on the other hand, the government is not prepared to interfere with parents' views on how to bring up their children. The government claims that attitudes are already changing and that younger parents are less ready to resort to smacking.[135] Nonetheless, although 'most children' consider that smacking is out of place in modern childhood,[136] it refuses to interfere more radically. It is difficult to defend this narrow interpretation of the law's proper role in society. Nor is such deference to parental discretion required by Article 8 of the ECHR, which ensures respect for family privacy.[137]

Research evidence demonstrating the harmful impact of physical punishment and the evident confusion as to the limits of the current law provide strong reasons for giving children equal protection from physical assault. Such a change would give children in England the same protection as those in Scotland and Wales. This is backed by an increasing international movement and by widespread recognition in international law of children's right to be protected from physical punishment. Unfortunately, the UK's dualist approach to international law means that this international law does not have direct effect on domestic law.[138] Whether the current law is consistent with Articles 3 and 8 of the ECHR, which does have such domestic impact, is more difficult to assess. It is true that, as discussed above, to date the ECtHR found that children do not have a right to protection from all forms of physical punishment, but only those that meet the minimum level of severity to attract the protection of Articles 3 and 8.[139] For this reason, when the Parliamentary Joint Committee on Human Rights (JCHR) conducted its pre-legislative scrutiny of the current law now contained in section 58 of the Children Act 2004, it considered that the changed law, combined with the new CPS charging standard, achieved just enough to comply with the existing ECtHR judgments.[140] Nonetheless, as the JCHR also pointed out, this does not mean

---

[132] Sweden banned all physical punishment in 1979.

[133] J. Durrant (2000) p. 9: while in 1965, 8 years after the law reform, 50 per cent of the Swedish population believed that corporal punishment was a necessary aspect of childrearing, by 1994, only 11 per cent supported corporal punishment in even its mildest form. See also A. Zolotor and M. Puzia (2010).

[134] R. Smith (2004) pp. 266–71.   [135] DfES (2007) paras 29–30.   [136] Ibid. para. 35.

[137] *Tlapak* v. *Germany* [2018] ECHR 262, discussed further below.

[138] As discussed in Chapter 2.

[139] *Costello-Roberts* v. *United Kingdom* [1994] 1 FCR 65 and repeated in *A* v. *United Kingdom (Human Rights: Punishment of Child)* [1998] 2 FLR 959.

[140] JCHR (2004).

the current law would survive a fresh challenge, either before the ECtHR or in the domestic courts under the HRA.

Interpretation of the ECHR is not static: the Convention is a 'living instrument' and its meaning takes account of prevailing social standards. The ECHR jurisprudence that forms the basis of current domestic law dates to the 1990s and there have been considerable changes in the court's approach and international attitudes to corporal punishment in that time. It is now the case that more than two-thirds of state parties to the ECHR have complete bans on corporal punishment; the vast majority, twenty-eight of thirty-four, of these states have enacted their bans since the decision in *A v. United Kingdom*. A fresh review of the law would be against a very different prevailing European attitude from that evident in 1998. This is an important point, as the ECtHR has been particularly sensitive to changing social attitudes in relation to matters concerning intimate family relationships and has been willing to adjust its interpretation of the ECHR to take account of those changes.[141] Similarly, the detailed position of the UN Committee on the Rights of the Child was established beyond doubt in 2006 when a General Comment on the subject was issued, and has since been reaffirmed.[142] The ECtHR has increasingly taken account of the CRC in interpreting its rights in relation to children, including in relation to corporal punishment. For example, in *Tlapak v. Germany*,[143] the ECtHR drew on the CRC, the General Comments and the European Social Charter in analysing their approach to corporal punishment. For these reasons, the Convention is open to reinterpretation in the light of the increasing European consensus on the issue and the developing international law.

A further reason for considering that the existing law is open to challenge is that the ECtHR has developed its jurisprudence on Article 3 further since *Costello-Roberts* and *A v. United Kingdom*. In particular, the Grand Chamber has emphasised the importance of dignity as an underlying principle in interpreting Article 3, drawing on a wide range of international instruments, including the CRC. The principle of dignity has, for example, allowed the ECtHR to conclude that a slap on the face of a detained person by a police officer was sufficient to breach Article 3, despite the relatively superficial injuries. The Grand Chamber took the view that:

> Ill-treatment that attains such a minimum level of severity usually involves actual bodily injury or intense physical or mental suffering. However, even in the absence of these aspects, where treatment humiliates or debases an individual, showing a lack of respect for or diminishing his or her human dignity, or arouses feelings of fear, anguish or inferiority capable of breaking an individual's moral and physical resistance, it may be characterised as degrading and also fall within the prohibition set forth in art.3. It should also be pointed out that it may

---

[141] E.g. *Goodwin v. United Kingdom*, App. No. 28957/95, [2002] 2 FLR 487.
[142] Committee on the Rights of the Child (2006), (2011).   [143] [2018] ECHR 262, at [58]–[62].

well suffice that the victim is humiliated in his own eyes, even if not in the eyes of others.[144]

While this case placed great importance on the context of detention by the state and so is not directly applicable to the context of corporal punishment by parents, the reasoning used is significant. It is clear that it is not the seriousness of injury alone that determines whether Article 3 is breached, but that relatively minor physical consequences may be sufficient if the victim feels humiliated or the treatment arouses feelings of fear and inferiority to break the person's resistance. On this basis, it is difficult to imagine that the beating of a 7-year-old with a slipper by a head teacher in *Costello-Roberts* would be decided the same way today. Given that much corporal punishment is designed precisely to humiliate the child, reinforce inferiority and break the child's will, it is arguable that even a 'mild smack' is sufficient to engage Article 3.[145] This is particularly so because the Grand Chamber in *Bouyid* put weight on the fact that one of the alleged victims was only 17. Drawing on the CRC, the Grand Chamber considered that 'ill-treatment is liable to have a greater impact – especially in psychological terms – on a minor than on an adult', such that treatment acceptable in relation to an adult might be a breach of Article 3 simply because the victim is a minor.[146] This observation is consistent with the research findings, discussed above, on the impact of violence on the mental health and psychological development of children. For these reasons, there is a good argument that Article 3 should now be interpreted as prohibiting any use of physical punishment of children and the positive obligation on the state to protect children from such treatment, as recognised in *Costello-Roberts*, would then require the current law to be amended. Article 3 is stated in absolute terms and, on this basis, no argument as to the desirability of retaining parental discretion would be relevant to justify retention of the current law.

The ECtHR has recognised the weight of these arguments, although it has not yet gone so far as to require that children be given equal protection from physical assault in law. In *Tlapak v. Germany*,[147] the court considered the case of children who had been removed from parents who used caning as corporal punishment. The parents in question were all members of a small religious community which taught that beating with rods was the correct punishment for children aged 3 or above. The parents sought to argue that the removal of the children and withdrawal of parental authority was a violation of the parents' Article 8 rights. Their claim was swiftly rejected by the ECtHR, which found the actions of the state were clearly justified on the basis of their careful assessment of the children's welfare and the need to protect the

---

[144] *Bouyid* v. *Belgium* (2016) 62 EHRR 32, at [87]; see also [105].

[145] E.g. in *M and M* v. *Croatia* (2017) 65 EHRR 9, at [133]–[135], the young age (9) of the child and her feelings of fear and shame were important in concluding that abusive behaviour by her father met the threshold of severity to engage Art. 3.

[146] *Bouyid* v. *Belgium* (2016) 62 EHRR 32, at [109] and [110].

[147] [2018] ECHR 262, at [58]–[62].

children from inhuman and degrading treatment contrary to Article 3. Drawing on the CRC, European Social Charter and the decision in *Bouyid*, the court recognised that the vulnerability of children, their age and the impact of humiliation and fear of physical punishment on their dignity, should all be taken into account in deciding whether punishment reached the severity required by Article 3. Nonetheless, it was not necessary for the ECtHR to decide whether Article 3 prohibited all forms of physical punishment. Instead, the court would only go so far as to say that it would be 'commendable if member States prohibit in law all forms of corporal punishment of children'.[148] In the light of the firm consensus in international law, it is disappointing that the ECtHR position has remained so equivocal. The case is a good example of the way in which the ECtHR resolves parental claims by relying on individual assessments of welfare rather than determining what is required by children's fundamental rights. The case does, however, show a significant narrowing of the treatment of children that is permissible under Article 3 and gives express approval to arguments which could form the basis of a future challenge to the current domestic law on physical punishment.

Given the mounting research evidence that physical punishment is harmful and counter-productive, the diverging approaches within the UK and the growing international movement to prohibit its use, the arguments in favour of retaining the current law look weak, particularly given the confusing message that it sends to parents, children and practitioners. The arguments in favour of the current law largely rely on protecting parental discretion to discipline as they wish. The strongest version of this argument is that criminalising parents for relatively minor actions is likely to have a greater detrimental effect on children than the punishment itself. In its General Comment, the Committee on the Rights of the Child recognises that prosecuting parents in such circumstances is unlikely to be in the child's best interests. Instead, it recognises the importance of ensuring that prosecution or care proceedings 'should only proceed when they are regarded both as necessary to protect the child from significant harm and as being in the best interests of the affected child'.[149] This principle is reflected in the fact that most countries that have prohibited all corporal punishment have also specifically limited prosecution to cases that meet a minimum threshold.[150] The primary aim of a change in the law would be to educate and encourage a change in cultural attitudes to parenting, as has been observed elsewhere, rather than to increase criminal or care proceedings. It might be argued that the state has no business interfering with the private discretion of parents, but this argument would be self-evidently weak given the positive obligations on the state to protect children from private behaviour that infringes their fundamental rights.

[148] Ibid. at [90].   [149] Committee on the Rights of the Child (2006) paras 40–1.
[150] A. Zolotor and M. Puzia (2010) p. 232.

(7) Conclusion

The law on corporal punishment of children is perhaps the clearest example of the breadth of freedom given to parents in domestic law. While there are good reasons for protecting the authority of parents and ensuring that children benefit from having decisions made by those who know and love them, shielding the parental role behind the private sphere can inhibit the protection of children's rights and the promotion of their welfare. The current law is deeply ambivalent as to the relationship between parental responsibilities and the rights and welfare of children. Nowhere is this clearer than in relation to physical punishment, where parental freedom is prioritised despite substantial evidence of its harmful effects and widespread recognition of children's right to equal protection from assault in international law. As the following chapters demonstrate, the law frequently draws the boundaries of parental discretion in a way that allows the rights and interests of children to be neglected.

The example of corporal punishment also demonstrates important lessons as to the power and limitations of children's human rights. The resistance of successive governments to fulfilling the obligations of the CRC highlights just how easy it is for those obligations to be manipulated and ignored. Further, the example of physical punishment demonstrates the limitations of the adult-focused ECHR as a vehicle for the rights of children. Despite these weaknesses, it has been rights-based litigation that has formed the basis for change. In the face of consistent political opposition to limiting parents' rights to discipline as they wish, litigation in cases such as *A* v. *United Kingdom* has been the catalyst for legal change and it is the development of these rights that offers the best hope for the future.

Crafting the law to recognise children's need for a family that nurtures and protects them and their need to, sometimes, be protected from that family is one of the greatest challenges in the law relating to children. As will be seen in the following chapters, at present, the law frequently draws that line in a way that gives generous discretion to parents, with too little attention to their potential to infringe the rights of children.

Bibliography

NB: Many of these publications can be obtained on the relevant organisation's website.

Archard, D. (2014) *Children: Rights and Childhood*, Routledge.
Brighouse, H. and Swift, A. (2014) *Family Values: The Ethics of Parent–Child Relationships*, Princeton University Press.
Choudhry, S. and Herring, J. (2010) *European Human Rights and Family Law*, Hart Publishing.
Committee of Ministers of the Council of Europe (2015) Resolution concerning Association for the Protection of All Children (APPROACH) Ltd v. Belgium, Complaint No. 98/2013 CM/ResChS(2015)12.
Commission on Children and Violence (1995) *Children and Violence*, Calouste Gulbenkian Foundation.

Committee against Torture (2013) *Concluding Observations on the 5th Periodic Report of the United Kingdom of Great Britain and Northern Ireland 2013*, CAT/C/GBR/CO/5, Centre for Human Rights, Geneva.

Committee on Economic, Social and Cultural Rights (2002) *Concluding Observations of the Committee on Economic, Social and Cultural Rights: United Kingdom of Great Britain and Northern Ireland – Dependent Territories 2002*, E/C 12/1/Add 79, Centre for Human Rights, Geneva.

(2009) *Concluding Observations of the Committee on Economic, Social and Cultural Rights: United Kingdom of Great Britain and Northern Ireland – Dependent Territories 2009*, E/C.12/GBR/CO/5, Centre for Human Rights, Geneva.

Committee on the Elimination of Discrimination against Women (2008) *Concluding Observations of the Committee on the Elimination of Discrimination against Women: United Kingdom of Great Britain and Northern Ireland*, CEDAW/C/GBR/CO/6, Centre for Human Rights, Geneva.

(2013) *Concluding Observations of the Committee on the Elimination of Discrimination against Women: United Kingdom of Great Britain and Northern Ireland*, CEDAW/C/GBR/CO/7, Centre for Human Rights, Geneva.

Committee on the Rights of the Child (2006) *General Comment No. 8 on the Right of the Child to Protection from Corporal Punishment and Other Cruel or Degrading Forms of Punishment*, Centre for Human Rights, Geneva.

(2011) *General Comment No. 13 on the Right of the Child to Protection from All Forms of Violence*, Centre for Human Rights, Geneva.

(2016) *Concluding Observations of the Committee on the Rights of the Child: United Kingdom of Great Britain and Northern Ireland*, CRC/C/GBR/CO/5, Centre for Human Rights, Geneva.

Department for Education and Skills (DfES) (2007) Cm 7232, *Review of Section 58 of the Children Act 2004*, The Stationery Office.

Department for Work and Pensions (DWP) (2011) Cm 7990, *Strengthening Families, Promoting Parental Responsibility: The Future of Child Maintenance*, The Stationery Office.

Department of Health (DH) (2000) *Protecting Children, Supporting Parents: A Consultation Document on the Physical Punishment of Children*, Department of Health.

(2001) *Analysis of Responses to the 'Protecting Children, Supporting Parents' Consultation Document*, Department of Health.

Durrant, J. (2000) *A Generation Without Smacking: The Impact of Sweden's Ban on Physical Punishment*, Save the Children.

Eekelaar, J. (1991) 'Parental Responsibility: State of Nature or Nature of the State?' 13 *Journal of Social Welfare and Family Law* 37.

(2015) 'Can There Be Family Justice without Law?' in Maclean, M., Eekelaar, J. and Bastard, B. (eds) *Delivering Family Justice in the 21st Century*, Bloomsbury.

Freeman, M. (2006) 'What's Right with Rights for Children?' 2 *International Journal of Law in Context* 89.

Gilmore, S. (2009) 'The Limits of Parental Responsibility' in Probert, R., Gilmore, S. and Herring, J. (eds) *Responsible Parents and Parental Responsibility*, Hart Publishing.

Guggenheim, M. (2005) *What's Wrong with Children's Rights?*, Harvard University Press.

HM Government (2014) *The 5th Periodic Report to the UN Committee on the Rights of the Child*.

Hale, B. (2006) 'Understanding Children's Rights: Theory and Practice' 44 *Family Court Review* 350.

Heilman, A., Kelly, Y. and Watt, R. (2015) *Equally Protected? A Review of the Evidence on the Physical Punishment of Children*, NSPCC Scotland.

Hoggett, B. (1994) 'Joint Parenting Systems: The English Experiment' 6 *Journal of Child Law* 8.

Human Rights Committee (2015) *Concluding Observations on the 7th Periodic Report of the United Kingdom of Great Britain and Northern Ireland 2015*, CCPR/C/GBR/CO/7, Centre for Human Rights, Geneva.

Joint Committee on Human Rights (JCHR) (2004) *Children Bill*, Nineteenth Report of Session 2003–04, HL Paper 161/ HC 537, The Stationery Office.

Law Commission (1988) Review of Child Law, Guardianship and Custody, Law Com No. 172, HC 594, Her Majesty's Stationery Office.

Minow, M. (1986) 'Rights for the Next Generation: A Feminist Approach to Children's Rights' 9 *Harvard Women's Law Journal* 1.

Northern Ireland Office of Law Reform (2001) *Physical Punishment in the Home – Thinking About the Issues, Looking at the Evidence*, A consultation paper for Northern Ireland, Office of Law Reform.

Smith, R. (2004) '"Hands-off parenting?" – Towards a Reform of the Defence of Reasonable Chastisement in the UK' 16 *Child and Family Law Quarterly* 261.

Sutherland, E. (2020) 'The Enigma of Article 5 of the United Nations Convention on the Rights of the Child: Central or Peripheral' 26 *International Journal of Children's Rights* 447.

Tobin, J. (2013) 'Justifying Children's Rights' 21 *International Journal of Children's Rights* 395.

UN General Assembly (2006) A/61/150, *Report of the Independent Expert for the United Nations study on Violence Against Children*, Geneva.

Zolotor, A. and Puzia, M. (2010) 'Bans against Corporal Punishment: A Systematic Review of the Laws, Changes in Attitudes and Behaviours' 19 *Child Abuse Review* 229.

5

The Child's Right to Identity

(1) Introduction

The concept of identity is fundamental to a person's sense of self and to their relationships with others. It includes internal and external aspects; describing both the expression of a person's individuality and the way in which that individual is recognised as a member of wider society and of groups defined by characteristics such as family, nationality and religious affiliation.[1] At its most basic, possession of a legal identity is essential for a person to be recognised as an individual with rights and obligations. This aspect of identity is particularly important for children, who are especially vulnerable to exploitation if they do not possess a legal identity. By requiring a system of mandatory birth registration, Article 7 of the UN Convention on the Rights of the Child (CRC)[2] ensures that children are made visible to the state and given a name and nationality. Birth registration identifies the child as a person to whom obligations are owed both by the state and by parents; in this way, it is foundational to the practical protection of all other rights. It is for good reason that the core aspects of a child's identity, including nationality, name, parenthood and kinship relationships, are put in place soon after birth. These markers of identity are recognised by the CRC as fundamentally important to the child. In response to the abuses committed by the military regime in Argentina, during which babies were abducted from mothers at birth and given to couples associated with the armed forces and the police,[3] illegally depriving the child of their identity is itself a violation of the CRC.[4] The markers of identity given to a child at birth are, however, not only of importance to the child in question. Adults often have powerful interests in the way in which a child's identity is determined and recorded. Allocation of legal parenthood tends to reflect adult intentions and perceptions of the relevance of biological and social relationships. The name given to a child is often a vehicle through which adults express their understanding of the child's cultural, religious and family identity. Minority groups may have a particular interest in identifying the child as a member of that group in order to preserve their continuation into the future.

[1] J. Eekelaar (2018).   [2] See also International Covenant on Civil and Political Rights, Art. 24.
[3] S. Detrick (1992) pp. 292–4.   [4] CRC, Art. 8.

Important decisions concerning the child's identity are inevitably made while the child is still too young to understand or influence those choices. For these reasons, claims based on young children's right to identity can be a convenient means to further adult interests. A particularly strong example can be seen in the way in which putative fathers have used the child's purported right to knowledge of their genetic identity to found claims to a social relationship with that child.[5]

As the child matures, their life experience and own evolving sense of internal identity may conflict with the decisions made for them at birth and with the legally recognised aspects of their identity. A child may, for example, wish to change a surname that reflects a connection to an abusive parent, or may reject fundamental aspects of the identity recorded at their birth, such as the sex entered on their birth certificate. In such cases, the identity legally recognised at birth may appear an oppressive imposition rather than a right to be cherished. The extent to which a child has a right to legal recognition of their own developing internal sense of identity is unclear.

This chapter will start by considering parenthood and identity. The identification of a child's legal parents is important in its own right and because it acts as a means of establishing further important aspects of a child's identity such as nationality. The chapter will then consider the child's right to knowledge of their origins and the identity of genetic and gestational parents. It will then look at fatherhood and identity. The distinction between the right to knowledge of origins and the identity of a child's legal parents has been drawn clearly in cases of assisted reproduction. For children born through sexual reproduction, identification of a genetic father will determine legal parenthood and, if the father seeks it, will usually lead to parental responsibility and a social relationship. Finally, the chapter will consider children's names and the distinct issues that naming and changes of names raise for children's identity. In each of these areas, important aspects of the child's identity are inevitably determined before the child is able to contribute to that decision. Children's identity rights required careful consideration to ensure that they are not lost, or misused, in adult decisions that will have such important consequences for the child's future and sense of self.

(2) Parenthood and Identity

(A) Introduction

As Sir James Munby has observed:

> The question of who, in law, is or are the parent(s) of a child . . . is a question of the most fundamental gravity and importance. What, after all, to any child, to any parent, never mind to future generations and indeed to society at large, can

---

[5] See discussion below.

be more important, emotionally, psychologically, socially and legally, than the answer to the question: Who is my parent? Is this my child?[6]

Answering this question has become increasingly complex. That complexity is due in part to social and scientific changes which mean that it is increasingly common for children to be brought up in families differing greatly from the traditional unit formed by an opposite-sex married couple and their biological children. Today, society accepts that parent–child relationships can be created through adoption, fostering, surrogacy, gamete donation or the blending of families, regardless of whether the parents are in a formal relationship with each other and whether they are of the opposite sex, the same sex or the parent is a single individual. Identifying a child's parents is also complex because the significance of parenthood has numerous facets. Parenthood can, for example, signify: a biological relationship; the location of legal responsibility for a child; a social relationship of primary care; and the route through which a child's membership of family, nation, religion and culture is determined. Each of these forms of parental significance is of independent importance to the child. Parenthood is important to children both because it provides the primary relationship of responsibility for the child and because it recognises the most fundamental aspects of a child's identity from birth. While the same adults will often perform both functions, the conceptual foundations of the child's right to identity are distinct from those that underlie the right to be cared for by their parents. The distinction between these rights is well illustrated by the decision of the European Court of Human Rights (ECtHR) in *Mennesson v. France*.[7] The case concerned French intended parents who had entered a surrogacy arrangement in California through which twins had been born. French law had not prevented the twins from living with their intended parents – indeed, they had done so for almost 14 years at the time of the judgment. There was, therefore, no breach of the rights of the parents or the children to enjoy *family* life together. France had, however, refused to recognise a legal relationship between them and it was this that was a breach of the children's right to *identity*, protected as an aspect of their private life under Article 8 of the ECHR. This right to private life required that the children were able to obtain legal recognition for their relationship with their parents and that they were not deprived of their nationality and inheritance rights that flowed from this legal recognition. This chapter will focus on this right to identity.[8]

---

[6] *Re The Human Fertilisation and Embryology Act 2008 (Cases A, B, C, D, E, F, G and H)* [2015] EWHC 2602 (Fam), [2017] 1 FLR 366, at [3].
[7] *Mennesson v. France*, App. No. 65192/11, Judgment of 26 June 2014.
[8] The distinct, but often related, right to family life and a social relationship between parents and children is considered in Chapter 6.

Parenthood[9] is relevant to a child's right to identity in two distinct ways. First, a child's knowledge of their genetic origins and the circumstances of their birth may be important to their sense of self and personal identity, as considered below. Second, parenthood is central to a child's legal identity, whether or not those legal parents have a biological relationship to the child. Through the legal status of parenthood, the law not only recognises a life-long[10] relationship of belonging between parent and child, but also provides the gateway through which other important aspects of the child's belonging, such as kinship and nationality,[11] are determined. The decision in *Mennesson* illustrates that legal recognition of the parent–child relationship is an important aspect of the child's right to identity. The case does not, however, give clear guidance on *which* parental relationships must be recognised in this way under Article 8 of the ECHR. In that case, the intended father was also the genetic father, while the intended mother had no biological connection to the children. Although the court found that the failure to recognise the legal relationship with *both* parents was relevant to the children's right to identity,[12] there was a 'special dimension' in the fact that the father was also the children's biological father and it was the failure to recognise that relationship that was outside of the state's margin of appreciation.[13] The Grand Chamber has, however, made it quite clear that the existence of 'private life' between 'parents' and children does not depend solely on biological ties, but can arise in other circumstances.[14] As yet, it is unclear how these different forms of parental recognition interact, especially in circumstances in which the children's right to a legal identity in Article 8 of the ECHR may require

---

[9] This chapter will focus on parenthood as birth; the question of transfer of legal parenthood through adoption is considered in Chapter 6 and adoption following child protection proceedings in Chapter 16.

[10] Save where that relationship is severed through adoption or a parental order.

[11] See *R (on the application of K (A Child))* v. *Secretary of State for the Home Department* [2018] EWHC 1834 (Admin): the rule in the British Nationality Act 1981 that the child of a married mother be conclusively treated as the child of her husband for the purpose of acquisition of nationality, despite proof that another man was her biological father, was a breach of the child's rights under ECHR, Art. 14, read with ECHR, Art. 8, and a declaration of incompatibility was made accordingly.

[12] *Mennesson* v. *France*, App. No. 65192/11, at [96]–[98].

[13] Ibid. at [100]. The egg had been provided by a donor. See A. Mulligan (2018), who argues that the right to identity in Strasbourg jurisprudence on surrogacy should not be understood as being confined to genetic identity and includes gestational parents and intended parents.

[14] *Paradiso* v. *Italy* (2017) 65 EHRR 2, at [161]: 'The Court considers that there is no valid reason to understand the concept of "private life" as excluding the emotional bonds created and developed between an adult and a child in situations other than the classic situations of kinship. This type of bond also pertains to individuals' life and social identity. In certain cases involving a relationship between adults and a child where there are no biological or legal ties the facts may nonetheless fall within the scope of "private life"'. In this case, there was no biological tie between the child and the applicants who had purported to enter a surrogacy agreement in Russia in violation of Italian law. In contrast to *Mennesson* v. *France*, the child was not an applicant and his right to identity was not directly before the court, at [195], as discussed further in Chapter 2.

recognition of a parent without the 'special dimension' of a biological relationship.

Many of the ECtHR cases concerning children's legal identity have, like *Mennesson*, been decided in the fast-developing area of international surrogacy. The multiple potential parents – gestational, genetic and intentional – mean that this area is particularly complex for the law to navigate. The ECtHR has been willing to grant a wide margin of appreciation given the sensitive moral and ethical issues raised by surrogacy and the lack of a European consensus as to how to resolve those issues.[15] This is especially important as many states have put in place regulation designed to protect women from exploitation, avoid child trafficking and provide legal certainty in identifying parents. Nonetheless, a narrow margin of appreciation is usually afforded to questions concerning fundamental aspects of personal identity, such as the child's legal relationship with their parents.[16] The contours of these competing considerations have been difficult to navigate. The ECtHR has been clearest in cases in which there is a genetic link between the child and intended parent, in which case a means of establishing legal parental recognition must be available, although states have a considerable margin of appreciation in deciding what form this recognition might take and the conditions attached to it.[17] The position of a non-genetic, intended parent is far more precarious. If she is raising the child with a genetic intended parent, then some means of legal recognition must be available, although states again have a wide margin of appreciation as to how this is to be achieved and a route to recognition through adoption will usually be sufficient.[18] If neither intended parent has a genetic link to the child, or the relationship with the genetic parent has broken down, the intended parent's position will be even more fragile. In *AM* v. *Norway*,[19] the intended parents continued to pursue a foreign surrogacy arrangement

---

[15] E.g. *Valdís Fjölnisdóttir and others* v. *Iceland*, App. No. 71552/17, Judgment of 18 August 2021, at [69]–[70].

[16] *Advisory opinion concerning the recognition in domestic law of a legal parent–child relationship between a child born through a gestational surrogacy arrangement abroad and the intended mother* (request no. P16-2018–001, French Court of Cassation, 10 April 2019) ('Advisory Opinion'), at [44]–[45].

[17] E.g. *D* v. *France*, App. No. 11288/18, Judgment of 16 July 2020, concerning a genetic and intended mother in a surrogacy arrangement conducted in Ukraine. There was no requirement that legal recognition took the form of recording the information on the Ukrainian birth certificate: adoption was permissible. In the domestic case of *R (H)* v. *Secretary of State for Health and Social Care* [2019] EWHC 2095 (Admin), the genetic, intended father could not be recognised as the legal father as the surrogate would not give her consent. There was no violation of the child's Art. 8 rights as a means of parental recognition was available and the requirement of consent was a justifiable part of the legislative scheme. In this case, the child was living with the intended parents, who had parental responsibility for her.

[18] *Advisory Opinion*, at [48]–[55]. The opinion was given in the context of a foreign surrogacy, achieved with donor eggs, in which the intended mother was recognised on the foreign birth certificate and the legal parent–child relationship with the intended father is recognised in domestic law. The opinion was not intended to apply outside of this context: at [32].

[19] App. No. 30254/18, Judgment of 24 March 2022.

after they had separated, resulting in the birth of a child who was genetically related to the intended father, but not the intended mother. Both intended parents were involved in the child's care until he was 17 months old, at which point the parenting relationship broke down and the father cut off all contact between them. The genetic father was recognised as the legal father under Norwegian law, but the intended mother's only route to domestic legal recognition was through adoption, which was unavailable as the father was unwilling to provide the necessary consent. While the ECtHR accepted that the bond of care between the intended mother and child meant that her private life, under Article 8 of the ECHR, was engaged,[20] there had been no violation of that right. The state had provided a route for legal recognition and included conditions that were designed to protect the interests of others, including the child. The fact that adoption was unavailable on the facts was due to the decision of the father and not the actions of the state.[21] The case demonstrates the additional barriers often faced by non-genetic intended parents to establishing legal status in domestic law and to bringing a successful claim under Article 8. It also demonstrates the difficulties in determining the child's identity rights in such complex cases. In *AM* v. *Norway*, the applicant was only able to raise her own Article 8 rights and not those of the child. With no one to represent the child's position, the court gave no view as to whether the child had a right to have a legal relationship with the intended mother who had provided primary care in the first months of his life and had embarked on the 'parental project' that led to his birth, albeit a project that was prohibited in Norwegian law. The court has been reluctant to identify the limits of the child's right to legal recognition of a non-genetic parent, even in cases in which those rights are directly before the court. For example, in *Valdís Fjölnisdóttir and others* v. *Iceland*,[22] neither intended parent had a genetic connection to the child who had been born through a foreign surrogacy agreement that was prohibited in Iceland. Although divorced, both intended parents had continued to raise the child, who had been granted Icelandic citizenship. Given the practical enjoyment of family life between them, the ECtHR found that failure to recognise the legal relationship between them was not a violation of the right to family life of the intended parents and child. It refused, however, to give any separate consideration to the right to private life.[23] In the absence of more detailed case law, it is difficult to determine the precise ambit of the child's right to private life and to legal recognition of a relationship with an intended parent, particularly if that parent does not have a biological connection to the child.

The CRC is similarly unclear as to which potential parents must be recognised as legal parents under Article 7 of the CRC, although it takes a broad approach to the range of relationships that may be of importance to a child's

---

[20] Ibid. at [110]–[111].   [21] Ibid. at [127]–[133].
[22] App. No. 71552/17, Judgment of 18 August 2021.   [23] Ibid. at [76].

development.[24] It does, however, recognise the risks to children's rights that can come from adult desires to become parents or to obscure the child's origins. As John Eekelaar has observed, 'the "truth" of parenthood has been, and still is, used to give adults power over children'.[25] The potential for abuse of this adult power is clearly recognised in the CRC. The right to preservation of a child's identity in Article 8 of the CRC was included as a direct response to the Argentinian Junta's removal of babies from political dissidents and their allocation to adults who supported the regime. Similarly, the potential for children, and parents, to be exploited for profit is recognised by the prohibition on the sale of children,[26] including in relation to adoption.[27] The CRC acknowledges the importance to children of recognising those adults who have an important role in the child's life, but also the potential for exploitation of children to meet adults' interests in becoming parents. It does not, however, give further guidance on which parents must be recognised in different circumstances. Given this ambiguity, the UK has made a specific declaration as to the meaning of parenthood in the CRC to clarify that it only applies to those regarded in domestic law as parents.[28]

(B) Domestic Law: Parenthood and Identity

Domestic law, like ECHR and CRC law, does not embody one particular 'truth' as to the meaning of parenthood; while genetics, intention to parent and child welfare all play different roles in setting the rules on parenthood, none provides the trump card that identifies the essence of legal parenthood.[29] The law will only recognise a maximum of two legal parents for a child, meaning that in circumstances such as surrogacy or gamete donation, where there are more than two adults who have a plausible parental link to the child, the law must lay down rules to choose between them. This choice has profound consequences for children, but children's rights have had a limited impact on the formation of those rules. Perhaps inevitably, this most important of relationships for children depends on decisions made by adults, usually before the child is conceived. Those rules tend to reflect adult perceptions of the interests that are most important in each form of conception. If a child is given

---

[24] See further discussion in Chapter 6.   [25] J. Eekelaar (2017) p. 148.

[26] CRC, Art. 35, supplemented by the Optional Protocol to the Convention on the Rights of the Child on the Sale of Children, Child Prostitution and Child Pornography.

[27] CRC, Art. 21. A principle that is of particular importance in the Preamble to the Hague Convention on Protection of Children and Co-operation in Respect of Intercountry Adoption. For an analysis of children's rights in this context, see C. Fenton-Glynn (2014).

[28] The UK interprets the references in the Convention to 'parents' to mean only those persons who, as a matter of national law, are treated as parents. This includes cases where the law regards a child as having only one parent, e.g., where a child has been adopted by one person only and in certain cases where a child is conceived other than as a result of sexual intercourse by the woman who gives birth to it and she is treated as the only parent.

[29] E. Jackson (2006).

new legal parents, through adoption or a parental order,[30] the individual child's welfare will be the paramount consideration in allocating parenthood. In contrast, allocation of parenthood at birth is dependent on the application of legal rules rather than a discretionary analysis of individual welfare, even in cases in which parenthood is disputed.[31] This means that there is no scope within the existing rules for a court to recognise, or refuse to recognise, a particular person as a parent on the basis of the child's best interests. This is not to say that the law on legal parenthood is contrary to children's rights or interests. The law tends to operate in a way that provides certainty and allocates legal parenthood to those most likely to care for the child. Nonetheless, the law on parenthood will often have a profound effect on the child's life, relationships and identity. By prioritising certainty over discretion, the application of that law will sometimes allocate legal parenthood in a way that does not reflect the child's upbringing or identity.

The one bright line rule on the allocation of parenthood is that the woman who gives birth to the child is the child's legal mother at birth. This rule applies whether or not she is genetically related to that child and regardless of whether she intends to bring the child up herself or to hand the child to intended parents under a surrogacy arrangement.[32] In *R (McConnell and another)* v. *Registrar General for England and Wales*,[33] the applicant was a transgender man who had conceived and given birth after obtaining a gender recognition certificate that recognised him as legally male, so raising the question of whether he should be registered as the mother, father or simply as a parent. As a matter of statutory construction, the Court of Appeal found that the parent who had given birth should always be registered as the child's mother, regardless of whether, or when, the parent had obtained a gender recognition certificate. The court accepted that this would be an interference with the ECHR Article 8 identity rights of both the parent and the child, but that this interference could be justified under Article 8(2). The case again raises the question of the respective relevance of biology and social relationships to the child's legal identity. The Court of Appeal had accepted that there was an interference with the child's Article 8 right to identity, as the birth certificate describing the parent as the mother was likely to conflict with the child's social experience of the parent as a father.[34] Nonetheless, the legislative scheme was found to serve a legitimate aim in providing a clear and coherent system of

---

[30] Adoption and Children Act 2002, s. 1. A parental order is defined in Human Fertilisation and Embryology Act (HFEA) 2008, s. 54 and is available in cases of surrogacy.

[31] Although a clinic providing assisted reproductive treatment must consider the welfare of any resulting child, including the need for supportive parenting: HFEA 1990, s. 13(5).

[32] Although the Law Commission has proposed a new pathway for surrogacy which would enable intended parents to be recognised as the child's legal parents at birth if the conditions of the pathway are fulfilled. If implemented, this would provide the first instance in which a woman could give birth to a child without being recognised as the child's mother in domestic law: Law Commission and Scottish Law Commission (2019) ch. 8.

[33] [2020] EWCA Civ 559, [2020] 3 WLR 683. See A. Margaria (2020).   [34] Ibid. at [56].

births that allowed children the right to know who had given birth to them.[35] In particular, Parliament was entitled to take the view that the best interests of children generally were served by a system that ensured that every child had a mother and could discover who that mother was. In this way, the case protected the biological 'truth' of children generally over the social 'truth' of the individual child. Whether this conclusion will survive scrutiny by Strasbourg remains to be seen. At present, there is no case law concerning the legal identity of children born to transgender men, but the first such case is pending before the ECtHR.[36] Given the lack of consensus within Europe on transgender parenthood, the Court of Appeal may well be right to suggest that Strasbourg is likely to grant a wide margin of appreciation to states on such issues, especially if there has been no impediment to family life between the parent and child.[37] In the absence of a ruling to the contrary, the domestic position is likely to continue to prioritise biological identity over social identity by requiring any gestational parent to be registered as a mother regardless of their legal gender.

The decision in *McConnell* makes it clear that all children will have a legal mother at birth. The question of whether the child has another legal parent, and who that might be, is the subject of a complex set of legal rules that can produce distinctions that appear almost entirely unrelated to the welfare and upbringing of the child. A good example of this can be seen in the context of gamete donation. If gamete donation takes place in a licensed clinic, the allocation of parenthood is primarily based on consent. Sperm donors who have provided consent in the correct form are exempt from the usual rule that fatherhood follows genetic paternity.[38] Instead, legal parenthood can be allocated to any partner, male or female, of the mother who has given appropriate consent in the prescribed form prior to treatment.[39] These rules combine to mean that legal parenthood is generally allocated to those who commit to the child's upbringing prior to conception.[40] This is in contrast to cases of sexual

---

[35] Ibid. at [58].   [36] *OH and GH* v. *Germany*, App. Nos 53568/18 and 54941/18.

[37] [2020] EWCA Civ 559, [2020] 3 WLR 683, at [73]–[80]. See discussion above of *Valdís Fjölnisdóttir and others* v. *Iceland*, App. No. 71552/17, Judgment of 18 August 2021.

[38] HFEA 2008, s. 41(1). See also HFEA 2008, s. 47 in relation to egg donors.

[39] The spouse or civil partner of the mother who conceived with donor gametes will be a legal parent unless it is shown that they did not consent to the procedure: HFEA 2008, s. 35 (marriage to a man) and s. 42 (marriage or civil partnership to a woman). If the intended parents are not in a status relationship, the partner may acquire parenthood by demonstrating consent in accordance with the agreed fatherhood conditions (HFEA 2008, ss 36–8) or agreed female parenthood conditions (HFEA 2008, ss 43–5). If no second parent has consented via these provisions, the child's only legal parent will be the mother.

[40] Although difficulties have occurred in cases in which that wish to parent has not been evidenced through informed consent in the prescribed form, e.g.: *Leeds Teaching Hospitals NHS Trust* v. *A* [2003] EWHC 259, [2003] 1 FLR 1091 (no consent to procedure that resulted from clinical error); *Re E (Assisted Reproduction: Parent)* [2013] EWHC 1418 (Fam), [2013] 2 FLR 1357 (forms downloaded from internet rather than provided by clinic with proper information). In a series of subsequent cases, the courts have been required to consider various errors in paperwork; not all flaws in consent forms will render consent ineffective, provided that that

conception, in which legal fatherhood is allocated on the basis of genetics, regardless of the genetic father's wish to be a parent or his commitment to the child. If the intended parents seek to make their own arrangements for informal donation outside of a clinic, the situation falls between these two regimes depending on the precise circumstances. For example, in *M v. F and H (Legal Paternity)*,[41] where a married woman made arrangements with a sperm donor through an internet site, it was common ground that attempts to conceive included both artificial insemination and sexual intercourse. Whether the 'donor' was the legal father of the resulting child depended on both the husband's consent and which of these methods had resulted in the eventual conception. Had the husband consented then he would have been the legal father of any child conceived through artificial insemination; although if the couple had been unmarried then his consent to informal artificial insemination would have been ineffective in conferring fatherhood. In fact, the court found that the child was conceived through natural intercourse and the question of whether the husband had consented was irrelevant. Instead, the common law reasserted itself and the 'donor' was the father regardless of his intentions and those of the mother. As this example shows, the allocation of legal parenthood can depend on complex questions of genetics, intention, marital status and means of conception, which may have little to do with the individual child's welfare or eventual upbringing. While the law on donated gametes applies in the same way regardless of the sex of the intended parents, these provisions have a particular impact on the parenthood of children born to lesbian couples, who will require sperm donation to conceive and appear more likely to utilise known donors than heterosexual couples.[42]

A further example of the way in which a child can be allocated legal parents that do not accord with the child's welfare or future upbringing can be seen in the context of surrogacy. At birth, the child's legal parenthood is allocated according to the ordinary rules of parenthood, without regard to the surrogacy context. As a result, the woman who gives birth will be the legal mother and, if she is married, her spouse will usually also be the child's legal parent. This means that at birth the child will have legal parents who will almost certainly have no wish to act as social parents and may have no genetic connection to the child. The law provides parental orders[43] as a means of transferring parenthood to align the child's legal identity with the intended parental relationship. Applications for parental orders are subject to an extensive list of legislative conditions, which appear to place significant restrictions on the ability of the

---

consent is given prior to treatment: *Re A (Human Fertilisation and Embryology Act 2008: Assisted Reproduction: Parent)* [2015] EWHC 2602 (Fam), [2016] 1 WLR 1325.

[41] [2013] EWHC 1901 (Fam), [2014] 1 FLR 352.

[42] L. Smith (2013). See esp. *MacDougall v. SW and others (Sperm Donor: Parental Responsibility or Contact)* [2022] EWFC 50, discussed further below, for a particularly concerning example of a 'sperm donor' offering informal donation through internet sites aimed at lesbian women who were seeking to conceive.

[43] HFEA 2008, s. 54 (two intended parents) and s. 54A (a single intended parent).

courts to grant parental orders.[44] The courts have been willing to adopt a strained interpretation of many of these conditions to allow them to make orders that reflect the child's best interests and Article 8 rights.[45] For example, the statutory language requiring applications to be made in the first 6 months of the child's life has been read down to allow parental orders to be made for much older children, and even a young adult, in order to secure their rights to identity and family life.[46] Similarly, the requirement that the 'child's home must be with the applicants' was found to be satisfied in a case in which the 3-year-old child had not had any form of direct contact with one of the applicants.[47] Nonetheless, it is not always possible to read down the requirements of the statute, even if it is clear that the child's future lies with the intended parents.[48] If a parental order cannot be made, the legal parenthood of the child remains as it was at birth. Unless the intended parents seek to adopt the child,[49] the court has no means of recognising them as legal parents and must instead use tools such as wardship and child arrangements orders to construct a form of legal relationship between the intended parents and the child.[50] Following the decision in *Mennesson*, discussed above, the failure to recognise a genetic intended parent as a legal parent might appear to be a breach of the children's right to identity. In *Mennesson*, however, there was

[44] Including that: the child was conceived through artificial reproduction; the application is brought within 6 months of the child's birth; the child's home is with the applicants; the consent of the mother, and any other legal parent, has been obtained; at least one of the applicants has a genetic connection to the child; and, in the case of an application by two intended parents, they are married, or in a civil partnership or enduing relationship: HFEA 2008, ss 54 and 54A.

[45] The courts are under a duty to treat the child's welfare as paramount when determining an application for a parental order: Human Fertilisation and Embryology Regulations 2018 (SI 2018/1412), reg. 2 and Sch. 1.

[46] In *X* v. *Z (Parental Order: Adult)* [2022] EWFC 26, the 'child' was 23 at the date of application, but the parental order was granted. See also *Re X (A Child) (Surrogacy: Time Limit)* [2014] EWHC 3135 (Fam), [2015] Fam 186, esp. at [61].

[47] *Re A (Surrogacy: s54 Criteria)* [2020] EWHC 1426 (Fam), [2021] 1 FLR 357: the parents had separated prior to the embryo transfer and the 'father' had initially wanted nothing to do with the child.

[48] E.g. in *Re Z (A Child) (Surrogate Father: Parental Order)* [2015] EWFC 73, [2015] 1WLR 4993, the requirement that there were two applicants could not be read down to allow an order to be granted to a single intended father. Subsequently, in *Re Z (A Child) (No. 2)* [2016] EWHC 1191 (Fam), it was conceded by the Secretary of State that this rule was incompatible with Art. 14 when read with Art. 8. A declaration of incompatibility was made on the basis of this concession, and the court did not consider whether it was also a breach of the child's right to identity under Art. 8. The incompatibility was addressed by the introduction of HFEA 2008, s. 54A, which permitted applications by single parents.

[49] The domestic courts have generally been reluctant to use adoption where there is already a biological relationship between the intended parents and the child; e.g. *M* v. *F and SM* [2017] EWHC 2176 (Fam), at [18].

[50] E.g. *AB* v. *CD* [2018] EWHC 1590 (Fam): twin children born via a surrogacy arrangement in India were handed to their genetic commissioning parents at birth, but it was not appreciated that a parental order was required until the children were 6 years old. By this time, the parents had separated and the 'father' had disengaged. As the law at the time required an application by a couple, it was not possible to make an order and legal parenthood remained with the Indian surrogate and her husband.

no means by which the intended parents could acquire legal parenthood: the ECHR does not prohibit conditions on the legal process for recognising legal parental status, particularly if that process is designed to protect the best interests of the child or the rights of others. For example, in *R (H)* v. *Secretary of State for Health and Social Care*,[51] the genetic intended father could not obtain a parental order as the surrogate mother and her husband refused to give their consent and that consent was a requirement that could not be dispensed with. The child lived with the intended father and his partner under a child arrangements order, meaning that there was no interference with her right to family life.[52] The inability to grant a parental order was an interference with her ECHR Article 8 right to private life, but there was no violation of that right. The requirement of consent was a justifiable part of the legislative scheme, which had been designed to give legal certainty and protect the rights of all participants. The fact that the scheme could not be used in this case was due to the actions of the surrogate mother and not the state. In this way, the domestic courts, like Strasbourg, have been willing to uphold legislative schemes for recognising legal parenthood, even if individual children are unable to secure their legal identity because of a justifiable condition to using the scheme. Further, the availability of adoption might be considered strictly sufficient to comply with Article 8,[53] although the domestic courts have considered it inappropriate to use adoption to recognise genetic commissioning parents as legal parents given that adoption is based on a change of the child's identity and not merely recognition of that identity.[54] While these points mean that the parental order scheme is likely to survive a challenge at Strasbourg, it is clear that at present the law operates in a way that leaves many children born through surrogacy in a precarious legal position in practice. The Law Commission has proposed a new parental pathway that, if followed, would enable the child's legal identity with the intended parents to be secured before birth. Such a scheme would reduce, but not eliminate, those cases in which the child's identity is left in limbo.[55]

It is clear that legal parenthood is not always allocated to those adults who will have the most important role in a child's upbringing, or to all of those adults who have played an important role in the child's origins. These children may find that their legal identity does not accord with their social relationships or internal sense of identity. This does not mean that there has *necessarily* been

---

[51] [2019] EWHC 2095 (Admin).   [52] Ibid. at [81].

[53] In *Mennesson* v. *France*, App. No. 65192/11, the case law of the Court of Cassation also prevented the intended parents from obtaining legal status through adoption: at [100]. In *Re Z (A Child) (No. 2)* [2016] EWHC 1191 (Fam), the Secretary of State argued that the availability of adoption meant that there was no violation of Art. 8. This point was not decided by the court.

[54] E.g. *M* v. *F and SM* [2017] EWHC 2176 (Fam), at [18].

[55] See Law Commission and Scottish Law Commission (2019). Whether surrogacy itself is compatible with children's rights, particularly if arranged on a commercial basis, remains a contentious question that is beyond the scope of this chapter. See K. Wade (2017) and J. Tobin (2014) for very different views as to the proper children's rights approach to surrogacy.

a breach of the child's rights. Both the ECtHR and the domestic courts have upheld legislative schemes that have a justifiable approach to allocating parenthood, even if those schemes are unable to give each and every child the legal identity that matches their social reality and personal identity.[56] Those conditions do, however, require careful scrutiny and are more likely to survive that scrutiny if the child's family life is protected.

(C) Biological Identity, Legal Identity and Family Life

The fragmentation of legal, social and biological identity means that different legal tools are needed to recognise the fact that the different facets of parenthood are not always accommodated by legal parenthood. Domestic law recognises that adults caring for children may have a social relationship with them which is far more important to the children themselves than any link with their biological progenitors.[57] In particular, child arrangements orders, which regulate the child's upbringing and relationships, are based on the welfare of the individual child. As will be seen in the following chapter, that law is primarily concerned with the realities of the child's relationships rather than the formal legal status of parenthood.[58] Conversely, the law also recognises that adults can play a role in the child's conception that is important to the child's identity, even if there will not be a parenting relationship between them. For example, if a couple are receiving fertility treatment and the partner dies prior to the embryo being transferred to the mother, the partner may still be entered onto the child's birth certificate, regardless of whether there is any genetic connection between them, provided that the partner gave the necessary consent prior to their death.[59] This is an extraordinary provision in that it recognises a form of parental link between a child and a person with no genetic, gestational or social link to that child, merely on the basis of their prior consent. The legal recognition of the deceased parent in these circumstances has no further legal consequences[60] and is a good example of the way in which the law can reflect the complexities of modern conception and the importance of different adults to a child's origins.[61]

---

[56] E.g. *R (H)* v. *Secretary of State for Health and Social Care* [2019] EWHC 2095 (Admin); *AM* v. *Norway*, App. No. 30254/18, Judgment of 24 March 2022, discussed above.

[57] Most importantly through Children Act (CA) 1989, s. 12(2), which enables a person legally unrelated to the child to acquire parental responsibilities over him or her through obtaining a child arrangements order directing that the child lives with that person. The court also has the discretion to grant parental responsibility to a person for the duration of a child arrangements order directing that they should have contact with the child: CA 1989, s. 12(2(A)).

[58] See e.g. *Re B (A Child)* [2016] UKSC 4, [2016] AC 606.

[59] Human Fertilisation and Embryology Act (HFEA) 2008, s. 40 (male partners) and s. 46 (female partners).

[60] HFEA 2008, s. 48(3) and (4).

[61] Although, as discussed below, birth certificates do not otherwise record the role of adults who are not the child's legal parents.

In cases of assisted reproduction, the law has been designed to draw a clear distinction between the child's interest in knowing their biological identity and their interest in having a legal identity and family relationship with their intended parents. In stark contrast, the law finds it much more difficult to recognise diverse forms of parenthood and parental relationships for children conceived through a sexual relationship. In respect of these children, genetic fatherhood leads to legal fatherhood, financial liability for the child and a presumption that it is in the child's best interests for that father to have parental responsibility and a social relationship with the child should he wish to do so, regardless of whether such relationship already exists.[62] As Jane Fortin has argued elsewhere, this:

> assumption that once the biological ties between father and child have been clearly identified, they should be fulfilled by a social relationship, produces an elision of the right to know the parent's identity, with the right to know and have a relationship with that parent.[63]

As a result, there is a deep ambivalence in the current law over the social significance that attaches to the biological tie between a child and genetic parents. That ambivalence means that protection of the child's right to know their origins can have far-reaching consequences for the child's legal identity and social relationships, depending on the circumstances of the child's conception.

(3) A Child's Right to Knowledge of Origins

(A) Background

It seems reasonably clear that the relative ease with which it is now possible to establish the identity of a person's genetic progenitors is one of the factors driving the developing societal view that everyone has an in-built need to know the genetic 'truth' of their origins.[64] It is undoubtedly provoking a dislike of secrecy being allowed to mask the true situation.[65] Freeman and Richards assert that the prevalent assumptions that 'our biological origins are a significant determinant of identity and kin relationships' have been heightened by a knowledge of genetic science.[66] Whether the need to know one's origins is indeed 'a basic human right' or 'the voguish language of cod-psychology'[67] is unclear. As O'Donovan has so wisely observed in the context of adoption, the search for identity does not exist in a vacuum: 'It is produced by legal and social structures which attach value to concepts of identity linked to genitors.'[68] Be this as it may, the lessons gained from adoption research are

---

[62] CA 1989, s. 1(2A), inserted by Children and Families Act 2014, s. 11.
[63] J. Fortin (2009). See further discussion below.
[64] T. Freeman and M. Richards (2006) p. 75. See also C. Smart (2007) p. 36.
[65] J. Eekelaar (2017) p. 161.   [66] T. Freeman and M. Richards (2006) p. 79.
[67] V. Groskop and C. Sarler (2007).   [68] K. O'Donovan (1990) p. 102.

compelling and it is tempting to apply them more generally. The research suggests that many adopted children benefit from discovering the true identity of those who brought them into the world and that this information should be provided early in life. It appears that information about children's origins gives them the ability to place themselves in a social context. They gain a continuity with the past and a complete and consistent biography.[69] Furthermore, concealment and secrecy contribute to children's sense of bewilderment if told later that they have been brought up in the incorrect belief that their present carers are their birth parents.[70] It was this research material which prompted the introduction of legislation giving adult adoptees a procedural right to discover the identity of their birth relatives.[71]

But there are other groups with similar claims, notably those born with the assistance of donor conception. Referring to the lessons learnt from adoption, Scott Baker J, in Rose v. *Secretary of State for Health and Human Fertilisation and Embryology Authority*,[72] fully sympathised with the needs of a woman conceived through sperm donation to know the identity of her father. Indeed, by the early twenty-first century, the inability of children conceived through sperm donation and other methods of reproductive technology to obtain any information identifying their biological parents[73] was becoming increasingly controversial,[74] given our more open society and the increasing numbers of children conceived in such a way.[75] Furthermore, the practical implications of donation, such as the need to discover an inherited genetic disorder before starting a family of their own, were given increasing weight.[76] Whether or not it is appropriate to use the analogy with adoptees, Scott Baker J's acknowledgement that such claims were backed by the right to identity in Article 8 of the ECHR[77] made change virtually inevitable.[78] By then, the Committee on the Rights of the Child had also criticised English law for withholding information

---

[69] E. Haimes (1987) p. 363.

[70] J. Triseliotis (1973) p. 20: those adoptees aged between 4 and 8 years when told of their adoption experienced the greatest satisfaction; those told in adolescence and adult life experienced the greatest distress and shock.

[71] The current, complicated system for obtaining such information was introduced by the Adoption and Children Act (ACA) 2002, ss 56–65. See C. Bridge and H. Swindells (2003) pp. 246–56.

[72] [2002] EWHC 1593 (Admin), [2002] 2 FLR 962, at [47].

[73] An adult could only apply to the Human Fertilisation and Embryology Authority for non-identifying information about a donor contained on its register.

[74] M. Freeman (1996).

[75] Human Fertilisation and Embryology statistics indicate that around 20,000 children are born annually through IVF treatment; of these, around 2,000 are conceived using donor gametes: www.hfea.gov.uk.

[76] E.g. Re H (Adoption: Disclosure of Information) [1995] 1 FLR 236: the High Court allowed information from a sibling to be passed on to an adopted adult, alerting him to the danger of having inherited a biological disorder.

[77] [2002] EWHC 1593 (Admin), [2002] 2 FLR 962, at [48].

[78] The resulting provisions, contained in Human Fertilisation and Embryology Authority (Disclosure of Donor Information) Regulations 2004 (SI 2004/1511), are discussed further below.

about the biological identity of donors from children born by donor conception.[79] But since parents using donor conception may be reluctant to tell their children the circumstances of their conception, further reforms are now urged ensuring that donor-conceived children have the method of their conception indicated on their birth certificates.[80]

The research on whether donor-conceived children and adults benefit from knowledge of their origins remains somewhat equivocal. Nonetheless, the argument that individuals possess a *right* to knowledge of their biological identity, regardless of its benefits, has gained increasing support. The changing landscape of fertility treatment continues to present new challenges in defining the scope of this right and to its protection in practice. In 2015, the law was altered to permit a child to be born from genetic material from three people in tightly defined cases of mitochondrial disease.[81] This change highlights the need for clarity on the basis and extent of the right to genetic knowledge: does such a right extend to *any* genetic contribution, no matter how limited that contribution and how detached from the individual's characteristics? At the same time, the increasingly global nature of the market in fertility treatment limits the extent to which any national government can regulate the information available to donor-conceived people within its jurisdiction. Alongside this, the ease with which individuals can now access DNA testing and the availability of online sites to connect people with genetic relatives means that it is much more difficult to maintain secrecy in practice. Each of these developments presents challenges to defining and implementing the right to knowledge of genetic origins.

(B) International Human Rights Law

Claims that children have a right to accurate information about their biological origins are substantially reinforced by international human rights law, although identifying the precise legal foundation for the right is not straightforward.[82] None of the three articles of the CRC normally quoted as supporting this argument directly substantiates such a claim. Article 7 of the CRC was inspired by a concern to redress children's statelessness. Its phrasing makes it clear that state parties must provide a method whereby children are 'labelled' or named immediately after birth and thereby linked accurately and quickly to those who brought them into the world. Article 8 responded to the abuses committed by the military regime in Argentina and requires states to provide a means whereby children retain their identity, a concept which includes name, family and nationality, thereby ensuring that they are easily

---

[79] Committee on the Rights of the Child (2002) paras 31 and 32.   [80] Discussed below.
[81] The Human Fertilisation and Embryology (Mitochondrial Donation) Regulations 2015, discussed further below.
[82] S. Besson (2007) esp. pp. 141–3. See also R. Blauwhoff (2008) pp. 105–12; D. Lyons (2018).

reunited with their parents if they become separated.[83] Article 9 was clearly intended to bar children from being removed from their parents by the state except in situations involving abuse or neglect. Despite none of these articles specifically promoting a child's right to knowledge of origins, the UN Committee on the Rights of the Child has interpreted Article 7 in precisely such a manner. The Committee criticises legal systems which withhold information from children born by donor conception and those which allow mothers to give birth anonymously and to keep their identity secret from their offspring.[84] Nonetheless, although the Committee has been increasingly clear that there is a right to knowledge of origins, there remain significant ambiguities in the Committee's interpretation of this right and its limits. In particular, there is a lack of clarity as to whether the donor-conceived *child* has a right to access information as to their origins, or whether that information need only be safeguarded to allow the right to be exercised in adulthood.[85] Further, the Committee has given little guidance on the limits of this right and how to resolve potential conflicts with the rights of others or the child's best interests.

It is the Strasbourg jurisprudence interpreting Article 8 of the ECHR which most clearly supports the view that children have a right to establish details of their parentage. As discussed earlier,[86] the right to respect for private life has been widely interpreted. The early decision in *Gaskin* v. *United Kingdom*[87] reached by the ECtHR secured for children the right to obtain information about themselves held by public agencies on their childhood and early development.[88] Later, in *Mikulic* v. *Croatia*,[89] this interpretation of Article 8 was taken further in the context of a child's claim that her father's identity should be established through DNA testing. The court considered that there appeared 'to be no reason of principle why the notion of "private life" should be taken to exclude the determination of the legal relationship between a child born out of wedlock and her natural father'.[90] Clearly, no rights under Article 8 are absolute, given that their infringement may be justified to promote the interests of others under Article 8(2). Here, the ECtHR concluded that Croatia should have had in place a procedure striking a fair balance between the needs of a child to have eliminated without unnecessary delay any uncertainty over her personal identity (arising from ignorance of a parents' identity) and those of the alleged father not to be forced into DNA testing.[91]

---

[83] S. Detrick (1992) pp. 292–4.   [84] As in France; R. Hodgkin and P. Newell (2007) p. 106.
[85] D. Lyons (2018).   [86] See Chapter 2.   [87] (1989) 12 EHRR 36.
[88] The Data Protection Act 1998 (as amended by the Freedom of Information legislation) imposed a general duty on local authorities (LAs) to provide full access to social work records.
[89] [2002] 1 FCR 720: a 5-year-old girl (through her mother) claimed successfully that the absence of any legal means of forcing a putative father to comply with court orders for DNA tests infringed her right to private life under ECHR Art. 8, given that there was no independent authority to which she could turn to adjudicate her paternity claim.
[90] Ibid. at [53].   [91] Ibid. and at [64]–[66].

In *Mikulic*, the court was fully aware of the potential tensions in such cases between the rights of the child and those of adult parties, more particularly, the alleged father's rights not to be forced into DNA testing in a disproportionate manner. Critics, agreeing with the powerful dissenting decision in *Odièvre* v. *France*,[92] argue that the majority of the ECtHR in that case got the balance entirely wrong between the rights of mother and child.[93] They had decided that given the flexibility introduced into the system,[94] it was within France's margin of appreciation[95] to continue allowing mothers to give birth anonymously and to retain their anonymity, even at the expense of their children being forced to remain in ignorance of their mother's identity. But, as the dissenting judges urged, this effectively made the mother's unilateral decision binding. Besson[96] argues that the significance of the dissenting judges' view in *Odièvre* was that the margin of appreciation should not prevent the ECtHR subjecting any system established for balancing competing interests to 'the fairest scrutiny' in cases where 'the very nature of the interest concerned [the right to identity]' or 'its inner core' is at stake.[97] Later decisions of the ECtHR have affirmed this understanding that the right to information on identity, including parentage, is integral to the notion of private life,[98] and that the circumstances of the child's birth form part of the *child's* right to identity as well as that of the future adult that the child will become.[99]

Clearly, the ECtHR's willingness to scrutinise carefully claims involving children's right to know their parents' identity is an important development. Nonetheless, Article 8 is a qualified right and case law continues to stress that a fair balance must be found between the child's right to identity and competing interests.[100] While states have some discretion in balancing these interests, the ECtHR has been increasingly willing to subject that balance to 'particularly rigorous scrutiny'[101] and find that limits placed on access to information are in breach of Article 8. A further complexity is how the right to information applies in different circumstances. The cases heard by the ECtHR to date have covered a variety of circumstances; including paternity claims, anonymous births and recognition of parenthood founded on surrogacy arrangements. The court has not yet heard a case concerning information about genetic

---

[92] [2003] 1 FCR 621; joint dissenting opinion by Judges Wildhaber *et al.*, esp. at [5]–[7].

[93] Inter alia: E. Steiner (2003); S. Besson (2007) pp. 150–2.

[94] Ibid. at [49]: France had established an independent body to consider requests from children to have the identity of their mothers disclosed, subject only to the mothers' own consent; absent such consent, they would obtain only non-identifying information.

[95] This term is discussed in Chapter 2.   [96] S. Besson (2007) p. 151.

[97] [2003] 1 FCR 621, joint dissenting opinion by Judges Wildhaber *et al.*, at [11].

[98] *Jäggi* v. *Switzerland*, App. No. 58757/00, at [37]; *Phinikaridou* v. *Cyprus*, App. No. 23890/02, at [45]; *Pascaud* v. *France*, App. No. 19535/08. For this reason, Besson argues that *Odièvre* might not be decided along the same lines today: S. Besson (2007) p. 154.

[99] *Phinikaridou* v. *Cyprus*, App. No. 23890/02, at [45]; *Mennesson* v. *France*, App. No. 65192/11, Judgment of 26 June 2014, at [100].

[100] *Jevremović* v. *Serbia* [2007] ECHR 612, at [106]–[111].

[101] *Phinikaridou* v. *Cyprus*, App. No. 23890/02, at [45].

donors following assisted reproduction or concerning the gestational mother in a surrogacy arrangement. It is not yet clear how wide a margin of appreciation the state has in such circumstances, nor how far the state has a positive obligation to ensure that the child may discover the circumstances of their birth. The fact remains, however, that the Strasbourg jurisprudence has played a significant role in establishing the right to information on biological origins.

(C) Assisted Reproduction and the 'Right to Know'

Many would argue that English law has more than adequately fulfilled its need to protect the right to knowledge of biological identity, both under Article 7 of the CRC and under the existing case law on Article 8 of the ECHR. Adopted children may discover the identity of their birth parents once they reach the age of 18.[102] This same system now extends to those children who were born through a surrogacy arrangement who wish to obtain information concerning their birth, including the identity of their gestational mother.[103] Similarly, adults who were born by donor conception through a domestic licensed clinic have also acquired the right to discover the identity of their gamete donors. As a result of these provisions, children aged over 16 may obtain non-identifying information about the genetic donor,[104] and upon reaching adulthood may obtain identifying information.[105] The removal of donor anonymity applies to those donations that took place on or after 1 April 2005, meaning that the first 18-year-olds eligible to exercise the right to discover the identity of their genetic donors could do so from 2023. It is not yet clear what proportion of donor-conceived people are likely to request such information or their motivation for doing so. Research from jurisdictions in which open-identity donations have been available for a longer duration suggests that a significant

[102] The current system, applicable to children adopted after 30 December 2005, is found in Adoption and Children Act (ACA) 2002, ss 56–65. The position of those adopted before this date is governed by The Adoption Information and Intermediary Services (Pre-commencement Adoptions) Regulations 2005. See also the provisions concerning the Adopted Children Register: ACA 2002, ss 77–81.

[103] The Human Fertilisation and Embryology (Parental Orders) Regulations 2018 (2018/1412), reg. 2 and Sch. 1. Although the Law Commission found that both legal and practical problems prevent people born through surrogacy from accessing information in this way or through court files: Law Commission and Scottish Law Commission (2019) paras 10.19–10.43.

[104] HFEA 1990, ss 31ZA–31ZB (as amended by the HFEA 2008, s. 24) gives 16-year-olds the right to obtain non-identifying information about their genetic parents; see DH (2007) para. 68.

[105] Human Fertilisation and Embryology Authority (Disclosure of Donor Information) Regulations 2004 (SI 2004/1511), reg. 2(2), enables donor-conceived adults (i.e. aged 18 and over) to obtain all information (other than identifying information) held by the Authority on its register of donors about the donor; reg. 2(3) enables donor-conceived adults to obtain all information (identifying and other) held by the Authority on its register supplied to clinics from 1 April 2005. I.e. as from that date, clinics were required to obtain identifying information from all sperm donors. The regulation changes were not retrospective, so children born through an earlier donation cannot access identifying information in this way unless the donor has chosen to supply additional identifying information after that date.

proportion of donor-conceived adults wish to obtain identifying information about their genetic donor.[106] The reasons given by those adults who do seek knowledge of their genetic origins reflect a wide variety of motivations: some merely seek information as to their medical history or genealogical origins; others consider that knowledge of the donor will assist them in forming their own identity; while some wish to form a social relationship with the donor and the donor's family, although this is not usually a desire for a parental relationship.[107] There is also increasing research demonstrating the interest of donor-conceived people in making contact with other genetic relatives, particularly 'donor siblings' who share a genetic parent.[108] As John Eekelaar notes, for these people the connection with donor 'family' is not merely a matter of seeking information or developing an internal sense of self-identity, instead the desire is to form a communal identity through the genetic connection.[109] It is clear that at least some donor-conceived people put great value on obtaining information about their donor, although others do not, and that the meaning placed on that information varies considerably between individuals.

The basis of the law's commitment to providing identifying information on genetic donors is brought into sharp focus by the decision to allow children to be conceived using genetic material from three 'parents'. This procedure is only permitted in cases in which the intended mother's eggs have mitochondrial abnormalities caused by mitochondrial DNA.[110] If there is a significant risk that a child conceived using those eggs would suffer from serious mitochondrial disease,[111] the law now permits the creation of an embryo using genetic material from the eggs of both the mother and a donor, alongside the father's sperm. In essence, the unhealthy mitochondria are removed from the mother's egg, or an embryo created using that egg, and replaced with the healthy mitochondria of the donor. The donor's genetic material allows the child to escape the potentially devastating impact of mitochondrial disease, but the extent to which that DNA contributes to the child's identity is a matter of controversy. The government took the view that such DNA transfer was in

---

[106] J. Scheib *et al.* (2017) found that over a 10-year period, around one-third of adults conceived through donation at a Californian clinic sought information about their donor's identity, although as the rate of request was lower among those children brought up by a heterosexual couple, the researchers suggest that some of those who did not request may well not have known of their origins as a donor-conceived child. The majority of applicants requested information at the age of 18, suggesting that the interest in contacting the donor starts before the age of majority.

[107] Nuffield Council on Bioethics (2013) paras 4.26–4.28; E. Blyth *et al.* (2012).

[108] Ibid., the Human Fertilisation and Embryology Authority now runs 'donor sibling link' to facilitate such searches: HFEA 1990, s. 31ZE.

[109] J. Eekelaar (2018).

[110] The Human Fertilisation and Embryology (Mitochondrial Donation) Regulations 2015 (SI 2015/572), discussed by R. Scott and S. Wilkinson (2017).

[111] The Human Fertilisation and Embryology (Mitochondrial Donation) Regulations 2015 (SI 2015/572), reg. 5.

no way comparable to the ordinary circumstances of egg donation, on the basis that mitochondrial DNA merely provided the 'power pack' for the cell. In contrast, it considered, it was the nuclear DNA from the intended parents that provided the material that would shape the child's individual personality and traits and would form the basis of the child's identity.[112] On this basis, the government considered that there was no reason to allow access to identifying information about the child's mitochondrial donor and, as a result, the 2015 Regulations that permit the procedure only allow access to non-identifying information about that donor.[113] This line of reasoning situates the 'right to know' a genetic donor in the donor's contribution to the individual character- istics of the future child.[114] In contrast, Thana de Campos and Caterina Milo argue that the fact that each of the three 'parents' makes a unique and permanent contribution to the child is enough to ground the child's right to know each of those who contributed genetic material, regardless of the value that others attribute to the particular genetic material.[115] The issue of mito- chondrial donation highlights the uncertainty as to the normative foundations of the 'right to know' the identity of the donor. While the 2015 Regulations appear to base that right on the assumed contribution of genetics to individual characteristics, it might be better seen as a claim to knowledge of personal history and for the individual to create their own understanding of their origins and communal identity. Neither the case law on the right to identity in ECHR Article 8 nor the UN Committee on the Rights of the Child's interpretation of the CRC offer a sufficiently developed understanding of the right to identity to offer a solution to this debate.

It is striking that in each of these areas the law demonstrates a willingness to facilitate *adults* who wish to obtain information about their biological origins. In respect of children, the law does not protect a right to knowledge of origins as such, but instead safeguards the information necessary to allow the child access to it as an adult.[116] Bainham[117] strongly asserts that children have a right to know the truth about their biological parentage and that as a result the law should oblige parents to tell their children that they are donor-conceived.[118] The government currently maintains that rather than the law being prescrip- tive, it is preferable for parents to be educated in the benefits of their children

---

[112] R. Scott and S. Wilkinson (2017) p. 898.

[113] The Human Fertilisation and Embryology (Mitochondrial Donation) Regulations 2015 (SI 2015/572), regs 11–15.

[114] Although R. Brandt (2016) argues that the evidence that mitochondrial DNA does not affect personal characteristics is not as certain as the government would suggest.

[115] T. de Campos and C. Milo (2018).

[116] Save for the fact that, as discussed above, at the age of 16 a donor-conceived person acquires the right to request non-identifying information about their donor.

[117] A. Bainham (2008a) pp. 335–6.

[118] Joint Committee on the Human Tissue and Embryos (Draft) Bill (2007) paras 268–71: summary of evidence provided by A. Bainham and others favouring a parental duty. See A. Bainham (2008b) pp. 262–7.

being told the truth about their birth. For this reason, clinics are required to inform potential parents of donor-conceived children of the importance of informing those children of their biological origins at an early age.[119] Similarly, parents of children born through surrogacy are advised to be open and transparent about that fact while the child is still of pre-school age.[120] The current approach encourages disclosure, but places that decision in the hands of the parents. In this way, the law allows an infertile couple who have used donor conception to conceive to 'pass the child off' as their genetic offspring.[121] While parents are under no obligation to heed government advice in favour of openness, there are good reasons for choosing to do so. There is certainly evidence that the effect of disclosure on donor-conceived people is related to the age at which disclosure takes place and the means by which that information is given. Disclosure at earlier ages tends to be associated with more positive outcomes for relationships and well-being,[122] while disclosure at older ages is more likely to be associated with negative feelings such as betrayal of trust.[123] Parents who choose to withhold information from their children are taking an increasingly risky decision. The availability of direct-to-consumer DNA testing and of DNA matching databases means that the genetic truth may be uncovered, either by the donor-conceived person actively seeking that information or through accidental discovery driven by curiosity for other reasons such as health or genealogy.[124] Given these risks, parents may be wise to follow the advice to speak to their child about their origins at an early age to avoid the consequences of a chaotic and hurtful later discovery by the child or their relatives.

Although there are good reasons to adopt policies to encourage early disclosure by parents, this does not mean there ought to be a legal *obligation* on parents to do so. Such an obligation would be difficult to enforce in practice, particularly as informing the child of their origins is likely to be a process that adapts to their growing understanding, rather than a single event. It is difficult to argue that a parental obligation is required by the international human rights law discussed above, as neither the ECHR nor the CRC has yet been interpreted to guarantee the right to disclosure of information during

---

[119] HFEA 2008, s. 14(3)(6C).   [120] Department of Health and Social Care (2018) p. 23.

[121] S. Golombok *et al.* (2006) p. 1921: 46 per cent of the donor insemination parents had decided against disclosing to their child the method of their conception. There is evidence of an increasing willingness to disclose biological origins to children: Nuffield Council on Bioethics (2013) paras 4.13–4.12. Although intentions to disclose do not always result in actual disclosure in practice, as parents encounter difficulty in the timing and means of doing so: L. Applegarth *et al.* (2016). The form of assisted conception and the type of family also affects disclosure: single parents and same-sex couples are more likely to disclose than heterosexual couples who are more able to hide the presence of the donor. Similarly, parents who used surrogacy seem much more likely to disclose than recipients of donor gametes: Readings *et al.* (2011).

[122] E.g. E. Ilioi *et al.* (2017), comparing disclosure before the age of 7 with subsequent disclosure in childhood.

[123] Nuffield Council on Bioethics (2013) ch. 4.   [124] J. Harper *et al.* (2016); M. Crawshaw (2017).

childhood.[125] Even if the right to identity is interpreted to include disclosure in childhood, it is not absolute, and both conventions support the primary role of parents in making decisions for their children.[126] It is very unlikely that either convention would be interpreted to require states to displace parental discretion in such a sensitive area.[127] It might be argued that an obligation to disclose is necessary in order to protect the child's best interests, but the empirical evidence on this point is contentious. The early claims in favour of openness with donor-conceived children were primarily based on research with adopted children. As Turkmendag *et al.* urge, analogies with adoption are not necessarily appropriate, given that adoption involves the creation of a family around an already existing individual, whereas donor conception is a form of procreation.[128] Empirical research on outcomes for children in families formed through donor-conception and surrogacy is more limited, although growing. The research that is available suggests that donor-conceived children show similar levels of psychological adjustment to those conceived by other means.[129] There is also little to suggest that children who are not told of their origins are at increased risk of psychological problems or of experiencing difficulties in their relationships with their parents.[130] On the other hand, there is evidence of some positive benefits to children's well-being from disclosure – for example, through more positive mother–child interaction.[131] There is also research to suggest that, in adolescence, a key time for the formation of identity, those who have been told about their conception tend not to show distress about their origins, but tend to be interested in finding out more about the donor or surrogate or are already in contact with them.[132] The research to date does not demonstrate sufficient evidence of benefit to children's well-being to *require* recognition of an obligation to disclose biological origins during childhood. Nonetheless, the research also demonstrates that there is no reason to fear that children will be harmed by disclosure: they may well experience some benefits from doing so.

It has been argued that the right to identity places a positive obligation on the state to alert the individual to information held on their origins and that this right is not satisfied by merely allowing access once that information is requested.[133] Although this obligation is not established in the current case law on ECHR Article 8, there are nonetheless good arguments for increasing openness of official information, particularly given the ease with which

---

[125] Although see D. Lyons (2018) for the argument that denying information to children is inconsistent with the CRC.

[126] See discussion in Chapter 4. Note esp. CRC, Art. 5.

[127] Nuffield Council on Bioethics (2013) ch. 4 considers some of the reasons for parents deciding not to disclose, including the fear of stigma in some communities and the impact that the parents fear that this could have on the child.

[128] I. Turkmendag *et al.* (2008) p. 289.

[129] Nuffield Council on Bioethics (2013) ch. 4 summarises the research.

[130] Ibid.; G. Pennings (2017).   [131] S. Golombok *et al.* (2011).   [132] S. Zadeh *et al.* (2018).

[133] M. Crawshaw *et al.* (2017).

home DNA testing can undermine any attempt at secrecy. One means of alerting people born through donor-conception to their origins would be to ensure that that fact is entered on their birth certificates.[134] The fact that the information would be discoverable would also be likely to encourage parental openness during childhood. At present, the purpose of the birth certificate is somewhat ambiguous; for children born through donor-conception, it provides evidence of social and legal parenthood, but not of genetic parenthood. It has been argued that this fact involves the state in 'colluding in a deception'[135] of the donor-conceived person. This argument is perhaps overstated given that it has probably always been the case that some birth certificates have recorded parents who do not have a genetic connection to the child.[136] Nonetheless, there are good arguments for reforming the Victorian law on certification to reflect the diversity of family forms and the fragmentation of genetic, gestational, social and legal parenthood that is now possible.[137] Various proposals have been put forward to reform that law to record the circumstances of the child's biological origins separately from their legal parenthood.[138] There are difficult issues of privacy as to who would have access to this information and at what stage the child would be entitled to it. A particularly contentious question is whether the donor should be identified by name on the original birth certificate. Such a change would remove anonymity for donors entirely and would allow children, and parents, to seek them out during childhood, perhaps to establish a form of 'identity contact' with the donor. This would be a significant shift from the original notion of anonymous donation, but any adult involved in the process is now aware of the ease with which home DNA testing can establish connections even during the child's minority.[139] A disadvantage of this approach is that it removes the right of the donor-conceived person *not* to know the identity of the donor. An alternative is to give sufficient information on the birth certificate to ensure that the individual concerned is alerted to the circumstances of their conception and so seek further information if they wish. For those born through the regulated system of domestic licensed clinics, the linking of information between the birth certificate and Human Fertilisation and Embryology Authority (HFEA) records would provide an independent and reliable source of information. For those born outside of that system, the reliability of the birth record would depend on the willingness of parents to provide that information and may provide an incentive for those wishing to conceal the child's origins to seek treatment elsewhere.

---

[134] Joint Committee on the Human Tissue and Embryos (Draft) Bill (2007) para. 276; DH (2007) paras 69–70.
[135] Joint Committee, ibid., para. 276.   [136] E. Blyth *et al.* (2009).
[137] J. McCandless (2017) considers the wider case for birth certificate reform.
[138] See e.g. E. Blyth *et al.* (2009); M. Crawshaw *et al.* (2017).
[139] A number of well-established DNA testing services allow parents to submit tests for their minor children, or permit older children to do so themselves.

The difficulty of enforcing a 'right to know' in practice is exacerbated by the increasing complexity of the means by which intending parents seek assistance with conception. While a person conceived through a licensed clinic in the UK might discover that fact by inquiring through the HFEA,[140] those conceived outside of the regulated regime may face considerable practical and legal barriers to doing so. Fertility treatment has become an increasingly global industry, with implications for the growing number of children born in this jurisdiction, but conceived through treatment abroad.[141] For some intending parents, the possibility of being treated with anonymously donated gametes is a motivating factor in seeking treatment abroad,[142] while for others it may be the unavoidable consequence of constraints imposed by affordability or availability of donor gametes domestically. Whether intentional or not, by seeking treatment in a country with anonymous donation, parents effectively create barriers to the child's right to access information about the donor. Even in a country with identifiable donors, the potential obstacles formed by language differences and different legal regimes mean that children may find it difficult to access information through formal means in the future. Similar problems are posed by the use of introduction websites which allow intending parents to connect with potential donors, co-parents and surrogates.[143] Such websites are entirely unregulated, leaving both the participants and any children conceived exposed to a wide range of risks, given the lack of screening or recording of information.[144] This lack of recorded information leaves the child with no record of the circumstances of their birth, the possibility of hereditary conditions, or of any genetic siblings.[145] As a result, however carefully constructed the disclosure regime applicable to domestic licensed clinics, children born through cross-border or informal donation are currently beyond the reach of regulation seeking to protect their right to identity. These children will instead rely on parental openness or the happenstance of informal means of obtaining genetic information.

As the right to knowledge of identity has gained increasing support and protection in the law, so the widening options for those seeking assistance with conception has highlighted the limits to the state's reach in regulating access to fertility treatment and to donor information. The ability of children to discover

---

[140] As explained above.   [141] E. Jackson (2015).

[142] F. Shenfield *et al.* (2010) found that 26.4 per cent of British patients in the records that they analysed cited 'wish for anonymous donation' as a reason for seeking treatment abroad.

[143] E. Jackson (2015).

[144] J. Harper *et al.* (2017). The pitfalls of using such sites are evident in *M* v. *F and H (Legal Paternity)* [2013] EWHC 1901 (Fam), [2014] 1 FLR 352.

[145] The number of such siblings may be considerable. One British donor has claimed to have fathered between 800 and 1,000 children through informal arrangements: 'World's Most Prolific Sperm Donor – with 800 Children – Finds Clients through Facebook', *The Telegraph*, 13 June 2016. While this claim is unverifiable, the potential for genetic siblings to become romantically involved in the future is considerable. In contrast, donors to licensed clinics may only donate to up to ten families.

their biological identity in cases of assisted reproduction is most likely to find effective protection through changes in social and parental attitudes to openness. Nonetheless, the existing system of birth registration and access to donor records appears increasingly out of step with social attitudes, the practical availability of genetic information and the developing law on the right to identity.

(4) Fatherhood: Identity and Parenthood

(A) Fatherhood: Introduction

In the law on assisted reproduction discussed above, it is the child's right to understand their identity that drives claims to access information on their biological origins. In these circumstances, the right to identity is clearly separated from any claim that there should be family life between the child and the biological parent. The law protects the interests of the donor-conceived person in seeking out identifying information on the donor, but gives no equivalent right to the donor who may wish to contact the child. The decision to seek out identifying information without parental assistance is reserved to adulthood and identification of the donor does not displace the law's recognition of the child's existing parental relationships. This focus on identity also reflects the fact that the gamete donor, or surrogate mother, has participated in the arrangement with the purpose of assisting others to become parents and is unlikely to be seeking a parental relationship with the child.[146] While superficially similar, claims that children have a right to know their biological origins play a very different role when deployed outside of the arena of regulated assisted reproduction. Such cases are most often brought by genetic fathers seeking a relationship with the child, rather than by the child themselves. In these cases, the 'right to know' is not merely advanced to allow the child to access information, but has the potential to act as a gateway to a social relationship and to legal recognition that disturbs the child's existing parental relationships. Fundamentally, courts considering these claims must contemplate the question: Does the biological tie's existence, in itself, justify the creation of a legal and social relationship between them where none existed before, or is it enough for the child to be given accurate information about the identity of an absent parent?

At one time, the absence of any foolproof method for establishing paternity led to the children of married women being protected against the stigma of an illegitimate status by the common law presumption of legitimacy and of

---

[146] Although, as discussed below, in a number of cases known donors who have had a relationship with the child have sought the court's assistance to continue that relationship against the wishes of the legal parents. See *Re G (Children: Sperm Donors: Leave to apply for Children Act Orders)* [2013] EWHC 134 (Fam), [2013] 1 FLR 1334.

marital paternity.[147] Indeed, the father–child relationship was thereby constructed through marriage.[148] Today, while this presumption can be rebutted on the balance of probabilities,[149] scientific testing has produced a situation where uncertainty is no longer necessary.[150] As Freeman and Richards comment:

> What is perhaps more disruptive for the traditional patriarchal order is the potential for DNA testing to challenge the ideological foundations of the marital framework itself by rendering the hidden paradoxes of paternal uncertainty visible to scrutiny ... It is evident that DNA testing has the potential both to reinforce and destabilise longstanding assumptions concerning the socio-legal status of paternity.[151]

While DNA testing increasingly undermines attempts to keep secrets within families,[152] changing social attitudes and legal reform have largely removed the social stigma and legal disadvantages that once attached to children born outside this marital framework and motivated much of that secrecy.[153] As increasing numbers of children are born to unmarried parents, so the formal relationship between a child's parents has become less important to the allocation and meaning of parenthood. Instead, as Sheldon remarks, there is a 'seeming inevitability of a movement towards formal equality between all parents and a greater reliance on the genetic connection in grounding legal fatherhood and its rights and responsibilities'.[154] As genetics becomes the primary means through which fatherhood is determined, the child's interest in knowledge of biological identity becomes entangled in questions of legal parenthood and parenting in practice. A man seeking a DNA test to identify himself as a child's father (opposed by the mother) will undoubtedly reinforce his claim by citing the child's own right to knowledge of his or her origins[155] and arguing that it is in the child's best interests to discover that knowledge.[156] Add this to what Lind calls a 'long-standing obsession with the idea that there should be a genetic link between those who raise children and the children they raise'[157] – and the argument that children have a right to knowledge of their origins becomes conflated with the argument that they need a social relationship with their biological fathers.[158] Not to be forgotten is the government's

---

[147] *The Ampthill Peerage Case* [1977] AC 547: the presumption of legitimacy rests on the assumption that a married woman only conceives a child through intercourse with her husband. This presumption does not extend to marriages between same-sex couples: Marriage (Same Sex Couples) Act 2013, Sch. 4, Pt 2.

[148] T. Freeman and M. Richards (2006) p. 72. See also C. Smart (2007) pp. 122–3.

[149] Family Law Reform Act (FLRA) 1969, s. 26: by evidence showing that it is more probable than not that the person in question is the child's father.

[150] *Re H and A (paternity: blood tests)* [2002] EWCA Civ 383, [2002] 1 FLR 1145, per Thorpe LJ, at [30].

[151] T. Freeman and M. Richards (2006) p. 74.   [152] C. Smart (2007) pp. 126–7.

[153] Family Law Reform Act 1987, s. 1.   [154] S. Sheldon (2007) p. 16.

[155] E.g. *Re T (Paternity: Ordering Blood Tests)* [2001] 2 FLR 1190, discussed below.

[156] J. Wallbank (2004) p. 253.   [157] C. Lind (2006) p. 584.   [158] J. Wallbank (2004) p. 253.

own interest in combating child poverty by ensuring that men identified as fathers pay child maintenance. As Eekelaar comments, 'the man who procreates as a result of a "one-night stand" is the legal father and will be liable to support the child, whether or not he expected a child to result'.[159] As a result, genetic fatherhood takes on multiple meanings: it is a route to financial responsibility,[160] legal parenthood and a social relationship, as well as a facet of the child's identity. These multiple meanings come under particular pressure in cases in which the child is being brought up by a lesbian couple, who may regard recognition of the genetic father as a threat to their family life and security as a nuclear family.

This heady cocktail of factors propels the courts into placing even greater faith on the value of biological links between children and parents. But the assumption that the birth tie automatically guarantees a beneficial in-built affinity between parent and child is surely naive. Adult claims to have a social relationship with their biological children are often cloaked in the language of children's rights, a tactic that has dubious merit and often has more to do with adults' rights than those of their children.

(B) DNA Testing

Today, courts seem fully aware of the way in which children's rights to know the truth about their origins are protected by human rights law. In some cases, as in *Re L (Family Proceedings Court) (Appeal: Jurisdiction)*,[161] doubt over a child's paternity is provoked by a man's desire to avoid financial responsibility for the child. There, a 15-year-old girl was devastated suddenly to discover that the man she had always thought to be her father was now denying it and was refusing to pay child support for her. Munby J deplored the way in which the magistrates had accepted the truth of the man's assertions and had made a declaration to that effect,[162] without the girl or her mother either being notified of the hearing, or being given a chance to attend and give evidence at it. Referring to domestic and Strasbourg case law,[163] he strongly asserted that the magistrates had infringed her fundamental human rights under Article 8 of

---

[159] J. Eekelaar (2006) p. 67.

[160] E.g. *Secretary of State for Work and Pensions* v. *Jones* [2003] EWHC 2163 (Fam), [2004] 1 FLR 282, per Dame Elizabeth Butler-Sloss P: the magistrates' finding that a named man was not a child's father for child-support purposes was faulty because: (i) it infringed the child's rights under Art. 8 of the European Convention for the Protection of Human Rights and Fundamental Freedoms (ECHR) and under the Convention on the Rights of the Child (CRC) to knowledge of the identity of his father; (ii) there was no clear scientific evidence to back up their finding; (iii) they could have drawn adverse inferences from the man's refusal to undergo DNA testing under the Family Law Reform Act (FLRA) 1969, s. 23(1).

[161] [2003] EWHC 1682 (Fam), [2005] 1 FLR 210.

[162] I.e. a declaration of non-parentage under Family Law Act 1986, s. 55A(1).

[163] *Rose* v. *Secretary of State for Health and Human Fertilisation and Embryology Authority* [2002] EWHC 1593 (Admin), [2002] 2 FLR 962; *Gaskin* v. *United Kingdom* (1989) 12 EHRR 36; *Mikulic* v. *Croatia* [2002] 1 FCR 720.

the ECHR to know the true identity of her biological father and her rights under Article 6 to a fair hearing.[164]

In *Re L*, the putative father's behaviour stemmed from his unwillingness to acknowledge his alleged daughter. Other children are left in ignorance of their fathers' identity not because fathers refuse to acknowledge them, but because their mothers refuse to tell them the truth.[165] Some children never discover that their mothers lied to them over the identity of their fathers. Others, however, do so when a dispute arises between the adults involved because the putative father very much wants to acknowledge his relationship with the child, but the mother objects. Then the role played by the courts, when interpreting the child's right to knowledge of origins, is crucial. Such issues arise where either of two men could have fathered the child,[166] but the mother refuses to acknowledge any doubt over the identity of her child's father and excludes the 'other man' – the putative father – from the child's life. If the putative father wishes to assert his paternity and to establish a relationship with the child, a vital first step is for him to establish his biological links with the child by asking the court to make a direction for DNA testing.[167]

It may not be too cynical to suggest that these disputes are primarily adult-centred.[168] The men concerned do not seek directions for DNA tests in order to fulfil the child's right to genetic truth as a right with an intrinsic value of its own. They are often motivated by the assumption that biological parentage carries with it a right to enjoy a social relationship with the child and that, once established, the court will assist in promoting such a right through court-ordered contact. In other words, the impetus for the putative father's application for paternity testing is his desire to follow this up with an application for

---

[164] [2003] EWHC 1682 (Fam), [2005] 1 FLR 210, at [23]–[24]. See also *MS v. RS and BT (Paternity)* [2020] EWFC 30, [2020] 2 FLR 689, discussed further below.

[165] C. Lind (2006) p. 584, fn 47: studies often maintain that the number of men hoodwinked into believing children to be their own offspring is much higher than society imagines. See *A v. B (Damages: Paternity)* [2007] 2 FLR 1051: a man fraudulently persuaded that he is a child's father and to support him or her financially can sue the woman for deceit, with those sums repayable in the form of general damages.

[166] E.g., inter alia: *Re F (A Minor) (Paternity Test)* [1993] 1 FLR 598; *Re G (A Minor) (Blood Test)* [1994] 1 FLR 495; *Re H (Paternity: Blood Test)* [1996] 2 FLR 65; *Re G (Parentage: Blood Sample)* [1997] 1 FLR 360; *Re T (Paternity: Ordering Blood Tests)* [2001] 2 FLR 1190; *Re H and A (Paternity: Blood Tests)* [2002] EWCA Civ 383, [2002] 1 FLR 1145.

[167] Under FLRA 1969, s. 20(1). In the past, the courts commonly directed 'blood tests', once DNA testing was established; the current legislation was amended to refer to 'scientific tests': Family Law Reform Act 1987, s. 23. In *Anderson v. Spencer* [2018] EWCA Civ 100, [2018] 3 WLR 972, the Court of Appeal found that there was a residual power under the inherent jurisdiction to direct scientific tests in cases that fell outside of the statutory scheme as the putative father was deceased. They affirmed the decision to direct such tests, noting the Art. 8 rights of the adult applicant and his interest in knowing whether he was likely to be the carrier of a genetic predisposition to the cancer that had caused his putative father's death.

[168] The decision as to whether or not to direct scientific tests is not governed by the welfare principle; instead, a test will be directed unless it would be *against* the child's interests to do so: *S v. S; W v. Official Solicitor (or W)* [1972] AC 24.

a child arrangements order.[169] Equally, the mother's desire to stop him is often motivated by her fear that if he establishes his paternity, the courts will force her to allow him contact and will grant him parental responsibility. Alternatively, the mother herself seeks a direction for paternity testing, hoping that it will show that a particular man is not the father and that she can *therefore* oppose his contact application, on the basis that there is no biological tie between them and consequently no merit in granting an order.[170] At one time, mothers who sought to prevent their children discovering the identity of their genetic fathers could attempt to sabotage a court's direction for paternity testing by refusing consent for a sample to be taken from the child.[171] In response to concerns that this allowed the child's rights to be disregarded,[172] the law was strengthened to allow the court to order samples to be taken from the child, without parental consent, to protect the child's best interests.[173] Using these powers, the courts quickly overcame their early reluctance to override mothers' refusal to agree to tests. As Wallbank predicted, the conjunction of the biological father's ability to claim paternity testing and the child's right to knowledge of origins has resulted in women who refuse to cooperate with testing being seen as opposing their children's best interests.[174]

One response to mothers who seek to resist such application is to emphasise that the child's right to know their father's identity is a separate matter to the possible outcome of an application for other orders, such as contact or parental responsibility. Indeed, the judiciary seem keen to deal with the issue of biological parentage as a preliminary issue, detached from the question of whether the applicant should in future be allowed to acquire a psychological or social relationship with the child. Thus, Ward LJ has pointed out that if a test excludes the applicant from paternity, this does not necessarily prevent a future contact application succeeding; he might then convince the court that the child would benefit from continued contact with a devoted stepfather.[175] Equally, Bodey J in

---

[169] At one time, there was a procedural basis for combing an application for DNA testing with an application for contact or parental responsibility as the court has no freestanding power to make an order for scientific tests: FLRA 1969, s. 20(1): the courts can *only* make a direction for scientific tests in the course of 'any civil proceedings in which the parentage of any person falls to be determined'. See *Re E (Parental Responsibility: Blood Tests)* [1995] 1 FLR 392. While this rule still applies, a less confrontational means of fulfilling it is to apply for a declaration of parentage: Family Law Act 1986, s. 55A: subject to restrictions (see s. 55A(3)–(5)), anyone can apply for a declaration of parentage regarding another person.

[170] See *O* v. *L (Blood Tests)* [1995] 2 FLR 930; *Re G (Parentage: Blood Sample)* [1997] 1 FLR 360.

[171] E.g. *Re F (A Minor) (Blood Tests: Parental Rights)* [1993] Fam 314; discussed by J. Fortin (1994) and C. Smart (2007) pp. 124–5.

[172] *Re O and J* [2000] 1 FLR 418, per Wall LJ, at 434.

[173] Under FLRA 1969, s. 21(3)(b) (as amended by Child Support, Pensions and Social Security Act 2000, s. 82), the court can direct that samples are taken if it 'considers that it would be in [the child's] best interests for the sample to be given', irrespective of his or her carer's lack of consent.

[174] J. Wallbank (2004) p. 253.

[175] *Re G (Parentage: Blood Sample)* [1997] 1 FLR 360, per Ward LJ, at 366. See also *Re H (Paternity: Blood Test)* [1996] 2 FLR 65, at 82.

Re T[176] emphasised that in the event of tests confirming the putative father's claims, it would not automatically follow that he would then succeed in obtaining a contact order or a parental responsibility order.[177] In the unusual case of *H* v. *R and another*,[178] MacDonald J similarly made it clear that if the genetic father were to be successful in obtaining a declaration of parentage, this would in no way lead to the court granting him an active role in the life of the child, who had been adopted. Nonetheless, in more commonplace cases, once the father is identified the courts will almost certainly disapprove of any attempt on the mother's part either to keep this information from the child or to prevent the father from having a relationship with the child. A court may well direct the mother to give the child information about his true identity[179] or will expect her to produce extremely cogent reasons why she should not be required to do so.[180] In *Re R (A Minor) (Contact)*,[181] the mother was even told that if she could not tell her daughter the truth herself, a child psychiatrist instructed by the Official Solicitor, who was acting as guardian *ad litem* for the child, would do so instead.[182] Notably, this mother was not only expected to identify the child's father, but also to introduce him to the child through gradually increasing contact. Clearly, these disputes over whether a child should be informed of the real identity of his or her biological father are almost inevitably underpinned by assumptions that the father *should* also have contact with the child, albeit only indirect contact in some cases.[183] Such applications have a strong prospect of success once the biological connection is established. The assumption that a biological father should have involvement in the child's life is now underlined by the statutory presumption that parental involvement will benefit the child's welfare,[184] meaning that while an application for a DNA test is legally distinct from an application for contact, the strong assumption that the child will benefit from such a relationship means that they can be more difficult to disentangle in practice.

Putative fathers often have little difficulty in obtaining directions for DNA tests on the basis that children have a 'right' to discover their biological origins or that such knowledge will be in their best interests.[185] Perhaps influenced by the research relating to adopted children,[186] the courts have been particularly

---

[176] [2001] 2 FLR 1190, at 1198.   [177] Ibid. at 1196.

[178] [2020] EWFC 74, [2021] 3 WLR 1147 and [2021] EWHC 1943 (Fam), [2021] 3 WLR 1175. In the event, the court considered that it had the jurisdiction to make the declaration of parentage, but declined to do so. While this did have consequences for the child's right to knowledge of her genetic origins, that right could be fulfilled through life story work.

[179] *Re F (Paternity: Jurisdiction)* [2007] EWCA Civ 873, [2008] 1 FLR 225, per Thorpe LJ, at [8] and [14], confirming that the courts have jurisdiction to make a specific issue order requiring the mother to tell her children the truth about their parentage.

[180] E.g. *Re K (Specific Issue Order)* [1999] 2 FLR 280; *Re J (Paternity: Welfare of Child)* [2006] EWHC 2837 (Fam), [2007] 1 FLR 1064.

[181] [1993] 2 FLR 762.   [182] Ibid. at 768.   [183] E.g. *A* v. *L (Contact)* [1998] 1 FLR 361.

[184] Children Act 1989, s. 1(2A), discussed further in Chapter 6.

[185] E.g. *Re D (Paternity)* [2006] EWHC 3545 (Fam), [2007] 2 FLR 26.   [186] Discussed above.

concerned about the dangers of a child discovering the true facts by accident. According to Holman J:

> To do and say nothing now is in truth storing up a potential bombshell for the future, which might be very damaging for J to learn and might indeed seriously undermine his sense of trust in his mother.[187]

Similarly, Ward LJ has maintained that 'every child has a right to know the truth unless his welfare clearly justifies the cover-up'.[188] The rights analysis in such cases is, however, far more complex than merely the child's right to 'know the truth'. Bodey J's decision in *Re T (Paternity: Ordering Blood Tests)*,[189] the first such case following the introduction of the HRA, was strongly rights-based. It demonstrates very clearly how, by articulating the various ECHR rights involved in these complex situations, the conflicting interests can be appropriately identified and weighed. As he indicated, the 7-year-old boy in question had a right to respect for his private life under ECHR Article 8 'in the sense of having knowledge of his identity, which encompasses his true paternity'.[190] But his rights might conflict with each other – his right to know the truth might conflict with his right to security with his present de facto family (his mother and her husband, whom he believed to be his biological father). Furthermore, the child's mother and her husband had a right to respect for their private and family life, free from interference from the man claiming to be the child's biological father. Such a right might be protected by refusing to direct blood tests against her wishes. Equally, the man claiming to be the boy's real father might himself have had a right to family life with his child, if he was proved to be the child's father – which, in turn, he wanted further promoted by a contact order.[191] In the circumstances of this case, Bodey J considered that greatest weight should be given to the boy's right to know 'perhaps with certainty, his true roots and identity'.[192] Consequently, any interference with the rights of the mother and her husband was justified under Article 8(2) of the ECHR, as being proportionate to the legitimate aim of furthering T's right to certainty as to his real paternity. The mother's refusal to agree to blood testing was therefore overridden by the court.[193] In cases such as *Re T*, there are clear advantages to the putative father in relying primarily on the child's Article 8 rights rather than his own. A man who is not in an existing social relationship with the child may struggle to establish that he has a family life with the child, particularly if he was not in a secure relationship with the mother at the time of conception.[194] He may have more success in advancing

---

[187] *A v. L (Contact)* [1998] 1 FLR 361, at 366.
[188] *Re H (Paternity: Blood Test)* [1996] 2 FLR 65, at 80.   [189] [2001] 2 FLR 1190.
[190] Ibid. at 1197.
[191] Bodey J quite correctly doubted the strength of this argument in this particular case.
[192] [2001] 2 FLR 1190, at 1198.   [193] I.e. under FLRA 1969, s. 21(3)(b).
[194] *Kautzor v. Germany*, App. No. 23338/09, at [61]–[62], in which the potential father failed to demonstrate family life with the child whom he had never seen, despite the child having been conceived while he was married to the mother.

the argument that the right to have paternity established is an aspect of his private life, protected by Article 8, but the ECtHR has stressed that the child's best interests are to be given particular weight in such cases and may outweigh the man's interest in paternity.[195] For these reasons, the putative father is more likely to succeed if he can establish the child's right to knowledge of his or her biological origins.

Subsequent cases have tended to stress the child's right to, or interest in, knowledge of genetic truth, without the same recognition that the child may possess conflicting rights and interests. In particular, little weight is often placed on the potential for upsetting a child's security in his or her existing family unit through a combination of a claim for DNA testing with a claim for contact.[196] It was the risk of losing this security that worried the trial judge in *Re H and A (paternity: blood tests)*.[197] He considered that it would be disastrous for the mother's husband to be excluded from paternity because the twin girls would lose their 'psychological father' and primary carer. The Court of Appeal disagreed, considering that the uncertainty over their father's identity would cause greater damage and that the court should be furnished with the best science available rather than presumptions and inferences.[198] A similar approach to the potential for disruption can be seen in *Re H (Contact with Biological Father)*,[199] in which the child had been conceived through an arrangement between a married couple and a friend, who had initially agreed to act as a sperm donor through artificial insemination, but then commenced a full sexual relationship with the mother. On the basis of DNA testing, the man had obtained a declaration of parentage and had been placed on the child's birth certificate, an act that the court found had conferred parental responsibility on him.[200] The district judge had, however, refused to order contact on the basis of the damage that it would do to the stability of the child's upbringing with his mother and her husband.[201] The Court of Appeal considered that the judge had fallen into error and it was instead 'a given' and a 'starting point' that children 'normally benefit from having a full and meaningful relationship with both of their parents as they grow up'.[202] It was

---

[195] *Kautzor* v. *Germany*, App. No. 23338/09, at [63]–[65].   [196] C. Smart (2009).
[197] [2002] EWCA Civ 383, [2002] 1 FLR 1145.   [198] Ibid., per Thorpe LJ, at [29].
[199] [2012] 2 FLR 627.
[200] Ibid. at [6], on the basis of the information given in the case report, it seems that the assumption that the re-registration conferred parental responsibility may have been incorrect. Re-registration of a birth following a declaration of parentage takes place under the Births and Deaths Registration Act 1953, s. 14A. Children Act 1989, s. 4(1)(a) only confers parental responsibility via registration for those fathers who are registered at birth under the Births and Deaths Registration Act 1953, s. 10(1)(a), (b) and (c) or those who are re-registered with the mother's consent and for whom no father was previously named under the Births and Deaths Registration Act 1953, s. 10A(1). Re-registration following a declaration of parentage is not in itself enough to confer parental responsibility. The connection between the birth certificate and parental responsibility is discussed further below.
[201] Particularly as the judge found that the biological father had acted violently to the husband on at least two occasions.
[202] [2012] 2 FLR 627, at [18].

that relationship that was to have priority, albeit balanced against the other issues in the case. Had the conception occurred in the manner that the adults had originally contemplated, the biological father would not have been the legal father and nor would he have been entitled to recognition on the birth certificate with its connected parental responsibility.[203] Nonetheless, the contact application would not *necessarily* have been unsuccessful. Even in cases in which the known biological father has acted as a sperm donor and is not the child's legal parent, the courts have been increasingly willing to order some form of contact on the basis that it will be beneficial to the child's understanding of his or her identity, particularly if there has already been some contact between the child and the donor.[204] As discussed below, these cases frequently involve children born to a lesbian couple who have conceived with a known donor. In such cases, the courts have struggled to accommodate both the importance of supporting the primary parenting relationship provided by the two women and the child's interest in knowing his or her genetic father.[205]

The potential conflict between the interests of the adults and those of the child is raised particularly acutely in those cases in which the child is old enough to have strong views of their own about their parents' identity.[206] Some children, like T, the troubled 11-year-old boy in *Re D (Paternity)*,[207] strongly reject adults' suggestions that they will be psychologically damaged without an accurate knowledge of their fathers' identity. T rejected the paternity claims of the putative father,[208] desiring to retain the view that he was being cared for by his paternal grandmother – and so did she. Hedley J considered that it would be against T's best interests to be forced to undergo DNA testing. But since, in his view, it was in T's long-term best interests to know the truth, he made a direction that T should undergo DNA testing, but stayed it for an unlimited time, with liberty to restore it.[209] T's guardian was asked to explain to T after the hearing that it was the view of the judge, social worker and guardian that 'this matter of paternity should be resolved and that in the end truth is easier to live with than doubt or fiction'.[210]

T's case produces a feeling of unease. Just as Munby J has asserted that it would smack 'too much of the Inquisition' to try to force a mother who has

---

[203] As HFEA 2008, s. 35 would have applied: see *M v. F and H (Legal Paternity)* [2013] EWHC 1901 (Fam), [2014] 1 FLR 352.

[204] *Re G (A Child) (Child Arrangements Order)* [2018] EWCA Civ 305, [2018] 1 WLR 2769, in which contact with the biological grandparents was also upheld. *Re G (Children: Sperm Donors: Leave to apply for Children Act Orders)* [2013] EWHC 134 (Fam), [2013] 1 FLR 1334, granting *leave* to apply for contact.

[205] L. Smith (2013).

[206] E.g. *Re L (Family Proceedings Court) (Appeal: Jurisdiction)* [2003] EWHC 1682 (Fam), [2005] 1 FLR 210, discussed above.

[207] [2006] EWHC 3545 (Fam), [2007] 2 FLR 26.

[208] The putative father had applied for a residence order (later withdrawn), a parental responsibility order and a contact order, combined with a request for a direction for scientific testing under FLRA 1969, Pt III.

[209] [2006] EWHC 3545 (Fam), [2007] 2 FLR 26, at [30].   [210] Ibid. at [31].

placed her child for adoption to identify the child's father,[211] so the courts should recognise that a right claimed for all children as a class may not always promote an individual child's best interests. Cases like *Re D (Paternity)* show that the view that *all* children should know their parents' identity may sometimes achieve more harm than good, given the danger of two issues being confused, at least in the child's mind – the child's need to know about his origins and his possible need for a social relationship with his biological parent. T neither wanted any knowledge of his putative father nor contact of any kind with him, but the latter's claims had already unsettled him considerably. Just like the boy in *Re T*, his right to stability with his putative grandmother could be jeopardised by his putative father's claims. Nonetheless, the ECtHR has upheld a similar approach by the French courts, in which the Article 8 'right' of a 15-year-old to knowledge of his biological paternity was prioritised over the child's own wish to preserve his legal relationship with his social father.[212] In the light of this case, it is likely that the approach in *Re D* would be found to be Convention-compliant. As Claire Fenton-Glynn notes, this approach 'transforms the right of the child into a duty'.[213] Given the emphasis plsced by the CRC on having regard to the child's evolving capacities, it is arguable that more weight should be placed on older children's own feelings and understanding of their relationships. In particular, a child may have a right *not* to know the identity of his or her father. This argument has had some recognition in the domestic courts as the courts have refused to exercise their power to compel older children to give samples for DNA testing.[214] In particular, in *L v. P (Paternity Test: Child's Objection)*, the court gave significant weight to the 'rational and cogent' views of a 15-year-old girl who had resisted testing both because of the impact that it would have on her mother and stepfather and because she did not wish to pursue a relationship with the putative biological father. Although the court found that the decision of a *Gillick*-competent child was not determinative, and the decision may affect the rights and obligations of others,[215] the reasonable views of a mature child carried great weight and the application was refused. Similarly, in *MS v. RS and BT (Paternity)*,[216] the court declined to direct *Gillick*-competent 13- and 15-year-old children to undergo testing against their will. The children were understandably angry that the man

---

[211] *Re L (Adoption: Contacting Natural Father)* [2007] EWHC 1771 (Fam), [2008] 1 FLR 1079, at [40].

[212] *Mandet v. France*, App. No. 30955/12, Judgment of 14 January 2016.

[213] C. Fenton-Glynn (2016).

[214] *Re P (Identity of Mother)* [2011] EWCA Civ 795; *L v. P (Paternity Test: Child's Objection)* [2011] EWHC 3399 (Fam). In the former of these cases, that court made it clear that they may draw inferences from the refusal to undergo testing under Family Law Reform Act 1969, s. 23(1): in this case, the child's maternity may have had consequences for her immigration status. In both of these cases, the girls were 15 years old.

[215] In *L v. P*, ibid., the putative father sought to resist enforcement proceedings for non-payment of child support, but the evidence that he might not be the father was rather flimsy.

[216] [2020] EWFC 30, [2020] 2 FLR 689.

who had brought them up as their father now sought a declaration of non-paternity and felt betrayed by the fact that he had previously tricked them into providing samples for a commercial DNA test. The children had clearly suffered serious emotional harm from these actions and the court considered that it would be both against their best interests and 'wrong in principle' to impose DNA testing against their wishes as *Gillick*-competent minors.[217] Although the children's views were decisive in this case, MacDonald J did not go so far as to decide that competent children have a *right* to make a determinative decision to refuse to submit to testing. Anyone aged 16 or over may refuse to give a sample for testing and that refusal may not be overridden by the court, although it may draw adverse inferences from the refusal.[218] While it is well established that *Gillick*-competent children may consent to medical procedures, the question of when their refusal can be overridden remains contentious.[219] Although the inherent jurisdiction permits judicial override of a competent refusal, the courts are increasingly aware that this should be used sparingly and only in the most serious of circumstances. A decision to submit a sample for testing is essentially concerned with the child's own private life and intimate identity.[220] In these circumstances, the decision not to consent to testing should fall into the category of cases on which the wishes of a *Gillick*-competent child 'where they are not objectively foolish or unreasonable, should normally be given effect'.[221]

The circumstances in which DNA tests are sought by biological fathers raise very different questions from those in which donor-conceived children may access information on the circumstances of their birth. The fact that such cases are brought during the child's minority and tend to carry with them the assumption that biological ties *should* usually carry social relationships means that the child's 'right to know' is invoked for very different reasons. These cases raise complex and multi-layered aspects of the child's identity, affecting legal and social parenthood as well as the mere transmission of biological information. The child's interest in knowledge of their genetic

---

[217] Ibid. esp. at [91]–[92].

[218] Family Law Reform Act 1969, s. 23(1): in this case, the court refused to draw any adverse inferences from the children's refusal, finding that 'for two *Gillick* competent children to object to further DNA testing at the request of an adult who they consider has fundamentally betrayed their trust is plainly an objectively valid, rational, logical and consistent position. Accordingly, it would not be appropriate for the court to draw any adverse inference from their position on further testing.' Ibid. at [86].

[219] Discussed further in Chapter 11.

[220] In contrast to the determination of the application for a declaration of parentage itself, which includes consideration of the rights and interests of others, as well as the public interest, rather than being a matter of the child's interests alone: *Re S (A Child) (Declaration of Parentage)* [2012] All ER (D) 140.

[221] *AS v. CPW (Inward Return Order)* [2020] EWHC 1238 (Fam), [2020] Fam Law 1019, at [51], in the very different context of an application for an inward return order, returning the child from Sierra Leone to the UK. See further discussion in Chapter 12.

identity should not be conflated with their interests, or those of their biological father, in their legal identity and parenting relationships.

(C) Fatherhood: Identity, Responsibility and Birth Registration

One method of ensuring that children have access to information about their fatherhood would be to require that information be listed on the birth certificate so that it is accessible to the child in the future. Under the current law, although most births are jointly registered, unmarried mothers are not obliged to register their children's birth jointly with the father and may not do so without his consent or court intervention.[222] Andrew Bainham argues that since the child has an independent right to know the identity of his or her parents, mothers should be under a duty to identify the child's father.[223] A scheme that would have gone some way to implementing this proposal was put on the statute book in the Welfare Reform Act 2009, but has not been brought into force.[224] Under the 2009 Act, mothers would have been required, subject to certain exceptions, to name the father on the child's birth certificate. The scheme was dropped as research suggested it was likely to have little impact on the government's aim of increasing these fathers' willingness to take responsibility for their children.[225] Although the scheme now seems unlikely to be implemented, the debate again brings to the fore ambiguity in the purpose of birth certification.

The right to registration of birth found in Article 7 of the CRC is foundational to children's legal identity, but gives no further indication as to which parents must be recorded. The purpose of the parental information recorded on the current domestic birth certificate is surprisingly difficult to define. As discussed above, in cases of assisted reproduction, the law facilitates a situation in which that parent–child relationship and the information recorded on the certificate does not reflect the child's genetic heritage and even outside of such cases, the law does little to guarantee that the 'right' men are identified and registered as fathers. For these reasons, it is difficult to argue that the current law regards the purpose of the birth certificate as providing an accurate record of biological information. This is not, however, to say that biological truth is

---

[222] The Office for National Statistics records that, in 2019, 5.2 per cent of births were not jointly registered. The existing law (Births and Deaths Registration Act 1953, ss 2 and 10) obliges only parents in a marriage or civil partnership and single mothers to register the child's birth within 42 days of its occurrence. The name of a father who is not married to, or in a civil partnership with, the mother can be entered only if both parents attend to register the child's birth, or if a court order or formal declaration exists indicating his paternity. A. Bainham (2008b) pp. 450–6 discusses the current system of birth registration.

[223] A. Bainham (2008a) p. 330, (2008b) p. 460.

[224] The scheme would require the mother to identify the father unless she fell under one of the broad categories of exemptions. If she identified the father's name against his wishes, the registrar would then contact the man she identified, requiring him to undergo a paternity test, followed by compulsory registration: Welfare Reform Act 2009, Sch. 6.

[225] J. Wallbank (2009).

irrelevant to the law on birth certification. It is an offence to give false information to the registrar,[226] for example, by registering a child as born to married parents while knowing that the child was actually the product of an affair. Further, while some countries place severe restrictions on the ability to challenge a child's paternity,[227] in this jurisdiction there are relatively few constraints on the availability of a declaration of parentage, or non-parentage, and re-registration of the birth to reflect that declaration.[228] This means that the birth certificate can be re-issued even if the child in question has now reached adulthood.[229] The importance of the registered father to the child's identity is also illustrated by the unusual case of *JK* v. *Registrar General for England and Wales*.[230] In that case, a transgender woman who had fathered two children through sexual intercourse wished to amend their birth certificates to replace the term 'father' with 'parent' to reflect her identity and to prevent her transgender status being revealed by production of those certificates.[231] The court upheld the refusal of her request on the basis that the undoubted interference with her rights was justified given that the identity of their biological father was an important aspect of the children's fundamental identity.[232] There is an ambiguity in the law: in some circumstances, the child's interest in biological truth is given a dominant role, while in others, it is absent from the birth certificate.

Reforming the law on birth certificate registration of legal fathers raises more complex questions than recording information about donors. As discussed above, there is a strong case for increasing the official information available to donor-conceived people and for using the birth certificate to do so. This case is primarily concerned with the right to identity. Recording the name of a father on a birth certificate not only conveys information, but also has significant implications for the child's legal identity and upbringing. Any proposal to alter the system for recording parental information on the birth certificate must address the multiple purposes that it fulfils. As Julie McCandless notes, the birth certificate is not merely a record of information, but is now used as 'a social policy tool that facilitates a parent–child

---

[226] Perjury Act 1911, s. 4.   [227] E.g. *Kautzor* v. *Germany*, App. No. 23338/09.

[228] Births and Deaths Registration Act 1953, s. 14A; Family Law Act 1986, s. 55A.

[229] See e.g. the case of Emma Cresswell, who at the age of 25 had her birth certificate amended to remove the man she had erroneously assumed to be her biological father: discussed by J. McCandless (2017).

[230] [2015] EWHC 990 (Admin), [2016] 1 All ER 354.

[231] The Gender Recognition Act 2004, s. 12 states that: 'The fact that a person's gender has become the acquired gender under this Act does not affect the status of the person as the father or mother of a child.' In this case, JK's application for a gender recognition certificate had not been finalised at the time of the hearing in any case.

[232] [2015] EWHC 990 (Admin), [2016] 1 All ER 354, at [109]–[110]. See also the McConnell case, discussed above, in which a similar conclusion was reached in respect of a transgender man who gave birth and challenged his registration as the child's mother: *R (McConnell and another)* v. *Registrar General for England and Wales* [2020] EWCA Civ 559, [2020] 3 WLR 683.

relationship'.[233] Naming a father on the birth certificate is not only prima facie evidence of his paternity,[234] but also confers parental responsibility on him.[235] It can also be used as easily accessible evidence in conferring further rights and obligations connected to paternity, including the child's right to British nationality[236] and the father's obligation of child support.[237] The conflation of these different purposes of birth registration can be seen in the government's claims that the mandatory joint registration in the doomed Welfare Reform Act 2009 would 'promote child welfare, parental responsibility and the right of every child to know who his or her parents are'.[238] Perhaps more to the point, the government undoubtedly saw the proposal, which first emerged in the context of child maintenance reform,[239] as having a fiscal impact. The Green Paper's reference to US research indicating that fathers who acknowledge paternity at the child's birth are more likely to pay child maintenance[240] suggested that the government's hopes were not entirely focused on children's welfare and their right to identify their fathers. The accompanying empirical research suggested that the government had been optimistic to assume that joint registration would lead to increased practical and financial responsibility among those fathers who did not already register and the government's enthusiasm for the reform waned.[241]

If mandatory joint birth registration were brought into force, it would for the first time allow fathers to gain parental responsibility without either approval from the mother or a court.[242] Under current law, the children whose parents jointly register their births, like children of married parents, have two parents with automatic parental responsibility for them.[243] This reform, introduced in 2003, was of enormous importance in extending parental responsibility for the growing numbers of children born to unmarried parents. Prior to the change in the law, relatively few unmarried fathers availed themselves of the legal procedures whereby they could acquire parental responsibility,[244] with many mistakenly assuming that because they lived with and took financial and practical responsibility for their children, they automatically enjoyed legal parental responsibility for them.[245] The current

---

[233] J. McCandless (2017) p. 53.   [234] *Brierley* v. *Brierley* [1918] P 257.
[235] Children Act 1989, s. 4(1)(a).
[236] British Nationality (Proof of Paternity) Regulations 2006 (SI 2006/1496), reg. 3(c), amended by British Nationality (Proof of Paternity) (Amendment) Regulations 2015 (SI 2015/1615).
[237] Child Support Act 1991, s. 26(2), Case A2.   [238] DWP (2008) para. 23.
[239] DWP (2006) paras 2.43–2.48.   [240] DWP (2007) para. 18.   [241] J. Wallbank (2009).
[242] I.e. by the mother agreeing to include the father on the birth certificate or entering into a parental responsibility agreement, or the court granting a parental responsibility order on the basis of the child's welfare. Re-registration following a declaration of parentage (which does not require a welfare analysis) is not in itself enough to confer parental responsibility: Children Act 1989, s. 4(1)(a).
[243] CA 1989, s. 4(1)(a), implemented as from 1 December 2003.
[244] I.e. under CA 1989, s. 4(1)(b) and (c): an unmarried father may enter into a parental responsibility agreement with the mother or apply for a parental responsibility order.
[245] R. Pickford (1999a) pp. 145–52. See also R. Pickford (1999b): 75 per cent of the fathers who knew that they were financially responsible for their non-marital children were unaware that they lacked parental responsibility.

law means that a large majority of children now have two parents with legal parental responsibility for them. Nonetheless, the law creates a complex picture, with three groups of children enjoying subtly different legal relationships with their parents.[246] The first are children born to parents who are married or in a civil partnership with each other; the second have parents who jointly register the birth, but are not in a formal relationship with each other; and the third have only the mother identified on their birth certificates.[247] The first group are the most secure, as both parents have automatic parental responsibility over them as from their birth.[248] Unlike the second, their father's parental responsibility cannot be terminated by court order.[249] The third group lack two parents with a legal parental responsibility for them, since only their mothers gain such legal recognition,[250] and will have no one with parental responsibility in the event of their mothers dying.

Nevertheless, the position of the third group is not as stark as this outline might suggest. First, unregistered fathers are not devoid of all legal status as by virtue of the FLRA 1987, section 1, references to 'parent' in legislation like the CA 1989[251] and the Child Support Act 1991[252] must be interpreted as if the difference in legal status between all married and unmarried fathers is irrelevant. Even if the man is not named on the birth certificate, a DNA test showing his connection to the child is accepted as evidence of fatherhood in areas of law such as nationality[253] and child

---

[246] J. Eekelaar (2001) pp. 426–8. The position of a female parent of a child born through assisted reproduction mirrors this law; i.e. if she is married to, or in a civil partnership with, the mother she will automatically acquire parental responsibility (CA 1989, s. 2(1A)); if she is not in a status relationship with the mother she may acquire it through registration, agreement or court order (CA 1989, s. 4ZA).

[247] In reality, because the reform conferring parental responsibility on registered parents was not retrospective, a fourth group was also created. These are the children born before the reforms, who, despite their parents' names appearing on their birth certificates, were treated in an identical manner to those in the third group. As this group only included those registered before the implementation of the reform on 1 December 2003, all of those affected are now adults. As parental responsibility terminates on the child reaching majority, this group is now obsolete.

[248] CA 1989, s. 2(1). See Chapter 4 for a discussion of the term 'parental responsibility'.

[249] CA 1989, s. 4(3): an unmarried father's parental responsibility can be terminated by court order on application by anyone with parental responsibility or by the child with court leave. In practice, it is extremely rare for parental responsibility to be terminated, although there are reported examples: *Re P (Terminating Parental Responsibility)* [1995] 1 FLR 1048; *DW (A Child) (Terminating Parental Responsibility)* [2014] EWCA Civ 315, [2015] 1 FLR 166. See S. Gilmore (2015) for an assessment of this case law and unreported cases on the same point.

[250] CA 1989, s. 2(2).

[251] E.g. *Re B (Care Proceedings: Notification of Father without Parental Responsibility)* [1999] 2 FLR 408: care order was set aside because the child's unmarried father was not served with notice of the care proceedings.

[252] Child Support Act 1991, s. 1 imposes liability on the non-residential parent irrespective of legal status.

[253] British Nationality (Proof of Paternity) Regulations 2006 (SI 2006/1496), reg. 3(c), amended by British Nationality (Proof of Paternity) (Amendment) Regulations 2015 (SI 2015/1615). See S. Sheldon (2007) pp. 3–7 for a historical assessment of the law in this area. See also *R (on the*

support.[254] Second, fathers who are not named on the birth certificate can take steps to acquire parental responsibility through obtaining a parental responsibility order (PRO).[255] Indeed, the assumption that the biological link between parent and child *normally* carries a social and legal relationship clearly underlies the ease with which many unmarried fathers obtain PROs, even when opposed by mothers. This assumption was implicit in the words of Ward LJ, who explained that the effect of such an order is to confer 'upon a committed father the status of parenthood for which nature has already ordained that he must bear responsibility'[256] – a position now reinforced by the application of the statutory presumption that parental involvement will benefit the child's welfare.[257] On the application of this approach, most unmarried fathers find that it is a relatively simple task to satisfy the requisite 'attachment and commitment to the child' test to obtain a PRO.[258] His merit, or lack of merit, as a father is largely irrelevant. Indeed, the woman struggling to bring up her child free from his violent attentions,[259] or without his financial help,[260] is expected to think 'calmly' about his gaining a PRO, because it merely carries the 'status of parenthood' and, furthermore, any misuse can be controlled by a section 8 order, if and when it occurs.[261] But, as various writers point out, there are some cases in which fathers receive very different judicial treatment.[262] At times, the courts have implicitly accepted that such an order does not merely carry parental status, but also the ability to become involved in the child's upbringing.[263] In these decisions, the courts have more critically appraised the father's application from the child's viewpoint, considering whether the PRO's potential for destabilising the child's

---

application of K (A Child)) v. *Secretary of State for the Home Department* [2018] EWHC 1834 (Admin), in which a declaration of incompatibility was made in respect of the rule that the child of a married mother was not permitted to adduce proof that another man was her biological father for the purpose of acquisition of nationality.

[254] Child Support Act 1991, s. 26(2), Case A3.   [255] CA 1989, s. 4(1)(c).

[256] *Re S (Parental Responsibility)* [1995] 2 FLR 648, at 657. See also *Re C and V (Contact and Parental Responsibility)* [1998] 1 FLR 392.

[257] CA 1989, s. 1(2A) and (7).

[258] *Re H (Illegitimate Children: Father: Parental Rights) (No. 2)* [1991] 1 FLR 214, per Balcombe LJ, at 218: the court must consider the unmarried father's degree of commitment to the child, the degree of attachment existing between him and the child, and his reasons for applying for the order.

[259] E.g. *Re B J (A Child) (Non-Molestation Order: Power of Arrest)* [2001] 1 All ER 235.

[260] E.g. *Re H (Parental Responsibility: Maintenance)* [1996] 1 FLR 867.

[261] *Re S (Parental Responsibility)* [1995] 2 FLR 648, per Ward LJ, at 657. See F. Kaganas (1996) for a critical discussion of this decision.

[262] J. Wallbank (2002) and S. Gilmore (2003) discuss the case law on parental responsibility orders, together with its inconsistencies.

[263] E.g. *Re P (Parental Responsibility)* [1998] 2 FLR 96: PRO withheld from a man who had not only behaved in a way strongly suggesting that he might be a paedophile, but whose behaviour to date indicated that he would interfere with the child's upbringing; *Re H (Parental Responsibility)* [1998] 1 FLR 855: PRO withheld from a father who, it appeared, had treated his 15-month-old son with deliberate cruelty and sadism.

current upbringing would impact deleteriously on him or her.[264] As noted below, the courts seem more attracted by this position when dealing with genetic fathers' applications for PROs, when opposed by lesbian parents.

Despite the reforms to date, there is a strong groundswell of opinion that the law should not withhold parental responsibility from any fathers, as to do so is discriminatory and requires the father to overcome hurdles not required of the mother.[265] Further, there remains a small group of children who, through no fault of their own, have fathers with no parental responsibility for them and who risk having no one with responsibility for them should their mothers die. On the other hand, the vast majority of fathers are recorded on their child's birth certificate and those who are not are a very diverse group, including: those who intended to act as informal 'sperm donors' and have no parental relationship with the child; those who had no intention of conceiving and subsequently have no contact with the child; but also those who intend to become a closely involved parent and are prevented from taking that role by the mother.[266] As Julie Wallbank argues, granting parental responsibility to those fathers who have no involvement in the life of their child risks undermining the parenting provided by sole-registering mothers, many of whom are already socially and economically vulnerable.[267] A further argument for the current position is that the law provides certainty in that any parent with parental responsibility is able to demonstrate that fact by producing the relevant certificate, agreement or court order.[268] To grant parental responsibility without documentary evidence of fatherhood would be to undermine this certainty. As this discussion demonstrates, there are cogent arguments for and against reforming the law yet again, providing all unregistered fathers with an equal status to mothers. Despite the potential discrimination, it does not

---

[264] E.g. *Re J (Parental Responsibility)* [1999] 1 FLR 784: PRO withheld from a father largely due to the 12-year-old child's evidence that he had sought little to no contact with her since her birth and she wanted none with him now; *Re M (Contact: Parental Responsibility)* [2001] 2 FLR 342: PRO withheld from a father largely because to date he had substantially interfered with his disabled daughter's upbringing and would misuse the PRO to interfere even more; and *PM v. MB* [2013] EWCA Civ 969: PRO withheld from a father in part due to opposition of his 11-year-old son who strongly resisted his father's involvement in, or knowledge of, his education given his previous abduction of his son from school.

[265] J. Clifton (2014). Although, as noted above, the same means of acquiring parental responsibility apply to female parents who obtain parenthood through the HFEA 2008.

[266] See J. Wallbank (2009), who notes that the empirical research carried out prior to the Welfare Reform Act 2009 found that only 45 per cent of unregistered fathers were in regular contact with their children, although whether registration would encourage the participation of the 55 per cent who were not is difficult to prove. See also S. Sheldon (2007) p. 12; *B v. United Kingdom* [2000] 1 FLR 1, at 5, discussed below.

[267] J. Wallbank (2009). Although a parent with parental responsibility is usually able to act alone (CA 1989, s. 2(7)), there are important areas in which parents with parental responsibility must consult with each other or obtain consent – e.g. in order to remove the child from this jurisdiction: Child Abduction Act 1984, s. 1(3)(a)(ii).

[268] Although on this argument there would be no objection to a father obtaining parental responsibility through re-registration of a birth following a declaration of parentage: Births and Deaths Registration Act 1953, s. 14A.

appear that the ECHR *requires* such reform. Article 8 of the ECHR does indeed impose a positive obligation on states to provide legal safeguards enabling the child to be integrated within his or her family from the moment of birth.[269] Nevertheless, although Article 8 protects various forms of 'de facto' family,[270] the biological connection between father and child is not enough per se to create family life protected by Article 8.[271] Even if family life is established, the protection of Article 8 does not create an absolute right to legal recognition, particularly if the court withholds that recognition to protect the child's best interests.[272] Further, while Articles 8 and 14 combined together form a powerful weapon against discriminatory practices which inhibit the right of unmarried parents to enjoy their children's company,[273] the ECtHR has rejected claims that unmarried fathers' biological relationship with their children must always be reinforced by parental responsibility.[274] The court clearly doubts the sense of automatically providing *all* fathers with parental responsibility, irrespective of their relationship with the child or mother. The fact that the relationship between unmarried fathers and their children 'varies from ignorance and indifference to a close stable relationship indistinguishable from the conventional family-based unit' justifies any differences in the means of acquisition of legal status. Thus, the court found that their rights under Articles 8 and 14 of the ECHR were not infringed by English law denying them automatic parental responsibility. Given that the majority of committed fathers now obtain parental responsibility automatically at the child's birth or registration, it is likely that this conclusion would be upheld were it to be challenged at Strasbourg again.

(D) Known Fathers and Lesbian Parents

These disputes take on a different dimension in relation to lesbian couples who conceive with the assistance of a known biological father. While legislation enables both women to be recognised as parents from birth, so excluding the

---

[269] *Marckx* v. *Belgium* (1979) 2 EHRR 330, at [31].

[270] E.g. *Johnston* v. *Ireland* (1986) 9 EHRR 203: the child of a cohabiting couple was entitled to protection of her family life under ECHR, Arts 8 and 14; *X, Y and Z* v. *United Kingdom* [1997] 2 FLR 892: the family unit existing between a transsexual, his partner and child was a de facto family warranting the protection of Art. 8.

[271] *Lebbink* v. *Netherlands* [2004] 2 FLR 463, at [36]–[38]: absent cohabitation between the parents, other factors must demonstrate that the father's relationship with the child had 'sufficient constancy and substance' to create de facto 'family ties'; mere biological kinship, without further legal or factual elements indicating the existence of a close personal relationship, is insufficient to ground a claim under Art. 8.

[272] *Yousef* v. *Netherlands* [2003] 1 FLR 210: the infringement of the father's rights (under Art. 8) to have his family ties between him and his daughter recognised was justified (under Art. 8(2)) by the domestic court's view that this would be against her best interests.

[273] *Keegan* v. *Ireland* (1994) 18 EHRR 342: Irish law had infringed an unmarried father's rights under Arts 8 and 14 by denying him a right to challenge his child's adoption. See also *Kroon* v. *Netherlands* (1995) 19 EHRR 263.

[274] *B* v. *United Kingdom* [2000] 1 FLR 1.

genetic father from legal parenthood,[275] the courts have struggled with the question of what to do when the legislation does not apply and the genetic father remains the legal father despite the intention behind the arrangement.[276] In a number of cases, the courts have sympathised with the view that a child raised by two female parents does not need a social father and that his involvement may undermine the stability of the child's upbringing. In a number of cases, parental responsibility has been used to give legal recognition to the intended female parent who is not able to obtain legal parenthood.[277] Conversely, the genetic father may either obtain a PRO hedged around by a list of stringent limitations,[278] or be refused a PRO entirely, on the basis that gaining one would be a 'threat to their [the lesbian couple's] autonomy as a family unit'.[279] He may be granted very limited contact[280] to enable the child to satisfy any natural curiosity over the father's identity, without thereby allowing the development of a parental relationship.[281] These cases demonstrate much more willingness to view parental responsibility as a threat to the child's primary parenting relationships than in cases involving separated opposite-sex parents. For example, in *MacDougall v. SW and others (Sperm Donor: Parental Responsibility or Contact)*,[282] a man had acted as 'donor' to a substantial number of women that he had contacted through a social media site aimed at lesbians who wished to conceive. He sought parental responsibility for, and contact with, some of those children, at least one of whom had had recent regular contact with him. The court refused his applications on the basis that it was not in the children's best interests, not least because he had acted aggressively and irresponsibly,[283] and was likely to use parental responsibility to try to control the mothers. Such concerns appear much more likely to succeed in this context than in the case of children conceived through a sexual relationship.

---

[275] HFEA 2008, s. 45(1): 'Where a woman is treated by virtue of section 42 or 43 as a parent of the child, no man is to be treated as the father of the child.'

[276] Either because conception occurred prior to the HFEA 2008 coming into force, or because the conception was arranged informally by two women who were not in a marriage or civil partnership together: see *M v. F and H (Legal Paternity)* [2013] EWHC 1901 (Fam), [2014] 1 FLR 352, which involved an opposite-sex couple, but would apply in the same way to a same-sex couple. See also *MacDougall v. SW and others (Sperm Donor: Parental Responsibility or Contact)* [2022] EWFC 50. Similar issues arise in relations to single women who arrange for informal donation.

[277] E.g. *FC v. MC* [2021] EWHC 154 (Fam).

[278] E.g. *Re D (Contact and Parental Responsibility: Lesbian Mothers and Known Father)* [2006] EWHC 2 (Fam), [2006] 1 FCR 556.

[279] *Re B (Role of Biological Father)* [2007] EWHC 1952 (Fam), [2008] 1 FLR 1015, per Hedley J, at [26]. See also *R v. E and F (Female Parents: Known Father)* [2010] EWHC 417 (Fam), [2010] 2 FLR 383.

[280] Ibid. at [30]: contact four times per annum of 2 hours' duration.   [281] Ibid. at [29].

[282] [2022] EWFC 50.

[283] Ibid. at [78]. In particular, he had failed to disclose that he had Fragile X, a heritable condition, when making the arrangements to donate his sperm. There were also some findings of aggressive behaviour.

Nonetheless, as Leanne Smith points out, different cases demonstrate very different judicial assumptions as to the role of the biological father in such arrangements,[284] particularly in the light of the Court of Appeal's view that these fathers should not be viewed as 'secondary parents' or necessarily as donors.[285] Whether a father is successful in an application for parental responsibility and contact will depend on the particular factual matrix, including the care given to the child, relationships between the adults and the pre-conception intentions of those involved.[286] The latter is likely to play an increasingly important role as people seek out new ways of forming families, including with the intention of more than two adults taking an active parenting role, whether or not the adults have been in a relationship with one another. One means of approaching these cases would be to amend the law so as to allow three, or more, legal parents to be registered on the child's birth certificate in cases in which the child was conceived with the intention of each adult fulfilling a parenting role.[287] Certainly, the current parental model, based on the heterosexual couple who have conceived together, is strained when seeking to accommodate the complexity of modern family life. A more effective and child-focused response will require a willingness to draw sharper lines between children's respective rights to family life, knowledge of their origins and a legal identity that reflects the child's own family structure.

(5) Identity and Names

Children's names carry a practical as well as symbolic importance. Names are important to a child's identity, both as a means of signifying the child as an individual and as a reflection of their belonging to family, culture, religion or nation. As Mr Justice Cobb has explained:

> A surname defines, and is defined by, familial heritage and genealogy. A person's forename invariably identifies gender, and often personifies culture, religion, ethnicity, class, social or political ideology. A forename and surname together represent a person's essential identity. From very earliest childhood, one's name is an intrinsic part of who you are, and who you become.[288]

---

[284] L. Smith (2013).

[285] *A v. B and C* [2012] EWCA Civ 285. Parental responsibility was not directly in issue in this case, as the 'donor' father had married the mother in order to present a marital relationship that would be acceptable to her religious parents.

[286] Ibid. at [44]–[48].

[287] Such arrangements have been permitted in other jurisdictions. E.g. in Canada, the Court of Appeal for Ontario recognised both the women and the known donor in such a relationship in *A. A v. B. B* [2007] ONCA 2. Similarly, in *Re CC* [2018] NLSC 71, the Supreme Court of Newfoundland and Labrador recognised the three partners in a polyamorous relationship as the legal parents of a child born to the woman in that relationship, in circumstances in which each of the men in that relationship intended to act as a parent, and it was not clear which was the biological father.

[288] *Re B and C (Change of Names: Parental Responsibility: Evidence)* [2017] EWHC 3250 (Fam), at [33].

It is important that children's existence is recognised in this way, as soon after birth as possible. Article 7 of the CRC specifically guarantees the child's right to a name 'from birth', while Article 8 of the CRC requires the state to respect the child's right to preserve their identity, including their name. Similarly, although the ECHR does not explicitly refer to names in its text, given the importance of names to personal identity and as a symbol of connection to family, any dispute concerning them will fall under Article 8 of the ECHR as an aspect of private and family life.[289] English law more than adequately fulfils these rights. Dame Elizabeth Butler-Sloss P has emphasised the importance to children of their names, both forename and surname. As she rightly observed, even a very young child is able to answer the question 'what's your name?'.[290] This led her to castigate foster parents for changing the forename of a 6-year-old foster child, because in so doing they were changing her identity.[291] The importance of a child's name is also recognised in statute. Legislation explicitly requires the written consent of all those with parental responsibility, or the leave of the court, to change a child's surname where there is a special guardianship order,[292] care order,[293] placement order for adoption[294] or child arrangements order determining with whom the child is to live.[295] The fact that a change of name is singled out in this way[296] highlights the fundamental importance with which it is regarded.

But what name should a child be given in the first place? The law gives parents considerable freedom as to the names that they give to the child; indeed, there is no requirement to register a forename at all.[297] This is not to say that parental choice is immune from court intervention. In the unusual case of *Re C (Children) (Child in Care: Choice of Forename)*,[298] a local authority applied, under the inherent jurisdiction, to prevent a mother from registering her twin children with the names 'Cyanide' and 'Preacher'.[299] The Court of Appeal made the orders requested, rejecting the mother's argument that the name Cyanide had positive connotations given that the poison had been instrumental in the deaths of Hitler and Goebbels. Instead, it found that the name would cause the child significant emotional harm, not least because her sense of identity and self-worth would be badly affected by being named after a deadly poison. While the name Preacher would not in itself warrant judicial

---

[289] E.g. *Znamenskaya* v. *Russia* (2007) 44 EHRR 293, at [23].

[290] *Re D, L and LA (Care; Change of Forename)* [2003] 1 FLR 339, at 346.   [291] Ibid.

[292] Children Act 1989, s. 14C(3)(a).   [293] Children Act 1989, s. 33(7)(a).

[294] Adoption and Children Act 2002, s. 28(3)(a).   [295] Children Act 1989, s. 13(1)(a).

[296] In each of these circumstances, the same requirements also apply to a decision to remove the child from the UK.

[297] Registration of Births and Deaths Regulations 1987 (SI 1987/2088), reg. 9(3)(a).

[298] [2016] EWCA Civ 374, [2016] 3 WLR 1557.

[299] The children were accommodated by the local authority under an interim care order. While the care order gave the local authority the power to control the mother's exercise of parental responsibility (Children Act 1989, s. 33(3)(b)), restricting the mother's ability to name the child as she wished was a serious interference with her rights under ECHR Art. 8 and the local authority were right to seek approval from the court to do so.

intervention, treating the children differently on this sensitive matter would also cause significant harm. It is clear, however, that this case was exceptional and it is unlikely that a court would intervene to prevent parents from registering names of choice unless those names would cause significant harm, particularly given that any such interference would require justification under Article 8 of the ECHR.[300] While *Re C* concerned forenames, the majority of cases concerning children's names have involved surnames. When describing the common practice in this country whereby married parents give a child the father's surname, Lord Jauncey of Tullichettle has suggested that this is a way of:

> demonstrating its relationship to him. The surname is thus a biological label which tells the world at large that the blood of the name flows in its veins.[301]

John Eekelaar has robustly described Lord Jauncey's views as a 'pathetic hangover from the patriarchal era'.[302] Hale LJ subsequently doubted that they accorded with the modern law.[303] She observed:

> It is also a matter of great sadness to me that it is so often assumed, and even sometimes argued, that fathers need that outward and visible link [through surnames] in order to retain their relationship with, and commitment to, their child. That should not be the case ... After all, that is a privilege which is not enjoyed by many mothers ... They have to rely on other more substantial things.[304]

As Eekelaar's words above suggest, the initial selection of a surname for children is often strongly influenced by the now outdated customs of a patriarchal society. There is, however, no requirement in law that such a practice should be adopted. Notably, the law gives no indication what surname the child should take on birth,[305] merely indicating who should register it and when.[306] Parents are free to give the child any surname that they wish, even one that has no family connection to either parent.

Many of the reported cases on children's names have not related to the initial registration, but to a subsequent parental dispute as to whether the child's name should be changed. As noted above, if there is a child arrangements order specifying with whom the child is to live, the child's surname cannot be changed without the written agreement of all those with parental responsibility, or the leave of the court.[307] There has been some dispute as to

---

[300] [2016] EWCA Civ 374, [2016] 3 WLR 1557, at [107].
[301] *Dawson v. Wearmouth* [1999] 2 All ER 353, at 361.   [302] J. Eekelaar (2017) p. 157.
[303] *Re R (Surname: Using Both Parents')* [2001] EWCA Civ 1344, [2001] 2 FLR 1358, at [13].
[304] Ibid. at [18].
[305] The Registration of Births and Deaths Regulations 1987 (SI 1987/2088), reg. 9(3), merely states that the surname to be entered 'shall be the surname by which at the date of the registration of birth it is intended that the child shall be known'.
[306] The Births and Deaths Registration Act 1953, s. 2, requires the child's birth to be registered within 42 days of its birth and if the parents are married, either should do so. If the parents are unmarried, the duty is on the mother to do so. See A. Bainham (2008b) pp. 450–7.
[307] CA 1989, s. 13(1)(a).

the position where no such order is in force. It is a general principle of the Children Act 1989 that a parent with parental responsibility is ordinarily able to meet his or her responsibilities regarding the child unilaterally, without consulting the other,[308] and certainly without obtaining court permission.[309] Nevertheless, the courts have found it difficult to accept the proposition that a parent is legally entitled to go ahead with such an important change as altering a child's surname, without first obtaining the other parent's consent or that of the court.[310] Through a series of self-referencing decisions, the courts have laid down the proposition that if parents cannot agree whether to change their child's surname, they must seek judicial authority first.[311] The requirement of mutual consent is only applicable to surnames, but it is also clear that a court may resolve a dispute that arises concerning forenames. There has been some suggestion that a change of forename is of less consequence than a surname, which 'denotes the family to which the child belongs', and that a forename may be treated with greater fluidity over the course of a child's life.[312] This perception has been challenged in later cases and the better view seems to be that preferred by King LJ in *Re C*,[313] that a forename may be of equal importance to a child's identity as a surname, particularly given that forenames are more widely used in everyday life and that it is now commonplace for family members to have different surnames to one another.

Where a dispute is before the court, a change in a child's name will only be authorised if it is considered to be in the child's best interests.[314] Many of the leading cases have concerned disputes between parents on separation, with a mother commonly deciding to mark her changed way of life by shedding her ex-partner's surname and seeking to apply her new name to her child, against the objection of the father, who will often see this as an attempt to cut his links with his children.[315] Hale LJ has characterised the court's task as one of finding

---

[308] CA 1989, s. 2(7): 'Where more than one person has parental responsibility for a child, each of them may act alone and without the other (or others) in meeting that responsibility.'

[309] J. Eekelaar (1998), (2001) pp. 428–9; N. Gosden (2003) pp. 186–8.

[310] *Re PC (Change of Surname)* [1997] 2 FLR 730, per Holman J, at 732–3.

[311] *Re PC*, ibid.; *Re C (Change of Surname)* [1998] 2 FLR 656; *Dawson* v. *Wearmouth* [1999] 2 All ER 353; *Re W, Re A, Re B (Change of Name)* [1999] 2 FLR 930.

[312] *Re H (A Child) (First Name)* [2002] EWCA Civ 190, [2002] 1 FLR 973, at [13]–[14] (Thorpe LJ).

[313] *Re C (Children) (Child in Care: Choice of Forename)* [2016] EWCA Civ 374, [2016] 3 WLR 1557, at [50].

[314] *Dawson* v. *Wearmouth* [1999] 2 All ER 353, per Lord Mackay, at 359. See also *Re W, Re A, Re B (Change of Name)* [1999] 2 FLR 930, per Butler-Sloss LJ, at 933. Strictly speaking, the welfare checklist in Children Act 1989, s. 1(3) will apply to applications for a specific issue order under s. 8, but not to disputes under s. 13(1)(a), i.e. where a child arrangements order determining with whom the child is to live is in force. In practice, as this latter case demonstrates, the factors listed in the checklist are likely to be a useful guide to the determination of welfare in s. 13 cases too.

[315] E.g. *Re PC (Change of Surname)* [1997] 2 FLR 730. Alternatively, the father may apply to force her to change the child's name back, she having made the change already, e.g. *Re C (Change of Surname)* [1998] 2 FLR 656.

a balance between the child's long-term interests in retaining an outward link with a parent with whom they may not be living, against the short-term benefits of avoiding any confusion and embarrassment that may be caused to the child by having a different surname from other members of the family.[316] The case law reflects the different judicial approaches to this balancing act. Some courts consider that a child's surname is a matter of fundamental importance because it may break the child's link with his or her father.[317] Consequently, they may give little weight to the fact that the child's surname is different from that of the applicant.[318] Others consider that the courts should concentrate on fostering the father's *actual* links with the child through good contact arrangements rather than on the symbolism of a shared surname.[319] Butler-Sloss LJ, summarising the case law on the factors to be considered, has also suggested that when deciding whether such a change is in the child's best interests, the courts are influenced by the parents' marital status.[320] Much of the case law on change of surname following parental separation is now rather old and some caution should be used in applying the assumptions of earlier ages to the welfare of a child in a modern dispute. The greater diversity of family forms, and particularly the increase in blended families, mean that there is no expectation that family members will share a surname. The concern in older cases that stigma would attach to a child in this situation may now be rather outdated, in the same way as the assumption that a child's surname will usually reflect paternity. Nonetheless, the essential point remains that the legal test to be applied is the welfare test and the importance of a child's name to their identity will be an important aspect of the welfare analysis for each child.

Many of the more recent reported cases of mothers applying to change children's names have involved the very different situation of children at risk of abduction or serious abuse at the hands of their father.[321] In these cases, the

---

[316] *Re R (Surname: Using Both Parents')* [2001] EWCA Civ 1344, [2001] 2 FLR 1358, at [15].

[317] E.g. *W* v. *A (Child: Surname)* [1981] Fam 14; *Re C (A Child) (Change of Surname)* [1999] 1 FCR 318. Such a view may be strengthened by circumstances in which changing a child's surname would risk his losing his links with his racial and religious identity, e.g. *Re S (Change of Names: Cultural Factors)* [2001] 2 FLR 1005.

[318] Per Butler-Sloss LJ in *Re W, Re A, Re B (Change of Name)* [1999] 2 FLR 930, at 933.

[319] E.g. *D* v. *B (Otherwise D) (Child: Surname)* [1979] 1 All ER 92; *A* v. *Y (Child's Surname)* [1999] 2 FLR 5. See also *Yousef* v. *Netherlands* [2003] 1 FLR 210: the ECtHR implicitly approved of the Dutch court's view that the child might be harmed by the automatic assumption of her father's surname were he allowed formally to recognise her as his daughter. She was being brought up by her mother's family under their surname and a different surname might set her apart from them.

[320] *Re W, Re A, Re B (Change of Name)* [1999] 2 FLR 930, at 933. In her view, in the case of a child born to married parents, the court expects strong reasons to justify changing the surname from that registered on the birth certificate (normally that of the father). In the case of a child born to unmarried parents, given that the child's name was determined by the mother on registration of birth, the court expects evidence of the father's commitment to the child, the quality of his relationship with his child and the existence or absence of parental responsibility.

[321] E.g. *Re B and C (Change of Names: Parental Responsibility: Evidence)* [2017] EWHC 3250 (Fam); *A (Children) (Restrictions on Parental Responsibility: Extremism and Radicalisation in Private Law)* [2016] EWFC 40, [2016] 2 FLR 977; *The C, D, E & F Children (through their*

application to change the child's forenames and surnames has formed part of an application for a wider set of protective orders designed to reduce the risk of the child being traced. As a result, the courts have had the difficult task of weighing the consequences of a change of name for the child's identity against their need for protection from serious harm. Perhaps unsurprisingly, the courts have frequently found that this balance falls in favour of changing the child's name to protect their safety,[322] especially given the ease with which the internet may be used to trace a child with a distinctive name. Similar concerns have also arisen outside of the context of private law parental disputes. For example, in *London Borough of Haringey* v. *Musa*,[323] the circumstances under which the children had been taken into care had been the subject of an extensive and high-profile internet campaign, through which the full names of the children were widely known. This publicity had caused great difficulty both in finding prospective adoptive parents and in shielding the children from attention and attempts to trace them once placement orders had been made. The court was particularly concerned about the change to the children's forenames, given that their surnames were likely to be changed in any case once the adoption order was made. As King LJ observed in a later case, a forename given to a child by a parent who will not be able to bring them up is likely to be of infinite value as a lasting gift from their birth family.[324] For this reason, the court in *Musa* was clearly reluctant to change the children's forenames, aware that it would be a fundamental change to their identity, 'their background, their history, their culture, their heritage; past, present and future'.[325] Nonetheless, the court had little choice but to make the orders sought under the inherent jurisdiction, given that it was only with the security of a new identity that the children were likely to have the protection needed to live a normal life.[326] These acute dilemmas between the protection of children's safety and the preservation of their identity are likely to intensify, given the ease with which social media and search engines can often allow individuals to be traced.[327]

Domestic law, both in legislation and judicial decision, demonstrates an acute awareness of the importance of children's names to their identity and of their right to preserve that identity. The cases are rather less clear on the role that children's own views play in these cases, and particularly on the question of whether *Gillick*-competent children have the right to change their own name. In the surprising case of *Re B (Change of*

Children's Guardian) [2013] EWHC 227 (Fam), [2014] 1 FLR 178; *A (Termination of Parental Responsibility)* [2013] EWHC 2963 (Fam), [2014] 1 FLR 1305.

[322] This was the case in each of the cases cited above.

[323] [2014] EWHC 2883 (Fam); see also an earlier stage of proceedings at [2014] EWHC 962 (Fam), [2015] 1 FCR 433.

[324] *Re C (Children) (Child in Care: Choice of Forename)* [2016] EWCA Civ 374, [2016] 3 WLR 1557, at [41].

[325] *London Borough of Haringey* v. *Musa* [2014] EWHC 2883 (Fam), at [25].   [326] Ibid.

[327] E.g. 'Facebook used to track down adopted children', *The Times*, 5 January 2012.

Surname),[328] the court refused to allow three children, aged 16, 14 and 12, to change their surname from that of their father, whom they no longer saw, to that of their stepfather, whose name their already used informally. It is difficult to imagine that this refusal would do anything other than create a greater feeling of resentment towards the father on the part of the children involved. In other cases, the courts have been more ready to take account of children's own views, although stressing that those views do not displace the welfare test.[329] The most recent cases have shown much greater sensitivity to the views of children in applying the welfare test, even where those children are relatively young.[330] Given the importance of names to a child's internal sense of self, this is surely the correct approach.

(6) Conclusion

The right to identity is crucial for children. A legal identity secures the child's place in society, nation and family, providing the foundations for the child's sense of self and relationships with others. It is for good reason that the CRC requires that core aspects of a child's identity are in place soon after birth. The fact that these crucial aspects of identity are put in place when the child is an infant means that particular care must be taken to ensure that the child's interests are not lost; not least because adults often have powerful interests in the way in which a child's identity is determined and recorded. There is increasing international and domestic recognition of the importance of children's identity rights in determining parenthood and preserving access to information on their origins. Nonetheless, securing these rights in practice remains complex. Technological and social change presents new challenges to realising children's identity rights in practice. In responding to these challenges, it is also important to recognise that children's identity rights can be employed by adults for their own interests. A particularly strong example can be seen in the way in which putative fathers have used the child's purported right to knowledge of their genetic identity to found claims to a social relationship with that child. As the child matures, their life experience and own evolving sense of internal identity may conflict with the decisions made for

---

[328] [1996] 1 FLR 791.

[329] E.g. *Re M, T, P, K and B (Care: Change of Name)* [2000] 2 FLR 645. Cf. *Re S (Change of Surname)* [1999] 1 FLR 672, in which Thorpe LJ criticised the judge at first instance for not perceiving that a 15-year-old girl was *Gillick*-competent and allowing an appeal against refusal of permission to change her surname from that of her father (against whom child sexual abuse allegations had been made by her elder sister) to that of her maternal uncle and aunt. This case concerned a child in care and so was decided under CA 1989, s. 33(7).

[330] *Re B and C (Change of Names: Parental Responsibility: Evidence)* [2017] EWHC 3250 (Fam), at [50]–[51], placing weight on the views of the 8-year-old child, but also noting that the risk to her safety was such that it is likely that the change would have to be made even against her objections.

them at birth and with the legally recognised aspects of their identity. The extent to which a child has a right to legal recognition of their own developing internal sense of identity while still a child is unclear. While courts are increasingly placing weight on children's views in cases of name change or DNA testing, children remain unable to access official records concerning their origins until adulthood. The scope and limits of the right to identity remain contested, as does its implementation in a changing world.

Bibliography

NB: Many of these publications can be obtained on the relevant organisation's website.

Applegarth, L., Kaufman, N., Josephs-Sohan, M., Christos, P. and Rosenwaks, Z. (2016) 'Parental Disclosure to Offspring Created with Oocyte Donation: Intentions versus Reality' 31 *Human Reproduction* 1809.

Bainham, A. (2008a) 'Arguments about Parentage' 67 *Cambridge Law Journal* 322.
  (2008b) 'What Is the Point of Birth Registration?' 20 *Child and Family Law Quarterly* 449.

Besson, S. (2007) 'Enforcing the Child's Right to Know Her Origins: Contrasting Approaches Under the Convention on the Rights of the Child and the European Convention on Human Rights' 21 *International Journal of Law, Policy and the Family* 137.

Blauwhoff, R. (2008) 'Tracing Down the Historical Development of the Legal Concept of the Right to Know One's Origins. Has "to Know or Not to Know" Ever Been the Legal Question?' 4 *Utrecht Law Review* 99.

Blyth, E., Crawshaw, M., Frith, L. and Jones, C. (2012) 'Donor-Conceived People's Views and Experiences of Their Genetic Origins: A Critical Analysis of the Research Evidence' 19 *Journal of Law and Medicine* 769.

Blyth, E., Frith, L., Jones, C. and Speirs, J. (2009) 'The Role of Birth Certificates in relation to Access to Biographical and Genetic History in Donor Conception' 17 *International Journal of Children's Rights* 207.

Brandt, R. (2016) 'Mitochondrial Donation and the "Right to Know"' 42 *Journal of Medical Ethics* 678.

Bridge, C. and Swindells, H. (2003) *Adoption – The Modern Law*, Family Law.

Clifton, J. (2014) 'The Long Road to Universal Parental Responsibility: Some Implications of Research into Marginal Fathers' 44 *Family Law* 858.

Committee on the Rights of the Child (2002) *Concluding Observations of the Committee on the Rights of the Child: United Kingdom of Great Britain and Northern Ireland*, CRC/C/15/Add 188, Centre for Human Rights, Geneva.

Crawshaw, M. (2017) 'Direct-to-Consumer DNA Testing: The Fallout for Individuals and Their Families Unexpectedly Learning of Their Donor Conception Origins' 21 *Human Fertility* 225.

Crawshaw, M., Blyth, E. and Feast, J (2017) 'Can the UK's Birth Registration System Better Serve the Interests of Those Born Following Collaborative Assisted Reproduction?' 4 *Reproductive Biomedicine and Society Online* 1.

De Campos, T. and Milo, C. (2018) 'Mitochondrial Donation and the Right to Know and Trace One's Genetic Origins: An Ethical and Legal Challenge' 32 *International Journal of Law Policy and the Family* 170.

Department of Health (DH) (2007) Cm 7209, *Government Response to the Report from the Joint Committee on the Human Tissue and Embryology (Draft) Bill*, The Stationery Office.

Department of Health and Social Care (2018) *The Surrogacy Pathway: Advice for Intended Parents and Surrogates in England and Wales*.

Department for Work and Pensions (DWP) (2006) Cm 6979, *A New System of Child Maintenance*, The Stationery Office.
  (2007) Cm 7160, *Joint Birth Registration: Promoting Parental Responsibility*, DWP.
  (2008) Cm 7293, *Joint Birth Registration: Recording Parental Responsibility*, DWP.

Detrick, S. (ed.) (1992) *The United Nations Convention on the Rights of the Child: A Guide to the 'Travaux Préparatoires'*, Martinus Nijhoff.

Eekelaar, J. (1998) 'Do Parents Have a Duty to Consult?' 114 *Law Quarterly Review* 337.

(2001) 'Rethinking Parental Responsibility' 31 *Family Law* 426.

(2006) *Family Law and Personal Life*, Oxford University Press.

(2017) *Family Law and Personal Life*, 2nd edn, Oxford University Press.

(2018) 'Family Law and Identity' 38 *Oxford Journal of Legal Studies* 1.

Fenton-Glynn, C. (2014) *Children's Rights in Intercountry Adoption: A European Perspective*, Intersentia.

(2016) 'Information on Origins: Right or Obligation?' 46 *Family Law* 946.

Fortin, J. (1994) 'The Gooseberry Bush Approach' 57 *Modern Law Review* 296.

(2009) 'Children's Right to Know Their Origins – Too Far Too Fast?' 21 *Child and Family Law Quarterly* 336.

Freeman, M. (1996) 'The New Birth Right?: Identity and the Child of the Reproductive Revolution' 4 *International Journal of Children's Rights* 273.

Freeman, T. and Richards, M. (2006) 'DNA Testing and Kinship; Paternity, Genealogy and the Search for the "Truth" of Our Genetic Origins' in Ebtehaj, F., Lindley, B. and Richards, M. (eds) *Kinship Matters*, Hart Publishing.

Gilmore, S. (2003) 'Parental Responsibility and the Unmarried Father – a New Dimension to the Debate' 15 *Child and Family Law Quarterly* 21.

(2015) 'Withdrawal of Parental Responsibility: Lost Authority and a Lost Opportunity' 78 *Modern Law Review* 1042.

Golombok, S., Murray, C., Jadva, V., Lycett, E., MacCallum, F. and Rust, J. (2006) 'Non-Genetic and Non-Gestational Parenthood: Consequences for Parent–Child Relationships and the Psychological Well-Being of Mothers, Fathers and Children at Age 3' 21 *Human Reproduction* 1918.

Golombok, S., Readings, J., Blake, L., Casey, P., Mellish, L., Marks, A. and Jadva, V. (2011) 'Children Conceived by Gamete Donation: The Impact of Openness about Donor Conception on Psychological Adjustment and Parent–Child Relationships at Age 7' 25 *Journal of Family Psychology* 230.

Gosden, N. (2003) 'Children's Surnames – How Satisfactory Is the Current Law?' 33 *Family Law* 186.

Groskop, V. and Sarler, C. (2007) 'Do We Need to Know our Parentage?' *The Observer*, 5 August.

Haimes, E. (1987) '"Now I Know Who I Really Am": Identity Change and Redefinitions of the Self in Adoption' in Honess, T. and Yardley, K. (eds) *Self and Identity*, Routledge and Kegan Paul.

Harper, J., Jackson, E., Spoelstra-Witjens, L. and Reisel, D. (2017) 'Using an Introduction Website to Start a Family: Implications for Users and Health Practitioners' 4 *Reproductive Biomedicine & Society* 13.

Harper, J., Kennett, D. and Reisel, D. (2016) 'The End of Donor Anonymity: How Genetic Testing Is Likely to Drive Anonymous Gamete Donation Out of Business' 31 *Human Reproduction* 1135.

Hodgkin, R. and Newell, P. (2007) *Implementation Handbook for the Convention on the Rights of the Child*, Unicef.

Ilioi, E., Blake, L., Jadva, V., Roman, G. and Golombok, S. (2017) 'The Role of Age of Disclosure of Biological Origins in the Psychological Wellbeing of Adolescents Conceived by Reproductive Donation: A Longitudinal Study from Age 1 to Age 14' 58 *Journal of Child Psychology and Psychiatry* 315.

Jackson, E. (2006) 'What Is a Parent?' in Diduck, A. and O'Donovan, K. (eds) *Feminist Perspectives in Family Law*, Routledge–Cavendish.

(2015) 'The Law and DIY Assisted Conception' in Horsey, K. (ed.) *Revisiting the Regulation of Human Fertilisation and Embryology*, Routledge.

Joint Committee on the Human Tissue and Embryos (Draft) Bill (2007) *Human Tissue and Embryos (Draft) Bill*, Volume I, HL 169-I, HC 630-I, The Stationery Office.

Kaganas, F. (1996) 'Responsible or Feckless Fathers? – *Re S (Parental Responsibility)*' 8 *Child and Family Law Quarterly* 165.

Law Commission and Scottish Law Commission (2019) *Building Families through Surrogacy: A New Law. A Joint Consultation Paper*, Law Commission Consultation Paper 244, Scottish Law Commission Discussion Paper 167.

Lind, C. (2006) '*Evans* v. *United Kingdom* – Judgments of Solomon: Power, Gender and Procreation' 18 *Child and Family Law Quarterly* 576.

Lyons, D. (2018) 'Domestic Implementation of the Donor-Conceived Child's Right to Identity in Light of the Requirements of the UN Convention on the Rights of the Child' 32 *International Journal of Law Policy and the Family* 1.

Margaria, A. (2020) 'Trans men Giving Birth and Reflections on Fatherhood: What to Expect' 34 *International Journal of Law, Policy and the Family* 225.

McCandless, J. (2017) 'Reforming Birth Registration Law in England and Wales' 4 *Reproductive Biomedicine and Society Online* 52.

Mulligan, A. (2018) 'Identity Rights and Sensitive Ethical Questions: The European Court of Human Rights and the Regulation of Surrogacy Arrangements' 26 *Medical Law Review* 449.

Nuffield Council on Bioethics (2013) *Donor Conception: Ethical Aspects of Information Sharing*, Nuffield Council on Bioethics.

O'Donovan, K. (1990) 'What Shall We Tell the Children?' in Lee, R. and Morgan, D. (eds) *Birthrights*, Routledge.

Pennings, G. (2017) 'Disclosure of Donor Conception, Age of Disclosure and the Well-Being of Donor Offspring' 32 *Human Reproduction* 969.

Pickford, R. (1999a) 'Unmarried Fathers and the Law' in Bainham, A., Day Sclater, S. and Richards, M. (eds) *What Is a Parent?: A Socio-Legal Analysis*, Hart Publishing.

(1999b) *Fathers, Marriage and the Law*, Family Policy Studies Centre.

Readings, J., Blake, L., Casey, P., Jadva, V. and Golombok, S. (2011) 'Secrecy, Disclosure and Everything In-between: Decisions of Parents of Children Conceived by Donor Insemination, Egg Donation and Surrogacy' 22 *Reproductive Biomedicine Online* 485.

Scheib, J., Ruby, A. and Benward, J. (2017) 'Who Requests Their Sperm Donor's Identity? The First 10 Years of Information Releases to Adults with Open-Identity Donors' 2 *Fertility and Sterility* 483.

Scott, R. and Wilkinson, S. (2017) 'Germline Genetic Modification and Identity: The Mitochondrial and Nuclear Genomes' 37 *Oxford Journal of Legal Studies* 886.

Sheldon, S. (2007) 'Unmarried Fathers and British Citizenship: The Nationality, Immigration and Asylum Act 2002 and British Nationality (Proof of Paternity) Regulations 2006' 19 *Child and Family Law Quarterly* 1.

Shenfield, F., de Mouzon, J., Pennings, G., Ferraretti, A. P., Nyboe Andersen, A., de Wert, G., Goossens, V. and the ESHRE Taskforce on Cross Border Reproductive Care (2010) 'Cross Border Reproductive Care in Six European Countries' 25 *Human Reproduction* 1361.

Smart, C. (2007) *Personal Life*, Polity Press.

(2009) 'Family Secrets: Law and Understandings of Openness in Everyday Relationships' 38 *Journal of Social Policy* 551.

Smith, L. (2013) 'Tangling the Web of Legal Parenthood: Legal Responses to the Use of Known Donors in Lesbian Parenting Relationships' 33 *Legal Studies* 355.

Steiner, E. (2003) '*Odièvre* v. *France* – Desperately Seeking Mother – Anonymous Births in the European Court of Human Rights' 15 *Child and Family Law Quarterly* 425.

Tobin, J. (2014) 'To Prohibit or Permit: What Is the (Human) Rights Response to the Practice of International Commercial Surrogacy?' 63 *International and Comparative Law Quarterly* 317.

Triseliotis, J. (1973) *In Search of Origins*, Routledge and Kegan Paul.

Turkmendag, I., Dingwall, R. and Murphy, T. (2008) 'The Removal of Donor Anonymity in the UK: The Silencing of Claims by Would-Be Parents' 22 *International Journal of Law, Policy and the Family* 283.

Wade, K. (2017) 'The Regulation of Surrogacy: A Children's Rights Perspective' 29 *Child and Family Law Quarterly* 113.

Wallbank, J. (2002) 'Clause 106 of the Adoption and Children Bill: Legislation for the "Good" Father?' 22 *Legal Studies* 276.

(2004) 'The Role of Rights and Utility in Instituting a Child's Right to Know Her Genetic History' 13 *Social and Legal Studies* 245.

(2009) 'Bodies in the Shadows: Joint Birth Registration, Parental Responsibility and Social Class' 21 *Child and Family Law Quarterly* 267.

Zadeh, S., Ilioi, E., Jadva, V. and Golombok, S. (2018) 'The Perspectives of Adolescents Conceived Using Surrogacy, Egg or Sperm Donation' 33 *Human Reproduction* 1099.

6

The Child's Right to Respect for Family Life

The Right to Know and Be Brought Up by Parents

(1) Introduction

The right to respect for family life is one of the most important and closely protected rights that children possess. The fundamental importance of family relationships for children's protection and well-being means that this right is perhaps the most widely litigated of all children's rights, offering protection in a diverse range of areas such as immigration,[1] state benefits[2] and the responsibility of the state to children in public care.[3] There are many good reasons for putting great weight on the protection of children's family relationships. The centrality of parental responsibility for children[4] means that parental relationships are the primary means by which the law anticipates that children will be cared for and their interests protected. Family relationships are also vital to a child's sense of identity and place in the world.[5] Perhaps most importantly, it is widely recognised that loving, secure and stable relationships with trusted carers are fundamental to a child's well-being and development.

Despite the undoubted importance of children's family relationships, the right to family life poses a number of important challenges. A defining feature of the Strasbourg conception of the right to respect for family life between parents and children is that it is mutual: the right of the child to a relationship with the parent is reinforced by the parent's corresponding right to a relationship with the child.[6] This is a powerful recognition of the reality of many parent–child relationships, but can obscure the child's own rights where they conflict with the interests of parents. This is particularly the case in situations where the child has formed a secure attachment with other carers, or the parental relationship poses risks for the child's welfare. This chapter is concerned with such situations and particularly the extent to which a child's right to respect for family life implies a right to know and be brought up by

---

[1] E.g. *ZH (Tanzania)* v. *Secretary of State for the Home Department* [2011] UKSC 4, [2011] 2 AC 166, discussed in Chapter 3.

[2] E.g. *Re McLaughlin* [2018] UKSC 48, [2018] 1 WLR 4250. See further Chapter 13 for discussion of using children's rights in cases concerning state benefits.

[3] See discussion in Chapter 16.   [4] See discussion in Chapter 4.

[5] See discussion in Chapter 5.   [6] E.g. *K and T* v. *Finland* [2001] 2 FLR 707, at [151].

their biological or legal parents.[7] The courts have long struggled with the extent to which the biological and legal relationship between children and parents should be regarded as of value, regardless of the quality of the underlying reality of the social relationship. The difficulties confronting the courts when dealing with disputes over children who form attachments with those who care for them and love them on a day-to-day basis, but who are not their birth parents are well captured by Wall J's observation in such a case:

> The case thus raises as a central issue the classic dilemma sadly so often found in children's cases. B has become attached to people who are not her natural parents. To break that attachment will undoubtedly cause her harm. Does the harm that will be caused outweigh the benefit which B will otherwise derive from being brought up by her parents in the cultural heritage and traditions into which she was born?[8]

Schaffer warns against assuming that these affectionate ties are somehow less important to the child:

> The widespread belief in the blood bond is based on the notion that there is a natural affinity between child and biological parents which makes the latter more fit to be responsible for the child's care and upbringing than any outsider. Such fitness is assumed to be due to the common heredity found in parent–child pairs; whatever experiences a child may share with some other adult and whatever affectionate ties then develop between them are considered to be of secondary importance to the blood bond which is said to exist from the moment of conception.[9]

Having summarised the well-documented research showing only too clearly the way in which children can form positive attachments with adopters and other carers,[10] Schaffer concludes:

> It is a history of social interaction, not kinship, that breeds attachment, and to break these bonds cannot be done lightheartedly – certainly not on the basis of a myth, namely a psychological blood bond.[11]

Very similar views led Goldstein *et al.* to coin their concept of the child's 'psychological parent'.[12] Schaffer's words make clear his disapproval of those who assume that the bonds between a child and his or her attachment figures can be broken simply because they are not linked to each other by biological relatedness. Children suffer severe psychological trauma when separated from such carers,[13] whether or not they are biologically related and whether or not the relationship has been recognised through legal parenthood.

---

[7] The case law and commentary on the question of whether there is a right to know and be brought up by birth parents sometimes conflates biological and legal parenthood. While the discussion is often framed in terms of the biological bonds between birth parents and children, the legal principles discussed in this chapter apply equally to legal parents who do not have a biological relationship with the child: see further Chapter 5.

[8] *Re B (Adoption: Child's Welfare)* [1995] 1 FLR 895, at 896.   [9] H. Schaffer (1998) p. 51.

[10] See also the research summarised by I. Weyland (1997) pp. 175–8.

[11] H. Schaffer (1998) p. 62.   [12] J. Goldstein *et al.* (1973) p. 19.

[13] H. Schaffer (1998) pp. 90–111.

Against this view has to be balanced the importance society places on the relationship between children and birth parents and a feeling of unease generated by laws which might allow alternative carers to keep children in their care despite the birth parents' strong opposition. As Eekelaar has pointed out:

> It would surely be legally wrong for a hospital to hand a child over to a stranger rather than to its mother, not simply because the child would (or might) do better with the mother, but because the mother is entitled to her child unless deprived of this right through proper legal procedures ... It is surely not a matter of embarrassment to hold that parents have a prima facie right to possess their children. This must be fundamental to our social ordering.[14]

It is difficult to quarrel with this comment or with the commonly held view, reflected in Articles 7, 8 and 9 of the UN Convention on the Rights of the Child (CRC), that, in ordinary circumstances, children have a corresponding right to be brought up by their birth parents. The law has, however, faced difficulties in finding the limits of this principle in circumstances outside of the ordinary, especially where the parents' 'prima facie right to possess their children' conflict with the child's own interests.

This chapter explores the extent to which the child's right to family life protects biological relatedness, legal parenthood or practical relationships of care and responsibility, particularly where these are in conflict with one another. It will do so in three contexts: first, disputes concerning child arrangements between parents who do not live together; second, disputes between parents and alternative carers with whom the child has built a psychological bond; and, finally, the weight put on the relationship with birth parents in placing a child for adoption and in post-adoption contact. While these are different forms of dispute with different legal consequences, each has the potential, at least in the most serious of cases, to severely limit or even sever the child's relationship with their birth parent and members of their wider birth family. In each of these areas, the law has struggled to maintain a consistent stance on the value of those relationships to the child's welfare and the weight, if any, to be placed on the parent's interest in the relationship with the child. Each area also demonstrates how the language of rights has at times been distorted to create simple principles that belie the complex reality of the rights involved.

(2) The Child's Right to Family Life

Family relationships are central to the conception of children's rights contained in the CRC[15] and protection of those relationships forms a core purpose of the CRC.[16] The child's right to family life receives close attention throughout the CRC, with different facets of the right to family life receiving specific attention.

---

[14] J. Eekelaar (1991) p. 388.   [15] See further discussion in Chapter 4.
[16] The right to family life is also protected by a range of other international instruments; see discussion in Chapter 2.

Article 9 is perhaps the most important of these rights, protecting the relationship between parents and children. It provides that children will not be separated from their parents against their[17] will, unless such separation is necessary for the best interests of the child and gives procedural protection for all parties in that assessment. Further, Article 9 protects the child's right to direct and regular contact with parents, again recognising that contact may be refused if it is contrary to the child's best interests.[18] Beyond Article 9, Articles 7 and 8 protect children's relationships as an aspect of their right to identity.[19] Article 7 obliges the state to ensure that the child will 'as far as possible' have a right from birth 'to know and be cared for by his or her parents',[20] while Article 8 extends beyond the parental relationship, requiring respect for the child's right to preserve 'family relations recognized by law without unlawful interference'. Detailed protection for relationship rights in particular circumstances, such as family reunification,[21] abduction[22] and adoption,[23] is found in further articles. As a result, the protection of family relationships is a vital thread that runs through the CRC.[24] In addition to the CRC itself, a wide range of international and regional instruments provide specific protection for elements of family life[25] and offer effective frameworks for the resolution of disputes that cross borders.[26]

Despite the importance given to family relationships in the CRC, there is no authoritative definition of the family in the text or elsewhere in international law, nor is a definition of 'parent' provided. This is an important issue as in many disputes about children's upbringing the essence of the dispute is concerned with competing claims to be regarded as the child's 'true' family. The UK has made a specific declaration as to the meaning of parenthood to clarify that it only applies to those regarded in domestic law as parents; so, for example, birth parents would not be able to invoke Article 9 of the CRC in order to bolster a claim for post-adoption contact.[27] There is no equivalent declaration for the term 'family', which is broad enough to cover extended family members and to encompass diverse conceptions of 'family' that may prevail in different member states. This breadth is clear from Article 5, which

---

[17] Art. 9 is ambiguous as to whether 'their will' refers to the will of the parents or that of the child. In the light of the emphasis that the CRC places on the child's participation in decisions, the better view is that the term 'their' refers to both parents and child; G. Van Bueren (1995) p. 80.

[18] Art. 9(3).   [19] See discussion in Chapter 5.

[20] This final version of the right replaced the original proposal that the child had a right to 'know and belong to his parents', a formulation that would have risked the view that the parent–child relationship was primarily a possessive right of the parents. The current formulation is clearly focused on the child's right to care and relationships.

[21] CRC, Art. 10.   [22] CRC, Art. 11.   [23] CRC, Art. 21.   [24] J. Tobin (2017).

[25] E.g. UN Guidelines for the Alternative Care of Children (2010) A/RES/64/142.

[26] E.g. The Hague Convention on the Civil Aspects of International Child Abduction.

[27] 'The United Kingdom interprets the references in the Convention to "parents" to mean only those persons who, as a matter of national law, are treated as parents. This includes cases where the law regards a child as having only one parent, for example where a child has been adopted by one person only and in certain cases where a child is conceived other than as a result of sexual intercourse by the woman who gives birth to it and she is treated as the only parent.'

not only recognises the rights and duties of parents, but also those of 'the extended family or community as provided for by local custom'. The Committee on the Rights of the Child has interpreted 'family' inclusively to include a range of forms of primary care, including those with whom the child does not share a biological relationship.[28]

The European Convention on Human Rights and Fundamental Freedoms (ECHR) gives protection to children's family relationships through the right to respect for family life in Article 8. The definition of family life has been the subject of extensive Strasbourg jurisprudence, the essence of which, although not always consistently applied, is that family life depends on the reality of close personal ties,[29] rather than biological or legal relationships alone. While children will usually have family life with their biological parents, a biological connection is neither a necessary[30] nor sufficient[31] condition of family life. For example, a genetic father who has had no contact with his child may be unable to establish 'family life' unless he can show that the child was born into a 'genuine relationship' or that he has shown sufficient interest in and commitment to the child before and after birth.[32] Similarly, while legal parenthood is a relevant factor,[33] family life may arise in the absence of a recognised legal relationship.[34] Family life can also be found in other relationships, including with grandparents,[35] siblings and foster carers.[36] In consequence, in many complex disputes Article 8 will be relevant in considering multiple relationships and will not simply reinforce the claims of the biological or legal parents. The focus on the reality of relationships means that Article 8 is often said to be concerned with the mutual relationships between children and

---

[28] J. Tobin (2017) pp. 56–7.   [29] *Paradiso* v. *Italy* (2017) 65 EHRR 2.

[30] In *Pini and Bertani; Manera and Atripaldi* v. *Romania* [2005] 2 FLR 596, at [136]–[148], the adoptive parents in a 'lawful and genuine' international adoption case had some measure of protection under Art. 8, despite the fact that they had not yet met the children. In the event, the adoptive parents' family life was outweighed by the strong opposition of the 12-year-old adoptees to leaving their existing home.

[31] In *G* v. *Netherlands* (1993) 16 EHRR CD38, the sperm donor did not have family life with the child, despite having spent some time caring for him. In *IS* v. *Germany* [2014] ECHR 577, the mother's consent to the adoption of her biological children severed her legal relationship and 'might' bring family life to an end, although any continuing relationship or intended relationship between them was capable of creating new rights to family or private life.

[32] *L* v. *Netherlands*, App. No. 45582/99, ECHR 2004, at [35]–[40].

[33] *Pini and Bertani; Manera and Atripaldi* v. *Romania* [2005] 2 FLR 596, at [136]–[148] (see above); legal adoption was of some value, even in the absence of a relationship with the children, although full family life had not arisen. In contrast, in *Paradiso* v. *Italy* (2017) 65 EHRR 2, intention to create a family relationship and 8 months of actual care for the child were insufficient to found family life in a case where the 'parents' had failed to comply with domestic law in relation to a child who was purportedly born through a surrogacy arrangement abroad, but with whom they had no genetic relationship.

[34] In *Mennesson* v. *France*, App. No. 65192/11, Judgment of 26 June 2014, at [87], failure to recognise the relationship between parents and children following a surrogacy relationship interfered with the family life of the parents and children. On the facts, the interference with family life was justified, although the interference with the children's private life was not.

[35] *Manuello and Nevi* v. *Italy*, App. No. 107/10, ECHR 2015.

[36] *Moretti and Benedetti* v. *Italy*, App. No. 16318/07, ECHR 2010.

their family members.[37] Nonetheless, there is a danger that this approach may imply interests of parents and children are co-extensive and obscure the fact that in many of the cases that get as far as the courts, the child's interests may conflict with those of their parents. This is exacerbated by the fact that the European Court of Human Rights (ECtHR) has often dealt with disputes in terms of adults' *rights* and children's *interests*, with the children's position being considered within the context of justifying an infringement of the adults' rights, rather than through independent consideration of the child's own rights.[38] When doing so, the ECtHR has stressed that there must be a fair balance between the interests of the child and those of the parent, with particular importance being attached to the child's best interests, which, depending on their nature and seriousness, may override those of the parent.[39] Despite the 'particular importance' placed on the interests of children, the interests of adults in having a relationship with their children remain an important factor,[40] even if the child does not want to see the parent.[41] This, together with the ECtHR's strong assumption that it is ordinarily in the child's interests to have a relationship with their parents, means that while the ECtHR is effective at protecting children's relationships from unwarranted interference, it can serve to obscure the individual child's rights.

Overall, the child's right to family life is well protected from unwarranted interference under the ECHR, CRC and wider international law. The breadth of the term 'family' in both the CRC and ECHR means that the right to respect for family life should be able to encompass the child's interest in a wide range of caring relationships and family structures rather than providing a myopic focus on biological or legal relationships. Nonetheless, in practice, the right can sometimes appear to act against the child's interests, especially in circumstances where those relationships threaten the child's safety or settled home with alternative carers. Further, even mature children may struggle to assert their right *not* to have a relationship with particular family members.

(3) Parental Relationships and Child Arrangements Orders

(A) A 'Right' to Contact?

A substantial number of children in the UK experience parental separation: around one in six are born into a family in which their birth parents do not live together, while one in three will experience parental separation in their

---

[37] E.g. *K and T v. Finland* [2001] 2 FLR 707, at [151].

[38] Discussed in Chapter 2. E.g. *Elsholz* v. *Germany* [2000] 2 FLR 486, at [43]. This approach is also often adopted in domestic law, e.g., *Re M (Children)* [2013] EWCA Civ 1147, at [24].

[39] E.g. *Hoppe* v. *Germany* [2003] 1 FLR 384, at [49]; *Elsholz* v. *Germany* [2000] 2 FLR 486, at [50]; *Sahin* v. *Germany; Sommerfeld* v. *Germany* [2002] 1 FLR 119, [2003] 2 FLR 671, at [66]; *Neulinger and Shuruk* v. *Switzerland* (2012) 54 EHRR 31, at [134]. As discussed in Chapter 2, the precise formulation used has not been consistent between cases.

[40] *Neulinger and Shuruk* v. *Switzerland* (2012) 54 EHRR 31, at [134].

[41] *K.B.* v. *Croatia*, App. No. 36216/13, unreported, Judgment of 14 March 2017, at [143].

childhood.[42] There is a voluminous body of research literature on the outcomes for children who experience parental separation,[43] although the potential for post-separation parenting to mitigate or exacerbate any adverse outcomes is less well understood.[44] One immediate outcome is that parents often disagree over their children's future upbringing. The high number of disputes about child arrangements very obviously reflects the need experienced by separated parents and children to spend time together and an assumption that it is their right to do so, by virtue of the biological and legal links between them. As Buchanan *et al.* observe, these disputes provoke profound debates within our society – in particular, there is the question of whether a biological tie per se entitles a parent to an ongoing relationship with his or her child or whether the role of parent has to be earned.[45] Few doubt that it is *normally* in children's best interests to maintain a relationship with both parents when a couple separate and international human rights law recognises this. The ECHR, CRC and European Convention on Contact Concerning Children[46] all emphasise the need for the child and parent to maintain direct and regular contact, except in circumstances where this would be against the child's best interests. Those disputes that come to court are often characterised by high conflict and allegations raising serious welfare concerns.[47] Whether contact is in the child's best interests in these cases is far more difficult to determine.

The use of rights 'talk' in the context of parental disputes in this country is not new. Wrangham J famously described the companionship of a parent being of such immense value to a child that it should be described as 'a basic right in the child rather than a basic right in the parent'.[48] It is also clear that Strasbourg jurisprudence has been a defining influence in the way in which domestic law has developed.[49] Despite this influence, the courts have moved away[50] from employing the language of *children's* rights in parental disputes, instead articulating children's interests in terms of welfare.[51] Instead, 'rights

---

[42] C. Bryson *et al.* (2017) p. 11.

[43] See summaries by: J. Fortin *et al.* (2006) pp. 212–13; G. Harold and M. Murch (2005) pp. 186–95; C. Bryson *et al.* (2017) pp. 12–13 and 28–9. The link between parental separation and adverse outcomes for children is not necessarily causal, but may be associated with the differences between families that separate and those that do not and with the post-separation circumstances: C. Bryson *et al.* (2017) pp. 53–4.

[44] A. Goisis *et al.* (2016).   [45] A. Buchanan *et al.* (2001) p. 1.

[46] Adopted and opened for signature in 2003, but not yet signed or ratified by the UK. See esp. Art. 1.

[47] Discussed further below: e.g. M. Harding and A. Newnham (2015).

[48] *M* v. *M (Child: Access)* [1973] 2 All ER 81, at 85.

[49] E.g. the influential summary of the law in *Re C (A Child) (Suspension of Contact)* [2011] EWCA Civ 521, [2011] 2 FLR 912, at [37]–[47].

[50] Inter alia: *Re S (Minors) (Access)* [1990] 2 FLR 166, per Balcombe LJ, at 170; *Re R (A Minor) (Contact)* [1993] 2 FLR 762, per Butler-Sloss LJ, at 767; *A* v. *Y (Child's Surname)* [1999] 2 FLR 5, per Judge Tyrer, at 8.

[51] E.g. *Re W (Contact: Joining Child as Party)* [2001] EWCA Civ 1830, [2003] 1 FLR 681, per Dame Elizabeth Butler-Sloss P, at 685; *Re L (A Child) (Contact: Domestic Violence) and other appeals* [2000] 4 All ER 609, per Thorpe LJ, at 633–8.

talk' has been more closely associated with fathers' pressure groups claims that fathers are treated unfairly by the court when dealing with parental disputes and campaigns to change the law; these references to rights largely focus on their own rights, not on those of their children.[52] This section will consider the extent to which children's rights and interests are protected in practice in parental disputes on child arrangements. It will first look at the reforms that have emerged from these campaigns for change, before examining the operation of the current law, including in relation to domestic abuse and enforcement of child arrangements orders, both areas in which children are at risk of harm. Protection of children in these cases depends not just on the substantive law, but also on the severe restrictions on public funding, which have made it more difficult to give independent representation to children's wishes and to secure independent assessment of their welfare.

(B) The Campaign for Reform: Shared Parenting to Child Arrangements Orders

The framework in which private parental disputes are determined was recast by the Children and Families Act 2014 (CFA 2014). The background to the CFA 2014 has its roots in the activism of the fathers' rights movement.[53] Much has been written about the fathers' rights movement in England and in other parts of the world.[54] Changes in attitudes towards parenting, with more mothers now working and more fathers spending increasing amounts of time with their children,[55] undoubtedly underlie some of the fathers' concerns. It is notable how the increasingly polarised and gender-based debate between the fathers' pressure groups and the women's groups has become very adult focused. Mothers often see the legal process as forcing them into apparently opposing fathers' claims to their 'legitimate' rights[56] and into asserting their own roles as 'good mothers'.[57] When opposing calls for equal parenting presumptions,[58] women's groups tend to focus on the dangers of unsafe contact, more particularly on the harm suffered by mothers and children as a result of fathers' domestic abuse.[59] Increasingly, the fathers' rights groups here and abroad[60] concentrate on issues of justice and fairness. Indeed, the research literature shows non-resident fathers' pervasive sense of being controlled by their ex-partners, their feeling of powerlessness and anger over the perceived injustice of their position.[61]

The changes eventually implemented by the CFA 2014 fall far short of the initial aim of fathers' rights groups to introduce a legal presumption of equal shared residence in the form of a 50/50 division of children's time between

---

[52] C. Smart (2004) p. 485; R. Collier and S. Sheldon (2006); F. Kaganas (2013).
[53] F. Kaganas (2013).
[54] Inter alia: H. Rhoades and S. Boyd (2004); R. Collier (2005); R. Collier and S. Sheldon (2006).
[55] DCA *et al.* (2004) paras 35–6.   [56] C. Smart and B. Neale (1999) p. 163.
[57] S. Day Sclater and F. Kaganas (2003) pp. 163–6.   [58] Discussed below.
[59] H. Reece (2006).   [60] H. Rhoades and S. Boyd (2004).   [61] B. Geldof (2003).

each parent.[62] This suggested solution was rejected by the government on the basis that:

> Children are not a commodity to be apportioned equally after separation. The best arrangements for them will depend on a variety of issues particular to their circumstances: a one-size-fits-all formula will not work.[63]

The Family Justice Review, which preceded the CFA 2014, reviewed the research evidence and similarly rejected modified proposals for a presumption of equal shared parenting.[64] Although a presumption of shared parenting[65] might address arguments about 'fairness', research suggests that such arrangements are not always a positive experience for the children concerned, with some finding them positively burdensome, particularly as they grow into adolescence.[66] The research suggests that successful shared parenting arrangements are characterised by parents who are able to adopt a cooperative and child-centred parenting style, so creating a low-conflict and flexible approach that is responsive to their children's changing needs.[67] Such low-conflict families are unlikely to be represented in the litigated cases on which a judicial presumption would primarily bite. The imposition of shared care on litigating parents almost inevitably means its use in high-conflict situations where there are often significant welfare concerns. Experience in Australia demonstrates that shared parenting orders in such circumstances are often associated with poor outcomes for children and in the worst cases can entail risks to their safety.[68] Worryingly, parents in those studies often misunderstood the legislation to create a parental *right* to shared time and felt that they had no choice but to agree to it, even in circumstances where the risk was such that the court was unlikely to have ordered it.[69] As Sonia Harris-Short argues, shared parenting is best achieved in an environment in which policy and practice encourage shared parenting from the start of a child's life and not by its artificial imposition at the point where the parents separate.[70] She points to the experience of Sweden, where

---

[62] F. Kaganas and C. Piper (2002); S. Day Sclater and F. Kaganas (2003) pp. 156–8; H. Rhoades (2006) p. 143.

[63] DCA *et al.* (2004) para. 42. See also DCA *et al.* (2005) para. 13.   [64] D. Norgrove (2011) ch. 4.

[65] The definition of 'shared care', 'shared parenting' or 'shared residence' often differs between studies, creating some difficulties in comparing the outcomes of research. The terms do not necessarily indicate an exact 50/50 split, but instead arrangements with a substantial time allocated to each parent, with some including 30 per cent of overnight stays as a benchmark; L. Trinder (2010).

[66] C. Smart (2004) esp. p. 495; H. Rhoades and S. Boyd (2004) p. 132; J. Hunt with C. Roberts (2004) pp. 6–7; S. Gilmore (2006) pp. 353–8.

[67] L. Trinder (2010).   [68] B. Fehlberg *et al.* (2011).

[69] The Australian legislation created a presumption of 'equal shared parental responsibility', which was often misinterpreted by parent to give a presumption of equal shared *time*: B. Fehlberg *et al.* (2011).

[70] S. Harris-Short (2011). Similarly, T. Haux and L. Platt (2015) found that fathers' pre-separation parenting was associated with greater frequency of contact and overnight stays after separation. J. Fortin *et al.* (2012) also found a similar connection between pre-separation parenting and the quality of post-separation contact.

a norm of shared parenting is underpinned by policies that support both parents in playing an active part in child care and in continuing in the workforce. It was the research evidence that convinced the Family Justice Review and, eventually, Parliament to step back from introducing any presumption of shared time or shared parenting in the CFA 2014.[71] Despite the absence of any legislative imperative to do so, the English courts had in any event changed their attitude to shared residence orders.[72] They had moved from confining them to exceptional circumstances,[73] via a mid-point position of considering their availability where the children are already spending substantial amounts of time with each parent,[74] to asserting that in such situations 'good reasons are required if a shared residence order is not to be made'.[75] This change of attitude was, at least in part, symbolic, with orders being used to signify equality of status between parents, even in circumstances in which the division of the child's time was very unequal in practice.[76] Indeed, the courts had enthusiastically endorsed the ability of such orders to educate parents over the need to cooperate over their parenting even in cases where the parents were on particularly bad terms.[77]

This symbolism can be seen as the underlying justification for the eventual reforms in the CFA 2014, which introduced a change of statutory language from residence and contact orders, with their corresponding connotations of a primary and secondary parent, to 'child arrangements orders' in which the equal status and responsibility of both parents is emphasised.[78] While this message may be a laudable one if acted upon, it may be rather optimistic to expect that a change in terminology will encourage parents to take equal responsibility in practice. Alongside these changes, courts must now operate on the presumption that the child's welfare will usually benefit from involvement of each parent in the life of the child.[79] It seems unlikely that either of these changes has had, or was intended to have, a significant impact on the way in which disputes are handled by the courts. Instead, the intended impact appears to be in restoring public faith in the neutrality of the family courts and bolstering

---

[71] L. Trinder (2014) pp. 42–5 explains the initial resistance of the government to the outcome of the Family Justice Review and the eventual drafting of the provisions in the CFA 2014.

[72] Under the former CA 1989, s. 11(4). S. Gilmore (2006) assesses the changing judicial approach to joint residence orders.

[73] *Re H (A Minor) (Shared Residence)* [1994] 1 FLR 717, per Purchas LJ, at 728.

[74] *D v. D (Shared Residence Order)* [2001] 1 FLR 495, per Hale LJ, at [32]. See also *Re F (Shared Residence Order)* [2003] EWCA Civ 592, [2003] 2 FLR 397: the fact that the parents' homes would be separated by a considerable distance (mother in Scotland and father in England) did not preclude a shared residence order.

[75] *Re P (Shared Residence Order)* [2005] EWCA Civ 1639, [2006] 2 FLR 347, per Wall LJ, at [22]. See also *Re K (Shared Residence Order)* [2008] EWCA Civ 526, [2008] 2 FLR 380: a shared residence order could be ordered in cases where the child's time was not shared between the parents equally; in this case, 40 per cent was to be with the father.

[76] P. Harris and R. George (2010).   [77] Ibid.

[78] CA 1989, s. 8(1), as amended by CFA 2014, s. 12; A. McFarlane (2014).

[79] CA 1989, s. 1, as amended by CFA 2014, s. 11.

public perception as to the 'right' way to go about parenting following relationship breakdowns. While this message may be beneficial to those children whose parents can cooperate in giving the child a safe and secure upbringing, the greatest concern is that the changing language of the law may make it more difficult for parents to keep their child safe from harmful relationships.

(C) Welfare and the Presumption of Parental Involvement

When making a child arrangements order, the court is required to treat the child's welfare as paramount, using the welfare checklist in determining the child's welfare.[80] As part of that welfare assessment, the court is required to apply the presumption of parental involvement, introduced by the CFA 2014.[81] The presumption might appear to make a decisive shift in favour of separated parents who seek greater involvement in their child's life, but in reality makes little more than a statement of existing practice. The presumption only applies to parents who 'can be involved in the child's life in a way that does not put the child at risk of suffering harm'.[82] Where the presumption does apply, the court must 'presume, unless the contrary is shown, that involvement of that parent in the life of the child concerned will further the child's welfare'.[83] However, involvement means 'involvement of some kind' and may be direct or indirect; in contrast to the original campaign for a presumption of equal time, it does not impose any particular starting point as to how the child's time should be divided.[84] Despite rather convoluted drafting, the presumption seems to do little more than make a rather anodyne statement that children will generally benefit from their parents each having some kind of involvement in their life, provided that there is no evidence that that involvement will cause them harm. The presumption appears to have been designed to do very little to alter the judicial approach in practice; indeed, the Minister's evidence to the Justice Committee in its pre-legislative scrutiny showed that the presumption was:

> included not to effect any change in Court orders but to tackle a perception of bias within the Courts that we have previously concluded has no basis in fact,[85]

---

[80] CA 1989, s. 1.   [81] Inserted by CFA 2014, s. 11.

[82] CA 1989, s. 1(6): evidence is required before a court can conclude that 'involvement of that parent in the child's life would put the child at risk of suffering harm whatever the form of involvement', given that involvement can include indirect, occasional contact, it will be rare that the presumption can be shown not to apply to a particular parent. Practice Direction 12J para. 7 directs the court to carefully consider this provision in cases involving domestic abuse, discussed further below.

[83] CA 1989, s. 1(2A).

[84] CA 1989, s. 1(2B) explicitly states that 'involvement' does not require 'any particular division of a child's time'.

[85] Research suggests that the Justice Committee was correct to find that the evidence does not support allegations of gender bias in the courts' decision-making; e.g. M. Harding and A. Newnham (2015) ch. 4 found that while there were small differences in success rates between mothers and fathers in their sample, these were largely attributable to the different factual circumstances and particularly the greater likelihood that the mother was already acting as the primary parent.

and in the hope of influencing parents to agree to make provision for shared parenting rather than risk entering the court process.[86]

While the courts had eschewed the language of presumptions before the CFA 2014,[87] in practice orders for no contact were already rare[88] and research on the attitudes of practitioners found an understanding that there was already a '*de facto* presumption that unless there are good reasons to the contrary there should be contact'.[89] This impression was borne out by a long-standing body of case law demonstrating a judicial understanding that it will 'almost always' benefit children to have as much contact with both parents as possible and that compelling evidence is required for contact to be refused.[90] It is therefore unsurprising that the introduction of the statutory presumption appears to have no real impact on judicial practice.[91]

The current approach of the judiciary not only reinforces the assumption that contact will almost always be in the best interests of children, but also emphasises that the courts have a positive duty to promote contact and to 'grapple with all the available alternatives before abandoning hope of achieving some contact'.[92] As a result, the court will not simply consider whether contact is beneficial on the available evidence, but is required to take proactive steps to try to establish beneficial contact and overcome obstacles to the relationship.[93] The importance placed on the parental relationship often appears to outweigh other important aspects of the child's welfare and is pursued even if the relationship might appear hopeless or even potentially harmful. For example, in *Re CB (International Relocation: Domestic Abuse)*,[94] the father had a conviction for harassment against the mother, and the court also found a pattern of domestic abuse that was likely to cause the child harm if not

---

[86] Justice Committee (2012) para. 153.

[87] E.g. *Re L (A Child) (Contact: Domestic Violence) and other appeals* [2000] 4 All ER 609, per Thorpe LJ, at 633–8: the language of 'rights' should be dropped and the word 'assumption', not 'presumption', better describes the judicial preparedness to award contact.

[88] E.g. J. Hunt and A. Macleod (2008) p. 250; M. Harding and A. Newnham (2015) ch. 4.

[89] J. Hunt and A. Macleod (2008) p. 222.

[90] E.g. *Re O (Contact: Imposition of Conditions)* [1995] 2 FLR 124; *Re P (Contact: Supervision)* [1996] 2 FLR 314; *Re O (A Child) (Contact: Withdrawal of Application)* [2003] EWHC 3031 (Fam), [2004] 1 FLR 1258; *Re Bradford; Re O'Connell* [2006] EWCA Civ 1199, [2007] 1 FLR 530, esp. at [70]; *Re C (A Child) (Suspension of Contact)* [2011] EWCA Civ 521, [2011] 2 FLR 912; *Re W (Children)* [2012] EWCA Civ 999, [2013] 1 FLR 494.

[91] In *Re J (Children)* [2018] EWCA Civ 115, [2018] 2 FLR 998, at [48], McFarlane J described the presumption as enacting a basic tenet of family law; on this view, the presumption merely codifies the existing law. This view appears to be borne out by empirical research: J. Harwood (2021).

[92] *Re C (A Child) (Suspension of Contact)* [2011] EWCA Civ 521, [2011] 2 FLR 912, at [47].

[93] E.g. in *Re A (Children) (Ultra-Orthodox Judaism: Transgender Parent)* [2017] EWCA Civ 2164, [2018] 4 WLR 60, the court suggested that the children may have to be removed from their mother's care if they were not able to have contact with their father, who was living as a transwoman, without encountering hostility within the ultra-orthodox Jewish community of which the mother and children were a part.

[94] [2017] EWFC 39, [2017] 3 FCR 273.

checked. His aggressive and intimidating behaviour meant that staff at social services and the local contact centre would no longer work with him to supervise or promote contact out of concern for their own safety. The mother, who on any outcome would be the sole carer for the child, wished to return home to Portugal to the support of her family and to find work rather than relying on benefits. Nonetheless, the court adjourned the case to give him at least another 5 months to try to access programmes to show he could be safely involved in the child's life, despite the court's own doubts that this could be achieved and the absence of any evidence that such programmes were available to him. The court's pro-contact stance means that risks associated with parental involvement are increasingly seen as obstacles for the court to address rather than reasons to refuse the order sought.

Many disputes between parents do not get as far as court. For a considerable time, private family law has been 'dominated by a general preference for reaching agreed outcomes',[95] leading to parents coming under considerable pressure to settle their disputes out of court, often with little knowledge of their legal position. The evidence to the Justice Committee suggested that the presumption was primarily aimed at these parents; as Kaganas argues, the presumption further embeds the norm of parental involvement, meaning that mothers who resist that message in negotiations risk being labelled as aberrant in doing so.[96] The removal of legal aid from most private family cases[97] means that many parents approaching negotiation over child arrangements do so without the benefit of legal advice and may feel compelled to agree to contact, even in circumstances in which there is a risk of harm sufficient to prevent a court making an order for direct contact. As discussed above, the research from Australia demonstrates that messages embedded in legislation can easily be misinterpreted and that mothers can feel coerced into agreeing arrangements even in circumstances in which they are unsafe. Although there is not yet any robust evidence as to the impact that the presumption has had on private agreements, there is a risk that it may have a similar impact here.

The law outlined above has been developed on the assumption that parental involvement will virtually always benefit the child; an assumption not supported by research, which presents a more nuanced picture. There is indeed a large body of research literature indicating not only that divorce and separation has a long-term impact on outcomes for many children, but also that this can be mitigated by both parents remaining easily accessible to the child and involved in the parenting

---

[95] J. Hunt and A. Macleod (2008) p. 187. The CFA 2014 has furthered this trend by introducing a statutory requirement to attend a mediation, information and assessment meeting before initiating relevant family proceedings, including child arrangements order applications: CFA 2014, s. 10.

[96] F. Kaganas (2013) pp. 288–93.

[97] Legal Aid, Sentencing and Punishment of Offenders Act 2012; as discussed below, exceptions exist in a narrow range of cases, including those in which the applicant can demonstrate that they are the victim of domestic abuse.

role.[98] If contact can occur happily, it will certainly provide the child with many benefits, including the relationship with the parent and wider family and reinforcing the child's sense of identity and knowledge of origins.[99] There is strong evidence that these beneficial effects depend on the nature and quality of the contact and not the mere fact that contact takes place. The benefits of involvement are clearly linked with the quality of the relationship between the parent and child and the degree of ongoing conflict between the parents, rather than the amount of contact itself.[100] Conversely, risks are associated with contact that is unreliable, acrimonious or poor quality.[101] Longitudinal studies suggest that it is impossible to generalise over what is best for children after parental separation, since this will depend on the diversity of experiences and family processes. Overall, the evidence tends to demonstrate that it is not the structure of contact, in terms of the number and pattern of days and nights, that is most influential on child outcomes, but the quality and stability of the relationships involved.[102]

Given this research, an assumption that *court-ordered* contact will generally be beneficial for children does not accord with the complexities of parental disputes.[103] The outcomes for children are related to the extent to which they are exposed to inter-parental conflict, which will inevitably increase if the parents go to court. Further, there is considerable evidence that those cases that do reach court are characterised by allegations raising serious welfare concerns, such as domestic abuse, drug/alcohol addiction or child protection concerns.[104] In these cases, there is a risk that ongoing parental involvement could pose a serious risk to the child. As a result, it appears that court-enforced contact arrangements may actually harm some children, given that they provide further opportunities for conflict between the parents, including domestic abuse.[105] There is also a concern that many court orders are far too inflexible to accommodate children's own developmental and practical needs.[106] Successful parental involvement is responsive to the child's changing needs over time,[107] but there is evidence that contact declines over time,[108] with that decline being stronger in those cases that have had court involvement.[109] Research with young adults who had experienced parental

---

[98] S. Gilmore (2008), A. Mooney *et al.* (2009) and A. Goisis *et al.* (2016) all provide useful summaries of the existing research.

[99] C. Sturge and D. Glaser (2000) pp. 616–17 and 627.

[100] G. Harold and M. Murch (2005); S. Gilmore (2008).   [101] S. Gilmore (2008).

[102] J. Fortin *et al.* (2012).

[103] See research summaries, inter alia: J. Hunt with C. Roberts (2004); J. Fortin *et al.* (2006) pp. 212–14; S. Gilmore (2006) pp. 347–53; G. Harold and M. Murch (2005) pp. 188–9.

[104] E.g. in J. Hunt and A. Macleod (2008), 54 per cent of cases concerned such allegations. M. Harding and A. Newnham (2015) found that 45 per cent of their sample involved allegations that the parent was unable to parent or risked harm to the child, and 49 per cent involved domestic violence.

[105] J. Hunt with C. Roberts (2004) pp. 7–8; the issue of domestic abuse is discussed below.

[106] C. Smart (2004) pp. 492–5.   [107] J. Fortin *et al.* (2012).   [108] T. Haux and L. Platt (2015).

[109] A. Goisis *et al.* (2016), although, as they note, this may reflect the cohort of cases that go to court rather than the impact of the court itself.

separation as children has also emphasised the importance of listening to the children and involving them in decision-making over time.[110]

The evidence to support an assumption that parental involvement will generally be in a child's best interests in contested cases is much more finely balanced than the presumption and the approach of the courts suggests. Instead, resources may be better targeted at improving parental involvement and parenting quality before separation takes place. Reece argues that, given the 'shaky empirical basis' for the degree of importance placed on maintaining parental involvement, the law is not primarily concerned with child welfare, but is instead designed to reinstate the biological father into potentially fatherless families, thereby containing social anxiety about the collapse of the family.[111] This impression is reinforced by the way in which the courts have struggled to safeguard children's welfare in the context of domestic abuse.

(D) Risks to Children: Domestic Abuse

It is now widely recognised that all forms of domestic abuse put children at a serious risk of a myriad of harmful consequences. As Practice Direction 12J (PD12J) explains:

> Domestic abuse is harmful to children, and/or puts children at risk of harm, whether they are subjected to domestic abuse, or witness one of their parents being violent or abusive to the other parent, or live in a home in which domestic abuse is perpetrated (even if the child is too young to be conscious of the behaviour). Children may suffer direct physical, psychological and/or emotional harm from living with domestic abuse, and may also suffer harm indirectly where the domestic abuse impairs the parenting capacity of either or both of their parents.[112]

A wealth of research shows that growing up in an abusive household can seriously damage children's physical, emotional and psychological health[113] and there is a strong correlation between domestic abuse of an adult and child abuse.[114] For this reason, the Domestic Abuse Act 2021 recognises children who are brought up in abusive households as victims of that abuse.[115] Research also shows that those child arrangements disputes that end up in court often involve allegations of domestic abuse.[116] In many cases, abuse does not cease

---

[110] J. Fortin *et al.* (2012).   [111] H. Reece (2006) p. 548; S. Gilmore (2008).

[112] Practice Direction 12J: Child Arrangements and Contact Orders: Domestic Abuse and Harm para. 4 (revised October 2017).

[113] Summarised by C. Sturge and D. Glaser (2000) pp. 617–21; S. Walby (2004) para. 7.2.

[114] See research summaries in J. Hunt with C. Roberts (2004) p. 7; S. Walby (2004) para. 7.3.

[115] Domestic Abuse Act 2021, s. 3.

[116] Inter alia: J. Hunt and A. Macleod (2008) p. 183: 54 per cent of the cases reviewed involved 'serious welfare issues' and 50 per cent of these involved domestic violence allegations. M. Harding and A. Newnham (2015): 49 per cent of cases involved allegations of domestic violence. A review of the empirical literature demonstrates that these findings are typical, with researchers generally finding that 49–62 per cent of private child law cases involve allegations of domestic abuse: A. Barnett (2020a) p. 20. *Re H-N and others (Children) (Domestic Abuse:*

on separation and contact may be a particular danger point for further abuse.[117] Court orders (including consent orders) imposing child arrangements may therefore endanger not only the women, but also the children, in further incidents of intimidation, control and abuse.[118] For all of these reasons, allegations of domestic abuse must be taken seriously and dealt with effectively if courts are to keep children safe and promote their welfare. Unfortunately, the courts have struggled to achieve and maintain such an approach within a system that treats parental involvement as almost always in the interests of the child.[119] As Marianne Hester observes, private family law's emphasis on promoting contact, encouraging parental agreement and focusing on the future meant that its treatment of domestic abuse often appears to be on a different 'planet' from the domestic violence and child protection spheres, which are focused on intervention to deal with risk of harm.[120] The President of the Family Division has observed that this leads to a

> contradiction between the approach taken in child protection proceedings where, in bald terms, the message may be that there is to be absolutely no contact between the perpetrator and the child, as compared with private law proceedings where the emphasis may be upon contemplating some contact notwithstanding that domestic abuse has taken place.[121]

The starting point for the current approach to contact in cases of domestic abuse was signalled by the Court of Appeal's decision in *Re L (A Child) (Contact: Domestic Violence)*.[122] In *Re L*, influenced by 'the experts' report',[123] the Court of Appeal considered that the courts should take greater account of the impact of abuse on the family and the psychological dangers to children of ordering contact in such cases.[124] The Court of Appeal emphasised both the importance of establishing the truth or otherwise of the allegations and also the need for an assessment of the benefits and risks of contact for the individual child. Controversially, however, the court rejected the notion that they should introduce a presumption against contact being granted to a violent perpetrator.[125] The court instead reiterated the importance of the assumption that contact is of benefit to the child, albeit a benefit that might be outweighed in an individual case – despite evidence in the experts' report that such an assumption was not supported in cases of domestic abuse.[126]

Fact-Finding Hearings) [2021] EWCA Civ 448, [2021] 2 FLR 1116, at [3] suggested that the number was at least 40 per cent of private law children cases.

[117] This research is evaluated in detail by A. Barnett (2020a) ch. 6. See also J. Hunt with C. Roberts (2004) p. 7.

[118] H. Reece (2006) pp. 542–5; J. Birchall and S. Choudhry (2018).   [119] R. Hunter *et al.* (2020).

[120] See also M. Hester (2011).   [121] A. McFarlane (2017).   [122] [2000] 4 All ER 609.

[123] C. Sturge and D. Glaser (2000).

[124] [2000] 4 All ER 609, per Dame Elizabeth Butler-Sloss P, at 616, and per Thorpe LJ, at 642–3.

[125] [2000] 4 All ER 609, per Dame Elizabeth Butler-Sloss P, at 616, and per Thorpe LJ, at 643.

[126] S. Gilmore (2008) persuasively argues that the Court of Appeal decision did not properly represent the expert report and the lack of evidence in favour of an assumption that contact can be beneficial in domestic abuse cases.

Despite repeated further attempts to address these issues, research has continued to find that children are frequently being put at risk of harm by contact that is ordered by the court or agreed to by parents who feel that the courts are unwilling to safeguard children from the risks posed by domestic abuse.[127] Further, victims of domestic abuse report that the court process adds to the trauma that they have suffered and itself offers an opportunity for further abuse.[128] The senior judiciary in the Family Division have taken these concerns seriously[129] and recent revisions to PD12J seek to address many of the problems. It seems, however, that the practice direction is not always followed[130] and that past attempts to implement change have found it difficult to challenge the deep-seated pro-contact approach of those involved in the system.[131] Added to this, the severe restrictions placed on legal aid[132] mean that many of these cases now take place with one or both parties unrepresented, posing immense difficulties for judges in trying to ensure that evidence can be properly tested while protecting abuse victims from further trauma.[133] Without additional resources and a change in approach at ground level, it may be difficult for legislation and practice directions to bring about positive change in practice. For example, the definition of domestic abuse contained in PD12J was widened in 2014 and again in 2017 to recognise coercive control[134] and the broad array of abusive conduct that goes far beyond physical violence. The definition used is now reflected in the Domestic Abuse Act 2021, and includes 'physical or sexual abuse, violent or threatening behaviour, controlling or coercive behaviour, economic abuse, and psychological, emotional and other abuse'.[135] Despite this broadening definition, there are

---

[127] R. Hunter et al. (2020); Women's Aid (2016).

[128] R. Hunter et al. (2020), J. Birchall and S. Choudhry (2018); APPG on Domestic Violence (2016).

[129] A. McFarlane (2017); Review of Practice Direction 12J FRP (2010) Child Arrangement and Contact Orders: Domestic Violence and Harm (2017) 'Cobb review'.

[130] A. Barnett (2020a) p. 113. E.g. Re D (Appeal: Failure of Case Management) [2017] EWHC 1907 (Fam), [2017] 3 FCR 451; Re CB (International Relocation: Domestic Abuse) [2017] EWFC 39, [2017] 3 FCR 273; J. Birchall and S. Choudhry (2018).

[131] R. Hunter et al. (2020); L. Trinder et al. (2006). E.g. Re H (Contact: Domestic Violence) [2005] EWCA Civ 1404, [2006] 1 FLR 943. See also Re V (Children) [2008] EWCA Civ 635, unreported.

[132] Legal Aid, Sentencing and Punishment of Offenders Act 2012; although there are exceptions for victims of domestic abuse, those victims have often found it difficult to satisfy these exceptions in practice. A successful challenge to the evidential requirements in R (on the application of Rights of Women) v. Lord Chancellor [2016] EWCA Civ 91, [2016] All ER (D) 177 has led to some improvement: Civil Legal Aid (Procedure) (Amendment) (No. 2) Regulations 2017.

[133] The problems are discussed by M. Coy et al. (2015). See e.g. Re J (Children) [2018] EWCA Civ 115, [2018] 2 FLR 998. A good example of the problems faced at the family court level can be seen in Mr JY v. Ms RY, Case No. MB17P00250 Middlesbrough Family Court (26 April 2018, unreported), esp. at [35].

[134] So aligning with the criminal law, which recognises coercive and controlling behaviour as domestic abuse; Serious Crime Act 2015, s. 76.

[135] Domestic Abuse Act 2021, s. 1.

repeated reports that courts focus on physical abuse, minimising other forms of abuse.[136] This approach has been reinforced by a fact-finding process that concentrates on discrete incidents and can impede the ability of the court to recognise patterns of abuse, especially coercion and control. The Court of Appeal has emphasised the importance of ensuring that fact-finding is conducted in a way that allows allegations of all forms of domestic abuse to be tested and proven, in particular by ensuring that the court is able to consider patterns of abusive behaviour.[137] Such a change is vital if courts are to be able to identify the wide range of abuse that is now recognised as harmful to children. Disappointingly, the Court of Appeal has given little guidance as to how this should be achieved in practice. Given the enormous resource pressure under which the family courts are operating, additional time for fact-finding will be very difficult to find without adding further delay, which is itself harmful to children. Without increased resources and improved judicial training, it will be difficult to protect children from the harmful situations that are now better recognised in the law and practice direction.

An important issue for children is the question of how the presumption of parental involvement applies in circumstances of domestic abuse. As explained above, the presumption only applies if the parent can be involved in the child's life without putting the child at risk of suffering harm. PD12J reminds the court that in each case there must be careful consideration of whether the presumption applies[138] and it might be thought that this will obviate the risk of a child being required to have contact with an abusive parent, although this is not always the case in practice.[139] Disapplying the presumption requires evidence, which is often difficult to achieve, especially outside of the arena of physical abuse. The difficulties of proof, particularly in an environment of reduced funding, mean that it can be difficult to establish the evidence base needed to displace the presumption in an abusive relationship.[140] Mothers who raise domestic abuse, but fail to prove it in court, have long risked being labelled as implacably hostile or seen as alienating their children from their father.[141] On the other hand, false allegations of domestic abuse can cause enormous damage to fathers and alienation can destroy relationships between parents and children. The ECtHR has found that failure to take steps to address

[136] Hunter *et al.* (2020); M. Coy *et al.* (2015); R. Hunter and A. Barnett (2013); A. Barnett (2017).
[137] *Re H-N and others (Children) (Domestic Abuse: Fact-Finding Hearings)* [2021] EWCA Civ 448, [2021] 2 FLR 1116.
[138] PD12J para. 7.
[139] J. Harwood (2021) found that there was little evidence that the presumption had had any significant impact in domestic abuse cases given the pre-existing practice of prioritising contact in almost all circumstances.
[140] In the sample of cases considered by M. Harding and A. Newnham (2015), steps to investigate the truth of the allegations were undertaken in fewer than a quarter of the cases in which allegations of domestic abuse were made, with only eight of the eighty-six cases progressing to a full fact-finding hearing: pp. 42–4.
[141] R. Hunter *et al.* (2020) ch. 5.

alienation can breach the rights of parents and children, particularly under Article 8.[142] There is evidence that alienation is being raised more frequently by fathers accused of abuse.[143] In such cases, courts are faced with serious allegations by both parties and any attempt to resolve those allegations will require careful findings of fact. For these reasons, PD12J emphasises the importance of early consideration of the need for fact-finding,[144] a point reinforced by the Court of Appeal in *Re J (Children)*.[145] As *Re J* makes clear, allegations of alienation also require fact-finding before they can be taken into account; accusations of 'alienation' should be confined to those cases of actual manipulation and not used loosely as a threat to be deployed whenever children show resistance to contact or allegations of abuse are not proven.[146] At present, there are high stakes for abuse victims who may run the gauntlet of a traumatic court battle, only to find themselves labelled as harming the child by 'alienating them' on the basis of that they have raised allegations of abuse. This creates real risks for children who find it difficult to make their voices heard if alienation is alleged and risk being moved to live with the abusive parent to counter the 'alienation'.[147] Given these risks, victims of domestic abuse may judge that it is better to agree to arrangements rather than risk adverse judgment in court. PD12J is emphatic that it also applies to consent orders and that no consent order should be made without careful scrutiny of its terms and consideration of all of the evidence, including whether to order welfare reports.[148] Nonetheless, researchers have long reported women feeling coerced into agreeing to unsafe contact arrangements in order to appear 'reasonable'.[149] Efforts to improve practice in the courts will come to naught if the women themselves feel unable to raise their experience of abuse and fears for their children.

If the allegations of domestic abuse are made out, the primary focus in the practice direction is on establishing contact that does not expose the child to an 'unmanageable'[150] risk of harm rather than prohibiting contact altogether.

---

[142] E.g. *I.S. and others* v. *Malta*, App. No. 9410/20, decided 18 March 2021. See Chapter 12 for discussion of the child's right to be heard in the context of parental alienation.

[143] A. Barnett (2020b).

[144] PD12J paras 18 and 29: if the court considers that fact-finding is not necessary, the order must record the reasons for that conclusion.

[145] In *Re J (Children)* [2018] EWCA Civ 115, [2018] 2 FLR 998, at [38]–[56], the case concerned a mother who made extensive allegations of physical violence, controlling behaviour and rape, and a father who denied those allegations and accused the mother of fabricating them to alienate the children from him. No fact-finding had been conducted, in part because the father was a litigant in person and the court had not been able to find a way of testing the evidence without subjecting the mother to cross-examination by her alleged rapist and abuser. The Court of Appeal considered that the children were at risk from at least one parent, either due to domestic abuse or alienation, but without fact-finding, the court was unable to determine which.

[146] S. Gilmore (2020).   [147] See Chapter 12 and discussion of enforcement below.

[148] PD12J paras 6 and 8.

[149] R. Hunter *et al.* (2020) pp. 144–5; J. Masson (2006) p. 1044; L. Trinder *et al.* (2006).

[150] PD12J para. 35.

PD12J directs that contact should only be ordered if the court is satisfied that the 'physical and emotional safety of the child and the parent with whom the child is living can, as far as possible, be secured before, during and after contact, and that the parent with whom the child is living will not be subjected to further domestic abuse by the other parent'.[151] The court should consider the effect of the abuse and future contact on the child and parent in the past, the perpetrator's ability to change and likely behaviour during future contact.[152] Although the guidance stresses the need for orders not to endanger the parent or child, in practice, this can come into tension with the Court of Appeal's direction that courts must 'grapple with all the available alternatives before abandoning hope of achieving some contact'.[153] Research by Cafcass found that in a substantial minority of cases in which domestic abuse was alleged, unsupervised contact was ordered from the first hearing.[154] There is continuing faith in indirect contact as a last resort, even in cases involving proved domestic abuse,[155] with an order for supervised or supported contact[156] with family members or at a contact centre being a preferred option.[157] Such arrangements are often far from ideal; many of the untrained volunteers maintain a pro-contact stance which prevents their paying sufficient heed to the need to protect mothers and children from abuse, even when alerted to the danger.[158] Supervised contact can be a means of fostering a relationship that is

---

[151] Ibid. paras 35 and 36.   [152] Ibid. para. 37.

[153] *Re C (A Child) (Suspension of Contact)* [2011] EWCA Civ 521, [2011] 2 FLR 912, at [47]; see above.

[154] Cafcass and Women's Aid (2017): 23 per cent of cases involving allegations of domestic abuse resulted in supervised contact at the first hearing, as opposed to 55 per cent of cases in which there were no such allegations. The research considered a representative sample of 216 cases with Cafcass involvement over a 12-month period 2015–16.

[155] E.g. *Re G (Domestic Violence: Direct Contact)* [2001] 2 FCR 134: indirect contact ordered (cards and presents at Christmas and birthdays) despite the fact that the father had murdered the mother, had no understanding of his child's needs and the child's own fear of him and reluctance to see him; *Re A (Contact: Witness Protection Scheme)* [2005] EWHC 2189 (Fam), [2006] 2 FLR 551: interim provision for indirect contact (by video contact) despite the father's violent treatment of the mother, and the risk of the child being harmed through abduction to Pakistan or by his mother being subjected to further violence by his father or his paternal extended family; *Re F (Indirect Contact)* [2006] EWCA Civ 1426, [2007] 1 FLR 1015: mother's appeal against an indirect contact turned down despite, inter alia: the children's guardian's recommendation against it; the father's history of serious and uncontrollable violence against the mother; his repeated failure to comply with non-molestation orders (sixty-eight breaches), leading to periods of imprisonment; findings of the risks to the mother and child if he tracked them down (the mother and child having been forced to move ten times over 5 years to escape his attentions); the further risks to the child and mother's physical safety and emotional stability involved in indirect contact. Indirect contact to be organised by Cafcass Legal.

[156] E.g. *Re CB (International Relocation: Domestic Abuse)* [2017] EWFC 39, [2017] 3 FCR 273, discussed above.

[157] 'Supervised contact' is provided by specialist contact centres involving contact between the non-resident parent and child in the presence of professionally trained qualified staff; cf. 'supported contact', which is usually provided (in non-dedicated buildings) in communal contact areas, staffed by untrained volunteers.

[158] J. Birchall and S. Choudhry (2018) pp. 38–40 record the experiences of victims of domestic abuse and the way in which supervised contact can lead to risk to safety and child welfare.

emotionally and psychologically damaging even if the child can be kept physically safe.[159] Arguably, the courts should place less weight on the need to 'grapple' with alternatives to allow contact to take place and more on the research evidence that such relationships can be immensely harmful.[160] Children surely have a right *not* to have contact of any kind with a parent who has been found to abuse them or their family members.[161]

(E) Enforcing Child Arrangements Orders

A common complaint of non-resident parents is that even if they obtain a favourable outcome from the courts, the other party may disobey the order with impunity. Enforcement of child arrangements orders has presented an ongoing problem for the courts. On the one hand, if the relationship is genuinely in the best interests of the child, failure to enforce the order could deprive the child of their right to that relationship and the benefits that go with it. On the other hand, research consistently shows that the most common reasons for failure to comply with such orders relate to serious welfare concerns, including domestic abuse, and high conflict on the part of both parents.[162] There are extreme examples of parents who, in the absence of welfare concerns, demonstrate implacable hostility towards the other and who behave entirely selfishly when opposing contact, although these cases are relatively infrequent.[163] While parents who raise genuine concerns about contact risk being classified as 'implacably hostile',[164] those parents who routinely fail to fulfil contact arrangements either at all, or punctually, are not castigated 'implacably irresponsible'.[165] The law does little, if anything, to

---

[159] Supervised contact is particularly dangerous in cases of child sexual abuse where it might be used to continue grooming of the child: C. Macaskill (2002) p. 60 provides a chilling description of supervised contact visits between a sexually abusive father and his 5-year-old daughter.

[160] C. Sturge and D. Glaser (2000) p. 624: contact would provide children with no advantage unless the non-resident parent showed, inter alia: acknowledgement of the domestic violence; an awareness of the inappropriate nature of their conduct; regret; and an understanding of the impact of their behaviour on their ex-partner, in the past and currently.

[161] E.g. *Re M and B (Children) (Contact: Domestic Violence)* [2001] 1 FCR 116: an order for indirect contact was replaced, on appeal, by an order for no contact and a moratorium (under CA 1989, s. 91(14)) on the violent father reapplying for contact within 2 years without court leave. Per Thorpe LJ: the trial judge should have considered the impact of indirect contact on the mother's mental health, she having been subjected to 6 years of serious domestic violence culminating in the father's imprisonment.

[162] Inter alia: A. Buchanan *et al.* (2001) pp. 15–18; H. Rhoades (2002) pp. 75–6; L. Trinder *et al.* (2005) ch. 7, (2006) p. 94; H. Reece (2006) p. 552; J. Hunt and A. Macleod (2008) p. 9; Trinder *et al.* (2013).

[163] J. Hunt and A. Macleod (2008) pp. 192–5. See also Trinder *et al.* (2013), discussed further below.

[164] In *Re A (A Child)* [2013] EWCA Civ 1104, [2014] 1 FLR 1185, at [4], this was described as a label familiar to all who practice in the family courts.

[165] C. Smart and B. Neale (1997) p. 336. See also H. Rhoades (2002) pp. 78–9.

require a reluctant parent to have contact with their child, however much the child might wish for that relationship.

Although the Strasbourg case law is far from clear cut, it does establish that the state has a positive obligation to take all necessary steps as can *reasonably* be demanded in the circumstances of the case to facilitate a reunion between child and parent and as swiftly as possible.[166] The ECtHR has, however, stressed that the domestic courts' duty in this respect is not absolute.[167] It accepts that if the child has been living for some years without contact with the non-resident parent, any reunion may require preparation, perhaps with the assistance of psychologists or psychiatrists.[168] The court has even acknowledged that reunion may be impossible: the state's obligation to apply coercion is limited by the need to take the best interests of the child into account and to strike a fair balance between the rights of the absent parent and those of the child.[169] Nor is the ECtHR entirely consistent in its approach to children who strongly resist the enforcement of adults' claims. It has stressed, on the one hand, that children's opinions should be taken into account once they attain the necessary maturity to express them.[170] But, on the other hand, it has warned of the ability of adults to manipulate children,[171] and has emphasised that there may be an obligation on the state to examine the reasons for the children's objections and to consider the possibility that the child is being 'alienated' by the resident parent.[172]

The domestic courts have recognised the importance of these obligations. For example, in *Re A (A Child)*,[173] the Court of Appeal found that there had been a breach of the Article 8 rights of a father and child in a situation where litigation over the course of 12 years, with over 100 hearings, had ended with no order for contact given the fierce opposition of the then 13-year-old child. Yet, as John Eekelaar notes, the case might be better seen as an example of the inherent difficulties that courts face in trying to respond to the shifting complexities of individual behaviour.[174] Far from being a case in which the courts had failed to act, the case was characterised by extensive, though ineffective, action. The case might better be seen as demonstrating the limits

---

[166] Inter alia: *Hokkanen v. Finland* (1994) 19 EHRR 139, at [58]; *Ignaccolo-Zenide v. Romania* (2001) 31 EHRR 7; *Sylvester v. Austria* [2003] 2 FLR 210; *Hansen v. Turkey* [2004] 1 FLR 142; *Aneva v. Bulgaria* (66997/13) unreported, Judgment of 6 April 2017.

[167] The classic exposition of this principle is set out in *Hokkanen v. Finland* (1994) 19 EHRR 139, at [58].

[168] *Ignaccolo-Zenide v. Romania* (2001) 31 EHRR 7, at [112]; *Hansen v. Turkey* [2004] 1 FLR 142, at [103].

[169] Inter alia: *Ignaccolo-Zenide v. Romania* (2001) 31 EHRR 7, at [94]; *Hansen v. Turkey* [2004] 1 FLR 142, at [98]; *Wdowiak v. Poland* [2017] ECHR 133.

[170] *Pini and Bertani; Manera and Atripaldi v. Romania* [2005] 2 FLR 596, at [164].

[171] E.g. *S and G v. Italy* [2000] 2 FLR 771, at 210.

[172] *K.B. v. Croatia*, App. No. 36216/13, unreported, Judgment of 14 March 2017.

[173] [2013] EWCA Civ 1104, [2014] 1 FLR 1185.

[174] J. Eekelaar (2014). The child had had contact with the father at times during this period, including living with him for a period of nearly a year.

of the courts' ability to forge meaningful relationships in highly contested cases. The complexity of enforcement cases is demonstrated by Trinder *et al.*'s research.[175] They found that only 4 per cent of cases in their sample[176] concerned implacably hostile parents. Instead, the majority of cases (55 per cent) involved high conflict, in which the parents were unable to work together to deal with everyday problems arising in the course of contact. Other disputes arose in the context of significant welfare concerns (31 per cent) or older children's hostility (10 per cent).[177] The researchers found that the courts primarily focused on solving the underlying problems impeding the relationships, rather than on punishing breaches of the order,[178] although there are inevitably limits to the ability of the courts to control the minutiae of hostile relationships.

Courts faced with an intractable dispute have a difficult task in working out the limits of the requirement to attempt to re-establish contact. In many cases, the problem-solving approach found in Trinder *et al.*'s study is likely to be more productive than a punitive approach. One difficulty with a punitive approach is that sanctions imposed on a recalcitrant parent are also likely to be damaging to the children. This is particularly true of imprisonment which, while available,[179] deprives the children of their primary carer and has traditionally been seen as a remedy of last resort.[180] Although the welfare of the child is not paramount in incarceration cases, the courts are clear that it should never be ordered without carefully considering the effect on the children.[181] Similarly, fining mothers already short of money merely results in children going without. Unpaid work orders offer a punitive alternative that may have less direct impact on the child,[182] although these too seem to have been rarely used.[183] While proposals for further punitive options, including curfews, passport and driving licence confiscation, have been suggested, none has

---

[175] Trinder *et al.* (2013).

[176] The research considered 205 cases, consisting of all of the enforcement applications made within a specified period.

[177] Trinder *et al.* (2013) pp. 29–36. The researchers distinguished children's opposition cases from implacable cases by considering whether the child's opposition to contact was independent from the views of the parent. In many of these cases, the researchers considered that the child's opposition was based on an understandable reaction to the behaviour of the non-resident parent; e.g. in one case, two teenagers resisted contact with their father after witnessing him assaulting his new partner.

[178] Trinder *et al.* (2013) ch. 6.

[179] *Re D (Intractable Contact Dispute: Publicity)* [2004] EWHC 727 (Fam), [2004] 1 FLR 1226, per Munby J, at [56]–[57]. See also *Re S (Contact Dispute: Committal)* [2004] EWCA Civ 1790, [2005] 1 FLR 812; *Richards* v. *Martin* [2017] EWHC 2187 (Fam), [2018] 1 FCR 256.

[180] *Re M (Contact Order: Committal)* [1999] 1 FLR 810, per Ward LJ, at 825.

[181] *Re V (Children)* [2008] EWCA Civ 635, unreported, per Wall LJ, at [36]. See also compensation orders, available under CA 1989, s. 11O.

[182] CA 1989, s. 11J–L: the court must be satisfied that an enforcement order is 'necessary' to secure compliance and that the impact of the enforcement order on the recipient is 'proportionate to the seriousness of the breach'. Welfare must be taken into account, but is not paramount.

[183] Trinder *et al.* (2013) ch. 10.

been introduced. Further, there is troubling evidence from abroad that an authoritarian approach to the enforcement of contact orders produces judicial decision-making that sometimes endangers children's safety.[184] The alternative of requiring parents to undergo therapeutic intervention such as 'contact activities', including receiving information, advice, counselling and/or guidance sessions,[185] may well improve their ability to work together, provided that intervention is aimed at addressing the underlying reasons for the dispute.[186]

One final approach that is sometimes attempted is to change the child's primary residence from the parent who is perceived to be obstructing contact, to the other parent, or alternative carer, who will support the relationship with both parents. Any order changing the child's residence will be determined on the basis of the welfare principle and will need to take into account the harm that can be done in moving a child from their established home, as well as the potential benefits of contact. A good example of the problems that can result in such cases can be seen in *Re S (Transfer of Residence)*,[187] in which the residence of 11-year-old S was transferred from his mother, with whom he had lived with since birth, to his father, whom he had not seen for 4 years. The court took this drastic action on the understanding that S's opposition was due to his 'alienation' from his father and that only by making a decisive break could that alienation be countered. Nonetheless, S continued to oppose contact, successfully applied to go into interim foster care rather than being transferred immediately to his father and refused to cooperate on any level with attempts to reintroduce a relationship with his father. Eventually, the father abandoned attempts to enforce the order, given S's continued resistance and evidence of the serious impact that the situation was having on S's mental health. The case is a good example of the way in which children's well-being can be harmed by attempts to enforce contact and the difficulty of coercing a relationship in the face of sustained opposition from an older child. While a change of residence may be appropriate in some cases, the potential risks from disruption mean that these cases will be relatively rare. At one time, change of residence was said to be a 'judicial weapon of last resort',[188] but recent cases have emphasised that this phrase should not be used to impose a 'gloss' on the welfare principle.[189] Decisions on change of residence should be made on the basis of the child's welfare and not as an attempt to enforce the order as such. Assessment of the child's welfare will require careful scrutiny of the risks of change, as well as the

---

[184] H. Rhoades (2002).   [185] CA 1989, s. 11A(5).

[186] A good example of a therapeutic approach to an intractable case can be seen in *Re Q (A Child)* [2015] EWCA Civ 991, [2016] 2 FLR 287.

[187] The various stages of the case are reported at: [2010] EWHC 192 (Fam), [2010] 1 FLR 1785 (initial order for transfer); [2010] EWCA Civ 325 (appeal against that order; and [2011] 1 FLR 1789 (eventual abandonment of attempt to transfer).

[188] *Re A (Residence Order)* [2009] EWCA Civ 1141, [2010] 1 FLR 1083, at [18].

[189] *Re H (Parental Alienation)* [2019] EWHC 2723 (Fam), [2020] 1 FLR 401, esp. at [5]. See also *Re L (A Child)* [2019] EWHC 867 (Fam), [2019] 2 FCR 864.

status quo, and the potentially conflicting rights of the child to relationships and family stability, and to be heard.

Overall, there remain real questions over the extent to which punitive enforcement powers are able to improve children's well-being in many cases. As Smart and Neale commented with some prescience, 'the law is beginning to look like a lever for the powerful to use against the vulnerable, rather than a measure to safeguard the welfare of children'.[190] This is particularly so in cases such as *Re S*, where the measures taken to enforce contact risk real harm. It also resonates in those high-conflict cases where research suggests that court-ordered contact may cause more harm than good.

(F) Conclusion: The Influence of Rights

The Strasbourg case law on Article 8 and parental contact has had a strong and explicit influence on the development of the courts' current approach to child arrangements orders. Whether this law offers true protection for children's rights is more uncertain. The Strasbourg approach of balancing children's interests against parents' rights, together with the emphasis put on the importance of parental relationships in assessing a child's welfare, means that the law is more effective at protecting children's right *to* a relationship than to be protected *from* that relationship. It is notable that children's rights, other than the right to family life, are rarely mentioned in the case law, even in cases involving domestic abuse, despite the established right of children to be protected from witnessing or being the victim of domestic abuse.[191] Where such rights are mentioned, they are rarely assessed in detail; instead, the child's rights are often all too easily subsumed into the rights of adult seeking contact, given the 'mutual enjoyment' approach.[192]

One important right of the child which is undoubtedly not adequately protected by current practice is the child's right to be heard in matters concerning them.[193] The severe restrictions on public funding of private family cases mean that both children and parents find it difficult to obtain legal advice or representation in child arrangements cases or to ensure that children's views are properly heard or their welfare properly assessed.[194] The push towards private resolution of family disputes can also marginalise the views of children. For example, the Family Mediation Council's Code of Practice for Family Mediators

---

[190] C. Smart and B. Neale (1997) p. 336.

[191] *Eremia* v. *Moldova* (2014) 58 EHRR 2 decided under Art. 8, although Art. 3 was applied in the case of their mother who had been the direct victim of the physical assaults.

[192] E.g. in *Re CB (International Relocation: Domestic Abuse)* [2017] EWFC 39, [2017] 3 FCR 273, at [66], the child's right to protection is briefly mentioned, as is that of the mother, but no further analysis of the extent of this right or how it should be balanced against the father's right to contact is given.

[193] CRC, Art. 12; see further discussion of children's participation in family proceedings in Chapter 12.

[194] JCHR (2018) paras 56–61.

requires mediators to have 'particular regard' to the welfare of the children and to encourage the parties to 'focus on the needs and interests of the children as well as on their own'.[195] This requirement falls far short of the paramountcy test that applies in domestic law. Similarly, the provisions on consulting children only require the mediator to 'encourage the Participants to consider the children's wishes and feelings',[196] making the child's participation as contingent on the willingness of their parents to hear them. The emphasis of mediation is on achieving parental agreement rather than directing the content of that agreement, making it difficult to accommodate a requirement on the mediator to ensure that the child's welfare is paramount or that particular weight is given to the child's views.[197] The current practice means that it is increasingly unlikely that children involved in disputes will have the opportunity to ensure that their views are heard or their welfare properly assessed.

Where children's views are heard before the court, there remains a difficult question as to what should be done where the child expresses a sustained and considered objection to continuing to have a relationship with their parent. It is difficult to imagine another situation in which a person can be required to have a relationship against their will, particularly under the guise of protecting their own rights. Certainly, reluctant parents are not required to see their children, however important that relationship might be to the child. The courts are alert to the potential for children to be manipulated or to feel compelled to express views that do not reflect their actual feelings.[198] For this reason, courts will often draw a distinction between the expressed views of the child and their 'ascertainable' views, which will take into account their actions and any expert evidence as to manipulation.[199] It is, however, important that children who object to contact are not assumed to be 'alienated' in circumstances in which they may have good reason not to want to see their parent. Research with young adults who had been the subject of contact disputes as children demonstrates that those who objected to contact usually did so on the basis of considered reasons such as lack of parental interest or feeling unsafe or neglected by the parent in question.[200] Distinguishing parental manipulation from genuine objections can be difficult in practice, given the absence of a sound empirical basis on which to do so.[201] While the views of a child are not determinative, the Strasbourg court has repeatedly observed, relationships

---

[195] FMC (2018) para. 5.3.

[196] Ibid. para. 6.6.1, although the code also states that children over 10 should be offered the opportunity to be heard.

[197] M. Maclean and J. Eekelaar (2016) pp. 87–91. Discussed further in Chapter 12.

[198] As discussed above, the ECtHR has emphasised that states have a positive obligation to investigate the reason for the child's views if manipulation is suspected: *K.B.* v. *Croatia*, App. No. 36216/13, unreported, Judgment of 14 March 2017.

[199] E.g. *Re H (Children)* [2014] EWCA Civ 733.

[200] J. Fortin *et al.* (2012); see also the similar findings of Trinder *et al.* (2013) pp. 29–36, discussed above.

[201] J. Doughty *et al.* (2020).

are at heart mutual. To force a relationship[202] against well-considered objections is unlikely to result in a successful relationship and reinforces the impression that the presumption of parental involvement is more concerned with the rights of the parents rather than those of the child.[203]

(4) The Right to Be Brought Up by Parents? Disputes between Parents and Other Carers

(A) Children's Upbringing Outside of Parental Relationships

There are many situations in which children are brought up outside of their parental family. In cases where the state has intervened to remove children and place them in alternative care, the process is subject to extensive regulation designed to safeguard the welfare of the child and to protect the rights of parents and children.[204] Where arrangements are made privately, without direct state intervention, they take place outside of this framework and the safeguards that it provides. Such arrangements take many forms. In some cases, family members, such as grandparents, have stepped in to care for a child in circumstances in which the parents are unable or unwilling to do so.[205] These arrangements may be formalised through a child arrangements order or a special guardianship order, or may be organised without formal recognition. Other children are cared for under private fostering arrangements,[206] with carers who are not related to them. No one really knows how many such private fostering arrangements exist up and down the country, largely because birth parents and fosterers alike fail to notify their local authority (LA) of the arrangements they are entering into.[207]

---

[202] See Munby P's view that a parent has an obligation to deal with a 'rebellious teenager' refusing to see her father 'by argument, persuasion, cajolement, blandishments, inducements, sanctions (e.g. "grounding" or the confiscation of mobile phones, computers or other electronic equipment) or threats falling short of brute force': *Re H-B (Children) (Contact: Prohibition on Further Applications)* [2015] EWCA Civ 389, [2015] 2 FCR 581. The breakdown in the relationship had started when the father's new wife had 'behaved inappropriately' to the then 9-year-old by grabbing her and holding her down, causing bruising. The father had failed to intervene and minimised its seriousness. It is not difficult to imagine why a young child in such circumstances might feel unsafe and unwelcome in the home, even if the incident might appear minor to an adult, and that the use of threats to force the relationship further would be unlikely to dispel those fears.

[203] *K.B. v. Croatia*, App. No. 36216/13, unreported, Judgment of 14 March 2017, at [143] makes it clear that the views of children are not necessarily sufficient to override the *parent's* interest in contact.

[204] Considered further in Chapter 15.

[205] E.g. *Re B (A Child) (Residence: Biological Parent)* [2009] UKSC 5, [2009] 1 WLR 2496, discussed further below.

[206] CA 1989, s. 66(1) and (2): a 'privately fostered child' is a child under the age of 16 who is cared for and provided with accommodation for more than 28 days by someone *other* than their parent, someone with parental responsibility or a relative.

[207] Children (Private Arrangements for Fostering) Regulations 2005 (SI 2005/1533), regs 3–4: foster carers are obliged to notify the LA of an intention to foster a child privately at least 6 weeks before the fostering arrangement starts. In 2014/15, the last year for which statistics are available, 1,560 children were reported as being in a private foster arrangement, although this

Consequently, LAs often find it difficult to exercise any real control over the placement or welfare of privately fostered children.[208] Private foster arrangements take place for a wide range of reasons, including situations where the child's parents are no longer able to care for them or where relationships between parents and older children have broken down.[209] The majority of private foster arrangements concern children who were born outside of the UK;[210] these children are in the UK without their parents for diverse reasons, from education to child trafficking.[211] Consequently, the needs of children in these arrangements vary considerably, from those who are in need of a relatively short-term home for a particular purpose, to long-term relationships of care, or situations of exploitation and abuse.

In circumstances of privately arranged alternative care, disputes can arise if the parents seek to have the child returned and meet opposition from the carer. In principle, there is nothing to prevent the parents visiting the carers in person and demanding that their child be handed over to them there and then. Unless they have already taken legal steps to protect their continued care of the child against the parents' wishes, carers confronted by parents in this way have no legal authority to retain the child. Where carers do have legal authority, or seek to obtain it, the dispute is resolved by the courts through private law orders[212] and determined under the welfare principle.[213] Thus, although the parents may risk losing the ability to raise the child, the dispute is framed in a very different way from public law cases, in which the state must first demonstrate significant harm before showing that it is in the child's best interests to be removed.[214] The courts have struggled to maintain a consistent approach to these disputes. Judicial approaches to the importance of the parental relationship to the child's welfare have changed over time, as have views on the relevance, if any, of the purported right of parents to raise their child or the right of children to be brought up by their parents. Some of the case law demonstrates how the language of children's rights can be distorted to

is likely to be a substantial underestimate; DfE (2015). Central government has ceased to collect statistics on reported private fostering arrangements, largely because so many arrangements are not notified.

[208] Ofsted (2014). CA 1989, s. 67 and Children (Private Arrangements for Fostering) Regulations 2005 (SI 2005/1533): the LA must visit the proposed foster carers to satisfy themselves of the suitability of the proposed arrangements, then visit every 6 weeks within the first year of the arrangement and thereafter every 12 weeks.

[209] Ofsted (2014).

[210] DfE (2015); only 37 per cent of children in reported private foster care were born in the UK.

[211] DCSF Advisory Group (2010).

[212] In the past, foster carers often utilised the wardship jurisdiction to gain authority for continued care of a foster child. Today, they would apply for a child arrangements order or special guardianship order under CA 1989, ss 8 and 14A.

[213] CA 1989, s. 1.

[214] Although the context of the dispute is different in that in the cases considered in this section, the child is usually already living with the alternative carers rather than being removed from their parents' care, nonetheless in both situations the parents may be deprived of the ability to bring their children up: see further Chapter 15.

mask concerns over parents being deprived of their children's care.[215] Indeed, the child's right to protection from psychological harm has, at times, been sacrificed to promoting the biological tie between children and their parents. The changing tides of judicial approach to these disputes well-illustrates the difficulty of reconciling the individual child's rights with the general understanding that in the ordinary case children will be best served by an upbringing with their parents.

(B) No Presumption Favouring the Birth Parents

Despite its venerable age, the House of Lords' decision in *J* v. *C*[216] has retained its significance. It remains one of the best factual examples of a dispute between birth parents and carers arising out of an informal fostering arrangement. The House of Lords considered it to be against the best interests of a 10-year-old boy to return him to his Spanish parents in Spain, after 7 years in the care of English foster parents. The decision established that all the evidence relating to where the child should live should be weighed together, with no presumption favouring his birth parents. Indeed, Lord MacDermott quoted with approval the words of Wilberforce J in an earlier adoption decision:

> The tie ... between the child and his natural father (or any other relative) may properly be regarded in this connexion, not on the basis that the person concerned has a claim which he has a right to have satisfied, but, only if, and to the extent that, the conclusion can be drawn that the child will benefit from the recognition of this tie.[217]

In evidential terms, the birth parents in *J* v. *C* were not deemed to occupy a more favourable position to retrieve their son than the foster carers. The decision established that although the claims of birth parents would often have great weight and cogency, they had to be 'assessed and weighed in their bearing on the welfare of the child in conjunction with all other factors relevant to that issue'.[218] The nearest that Lord MacDermott went to suggesting that birth parents occupied a special position in such disputes was to comment:

> While there is now no rule of law that the rights and wishes of unimpeachable parents must prevail over other considerations, such rights and wishes, recognised as they are by nature and society, can be capable of ministering to the total welfare of the child in a special way, and must therefore preponderate in many cases.[219]

The decision in *J* v. *C* was controversial for a number of reasons. In particular, it suggested that the special relationship and tie between birth parents and

---

[215] K. Everett and L. Yeatman, L (2010) chart the changing approach of the courts.
[216] [1970] AC 668.
[217] *Re Adoption Application No. 41/61 (No. 2)* [1963] 2 All ER 1082, at 1085.
[218] [1970] AC 668, per Lord MacDermott, at 713.   [219] Ibid. at 715.

children carried no significant weight.[220] Consequently, in disputes of this kind, there was no onus on the foster carers to overturn a legal presumption favouring continuation of the birth parents' care; rather, it was the job of the court to assess which course of action would promote the child's best interests. As Eekelaar commented, 'parental claims have no independent weight but are relevant only as evidence as to what course is best for the child'.[221] *J* v. *C* was subsequently applied to other disputes of this kind, with birth parents being denied special treatment. The courts did not confine themselves to assessing the disruption that children would suffer when being uprooted from their homes with their foster carers after some years. They also considered it perfectly appropriate to compare the advantages of family life offered by the foster carers, with the natural care and affection that birth parents were able to offer.[222] Indeed, case law indicated the judiciary placing the blood tie between a child and his or her birth parents in the context of a variety of other factors.[223]

(C) The Child's 'Prima Facie Right' to an Upbringing by Birth Parents?

The unemotional way in which the judiciary considered the value of maintaining the blood tie between parent and child was soon to give way to a rather different approach. This utilised the concept of children's rights to promote what, in reality, appeared to be concerns about parents' rights. Indeed, the Court of Appeal now seemed to see the child–parent tie in an entirely different light, carrying a far greater significance. It produced an evidential formula which considerably favoured birth parents. In a new line of cases, starting with *Re K (A Minor) (Ward: Care and Control)*,[224] the judiciary made it clear that it was wrong for courts to weigh up the evidence relevant to the child's future life with one family rather than the other, before deciding whether to order the child's return to his or her birth parents:

> The question was not: where would R get the better home? The question was: was it demonstrated that the welfare of the child positively demanded the displacement of the parental right? The word 'right' is not really accurate in so far as it might connote something in the nature of a property right (which it is not) but it will serve for present purposes. The 'right', if there is one, is perhaps more that of the child.[225]

---

[220] J. Eekelaar (1973) p. 217.   [221] Ibid. p. 216.

[222] E.g. *Re H (A Minor) (Custody)* [1990] 1 FLR 51: an English father brought his 8-year-old son to England from India and placed him in the care of his paternal uncle and aunt. His Indian mother failed to recover his care because he had been settled happily with his English foster carers for 2.5 years and a change would be disruptive both to his home and education.

[223] E.g. *Re M (A Minor) (Custody Appeal)* [1990] 1 FLR 291: a dispute involving an adoption application.

[224] [1990] 3 All ER 795: after his mother's suicide, a boy, now aged 4.5 years, had been placed by his father with his maternal aunt and uncle. After he had been in their care for 1 year, the foster parents refused to return him to his father.

[225] Ibid. per Fox LJ, at 798.

This mysterious change of attitude may have been influenced by the developing adoption law.[226] The judiciary's anxiety to avoid accusations of 'social engineering', when considering evidence relating to a child's future well-being with prospective adopters,[227] may have coloured their approach to similar disputes between foster carers and birth parents. It also appears that the then recent decision of the House of Lords in *Re KD (A Minor) (Ward: Termination of Access)*[228] had a powerful impact on judicial decision-making. Their Lordships voiced some stirring views about the concept of parenthood. Indeed, it was probably Lord Templeman's eminently quotable and emotive phrases that invoked a new willingness to give the biological tie between child and parent a far greater significance:

> The best person to bring up a child is the natural parent. It matters not whether the parent is wise or foolish, rich or poor, educated or illiterate, provided the child's moral and physical health are not endangered.[229]

Lord Oliver also said:

> Parenthood, in most civilised societies, is generally conceived of as conferring on parents the exclusive privilege of ordering, within the family, the upbringing of children of tender age, with all that that entails. That is a privilege which, if interfered with without authority, would be protected by the courts.[230]

Despite this recognition of the privileges of parenthood, Lord Oliver stressed, contrary to the mother's claims in *Re KD*, that no provision in the ECHR required a reassessment of the principles established by *J v. C*[231] regarding parents' 'rights'. Indeed, he made it plain that the mother was to be given no special preference when it came to weighing the evidence regarding her claimed 'right' to access to her child. This would be determined by the child's welfare.[232] As Eekelaar comments of this outcome: 'Neither party, it seems, starts with an inherent *legal* advantage. If he or she is to "win", the erstwhile "right-holder", as much as the challenger, must establish that his or her proposals are better for the child than the competing set.'[233] Although concerned with the court's public law functions in wardship, *Re KD* clearly

---

[226] J. Fortin (1999) pp. 436–9.

[227] E.g. Butler-Sloss LJ, in *Re K (A Minor) (Wardship: Adoption)* [1991] 1 FLR 57, at 62; *Re O (A Minor) (Custody: Adoption)* [1992] 1 FLR 77, at 79.

[228] [1988] AC 806: an application in wardship by a mother claiming that the LA was acting in breach of her parental 'right' to visit her baby while in LA care.

[229] Ibid. at 812.

[230] Ibid. at 825. He then qualified this statement with the following words: 'but it is a privilege circumscribed by many limitations imposed both by the general law and, where the circumstances demand, by the courts or by the authorities on whom the legislature has imposed the duty of supervising the welfare of children and young persons.'

[231] [1970] AC 668. The question of whether the ECHR requires modification to the welfare principle is considered in Chapter 3.

[232] [1988] AC 806, at 827.   [233] J. Eekelaar (1988) p. 632 (emphasis in the original).

influenced the future treatment of private law disputes between birth parents and foster carers.

Their Lordships' remarks in *Re KD* were later enthusiastically adopted by the Court of Appeal in *Re K (A Minor) (Ward: Care and Control)*.[234] They were taken to mean that the court should not oppose the claims of a birth parent, unless there was some evidence relating to the child's welfare which positively required that the parental rights should be suspended or superseded. The assumption was that the child had a 'prima facie right' to an upbringing by his or her birth parents and this right survived any subsequent changes in the child's care. This subtly downgraded the principle in *J* v. *C*, since foster carers were now required to produce evidence showing that the child's best interests required the *displacement* of the parents' prior claims. The court's job was not to assess the child's potential welfare in the two households, since the onus was on the foster carers to provide the court with evidence that there were 'compelling factors which required him [the learned judge] to override the prima facie right of this child to an upbringing by its surviving natural parent'.[235] It was unfortunate that the evidential presumption favouring the birth parents was concealed behind the language of children's rights, given that its effect was to endanger children's right to protection from psychological harm and their relationships within the home where they were being brought up. The new presumption encouraged the courts to give far less serious consideration to the dangers of psychological and emotional damage being caused by removing the child from his or her present home, than to the benefits of being brought up by birth parents.[236]

Judicial unease over the direction being taken by the case law was soon evident; Lord Donaldson MR admitted being:

> slightly apprehensive that *Re K (a minor) (ward: care and control)*[237] may be misconstrued . . . it is not a case of parental right opposed to the interests of the child, with an assumption that parental right prevails unless there are strong reasons in terms of the interests of the child . . . all that *Re K* is saying, as I understand it, is that of course there is a strong supposition that, *other things being equal*, it is in the interests of the child that it shall remain with its natural parents. But that has to give way to particular needs in particular situations.[238]

This decision was delivered just a few months before the CA 1989 came into force. The Law Commission, in its work preceding the Act, had explicitly endorsed the *J* v. *C* approach of determining disputes on the basis of welfare, with no presumption in favour of birth parents.[239] In the Law Commission's view, the 'welfare test itself is well able to encompass any special contribution

---

[234] [1990] 3 All ER 795. See also *Re K (A Minor) (Wardship: Adoption)* [1991] 1 FLR 57.
[235] Ibid. per Waite J, at 800.   [236] J. Fortin (1999) pp. 439–40; I. Weyland (1997) pp. 180–4.
[237] [1990] 3 All ER 795.
[238] *Re H (A Minor) (Custody: Interim Care and Control)* [1991] 2 FLR 109, at 112–13 (emphasis added).
[239] Law Commission (1986) paras 6.20–6.22.

which natural parents can make to the emotional needs of their child, in particular to his sense of identity and self-esteem, as well as the added commitment which knowledge of their parenthood may bring'.[240] Given that this was the basis on which the CA 1989 was based, one might have expected a return to the straightforward welfare approach of *J* v. *C*. Nonetheless, there was little discernible change in the approach adopted; the courts remained unshaken in their assumption that a change in the child's care made little or no difference to the child's 'right' to be brought up by the birth parents. Consequently, there was a marked reluctance to assess and weigh all the evidence from each 'side', in order to decide what course of action would be in the child's best interests.[241] It is surprising that decisions like *Re M (Child's Upbringing)*[242] did not provoke judicial doubts about the wisdom of assuming that the tie between a child and his or her parent would always produce a relationship valuable to *both*. In this case, the child was removed from his carer of 4 years and returned to his parents despite the 10-year-old boy's own strong opposition to such a step. Neill LJ stated: 'he has the *right* to be reunited with his Zulu parents and with his extended family in South Africa'.[243] The Court of Appeal ignored the psychiatrist's warnings that the damage to the boy's emotional well-being, by being forced to return to his birth parents, might wholly undermine his ability to benefit from his renewed links with his Zulu heritage. Unfortunately, court orders cannot magically transform children's affections. The boy's unhappiness in South Africa forced his parents to admit defeat and to return him to his foster mother's care in England. This is again a good example of the deployment of the language of children's rights in circumstances that appear to benefit the parents, but harm the child.

(D) Welfare Triumphant?

Given the persistence of the language of rights in these disputes and the continued uncertainty as to how the parental relationship was relevant to the child's welfare, the intervention of the House of Lords into the arena was perhaps inevitable. *Re G (Children) (Residence: Same-Sex Partner)*[244] concerned a dispute between two women (CG and CW) who had previously been in relationship together. In the course of that relationship, CG had given birth to two children using donor sperm and CG and CW had parented the children together. Following the relationship breakdown, the children, then aged 1 and 3, had remained with CG, with a contact order in favour of CW. CG had, the court found, remained hostile to the children's contact with

---

[240]   Ibid. (1986) para. 6.22.
[241]   E.g. *Re W (A Minor) (Residence Order)* [1993] 2 FLR 625; *Re N (Residence: Appointment of Solicitor: Placement with Extended Family)* [2001] 1 FLR 1028; *Re D (Care: Natural Parent Presumption)* [1999] 1 FLR 134. See J. Fortin (1999).
[242]   [1996] 2 FLR 441.   [243]   Ibid. at 454 (emphasis added).
[244]   [2006] UKHL 43, [2006] 4 All ER 241.

CW and sought to marginalise her role in their lives. Fearing that she would lose her relationship with the children, CW applied for the children's primary residence to be transferred to her, an application that succeeded at first instance and was upheld by the Court of Appeal. The case raised the vexed issue of the relevance of legal and biological parenthood in residence disputes, but had two important factual differences from most of the cases considered so far. First, the case concerned an attempt to change the children's residence from their settled home with a parent, rather than returning them to parents from an established home elsewhere. Second, while in terms of legal status the dispute was between a parent and a non-parent, the children had been born into the relationship and CW had played a full parental role from the time of the children's birth. In this sense, the dispute was better characterised as a parental dispute rather than one between a parent and an alternative carer. In the House of Lords, Baroness Hale's leading judgment made it clear that the only question for the court was the welfare of the children and that there was no presumption in favour of 'natural' parents,[245] but then immediately muddied the waters in discussion of how 'natural' parenthood relates to children's welfare. Baroness Hale noted that 'natural' parenthood[246] had at least three meanings, each of which could be very significant in assessing welfare: genetic parenthood; gestational parenthood; and social or psychological parenthood. For this reason, both CG and CW were natural parents, but:

> While CW is their psychological parent, CG is . . . both their biological and their psychological parent. In the overall welfare judgment, that must count for something in the vast majority of cases. Its significance must be considered and assessed.[247]

Although this did not create a presumption in favour of the biological parent, it gave the impression that the biological parent would be at an advantage in the welfare assessment.[248] This impression was reinforced by Lord Scott's comment that 'mothers are special'[249] and Lord Nicholl's view that in assessing welfare:

> the court should always have in mind that in the ordinary way the rearing of a child by his or her biological parent can be expected to be in the child's best interests, both in the short term and also, and importantly, in the longer term. I decry any tendency to diminish the significance of this factor. A child should not be removed from the primary care of his or her biological parents without compelling reason. Where such a reason exists the judge should spell this out explicitly.[250]

---

[245] Ibid. at [30]–[31] and [34].

[246] As opposed to legal parenthood; see ibid. at [32] and discussion in Chapter 5.

[247] Ibid. at [38].

[248] Baroness Hale has, writing extra-judicially, accepted that this may have given the impression of attaching too much weight to CG's biological role: B. Hale (2014) p. 30.

[249] *Re G* [2006] UKHL 43, [2006] 4 All ER 241, at [3].   [250] Ibid. at [2].

Given the emphasis on biological parenthood, it was perhaps unsurprising that the courts below quickly returned to emphasising the importance of this facet of parenthood.[251] The Court of Appeal summarised the position by finding that there was a 'fundamental proposition that children have a right to be brought up by their natural parents unless their welfare positively demands the replacement of that right'.[252]

The issue was soon before the newly formed Supreme Court in *Re B (A Child) (Residence: Biological Parent)*,[253] in which a father sought a residence order in respect of his 4-year-old son, who had been cared for by his maternal grandmother since his birth. The father had succeeded in the Family Division, with the judge once again basing his judgment on the child's 'right' to be brought up with his natural parent. In a forcefully worded, unanimous judgment, the Supreme Court found for the grandmother, rejecting talk of either the child's or parent's rights[254] in this context and stating unambiguously that:

> All consideration of the importance of parenthood in private law disputes about residence must be firmly rooted in an examination of what is in the child's best interests. This is the paramount consideration. It is only as a contributor to the child's welfare that parenthood assumes any significance. In common with all other factors bearing on what is in the best interests of the child, it must be examined for its potential to fulfil that aim.[255]

The Supreme Court in *Re B* gives no room for doubt that residence cases should be decided according to the child's welfare. Parenthood is relevant so far as it contributes to the child's welfare, but is not a factor in its own right. Subsequent cases seem to have at last followed this approach. A good example is the protracted litigation in *Re E-R*,[256] concerning a child who lived with family friends who were caring for her terminally ill mother, and continued to live with them following the mother's death. The father, who had not had contact with the child for some years, initially succeeded in obtaining an order that the child should live with him on the basis that there was a 'broad natural parent presumption in existence under our law'. The Court of Appeal firmly rejected this approach, restated the paramount importance of welfare and ordered that the child remain with her carers, with contact with the father.[257] An important aspect of the case was the fact that the new carers had become her psychological parents[258] and that the evidence strongly

---

[251] K. Everett and L. Yeatman (2010).

[252] *Re R (Residence)* [2009] EWCA Civ 358, [2009] 2 FLR 819, at [116].

[253] [2009] UKSC 5, [2009] 1 WLR 2496.   [254] Ibid. at [19]–[20] and [33].   [255] Ibid. at [37].

[256] *Re E-R (A Child)* [2015] EWCA Civ 405, [2016] 1 FLR 521; *Re E-R (Children) (Child Arrangements)* [2016] EWHC 805 (Fam), [2017] 2 FLR 501; *E-R (Child Arrangements)* [2017] EWHC 2382 (Fam), [2018] 1 FCR 1; *E-R (Children) (Child Arrangements Order: Costs)* [2017] EWHC 2535 (Fam), [2018] 1 FCR 23.

[257] *E-R (A Child)* [2015] EWCA Civ 405, [2016] 1 FLR 521.

[258] Although being a 'psychological parent' is also not a factor that raises any presumption in favour of the applicant. See e.g. *Re A (A Child: Application for Leave to Apply for a Child Arrangements Order)* [2015] EWFC 47, where a past 'psychological parent' was unable to even

indicated that separation from them would be 'psychologically catastrophic' in view of the bereavement that she had already suffered,[259] although this finding did little to dissuade the father from seeking to pursue his 'rights' in further litigation.[260] Further cases have similarly emphasised the importance of the child's caring relationships to determining their welfare and applied the principle that biological parenthood is not a 'stand-alone factor', but is only relevant in so far as it impacts on the welfare of the child.[261] As a result, parents have found it difficult to disrupt established and caring relationships with alternative carers.

The intervention of the Supreme Court appears, at least for now, to have unambiguously restored the position in *J* v. *C*:[262] welfare is paramount and neither legal nor biological parenthood creates a presumption or right to bring the child up. The persistence of the view that there should be a special status for parental upbringing is perhaps testament to the fact that, for most parents and children, to contemplate losing that relationship is unbearable. If parents are caring for their children in the ordinary way, it is very unlikely to be in the child's best interests to disrupt that relationship at the behest of a third party.[263] However, as cases such as *Re E-R* demonstrate, the cases that come before court tend not to 'follow the ordinary way'[264] and the assumptions that apply to ordinary relationships cannot simply translate into principles to apply in the conflicted cases before the courts.[265]

(E) Conclusions: Rights Rejected?

The rise and fall of the child's 'right' to be brought up by their parents demonstrates much that is often said to be wrong with the use of rights in children's cases. The invocation of the child's 'right' has often appeared as

---

obtain leave to apply for contact given the disruption that it would cause to the child's life. Note too the possibility that psychological parenthood could be lost over time at [56].

[259] *Re E-R (Children) (Child Arrangements)* [2016] EWHC 805 (Fam), [2017] 2 FLR 501, esp. at [43], [51] and [55]. Strikingly, when asked to draw a 'genogram' showing those closest to her, she put her mother and carers at the centre, but the father and his family some way beyond her friends, her deceased dog and a mulberry tree, at [54].

[260] *E-R (Child Arrangements)* [2017] EWHC 2382 (Fam), [2018] 1 FCR 1.

[261] E.g. *Re T* [2010] EWCA Civ 1644, in which the mother failed to recover her two children who had lived for 6 years with the paternal grandparents of one of them. The fact that one of the children was not biologically related to the 'grandparents' was not relevant as there was no evidence to suggest that this had in any way impacted on the care offered to them, at [20].

[262] [1970] AC 668.

[263] E.g. *B (A Child)* [2012] EWCA Civ 858, in which the Court of Appeal overturned the initial decision to transfer residence from the mother to the paternal grandmother in order to enforce contact with the paternal family, regarded by the mother as 'abusive and dangerous'. While such measures had been taken in cases between parents, Thorpe LJ observed at [13] that he knew 'of no case in which such a dire sanction has been exercised against an obdurate parent to transfer the primary care to a grandmother. Manifestly grandparents are not on equal footing with parents.'

[264] *Re B (A Child) (Residence: Biological Parent)* [2009] UKSC 5, [2009] 1 WLR 2496, at [35].

[265] J. Herring (2014).

a smokescreen for the interests of parents and has operated with little regard to the feelings, welfare or relationships of the child in question.[266] Further, in cases in which parents appear convinced of their own right to raise their child, protecting that 'right' appears to fuel conflict and blunt sensitivity to the interests of the child.[267] In sum, where rights have been deployed they have operated in a way that makes a solution that maximises the child's interests less likely. As such, residence disputes between parents and other carers seem to offer a textbook example of why rights should be kept firmly away from children's cases, at least within private law.

While there is much force in these observations, the purported 'rights' asserted in these cases have not been those protected by the CRC or ECHR, but have instead taken the form of proprietorial rights over children. The courts have been quite right to banish these asserted 'rights' from children's cases. Nevertheless, as Andrew Bainham notes,[268] this does not change the fact that as a matter of international and ECHR law, these cases do involve the human rights of children and adults. Those human rights offer a far more nuanced understanding of the child's position than the blunt assertion of a prima facie right to upbringing by natural parents. Instead, they recognise the child's family life with significant carers beyond parents and that the rights of adults are qualified by the need to protect the rights and welfare of children.[269] These factors are also recognised by the application of the welfare principle in cases such as the Supreme Court decision in Re B,[270] meaning that children's human rights will usually receive practical protection through the use of welfare, without the need for explicit reference to those rights.[271] The child's welfare is also highly likely to outweigh any Article 8 right of the parents in most cases, particularly if the parent is trying to recover their child from a settled home with alternative carers.

A parent faced with losing care of their child in private proceedings may, however, be surprised at the sharp contrast with the position in public law. In public law proceedings, the court would have to find that the significant harm threshold[272] had been surmounted and the order proportionate to the inter-ference with the rights involved before a compulsory order, permitting the child to be removed, could be made to protect the child's welfare. Faced with such a case, the parents would be entitled to legal aid and the child separately represented, both increasingly rare in private proceedings. This difference is often justified on the basis that public law cases involve an exercise of state

---

[266] E.g. *Re M (Child's Upbringing)* [1996] 2 FLR 441.

[267] A good example of this problem can be seen in the *Re E-R* saga, esp. *Re E-R (Child Arrangements)* [2016] EWHC 805 (Fam), [2017] 2 FLR 501, at [52], and [58]–[59], where the father was described as verging 'on the belligerent in his assertion of his rights'.

[268] A. Bainham (2010).   [269] See discussion above.   [270] [2009] UKSC 5, [2009] 1 WLR 2496.

[271] As discussed in Chapter 3, the Human Rights Act 1998 does not usually require courts to reason by direct reference to the protected rights where the ordinary operation of domestic law offers effective protection.

[272] CA 1989, s. 31, discussed in Chapter 15.

power, but the consequences for parents and children separated by court order in private proceedings can be materially identical to those under a care order. The line between the two becomes increasingly blurred where private law proceedings arise in the context of LA involvement with the family. This appears to be increasingly the case, as LAs seek to avoid care proceedings by encouraging placement in the family.[273] For example, in Maebh Harding and Annika Newnham's research on county court cases, the LA had been involved in more than half of residence applications by non-parents – often having encouraged, or even insisted on, that application.[274] A good example of the blurring of the distinction[275] and the difficulties that can arise can be seen in *Northamptonshire County Council* v. *M*,[276] in which the LA was in 'egregious breach' of its duties towards the child and his parents and of their rights under Articles 6 and 8. The authority had placed the child, then aged 1, with his grandmother, ostensibly through consent,[277] at a point where the threshold criteria would probably not have been met to a degree that would warrant his long-term or compulsory removal from his mother. The LA then failed to assess the parents or start care proceedings, but acted as if it already had a care order, and imposed significant restrictions on contact with the child in the absence of care proceedings. Further, no legal aid was available to aid the parents in taking legal advice or challenging the position. The matter eventually came to court in an application, instigated by the LA, for a private order in favour of the grandmother. By this point the child was 4 years old and it was clearly in his best interests to remain with his grandmother under a special guardianship order, despite the injustice caused by the LA's failures. The case demonstrates the complexity of many of the cases that come under private proceedings and the difficulties faced by parents in using those proceedings to recover their children, particularly given the constraints on public funding. While welfare remains the sole consideration in deciding on the child's future, if the order effectively severs the relationship between parent and child, it is arguable that the court should explicitly consider the proportionality of the interference with their rights, in the same way as it would in public law proceedings.

Despite these concerns, the law on disputes between parents and alternative carers appears to have been returned to a position that decisively puts children at the centre by focusing on the reality of the child's relationships rather than through abstract assumptions as to the value of legal or biological parenthood.

---

[273] F. Kaganas and C. Piper (2018); R. Taylor (2018).
[274] M. Harding and A. Newnham (2015) ch. 6.   [275] A. Bainham (2010).
[276] [2017] EWHC 997 (Fam), [2017] 2 FLR 1250.
[277] CA 1989, s. 20; the father had not been asked for his consent and the legality of the placement was in serious doubt.

(5) Birth Parents, Kinship and Adoption

(A) Adoption: Welfare and Rights

Of all the possible orders that a court might make, it is adoption that poses the most serious consequences for a child's relationship with their birth family. Adoption not only deprives children of an upbringing with their birth parents, but irrevocably[278] severs their legal ties to their entire birth family, replacing them with permanent legal ties to the adoptive parents and their family.[279] Adoption raises the same fraught questions of how children's family life relates to their rights and welfare and how that welfare should be measured against parental rights to a relationship with their child as the disputes with alternative considered above. The context and consequences of the two scenarios are, however, very different, not least because in private law cases the child retains their legal, and often social, relationship with their birth family.[280] Further, although adoption may be used to give children security with their current carers,[281] in a typical case children will be placed for adoption with parents who were previously strangers to them, so creating a new social relationship rather than recognising one that has already formed.

While at one time adoption was primarily aimed at finding new homes for relinquished babies, the majority of adoptions now concern children who have previously been looked-after children within the care system.[282] Decisions made about the future of children in care[283] should be seen in the context of repeated efforts by governments to overhaul the adoption system. The current

---

[278] While it is possible to apply to set aside an adoption order that has been lawfully and properly made, these applications will only be successful in limited exceptional circumstances. In *Webster* v. *Norfolk* [2009] EWCA Civ 59, the birth parents applied to set aside adoption orders made in respect of three of their children on the basis that fresh medical evidence demonstrated that the injuries that had caused the children to be removed had an innocent medical explanation. Despite recognising that, if admitted, the evidence appeared to show that the parents were innocent and that the family had suffered a serious miscarriage of justice, the Court of Appeal refused to set aside the orders as this would undermine the policy of permanence underlying adoption and would be disruptive for the children who had lived with their adoptive parents for 4 years. A rare example of a successful application is *PK* v. *K* [2015] EWHC 2316 (Fam), [2016] 2 FLR 576, in which a 14-year-old girl applied to have the adoption order set aside after she had been subject to significant abuse by her adopters' extended family and was now happily living with her biological family.

[279] ACA 2002, ss 46 and 67.

[280] The outcome of a private dispute is usually a child arrangements order or an SGO, both of which will give the holder parental responsibility, but will not remove it from the existing legal parents. An SGO also allows the guardian to exclude the child's birth parents from decision-making regarding his or her upbringing: CA 1989, s. 14C(1)(a). NB: see *Re AJ (Adoption Order or Special Guardianship Order)* [2007] EWCA Civ 55, [2007] 1 FLR 507, at 524: schedule listing the differences between adoption orders and SGOs.

[281] A step-parent may adopt a child with whom they have lived for the past 6 months (ACA 2002, ss 51(2) and 42(3)), although such applications are declining; N. Lowe and G. Douglas (2014) p. 687. Private foster carers may also seek to adopt, but only once the child has been living with them for 3 of the past 5 years (ACA 2002, s. 42(5)).

[282] J. Lewis (2004) p. 239.   [283] See Chapter 16.

law, found in the Adoption and Children Act (ACA) 2002, has its roots in government policy that was extremely critical of the extent to which large numbers of children being looked after by LAs were 'drifting in care', often with very poor outcomes in their future life.[284] The 'solution' was to ensure that far more children gained permanent adoptive families who would give them safety, stability and lifelong support.[285] By introducing a new, highly regulated adoption service and by amending the law to introduce a more efficient and rapid legal process, the government hoped that more children could be adopted faster. Successive governments have similarly adopted policies targeted at increasing the numbers of children in care who are adopted and the speed at which that is achieved.[286] These reforms have, however, attracted severe misgivings as to whether more and quicker adoptions necessarily benefit large numbers of children entering the care system.[287] Children within the care system often have extremely complex needs and finding the 'right' adoptive parents for them may not be easy, appropriate or even practicable.[288] Furthermore, adoption targets,[289] combined with legislation making it easier to dispense with parental consent to adoption and cuts to support services, can pose a threat to disadvantaged and impoverished parents, who with more social work support, might eventually manage to provide a stable home for their children.[290]

A defining feature of the ACA 2002 was the decision to put the 'child's welfare throughout his life' at the heart of adoption decisions by making it the paramount consideration for both courts and adoption agencies.[291] The CRC, in Article 21, directs that the child's best interests will be the paramount consideration in adoption;[292] while the ECHR does not refer to adoption specifically, the ECtHR has also adopted the paramountcy test in assessing whether adoption breaches Article 8 of the ECHR.[293] This apparent unanimity masks the complexity of determining what the rights and best interests of the child might be in any adoption decision. As the ECtHR observed in *YC v. United Kingdom*:

> In identifying the child's best interests in a particular case, two considerations must be borne in mind: first, it is in the child's best interests that his ties with his family be maintained except in cases where the family has proved particularly unfit; and secondly, it is in the child's best interests to ensure his development in a safe and secure environment. It is clear from the foregoing that family ties may

---

[284] PIU Report (2000). The report notes that adults who had grown up in care were four times as likely to be unemployed as the general population, sixty times more likely to be homeless and made up a quarter of the adult prison population; ibid. p. 16.

[285] Ibid. para. 4.9.   [286] C. Fenton-Glynn (2015) pp. 22–3.

[287] S. Harris-Short (2001) pp. 417–20 and 421.

[288] Family Policy Studies Centre (2000) pp. 2–3.   [289] C. Fenton-Glynn (2016).

[290] British Agencies for Adoption and Fostering (2001) para. 11.3.   [291] ACA 2002, s. 1(3).

[292] In contrast to the general requirement in Art. 3 that best interests are the 'primary consideration'.

[293] *YC v. United Kingdom* (2012) 55 EHRR 33, at [134].

only be severed in very exceptional circumstances and that everything must be done to preserve personal relations and, where appropriate, to 'rebuild' the family. It is not enough to show that a child could be placed in a more beneficial environment for his upbringing.[294]

This tension between these factors is broadly reflected in the welfare checklist contained in the ACA 2002,[295] but listing these considerations is far easier than resolving them in practice. In many cases, the alternative to adoption for the child is not a return to the birth parents in the foreseeable future, but continuing within the care system or being placed with kinship carers.[296] The judge or adoption agency faced with assessing the different facets of a child's welfare 'throughout his life' in each of these options is engaging in an almost impossible task. A particular difficulty, noted by Sir Andrew McFarlane, is that there is very little in the way of robust data or research that informs judges on the likely impact of their decision on children's future adulthood.[297] As adoption is now considered a solution for more children, many of whom have experienced significant trauma before being adopted, so research on previous generations may not be a reliable guide for the future of children adopted today, particularly given that the closed nature of adoption is being made more precarious by the ease of making contact via the internet. A judge assessing welfare under the ACA must consider both the importance of the child's ties to the birth family and the need for a safe and secure environment, but the Act itself gives little indication as to how that balance is to be drawn.

A further problem for the application of the welfare model is the tension between the government's policies to drive forward adoption and the undoubted emphasis that both the CRC and ECHR also place on the importance of the family to children's rights.[298] Simply adopting the principle that welfare is paramount is not enough in itself to achieve compliance with either the CRC or the ECHR: assessment of welfare must reflect and comply with the full range of children's rights, including those rights that protect family relationships. The problem is made still more complex by the fact that under the ECHR the child's birth parents, wider birth family and sometimes the adopters themselves will also have rights to family life, which are arguably not properly protected by a simple assessment of welfare. As reflected in the case of *YC* v. *United Kingdom*, quoted above, the Strasbourg jurisprudence stresses that welfare agencies that remove children from their parents into care should treat such a measure as a temporary one; they must take all steps

---

[294] Ibid.

[295] ACA 2002 s. 1(4). In particular, the checklist requires that consideration is given to 'the likely effect on the child (throughout his life) of having ceased to be a member of the original family and become an adopted person' and to the child's relationships with relatives, including prospective adopters.

[296] In cases of adoption from care, potential kinship carers should be assessed before a plan for adoption is made (see Chapter 16), but, as discussed below, such carers may emerge during the adoption process.

[297] A. McFarlane (2017).   [298] B. Sloan (2013).

which could reasonably be expected of them to re-establish the parent–child relationship as soon as possible.[299] Nevertheless, the ECtHR also acknowledges that measures depriving a birth parent of his or her family life with their child can be taken, but only in exceptional circumstances 'motivated by an overriding requirement pertaining to the child's best interests'.[300] An adoption order may eventually be an appropriate means of giving a child security, rather than in a state of uncertainty in temporary placements in public care, but must be a proportionate response.[301] The law must negotiate the tightrope designed by this Strasbourg jurisprudence. On the one hand, children cannot be expected to wait for new families indefinitely, so LAs must take adequate steps to secure for a child who has been deprived of family life with his birth family, 'a life with a new family who can become his new "family for life" to make up for what he has lost'.[302] On the other hand, the court should consider carefully whether an adoption order is a proportionate response to the child's need for permanency, given that an adoption order is the most radical form of interference with family life.[303] Determining the rights and welfare of children and family members within this framework is complex; this section considers its application in adoption cases in three contexts: parental consent and objections to adoption; challenges from the wider birth family; and post-adoption contact.

(B) Parental Opposition and 'Non-Consensual' Adoptions

The balance maintained by the law between the interests of child and parents is seen in the legal principles governing parental consent to adoption. Despite the momentous consequences for the child's future, the child's consent to adoption is not required at any age.[304] In contrast, parental[305] consent must be

---

[299] Inter alia: *Johansen* v. *Norway* (1996) 23 EHRR 33, esp. at [78]; *EP* v. *Italy* (2001) 31 EHRR 17, esp. at [62]. See also *Olsson* v. *Sweden* (1988) 11 EHRR 259; *K and T* v. *Finland* [2001] 2 FLR 707; *S and G* v. *Italy* [2000] 2 FLR 771; *Haase* v. *Germany* [2004] 2 FLR 39.

[300] *Johansen* v. *Norway* (1996) 23 EHRR 33, at [78]; *Gnahore* v. *France* (2002) 34 EHRR 38, at [59]; discussed by A. Bainham (2003) pp. 81–3.

[301] *Johansen* v. *Norway* (1996) 23 EHRR 33, at [80]; *Scott* v. *United Kingdom* [2000] 1 FLR 958, at 970.

[302] Per Hale LJ, in *Re W and B; Re W (Care Plan)* [2001] EWCA Civ 757, [2001] 2 FLR 582, at [55]. Although this decision was reversed by the House of Lords in *Re S and Re W* [2002] UKHL 10, [2002] AC 291, Hale LJ's views, in this respect, remain relevant.

[303] *Re B (Adoption by One Natural Parent to Exclusion of Other)* [2001] 1 FLR 589, per Hale LJ, at [37]. This decision was reversed by the House of Lords, but the principle referred to by Hale LJ remains an important one. See also *Down Lisburn Health and Social Services Trust* v. *H* [2006] UKHL 36, [2007] 1 FLR 121, per Baroness Hale of Richmond, at [34].

[304] In contrast, in Scotland a child aged 12 or over must give their consent, unless they are incapable of doing so, before the adoption can proceed: Adoption and Children (Scotland) Act 2007, s. 32. A proposal to introduce a similar provision in ACA 2002 was unsuccessful, although the child's ascertainable wishes and feelings will be considered as an aspect of their welfare: ACA 2002, s. 1(4)(1).

[305] 'Parent' in this context means parent with parental responsibility; ACA 2002, ss 47(2) and 52(6). The consent of a parent without responsibility is not required; nevertheless, such

given, or dispensed with by the court, for the child to be placed for adoption[306] and for the final adoption order to be made.[307] Under the ACA 2002,[308] the courts must ask a simple question when deciding whether a parent's consent should be dispensed with: does the child's welfare require the adoption order to be made?[309] The introduction of the welfare formula as a basis for dispensing with parental consent was extremely controversial; under the previous law, the court would normally only consider doing so on the basis that the parents were withholding consent unreasonably.[310] In truth, given that the reasonable parent would be expected to have regard to the welfare of their child,[311] the concept of the reasonable parent was a fiction designed to find an appropriate balance between the child's welfare and the parents' own wishes and concerns.[312] But while few maintained that the old formula was ideal, it reminded the courts of the need to maintain that balance as far as possible. The introduction of a welfare formula as a basis for dispensing with parental consent attracted considerable opposition when adoption law reform was first mooted.[313] Critics urged that such a formula would not necessarily accommodate the complexities of adoption and would mean that children could be removed from their families and have the legal relationship with their parents irrevocably severed 'simply because an adoption agency and court are satisfied that another family could do a better job',[314] which 'could lead to social engineering of the worst kind'.[315] Further, given the draconian nature of the adoption order and its serious implications for the rights of parents and children, there was also a strong argument that explicit consideration of the interference with those rights was required to ensure that it was proportionate and complied with the rights outlined above.[316] These concerns have not abated as experience with the legislation has progressed, particularly as the vast majority of adoption placements now occur without parental consent.[317] The issue has acquired an international dimension, as a number of EU

---

a parent is normally notified of the adoption proceedings and may be joined as a party; see discussion below. The child's consent is not required.

[306] ACA 2002, s. 19.   [307] ACA 2002, ss 20 and 47(1)–(4).

[308] Unless the parent cannot be found or is incapable of consenting to the adoption; ACA 2002, s. 52(1)(a).

[309] ACA 2002, ss 52(1)(b) and 1(2) and (4).

[310] Adoption Act 1976, s. 16(2)(b) (now repealed). The other grounds (the parent could not be found; was incapable of signing the agreement; had abandoned or neglected the child; or had persistently or seriously ill-treated the child) were very seldom used.

[311] *Re W (An Infant)* [1971] 2 All ER 49, per Lord Hailsham, at 55.

[312] *Re C (A Minor) (Adoption: Parental Agreement: Contact)* [1993] 2 FLR 260, per Steyn and Hoffmann LJJ, at 272.

[313] J. Lewis (2004) pp. 240ff.   [314] BASW (2001) para. 1.

[315] National Organisation for the Counselling of Adoptees and Parents (2001) Summary.

[316] Inter alia: A. Bainham (2003) pp. 82–3; S. Harris-Short (2001) pp. 423–4; S. Choudhry (2003) pp. 123–34; S. Harris-Short (2008) esp. p. 37.

[317] C. Fenton-Glynn (2015) notes that 96 per cent of adoption placements in 2014 were made without parental consent.

countries have raised concerns that non-consensual adoption has been used to remove children from their citizens resident in this jurisdiction.[318]

One answer to these concerns lies in the statutory language for dispensing with consent: the ACA 2002 states that parental consent *cannot* be dispensed with unless the welfare of the child *requires* it to be dispensed with.[319] This language suggests that there may be circumstances in which the child's welfare would be served by adoption, but that the impact would not be sufficient to 'require' such an extreme measure as non-consensual adoption, with the consequential interference with the rights of family members under Article 8. Yet, at the same time, the Act also requires the courts to treat the child's welfare as paramount, suggesting that the court should make the order that best enhances the child's welfare, regardless of the impact on the rights of others. The potential conflict between these provisions was considered by the Court of Appeal in the leading case of *Re P (Placement Orders: Parental Consent)*.[320] Wall LJ, delivering the judgment of the court, dealt in detail with the concerns that to dispense with parental consent on the simple criterion of the child's best interests would jeopardise the balance between the rights of parents and children. He asserted that as long as the statutory language is followed carefully, the Strasbourg jurisprudence does not prevent a court dispensing with a parent's consent if it is convinced that adoption is what the child's welfare requires.[321] He categorically rejected the mother's claim that the court should apply an enhanced welfare test;[322] instead the court must consider the statutory test of whether the child's welfare 'throughout his life'[323] requires that he or she be adopted.[324] At the same time, he acknowledged that an adoption order against the parent's wishes will be an unjustifiable infringement of her Article 8 rights under the ECHR unless such a step is proportionate to the legitimate aim of protecting the child.[325]

> In assessing what is proportionate, the court has, of course, always to bear in mind that adoption without parental consent is an extreme – indeed the most extreme – interference with family life. Cogent justification must therefore exist if parental consent is to be dispensed with.[326]

The answer to this apparent conflict between the child's welfare and the adult's right to family life was found in the term 'requires', which had been used to reflect the Strasbourg jurisprudence and has the 'connotation of the imperative, what is demanded rather than what is merely optional or reasonable or desirable'.[327] Whether this approach fully resolves the conundrum of the tension

---

[318] See ibid., who demonstrates that every country in Europe has a mechanism for allowing adoption without parental consent, although the numbers of such cases appear to be much higher within this jurisdiction.
[319] ACA 2002, s. 52(1)(b).
[320] Also called *SB v. County Council* [2008] EWCA Civ 535, [2008] 2 FCR 185.
[321] Per Wall LJ, at [113]–[133].   [322] Ibid. at [127].
[323] ACA 2002, s. 1(2), which also governs s. 52(1)(b).   [324] Per Wall LJ, at [128].
[325] Ibid. at [119]–[123].   [326] Ibid. at [124].   [327] Ibid. at [125].

between the ECHR rights of adults and the welfare principle is debatable, but it now appears well-settled that the term 'requires' should be interpreted to reflect the Strasbourg jurisprudence discussed above.[328]

In addition to parental consent to placement of a child for adoption, parental opposition may also be relevant at the point at which the application for the adoption order itself is determined. Once a child has been placed for adoption, the prospective adopters may only apply for the final order once the child has lived with them for the specified period of time.[329] At this point, the child may well have formed a strong bond with the prospective adopters and this itself may be protected by Article 8 of the ECHR. Parental objections operate in a very different context at this stage of the process and the leave of the court is needed for a parent to oppose the order at this final stage.[330] Leave to oppose was at one time extremely difficult to obtain,[331] but the controversial decision of the Court of Appeal in *Re B-S (Adoption: Application of s 47(5))*[332] appears to have created a significant change in practice.[333] The case was a response to *Re B (Care Proceedings: Appeal)*,[334] in which the Supreme Court had emphasised the importance of ensuring that decisions made on adoption complied with ECHR law. This law was summed up in Baroness Hale's observation that:

> it is quite clear that the test for severing the relationship between parent and child is very strict: only in exceptional circumstances and where motivated by overriding requirements pertaining to the child's welfare, in short, where nothing else will do.[335]

In *Re B-S*, the Court of Appeal expanded on this approach, making clear that they were aware of serious concerns about the way in which non-consensual adoptions were handled by the courts. Building on the ECtHR case law discussed above, the court stressed the need for proper evidence that carefully considered all of the realistic options for the child's future and the need for properly reasoned judgments that also did so.[336] In relation to leave to oppose

---

[328] E.g. *Re Q (A Child)* [2011] EWCA Civ 1610, at [58]. In *Re B-S (Adoption: Application of s 47(5))* [2013] EWCA Civ 1146, [2014] 1 WLR 563, this was reaffirmed and it was stressed that the test was 'stringent and demanding' at [20].

[329] ACA 2002, s. 42; the period of time in question will depend on the type of adoption, but the minimum period is 10 weeks in cases where the child has been placed by an adoption agency or in pursuance of a court order.

[330] ACA 2002, s. 47(3) and (5); s. 47(7) makes it clear that: 'The court cannot give leave under subsection (3) or (5) unless satisfied that there has been a change in circumstances since the consent of the parent or guardian was given or, as the case may be, the placement order was made.'

[331] E.g. *Re W (Adoption Order: Set Aside and Leave to Oppose)* [2010] EWCA Civ 1535, [2011] 1 FLR 2153.

[332] [2013] EWCA Civ 1146, [2014] 1 WLR 563.   [333] J. Masson (2017).

[334] [2013] UKSC 33, [2013] 1 WLR 1911.

[335] In *Re B (Care Proceedings: Appeal)* [2013] UKSC 33, [2013] 1 WLR 1911, at [198], Baroness Hale dissented on the facts, but not the applicable law.

[336] These aspects of the judgment and their subsequent impact in practice are considered further in Chapter 15.

adoption specifically, the court stressed that in applying the statutory tests the judge should have at the 'forefront of his mind' that adoption was a 'last resort' and that the 'child's interests include being brought up by the parents or wider family unless the overriding requirements of the child's welfare make that not possible'.[337] Although the Court of Appeal has subsequently clarified that *Re B-S* was not intended to change the law or to make adoption more difficult,[338] the case appears to have caused significant disruption in practice, including an increase in applications for leave to oppose by parents.[339] The courts have shown themselves to be acutely aware of the potential conflict between the rights of family members to family life with one another and the need to ensure that the child has a safe and secure environment in which to develop. Unfortunately, these attempts to reconcile the welfare of the child with the human rights of those involved have generated considerable confusion in practice. At base, this reflects a lack of clarity both as to how children's biological relationships are relevant to their welfare and also how rights of all involved relate to the welfare analysis for the child. This lack of clarity is exacerbated by the tension between government policies promoting adoption and the ECtHR case law emphasising the seriousness of this step.

(C) Kinship Care and Adoption

The legal obligations on LAs puts considerable emphasis on placing looked-after children within their existing family and kinship networks where practicable and consistent with the child's welfare.[340] As *Re B-S* emphasises, in considering whether a child should be placed for adoption, LAs and the courts are required to give careful consideration to alternative placements, including those within the wider family. Particular difficulties arise where kinship carers emerge as an alternative to adoption after the initial placement has been made and when relationships with the potential adopters have been formed. These cases again demonstrate the difficulties that the courts have had in resolving the relative importance of biological relatedness and caring relationships. The tangled question of how the law values parenting relationships as against the preservation of links with the biological family was demonstrated particularly sharply in the case of *Re W*,[341] a case worth careful consideration both for this reason and for the way in which it illustrates the problems arising from *Re B-S*.

Re W concerned a child, A, whose natural parents, both of whom had significant learning disabilities, had never cared for her and had no wish to

---

[337] [2013] EWCA Civ 1146, [2014] 1 WLR 563, at [74].

[338] *Re R (A Child) (Adoption: Judicial Approach)* [2014] EWCA Civ 1625, [2015] 1 WLR 3273, esp. at [41]–[44].

[339] J. Masson (2017) reports one dedicated family judge as saying that 20 per cent of his time was spent hearing such cases and that they were often 'hopeless'.

[340] CA 1989, s. 22C.

[341] *Re W* [2016] EWHC 2437 (Fam); *Re W (A Child)* [2016] EWCA Civ 793, [2017] 1 WLR 889; *Re W (Adoption: Contact)* [2016] EWHC 3118 (Fam). See J. Masson (2016).

do so. She had been placed in care at birth and was placed with prospective adopters at 7 months. Her paternal grandparents, who were estranged from the parents, only became aware of A's existence when they took on the care of the birth parents' subsequent child shortly after his birth. The grandparents quickly sought the care of A under a child arrangements or special guardianship order. In the meantime, the prospective adopters had lodged their adoption application. By this time, A was 2 years old and a close and loving attachment had clearly been built between them. The court[342] was faced with a 'judgment of Solomon' to decide between two prospective secure homes: one offering an upbringing within the biological family; and the other providing the only parenting relationship that A had ever known. At first instance, in deciding for the grandparents, the court was clearly influenced by the reports of the children's guardian and the independent social worker, both of whom worked from the assumption that if the grandparents were willing and able to provide a secure home for A, she ought to be placed with them – indeed, that she had a *right* to be placed with them. The Court of Appeal,[343] setting aside the decision, was determined to dispel any notion that there was a right or presumption that A should be brought up within her 'natural' family. McFarlane LJ was clear that this was a dangerous misunderstanding of the *Re B/Re B-S* 'nothing else will do' approach:

> The phrase is meaningless, and potentially dangerous, if it is applied as some freestanding, shortcut test divorced from, or even in place of, an overall evaluation of the child's welfare. Used properly, as Baroness Hale explained, the phrase 'nothing else will do' is no more, nor no less, than a useful distillation of the proportionality and necessity test as embodied in the ECHR and reflected in the need to afford paramount consideration to the welfare of the child throughout her lifetime ... The phrase 'nothing else will do' is not some sort of hyperlink providing a direct route to the outcome of a case so as to bypass the need to undertake a full, comprehensive welfare evaluation of all of the relevant pros and cons.[344]

When considering the welfare evaluation at the placement stage, that assessment would naturally tilt to good quality care within the family, as no relationship with the potential adopters would yet have been established. Where this relationship had been established and the child had formed a secure attachment to the potential adopters, that balance would naturally change and the child's welfare could not be determined simply by looking at the existence of the viable family placement. Instead, the status quo and the child's existing attachment to their primary carers would play a significant part in the welfare assessment. This was evident when the case was reheard[345] on the basis of the law explained by the Court of Appeal and with the benefit of new and

---

[342] *Re W* [2016] EWHC 2437 (Fam).
[343] *Re W (A Child)* [2016] EWCA Civ 793, [2017] 1 WLR 889.   [344] Ibid. at [68].
[345] *Re W (Adoption: Contact)* [2016] EWHC 3118 (Fam).

extensive expert reports. In the light of these reports, it was clear that there was a 'serious possibility of medium-term and long-term emotional and psychological damage to A by the traumatic severing of the secure attachment' if she were moved to the grandparents. On the other hand, while it was recognised by all parties that contact with the paternal grandparents and the creation of a relationship would be of benefit to A in the future, that relationship did not yet exist and it was unlikely that the paternal grandparents had Article 8 rights through their blood relationship with A alone. For these reasons, A's welfare required her adoption with the parents who were already her primary carers.

Re W is important for its firm restatement of the importance of a full welfare analysis, unimpeded by presumptions as to the value to be placed on biological relationships alone. It is also important for the recognition that, from the child's perspective, the relationships of care and psychological bonds formed with prospective adopters may be far more important than biological ties that are as yet not formed into an actual relationship. The importance of the relationship with prospective adopters has now been given explicit statutory recognition as part of the welfare checklist.[346] From the grandparents' perspective, the outcome may appear unjust, but protection for the birth family is not primarily found in this final welfare assessment, but in the statutory structures and guidance around parental consent and the priority given to kinship care. The tragedy for the grandparents was that the delay, entirely unattributable to them, in informing them of A's birth deprived them of the opportunity to demonstrate themselves to be suitable carers for A. While all family cases depend on their facts, *Re W* has had a pivotal role in reminding judges that a full assessment of the options for the child's future was required and could not be replaced by abstract notions of a 'right' to an upbringing with the biological family.[347]

(D) Post-Adoption Contact

In *Re W*,[348] just discussed, it was recognised by all parties, including the prospective adopters, that contact with the paternal grandparents and the creation of a relationship would be of benefit to A in the future. While adoption severs legal ties to the birth family, many adopted children have some form of contact with members of their birth family[349] and, in this way, there is a continuing recognition of the importance of biological relatedness even after adoption has taken place. Nonetheless, even though the court in *Re W* recognised the benefit of contact for A, it considered that the prospective

---

[346] ACA 2002, s. 1(4)(f), inserted by Children and Social Work Act 2017, s. 9.
[347] Nevertheless, it seems that the 'nothing else will do' approach is still misapplied in the family courts. See e.g. in *Re R (A Child)* [2021] EWCA Civ 1019, [2021] 3 FCR 590.
[348] *Re W (Adoption: Contact)* [2016] EWHC 3118 (Fam).
[349] E. Neil (2009): this contact will often be indirect contact such as letterbox contact, although it may also take the form of direct contact.

adopters should be in control of that contact and so declined to order that contact take place.[350] Although *Re W* was unusual, in that the grandparents did not have an existing relationship with A, it is typical of the courts' approach to post-adoption contact: while there is increasing recognition that contact with birth families can be positive for adopted children, there remains a reluctance to override the discretion of adoptive parents and to require that contact takes place.

At one time, any form of ongoing contact with the birth family was considered inconsistent with the very nature of adoption and the child's new status as a member of their adoptive family.[351] The changing nature of adoption means that children are now more likely to have existing relationships with members of their birth family, which may have ongoing importance to the child even after the adoption has been made. Research on post-adoption contact, perhaps unsurprisingly, demonstrates that the risks and benefits vary considerably between different situations and that decisions on contact should be individualised to the particular child and responsive to changes based on their experiences.[352] At the most serious, contact with abusive birth parents may perpetuate the trauma experienced by the child; contact with birth family members who resent the adoption may also lead to disruption in the child's attachment in the adoptive family.[353] Contact can, however, give positive benefits to children, birth parents and adoptive parents. In particular, it can assist the child in understanding their dual identity and the reasons for their removal from the birth family; the openness that this brings may also enhance relationships and security within the adoptive family.[354] Contact with wider birth family members, such as siblings and grandparents, is particularly associated with positive experiences, especially where the child had lived with those birth family members before being placed for adoption.[355] A further dimension is added by the ease with which social media can be used by adopted children and birth families to track down and make contact with one another. There is considerable anecdotal evidence of serious damage being done to adopted children and their relationships with their adoptive families by unregulated, unsupported contact being made through social media.[356] The risk of such a chaotic, secretive reintroduction of the birth family during the child's adolescence means that there is a good pragmatic argument for introducing managed contact from early childhood.

Despite this changing landscape, there is still considerable judicial ambivalence to ordering post-adoption contact. When making an adoption order, the court is directed to consider the value of the child maintaining links with his or her birth family and whether to order contact.[357] There is also now specific

---

[350] *Re W (Adoption: Contact)* [2016] EWHC 3118 (Fam), at [67]–[68].
[351] *Re V (A Minor) (Adoption: Dispensing with Agreement)* [1987] 2 FLR 89.
[352] E. Neil *et al.* (2013) esp. pp. 290–3.   [353] C. Boyle (2017).
[354] E. Neil *et al.* (2013) esp. ch. 6.   [355] C. Boyle (2017).
[356] E. King (2013); H. Oakwater (2012).   [357] ACA 2002, ss 1(4)(f) and 46(6).

provision, in section 51A of the ACA 2002,[358] for the court to make a post-adoption contact order requiring or prohibiting contact with a range of people, including the child's birth relatives.[359] There is some support for the need to promote contact between siblings who cannot be found a placement together. In *Re P (Placement Orders: Parental Consent)*,[360] there was weighty evidence that the relationship between two siblings was of great value to them both and the children's guardian was particularly worried that the relationship would be jeopardised if they were to be placed with separate adopters. Wall LJ considered that contact between them was so important that the mother would almost certainly gain leave to apply for a revocation of the placement order if the adopters or foster carers with whom the child was placed failed to facilitate contact between them.[361] In this case, the contact was of such fundamental importance that it was right that the court remained in control of that contact rather than leaving it to the discretion of the adoption agency or prospective parents.[362] While *Re P* seems to indicate a positive approach to the court's role in maintaining contact, it was concerned with the placement stage; cases arising post-adoption have been far more sceptical of the court's role in maintaining contact. For example, in *Oxfordshire County Council* v. *X*,[363] the Court of Appeal overturned a decision to allow the birth parents to retain an annual photograph of the child against the wishes of the adoptive parents, who feared that it may be used to trace the child. The Court of Appeal found that it was not enough to simply give considerable weight to the adoptive parents' views; instead, the judge should have reminded himself that it would be 'extremely unusual' to make an order that the parents did not agree with, although their wishes were not dispositive. The child's welfare[364] was primarily found in the security of the adoptive placement and, as such, unless they had no reasonable basis, the court should respect the parents' fears. There is, nonetheless, a good argument that this approach risks conflating the welfare of the child with the interests of the parents by neglecting the fact that the child

---

[358] Inserted by Children and Families Act 2014.

[359] An application for a s. 51A order requires leave unless brought by the child or the adopters: ACA 2002, s. 51A(4). The s. 51A order only applies to agency adoptions: for other adoptions, applications would proceed as applications for a child arrangements order under CA 1989, s. 8.

[360] [2008] EWCA Civ 535, [2008] 2 FCR 185, also discussed above in relation to dispensing with parental consent.

[361] Ibid. at [150].

[362] Ibid. at [153]–[154]. For a good example of a family court case that placed similar emphasis on the importance of sibling contact at the placement stage, see *Re A, B, C, D, E (Children: Placement Orders: Separating Siblings)*, Case No. DE16CO0355 (15 March 2018).

[363] [2010] EWCA Civ 581, [2011] Fam 11.

[364] This case was decided before s. 51A was inserted into ACA 2002 by Children and Families Act 2014. As a result, the case was decided under the CA 1989 and its approach to welfare. There is a plausible argument that a decision made under s. 51A ought to be treated differently as the ACA 2002 specifically directs the court to consider the child's welfare over the whole of their life, but the Court of Appeal has rejected such arguments and continued to take the view that it is 'extremely unusual' for contact to be ordered against the wishes of adopting parents: *Re B (A Child) (Post-Adoption Contact)* [2019] EWCA Civ 29.

may have an independent interest in the relationship with their birth family.[365] The case also demonstrates why post-adoption contact orders are so rarely made: if it is 'extremely unusual' to grant contact against the wishes of the adoptive parents in cases such as *Oxfordshire CC* v. *X*, yet unnecessary to grant orders in cases such as *Re W*, where they are supportive of contact, this leaves a very narrow band of unusual cases in which contact orders might be made.

Harris-Short cogently maintains that both birth families and children have a right under Article 8 of the ECHR to retain their familial links through some kind of contact, if all agree that this is beneficial to them.[366] Certainly, it is arguable that 'the ability of birth parents to retain some contact with their child may also help to make compulsory adoption more Convention compliant'.[367] Although, as Harris-Short observes, if the courts were to favour post-adoption contact orders more commonly, the support services currently offered to adoptive parents would have to improve greatly.[368] These arguments were, however, substantially rejected in *Seddon* v. *Oldham Metropolitan Borough Council*,[369] in which a birth mother, who had had letterbox contact, sought to argue that failure to order direct contact, against the wishes of the adoptive parents, was a breach of Article 8. Crucially, the court found that the severance of the legal ties between birth parent and child also brought to an end their family life for the purposes of Article 8, so meaning that it was not applicable to an application for post-adoption contact.[370] A similar difficulty might be found in any attempt to use the CRC provisions to bolster a claim that the child has a right to post-adoption contact, given that the UK interprets the word 'parent' in the CRC to mean only those recognised in national law as parents.[371] The conclusion that Article 8 has no relevance to post-adoption contact may, however, be premature. The ECtHR jurisprudence on the question is very sparse and does not support an unequivocal conclusion that adoption brings all family life with the birth family to an end.[372] The existence

---

[365] See K. Hughes and B. Sloan (2011), although they make it clear that they do not dispute the outcome in this particular case.

[366] S. Harris-Short (2008) pp. 38–41.   [367] B. Hale and J. Fortin (2008) p. 102.

[368] S. Harris-Short (2008) pp. 43–51.   [369] [2015] EWHC 2609 (Fam), [2016] Fam 171.

[370] In *Re TJ (Relinquished Baby: Sibling Contact)* [2017] EWFC 6, at [27], it was held that adoption also brought pre-existing family life between siblings to an end, although in this case the siblings in question had not met and in fact did not know of each other's existence, and so there was no factual element of family life.

[371] Upon ratification, the UK made the following declaration: 'The United Kingdom interprets the references in the Convention to "parents" to mean only those persons who, as a matter of national law, are treated as parents. This includes cases where the law regards a child as having only one parent, e.g. where a child has been adopted by one person only and in certain cases where a child is conceived other than as a result of sexual intercourse by the woman who gives birth to it and she is treated as the only parent.'

[372] S. Hansen (2019); K. Hughes and B. Sloan (2011) consider the current case law. See also the subsequent case of *IS* v. *Germany* [2014] ECHR 577, in which the court only went so far as to say that 'biological kinship between a natural parent and a child alone, without any further legal or factual elements indicating the existence of a close personal relationship, *might be* insufficient to attract the protection of Article 8', at [68] (emphasis added).

of family life in Article 8 has long been held to include de facto family relationships and not merely those that are recognised by legal structures. This means that while the biological ties themselves will not be sufficient to sustain family life beyond adoption, the fact of a close and personal relationship may do so, particularly if it has continued after adoption, a point recognised in *Seddon* itself.[373] This may be a particularly persuasive argument in relation to siblings,[374] or other family members, who may have had a close relationship, but no part in the decisions and circumstances leading up to the adoption. Finally, even if a post-adoption relationship is not sufficient to qualify as 'family life', the ECtHR appears to have accepted that it may qualify as 'private life' for the purposes of Article 8.[375] Recognising the 'private life' aspects of post-adoption contact would give particular protection to its role in a child's identity. For all of these reasons, while *Seddon* may well be correct to hold that the biological relationship is not enough in itself to found Article 8 family life post-adoption, there may well be other human rights implications to post-adoption contact, particularly where a close relationship exists in practice. Of course, as in *Seddon* itself, the interest that the child has in a secure home with their adoptive parents will often be enough to outweigh the interests of the child and birth family to contact, particularly direct contact. This is, however, a fact-dependent balance that should be recognised for its important implications for the child. At present, the judicial approach puts the decision almost entirely in the hands of the adoptive parents, in contrast to non-adoption contact cases, in which parents are frequently obliged to support their children's relationships against their own will.

(6) Conclusion

It is undoubtedly the case that for the majority of children their relationship with their birth parents and wider family is of vital importance to their lives and well-being and merits assiduous protection in law. Yet, as each of the areas considered in this chapter shows, those relationships can also be a source of harm. In these cases, other relationships provide the care and responsibility that might commonly be expected from the birth parents. The disputes considered in this chapter are complex and fact-sensitive: there is no simplistic formula that can be used to encapsulate the value that should be attributed to family relationships across the myriad situations raised before the courts. Unfortunately, in each of the areas of law considered in this chapter, influential statements of the *general* importance of birth family relationships to children's

---

[373] [2015] EWHC 2609 (Fam), [2016] Fam 171, at [54].

[374] See D. Monk and J. Macvarish (2018) for consideration of both the importance of sibling relationships and the obstacles to maintaining sibling relationships following adoption. In particular, social workers expressed concern that the pool of potential adopters would diminish if they were required to maintain sibling contact.

[375] *IS* v. *Germany* [2014] ECHR 577.

lives have had a distorting impact on the case law, making it more difficult to achieve protection for *individual* children to find protection for their wider needs and relationships. These general statements have often been clothed in the language of children's rights to know and be brought up by their parents, although in truth, they often disguise claims to adults' rights to care for their children. The distortion of children's rights is made easier by the way in which Strasbourg allows the Article 8 rights of children to be fused with those of adults. Ironically, when adopting this approach, the courts appear more likely to neglect making a proper assessment of the child's psychological needs or wider rights, than in cases where this 'rights language' is not used.

In each area considered, the law has oscillated between reliance on broad principles based on the child's right to be brought up by birth parents, and a return to an approach rooted in a highly individualised welfare assessment that recognises their wider interests. The discretionary nature of judicial decision-making in these areas of child law masks a lack of clarity over the issues at stake and the attraction of such principles is their ability to give a veneer of consistency and rigour. This is particularly so in the context of funding cuts, in which the resources available for nuanced legal advice, rigorous welfare assessment and judicial fact-finding are in short supply. While it cannot remedy these limitations on resources, a well-founded children's rights framework for decision-making, based on the full range of rights that children possess, might lead to a more beneficial outcome for the children who are the subject of these disputes. While children's right to family life with their birth family is undoubtedly important, a myopic focus on that right can neglect the wider relationships recognised in the CRC and children's full rights to a safe and secure upbringing.

Bibliography

NB: Many of these publications can be obtained on the relevant organisation's website.

All-Party Parliamentary Group (APPG) on Domestic Violence (2016) *Domestic Abuse, Child Contact and the Family Courts*, APPG on Domestic Violence.

Bainham, A. (2003) 'Contact as a Right and Obligation' in Bainham, A., Lindley, B., Richards, A. and Trinder, L. (eds) *Children and Their Families: Contact, Rights and Welfare*, Hart Publishing.

(2010) 'Rowing Back from *Re G*? The Natural Parent Presumption in the Supreme Court' *Family Law* 394.

Barnett, A. (2017) '"Greater than the Mere Sum of Its Parts": Coercive Control and the Question of Proof' 29 *Child and Family Law Quarterly* 379.

(2020a) *Domestic Abuse and Private Law Children Cases: A Literature Review*, Ministry of Justice.

(2020b) 'A Genealogy of Hostility: Parental Alienation in England and Wales' 42 *Journal of Social Welfare and Family Law* 18.

Birchall, J. and Choudhry, S. (2018) '*What about My Right Not to Be Abused?' Domestic Abuse, Human Rights and the Family Courts*, Women's Aid.

Boyle, C. (2017) 'What Is the Impact of Birth Family Contact on Children in Adoption and Long-Term Foster Care? A Systematic Review' 22 *Child and Family Social Work* 22.

British Agencies for Adoption and Fostering (2001) *Memorandum of Evidence Submitted to the House of Commons Special Select Committee on the Adoption and Children Bill*, BAAF.

British Association of Social Workers (BASW) (2001) *Memorandum of Evidence Submitted to the House of Commons Special Select Committee on the Adoption and Children Bill*, BASW.

Bryson, C., Purdon, S. and Skipp, A. (2017) *Understanding the Lives of Separated and Separating Families in the UK: What Evidence Do We Need?*, Nuffield Foundation.

Buchanan, A., Hunt, J., Bretherton, H. and Bream, V. (2001) *Families in Conflict: Perspectives of Children and Parents on the Family Court Welfare Service*, The Policy Press.

Cafcass and Women's Aid (2017) *Allegations of Domestic Abuse in Child Contact Cases*, Cafcass.

Choudhry, S. (2003) 'The Adoption and Children Act 2002, the Welfare Principle and the Human Rights Act 1998 – a Missed Opportunity?' 15 *Child and Family Law Quarterly* 119.

Collier, R. (2005) 'Fathers 4 Justice, Law and the New Politics of Fatherhood' 17 *Child and Family Law Quarterly* 511.

Collier, R. and Sheldon, S. (2006) *Fathers' Rights Activism and Law Reform in Comparative Perspective*, Hart Publishing.

Coy, M., Scott, E., Tweedale, R. and Perks, K. (2015) 'It's Like Going through the Abuse Again' 37 *Journal of Social Welfare and Family Law* 1.

Day Sclater, S. and Kaganas, F. (2003) 'Mothers, Welfare and Rights' in Bainham, A., Lindley, B., Richards, A. and Trinder, L. (eds) *Children and Their Families: Contact, Rights and Welfare*, Hart Publishing.

Department for Children Schools and Families (DCSF) Advisory Group (2010) *No Simple Answers: DCSF Advisory Group Report on Private Fostering 2008–2010*, DCSF.

Department for Constitutional Affairs (DCA)/Department for Education and Skills/Department for Trade and Industry (2004) Cm 6273, *Parental Separation: Children's Needs and Parents' Responsibilities*, The Stationery Office.

(2005) Cm 6452, *Parental Separation: Children's Needs and Parents' Responsibilities: Next Steps*, The Stationery Office.

Department for Education (DfE) (2015) *Notifications of Private Fostering Arrangements in England: Year Ending 31 March 2015*, DfE.

Doughty, J., Maxwell, N. and Slater, T. (2020) 'Professional Responses to "Parental Alienation": Research-Informed Practice' 42 *Journal of Social Welfare and Family Law* 68.

Eekelaar, J. (1973) 'What Are Parental Rights?' 89 *Law Quarterly Review* 210.

(1988) 'Access Rights and Children's Welfare' 51 *Modern Law Review* 629.

(1991) 'The Wardship Jurisdiction, Children's Welfare and Parents' Rights' 107 *Law Quarterly Review* 386.

(2014) 'Family Justice on Trial' *Family Law* 473.

Everett, K. and Yeatman, L. (2010) 'Are Some Parents More Natural than Others?' 22 *Child and Family Law Quarterly* 290.

Family Mediation Council (FMC) (2018) *Code of Practice for Family Mediators* (revised May 2018).

Family Policy Studies Centre (2000) Families and Adoption, Family Briefing Paper 14, Family Policy Studies Centre.

Fehlberg, B., Smythe, B., Maclean, M. and Roberts, C. (2011) 'Legislating for Shared Time Parenting after Separation: A Research Review' 25 *International Journal of Law, Policy and the Family* 318.

Fenton-Glynn, C. (2015) *Adoption without Consent*, European Parliament Policy Department.

(2016) 'Adoption Targets: The Good, the Bad and the Ugly' *Family Law* 148.

Fortin, J. (1999) 'Re D (Care: Natural Parent Presumption)' 11 *Child and Family Law Quarterly* 435.

Fortin, J., Hunt, J. and Scanlan, L. (2012) *Taking a Longer View of Contact: The Perspectives of Young Adults Who Experience Parental Separation in Their Youth*, Project Report. School of Law, Brighton.

Fortin, J., Ritchie, C. and Buchanan, A. (2006) 'Young Adults' Perceptions of Court-Ordered Contact' 18 *Child and Family Law Quarterly* 211.

Geldof, B. (2003) 'The Real Love that Dare Not Speak Its Name' in Bainham, A., Lindley, B., Richards, A. and Trinder, L. (eds) *Children and Their Families: Contact, Rights and Welfare*, Hart Publishing.

Gilmore, S. (2006) 'Contact/Shared Residence and Child Well-Being: Research Evidence and its Implications for Legal Decision-Making' 20 *International Journal of Law, Policy and the Family* 478.

(2008) 'Disputing Contact: Challenging Some Assumptions' 20 *Child and Family Law Quarterly* 285.

(2020) 'Justice and Implacable Hostility to Contact: Parental Beliefs, Factual Foundation and Justification' 136 *Law Quarterly Review* 136.

Goisis, A., Ozcan, B. and Sigle, W. (2016) *Child Outcomes after Parental Separation: Variations by Contact and Court Involvement*, Ministry of Justice.

Goldstein, J., Freud, A. and Solnit, A. (1973) *Beyond the Best Interests of the Child*, Free Press.

Hale, B. (2014) 'New Families and the Welfare of Children' 36 *Journal of Social Welfare and Family Law* 26.

Hale, B. and Fortin, J. (2008) 'Legal Issues in the Care and Treatment of Children with Mental Health Problems' in Rutter, M., Bishop, D., Pine, D., Scott, S., Stevenson, J., Taylor, E. and Thapar, A. (eds) *Rutter's Child and Adolescent Psychiatry*, Blackwell Publishing.

Hansen, S. (2019) 'Birth Relationships after Adoption: Is There a Role for Article 8?' 31 *Child and Family Law Quarterly* 211.

Harding, M. and Newnham, A. (2015) *How Do County Courts Share the Care of Children Between Parents? Full Report*, Nuffield Foundation.

Harold, G. and Murch, M. (2005) 'Inter-Parental Conflict and Children's Adaptation to Separation and Divorce: Theory, Research and Implications for Family Law, Practice and Policy' 17 *Child and Family Law Quarterly* 185.

Harris, P. and George, R. (2010) 'Parental Responsibility and Shared Residence Orders: Parliamentary Intentions and Judicial Interpretations' 22 *Child and Family Law Quarterly* 151.

Harris-Short, S. (2001) 'The Adoption and Children Bill – a Fast Track to Failure?' 13 *Child and Family Law Quarterly* 405.

(2008) 'Making and Breaking Family Life: Adoption, the State and Human Rights' 35 *Journal of Law and Society* 28.

(2011) 'Building a House upon Sand: Post-Separation Parenting, Shared Residence and Equality – Lessons from Sweden' 23 *Child and Family Law Quarterly* 344.

Harwood, J. (2021) 'Presuming the Status Quo? The Impact of the Statutory Presumption of Parental Involvement' 43 *Journal of Social Welfare and Family Law* 119.

Haux, T. and Platt, L. (2015) *Parenting and Contact before and after Separation*, Nuffield Foundation.

Herring, J. (2014) 'The Welfare Principle and the Children Act: Presumably It's about Welfare?' 36 *Journal of Social Welfare and Family Law* 14.

Hester, M. (2011) 'The Three Planet Model: Towards an Understanding of Contradictions in Approaches to Women and Children's Safety in Contexts of Domestic Violence' 41 *British Journal of Social Work* 837.

Hughes, K. and Sloan, B. (2011) 'Post-Adoption Photographs: Welfare, Rights and Judicial Reasoning' 23 *Child and Family Law Quarterly* 393.

Hunt, J. and Macleod, A. (2008) *Outcomes of Applications to Court for Contact Orders after Parental Separation or Divorce*, Ministry of Justice.

Hunt, J. with Roberts, C. (2004) Child Contact with Non-Resident Parents, Family Policy Briefing 3, University of Oxford.

Hunter, R. and Barnett, A. (2013) *Fact-Finding Hearings and the Implementation of the President's Practice Direction: Residence and Contact Orders: Domestic Violence and Harm*, Family Justice Council.

Hunter, R., Burton, M. and Trinder, L. (2020) *Assessing Risk of Harm to Children and Parents in Private Law Children Cases: Final Report*, Ministry of Justice.

Joint Committee on Human Rights (JCHR) (2018) *Enforcing Human Rights*, HL Paper 171, HC 669, The Stationery Office.

Justice Committee (2012) *Fourth Report, Pre-Legislative Scrutiny of the Children and Families Bill*, The Stationery Office.

Kaganas, F. (2013) 'A Presumption that "Involvement" of Both Parents Is Best: Deciphering Law's Messages' 25 *Child and Family Law Quarterly* 270.

Kaganas, F. and Piper, C. (2002) 'Shared Parenting – a 70% Solution?' 14 *Child and Family Law Quarterly* 365.

(2018) 'Looking after Grandchildren: Unfair and Differential Impacts?' in Clough, B. and Herring, J. (eds) *Ageing, Gender and Family Law*, Routledge.

King, E. (2013) '"May I Be Your Facebook Friend?" Life Stories and Social Media' *Family Law* 1399.

Law Commission (1986) *Working Paper No. 96, Family Law, Review of Child Law: Custody*, Her Majesty's Stationery Office.

Lewis, J. (2004) 'Adoption: The Nature of Policy Shifts in England and Wales, 1972–2002' 18 *International Journal of Law, Policy and the Family* 235.

Lowe, N. and Douglas, G. (2014) *Bromley's Family Law*, Oxford University Press.

Macaskill, C. (2002) *Safe Contact? Children in Permanent Placement and Contact with Their Birth Relatives*, Russell House Publishing.

Maclean, M. and Eekelaar, J. (2016) *Lawyers and Mediators: The Brave New World of Services for Separating Families*, Bloomsbury Publishing.

Masson, J. (2006) 'Consent Orders in Contact Cases: A Survey of Resolution Members' 36 *Family Law* 1041.

(2016) 'Relationships vs Relatedness in Family Justice' 38 *Journal of Social Welfare and Family Law* 456.

(2017) 'Disruptive Judgments' 29 *Child and Family Law Quarterly* 401.

McFarlane, A. (2014) 'Making Parental Responsibility Work' *Family Law* 1264.

(2017) 'Holding the Risk: The Balance between Child Protection and the Right to Family Life' *Family Law* 610.

Monk, D. and Macvarish, J. (2018) *Siblings, Contact and the Law: An Overlooked Relationship?*, Birkbeck.

Mooney, A., Oliver, C. and Smith, M. (2009) *Impact of Family Breakdown on Children's Being*, Department for Children, Schools and Families.

National Organisation for the Counselling of Adoptees and Parents (2001) *Memorandum of Evidence Submitted to the House of Commons Special Select Committee on the Adoption and Children Bill*, NORCAP.

Neil, E. (2009) 'Post-Adoption Contact and Openness in Adoptive Parents' Minds: Consequences for Children's Development' 39 *British Journal of Social Work* 5.

Neil, E., Beek, M. and Ward, E. (2013) *Contact after Adoption: A Follow-up in Late Adolescence*, University of East Anglia.

Norgrove, D. (2011) *Family Justice Review*, Department of Education.

Oakwater, H. (2012) *Bubble Wrapped Children, How Social Networking Is Transforming the Face of 21st Century Adoption*, Andrews UK.

Ofsted (2014) *Private Fostering: Better Information, Better Understanding*, Ofsted.

Performance and Innovation Unit (PIU) Report (2000) *The Prime Minister's Review of Adoption*, Cabinet Office.

Reece, H. (2006) 'UK Women's Groups' Child Contact Campaign: "So Long as It Is Safe"' 18 *Child and Family Law Quarterly* 538.

Rhoades, H. (2002) 'The "No-Contact Mother": Reconstructions of Motherhood in the Era of the "New Father"' 16 *International Journal of Law, Policy and the Family* 71.

(2006) 'Yearning for Law: Fathers' Groups and Family Law Reform in Australia' in Collier, R. and Sheldon, S. (eds) (2006) *Fathers' Rights Activism and Law Reform in Comparative Perspective*, Hart Publishing.

Rhoades, H. and Boyd, S. (2004) 'Reforming Custody Laws: A Comparative Study' 18 *International Journal of Law, Policy and the Family* 119.

Schaffer, H. (1998) *Making Decisions about Children*, Blackwell.

Sloan, B. (2013) 'Confliction Rights: English Adoption Law and the Implementation of the UN Convention on the Rights of the Child' 25 *Child and Family Law Quarterly* 40.

Smart, C. (2004) 'Equal Shares: Rights for Fathers or Recognition for Children?' 24 *Critical Social Policy* 484.

Smart, C. and Neale, B. (1997) 'Arguments Against Virtue: Must Contact be Enforced?' 27 *Family Law* 332.

(1999) *Family Fragments?*, Polity Press.

Sturge, C. and Glaser, D. (2000) 'Contact and Domestic Violence – the Experts' Court Report' 30 *Family Law* 615.

Taylor, R. (2018) 'Grandparents and Grandchildren: Relatedness, Relationships and Responsibility' in Clough, B. and Herring, J. (eds) *Ageing, Gender and Family Law*, Routledge.

Tobin, J. (2017) 'Fixed Concepts But Changing Conceptions: Understanding the Relationship between Parents and Children under the CRC' in Ruck, M., Peterson-Badali, M. and Freeman, M. (eds) *Handbook of Children's Rights: Global and Multidisciplinary Perspectives*, Routledge.

Trinder, L. (2010) 'Shared Residence: A Review of Recent Research Evidence' 22 *Child and Family Law Quarterly* 475.

(2014) 'Climate Change: The Multiple Trajectories of Shared Care Law, Policy and Social Practices' 26 *Child and Family Law Quarterly* 30.

Trinder, L., Connolly, J., Kellett, J. and Notley, C. (2005) A Profile of Applicants and Respondents in Contact Cases in Essex, DCA Research Series 1/05, DCA.

Trinder, L., Connolly, J., Kellett, J., Notley, C. and Swift, L. (2006) Making Contact Happen or Making Contact Work? The Process and Outcomes of In-court Conciliation, DCA Research Series 3/06, DCA.

Trinder, L., Hunt, J., Macleod, A., Pearce, J. and Woodward, H. (2013) *Enforcing Contact Orders: Problem-Solving or Punishment?*, University of Exeter and Nuffield Foundation.

Van Bueren, G. (1995) *The International Law on the Rights of the Child*, Martinus Nijhoff Publishers.

Walby, S. (2004) *The Cost of Domestic Violence*, Women and Equality Unit, DTI.

Weyland, I. (1997) 'The Blood Tie: Raised to the Status of a Presumption' 19 *Journal of Social Welfare and Family Law* 173.

Women's Aid (2016) *Nineteen Child Homicides*, Women's Aid.

7

Parents' Decisions and Young Children's Health Rights

(1) Introduction

The Convention on the Rights of the Child (CRC) recognises that without good health, children have little hope of fulfilling their potential. Article 24(1) requires states to:

> recognise the right of the child to the enjoyment of the highest attainable standard of health and to facilities for the treatment of illness and rehabilitation of health. States Parties shall strive to ensure that no child is deprived of his or her right of access to such health care services.

Article 3 requires anyone reaching a decision relating to a child to give primary consideration to his or her best interests and Article 6 requires states to recognise every child's right to life, and to promote their survival and development. These requirements should not be too onerous for the UK to fulfil, with its well-established health service and comparatively good hygiene and living conditions by global standards. Nevertheless, advances made by medical technology sometimes confront parents and doctors alike with difficult dilemmas over what is the appropriate decision to reach. For those children too young to make medical decisions themselves,[1] their parents will act as primary decision-makers and guardians of their child's rights and interests. But parents may not always be best placed to judge those interests. The complexity of some medical decisions means that parents face difficulties in evaluating evidence and assessing risk. Parents may act from self-interest or idiosyncratic beliefs, or be blinded by their own fears of losing their much-loved child. For these reasons, the decision of parents cannot be absolute, particularly given the importance of the child's rights to life, health and bodily integrity. The point at which the state can step in to require or withhold treatment, against the wishes of parents, is one of the most contentious areas in child law.

---

[1] This chapter is concerned with children who are not considered competent to make their own medical decisions, although, as discussed below, the views of those children remain important in determining their best interests. The issue of adolescent decision-making and competence to take medical decisions is considered in Chapter 11.

This assessment of these complex issues is primarily concerned with two very different aspects of this area of law, both of which have serious implications for children's rights. The first deals with life and death decisions and the extent to which children's right to life can be endangered by decisions relating to their health. The second deals with the extent to which parents have the right to consent to practices, such as circumcision and tissue donation, which are not motivated by the child's medical needs, but for non-therapeutic reasons. These cases may represent a serious invasion of the child's bodily integrity and are particularly susceptible to the conflation of the interests of parents and children. The chapter starts with a brief assessment of the general principles which recur in much of the case law regarding children's medical care.

(2) General Principles

(A) Children's Healthcare

Advances in medical technology, the availability of antibiotics and immunisation, together with a higher standard of living, have led to British children today enjoying far better general health than did their counterparts a century ago. The two main measures of health in early childhood, infant mortality and life expectancy at birth, have improved dramatically over this period, with a particularly striking reduction in the number of children's lives being lost to infectious diseases.[2] Thus, the downward trend in infant mortality has continued into the twenty-first century, largely due to improvements in diet and sanitation, ante and post-natal medical care, infant medical care and vaccines and immunisation programmes.[3] Similarly, the rate of life expectancy has steadily increased.[4] Nonetheless, there are signs that this progress is slowing or even reversing.[5] Further, there are significant concerns about the way in which poverty and social class affect children's health and their chances of surviving to a healthy adulthood. There is, for example, a greater chance of children in deprived families suffering from low birth weight,[6] mental health problems, obesity and diabetes.[7] Furthermore, the rates of infant mortality[8]

---

[2] Between 1685 and 1801, the annual incidence of smallpox peaked at 2,355 per 100,000 population and never fell below 313 per 100,000.

[3] ONS (2008) p. 96: between 1930 and 2006, the rate of infant deaths (prior to the age of 1) per 1,000 live births reduced from 60 to 5. This rate further reduced to its lowest recorded rate of 3.6 per 1,000 live births in 2014, before increasing to 3.9 in 2017. This increase may be explained, at least in part, by a reduction in the rate of still births: ONS (2019) pp. 3–4.

[4] ONS (2008) p. 94: between 1901 and 2006, male life expectancy increased from 45 to 77 and female life expectancy from 49 to 82.

[5] ONS (2019).   [6] J. Maher and A. Macfarlane (2004) p. 40.

[7] Healthcare Commission (2007) pp. 68–9.

[8] ONS (2019): in 2017, mortality rates in the most deprived areas were 5.2 per 1,000 live births compared to 2.7 in the least deprived areas.

and accidental child deaths[9] vary significantly according to the parents' socio-economic circumstances. Indeed, it appears that rather than achieving government targets to reduce health inequalities in infant mortality and life expectancy at birth, the inequalities gap is actually widening.[10] Despite overall improvements, UK rates of infant mortality and low birth weight compare very poorly with other OECD countries.[11]

The fact that children and young people have different health needs from adults means that it is critically important to ensure that their health needs are given careful consideration in policy-making and resource planning 'if further progress is to be made in improving the nation's quality of life'.[12] In addition to national strategies, local authorities (LAs) are further legally obliged to improve the well-being of young children in their areas and to reduce inequalities in their 'physical and mental health and emotional well-being'.[13] Nevertheless, the extent to which children's health can be improved on a national or local level not only depends on better healthcare facilities and financial support for families with children. It also depends on parents being educated about their children's health needs and the state's willingness to intervene to ensure that these needs are met. There is currently no legal compulsion on parents to allow health agencies to monitor their children's health. Indeed, the government assumes that parents are the best judges of their children's medical needs. Parents are not obliged to allow health visitors into their homes to examine their babies.[14] Similarly, although compulsory immunisation would help prevent the periodic outbreaks of serious childhood diseases,[15] there is no legal obligation on parents to ensure that their children receive vaccinations.[16] The question of whether there should be mandatory[17] or compulsory vaccination programmes that require parental compliance is one that sharply raises the respective health responsibilities of parents and the state. The problem is particularly difficult to address on usual principles of best interests, given that the purpose of vaccination is not simply to protect the

---

[9] Healthcare Commission (2007) p. 68: children of parents who had never worked or were long-term unemployed were 13 times more likely to die from unintentional injury than children of parents in higher managerial and professional occupations.

[10] RCPCH (2017).   [11] R. Viner *et al.* (2018).   [12] Healthcare Commission (2007) p. 63.

[13] Childcare Act 2006, s. 1.

[14] R. Dingwall *et al.* (1995) pp. 218–21 discuss 'the liberal compromise' between state surveillance and non-intervention.

[15] ONS (2008) p. 96. E.g. the mumps outbreaks in a number of UK universities in 2019.

[16] Cf. the Compulsory Vaccination Acts 1853 and 1867, which compelled parents to have their children vaccinated against smallpox within the first years of their lives and imposed fines or imprisonment for default. This was so unpopular that the Anti-Vaccination League was founded in 1867 to spearhead opposition.

[17] Some states have introduced mandatory vaccination programmes which do not criminalise parents, but instead withhold access to services or benefits from those families who have not vaccinated their children (without reasonable excuse). E.g. in Australia, eligibility for certain welfare benefits has been tied to compliance with vaccination programmes: 'Benefits to be cut for Australian parents who reject children's vaccines in "no jab, no pay" plan', *The Independent*, 20 April 2015.

child in question, but also to establish collective, herd immunity. This question has become pressing in the light of the fall in the number of children vaccinated against measles, mumps and rubella and the resurgence of measles cases across the UK. Despite reassurance from the government and medical professionals, a substantial number of parents remain concerned about the safety of the MMR vaccine, a concern that appears to be fuelled by misinformation online and through social media.[18] Similar concerns have been raised in relation to the Covid-19 vaccination programme, with parents citing concerns about the novel nature of the vaccine and the balance of risks for children, given the relatively low risks that Covid-19 poses to them.[19] Those parents who strenuously oppose immunisation[20] would undoubtedly claim not only that compulsion would infringe their own rights to respect for their family life under Article 8 of the European Convention for the Protection of Human Rights and Fundamental Freedoms (1950) (ECHR), but also their children's right to family life and bodily privacy and integrity.[21] Given that the state has an evident responsibility for public health, including establishing collective protection from infectious diseases, as well as a responsibility to individual children, it is likely that any such challenge would fail provided that the features of the compulsory regime met the requirement of proportionality.[22]

There is an obvious concern on the part of the government not to interfere with parents' own views regarding the medical treatment of their children. Nevertheless, as the criminal law recognises, inactivity regarding healthcare may endanger children's lives.[23] Parents may be guilty of criminal neglect if

[18] E.g. *Re H (A Child) (Parental Responsibility: Vaccination)* [2020] EWCA Civ 664, [2021] Fam 133, concerning a child in LA care whose parents objected to routine vaccinations, including MMR. The Court of Appeal found that routine vaccinations would usually be in the child's best interests. The court also found that the decision to give routine vaccinations against parental objection for a child in care would not usually be within the category of 'grave' decisions that required court approval. Instead, the LA could give consent under CA 1989, s. 33(3)(b), although the views of the parents should be considered. J. Bridgeman (2007) pp. 108–17 discusses childhood immunisation.

[19] E.g. *Re C (Looked After Child) (Covid-19 Vaccination)* [2021] EWHC 2993 (Fam), which concerned parental objection to Covid-19 vaccination for a child in care. The child was 12 years old and wished to have the vaccine. The court applied the same principles as in *Re H* (ibid.) and took the view that any vaccination in the national programme would ordinarily be in the child's best interests in the absence of specific concerns related to their individual circumstances.

[20] E.g. *Re C (Welfare of Child: Immunisation)* [2003] EWHC 1376 (Fam), [2003] 2 FLR 1054 (decision confirmed by the Court of Appeal in *Re C (Welfare of Child: Immunisation)* [2003] EWCA Civ 1148, [2003] 2 FLR 1095); discussed by R. Huxtable (2004).

[21] *Wain* v. *United Kingdom* (1987) 9 EHRR 122, per the European Commission of Human Rights: despite his son's serious reaction to the diphtheria, tetanus and whooping cough vaccination, a father's rights under Art. 8 had not been infringed by the government's failure to provide parents with detailed information about the risks of particular vaccines, since the vaccination scheme was voluntary. See also the European Commission of Human Rights' decision in *Association X* v. *United Kingdom*, App. No. 7154/75, (1978) 14 DR 31.

[22] See e.g. *Re H (A Child) (Parental Responsibility: Vaccination)* [2020] EWCA Civ 664, [2021] Fam 133, at [98]. E. Cave (2017) considers these arguments in more detail.

[23] Children and Young Persons Act (CYPA) 1933, s. 1(1). Discussed in R. Taylor and L. Hoyano (2012).

they wilfully fail to provide their child with adequate medical aid.[24] Indeed, the criminal law has shown little sympathy for parents whose failure to ensure that their child receives medical attention has been motivated by religious convictions,[25] or those who refuse to consent to what is deemed to be essential medical care.[26] Criminal sanctions may, however, be too late to protect the child's health. Furthermore, the House of Lords' strict interpretation of the wilful element of the offence of child neglect[27] has left children vulnerable to the 'stupidity or fecklessness' of their parents.[28] Child protection laws can probably achieve far more than the criminal law in terms of ensuring that a child's right to healthcare is fulfilled. LAs are legally obliged to ensure that they seek out and protect children who are suffering or are likely to suffer 'significant harm' for any reason, and this will obviously include a duty to investigate cases of ill-health due to parental inattention.[29] Young children, particularly babies, die very quickly if they become ill and are not provided with medical attention. Depending on the urgency of the situation, parental failure to seek medical attention can be dealt with by the LA seeking a child assessment order[30] or an emergency protection order.[31] Alternatively, they may seek a specific issue order regarding the child's further assessment or treatment.[32]

(B) Principles of Common Law

Given that the law generally adopts a non-interventionist approach to family life, can parents be trusted to protect adequately their young children's right to good health? English common law requires parents to reach all decisions regarding their children's upbringing, more particularly regarding medical

---

[24] CYPA 1933, s. 1(2)(a).

[25] E.g. *R* v. *Senior* [1899] 1 QB 283. See J. Bridgeman (2007) pp. 85–95 for a discussion of the criminal law's approach to parents who neglect their children's medical care.

[26] E.g. *Oakey* v. *Jackson* [1914] 1 KB 216.

[27] *R* v. *Sheppard* [1981] AC 394, per the House of Lords (majority): CPYA 1933, s. 1(1) (which imposes liability on anyone who '*wilfully* assaults, ill-treats, neglects, abandons or exposes him' – emphasis added) includes only parents able to appreciate the need to obtain medical care for their child and not parents who through stupidity, ignorance or personal inadequacy fail to do so. Discussed in R. Taylor and L. Hoyano (2012).

[28] [1981] AC 394. See Lord Fraser's dissenting judgment, at 416–17.

[29] CA 1989, s. 47, discussed in Chapter 15.

[30] CA 1989, s. 43. A child assessment order would enable the LA to establish whether the child needs medical attention and, if so, what form it should take. But such an order is inappropriate in emergencies, since it can only be obtained on notice to the parents, and it does not confer parental responsibility on the LA.

[31] CA 1989, s. 44: an emergency protection order can be obtained rapidly ex parte and confers on the holder parental responsibility, thereby entitling the LA to consent to medical treatment. Discussed in Chapter 15.

[32] E.g. *Re C (HIV Test)* [1999] 2 FLR 1004: the LA obtained a specific issue order authorising the testing for HIV of a baby against the wishes of both her parents.

care, in accordance with their best interests.[33] Any decisions reached which manifestly infringe such a principle can be challenged, even overridden.[34] Indeed, case law demonstrates that the best interests test, as interpreted by parents, does not always protect children's rights, without the intervention of doctors or the courts. The real difficulty is that most parents find it relatively easy to justify their decisions by reference to their children's best interests. Since it is virtually impossible to interpret such a term objectively, it is questionable whether it provides the child with adequate protection. As Gerald Dworkin has observed, the personal views of individual parents may define the 'best interests' of their child in terms of the parent's best interests.[35]

Once a doctor is consulted, he or she must comply with the principles of common law, which are little different from those applying to adults.[36] Both legislation[37] and case law[38] acknowledge that it is unlawful for doctors to treat children without consent, unless it is to avoid serious harm or death, in an emergency.[39] In the case of a child too young and immature to be deemed *Gillick*-competent,[40] doctors will seek consent from the child's parents, as his or her proxies.[41] It is they who brought their child into the world and they are assumed to be the adults most likely to have his or her interests at heart.[42] In general terms, since any single adult with parental responsibility (PR)[43] can consent to a child's medical treatment,[44] consent can be obtained from either

---

[33] Discussed further in Chapter 4. It is arguable that, for essentially trivial non-therapeutic procedures, the test is the less rigorous 'not against the child's best interests'. See *S v. S; W v. Official Solicitor (or W)* [1972] AC 24.

[34] *Gillick v. West Norfolk and Wisbech Area Health Authority* [1986] AC 112, per Lord Scarman, at 184.

[35] G. Dworkin (1982) p. 200. See also *NHS Trust v. A* [2007] EWHC 1696 (Fam), [2008] 1 FLR 70, per Holman J, at [40] (x): parents' wishes are 'wholly irrelevant to consideration of the objective best interests of the child save to the extent in any given case that they may illuminate the quality and value to the child of the child–parent relationship'.

[36] *Re F (Mental Patient: Sterilisation)* [1990] 2 AC 1, per Lord Goff, at 74; *Sidaway v. Board of Governors of the Bethlem Royal Hospital and the Maudsley Hospital* [1985] AC 871, per Lord Scarman, at 882: medical treatment of an adult without consent will normally, unless life-saving treatment is required in an emergency when it can be carried out under the doctrine of necessity, amount to a trespass to the person and to a criminal assault. Also discussed in Chapter 11.

[37] Family Law Reform Act (FLRA) 1969, s. 8(1); discussed in Chapter 11.

[38] *Gillick v. West Norfolk and Wisbech Area Health Authority* [1986] AC 112.

[39] Ibid., per Lord Scarman, at 189.

[40] As discussed further below, even if the child is not yet competent to make decisions concerning their treatment, their views will nonetheless be important in determining their best interests.

[41] Ibid. at 184: 'It is abundantly plain that the law recognises that there is a right and a duty of parents to determine whether or not to seek medical advice in respect of their child, and, having received advice, to give or withhold consent to medical treatment.'

[42] G. Dworkin (1982) p. 204.

[43] But NB, in the event of any parental dispute over immunisation (*Re C (Welfare of Child: Immunisation)* [2003] EWCA Civ 1148, [2003] 2 FLR 1095) or circumcision (*Re J (Specific Issue Orders: Child's Religious Upbringing and Circumcision)* [2000] 1 FLR 571), consent from a single parent is insufficient: judicial authority must be obtained.

[44] But NB CA 1989, s. 3(5): any person with care of a child, but without PR (e.g. a childminder or foster carer) can do 'what is reasonable in all the circumstances of the case for the purpose of

parent with PR, even if the other objects. Nonetheless, given the importance of both parents' responsibility, if parents cannot agree on a very serious matter of medical treatment, the medical team may decide to seek the court's view as to the child's best interests rather than relying on the consent of one parent to override the objections of the other.[45] Similarly, LAs have been required to obtain judicial approval in disagreements with parents over grave decisions concerning the medical treatment of children in care[46] despite the fact that the LA has PR and may control that of the parents.[47] These cases underline the fact that the law encourages collaboration between those with parental responsibility in making important medical decisions. Further, the parental role is considered to be of great importance, even in cases where there has been a risk of significant harm, both because the parent is often best placed to know the child and because the parent–child relationship is protected through Article 8 of the ECHR.

The importance of collaboration to protect the child's best interests is also recognised in cases in which parents and doctors disagree over a child's medical treatment. In such cases, both parents and doctors owe duties to act in the child's best interest. Jo Bridgeman has argued that this gives rise to an obligation on both parents and the medical team to act in partnership, recognising the parents' unique knowledge of the individual child and the doctors' medical expertise.[48] In responding to chronic conditions, this partnership will be of particular importance, given that the parents are likely to play a significant role in the child's ongoing care and that that care is likely to change over time. If the partnership between parents and medical professionals breaks down and they are unable to agree on the best course of action

---

safeguarding or promoting the child's welfare'. This might include consenting to therapeutic medical treatment.

[45] *An NHS Trust* v. *SR* [2012] EWHC 3842, at [2]. In this case, a dispute arose as to the post-operative treatment of a child following surgery to remove a malignant brain tumour. The mother strongly opposed the conventional treatment of radiotherapy and chemotherapy on the basis of the acknowledged risk of serious detrimental side effects from the radiotherapy. At one point, the mother had 'gone missing' with the child in order to prevent such treatment from taking place. The father accepted the advice of the child's doctors that the conventional treatment gave the best chance of saving his life, despite the risks associated with it. The court approved the treatment and specifically ordered that the father's consent would be sufficient for future medical decisions, provided that the issue had been discussed with the mother where reasonable and practicable. The court considered that the seriousness of the child's treatment and depth of disagreement between the parents meant that the NHS Trust was right to bring the case to the court, despite the father's consent.

[46] *Re Jake (A Child)* [2015] EWHC 2442 (Fam), [2016] 2 FCR 118; see also *Re AB* [2018] EWFC 3, in which the application for a care order was withdrawn with the approval of the court, which made it clear that it would usually be inappropriate and ineffective for an LA to apply for a care order for the purpose of consenting to medical treatment against the wishes of parents, esp. at [24]. But see *Re H (A Child) (Parental Responsibility: Vaccination)* [2020] EWCA Civ 664, [2021] Fam 133: routine vaccinations are not 'grave' decisions requiring court decision in cases of parental objection.

[47] Children Act 1989, s. 33(3) and (4): the LA may control the PR of the parents if 'satisfied that it is necessary to do so in order to safeguard or promote the child's welfare'.

[48] J. Bridgeman (2017).

for the child, the resulting dispute can be extremely damaging. Mediation and other forms of alternative dispute resolution are increasingly being used in order to attempt to resolve disputes while upholding this important partnership.[49] If this is not possible, the dispute must be taken to court,[50] with a decision being reached over what most accords with the child's best interests. But this is an indeterminate standard which seldom produces any clear-cut answers. The court will make its own judgment as to the child's best interests, but will seek the views of both the medical team and the parents, which, as the case law shows,[51] will often fundamentally differ. These common law principles are now reinforced by the protection provided by human rights law, which requires practitioners to approach children's healthcare from a subtly different perspective.

(C) A Rights-Based Approach?

Overall, the Human Rights Act (HRA) 1998 has not had a substantial impact on the framework of the law concerning young children's healthcare. While judges are now more likely to cite children's rights in medical decisions than they were in the past,[52] the courts have tended to view children's rights as reinforcing, rather than challenging, the pre-existing approach to children's medical treatment.[53] In a sense, this is not surprising, given the centrality of the concept of best interests to domestic medical law and to children's rights cases under both the ECHR and CRC.[54] Nonetheless, some writers, such as Bridgeman, argue that invoking rights in complex medical scenarios is not helpful. When parents and professionals are seeking to do their best for the child:

> rights are not the most appropriate instrument for structuring relationships and resolving disputes. Rights make abstract claims when particular needs require

---

[49] E. Harrop (2019). A number of proposals to make mediation compulsory in such cases have been made. These include the private members' bill, Access to Palliative Care and Treatment of Children Bill 2019–21.

[50] By application to the High Court for a declaration under the inherent jurisdiction, or by application for a specific issue order under the CA 1989, s. 8. In *Re JM (A Child)* [2015] EWHC 2832 (Fam), [2016] 2 FLR 235, Mostyn J reaffirmed that specific issue orders provided the appropriate route for the resolution of disputes between parents and healthcare professionals over children's medical treatment. For procedural reasons, the court recommended that serious cases, especially those involving deprivation of liberty, should be pursued through both the inherent jurisdiction and s. 8; see esp. [25]–[28].

[51] Discussed below.

[52] E.g. *Re King* [2014] EWHC 2964 (Fam), [2014] 2 FLR 855, at [30]. Contrast *Re T (Wardship: Medical Treatment)* [1997] 1 FLR 502, at 512, discussed below.

[53] *Portsmouth NHS Trust v. Wyatt and Wyatt, Southampton NHS Trust intervening* [2004] EWHC 2247 (Fam), [2005] 1 FLR 21, at [25]. See also *NHS Trust v. A* [2007] EWHC 1696 (Fam), [2008] 1 FLR 70, per Holman J, at [44].

[54] In the Matter of Alfie Evans, Permission to Appeal Determination, Supreme Court, 20 March 2018, at [14]. *Gard v. United Kingdom* (2017) 65 EHRR SE9, at [107]. As noted in Chapter 3, the Supreme Court has stressed that the development of domestic law should be the first means by which human rights are given protection.

investigation. They force the parties to express their positions in ways which polarise and position them in conflict when, in relation to children's healthcare, they share a goal.[55]

This criticism might be thought to have particular resonance in those cases in which parents have sought to use their own human rights to protect their decisions concerning their child's medical treatment from court challenges based on the child's best interests.[56] In these cases, the language of rights has been used in a way which appears to exacerbate and prolong conflict between parents and medical professionals, to the detriment of the child. These parental claims have, however, consistently been rejected by the domestic courts and the European Court of Human Rights (ECtHR). Instead, the courts have interpreted the rights of children and parents in a manner which reinforces the central common law framework. While parents' Article 8 rights include the right to respect for decisions concerning the child's medical treatment,[57] this right is not unlimited and does not entitle parents to take measures that would harm the child's health and development.[58] Further, the courts have consistently upheld the principle that any conflict between the parent's decision-making rights and the child's rights must be resolved according to the child's best interests.[59] Strasbourg's interpretation of children's rights has also emphasised the importance of a collaborative approach between parents and medical professionals. This can be seen in the ECtHR decision in *Glass* v. *United Kingdom*,[60] which acknowledged that Article 8 of the ECHR gave David Glass, a severely disabled child, the right to challenge his doctors for treating him without the consent of his mother, as his legal proxy. The ECtHR's confirmation that children have a right to physical integrity under Article 8, which will be infringed by treatment without consent, has played a part in reinforcing the importance of cooperation between parents and medical professionals in treating young children.[61] The principles of human rights law concerning medical treatment of young children have largely been interpreted in a way that is harmonious with the common law described above. Further, courts applying the common law have taken account of ECHR rights to inform their interpretation of children's best interests.[62]

Although the human rights framework primarily reinforces existing common law principles, it has a valuable role in reminding parents and medical practitioners alike that child patients have an independent status of their own. Further,

---

[55] J. Bridgeman (2007) p. 234.

[56] E.g. *Great Ormond Street Hospital for Children NHS Foundation Trust* v. *Yates* [2017] EWCA Civ 410, [2018] 4 WLR 5; *Re E (A Child)* [2018] EWCA Civ 550, [2019] 1 WLR 594. Discussed further below.

[57] *Nielsen* v. *Denmark* (1988) 11 EHRR 175.

[58] *Johansen* v. *Norway* (1996) 23 EHRR 33, at [78].

[59] *Gard* v. *United Kingdom* (2017) 65 EHRR SE9, at [107].   [60] [2004] 1 FLR 1019, at [70].

[61] See also *MAK and RK* v. *United Kingdom*, App. Nos 45901/05 and 40146/06, [2010] 2 FLR 451.

[62] *Portsmouth NHS Trust* v. *Wyatt and Wyatt, Southampton NHS Trust intervening* [2004] EWHC 2247 (Fam), [2005] 1 FLR 21, at [25].

human rights law provides a clear framework for evaluating the full range of interests and rights impacted by medical decisions. The CRC contains a number of relevant rights. As noted above, Article 24 entitles children to the highest attainable standard of health and all treatment decisions should be taken bearing in mind the child's best interests, as a primary consideration.[63] Furthermore, Article 6 of the CRC requires states to recognise every child's right to life, and to promote their survival and development, while Article 12 provides for children's right to be heard in decisions concerning them. The ECHR also contains a range of relevant rights, most importantly, the right to life in Article 2, protection from inhuman and degrading treatment in Article 3 and the right to bodily integrity in Article 8.[64] These rights have been particularly relevant in setting the standards by which medical decisions must be made, rather than in directing the outcome of those decisions. For example, it is clear that Article 2 of the ECHR does not require doctors to provide treatment where to do so would, in their view, be futile and not in the best interests of the child.[65] Any decision to withdraw treatment must, however, take place within a regulatory system that complies with Article 2, incorporating consultation with the child and her parents and allowing application to the court to determine the child's best interests in cases of doubt.[66] In this way, human rights law is not only relevant to the individual decision, but also to setting the regulatory framework and values in which those decisions are taken.

The value of a rights approach is that it reminds parents and medical practitioners of the child's independent status, with rights of his or her own. The rights approach is a valuable counterpoint to the best interests test: it provides a framework against which a best interests test can be evaluated to ensure that it genuinely serves the child and not the adults surrounding the decision. A rights-based approach can also provide a powerful way of challenging existing orthodoxies and setting the standards by which decisions are made in order to find a treatment plan that is best for the individual child.

(D) Legal Competence to Consent and the Right to Be Consulted

One of the guiding principles of international children's rights law is the child's right to be heard and to contribute to decisions concerning them.[67] In medical decisions, this right is important both to respecting the dignity of the child and to tempering the risk that the 'best interests' test will result in a paternalistic

---

[63] CRC, Art. 3. See further: Committee on the Rights of the Child (2013).

[64] See *Glass v. United Kingdom* [2004] 1 FLR 1019, at [70].

[65] *NHS Trust A v. M; NHS Trust B v. H* [2001] 1 All ER 801, per Dame Elizabeth Butler-Sloss P, at [37]. See also *Re Y (No. 1)* [2015] EWHC 1920 (Fam), at [37].

[66] *Lambert and others v. France* (Grand Chamber) (2016) 62 EHRR 2, concerning an adult patient in a persistent vegetative state. Applied to decisions concerning children in *Gard v. United Kingdom* (2017) 65 EHRR SE9 and *Afiri and Biddarri v. France* (dec.), No. 1828/18, 23 January 2018.

[67] CRC, Art. 12.

assessment that fails to recognise the individual child concerned. When treating an older child, doctors will turn, in the first place, to the child for consent to treatment. Despite the legislative presumption that those over the age of 16 can legally consent to treatment,[68] according to the *Gillick*[69] principle, many young people under that age may also be legally capable of consenting for themselves. The boundary at which children are competent to consent to medical treatment is contentious and considered in more detail in a later chapter.[70] Some argue that even very young children are capable of making far-reaching decisions about their health.[71] In Alderson's research, medical staff considered that some 3- and 4-year-old children were able to understand medical information 'as well as the average adult', and that 'exceptional' 5- and 6-year-olds were thought to be able to make complex, wise decisions.[72] This led Alderson and Montgomery to suggest the introduction of a new code governing healthcare for children which incorporated a legal presumption that all 5-year-olds should be deemed competent to consent to all healthcare.[73] This suggestion is unlikely to be successful given the research on children's cognitive development, which suggests that before early adolescence, younger children are far less likely to be able to weigh up alternatives and cope rationally with complex decisions affecting their upbringing.[74] While a universal young age of presumed consent is unlikely to reflect the maturity and understanding of most children, *some* young children are able to make *some* decisions effectively. Not only do individual children vary, but decisions concerning medical treatment cover a wide range of circumstances, from routine care of common grazes to end-of-life decisions for children with terminal conditions. For example, children living with chronic conditions will be able to draw on their own experiences to gain a unique depth of understanding of their own situation.[75] For these reasons, the point at which a child may consent to treatment is nuanced and individual.

Many younger children will not have the competence to consent to important medical decisions, but this does not mean that they do not have a right to be consulted. Article 12 of the CRC does not require children to be given the right to autonomy before they have acquired the capacity to exercise it; instead, it protects the right for children to be involved in decisions relating to their future and for their views to be given weight in those decisions. Such involvement is, however, crucial, wherever possible. Although children are often too immature to *decide* such matters, even very young children may be able to communicate their perspective[76] and have important views over the costs and benefits to them

---

[68] FLRA 1969, s. 8(1).

[69] *Gillick* v. *West Norfolk and Wisbech Area Health Authority* [1986] AC 112.

[70] Discussed in Chapter 11.   [71] P. Alderson and J. Montgomery (1996) ch. 2.

[72] P. Alderson (1993) p. 193.

[73] P. Alderson and J. Montgomery (1996) ch. 5. The authors' proposed code of practice contained guidance on the factors to consider when attempting to rebut such a presumption.

[74] Discussed in Chapter 9.   [75] K. Moreton (2020).

[76] P. Alderson *et al.* (2005) consider that even premature babies may be able to communicate their experiences of care.

of the proposed treatment. It insults their dignity and self-respect for parents and doctors to make decisions which infringe their right to bodily integrity without consulting them. By the same token, they will respond to medical treatment much better if they have been fully involved in it, understand it and have confidence in it. Current medical guidance acknowledges this and states:

> Children and young people are individuals with rights that should be respected. This means listening to them and taking into account what they have to say about things that affect them. It also means respecting their decisions and confidentiality.[77]

This guidance should mean that children are informed, respected and involved in decisions taken with medical professionals. A prominent example of such a case is that of Hannah Jones, whose decision, at 12 years old, that she did not want to receive a potentially life-saving heart transplant was respected by her doctors in the light of her extensive experience of invasive medical treatment throughout her young life.[78] In Hannah's case, the NHS Trust did not take the case to court to challenge her wishes. Those cases that do reach court show a rather variable approach to the importance of children's views. In *Re X (A Child)*,[79] the views of a pregnant 13-year-old girl were given great weight despite the fact that she was found not to be competent to decide whether to have an abortion. The seriousness of either imposing an abortion against her will, or compelling her to continue with a pregnancy she did not want, meant that only the most compelling arguments could justify a best interests assessment that did not accord with the child's own views.[80] In other cases, the courts seem much more willing to discount the views of even relatively mature children. For example, in *F* v. *F*,[81] the objections of L, a 15-year-old, and her 11-year-old sister to receiving the MMR vaccine were dismissed as naïve and overridden. Those views were outweighed in the court's assessment of best interests, despite the relatively minimal advantages of receiving the vaccine to the individual children concerned and the seriousness of L's principled objections, as a vegan, to the use of gelatine in the vaccine. As Emma Cave notes, it is not clear that such an approach to the views of mature children is sufficient to give them the 'due weight' required by Article 12 of the CRC.[82]

---

[77] GMC (2007) para. 7. See also RCPCH (2015).

[78] Discussed in detail by K. Moreton (2020). In the event, Hannah changed her mind and later received a successful heart transplant at age 14.

[79] [2014] EWHC 1871 (Fam).

[80] Ibid. at [9]–[10]: 'A child or incapacitated adult may, in strict law, lack autonomy. But the court must surely attach very considerable weight indeed to the albeit qualified autonomy of a mother who in relation to a matter as personal, intimate and sensitive as pregnancy is expressing clear wishes and feelings, whichever way, as to whether or not she wants a termination.' In this case, the child wished to have an abortion, although she had initially decided to continue the pregnancy and arguments had been prepared on that basis.

[81] [2013] EWHC 2683 (Fam).   [82] E. Cave (2014).

(3) A Child's Right to Life: Withholding or Withdrawing Treatment from Desperately Ill Children

(A) Life-Sustaining Treatment for Babies and Young Children

The most difficult cases in which these principles are applied are often those concerning life-sustaining treatment for babies and young children. The increasingly sophisticated technology available to neonatal intensive care units has transformed the chances of survival of many desperately ill newborns. While the percentage of babies born prematurely and with a low birthweight has gradually increased in recent years, the rate of neonatal infant mortality among these babies has steadily decreased.[83] These babies may, however, require intensive intervention to survive more than a few days or weeks. Some survive beyond a few months, but with conditions that are incompatible with independent life, or with such a low quality of life that decisions must be made as to whether to continue the aggressive interventions keeping them alive. Obvious dilemmas are posed by the fact that although the lives of some extremely premature or desperately ill babies[84] can be saved by resuscitation and intensive care, life-saving therapies may themselves cause pain and distress and may mean lifelong severe disabilities, or they may 'only prolong inevitable death'.[85]

However bleak the prognosis, even the youngest premature baby possesses the same right to life under Article 2 of the ECHR as any other person.[86] Legal protection for the right to life attaches to any legal person, from the moment of being born alive and separate from the mother.[87] During the 1960s and 1970s, influenced by the poor quality of life of those treated, some doctors followed a deliberate policy of selective non-treatment of infants with severe medical conditions.[88] As Mason and Laurie comment, such conduct came 'perilously close to breaking the law'[89] since it ensured that at least some of these newborns failed to survive who could have been kept alive.[90] In the early 1980s, the trial of Dr Arthur made plain that to end the life of a newborn baby, irrespective of his

---

[83] M. Brazier (2006) pp. 30–2.

[84] Ibid. para. 5.1 describes those extremely premature babies who are born alive at or before the gestational age of 25 weeks and 6 days as babies born at 'the borderline of viability'.

[85] Ibid. paras 3.9–3.10.

[86] There remains some ambiguity as to whether ECHR, Art. 2 can have any application prior to birth: *Vo* v. *France* [2004] ECHR 326.

[87] *Rance* v. *Mid-Downs Health Authority* [1991] 1 All ER 801, per Brooks J, at 817: the criminal law protects any child 'born alive', i.e. capable of breathing and existing independently of its mother.

[88] J. Read and L. Clements (2004) pp. 489–94 discuss the practice developed by Dr Lorber, relating to the selective non-treatment of infants born with severe spina bifida and hydrocephalus. See also M. Brazier (2006) p. 135, Box 8.1 on current Dutch guidelines on the practice of ending the life of severely ill new-born infants.

[89] J. Mason and G. Laurie (2006) p. 545.

[90] It was estimated that in the mid-1980s, anything up to 30 per cent of deaths occurred in neonatal intensive care units due to the deliberate withdrawal of life support. Ibid. p. 546, citing A. Whitelaw (1986).

disabilities, by deliberate action carries the same criminal sanctions as killing an adult.[91] This principle was later reinforced by the Court of Appeal's decision in *Re A (Conjoined Twins: Medical Treatment)*,[92] that the immensely mentally and physically disabled Mary[93] had as much right to life as her sister, Jodie.[94]

The fact that a seriously ill child has the right to life does not mean that doctors are obliged to provide life-saving treatment, irrespective of the fact that he or she has no realistic prospect of survival and whose future life is considered to be full of suffering.[95] In *Re C (A Minor) (Wardship: Medical Treatment)*,[96] the Court of Appeal confirmed that a dying baby's life does not have to be extended by artificial means, irrespective of the circumstances. The utility of the treatment is to be judged by the child's best interests, which in turn depend on the quality of life which might be achieved for the child through the proposed treatment. Many would agree with the view that if nothing is to be gained by further intervention, a dying baby has a right to die with dignity.[97] While this case was decided prior to the HRA 1998, it is consistent with the interpretation of the right to life in Article 2, which does not impose an absolute obligation to treat, where to do so would be futile and against the best interests of the child.[98] Article 2 also permits the *removal* of the child's life-sustaining treatment, despite the fact that death will almost certainly follow, provided that the decision is made within a regulatory system

---

[91] *R* v. *Arthur* (1981) 12 BMLR 1: Dr Arthur, a well-known and respected paediatrician, placed a newly born baby with Down's syndrome (whose parents did not want him to survive) on a regime described as 'nursing care only' involving suppressing his appetite with a large dose of a sedating drug and thereafter being kept comfortable. The baby died soon after birth. Dr Arthur was tried for murder, the charge being later reduced to attempted murder. Discussed by M. Gunn and J. Smith (1985) and J. Read and L. Clements (2004) pp. 484–6.

[92] [2001] 1 FLR 1.

[93] She had a very poorly developed 'primitive' brain, a very poorly functioning heart and no functioning lung tissue.

[94] The Court of Appeal confirmed the authorisation by the court below of surgery separating the twins, despite the fact that it would effectively kill Mary.

[95] Ibid. at [8.21]–[8.22].

[96] [1989] 2 All ER 782, per Lord Donaldson MR, at 787: confirmed the order of court below that the medical staff were not obliged to administer antibiotics and use intravenous feeding in the event of C (a 4-month-old massively handicapped and terminally ill baby) acquiring an infection or becoming unable to take feeds by mouth; they could care for her in a way which would relieve her suffering and allow her to die peacefully and with dignity.

[97] Ibid.

[98] *Admissibility decision, Application no. 61827/00 by David and Carol Glass* v. *United Kingdom*, unreported. See also *NHS Trust A* v. *M; NHS Trust B* v. *H* [2001] 1 All ER 801, per Dame Elizabeth Butler-Sloss P, at [37], in relation to two adult permanent vegetative state (PVS) patients: the positive obligation imposed by ECHR, Art. 2 only obliges medical teams to keep a terminally ill patient alive if, according to responsible medical opinion, this would be in the patient's best interests. It 'does not impose an absolute obligation to treat if such treatment would be futile'. See also *A National Health Service Trust* v. *D* [2000] 2 FLR 677, per Cazalet J, at 695: a declaration authorising the medical team not to continue with mechanical ventilation or to resuscitate a dying infant with an irreversible and worsening lung condition was not counter-indicated by ECHR, Art. 2.

that is compatible with the Convention.[99] Most importantly, the decision must be made in consultation with the parents[100] and application to court to determine the child's best interests must be available in cases of dispute that cannot otherwise be resolved.[101] These twin requirements of parental involvement and possibility of court resolution each require careful consideration.

(B) The Doctor/Parent Partnership

The collaborative relationship between parents and doctors, discussed above, is of particular importance in cases in which the child is dependent on life-sustaining treatment and so in the constant care of a medical team. Doctors treating these children, who are too young to speak for themselves,[102] must seek consent to treatment, or its withdrawal, from their parents, who have primary responsibility for their child's health.[103] The ECtHR's decision in *Glass* v. *United Kingdom*[104] reinforces this need for parental involvement. The court made it clear that in all but the most urgent situations, the objections of a child's parent to a particular form of treatment could only be overridden by a court acting in the best interests of the child.[105] Otherwise, as in *Glass* itself, a medical team will be unable to justify infringing the child's rights under Article 8, by reference to the 'necessity' of the interference.[106] Nonetheless, doctors traditionally wield considerable power in such situations, since ultimately it is they, as the gatekeepers to treatment resources, who decide what treatment, if any, is medically indicated. The developing medical technology has also become increasingly difficult for parents to comprehend, undermining their ability to evaluate the doctors' advice. At the same time, particularly with the assistance of the internet, parents are able to access a greater range of information from diverse sources[107] and more often disagree with the doctors over the proper interpretation of their view of what is in the child's best interests.[108] Many commentators on medical law consider that the increasing

---

[99] *Lambert and others* v. *France* (Grand Chamber) (2016) 62 EHRR 2, concerning an adult patient in a persistent vegetative state. Applied to decisions concerning children in *Gard* v. *United Kingdom* (2017) 65 EHRR SE9 and *Afiri and Biddarri* v. *France* (dec.), No. 1828/18, 23 January 2018.

[100] The child's wishes will, of course, also be important in cases in which the child is able to communicate those wishes or has been able to do so in the past.

[101] *Gard* v. *United Kingdom* (2017) 65 EHRR SE9.

[102] Although P. Alderson *et al.* (2005) suggest that even very young babies can communicate preferences and personality.

[103] *Re King* [2014] EWHC 2964 (Fam), [2014] 2 FLR 855.

[104] *Glass* v. *United Kingdom* [2004] 1 FLR 1019: the Official Solicitor had advised the medical team at Portsmouth hospital that no judge had ever overturned a doctor's decision to withdraw treatment/alleviate symptoms. The medical team concluded that they could give morphine to David Glass even against his mother's wishes.

[105] Ibid. at [79].   [106] I.e. under Art. 8(2). Ibid. at [78]–[81].

[107] M. Brazier (2006) para. 3.18.

[108] Sometimes pro-life groups support parents' applications. See e.g. the cases of Charlie Gard and Alfie Evans, discussed further below.

availability of information has contributed to a shift in the relationship between patients and doctors: patients are increasingly recognised as autonomous rights-holders and treated as active participants in decisions rather than passive recipients of care.[109] As Bridgeman argues, this shift is evident in cases concerning the medical treatment of children, where it is 'parents who are claiming rights and making choices'.[110] As a result, there is an increasing emphasis in paediatric practice on sharing information with parents and working with them at an early stage to facilitate informed decision-making, recognising the importance of this collaborative relationship.[111]

Despite efforts to work with parents in decision-making, tensions can arise, especially in the emotionally charged context of withdrawal of treatment. On the one hand, the medical team may consider that parents who object to withdrawal of life-sustaining treatment are being unrealistic. They may urge that when a child is suffering a serious fatal condition, constant intervention may not only be futile but cruel, since it will cause the child distress, not balanced by any real benefit, in terms of quality of life. On the other hand, the parents may argue that they are closer to their child than the doctors, and can detect improvements which others cannot see. They might also argue that the child derives pleasure from experiences and relationships and so has a greater quality of life than the doctors are able to discern.[112] The very different perspectives of doctors and parents was well-expressed by MacDonald J:

> For the treating doctors involved in such cases, seen through the prism of medical best interests life is at best a barely wakeful shadow burdened by futile medical treatment or, at worst, mere oblivion. For parents, seen through the prism of abiding love and fierce devotion and the amplifying effect on those emotions of the flattering voice of hope, life is still a faded jewel that has not yet been robbed away from the body and one that may yet regain its lustre.[113]

The common dilemma is that these desperately ill children sometimes suffer numerous episodes of respiratory failure requiring ventilation to keep them alive – but it is unclear whether this is a steady downward process. In cases like this, the fact that the child is not dying in the short term may encourage his or her parents to reject the medical team's pessimistic medical prognosis; they hope for a miracle and argue that their child is not ready to die.[114] Rapid

---

[109] *Montgomery (Appellant)* v. *Lanarkshire Health Board (Respondent) (Scotland)* [2015] UKSC 11, [2015] AC 1430 has been widely, although not universally, regarded as such a case.

[110] J. Bridgeman (2019) pp. 150–1.   [111] E. Harrop (2019).

[112] E.g. *King's College Hospital NHS Foundation Trust* v. *Thomas* [2018] EWHC 127 (Fam), at [91].

[113] *Barts NHS Foundation Trust* v. *Shalina Begum, Muhhamed Raqeeb and Tafida Raqeeb (by Her Children's Guardian)* [2019] EWHC 2531 (Admin) and [2019] EWHC 2530 (Fam), [2020] 3 All ER 663, at [1].

[114] E.g. Charlotte Wyatt, born prematurely at 26 weeks with serious medical problems, survived to over 4 years old, and Luke Winston-Jones, diagnosed with Edward's syndrome, causing multiple defects, with a predicted life expectancy of 1 year, on birth was only expected to live for a few days; he survived to 10 months. Discussed by L. Jackson and R. Huxtable (2005).

advances in medical technology undoubtedly encourage parents to hope that treatment will be found to keep their ill children alive or improve their condition.

Most doctors will go to considerable lengths to resolve such a dispute without going to court,[115] but they must act in their young patient's best interests. The law only expects them to accommodate parental wishes 'as far as professional judgment and conscience will permit'.[116] They might feel obliged to reject parental requests for treatment if they consider it to be inappropriately invasive or outside the range of viable treatments for the child. If alternative forms of dispute resolution fail, there may be no alternative but to turn to court for judicial determination of the child's best interests and authorisation for treatment or its withdrawal.

(C) Court Decisions, Best Interests and Withdrawal of Medical Treatment

While the courts have stressed that there is no legal difference between withholding or withdrawing life support,[117] disputes most often arise over the withdrawal of life-sustaining treatment from a child who has survived for many months or even longer. Although such decisions are difficult in practice, given the complexity of the medical evidence and the high stakes for the child and parents, the legal framework in which the decision is made is relatively straightforward and has been remarkably stable.

Lord Donaldson MR's decision in *Re J (A Minor) (Wardship: Medical Treatment)*[118] remains an influential starting point. Although decided prior to the HRA, the approach that derives from the case has been found to be consistent with the requirements imposed by Article 2 of the ECHR in withdrawing life-sustaining treatment.[119] In *Re J*, the Court of Appeal held that the doctors were not obliged to resuscitate J again, having done so twice already, bearing in mind that resuscitation was an invasive process and would cause him distress. The decision in *Re J* was important in that it established that a child does not need to be actually dying before a medical team can contemplate withholding treatment. While confirming the important difference between taking no steps to extend artificially the child's life, which might be lawful, and taking steps to terminate the child's life, which will never be,[120] the

---

[115] L. Austin and R. Huxtable (2019).

[116] *Re Wyatt* [2005] EWHC 2293 (Fam), [2005] 4 All ER 1325, per Hedley J, at [41].

[117] *Re MB* [2006] EWHC 507 (Fam), [2006] 2 FLR 319, per Holman J, at [18]–[23].

[118] [1990] 3 All ER 930: apart from severe and permanent brain damage at birth, 4.5-month-old J (born very prematurely) had other disabilities suggesting an extremely poor quality of life, with predicted paralysis in all his limbs, deafness, limited intellectual abilities and no speech. Although not dying, his life expectancy was uncertain, but might extend to his late teens.

[119] *Gard* v. *United Kingdom* (2017) 65 EHRR SE9, applying *Lambert and others* v. *France* (Grand Chamber) (2016) 62 EHRR 2. See also *Re Y (No. 1)* [2015] EWHC 1920 (Fam), at [37].

[120] *Re J (A Minor) (Wardship: Medical Treatment)* [1990] 3 All ER 930, per Taylor LJ, at 943.

court rejected any absolute notion of the sanctity of life. Lord Donaldson MR's words are often cited:

> But in the end there will be cases in which the answer must be that it is not in the interests of the child to subject it to treatment which will cause increased suffering and produce no commensurate benefit, giving the fullest possible weight to the child's, and mankind's, desire to survive.[121]

The decision affirms the very strong presumption in favour of prolonging life,[122] but that continued intervention is not essential if the benefit available to the child would be so limited that it would be against the child's best interests to strive to keep him or her alive. Indeed, continued medical intervention will only be lawful if it is in the child's best interests, meaning that the question for the court is whether continued treatment is in the child's best interests, rather than whether withdrawal can be justified.[123] A balancing exercise has to be performed between what can be achieved by active intervention to keep the child alive and the burdens of such invasive procedures, as well as the extremely poor quality of life that survival may bring.[124] This approach has been distilled into 'ten propositions' by Holman J in *Re MB*,[125] which summarise the correct approach to such cases and have been widely drawn upon in subsequent decisions. The propositions stress that each case should be considered on its own facts, often by drawing up a balance sheet of the benefits and burdens of continuing and withdrawing treatment.[126] While the views of the doctors and parents will be influential and must be carefully considered, the role of the court is not to choose between them, but to come to its own independent assessment of the child's best interests; in so far as possible, it ought to view those interests from the perspective of the child concerned.[127]

Case law indicates that the courts still very seldom disagree with doctors' views over what treatment is in a child's best interests,[128] although this may reflect the fact that doctors are reluctant to take cases to court unless the

---

[121] Ibid. at 938.   [122] Ibid.

[123] *Re A (A Child)* [2016] EWCA 759, at [31], drawing on *Aintree University Hospital NHS Foundation Trust v. James* [2013] UKSC 67, [2014] AC 591.

[124] *Re J (A Minor) (Wardship: Medical Treatment)* [1990] 3 All ER 930, at 939.

[125] *Re MB* [2006] EWHC 507 (Fam), [2006] 2 FLR 319, at [16]. See also *NHS Trust v. A* [2007] EWHC 1696 (Fam), [2008] 1 FLR 70, at [40]; *Re A (A Child)* [2016] EWCA 759, at [33]–[34]; *King's College Hospital NHS Foundation Trust v. Thomas* [2018] EWHC 127 (Fam), at [69].

[126] *Wyatt v. Portsmouth NHS Trust* [2005] EWCA Civ 1181, [2006] 1 FLR 554, per Wall LJ, at [87]; *Re MB* [2006] EWHC 507 (Fam), [2006] 2 FLR 319, per Holman J, at [58]–[62]; *NHS Trust v. A* [2007] EWHC 1696 (Fam), [2008] 1 FLR 70, per Holman J, at [61]–[67].

[127] *Re MB* [2006] EWHC 507 (Fam), [2006] 2 FLR 319, per Holman J, at [69].

[128] Examples include: *Alder Hey Children's NHS Foundation Trust v. Evans* [2018] EWHC 818 (Fam); *King's College Hospital NHS Foundation Trust v. Thomas* [2018] EWHC 127 (Fam); *Great Ormond Street Hospital for Children NHS Foundation Trust v. Yates & Gard* [2017] EWHC 972. This tendency can also be seen in the older case law. *Re J (A Minor) (Wardship: Medical Treatment)* [1990] 3 All ER 930, per Lord Donaldson MR, at 934; *Re J (A Minor) (Wardship: Medical Treatment)* [1992] 4 All ER 614, per Lord Donaldson MR, at 622 and Balcombe LJ, at 625; *Re R (A Minor) (Wardship: Medical Treatment)* [1991] 4 All ER 177, per

consequences for the child are grave.[129] Nonetheless, although it is true that judges are often strongly influenced by the medical evidence, assessing the child's best interests is not merely a medical exercise, but encompasses the child's interests in the widest sense. A typical example can be seen in Russell J's consideration of the best interests of C, a 2-month-old baby with severe lissencephaly, resulting in profound disabilities and a life expectancy of less than a year:

> when considering his best interests, I include C's medical, emotional, sensory perceptions (including his ability to give and, in C's case as a small baby, especially to receive love and affection, his awareness of his surroundings, and his pain and suffering) and the human instinct to survive and prolong life.[130]

Full consideration of a child's best interests might justify sustaining treatment despite medical consensus that the long-term prognosis is bleak. Holman J's decision in *Re MB*[131] is perhaps a good example of such an approach. There, the parents opposed the withdrawal of life support, arguing that 18-month-old M could see, hear and respond positively and with pleasure to family visits and familiar television programmes and music. Holman J acknowledged that parents' views on treatment are particularly valuable, bearing in mind that they spend a great deal of time with their child and know him well. While their own wishes are irrelevant to an objective view of the child's best interests, they may 'illuminate the quality and value <u>to the child</u> of the child/parent relationship'.[132] Holman J proceeded on the basis that M, with age-appropriate cognition, hearing and some residuary vision, had a relationship of value to him with his family and continued to gain other pleasures from touch, sight and sound. While Holman J could not value these benefits mathematically, he considered that 'they are precious and real and they are the benefits, and only benefits, that M was destined to gain from his life'.[133] Since he did not consider that the routine discomfort, distress and pain caused by procedures used to keep M alive outweighed these benefits, he could not conclude that it was in M's best interests for those benefits, and life itself, immediately to end.[134]

Lord Donaldson MR, at 187; *Re C (Medical Treatment)* [1998] 1 FLR 384, per Sir Stephen Brown P, at 389–90. J. Fortin (1998) p. 416.

[129] I. Goold (2019) p. 42.

[130] *An NHS Trust* v. *A & B & C* [2018] EWHC 2750, at [27]. Similar examples can be seen in the older case law: *Re L (Medical Treatment: Benefit)* [2004] EWHC 2713 (Fam), [2005] 1 FLR 491, per Dame Elizabeth Butler-Sloss P, at [12]; *Wyatt* v. *Portsmouth NHS Trust* [2005] EWCA Civ 1181, [2006] 1 FLR 554, per Wall LJ, at [87].

[131] [2006] EWHC 507 (Fam), [2006] 2 FLR 319 (discussed by J. Bridgeman (2007) pp. 162–4): 18-month-old M suffered from a severe form of spinal muscular atrophy, a degenerative and progressive condition, who needed mechanical ventilation to breathe and was tube fed. Despite a limited life expectancy (probably not more than 1 year), he was conscious and was assumed to have normal cognitive function, including sensory awareness, but had lost the power to communicate orally, and had lost most movement.

[132] Ibid. at [16] (x) (emphasis in the original).   [133] Ibid. at [102].   [134] Ibid.

While the law is relatively clear, the task required of judges in these cases is extraordinarily difficult. The best interests test has been criticised in other contexts.[135] Its indeterminacy also causes difficulties in disputes of this kind. The broad nature of the best interests test espoused by the courts requires judges to enter into an evaluation of incommensurable values. Cases usually come before the court because the parents and doctors fundamentally disagree on precisely the question of whether the life available to the child is worth the burden of imposing treatment to sustain that life. While the best interests test gives a veneer of objectivity, it is impossible for courts to decide these disputes without taking a position on the deeply contested question of what it means to live a meaningful life.

In the face of this difficulty, the courts have increasingly considered professional guidance produced to guide doctors on the ethics of end-of-life care, especially that produced by the Royal College of Paediatrics and Child Health (RCPCH).[136] That guidance considers that continuing life-sustaining treatment may not be in the child's best interests where life is limited in quantity or in quality and gives detailed guidance to doctors faced with such cases.[137] Valuable as the guidance is, it cannot avoid the necessity for the courts to take a position on these contested ethical questions. In cases in which death is not imminent, but will inevitably follow in a short time frame, reasonable people would disagree on the extent to which they are willing to endure pain and suffering to prolong the life available to them. Parents too may take different approaches on behalf of their children,[138] and may question why their view should be superseded by that of the court. The role of the court is not, however, to assess the reasonableness of the parents' decision, but to take its own view of the child's best interests, even if it is different from that of the reasonable parents.[139] Even more difficult are those cases in which the child may survive for some time if treatment is maintained, but the quality of life is thought to be so poor that the medical team consider that withdrawal of treatment is justified. Evaluating the quality of life of a seriously ill child who is not able to explain their own view is fraught with difficulty. As MacDonald J observed in *Barts NHS Foundation Trust* v. *Shalina Begum, Muhhamed Raqeeb and Tafida Raqeeb (by Her Children's Guardian).*[140]

---

[135] Discussed in Chapter 3.

[136] RCPCH (2015). E.g.: *An NHS Trust* v. *A & B & C* [2018] EWHC 2750, at [39]–[43]; *King's College Hospital NHS Foundation Trust* v. *Thomas* [2018] EWHC 127 (Fam), at [43], [110] and [112]; *Great Ormond Street Hospital for Children NHS Foundation Trust* v. *Yates & Gard* [2017] EWHC 972, at [60]; *Great Ormond Street Hospital for Children NHS Foundation Trust* v. *Yates* [2017] EWCA Civ 410, [2018] 4 WLR 5, at [75] and [76].

[137] RCPCH (2015) pp. 4–5.

[138] See e.g. *GOSH* v. *NO & KK & MK* [2017] EWHC 241, at [10] and [17], in which the parents of a 'responsive, inquisitive and smiley' 8-month-old who was dying but not in constant pain felt that she should be given any procedure available if that would prolong her life for one day.

[139] *Re T (A Minor)* [1997] 1 WLR 242.

[140] [2019] EWHC 2531 (Admin) and [2019] EWHC 2530 (Fam), [2020] 3 All ER 663, at [191] (*Raqeeb*).

Absent the fact of pain or the awareness of suffering, the answer to the objective best interests tests must be looked for in subjective or highly value laden ethical, moral or religious factors extrinsic to the child, such as futility (in its nontechnical sense), dignity, the meaning of life and the principle of the sanctity of life, which factors mean different things to different people in a diverse, multicultural, multifaith society.

As was the case in *Raqeeb*, many of the most contested cases involve children born into families with deeply held religious, cultural or ethical beliefs that determine the value-laden lens through which the parents view their child's treatment.[141] The courts have repeatedly been faced with claims that these beliefs should play a greater, or even determinative, role in the courts' decisions, both because the parents have primary responsibility for the child and because it can be assumed that the child herself would go on to adopt those values. In *Raqeeb* itself, the parents' opposition to withdrawal of treatment was informed by the value that they placed on sanctity of life as an aspect of their Islamic faith. The facts of the case were, however, unusual. The court found that Tafida was unlikely to be suffering any pain or have awareness of her condition. The parents had obtained funding to have her treated at a well-respected hospital in Italy, where the clinicians were of the view that her life could be sustained for 10 to 20 years. In these finely balanced circumstances, in which the parents' views aligned with a responsible body of medical opinion, MacDonald J found that the decision lay:

> towards the end of the scale where the court should give weight to the reflection that in the last analysis the best interests of every child include an expectation that difficult decisions affecting the length and quality of the child's life will be taken for the child by a parent in the exercise of their parental responsibility.[142]

In itself, this conclusion was uncontroversial and can be seen as an application of the well-established principle that parental views should be considered in the court's determination of the child's best interests. Nonetheless, the case has been criticised for reintroducing parental rights by the back door.[143] Although HRA arguments did not play a prominent role in the judgment, MacDonald J raised the suggestion that withdrawing life support in these circumstances would be a breach of the parents' Article 8 rights.[144] The court also considered that 4-year-old Tafida would benefit from being treated in accordance with the religious tenets in which she was being raised, but did not explain how a child who has minimal awareness, and who had not contemplated her views on the decision in hand, could benefit from the fact that treatment aligned with her

---

[141] E.g. *Fixsler* v. *Manchester University NHS Foundation Trust* [2021] EWHC 1426 (Fam), [2021] 4 WLR 95 and [2021] EWCA Civ 1018, [2021] 4 WLR 123; *Re ABC* [2021] EWHC 2574 (Fam).
[142] Ibid. at [182].   [143] E. Cave *et al.* (2020).
[144] [2019] EWHC 2531 (Admin) and [2019] EWHC 2530 (Fam), [2020] 3 All ER 663, at [182]. Weight was also given to the Art. 9 rights of Tafida and her parents: [184].

parents' religious conscience.[145] While the decision in *Raqeeb* was justifiable on conventional principles, these observations strengthened the argument that parents should have the right to determine their child's treatment in accordance with their own beliefs.[146] This argument was developed further in *Fixsler v. Manchester University NHS Foundation Trust*,[147] in which it was argued that the requirement to consider the child's best interests from her own perspective required the court to approach the decision from the values of the orthodox Jewish community into which she had been born. Within this community, it was argued, religion was a matter of identity rather than simply cognitive belief, meaning that the perspective of this very young child should reflect her religious and community identity.[148] The court refused to accept that the child's religious and cultural background should be the 'key driver' of the decision, holding instead that it was an important factor to be taken into account in the overall best interests analysis.[149] The court was also concerned not to attribute the parents' religious beliefs to a child who had not had the cognitive ability to understand and accept them.[150] This is an important decision in ensuring that the child's interests do not simply elide with those of the parents. It does, however, leave family court judges with the difficult problem of how to evaluate and weigh the importance of religious background to a child's best interests in circumstances in which the child will sadly never be able to understand that background.

It is perhaps inevitable that any resolution of these cases will involve judges entering into profound questions that ultimately require value-laden assessment. The best interests test cannot avoid this problem, but does at least have the merit of focusing the attention of the court on the child at the centre of the decision. Recognition of the fact that the child has important rights at stake, most notably the right to life, reinforces this approach, but does not resolve the ethical dilemmas at its heart. If courts exercising this draconian discretion are to retain the confidence of the public, and most importantly the parents, it is vital that they do as much as possible to explain and justify the value judgments inherent in each case.

---

[145] Ibid. at [172]–[174]. The court took the view that Tafida herself was too young to have formed a view on the religious implications of the decision before the court. Although she had demonstrated a basic affinity for the tenets of the religion in which she was being raised, that did not extend to an appreciation of the religious, moral and ethical implications of the situation in which she now found herself: ibid. at [166]–[167].

[146] C. Auckland and I. Goold (2020) argue that *Raqeeb* supports their argument that a significant harm threshold should be imposed for judicial intervention in parental decisions.

[147] [2021] EWHC 1426 (Fam), [2021] 4 WLR 95 and [2021] EWCA Civ 1018, [2021] 4 WLR 123.

[148] [2021] EWCA Civ 1018, [2021] 4 WLR 123, at [65]–[70].

[149] Ibid. at [79]–[85]. In particular, the court was concerned not to replace the objective best interests test with a test of substituted judgment, as applied to decisions concerning adults under the Mental Capacity Act 2005, s. 4, although the child's views would be an important aspect of determining her best interests.

[150] Ibid. at [85]–[86].

(D) Parental Choice, Alternative Treatments and Medical Tourism

A judicial decision that permits withdrawal of life-sustaining treatment from a child, against the wishes of the parents, is one of the most serious decisions that a court can be asked to make. The exercise of authority that has such significant consequences requires robust justification, particularly as the interests of children are primarily entrusted to their parents. If the court's jurisdiction is invoked in a dispute between parents, each of whom has a duty to act in the welfare of the child, the normative basis for the court's intervention is readily found. The court can only resolve the dispute by giving an authoritative determination of the child's welfare, the basis on which the parents are obliged to carry out their responsibilities to their children. The same normative basis can be found in disputes between parents and healthcare professionals on whom the child is dependent, as they also owe duties to act in the child's best interests. If parents and medical practitioners advance incompatible treatment plans for the child, each may seek the guidance of the court to resolve disagreement on how those duties should be discharged in the child's best interests. A number of high-profile court cases have involved parents who do not simply disagree with the child's current medical team, but seek to change the child's care to doctors who are willing to provide the parents' preferred course of action. It is now increasingly easy for parents to learn of new and experimental treatments through the internet and to make contact with doctors and researchers throughout the world who may be able to offer hope to the child. In this way, parents may be able to access possible treatments that are not available through the child's current medical team or which they would not be prepared to support. Similarly, the parents may wish to move their child to a different jurisdiction in which the approach to life-sustaining treatment is different from that prevailing here.[151] Problems arise in those cases in which the child's current medical team consider that the proposed treatment is contrary to the child's interests and refuse to facilitate the move or are willing to go to court to prevent the parents from carrying out their plan. In these cases, the courts are not merely asked to authorise a doctor's refusal to treat, but are intervening to prevent parents from transferring the child to a doctor who *is* willing to treat. This appears to be a draconian interference in parents' freedom to act as they see fit for their child and so sharply raises the question of where the boundary is drawn between state and parental responsibility for children's medical interests.

The starting point of the law is that medical professionals offer treatment that is in the child's best interests[152] and ordinarily there is nothing to prevent parents from choosing to move their child to a new medical team or taking them abroad for treatment. This point, and the difficulties caused by the breakdown of collaboration between parents and doctors, are well illustrated

---

[151] N. Bhatia and G. Birchley (2020).   [152] I. Goold (2019) p. 37.

by the case of 5-year-old Ashya King, who suffered from a serious form of brain tumour.[153] In that case, the relationship between the parents and medical team broke down over the question of whether he ought to receive conventional radiotherapy, as the hospital recommended, or the parents' preferred option of proton therapy, which was not opposed by his doctors, but was not available in the UK. In response to the disintegrating relationship with the medical team, the parents removed him from the hospital without warning[154] and took him to Spain while they sought funding for his treatment. In response, Ashya was made a ward of court while his whereabouts was ascertained. By the time the medical issue came to court, there was no opposition to the parents' plan, but the court's authorisation was required given that Ashya remained a ward. In approaching the case, Baker J considered that:

> it is a fundamental principle of family law in this jurisdiction that responsibility for making decisions about a child rest with his parents. In most cases, the parents are the best people to make decisions about a child and the state – whether it be the court, or any other public authority – has no business interfering with the exercise of parental responsibility unless the child is suffering or is likely to suffer significant harm as a result of the care given to the child not being what it would be reasonable to expect a parent to give.[155]

Rather than evaluating the evidence and making an entirely independent analysis of Ashya's welfare as would be the case in resolving a dispute, Baker J found that 'there was no reason to stand in the way of the parents' proposal'.[156] Contrasting the case with those where parents sought a 'wholly unreasonable course of treatment', Baker J justified his approach on the basis that:

> Both courses are reasonable and it is the parents who bear the heavy responsibility of making the decision. It is no business of this court, or any other public authority, to interfere with their decision.

In this way, the court's own obligation to act in Ashya's best interests was discharged by recognising the parents' primary responsibility[157] and respecting their reasonable decision on his welfare.

At first sight, this case sits uneasily with a series of other cases in which parents have sought to resist hospital applications to remove life-sustaining treatment from their children by instead proposing alternative treatment with a different medical team[158] or by seeking to remove the child to a hospital that is willing to

---

[153] *Re King* [2014] EWHC 2964 (fam), [2014] 2 FLR 855.

[154] Parents have similarly removed their children to avoid state intervention and to implement their preferred treatment in a number of high-profile cases: discussed in J. Bridgeman (2017) p. 376.

[155] *Re King* [2014] EWHC 2964 (Fam), [2014] 2 FLR 855, at [31].   [156] Ibid. at [34].

[157] E.g. *In the matter of E (A Child) (Medical Treatment)* [2016] EWHC 2267. See discussion above on the primary role of parents.

[158] *Great Ormond Street Hospital for Children NHS Foundation Trust* v. *Yates & Gard* [2017] EWHC 972; *Great Ormond Street Hospital for Children NHS Foundation Trust* v. *Yates* [2017] EWCA Civ 410, [2018] 4 WLR 5.

continue to offer life support and palliative care.[159] In these cases, the child is dependent on the current hospital for life-sustaining treatment, meaning that the parents cannot remove their child to alternative provision without the intimate involvement and support of the current medical team. If the current medical team feel that the transfer is not in the child's best interests, the dispute may be resolved in court. The case of Charlie Gard provides a good example of such cases, which sharply raise the problem of the limits of parental responsibility for children's medical decisions.[160] Charlie suffered from a severe and progressive form of mitochondrial depletion syndrome, which affected his brain, muscles and ability to breathe. His parents wished to take him to the US to receive experimental nucleoside therapy, which offered the 'theoretical possibility' of benefit to Charlie, but had not yet been trialled on children, or even mice, with his condition. His current medical team considered that Charlie's condition had deteriorated to the point at which he was extremely unlikely to benefit from treatment and that his quality of life was so poor that it was not in his interests to endure the pain and suffering of ventilation or being transferred for the treatment. As such, they considered that the best outcome for Charlie would be to withdraw life-sustaining treatment to allow him to die with dignity. His parents strongly rejected this assessment of his condition and refused consent to the withdrawal of ventilation. They remained convinced that he should have the opportunity to test whether he would benefit from nucleoside therapy and had raised funds to allow this to occur. At first instance, the court considered that further treatment was not in Charlie's best interests and authorised withdrawal of life-sustaining treatment.[161] The principles applied by the court were based on the conventional approach that the court was to determine the decision by taking its own view of Charlie's best interests.

On appeal, the parents challenged the application of this conventional approach to the case, arguing that in cases in which the parents proposed a viable alternative treatment, the court had no jurisdiction to intervene unless the parents' proposed treatment was likely to cause significant harm.[162] This approach, the parents argued, reflected the principle affirmed in *King*: it is parents who have the primary responsibility for their child's healthcare and the state has no business in policing a joint parental decision to transfer to a new

[159] *Alder Hey Children's NHS Foundation Trust* v. *Evans* [2018] EWHC 818 (Fam); *Re E (A Child)* [2018] EWCA Civ 550, [2019] 1 WLR 594.

[160] *Great Ormond Street Hospital for Children NHS Foundation Trust* v. *Yates & Gard* [2017] EWHC 972; *Great Ormond Street Hospital for Children NHS Foundation Trust* v. *Yates* [2017] EWCA Civ 410, [2018] 4 WLR 5.

[161] *Great Ormond Street Hospital for Children NHS Foundation Trust* v. *Yates & Gard* [2017] EWHC 972.

[162] *Great Ormond Street Hospital for Children NHS Foundation Trust* v. *Yates* [2017] EWCA Civ 410, [2018] 4 WLR 5, at [54]–[114]. Contrast I. Goold (2019) and R. Taylor (2019) for different views on whether this argument should have succeeded. The private members' bill, Access to Palliative Care and Treatment of Children Bill 2019–21, would introduce a requirement that courts assume that any treatment put forward by a person with parental responsibility is in the child's best interests, unless the contrary is clearly established.

medical team unless doing so would meet the child protection threshold of significant harm. Up until this point, the parents argued, they had the *right*, protected by Article 8 of the ECHR, to raise their child as they saw fit. To intervene where there was no parental dispute and no risk of harm would be a breach of this right and a decisive shift from recognising parents as having primary responsibility for their children. The Court of Appeal rejected this argument, reaffirming that once its protective jurisdiction had been invoked, the court's duty was to act in the child's best interests, and that while the views of parents would be given great weight in assessing those interests, the rights and best interests of the child would outweigh any parental right. It was not necessary to demonstrate significant harm or a dispute in order for the child's treatment to be brought to the court's attention.[163] The Supreme Court affirmed these principles in refusing permission to appeal, while the ECtHR considered the case inadmissible,[164] finding that the careful court process to determine Charlie's best interests justified any interference with the parents' Article 8 rights.[165]

In reality, medical professionals are very reluctant to take parental decisions to court unless they fear that the decision will cause harm to the child.[166] For this reason, the dispute in *Gard* may be of greater symbolic, rather than practical, value. That symbolism is important: *Gard* and the cases that followed it[167] reaffirm that it is children's interests, not parental rights, that are at the centre of decisions on children's medical treatment. These cases do, however, raise difficult questions as to the nature of the collaboration between parents and the state in raising children. The force of the parents' argument is found in the fact that children's best interests are often matters on which reasonable people disagree. In those cases of reasonable disagreement, there is a good argument that it is the decision of the parents, who love the child and who will have to bear the consequences of the decision, that should prevail. The leading role of parents in collaborative responsibility for the child is best recognised through parental involvement in decision-making and in respect for parental views in court,[168] rather than by reframing medical decisions about children as matters of parental

---

[163] *Re D (A Minor) (Wardship: Sterilisation)* [1976] 1 All ER 326; R. Taylor (2019).

[164] *Gard* v. *United Kingdom* (2017) 65 EHRR SE9: the court did not consider it necessary to determine whether the appropriate test for interference with the parents' Art. 8 rights was best interests or significant harm at [118]–[119].

[165] See also *Parfitt* v. *United Kingdom* (2021) 73 EHRR SE1, at [51], in which the ECtHR made clear that the UK was within its margin of appreciation in applying a best interests test to such cases.

[166] See: Birchley (2019); Wilkinson (2019). The Court of Appeal in *Gard* considered that it was likely that the significant harm test would have been passed in this case, although the judge had not made any finding on that point: *Great Ormond Street Hospital for Children NHS Foundation Trust* v. *Yates* [2017] EWCA Civ 410, [2018] 4 WLR 5, at [114].

[167] *King's College Hospital NHS Foundation Trust* v. *Thomas* [2018] EWHC 127 (Fam); *Alder Hey Children's NHS Foundation Trust* v. *Evans* [2018] EWHC 818 (Fam); *Re E (A Child)* [2018] EWCA Civ 550, [2019] 1 WLR 594.

[168] As illustrated by the decision in *Barts NHS Foundation Trust* v. *Shalina Begum, Muhhamed Raqeeb and Tafida Raqeeb (by Her Children's Guardian)* [2019] EWHC 2531 (Admin) and [2019] EWHC 2530 (Fam), [2020] 3 All ER 663, discussed above.

rights, to be defended unless forfeited. Whether this principled stance can survive in an increasingly globalised health market remains to be seen.[169]

(E) Can Parents Deny Children the Right to Life?

Most of the cases concerning the medical treatment of seriously ill children involve parents who are desperate to ensure that the child continues to receive treatment to give them the best chance of survival for as long as possible. A smaller number of cases concern parents who refuse to consent to recommended treatment, despite the risk that the child may not survive without it. Some of these cases arise because the parents believe that it would be better for the child to die, rather than to suffer the burdens of continued treatment. In other cases, the parents may have strong convictions which lead them to object to the specific treatment offered. The courts most commonly encounter cases of this kind where the parents' opposition to treatment stems from their religious convictions. Legally, of course, there is no need for medical staff to obtain judicial consent before giving emergency life-saving treatment to children against the wishes of their parents. Life-saving treatment can be justified under the common law principle of necessity, backed up by the need to promote a child's right to life under Article 2 of the ECHR. Nevertheless, given the uncertain scope of the defence of necessity,[170] it would be wise always to seek judicial authority for treatment which ignores parental objections.[171] This approach would accord with the ECtHR's obvious lack of sympathy with the medical team in *Glass* v. *United Kingdom*[172] for not having obtained prior emergency judicial approval for treating David in a way they knew his mother opposed. Despite some sympathy with parents who carry a substantial burden of care for a seriously ill or disabled child, the law has increasingly protected the child's right to life against the objections of their parents.

Society has at times seemed more tolerant of parents who rejected children born with disabilities. The response of the doctors caring for two babies with Down's syndrome in the early 1980s indicates that considerable sympathy then existed for parents who rejected otherwise healthy babies on the grounds of this condition alone. A reading of decisions like *Re B (A Minor) (Wardship: Medical Treatment)*[173] and of accounts of the trial in *R* v. *Arthur*[174] shows that

---

[169] N. Bhatia and G. Birchley (2020).

[170] *Re F (Mental Patient: Sterilisation)* [1990] 2 AC 1, per Lord Goff, at 74.

[171] The hospital trust may seek leave from the court under the CA 1989, s. 10 to apply for a specific issue order under the CA 1989, s. 8 or seek a declaration under the inherent jurisdiction: *Re JM (A Child)* [2015] EWHC 2832 (Fam), [2016] 2 FLR 235.

[172] [2004] 1 FLR 1019, at [79].

[173] [1990] 3 All ER 927: her Down's condition apart, child B had no handicaps, bar an intestinal blockage urgently requiring uncomplicated surgery, which, if successful, would give her a life expectancy of 20 to 30 years. The parents refused consent, considering it kinder to allow her to die. The LA warded her and obtained judicial authorisation for the surgery.

[174] *R* v. *Arthur* (1981) 12 BMLR 1.

such parental rejection was neither uncommon, nor considered surprising. There was the strong view that families were entitled to family privacy, with a right to raise their children as they saw fit, free from state intervention. The lives of people with disabilities generally were viewed as being poor in quality.[175] Indeed, as Read and Clements observe:

> disabled babies and children were implicitly placed in a separate category from their non-disabled peers with the consequence that they need not be afforded the same rights or protections.[176]

Interlaced with such ideas may have been the notion that babies, particularly babies with cognitive impairments, lacked the characteristics and attributes commonly associated with a worthwhile existence, thereby justifying a lower order of protection.[177]

These views were underpinned by the assumption that parents had the right to determine the fate of their babies with disabilities. It was urged that the law is incapable of effectively managing the delicate and complex relationship between parent and child and that if parents refused routine but life-saving treatment for their children, the doctors should comply with their wishes. In *Re B*, decided in 1981,[178] the surgeon who was to have performed straightforward but life-saving surgery on baby B declined to do so when informed of her parents' objections. Even Ewbank J, at first instance, concluded that their wishes had to be respected and refused to authorise the procedure. The Court of Appeal's decision overruling the parents' views was itself criticised by members of the general public, who considered it unfair to foist on parents the care of children with cognitive impairment against their wishes.[179]

These two cases established that parents do not have the power to dictate whether their children should live or die. The law prohibits doctors from allowing healthy babies to die by withholding normal sustenance, regardless of any likely disability. Furthermore, parents' decisions to reject straightforward life-saving surgery may be overridden. Public opinion has changed considerably since the early 1980s.[180] Although many parents still consider they have considerable power over their children's lives, the concept of children having rights to protection *from* their parents has now gathered pace. Further, the rights of children with disabilities are now firmly embedded in international human rights law. The CRC was innovative in giving specific protection for children with disabilities,[181] rights which were further strengthened by the Convention on the Rights of Persons with Disabilities.[182] These

---

[175] J. Read and L. Clements (2004) pp. 495–500.   [176] Ibid. p. 506.

[177] C. Wells (1989) pp. 202–3.   [178] But not officially reported until 1990: [1990] 3 All ER 927.

[179] J. Read and L. Clements (2004) pp. 501–4.   [180] Ibid. pp. 504–5.

[181] CRC, Arts 2 and 23, discussed by B. Byrne (2019). See further: Committee on the Rights of the Child (2006).

[182] See esp. Arts 7 (children) and 25 (health). The Convention entered into force on 3 May 2008 and was ratified by the UK on 8 June 2009.

provisions not only give children with disabilities equal rights to healthcare, but also put positive obligations on the state to support children and their families. Recognition of children with disabilities as equal rights-holders has an important role in changing public and official attitudes. Nonetheless, abortion legislation continues to permit termination right up to full term, if 'there is a substantial risk that if the child were born it would suffer from such physical or mental abnormalities as to be seriously handicapped', regardless of whether that 'abnormality' is incompatible with life.[183] Campaigners have long argued that the application of this provision embodies an implication that the lives of children with disabilities are of less value than others and that becoming a parent of a child with disabilities is something to be avoided. Nonetheless, attempts to challenge these provisions under the HRA have failed, not least because the protection of the ECHR is generally understood to start at birth.[184] A further concern raised in respect of equal treatment for children with disabilities is the argument that in evaluating the child's best interests in withdrawal of treatment cases, quality of life assessments favour children with higher cognitive abilities.[185] This creates the concern that the test may be applied to the detriment of children with particular disabilities,[186] especially as research demonstrates that health professionals significantly underestimate the quality of life of people with disabilities.[187] Judges applying the best interests test must be vigilant to the risk of it implying that parents are entitled to refuse life-saving treatment not because the child is ill or dying, but because of the child's disabilities.

Cases involving refusal of treatment also reach the courts because the parents have strong objections to the treatment in question, often on grounds of religious belief. The children concerned are often too young to have formed their own convictions. Although when they are older they might agree with their parents,[188] the outcome of their parents' decisions would prevent them living long enough to develop their own ideas. Justice Holmes in *Prince v. Massachusetts* put it well when he said:

> Parents may be free to become martyrs themselves. But it does not follow they are free, in identical circumstances, to make martyrs of their children before they

---

[183] Abortion Act 1967, s. 1(1)(d). See F. Bruce (2013): e.g. the evidence presented to this parliamentary inquiry suggested that 90 per cent of pregnancies with a definite diagnosis of Down's Syndrome resulted in termination, p. 15.

[184] *R (Crowther) v. Secretary of State for Health and Social Care* [2021] EWHC 2536 (Admin), in which a challenge to this provision under Arts 2, 3, 8 and 14 failed. The applicant argued that the ECtHR has not considered whether a viable foetus could possess rights under the ECHR. The High Court considered that it was not for the domestic courts to decide this matter and in the absence of a ECtHR case to the contrary the ECHR was not to be applied to the unborn.

[185] E.g. M's *Re MB* [2006] EWHC 507 (Fam), [2006] 2 FLR 319.

[186] M. Brazier (2006) para. 8.36. This concern is addressed at RCPCH (2015) s. 12.

[187] Discussed by B. Byrne (2019) at p. 887.

[188] E.g. *Re E (A Minor) (Wardship: Medical Treatment)* [1993] 1 FLR 386, discussed in Chapter 11.

have reached the age of full and legal discretion when they can make that choice for themselves.[189]

Case law indicates a general willingness on the part of the judiciary to accept medical advice that the treatment proposed is the only means of saving a sick child, even when it means overriding the religious tenets of his or her parents.[190] The wishes of parents are entitled to 'very great respect', but are subordinate to welfare, meaning that even a small risk of death will 'point powerfully' to authorisation of treatment.[191]

However, the much criticised decision of the Court of Appeal in *Re T (A Minor) (Wardship: Medical Treatment)*[192] seemed for a time to undermine the courts' protective role. There, the mother, having seen how 18-month-old C (born with a life-threatening condition) had suffered after the failure of earlier surgery, opposed his undergoing a liver transplant despite the high prospects of its success. As many critics pointed out, by suggesting that C's welfare depended on his mother[193] and that mother and child 'are one',[194] the Court of Appeal's decision carried the underlying message that the best interests test should be interpreted from the mother's perspective. More to the point, the effect of its decision not to authorise life-saving surgery, given his mother's strong objections, was that C would die. In his decision, which predated the HRA, Waite LJ considered it inappropriate 'even in an age preoccupied with "rights" – to talk of the rights of a child, or of a parent, or the rights of the court'.[195] Had the court been prepared to approach the case from a rights-based perspective, it would surely have acknowledged, more honestly than the Court of Appeal ever did, the outcome of their decision to abide by the mother's wishes. This was that C's right to life was to be set aside. Instead, they chose death for him – on the basis that it would be better than the post-operative pain and suffering and potential complications attending the proposed surgery, bearing in mind his mother's own reluctance to cope with his post-operative care. The case illustrates the dangers of applying the best interests test without regard to the fact that the child has independent rights.

Holman J's decision in *NHS Trust* v. *A*,[196] which involved the possibility of very invasive treatment, suggests that the judiciary remain well aware of the need to protect children against their parents' rejection of life-saving treatment. There, strongly Christian parents opposed a bone marrow transplant

---

[189] 321 US 158, at 165 (1944).
[190] In both *Re O (A Minor) (Medical Treatment)* [1993] 2 FLR 149 (3-month-old very low weight premature baby) and *Re R (A Minor) (Medical Treatment)* [1993] 2 FLR 757 (10-month-old baby suffering from leukaemia), the courts authorised the use of blood transfusions. *Re S (A Minor) (Medical Treatment)* [1993] 1 FLR 376 (child aged 4.5 suffering from leukaemia).
[191] *An NHS Trust* v. *B* [2014] EWHC 3486 (Fam), at [18] and [19].
[192] [1997] 1 All ER 906. Discussed by M. Fox and J. McHale (1997) and J. Bridgeman (2007) pp. 137–42.
[193] [1997] 1 All ER 906, per Butler-Sloss LJ, at 915.   [194] Ibid. at 914.   [195] Ibid. at 916.
[196] [2007] EWHC 1696 (Fam), [2008] 1 FLR 70.

(BMT) as the only form of possible cure for their seriously ill daughter A,[197] now aged 6 months. Like the mother in *Re T*, they had witnessed A suffering pain and distress when undergoing very strong drug treatment and wished to spare her a similar ordeal. Furthermore, they knew that the BMT might not succeed,[198] the treatment would be lengthy, painful (possibly very painful) and distressing and it would render A infertile.[199] As strong and committed Christians, they hoped that God would heal their daughter without a BMT.

Noting that the rights-based perspective was consistent with the existing domestic law,[200] Holman J reapplied the 'ten propositions' established by existing case law.[201] These include the fact that each case depends on its own facts,[202] so in A's case, *Re T* could safely be distinguished.[203] He also stressed that although parents' views are particularly valuable, because they know their own child, their wishes are wholly irrelevant to an objective consideration of the child's best interests 'save to the extent in any given case that they may illuminate the quality and value to the child of the child–parent relationship'.[204] That being the case, in his view, Holman J could set aside the parents' religious views.[205] Having weighed up the benefits and burdens of the BMT, he concluded that a 50 per cent prospect of A living a full, normal life, albeit infertile, outweighed the certainty of death before the age of 1 to 1.5. A 'is a living human being, with a future as well as a present, to whom, despite her disease, modern medicine and science may be able to give a full life'.[206] The decision in *Re T* had dangerously undermined the clear principle that parents have no absolute right to parental autonomy, nor the final say over whether their children should live or die. *NHS Trust* v. *A* and subsequent cases have restored this principle, making it clear that children's lives are too precious to be sacrificed to their parents' religious faith, personal convictions or fears for the future.

(4) Children's Healthcare and Non-Therapeutic Treatment

(A) Parental Consent and Non-Therapeutic Treatment

Although the proprietorial attitude of Victorian parents towards their children is objectionable to modern eyes, many of today's parents unconcernedly exhibit a similar approach. They quite commonly arrange for their young

---

[197] A suffered from haemophagocytic lymphohistiocytosis (HLH), a fatal genetic defect in the immune system.

[198] [2007] EWHC 1696 (Fam), [2008] 1 FLR 70, per Holman J, at [1]: the BMT might achieve, inter alia: approximately a 50 per cent prospect of effecting a lasting cure with a normal life expectancy; a 10 per cent prospect of ensuring her survival, but with some significant impairment; a 10 per cent prospect of killing her; and a 30 per cent prospect of failing, in which case A would die of HLH.

[199] Ibid. at [45].   [200] Ibid. at [44].

[201] Ibid. at [40]. See also *Re MB* [2006] EWHC 507 (Fam), [2006] 2 FLR 319, per Holman J, at [16], discussed above.

[202] [2007] EWHC 1696 (Fam), [2008] 1 FLR 70, at [40] (ix).   [203] Ibid. at [43].

[204] Ibid. at [40] (x).   [205] Ibid. at [42].   [206] Ibid. at [70].

children to undergo procedures which infringe their children's right to bodily integrity under Article 8 of the ECHR, without always considering whether this can be justified. The ambit of parental authority to consent to such procedures appears to have narrowed, particularly with a greater appreciation of the position of children as independent rights-holders. *Re D (A Minor) (Wardship: Sterilisation)*[207] showed that, in the late 1970s, even very young children were being sterilised for non-therapeutic purposes. Other young girls were presumably undergoing similar surgery without intervention, on the assumption that parents had the right to consent on their behalf. It is now beyond doubt that such cases require judicial authorisation and that the courts are becoming more critical of the rare requests for sterilisation of girls that do reach them.[208] In contrast, parents are unlikely to face any legal difficulty in arranging for children to undergo relatively uncomplicated, non-therapeutic procedures, such as ear-piercing and minor cosmetic surgery. There is, however, some doubt as to the scope of parental authority to consent to procedures that are not of therapeutic benefit to the child.

While there is no absolute legal distinction between therapeutic and non-therapeutic treatment,[209] a procedure that is medically advised will usually fall clearly within the 'zone of parental responsibility' allowing parents to consent on their child's behalf to further the child's best interests. The child's best interests are not merely medical, but encompass all aspects of the child's life, including social, relational and cultural interests; these interests may be sufficient to justify an interference with the child's bodily integrity despite the lack of therapeutic benefit. Nonetheless, non-therapeutic interventions raise particularly difficult questions as to when interference with the child's bodily integrity can be justified, especially as the parents' own interests are often entangled in their perception of the child's social, cultural and relationship interests. The sections below explore these dilemmas in the contexts first of organ and tissue donation and then cultural practices, particularly female genital mutilation and circumcision. While children's bodily integrity is recognised and protected from the most serious forms of intervention, parents are still given significant discretion to authorise practices which may be of greater benefit to the parents themselves than the child on whom they are imposed.

---

[207] [1976] 1 All ER 326: a mother had arranged for her 12-year-old daughter, who had a mental impairment, to undergo a sterilisation; this was stopped by an application brought under the wardship jurisdiction.

[208] The development of the law in this area is covered in more detail in the 3rd edition of this book at Chapter 10.

[209] The House of Lords rejected the distinction in *Re B (A Minor) (Wardship: Sterilisation)* [1988] AC 199, but it has been widely used in subsequent cases. E.g. *Re GF (Medical Treatment)* [1992] 1 FLR 293, per Sir Stephen Brown P, at 294: an application for leave to carry out a sterilisation is unnecessary providing two medical practitioners are satisfied that it is necessary for therapeutic purposes, it is in the patient's best interests and that there is no practicable, less intrusive means of treatment; *Re E (A Minor) (Medical Treatment)* [1991] 2 FLR 585: no judicial authority required for the performance of a therapeutic hysterectomy on a 17-year-old mentally impaired girl who suffered from serious menorrhagia.

(B) Organ and Tissue Donation

The prospect of having to watch a child die is one that no parent would wish to contemplate. In some cases, a seriously ill child's life might be saved by the donation of an organ, tissue or bone marrow provided by a healthy living donor. The advantages of genetic compatibility may lead parents to consider arranging for one of their healthy children to act as donor for the dying child. They may even produce a baby who can provide tissue to save an older child – the 'saviour sibling' scenario.[210] The possibility of a child acting as a donor for a sibling presents an ethical and legal dilemma. The donor-child is asked to go through an invasive medical procedure which carries with it, sometimes substantial, risks but no physical advantage to the donor. The parents are faced with the unenviable task of trying to assess the interests of the donor-child, in the knowledge that donation may be the best hope for the survival of their seriously-ill child. The framework for resolving these issues is found in the legislation,[211] regulations[212] and codes of practice[213] governing this area of practice. Despite this extensive regulation, in practice there is concern that not enough is done to recognise the rights of donor-children and to protect them from the pressures inherent in the emotive family circumstances surrounding donation.[214]

Assessment of the child's best interests will depend, in part, on the nature of the proposed donation. Most practitioners have very grave reservations about children and young people being used as living donors of non-regenerative organs, such as a kidney.[215] The Human Tissue Authority (HTA) nevertheless implicitly assumes that children do exceptionally provide organs, commenting: 'Children can be considered as living organ donors only in extremely rare circumstances.'[216] In its guidance,[217] the HTA suggests that, in addition to complying with the common law requirements relating to consent for removal of the organ, medical practitioners and parents must overcome two hurdles. First, although the actual *removal* of the organ is not within the scope of the HT Act 2004 (it governs the *use* of the organ, with removal still being governed by the common law), the HTA suggests that court approval should be obtained

---

[210] R. Brownsword (2005). See further *Quintavalle (On behalf of Comment on Reproductive Ethics)* v. *Human Fertilisation and Embryology Authority* [2005] UKHL 28. Legislation permits embryo testing to identify potential 'saviour siblings' who might donate 'umbilical cord blood stem cells, bone marrow or other tissue', but excludes whole organ donation from this provision: Human Fertilisation and Embryology Act 1990, Sch. 2, para. 1ZA(1)(d) and (4).

[211] Human Tissue (HT) Act 2004.

[212] Inter alia, the Human Tissue Act 2004 (Persons who Lack Capacity to Consent and Transplants) Regulations (HT Act 2004 (PLCCT) Regs) 2006 (SI 2006/1659).

[213] Issued by the Human Tissue Authority (established by the HT Act 2004, Pt 2).

[214] S. Then (2017); L. Cherkassky (2015).

[215] J. Mason and G. Laurie (2006) p. 488: their inquiries indicated that only one transplant involving an identical twin aged 17 has occurred in the previous 20 years.

[216] HTA (2020) para. 44.

[217] Ibid. paras 45–46. This guidance has been updated on a number of occasions, but retained the same approach to children in each update.

before the removal of a solid organ from a child.[218] Although sensible, in the absence of any reported domestic case law on this matter, it is difficult to know how this advice originated. The only reported judicial comment on children donating organs came from Lord Donaldson, who considered it 'highly improbable' that an adolescent under the age of 18 wishing to become an organ donor could ever be sufficiently competent to consent on his own behalf.[219] But in any event, given the concerns over children donating tissue such as regenerative bone marrow,[220] most courts in this country would surely refuse to rule that it is in a healthy child's best interests to donate an organ or even part of an organ. Second, in the event of a court authorising such a donation, the regulations require that before the donation can go ahead, it must be drawn to the attention of the HTA[221] and be approved by a panel of no fewer than three of its members.[222] Before the HTA panel approves the donation, it must be satisfied that no reward was provided for the donation and that the removal of the organ was otherwise lawful.[223] These complicated provisions, together with criminal sanctions,[224] reinforce the general view that to use children for the donation of organs is unethical.

The implications of donating regenerative tissue, such as bone marrow, are far less serious for child-donors than donation of an organ. For this reason, the law and practice on tissue donation is much more permissive than that concerning organ donation. Nonetheless, donation carries with it risks of physical and psychological harm and remains a significant invasion of bodily integrity.[225] Assessing the child's best interests in the emotive context of family donation is complex, especially as there is no case law in this country testing the legality of using children as donors of bone marrow or other regenerative tissue.[226] There is a risk that the child's independent rights and interests can be obscured by focusing on the assumption that the child will benefit from the relationship with the seriously ill family member.

The procedure for tissue donation by a child-donor who is not yet competent to consent requires a two-stage process. First, 'appropriate consent' must be obtained from a person with PR for that child.[227] If there is disagreement

---

[218] Ibid. para. 45.

[219] *Re W (A Minor) (Medical Treatment: Court's Jurisdiction)* [1993] Fam 64, per Lord Donaldson, at 79.

[220] Discussed below.

[221] HT Act 2004 (PLCCT) Regs 2006, reg. 11(2): the registered medical practitioner who has clinical responsibility for the donor must bring the proposed transplant to the attention of the HTA.

[222] HT Act 2004 (PLCCT) Regs 2006, reg. 12(1) and (2).   [223] Ibid. reg. 11(3).

[224] HT Act 2004, s. 33.   [225] S. Then (2017).

[226] Although the decision of the House of Lords on *screening* embryos for suitability for future donation would seem to imply that donation is permissible: *Quintavalle (On behalf of Comment on Reproductive Ethics)* v. *Human Fertilisation and Embryology Authority* [2005] UKHL 28, esp. at [37] and [38] (Lord Hoffmann).

[227] HT Act 2004, s. 2. Children may consent on their own behalf to the procedure if they can show *Gillick* competence for these purposes. The guidance states that parental consent will not be

between those with PR, or the clinicians and parents, an application should be made to court for determination of the child's best interests, but, in contrast to the position on organ donation, there is no routine court involvement in such cases.[228] Second, once consent has been given for an *incompetent* child to be used as a live donor, there is an additional layer of supervision by the HTA, which must consent to the process.[229] This process appears to create safeguards to ensure that the donor-child's rights receive protection, although it is not clear that this is achieved in practice.

Parents who are asked to give consent for one of their children to donate to provide treatment for another face an obvious conflict of interests. The guidance skates over these problems involved in assessing the best interests of a healthy child with a desperately ill sibling. The guidance points out that neither the medical practitioner nor the parent with PR should allow a child to act as a donor unless they are convinced that such a procedure is in the child's best interests. Furthermore, it states that this test is not confined to the child's medical interests, but should include 'emotional, psychological and social benefits'.[230] The guidance suggests, albeit in passing, that the parents should take account the *risks* of the procedure for the child-donor.[231] But, astonishingly, there is no clear warning that parents may be unable to take a dispassionate view of the donor's best interests where tissue is required to save the life of a seriously ill sibling. In contrast, earlier official guidance had specifically considered this problem and suggested that to counter such a risk, there should be independent scrutiny of the parents' decision by an independent assessor or by a hospital ethics committee.[232] By failing to draw specific attention to the parents' ambivalent position in cases like this, the HTA side-steps widely expressed doubts over whether the donation of bone marrow can ever be in the best interests of a healthy child. Parents may argue that the psychological benefits to the donor of saving his or her sibling's life will outbalance the dangers involved. Indeed, they might adopt Eekelaar's approach and claim that the potential donor, when mature, would have chosen retrospectively to save a dying sibling.[233] Furthermore, they might suggest that if they refused to allow their healthy child to be used as a donor, he or she might feel distressed on being told, when older, that the sibling had died because of the absence of a suitable donor. These arguments, while speculative, may be persuasive, but do they give sufficient weight to the rights of the healthy potential donor? To suggest that there are no medical or ethical problems involved because the tissue is regenerative is surely to over-simplify the issues.

regarded as lawful consent if the child is competent, although parental involvement is encouraged: HTA (2017) paras 41–44.

[228] HTA (2017) para. 48. As yet, no such case has been reported.

[229] HT Act 2004 (PLCCT) Regs 2006, reg. 10(1)(b) and (3)(b): 'transplantable material' for the purposes of the HT Act 2004, s. 33 (restrictions on transplants involving live donors), is defined as including bone marrow when it is removed from an incompetent child.

[230] HTA (2017) para. 74.   [231] Ibid.   [232] DH (2001) pp. 20–1.

[233] J. Eekelaar (1986) p. 170.

The procedure often involves some risk to the donor-child. For example, for bone marrow donation, he or she will undergo a general anaesthetic, which in itself carries risk, will undergo multiple punctures leading to pain and potential infection, may require blood transfusion and will risk further complications, including anaemia, cardiovascular complaints and the possibility of an elevated risk of leukaemia.[234] A donor-child may gain little real psychological benefit from helping a dying sibling where he or she is too young to have established any emotional bond with the proposed recipient.[235] Indeed, it is unclear whether siblings truly benefit from acting as donors, particularly if the procedure does not save the ill child.

The HTA guidance suggests that if in doubt about the legality of a donation from a child, a medical practitioner should consult the courts.[236] But there is little domestic authority as to how they would react to such an application. The first reported English case, *Re Y (Mental Incapacity: Bone Marrow Transplant)*,[237] involved an adult donor. As Feenan points out, Connell J's decision approving the donation is a weak one.[238] He had little difficulty in deciding that it would benefit Y, a severely mentally and physically disabled woman, to provide bone marrow for her sister who was suffering from a potentially fatal degenerative bone marrow disorder. Without any detailed analysis of the dangers involved in the harvesting procedure,[239] he considered that the risks were very slight and were more than counter-balanced by the benefits to her of being able to retain close contact with her mother, given that this was a very close-knit family. There was an extremely tenuous logical connection between Y's donation to her sister and her retaining contact with their mother – the argument being that, if the sister died, the mother's state of health would deteriorate, making it unlikely that she would be able to continue visiting Y in her residential home. To prevent Y suffering the loss of her mother's visits, she should provide her sister with bone marrow. The looseness of this judicial reasoning would be alarming if the decision was adopted as guidance for use in children's cases. It demonstrates how easily doubts over the dangers to the donor of undergoing a bone marrow harvesting procedure can be assuaged by vague assurances of it being virtually risk free. More recently, the Court of Protection revisited the same question in *A NHS Foundation Trust* v. *MC*.[240] The case concerned *MC*, an 18-year-old who lacked capacity to make the decision to act as a donor of peripheral blood stem cells to benefit her mother, who had chronic leukaemia. While the circumstances were similar to those in *Re Y*, the intervening introduction of the Mental Capacity Act (MCA) 2005 and creation of the HTA meant that the legal and regulatory framework was very different. In considering that MC's best interests were

---

[234] S. Then (2017) p. 5; L. Cherkassky (2015) p. 43.   [235] S. Then (2017) pp. 13–14.

[236] HTA (2017) para. 48.   [237] [1996] 2 FLR 787.   [238] D. Feenan (1997) pp. 309–10.

[239] [1996] 2 FLR 787, per Connell J, at 793: the risks of a general anaesthetic were 'extremely low', being 1 per 10,000.

[240] [2020] EWCOP 33.

overwhelmingly in favour of permitting her to donate, Cohen J avoided many of the pitfalls present in *Re W*. First, he was careful to outline the medical process and to note that it was not without risks to MC. Nonetheless, MC would derive emotional, social and psychological benefits from her mother's life being extended, and these relationship benefits were much less tenuous than those in *Re Y* as MC lived with her mother and wished to help her. More troublingly, some weight was placed on the view that MC 'may be seen by others positively by acting altruistically'.[241] It is questionable whether a person who does not fully understand an act can be seen as altruistic in performing it. Further, placing value on the perceptions of others risks reinforcing family expectations of the donor and could obscure the interests of the child-donor if the same reasoning were to apply to them. As Cohen J noted with concern, in fact the position for child-donors is much weaker than that for adults without capacity, leaving them in something of a regulatory vacuum which is only partially filled by the HTA.[242]

Some independent protection for the donor-child's interests is given by the requirement for approval from the HTA for donations involving an incompetent child.[243] The HTA must be satisfied that appropriate consents have been given and that the procedure is lawful.[244] In doing so, the HTA should take account of a report prepared by an Accredited Assessor (AA),[245] who must interview the child and the person with PR over the child to ensure, inter alia, that: the donor's best interests have been properly considered; the donor and recipient understand the procedure's risks and implications; and the person with PR has consented to the procedure understanding that 'they have to be solely focused on the best interests of the donor child'.[246] The AA should ensure that the child-donor has an age-appropriate understanding of the procedure and has not been coerced, and that their views have been taken properly into account.[247] Together, these provisions could provide a safeguard for the child-donor's rights, despite the obvious conflict of interest faced by their family. The Court of Protection in *MC* was informed that around sixty-five cases of donations by under 18s are taken to the HTA each year.[248] It seems that the HTA has approved every case of donation by an incompetent minor that has come before it.[249] Although no further details on these cases are available, there must be a concern that this represents an uncritical pro-donation approach by AAs and the HTA.

It is unfortunate that the HTA's guidance does not deal more rigorously with the conflict of interests underlying situations of this kind. A more robust

---

[241] Ibid. at [17].   [242] Ibid. at [19]–[22].   [243] HT Act 2004 (PLCCT) Regs 2006, reg. 11.

[244] Ibid. reg. 11(3)(b). NB: HT Act 2004, s. 2(3): 'appropriate consent' in relation to an incompetent child is a person with PR.

[245] HTA (2017) paras 88–118. AAs are usually based in hospitals with bone marrow transplant units.

[246] Ibid. paras 102(b) and 54–55.   [247] Ibid. paras 95–100.

[248] *A NHS Foundation Trust* v. *MC* [2020] EWCOP 33, at [19].

[249] L. Cherkassky (2015) p. 50.

basis for assessment, suggested by Cohen J in *MC*, would be for the HTA and AAs to use the same considerations set out in the MCA 2005 to consider the best interests of children without capacity to decide for themselves.[250] Meanwhile, it is unclear how the HTA currently deals with applications involving live children as bone marrow donors for close relatives, often their own siblings. Hopefully, its supervision is not purely tokenistic on the basis that the procedure 'merely' involves the removal of regenerative tissue. The pressures on parents in such cases mean that safeguards are required that recognise the invasion of bodily integrity for the child and the complex conflicts of interests that arise in this emotive family situation.

(C) Parents' Culture and Children's Bodies

The ambit of parental authority to take decisions that permanently alter a child's body has been particularly contentious in relation to cultural, social and religious practices. Some parents obviously feel free to arrange for their children to undergo what Feldman describes as various forms of 'mutilation' carried out for religious or social reasons, such as ear piercing, male circumcision and clitorectomy (female genital mutilation, or FGM), all of which represent a prima facie violation of children's right to bodily integrity.[251] The argument that such practices can be justified on the basis of cultural practice or parental religious belief has come under increasing scrutiny internationally. Those defending parental freedom tend to emphasise the importance of the child's social, relational and cultural interests, which may be said to be advanced by adhering to practices that signify belonging to the community. Further, it might be argued that attempts to regulate such practices represent an arrogant refusal to acknowledge or understand long-held cultural beliefs. In relation to FGM, there has been a strong movement, both internationally and domestically, to rejecting these arguments on the basis that they cannot justify the imposition of harmful practices that often cause permanent physical and psychological damage. In contrast, parents who agree to circumcise their sons face no legal barrier to doing so, despite the potential harm and permanent physical change that the practice imposes.

The practice of FGM is not only a cultural tradition going back centuries and pre-dating Islam, but one which is still widely performed on women and girls in various communities, primarily in Africa and the Middle East.[252] This topic proved a controversial one at the drafting stage of the CRC, with delegates

---

[250] *A NHS Foundation Trust* v. *MC* [2020] EWCOP 33, at [22]. These factors are found in MCA 2005, s. 4.

[251] D. Feldman (2002) pp. 270–2.

[252] UNICEF provides frequently updated statistics on FGM on their website at www.unicef.org /protection/female-genital-mutilation: current estimates suggest that some 3 million girls and women who live in some thirty countries, primarily in Africa and the Middle East, are cut each year.

from the UK and the US wanting an outright condemnation of the practice, and delegates from countries such as Senegal wanting a more general formula.[253] The compromise which emerged is seen in the wording of Article 24(3). While states are obliged to take measures 'with a view to abolishing traditional practices prejudicial to the health of children', there is no specific reference to the prohibition of FGM. Subsequent developments in international human rights law have taken an increasingly firm stand against the practice and the UN Committee on the Rights of the Child is clear that the practice is included within Article 24(3) of the CRC, despite the ambiguity introduced in the drafting process.[254] Concerns regarding community sensitivities have not weakened an international resolve to stamp out FGM.[255] The practice often involves girls in extreme pain and often carries long-term and serious side effects on mental and physical health.[256] There is widespread condemnation of the practice on the basis that it not only infringes girls' rights under the CRC, but also their rights under a range of other international conventions.[257] Legal prohibition alone is unlikely to be successful at eliminating the practice. As the UN Committees explain, 'an underlying challenge that must be confronted is the fact that harmful practices may be perceived as having beneficial effects for the victim and members of their family and community'.[258] In many communities, genital cutting is considered to be an essential sign of a girl's virginity and without it she has no chance of marriage, her only route to security and prosperity. A single family cannot reject the customs of their own community if they consider that their daughters will suffer socially as a result.[259] International development agencies now widely consider that the only way to eradicate the practice is to challenge existing social norms, educate communities from within and persuade them of the dangers, rather than simply condemning FGM.[260]

Migration has also brought the challenge of combatting FGM to Europe.[261] The ECHR does not explicitly mention FGM, but, as Baroness Hale explained, 'FGM will almost inevitably amount either to torture or to other cruel,

---

[253] L. LeBlanc (1995) pp. 85–9.

[254] Committee on the Elimination of Discrimination Against Women and Committee on the Rights of the Child (2014).

[255] See UNICEF's work on monitoring developments at: www.unicef.org/protection/female-genital-mutilation.

[256] See *K* v. *Secretary of State for the Home Department, Fornah* v. *Secretary of State for the Home Department* [2006] UKHL 46, [2007] 1 AC 412, per Baroness Hale of Richmond, at [91]–[92], for a short, but graphic, summary of the methods used in FGM and its effects.

[257] Ibid. at [94]. See also *A Local Authority* v. *M and N (Female Genital Mutilation Protection Order)* [2018] EWHC 870 (Fam), at [22].

[258] Committee on the Elimination of Discrimination Against Women and Committee on the Rights of the Child (2014) para. 59.

[259] N. Ford (2005) p. 188. See also UNICEF Innocenti Research Centre (2005) ch. 3.

[260] Committee on the Elimination of Discrimination Against Women and Committee on the Rights of the Child (2014) para. 59; N. Ford (2005) p. 188.

[261] UNICEF Innocenti Research Centre (2005) p. 4.

inhuman or degrading treatment' contrary to Article 3 of the ECHR.[262] This is significant both because Article 3 is an absolute right and because it carries with it a positive obligation on the state to 'do that which is reasonable in all the circumstances to protect children from real and immediate risk of harm' imposed by third parties, including parents.[263] Until recently, it seemed unlikely that the UK was fulfilling these obligations and providing sufficient protection from what has been described as 'an extreme and ghastly manifestation' of discrimination and subjugation.[264] Although legislation specifically criminalising the practice had been in place since 1985,[265] no prosecutions were brought under it. That legislation was replaced with the Female Genital Mutilation Act 2003, itself significantly updated in 2015.[266] There is now a more comprehensive set of criminal laws, including offences designed to protect girls resident in the UK from being sent abroad to undergo the procedure[267] and to prosecute parents who fail to protect their child from FGM.[268] Teachers and health and social work professionals are now required to report to the police any cases of FGM on children that come to their attention,[269] an important duty given the understandable reluctance to report family members to the police.[270] While prosecutions are still rare, they have started to take place and the first conviction was reported in 2019.

Preventing mutilation in the first place is preferable to prosecution after the harm has been done. The 2015 Act also introduced FGM prevention orders, giving the courts the power to impose wide-ranging restrictions to protect girls from FGM.[271] The initial cases on these orders have centred the Article 3 rights of girls to state protection from credible threats of FGM.[272] As a result, significant restrictions can be imposed even if they prevent the child from developing relationships with close family members, protected by Article 8 of the ECHR, provided that they are proportionate to the threatened harm.[273]

---

[262] *K v. Secretary of State for the Home Department, Fornah v. Secretary of State for the Home Department* [2006] UKHL 46, [2007] 1 AC 412, per Baroness Hale of Richmond, at [94].

[263] *A Local Authority v. M and N (Female Genital Mutilation Protection Order)* [2018] EWHC 870 (Fam), at [38]; see discussion of the nature of the obligation from [26]–[47].

[264] [2006] UKHL 46, per Lord Brown of Eaton-Under-Heywood, at [119].

[265] Prohibition of Female Circumcision Act 1985 (repealed and replaced by later legislation in 2003).

[266] Serious Crime Act 2015, ss 70–5.

[267] Female Genital Mutilation Act 2003, s. 1: criminal offence of FGM; s. 3: criminal offence of assisting a non-UK resident to carry out FGM overseas.

[268] Female Genital Mutilation Act 2003, s. 3A, inserted by Serious Crime Act 2015, s. 72(2).

[269] Female Genital Mutilation Act 2003, s. 5B, inserted by Serious Crime Act 2015, s. 74.

[270] Although R. Gaffney-Rhys (2017) p. 426 notes the potential for this duty to discourage parents from seeking medical attention for their daughters.

[271] Female Genital Mutilation Act 2003, Sch. 2, inserted by Serious Crime Act 2015.

[272] *A Local Authority v. M and N (Female Genital Mutilation Protection Order)* [2018] EWHC 870 (Fam), at [24].

[273] *A Local Authority v. M and N (Female Genital Mutilation Protection Order)* [2018] EWHC 870 (Fam); *M v. F, Z (A Child)* [2017] EWHC 3566 (Fam). See also *Re X (A Child) (FGMPO)* [2018] EWCA Civ 1825, in which the Court of Appeal found that there was not sufficient reasoning in the initial decision to demonstrate that an absolute travel ban was proportionate to the risk.

Further, FGM is clearly recognised as a child protection issue.[274] If there are concerns that FGM is to be carried out on a child, the police and children's social care should be involved, with a section 47 investigation taking place and consideration given to obtaining an emergency protection order.[275] In an important decision in *B and G (Children) (No. 2)*,[276] the President made it clear that any form of FGM constitutes 'significant harm' for the purposes of child protection law and that no reasonable parent could allow it to be inflicted, despite the cultural context,[277] so allowing the court to make child protection orders for FGM victims if their welfare requires it. Together, these legal developments provide a comprehensive framework of legal protection that can be utilised to protect victims and potential victims of FGM. While it remains to be seen whether this will result in effective protection in practice, the clear message from the courts and Parliament is that FGM is a serious violation of a child's rights, requiring the state to act to protect the child.

In contrast to the increasingly clear condemnation of FGM, male circumcision is widely tolerated, socially and legally. The courts have shown little stomach for tackling the fraught question of whether male circumcision can be justified as being in the child's best interests. Until the decision in *Re J (Specific Issue Orders: Muslim Upbringing and Circumcision)*,[278] there had been no legal ruling on its legality. While acknowledging that much of the medical literature adopts the view that such a procedure without medical necessity is an assault on the child's bodily integrity,[279] Wall J concluded that the procedure is lawful because 'there have, historically, been a number of medical justifications put forward for male circumcision' and because 'it is insisted on by Muslim and Jews', and further that it has 'over the years, become an accepted practice amongst a significant number of parents in England'.[280] The decision, confirmed by the Court of Appeal,[281] is authority for the proposition that as long as parents agree, the law allows them to arrange for their children to be circumcised, but if they disagree over such a matter, judicial authority must be obtained from the courts.

It is questionable whether Wall J's reasoning suffices as a good legal justification. Popularity of a parental practice should not prevent the judiciary from declaring it to be unlawful, if they consider it to be against children's best interests. Because in *Re J*, the divorced parents disagreed over whether their son should be circumcised, Wall J was able to weigh up the pros and cons of the procedure being carried out on their small son aged 5. He concluded that the boy was unlikely to have sufficient involvement with his Muslim father's community to justify circumcising him, given the potential medical and psychological risks, its irreversible nature and his mother's opposition.[282] But, as Fox and Thomson

---

[274] HM Government (2016).   [275] Ibid. p. 63.   [276] [2015] EWFC 3, [2015] 1 FLR 905.
[277] Ibid. at [67]–[71].   [278] [1999] 2 FLR 678.   [279] Ibid. at 690.   [280] Ibid.
[281] *Re J (Specific Issue Orders: Child's Religious Upbringing and Circumcision)* [2000] 1 FLR 571. See also *Re S (Specific Issue Order: Religion: Circumcision)* [2004] EWHC 1282 (Fam), [2005] 1 FLR 236, per Baron J, at [76]–[78], adopting Wall J's view of the law in *Re J* [1999] 2 FLR 678.
[282] [1999] 2 FLR 678, at 699–700.

point out, such an approach avoids the crucial question – why should circumcision be left to parental decision?[283] It leaves the children of united parents unprotected against a practice on which they are not consulted and over which they have no control. Indeed, these authors criticise the courts for assuming that the socioreligious benefits to a child of being brought up in a Muslim or Jewish environment can outweigh the medical risks, without those medical risks ever being properly analysed.[284] They argue that the whole range of 'ethico-legal texts' on this procedure portray infant male circumcision as of low risk and therefore a matter of parental choice:

> Only limited consideration is given to the seemingly obvious fact that circumcision is the excision of healthy tissue from a child unable to give his consent for no demonstrable medical benefit.[285]

Nor does the case law show any judicial consideration of the child's own rights in such cases. Although the court in *Re J* considered and rejected the father's claimed right under Article 9 of the ECHR, to arrange for his son's circumcision according to the tenets of his religion, there was no analysis of the child's own rights, either to bodily integrity or respect for his religious identity, both now and in the future.

The stark difference between the law's treatment of FGM and male circumcision was addressed directly in *B and G (Children) (No. 2)*.[286] The care proceedings in that case were brought in relation to a 3-year-old girl and her 4-year-old brother, on the basis that the girl had been subject to FGM. Had that allegation been proven, the threshold of significant harm would have been crossed and the court would have had the power to grant the LA the care order that they sought, if shown to be in the children's best interests, with a plan for adoption for both children.[287] Although the point was not directly before the court, as the family were Muslims it was likely that the boy in this case had been circumcised or would be if returned to the care of the parents. As Munby P observed, this led to the 'curious' result that the law would permit the parents to circumcise their son, but would regard FGM as sufficient to justify the adoption of *both* children.[288] Most forms of FGM are clearly far more invasive and entail far more serious consequences than male circumcision,[289] but in this particular case, the form of FGM alleged was the least intrusive[290] and,

---

[283] M. Fox and M. Thomson (2005) pp. 165–6.   [284] Ibid. p. 166.   [285] Ibid. p. 170.

[286] [2015] EWFC 3, [2015] 1 FLR 905.

[287] Discussed above. On the facts of this case, the LA was unable to prove that FGM had taken place.

[288] [2015] EWFC 3, at [63].

[289] *K* v. *Secretary of State for the Home Department, Fornah* v. *Secretary of State for the Home Department* [2006] UKHL 46, [2007] 1 AC 412, per Baroness Hale of Richmond, at [93].

[290] The World Health Organization commonly classifies four types of FGM. The allegations in this case concerned type IV, defined as: 'All other harmful procedures to the female genitalia for non-medical purposes, for example, pricking, piercing, incising, scraping and cauterization.' The classifications are set out in [2015] EWFC 3, at [7].

Munby P considered, was less invasive than male circumcision and entailed no more traumatic or serious long-term consequences.[291] As a result, he concluded, if *all* forms of FGM constitute 'significant harm', then male circumcision must *also* be regarded as inflicting significant harm.[292] For the threshold criteria for care proceedings to be made out, the law also requires that harm is attributable to parental care which is not what it would be 'reasonable to expect' of a parent.[293] It was at this point that Munby P found that the law's approach to FGM and male circumcision differed in that:

> Whereas it can never be reasonable parenting to inflict *any* form of FGM on a child, the position is quite different with male circumcision. Society and the law, including family law, are prepared to tolerate non-therapeutic male circumcision performed for religious or even for purely cultural or conventional reasons, while no longer being willing to tolerate FGM in any of its forms.[294]

The fact that society is willing to tolerate a practice is not in itself a justification for allowing parents to inflict significant harm on a child. Nor is it sufficient to justify interference with the child's right to bodily integrity under Article 8 of the ECHR. The implication of the argument must be that society is willing to regard male circumcision as reasonable parenting on the basis that it is capable of furthering the child's best interests. Munby P goes on to suggest the following distinctions between the two practices:

> FGM has no basis in any religion; male circumcision is often performed for religious reasons. FGM has no medical justification and confers no health benefits; male circumcision is seen by some (although opinions are divided) as providing hygienic or prophylactic benefits.[295]

Each of these reasons is itself debatable. Medical opinion seems divided over whether non-therapeutic male circumcision is beneficial or harmful.[296] Like any surgical procedure, it is certainly not risk free, even when carried out expertly, under medical conditions. The British Medical Association warns that the practice should not be justified solely by reference to evidence of its health benefits – such evidence is simply insufficient.[297] The view that male circumcision is a religious practice while FGM is merely cultural is also not as clear cut as is often assumed, for three reasons. First, both male circumcision and FGM are performed across a range of different cultures and carry with them different meanings across those socio-cultural contexts that fall outside

---

[291] Ibid. at [63].   [292] Ibid. at [69].

[293] Children Act 1989, s. 31(2)(b)(i). Alternatively, the threshold can be made out on the basis that the harm is attributable to the child being beyond parental control, a point that was not relevant in this case.

[294] [2015] EWFC 3, at [72] (emphasis in the original).   [295] Ibid. at [72].

[296] B. Earp *et al.* (2017) review the evidence concluding that they are 'modest at best', especially when viewed against the risks of circumcision and the safe means of obtaining the same benefits (e.g. good hygiene).

[297] BMA (2019) p. 11.

of the dichotomy of religious circumcision and cultural FGM.[298] Second, human rights law does not merely protect beliefs and practices that derive from religious tradition, but all beliefs of sufficient cogency and seriousness, including those with cultural origins.[299] Finally, parental religious belief is not usually considered sufficient to inflict harm on children.[300] While it is the case that boys may be more easily integrated into the community if they have been circumcised, the same argument has not prevented criminalisation of FGM.

Although most forms of FGM are undoubtedly more harmful and a more serious violation of bodily integrity than male circumcision, the judgment in *B and G (Children) (No. 2)*[301] demonstrates the difficulties in justifying a permissive approach to male circumcision while offering robust legal protection to the rights of girls. In practice, it has proved much more difficult for the international community to reach consensus on circumcision of boys or for national legal systems to prohibit it.[302] A compromise would be to introduce greater protection for children by passing strict regulations requiring the procedure to be performed only by the medically qualified.[303] In more general terms, there is a need to encourage parents to think more about their children's right to bodily integrity, rather than treating them like mere family appendages. They should avoid making any arrangements for their young children to undergo procedures, however apparently trivial, which may damage their health and bodily integrity. Instead, they should respect their children's individuality and leave them to decide for themselves when older how to treat their own bodies.

(5) Conclusion

Although doctors have the expertise and training to promote children's healthcare, they do not have the primary responsibility for decisions concerning children and are not necessarily in the best position to advise how children's rights should be protected. But then, nor are children's parents always well equipped to protect the rights of their desperately ill children; not surprisingly, they may find it impossible to be objective over the decisions to be made. These problems are exacerbated when tiny babies are the focus of decision-making, given their inability to speak on their own behalf. Indeed, it is in the context of the medical care of young children that we find parents and doctors

---

[298] B. Earp *et al.* (2017) pp. 609–13.
[299] E.g. *Campbell and Cosans* v. *United Kingdom* (1982) 4 EHRR 293.
[300] See discussion of *Prince* v. *Massachusetts*, 321 US 158, at 165 (1944), above.
[301] [2015] EWFC 3, [2015] 1 FLR 905.
[302] M. Fox and M. Thomson (2017) discuss developments in the Council of Europe, Germany and the Netherlands.
[303] See Parliamentary Assembly of the Council of Europe, 'Children's right to physical integrity', Resolution 1952 (2013), which recognises male circumcision as a violation of physical integrity, but limits its proposal to defining 'the medical, sanitary and other conditions' for male circumcision, in contrast to the requirements to prohibit and prevent FGM.

alike assuming that parents are entitled to reach decisions without judicial supervision, in a way that would be unthinkable in relation to older children and adults. These problems are also evident in non-therapeutic decisions in which parents may lose sight of their duty to protect the child's own rights from being infringed by decisions which appear to be in a child's best interests, but which may be more to do with those of his or her carers. While professional guidance, legislation and court decisions are now more likely to recognise children's independent rights to bodily integrity and life, there remain areas in which the law is content to tolerate significant intervention without adequate protection for the child. Children's rights should not be lost somewhere in the middle, between parental, medical and judicial paternalism.

Bibliography

NB: Many of these publications can be obtained on the relevant organisation's website.

Alderson, P. (1993) *Children's Consent to Surgery*, Oxford University Press.

Alderson, P., Hawthorne, J. and Killen, M. (2005) 'The Participation Rights of Premature Babies' 13 *International Journal of Children's Rights* 31.

Alderson, P. and Montgomery, J. (1996) *Health Care Decisions: Making Decisions with Children*, IPPR.

Auckland, C. and Goold, I. (2020) 'Re-evaluating "Best Interests" in the Wake of *Raqeeb* v. *Barts NHS Foundation Trust & Anor*' 83 *Modern Law Review* 1328.

Austin, L. and Huxtable, R. (2019) 'Resolving Disagreements about the Care of Critically Ill Children: Evaluating Existing Processes and Setting the Research Agenda' in Goold, I., Herring, J. and Auckland, C. *Parental Rights, Best Interests and Significant Harms: Medical Decision-Making on Behalf of Children Post-Great Ormond Street Hospital* v. *Gard*, Hart Publishing.

Bhatia, N. and Birchley, G. (2020) 'Medical Tourism and the Best Interests of the Critically ill Child in the Era of Healthcare Globalisation' 28 *Medical Law Review* 696.

Birchley, G. (2019) 'The Harm Threshold: A View from the Clinic' in Goold, I., Herring, J. and Auckland, C. (eds) *Parental Rights, Best Interests and Significant Harms: Medical Decision-Making on Behalf of Children Post-Great Ormond Street Hospital* v. *Gard*, Hart Publishing.

Brazier, M. (Chair) (2006) *Critical Care Decisions in Fetal and Neonatal Medicine: Ethical Issues*, Nuffield Council on Bioethics.

Bridgeman, J. (2007) *Parental Responsibility, Young Children and Healthcare Law*, Cambridge University Press.

(2017) 'The Provision of Healthcare to Young and Dependent Children: The Principles, Concepts, and Utility of the Children Act 1989' 25 *Medical Law Review* 363.

(2019) 'Beyond Best Interests: A Question of Professional Conscience' in Goold, I., Herring, J. and Auckland, C. (eds) *Parental Rights, Best Interests and Significant Harms: Medical Decision-Making on Behalf of Children Post-Great Ormond Street Hospital* v. *Gard*, Hart Publishing.

British Medical Association (BMA) (2019) *Non-Therapeutic Male Circumcision (NTMC) of Children – Practical Guidance for Doctors*, BMA.

Brownsword, R. (2005) 'Happy Families, Consenting Couples, and Children with Dignity: Sex Selection and Saviour Siblings' 17 *Child and Family Law Quarterly* 435.

Bruce, F. (2013) *Parliamentary Inquiry into Abortion on the Grounds of Disability*, UK Parliament.

Byrne, B. (2019) 'Article 23: Children with disabilities' in J. Tobin (ed.) *The UN Convention on the Rights of the Child: A Commentary*, Oxford University Press.

Cave, E. (2014) 'Adolescent Refusal of MMR Inoculation: *F (Mother)* v. *F (Father)*' 77 *Modern Law Review* 619.

(2017) 'Voluntary Vaccination: The Pandemic Effect' 37 *Legal Studies* 279.

Cave, E., Brierley, J. and Archard, D. (2020) 'Making Decisions for Children – Accommodating Parental Choice in Best Interests Determinations: *Barts Health NHS Trust* v. *Raqeeb* [2019] EWHC 2530 (Fam); *Raqeeb and Barts Health NHS Trust* [2019] EWHC 2531 (Admin)' 28 *Medical Law Review* 183.

Cherkassky, L. (2015) 'The Wrong Harvest: The Law on Saviour Siblings' 29 *International Journal of Law, Policy and Family* 36.

Committee on the Elimination of Discrimination Against Women and Committee on the Rights of the Child (2014) *Joint General Recommendation/General Comment No. 31 of the Committee on the Elimination of Discrimination Against Women and No. 18 of the Committee on the Rights of the Child on Harmful Practices*, CEDAW/C/GC/31-CRC/C/GC/18.

Committee on the Rights of the Child (2006) *General Comment No. 9 on the Rights of Children with Disabilities*, CRC/C/GC/9, Centre for Human Rights, Geneva.

  (2013) *General Comment No. 15 on the Right of the Child to the Enjoyment of the Highest Attainable Standard of Health (Art. 24)*, CRC/C/GC/15, Centre for Human Rights, Geneva.

Department of Health (DH) (2001) *Seeking Consent: Working with Children*, Department of Health Publications.

Dingwall, R., Eekelaar, J. and Murray, T. (1995) *The Protection of Children*, Avebury.

Dworkin, G. (1982) 'Consent, Representation and Proxy Consent' in Gaylin, W. and Macklin, R. (eds) *Who Speaks for the Child: The Problems of Proxy Consent*, Plenum Press.

Earp, B., Hendry, J. and Thomson, M. (2017) 'Reason and Paradox in Medical and Family Law: Shaping Children's Bodies' 25 *Medical Law Review* 604.

Eekelaar, J. (1986) 'The Emergence of Children's Rights' 6 *Oxford Journal of Legal Studies* 161.

Feenan, D. (1997) 'A Good Harvest? *Re Y (Mental Incapacity: Bone Marrow Transplant)*' 9 *Child and Family Law Quarterly* 305.

Feldman, D. (2002) *Civil Liberties and Human Rights in England and Wales*, Oxford University Press.

Ford, N. (2005) 'Communication for Abandonment of Female Genital Cutting: An Approach Based on Human Rights Principles' 13 *International Journal of Children's Rights* 183.

Fortin, J. (1998) '*Re C (Medical Treatment)*: A Baby's Right to Die' 10 *Child and Family Law Quarterly* 411.

Fox, M. and McHale, J. (1997) 'In Whose Best Interests?' 60 *Modern Law Review* 700.

Fox, M. and Thomson, M. (2005) 'Short Changed? The Law and Ethics of Male Circumcision' 13 *International Journal of Children's Rights* 161.

  (2017) 'Bodily Integrity, Embodiment and the Regulation of Parental Choice' 44 *Journal of Law and Society* 501.

Gaffney-Rhys, R. (2017) 'From the Offences Against the Person Act 1861 to the Serious Crime Act 2015 – the Development of the Law relating to Female Genital Mutilation in England and Wales' 39 *Journal of Social Welfare and Family Law* 417.

General Medical Council (GMC) (2007) *0–18 Years: Guidance for all Doctors*, GMC.

Goold, I. (2019) 'Evaluating Best Interests as a Threshold for Judicial Intervention in Medical Decision-Making on Behalf of Children' in Goold, I., Herring, J. and Auckland, C. (eds) *Parental Rights, Best Interests and Significant Harms: Medical Decision-Making on Behalf of Children Post-Great Ormond Street Hospital* v. *Gard*, Hart Publishing.

Gunn, M. and Smith, J. (1985) 'Arthur's Case and the Right to Life of a Down's Syndrome Child' *Criminal Law Review* 705.

Harrop, E. (2019) 'Setting the Scene – Supporting and Informing Shared Decision-Making at the Bedside' in Goold, I., Herring, J. and Auckland, C. (eds) *Parental Rights, Best Interests and Significant Harms: Medical Decision-Making on Behalf of Children Post-Great Ormond Street Hospital* v. *Gard*, Hart Publishing.

Healthcare Commission (2007) HC 97 *State of Healthcare 2007*, The Stationery Office.

HM Government (2016) *Multi-agency Statutory Guidance on Female Genital Mutilation*, Open Government.

Human Tissue Authority (HTA) (2017) *Code of Practice G – Donation of Allogeneic Bone Marrow and Peripheral Blood Stem Cells for Transplantation*, HTA.

  (2020) *Code of Practice F – Donation of Solid Organs and Tissue for Transplantation: Part 1 Living Organ Donation*, HTA.

Huxtable, R. (2004) 'Re C (A Child) (Immunisation: Parental Rights) [2003] EWCA Civ 1148' 26 *Journal of Social Welfare and Family Law* 69.

Jackson, L. and Huxtable, R. (2005) 'The Doctor-Parent Relationship: As Fragile as *Glass*?' 27 *Journal of Social Welfare and Family Law* 369.

LeBlanc, L. (1995) *The Convention on the Rights of the Child: United Nations Lawmaking on Human Rights*, University of Nebraska Press.

Maher, J. and Macfarlane, A. (2004) 'Trends in Live Births and Birthweight by Social Class, Marital Status and Mother's Age, 1976–2000' 23 *Health Statistics Quarterly* 34.

Mason, J. and Laurie, G. (2006) *Mason and McCall Smith's Law and Medical Ethics*, Oxford University Press.

Moreton, K, (2020) 'Reflecting on "Hannah's Choice": Using the Ethics of Care to Justify Child Participation in End of Life Decision-Making' 28 *Medical Law Review* 124.

Office of National Statistics (ONS) (2008) *Social Trends* No. 38, Palgrave Macmillan.

(2019) *Child and Infant Mortality in England and Wales: 2017*, ONS.

Read, J. and Clements, L. (2004) 'Demonstrably Awful: The Right to Life and the Selective Non-Treatment of Disabled Babies and Young Children' 31 *Journal of Law and Society* 482.

Royal College of Paediatrics and Child Health (RCPCH) (2015) 'Making Decisions to Limit Treatment in Life-Limiting and Life-Threatening Conditions in Children: A Framework for Practice' 100 *Archives of Disease in Childhood* s1.

(2017) *State of Child Health Report 2017*, RCPCH.

Taylor, R. (2019) 'Parental Decisions and Court Jurisdiction: Best Interests or Significant Harm' in Goold, I., Herring, J. and Auckland, C. (eds) *Parental Rights, Best Interests and Significant Harms: Medical Decision-Making on Behalf of Children Post-Great Ormond Street Hospital v. Gard*, Hart Publishing.

Taylor, R. and Hoyano, L. (2012) 'Criminal Child Maltreatment: The Case for Reform' *Criminal Law Review* 871.

Then, S. (2017) 'Best Interests: The "Best" Way for Courts to Decide if Young Children Should Act as Bone Marrow Donors?' 17 *Medical Law International* 3.

UNICEF Innocenti Research Centre (2005) *Changing a Harmful Social Convention: Female Genital Mutilation/Cutting*, UNICEF.

Viner, R., Ward, J., Cheung, R., Wolfe, I. and Hargreaves, D. (2018) *Child Health in 2030 in England: Comparisons with Other Wealthy Countries*, State of Child Health Short Report Series, October 2018, Royal College of Paediatrics and Child Health.

Wells, C. (1989) '"Otherwise Kill Me": Marginal Children and Ethics at the Edges of Existence' in Lee, R. and Morgan, D. (eds) *Birthrights: Law and Ethics at the Beginnings of Life*, Routledge.

Whitelaw, A. (1986) 'Death as an Option in Neonatal Intensive Care' 328 *The Lancet* 328–31.

Wilkinson, D. (2019) 'In Defence of a Conditional Harm Threshold for Paediatric Decision-Making' in Goold, I., Herring, J. and Auckland, C. (eds) *Parental Rights, Best Interests and Significant Harms: Medical Decision-Making on Behalf of Children Post-Great Ormond Street Hospital v. Gard*, Hart Publishing.

8

The Child's Right to Education
Parental Choice and Plural Values

(1) Introduction

The right to education is one of the most important rights for children, providing the foundation upon which the child's future is built.[1] As the Committee on the Rights of the Child explains, the purposes of education are broad and aim to:

> empower the child by developing his or her skills, learning and other capacities, human dignity, self-esteem and self-confidence ... [enabling] children, individually and collectively, to develop their personalities, talents and abilities and to live a full and satisfying life within society.[2]

Determining and guiding the child's education is also one of the most important responsibilities for parents. That responsibility takes on particular significance in circumstances in which the convictions of the parents, or the child, are at variance with those held by the majority in society. If the child is to be equipped with the ability to 'live a full and satisfying life within' wider society, then the education they receive will need to provide the skills, knowledge and values that will enable them to do so. Yet, this education may be in tension with the values and teaching of the child's parents and the community in which they live. In the most difficult cases, there may be a direct conflict between the child's right to an 'open future' within wider society and their integration into that community.

Many of the international human rights treaties that protect the child's right to education also recognise the dilemma that state-controlled education can be used to impose ideology and suppress minority views. Religious and ethnic minority groups[3] contribute to the richness of a pluralistic society. One of the

---

[1] The meaning of the right to education and the extent to which children's rights in education are realised in domestic law is further explored in Chapter 14.

[2] Committee on the Rights of the Child (2001) para. 2.

[3] Finding an acceptable definition of the term 'minority group' is fraught with difficulty; P. Thornberry (1991) esp. pp. 164–72. For the purposes of this work, it is assumed that a 'minority group' is numerically smaller than the majority, whose members possess distinctive ethnic, religious or linguistic characteristics and who show a sense of solidarity directed towards preserving their culture, traditions, religion or language.

most important rights for such a group is to preserve its separate identity. It cannot do so unless it maintains its continuity by educating its children to understand and respect its own customs, religion and culture. They can then mature into adult members of the group, with a commitment to its future preservation. Nevertheless, when the educational rights of the children of minority groups are considered, a number of competing considerations become apparent. Indeed, a familiar dilemma arises: how to find a suitable means of ensuring that parents' rights do not override those of their children. Alongside this dilemma is the question of the content of the child's own rights to freedom of thought and belief. While the child might express commitment to the values of the community, the weight that should be placed on that commitment may be limited if the child has not had an education that allows her to question and evaluate those views.

Overarching this discussion is a more fundamental question regarding minority groups' relationships with wider society. An acceptable compromise must always be found between the views of extreme pluralists who maintain the absolute right of minority groups to preserve all the elements of their cultural traditions, and those of assimilationists who expect minorities to be absorbed into the culture of the mainstream community.[4] As Poulter comments, the compromise adopted in Britain has been to promote a 'cultural pluralism within limits'.[5] This reflects the pervading view that a democratic pluralist society should support the cultures and lifestyles of its different groups, while expecting all groups to accept a set of shared values distinctive of that society as a whole. This approach has underpinned the way in which education has been delivered, since it was embraced by the Swann Report in the 1980s, which argued that the education system should reflect the fact that a policy of pluralism must be limited by the need for a cohesive society founded on shared fundamental values.[6] This deliberate policy of pluralism was the foundation for an expansion in the number and variety of 'schools with a religious character' from the start of the New Labour government in the late 1990s.[7] Nevertheless, across the political spectrum, anxiety has been expressed that this pluralist approach to accommodation of diverse communities has risked fragmentation and segregation. These concerns gained particular prominence in the aftermath of the 2001 riots in the North of England. The Cantle Report into the causes of the riots found that communities had segregated along ethnic, cultural and religious lines, including in their educational arrangements. For Cantle, a key aspect of the response to such division was, again, to build community cohesion on the basis of shared values.[8] The concept of cultural pluralism within limits provides no clear answers as to how to define the fundamental values around which limits should be set. This question has become increasingly fraught as opposition to shared 'British

---

[4] S. Poulter (1998) ch. 1.   [5] Ibid. p. 21.   [6] M. Swann (1985) p. 6.
[7] Department for Education and Skills (2001) esp. ch. 5.   [8] T. Cantle (2001) pp. 18–21.

Values' has been defined as 'extremism' within the government's anti-terrorism strategy.[9] Educational institutions have been placed under extensive obligations to 'actively promote' 'fundamental British values' to the children within their care in order to prevent them from being drawn into extremism and terrorism.[10] It is then the state interest in community cohesion and security, rather than the educational rights of children, that has been key to setting the acceptable limits of diverse values within education.

One might claim that it is in the best interests of children, as well as society, for all children to be educated in multicultural and multi-faith state schools. Such a system would undoubtedly enable children to learn about and respect the beliefs of others and equip them better to take their place in the outside world. However, by refusing to allow the establishment of separate schools, the government would risk undue interference with the freedom of parents and minority groups, as secured by the human rights instruments referred to below. Nonetheless, the continued existence of faith schools provokes a number of questions. For example, should society acknowledge that parents and minority groups have an absolute right to educate their children as they wish, even if they adopt educational methods that the state considers to be inward looking or even contrary to 'British Values'?[11] How should it respond if the education provided is considered to be inadequate and stultifyingly narrow? If children receive an education which is too restricted to enable them to leave their community and compete for a place outside its confines, then they may justifiably accuse the state of failing in its duty to ensure that they have equality of opportunity in the education they receive. Yet, parents or members of minority groups may also see any attempt to interfere with their freedom to educate their children according to their own beliefs not only in terms of a threat to their own convictions, but as an infringing of their own fundamental human rights.[12]

This chapter considers these questions from four educational perspectives. First, it considers the concept of separate education from a rights perspective, looking at the international human rights context and, in particular, the handling of parents' and children's rights. Second, the chapter considers the extent to which the state does, and should, regulate the limits of educational choice in order to ensure that children are prepared for life within a wider society. The chapter then turns to the third section to consider the degree to which parents should be permitted to remove their children from aspects of schooling which may most offend their own principles, notably collective worship and religious education. Finally, the chapter considers the way in which the law deals with pupils' appeals to their own religious rights in the context of current school uniform policies.

---

[9] HM Government (2011) Annex A. To be classed as extremism under the Prevent Strategy, the opposition to British values must be 'vocal or active'.

[10] Counter-terrorism and Security Act 2015, s. 26(1).

[11] K. Ajegbo (2007) pp. 90–3: the concept of 'Britishness'; R. Taylor (2015).

[12] Discussed below.

(2) Children's Education and Parental Convictions: A Rights Perspective

(A) The International Human Rights Context

The right to education is recognised in all core human rights instruments, underscoring its importance as a fundamental human right that crosses the traditional divide between civil and political rights.[13] The foundational human rights treaties were drafted at a time when religious and racial persecution before and during the Second World War was still recent history; in consequence, they emphasise the need to avoid educational institutions being used by states to indoctrinate children in ways that undermine their allegiance to their families and their own culture and religion. This, together with the fact that the notion of children's rights was still in its infancy, means that the provisions dealing specifically with children's right to education do so in a particularly adult-focused way, protecting parents' freedom to have their children educated according to their own beliefs. For example, Article 26(3) of the Universal Declaration of Human Rights states that: 'Parents have a prior right to choose the kind of education that shall be given to their children.' Similarly, during the drafting of the twin international covenants, many states recalled the Nazis' abuse of the education system for propaganda purposes,[14] and stressed the importance of respecting the liberty of parents to direct their children's education as a means to resist indoctrination. This is reflected in the International Covenant on Economic, Social and Cultural Rights in Article 13(3), which requires the state parties to:

> have respect for the liberty of parents and, when applicable, legal guardians to choose for their children schools, other than those established by the public authorities, which conform to such minimum educational standards as may be laid down or approved by the State and to ensure the religious and moral education of their children in conformity with their own convictions.[15]

While the intention behind the drafting of these provisions is laudable, they are written from an entirely adult perspective. The underlying assumption is that the interests of children can be identified with those of their parents, albeit within the limits of the 'minimum educational standards' that the state may choose to provide.[16] In doing so, it appears to give no consideration to the evolving capacity of the child or her right to have her own convictions respected and voice heard.

The Convention on the Rights of the Child (CRC) gave an opportunity to consider the right to education from the perspective of the child. The initial

---

[13] The detailed meaning of this right and the positive obligations that it places on the state are considered further in Chapter 14.

[14] G. Van Bueren (1995) p. 240.

[15] See also International Covenant on Civil and Political Rights, Art. 18(4), which requires state parties to 'have respect for the liberty of parents and, when applicable, legal guardians to ensure the religious and moral education of their children in conformity with their own convictions'.

[16] Committee on Economic, Social and Cultural Rights (1999) paras 28–29.

draft of the right to education would have done this by requiring states to respect both the liberty of the *child* and of the parents to an education in conformity with the convictions of *their* choice.[17] The question of children's religious freedom was one of the most contentious in the drafting of the CRC,[18] and this provision did not survive to the final text. Instead, the child's right to education in the CRC omits any direct reference to the rights of parents or to their religious convictions as protected by the instruments discussed above. The Convention takes an important step in moving away from an adult focus by clearly stating that education is the right of the child.[19] The question of state indoctrination is dealt with by requiring that one of the aims of that education shall be 'the development of respect for the child's parents, his or her own cultural identity, language and values'.[20] In this way, the problem is viewed through the prism of the child's right to be educated in a way that does not isolate her from her family and community, rather than through the rights of parents to direct that education. Together with the recognition of the child's own right to freedom of thought, conscience and religion in Article 14, this provides an important counterweight to the rights of parents within the documents discussed above. It is arguable that the respect that is owed to parents in educating their children in conformity with their own convictions under the international covenants is limited to circumstances in which those convictions do not conflict with the rights of the child to education and to freedom of thought. Nonetheless, there remain ambiguities within the CRC that mean that the problem is not fully resolved. In particular, Article 14 is an uneasy compromise between the child's right to freedom of thought and the rights of parents to provide direction to the child in exercising that freedom.[21] While children who have evolved capacity to decide for themselves may be able to assert their Article 14 rights without parental interference, they may never develop the capacity required to exercise freedom of thought, conscience or religion, unless the state intervenes to prevent their parents educating them in such a way that undermines their capacity for independent thought in the first place.

(B) The European Convention on Human Rights

Although the CRC contains compromises regarding children's rights, which could endanger a child's ability to break away from his or her parents' narrow beliefs through receiving a liberal education, it centres the right to education on the rights of the child rather than the beliefs of the parents. In contrast, the provision on education in the European Convention on Human Rights and

---

[17] G. Van Bueren (1995) pp. 159–60.   [18] See Chapter 2.   [19] CRC, Art. 28(1).
[20] CRC, Art. 29(1)(c).
[21] See Chapter 2 for discussion of the differing interpretations and reservations given to this right by state parties.

Fundamental Freedoms (ECHR) was drafted in an adult-focused manner. Article 2 of Protocol 1 (hereafter A2P1) provides:

> No person shall be denied the right to education. In the exercise of any functions which it assumes in relation to education and teaching, the state shall respect the right of parents to ensure such education and teaching in conformity with their own religious and philosophical convictions.

It is notable that the first sentence of this provision is not phrased as a positive right to be educated, but rather as a grudging statement that any education that the state does provide will not be denied to the individual.[22] The absence of any mention of the child in the first sentence contrasts with the focus on the rights of parents in the second sentence. The state must respect the right of *parents* to ensure that the education is in conformity with their own religious and philosophical convictions, but no mention is made of the convictions of children. The imbalance in the wording of the provision appears to give decisive control to parents, with very little safeguard for children. Nonetheless, subsequent interpretation of A2P1 has made it clear that the parental convictions covered by the provision are limited, as is the obligation to 'respect' them. Most importantly, the European Court of Human Rights (ECtHR) has consistently held that A2P1 is dominated by the right to education and that the second sentence is an adjunct to the first.[23] This means that a parent cannot demand respect for a conviction that would deny the child an education within the meaning of the first sentence.[24] Further, the convictions must be sufficiently cogent and serious to qualify for protection and must be 'worthy of respect in a democratic society' and 'not incompatible with human dignity'.[25] Finally, the obligation to *respect* parental convictions does not mean that those convictions must be *complied* with: the state is not obliged to provide a form of education that satisfies each parent's convictions. Together, these restrictions mean that, if it wishes, the state is given considerable latitude to regulate education to promote the right to education and to provide a plural approach to it, despite any conflict with the convictions of parents. The position of children in A2P1, however, remains very weak; their convictions are rarely considered and it seems doubtful that the state has a positive obligation to ensure that each child obtains a plural education.

The case law on precisely what A2P1 does require is convoluted and not always consistent. Its primary purpose is often said to be to prevent the state from indoctrinating children through the education system,[26] and parents have been most successful in cases in which they have objected to

---

[22] Although the ECtHR has found that despite this negative formulation the provision should be interpreted as a right to education: *Belgian Linguistics Case (No. 2)* (1968) 1 EHRR 252.

[23] E.g. *Kjeldsen, Busk and Pedersen* v. *Denmark* (1976) 1 EHRR 711, at [50] and [52]; *Campbell and Cosans* v. *United Kingdom* (1982) 4 EHRR 293, at [40].

[24] E.g. *Leuffen* v. *Germany*, App. No. 19844/92, Commission decision of 9 July 1992, unreported.

[25] *Campbell and Cosans* v. *United Kingdom* (1982) 4 EHRR 293, at [36].

[26] *Kjeldsen, Busk and Pedersen* v. *Denmark* (1976) 1 EHRR 711, at [53].

a curriculum that is not delivered in line with the principles of pluralism and objectivity.[27] Parents have been much less successful in seeking to use the right to obtain exemption from education that does meet those criteria. When interpreting A2P1 of the ECHR, the ECtHR obviously appreciates the need to maintain a balance between protecting pluralism and upholding the state's right to run an efficient education system reflecting society's shared values. Thus, in *Kjeldsen, Busk and Pedersen* v. *Denmark*,[28] it upheld the Danish state's right to set the curriculum and to impart information or knowledge of 'a directly or indirectly religious or philosophical kind'. This, the court considered, was acceptable, as long as the information was conveyed in an 'objective, critical and pluralistic manner', without attempting to indoctrinate pupils in a way which does not respect their parents' religious convictions.[29] It decided that the inclusion of compulsory sex education in all primary schools' curriculum did not infringe Danish parents' rights under A2P1 of the ECHR, given the scientific and factual manner in which it was taught,[30] and given that they could dissociate their children from sex education by sending them to private schools or educating them at home.[31] There is then no parental right to prevent the child from being exposed to teaching that conflicts with the parents' convictions, provided that the teaching is carried out in an objective and pluralistic manner. This principle also applies to activities as well as teaching; parents may not, for example, use A2P1 to require that their child is exempt from mixed swimming lessons[32] or drama workshops raising awareness of sexual abuse.[33]

In contrast, in *Folgerø* v. *Norway*,[34] humanist parents successfully objected to a curriculum on religion and philosophy that was dominated by Evangelical Lutheran Christianity. While it was permissible for a state to give greater prominence to religious traditions that had played an important role in the nation's development, in this case there was also a qualitative difference: children were being prepared for a Christian upbringing rather than merely informed about it. For this reason, the state had breached the requirements of objectivity and pluralism. This breach could not be remedied by the partial

---

[27] It should be noted a state may fall foul of A2P1 by failing to provide a sufficiently objective and pluralistic education, even in circumstances in which it does not seek to indoctrinate children; *R (Fox)* v. *Secretary of State for Education* [2015] EWHC 3404 (Admin), at [29] and [31].

[28] (1976) 1 EHRR 711. See also: *Angelini* v. *Sweden* (1988) 10 EHRR 123; *Folgerø and others* v. *Norway* [2007] ELR 557.

[29] Ibid. at [53]–[54].   [30] Ibid. at [54].

[31] Ibid.; some weight was put on the fact that the Danish private education system was heavily subsidised. See also *Dojan* v. *Germany* [2011] ELR 511, in which attendance at compulsory sex education classes and workshops was not a breach of A2P1 despite the fact that the parents did not have the option of home schooling given that it is prohibited in Germany.

[32] *Osmanoglu* v. *Switzerland*, App. No. 29086/12, decision of 10 January 2017. Technically, the case was decided under Art. 9 as Switzerland has not ratified Protocol 1; the same reasoning would be likely to apply under a case directly decided under A2P1 as it is regarded as the *lex specialis* in relation to Art. 9 in education cases.

[33] *Dojan* v. *Germany* [2011] ELR 511.   [34] [2007] ELR 557.

opt-out granted to parents or the possibility of private education. Similarly, in *Hasan* v. *Turkey*,[35] the same conclusion was reached in relation to the teaching of Hanafism, the dominant form of Sunni Islam in Turkey, with insufficient objectivity or parental exemptions. The exact limits of the requirements of pluralism are nonetheless difficult to discern. In *Lautsi* v. *Italy*,[36] the Grand Chamber controversially decided that it was within the state's margin of appreciation to allow crucifixes to be displayed in classrooms of state schools, considering the crucifix to be 'essentially a passive symbol'[37] that would not influence children in the same way as teaching might. It seems that there is no requirement that education is delivered in an environment that is entirely free from partiality to a particular religion or belief.

A2P1 is most effective as a means of protecting children from state indoctrination and ensuring that teaching is delivered in an objective and pluralistic manner. Where, conversely, the parent seeks to limit the child's exposure to plural ideas, they are likely to find it much more difficult to enlist A2P1 to assist them in doing so. The wide margin of appreciation given to states in how they 'respect' the convictions of parents has become particularly important as society has become more diverse and children are exposed to a wide variety of ideas in school, media, social media and elsewhere. As Judge Rozakis noted in his concurring judgment in *Lautsi*:[38]

> it is increasingly difficult for a state to cater for the individual needs of parents on educational issues. I would go as far as saying that its main concern, and this is a valid concern, should be to offer children an education which will ensure their fullest integration into the society in which they live and prepare them, in the best possible way, to cope effectively with the expectations that that society has of its members ... the duties of the state have largely shifted from concerns of parents to concerns of society at large, thus reducing the extent of the parents' ability to determine, outside the home, the kind of education that their children receive.

The state is clearly entitled to place great importance on educating children for life in a plural society and seeking to promote understanding between different groups within that society. Whether this amounts to a *right* for children to be given a plural education or to be educated in a way that respects their own beliefs, separately from their parents, is much more difficult to determine. The ECtHR has attempted to mitigate the weak language of A2P1 for children by insisting that it is interpreted in line with international law, including the CRC, which does state that education is the right of the child.[39] The Grand Chamber has also spoken of the ECHR as recognising the right of the child 'to education

---

[35] (2008) 46 EHRR 1060.   [36] (2012) 54 EHRR 3.

[37] Ibid. at [72]. In contrast, the wearing of an Islamic headscarf by a teacher has been found to be a 'powerful external symbol': *Dahlab* v. *Switzerland* [2001] ECHR 42393/98.

[38] *Lautsi* v. *Italy* (2012) 54 EHRR 3, at [O-I3].

[39] *Catan* v. *Moldova* (2013) 57 EHRR 4, at [136].

in a form which respects their right to believe or not to believe'.[40] This right is recognised to the extent that the state is entitled to regulate education to achieve it, but there is no case law to suggest that there is a positive obligation to ensure that the child receives such an education against the wishes of their parents. Given the negative wording of the right to education in A2P1 and the ECtHR's recognition of education as primarily the responsibility of parents,[41] it is not at all clear that a child could use A2P1, or Article 9, to object to being provided with a limited education by her parents, if national law allowed that. This is particularly so as the court has stated that the Convention recognises the rights of parents to promote their world view to their child even in an 'insistent or overbearing manner'.[42] For example, if parents wished to home educate their child within a restrictive world view then, while the state would be permitted to regulate that education,[43] it is unlikely that the child would have a successful claim against the state if it chose not to do so. Once again, the adult-centred nature of the Convention means that case law focuses on the relationship between state and parents rather than on the child. Children's rights to a plural education tend to be protected as a by-product of the rights of parents or the actions of the state, rather than as a right of independent importance.

This blindness to the child's own right to education is evident throughout the case law of the ECtHR. Where parents and children are both applicants in a case, the court rarely gives substantive consideration to the position of children. For example, in *Valsamis* v. *Greece*,[44] the ECtHR decided that neither the parents' religious convictions under Article 9 nor their pacifist views under A2P1 of the ECHR had been infringed when their daughter was disciplined for refusing to participate in a school parade. Having rejected the arguments focusing on the parents' religious rights under Article 9, the court thought it unnecessary to consider their daughter's own perspectives despite the fact that it was the daughter who had been disciplined and who would have been required to take part in the parade.[45] Similarly, in *Lautsi*, the Grand Chamber dismissed the children's claims with nothing more than a brief reference to the finding that there had been no interference with the right of the parent.[46] Again, in *Campbell and Cosans* v. *United Kingdom*,[47] the court found that the use of corporal punishment in schools was a breach of the parents' right to respect for their convictions that opposed its use, but there was no consideration of the question of whether children had similar convictions and a right to be educated in line with them. The same observation could be made about almost all of the A2P1

---

[40] *Lautsi* v. *Italy* (2012) 54 EHRR 3, at [78].   [41] *Catan* v. *Moldova* (2013) 57 EHRR 4, at [38].

[42] *Vojnity* v. *Hungary* [2013] 2 FCR 495, at [37]. The right to do so was said to apply unless it exposed the child to dangerous practices or caused the child physical or psychological harm. The case itself was concerned with religious upbringing in general, rather than education, but this principle was said to result from ECHR, Arts 8 and 9, and A2P1.

[43] Or to prohibit it: *Konrad and others* v. *Germany* [2007] ELR 435.   [44] (1996) 24 EHRR 294.

[45] U. Kilkelly (1999) pp. 73–5 and 134–5.   [46] *Lautsi* v. *Italy* (2012) 54 EHRR 3, at [78].

[47] (1982) 4 EHRR 293.

cases that come before the court:[48] the court tends to assume that a child's interests are identical to those of the parents, with no consideration of the differential impact on the child or the fact that the right to education in the first sentence of A2P1 is very different from the rights of parents in the second sentence.

This approach overlooks the fact that when upholding parents' claims to have their own religious convictions respected, the state quite possibly infringes the child's own rights. This was seen only too clearly during the litigation in *R (on the application of Williamson and others)* v. *Secretary of State for Education and Employment and others.*[49] Admittedly, the House of Lords rejected the claim of a group of fundamentalist Christians that their rights under both Article 9 and A2P1 of the ECHR had been infringed by the law prohibiting corporal punishment in the school to which they sent their children. Nevertheless, with the exception of a passing reference by Baroness Hale of Richmond,[50] the children's own right to an education in a non-violent atmosphere was not discussed. Indeed, the case is a prime example of parents exploiting their own position as rights-holders under the ECHR in an attempt to influence their children's education.

The application of A2P1 promotes freedom of thought and religion and the right to an education free from state indoctrination from an almost entirely adult perspective. There is rarely recognition of children's own convictions or the fact that their experiences of education engage their rights in a very different way from those of their parents. That said, where adults, whether parents or the state, seek to ensure that the child receives a pluralistic education, then A2P1 will assist them in doing so. Nonetheless, where those adults do not do so, the position of the child is much more equivocal, with little recognition of children's individual rights or the fact that education could have an extremely important part to play in ensuring that children develop their own views, free of any indoctrination from their parents or, indeed, from the group into which they were born.

(C) Parental Choice and Children's Right to Education

The potential conflict between the right of children to education and the rights of their parents to direct that education in line with their own convictions is perhaps best illustrated by the decision of the US Supreme Court in *Wisconsin* v. *Yoder.*[51] In this well-known case, the State of Wisconsin challenged the right

---

[48] E.g. *Efstratiou* v. *Greece* (1997) 24 EHRR 298. Perhaps the best example of a case in which there is recognition of the fact that children's experiences are different from those of their parents is *Grezelak* v. *Poland*, App. No. 7710/02 (2010). See also the more limited consideration of children's interests as distinct from their parents in *Catan* v. *Moldova* (2013) 57 EHRR 4, at [143].

[49] [2005] UKHL 15, [2005] 2 All ER 1; discussed in Chapter 4.   [50] Ibid. at [85].

[51] 406 US 205 (1972).

of the Amish community to deny education to their children beyond the eighth grade.[52] At the time of the decision, the Supreme Court had already established case law recognising that states had a right to interfere with parental authority over children, even in situations involving parents' religious convictions. Thus, in the celebrated decision in *Prince* v. *Massachusetts*,[53] the Supreme Court made the following observations:

> On one side is the obviously earnest claim for freedom of conscience and religious practice. With it is allied the parent's claim to authority in her own household and in the rearing of her children ... Against these sacred private interests, basic in a democracy, stand the interests of society to protect the welfare of children, and the state's assertion of authority to that end ... It is the interest of youth itself, and of the whole community, that children be both safeguarded from abuses and given opportunities for growth into free and independent well-developed men and citizens ... neither rights of religion nor rights of parenthood are beyond limitation.[54]

Despite this strong justification for state intervention to protect minority children against their parents' authority,[55] nearly 40 years later the Amish community finally gained the right to exempt their children from school after the eighth grade, contrary to Wisconsin state laws, which imposed compulsory schooling up to the age of 16. In *Wisconsin* v. *Yoder*, the Supreme Court accepted that, although the state had a compelling interest in the education of all its children, in this instance the state's law infringed the free exercise of Amish parents' religion as guaranteed by the First Amendment of the American Constitution. If their children attended school for two more years, instead of learning the skills and customs of the Amish community through farm and household tasks, the identity of the community would suffer. Further, the majority considered that exposure to 'worldly influences' contrary to Amish beliefs would interfere with the children's 'religious development' and integration into the Amish community. In a powerful dissenting judgment, Justice Douglas asserted that the state should be concerned with the children's religious freedoms and not those of their parents.[56] He was particularly concerned that these restrictions on an Amish child's education might damage his or her adult prospects in the outside world.

> It is the future of the student, not the future of the parents, that is imperilled by today's decision. If a parent keeps his child out of school beyond the grade

---

[52] Ibid.

[53] 321 US 158 (1944): the Supreme Court upheld a conviction against a Jehovah's Witness mother for allowing her two children and her 9-year-old ward to help her distribute Jehovah's Witness literature on the streets, in violation of a state child labour law.

[54] Ibid. at 165–6.

[55] Limiting previous case law such as *Meyer* v. *Nebraska* 262 US 390 (1923) and *Pierce* v. *Society of Sisters* 268 US 510 (1925), which had protected the right of parents to direct the religious upbringing of their children.

[56] Ibid. at 242.

school, then the child will be forever barred from entry into the new and amazing world of diversity that we have today. The child may decide that is the preferred course, or he may rebel . . . If he is harnessed to the Amish way of life by those in authority over him and if his education is truncated, his entire life may be stunted and deformed.[57]

Justice Douglas suggested that the answer was to consult these pupils themselves. He considered that 14- to 15-year-old teenagers were quite old enough to speak for themselves over whether they wished to attend high school, rather than their parents being allowed to speak for the entire family. Although ostensibly sensible, this suggestion overlooked the fact that children brought up in a strict and enclosed community might be too indoctrinated to have independent views, or to express them confidently. The same problem would undoubtedly have arisen had any separate representation been arranged for the children involved in *R (on the application of Williamson and others) v. Secretary of State for Education and Employment and others*.[58] It is, after all, how inward-looking minority groups renew themselves – by indoctrinating fresh generations of children.

It certainly seems unlikely that a religious group in this country would be allowed to exempt its children from the last two years of compulsory education, as the Amish were allowed to do in Wisconsin.[59] Nonetheless, its wider implications are obvious; it demonstrates well the tensions that arise when attempting to mediate between the needs of a minority religious group and those of the state over the education of a new generation of children.[60] It also demonstrates the ease with which courts identify the interests of children with those of their parents and assume that the child will remain part of the community of which their parents are members. Finally, it illustrates the way in which parental convictions can overshadow the child's independent right to education.

The foundations of domestic law on education are based on parental responsibility rather than children's rights. As the leading text on education law bluntly observes: 'education law fails to recognise the independent rights of children'.[61] Instead, domestic law is fundamentally based on the primary duty of parents to educate their children. Parental choice in education has historically been closely linked to the right of parents to determine their children's religious upbringing. The importance of education as a means of inculcating religious principles meant that, at least since the early nineteenth century,[62]

---

[57] Ibid. at 245–6; see C. Hamilton (1995) pp. 265–71.

[58] [2005] UKHL 15, [2005] 2 All ER 1, discussed above.

[59] *Yoder* has also been distinguished in many decisions within the US; N. Harris (2007) pp. 393–6.

[60] Ibid. pp. 393–4.   [61] Ford *et al.* (2016) para. 2.41.

[62] See L. M. Friedman (1916), who considers that, de facto if not de jure, this approach was established in judicial practice by the mid-eighteenth century. In contrast, the deep religious conflicts of the sixteenth and seventeenth centuries gave rise to draconian state interference in religious belief, including parental religious freedom; e.g. *Shaftsbury* v. *Hannam Finch* 323 (1677).

choice of education was largely treated as a private matter, usually determined by the father's own religious conviction.[63] The modern duty is contained in section 7 of the Education Act 1996, which requires parents[64] of children of compulsory school age to ensure that they receive an 'efficient full-time education' suitable to their circumstances, 'either by regular attendance at school or otherwise'. Parents have considerable freedom in how they choose to discharge this duty: through state-funded education, independent schools or home education. This means that in principle the ability of parents to choose an education that aligns with their convictions is relatively unconstrained, at least to the extent that they possess the resources and opportunities to exercise that choice in a meaningful way. If parents object to the regulation of schools by the state, the option of home education offers a very lightly regulated means of avoiding that oversight.

Where parents disagree on the future of their child's education, they may take that disagreement to court to be determined on the basis of the child's welfare.[65] Identifying the values by which a child's welfare should be judged was the central point in the Court of Appeal's judgment in *Re G (Children)*.[66] The case concerned the education of five children who had been brought up in the ultra-orthodox Jewish Chareidi community of their parents. This way of life included single-sex education, focused on the role that the child was expected to fulfil as an adult within the Chareidi community, and gave children limited opportunity to develop careers in the secular world. The mother had left that community and wished to move the children to co-educational Modern Orthodox schools to give them the educational opportunities and future career prospects that were not available in their current schools. The father was deeply opposed to the change of schools, arguing that this was a fundamental change in the children's way of life, relationships and community. In deciding that the children should be educated in line with the mother's proposal, Munby LJ, giving the leading judgment, set out the values by which the children's welfare would be assessed, holding these to be the values of 'reasonable men and women'. He found these values to be: equality of opportunity; the encouragement and fostering of aspiration; and 'to maximise the child's opportunities in every sphere of life as they enter adulthood'. Although each case will turn on facts specific to the child,[67] the case stands for the proposition that children's welfare will be well served by an education that allows the child to develop the skills and outlook that will equip them to pursue opportunities in the wider world, should they choose to do so. It is not,

---

[63] D. Monk (2009a).

[64] Defined by Education Act 1996, s. 576, this includes non-parents who have parental responsibility.

[65] Children Act 1989, s. 1(1); see further Chapter 4.

[66] *Re G (Children)* [2012] EWCA Civ 1233, [2012] 3 FCR 524. See R. Taylor (2013).

[67] E.g. in a similar dispute in *Re A (Children)*, Case No. FD13P01649, unreported, as the children were to remain in the community with their mother, and given the lack of suitable alternative schools, the court found that it would be in their welfare to be educated within that community.

however, premised on the view that the child has a *right* to such an education; indeed, the court was quite clear that if the parents had agreed on the narrow education offered in the Chareidi schools, the court would have no place in intervening.[68] Parents are largely free to educate in a way that rejects Munby LJ's values of aspiration and maximum opportunity provided that they are in agreement to do so. Legal regulation of education in this country has, until recently, placed very little constraint on that parental choice. There has, however, been a recent tightening of regulation of education to require schools to prepare children for life in wider society and it is this regulation that is considered in the next section.

(3) State Regulation of Education: Pluralism, British Values and Extremism

(A) Pluralism in Education

The historic role of the Christian churches in providing education[69] means that, rather than adopting a purely secular state education system, the domestic state sector actively supports faith-based schools. As society has become more diverse, the state has responded by increasing the number and variety of 'schools with a religious character',[70] based on a deliberate policy of pluralism[71] and respect for parents' rights to choose a faith-based education.[72] The first state-funded Muslim schools were introduced in 1998 along with a 7th Day Adventist School, followed by the first Sikh school in 1999 and Greek Orthodox in 2000. Around a third of state-funded schools are now faith schools, although it is still the case that the vast majority have a Christian ethos. The government has continued to pursue this policy of seeking to expand faith-based education, despite evidence that such schools predominantly attract students of similar ethnic backgrounds, so raising concerns that they contribute to segregation in communities.[73] In addition to those state-funded religious schools, some parents may feel obliged to fund their children's education themselves in order to obtain an education that accords with their values and convictions. The right to do so is recognised in A2P1 of the ECHR, which guarantees the right to start and run a private school, subject to any regulation by the state to ensure the proper functioning of the education system.[74]

---

[68] *Re G (Children)* [2012] EWCA Civ 1233, [2012] 3 FCR 524, at [90]–[94].
[69] For detailed history, see J. Rivers (2010) ch. 8.
[70] For explanation of the different forms of school in England and the consequences of that classification, see R. Sandberg (2011) ch. 8.
[71] Department for Education and Skills (2001).
[72] See Estelle Morris, Secretary of State for Education, speaking to the General Synod on 14 November 2001.
[73] DfE (2016) pp. 30–4.   [74] *Jordebo v. Sweden*, App. No. 11533/85, 52 DR 125.

The fact that a school is independent, or has a designated religious character, does not absolve it from state regulation. English law empowers the state to supervise closely and, if necessary, interfere with the operation of all schools in the country, whether they are state-funded or independent and whether or not they cater for a particular religious or ethnic group.[75] The right of the state to impose 'minimum standards of education' is recognised by the ECHR and in international human rights law.[76] It is obviously important for any liberal democracy to clarify the aims of its educational system when laying down the 'minimum standards' it requires of the education provided. Otherwise, it could be accused of attempting to achieve an authoritarian standardisation at the expense of diversity of religious freedom. As such, questions inevitably arise over the legitimacy of state intervention to ensure that their children obtain a well-balanced education and the limits of that intervention, especially where the school in question is funded by parents rather than through state provision. For schools that primarily cater to a particular group, there is an important question of whether the state is entitled to require that children are prepared for life within wider society, as opposed to within the group in question.

These tensions are well illustrated by the litigation in *R* v. *Secretary of State for Education and Science, ex p Talmud Torah Machzikei Hadass School Trust*.[77] A critical HMI report had led to an independent boys' school run by the Belz section of the orthodox Hasidic Jewish community in Hackney being threatened with closure.[78] The report had criticised the inadequacy of the buildings, the narrowness of the curriculum, the lack of encouragement of imaginative work, the staff's failure to provide a stimulating learning environment and the failure to ensure that pupils were sufficiently prepared for life outside the community.[79] In response, the school challenged the competence of HMI to review its work, asserting, in judicial review proceedings, that it could only be assessed in the context of the traditions it served. Only one of the inspectors on the team understood Yiddish, the language in which many of the lessons were conducted, and even his grasp of the community's cultural traditions were insufficient for him to comprehend fully the significance of the pattern of the lessons. More fundamentally, the school argued that the standard by which it had been assessed had been wrong. On this point, Woolf J,

---

[75] The precise regulations applicable and supervision arrangements do depend on the type of school in question. This has become more complex with the advent of academies which take the form of state-funded independent schools, bound by their funding agreements. The different arrangements for inspection are explained in Ford *et al.* (2016) paras 4.55–4.65.

[76] E.g. ICESCR, Art. 13(3). CRC, Art. 29(1) also expects the education provided to develop the child's personality, talents and abilities to their fullest potential.

[77] (1985) *Times*, 12 April.

[78] Under the inspection system then operating, as governed by the Education Act 1944, s. 71.

[79] A. Bradney (1987) provides a full discussion of the HMI report on the Talmud Torah Machzikei Hadass School. See A. Bradney (2009) for a discussion of Ofsted's inspection findings when inspecting the same school in 2007.

as he then was, accepted the concession of the counsel for the Department of Education, stating that a suitable education is one that:

> primarily equips a child for life within the community of which he is a member, rather than the way of life in the country as a whole, as long as it does not foreclose the child's options in later years to adopt some other form of life if he wishes to do so.

Although the judicial review application failed, the decision in the *Talmud Torah Machzikei Hadass* case is an important one. The Secretary of State's concession indicated that such schools may primarily focus on the child's future within the community, albeit with the limit that that education must not prevent the child from pursuing life within wider society. This latter point echoes the concerns of Justice Douglas in the *Yoder* case,[80] that the Amish children might be barred from 'the new and amazing world of diversity' provided by society today. Nonetheless, those two aims will frequently be in tension with each other; a person who has been educated without access to a full secular education and understanding of the diversity of modern life is likely to encounter great difficulties in forging a life outside of that community. This is particularly so if, as was the case for *Talmud Torah Machzikei Hadass*, much of the teaching is not in English. Despite these tensions, the approach of prioritising the child's future within the community over their opportunities within wider society, albeit not foreclosing those opportunities, long remained the dominant approach in regulating separate schools.[81] There has, however, been a notable recent reversal in the government's approach to regulating such schools. There is little evidence that the impetus for this change is based on a government concern to protect the right of children to education. Instead, it has been primarily driven by concerns over community cohesion and preventing extremism.

(B) Increased Regulation: British Values, Equality and Protection from Terrorism

An important catalyst for the increased scrutiny of separate schools was the so-called Trojan Horse affair. In November 2013, a letter was received by Birmingham City Council purporting to contain the details of a plot to take over schools in the Birmingham area and run them along strict Islamic lines. While the authenticity of the letter has not been established, the Clarke Report into the allegations found:

> a sustained and coordinated agenda to impose upon children in a number of Birmingham schools the segregationist attitudes and practices of a hardline and politicised strand of Sunni Islam. Left unchecked, it would confine school

---

[80] *Wisconsin* v. *Yoder* 406 US 205 (1972).
[81] For more detail, see the 3rd edition of this book at pp. 421–4.

children within an intolerant, inward-looking monoculture that would severely inhibit their participation in the life of modern Britain.[82]

Regardless of the veracity of the allegations in this case, the affair was important in shifting perceptions of such schools to one of posing a threat. The nature of this perceived threat was evident in the choice of Peter Clarke, former national head of counter-terrorism, to conduct the inquiry. The view that extremist ideas are a key driver of terrorism, whether or not those ideas themselves support violence, had already been put at the heart of the 2011 revision of the government's anti-terrorism 'Prevent Strategy'.[83] In this light, schools that allow children to be educated in an 'intolerant, inward-looking monoculture' are not only a threat to children, in engendering intolerance and narrowing opportunities, but also a threat to society in creating the conditions for radicalisation and violent extremism. The resulting tightening of regulation of schools has largely been derived from government policy on anti-terrorism rather than from children's right to a plural education.[84] Schools of all kinds are now under an obligation to 'actively promote' fundamental 'British values', namely 'democracy, the rule of law, individual liberty and mutual respect and tolerance of those with different faiths and beliefs'.[85] This definition of British values is derived from the 'Prevent Strategy', which defines active or vocal opposition to these values as extremism.[86] Further, all schools, whether independent or state-funded, are now under a statutory duty to have 'due regard to the need to prevent people from being drawn into terrorism' in carrying out their functions,[87] and as part of this duty are to teach children how to challenge extremist ideas.[88] Together, these changes put increasingly firm outer limits on the beliefs and practices promoted within all schools.

A particularly contentious aspect of this tightening regulation has been the obligations placed on schools in relation to equality. All schools are now explicitly required to promote respect for people of all faiths, races, genders, ages, disability, sexual orientations and other protected characteristics.[89] In addition, state-funded schools are subject to the Public Sector Equality Duty,

---

[82] P. Clarke (2014) p. 13.

[83] HM Government (2011). David Cameron's Munich Speech on Radicalisation and Islamic Extremism (5 February 2011) is often cited as signalling the start of this policy.

[84] R. Taylor (2015).

[85] The Education (Independent School Standards) Regulations 2014 (SI 2014/3283), Sch. 1, reg. 5(a). The Independent School Standards were altered in 2012, following the 2011 revision of the Prevent Strategy, to require schools to encourage pupils to respect such values. The 2014 revision of the standards strengthened the requirement to active promotion. For maintained schools, see Ofsted (2018) paras 145 and 148. See also Independent Education Provision in England (Prohibition on Participation in Management) Regulations 2014 (SI 2014/1977), para. 2(5)(a) and Local Authority (Duty to Secure Early Years Provision Free of Charge) Regulations 2014/2147, reg. 2(2)(b).

[86] HM Government (2011) p. 107.   [87] Counter-terrorism and Security Act 2015, s. 26(1).

[88] HM Government (2015) para. 64.

[89] Ofsted (2018) para. 148. For independent schools, see The Education (Independent School Standards) Regulations 2014 (SI 2014/3283), Sch. 1, regs 2(2)(d)(ii) and 5(b)(vi).

which requires them to give due regard to the need to eliminate discrimination, advance equality of opportunity and foster good relations between different groups.[90] Collectively, these obligations have the potential to conflict with the teachings of some religious groups, especially in relation to sex, gender identity and sexual orientation. Evidence on Ofsted's application of this standard has, however, suggested that schools are not prohibited from explaining their own religious teaching on these matters, provided that they promote respect for others who do not follow those teachings.[91] Nonetheless, equality obligations can require significant change for some religious schools. This was vividly demonstrated by the Court of Appeal's decision in *Chief Inspector of Education, Children's Services and Skills* v. *Interim Executive Board of Al-Hijrah School*.[92] The Al-Hijrah school was a voluntary aided, Islamic faith school. The school admitted both boys and girls, but operated a strict segregation policy, which prevented any contact between boys and girls over the age of 9, not only in lessons, but also at break times and in all extracurricular activities. There was no evidence to suggest that the quality or content of the teaching given to girls differed from that given to boys; however, Ofsted considered that the fact of segregation itself failed to prepare the children for their future social interactions and that the school had failed to fulfil its Public Sector Equality Duty. This finding, among others, led to the school being given an inadequate rating. The Court of Appeal rejected the school's judicial review application, finding that the complete segregation of pupils itself constituted direct discrimination,[93] and that it was not necessary to show that girls as a class received inferior treatment. Instead, it was sufficient to show that girl pupils were denied the opportunity that boy pupils had to mix with other boys and vice versa. This was in itself sufficient to find the school in breach of the Equality Act 2010. The fact that the school's motivation was based on their interpretation of Islam and that many of the parents had chosen the school for precisely this reason, was irrelevant and could not justify the discrimination.[94] Lady Justice Gloster went further, finding that segregation at the school had to be viewed in the context of sex discrimination both in wider society and in the culture and community of this particular school. Ofsted had found books in the school library and work by the children that reinforced gender stereotypes and the inferiority of women and girls – for example, in justifying violence against wives. For Gloster LJ, segregation in such an environment *did* subject girls to less favourable treatment both in practice and in its expressive role in reinforcing gender stereotypes and inferiority. While the majority found that in this case there was insufficient evidence to support Gloster LJ's conclusions on these additional grounds, her judgment

---

[90] Equality Act 2010, s. 149.   [91] R. Vanderbeck and P. Johnson (2016).

[92] [2017] EWCA Civ 1426, [2018] 1 WLR 1471.

[93] Contrary to Equality Act 2010, ss 13 and 85. Sch. 11 of the Act contains specific exemptions from these duties with regard to single-sex schools.

[94] [2017] EWCA Civ 1426, [2018] 1 WLR 1471, at [81]–[82].

demonstrates how, far from justifying inequality, the belief systems supported by a school may subject its decisions to more intense scrutiny. Her judgment is rooted in a clear commitment to the role of schools in supporting all pupils to make free and informed choices about their future in British society, regardless of whether those choices reflect the child's cultural, community and religious background.

Collectively, the obligations on schools concerning British values, extremism and equality have brought greater scrutiny of the beliefs and values taught within all schools. Although the schools at the heart of the Trojan Horse allegations were primarily non-faith maintained schools, the consequences have been particularly notable for faith-based independent schools, which have suffered a sharp decline in inspection results, with nearly half of inspected independent faith schools judged as inadequate or requiring improvement since the changed standards.[95] As a result, such schools are no longer able to focus on equipping the child for life within the community 'rather than the way of life in the country as a whole', as was the case in *Talmud Torah Machzikei Hadass*. In that case, Woolf J considered that a suitable education would not foreclose a child's future option to live outside of the community, but independent schools must now go much further and instead ensure 'effective preparation of pupils for the opportunities, responsibilities and experiences of life in British society'.[96] This change of emphasis is well illustrated by the experience of the *Talmud Torah Machzikei Hadass* itself. The school was found not to meet the revised standards when inspected in 2015, despite a glowing report which found it to be good with outstanding features just a few months earlier. Among other failings, the school: had failed to develop policies to protect the children from radicalisation; gave insufficient education on other faiths or beliefs; had not developed respect for protected characteristics, including sexual orientation; and did not give guidance on careers outside of further religious study.[97] The dramatic fall in the school's fortunes demonstrates the new importance of educating children on the values and opportunities in life outside of their community.

Many minority and religious communities will have no difficulty in complying with the tighter regulations and will indeed find that those values are supported by their own religious and cultural beliefs. There will, however, be some schools that find a direct conflict between their religious convictions and

---

[95] Ofsted (2017) paras 63–71. In addition to the British values requirements, the 2014 revision of the Independent School Standards introduced a range of new requirements. Of the independent faith schools judged inadequate or requiring improvement between 2015 and 2017, 18 per cent failed to meet reg. 5(a) concerning British values and the spiritual, moral, social and cultural development of pupils. In addition, 10 per cent failed to reflect British values in their written curriculum policies (reg. 2(1)(b)(ii)) and 10 per cent failed to reflect them in their teaching (reg. 3(i)).

[96] The Education (Independent School Standards) Regulations 2014, Sch. 1, reg. 2(2)(i). For maintained schools, see the similar requirement Education Act 2002, s. 78.

[97] Ofsted (2015).

the values embedded in the regulation of schools.[98] The parents and teachers in these schools may object that this regulation is intolerant of freedom of belief and the rights of minority communities to maintain their identity. It is, however, very unlikely that those parents would be successful in arguing that the state had failed in its ECHR A2P1 obligation to respect their rights to ensure that the education and teaching of their children was in conformity with their own religious and philosophical convictions. As discussed above, this right is primarily concerned with protecting children from state indoctrination and safeguarding pluralism. Admittedly, the requirement that schools 'actively promote' values derived from government policy could be applied in a manner that risked state indoctrination. The right is, however, unlikely to be breached by requiring that children are given objective information and encouragement to: respect the rights of others; understand the foundational values of democracy and the rule of law; and prepare themselves for life within a pluralistic society.

Just as the ECtHR has tended to approach A2P1 claims as disputes between parents and the state, with little discussion of the education rights of children, so the increased domestic regulation of schools has given little explicit recognition to children's education rights. This is particularly evident in the way in which British values have entered schools, through the security agenda and the government's controversial anti-terrorism strategy, rather than through consideration of the educational rights and needs of children. The derivation of 'British values' from government policy, with no genuine process of consultation, undermines their ability to act as collective, normative values. The interests of children are also obscured by this security focus. The regulations are partly concerned with children's education, but also safeguarding children from extreme ideas and limiting the perceived threat to society from children with such ideas. An explicit focus on children's rights would provide a much more secure basis for child-focused values in education and provide a positive grounding in understanding human rights.[99] A children's rights approach to the values in education can be found in Article 29 of the CRC, which recognises that the child's right to education shall be directed to specified purposes, including preparing the child for a responsible life in a free society and developing respect for: human rights; the child's parents; his or her own cultural identity; the national values of the child's country; and civilisations different from his or her own. The existing law will no doubt go some way to

---

[98] E.g. in *Beis Aharon Trust* v. *Secretary of State for Education* [2016] UKFTT 270, the First-tier tribunal rejected a challenge to an order of the Secretary of State that prevented the school from admitting new pupils on the basis that it did not meet the Independent School Standards, including those concerning equality and British values. The school argued that its beliefs prevented adherents from turning their mind to matters forbidden by their understanding of the Jewish faith, including other religions, sexual orientation and gender identity at [55] and [92]. The First-tier tribunal found that these beliefs did not absolve the school of the obligation to comply with the standards.

[99] A. Struthers (2017).

achieving these aims, but an explicit rights-based approach would require sharper attention to enabling children to understand their overlapping membership of family, community, nation and humanity. In doing so, it would require a more nuanced approach that would acknowledge the tensions that can arise between these different spheres of belonging. Such an approach would also recognise the entitlement of all children to an education that equips them for life in wider society and the future opportunities that this offers.[100]

(C) Home Education and Unregistered Schools

If *all* children possess a right to be educated in a manner that allows them access to the opportunities of wider society, action to guarantee that right may need to extend beyond regulation of schools. Parents are obliged to ensure that their school-aged children receive an 'efficient full-time education' that is 'suitable' to their needs. There is no requirement that this education is received in school; the obligation can be fulfilled 'either by regular attendance at school or otherwise'.[101] Parents who wish to educate their children outside of the school system are free to do so, with very little regulation or state supervision. There is no requirement that parents register or inform the local authority (LA) that they intend to educate their child at home.[102] As a result, there are no official figures as to how many children are receiving their education at home, although there is widespread agreement that the number is increasing.[103] For many parents, home education offers a positive choice to give their children an education that best meets their children's needs, although for some the decision is more accurately seen as a response to the failure of the school system to meet those needs.[104] The wider debates on the relative role of parents and the state in securing the interests and rights of children are raised sharply by the question of whether home education should be subject to greater state oversight.

At present, home education is subject to some regulation, although that regulation is minimal, uncertain in scope and difficult to enforce. The law gives

---

[100] R. Taylor (2015).   [101] Education Act 1996, s. 7.

[102] If parents remove their child from school in order to educate them at home, then the parents are required to inform the school and the school to inform the LA of that decision: Education (Pupil Registration) (England) Regulations 2006 (SI 2006/1751), reg. 8(1)(d) and 12(7)(f). Parents of children in other circumstances (e.g. those who have never entered school or have been home educated having completed one stage of their schooling) are not under an obligation to report their decision.

[103] House of Commons Education Committee (2021) p. 17: the number of children being home educated appears to have increased significantly during the Covid-19 pandemic, although it is not yet clear whether this increase will be sustained. There had already been an upward trend in the number of children being home educated for some time prior to the pandemic: Children's Commissioner (2017) p. 12.

[104] Children's Commissioner (2017) p. 11, noting too the practice of some schools to put pressure on parents of 'challenging or low-achieving children' to home educate those children as an alternative to exclusion. This practice of 'off-rolling' is discussed in Chapter 14.

parents considerable freedom to choose the nature of the education that their children receive: they do not have to follow the national curriculum and there are no prescribed requirements as to the content or format of the education. Parents are obliged to ensure that their children receive an 'efficient', 'full-time' and 'suitable'[105] education, but, as Daniel Monk notes, the meaning of these terms depends on cultural, philosophical and political assumptions rather than precise, objective definition.[106] This uncertainty causes great difficulty for LAs in discerning the limits of their statutory role. The changing nature of the regulation of schools adds further uncertainty here. The *Talmud Torah Machzikei Hadass* definition of a suitable education as one which 'primarily equips a child for life within the community of which he is a member' has been taken to apply to home education as well as schooling. As the demands on schools move further away from that understanding, so it might be said that what is considered to be a 'suitable' education for home-educated children has also changed. There is, however, no current judicial guidance to provide clarity on this point. The government has, however, issued guidance to LAs and parents on their duties under the current law.[107] This guidance does not seek to set any minimum standards as to what constitutes a suitable education, although it does state that the education should enable the child to 'function as an independent citizen in the UK' in later life.[108] This guidance is clear that the child should be equipped with the means to live a life outside of the community in which they were raised, should they choose to do so. It is also clear that an education is unlikely to be suitable if it conflicts with 'British values', although there is no obligation on parents to actively promote such values.[109] Although this guidance goes some way to recognising the importance of equipping children for an open future, the government has maintained its focus on parental choice. Although the guidance contains a brief section on the children's rights, bizarrely this includes no reference at all to the child's right to education or to the aims of education contained in the CRC. The guidance merely references the child's right to express their views under Article 12 of the CRC, before restating that this 'does not give children authority over parents' and reassuring parents that 'a decision to educate a child at home is a matter for you as parents'.[110] Once again, the child's right to education is obscured by the narrative of parental choice.

The meaning of 'suitable' is important because it is both the defining point of parental obligation and the hinge on which LA duties and powers of enforcement depend.[111] If it appears to the LA that a child is not receiving a suitable education, they must serve notice on the child's parents requiring

---

[105] The education must be suitable to the child's 'age, ability and aptitude' and to 'any special educational needs': Education Act 1996, s. 7.
[106] D. Monk (2009b) p. 175.   [107] DfE (2019a), (2019b).
[108] DfE (2019b) p. 7. See also (2019b) p. 30, discussed by N. Harris (2020) p. 445.
[109] DfE (2019b) pp. 8 and 31.   [110] Ibid. p. 9.
[111] House of Commons Education Committee (2021) pp. 4–5.

them to satisfy the LA that such an education is being received.[112] Failure by the parents to do so is likely to lead to a school attendance order, requiring that the child is registered at a specified school.[113] While this is a potentially powerful order, the uncertain meaning of 'suitable', together with the fact that LAs may well be unaware that a child is being educated at home, create difficulties for LAs in using the order in practice. To date, proposals to regulate home education more tightly have been unsuccessful.[114] Following consultation, the government is now committed to creating a register of children who are not in school.[115] The purpose of this register would be to assist LAs in fulfilling their existing duties to children. The government remains committed to parental freedom to choose home education and does not intend to bring forward any change to the existing legislation on when such education is 'suitable'.

The renewed pressure for reform of home education has come in part from concerns over British values and radicalisation. Children who are home educated are a diverse group, with widely differing forms of provision and reasons for educating outside of schools. There have, however, been suggestions that some parents have sought to educate their children outside of a school environment to avoid exposure to values that conflict with their beliefs. Dame Louise Casey, in her review of opportunity and integration in the UK, found that the current law was allowing some children to be home educated in a totally secluded environment, without preparation for life in wider society.[116] In some extreme cases, the courts have found that home education has formed part of the environment in which children have been isolated from wider society and radicalised.[117] Further, Ofsted have found that some children who appear to be home educated are actually being sent to schools that have been left unregistered specifically to avoid regulation around educational standards, safeguarding and British values that appear to be in tension with the belief systems of the community.[118] These unregistered settings are already illegal, although discovering their existence can be difficult, so posing an obstacle to enforcement.[119] Parents, however, are not bound by the legislation on equality, British values and

---

[112] Education Act 1996, s. 437(1). See further DfE (2019a).

[113] If the opinion of the LA in such circumstances is that it is expedient that the child should attend school, the authority is obliged to serve the order; Education Act 1996, s. 437(3).

[114] See N. Harris (2020) p. 442. In particular, the 2009 review of home education by Graham Badman recommended compulsory registration of home education. This proposal was initially included in the draft Children, Schools and Families Bill 2009, but proved controversial and so was dropped from the Bill as it went through in the 'wash-up' period prior to the 2010 general election. A private members' bill seeking to achieve a registration scheme and further guidance on 'suitable' education also failed to become law: Home Education (Duties of Local Authorities) Bill 2017–19.

[115] DfE (2022).   [116] L. Casey (2016) para. 7.69.

[117] *A Local Authority* v. *M, F, C, D, E, F* [2016] EWHC 1599 (Fam), at [49]; *London Borough of Tower Hamlets* v. *B* [2016] 2 FLR 887, at [17].

[118] Ofsted (2017) p. 16.

[119] Ibid. For further discussion, see: D. Monk (2016); N. Harris (2020) pp. 434–5.

radicalisation that apply to schools and are free to educate their children within a narrow range of values and beliefs if they wish to do so.[120] LAs are now required to have 'due regard to the need to prevent people from being drawn into terrorism' in carrying out their functions,[121] and as such will need to be alert to the possibility of radicalisation in monitoring home education. Beyond this duty, home education has so far been left largely untouched by the changes that have been applied to schools.

In the absence of effective minimum standards, there is a compelling argument that the state is failing in its international obligations to protect the right of *all* children to an education that prepares them for a life within wider society and which meets the purposes set out in Article 29 of the CRC. Given the negative formulation of the right to education in ECHR law and its limited recognition in domestic law, it might be difficult to enforce this obligation in the domestic courts, although arguably a 'suitable' education is one that meets internationally agreed minimum purposes. Equally, it seems clear that if the state does choose to regulate home education more rigorously, parents are unlikely to be able to use A2P1 or Article 8 of the ECHR to object, even if that regulation were to intrude on the content of the education provided.[122] In *Konrad and others* v. *Germany*,[123] the ECtHR upheld a total ban on home education in Germany, finding that the ban was within the state's margin of appreciation. The ECtHR accepted as legitimate Germany's justification for the ban that it was in the 'general interest of society to avoid the emergence of parallel societies based on separate philosophical convictions and the importance of integrating minorities into society'. This justification has clear echoes of the similar concerns that have motivated the use of British values and equality in schools and it is likely that a move to monitor the content of home education in this way would also be justified on the same grounds. Whether the state ought to take this step is a controversial question, not least because it engages wider debates on the relative roles of parents and the state in protecting the rights and interests of children. Many home-educating parents resist state intervention on the basis that it would erode the principle that they have primary responsibility for their child's education in domestic law, particularly given that many of those children are being home educated precisely because they have already been failed by the state. Nevertheless, the state clearly has an international obligation to ensure that the rights of all children to an education that enables them to fulfil their individual potential and it is difficult to see how this can be achieved without some increase in the degree of state supervision.

---

[120] DfE (2019b) p. 8. Although radicalisation of children, whether home educated or not, may amount to significant harm and so invite care proceedings under Children Act 1989, Pt IV. See R. Taylor (2018).

[121] Counter-terrorism and Security Act 2015, s. 26(1).

[122] *Family H* v. *United Kingdom*, App. No. 10233/83, [1984] DR 105.

[123] [2007] ELR 435. See also *Wunderlich* v. *Germany* [2019] ELR 435, in which the ECtHR found that removal of four children from parental care was justified under ECHR, Art. 8(1) following prolonged parental refusal to send the children to school.

(4) Collective Worship and Religious Education

Given the decline in religious observance throughout the country,[124] some would be surprised to find that English law obliges all maintained schools to promote religious observance, through a daily act of collective worship.[125] Although parents may withdraw their children,[126] the current legislation retains provisions introduced in 1988 with the specific intention of forcing all maintained schools to increase the Christian content of their religious education and collective worship.[127] Thus, community schools and foundation schools without a religious character must arrange a daily act of collective worship which is 'wholly or mainly of a broadly Christian character'.[128] Although schools are entitled to interpret the 'broadly Christian' requirement quite loosely, to enable pupils of a non-Christian background to take part,[129] the act of corporate worship must contain some elements which can be related specifically to the traditions of Christian belief.[130] Foundation and voluntary schools with a religious character must provide a daily act of collective worship in accordance with their trust deed or religious denomination.[131] Furthermore, although as a general principle, it is unlawful for an LA or school to discriminate against pupils on the grounds of their religion or belief, this prohibition does not apply to the provision of religious education or acts of collective worship.[132] The government seems reluctant to abolish this widely flouted legal provision,[133] despite influential calls for it to be removed or reformed, say by reducing the required frequency.[134] If it is to be retained, the rationale for its continued relevance in an increasingly secular and diverse

[124] The British Social Attitudes Survey 28 (2010) found that half of people in Britain had no religious affiliation. Of those who did belong to a religion, 56 per cent never attended religious services or meetings and just 14 per cent attended weekly.

[125] First introduced by the Education Act 1944.

[126] School Standards and Framework Act 1998 (SSFA), s. 71(1), discussed below.

[127] Introduced by the Education Reform Act 1988; C. Hamilton (1995) pp. 271–309.

[128] SSFA 1998, s. 70 and Sch. 20, para. 3(2). See also Sch. 20, para. 3(4): not *every* act of worship need comply with this requirement, providing that, taking any term as a whole, *most* do. The requirement of collective worship is also imposed on academies and free schools through their funding agreements.

[129] *R v. Secretary of State for Education, ex p R and D* [1994] ELR 495, per McCullough J, at 502: the legislation permits some non-Christian elements in the collective worship, as long as those do not deprive it of its broadly Christian character and this character would not be lost by the inclusion of elements common to Christianity and to one or more other religions.

[130] SSFA 1998, Sch. 20, para. 4(1) and Education Act 1996, s. 394: a head teacher of a school with largely non-Christian pupils may be permitted by the local Standing Council on Religious Education (SACRE) not to provide a form of collective worship at all or to provide a form more appropriate to the pupils' family backgrounds.

[131] SSFA 1998, Sch. 20, para. 3(3).   [132] Equality Act 2010, s. 65 and Sch. 11, Pt 2, para. 6.

[133] Discussed by N. Harris (2020) pp. 408–15. See Lord Nash's confirmation that the government has no plans to change the law on collective worship: HL 26 January 2016, vol. 769, WA5274.

[134] As suggested by David Bell, then head of Ofsted, on 21 April 2004, in an unpublished speech in the House of Commons. He said that 76 per cent of secondary schools were breaking the law by not complying with this legal requirement and that Ofsted inspectors struggled to enforce it.

society must be clear. The government should also heed the suggestion that head teachers and teaching staff need training to run more effective religious assemblies.[135]

The same features are present in the legal principles governing religious education (RE), which must be provided for all registered pupils by all state-maintained schools.[136] As in the case of the provisions governing collective worship, the legislation puts particular emphasis on Christianity, specifying that every agreed syllabus:

> shall reflect the fact that the religious traditions in Great Britain are in the main Christian whilst taking account of the teaching and practices of the other principal religions represented in Great Britain.[137]

The objectives of that legislation may now seem anachronistic to a society in which a great variety of religious and non-religious views are widely held. Nevertheless, A2P1 of the ECHR permits greater attention to be given to those religious traditions that have played an important part in the country's development, provided that there is no qualitative difference in the treatment given to the beliefs.[138] This means that, at least for schools without a designated religious character, RE must be taught in an impartial manner, which gives equal respect to different forms of belief, even if they do not all receive equal time.[139] Despite the term 'religious education', this equal respect must also be extended to non-religious beliefs and, as a result, it has been held to be unlawful to seek to fulfil the requirements for RE solely through the provision of a GCSE religious studies course that only considers religious beliefs.[140] For this reason, most agree that when these objectives are interpreted broadly, through schools adopting a broadly multi-faith approach, the teaching of RE, if well taught, can achieve a great deal. It not only promotes pupils' spiritual and moral development, with a focus on 'ultimate questions and ethical issues', but also teaches them 'to appreciate their own and others' beliefs and cultures and how these

---

[135] *The Guardian*, 13 June 2006: joint letter from senior representatives of the Anglican, Catholic and Baptist churches to Alan Johnson, Education Secretary, stating that although most primary schools fulfil their obligation to organise daily acts of worship, many state secondaries do not, and calling for better training for head teachers and teaching staff.

[136] Education Act 2002, s. 80; SSFA 1998, s. 69(1). It is therefore a compulsory subject, but because it is not included in the national curriculum, it is not subject to national assessment.

[137] Education Act 1996, s. 375(3); C. Hamilton (1995) pp. 298–300.

[138] See *Folgerø and others* v. *Norway* [2007] ELR 557, discussed above. For this reason, it is unlikely that Education Act 1996, s. 375(3) is itself in breach of ECHR, A2P1: *R (Fox)* v. *Secretary of State for Education* [2015] EWHC 3404 (Admin), at [74].

[139] The precise syllabus arrangements depend on the nature of the school in question. See Ford *et al.* (2016) paras 4.32–4.44 for detail. A locally agreed syllabus, approved and monitored by the local SACRE, is produced for each LA and this must be followed by those maintained schools without a designated religious character.

[140] *R (Fox)* v. *Secretary of State for Education* [2015] EWHC 3404 (Admin). The GCSE syllabus in itself was not unlawful, but the implication that it could fulfil the RE requirements through solely teaching religious beliefs was unlawful. This case was only concerned with schools without a designated religious character.

impact on individuals, communities, societies and cultures'.[141] Unfortunately, it seems that RE is often not well taught. Ofsted has long expressed concern that RE teaching is often neglected in comparison to those subjects that form part of the national curriculum and suffers from a lack of clarity as to its purpose.[142] Poor teaching is still only too common,[143] with even poorer assessment and planning.[144] As Ajegbo observes, it is often simpler for teachers to fall back on 'the mechanics of religion instead of tackling the reality of being religious'.[145] This is backed up by Ofsted's finding that students often had basic factual information about different beliefs, but little depth of understanding or ability to give informed responses to religious, philosophical or ethical questions.[146] There is also evidence that some schools, particularly secondary academies, are simply failing to give any RE teaching despite the obligation to do so.[147] The poor standards in the subject are of real concern as there is wisdom in the assertion that current developments in RE are taking place:

> within the context of the extraordinary increase in the political, social and cultural importance of religion in Britain in this century. Recent world events, the rise of more fundamentalist forms of religion, the growth of faith schools and the debates about the relationship between religion and British identity have given a new impetus and urgency to the subject ... The notions, common until recently, that religion was quietly declining and RE had little relevance to modern life now look naïve ... children and young people need to develop a more profound understanding of the importance of religious commitment and diversity. They need the opportunity to reflect on issues about personal identity, meaning and truth.[148]

English law gives parents the right to withdraw their children from both collective worship and RE.[149] It is clear that in adopting this stance, the law has been influenced by international human rights law obliging the state to respect the right of parents to educate their children according to their own convictions and beliefs.[150] Indeed, the right to withdraw a child in domestic law gives greater concession to parental convictions than is strictly required by A2P1 of the ECHR,

---

[141] QCA (2004) p. 8.

[142] Ofsted (2013). RE is compulsory and forms part of the basic curriculum, but does not form part of the national curriculum.

[143] Ibid. pp. 9–12 and 38: the teaching of RE in the primary schools visited was less than good in more than 50 per cent and outstanding in only one of ninety schools; the teaching of RE in secondary schools visited was good and better in just over half the schools visited.

[144] Ibid.: in the primary schools visited, assessment was good or better in approximately two out of ten schools and inadequate in nearly a third; in the secondary schools visited, assessment was good or better in only three in ten schools and inadequate in nearly a fifth.

[145] K. Ajegbo (2007) p. 68.   [146] Ofsted (2013) p. 8.

[147] See research reported at: 'Up to a quarter of secondary schools break the law by failing to teach religious education, survey finds', *The Telegraph*, 17 September 2017.

[148] Ofsted (2007) para. 132.

[149] SSFA 1998, s. 71(1). See Chapter 14 for discussion of the similar provisions concerning withdrawal from sex education.

[150] Discussed above.

giving parents the right to withdraw even from RE that is presented in a factual and plural manner.[151] From a legal perspective, it is regrettable that the principles of law applying to collective worship and RE assume that parents' right to religious freedom is identical with that of their children.[152] Sixth formers are now exempted from the parental power of withdrawal[153] and are also entitled to excuse themselves from both religious worship and RE.[154] But these concessions do not dispel the general principle's overall message. It suggests to pupils that, until they reach the sixth form, their own views are unimportant. Withdrawing children from school activities participated in by the majority potentially marginalises them from their contemporaries and makes them feel different. By entitling parents to withdraw them with no explanation, the law reinforces parents' perceptions that they have a right to dictate religious matters to their children.[155] There is also a greater risk of their children becoming forced further into the confines of the family and their parents' beliefs – on the basis that although the state must not indoctrinate children, parents can. Similarly, children who wish to withdraw against the wishes of their parents cannot do so, placing them in the extraordinary position of being forced to participate in worship that may conflict with their own fundamental beliefs and convictions. At first sight, the intertwining of children's right to freedom of thought and religion with the right of parents to provide direction to the child in that belief, may appear to justify this rule.[156] Nonetheless, the rights of parents to direct the child cannot negate the child's primary right to freedom of belief, particularly in respect of mature children. The Committee on the Rights of the Child has made it clear that they regard the inability of children to withdraw themselves from religious worship without parental permission as inconsistent with their CRC rights and has recommended that the law on compulsory attendance is amended.[157] The Joint Committee on Human Rights has also taken the view that the rights of mature children to freedom of belief mean that those who are *Gillick*-competent should have the right to make their own decision on withdrawal and that failure to do so cannot be justified on the basis of administrative convenience.[158] While the government has so far resisted this analysis, it is difficult to imagine another situation in which a person might be compelled by law to participate in veneration of a divine being in whom they did not believe.

(5) School Uniforms and Pupils' Rights

Whether a school has a uniform policy and, if so, what that policy entails, is a matter for the governing body of that school. The government does, however, strongly encourage schools to have a uniform, on the basis that it can 'play

---

[151] *Appel-Irrgang* v. *Germany*, App. No. 45216/07 (20 October 2009).
[152] N. Harris (2020) pp. 402–8 and 414–15.   [153] SSFA 1998, s. 71(1A).   [154] Ibid. s. 71(1B).
[155] C. Hamilton (1995) pp. 303–9.   [156] Esp. CRC, Art. 14.
[157] Committee on the Rights of the Child (2016) paras 35–6.
[158] JCHR (2008) paras 1.40–1.45.

a key role in promoting the ethos of a school, providing a sense of belonging and identity, and setting an appropriate tone'.[159] But despite the comparative liberality of school uniform policies adopted by most schools in this country,[160] some pupils have litigated to gain the right to wear clothing, uniform or hairstyles that reflects their religious beliefs or racial heritage. Such challenges raise difficult problems for schools. While the school may be concerned that ad hoc exemptions will undermine the purpose of the uniform policy, as discussed above, schools must consider the need to promote equality in all of their decisions and must give careful consideration to reasonable requests.[161] The reported cases have tended to concern children of secondary school age who are in the process of developing opinions of their own on their beliefs and heritage, something that schools must surely encourage and support. In *R (on the application of Begum)* v. *Head Teacher and Governors of Denbigh High School* (hereafter *Begum*),[162] Baroness Hale of Richmond was not surprised that having attended her secondary school for two years wearing the shalwar kameez without complaint, Shabina Begum, at the age of nearly 14, decided that this form of dress was not acceptable for Muslim women. The fact that Shabina's parents had apparently accepted the school's uniform policy when they enrolled her at Denbigh High School was neither here nor there; 'it is not at all surprising to find adolescents making different moral judgments from those of their parents. It is part of growing up'.[163]

The House of Lords' decision in *Begum* appeared to set formidable obstacles before any pupil seeking to use the Human Rights Act 1998 to challenge uniform policies. The court rejected Shabina Begum's claim that her rights under Article 9 and A2P1 of the ECHR entitled her to attend school dressed in a jilbab. In the view of the majority,[164] she failed at the first hurdle as her religious rights under Article 9 had not been interfered with. As Lord Hoffmann stressed, 'Article 9 does not require that one should be allowed to manifest one's religion at any time and place of one's own choosing'.[165] Lord Bingham explained that the ECtHR had been reluctant to find an interference with Article 9 where the applicant had 'voluntarily accepted' a position and there were 'other means open to the person to practise or observe his or her religion without undue hardship or inconvenience'.[166] On this basis, there was no interference with Shabina's rights as she had enrolled at the school knowing the policy and could have simply transferred to another school which allowed pupils to wear a jilbab. As Baroness Hale observed, treating the question as determined by Shabina's 'choice' failed to capture the reality of the situation, not least because it is parents, not children, who have the final say in choosing

---

[159] DfE (2021).

[160] D. McGoldrick (2006) pp. 176–7: many British schools have allowed Muslim girls to wear the Islamic headscarf for many years and, more recently, the shalwar kameez.

[161] DfE (2021).   [162] [2006] UKHL 15, [2007] AC 100.   [163] Ibid. at [93].

[164] Lord Bingham of Cornhill, Lord Hoffmann and Lord Scott of Foscote.

[165] [2006] UKHL 15, [2007] AC 100, at [50].   [166] Ibid. at [23]–[24].

which school to apply to.[167] In any case, it is to be expected that an adolescent of 14 may have very different views from those held at 11, not least where the decision is related to religious obligations that may arise on puberty. Further, pupils may encounter practical difficulties and disruption to education in seeking to move to an alternative school with different uniform requirements. For these reasons, the minority[168] considered that the school's refusal to allow Shabina to attend school in a jilbab had interfered with her Article 9 rights. Subsequent developments in ECHR law mean that the minority view is likely to be preferred in any future case. The ECtHR has explicitly responded to Lord Bingham's analysis, finding that the fact that an applicant could move elsewhere in order to avoid restrictions on dress is not itself a reason for finding that there had been no interference with religious rights, but is instead relevant to whether that interference can be justified.[169] In future cases, it is likely that this would be followed, meaning that the question of whether interference with the pupil's religious beliefs could be justified under Article 9(2) is likely to become crucial to the outcome of the case. Nevertheless, in *Begum*, all agreed that the refusal to allow Shabina to wear the jilbab could be justified, finding that the school's uniform policy was a proportionate response to accommodating the needs of all the pupils. Their Lordships were clearly impressed by the care the school had taken to ensure that their uniform policy satisfied the requirement of modest dress for Muslim girls.[170] Particularly influential was the head teacher's view that adherence to the school uniform policy promoted inclusion and social cohesion and that to allow new variants would encourage the formation of groups or cliques identified by their clothing.[171] Account was also taken of the girls' own concern that they might face pressure to adopt the jilbab themselves if it was allowed.[172]

Critics of the *Begum* decision have largely focused on the issues underlying Shabina's claim – more particularly the international debates over Muslim women wearing the Islamic headscarf.[173] The approach to religious dress adopted by schools and universities here is far more liberal than the controversial ban on the headscarf by some European countries[174] – a ban not condemned by the ECtHR.[175] As such, it is unlikely that Shabina Begum would have succeeded had her case gone to Strasbourg.[176] Nevertheless, critics argue that *Begum* not only ignores children's autonomy rights – their right to

---

[167]   Ibid. at [92]–[93].   [168]   Lord Nicholls of Birkenhead and Baroness Hale of Richmond.

[169]   *Eweida and others* v. *United Kingdom* [2013] ECHR 37, at [83].

[170]   The school governors had consulted parents, students, staff and the Imams of the three local mosques.

[171]   [2006] UKHL 15, [2007] AC 100, ibid., per Lord Bingham, at [18].

[172]   Ibid., per Baroness Hale, at [98].

[173]   Inter alia: E. Brems (2006); S. Edwards (2007); A. Pimor (2006).

[174]   D. McGoldrick (2006) chs 2–5.

[175]   *SAS* v. *France* [2015] 60 EHRR 11; *Sahin* v. *Turkey* [2006] ELR 73; *Dahlab* v. *Switzerland* [2001] ECHR 42393/98.

[176]   *Dogru* v. *France* (2009) 49 EHRR 8.

make religious choices – but also their right to education, since very orthodox believers will feel obliged to drop out of school if barred from wearing the dress they consider to be demanded by their religion.[177] Furthermore, the Committee on the Rights of the Child has itself criticised countries like France for preventing Muslim girls and teachers from wearing the Islamic headscarf.[178] But Baroness Hale of Richmond's judgment in *Begum* reflects her awareness of these broader issues underlying Shabina's application.[179] She appreciated that, on the one hand, Muslim women may genuinely choose to wear the headscarf, but that on the other, they may be pressured to do so by a male-dominated code of dress.[180] For Baroness Hale, schools could play an important role in helping girls to understand and respond to these pressures:

> A uniform dress code can play its role in smoothing over ethnic, religious and social divisions. But it does more than that. Like it or not, this is a society committed, in principle and in law, to equal freedom for men and women to choose how they will lead their lives within the law. Young girls from ethnic, cultural or religious minorities growing up here face particularly difficult choices: how far to adopt or to distance themselves from the dominant culture. A good school will enable and support them. This particular school is a good school.[181]

These words suggest that Baroness Hale took very seriously the head teacher's fears that Muslim pupils in her school would come under pressure from family members or extremist groups to wear the jilbab were it to be introduced into the uniform code.[182] The *Begum* decision and subsequent case law suggests that schools may fight off challenges under Article 9 of the ECHR, by arguing that a strict uniform policy can be justified under Article 9(2).[183] Although each case is fact-sensitive, the school is more likely to be successful in doing so if they can show, as in *Begum* itself, that the decision on the uniform has been made with careful consideration both of the rights of the pupil objecting to the policy and of the wider school community.

[177] E. Brems (2006) pp. 129–33.   [178] Ibid. See also D. McGoldrick (2006) pp. 281–2.
[179] See generally D. McGoldrick (2006).
[180] [2006] UKHL 15, [2007] AC 100, at [94]–[96]. Baroness Hale also relied on the work of Professor Frances Radnay in 'Culture, Religion and Gender' [2003] 1 *International Journal of Constitutional Law* 663, who considered that: 'A mandatory policy that rejects veiling in state educational institutions may provide a crucial opportunity for girls to choose the feminist freedom of state education over the patriarchal dominance of their families.'
[181] Ibid, at [97].
[182] In *Begum*, the court appeared concerned that Shabina Begum's older brother may be particularly influential in the stance she had adopted. Shabina Begum has subsequently, as an adult, stated that her decision was her own and not made under pressure from her brother: N. Ferreira (2017).
[183] *R (X)* v. *Head Teacher and Governors of Y School* [2007] EWHC 298, [2008] 1 All ER 249: Muslim pupil unsuccessfully claimed the right to wear a niqab, not a headscarf; *R (on the application of Playfoot)* v. *Governing Body of Millais School* [2007] EWHC 1698 (Admin), [2007] ELR 484: Christian pupil unsuccessfully claimed the right to wear a 'purity ring' despite the uniform policy prohibiting jewellery (S. Bacquet (2008)).

Subsequent litigation suggests that a claimant may find an alternative route to challenge in equality legislation. As Harris points out, Shabina Begum could not have brought herself within the protection of the then race relations legislation[184] because Muslims are not regarded as an ethnic group per se;[185] nor was religious belief a protected characteristic as it is now.[186] Today, a pupil may argue that by refusing to allow him or her to attend school wearing a distinctive item of clothing as a visible sign of membership of that group or faith, the head teacher is guilty of indirect racial and/or religious discrimination under the Equality Act 2010.[187] Just as infringement of Article 9 can be justified under Article 9(2), so a school may defend its discriminatory uniform policy by showing that the ban is a proportionate means of achieving a legitimate aim.[188] Silber J's decision in *R (Watkins Singh) v. The Governing Body of Aberdare Girls' High School and Rhondda Cynon Taf Unitary Authority*[189] is a good example of a successful challenge under equality legislation. The case concerned a challenge to the school's refusal to exempt Sarika Watkins-Singh (a 14-year-old Sikh girl) from the school's jewellery ban, in order to allow her to wear the Kara (a narrow plain steel bangle). The school argued that Sarika had not been subject to a 'particular disadvantage' as wearing the Kara was not a compulsory requirement for Sikhs. Having heard expert evidence on the importance to Sikhs of wearing the Kara and of the importance attached to it by Sarika herself, Silber J rejected this argument, finding that wearing it need not be a compulsory requirement of the group or faith.[190] It was sufficient to show that the wearing of the Kara was of exceptional importance to Sarika's religious belief and that objectively to be of exceptional importance to Sikhs in order for the ban to constitute a particular disadvantage to her.[191] The school's attempt to justify the decision on the basis of the need to treat all the pupils in the same way failed, in part because Silber J was not satisfied that the school had ever considered the Kara's exceptional significance to Sarika's religious belief.[192] Furthermore, he emphasised that the bangle is very small and unostentatious and is normally hidden from view by the claimant wearing a long-sleeved garment.[193] Consequently, the school's refusal to exempt her from the ban on jewellery was not proportionate and could not be justified.[194] The case suggests that it will be more

---

[184] E.g. *Mandla v. Lee and others* [1983] 2 AC 548: per the House of Lords, a headmaster's unjustifiable refusal to allow a Sikh boy to wear a turban to school amounted to unlawful discrimination under the Race Relations Act (RRA) 1976 (now repealed and replaced by Equality Act 2010).

[185] N. Harris (2007) p. 155.   [186] Equality Act (EA) 2010, s. 10.   [187] Ibid. s. 19.

[188] Ibid. s. 19(2)(d).

[189] [2008] EWHC 1865 (Admin), [2008] ELR 561. The case was decided prior to the EA 2010, under the Equality Act 2006.

[190] Ibid., per Silber J, at [50]–[55].

[191] Ibid. at [56B]. Although in *G (By His Litigation Friend) v. The Head Teacher and Governors of St Gregory's Catholic Science College* [2011] ELR 446, at [36]–[38], Collins J considered that the term 'exceptional' may itself be too high a threshold; see below.

[192] Ibid. per Silber J, at [112]–[114].   [193] Ibid. at [77]–[78].   [194] Ibid. at [92].

difficult to justify restrictions on discreet items of dress than those that are more obvious, such as the jilbab in *Begum*. These cases are, however, very much dependent on their facts and do not seek to set down any rules as to the forms of dress that a school should permit.[195] While it will be easier for a school to justify restrictions that are the product of careful consideration and which impact on very visible practices, this is not inevitably the case. For example, in *G (By His Litigation Friend)* v. *The Head Teacher and Governors of St Gregory's Catholic Science College*,[196] an 11-year-old boy of African-Caribbean ethnicity succeeded in challenging a policy on haircuts that would prevent him from wearing his hair in cornrows, a cultural practice of 'particular importance' to him. The school had designed its policy with reflection on the diverse population that it served and imposed clear restrictions on haircuts in order to prevent those associated with local gang culture. There was, however, no evidence that cornrows were in any way connected with this gang culture and the reason given could not justify the restriction. The case demonstrates that even schools that base their policy on considered reasons, may find themselves unable to justify that policy if they do not give sufficient consideration to reasonable requests for exemptions.

The case law on pupils' dress demonstrates the difficulty for schools in accommodating the rights of individual pupils and the interests of the wider school community. The government guidance to schools recognises the dilemma that this gives to schools, but does little to help schools to resolve that dilemma, besides reminding them of their duties under equality and human rights law and the importance of maintaining flexibility to deal with exceptions.[197] Although the *Begum* case appeared to create a formidable obstacle to pupils wishing to challenge their school, the subsequent developments now require far greater respect to be given to the cultural practices and beliefs of individual children. Schools must treat those beliefs and practices with respect and individual consideration to avoid falling foul of the law, but need not accede to every request if there is sufficient justification for refusal.

(6) Conclusion

The methods adopted by the state in maintaining the balance between parents' rights and children's rights should always be exercised with sensitivity. The law must respect the right of parents to instruct their children on their culture, beliefs and traditions. But although aggressive interference with their educational methods can very easily be seen as religious persecution, all children are entitled to equality of educational opportunity; further to an education which broadens their horizons, rather than narrowing their potential. The law has

---

[195] *R (X)* v. *Head Teacher and Governors of Y School* [2007] EWHC 298, [2008] 1 All ER 249, at [1]; *R (Watkins Singh)* v. *The Governing Body of Aberdare Girls' High School and Rhondda Cynon Taf Unitary Authority* [2008] EWHC 1865 (Admin), [2008] ELR 561, at [1].
[196] [2011] ELR 446.   [197] DfE (2021).

traditionally given parents wide discretion in the choice of education that they give their children, at least for those who have the resources available to exercise that choice. That parental freedom has come under increased pressure, not primarily from a desire to promote children's educational rights, but from a concern that certain forms of separate education can lead to fragmented communities and extremism, and even lay the foundations for future security risks. A focus on these concerns, important as they are, politicises the beliefs and education of children in a manner that can detract from the interests of the children themselves. Education can play a vital role for children in developing their understanding of and opportunities for life in wider society and helping them to navigate between the spheres of family, community and that wider society. The obligations that have been placed on schools in relation to uniforms demonstrate how difficult this can be to implement in practice. There are no simple answers to how diversity of culture and belief should be accommodated within education, but a children's rights approach would ensure that the children whose education is at stake are placed at the centre of a debate which is often dominated by tensions between parental freedoms and state interests.

Bibliography

NB: Many of these publications can be obtained on the relevant organisation's website.

Ajegbo, K. (Chairman) (2007) *Diversity and Citizenship: Curriculum Review*, DfES.
Bacquet, S. (2008) 'School Uniforms, Religious Symbols and the Human Rights Act 1998: The "Purity Ring" Case' 8 *Education Law Journal* 11.
Bradney, A. (1987) 'Separate Schools and Ethnic Minorities and the Law' 13 *New Community* 412.
    (2009) 'The Inspection of Ultra-Orthodox Jewish Schools: "The Audit Society" and "The Society of Scholars"' 21 *Child and Family Law Quarterly* 131.
Brems, E. (2006) 'Above Children's Heads: The Headscarf Controversy in European Schools from the Perspective of Children's Rights' 14 *International Journal of Children's Rights* 119.
Cantle, T. (2001) *Community Cohesion: A Report of the Independent Review Team*, Home Office.
Casey, L. (2016) *The Casey Review: A Review into Opportunity and Integration*, Department for Communities and Local Government.
Children's Commissioner (2017) *Briefing: Falling through the Gaps in Education*, Office of the Children's Commissioner.
Clarke, P. (2014) *Report into Allegations Concerning Birmingham Schools Arising from the 'Trojan Horse' Letter*, HC 576, The Stationery Office.
Committee on Economic, Social and Cultural Rights (1999) *General Comment No. 13 on the Right to Education*, Centre for Human Rights, Geneva.
Committee on the Rights of the Child (2001) *General Comment No. 1 on Article 29(1): The Aims of Education*, Centre for Human Rights, Geneva.
    (2016) *Concluding Observations of the Committee on the Rights of the Child: United Kingdom of Great Britain and Northern Ireland*, CRC/C/GBR/CO/5, Centre for Human Rights, Geneva.
Department for Education (DfE) (2016) *Schools that Work for Everyone*, DfE.
    (2019a) *Elective Home Education: Departmental Guidance for Local Authorities*, DfE.
    (2019b) *Elective Home Education: Departmental Guidance for Parents*, DfE.
    (2021) *School Uniform: Guidance for Governing Bodies, School Leaders, School Staff and Local Authorities*, DfE.
    (2022) *Children Not in School: Government Consultation Response*, DfE.

Department for Education and Skills (2001) Cm 5230, 2001, *Schools: Achieving Success*, The Stationery Office.

Edwards, S. (2007) 'Imagining Islam ... of Meaning and Metaphor Symbolising the Jilbab – R (Begum) v. Headteacher and Governors of Denbigh High School' 19 *Child and Family Law Quarterly* 247.

Ferreira, N. (2017) '*R (on the application of Begum)* v. *Headteacher and Governors of Denbigh High School*: Commentary' in Stalford, H., Hollingsworth, K. and Gilmore, S. (eds) *Rewriting Children's Rights Judgments: From Academic Vision to New Practice*, Hart Publishing.

Ford, J., Hughes, M., May, K., Shaughnessy, M. and Gill, H. (2016) *Education Law and Practice*, 4th edn, LexisNexis.

Friedman, L. M. (1916) 'The Parental Right to Control the Religious Education of the Child' 29 *Harvard Law Review* 485.

Hamilton, C. (1995) *Family, Law and Religion*, Sweet & Maxwell.

Harris, N. (2007) *Education, Law and Diversity*, Hart Publishing.

  (2020) *Education, Law and Diversity*, 2nd edn, Hart Publishing.

HM Government (2011) Cm 8092, *Prevent Strategy*, The Stationery Office.

  (2015) *Revised Prevent Duty Guidance for England and Wales*, The Stationery Office.

House of Commons Education Committee (2021) Strengthening Home Education, Third Report of Session 2021–22, HC 84, House of Commons.

Joint Committee on Human Rights (JCHR) (2008) *Nineteenth Report of Session 2007–08, Legislative Scrutiny: Education and Skills Bill*, HC553, The Stationery Office.

Kilkelly, U. (1999) *The Child and the European Convention on Human Rights*, Ashgate.

McGoldrick, D. (2006) *Human Rights and Religion: The Islamic Headscarf Debate in Europe*, Hart Publishing.

Monk, D. (2009a) 'Parental Responsibility and Education: Taking a Long View' in Probert, R., Gilmore, S. and Herring, J. J. W. (eds) *Responsible Parents & Parental Responsibility*, Hart Publishing.

  (2009b) 'Regulating home education: Negotiating standards, anomalies and rights' 21 *Child and Family Law Quarterly* 155.

  (2016) '"Out of School Education" and Radicalisation: Home Education Revisited' *Education Law Journal* 17.

Office for Standards in Education (Ofsted) (2007) *Reference No 070045, Making Sense of Religion: a Report on Religious Education in Schools and the Impact of Locally Agreed Syllabuses*, Ofsted.

  (2013) *Religious Education: Realising the Potential*, Ofsted.

  (2015) *Emergency Inspection Report on the Talmud Torah Machzikei School*, Ofsted.

  (2017) *Annual Report of Her Majesty's Chief Inspector for Education, Children's Services and Skills 2016/17*, HC 618, Ofsted.

  (2018) *School Inspection Handbook*, Ofsted.

Pimor, A. (2006) 'The Interpretation and Protection of Article 9 ECHR: Overview of the Denbigh High School (UK) Case' 28 *Journal of Social Welfare and Family Law* 323.

Poulter, S. (1998) *Ethnicity, Law and Human Rights: The English Experience*, Oxford University Press.

Qualifications and Curriculum Authority (QCA) (2004) *Religious Education: The Non-statutory Framework*, QCA Publications.

Rivers, J. (2010) *The Law of Organised Religions: Between Establishment and Secularism*, Oxford University Press.

Sandberg, R. (2011) *Law and Religion*, Cambridge University Press.

Struthers, A. (2017) 'Teaching British Values in Our Schools: But Why Not Human Rights Values?' 26 *Social and Legal Studies* 89.

Swann, M. (Chairman) (1985) Cmnd 9453, *Education for All Report of the Committee of Inquiry into the Education of Children from Ethnic Minority Groups*.

Taylor, R. (2013) 'Secular Values and Sacred Rights: Re G (Education: Religious Upbringing)' 25 *Child and Family Law Quarterly* 336.

  (2015) 'Responsibility for the Soul of the Child: The Role of the State and Parents in Determining Religious Upbringing and Education' 29 *International Journal of Law, Policy and the Family* 15.

(2018) 'Religion as Harm? Radicalisation, Extremism and Child Protection' 30 *Child and Family Law Quarterly* 41.

Thornberry, P. (1991) *International Law and the Rights of Minorities*, Clarendon Press.

Van Bueren, G. (1995) *The International Law on the Rights of the Child*, Martinus Nijhoff Publishers.

Vanderbeck, R. and Johnson, P. (2016) 'The Promotion of British Values: Sexual Orientation Equality, Religion and England's Schools' 30 *International Journal of Law, Policy and the Family* 292.

9

Adolescent Autonomy

(1) Introduction

Adolescents are fast approaching adulthood, but they cannot be expected to make the transition from childhood to an adult legal status successfully without assistance. They need to develop complex skills for independent life in our relatively wealthy and technologically sophisticated society. Although parents have an essential part to play in this process, the law should also assist by ensuring that an adolescent's decisions are, as far as possible, respected. The growing emphasis on adult autonomy encouraged by the implementation of the Human Rights Act (HRA) 1998 has produced a judicial willingness to accommodate such ideas when interpreting adolescents' interests. The words of Baroness Hale of Richmond exemplify such an approach:

> Important physical, cognitive and psychological developments take place during adolescence. Adolescence begins with the onset of puberty; from puberty to adulthood, the 'capacity to acquire and utilise knowledge reaches its peak efficiency'; and the capacity for formal operational thought is the forerunner to developing the capacity to make autonomous moral judgments. Obviously, these developments happen at different times and at different rates for different people. But it is not at all surprising to find adolescents making different moral judgments from those of their parents. It is part of growing up.[1]

It is, however, unrealistic to expect children of any age to make decisions for themselves before they are developmentally ready to do so. Those who argue over the extent to which children should be allowed greater legal responsibilities seldom refer to the extensive body of research on children's mental processes and cognitive powers. This chapter briefly summarises some of this material and explores how it might inform decision-making relating to children as they mature into adolescence.

The second part of the chapter considers, in general terms, the confused legal principles now governing the relationship between adolescents and their parents. In practice, parents play an enormously influential role in their

---

[1] *R (on the application of Begum)* v. *Head Teacher and Governors of Denbigh High School* [2006] UKHL 15, [2007] AC 100, at [93].

children's lives. Parents are the people who can most effectively encourage them to develop a capacity for independence. Parents are also excellently placed to undermine the self-confidence of their teenage offspring so effectively that they emerge into adulthood quite unable to fend happily for themselves. The law is ambivalent both over the extent to which parents should be encouraging their children to become independent and over the legal limits to their own authority. It is also ambivalent over the circumstances in which mature adolescents should be recognised as having the ability to make decisions over their own lives, regardless of the views of their parents. The chapter concludes by considering the application of these general principles in the fraught context of deprivation of liberty. Despite recent rights-based judgments, the law's confused approach to adolescent decision-making and to relationships between parents and older children adds uncertainty to this complex area of law. As a result, adolescents find themselves at risk of being deprived of this most important of rights without access to the legal safeguards that protect adults. This area of law is an excellent example of the practical consequences of the law's ambivalence on adolescent autonomy and the role of parents.

(2) Child and Adolescent Developmental Capacity for Decision-Making: The Research Evidence

Ideas about children's competence for various tasks are formed by practitioners and academics alike in a variety of different contexts, but often without any cross-referencing, or exploration of common themes. Thus, those involved in the field of youth crime are well aware that they should have some understanding of children's ability to take responsibility for their wrongdoing. Equally, no practitioner should consider calling a child as a witness in a criminal trial without a good understanding of children's mental processes and capacity to recall events. Similarly, doctors treating children and adolescents require a reasonably accurate idea of their young patients' ability to comprehend and consent to treatment.[2] Legal practitioners may have to decide whether a young person has the legal capacity to instruct his or her own solicitor in litigation involving their parents.[3] There is a huge body of research literature on developmental psychology which provides information about children's decision-making processes. Nevertheless, its very complexity defies those wishing to find straightforward answers to specific questions about a particular child's competence in any given context. Indeed, different aspects of the research may be exploited for different purposes. Thus, critics of the punitive aspects of the law on youth crime point to the developmental research indicating that adolescents' ability to take responsibility for their criminal acts may develop far later than their physical and intellectual ability suggests.[4] By contrast, those

---

[2] See Chapter 11.   [3] See Chapter 12.   [4] E.g. Royal College of Psychiatrists (2006).

arguing that children and young people should be allowed to take earlier responsibility for a variety of activities, including voting and medical decision-making, emphasise the research indicating the development of cognitive and social skills in some children at relatively early ages.[5]

Generalisations are, of course, always misleading. Ideally, a child's capacity for decision-making should always be considered on an individual case-by-case basis, since it will hinge largely on the type of decision, its context and the child's own personal circumstances.[6] Nevertheless, scientific research provides a valuable basis for understanding the development of cognitive and decision-making skills throughout childhood and into adolescence and adulthood. This understanding is an important tool in evaluating the law's assumptions about the value to be attributed to children's decisions and the point at which competence to make those decisions should be attributed. The answers that this research provides are themselves complex and developing. Competence to make a decision is not merely a matter of being able to understand and process information, but also requires social and emotional maturity. As these skills are acquired at different rates, so children may be able to exhibit some of the skills necessary to engage in a particular decision, but lack the full range of abilities needed to approach it with full maturity.[7] Further, while research can provide information to assist in developing the law, it cannot provide simple answers as to how that should be done. Moral, social and political choices are made in interpreting that research and translating it into legal rules; these choices may be informed by research, but not determined by it. A particularly good example can be seen in the way in which the law imposes a bright-line cut-off of 18 as the age at which the legal status of adulthood is acquired,[8] despite a lack of consensus in the research literature as to when adolescence ends and evidence that important developmental changes continue after this age.[9] Scientific research into the capacities and brain development of children and adolescents is becoming increasingly sophisticated and nuanced and may require us to re-evaluate the way in which the law understands competence and development.

In order to be competent to make a decision, it is essential to have the decision-making capacity to do so.[10] Decision-making capacity itself requires a number of neurological skills; each of these skills typically develop at different rates and stages, but are largely in place by early adolescence. These skills

[5] E.g. P. Alderson (1993); L. Ferguson (2004).   [6] M. Rutter and M. Rutter (1993) p. 197.
[7] L. Steinberg (2013); see further discussion below.
[8] Although, as discussed below and in Chapter 10, certain rights and competencies are acquired before this date.
[9] S. Blakemore (2012); S. Blakemore and T. Robbins (2012).
[10] Decision-making *capacity* is not the only component of decision-making *competence*. E.g. a child might have the intellectual capacity to make a decision, but lack the information or the emotional maturity to do so, as discussed below. Decision-making capacity is therefore a necessary but not sufficient condition for decision-making competence: P. Grootens-Wiegers *et al.* (2017).

are often considered through four standards for decision-making capacity: ability to express a choice; understanding; reasoning; and appreciation.[11] Expression of choice is the earliest of these standards to be met: even pre-verbal children may have the communication skills necessary to be able to express a choice.[12] More complex communication usually relies on verbal skills; the core verbal skills are developed in relatively early childhood and are largely in place by the age of 4, although they will refine further beyond this age.[13] The second standard, understanding, requires a far more complex set of neurological skills. Not only must a child have the intelligence and language skills to be able to understand information, but they must then have the ability to direct attention to that information and retain it in their working memory in order to process it. These skills are, however, substantially developed by adolescence: children's ability to direct attention develops rapidly between the ages of 7 and 10; while memory increases between the ages of 6 and 12, with 10–12-year-olds demonstrating similar recall skills to those of adults.[14] Reasoning, the third standard, builds on the ability to understand information, but also requires the skills to apply logical reasoning and to assess the relative risks and benefits of the decision in question. The nature of reasoning required to make a decision will vary with the type of decision being made, meaning that it is difficult to give a simple answer as to when the relevant skills are usually acquired. Children develop basic logical reasoning between the ages of 6 and 8, with significant improvement by the end of primary school at age 11.[15] More complex forms of advanced, abstract reasoning emerge in early adolescence and improve during mid-adolescence, although many continue to struggle with these forms of reasoning even into adulthood, meaning that there is considerable variation in the standard achieved by a particular age.[16] The final standard, appreciation, requires the individual to be able to appreciate the significance of different outcomes for their own personal circumstances. A number of skills are necessary to be able to do so. In particular, the decision-maker must have the ability to engage in abstract thinking and to understand their own goals and values. It is clear that the neurological skills necessary to meet these four standards and to demonstrate decision-making capacity grow over time. The age at which the skills are typically acquired can be stated in broad terms, but decision-making capacity is not purely a function of age; instead, for each person, its acquisition will depend on individual and environmental factors. Further, capacity to make a particular decision will also depend on the complexity of that decision: a child may have capacity to make one form of decision, but not another. Despite these caveats, it is broadly the case that the skills required to obtain decision-making capacity develop substantially during the period of childhood from age 6 to 11 and are largely in

---

[11] P. Appelbaum and T. Grisso (2001).
[12] See discussion in Chapter 12 on children's views in court proceedings.   [13] E. Hoff (2013).
[14] P. Grootens-Wiegers *et al.* (2017).   [15] H. Markovits (2013) pp. 71–94.   [16] Ibid.

place by early to mid-adolescence, although development in the most complex forms of abstract reasoning continues after this time. Indeed, most researchers seem agreed that 'a considerable degree of intellectual maturation may have occurred by 14 years',[17] with the ability to make certain decisions occurring before adolescence begins.[18]

The acquisition of decision-making capacity is not the only aspect of development that is important to assessing the ability of adolescents to make mature decisions. As the Royal College of Psychiatrists puts it:

> Improved cognitive or thinking capacities are only one aspect of the maturational and learning processes which need to occur to turn the naturally impulsive, self-centred, short-term thinking toddler into a reasonably self-controlled, reflective young adult, able to take a long-term view.[19]

As critics of the harsh juvenile justice system emphasise, cognitive capacity to reach decisions does not necessarily correlate with mature judgment. Most agree that 'mature' decision-making is greatly influenced by such matters as context and by an individual's emotional and social development.[20] The rapidly developing neuroscientific research on adolescence demonstrates that it is a period of significant changes in brain structure and function and that the brain in adolescence is different both from the brain in childhood and in adulthood.[21] These differences have important consequences for the way in which adolescents make decisions and the conditions most conducive to good decision-making. The areas of the brain that undergo particularly significant changes, from around the age of 12, are those associated with self-regulation or control and those associated with sensitivity to rewards.[22] In particular, there are relatively slow, protracted changes to the pre-frontal cortex that continue throughout adolescence and into early adulthood.[23] These changes are closely connected with impulse control and high cognitive functioning.[24] Adolescence is also a time of heightened sensitivity to dopamine, which results in greater responses to rewards.[25] Many researchers associate this aspect of development with an adolescent propensity to engage in risky decisions in pursuit of rewards and sensation seeking.[26] Importantly, the control and reward systems do not follow a linear path, leading some researchers to speak of a 'mismatch' in development as the control aspects of development take more time to

---

[17] M. Rutter (2005) p. 33; L. Steinberg (2013) p. 265. See also L. Ferguson (2004) p. 43, who notes general agreement among researchers that minors become 'mature abstract cognitive thinkers' from age 14 onwards.

[18] I. Hein *et al.* (2014) found that by the age of 11.2 competence to consent to participation in research trials was probable. See also P. Grootens-Wiegers *et al.* (2017), who suggest that by around the age of 12 children may have competence to make medical decisions.

[19] Royal College of Psychiatrists (2006) p. 33.

[20] L. Steinberg (2013); L. Ferguson (2004) pp. 43–50: research summary.

[21] P. Grootens-Wiegers *et al.* (2017).   [22] Ibid.   [23] L. Steinberg (2013) pp. 259–60.

[24] S. Blakemore and T. Robbins (2012) p. 1184.   [25] L. Van Leijenhorst *et al.* (2010).

[26] S. Blakemore and T. Robbins (2012) p. 1184; L. Steinberg (2013).

mature, perhaps leading to difficulty for some adolescents in restraining risky behaviour.[27] There is also considerable support for the view that adolescents are more likely to engage in risk-taking in emotionally 'hot' circumstances, particularly involving peer approval, than 'cold' situations with low emotional arousal.[28] Further, in addition to physical changes in the brain structure, adolescents often undergo dramatic hormonal and emotional changes.[29] There may, therefore, be good reason to consider that 'adolescents mature intellectually before they mature socially and emotionally'.[30]

When considering the capacity of children and adolescents to reach decisions for themselves, writers, practitioners and the judiciary often use imprecise terms such as 'competence', 'maturity' and 'understanding'. The body of research on children's developmental processes is vitally important in translating these terms into meaningful standards. Nonetheless, the scientific research on adolescent development cannot give a complete answer as to how society should respond to these findings. For example, if it is the case that adolescents are more likely to engage in risky behaviour than adults, this does not necessarily mean that adolescent decision-making should be constrained until an adult approach to risk is achieved. While young people, and others within society, might need protection from some forms of risky adolescent behaviour, experimentation can be an important educational element on the path to adulthood.[31] Adolescence is a time for experimenting with new ideas, clothes and behaviour; it is a time in which many adolescents start questioning the belief-system with which they were brought up and forging their own approach to adulthood. Adolescents need the freedom to make decisions and explore new ways of living, not only because it is intrinsically valuable to direct one's own life, but also for the pragmatic reason that experimentation at this stage in life will allow the individual to practice decision-making and form their own goals and values. The law must accommodate the value of adolescent decision-making, while also recognising the risks it may entail.

(3) Child and Adolescent Capacity for Decision-Making: Liberalising the Law on Minority Status?

Children in this country remain minors until they reach the age of 18,[32] although they obtain some legal competencies at an earlier age.[33] Whether the law is right to draw this line between adulthood and minority status and

---

[27] P. Grootens-Wiegers et al. (2017). K. Mills et al. (2014) express some caution as to whether there is actually a correlation between brain maturation and risky behaviour in practice, but note that their research considers a small sample (twenty-four participants) and cannot be relied upon to draw any firm conclusions on the relationship between the two.

[28] S. Blakemore and T. Robbins (2012).   [29] Juvenile Justice Center (2004) p. 2.

[30] L. Steinberg (2013) p. 261.   [31] J. Coleman and L. Hendry (1999) p. 135.

[32] Family Law Reform Act (FLRA) 1969, s. 1.

[33] E.g. at 16, the consent of a minor to consent to medical treatment is recognised by statute: FLRA 1969, s. 8(1), discussed in Chapter 11. See further Chapter 10 for discussion of the ages at which various legal rights are acquired.

whether it does so in the correct way has been a continuous point of disagreement among writers on childhood. In particular, there remains an active question as to whether adolescents should obtain the legal right to make significant decisions at a different stage than is the case at present. Outside of the legal realm, the end of adolescence is often defined not by age, but by the point at which the individual makes a transition into adult roles.[34] The complexity of modern society means that this social milestone is often not achieved until a person is in their early to mid-20s, coincidentally a time which some authors see as reflecting the point at which the brain reaches maturity.[35] On this basis, it could be argued that the age at which the law confers adult status should be raised. On the other hand, the ability of adolescents to transition into adult roles is not merely constrained by cognitive development, but is often limited by legal rules that prevent them from leaving education, entering the workforce or living independently.[36] Some writers consider that the activities of children who take on adult-like responsibilities demonstrate that they are capable of considerable competence and deserve greater respect for their decision-making abilities than is recognised in the current law.[37] They point to the many children under the age of 18 who care for ill or disabled parents with little or no help, the street children in the world's major cities who exhibit survival strategies equal to those of many adults, and the children who happily take on a responsible role in working parents' households, if properly involved in the division of labour.[38] Alderson's research with children in hospital led her to conclude that children develop the competence to make complex decisions about their medical treatment at far earlier ages than adults realise or accept. Indeed, she argues that since many children exceed many adults in qualities such as intelligence, ability and prudence, differences between adults and children lie mainly in social beliefs about childhood, rather than in children's actual abilities.[39] On this view, it is arguable that by keeping adolescents and young adults in a dependent condition, the law prevents them from gaining experience and practising skills that may be necessary to acquire competence in a particular area and artificially delays adulthood.[40]

The developing scientific research discussed above is important in informing the law's approach to these debates, but it cannot determine that approach. As Martha Minow has argued:

> competence and incompetence are used as proxies for a variety of concerns about what societal decision-makers think children may need, and about what they simultaneously think allows adults to choose for themselves . . . There are

[34] L. Steinberg (2016) p. 4.

[35] L. Steinberg (2016). To some extent, those aged 18–25 are treated differently in law at present; e.g. payment of the living wage is not required until a person reaches 25. Similarly, the Children and Social Work Act 2017 places obligations on local authorities to support young adults formerly under their care until the age of 25.

[36] Discussed in Chapter 10.   [37] G. Lansdown (2005) pp. 24–31: research summary.   [38] Ibid.

[39] P. Alderson (1993) p. 190.   [40] L. Rosenbury (2015).

no uncontroversial principles to pinpoint the kinds of competencies crucial to accord an individual independent decision-making power and to relinquish paternalist control. Granting someone independence is a political or moral choice made by each society to fulfil its own purposes – not a rational decision gauged by psychological or other scientific measures.[41]

Even if science were to provide a perfect understanding of the adolescent brain, these political and moral choices would remain contentious. There are some principles that are likely to be considered more important than fidelity to scientific research in developing the law. It is likely, for example, that even if there were incontrovertible evidence that male and female adolescents typically developed competence at different ages to one another, the principle of equal treatment would be considered too important to introduce different ages of majority for men and women.[42] Similarly, it is unlikely that there would be political will to *raise* the age of majority on the basis that structural changes in the brain that affect risk-taking and self-regulation continue into early adulthood.[43] Much of the law on adolescent competence might be better seen as a reflection of the risks that society is willing to allow young people to take, rather than being rooted in a consistent approach to the scientific analysis of adolescent capacity for autonomous choice.[44] Adolescence is often viewed as a critical period for future life chances[45] and the law reflects a willingness to limit the choices that adolescents make in the present in order to prioritise their future adult self.[46] The Convention on the Rights of the Child (CRC) uses the concept of the evolving capacities of the child to mediate this tension between respecting adolescent decision-making and protecting children from harm.[47] The Committee on the Rights of the Child has issued a General Comment to give further guidance on its interpretation and recommends that states should ensure that laws on age limits are 'consistent with the right to protection, the best interests principle and respect for the evolving capacities of adolescents',[48] but does little to explain how to accommodate these competing rights in practice.

The developing scientific research on adolescent capacity and brain development cannot give an answer to these normative dilemmas; it can, however, inform the way in which the law should respond. An important principle is

---

[41] M. Minow (1986) p. 5.

[42] S. Blakemore (2012) summarises the current research on sex differences in brain development. Although the Committee on the Rights of the Child acknowledges that there is suggestion of such differences in the research literature, it considers that different ages of majority for boys and girls would be prohibited by the CRC in any event; Committee on the Rights of the Child (2016) paras 5 and 38.

[43] L. Steinberg (2013) pp. 259–61.

[44] This is seen particularly clearly in the law on mature minors who refuse medical treatment, discussed in Chapter 11.

[45] Committee on the Rights of the Child (2016) para. 11.

[46] See Chapter 1 for discussion of theoretical approaches to accommodating autonomy and protection rights.

[47] CRC, Art. 5.   [48] Committee on the Rights of the Child (2016) para. 39.

that children should not be asked to make decisions before they are developmentally ready to do so. The research material discussed above shows that there are significant and subtle differences between the development of young children and adolescents, and between younger and older adolescents. It appears that before early adolescence, the *majority* of children do lack the cognitive abilities and judgmental skills to make major decisions that might seriously affect their lives. Although some children may, through experience, become competent to deal with the challenges that life throws up and able to make decisions in the face of pain, hardship and ill-health, this may be at considerable psychological cost. Indeed, it is surely appropriate to shield the average child from making significant choices before he or she acquires the cognitive tools to do so adequately. Such an approach readily accords with the interest theory of rights, which presupposes that although children may have an interest in making choices, they do not necessarily have a moral right to do so. Under MacCormick's test, an interest in choice could only be deemed a moral right if it is so important to the child that it would be wrong in itself to deny or withhold it from him or her.[49] Children's interest in decisions concerning them is usually acknowledged through the right to participate in those decisions rather than the right to make the decision.[50] For example, even very young children may be able to express views on their living arrangements following parental separation, even if they are not able to weigh the full consequences of the options available. It is perfectly appropriate for society to protect children from being required to make significant choices if it considers that they may suffer unnecessarily from being involved in decision-making before they are sufficiently mature.

The research on the adolescent's psychological development suggests that a different approach is justified, particularly for those at the upper end of adolescence, and offers some support to those who argue that the current law is too restrictive in its approach to teenagers. As the discussion above shows, by early to mid-adolescence, most have acquired the intellectual skills necessary to engage in relatively complex decision-making. The recent research on adolescent brain development does, however, suggest that the context in which these decisions are made is important. Teenagers are likely to benefit from careful support, information and time to make best use of these intellectual skills, especially in complex or emotionally significant decisions. In contrast, they may make poor use of their skills and take risky decisions in 'hot' situations where decisions are made under the influence of peers or with considerable emotional or time pressure. This research supports the view that the law may be right to recognise some forms of adolescent autonomy while withholding the full range of legal rights that come with adulthood. Although different age restrictions may sometimes appear inconsistent, the context in which the decision is made is important. The law can rationally

---

[49] N. MacCormick (1982) p. 160; see Chapter 1.   [50] CRC, Art. 12, discussed in Chapter 12.

recognise the ability of adolescents to make difficult medical decisions with the support of professionals and parents, while also considering them unable to exercise the judgment and self-control needed to drive independently on public roads.[51]

A further question then arises as to how the law should determine competence to make a particular decision or engage in a particular activity. Competence for decision-making will vary enormously depending on a variety of factors, such as peer pressure and family environment. It not only depends on the maturity and social circumstances of the person reaching the decision, but also on the content and context of the decision in question. In some areas, such as consent to medical intervention, competence is assessed on an individual basis so allowing consideration of these factors; whereas in others, such as capacity to consent to marriage,[52] the minimum age is fixed by law and cannot be waived for individual children on the basis of their personal competence. It might be considered that such fixed age limits violate the rights of precocious children by preventing them from demonstrating their ability to take such decisions. This argument is strongest in circumstances in which the decision affects the child's fundamental rights. It is notable that the circumstances in which the law assesses individual competence tend to relate to fundamental rights such as liberty,[53] bodily autonomy[54] and the severance of family relationships.[55] Where the law merely acts to delay participation in such activities as purchasing alcohol, driving and marrying, the imposition of age limits is much more easily justified. This is particularly so where children as a class are likely to suffer harm from the activity in a manner, or to a degree, not experienced by adults.[56] Further, while individual children will demonstrate different abilities, the average child will develop along similar lines to his or her contemporaries. This is not to say that all of the current age limits found in law are rational or supported by research: there are clear arguments in favour of giving 16-year-olds voting rights,[57] but also in favour of raising the age of criminal responsibility.[58] Nonetheless, although the significance given

---

[51] L. Steinberg (2013).

[52] The Marriage and Civil Partnership (Minimum Age) Act 2022 raised the minimum age for entry into marriage or civil partnership to 18. Prior to this amendment, marriage was void if either party were aged under 16: Matrimonial Causes Act 1973, s. 11(a)(ii). Parental consent was required for a person aged 16 or 17 to marry, but the absence of such consent did not render the marriage void: Marriage Act 1949, s. 3.

[53] *A Local Authority* v. *D* [2016] EWHC 3473 (Fam); see also discussion in *Re T (A Child)* [2021] UKSC 35, [2021] 3 WLR 643, esp. from [156] onwards.

[54] *Gillick* v. *West Norfolk and Wisbech Area Health Authority* [1986] AC 112; *R (Axon)* v. *Secretary of State for Health and the Family Planning Association* [2006] EWHC 37 (Admin), [2006] 2 FLR 206.

[55] *Re S (Child as Parent: Adoption: Consent)* [2017] EWHC 2729 (Fam), [2018] 2 WLR 1029.

[56] E.g. the serious harm that can be done to children through early marriage means that children are recognised as having a right to be protected *from* marriage rather than being deprived of a right to marry: Convention on the Elimination of All Forms of Discrimination Against Women, Art. 16(2).

[57] See Chapter 10.   [58] See Age of Criminal Responsibility Act (Scotland) 2019.

by society to chronological age is probably excessive, the relative youth of a child is very relevant to the reasonableness of the choices put to him or her,[59] and age limits will often serve as useful indicators of probable competence.[60]

(4) Adolescents and Parents: Legal Boundaries?

(A) Legislative Persuasion

The law provides a series of mixed messages about the limits to parental authority once children reach adolescence.[61] No doubt this incoherence springs from the fact that society itself is uncertain about how parents should adapt to their children's growing maturity. Although children mature at different rates, the law withholds the right to full adult autonomy from all adolescents until they attain the age of 18.[62] But on attaining that age, adolescents are expected to make an immediate successful transition from the legal status of childhood to responsible citizenship.[63] Giving them a chance to develop the skills needed for adulthood is therefore essential. Whether they get it depends enormously on their parents' willingness to encourage in their children a capacity to take responsibility for their own future. But should the law make parents undertake this task? Research provides practical support for the views of the theorists who argue that parents have a duty to encourage children to develop decision-making capacities from as early an age as possible. It suggests not only that family environment and family dynamics are major factors in adolescent psychological development,[64] but also that parents help shape adolescents' capacity for reaching decisions competently and influence the extent to which they participate in decision-making.

Most parents agree that they have an important part to play in helping their children gain emotional independence,[65] but this may not always be as easy as it sounds. While many parents subscribe to the idea of the family becoming an increasingly democratic unit, they often find that life with teenagers 'presents fundamental contradictions between ideals and lived reality'.[66] The following words have a ring of truth for parents with teenage children:

> The teenage years herald a period of re-negotiation as budding adults take up the banner of freedom – freedom to make choices, such as what to wear, who to associate with or when to engage in sexual relations. On the other side, parents and carers wave the flag of responsibility, struggling to push recalcitrant adolescents towards maturity, sobriety, practical skills and 'appropriate' behaviour.[67]

Parents' proximity to their children may lead them to underestimate their children's maturity and abilities, particularly their ability to discuss sensibly

---

[59] J. Hughes (1989) p. 38.   [60] D. Archard (2014) ch. 6.   [61] J. Fortin (2001) pp. 247–50.
[62] FLRA 1969, s. 1.   [63] M. de Winter (1997) p. 26.
[64] See J. Coleman and L. Hendry (1999) ch. 5.   [65] W. Langford *et al.* (2001) p. 25.
[66] Ibid. p. 47.   [67] DH (1996) p. 18. See also W. Langford *et al.* (2001) ch. 4.

decisions relating to their own future. They may effectively undermine their children's self-confidence and hamper their decision-making skills by involving them very little in family decisions.[68] In particular, many parents find it extremely difficult to allow even quite mature children to make up their own minds on major matters affecting their upbringing and future. Knowledgeable parents might argue that they are supported in such an approach by Article 5 of the CRC. This requires governments to respect parents' rights and duties to provide 'appropriate direction and guidance in the exercise by the child of the rights recognised'. Nevertheless, parents should not overlook the article's qualifying phrase, which emphasises that parental direction and guidance should only be provided 'in a manner consistent with the evolving capacities of the child'. Furthermore, Articles 12, 13 and 14 of the Convention all emphasise the child's right to develop a capacity for independent thought and action. While Article 12 guarantees the right of all children who are capable of forming their own views, the right to express those views over matters to do with their upbringing,[69] Articles 13 and 14 secure their freedom of expression and their freedom of thought, conscience and religion.

Although domestic legislation could usefully guide parental attitudes, the Children Act (CA) 1989 and subsequent amending legislation signally failed to seize the opportunity to do so. Admittedly, the substitution of 'parental responsibility' for the old 'parental rights and duties' 'reflect[s] the everyday reality of being a parent';[70] it also discourages the idea that children are under parents' absolute control. Nevertheless, the failure to impose a duty on parents to consult their children over important matters regarding their own future is disappointing. Indeed, given the Law Commission's view that requiring the courts to consider children's views[71] would reflect 'the increasing recognition given both in practice and in law to the child's status as a human being in his own right, rather than the object of the rights of others',[72] it is surprising that no one apparently thought of requiring parents to do the same. Equally surprising was the failure to remedy this gap in the law when the CA 1989 was amended by later legislation. Thus, although the duty imposed on local authorities to consult children before reaching decisions relating to them[73] was extended by the CA 2004,[74] the legislative opportunity then to impose consultative duties on parents was missed.

This gap in the English legislation compares unfavourably with the Children (Scotland) Act 1995, section 6(1), which requires any parent, when reaching 'any major decision' involving his child's upbringing, to 'have regard so far as is practicable to the views (if he wishes to express them) of the child concerned'.[75]

---

[68] E.g. many divorcing parents fail to consult even quite mature children over their proposed arrangements for their children's future upbringing; see discussion in Chapter 12.
[69] See Chapter 12.   [70] Law Commission (1988) para. 2.4.   [71] CA 1989, s. 1(3)(a).
[72] Law Commission (1988) para. 3.24.   [73] CA 1989, s. 22(4)(a) and (5)(a).
[74] CA 2004, s. 53(1) and (3).
[75] Children (Scotland) Act 1995, s. 6(1) provides: 'A person shall, in reaching any major decision which involves –

Many parents aspire to moving into a more democratic, negotiated and 'open' style of communication with their teenage children,[76] but find it difficult to put this into practice.[77] Unlike their English counterparts, Scottish parents are under a legislative duty to do so. Furthermore, the legal presumption that a child of 12 years of age or more is 'of sufficient age and maturity to form a view' on such decisions requires a Scottish parent to justify reaching a decision without consulting his child, if the latter has attained such an age.[78] Interestingly, the Scottish Law Commission considered that the age limit of 12 was in line with psychological evidence on children's intellectual development, but recommended that the word 'maturity' was used, rather than 'understanding', to ensure that it is not merely a child's cognitive development which is considered.[79] Although this recommendation was not supported by reference to any particularly weighty psychological research, such a view seems reasonably consistent with the research evidence discussed above. Indeed, given that the provision does not give children the right to make decisions, but merely to require parents to consider their views, it seems rather conservative in its approach. After all, all children are rights-holders under Article 12 of the CRC and even very young children are often capable of forming and expressing a view.[80]

The imposition of a duty on Scottish parents to consult their children was prompted by the Scottish Law Commission's view that such a provision would emphasise 'that the child is a person in his or her own right and that his or her views are entitled to respect and consideration'.[81] It also noted that legislation incorporating such a provision would be consistent with Article 12 of the CRC and that a number of other legal systems had already introduced a similar provision, including Germany, Sweden, Norway and Finland. The Scottish Law Commission openly acknowledged the difficulties involved in introducing such a 'vague and unenforceable' provision, in particular the fact that there is no obvious sanction. It also admitted that it would not always be easy to distinguish 'major' decisions from 'minor' ones. Nevertheless, it considered that the benefits of introducing such a provision outweighed the difficulties, particularly because it could influence behaviour.[82]

(a) his fulfilling a parental responsibility or the responsibility mentioned in section 5(1) of this Act; or

(b) his exercising a parental right or giving consent by virtue of that section, have regard so far as practicable to the views (if he wishes to express them) of the child concerned, taking account of the child's age and maturity . . . and without prejudice to the generality of this subsection a child twelve years of age or more shall be presumed to be of sufficient age and maturity to form a view.'

[76] W. Langford *et al.* (2001) p. 36.   [77] Ibid. chs 7 and 8.
[78] Scottish Law Commission (1992) paras 2.63–2.65.   [79] Ibid.
[80] See discussion in Chapter 12.   [81] Scottish Law Commission (1992) para. 2.62.
[82] The use of legislation as an educative tool and a means to influence parental behaviour can also be seen elsewhere in domestic law. See e.g. the presumption of parental involvement introduced by Children and Families Act 2014, s. 11, discussed in Chapter 6.

The failure of the English legislation to introduce a similar provision suggests to parents here that there is no need for them to consult their children, whatever their age and irrespective of the importance of the decision. This omission reflects the government's assumption in this context that parents will comply with their parental responsibilities, with no guidance on how to do so. One might excuse the English legislation by pointing out that, unlike the Children (Scotland) Act 1995, the CA 1989 was drafted before the publication of the CRC; consequently, its draftsmen were not privy to the terms of Article 12, which was to become so influential throughout the world. But this excuse overlooks not only the wider implications of the decision in *Gillick v. West Norfolk and Wisbech Area Health Authority*,[83] decided well before the introduction of the CA 1989, but also the much later CA 2004, which, as noted above, tacked onto the CA 1989 various duties on local authorities, but omitted any mention of parents. Indeed, the extent of legal parental authority over their adolescent children remains very uncertain.

(B) *Gillick*: Autonomy and Best Interests

The House of Lords' decision in *Gillick v. West Norfolk and Wisbech Area Health Authority*[84] remains the pivotal case on adolescent autonomy and parental authority. The decision appeared to herald an enlightened approach to the parental role and to establish new legal boundaries for parents' relationships with their adolescent children. Much of the language used in the case seemed to endorse the view that mature adolescents had the legal capacity to make important decisions on their own lives even against the objection of their parents. Both Lord Fraser and Lord Scarman cited with approval Lord Denning's famous words in *Hewer v. Bryant*,[85] in which he emphasised that:

> the legal right of a parent to the custody of a child ends at the 18th birthday: and even up till then, it is a dwindling right which the courts will hesitate to enforce against the wishes of the child, and the more so the older he is. It starts with a right of control and ends with little more than advice.[86]

Similarly, Lord Scarman was uncompromising regarding the position of parents. In his view:

> [the] parental right yields to the child's right to make his own decisions when he reaches a sufficient understanding and intelligence to be capable of making up his own mind on the matter requiring decision.[87]

---

[83] [1986] AC 112.

[84] Ibid. The particular issue considered in the *Gillick* case concerned adolescent access to contraceptive advice and treatment without parental knowledge or consent. This aspect of the case and its application in medical decision-making is considered in Chapter 11.

[85] [1970] 1 QB 357.   [86] Ibid. at 369.   [87] [1986] AC 112, at 186.

These words indicate very plainly that he was concerned with the broad issue of potential conflicts between parent and child, in the light of adolescents' developing capacity for adult autonomy. There seemed little doubt in his mind that parents had no right to oppose their children once they had reached sufficient understanding and intelligence to make up their own minds on the matter in question. Lord Fraser's views were, in the main, restricted to the narrow confines of consenting to contraceptive treatment and advice. Nevertheless, he too made some general remarks about the need to encourage adolescents' capacity for independence:

> It is, in my view, contrary to the ordinary experience of mankind, at least in Western Europe in the present century, to say that a child or young person remains in fact under the complete control of his parents until he attains the definite age of majority ... In practice most wise parents relax their control gradually as the child develops and encourage him or her to become increasingly independent.[88]

Such an approach was remarkably enlightened, particularly bearing in mind that their Lordships were dealing with the legal capacity of adolescents under the age of 16 to reach decisions for themselves. Their finding that doctors could provide mature teenage girls with contraceptive treatment without requiring parental consent was timely.[89] But it went much further and translated into law what their Lordships clearly perceived to be the moral right of adolescents to take responsibility for *all* important decisions in their lives, when competent to do so. It also went considerably further than Article 12 of the CRC, which merely requires participation in decision-making, not that children's choices should be complied with. At the most, Article 12(1) requires a child's views to be given 'due weight', depending on his or her age and maturity.

In some senses, the decision in *Gillick* has proved to be remarkably successful. The principle that competent minors may take effective decisions, regardless of their parents' ignorance or even opposition, is firmly established in law. This principle has liberalised their legal position across a wide range of areas, far beyond the original medical context. The decisions of mature minors have been recognised in such diverse fields as adoption,[90] media publicity,[91] relocation,[92] restrictions on liberty[93] and participation in court proceedings.[94] Nevertheless, despite its enormous influence, *Gillick* has not delivered the far-reaching form of

---

[88] Ibid. at 171.   [89] Discussed in Chapter 11.

[90] *Re S (Child as Parent: Adoption: Consent)* [2017] EWHC 2729 (Fam), [2018] 2 WLR 1029: concerning the question of whether the mother, aged under 16, was competent to consent to the adoption of her child.

[91] *Re Roddy (A Child) (Identification: Restriction on Publication)* [2003] EWHC 2927 (Fam), [2004] 2 FLR 949.

[92] *AS v. CPW (Inward Return Order)* [2020] EWHC 1238 (Fam), [2020] Fam Law 1019, in the context of an inward return application. See also *S v. S (Relocation)* [2017] EWHC 2345 (Fam), [2018] 1 FLR 825.

[93] *A Local Authority v. D* [2016] EWHC 3473 (Fam).

[94] *Mabon v. Mabon* [2005] EWCA Civ 634, [2005] 2 FLR 1011.

adolescent autonomy that it initially appeared to promise.[95] The shortcomings of *Gillick* fall into two broad categories. First, the decision itself contains ambiguities and inconsistencies both within and between judgments. In particular, there is a lack of clarity as to how competence should be assessed. More fundamentally, it is unclear whether the rationale for the decision in *Gillick* is found in respect for adolescent autonomy, or in paternalism, albeit tempered by acknowledgement that the strongly held views of adolescents will often be crucial in determining their best interests. Second, while *Gillick* appeared radical and forward-thinking when it was decided, the case is now showing its age and is increasingly showing strain in its relationship with the wider law on human rights and capacity. The case was decided before much of the research on adolescent development discussed above was carried out. It also pre-dates the CRC and HRA, as well as the Children Act 1989 and the changes in approach to adult[96] capacity in the Mental Capacity Act (MCA) 2005. While the case law has explored some of these tensions, there remain conflicts between them and a risk that subsequent interpretation of *Gillick* means that *Gillick* competence can act as a break on respect for adolescent decisions despite its initial promise.

(C) *Gillick*: Ambiguities and Limitations

The passages from *Gillick* quoted above suggest that once a minor demonstrates competence in relation to a particular decision, they obtain the right to make that decision and that their parents lose *all* rights in respect of it, even if the parent considers that the child's best interests would be best served by overriding their decision. On this reading of *Gillick*, John Eekelaar considered that mature minors had 'in wider measure than ever before, that most dangerous but most precious of rights: the right to make their own mistakes'.[97] If this were correct, then *Gillick* would indeed have granted mature children autonomy: legal capacity would be defined by competence to decide the matter and not by the wisdom of the child's choice. This reading of *Gillick* was, however, controversial and primarily based on the judgment of Lord Scarman. The judgment of Lord Fraser[98] could be read as allowing for a far greater degree of paternalism. For Lord Fraser, the child could only be treated in accordance with her wishes if a series of conditions were met. These conditions included a finding that it was in the child's best interests to receive advice or treatment without parental consent. On this reading, the child's ability to consent to treatment remained subject to an external check on her best interests, albeit one reached by a doctor rather than her parents. As a consequence, there has

---

[95]　J. Eekelaar (1986).

[96]　The MCA 2005 applies to those over 16 who lack capacity at a particular time 'because of an impairment of, or a disturbance in the functioning of, the mind or brain': MCA 2005, s. 2(1).

[97]　J. Eekelaar (1986) p. 182.　　[98]　With whom Lord Scarman agreed.

been a long running debate as to the extent to which *Gillick*'s promise of autonomy is tempered by paternalism.[99]

Only a short time elapsed before the Court of Appeal, in *Re R (A Minor) (Wardship: Consent to Treatment)*[100] and *Re W (A Minor) (Medical Treatment: Court's Jurisdiction)*,[101] comprehensively undermined their Lordships' attempt to ensure that parents respected their adolescents' capacity for autonomy. In each case, the subject of the application was resisting life-saving medical treatment and in each the Court of Appeal held that under its inherent jurisdiction, a court can override a young patient's wishes and authorise life-saving treatment.[102] While it is arguable that judicial scrutiny of a minor's decision to imperil their own life can be justified as a means of protecting the child's Article 2 right to life, the Court of Appeal's approach was controversial. Rather than confining their reasoning to the courts' own powers to override the wishes of a teenage patient,[103] the Court of Appeal appeared to establish the principle that *anyone* with parental responsibility can provide legal authority to authorise medical treatment, despite the child's own clear opposition.[104] Accordingly, Lord Scarman's view in *Gillick* that 'the parental right *yields* to the child's right to make his own decisions when he reaches a sufficient understanding and intelligence to be capable of making up his own mind on the matter requiring decision'[105] apparently has no effect on parents' right to consent on the child's behalf. Since their right to consent survives the child's achieving *Gillick* competence,[106] that phrase merely means that parents cannot veto *affirmative* decisions reached by such a child. According to *Gillick*, whatever his or her age, parents cannot overrule an adolescent's consent to any procedure that he or she has the competence to comprehend fully. But, according to the Court of Appeal, those very same parents can themselves consent to any procedure on behalf of an adolescent of any age or competence, as long as they consider it to be in his or her best interests, and even if the adolescent objects violently. In this respect, the law not only created inordinate

---

[99] Discussed by S. Gilmore (2009) and J. Fortin (2011).

[100] [1992] Fam 11: the Court of Appeal authorised the compulsory use of anti-psychotic drugs to treat a 15-year-old suffering from increasingly paranoid and disturbed behaviour.

[101] [1993] Fam 64: the Court of Appeal authorised the compulsory treatment of a 16-year-old in a dangerously anorexic state. The legal competence of 16-year-olds to consent to medical treatment is recognised by statute (FLRA 1969, s. 8(1)), but this was held not to extend to *refusal* of treatment: this aspect of the case is discussed further in Chapter 11.

[102] *Re R (A Minor) (Wardship: Consent to Treatment)* [1992] Fam 11, per Lord Donaldson of Lymington MR, at 25. These cases are considered in further detail in the medical context in Chapter 11.

[103] See below.

[104] This proposition was introduced in *Re R (A Minor) (Wardship: Consent to Treatment)* [1992] Fam 11 and fully developed in *Re W (A Minor) (Medical Treatment: Courts' Jurisdiction)* [1993] Fam 64.

[105] [1986] AC 112, at 186 (emphasis added).

[106] *Re W (A Minor) (Medical Treatment: Courts' Jurisdiction)* [1993] Fam 64, per Lord Donaldson MR, at 78 and Balcombe LJ, at 87.

confusion, but retreated significantly from *Gillick*. Predictably, this case law attracted a storm of criticism.[107]

Both Lord Donaldson MR and Balcombe LJ seemed clearly aware of the implications of undermining *Gillick* in this way and were keen in *Re W* to stress that the wishes of a mature adolescent should always be given great weight. Lord Donaldson MR made this clear when he said:

> Adolescence is a period of progressive transition from childhood to adulthood and as experience of life is acquired and intelligence and understanding grow, so will the scope of the decision-making which should be left to the minor, for it is only by making decisions and experiencing the consequences that decision-making skills will be acquired ... 'good parenting involves giving minors as much rope as they can handle without an unacceptable risk that they will hang themselves'.[108]

He and his colleagues in the Court of Appeal suggested that the courts would be extremely slow to overrule the decisions of adolescents who had already attained the age of 16. But they appeared to overlook the fact that such moderation in the hands of the judiciary is of little relevance to an adolescent whose tyrannical and obsessive parents are endeavouring to force on him or her a wholly unwanted course of action. Lord Donaldson MR and Balcombe LJ acknowledged in *Re W* that parents might endeavour to force adolescents to undergo procedures against their will. But they only envisaged this happening in a medical context, more particularly in the context of a teenage girl being forced by her parents to have an abortion against her wishes. This overlooks the fact that the principle they established is not confined to medical matters and has a general application. More remarkably, the principle applies to all adolescents up to their 18th birthdays. The legal limitation on the parents' activities is that their choices for their child must be consistent with the child's best interests. But the best interests test is too subjective[109] to deter bullying parents from seeing only their own point of view. While it is arguable that the judiciary should be able to override those minors who refuse life-saving treatment, the Court of Appeal did not perceive the dangers of handing back to parents so much of the power removed from them by the House of Lords in *Gillick*. Only a radical reassessment of the law can address the complete lack of coherence between the *Gillick* principle and that contained in the later case law. The *Gillick* decision contained a powerful message to parents intent on maintaining a repressive and authoritarian family regime. They should heed the law which acknowledges adolescents' increasing ability to make important decisions for themselves. The later decisions appeared to be saying the opposite. The fact that a court is unlikely to uphold the repressive decisions of domineering parents is neither here nor there. Unlike the exercise of

---

[107] Inter alia: G. Douglas (1992); M. Freeman (2005); discussed in more detail in Chapter 11.

[108] *Re W (A Minor) (Medical Treatment: Courts' Jurisdiction)* [1993] Fam 64, at 81.

[109] See discussion in Chapter 4.

paternalism by the judiciary, which is at least open to public scrutiny, parental paternalism is restrained only by the indeterminacy of the best interests test and hidden from view by the curtain of family privacy. Judicial unease with this position is evident from the lack of subsequent case law reconfirming the power of parents to overrule their competent children and from obiter observations doubting that parental responsibility includes the power to do so.[110]

In both *Re R* and *Re W*, the Court of Appeal's findings that the courts and parents could overrule the refusal of a competent child were in fact obiter: the children in question were found not to have the necessary *Gillick* competence to refuse treatment. Similarly, in subsequent cases, courts have often found adolescents to lack competence when making decisions that might be considered to be against their best interests, rather than finding them competent but then overruling them on the basis of their best interests.[111] The reasons given for lack of competence in many of these cases seem somewhat flimsy. For example, in *F* v. *F*,[112] a 15-year-old vegan who objected to having the MMR vaccine, in part because it contained animal products, was treated as incompetent on the basis that adopting such a fixed stance demonstrated a lack of maturity.[113] Yet, as Jonathan Herring points out, many people hold strong moral principles that they believe to be absolute and it is not clear why adopting a considered value system should indicate lack of capacity.[114] Incredibly, the court did not make an explicit finding as to the girl's competence or capacity, but treated the matter as a parental dispute. To give a non-consensual vaccination against the considered objections of an 'intelligent, articulate and thoughtful' 15-year-old, without a proper finding as to her capacity or consideration of the harm that might be caused by acting without her consent, demonstrates the ease with which adolescent autonomy is sidelined by the courts despite the strong statements in *Gillick*. Similarly, in other cases,[115] adolescents have been found to lack capacity because they have not been furnished with the information necessary to understand the consequences of their decision,[116] have led a sheltered life,[117] or may not fully appreciate the emotional consequences of the decision for their family.[118] Much of the case law on *Gillick* competence appears focused on finding

---

[110] *AB* v. *CD* [2021] EWHC 741 (Fam), at [52]–[70]. See Chapter 11 for a fuller argument, in the context of medical treatment, that parental responsibility should no longer be regarded as including the legal capacity of parents to overrule the decisions of their competent offspring.

[111] A. McFarlane (2011). Although see *Re E (Children: Blood Transfusion)* [2021] EWCA Civ 1888, discussed further in Chapter 11, for an example of a case of overruling adolescents who had been found to be competent.

[112] [2013] EWHC 2683 (Fam).

[113] The finding of lack of competence is implied by Theis J's conclusion that the girl's reasons displayed a lack of maturity and balance: [2013] EWHC 2683 (Fam), at [22].

[114] J. Herring (2016) p. 51.

[115] These cases are primarily concerned with medical treatment and are considered in more detail in Chapter 11.

[116] *Re L (Medical Treatment: Gillick Competency)* [1999] 2 FCR 524.   [117] Ibid.

[118] *Re E (A Minor) (Wardship: Medical Treatment)* [1993] 1 FLR 386.

reasons not to respect the views of children rather than seeking to take them seriously.

The ease with which adolescent competence can be avoided by the courts is in part a reflection of the uncertainty inherent in the concept of *Gillick* competence. Making an adolescent's legal capacity hinge on notions as debatable as 'understanding' and 'maturity' fundamentally hampers its effectiveness and clarity. This is particularly true of 'maturity', which goes beyond intellectual capacity and may include appreciation for a broad range of emotional, social and psychological factors. Given the subjectivity inherent in assessing any of these factors for a given decision, the *Gillick* test of competence can easily morph into a paternalistic assessment of whether the minor has made a wise decision rather than an assessment of competence to make the decision.[119] Further, the *Gillick* test contains no guidance over the extent to which an adjustment should be made for factors affecting the adolescent's decision, such as peer pressure, drug and substance abuse, family stress, emotional disturbance, or physical and mental illness. The difficulties of applying the *Gillick* test not only mean that it can be problematic for courts and for professionals such as clinicians,[120] but also that it creates considerable uncertainty for parents and for the adolescent themselves. The law provides little clarity on the ambit of parental responsibility for the mature child. In practice, a definitive ruling on an adolescent's legal competence in various situations can only emerge through applying for the courts' assistance over the matter, but this is haphazard and dependent on relevant cases reaching the courts. In the absence of clear guidance, many parents might assume that their offspring have no legal right to reach major decisions regarding their lives.

(D) *Gillick*, the HRA 1998 and Facilitating Competence

The decision in *Gillick* was made more than a decade before the HRA 1998 was enacted. Although children possess rights under the HRA, there was a strong argument that the Act would actually erode the position of teenagers, by enhancing parents' ability to control their teenage offspring by reference to their own rights under Article 8. How would Mrs Gillick have fared had she gone to court after the implementation of the HRA 1998, instead of when she did, in the mid-1980s? Some of these issues were clarified when Ms Axon adopted a very similar position to that of Victoria Gillick in 2006. *R (Axon) v. Secretary of State for Health and the Family Planning Association*[121] provided Silber J with a good opportunity to show how the *Gillick* principles regarding the interrelationship between parents and adolescents can be aligned within the European Convention on Human Rights and Fundamental Freedoms (ECHR) framework of rights. Ms Axon had claimed that parents are legally responsible for all aspects of their children's welfare, including matters to do

---

[119] E. Cave (2014).   [120] See Chapter 11.   [121] [2006] EWHC 37 (Admin), [2006] 2 FLR 206.

with their health and sexuality, and that if doctors keep consultations with children secret, this undermines parents' ability to advise and help them on sexual matters.[122] She also claimed that such rights and responsibilities are reinforced by Article 8 of the ECHR. While the narrow focus of medical confidentiality, alongside the *Gillick* decision,[123] is discussed elsewhere in this text,[124] Silber J's treatment of the more general aspects of the parent–child relationship in the light of the HRA 1998 is instructive.

In Silber J's view, a close reading of the *Gillick* decision refuted all of Ms Axon's claims; it remained good law and was unaffected by Ms Axon's right under Article 8 of the ECHR to have her family life respected by the state. That being so, he attempted valiantly to translate the scope of parents' rights, as delineated by *Gillick*, into Convention-compatible terms. His conviction that any parental right or power under Article 8 is no wider than that delineated by the common law[125] led to his translating their Lordships' idea that parental authority dwindles as the child develops decision-making skills into the confines of Article 8. Thus, in his view, a parent's right to exercise control over his child, including the right to be notified over medical consultations, dwindles and then comes to an end as her teenage offspring reaches an age when (in Lord Scarman's words) 'he reaches a sufficient understanding and intelligence to be capable of making up his own mind on the matter requiring decision'.[126] Ms Axon's parental rights under Article 8 to advise and guide her daughters had therefore terminated on their attaining *Gillick* competence. This idea of parents simply *losing* their right to respect for family life, as soon as their children gain sufficient understanding to reach decisions for themselves, is not supported by Strasbourg jurisprudence,[127] despite its representing the House of Lords' view in *Gillick* of the common law.[128] There is, however, a cogent argument that the parent's right to enjoy family life under Article 8 does not necessarily carry a right to control his or her children throughout their minority. Family life exists between parents and children, but 'respecting' that family life will require diminishing recognition of parental rights of control as the child matures.[129]

It would surely have been more plausible for Silber J to approach a situation of this kind, where parent and child obviously have conflicting Convention rights, on the basis that an appropriate balance must be found between them.[130] The balance will tip in the child's favour as he or she grows in understanding and intelligence – at which point, the state can justify (under Article 8(2)) infringing the mother's rights under Article 8(1) by reference to the child's own rights under Article 8(1). But Silber J did not pursue such an approach when he dealt with the alternative argument – that (in the event of

---

[122] Ibid. at [44]–[45].
[123] *Gillick v. West Norfolk and Wisbech Area Health Authority* [1986] AC 112.
[124] In Chapter 11. [125] [2006] EWHC 37 (Admin), [2006] 2 FLR 206, at [132].
[126] Ibid. at [130]. [127] R. Taylor (2007) pp. 90–2. [128] Ibid. p. 90. [129] Ibid. p. 91.
[130] For a discussion of the 'ultimate balancing test', see J. Fortin (2006b) pp. 306–10.

his being wrong in his view that Ms Axon's Article 8 rights had simply terminated) the state could justify infringing her rights by reference to Article 8(2). When considering this issue, he referred rather generally to a variety of reasons justifying the state infringing her right to family life. Admittedly, he stated that young people have the same rights under Article 8(1) to medical confidentiality as adults,[131] but he made no real attempt to analyse all the specific Convention rights enjoyed by Ms Axon's daughters which might conflict with those of their mother. The judiciary not uncommonly analyse the rights that *adults* have, but fail to articulate those of the children.[132] In this instance, *Axon* was an important decision affecting the lives of teenage girls generally which failed to clarify exactly what Convention rights they have and how they might be balanced against those of their mother. This suggests a reluctance to engage with the notion that children have rights under the ECHR which may actually override those of their parents.[133]

Such an omission is odd given Silber J's careful assessment of the developing recognition of children's rights generally. Having reviewed the extensive protection of children's rights provided by the CRC,[134] he referred to the case law endorsing the view that:

> the right of young people to make decisions about their own lives by themselves at the expense of the views of their parents has now become an increasingly important and accepted feature of family life.[135]

He referred also to 'this change in the landscape of family matters, in which the rights of children are becoming increasingly important'.[136] Despite its failure to engage with the specific rights of the girls involved in the case, this aspect of Silber J's decision is important for the way that it can be seen as part of a 'growing movement towards greater recognition and autonomy of children'.[137] Alongside these developments for adolescents, there has been a similar 'rights-based paradigm shift'[138] to capacity in adults,[139] which may inform developing approaches to adolescent decision-making.

The law on adults who may lack capacity is found in the Mental Capacity Act (MCA) 2005, which seeks to facilitate and support decision-making by giving all appropriate support to enable the individual to make their own

---

[131] [2006] EWHC 37 (Admin), [2006] 2 FLR 206, at [127].   [132] J. Fortin (2006b) pp. 302–3.

[133] J. Fortin (2006a) p. 764.

[134] *R (Axon)* v. *Secretary of State for Health and the Family Planning Association* [2006] EWHC 37 (Admin), [2006] 2 FLR 206, at [76]–[79].

[135] Ibid. at [79]. The case law he referred to was *Mabon* v. *Mabon* [2005] EWCA Civ 634, [2005] 2 FLR 1011, per Thorpe LJ, at [26] and [28]; *R (on the application of Williamson and others)* v. *Secretary of State for Education and Employment and others* [2005] UKHL 15, [2005] 2 All ER 1, per Baroness Hale of Richmond, at [80].

[136] *R (Axon)*, ibid. at [80].   [137] R. Taylor (2007) p. 93.   [138] E. Cave (2014) pp. 112–13.

[139] The MCA 2005 primarily governs adult decision-making (including medical decision-making), but also governs decision-making on behalf of minors aged between 16 and 18 whose incapacity to reach decisions for themselves is attributable to an impairment of or a disturbance in the functioning of his or her mind or brain.

decision or maximise their participation in the decision-making process.[140] The MCA 2005 applies to people over 16, who therefore benefit from the presumption that they have capacity, and is concerned with difficulties in decision-making attributable to an impairment of or a disturbance in the functioning of the mind or brain.[141] The context of a younger adolescent, to whom the presumption of capacity does not apply and who is not suffering from such impairment, is rather different. Notably, for those under 16, the burden of proof is different in that they must prove their competence rather than relying on the presumption of capacity.[142] The MCA 2005 cannot be applied directly to minors; nonetheless, the ethos of facilitating capacity and underlying principles might usefully be drawn upon to inform assessments of *Gillick* competence.[143] The MCA 2005 stresses that a person should not be treated as lacking capacity in the absence of practicable help to assist in reaching a decision,[144] nor simply because the decision reached appears unwise,[145] nor because the person can only retain information relevant to the decision for short periods only.[146] Arguably, the principles underlying the MCA 2005 could be helpful in making the *Gillick* competence formula more workable and address some of the weaknesses and subjectivity in the current case law considered above. It has been suggested that as the judiciary gain experience of the principles of the MCA 2005, so there is an increased willingness to utilise this experience of balancing autonomy and best interests and read across this ethos to cases involving minors.[147]

The use of the MCA 2005 to inform *Gillick* competence has been endorsed in *Re S (Child as Parent: Adoption: Consent)*.[148] The case concerned a child mother, S, aged under 16, who suffered from developmental delay and learning difficulties. She wished to have nothing to do with her young baby, but instead to consent to the baby being placed for adoption; the question for the court was whether she had competence to do so. The answer to that question depended on whether she possessed *Gillick* competence, but in order to assess that competence Cobb J drew on the MCA 2005, which he found to be complementary and helpful to the *Gillick* assessment.[149] As adoption is one of the most serious orders that a court can make, the difficulty for the court was in

---

[140] DCA (2007) para. 1.2.   [141] MCA 2005, s. 2.

[142] Ibid., s. 2(5). There are difficulties in straightforwardly drawing on the MCA 2005 to develop the law for those under 16, given that the MCA 2005 is based on the presumption that adults possess capacity (MCA 2005, s. 1(2)), which is not applicable to those under 16s. Further, the MCA 2005 is concerned with those for whom incapacity is attributable to an impairment of or a disturbance in the functioning of his or her mind or brain, and so cannot be applied wholesale for those under 16 who do not have such a diagnosis.

[143] A. McFarlane (2011); V. Chico and L. Haggar (2011); E. Cave (2014).

[144] MCA 2005, s. 1(3). See also s. 3(2) and (4), which stress that the person should be given an explanation of the information relevant to the decision in a way appropriate to his circumstances (e.g. using simple language or visual aids), including information about the reasonably foreseeable consequences of deciding one way or the other or of failing to decide.

[145] Ibid., s. 1(4).   [146] Ibid., s. 3(3).   [147] A. McFarlane (2011).

[148] [2017] EWHC 2729 (Fam), [2018] 2 WLR 1029.   [149] Ibid. at [15]–[19].

ensuring that S had a full understanding of the decision, without setting the requisite level of understanding so high that it would artificially restrict S's ability to participate in the decision. The approach based on the MCA 2005 favoured an answer that facilitated S's involvement and ensured she understood the fundamental legal consequences, without requiring intricate understanding of the niceties of the complex statutory framework. Further, again drawing on the MCA 2005, all practicable steps were to be taken to give this information to S in an appropriate way that she could understand. In adopting this approach, the court stressed that S's right to autonomous decision-making under Article 8 of the ECHR would be enhanced.[150]

Re S is a good example of the way in which the *Gillick* framework can be adapted to incorporate a rights-based approach to adolescent decision-making. It is, however, not clear whether this approach will become widely used in *Gillick* assessments,[151] particularly as Cobb J was careful to note that his approach was desirable, but not mandatory. In *Re S*, the legislative framework for adoption included express reference to the MCA 2005[152] and Cobb J was clearly influenced by the benefits of a consistent approach to those who were just before and just after their 16th birthday; for this reason, it is not necessarily clear that the same approach would be applied outside of this statutory context. Further, all parties involved were agreed that it was overwhelmingly likely that adoption would be the best outcome; a finding of competence would therefore assist, rather than impede, the result the court considered in both children's best interests. Whether a similar facilitative approach will be taken in cases where the child's wishes conflict with the court's assessment is rather more doubtful. The principle that a person is not to be treated as unable to make a decision merely because the decision that they wish to make is unwise,[153] would require a far more rigorous approach to children's capacity than that adopted in much of the case law. While this would be desirable, the paternalism evident in much of the post-*Gillick* case law suggests that the judiciary is reluctant to allow adolescents the freedom to make unwise decisions. Indeed, as Cave argues, without the benefit of the presumption of capacity that applies to adults, the MCA 2005 may be applied to make more stringent demands on children than is the case under *Gillick*. In particular, the requirement to be able to retain, use and weigh information may set a rather higher standard that *Gillick* envisaged in relation to relatively straightforward decisions, and so in these cases may make it more difficult

---

[150] Ibid. at [41]–[43].

[151] *Re S* has been cited with apparent approval in *Bell* v. *Tavistock and Portman NHS Trust* [2020] EWHC 3274 (Admin), [2022] 1 FLR 30, at [116]–[118], but doubted in *Re X (A Child) (No. 2)* [2021] EWHC 65 (Fam), [2021] 4 WLR 11, at [70]–[76]. Similarly, in *Barts NHS Foundation Trust* v. *Shalina Begum, Muhhamed Raqeeb and Tafida Raqeeb (by Her Children's Guardian)* [2019] EWHC 2530 (Fam), at [123], McDonald J, speaking in the context of a much younger child, warned against importing wholesale the MCA 2005 principles into cases under the Children Act 1989.

[152] Adoption and Children Act 2002, s. 52(1)(a).   [153] MCA 2005, s. 1(4).

for a minor to prove the ability to give effective consent.[154] For these reasons, the MCA 2005 is unlikely to provide a full answer to the limitations of the *Gillick* test. Nonetheless, its principles are useful in emphasising the importance of giving appropriate support to facilitate and develop the capacity of young people to make their own decisions. In this way, the experience of the MCA 2005 can be useful in applying a rights-based framework to children's capacity that reflects children's evolving capacities and participation rights.[155]

(5) Deprivation of Liberty

The law on deprivation of liberty provides a particularly good example of the law's increased emphasis on autonomy, and of the ambiguities in the nature and extent of parental responsibility for adolescents. Children and young people may find themselves subject to restrictions on their liberty in order to protect their safety and well-being for a variety of reasons, including: mental health needs; learning disabilities; behaviour that poses a serious risk to themselves or others; or, in extreme cases, as protection from some forms of harm such as child sexual exploitation.[156] Restrictions on the liberty of children and young people in these circumstances may well be necessary for their protection and best interests, but the mere fact that restrictions are motivated by a benign intention to protect the individual concerned is not enough to justify such a serious limitation on their human rights.[157] The ECtHR[158] and the Supreme Court[159] have developed a detailed case law on the requirements of the right to liberty in Article 5 of the ECHR and the need for proper safeguards for those deprived of their liberty to ensure that the restrictions are justified, follow a procedure prescribed by law and are kept under review. The application of this case law to adults is far from straightforward,[160] but in relation to minors it is extraordinarily complex and inconsistent. While Article 5 of the ECHR clearly applies to everyone, regardless of age, the uncertain limits of parental responsibility have posed difficulties for children and young people in establishing that they have been deprived of their liberty in the first place.

---

[154] E. Cave (2014).   [155] See A. Daly (2020) for an approach to capacity based on the CRC.

[156] E.g. *Re W (A Child) (Secure Accommodation Order)* [2016] EWCA Civ 804, [2016] 4 WLR 159: imposition of a secure accommodation order on a young woman aged 17 years and 8 months who the court found to be the victim of child sex exploitation.

[157] The focus of the litigation in this area has been on the right to liberty under ECHR, Art. 5, although other rights may well be relevant, most notably where there are restrictions that affect the child's relationships under ECHR, Art. 8.

[158] Most notably in *Storck* v. *Germany* (2006) 43 EHRR 6.

[159] *Cheshire West and Chester Council* v. *P* [2014] UKSC 19, [2014] AC 896; *Re D (A Child)* [2019] UKSC 42, [2019] 1 WLR 5403.

[160] Law Commission (2017). The government accepted most of the Law Commission's recommendations, which are to be implemented through the Mental Capacity Amendment Act 2019.

The application of Article 5 to children has been stymied by the ECtHR's controversial decision in *Nielsen v. Denmark*,[161] which remains one of its leading cases on children's right to liberty and which cannot be ignored when considering the boundaries between parents' rights and those of their children. In *Nielsen*, a 12-year-old boy was placed, at his mother's request, under almost constant surveillance in the closed psychiatric ward of a state hospital for 5.5 months. The fact that the restrictions placed on the boy in *Nielsen* were at his mother's request had clearly presented the ECtHR with a problem. Despite the fact that the child was not suffering from any form of mental illness,[162] the majority of the ECtHR decided that his rights under Article 5 were not even engaged, let alone breached, as the restrictions were authorised by the mother's exercise of her parental rights, which were in turn protected by Article 8. The ECtHR accepted that parents' rights cannot be unlimited and that children must be protected from abuse,[163] but the majority concluded that the mother's authorisation of the lengthy restrictions on her son was for 'a proper purpose'[164] and well within the normal exercise of parental authority. It is notable that the Strasbourg judiciary were far from united in their treatment of the boy's application.[165] Their conclusion that the mother's decision had been for a 'proper purpose' also reflected the view that parental decision-making is not unlimited, but has clear boundaries – albeit rather more widely drawn than the minority thought appropriate. Furthermore, the boy concerned was only 12 years old; the strong implication of the majority decision of the ECtHR being that had he been older, they would not have considered the mother's actions to be so reasonable.[166] Nevertheless, the majority of the judges had a peculiarly authoritarian view of the parental role[167] and in reasoning that the child's rights were not engaged, their decision appeared to deprive children of all protection for their right to liberty if detained with the consent of parents acting within these extraordinarily broad powers. Nonetheless, there are strong reasons for caution in using *Nielsen* to determine the ambit of parental control. Notably, the case was decided before the CRC was concluded. Given the ECtHR's enthusiasm for drawing on the CRC in determining the extent of children's rights,[168] it is almost inconceivable that such a case would be decided today without careful consideration of the importance of the child's evolving capacities, best interests and views in determining the extent of parental powers.[169] This, together with

---

[161] (1988) 11 EHRR 175.

[162] It appears that he suffered from a 'nervous condition'; the problems appear to have originated in a bitter custody battle between the child's parents.

[163] (1988) 11 EHRR 175, at [72].   [164] Ibid. at [69].

[165] The European Commission of Human Rights had favoured the boy's claim, finding, eleven votes to one, a violation of Art. 5(1) and ten votes to two, a violation of Art. 5(4). The ECtHR concluded by only nine votes to seven that Art. 5 was inapplicable.

[166] (1988) 11 EHRR 175, at [72].   [167] J. Fortin (2004) p. 255.   [168] See Chapter 2.

[169] CRC, Arts 5, 3 and 12; see also Art. 37 on the right to liberty.

the ECtHR's greater emphasis on adult autonomy,[170] mean that the court is likely to depart from its now anachronistic interpretation of parental rights. Certainly, the domestic judiciary have expressed doubts as to its scope.[171]

Despite these doubts as to the ability of *Nielsen* to determine the outer limits of parental rights, the case remains authority for the proposition that there are circumstances in which parents can authorise their child's confinement. The courts have struggled to reach consensus as to how this conclusion should be reconciled with the developing law on Article 5. The ECtHR case law has provided a three-part test (the '*Storck* criteria') to assess whether there has been a deprivation of liberty:

(a) the objective component of confinement in a particular restricted place for a not negligible length of time;
(b) the subjective component of lack of valid consent; and
(c) the attribution of responsibility to the state.[172]

The *Storck* criteria play a pivotal role in the modern law by delineating the circumstances in which a person will be deprived of their liberty and the requirements of Article 5 apply. As *Nielsen* pre-dated *Storck* by nearly two decades, the question of how *Nielsen* fits into this framework is somewhat anachronistic, but important for establishing the operation of Article 5 for children. On one reading of *Nielsen*, the restrictions imposed upon him were within the reasonable boundaries of parental control for children of his age, meaning that component (a) was not satisfied. This reading was favoured by Lady Hale in her leading judgment in the seminal case of *Re D*.[173] An alternative reading, favoured by the minority and Court of Appeal in the same case, is that parental consent operated to prevent *Storck* criteria (b) from being fulfilled, such that the child was not legally regarded as being deprived of his liberty and so was not entitled to the safeguards attaching to Article 5.[174] Each of these components poses particular problems for the application of Article 5 to children.

The first problem for children and young people is found in the question of whether they have been subject to confinement in the first place. The 'acid test'

---

[170] E.g., inter alia: *YF* v. *Turkey* (2004) 39 EHRR 34, at [33]; *Storck* v. *Germany* (2006) 43 EHRR 6, at [150]–[152]; *Pretty* v. *United Kingdom* [2002] 2 FLR 45, at [41].

[171] *R (Axon)* v. *Secretary of State for Health and the Family Planning Association* [2006] EWHC 37 (Admin), [2006] 2 FLR 206, at [126]; *D (A Child)* [2017] EWCA Civ 1695, at [23].

[172] *Cheshire West and Chester Council* v. *P* [2014] UKSC 19, [2014] AC 896, at [37]. The case law discussed here is concerned with deprivation of liberty under the responsibility of the state rather than in a private setting. Nonetheless, the state also has positive obligations to protect children in cases where parents have imposed draconian restrictions on their children if the state knew, or ought to have known, of the confinement: *Re A and C (Equality and Human Rights Commission Intervening)* [2010] EWHS 978 (Fam), [2010] 2 FLR 1363. See also *Re D (A Child)* [2019] UKSC 42, [2019] 1 WLR 5403, at [43] and [47].

[173] *Re D (A Child)* [2019] UKSC 42, [2019] 1 WLR 5403, at [35]–[42].

[174] Ibid. at [147]–[156] (Lord Carnwath); he also suggests the case may be seen as an exception to the *Storck* categories.

for confinement in *Storck* criteria (a) is 'whether a person is under the complete supervision and control of those caring for her and is not free to leave the place where she lives'.[175] The obvious problem with this test for children is that it essentially describes the ordinarily expected circumstances of life, at least for young children. Indeed, a parent of a very young child may well be considered guilty of neglect were they not to impose such conditions. To describe a child as subject to 'confinement' in such ordinary circumstances is a stretch of language and may well cause difficulties for the care of young children who are in family settings, such as foster care, under the responsibility of the state.[176] For this reason, the test of whether a child is subject to confinement is assessed by reference to the freedom ordinarily enjoyed by children of the same age and maturity.[177] In applying this test, the appropriate comparator for a child with a mental disability is the restrictions placed on a child of the same age without such disabilities. This is crucial to ensure that children with disabilities are entitled to the same human rights as all children and are entitled to Article 5 protection for any additional restrictions, no matter whether those restrictions are in their best interests.[178] While the test of ordinary freedom may be unproblematic for very young children, who are in clear need of close supervision, it becomes much more difficult for older children and adolescents for whom there is a wider spectrum of opinion as to how much freedom is reasonable and expected.[179] For these older children, the degree of freedom that is ordinarily experienced will not depend solely on their age and maturity, but also on family circumstances, the nature of the local area and the family's values and culture. In *Cheshire West*, Lord Kerr suggested that the 'age', 'station' and 'familial background' of the child would be relevant in determining the relevant comparator.[180] It is not quite clear what Lord Kerr means by the terms 'station' and 'familial background', but it would clearly create undesirable discrepancies in protection for young people were the test of confinement to vary depending on, for example, whether their family background was within a restrictive religious community or a more liberal environment. Although there is inevitable uncertainty in any test that looks to ordinary socially acceptable standards, a greater consistency of judgment is

---

[175] *Cheshire West and Chester Council* v. *P* [2014] UKSC 19, [2014] AC 896, at [54].

[176] *D (A Child)* [2017] EWCA Civ 1695, at [30]–[39].

[177] The issue is discussed in *D (A Child)* [2017] EWCA Civ 1695, at [31]–[39] and [158], drawing esp. on the judgment of Lord Kerr in *Cheshire West and Chester Council* v. *P* [2014] UKSC 19, [2014] AC 896, at [77]–[79]. While this discussion is obiter, the President affirmed the approach in *A-F (Children)* [2018] EWHC 138 (Fam), [2018] 3 WLR 1905, at [29]. See also *Re D (A Child)* [2019] UKSC 42, [2019] 1 WLR 5403, at [39].

[178] *Re D (A Child)* [2019] UKSC 42, [2019] 1 WLR 5403, at [40]–[41].

[179] As Munby P points out in *A-F (Children)* [2018] EWHC 138 (Fam), [2018] 3 WLR 1905, at [31], it is probably unrealistic to consider any young person under 16 as 'free to leave' the family home given the difficulties that would be experienced in seeking to become financially independent and to secure housing. For further discussion, see Chapter 10.

[180] *Cheshire West and Chester Council* v. *P* [2014] UKSC 19, [2014] AC 896, at [77].

likely if the court looks primarily to age and maturity rather than these wider factors in seeking to find a notionally objective comparator.[181]

If the child is subject to confinement under *Storck* criteria (a), the question of consent under criteria (b) then arises. If valid consent is given by a parent or competent child, there will be no deprivation of liberty for the purposes of Article 5. Given the serious consequences for children, it is imperative that the proper scope of this consent is clearly defined. The scope of parental rights is determined by domestic law,[182] but as shown in this chapter, there is considerable uncertainty on where those limits lie, especially for adolescents. The decision of the Supreme Court in *Re D*[183] has brought clarity to those aged 16 and 17. In her detailed analysis of the limits of parental responsibility, Lady Black reached the conclusion that the parents of 16- and 17-year-olds had no authority at common law to consent to the confinement of their children in circumstances that would otherwise amount to a deprivation of liberty.[184] This conclusion reinforced Lady Hale's analysis of Article 5 and her finding that it would be a 'startling proposition' for parents to be able to license the state to deprive their child of liberty and so remove them from the safeguards provided by human rights law.[185] While *Re D* settles the position for 16- and 17-year-olds, the position for younger adolescents remains uncertain. In particular, while *Gillick*-competent children can consent to their confinement, the cases of *Re R*[186] and *Re W*,[187] discussed above, mean that it is not clear whether parental rights can be used to override the refusal of a competent child to accept confinement and so deprive them of their Article 5 safeguards. Further, as Lady Hale observed in *Re D*, her reasoning that parents were not able to authorise the state to impose restrictions on children beyond those normal for their age, applied with equal force to younger children whether or not they lack competence.[188] Given that the question of under-16s did not arise in the case, she declined to express a firm view on the subject, an unwillingness reflected by each of the majority judges.[189] Earlier case law had concluded that parents could consent to such confinement for under-16s, at least if they were not competent to do so themselves.[190] Whether authority survives the decision in *Re D* remains to be decided. If parents can consent, *Gillick* makes clear that parental rights exist for the benefit of the child and for their best

---

[181] In *A-F (Children)* [2018] EWHC 138 (Fam), [2018] 3 WLR 1905, the court considered that as a 'rule of thumb', age 12 is the point at which constant supervision is likely to result in a finding of confinement.

[182] *D (A Child)* [2017] EWCA Civ 1695, at [51].

[183] *Re D (A Child)* [2019] UKSC 42, [2019] 1 WLR 5403.   [184] Ibid. at [55]–[90].

[185] Ibid. at [48]–[49].   [186] *Re R (A Minor) (Wardship: Consent to Treatment)* [1992] Fam 11.

[187] *Re W (A Minor) (Medical Treatment: Courts' Jurisdiction)* [1993] Fam 64.

[188] *Re D (A Child)* [2019] UKSC 42, [2019] 1 WLR 5403, at [50].

[189] Ibid. at [50], [88]–[90], [117] and [159].

[190] *Re D (A Child) (Deprivation of Liberty)* [2015] EWHC 922 (Fam), [2016] 1 FLR 142, a case concerning the same child as the decision of the Supreme Court in *Re D*. Lord Carnwath, dissenting, considered that this case continued to represent the law: ibid. at [159].

interests. This provides some reassurance for children in that their parents cannot authorise their confinement in circumstances that clearly fall outside of their best interests; however. the vagueness of the term 'best interests' and the fact that parents are not obliged to consider the child's views in determining their interests means that this safeguard may be of more limited utility than it first appears. The courts have attempted to inject some degree of objectivity into the best interests test by finding that the 'zone of parental responsibility'[191] is to be determined by reference to 'general community standards',[192] but such standards are extremely difficult to discern given the diversity of views within society on the proper limits of parental control over their adolescent children. As a result, the 'zone of parental responsibility' remains a 'poorly understood and ill-defined concept':[193] adolescents may find themselves subject to draconian limits on their autonomy and deprived of independent oversight, based on the poorly defined powers of their parents.

The uncertainties surrounding the extent of adolescent freedom and the proper ambit of parental authority have resulted in a confusing set of standards by which to assess this most important of rights. Where young people are found to have been deprived of their liberty, they have also faced considerable difficulties in accessing the safeguards that should be guaranteed to them. In order to meet the requirements of Article 5, any deprivation of liberty must be subject to a procedure prescribed by law. Protection for children and young people is reliant on a confusing hotchpotch of legal regimes,[194] each dependent on statutory criteria. Further, as discussed later in this book, the woeful lack of resources available to provide for children in desperate need of urgent care has led to an increased use of the inherent jurisdiction to fill the gaps in provision and lacuna in the statute.[195] Particular problems have been evident due to the

---

[191] The term 'zone of parental responsibility' appears to draw on the similar notion of 'zone of parental control' used in the original Mental Health Code of Practice: DH (2008) para. 36.10. The current Code of Practice replaces the term 'zone of parental control' with 'scope of parental responsibility': DH (2015) p. 168. In determining whether a matter is within the 'scope of parental responsibility', the Code asks whether the decision is one that 'a parent should reasonably be expected to make': DH (2015) paras 19.41–19.43.

[192] *D (A Child)* [2017] EWCA Civ 1695, at [76] and [85].

[193] Law Commission (2017) para. 7.24.

[194] A secure accommodation order made under Children Act 1989, s. 25 provides an important statutory mechanism for those who fall within their scope (discussed further in Chapter 16), but the regime is limited to looked-after children who fulfil the statutory criteria and is not suitable for general authorisation of deprivation of liberty: *AB (A Child: Deprivation of Harm)* (2015) EWHC 3125 (Fam). Further, the extreme shortage of accommodation for those who are within the scope of the statute means that the system is already extremely stretched and often unable to provide for those children who do need care within secure accommodation: *Re M (A Child: Secure Accommodation)* [2017] EWHC 3021 (Fam). Similarly, the Mental Health Act 1983 may be used to authorise detention of children who fall within those statutory provisions. Further, the detention of 16–17-year-olds who lack capacity may be authorised by the Court of Protection, but not that of those under 16.

[195] The use of the inherent jurisdiction to authorise deprivation of liberty is putting some strain on court time and, more importantly, is being used as a means of plugging the gap in resources for

inconsistency in the legal treatment of 16- and 17-year-olds,[196] which creates cases of enormous complexity, with evidence that some public authorities are simply failing to bring cases to court, so depriving young people of their legal rights.[197] The situation for those of this age group who lack capacity should be improved by the introduction of Liberty Protection Safeguards, which replace the former Deprivation of Liberty Safeguards (DoLS). In contrast to DoLs, which only applied to adults, the new regime is available for 16- and 17-year-olds and is intended to provide a more streamlined form of safeguards.[198] Together with the decision in *Re D*, this provides older adolescents with greater protection for their Article 5 rights and demonstrates serious judicial and political engagement with those rights.[199] Despite this progress, the law on deprivation of liberty is an excellent example of the difficulties in translating commitment to children's rights into practical protection without clarity on the central principles governing the lives of adolescents and the responsibilities of their parents.

(6) Conclusion

The research evidence discussed at the beginning of this chapter suggests that children should not be expected to reach decisions for themselves before they are developmentally ready to do so. By then, however, despite starting to develop the skills they need for independent life, they often need their parents' assistance to establish the confidence and maturity to exercise them. As they develop, adolescents acquire greater capacity to achieve growing independence, although still need support to exercise that capacity in conditions that allow them to make best use of their growing maturity. The *Gillick* decision acknowledged that adolescents' sense of responsibility and ability to take control of their own lives are qualities which should be respected. Most parents will happily, or grudgingly, comply with the law's expectations and provide adolescents with an increasing measure of independence. Nevertheless, for those adolescents caught up in family disputes and crises, the law does not provide an effective framework for dealing with their problems. There is a need for considerably greater clarity in the legal principles applying to adolescents

those who would be more appropriately placed under a secure accommodation order. The Supreme Court has confirmed that the inherent jurisdiction can be used to authorise deprivation of liberty for the purposes of Art. 5, but has expressed concerns as to its use: *Re T (A Child)* [2021] UKSC 35, [2021] 3 WLR 643, discussed further in Chapter 16.

[196] *Re W (A Child) (Secure Accommodation Order)* [2016] EWCA Civ 804, [2016] 4 WLR 159 is a good example of a case where different provisions of the Children Act 1989 appeared to apply inconsistently to a 17-year-old.

[197] Law Commission (2017) para. 7.30.

[198] To be implemented by Mental Capacity Amendment Act 2019. The new regime and its extension to 16- and 17-year-olds was proposed by the Law Commission (2017).

[199] Although uncertainty remains for those in this age group who do not lack capacity due to a mental disorder, but are not competent to consent to a deprivation of liberty, or who are competent and refuse to do so.

and for the law to maintain a better balance between allowing young people as much freedom as they have the capacity for and recognising the responsibilities of parents to guide them. While the decision in *Gillick* still provides important guidance on these fundamental principles, the ambiguities within it have been exacerbated by later case law and the case is showing signs of its age as the legal principles surrounding capacity develop. This is clearly seen in the important area of deprivation of liberty, where the legal safeguards for children are dependent on an uncertain and ill-defined law concerning adolescent decisions and parental power. A growing realisation that children have rights to be respected may augur a new judicial approach to this sensitive balance between parents' rights and those of their maturing children.

Bibliography

NB: Some of these publications can be obtained on the relevant organisation's website.

Alderson, P. (1993) *Children's Consent to Surgery*, Oxford University Press.
Appelbaum, P. and Grisso, T. (2001) *The MacArthur Competence Assessment Tool for Clinical Research (MacCAT-CR)*, Professional Resource Press.
Archard, D. (2014) *Children: Rights and Childhood*, Routledge.
Blakemore, S. (2012) 'Imaging Brain Development: The Adolescent Brain' 61 *NeuroImage* 397.
Blakemore, S. and Robbins, T. (2012) 'Decision-Making in the Adolescent Brain' 15 *Nature Neuroscience* 1184.
Cave, E. (2014) 'Goodbye *Gillick*? Identifying and Resolving Problems with the Concept of Child Competence' 34 *Legal Studies* 103.
Chico, V. and Haggar, L. (2011) 'The Mental Capacity Act 2005 and Mature Minors: A Missed Opportunity?' 33 *Journal of Social Welfare and Family Law* 157.
Coleman, J. and Hendry, L. (1999) *The Nature of Adolescence*, Routledge.
Committee on the Rights of the Child (2016) *General Comment No. 20 on the Implementation of the Rights of the Child During Adolescence*, CRC/C/GC/20, Centre for Human Rights, Geneva.
Daly, A. (2020) 'Assessing Children's Capacity. Reconceptualising Our Understanding through the UN Convention on the Rights of the Child' 28 *International Journal of Children's Rights* 471.
Department for Constitutional Affairs (DCA) (2007) *Mental Capacity Act 2005: Code of Practice*, The Stationery Office.
de Winter, M. (1997) *Children as Fellow Citizens: Participation and Commitment*, Radcliffe Medical Press Ltd.
Douglas, G. (1992) 'The Retreat from *Gillick*' 55 *Modern Law Review* 569.
Department of Health (DH) (1996) *Focus on Teenagers: Research into Practice*, HM Stationery Office.
(2008) *Code of Practice: Mental Health Act 1983*, The Stationery Office.
(2015) *Code of Practice: Mental Health Act 1983*, The Stationery Office.
Eekelaar, J. (1986) 'The Emergence of Children's Rights' 6 *Oxford Journal of Legal Studies* 161.
Ferguson, L. (2004) *The End of an Age: Beyond Age Restrictions for Minors' Medical Treatment Decisions*, Law Commission of Canada.
Fortin, J. (2001) 'Children's Rights and the Use of Physical Force' 13 *Child and Family Law Quarterly* 243.
(2004) 'Children's Rights: Are the Courts Now Taking Them More Seriously?' 15 *King's College Law Journal* 253.
(2006a) 'Children's Rights – Substance or Spin?' *Family Law* 759.
(2006b) 'Accommodating Children's Rights in a Post Human Rights Act Era' 69 *Modern Law Review* 299.

(2011) 'The *Gillick* Decision – Not Just a High Watermark' in Gilmore, S., Herring, J. and Probert, R. (eds) *Landmark Cases in Family Law*, Hart Publishing.

Freeman, M. (2005) 'Rethinking *Gillick*' 13 *International Journal of Children's Rights* 201.

Gilmore, S. (2009) 'The Limits of Parental Responsibility' in Probert, R., Gilmore, S. and Herring, J. (eds) *Responsible Parents and Parental Responsibility*, Hart Publishing.

Grootens-Wiegers, P., Hein, I., van den Broek, J. and de Vires, M. (2017) 'Medical Decision-making in Adolescents: Developmental and Neuroscientific Aspects' 17 *BMC Pediatrics* 120.

Hein, I. M., Troost, P. W. and Lindeboom, R. (2014) 'Accuracy of MacArthur Competence Assessment Tool for Measuring Children's Competence to Consent to Clinical Research' 168 *JAMA Pediatrics* 1147.

Herring, J. (2016) *Vulnerable Adults and the Law*, Oxford University Press.

Hoff, E. (2013) *Language Development*, 5th edn, Wadsworth Publishing.

Hughes, J. (1989) 'Thinking about Children' in Scarre, G. (ed.) *Children, Parents and Politics*, Cambridge University Press.

Juvenile Justice Center (2004) *Adolescence, Brain Development and Legal Culpability*, American Bar Association.

Langford, W., Lewis, C., Soloman, Y. and Warin, J. (2001) *Family Understandings: Closeness, Authority and Independence in Families With Teenagers*, Joseph Rowntree Foundation.

Law Commission (1988) *Family Law Review of Child Law, Guardianship and Custody*, Law Com. No. 172, HC 594, HM Stationery Office.

(2017) Mental Capacity and Deprivation of Liberty, Law Com No. 372, HC 1079, HM Stationery Office.

Lansdown, G. (2005) *The Evolving Capacities of the Child*, Innocenti Insight, UN Children's Fund (Unicef).

MacCormick, N. (1982) *Legal Right and Social Democracy: Essays in Legal and Political Philosophy*, Clarendon Press.

McFarlane, A. (2011) 'Mental Capacity: One Standard for All Ages' *Family Law* 479

Markovits, H. (2013) 'The Development of Abstract Conditional Reasoning' in Barrouillet, P. and Gauffroy, C. (eds) *The Development of Thinking and Reasoning*, Psychology Press.

Mills, K. L., Goddings, A. L., Clasen, L. S., Giedd, J. N. and Blakemore, S. J. (2014) 'The Developmental Mismatch in Structural Brain Maturation During Adolescence' 36 *Developmental Neuroscience* 147.

Minow, M. (1986) 'Rights for the Next Generation: A Feminist Approach to Children's Rights' 9 *Harvard Women's Law Journal* 1.

Rosenbury, L. (2015) 'A Feminist Perspective on Children and Law: From Objectification to Relational Subjectivities' in Gal, T. and Duramy, B. F. (eds) *International Perspectives and Empirical Findings on Child Participation*, Oxford University Press.

Royal College of Psychiatrists (2006) *Child Defendants*, Occasional Paper OP 56, Royal College of Psychiatrists.

Rutter, M. (Chairman) (2005) *Commission on Families and the Wellbeing of Children, Families and the State: Two-way Support and Responsibilities*, The Policy Press.

Rutter, M. and Rutter, M. (1993) *Developing Minds: Challenge and Continuity across the Life Span*, Penguin.

Scottish Law Commission (1992) *Report on Family Law*, Scot Law Com No 135, HM Stationery Office.

Steinberg, L. (2013) 'Does Recent Research on Adolescent Brain Development Inform the Mature Minor Doctrine?' 38 *Journal of Medicine and Philosophy* 256.

(2016) *Adolescence*, 11th edn, McGraw-Hill Higher Education.

Taylor, R. (2007) 'Reversing the Retreat from *Gillick*? *R (Axon)* v. *Secretary of State for Health*' 18 *Child and Family Law Quarterly* 81.

Van Leijenhorst, L., Zanolie, K., Van Meel, C. S., Westenberg, P. M., Rombouts, S. A. and Crone, E. A. (2010) 'What Motivates the Adolescent? Brain Regions Mediating Reward Sensitivity across Adolescence' 20 *Cerebral Cortex* 61.

10

Leaving Home, Rights to Support and Emancipation

(1) Introduction

One of the most emphatic ways in which children and young people can assert their right to take responsibility for their own lives is by simply walking out – leaving their home and parents behind them. This is a drastic step. Many children, particularly teenagers, sometimes find their parents' ideas outdated and their attempts to discipline them tedious. In turn, parents may be reluctant to allow their offspring greater independence before they consider them ready to cope with it. Nevertheless, in well-functioning families, negotiation and compromise will ensure that both 'sides' emerge relatively unscathed. Sadly, increasing numbers of children and young people find life at home so unbearable that they vote with their feet and leave. The law presents them with a contradictory set of principles. There is confusion over whether they have the right to leave home at all, at what age they may do so, what rights they have on leaving and what rights their parents have to force their return.

While it is currently impossible to obtain accurate estimates of the number of children and young people running away from home,[1] it is clear that too many take this step.[2] Young people leave for a variety of reasons: to escape 'maltreatment';[3] arguments and family conflict;[4] general unhappiness at home;[5]

---

[1] Children's Society (2007) pp. 9–10: exacerbated by the definitional confusion between 'running away' and 'missing'; G. Rees (2011) pp. 18–19 found that at least 70 per cent of young 'runaways' are not reported to the police as 'missing persons', a figure consistent with previous research.

[2] G. Rees (2011) ch. 2: 8.9 per cent of teenagers surveyed had run away for one night or more; an estimated 84,000 young people run away each year in England and an estimated 100,000 do so in the UK as a whole. Over a third of runaways had first run away before the age of 13.

[3] G. Rees and J. Lee (2005) p. 16: approximately 12 per cent of young people surveyed gave 'maltreatment' (physical abuse or violence, emotional abuse or neglect, domestic violence, sexual abuse or feeling scared) as the reason for running away. See also N. Pleace et al. (2008) para. 12.52: 45 per cent of statutorily homeless 16–17-year-olds reported violence. See also, ibid., Table 12.4.

[4] G. Rees and J. Lee (2005) p. 16.

[5] Family formation underlies variations in rates of running away. See, inter alia: G. Rees et al. (2005) pp. 23–6: 10 per cent of young people who were living between two homes (one with each parent) were likely to have run away, cf. 3 per cent of those living with both birth parents. These rates were affected by the dynamics of the family situation, with young people being more likely to run away in situations where there were changes in family structure; e.g. 20.9 per cent of

and problems at school, including bullying and exclusions.[6] Surprisingly large numbers are quite simply told by their parents or step-parents to leave,[7] or they feel forced to go.[8] 'Looked-after children'[9] and young people cared for in children's homes or foster care also form a significant proportion of young runaways and are far more likely to run away than children outside of the care system.[10] They often have slightly different reasons for leaving, including bullying or abuse, being separated from siblings and parents, and frequent changes of placement.[11] Young people who are victims of exploitation, including child trafficking and child sexual exploitation, have particularly high levels of going missing from care and it is only fairly recently that the connections between these forms of exploitation and missing children has begun to be better understood.[12] The broad umbrella of 'runaway children' contains within it a diverse range of circumstances with very different underlying causes.

Although, outwardly, those who leave home may appear to demonstrate their capacity for independence, the fact that they do so does not necessarily indicate that they are sufficiently mature to look after themselves or that they have the resources to do so. Indeed, they are often at their most vulnerable and need considerable support. Many leave home with nowhere to go and some end up sleeping rough,[13] with a significant proportion turning to risky strategies to survive.[14] Young people who have run away are particularly at risk of sexual exploitation, violent crime, substance misuse and exploitation by gangs.[15] A series of child exploitation scandals have forcefully brought these risks to public attention and highlighted the ease with which the vulnerabilities of runaway children can be masked by an assumption that they are acting through choice, rather than as victims of exploitation.

young people living with a parent and step-parent where the change had occurred in the last year had run away, as compared to 5.9 per cent where that structure had been in place for more than a year.

[6] G. Randall and S. Brown (2001) pp. 15–16 and 2: many homeless young people mention problems at school. G. Rees (2011) pp. 33–4 found that young people who ran away were significantly less connected with school and felt themselves to be doing less well at school than the general population.

[7] N. Pleace *et al.* (2008) Table 12.2: 70 per cent of statutorily homeless 16–17-year-olds reported relationship breakdown as the reason for their homelessness.

[8] G. Rees (2011): a quarter of overnight runaways had been forced to leave home.

[9] Children Act (CA) 1989, s. 22(1) and (2): a 'looked after child' is either a child who is the subject of a care order or a child being provided with accommodation under s. 20 for a continuous period of more than 24 hours.

[10] G. Rees (2011) pp. 22–3. The law concerning looked-after children is considered in more detail in Chapter 16.

[11] APPG (2012).   [12] Ibid. pp. 12–14.

[13] G. Rees (2011) p. 16: one in six of the sample group had slept rough or with a stranger while away, while the most common place for the remainder to stay was with friends or relatives.

[14] Ibid. p. 18: one in eight of the sample group had turned to theft and one in eleven to begging. A further one in nine indicated that they had done 'other things' to survive, although the researchers considered it unethical to explore this category further. In total, one in five had resorted to one or more of these risky strategies.

[15] DfE (2014) para. 2.

Young people who do seek to support themselves are hampered by the fact that law and policy largely reflect an official view that all young people under the age of 18 should be living at home and that, if they are not, they only have themselves to blame. Matters are, however, confused by the way in which many legal principles distinguish between minors under the age of 16 and those aged between 16 and 18. But while this older group are, in many ways, treated like adults, in others, they are still treated like children. Difficulty in obtaining state benefits, a lower minimum wage and a requirement that they are in education or training[16] all place obstacles in the way of those who are unable or unwilling to access parental support and instead seek to forge a path to independence. The following chapter considers these tensions between recognising both young people's growing independence and the vulnerabilities that this often entails. In doing so, it considers the inconsistencies in the treatment of young people and the significant problems faced by those who fall outside of the expectation that they will continue to be dependent on their parents.

(2) Legal Age Limits

The law reflects a sense of deep confusion regarding the point at which children should be allowed to take full responsibility for their activities. Section 1 of the Family Law Reform Act 1969 bars all those under the age of 18 from full legal 'emancipation'. A range of disqualifications makes all minors of any age broadly incapable of entering into a legally binding contract, holding a legal estate in land, making a will or voting. Nevertheless, as discussed below, a number of adult freedoms are available to 16- and 17-year-olds, leaving those under the age of 16 the subject of much wider restrictions.

(A) Under 16: Supplementing Pocket Money?

For those under 16, a series of legislative provisions have, over the years, thrown up a collection of bizarrely arbitrary age limits governing a range of activities, such as riding an electric bike[17] and riding a horse without a safety helmet.[18] These are more a source of amusement than of any practical utility and often have little logical rationale. The simple explanation for this legislative hotchpotch is that the qualifying ages have been adopted on an ad hoc and piecemeal basis. Of more practical significance are the provisions of the criminal law making the age of 16 govern the point at which young people can agree to sexual intercourse[19] and of the child abduction legislation, which makes it so difficult for those under 16 to gain assistance in

---

[16] Education and Skills Act 2008.   [17] Allowed at age 14: Road Traffic Act 1988, s. 32.

[18] Allowed at age 14: Horses (Protective Headgear for Young Riders) Act 1990. A 16-year-old can, inter alia, buy lottery tickets and aerosol paint, sell scrap metal and join the army.

[19] Sexual Offences Act 2003.

leaving home.[20] Those under 16 must also remain in school on a full-time basis, and are thereby prevented from gaining financial independence through full-time employment. Despite this, large numbers of children and young people under that age supplement their pocket money, or provide their own, by working in their spare time out of school, often for very low rates of pay.[21]

The rules presently governing the extent to which schoolchildren under the age of 16 can take on part-time work are not only extremely confusing, but also fail to protect them adequately. Article 32(1) of the UN Convention on the Rights of the Child (CRC) requires states to protect children against economic exploitation and work that is likely to harm their safety, health or development, or jeopardise their education. Article 32(2) details the measures states should take to regulate ages and hours for admission to employment. Such duties would be fulfilled were employers in the UK to follow the EU requirements[22] protecting children from being employed for over-long hours and in unsuitable conditions.[23] Unfortunately, the domestic regulations introduced to implement these measures simply ensure that even fewer prospective employers than before understand the complicated laws limiting the part-time work of children under the age of 16. These now differ considerably, depending on a child's precise age and the type of work he or she is undertaking.[24] The confusing nature of the provisions restricting the hours and days of the week on which young people below 16 may work[25] enables them to be widely flouted, not only by employers, but also by the local authorities (LAs) who are responsible for their enforcement.[26] The resulting confusion leaves those under 16 particularly open to exploitation, with little chance of effective redress.[27]

---

[20] Discussed below.

[21] The national minimum wage only applies to those who have 'ceased to be of compulsory school age': National Minimum Wage Act 1998, s. 1(2)(c).

[22] Directive on the Protection of Young People at Work (94/33/EC).

[23] Children (Protection at Work) Regulations 1998 (SI 1998/276); Children (Protection at Work) Regulations 2000 (SI 2000/1333); the Children (Protection at Work) (No. 2) Regulations 2000 (SI 2000/2548).

[24] Children and Young Persons Act (CYPA) 1933, s. 18 (as amended) regulates children's part-time work, regarding the hours they can work and the type of work they can undertake, depending on whether they are aged 13, 14 or 15.

[25] CYPA 1933, ss 18–21 (as amended by the Children (Protection at Work) Regulations 1998–2000), *broadly* prohibit employers from employing children under 14 at all (unless employed by a parent or guardian in specified light work). Those between 14 and 16 cannot be employed before 7 a.m. and after 7 p.m. on any day and on school days, they can only be employed for a maximum of 2 hours, only one of which can be before school, or a maximum of 12 hours in any school week. In the school holidays, a 14-year-old may not work for more than 25 hours in any week, or more than 4 hours in any day without a rest break of 1 hour. These provisions are all subject to the provisions of local byelaws, themselves amended to comply with EU Directive 94/33/EC. See DCSF (2008) for a reasonably clear explanation of the existing law.

[26] J. McKechnie *et al.* (2011).   [27] S. Hobbs *et al.* (2017).

(B) Over 16 and under 18

This age group of adolescents is treated in a strangely ambivalent way. They face a number of formal legal barriers which, inter alia, exclude them from voting, standing for Parliament, being a school governor, acquiring a legal estate in land or making a will. Furthermore, as discussed below, those contemplating leaving home will find that there are further severe legal restrictions on their financial independence. They can claim only very limited social security benefits and, with the exception of contracts for the supply of 'necessaries' and beneficial contracts of service, they cannot enter into any legally binding contract.[28] Further, they are required to be in in education or training, with limited access to benefits.[29] Meanwhile, certain important and potentially life-changing freedoms become available to 16-year-olds. They may consent to surgical, medical or dental treatment,[30] marry with the consent of their parents, join the army and consent to sexual intercourse.[31]

No clear policy is discernible in the law presently governing those aged between 16 and 18 who seek employment. By and large, it treats them like adults, requiring them to pay national insurance contributions and taxes. But, in practice, even at 16, they are far more vulnerable than adult employees. The government recognises this vulnerability through protective employment restrictions,[32] which place specific obligations on employers to protect young people from risks that may arise from lack of experience or maturity.[33] Nonetheless, young people are treated very differently from adults in respect of pay. On its introduction, the government was reluctant to extend the statutory minimum wage scheme to 16–17-year-olds, only doing so following international criticism,[34] and persists in setting substantially lower rates of minimum

---

[28] The anachronistic rules of contract ensuring that minors can only enter into binding contracts for the supply of 'necessaries' and beneficial contracts of service are widely misunderstood. E.g. *Proform Sports Management Ltd* v. *Proactive Sports Management Ltd and another* [2006] EWHC 2812 (Ch), [2007] 1 All ER 542: since an agreement entered into by Wayne Rooney, a professional footballer, at the age of 15 was a voidable contract and not a contract for necessaries, it could be avoided.

[29] Education and Skills Act 2008; discussed further below.

[30] Family Law Reform Act 1969, s. 8(1), discussed in more detail in Chapter 11.

[31] Sexual Offences (Amendment) Act 2000 ensured that homosexual males finally acquired sexual parity with their heterosexual male and lesbian female counterparts.

[32] These regulations were put in place to comply with European Council Directive on the Protection of Young People at Work (94/33/EC), which requires, inter alia, strict regulation and protection of work done by 'adolescents' (those between minimum school leaving age and 18). Management of Health and Safety at Work Regulations 1999 (SI 1999/3242) require employers to make a risk assessment of certain types of employment for employees between the ages of 16 and 18. Explained by LAC 92/3 Rev and discussed by C. Hamilton and B. Watt (2004) pp. 147–8. Failure to comply with these regulations is common; e.g. in 2005, a verdict of unlawful killing was reached by a Newport inquest into the death of a 17-year-old employed by a roofing company, who within a week of starting his job fell through a skylight. He had received no prior safety training.

[33] Management of Health and Safety at Work Regulations 1999 (SI 1999/3242), esp. reg. 19.

[34] Committee on Economic, Social and Cultural Rights (2002) paras 15 and 33; Committee on the Rights of the Child (2002) paras 55 and 56.

wage for those under 18.[35] Even upon reaching the age of 18, young adults are entitled to relatively low minimum wage rates; it is only at age 25 that they are entitled to be paid the National Living Wage. The low rate payable to 16–17-year-olds has been officially justified as striking a balance between stopping exploitation and avoiding young people being priced out of the jobs market.[36] The current position is, however, open to substantial criticism in that it condones discrimination against young people by failing to guarantee equal pay for equal work. Further, while many young people are supported by their parents, for those who are not the low minimum wage payments are likely to leave them in severe poverty, particularly given the restrictions placed on 16- and 17-year-olds accessing benefits.[37] Despite continuing criticisms that the present arrangements are discriminatory and encourage the use of younger employees as a source of cheap labour, there seems little official enthusiasm for bringing their statutory minimum wage into line with that for 18–21-year-olds or that of older adults.

(C) Liberalising the Law for 16-18-Year-Olds?

The legal position of 16- and 17-year-olds is often inconsistent, reflecting ad hoc policy decisions rather than a coherent approach to this age group. Aspects of the law respect young people's autonomy and ability to take life-changing decisions, such as those relating to medical treatment. The Children Act 1989 also recognises that it will usually be inappropriate and futile to make orders concerning the living arrangements and upbringing of this age group, prohibiting the court from making such orders for 16- and 17-year-olds save in exceptional circumstances.[38] At the same time, the requirement that young people stay in education or training until the age of 18 treats this period as a final stage of preparation for adulthood. This further reflects an assumption that these young people will usually be dependent on their parents to at least some degree. Those who lack parental support, or find it intolerable to remain at home, find that both law and government policy place considerable barriers to the path to independence. Greater clarity might be achieved by lowering the age of majority to 16 years, although at present this appears unlikely to attract significant support, particularly given the widespread influence of the CRC's use of 18 as the appropriate standard.[39] Similarly, there has been a tendency in

---

[35] At the time of writing, those under 18 are entitled to £4.81 an hour. Those aged 18–20 are entitled to £6.83 an hour and 21–4 £9.18. It is only after the age of 25 that the National Living Wage is applicable (£9.50 an hour).

[36] Low Pay Commission (2019) p. viii.   [37] Discussed below.

[38] CA 1989, s. 9(7), although the court may still make orders under the inherent jurisdiction. See *Re D (A Child)* [2019] UKSC 42, [2019] 1 WLR 5403, at [26]–[27].

[39] The text of the CRC, Art. 1 permits member states to adopt differing ages of majority, stating that: 'a child means every human being below the age of eighteen years unless under the law applicable to the child, majority is attained earlier'. The Committee has, however, made it increasingly clear that they regard 18 as the appropriate standard and that those under 18 are

domestic law to raise, rather than lower, ages at which restrictions and protections are imposed on young people.[40] Indeed, it has been argued that the evolving research concerning brain development would support increasing, rather than lowering, the age of majority.[41]

While it is unlikely that the age of majority itself will be lowered, there are strong arguments to revise particular aspects of the law relating to 16- and 17-year-olds. Liberalising the law by extending the right to vote to 16-year-olds would reflect their growing ability to play a part in the community and give young people a greater voice in shaping the laws that affect them. This is of particular importance for those policies that concern intergenerational equality; for example, those policy areas that currently treat younger people less favourably than their older counterparts,[42] and those, such as environmental policy, which are likely to have a long-term impact and so will on average have the greatest consequence for the lives of younger voters. Further, as Tommy Peto argues, in a democracy, it 'must be wrong to deny the vote to any particular individual who is competent and whose interests are affected by the government',[43] particularly given that those 16- and 17-year-olds who are in employment will be contributing financially through tax and national insurance payments. One response to this reasoning would be to argue that some 16- and 17-year-olds lack the maturity and knowledge to make the complex political judgments necessary to vote wisely, although the same might be said of voters in older age groups. Certainly, the emerging research on adolescent development suggests that young people of this age group have typically reached the same cognitive and reasoning abilities of adults.[44] Evidence from those countries that have lowered the voting age to 16 suggests that younger first-time voters are more likely to vote than those who reach voting age after 18, especially once they have left school and family.[45] The 2014 referendum on Scottish independence demonstrated similar results, with 75 per cent of eligible 16–17-year-olds reporting that they had voted, a far higher proportion than the 54 per cent of 18–24-year-olds who had done so.[46] As first-time voting influences the likelihood of future voting, this has positive implications for future political engagement.

---

entitled to the protection of the rights contained in the CRC, placing particular emphasis on the protection of under 18s from exploitation and abuse: Committee on the Rights of the Child (2016) esp. paras 1, 5 and 40.

[40] Notably in the introduction of the requirement to be in training or education until 18: Education and Skills Act 2008. Other examples include: raising the age at which cigarettes might be purchased from 16 to 18 (Children and Young Persons (Sale of Tobacco etc.) Order 2007); and altering the offence concerning indecent images of children to include images of 16- and 17-year-olds (Sexual Offences Act 2003, s. 49(1)(2)).

[41] Discussed in Chapter 9. See esp. L. Steinberg (2016).

[42] E.g. the age-based thresholds that apply to eligibility for certain benefits and minimum wage entitlements, as discussed in this chapter.

[43] T. Peto (2018) p. 288.   [44] Discussed in Chapter 9. See also T. Peto (2018).

[45] T. Peto (2018) p. 292.   [46] Electoral Commission (2014).

Support for the enfranchisement of 16–17-year-olds in the UK is increasing. Following the positive experience of the 2014 referendum on independence, 16- and 17-year-olds are now eligible to vote in Scottish Parliament and local council elections.[47] The same approach was adopted in Wales in 2020.[48] The picture in England and the UK as a whole is more cautious. Given the long-term implications of the 2016 EU Referendum, there were strong arguments for including young people in that vote, an argument that persuaded the House of Lords, but was reversed in the House of Commons.[49] That said, an increasing number of UK political parties now support extension of the franchise to young people and there is growing pressure for change in English and UK-wide elections.[50] Such a change would be an important step forward for recognition of young people's citizenship, as well as having a practical impact on the way in which their views are considered in relation to law and policy affecting them.

(3) Legal Rights to Leave Home

(A) Can Parents Stop Young People Leaving?

'When can I leave home?' Unfortunately, those working with young people can give them no simple answer. Of greater relevance are two further questions: do their parents have a legal right to stop them leaving in the first place; and can their parents force them to return home if they do leave?[51] The answer is not always clear due to the law's ambivalence over the limits to parental control. In relation to the first question, there has always existed a principle of common law that parents have a power to control the person and property of their children, a power now included as an aspect of parental responsibility. The exercise of this power is, however, not unlimited: as with all parental rights, it is bounded by the welfare principle.[52] Further, the courts have long recognised that parental control often ends in practice before the young person reaches the legal age of majority.[53] In the memorable words of Lord Denning, the parental right to custody of the child is 'a dwindling right which the courts will hesitate to enforce against the wishes of the child, and the more so the older he

---

[47] Scottish Elections (Reduction of Voting Age) Act 2015. This right does not extend to UK elections for the Westminster Parliament as the franchise for such elections remains a reserved matter.

[48] Senedd and Elections (Wales) Act 2020.

[49] HL Deb on the European Union (Referendum) Bill, *Hansard*, col. 180, 18 November 2015.

[50] At the time of writing, the Labour, Liberal Democrat, Green and Scottish Nationalist Parties have all expressed such support.

[51] Discussed in more detail by J. Fortin (2001) pp. 247–50.   [52] Discussed further in Chapter 9.

[53] At common law, the court would refuse to use habeas corpus to return a child to parental control against the child's will once the child had reached the 'age of discretion': *R* v. *Howes* (1860) 3 EB & E 332. Discussed further below. See the different interpretations of this case law in *D (A Child)* [2017] EWCA Civ 1695 (Munby P), [2018] 2 FLR 13, at [54]–[65] and *Re D (A Child)* [2019] UKSC 42, [2019] 1 WLR 5403, at [55]–[68] (Lady Black).

is. It starts with a right of control and ends with little more than advice'.[54] Similarly, as Lord Scarman pointed out in *Gillick*,[55] although the parental 'right or power' exists, it does so 'primarily to enable the parent to discharge his duty of maintenance, protection, and education until he reaches such an age as to be able to look after himself and make his own decisions'.[56] These principles remain the foundation of the modern law, meaning that whether a parent seeking to control a young person's freedom to leave is acting in the 'ambit of parental responsibility' will not merely depend on age, but also on the individual circumstances and maturity of the young person.[57] Nonetheless, the point at which an adolescent reaches sufficient maturity to make their own decisions is often unclear and likely to be precisely the matter of dispute between the parents and young person. Recent judicial decisions have made it clear that the permissible restraint imposed by a parent on an adolescent child will be judged by the prevailing standards in modern society. As modern society puts considerable barriers in the way of young people who seek to become economically active or to live independently,[58] it is particularly difficult for those under 16 to demonstrate that they have reached a point where they are free to leave the parental home according to those prevailing standards.[59] This conclusion does not, however, mean that parents are entitled to resort to any means necessary to prevent young people in this position from leaving. The criminal law has, like the civil law, maintained a disapproving attitude towards parents who assume a right to control their children by force.[60] But there is no real clarity over the point at which parental behaviour changes from being a reasonable form of discipline to abusive behaviour amounting to false imprisonment.[61]

At first sight, one might have assumed that children faced by authoritarian parents seeking to prevent their leaving would gain assistance from the Human Rights Act (HRA) 1998, more particularly from Article 5 of the European Convention for the Protection of Human Rights and Fundamental Freedoms (1950) (ECHR),[62] which provides children with protection against deprivation of

---

[54] *Hewer* v. *Bryant* [1970] 1 QB 357, at 369.

[55] *Gillick* v. *West Norfolk and Wisbech Area Health Authority* [1986] AC 112.   [56] Ibid. at 185.

[57] In *Re D (A Child)* [2019] UKSC 42, [2019] 1 WLR 5403, Lady Black rejected the argument that *Gillick* competence could be applied to extend parental powers to confine young people aged 16 or 17 who lacked competence. She nonetheless accepted that there was an argument that this parental power ceased in relation to young people aged under 16 who had achieved competence at [88]–[89].

[58] Discussed further below.

[59] *Re A-F (Children)* [2018] EWHC 138 (Fam), [2018] 3 WLR 1905, at [31].

[60] E.g. *R* v. *D* [1984] 2 All ER 449: the House of Lords confirmed that a parent could be charged with the common law offence of kidnapping if he 'stole and carried away' a child against that child's consent.

[61] E.g. in *R* v. *Rahman* (1985) 81 Cr App Rep 349, Lord Lane CJ disapproved of a father who had bundled his teenage daughter into a car against her will in order to return her to Bangladesh. Such behaviour could amount to false imprisonment if, as in this case, it was outside the realms of reasonable parental discipline. But such a qualification creates further uncertainty: what is 'reasonable parental discipline'?

[62] Art. 8 might also assist, protecting the child's private life and physical integrity.

liberty.[63] Nevertheless, the European Court of Human Rights (ECtHR) in *Nielsen* v. *Denmark*[64] emphasised that a parent's right to family life under Article 8 includes a broad range of parental rights and responsibilities, including the right to decide where the child must reside and to 'impose, or authorise others to impose, various restrictions on the child's liberty'.[65] Although the ECtHR acknowledged that a parent's rights 'cannot be completely unlimited and that it is incumbent on the State to provide safeguards against abuse',[66] it was satisfied that this 12-year-old child was still of an age when it was 'normal' for a decision to be made by a parent even against his wishes. Consequently, the boy's challenge fell completely outside the ambit of Article 5 of the ECHR.[67] Crucially, the ECtHR failed to clarify the outer limits of parental behaviour or what might amount to an 'improper' purpose or 'bad faith', thereby excluding Article 8 protection. Given the extreme nature of the restrictions placed on the child in *Nielsen*,[68] the case appears to adopt a complacent approach to the ambit of parental power, so leaving children with very narrow and uncertain protection from authoritarian parents.

Children arguing that their rights under Article 5 of the ECHR have been infringed by parents obstructing their efforts to leave home may seek to persuade the domestic courts to set aside, or distinguish, *Nielsen* v. *Denmark*[69] as being anachronistic. Certainly, the domestic courts have expressed disquiet about its reach, although they have struggled to agree its basis and relevance to the modern law.[70] The Court of Appeal in *Re K (Secure Accommodation Order: Right to Liberty)*[71] suggested that its authority was restricted to normal parent–child relationships; both Judge LJ and Dame Elizabeth Butler-Sloss P signalled that the domestic courts might withdraw Article 8 protection from parents who behave in an outrageously over-authoritarian manner. Judge LJ thought he could easily distinguish between parents disciplining their children 'as necessary and appropriate' and parents behaving in a cruel or abusive way.[72] Similarly, Dame Elizabeth Butler-Sloss P considered that a court's response should depend on whether the parent's actions were 'within ordinary acceptable parental restrictions upon the movements of a child'.[73] In *Re D (A Child)*,[74] Lady Hale agreed that the judgments in *Re K* had identified the 'crux of the matter' and that

---

[63] Art. 5 is concerned with deprivation of liberty attributable to the state, but this includes the state's positive obligations to protect against confinement imposed by individuals: *Storck* v. *Germany* (2006) 43 EHRR 6, at [89] and [149].

[64] (1988) 11 EHRR 175. Discussed in more detail in Chapter 9.   [65] Ibid. at [61].

[66] Ibid. at [72].   [67] Ibid.

[68] The child was confined to a psychiatric ward for several months against his will despite the fact that he was not mentally ill.

[69] (1988) 11 EHRR 175.

[70] Discussed further in Chapter 9. *R (Axon)* v. *Secretary of State for Health and the Family Planning Association* [2006] EWHC 37 (Admin), [2006] 2 FLR 206, at [126]; *D (A Child)* [2017] EWCA Civ 1695, at [23]; *Re D (A Child)* [2019] UKSC 42, [2019] 1 WLR 5403.

[71] [2001] 1 FLR 526.   [72] Ibid. at [99].   [73] Ibid. at [28].

[74] [2019] UKSC 42, [2019] 1 WLR 5403, at [38]–[39]. See Lord Carnwath (dissenting), at [147]–[156], who took the view that the case was not only concerned with this point, but also the scope of parental rights.

the relevant question was whether the restriction at issue fell within normal parental control for a child of that age. Determining the limit of this 'normal parental control' poses further problems for young people relying on Article 5, not least because of the severe restrictions accepted in *Nielsen* itself. In *Re K*, Dame Butler-Sloss surprisingly considered that '[i]t might be permissible' for a parent to detain a child 'for a few days'.[75] This is regrettable; surely 'ordinary acceptable parental restrictions' would exclude restricting the liberty of an older child for more than a few *hours*? Nonetheless, in subsequent cases, the courts have recognised that the lives of young people are increasingly regulated and controlled so that 'ordinary acceptable parental restrictions' may be becoming more, rather than less, restrictive.[76] The current state of the case law gives young people and their parents very little guidance as to the scope of protection offered by Article 5 against excessive parental control.

(B) Can Parents Force a Child or Young Person to Return Home?

Once a child leaves the premises, the law remains confused over whether the parent can force him or her to return. The eighteenth- and nineteenth-century judiciary were unexpectedly liberal, refusing to issue writs of habeas corpus ordering children to return home against their will once they had attained the 'age of discretion' – at one time, 14 for boys and 16 for girls.[77] Today, the common law notion of a fixed 'age of discretion' is no longer applied in this way, but has not been replaced by a clear set of legal principles.[78] While it is arguable that a teenager returned home against her will could now seek to claim the protection of the ECHR, there is little case law supporting such an approach. In two very early cases, the European Commission of Human Rights responded inconsistently to runaway teenagers. In *X* v. *Netherlands*, it rejected the claim of a 14-year-old Dutch runaway that her rights under Article 8 had been infringed by the actions taken by the welfare authorities to return her home. Any infringement of her rights was justified by their need to protect her health and morals under Article 8(2).[79] But in a later decision, the European Commission rejected the parents' arguments that by refusing to force their 14-year-old daughter to return home against her will, the Danish welfare authorities had infringed the parents' own rights under Article 8.[80] Today, those

---

[75] Ibid. at [29].   [76] *Re A-F (Children)* [2018] EWHC 138 (Fam), [2018] 3 WLR 1905, at [31].

[77] Lord Scarman summarises this old case law in *Gillick* v. *West Norfolk and Wisbech Area Health Authority* [1986] AC 112, at 187–8. *Krishnan* v. *London Borough of Sutton* [1970] Ch 181 provides a twentieth-century example of the age of discretion cases. There, the court refused to order the LA to require a girl of nearly 18 to return to her father against her will, since, in practical terms, such an order could not be enforced.

[78] In particular, the interaction of this older case law and the more flexible, individual assessment of '*Gillick*' capacity is contentious. Cf. Lady Black in *Re D (A Child)* [2019] UKSC 42, [2019] 1 WLR 5403, at [55]–[90] and Sir James Munby in *D (A Child)* [2017] EWCA Civ 1695, at [51]–[95].

[79] *X* v. *Netherlands* (1974) 2 DR 118.   [80] *X* v. *Denmark* (1977–78) 7–9 DR 81.

advising a runaway would seek to convince a domestic court that he or she has a right to respect for his or her private life under Article 8, free from parental interference and to freedom from restraint under Article 5. But in the absence of any clearer guidance from Strasbourg, the domestic courts might instead turn to the common law principles, which, while not imposing a fixed age limit, broadly distinguish between those below and above the age of 16.

(i) Under 16s

Even relatively young children run away from home,[81] often for very good reasons. Indeed, as discussed above, due to family disruption, neglect, conflict and abuse, children are often told by their parents to leave or feel forced to do so. Nevertheless, the provisions of criminal law and those contained in the CA 1989 reflect a view of family life which is radically out of step with this reality experienced by so many. The law implicitly assumes that those assisting runaways under the age of 16 are breaking up happy family units – a situation which can be simply solved by the child's rapid return. While returning such children to the source of their unhappiness solves nothing, the child care agencies know that parents are those with parental responsibility for their children. The primary role of parents is emphasised by the criminal law which is clear that, until their children attain their 16th birthday, parents are subject to criminal sanctions if they neglect them,[82] or more specifically, fail to provide them with adequate food, clothing, medical aid or lodging.[83]

While it is important to recognise that many child runaways will be running from harmful or unpleasant home lives, it is also the case that children who run away are particularly vulnerable to harm, abuse and exploitation.[84] In particular, children may leave home and put themselves in risky situations as a result of child trafficking or through grooming by criminal gangs, including those intent on child sexual exploitation. The majority of children who run away do not seek help, while those who do are much more likely to turn to friends and relatives for that help than to the authorities.[85] Many children either do not know of the potential help available or fear that they will be returned home if they seek help. As a result, many children who run away are not visible to the services designed to protect and help them, and only a minority are reported as missing to the police.[86]

---

[81] This chapter is concerned with all children who run away from home, particularly those who run away from the family home. Children in LA care are disproportionately likely to run away from home, although the majority of children who run away are not in LA care. The distinct duties that apply to looked-after children are considered in more detail in Chapter 16.

[82] CYPA 1933, s. 1(1).   [83] CYPA 1933, s. 1(2)(a).

[84] G. Rees (2011) pp. 16–17 found that 26 per cent of child runaways (under 16 years old) engaged in one or more forms of risky or harmful behavior while away from home, including: suffering harm; sleeping rough or with someone that the child had not previously met; and adopting risky survival strategies such as stealing or begging.

[85] G. Rees (2011) pp. 17–18 found that 75 per cent of those interviewed had not sought help and that in total only 5 per cent of those running away overnight had approached a professional source of help.

[86] G. Rees (2011) found that a maximum of 30 per cent were reported as missing.

Anyone offering shelter or assistance to runaways under the age of 16 may be subject to the criminal law on 'harbouring', which prohibits those unconnected with a child from removing or keeping them from parental[87] control. The scope of section 2 of the Child Abduction Act 1984 is extremely wide.[88] Even providing a child under the age of 16 with advice or assistance over running away from home could theoretically amount to an offence. The offence is particularly useful in circumstances in which it is suspected that the child has been groomed for sexual exploitation or other forms of criminal exploitation. Children in this situation may well not perceive themselves to be victims of grooming, but instead see themselves as acting of their own free choice, but the child's wishes are no defence to a charge of abduction or harbouring.[89] Police forces are increasingly making use of Child Abduction Warning Notices (CAWN) to attempt to disrupt situations in which a child appears to be at risk of running away as a result of a potentially exploitative association with an adult.[90] While CAWNs have no specific statutory basis or penalty attached to them, they put the potential offender on notice that the police are aware of the situation and the potential for a harbouring charge. They also provide clear evidence that there is no defence of lawful authority or reasonable excuse if the offender does encourage the child to abscond. In this way, the existence of the offence is a route to early intervention and disruption to situations in which children are being groomed to run away. The breadth of the offence may also put off those who seek to give benign assistance and shelter to children who have left home for good reason, including children's charities. It is, however, unlikely that an offence could be proved against someone providing supportive assistance to a *Gillick*-competent child, given the statutory defence of 'reasonable excuse'. Furthermore, a prosecution is unlikely to succeed if the adult has merely responded to a child's plea for support, rather than actively encouraging him or her to run away.[91] Nonetheless, the 1984 Act has produced a situation in which child runaways under the age of 16 come under considerable pressure from aid workers and

---

[87] Or other person with 'lawful control'.

[88] Child Abduction Act 1984, s. 2(1) provides that a person unconnected with the child (i.e. not a parent or guardian) commits an offence 'if, without lawful authority or reasonable excuse, he takes or detains a child under the age of 16 – (a) so as to remove him from the lawful control of any person having lawful control of the child; or (b) so as to keep him out of the lawful control of any person entitled to lawful control of the child.'

Section 2(3) provides a statutory defence in the event of the person charged showing that he believed the child to have attained the age of 16 or in the case of a non-marital child of whom he reasonably believed himself to be the father.

See also the CA 1989, s. 49, which creates an offence for any person knowingly and without lawful authority or reasonable excuse to take away and keep children or induce or incite them to stay away from those responsible for their care under a care or emergency protection order, or police protection.

[89] E.g. *R* v. *Mortimore* [2013] EWCA Crim 1639; *Foster and Rutherford* v. *DPP* [2004] EWHC 2955 (Admin), [2005] 1 WLR 1400.

[90] See e.g. *R (Ghuman)* v. *Thames Valley Police* [2018] EWHC 2059 (Admin).

[91] C. Hamilton (2005) p. 43.

the police to return home. It was hoped, following implementation of the CA 1989, that as a last resort, runaways under the age of 16 could avoid being returned home by seeking accommodation at a 'child refuge'. Exempted from the harbouring laws,[92] refuges are authorised to provide children with a place if it appears that they are at risk of harm if not taken in.[93] Although immensely valuable, these establishments proved expensive and difficult to maintain and have practically ceased to operate.[94]

The way in which children are treated once located can have a significant impact on the chances that they go missing again and on addressing the causes of the decision to leave. As there are often serious safeguarding concerns behind the decision to run away and significant risks to children who do so, listening to children and responding effectively is vital. The guidance given to children's services is clear that those who go missing from LA care should not be peremptorily returned to a placement that they may find intolerable.[95] In contrast, in the absence of child protection concerns, LAs tend to place a relatively low priority on the child who runs away from his or her own family. The child is, normally, simply returned home by the police.[96] Statutory guidance now requires that all children who have been missing are offered an independent return interview,[97] to take place within 72 hours[98] of their return. The interview should be an in-depth opportunity for an independent person to seek to establish the trust of the child and explore both the reasons for the decision to run away and any harm or risk of harm that the child was exposed to while away. If conducted effectively, such interviews can have a vital role in uncovering risks to children and in providing information and services to keep the child safe and to reduce the risk of further episodes of the child going missing.[99] Young runaways themselves endorse the importance of their being supported on return and being given an opportunity to talk confidentially about their problems.[100] Given the strong association between running away and risks such as child sexual and criminal exploitation, there is immense value

---

[92] CA 1989, s. 51.

[93] A child can only stay for a maximum of 14 days. See the Refuges (Children's Homes and Foster Placement) Regulations 1991 (SI 1991/1507).

[94] G. Rees (2011) p. 6 reports that refuge closures mean that there were only five refuge bed spaces for children who run away in the whole of the UK.

[95] DfE (2014) esp. para. 68.

[96] Some are initially removed into police protection. Children cannot be held under these provisions for more than 72 hours, and the police must inform the LA and the child's parents of the steps taken. See CA 1989, s. 46, esp. s. 46(3)(a) and (4)(a). The police protection powers are often used to deal with runaways located 'out-of-hours', when the short-staffed children's social care Emergency Duty Teams are unable to help.

[97] DfE (2014) pp. 14–16 sets out the requirements for giving independent return interviews.

[98] The guidance specifies that the interview must *take place* within 72 hours of return: DfE (2014) para. 32. While a prompt response is important, there is some concern among professionals working with missing children that the deadline can be prioritised at the expense of the quality of the interview, particularly if the child is found at the weekend, thus giving relatively little time to make effective arrangements: Missing People (2019) p. 35.

[99] Missing People (2019).   [100] R. Morgan (2006a) pp. 16–17.

in offering this opportunity to all children, and not merely those who initially appear to the police to be at high risk of harm.[101] Initial 'safe and well' checks by police often find it difficult to establish the true reasons for the child leaving, especially as children may be mistrustful of the police and reluctant to disclose the true reasons to them.[102] Despite the statutory guidance and clear utility of return interviews, many authorities are failing to provide interviews to all missing children and there are clear geographical differences in the way in which returning children are treated.[103] Poor recording of information and sharing with police and other agencies can also impede the utility of interviews as a means of identifying problems and taking effective action.[104]

Children who are returned to a neglectful or abusive home environment may find little has changed unless the child's reluctance to return home (leading to repeat running away) triggers child protection concerns. The LA will then investigate his or her home circumstances[105] to establish any evidence of parental ill-treatment which might justify an application for a care order or emergency protection order,[106] or even for criminal proceedings to be instituted. But unless and until the LA acquires a court order authorising them to care for the child, they are under no legal duty to accommodate them unless the child is orphaned, lost or abandoned, or their present carers are prevented from doing so themselves.[107] More to the point, they are powerless to do so against the parents' wishes.[108] Social workers know that parents are legally responsible for accommodating their children aged under 16 themselves and, additionally, that there is a serious lack of emergency accommodation for this age group. In any event, LAs may be reluctant to accommodate young people in all but the most extreme circumstances. Researchers found that young runaways were being urged to return home by social workers, despite it being unsuitable for them to do so, in order to avoid activating LAs' leaving care obligations by the provision of accommodation. Indeed, the Children's Society reports 'many' LAs operating 'unwritten policies' to avoid accommodating 14- and 15-year-olds, and even 13-year-old runaways.[109] As discussed below, in their anxiety to avoid longer-term legal responsibilities, LAs often fail to provide vulnerable teenagers with appropriate support.

(ii) Over 16s

Once over the age of 16, young people may gain the false impression that parental responsibility has terminated, that they are therefore legally 'emancipated' and can behave as adults. Nevertheless, it is quite incorrect to give them

---

[101] Missing People (2019).   [102] Ibid. p. 18.   [103] Children's Society (2017a) pp. 25–31.
[104] Ofsted (2013) pp. 15–17.
[105] Under the CA 1989, s. 47(1). Discussed in more detail in Chapter 15.   [106] Ibid. s. 31 or 44.
[107] Ibid. s. 20(1).
[108] Ibid. s. 20(7). See also s. 20(8): the child's parents may remove him or her from LA accommodation at any time.
[109] Children's Society (2007) pp. 34 and 52.

such advice – the law is clear that they do not attain full legal independence until their 18th birthday. Until then, parents retain parental responsibility and the young person, as a legal minor, is subject to all the confusing legal incapacities affecting his or her ability to follow an independent existence.[110] Despite this, attaining the age of 16 does have considerable legal significance, so far as leaving home is concerned.[111] The criminal provisions and the criminal sanctions available against neglectful parents drop away from children once they attain the age of 16. Indeed, it appears that for these reasons, some parents regard 16 as the point at which they can reasonably 'kick out' their offspring if they are causing trouble in the home.[112] Strangely, the government does not appear to have considered changing the law by extending the scope of such criminal sanctions to the age of 18, thereby ensuring the law's consistency with the requirement that young people remain in education or training until they attain such an age.[113] At the same time, as the government has recognised, '[w]hen a 16- or 17-year-old runs away or goes missing they are no less vulnerable than younger children and are equally at risk, particularly of sexual exploitation or involvement with gangs'.[114] Nonetheless, the legal framework aimed at protecting younger children from such exploitation applies inconsistently to young people aged 16 and 17, with much of it falling away once a child reaches 16. The law struggles to accommodate both the growing independence of 16- and 17-year-olds and their continued vulnerability, which may be heightened, rather than diminished, by that growing freedom. In particular, the criminal law on 'harbouring' ceases to apply once a child reaches 16,[115] with the consequence that CAWNs cannot be used to protect them from harmful situations, unless the young person in question is in care.[116] Similarly, as young people reach the legal age of consent to sexual activity, it becomes increasingly difficult for the law to recognise and respond to sexual exploitation of 16- and 17-year-olds. The age-specific criminal offences apply to those under 16,[117] save where the offender is in a position of trust or a family member in relation to the child,[118] or in circumstances involving payment.[119] Outside of these offences, victims of sexual abuse who are aged 16–17 are protected by the same criminal law as adult victims. This adult-focused law may fail to recognise the particular vulnerabilities of young people who have experienced grooming and coercive relationships. The line between freely formed relationships and those that amount to sexual

---

[110] Discussed above. A point confirmed in *D (A Child)* [2017] EWCA Civ 1695, esp. at [128].

[111] See *Re D (A Child)* [2019] UKSC 42, [2019] 1 WLR 5403, esp. Lady Black, who at [72] considered that 16 now represented the age at which young people are free from parental physical control, replacing the common law differential ages of discretion for boys and girls.

[112] G. Randall and S. Brown (2001) p. 11.   [113] Education and Skills Act 2008.

[114] DfE (2014) para. 42.   [115] Child Abduction Act 1984, s. 2(1).

[116] CA 1989, s. 49 (abduction of children in care) extends protection from abduction to those over 16 if they are in care, the subject of an emergency protection order or under police protection. A CAWN may be used in these circumstances for young people under the age of 18.

[117] Sexual Offences Act 2003, ss 9–15A.   [118] Ibid. ss 16–24 and 25–6.   [119] Ibid. ss 48–9.

exploitation can be difficult for both young people and those working with them to recognise.[120]

Parents who wish to persuade sons and daughters over the age of 16 to return home will have an uphill battle. The courts' power to make any section 8 orders normally ends on a child attaining such an age[121] – reflecting the realistic view that it is pointless for courts to make orders concerning residence contrary to the wishes of those over 16. It is also unlikely that parents can force a 16-year-old to return home by involving the LA. If the LA considers that they are suffering significant harm, it can apply for a care order for a young person under 17,[122] but it is unlikely that an LA would contemplate seeking such an order against the wishes of an 'elderly' child, unless exceptional circumstances existed.[123] Admittedly, a young person over the age of 16 who is opposed to returning home might avoid doing so by persuading the LA to provide him or her with accommodation, as the LA is entitled to do,[124] even against his or her parents' wishes. The parents would then have no right to remove the young person from that accommodation.[125] In practice, however, as noted below, children's services may be cautious about doing so since the provision of accommodation might activate costly leaving care obligations towards such a child. Whether the young person is being looked after by the LA has significant implications for the way in which the state responds to 16- and 17-year-olds who abscond from home and appear at risk of serious exploitation and harm. Those who are 'looked after' by the LA may find themselves subject to draconian restrictions imposed in secure accommodation,[126] designed to protect them from harm even as they sit on the cusp of adulthood.[127] Such restrictions go far beyond those that it would be permissible for a parent to impose on their child in the same circumstances. In contrast, such orders are not available in respect of young people who are outside of LA care,[128] even if the risk is equally severe. For those who are 17 and so beyond the reach of care orders, there is little that the LA can do without the consent of the young

---

[120] Children's Commissioner (2012).

[121] CA 1989, s. 9(6) and (7): unless the circumstances are exceptional.

[122] Ibid. s. 31(3): 'No care order or supervision order may be made with respect to a child who has reached the age of seventeen.'

[123] E.g. *Re V (Care or Supervision Order)* [1996] 1 FLR 776.

[124] CA 1989, s. 20(3), discussed further below.

[125] CA 1989, s. 20(11). See also *Krishnan* v. *London Borough of Sutton* [1970] Ch 181.

[126] Through a secure accommodation order obtained under CA 1989, s. 25. The extent to which the inherent jurisdiction can be used to provide secure accommodation is considered in *Re T (A Child)* [2021] UKSC 35, [2021] 3 WLR 643.

[127] *Re W (A Child) (Secure Accommodation Order)* [2016] EWCA Civ 804, [2016] 4 WLR 159: imposition of a secure accommodation order on a young person aged 17 years and 8 months who appeared to be the victim of ongoing child sexual exploitation.

[128] *A City Council* v. *LS* [2019] EWHC 1384 (Fam): no jurisdiction in respect of a 17-year-old who appeared to be the subject of criminal exploitation through organised criminal gangs involved in 'county lines' drug dealing, knife crime and firearms offences. In this case, he had not been accommodated by the LA and both he and his parent objected to any accommodation under CA 1989, s. 20.

person or their parents. The ambiguous legal position of 16- and 17-year-olds is exacerbated by the substantially different role of the state in respect of those who fall into these different categories.

(4) Leaving Home: State Assistance with Financial Support

The list of rights contained in the CRC reflects the view that it is not enough to identify certain liberties essential to a child's capacity for eventual autonomy, such as freedom of speech. These are of no value to those too poor or ill to benefit from them, particularly if their time is taken up surviving from day to day. These rights must therefore be complemented by more positive action on the part of the state to enable children to enjoy fully their basic liberties.[129] Article 26 reserves the right of every child 'to benefit from social security, including social insurance', and Article 27(1) states that governments should 'recognise the right of every child to a standard of living adequate for the child's physical, mental, spiritual, moral and social development'. The obligations that these provisions impose on the state are, however, envisaged as secondary duties that support and supplement the primary role of parents in providing for their children.[130] As a result, there is considerable ambiguity as to the required role of the state when dealing with children who leave home and are not receiving parental support.[131]

Children who leave their homes before attaining adulthood quickly discover that, although the law may recognise their rights to express their views and to reach certain decisions, such rights may be of little value to them. Freedom from the restrictions of family life is often a bleak experience for those who have no correlative rights to financial help or accommodation. Homelessness and poverty combine to produce a host of practical difficulties, so that those without a home have no address and therefore no obvious credentials to offer prospective employers. Those who leave home hurriedly may have no formal identification documents with which to satisfy the demands of the benefits system. Those who are still under the age of 16 will find life particularly difficult, with no legal means of support. They should be in full-time school and so are not entitled to take substantial employment. They have no right to welfare benefits and are not entitled to work-based training places or apprenticeships. If they are determined to stay away from home and the LA fails to assist them, they will have no alternative but to find friends and relatives to care for them, or take to the streets.

Those over 16 may turn to the benefits system for financial assistance. The 16- and 17-year-olds who manage to obtain state support are the lucky few who find their way through a bizarrely complex system of interrelated benefits. It continues

---

[129] Discussed in Chapter 2.   [130] Discussed in Chapter 13.

[131] Although the Committee on the Rights of the Child has given specific consideration to the implementation of the CRC in adolescence, this does not give detailed advice on the implementation of these rights to young people living independently: Committee on the Rights of the Child (2016).

to attract considerable criticism for its harsh discrimination against those under the age of 18. Successive governments have maintained the view that this age group should either be capable of supporting themselves through work or training, or should be supported by their parents while remaining in full-time education.[132] The system of universal credit retains a standard minimum age of 18 for claimants,[133] on the basis of the government's view that 'it would be both inconsistent and regressive for the benefits system to treat 16 and 17-year-olds as ordinarily independent from their parents'.[134] The expectation of dependency on parents is also reinforced by the fact that parents remain able to claim universal credit for their dependent children who are in qualifying education and training between the ages of 16 and 19.[135] Young people who are not able to rely on the support of their parents in the way expected by the government will find it difficult to obtain benefits unless they fall into a narrow range of exceptions. Claims can be made by 16- and 17-year-olds who are pregnant or are themselves responsible for a child, have limited capacity to work, or have substantial caring responsibilities for a severely disabled person.[136] In addition, those who are without parental support can claim in tightly defined circumstances, including that they are estranged from their parents and that they would be at risk of significant harm if remaining at home.[137] This category is, however, treated as a limited exception from the normal expectation that parents will support their adolescent children. Those young people who have been accommodated in the care system are eligible for 'leaving care' support[138] and the expectation that the LA will continue to support them as a reasonable parent.[139] As a result, these young care leavers are only entitled to access the benefits system in even more limited circumstances, essentially requiring the young person to be responsible for a child or to have limited capability for work.[140]

Eligibility to apply for benefits does not necessarily equate to ease of access in practice. Claiming benefit payments is often a harrowing experience for 16–17-year-olds, particularly given that young people who require state support often face far more complex challenges than their peers nationally.[141] Those assisting

---

[132] This approach was first introduced by the Social Security Act 1986 (implemented in 1988), which withdrew the automatic right to draw supplementary benefit (later income support) from those aged 16 and 17.

[133] Welfare Reform Act 2012, s. 4(1)(a).

[134] Chris Grayling MP, speaking as Minister for Employment: *Hansard*, Public Bill Committee, 5th Sitting, col. 191, 29 March 2011.

[135] Universal Credit Regulations 2013 (SI 2013/376), reg. 5.

[136] Ibid. reg. 8. Care leavers are treated differently from those young people who are not leaving care (see below).

[137] Ibid. reg. 8(1)(g) and (3); this provision does not apply to care leavers.

[138] CA 1989, ss 22–4 and Sch. 2, para. 19.

[139] Care Leavers (England) Regulations 2010 (SI 2010/2571).

[140] Universal Credit Regulations 2013 (SI 2013/376), reg. 8(2).

[141] N. Pleace *et al.* (2008) para. 12.116. See also p. 280: 52 per cent of statutorily homeless 16–17-year-olds reported having had anxiety, depression or other mental health problems; 33 per cent had current mental health problems – three times that of young people of the same age in the general population.

young people find that some young claimants never complete the process of claiming benefits; those who do find that what they receive is very hard to live off,[142] with many suffering from financial difficulties.[143] This is exacerbated by the fact that young people are unlikely to have had the education and experience to acquire the skills needed to live within such austere means.[144] Young people with complex needs or chaotic lives may also find it difficult to abide by the stringent requirements for claimants to attend Job Centre commitments in order to claim. While those under 18 are protected from the full weight of the sanctions regime,[145] even a short suspension of benefits can cause extreme hardship given the precarious position in which such young people are placed. Once over 18, young adults living independently have far higher rates of sanction than other claimants, with 18–24-year-olds sanctioned at four times the rate of older claimants.[146] This problem is particularly acute for care leavers who are sanctioned at three times the rate of their peers.[147] These sanctions not only cause hardship, but also impede the supportive role that the Job Centre might otherwise provide in assisting the young person to future adulthood.

The expectation that young people will be supported to at least some degree by their parents is one that underlies both international law and domestic government policy. Those who fall outside of that expectation face considerable legal and practical hurdles in obtaining financial support to provide an adequate standard of living. To meet the right that the CRC guarantees to all children, it is not sufficient to provide subsistence alone, but a standard of living which is adequate for physical, mental, spiritual, moral and social development.[148] While the government has an understandable concern that it should not provide incentives for young people to leave the family home unnecessarily, at present it is difficult for young people living independently to access the support they need to provide for their development in this crucial period of life.

(5) Leaving Home: Assistance with Housing

There are no accurate national statistics measuring the extent of youth homelessness. The official statistics on the numbers of homeless young people relate only to those accepted as statutorily homeless. These figures do not, however, provide a true picture of the problem, since many young people do not approach the statutory agencies.[149] Some homeless young people find accommodation with friends and relatives, and others, perhaps inevitably, spend time

---

[142] Social Security Advisory Committee (2018) p. 18 provides a summary of the current position across a range of benefits. In general, those 16- and 17-year-olds who are eligible are entitled to the same provision as those under 25, but this amount is itself very low to reflect the assumed lower responsibilities of younger adults and the possibility of some level of familial support.
[143] N. Pleace et al. (2008) para. 12.127.   [144] Social Security Advisory Committee (2018) p. 25.
[145] Universal Credit Regulations 2013 (SI 2013/376), regs 102(2)(b), 103(2)(b) and 104(3).
[146] Social Security Advisory Committee (2018).   [147] Children's Society (2017b).
[148] CRC, Art. 27(1).   [149] D. Quilgars et al. (2008).

living rough on the streets.[150] Many children and young people who leave home are caught in a vicious spiral of no home, no address, no job prospects. Although significant advances have been made in the legal framework that applies to homeless young people, the system remains complex, leaving many young people to fall through the cracks between different legal duties to assist them. Further, many of those who are housed are still placed in unsafe or unsuitable conditions. Despite the positive advances in this area, more needs to be done to protect this vulnerable group and assist them in the difficult transition to adulthood.

(A) Homelessness Provision

As long as they are over the age of 16, young people who leave home today are better catered for by the law than they were in the past. For those under 16, even if the children's services authority are prepared to assist, parental objections may prevent such a move.[151] In relation to the older group, since 2002, the categories of 'priority need' include homeless 16- and 17-year-olds and care leavers aged between 18 and 21,[152] thereby imposing a legal obligation on housing authorities to provide them with accommodation.[153] Further, 16- and 17-year-olds remain 'children' for the purposes of the Children Act and as such many benefit from significant legal duties owed by children's services to those who are 'in need', including a duty to accommodate.[154] Despite this network of protective duties, many young people do not receive the help to which they are entitled; indeed, some research suggests that only one in five young people who present as homeless to their LA will actually receive accommodation.[155]

Not all young people who present as homeless will be best served by being accommodated by the LA. Many of this older group will have left home precipitately.[156] Indeed, housing authorities are increasingly finding that a major cause of homelessness throughout the country is young people being asked to leave by their parents.[157] Official guidance states that since it is generally in the best interests of 16- and 17-year-olds to live at home, the possibility of a reconciliation should be explored through family mediation strategies, unless relations have broken down irretrievably or it would not be

---

[150] Social Security Advisory Committee (2018) p. 16.
[151] CA 1989, s. 20(7) and (8); discussed above.
[152] Homelessness (Priority Need for Accommodation) (England) Order 2002 (SI 2002/2051).
[153] I.e. under the Housing Act 1996, s. 193(2).
[154] CA 1989, s. 20(3); the circumstances in which this duty arises are considered further below.
[155] I. Pona and R. Crellin (2015) esp. Pt 4.
[156] Young care leavers are also at particular risk of homelessness. Care leavers aged 16 and 17 are 'relevant children' and entitled to be provided with accommodation by the LA (CA 1989, s. 23B(8)) and to be provided with ongoing 'leaving care' support into early adulthood.
[157] Centrepoint report that 59 per cent of young people accessing their services have been asked to leave home due to breakdown of their family relationships: A. Gill (2016).

safe for the young person to return.[158] Research suggests that mediation is very commonly used as part of the homelessness assessment process for 16- and 17-year-olds,[159] and that it can be effective.[160] While ostensibly sensible, there is a real danger that some young people feel pressurised into returning to an unsafe home as a short-term 'fix',[161] or that support ceases at the point of return, leaving the relationship vulnerable to future deterioration.[162]

The accommodation needs of homeless 16- and 17-year-olds are now well recognised. If estranged from their families, they will be particularly vulnerable and may need a range of extra support.

> These young people's childhoods were very often marred by extremely difficult and fractured family relations – with family restructuring, violence, parents with mental health problems, and frequent moves commonly experienced – and many had also had a very disrupted education. Large proportions had experienced mental health and/or substance misuse problems.[163]

Accommodation alone is seldom sufficient, since they will often lack skills at managing their affairs and will need the advice and support normally available to that age group from their own families. For these reasons, it is clear that the majority of young people who are homeless, or at risk of homelessness, will be children 'in need'[164] and so should receive a full range of support services from children's services to safeguard them and promote their welfare. These duties owed by children's services to children in need also include a duty to provide accommodation to those who meet the criteria under section 20 of the CA 1989. Section 20(3) of the CA 1989 does not impose an *absolute* legal obligation on children's services to accommodate this group of older teenagers, as it only arises in relation to those over the age of 16 *if* their welfare is considered 'likely to be seriously prejudiced' without it. Nonetheless, the majority of young people who are homeless, including those 'sofa surfing' or in insecure accommodation, are very likely to fulfil this test.[165] There are, however, some who will not, either because they are able to access other safe accommodation with assistance or because they refuse to be accommodated by children's services in this way.[166]

---

[158] Ministry of Housing, Communities and Local Government (2018) para. 2.1.

[159] D. Quilgars *et al.* (2008) pp. 65–8; A. Gill (2016).

[160] I. Pona and R. Crellin (2015) p. 34 found that in two-thirds of cases in their sample, mediation was effective in rebuilding the family and preventing homelessness. They also emphasise the importance of ongoing support for the family relationships once the child has returned home.

[161] Inter alia: Shelter (2005) pp. 9–10; D. Quilgars *et al.* (2008) pp. 66–8.

[162] Effective mediation services for those young people who are *at risk* of homelessness may also be an effective means of fulfilling the duty to prevent homelessness introduced by the Homelessness Reduction Act 2017.

[163] N. Pleace *et al.* (2008) para. 12.134.

[164] The term 'child in need' is defined by CA 1989, s. 17(1).

[165] Baroness Hale regarded it as 'quite obvious' that a 'sofa surfing' child was in need and would require accommodation under s. 20: *R (G)* v. *Southwark London Borough Council* [2009] UKHL 26, [2009] 1 WLR 1299, at [28].

[166] Ibid.

A continuing problem has been ensuring that housing and children's services cooperate in providing these young people with an appropriate package
of services.[167] The relationship between the duties owed under the Children
Act and those contained in housing legislation is now quite clear in law but
persists in causing problems in practice. Although the relationship between
different statutory duties to house children might appear rather dry and
technical at first sight, it is of enormous practical significance to the young
people affected. Those young people who are housed under section 20 of the
CA 1989 are 'looked-after children' and as such are entitled to a wide range of
support services, including the leaving care obligations, which continue into
their early adulthood.[168] Those accommodated under housing legislation are
not entitled to this wider or longer-term support and find themselves reliant on
the benefit system to meet their costs. As such, the statutory regime through
which young people are accommodated is of vital importance to the support
they receive throughout this period and in their transition to independence.[169]
The cost of providing such support has in the past led to LAs trying to avoid
using section 20 of the CA 1989 by turning to other provisions instead. The law
is now clear that if section 20 applies, it takes priority over alternative obligations. The legal starting point is the 2002 Order which extended 'priority need'
housing obligations to 16- and 17-year-olds, while expressly excluding those
accommodated under section 20 of the CA 1989 from its remit.[170] As Baroness
Hale of Richmond observed in *R (M)* v. *Hammersmith and Fulham London
Borough Council*,[171] the Order clearly contemplates that 'social services rather
than housing should take the long term responsibility' for those young people
who fulfil the criteria in section 20 of the CA 1989. In this case, there was no
doubt that the housing authority should have referred the homeless 17-year-
old to children's services and that they should have accepted responsibility for
her, given her deeply troubled background and her need for far more than
a roof over her head.[172] Any doubt on this point was removed by the House of
Lords' decision in *R (G)* v. *Southwark London Borough Council*.[173] In that case,
the LA argued that they had met a 'sofa surfing' child's needs through help with

---

[167] CA 2004, ss 10–11 reinforce this duty to cooperate.

[168] A child becomes eligible for leaving care services if he or she is aged between 16 and 17 and has
been looked after (i.e. provided with accommodation under CA 1989, s. 20) for at least 13
weeks since the attainment of 14. These services were first introduced in Children (Leaving
Care) Act 2000, and are designed to recognise both the poor outcomes for many care leavers
and that young adults outside of the care system often receive ongoing support from their
families after the age of 18. Care leavers' entitlement to financial support and accommodation
continues until at least 21; for those in tertiary education it may extend beyond their 25th
birthday.

[169] I. Pona and R. Crellin (2015).

[170] Homelessness (Priority Need for Accommodation) (England) Order 2002 (SI 2002/2051), Art.
3. The duty also excludes 'relevant children', i.e. a care leaver, entitled to accommodation
under the leaving care legislation.

[171] [2008] UKHL 14, [2008] 1 WLR 535, at [31].   [172] Ibid. at [33].

[173] [2009] UKHL 26, [2009] 1 WLR 1299.

accommodation under housing legislation and that he did not require the more extensive obligations owed under section 20. The House of Lords unanimously rejected this argument: a child in this position was clearly 'in need' and met the criteria under section 20 of the CA 1989. As such, the LA could not side-step its obligations by claiming to be acting under alternative legislation.[174] This clear legal position is underlined by the guidance, which unambiguously states that section 20 takes precedence when it applies.[175]

While the duties owed in section 20 clearly take priority over housing legislation, an effective response to homelessness requires close cooperation between the two services, especially as not all young people will be eligible under section 20 and that children's services may need the assistance of the housing authority in providing accommodation for those that do. It is also important that children receive the same assessment and treatment regardless of which service they first approach, particularly in assessing their needs and entitlements. The housing guidance has consistently directed both services to establish joint protocols for liaising over this group of applicants, to ensure that joint assessments of the young person's needs are carried out[176] and that young people are not needlessly 'passed back and forth between services'. Research for the Children's Society found that in half of the cases reviewed, young people presenting to the local LA as homeless did not receive any formal assessment and that, of those that did, a substantial minority were assessed without reference to children's services.[177] The same research reveals that assessments carried out by children's services most often result in the child being returned home having been found not to be in need, with only 20 per cent of assessments resulting in accommodation under section 20.[178] These numbers must raise the concern that children's services are anxious to avoid triggering long-term and expensive leaving care liabilities.[179]

Although the legal obligations owed to homeless young people have become more extensive and certain, the law remains complex and often confusing for those trying to navigate it without sufficient advice and assistance. Many face obstacles to proper assessment and provision of services. A further concern is that young people seeking to become independent may resist becoming 'looked-after' children without understanding the significant consequences that this may have for their future. For those that do receive help, it is crucial that 16- and 17-year-olds are placed in appropriate accommodation. As noted below, it is still somewhat of a lottery whether this occurs.

---

[174] Including CA 1989, s. 17.

[175] Ministry of Housing, Communities and Local Government (2018) paras 1.1–1.3.

[176] Ibid. ch. 6.   [177] I. Pona and R. Crellin (2015).   [178] Ibid. Pt 4.

[179] A child becomes eligible for leaving care services if he or she is aged between 16 and 17 and has been looked after (i.e. provided with accommodation under CA 1989, s. 20) for at least 13 weeks since the attainment of 14. If a child ought to have been accommodated under CA 1989, s. 20, the obligations will still apply, even if the LA has purported to accommodate under a different provision: *R (on the application of TG)* v. *London Borough of Lambeth* [2011] EWCA Civ 526, [2011] 2 FLR 1007.

(B) Supported Accommodation

> Housing emerged as the life area most closely associated with mental well-being, outstripping the contribution made by involvement in education and training.[180]

The need to develop more suitable supported accommodation for the 16–18-year age group has been recognised for many years. As long ago as 2002, housing authorities were required to formulate an over-arching homelessness strategy within their areas, to prevent homelessness and to secure that appropriate accommodation is available.[181] The guidance on implementing this duty emphasises that 16- and 17-year-olds must be provided with support alongside accommodation, to recognise the vulnerabilities prevalent in this age group and to support the young person's positive transition towards independence.[182]

Most LAs make use of a range of accommodation for 16- and 17-year-olds, including supported lodgings, trainer flats, hostels and foyers.[183] While improvements in provision have taken place,[184] progress is patchy.[185] Young people are still being placed in very unsuitable accommodation in rough areas, in which they sometimes feel very unsafe,[186] and/or far from their support networks.[187] Official guidance is clear that bed and breakfast (B & B) accommodation is unsuitable and should not be used.[188] It is similarly clear that young people are often at risk in mixed-age hostels and that all-age night shelters should not be used, even in an emergency.[189] Despite this clarity in the guidance, a surprisingly high number of 16–17-year-olds are still being placed in B & B 'hotels' and other unsuitable accommodation.[190] Complaints to the Local Government and Social Care Ombudsman concerning unsuitable accommodation are depressingly common and frequently upheld.[191] These complaints reveal young people who are wrongly denied housing, left in unsafe B & B accommodation, or even abandoned with only a tent for shelter.[192]

---

[180] J. Wade and J. Dixon (2006) p. 203.   [181] Homelessness Act 2002, ss 1–4.

[182] Ministry of Housing, Communities and Local Government (2018) esp. paras 5.9 and 5.14.

[183] J. Wade and J. Dixon (2006) p. 202.

[184] D. Quilgars et al. (2008) pp. 30–1: in some areas, the Supporting People programme (established in 2003) has helped provide housing-related support services for vulnerable groups, such as young homeless people.

[185] J. Wade and J. Dixon (2006) p. 203; B. Broad (2005) pp. 377–8.

[186] D. Quilgars et al. (2008) pp. 52–3.

[187] J. Wade and J. Dixon (2006) p. 204. See also R. Morgan (2006b) p. 12.

[188] Ministry of Housing, Communities and Local Government (2018) para. 5.10.

[189] Ibid. para. 5.12.

[190] I. Pona and R. Crellin (2015) p. 40 found that 8 per cent of young people were placed in B & B accommodation despite the clear prohibition on its use.

[191] Local Government and Social Care Ombudsman (2017) notes that 70 per cent of such complaints are upheld, although this number does not distinguish complaints by lone young people and those by families with children.

[192] See e.g. the respective reports by the Local Government and Social Care Ombudsman: Investigation into a complaint against London Borough of Islington (reference number: 17 011 285) 31 May 2018 (wrongful refusal to provide accommodation to 16-year-old at risk of homelessness); Investigation into a complaint against Lancashire County Council (reference number: 13 020 158) 5 August 2015 (teenager with complex needs wrongly accommodated in

The resulting investigations often reveal a lack of understanding of duties owed to young people in some LAs and a crisis in available accommodation in many areas.

Those who are accommodated in accordance with the law and guidance still often find themselves facing significant risks. A particular concern arises in respect of those young people placed by children's services in supported accommodation rather than in foster care or children's homes.[193] This is because supported accommodation provided to looked-after 16- and 17-year-olds is not subject to the same system of regulation and registration as that required of children's homes which provide care and accommodation for younger children.[194] While LAs are under a duty to ensure that this accommodation is 'suitable',[195] it is clear that in many cases it is not. There is substantial evidence that young people in such accommodation are often exposed to significant risks, including drug-taking, sexual exploitation, violence and involvement with gangs.[196] As many of these young people have already experienced abuse, neglect and poor mental health, they are often particularly vulnerable to these risks, a fact that does not escape the notice of those who target these young people for sexual and criminal exploitation.[197] Far from providing support on the path to independent living, some of these settings expose young people to further risks to the detriment of their safety and life chances. While regulation itself cannot eliminate all of these risks, there are compelling reasons to extend regulation to these settings to safeguard these young people at a crucial stage of life. The government is committed to introducing new standards to regulate supported accommodation, with Ofsted overseeing the inspection of providers.[198] The proposed regime is undoubtedly an improvement on the current system that fails so many young people. It does, however, fall some way short of the tighter regulation for younger

---

bed and breakfast); and Investigation into a complaint against Cornwall Council (reference number: 17 005 652) 31 August 2018 (vulnerable 17-year-old provided with accommodation in static caravan and later a tent).

[193] It is estimated that around 22 per cent of looked-after 16- and 17-year-olds are accommodated in such 'other arrangements', although many more spend a period of time in such accommodation before returning home or transferring elsewhere: R. Crellin and I. Pona (2015).

[194] Children's homes must be registered and are regulated by Ofsted under the Care Standards Act 2000 and The Children's Homes (England) Regulations 2015 (SI 2015/541). It is illegal to operate a children's home without registration; this extends to the provision of care provided to 16- and 17-year-olds who are not able to live independently. Discussed further in Chapter 16.

[195] In relation to looked-after children, this obligation is contained in CA 1989, s. 22(6)(d) and Care Planning, Placement and Case Review (England) Regulations 2010 (SI 2010/959), reg. 27 and Sch. 6. Housing authorities providing accommodation are also required to ensure that that accommodation is suitable under Housing Act 1996, s. 206.

[196] Children's Commissioner (2020); R. Crellin and I. Pona (2015).

[197] R. Crellin and I. Pona (2015). Children's Commissioner (2020) p. 21 includes reports from the police that some providers of unregulated accommodation are affiliated to major organised crime networks and use the unregulated nature of provision in order to exploit children.

[198] DfE (2021).

children in care.[199] Although 16- and 17-year-olds benefit from a regime that guides them towards independence, many are not yet ready to take this step without the provision of care that is absent in both the current regime and the proposed standards.[200]

The lack of appropriate accommodation for homeless young people is exacerbated by the scarcity of affordable accommodation in the rented sector. Furthermore, the little understood principle of property law barring those under 18 from executing a legal lease greatly exacerbates the difficulties of homeless 16- and 17-year-olds seeking housing authority accommodation. A widespread misunderstanding of the law prevents this principle being avoided by relatively simple expedients.[201] For example, since a minor can hold an equitable tenancy in any property,[202] if a minor arranges to take a tenancy, it will operate as a contract for a lease,[203] binding on him or her, unless and until repudiated.[204] Nevertheless, housing authorities often refuse to offer tenancies to under 18-year-olds unless the children's services authority act as guarantor, which they may not wish to do.[205] For those who do obtain accommodation, the shared accommodation rate puts a ceiling on the benefits for which they are eligible, which in many areas means that very little accommodation is affordable to those in this position.[206] Young people fending for themselves for the first time may, in any event, be far more appropriately accommodated in supported accommodation, provided that that accommodation is of an appropriate standard.

(6) Children 'Divorcing' Their Parents

(A) The Child Applicant

A child leaving home will often turn to friends or relations for accommodation and help. In such circumstances, obtaining a court order approving such an arrangement clarifies the carer's legal position. Indeed, obtaining a child arrangements order under section 8 of the CA 1989 is a simpler way of

---

[199] A prohibition on placing under 16s in this form of accommodation was introduced by the Care Planning, Placement and Case Review (England) (Amendment) Regulations 2021 (SI 2021/161).

[200] Children's Commissioner (2020).

[201] D. Cowan and N. Deardon (2002) pp. 173–82: a detailed exposition of the legal pitfalls and remedies regarding the grant of tenancies to under-age tenants.

[202] Taking effect under the Trusts of Land and Appointment of Trustees Act 1996, Sch. 2, para. 2. See D. Cowan and N. Deardon (2002) pp. 173–82; J. Morgan (2000).

[203] Suitable accommodation for a minor will also inevitably be deemed 'a necessity'.

[204] See Hale J's explanation of a minor's position regarding leases of land in *Kingston upon Thames Borough Council* v. *Prince* [1999] 1 FLR 593.

[205] Shelter (2006) pp. 25–6.

[206] The shared accommodation rate applies to those under 35 (assuming that they are single and without dependent children) and is limited to the average rent for a room in a shared house. Social Security Advisory Committee (2018) pp. 37–42 demonstrates the difficulties faced in finding affordable accommodation for those subject to the rate.

obtaining a judicial stamp of approval for a child now living with someone outside his or her immediate family. Children may take the initiative and apply for such orders themselves.[207] A child arrangements order confirming the new carer's parental responsibility for the child[208] not only avoids the risk of criminal charges under the Child Abduction Act 1984,[209] but also persuades schools and other agencies that the carer has authority to make decisions regarding the child.[210]

It is a remarkably liberal aspect of English law that the CA 1989, by permitting children to apply for section 8 orders, enables them to instruct their own solicitors and initiate proceedings, thereby forcing their parents to answer their claims. It in no way detracts from the liberality of these provisions that they do not guarantee that the outcome will necessarily be what these children want. The court may ultimately decide that an order complying with a child's own wishes would not be in his or her best interests. Despite this, embarking on litigation is, in itself, a dramatic way of taking independent action. The fact that a solicitor who considers a child competent to give instructions is able to respect that child's wishes on this, and treat him or her as a client, indicates the extent to which English law currently acknowledges children's capacity for making important choices in their lives and taking the responsibility to pursue them.

It is unlikely that many solicitors would take instructions from a child very much below adolescence.[211] Indeed, children face at least two procedural hurdles before the courts hear their applications for section 8 orders under the CA 1989. They must first convince their solicitors that they have sufficient understanding to instruct them without a guardian or litigation friend.[212] Next, they must obtain leave from the court under section 10(8) to proceed with the application. Leave can only be obtained if they convince the court that they have 'sufficient understanding' to apply for the section 8 order in question.

A solicitor considering that the child would pass this test may nevertheless suggest that the adult with whom the child intends to live makes the application instead, perhaps to avoid the child being closely involved in potentially unpleasant litigation. But there are tactical reasons why an application by the

---

[207] Having first obtained leave to do so under CA 1989, s. 10(8).

[208] CA 1989, s. 12(2): anyone named in the order as a person with whom the child is to live will have parental responsibility for the duration of that order. This provision does not remove the parents' existing parental responsibility.

[209] Discussed above.

[210] E.g. *B v. B (A Minor) (Residence Order)* [1992] 2 FLR 327: the High Court agreed that, although under the CA 1989, s. 3(5), the child's grandmother could, as her carer, take decisions necessary to safeguard her welfare, a residence order (now known as a children arrangements order) would provide her granddaughter's school with legal confirmation of her authority to do so.

[211] Further, orders under CA 1989, s. 8 may not be made in respect of children aged 16 or over unless the court is satisfied that the circumstances are exceptional: CA 1989, s. 9(7).

[212] Both solicitor and court must be convinced on this score; discussed further in Chapter 12.

child might be preferable. In the first place, applications by children have received some protection from the removal of legal aid from most private family proceedings, meaning that it may be more likely that a child will receive public funding.[213] Second, the child might be more successful in obtaining leave to proceed because the qualifying formula applicable to a child under section 10(8) is different from the checklist of factors to be considered under section 10(9) on the application of an adult to obtain leave.[214] The legal outcome will be no different, whether the child takes the initiative and obtains leave under section 10(8) to apply for a child arrangements order, or the third-party residential carer does so under section 10(9).[215] As noted below, in each case, the order will be in the adult's 'favour', in so far as it vests parental responsibility in the person with whom the child now wishes to live.

(B) Applying for Court Leave

Despite the potential offered by section 10(8), there has been a relative dearth of case law testing out these provisions, which may suggest that they are little used in practice. Those that have reached the courts have received a mixed judicial response. This method of resolving family disputes very obviously challenges well-established perceptions about the appropriate roles of parent and child. There is a variety of misgivings about children's ability to litigate in this fashion. It can be particularly damaging for a child to become drawn into what may essentially be a dispute between the child's own parents over the child's future care. Furthermore, those with a specialised knowledge of child development often doubt their ability to maintain a sense of proportion if they get involved in their parents' disputes.[216] In the more typical running away scenario, where the child has fallen out with *both* parents,[217] the parents may

---

[213] Legal Aid, Sentencing and Punishment of Offenders Act 2012, Sch. 1, para. 15.

[214] E.g. *Re SC (A Minor) (Leave to Seek Residence Order)* [1994] 1 FLR 96: the foster carer with whom the child, S, wished to live had been considered and rejected by the LA as a prospective foster parent for S and so was unlikely to satisfy the test under s. 10(9) for obtaining leave to apply for a residence order. The factors listed in s. 10(9) are not exhaustive and do not constitute a test to be passed; instead, they are matters of particular relevance to the court's decision: *Re B (Grandmother: Joinder as Party)* [2012] EWCA Civ 737, [2012] 2 FLR 1358.

[215] E.g. *Re O (Minors) (Leave to Seek Residence Order)* [1994] 1 FLR 172: a distant cousin of two boys aged 13 and 10 was persuaded by them to go to the magistrates' court to seek a residence order authorising them to stay with him rather than returning to their mother and their alcoholic stepfather. In some circumstances, the carer may be entitled to apply for an order without leave, e.g. a relative with whom the child has lived for at least a year: CA 1989, s. 10(5B).

[216] See the child psychiatrist's doubts about the boy, N's, ability to instruct his own solicitor in *Re N (Contact: Minor Seeking Leave to Defend and Removal of Guardian)* [2003] 1 FLR 652, at 658.

[217] E.g. *Re CE (Section 37 Direction)* [1995] 1 FLR 26: CE, a girl of 14, ran away to live with her boyfriend and his parents, against the wishes of her own parents. Her parents applied for a residence order to determine where she should live. Their application was countered by CE herself instructing a solicitor to do the same on her own behalf.

argue that strangers to the family are unaware of the dangers of allowing a young person's wishes to cloud adult perceptions of their safety.

Case law has clarified the fact that the leave application under section 10(8) is not governed by the paramountcy criterion.[218] Thus, it is the court hearing the substantive application which must determine whether an order would be in the child's best interests, not the court hearing the leave application itself. Nevertheless, concerns over the wisdom of allowing children's applications for section 8 orders continue to colour the way in which leave applications are themselves dealt with.[219] For example, refusing to allow S, a highly intelligent 12-year-old boy, to proceed with his application for a section 8 order is open to criticism on a number of fronts.[220] Despite concluding that S had 'sufficient understanding' for the purposes of the CA 1989, section 10(8),[221] Johnson J did not consider that his evidence would add anything to the evidence provided by S's father in support of his own application.[222] Admittedly, the court would inevitably hear the evidence supporting these parents' respective applications, whether or not S provided his own interpretation of the situation. Nevertheless, the legislative formula contained in section 10(8) does not obviously allow the judiciary to refuse leave merely because the child intends to give similar evidence to his parent. More seriously, such an approach discounted the boy's own perspectives. Nor would such a refusal enhance his respect for the judicial process given the legislation apparently providing him with a procedural right to give his side of the picture, once he had established sufficient maturity to do so. This approach adds an extra obstacle in the way of children seeking leave under section 10(8).[223] Although it now seems unlikely that children need persuade the court that their applications are likely to succeed,[224] they must convince the court that their prospects of success are not so remote as to be unsustainable;[225] they must have sufficient understanding to apply; and their own case must be different from that of any other party in the dispute.

---

[218] *Re SC (A Minor) (Leave to Seek Residence Order)* [1994] 1 FLR 96; *Re C (Residence: Child's Application for Leave)* [1995] 1 FLR 927; *Re H (Residence Order: Child's Application for Leave)* [2000] 1 FLR 780.

[219] E.g. *Re C (A Minor) (Leave to Seek Section 8 Orders)* [1994] 1 FLR 26: a 15-year-old was refused leave to apply for a specific issue order to gain judicial authority to go to Bulgaria for a 2-week holiday with another family against her parents' wishes. Per Johnson J, a disagreement over a holiday was not sufficiently important to justify litigation.

[220] *Re H (Residence Order: Child's Application for Leave)* [2000] 1 FLR 780.

[221] Perhaps predictable, given that the boy had been placed by an educational psychologist in the 99th intelligence percentile.

[222] *Re H (Residence Order: Child's Application for Leave)* [2000] 1 FLR 780, at 783.

[223] C. Sawyer (1995) p. 205.

[224] *Re J (Leave to Issue Application for Residence Order)* [2003] 1 FLR 114, per Thorpe LJ, at [18].

[225] *Re B (Grandmother: Joinder as Party)* [2012] EWCA Civ 737, [2012] 2 FLR 1358. See also *Re W (Care Proceedings: Leave to Apply)* [2004] EWHC 3342 (Fam), [2005] 2 FLR 468, per Sumner J, at [28], in the context of a s. 10(9) application.

Not all section 10(8) applications brought by children are interpreted so restrictively. Stuart-White J approached a teenager's application for leave very differently in *Re C (Residence: Child's Application for Leave)*.[226] There, despite her father's claims that C lacked objectivity and insight, the court accepted evidence indicating that she had the understanding needed by section 10(8). She was aged 14, articulate, with very decided views of her own, and she was not content with these being presented for her by the court welfare officer. Stuart-White J appreciated that if he now refused her leave she would be unable to explain what her real views were.

The limited reporting of children's leave applications suggests that there are very few children troubled enough, bold enough or with the resources to seek judicial assistance over establishing where they should live. When they do, their way should be cleared rather than obstructed. Their ability to initiate an application for a section 8 order to resolve a situation which they find unbearable may prevent them from simply disappearing from view.

(C) Effect of a Section 8 Order Obtained on a Child's Application

Having granted a child leave to apply for a section 8 order, the court must decide the substantive application; at that stage, it must arbitrate between a child totally opposed to returning home and parents strongly opposed to the child staying away. Despite media comment when the Children Act 1989 was first introduced, if the child is successful the result achieved does not involve that child 'divorcing' his or her parents.[227] As Freeman points out, unlike the situation on divorce, which enables the parties to remarry with the possibility of an entirely new legal relationship, the child–parent legal relationship persists.[228] Given its drastic effect, few would advocate allowing young people here to obtain declarations of emancipation from their parents, as in some states of the US.[229] Nevertheless, in the event of a child arrangements order being granted, its subject is left in a kind of legal limbo. While the order remains in being, responsibility for all major decisions remain within the purview of adults – the child's present carers, but shared with his or her natural parents. The child has no greater legal status than before and remains under his or her parents' responsibility, despite their having been rejected by the child and the court as suitable carers. This must appear incomprehensible to child applicants, since it is intrinsically unlikely that a court will willingly grant a residence order on their application, unless their home circumstances have deteriorated very seriously.

---

[226] [1995] 1 FLR 927.

[227] The effect of CA 1989, ss 2(6) and 12 is that the adult acquiring parental responsibility through a child arrangements order shares parental responsibility for the child with the child's parents.

[228] M. Freeman (1996) p. 159.

[229] J. Fortin (2003) pp. 115–16 discusses the American system of emancipation. Once child petitioners in the US obtain declarations of emancipation, their parents have no further obligation to provide moral or financial support for them of any kind at all.

If the relationship between the young person and the parents has broken down to the extent that the young person objects to the parents retaining parental authority over decisions, it may be possible to persuade a court to take further action to restrict that authority. In theory, a child has the means of persuading a court to terminate her unmarried father's parental responsibility,[230] but the law retains the anomalous position that there is no means by which a child might ensure that an abusive mother or married father's parental responsibility is similarly terminated.[231] While this distinction is difficult to justify, successful applications to remove parental responsibility are vanishingly rare.[232] In extreme cases in which the relationship is beyond repair, a more pragmatic solution may be for the carer to apply for a special guardianship order, allowing the carer to control the parents' use of parental responsibility.[233] Alternatively, the child may themselves apply to the court for an order to control the parents' exercise of authority. For example, in *PD* v. *SD, JD and X County Council*,[234] the relationship between a 16-year-old and his parents had completely broken down as they struggled to accept his gender identity and new name. He was living separately from his parents[235] and able to give valid consent to his own medical treatment,[236] but sought to prevent his parents obtaining any further information about that treatment or his welfare. The court readily agreed to his application, finding that the balance of the case fell 'decisively' in favour of P's privacy rights under Article 8 of the ECHR given his age and complete disengagement from his parents. This liberal approach recognised both the importance of P's growing autonomy rights and the pragmatic fact that failure to respect his privacy was likely to further impede any hope of reconciliation. Whether the courts would be willing to apply this approach to younger children remains to be seen.

---

[230] CA 1989, s. 4(3)(b): a child can apply for an order terminating the father's parental responsibility provided he or she first obtains leave of the court. Similar provisions apply in respect of 'second female parents' and step-parents: CA 1989, s. 4ZA(6)(b) and 4A(3)(b).

[231] *Re B (A Minor) (Adoption: Natural Parent)* [2001] UKHL 70, [2002] 1 WLR 258. In *H* v. *A (No. 1)* [2015] EWFC 58, the court briefly considered the argument that this law violates the rights of marital children under ECHR Arts 8 and 14 as they have less protection than those of unmarried fathers. In this case, an order prohibiting a married father from using his parental responsibility was made following his callous disregard for the safety and well-being of the children, including his actions in setting fire to his car and driving it into the home where the children and their mother were present.

[232] *DW (A Child) (Terminating Parental Responsibility)* [2014] EWCA Civ 315, [2015] 1 FLR 166: in one of rare reported cases in which parental responsibility has been removed, the father had inflicted 'devastating acts of abuse on the family' through his sexual abuse of the child's half-siblings.

[233] CA 1989, s. 14C(1)(b).   [234] [2015] EWHC 4103 (Fam).

[235] At the time of the application, he was looked after by the LA under CA 1989, s. 20.

[236] As he had attained 16 years old: Family Law Reform Act 1969, s. 8(3). Discussed further in Chapter 11.

(7) Children's Right to Parental Money

The young person who becomes estranged from his or her parents and leaves home under the age of 18 is in an anomalous position. Even those who, through a court order, have gained judicial permission to live with someone other than their parents have no means of gaining complete financial independence without considerable assistance from some well-meaning adult. As noted above, they have very limited entitlement to social security benefits and will therefore suffer severe poverty, unless they can obtain reasonably paid employment or financial support from their parents or other carers.

A young person wishing to extract financial support from a parent will find that the legal principles governing the child–parent relationship produce a bizarre situation, even in the event of that parent being exceptionally wealthy. These principles reflect the assumption that if money is to be extracted, it should be done by an adult and not by the child. If parents are separated, it is, of course, perfectly feasible for one parent to apply for child maintenance from the other parent. But a parent cannot do so unless the child has remained at home in the parent's care. So those who refuse to live with either parent are in an anomalous position. One might assume that an older child could independently initiate maintenance proceedings against a parent, particularly if the parent is extremely wealthy and the teenager is living in impoverished circumstances. But unlike Scottish law, which allows any child having attained the age of 12 to initiate an application under the Child Support Act 1991,[237] children in England and Wales are not provided with any direct method of doing so. This gap in the English law seems odd, particularly given Baroness Hale of Richmond's conviction that children themselves have a civil right to be maintained by their parents and that this survives the child support legislation.[238]

The child support legislation only allows maintenance proceedings to be taken by an adult who is providing the child with a home and day-to-day care.[239] If an adult with whom an older child has taken refuge is prepared to take such a step, the child maintenance will obviously provide the child with much-needed financial assistance. Furthermore, an adult who has first obtained a child arrangements order authorising him or her to provide the child with a home can then apply to the courts for an additional order, forcing the parents to assist even more generously with the child's maintenance.[240] But adults with whom a runaway takes refuge may simply decide that they do not want the unpleasantness of initiating either set of proceedings against the parents – in which case, the child has no means at all of taking the matter into their own hands.

---

[237] CSA 1991, s. 7(1) enables children habitually resident in Scotland, having attained the age of 12 years, to apply for a maintenance assessment under the Act.

[238] *R (Kehoe)* v. *Secretary of State for Work and Pensions* [2005] UKHL 48, [2006] 1 AC 42, at [71] and [73].

[239] CSA 1991, s. 3(3). The person with care does not need to be a parent of the child, as long as they usually provide day-to-day care for the child and the child has a home with that person.

[240] I.e. under CA 1989, Sch. 1, para. 1.

Only elderly 'children' over the age of 18 seem to attract legislative attention in so far as they can utilise the legislative methods available to separating parents[241] and divorcing parents[242] to force their parents to maintain them. But applicants must justify such claims by reference to their educational or other special needs,[243] and can only apply at all if their parents are already living separately.[244] It seems unsupportable that despite children being able to 'divorce their parents', there is no obvious way for a child under the age of 18 to initiate maintenance proceedings against such parents, unless those parents divorce each other. This gap in the law suggests that the legislation is not designed for teenagers trying to sort out financial disputes with their parents themselves.

The type of family conflict which results in parents refusing to support their offspring might continue beyond the grave. A wealthy parent may die leaving a will excluding their estranged children entirely. The terms of the will could, of course, be disputed by the disinherited child (assisted by an adult litigation friend) bringing an application for reasonable provision out of the parent's estate.[245] Although the success of such an application is by no means a foregone conclusion, since it will depend on the court's view of the merits of the child's case, it seems unlikely that the court would refuse such an application entirely.[246] The dearth of relevant case law concerning minor children suggests that these situations rarely occur. If the parent dies intestate, the principles of law governing the distribution of his or her estate ensure that there is often little or nothing left from the estate for any issue after the surviving widow or widower takes their share.[247] Well-established case law demonstrates the inequities that such rules can produce.[248]

---

[241] CA 1989, Sch. 1, para. 2(1). But under para. 2(3), a child can only apply on attaining the age of 18 if a periodical payments order has not been in force with respect to him prior to his attaining the age of 16. The teenager who has been the subject of a periodical payments order prior to attaining 16 can himself apply for a variation of that order, on attaining that age.

[242] Matrimonial Causes Act 1973, s. 23(1).   [243] CA 1989, Sch. 1, para. 2(1).

[244] Ibid. para. 2(4).

[245] A child of married or unmarried parents can claim, under the Inheritance (Provision for Family and Dependants) Act 1975, a share in a deceased parent's estate on the basis that the will did not make reasonable provision for him or her. Claims are not restricted to the child's minority and may also be made by adult children: e.g. *Ilott* v. *Mitson* [2017] UKSC 17, [2018] AC 545.

[246] See Inheritance (Provision for Family and Dependants) Act 1975, s. 3, for the factors relevant to such an application, such as the financial resources and needs of the applicant. The child's potential need for education and training would be particularly relevant.

[247] Under the Administration of Estates Act 1925, s. 46, the surviving spouse is treated generously – i.e. a statutory legacy and half of any residue. Although legally, the remaining half of the residue is held on trust for the children, the surviving spouse's statutory legacy may entirely drain the estate.

[248] E.g., inter alia: *Sivyer* v. *Sivyer* [1967] 1 WLR 1482 (the intestate's entire estate went to his widow, who had been his second wife, with nothing left for his 13-year-old daughter by a previous marriage); *Re Collins (Decd)* [1990] Fam 56 (the deceased died having obtained a decree nisi [but not a decree absolute] of divorce against her husband; her husband was duly entitled to the whole of her estate on her intestacy, with nothing left for their son and her illegitimate daughter).

(8) Conclusion

Children and young people living in well-functioning families are not particularly affected by the confused hotchpotch of legal principles governing their gradual attainment of legal autonomy. These principles, though bewildering, do not impinge greatly on their everyday life. In the event of family life going badly wrong, however, young people are left in a complex web of, often inconsistent, laws and policies. That law is increasingly based on an assumption that most young people will be dependent on their parents, but is not accompanied by a financial safety net for those who are not able to do so. In practice, leaving home is often accompanied by considerable financial and emotional hardship. The law neither protects their wage-earning nor provides them with appropriate welfare benefits or a route to financial support from their parents. The destitution and despair experienced by minors of all ages who run away from home shows the extent to which English law is failing to live up to its international obligations under the CRC. While the law provides that those in need of a place to live should find themselves supported in safe accommodation, in practice, many are turned away and those that are housed frequently find themselves in risky, unregulated placements. Indeed, this group of children slip through the net at every turn and simply do not obtain the special protection and support that should attend the legal status of minority.

Overall, it appears that the law is attempting to have its cake and eat it. On the one hand, it withholds an adult legal status from all children under the age of 18, on the basis that they require special protection. But on the other hand, it also assumes that the source of this protection will be provided by parents and withholds it from those children who inconveniently refuse to fit into family life.

Bibliography

NB: Many of these publications can be obtained on the relevant organisation's website.

All-Party Parliamentary Group for Runaway and Missing Children (APPG) (2012) *Report from the Joint Inquiry into Children Who Go Missing from Care*, APPG.

Broad, B. (2005) 'Young People Leaving Care: Implementing the Children (Leaving Care) Act 2000?' 19 *Children and Society* 371.

Children's Commissioner (2012) *I Thought I was the Only One in the World: Inquiry into Child Sexual Exploitation in Gangs and Groups*, Office of the Children's Commissioner.

   (2020) *Unregulated: Children in Care Living in Semi-independent Accommodation*, Office of the Children's Commissioner.

Children's Society (2007) *Stepping Up: The Future of Runaways Services*, Children's Society.

   (2017a) *Making Connections: Understanding how Local Agencies Can Better Keep Missing Children Safe*, Children's Society.

   (2017b) *Claiming after Care*, Children's Society.

Committee on Economic, Social and Cultural Rights (2002) *Concluding Observations of the Committee on Economic, Social and Cultural Rights: United Kingdom of Great Britain and*

Northern Ireland – Dependent Territories 2002, E/C12/1/Add 79, Centre for Human Rights, Geneva.

Committee on the Rights of the Child (2002) *Concluding Observations of the Committee on the Rights of the Child: United Kingdom of Great Britain and Northern Ireland*, CRC/C/15/Add 188, Centre for Human Rights, Geneva.

(2016) *General Comment No. 20 on the Implementation of the Rights of the Child During Adolescence*, CRC/C/GC/20, Centre for Human Rights, Geneva.

Cowan, D. and Deardon, N. (2002) 'The Minor as (a) Subject: The Case of Housing Law' in Fionda, J. (ed.) *Legal Concepts of Childhood*, Hart Publishing.

Crellin, R. and Pona, I. (2015) *On Your Own Now: The Risks of Unsuitable Accommodation for Older Teenagers*, The Children's Society.

Department for Children, Schools and Families (DCSF) (2008) *Guidance on the Employment of Children*, DCSF.

Department for Education (DfE) (2014) *Statutory Guidance on Children Who Go Missing from Home or Care*, DfE.

(2021) *Introducing National Standards for Independent and Semi-Independent Provision for Looked-After Children and Care Leavers Aged 16 and 17: Government Consultation Response*, DfE.

Electoral Commission (2014) *Scottish Independence Referendum*, Electoral Commission.

Fortin, J. (2001) 'Children's Rights and the Use of Physical Force' 13 *Child and Family Law Quarterly* 243.

(2003) *Children's Rights and the Developing Law*, LexisNexis Butterworths.

Freeman, M. (1996) 'Can Children Divorce Their Parents?' in Freeman, M. (ed.) *Divorce – Where Next*, Dartmouth Publishing Co.

Gill, A. (2016) *Families under Pressure: Preventing Family Breakdown and Youth Homelessness*, Centrepoint.

Hamilton, C. (2005) *Working with Young People: Legal Responsibility and Liability*, Children's Legal Centre.

Hamilton, C. and Watt, B. (2004) 'The Employment of Children' 16 *Child and Family Law Quarterly* 135.

Hobbs, S., McKechnie, J. and Simpson, A. (2017) 'The Economic Exploitation of Child Workers in the United Kingdom' 24 *Childhood* 36.

Local Government and Social Care Ombudsman (2017) *Still No Place Like Home?*, Local Government and Social Care Ombudsman.

Low Pay Commission (2019) Cm 9717, *National Minimum Wage: Low Pay Commission Report 2019*, The Stationery Office.

McKechnie, J., Hobbs, S., Simpson, A., Howieson, C. and Semple, S. (2011) *The Regulation of Child Employment and Options for Reform*, Department for Education.

Ministry of Housing, Communities and Local Government (2018) *Prevention of Homelessness and Provision of Accommodation for 16 and 17 Year Old Young People Who May Be Homeless and/or Require Accommodation*, Ministry of Housing, Communities and Local Government.

Missing People (2019) *A Safer Return*, Missing People.

Morgan, J. (2000) 'Kingston upon Thames Borough Council v. Prince: "Children Are People Too"' 12 *Child and Family Law Quarterly* 65.

Morgan, R. and Children's Rights Director for England (2006a) *Running Away: A Children's Views Report*, Commission for Social Care Inspection.

(2006b) *Young People's Views on Leaving Care*, Commission for Social Care Inspection.

Ofsted (2013) *Missing Children*, Ofsted.

Peto, T. (2018) 'Why the Voting Age Should Be Lowered to 16' 17 *Politics, Philosophy and Economics* 277.

Pleace, N., Fitzpatrick, S., Johnsen, S., Quilgars, D. and Sanderson, D. (2008) *Statutory Homelessness in England: The Experience of Families and 16–17 Year Olds*, Department for Communities and Local Government.

Pona, I. and Crellin, R. (2015) *Getting the House in Order: Keeping Homeless Older Teenagers Safe*, The Children's Society.

Quilgars, D., Johnsen, S. and Pleace, N. (2008) *Youth Homelessness in the UK: A Decade of Progress?*, Joseph Rowntree Foundation.

Randall, G. and Brown, S. (2001) *Trouble at Home: Family Conflict, Young People and Homelessness*, Crisis.

Rees, G. (2011) *Still Running III: Early Findings from our Third National Survey of Young Runaways*, The Children's Society.

Rees, G., Franks, M., Raws, P. and Medforth, R. (2005) *Responding to Young Runaways: An Evaluation of 19 Projects, 2003 to 2004*, DfES Research Report RR 634, Children's Society/ University of York.

Rees, G. and Lee, J. (2005) *Still Running II: Findings from the Second National Survey of Young Runaways*, The Children's Society.

Sawyer, C. (1995) 'The Competence of Children to Participate in Family Proceedings' 7 *Child and Family Law Quarterly* 180.

Shelter (2005) *More Priority Needed: The Impact of Legislative Change on Young Homeless People's Access to Housing and Support*, Shelter.

   (2006) *How Registered Social Landlords Can Work With Young People: A Good Practice Guide*, Shelter.

Social Security Advisory Committee (2018) *Young People Living Independently*, Social Security Advisory Committee.

Steinberg, L. (2016) *Adolescence*, 11th edn, McGraw-Hill Higher Education.

Wade, J. and Dixon, J. (2006) 'Making a Home, Finding a Job: Investigating Early Housing and Employment Outcomes for Young People Leaving Care' 11 *Child and Family Social Work* 199.

11

Adolescent Decision-Making and Healthcare

(1) Introduction

It is no accident that many of the boundaries to adolescent legal independence have been mapped out by the courts in the context of healthcare. Medical treatment often involves an invasion of bodily and personal privacy which would be intolerable if patients had no right to control its delivery. International human rights law recognises that an important aspect of adults' right to self-determination includes the right to decide what should happen to their own body.[1] Long before the Human Rights Act (HRA) 1998 was implemented, the common law had emphasised that adult patients enjoy such a right.[2] Adolescents can justifiably argue that they too should have the right to make choices over their medical treatment if competent to do so.[3]

At one time, the accepted approach was to assume that parents were the appropriate people to determine what happened to their children's bodies when receiving medical treatment. Consequently, parents were automatically treated by the medical profession as proxy consent-givers. This was convenient, in so far as doctors could avoid asking their young patients their own views on the matter. But the law has gradually adapted its approach to adolescents to give greater recognition to their rights and the importance of their involvement in decision-making. Thus, the Family Law Reform Act (FLRA) 1969, section 8(1) established that on attaining the age of 16, adolescents could be assumed to have sufficient capacity to consent to treatment concerning their

---

[1] E.g. inter alia: *YF* v. *Turkey* (2004) 39 EHRR 34, at [33]: Art. 8 of the European Convention for the Protection of Human Rights and Fundamental Freedoms (1950) (ECHR) protects against compulsory medical intervention, even if that intervention is of minor importance. 'A person's body concerns the most intimate aspect of one's private life'; *Storck* v. *Germany* (2006) 43 EHRR 6: an adult's rights to liberty under ECHR, Art. 5 had been infringed by her being detained in a psychiatric clinic against her will on her father's authorisation alone, without a court order.

[2] See inter alia: *Re F (Mental Patient: Sterilisation)* [1990] 2 AC 1, per Lord Goff, at 72. There 'is the fundamental principle, long established, that every person's body is inviolate'. See also *Sidaway* v. *Board of Governors of the Bethlem Royal Hospital and the Maudsley Hospital* [1985] AC 871, per Lord Scarman, at 882; and *Re B (Adult: Refusal of Medical Treatment)* [2002] EWHC 429 (Fam), [2002] 2 All ER 449, per Dame Elizabeth Butler-Sloss P, at [94] and [100].

[3] See Chapter 7 for a discussion of the medical treatment of children too young to consent for themselves.

own healthcare.[4] For those under 16, the decision of the House of Lords in *Gillick* v. *West Norfolk and Wisbech Area Health Authority*[5] signified a much more liberal approach. Although it specifically dealt with the issue of adolescent competence to consent to contraceptive advice and treatment, the principles it established have a general application to all forms of medical treatment and assistance.[6] It introduced the idea that adolescents' rights over their own bodies grow with their competence to understand the implications of the procedure involved. As Feldman has pointed out, this approach is 'consistent with the theory that autonomy is the value at the root of the moral justification of freedom: the greater one's capacity to exercise a choice in an informed way, the stronger is one's claim to be free to exercise it'.[7]

While the law has developed greater protection for the growing competence of adolescents, they have not been recognised as autonomous in the same way as adults. The law has been willing accord young people the right to consent to treatment that has been found to be in their best interests, but courts have been far more reluctant to accept adolescents' decisions to refuse such treatment. This position has been defended on the basis that it strikes the right balance between recognising both the young person's right to bodily autonomy and the state's responsibility to protect their right to health and their best interests. The argument that the state has a responsibility to protect adolescent health, despite the wishes of the young person themselves, is strongest in relation to decisions that risk serious health consequences or death. The law is, however, not limited to such serious cases. Instead, it appears that *any* decision by a young person to refuse treatment can be overridden, even if the health consequences appear relatively trivial.[8] At present, the law permits the imposition of invasive medical treatment against the considered wishes of mature adolescents in ways that would be considered a significant violation of the rights of an adult with capacity. This approach looks increasingly out of step with the emphasis placed on patient autonomy in medical law and with the respect given to adolescent decisions in other contexts.

This chapter starts by assessing the extent to which the general principles of law recognise the capacity of adolescents to consent to medical treatment. It then goes on to consider the application of these principles in the context of young people who refuse treatment, including life-saving treatment, arguing that these principles require reassessment to reflect the rights of young people

[4] FLRA 1969, s. 8(1): 'The consent of a minor who has attained the age of sixteen years to any surgical, medical or dental treatment which, in the absence of consent, would constitute a trespass to his person, shall be as effective as it would be if he were of full age; and where a minor has by virtue of this section given an effective consent to any treatment it shall not be necessary to obtain any consent for it from his parent or guardian.' Whether this section gives an adolescent over 16 the right to *refuse* treatment is discussed further below.

[5] [1986] AC 112 (hereafter '*Gillick*'); also discussed in Chapter 9.

[6] It has also been influential outside of the medical context, as discussed in Chapter 9.

[7] D. Feldman (2002) p. 287.

[8] *F* v. *F* [2013] EWHC 2683 (Fam), discussed further below and in Chapter 9.

to bodily integrity and participation in decision-making. The chapter then considers the application of these principles in the context of adolescent decisions concerning fertility, an area which has been instrumental in the development of the law and in which the law has often operated to facilitate adolescent decisions. Finally, the extent to which medical professionals owe a duty of confidentiality to their young patients is assessed.

(2) Adolescents' Legal Right to Consent to Medical Treatment

(A) Legal Competence to Consent: Adolescents under 16

English law recognises the right of minors under the age of 16 to consent on their own behalf to a variety of medical procedures, as long as they are competent to do so. This principle was firmly established by the decision of the House of Lords in *Gillick*,[9] which clearly rejected the view that capacity to consent was only acquired on attaining a fixed age limit. Lord Fraser and Lord Scarman[10] both rejected Mrs Gillick's claim that section 8(1) of the FLRA 1969 implicitly precluded adolescents under the age of 16 from giving a valid consent to medical treatment. According to Lord Fraser:

> It seems to me verging on the absurd to suggest that a girl or a boy aged 15 could not effectively consent, for example, to have a medical examination of some trivial injury to his body or even to have a broken arm set. Of course the consent of the parents should normally be asked, but they may not be immediately available. Provided the patient, whether a boy or a girl, is capable of understanding what is proposed, and of expressing his or her own wishes, I see no good reason for holding that he or she lacks the capacity to express them validly and effectively and to authorise the medical man to make the examination or give the treatment which he advises.[11]

Instead, the majority accepted that the legislation had left intact the existing principles of common law[12] and that these allowed adolescents under 16 to consent to medical procedures once they were competent to do so. Lord Scarman explained that this competence was reached at the point at which:

> the child achieves a sufficient understanding and intelligence to enable him or her to understand fully what is proposed. It will be a question of fact whether a child seeking advice has sufficient understanding of what is involved to give a consent valid in law.[13]

---

[9] *Gillick* v. *West Norfolk and Wisbech Area Health Authority* [1986] AC 112.

[10] Lord Bridge agreed with both Lord Fraser and Lord Scarman, so forming a 3–2 majority against Mrs Gillick.

[11] [1986] AC 112, at 169. See also Lord Scarman, at 186: if the law imposed fixed limits 'where nature knows only a continuous process, the price would be artificiality and a lack of realism in an area where the law must be sensitive to human development and social change'.

[12] Lord Fraser [1986] AC 112, at 167 and Lord Scarman, ibid. at 182: FLRA 1969, s. 8(3) preserved existing means of giving effective consent.

[13] Ibid. at 189. Lord Fraser, at 170, similarly linked competence to the young person having sufficient understanding and intelligence to know what the treatment involved.

The question of whether this test also allows an adolescent to *reject* much-needed medical treatment remains controversial,[14] but this test of *Gillick* competence remains authoritative at least so far as *consent* to treatment is concerned. The *Gillick* competence formula was innovative in providing a method by which doctors could identify those young patients who are sufficiently mature to reach responsible decisions for themselves. The test is both child-specific and decision-specific: whether the minor has capacity to consent depends on *this* child's understanding of the particular procedure that is proposed. In this way, it allows a far more nuanced approach to the concept of capacity than one merely relying on age or generalised research evidence on children's cognitive development.[15]

Nonetheless, the test for assessing *Gillick* competence is deceptive in its simplicity. It was only in the context of the provision of contraceptive advice and treatment that further guidance on how to apply it was given in *Gillick* itself.[16] In more general medical contexts, *Gillick* left doctors with no clear guidelines over how to interpret such malleable concepts as 'maturity', 'intelligence' and sufficiency of understanding.[17] Nor is it clear on the extent to which the minor should be provided with advice and information to assist in attaining the understanding necessary to become competent.[18] *Gillick* appears to have influenced practice in so far as young patients are sometimes being given considerable responsibility for reaching medical decisions on their own behalf at relatively early ages.[19] But the uncertainty underlying the concept of *Gillick* competence undoubtedly weakens both its practical usefulness and its ability to give sufficient protection to the autonomy of mature minors. It places even the most mature adolescent almost entirely in the hands of the medical profession. Doctors are given considerable power, in that they must decide not only whether treatment is medically indicated, but also whether the adolescent patient is competent to consent to the procedure. The fact that such decisions must be taken on a case-by-case basis, according to the circumstances of each patient and each procedure, produces uncertainty for the adolescent patient and the medical professionals involved. In the face of that

---

[14] Discussed below.   [15] Discussed in Chapter 9.

[16] These 'Fraser Guidelines' are discussed further below.

[17] M. Brazier and C. Bridge (1996) pp. 91–2.

[18] E. Cave and C. Purshouse (2020). The GMC recommends that all relevant information is disclosed and discussed thoroughly before the competence decision is made: GMC (2018) para. 24. In *Bell* v. *Tavistock and Portman NHS Trust* [2020] EWHC 3274 (Admin), [2022] 1 FLR 30, at [130], the Divisional Court considered that the test of *Gillick* competence did not require a child to understand all of the information that would be disclosed by a clinician seeking to comply with the Supreme Court's decision in *Montgomery* to obtain informed consent from an adult patient (discussed below). As discussed below, the Divisional Court's decision was reversed on appeal, but the Court of Appeal made no adverse observation on this point.

[19] E.g. *An NHS Trust* v. *A, B, C, A Local Authority* [2014] EWHC 1445 (Fam), in which a girl who had just turned 13 was found to be competent to consent to an abortion. See also the case of Hannah Jones, discussed below, in which doctors respected the wishes of a 12-year-old girl to refuse a life-saving heart transplant.

uncertainty, medical professionals may adopt an over-protective attitude towards adolescents, fearful that if a child is judged competent and treated without parental consent, the parents may later challenge the assessment of their child's competence by suing in tort.[20] A further problem is that the malleable terms used in *Gillick* permit so much flexibility that practitioners may be tempted to focus on the outcome of the decision rather than the child's competence to make it. A child reaching a decision that fits with mainstream medical opinion is likely to find it much easier to persuade a doctor that she is competent than a child who reaches a more questionable decision.[21] Certainly, the case law on *Gillick* competence suggests that the *courts* strive to find that a child making a 'wise' decision is competent, but erect barriers to those that do not.[22]

It might be thought that one answer to the uncertainties of the *Gillick* test would be greater judicial guidance on its application and the factors to be considered by practitioners. Greater conceptual clarity on the meaning of the concepts used in *Gillick* would undoubtedly be helpful; however, the provision of specific judicial guidance is fraught with difficulty. Few medical decisions reach the courts, and those that do will tend to focus on the individual circumstances and the reason for doubt or dispute in the particular case. It is only rarely that the courts have the opportunity to give more general guidance on matters of policy as they did in *Gillick* on the question of contraceptive advice and treatment. One unusual case in which such a challenge was made demonstrates the difficulties of judicial guidance. In *Bell* v. *Tavistock and Portman NHS Trust*,[23] the claimants sought judicial review of the practice of the NHS Trust in prescribing puberty blockers as treatment for children with gender dysphoria. As the Court of Appeal noted, this was a highly contentious area of practice that divided medical opinion and the ethics of which were the subject of public and professional debate.[24] At first instance, the Divisional Court rejected the submission that under 18s were not capable of giving consent to puberty blockers, but expressed significant concern about the evidence base and uncertainty of the treatment.[25] In particular, the court was concerned that puberty blockers put children on a treatment path which would have significant consequences for their fertility and sexual functioning in adulthood that they were unlikely to fully understand as minors. In consequence, the court gave extensive guidance as to the factors that a child would have to understand to be competent to consent.[26] As the court considered that those under 13 were 'highly unlikely' to be *Gillick*-competent to make a decision concerning puberty blockers and it was 'very

---

[20] E. Cave and C. Purshouse (2020).   [21] E. Cave (2014) p. 109.

[22] Contrast *An NHS Trust* v. *A, B, C, A Local Authority* [2014] EWHC 1445 (Fam) with the refusal cases such as *Re X (A Child) (No. 2)* [2021] EWHC 65 (Fam), [2021] 4 WLR 11, discussed below.

[23] [2020] EWHC 3274 (Admin), [2022] 1 FLR 30, reversed on appeal [2021] EWCA Civ 1363, [2022] 1 FLR 69.

[24] [2021] EWCA Civ 1363, [2022] 1 FLR 69, at [3].

[25] [2020] EWHC 3274 (Admin), [2022] 1 FLR 30.   [26] Ibid. at [138].

doubtful' that 14- and 15-year-olds would be able to weigh the long-term consequences,[27] meaning that court approval should be sought before such treatment could be prescribed.[28] The Court of Appeal disagreed, finding that the Divisional Court had been wrong to give detailed guidance on clinic matters and that the ratio in *Gillick* was that it was for clinicians, not courts, to decide on competence.[29] In giving detailed guidance, creating age categories and requiring court approval, the court had taken upon itself a role that should be performed by clinicians subject to professional regulation and oversight.[30] The decision in *Bell* reaffirms the importance of individual clinician-led assessment of competence and so places emphasis on the importance of professional regulation and evidence-based guidance for clinicians.

Specialised guidance produced for medical practitioners has sought to amplify the *Gillick* test by introducing more practical considerations.[31] Although that guidance cannot supplant or change the legal tests, it is vital in guiding the application of the *Gillick* test in a changing legal and professional environment. In the years since *Gillick* was decided, there have been significant developments in medical practice, human rights law and research on adolescent development, all of which pose challenges to its application.[32] The case was decided before the CRC and HRA and the greater protection for children's rights and autonomy that have followed in their wake. Similarly, developments in medical law for adult patients have moved towards a greater emphasis on patient autonomy and the importance of informed consent.[33] In particular, the treatment of adults who may lack capacity has shifted from a paternalistic to a more strongly rights-based approach, first through case law[34] and then through the Mental Capacity Act (MCA) 2005. While *Gillick* may have been radical in its time, in an era concerned with rights and autonomy, it has begun to show its age.

---

[27] Ibid. at [145] and [151].

[28] Ibid. at [149]. While the court recognised that the position of those aged 16 and 17 was different by virtue of FLRA 1969, s. 8, it also suggested that clinicians may also wish to obtain court approval for this age group given the 'innovative and experimental' nature of the treatment: at [152].

[29] [2021] EWCA Civ 1363, [2022] 1 FLR 69, at [87]. The Court of Appeal contrasted the Divisional Court decision with the open-ended guidance given in *Gillick*, which identified relevant factors without being prescriptive as to how a clinician should regard them: at [80].

[30] A particular difficulty in this field of practice appears to have been that doubts had been raised as to the effectiveness of clinical practice and regulatory oversight, but the Court of Appeal considered that these failures were not to be addressed by restricting *Gillick* competence: ibid. at [93]. See also *AB* v. *CD* [2021] EWHC 741 (Fam), at [122]–[124].

[31] BMA (2019); DH (2009); GMC (2018) esp. paras 24–26.

[32] These challenges are discussed in more detail in Chapter 9.

[33] E.g. *Montgomery (Appellant)* v. *Lanarkshire Health Board (Respondent) (Scotland)* [2015] UKSC 11, [2015] AC 1430.

[34] *Re C (Refusal of Medical Treatment)* [1994] 1 FLR 31, per Thorpe J, at 33. The test (as later refined by Butler-Sloss LJ, in *Re MB (Medical Treatment)* [1997] 2 FLR 426, at 437) requires an ability to comprehend and retain treatment information relevant to the decision, especially as to the likely consequences of having or not having the treatment in question, to use it and to weigh it in the balance when arriving at a decision. This test of capacity influenced the test of *in*capacity adopted by the MCA 2005, s. 3(1).

Some of the limitations of the *Gillick* test of medical competence could be addressed by reference to the developing legal principles governing adult capacity to consent to medical procedures contained in the MCA 2005.[35] The MCA 2005 stresses that a person should not be treated as lacking capacity in the absence of practicable help to assist in reaching a decision,[36] nor simply because the decision reached appears unwise,[37] nor because the patient can only retain information relevant to the decision for short periods only.[38] The value of these additional refinements is that they would make the *Gillick* competence formula more sensitive to the rights of adolescents by seeking to facilitate their decision-making.[39] Such use of the MCA 2005 to inform *Gillick* competence has been endorsed in the different context of consent to adoption.[40] The influence of the MCA 2005 is also evident in professional guidance, meaning that, even in the absence of case law, professional practice surrounding adolescent consent is likely to be influenced by these developments in interpreting the *Gillick* test.[41] The General Medical Council's (GMC's) advice that the capacity of a minor to consent is shown by the ability to 'understand retain, use and weigh' information, and to communicate the decision, appears to be drawn directly from the test contained in the MCA 2005.[42] There are, however, risks that too enthusiastic a use of the MCA 2005 could have negative consequences for mature minors.[43] The MCA 2005 applies to people over 16, who therefore benefit from the presumption that they have capacity, and is concerned with difficulties in decision-making attributable to an impairment of or a disturbance in the functioning of the mind or brain.[44]

---

[35] The MCA 2005 primarily governs adult decision-making (including medical decision-making), but also governs decision-making on behalf of minors aged between 16 and 18 whose incapacity to reach decisions for themselves is attributable to an impairment of or a disturbance in the functioning of his or her mind or brain.

[36] MCA 2005, s. 1(3). See also s. 3(2) and (4), which stress that the person should be given an explanation of the information relevant to the decision in a way appropriate to his circumstances (e.g. using simple language or visual aids), including information about the reasonably foreseeable consequences of deciding one way or the other or of failing to decide.

[37] MCA 2005, s. 1(4).   [38] MCA 2005, s. 3(3).

[39] A. McFarlane (2011); V. Chico and L. Haggar (2011).

[40] *Re S (Child as Parent: Adoption: Consent)* [2017] EWHC 2729 (Fam), [2018] 2 WLR 1029, discussed in Chapter 9.

[41] See e.g. *An NHS Trust* v. *A, B, C, A Local Authority* [2014] EWHC 1445 (Fam), in which the professional evidence concerning the *Gillick* competence of a 13-year-old girl was given in terms that were strikingly similar to an assessment of capacity under the MCA 2005: K. Moreton (2015).

[42] MCA 2005, s. 3(1). See GMC (2018) para. 24; the guidance uses the term 'young people' to include all 'older or more experienced children' and not merely those who are over 16 and so covered by the MCA 2005.

[43] Sir James Munby expressed doubts about the use of the MCA 2005 in assessing *Gillick* competence in *Re X (A Child) (No. 2)* [2021] EWHC 65 (Fam), [2021] 4 WLR 11, at [70]–[76]. Similarly, in *Barts NHS Foundation Trust* v. *Shalina Begum, Muhhamed Raqeeb and Tafida Raqeeb (by Her Children's Guardian)* [2019] EWHC 2530 (Fam), at [123], McDonald J, speaking in the context of a much younger child, warned against importing wholesale the MCA 2005 principles into cases under the Children Act 1989. These points are considered further in Chapter 9.

[44] MCA 2005, s. 2.

The context of a younger adolescent, to whom the presumption of capacity does not apply and who is not suffering from such impairment, is rather different. Notably, for those under 16 the burden of proof is different in that they must prove their competence rather than relying on the presumption of capacity. There is a concern that the requirement to be able to retain, use and weigh information may set a rather higher standard that *Gillick* envisaged in relation to relatively straightforward decisions, and so in these cases may make it more difficult for a minor to prove the ability to give effective consent.[45] The very different context gives reason to be cautious in borrowing indiscriminately from the MCA 2005, particularly in the absence of authoritative case law relating to its use in cases concerning medical treatment. The principles of the Act can, however, be helpful in emphasising the importance of giving all appropriate support to facilitate and develop the capacity of young people to make their own decisions, rather than disregarding those decisions for paternalistic reasons.

(B) Legal Competence to Consent: Adolescents over 16

The research evidence on developmental growth suggests that later adolescence brings a more developed ability to deal with major decisions over healthcare. By this time, adolescents are typically more able to identify a range of risks and benefits, foresee the consequences of alternatives and gauge the credibility of information provided by experts.[46] Section 8(1) of the FLRA 1969 recognises this by assuming that on attaining the age of 16, but before they attain 18 (the age of majority), young people have the capacity and therefore the legal right to consent on their own behalf to 'any surgical, medical or dental treatment'. Thus, while the decision in *Gillick*[47] indicated that the law should recognise the decision-making rights of adolescents below that age, but on a case-by-case basis, section 8 introduces the presumption that all adolescents over that age have capacity to consent for themselves.

The consent rights of the adolescent over the age of 16 are nevertheless more limited than those of an adult patient simply because the scope of section 8 is relatively narrow. It only authorises adolescents over the age of 16 to consent to surgical, medical or dental treatment and diagnostic procedures. Blood and organ donations are, for example, outside the scope of section 8. Nevertheless, in Lord Donaldson's view, the donation of blood would not present problems, since '"a *Gillick* competent" minor of any age would be able to give consent [to giving blood] under the common law'.[48] But, he warned, organ donations are quite different. They are not only excluded from the scope of section 8, but, in his view, it would be 'highly improbable' that an adolescent under the age of 18 wishing to become an organ donor could be *Gillick*-competent 'in the context

---

[45] E. Cave (2014).   [46] Discussed in Chapter 9.
[47] [1986] AC 112, per Lord Scarman, at 184.
[48] *Re W (A Minor) (Medical Treatment: Courts' Jurisdiction)* [1993] Fam 64.

of so serious a procedure which could not benefit the minor'.[49] That being the case, a doctor should not proceed with an organ donation without securing the consent of a parent on the adolescent's behalf.[50]

There is, of course, nothing to prevent adolescents over the age of 16 consenting to any other procedure outside the section's scope, as long as they are *Gillick-competent*. But in those circumstances, the adolescent's competence is not presumed and must be assessed on a case-by-case basis, depending on the seriousness of the procedure involved. It should be noted, however, that in many cases, adolescents over the age of 16 considered to be *Gillick in*competent will *also* be deemed to lack capacity by the MCA 2005. This will almost certainly be the case if the adolescent's lack of capacity is attributable to an impairment of or a disturbance in the functioning of his or her mind or brain.[51] Although in such circumstances, the medical team may still gain authority to treat such a patient from his or her parents,[52] they can only consent to the treatment if it is deemed to be in the patient's best interests, as determined by the MCA 2005[53] and its accompanying Code of Practice.[54] But, as discussed below, the Code suggests that there may be situations where a young patient is unable to make a decision for some other reason, for example, because they are overwhelmed by the implications of the decision.[55] Since the MCA 2005 does not then govern the situation, the parents (or those with parental responsibility for the child) must decide for themselves what is in their child's best interests, assisted by the medical team.[56]

(3) Adolescents' Legal Right to Refuse Medical Treatment

(A) Legal Competence to Refuse Life-Saving Treatment

The decision in *Gillick* appeared to give young patients the right to martyr themselves by refusing life-saving medical treatment, providing they possessed sufficient maturity to be considered *Gillick*-competent. The judiciary, however, found it impossible to stand aside and allow young patients to endanger their lives in such a way. Subsequent case law preserved judicial discretion to override their more dangerous choices.[57] Despite this, the courts have explored

---

[49] Ibid.

[50] Ibid. at 79. Medical practitioners in the UK do not in practice countenance organ donation by minors; discussed in Chapter 9.

[51] MCA 2005, s. 2(1); DCA (2007) para. 12.13.

[52] Unless there is a disagreement over this, in which case a decision may be sought from the Court of Protection.

[53] MCA 2005, s. 4.   [54] DCA (2007) chs 4 and 12. See esp. para. 12.16.   [55] Ibid. para. 12.13.

[56] See further *Re D (A Child)* [2019] UKSC 42, [2019] 1 WLR 5403, at [71], where Lady Black confirmed that the MCA 2005 was not intended to be a complete decision-making framework for 16- and 17-year-olds or to exclude the existing common law and CA 1989.

[57] See esp.: *Re R (A Minor) (Wardship: Consent to Treatment)* [1992] Fam 11; *Re W (A Minor) (Medical Treatment: Court's Jurisdiction)* [1993] Fam 64; *Re X (A Child) (No. 2)* [2021] EWHC 65 (Fam), [2021] 4 WLR 11, discussed below. The concept of overriding the wishes of adolescents is discussed at a more theoretical level in Chapter 1, and more generally in Chapter 9, regarding adolescents and their legal relationship with their parents.

what level of competence an adolescent *theoretically* requires in order to refuse treatment. A finding that a young patient has the legal competence to refuse consent to the treatment under consideration results in the court giving an increased weight to his or her views, while recalling that they are not determinative.[58] But as Downie comments:

> the application of the principle in *Re W (a minor) (medical treatment)*[59] that the court can always override a refusal of consent even by a *Gillick* competent minor, means that the assessment of his competence is almost a pretence.[60]

Nevertheless, if, as argued below, Articles 3, 5 and 8 of the ECHR provide adolescents with greater protection from being forced to have medical treatment against their will, their competence to refuse consent becomes far more relevant than hitherto. A court might hesitate before asserting its own duty to preserve the life of a resisting patient if it considers that the patient is legally capable of making up his or her own mind over the matter. On this basis, the case law analysing an adolescent's competence to refuse treatment is of considerable current interest.

On the face of it, there seems no logical reason why any adolescent patient should need a higher level of competence to refuse to undergo treatment than to consent to it.[61] Although the courts have sometimes adopted similar criteria to those used when assessing an adult's capacity,[62] in most cases they require much higher levels of competence from uncooperative adolescents – thereby ensuring that they receive the medical treatment deemed essential to safeguard their health. In other words, the courts simply adjust the level of competence required, in the light of the implications of the minor's decision. The more dangerous the outcome, the more likely it is that the court will find that the child lacks competence. The outcome in *Re R (A Minor) (Wardship: Medical Treatment)*[63] was that, without treatment, R would again lapse into a dangerously psychotic state. Lord Donaldson MR did not consider her to be *Gillick*-competent. To qualify as competent, he demanded:

---

[58] *An NHS Foundation Trust* v. *A, M, P, A Local Authority* [2014] EWHC 920 (Fam), at [12].
[59] [1993] Fam 64.   [60] A. Downie (1999) p. 819.
[61] See S. Gilmore and J. Herring (2011), discussed further below, for a partial defence of differential competence between consent to a treatment and refusal of *all* treatment. Although in *Re X (A Child) (No. 2)* [2021] EWHC 65 (Fam), [2021] 4 WLR 11, at [2], Sir James Munby suggested that a court could also veto the consent of a child even if that child was over 16 and so benefited from FLRA 1969, s. 8.
[62] E.g. Wall J in *Re C (Detention: Medical Treatment)* [1997] 2 FLR 180, at 195, assessed the competence of C, a severely anorexic girl of 16, using the criteria established for adult patients by Thorpe J in *Re C (Refusal of Medical Treatment)* [1994] 1 FLR 31, at 33 – i.e. the patient should have an ability to comprehend and retain treatment information, believe it and weigh it in the balance to arrive at a decision. In his view, C lacked competence due to her inability to consider the long-term impact of refusing treatment for her anorexia. See also *An NHS Trust* v. *A, B, C and a Local Authority* [2014] EWHC 1445 (Fam), apparently using similar criteria, now contained in MCA 2005, s. 3, discussed further above.
[63] [1992] Fam 11.

not merely an ability to understand the nature of the proposed treatment . . . but a full understanding and appreciation of the consequences both of the treatment in terms of intended and possible side effects and, equally important, the anticipated consequences of a failure to treat.[64]

Such a test demands a higher threshold than the test of competence established by case law for adults with mental disorders.[65] It also remains more demanding than that required by the MCA 2005,[66] which stresses that an unwise decision does not connote incapacity.[67] Lord Donaldson's test of competence in *Re R* becomes even more onerous when combined with his other demand that *Gillick* competence must be a permanent aspect of an adolescent's development and not a form of competence which exists on some days and not on others. Since the adolescent in *Re R* was subject to 'fluctuating mental disability', being not only *Gillick* 'incompetent', but 'sectionable' on some days,[68] she could not satisfy the requirements of *Gillick* competence.[69] Given that the state of mind of many adolescents with mental disorders fluctuates from day to day, this requirement is particularly demanding. Again, this approach is very different from that towards adults with fluctuating capacity, who should be supported in decision-making at the point at which they do have capacity rather than denied all capacity on the basis of that fluctuating state.[70]

A similar approach can be seen in cases concerning young Jehovah's Witness patients, who, regardless of age, normally refuse treatment involving the use of blood products. In a series of cases, the courts found it impossible to stand aside and allow such patients to bring about their own deaths. So, instead, they simply decided that the adolescent involved had insufficient capacity to be *Gillick*-competent, that therefore his or her refusal could be ignored and a decision substituted by the court, in the minor's best interests. A finding of *Gillick* incompetence became readily available, given the courts' insistence on the patient not only understanding his or her impending death, but also possessing 'a greater understanding of the manner of the death and pain and the distress'.[71] *Re E (A Minor) (Wardship: Medical Treatment)*,[72] remains the most well-known of these cases, possibly because of its tragic sequel.[73] Although he was of sufficient intelligence to be able to take decisions

---

[64] Ibid. at 26.

[65] E.g. *Re JT (Adult: Refusal of Medical Treatment)* [1998] 1 FLR 48: the High Court refused to overrule a woman patient's refusal to undergo dialysis for renal failure, despite her learning difficulties and extremely severe behavioural disturbance, considering her capable of refusing agreement to treatment under the test in *Re C (Refusal of Medical Treatment)* [1994] 1 FLR 31.

[66] Discussed above.   [67] MCA 2005, s. 1(4).

[68] I.e. liable to compulsory admission under the Mental Health Act (MHA) 1983, s. 2 or 3.

[69] Per Lord Donaldson MR, [1992] Fam 11, at 26.   [70] DCA (2007) esp. paras 4.26–4.27.

[71] *Re E (A Minor) (Wardship: Medical Treatment)* [1993] 1 FLR 386, per Ward J, at 394.

[72] Ibid.

[73] Although the 16-year-old patient was forced to undergo treatment, tragically, when he reached the age of 18, he exercised his right as an adult to refuse treatment and died. This sequel to the decision was revealed in *Re S (A Minor) (Consent to Medical Treatment)* [1994] 2 FLR 1065.

about his own well-being, the court overrode the refusal of a 16-year-old Jehovah's Witness to receive blood transfusion treatment for his leukaemia. Ward J did not deem him to be *Gillick*-competent because there was a range of decisions facing him outside his full comprehension; furthermore, he lacked a full understanding of the implications of refusing treatment and the manner of his own death. Subsequent courts confronted by young uncooperative Jehovah's Witness patients[74] were similarly reluctant to allow 'an infant to martyr himself'.[75] But as critics have pointed out, it seems particularly inappropriate to judge adolescent patients incapable of comprehending the detailed manner of their death, when information about this is deliberately withheld from them by their doctors because of its distressing nature.[76] Indeed, neither case law[77] nor legislation[78] allows medical teams to overrule adults' refusal to undergo treatment for similar reasons. The MCA 2005 makes it clear that a person's capacity for decision-making should only be determined once he has been given 'the information relevant to the decision'.[79]

Children brought up within insular religious communities, or by parents who hold strong beliefs, often find it particularly difficult to convince the court that the decision is their own and not merely a reflection of their parents' views.[80] The courts have been very willing to assume that children brought up in such environments[81] are unable to reach an independent view given their limited exposure to other viewpoints, even if the child in question is able to give a clear and articulate account of their views.[82] Similarly, adolescents who

---

[74] *Re S*, ibid.: a 15.5-year-old Jehovah's Witness patient suffering from thalassaemia, virtually since birth, was kept alive by monthly blood transfusions and daily injections. The court authorised continued treatment despite her expressed wish to the contrary. See also *Re L (Medical Treatment: Gillick Competency)* [1999] 2 FCR 524: a deeply religious 14-year-old Jehovah's Witness patient suffered life-threatening scalds sustained while bathing. The court authorised blood transfusion treatment alongside the required surgical intervention, despite her strong opposition. See also *Re X (A Child) (No. 2)* [2021] EWHC 65 (Fam), [2021] 4 WLR 11, discussed further below, in which it appeared that the nearly 16-year-old had competence, but was nonetheless overruled.

[75] [1993] 1 FLR 386, per Ward J, at 394. See e.g. *Re P* [2003] EWHC 2327 (Fam).

[76] As in *Re E (A Minor) (Wardship: Medical Treatment)* [1993] 1 FLR 386 and *Re L (Medical Treatment: Gillick Competency)* [1999] 2 FCR 524. See C. McCafferty (1999).

[77] E.g. *Re C (Refusal of Medical Treatment)* [1994] 1 FLR 31: the court respected the right of a paranoid schizophrenic to refuse an amputation of his leg to cure potentially fatal gangrene. There was no indication that he fully realised the implications which lay before him as to the process of dying.

[78] MCA 2005.   [79] Ibid. s. 3(1)(a).

[80] E.g. in *Re S (A Minor) (Consent to Medical Treatment)* [1994] 2 FLR 1065, a 15.5-year-old Jehovah's Witness was unable to persuade the court that the decision was her own.

[81] This point not only applies to children from religious backgrounds, but also to other children whose families hold views that are outside of mainstream thinking or reject scientific orthodoxy: e.g. *Re JA (A Minor)* [2014] EWHC 1135 (Fam): a 14-year-old boy with HIV was heavily influenced by his parents' rejection of scientific consensus concerning HIV and its treatment and therefore was not competent to make decisions on his HIV treatment despite being intelligent, articulate and competent to consent to other elements of his medical treatment.

[82] E.g. in *Re L (Medical Treatment: Gillick Competency)* [1999] 2 FCR 524, the expert witness felt able to dismiss the 14-year-old girl's views as those of her parents and religious community

hold views that fall outside of the mainstream are far more likely to be found to lack competence even if those views are not shared by their parents.[83] Although there are legitimate arguments that seriously ill adolescents have a right to greater protection than adult patients, it remains questionable whether the levels of legal competence should be adjusted so blatantly. If an adolescent refuses to undergo life-saving treatment, it may be more honest to do as Sir James Munby did in *Re X (A Child) (No. 2)*:[84] accept that the patient is *Gillick*-competent and then consider whether the court will permit the decision to be overridden. This approach does not demean the minor by suggesting that his or her emotional maturity is fundamentally flawed. Further, such an approach allows explicit balancing of the child's rights to health, bodily integrity and autonomy, rather than veiling that decision behind a finding of incompetence.

(B) Overriding an Adolescent's Refusal to Be Treated

Lord Scarman, in his following words, implied that *Gillick* competence carries the right both to refuse and consent to medical treatment:

> In the light of the foregoing I would hold that as a matter of law the parental right to determine *whether or not* their minor child below the age of 16 will have medical treatment terminates if and when the child achieves a sufficient understanding and intelligence to enable him or her to understand fully what is proposed.[85]

But, as the Court of Appeal in *Re R (A Minor) (Wardship: Medical Treatment)*[86] and *Re W (A Minor) (Medical Treatment: Court's Jurisdiction)*[87] pointed out, such a statement was not made in the context of a desperately ill minor intent on rejecting essential medical treatment. Lord Donaldson MR argued that Lord Scarman had never intended to suggest that parents lost their right to consent to their child's treatment; but if Lord Scarman had so intended, he considered such a view to have been obiter.[88] According to the Court of Appeal in these later decisions, a medical team can obtain legal authority to treat a dissenting minor patient, whatever his or her age or legal competence, from anyone with

---

despite the fact that he had not met her. See also *Re E (A Minor) (Wardship: Medical Treatment)* [1993] 1 FLR 386.

[83] E.g. the moral objections of a 15-year-old vegan to a vaccine containing animal products were viewed as indicating immaturity rather than a mature appreciation for the moral context in *F v. F* [2013] EWHC 2683 (Fam), esp. at [22], discussed further in Chapter 9.

[84] [2021] EWHC 65 (Fam), [2021] 4 WLR 11. See also *Re E (Children: Blood Transfusion)* [2021] EWCA Civ 1888.

[85] *Gillick* v. *West Norfolk and Wisbech Area Health Authority* [1986] AC 112, at 188–9 (emphasis added). Although, as discussed in Chapter 9, Lord Fraser's speech could be read as permitting a far greater degree of paternalism.

[86] [1992] Fam 11.   [87] [1993] Fam 64.

[88] *Re R (A Minor) (Wardship: Medical Treatment)* [1992] Fam 11, at 23–4; *Re W (A Minor) (Medical Treatment: Court's Jurisdiction)* [1993] Fam 64, at 76.

parental responsibility (normally parents), or from the court itself.[89] The Court of Appeal emphasised that the courts would normally assume that it is in the best interests of *Gillick*-competent children to respect their wishes 'and not lightly override its decision on such a personal matter as medical treatment, all the more so if that treatment is invasive'.[90] Despite these sentiments, the court felt obliged to override the strong objections of the seriously ill teenage patients in *Re R* and *Re W*, to ensure that they received the treatment they needed. In *Re R*, the court authorised compulsory treatment for R, a 15-year-old, in the form of anti-psychotic drugs for her increasingly paranoid and disturbed behaviour. In *Re W*, the patient was so dangerously ill with anorexia that the court considered it essential to override her refusal of treatment, despite her being over 16 and apparently being of sufficient understanding to make an informed decision.[91]

These two Court of Appeal decisions contrived a situation whereby legal authority for such treatment could readily be obtained from the courts[92] or from well-intentioned parents desperate to save the life of their son or daughter. They produced great confusion, in that the legal principles appear to depend entirely on whether an adolescent refuses to undergo medical treatment, or consents, even when the proposed treatment is precisely the same.[93] According to *Gillick*, a minor patient of any age can consent to treatment, without parental involvement and however dangerous that treatment may be, as long as he or she passes the *Gillick* competence test. But according to the principles explored in *Re R* and more fully developed in *Re W*, a young patient's refusal to undergo treatment can be overridden, if legal authorisation can be secured from his or her parents or from the court. As Brazier and Bridge comment, according to this case law 'the right to be wrong applies only where minors say yes to treatment'.[94]

In relation to judicial powers, this exercise in paternalism on the part of the Court of Appeal was perhaps not surprising, given that a court may find it

---

[89] The High Court deals with such requests in the exercise of its inherent jurisdiction.

[90] *Re W (A Minor) (Medical Treatment: Court's Jurisdiction)* [1993] Fam 64, per Balcombe LJ, at 88.

[91] Ibid. at 80: Lord Donaldson MR doubted the correctness of Thorpe J's view (at first instance) that, despite her anorexic condition, W was sufficiently competent to reach an informed decision. But in any event, the courts' powers were sufficient to override her wishes, irrespective of her age (over 16) and her competence to refuse treatment; [1992] Fam 11, at 26.

[92] E.g. *Re C (Detention: Medical Treatment)* [1997] 2 FLR 180: Wall J overrode the anorexic girl's refusal to accept treatment irrespective of her capacity to consent on her own behalf to medical treatment.

[93] NB: the MCA 2005 has introduced further confusion. If a 16- or 17-year-old patient lacks capacity to consent, as determined by the MCA 2005, ss 2–3, his parents can only override his refusal to undergo treatment if such treatment fulfils the requirements of the best interests test set out by s. 4 and DCA (2007) ch. 4. See also DCA (2007) para. 12.17: if the parents of such a patient are unavailable or refuse to consent, the medical team can still treat the young patient without incurring medical liability (s. 5), as long as the treatment is deemed to be in the patient's best interests (s. 4).

[94] M. Brazier and C. Bridge (1996) p. 88.

impossible to conclude that a child should be allowed to die in circumstances in which that outcome could be prevented.[95] In *Re W*, Balcombe LJ considered that a child's refusal should be overridden to avoid 'death or severe permanent injury'.[96] In such circumstances, it is obviously extremely tempting for a court to authorise the treatment available. As Nolan LJ stated in *Re W*:

> In general terms, however, the present state of the law is that an individual who has reached the age of 18 is free to do with his life what he wishes, but it is the duty of the court to ensure so far as it can that children survive to attain that age.[97]

Furthermore, despite its outward appearance of illogicality, it has been argued that the distinction between consent to and refusal of treatment is sustainable, since doctors ought only to recommend treatment which they consider to be necessary and in the patient's best interests. Lowe and Juss point out that it is reasonable to withhold an adolescent's right to veto treatment designed for his or her benefit, particularly if refusal would lead to death or permanent damage.[98] Refusal of medical treatment not only rejects the advice of qualified doctors who know more about treatment than children, but closes down options, rather than opening them up, in such a way which may be regretted later.[99] To the extent that the role of the law is to promote the long-term best interests of the minor, as defined by mainstream medical opinion, the distinction between consent and refusal might be sustainable. The extent to which this approach can also be supported by an analysis based on the child's *rights* is considered further below.

A more limited defence of this line of cases has been put forward by Gilmore and Herring,[100] who draw a distinction between refusal of *a* treatment and refusal of *all* treatment. In relation to a *particular* treatment, they argue, it may be correct to view refusal as the obverse of consent and to treat both as requiring the same level of competence. Refusal of *all* treatment, however, requires a higher degree of competence as the minor would have to understand the consequences of a complete failure to treat. If this argument is accepted, there will be some situations in which a child has competence to decide whether to have a *particular* treatment, but not to refuse *all* treatment. In such cases, they argue, a parent faced with a refusing child would retain the right to consent on the child's behalf and to choose from all treatment options, including those that the child would have been competent to consent to. In these limited

[95] B. Hale and J. Fortin (2008) p. 106.

[96] *Re W (A Minor) (Medical Treatment: Courts' Jurisdiction)* [1993] Fam 64, per Balcombe LJ, at 88.

[97] Ibid. at 94.   [98] N. Lowe and S. Juss (1993) pp. 871–2.

[99] In some cases, an adolescent may welcome matters being taken out of his own hands: R. Lansdown (1998) p. 460: 'a very large fifteen-year-old' needle-phobic patient, who having been counselled, but then held down to undergo a blood test, told his doctor: 'That's better. Next time I have to have a needle you hold me down, forget all that psychological rubbish.'

[100] S. Gilmore and J. Herring (2011).

circumstances, they contend, it is logically possible that a child could be competent to consent to a particular treatment, but not to veto that treatment against parental consent. This argument has the advantage that it does not resort to paternalism to override competent decisions, although it has been criticised by Cave and Wallbank as an artificial approach to medical decision-making that does not reflect clinical experience.[101]

Although it is possible to argue that the reasoning is logically sustainable, the decisions in *Re R* and *Re W* have provoked considerable criticism.[102] While it may be morally justifiable to override the wishes of an adolescent to prevent his or her death or severe permanent injury, doing so where failure to treat will not produce such dire consequences is far less justifiable.[103] This is particularly so for decisions, such as abortion, in which overriding competent refusal is just as harmful as overriding competent consent, meaning that the distinction between the two is even more difficult to justify.[104] Furthermore, critics argue that it is an arbitrary and status-driven form of decision-making which allows the patient's legal competence to be treated as irrelevant, solely because he or she is under the age of 18.[105] They urge the courts to adopt a more critical approach to the assumption that minors, unlike adults, must always be forced to live. Thus, as Lewis argues:

> It may be that in a small minority of cases, an adolescent will be able to make a competent, maximally autonomous choice to refuse life-saving treatment. Respecting such a choice will be difficult, but it is preferable to arbitrary discrimination on the basis of age alone.[106]

The courts might, for example, justifiably distinguish the case where doctors are seeking to force an adolescent to continue with years of regular invasive treatment,[107] from that involving a one-off blood transfusion or even major surgery. As Bridge argues, 'there must come a time when a mature adolescent,

---

[101] E. Cave and J. Wallbank (2012).

[102] Inter alia: G. Douglas (1992); J. Masson (1993); J. Eekelaar (1993); R. Huxtable (2000); M. Freeman (2005).

[103] E.g. *Re K, W and H (Minors) (Medical Treatment)* [1993] 1 FLR 854: a psychiatric treatment unit obtained legal authority for the use of 'emergency medication' when treating three mentally disturbed teenagers; *South Glamorgan County Council* v. *W and B* [1993] 1 FLR 574: an LA obtained judicial authority for the forcible removal of a disturbed 15-year-old from home and her transfer to a specialised psychiatric unit for assessment and treatment.

[104] *Re X (A Child)* [2014] EWHC 1871 (Fam), at [9] and [10]: although the 13-year-old in this case was not competent to decide whether or not to continue her pregnancy, the seriousness of either compelling or prohibiting a lawful termination against her wishes meant that they would only be overridden in compelling circumstances. As discussed below, the decision of a *Gillick*-competent girl concerning abortion is best regarded as being determinative: *Re X (A Child) (No. 2)* [2021] EWHC 65 (Fam), [2021] 4 WLR 11, at [30].

[105] R. Huxtable (2000) pp. 84–6; P. Lewis (2001) p. 159; L. Ferguson (2004) Pt Five.

[106] P. Lewis (2001) p. 159.

[107] In *Re S (A Minor) (Consent to Medical Treatment)* [1994] 2 FLR 1065, the 15-year-old sufferer of thalassaemia was to be forced to undergo monthly blood transfusions for a further two-and-a-half years until, at the age of 18, she could refuse treatment.

like an adult suffering from chronic disability, can say "enough is enough" and reject treatment'.[108]

Perhaps the most worrying aspect of this case law, however, relates not to the *courts'* ability to override the objections of seriously ill adolescents, but to *parents'* power, in consultation with the doctors, to do so, irrespective of their age (over or under 16) and competence. As a matter of good practice, medical teams now try to involve all children in medical decisions and do not generally feel it appropriate to force treatment on unwilling patients, however young.[109] Nevertheless, a doctor, considering it essential for a young patient to receive the treatment he recommends, can simply appeal to the parents for authority to go ahead, in circumstances far less serious than those described by the judiciary in *Re W*. In such circumstances, a court will not be involved and so cannot withhold authority for treatment on the basis that an adolescent's wishes should *only* be overridden to avoid death or severe permanent injury. Imposing treatment on the basis of parental consent in this way risks a disproportionate interference with the child's rights, with no recourse to judicial oversight.

(C) Parental Consent: Time for Reassessment?

The legal principles underpinning *Re R* and *Re W* require reassessment now that developments in medical practice and human rights law have heightened a general awareness of rights entitlement, both for adults and children. Without a changed approach, an increasingly stark divide will emerge between the legal principles governing the treatment of adolescent patients and those governing adult patients.[110] Perhaps the most cogent reason for reassessing these principles is that overriding refusal inevitably involves interfering with a person's bodily and intellectual autonomy.[111] In these circumstances, the approach laid down in *Re R* and *Re W* in the early 1990s, prior to the HRA, looks increasingly out of step with medical practice and judicial respect for children's rights. While the courts have consistently upheld their jurisdiction to override the decision of a competent minor,[112] the ability of *parents* to do so has not received significant judicial attention since *Re R* and *Re W*.[113] There is a strong argument that the assumption in these cases that parents could override the refusal of their competent child was wrong and inconsistent with the decision in *Gillick*. Further, even if the decisions were correct at the time they were decided, subsequent developments in the professional, social and legal landscape mean that parents should no longer be

---

[108] C. Bridge (1999) p. 593. See e.g. the case of Hannah Jones, discussed below and in Chapter 7.
[109] Discussed further below.   [110] J. Fortin (2006) pp. 324–5.   [111] G. Douglas (1992) p. 576.
[112] *Re X (A Child) (No. 2)* [2021] EWHC 65 (Fam), [2021] 4 WLR 11, esp. at [61]. See also *Re E (Children: Blood Transfusion)* [2021] EWCA Civ 1888. These cases are discussed further below.
[113] In reviewing the role of the courts in such cases in *Re X (A Child) (No. 2)*, ibid. at [32], Sir James Munby was careful to state that he was not concerned with the parent's ability to override the decision of a competent minor.

regarded as having the authority to consent to medical treatment against the wishes of their competent child.

The guidance available to medical professionals reflects this uncertainty as to whether the law set out in *Re R* and *Re W* can still be relied upon in relation to parental decisions. The GMC advises doctors that the law concerning parental consent contrary to the refusal of a competent minor is 'complex' and recommends that legal advice is sought in such cases.[114] Similarly, the Department of Health guidance notes that there is no post-HRA case law to support the proposition that parents may override the refusal of their competent child and advises that a court decision is obtained in such circumstances.[115] The government's view that the legal principles established by the Court of Appeal in *Re R* and *Re W* are no longer reliable can also be seen in relation to the admission to hospital for treatment of children for a mental disorder. Legislation ensures that doctors can only admit 16- and 17-year-olds for treatment as 'voluntary' or 'informal' patients,[116] if they themselves consent to such admission, unless they lack capacity do so under the MCA 2005.[117] If they oppose such a step, doctors cannot obtain legal authority for admission from their parents, but must instead use the procedures provided in mental health legislation, as in the case of adult patients.[118] While the legislation is confined to those over 16, the Mental Health Code also states that it is not advisable to rely on parental consent to detain competent younger children who refuse admission, nor to provide medical treatment for competent children whether under or over 16.[119] Collectively, these documents reflect both official uncertainty as to the current state of the law and a reluctance to rely on parents to override the refusal of competent minors and those over the age of 16.

This guidance should be read against the backdrop of a broader shift in medical law and practice towards a greater respect for patient autonomy,[120] patient rights and the importance of informed consent.[121] The cases of Hannah Jones and Joshua McAuley provide vivid examples of medical teams respecting the views of mature minors. Hannah Jones was 12 years old when she refused a potentially life-saving heart transplant. Having already endured extensive experience of intrusive and painful medical treatment, she considered that she would rather spend her remaining time at home with her family than suffer another risky and intrusive operation. Hannah was supported in this decision

---

[114] GMC (2018) para. 31.   [115] DH (2009) p. 34.

[116] I.e. as a patient who consents to treatment, thereby obviating the need to comply with the requirements of the mental health legislation when treating patients against their wishes.

[117] Mental Health Act (MHA) 1983, s. 131(2), as amended by MHA 2007, s. 43.

[118] MHA 1983, s. 131(4).   [119] DH (2015) 19.39.

[120] *King's College Hospital NHS Foundation Trust* v. *C* [2015] EWCOP 80, esp. at [97]: the decision of an adult to refuse life-saving treatment because she feared a life in which she had lost her 'sparkle' may have been unwise, but was not evidence of lack of capacity. See also *Re B (Adult: Refusal of Medical Treatment)* [2002] EWHC 429 (Fam), [2002] 2 All ER 449, at [94] and [100].

[121] E.g. *Montgomery (Appellant)* v. *Lanarkshire Health Board (Respondent) (Scotland)* [2015] UKSC 11, [2015] AC 1430.

by her mother and by the treating medical team and no application was made to court to override her refusal. Happily, Hannah later received a changed prognosis and consented to a transplant; the response to her first decision demonstrates the respect given to the considered views and experiences of a relatively young adolescent.[122] Similarly, Joshua McAuley was 15 years old when he refused a blood transfusion following a car accident. He was a committed Jehovah's Witness and was supported in his decision by his parents. The medical team did not seek authorisation to treat Joshua against his wishes and sadly he died as a result of his injuries.[123] In both cases, the decisions of the young people, made with the support of their parents, were accepted by the medical professionals around them despite the life-threatening potential of those decisions. In neither case was there an application to court to compel treatment and in neither case was there any suggestion that the medical team had acted illegally or in breach of professional practice. It is not clear whether the medical teams considered Hannah and Joshua to be competent to refuse the treatment that was offered,[124] or whether they took the view that forced treatment was not in their best interests in any case. The fact that a child does not want an intrusive treatment will be an important aspect of assessing the child's best interests, regardless of competence. This is in part because of the greater recognition of children's participation rights in medical decisions, reflected in Article 12 of the CRC.[125] It is also because of the assault on a young person's dignity that comes from forced treatment against their express wishes.[126] More pragmatically, treatment imposed on a resistant child is less likely to be successful[127] and may require physical force in cases involving the treatment of an uncooperative but a fully grown adolescent.[128] For these reasons, the prospect of forcing treatment on an unwilling minor may mean that treatment that would otherwise be of benefit to them is no longer regarded as being in their best interests.[129] The courts have recognised this and been

---

[122] Discussed further in Chapter 7 and in detail by K. Moreton (2020). The decision was not initially supported by the Primary Care Trust, but upon receiving the initial evidence, the PCT dropped its initial threat of court action. In the event, Hannah survived this period and consented to a heart transplant at the age of 14 following a change in prognosis; fortunately, this transplant was successful and Hannah survived.

[123] Discussed by S. Gilmore and J. Herring (2011).

[124] Although K. Moreton (2020) states that the child protection nurse who visited Hannah concluded that she was competent.

[125] Discussed in Chapter 7.

[126] L. Gostin (1992) p. 76. See e.g. *An NHS Foundation Trust* v. *A, M, P, A Local Authority* [2014] EWHC 920 (Fam), at [17].

[127] E.g. *Re JA (A Minor)* [2014] EWHC 1135 (Fam), in which the proposed antiretroviral therapy required a high degree of commitment and adherence in order to be effective. While the treatment was in his best interests, compelling the reluctant, but not competent, 14-year-old to take it was unlikely to result in effective compliance.

[128] In *Re S (A Minor) (Consent to Medical Treatment)* [1994] 2 FLR 1065, at 1074, Johnson J acknowledged that the possible use of force was 'extremely distasteful'.

[129] E.g. *NHS Trust* v. *SK* [2016] EWHC 2860 (Fam), at [58]–[60]: the court found that palliative chemotherapy was in the best interests of a dying 11-year-old if he agreed to it, but not if it

willing to give approval to planned medical treatment that accords with a mature minor's wishes, even if complying with those wishes carries additional risks. For example, in *DV (A Child)*,[130] a 17-year-old Jehovah's Witness was only willing to consent to surgery if the medical team agreed that there would be no circumstances in which blood products would be used. Although there was an increased risk with this plan, the treating team was willing to agree to it as they considered it most important that he agree to have surgery. The court made a declaration that this plan would be in the child's best interests, so giving the treating team assurance that it would be lawful to proceed in the way he wished despite the increased risk. This is a further example of the increased weight placed on the consent of the mature minor.

Despite these developments, there has not yet been a direct legal challenge to the principles in *Re R* and *Re W* that appear to allow the refusal of a competent child, or a young person over 16, to be overruled by their parents. Nonetheless, Lady Hale, speaking in the Supreme Court, has suggested that the law on this point is open to doubt.[131] There are three grounds on which such a challenge might be made. First, as discussed above, there is a strong argument that the obiter comments in *Re R* and *Re W* were incorrect and inconsistent with the decision in *Gillick*, to the extent that they allowed parental consent to trump the refusal of a competent minor.[132] Second, even if the comments were correct at the time that the cases were decided, an argument for reassessment can be made on the basis that the scope of parental responsibility has shifted and should now be regarded as more limited in relation to competent minors. The extent of parental responsibility is not fixed, but is sensitive to social change,[133] and its ambit reflects the 'general community standards' of the time in which it is applied.[134] The changes in professional approaches to the decisions of competent adolescents, discussed above, arguably reflect a wider societal disapproval of the view that parents can legitimately impose intrusive treatment on their unwilling and competent child.[135] On this basis, it can be argued that parental responsibility should no longer be regarded as extending to authorising medical treatment against the decision of a competent minor. This argument

---

were compelled, as forced treatment was likely to exacerbate conflict and distress in his final weeks.

[130] [2021] EWHC 1037 (Fam): the boy had suffered post-traumatic stress disorder following previous treatment with blood products when he was 13 years old. As all parties were agreed that the surgery should take place in the way he wished, there was no necessity for a court order, but it was open to the NHS Trust to seek the order to confirm to the treating team that it was lawful and in the child's best interests.

[131] *Re D (A Child)* [2019] UKSC 42, [2019] 1 WLR 5403, at [26]: noting that: 'Whether the consent of a parent remains effective even if a child, with capacity, has refused consent is a more controversial question (which fortunately does not arise in this case).'

[132] This argument was accepted in *AB* v. *CD* [2021] EWHC 741 (Fam), at [52]–[67], but did not arise directly in that case as the child and parent were in agreement.

[133] *Gillick* v. *West Norfolk and Wisbech Area Health Authority* [1986] AC 112, at 186.

[134] *D (A Child)* [2017] EWCA Civ 1695, at [76]–[78].   [135] E. Cave and C. Purshouse (2020).

is particularly strong in relation to 16- and 17-year-olds,[136] given the deliberate decision of the legislature to treat this age group differently, in particular by extending the safeguards of the MCA 2005 to those over 16.[137]

The final ground on which the principles in *Re R* and *Re W* can be challenged is that the rights of the child also limit the ambit of parental responsibility. The application of this argument will depend on the circumstances of the proposed treatment and the rights that it engages. If the treatment requires forced admission to a hospital ward for treatment or restraint to administer medication, it may well amount to a deprivation of liberty under Article 5, depending on its degree and intensity.[138] The Supreme Court have confirmed, in *Re D*,[139] that parents have no authority to authorise the deprivation of liberty of a 16- or 17-year-old, regardless of the young person's capacity, meaning that judicial authorisation for such confinement should be sought to provide the safeguards required by Article 5. While the Supreme Court's decision concerned young people aged 16 and over, the same principles logically apply to younger children too,[140] suggesting that if a child is confined beyond the restrictions generally accepted for their age group, parental consent will not be effective to protect their Article 5 rights. The constraints on parental responsibility confirmed in *Re D* were specific to Article 5, but this is not the only right that may be engaged in medical treatment against the child's will. As Lady Hale has observed: 'it would be a startling proposition that it lies within the scope of parental responsibility for a parent to license the state to violate the most fundamental human rights of a child'.[141] While not all forms of medical treatment will involve the 'most fundamental' human rights, it is certainly the case that some forms of intrusive treatment, such as abortion, clearly do so. Indeed, it is arguable that the

---

[136] See *An NHS Foundation Trust Hospital* v. *P* [2014] EWHC 1650 (Fam), in which the mother consented to urgent life-saving treatment for her 17.5-year-old child who had taken an overdose. The hospital were reluctant to rely on parental consent and applied for a court order to do so.

[137] The MCA 2005 does not form a complete decision-making framework for this age group and does not oust the existing common law and statutory provisions: *Re D (A Child)* [2019] UKSC 42, [2019] 1 WLR 5403, at [71] (Lady Black). Nonetheless, the MCA 2005 provides evidence of the assumption that 16- and 17-year-olds will ordinarily have decision-making capacity.

[138] Non-consensual medical treatment will not necessarily amount to a deprivation of liberty under Art. 5, but may do so depending on the nature and duration of the detention: discussed in *Re X (A Child) (No. 2)* [2021] EWHC 65 (Fam), [2021] 4 WLR 11, at [122]–[130]. Even very short periods of restraint have been held to infringe Art. 5, e.g. *X* v. *Austria*, App. No. 8278/78, (1979) 18 DR 154 – detention in order to subject the detainee to a blood test, though short, could, in principle, amount to a breach of Art. 5.

[139] *Re D (A Child)* [2019] UKSC 42, [2019] 1 WLR 5403, discussed further in Chapter 9.

[140] Ibid. esp. at [46]–[50] (Lady Hale).

[141] Ibid. at [48] in relation to deprivation of liberty. While Lady Hale was careful to note that her judgment did not extend to considering the extent of parental responsibility in relation to medical treatment (at [50]), the observations made on this point are applied beyond the context of deprivation of liberty and are clearly apt to serious medical treatment.

imposition of serious medical treatment against the wishes of a competent person will almost inevitably involve a significant intrusion of the most serious human rights; as Gostin says:

> Nothing degrades a human being more than to have intrusive treatment thrust upon him despite his full understanding of its nature and purpose and his clear will to say 'no'.[142]

In particular, if forced treatment is serious enough, it may amount to a violation of the absolute prohibition on 'inhuman or degrading treatment' under Article 3 of the ECHR.[143] For adults, the fact that a treatment has been imposed without free and informed consent can be sufficient to violate Article 3, even if the procedure would otherwise be medically advised.[144] In the absence of authoritative judicial guidance on the application of this case law to mature minors,[145] there are good reasons to argue that parental consent alone should be insufficient, particularly as competent young people are likely to experience the violation of their dignity and choice in just the same way as adults. A similar argument may be made in relation to treatment that does not meet the severity required for Article 3, but engages the right to bodily integrity under Article 8 and so requires a careful assessment of the proportionality of any action imposed on the basis of an assessment of the young person's best interests. The mere fact of parental consent is insufficient to demonstrate proportionality. For these reasons, there is a strong case that parental responsibility should no longer be regarded as sufficient to impose medical treatment against the refusal of a competent minor. The professional guidance, considered above, is right to advise that judicial authority is sought in such cases in order to provide safeguards for the rights of mature minors and ensure that any treatment is proportionate to those rights.

In conclusion, the changing professional, social and legal landscape means that are strong reasons to conclude that parental responsibility no longer extends, if it ever did, to overriding the decision of a mature minor to refuse medical treatment. This does not mean that parents can never consent to treatment on behalf of their competent child. In circumstances in which the child is unable or unwilling to make the decision, the parent retains the legal

---

[142] L. Gostin (1992) p. 76.

[143] Forcing an adult patient to undergo medical treatment can involve 'inhuman or degrading treatment', even if he or she is mentally incompetent, unless the treatment is perfectly orthodox medically, deemed essential by the medical experts consulted and subject to procedural safeguards: *Jalloh* v. *Germany* [2007] 44 EHRR 32, esp. at [67]–[74].

[144] *VC* v. *Slovakia* [2014] 59 EHRR 29: sterilisation of a Roma woman without her free and informed consent amounted to a violation of Art. 3 even though there were medical reasons to advise that future pregnancy would be risky and the woman had signed a consent form (under pressure).

[145] *IG* v. *Slovakia* [2012] ECHR 1910 concerned sterilisation of mature minors without their informed consent or that of their parent or guardian. The ECtHR found a violation of Art. 3, but did not distinguish between the lack of consent of the applicants and their parents/ guardians.

capacity to do so.[146] That capacity does not extend to overruling a decision against the wishes of a competent child. The current uncertainty creates difficulties for professionals and also for young people, who are left unsure as to whether their decisions will be taken seriously. A reassessment of the law would provide clarity and address the concerns of those who so strongly condemned the way in which the Court of Appeal had undermined the House of Lords' attempt in *Gillick* to provide adolescents with a degree of legal autonomy.

(D) Judicial Consent: Time for Reassessment?

The conclusion that parents lack the ability to override their child's competent refusal does not necessarily mean that courts also lack the power to do so. It is well-established that the inherent powers of the courts under the *parens patriae* jurisdiction extend beyond the limits of parental responsibility.[147] In contrast to the dearth of post-HRA case law concerning parents, the courts have consistently found that they have a protective jurisdiction that extends to imposing treatment against the refusal of competent minors.[148] Further, independent scrutiny by the courts provides an important safeguard for the rights of minors that is not available if parental consent is relied upon alone. For these reasons, a challenge to the *courts'* jurisdiction to override a minor's competent refusal is much more difficult to sustain than a challenge to the power of parents to do so.

Despite the formidable authority supporting the courts' jurisdiction to impose treatment on unwilling, competent minors, young people may challenge its continued existence as incompatible with their rights and with changing social values. *Gillick*-competent adolescents resisting treatment might argue that they are as intellectually mature as many adults and are therefore entitled to the same rights to freedom from forcible treatment as those available to adult patients. A denial of such rights, they might argue, would not only infringe their rights under Article 8 of the ECHR and potentially Articles 3 and 5, but would also unlawfully discriminate against them on the grounds of age alone, under Article 14. In *Re X (A Child) (No. 2)*,[149] these arguments were forcefully made on behalf

---

[146] *AB* v. *CD* [2021] EWHC 741 (Fam), at [68]–[69].

[147] *Re W (A Minor) (Medical Treatment: Courts' Jurisdiction)* [1993] Fam 64, at 81; *Re JM (A Child)* [2015] EWHC 2832 (Fam), [2016] 2 FLR 235, at [24]; *Re X (A Child) (No. 2)* [2021] EWHC 65 (Fam), [2021] 4 WLR 11. See also *Re D (A Child)* [2019] UKSC 42, [2019] 1 WLR 5403.

[148] E.g. *An NHS Foundation Trust Hospital* v. *P* [2014] EWHC 1650 (Fam), in which the court consented to life-saving treatment against the wishes of a 17.5-year-old with capacity in relation to the decision. *Re X (A Child) (No. 2)* [2021] EWHC 65 (Fam), [2021] 4 WLR 11, at [61], gives a list of cases in which courts have exercised this jurisdiction subsequent to *Re R* and *Re W*. The Court of Appeal in *Re E (Children: Blood Transfusion)* [2021] EWCA Civ 1888, at [44], regarded the availability of the inherent jurisdiction in such cases to be well-established and considered that any change would be for Parliament.

[149] [2021] EWHC 65 (Fam), [2021] 4 WLR 11.

of X, a nearly 16-year-old who was found to be 'mature and wise beyond her years'. X, a committed Jehovah's Witness, had refused to consent to blood transfusions that were considered by her medical team to be necessary for the treatment of her sickle cell disease. The court had twice authorised transfusions against her wishes and the NHS Trust now sought a rolling order to allow transfusions to take place when required throughout her minority. X resisted the application, arguing that as a *Gillick*-competent[150] minor, her decision should be regarded as determinative just as it would be for a capacious adult, and that this conclusion was supported by Articles 3, 5, 8, 9 and 14 of the ECHR. These arguments were comprehensively rejected by Sir James Munby. While he accepted that Articles 3, 8, 9 and 14 were engaged[151] by the imposition of treatment on X against her competent refusal, nonetheless they were not breached. It was, he found, legitimate for the state to have regard to the preservation of life in assessing whether treatment violated Article 3 and whether it was justified under Articles 8 and 9. Further, he considered that the difference in treatment of minors, as compared to adults with capacity, was also justified under Article 14 by the aim of protecting the welfare of minors. The reasoning is perhaps unsurprising, given that the courts have long placed considerable weight on the importance of safeguarding life,[152] and maintained that this justifies treatment to save the life of a desperately ill adolescent, despite his or her own strong opposition.[153] Nonetheless, a competent adolescent such as X will undoubtedly find such an approach objectionable, particularly as the same argument would not permit the imposition of treatment on an adult with capacity.[154] Further, it involves the courts promoting the dubious proposition that by overriding an adolescent's autonomy rights, through enforced medical treatment, they are in fact safeguarding her rights to future health and self-fulfilment.[155] The question of whether court-imposed life-saving treatment protects, or violates, the rights of a mature minor is difficult to answer precisely because it raises fundamental theoretical questions as to the foundation of children's rights and the conflict that can arise between protecting the child

[150] It was common ground that X was *Gillick*-competent in respect of the treatment before the court.

[151] On the facts of the case, Art. 5 was not engaged as no order authorising restraint or preventing her from leaving the hospital had been made; further, she had acquiesced to treatment once ordered. Nonetheless, Sir James accepted that in other cases Art. 5 may be engaged and that there remained an open question as to whether there was a 'carve out' from Art. 5 for immediately necessary life-saving treatment: ibid. at [122]–[130].

[152] In some circumstances, Art. 2 imposes a positive obligation to protect life: *Osman* v. *United Kingdom* [1999] 1 FLR 193, at [115]–[116]; *Savage* v. *South Essex Partnership NHS Foundation Trust* [2008] UKHL 74, [2009] All ER 1053, per Lord Rodger of Earlseferry, at [45]; *Rabone* v. *Pennine Care NHS Foundation Trust* [2012] UKSC 2. While there was no such duty here that required court intervention, this did not prevent the court from regarding the preservation of life as an important factor in evaluating X's rights: ibid. at [107]–[108].

[153] E.g. *An NHS Foundation Trust Hospital* v. *P* [2014] EWHC 1650 (Fam), esp. at [15]: the court's positive duty under Art. 2 outweighed the refusal of a 17.5-year-old to accept life-saving treatment.

[154] *A NHS Trust* v. *Dr A* [2013] EWHC 2442 (COP).   [155] J. Fortin (2006) pp. 323–5.

and promoting her autonomy.[156] The approach to children's rights adopted in *Re X* is clearly based on the view that the state has a duty to bring children safely to adulthood, but not beyond.[157] As Emma Cave notes, in adopting this stance, the 'judgment lays bare the adoption of a future-orientated version of autonomy and a protectionist stance that will apply up to adulthood'.[158]

In the wake of *Re X*, it appears to be established that while a minor patient is certainly entitled to the basic freedoms guaranteed by Articles 3, 8, 9 and 14, these rights might be outweighed by judicial assessment of his or her best interests and value of life itself.[159] Even if the courts are ultimately unwilling to renounce their protective function for mature minors, the importance of the rights involved means that the jurisdiction should be exercised sparingly. A young person resisting a court application for medical treatment is likely to find it more fruitful to argue that treatment is disproportionate in their case than to challenge the existence of the jurisdiction itself. Indeed, in *Re X* itself, the court refused to make a rolling order to authorise further transfusions during her minority, finding that such an order would prevent careful analysis of the specific facts and would prioritise medical paternalism over judicial protection.[160] Although the courts' jurisdiction is not strictly limited to cases of serious risks to life or health, it will be much more difficult to justify imposing treatment outside of such cases.[161] Similarly, if a decision can safely be left until the minor reaches adulthood, the imposition of treatment is unlikely to be proportionate. The increasing professional and judicial sympathy with the notion of adolescent autonomy[162] requires that the decisions of mature minors are taken seriously, even if they appear to others to be unwise. As the Court of Appeal noted in *Re E (Children: Blood Transfusion)*,[163] the decision of a minor to refuse medical treatment would be effective in the absence of court intervention and the court must approach the child's decision alert to the seriousness of overriding it. This does not create a presumption in favour of following the child's wishes, but does mean that the court should give rigorous analysis and anxious scrutiny to the adequacy of the reasons for intervening.[164]

---

[156] See Chapter 1.

[157] See esp. *Re X (A Child) (No. 2)* [2021] EWHC 65 (Fam), [2021] 4 WLR 11, at [21], [119], [134] and [143].

[158] E. Cave (2021).

[159] Although *Re X* was decided in the High Court, the Court of Appeal refused an application for permission to appeal and has subsequently treated the law as settled: *Re E (Children: Blood Transfusion)* [2021] EWCA Civ 1888, at [5] and [44].

[160] *Re X (A Child) (No. 2)* [2021] EWHC 65 (Fam), [2021] 4 WLR 11, at [168]–[169].

[161] *Re E (Children: Blood Transfusion)* [2021] EWCA Civ 1888, at [61]–[64].

[162] Inter alia: *Re Roddy (A Child) (Identification: Restriction on Publication)* [2003] EWHC 2927 (Fam), [2004] 2 FLR 949; *Mabon v. Mabon* [2005] EWCA Civ 634, [2005] 2 FLR 101; *R (Axon) v. Secretary of State for Health and the Family Planning Association* [2006] EWHC 37 (Admin), [2006] 2 FLR 206, discussed by R. Taylor (2007); *AS v. CPW (Inward Return Order)* [2020] EWHC 1238 (Fam), [2020] Fam Law 1019.

[163] *Re E (Children: Blood Transfusion)* [2021] EWCA Civ 1888, at [6].

[164] Ibid. at [63]–[66]; *Re X (A Child) (No. 2)* [2021] EWHC 65 (Fam), [2021] 4 WLR 11, at [23]–[26].

Nonetheless, it remains rare for the court to accept the refusal of a minor in cases involving serious risks to health or life.[165]

In summary, in the changing professional, social and legal climate, the principles established in *Re R* and *Re W* must now be seen through the prism of the child's rights under Articles 3, 5 and 8 of the ECHR, combined with Article 14. Although the argument that these rights require the decision of a mature minor to be treated as determinative has so far failed, the rights context remains vital to the courts' exercise of their jurisdiction. Given the importance of the rights in question, and the difficulty of justifying prioritising the child's future self over their current capacious decision, the courts must conduct a rigorous analysis of any justification for overruling the decision of a minor with careful attention to all the circumstances of the case.

(4) The Control of Fertility

(A) Contraception

In contrast to the case law concerning young people who reject medical treatment, the courts have been much more willing to facilitate the decisions of girls who seek to control their fertility. This does not necessarily indicate approval for adolescent sexual activity, but a recognition that if a girl has sought contraceptive advice or treatment it is almost certainly better for her to receive it than to become sexually active without making an informed decision on her contraceptive choices. The contrast between these two areas of law reinforces the conclusion that the law on adolescent decision-making is more often concerned to promote outcomes that the court considers to be best, rather than to recognise the importance of adolescent autonomy for its own sake.

There seems to be general agreement that the outcomes for teenagers who complete their pregnancies and for their babies[166] are poorer than for older mothers, both in health and in socioeconomic terms.[167] Research indicates that the adverse outcomes frequently pass to the next generation who, in turn, are more likely to become teenage mothers themselves, and more likely to experience poverty, poor housing and poor nutrition. Although researchers stress that these disadvantages are in part a function of the conditions in which these mothers grow up themselves and are not necessarily related to their age

---

[165] See *DV (A Child)* [2021] EWHC 1037 (Fam), discussed above, for a rare example of the courts agreeing to treatment in accordance with the child's wishes, although in this case he was supported by the medical team who considered that the small but serious increased risk was worth taking to secure his agreement to surgery.

[166] Healthcare Commission (2007) p. 65: infant mortality for babies with mothers under 20 is 60 per cent higher than for babies of older mothers aged 20–39.

[167] Research summaries: J. Bynner and M. Londra (2004) para. 3.2.1; J. Bradshaw *et al.* (2004) para. 5.4; Health Development Agency (2004) p. 7; DCSF and DH (2008) s. 1. Much of the earlier research on teenage pregnancy is usefully summarised in Health Development Agency (2004).

per se,[168] it is clear that there are strong reasons to pursue policies that aim to reduce teenage pregnancy. Rates of teenage pregnancy in the UK have shown a substantial and sustained decline over the past decade.[169] While the precise reasons for this fall are complex, it seems likely that improved sex education and access to contraceptive treatment and advice have played an important part.[170] The law has long supported these developments through an essentially pragmatic stance; as Lord Scarman noted:

> women have obtained by the availability of the pill a choice of life-style with a degree of independence and of opportunity undreamed of until this generation ... The law ignores these developments at its peril.[171]

The decision in *Gillick* v. *West Norfolk and Wisbech Area Health Authority*[172] was a victory of realism over idealism. The House of Lords accepted the common-sense advice from the Department of Health that increased pregnancy and sexually transmitted diseases would result from a law requiring adolescents under 16 to obtain parental permission before seeking contraceptive advice and treatment. The decision legally affirmed that adolescents are entitled to act responsibly by seeking support and help outside their families, even if doing so offends their parents' own convictions. Moreover, their Lordships held that a doctor does not incur criminal liability[173] by providing such help, if the prescription of contraceptive treatment is medically indicated. This position is now confirmed by legislation, which makes it clear that a doctor acting to protect the adolescent's health will not be guilty of being an accessory to any criminal offence against the child by providing contraceptive advice or treatment.[174]

Despite the *Gillick* decision being regarded as the high-water mark for recognising adolescent decision-making rights, within its own context its demands are relatively rigorous. A teenage girl cannot demand contraceptive services from her doctor, irrespective of her circumstances. Both Lord Scarman and Lord Fraser stressed the complexities she must comprehend before a doctor can judge her competent to receive contraceptive advice and treatment. Lord Scarman emphasised that it is not enough for her to simply

---

[168] M. Wiggins *et al.* (2005) p. 9. See also S. Cater and L. Coleman (2006) ch. 4.

[169] ONS (2019): in 2017, there were 17.9 conceptions per 1,000 women aged 15–17, a 57 per cent decrease since 2007. For those aged under 16, there has been a 66.7 per cent drop in the rate of pregnancy over this 10-year period.

[170] ONS (2019).

[171] *Gillick* v. *West Norfolk and Wisbech Area Health Authority* [1986] AC 112, at 183.

[172] Ibid.

[173] I.e. aiding and abetting unlawful intercourse with a girl under 16 under the sexual offences legislation.

[174] Sexual Offences Act 2003, s. 73. Although doctors giving contraceptive advice or treatment are themselves protected from criminal liability, they need to be alert to the possibility that a child engaged in sexual activity may be the victim of sexual abuse or exploitation: GMC (2018) paras 57–60. This point is considered further below in the context of the relationship between the duty to disclose suspicion of abuse and the duty of confidentiality to the child.

understand the nature of the advice given: she must also have sufficient maturity to 'understand what is involved'. A doctor must be satisfied that she understands the long-term problems and risks associated with sexual intercourse, pregnancy and its termination.[175] Lord Fraser's judgment provided doctors with detailed practical advice which became immediately influential (known as the 'Fraser guidelines'). A doctor should only provide a girl with treatment or advice without involving her parents if fully satisfied over five rigorous requirements:[176] (1) that the girl must understand his advice; (2) she cannot be persuaded to inform her parents of the matter; (3) she is likely to have sexual intercourse with or without contraceptive treatment; (4) it is likely that her physical or mental health will suffer should she not receive the treatment; and, (5) her best interests require her to receive the treatment without her parents' consent. All five requirements were adopted by the revised government guidance[177] and by the medical profession and are regarded as the rules governing those prescribing teenagers with contraceptive services.[178]

The decision in *Gillick* would never have reached the House of Lords had Mrs Gillick not been so determined to prevent her adolescent daughters obtaining contraceptive advice and treatment without her consent. Many years later, Ms Axon, a mother with similarly strong views, received similarly robust judicial treatment.[179] Silber J rejected her argument that a mother's own Article 8 rights are unjustifiably infringed by her daughter being allowed to gain contraceptive advice from a doctor without her prior knowledge. His decision confirmed that the HRA 1998 had not affected the principles established by *Gillick* in this context. Adolescents remain entitled to seek contraceptive advice and treatment and to medical confidentiality, provided they comply with the tests of legal competence established by Lord Scarman and Lord Fraser.

(B) Abortion

The majority of adolescent pregnancies end in abortion, meaning that teenagers are more likely to end their pregnancy through abortion than women in any other age group.[180] Despite these figures, the question of whether a young person is competent to make a decision concerning abortion is more complex than that concerning contraception. Both the consequences of continuing the pregnancy and the decision to terminate may have profound social, moral and physical implications for the pregnant girl. In *Axon*, Silber J considered that *Gillick*

---

[175] *Gillick* v. *West Norfolk and Wisbech Area Health Authority* [1986] AC 112, at 189.
[176] Ibid. at 174.   [177] DH (1986) replaced by subsequent guidance.
[178] GMC (2018) para. 63.
[179] *R (Axon)* v. *Secretary of State for Health and the Family Planning Association* [2006] EWHC 37 (Admin), [2006] 2 FLR 206.
[180] ONS (2019): 60.7 per cent of pregnancies of girls under 16 and 51.7 per cent of those aged 16 and 17 ended in abortion. Despite these figures, as teenage pregnancy rates have declined, so the *rate* of abortion among teenagers has also declined.

competence to make a decision concerning abortion required a higher threshold of capacity than that for receiving contraceptive advice and treatment.[181] Unlike contraceptive treatment, abortion involves an invasive and irreversible surgical procedure with greater potential risks and side effects.[182] Even so, according to Silber J, the guidance on legal competence provided by Lord Scarman and Lord Fraser in *Gillick*[183] can be used in the context of abortion, but with some adaptation, given that abortion raises more serious and complex issues.[184] Consequently, a doctor providing an adolescent under the age of 16 with abortion services must fulfil Lord Fraser's five guidelines, but also taking additional account of Lord Scarman's requirement that the young person 'understands properly "what is involved"',[185] a requirement which in itself involves a 'high threshold' of legal competence.[186] A doctor providing abortion services without complying with such guidance must expect to be professionally disciplined.[187] The decision in *Axon* also confirmed the common assumption that if a doctor considers the girl to be sufficiently competent to consent to an abortion and that an abortion is medically advised, she need not consult her parents over the matter, although it will usually be preferable for her to do so.[188]

Although *Axon* stresses the onerous requirements of competence in this area, in *An NHS Trust* v. *A, B, C and a Local Authority*,[189] a girl who had just passed her 13th birthday was found to possess sufficient competence to consent to an abortion. Two particular features of the case demonstrate the reluctance of courts to intervene to oppose the views of adolescents in such a sensitive and personal area. First, as Kirsty Moreton notes,[190] in assessing competence the court focused on the girl's ability to understand the biological aspects of the decision, rather than engaging with the full moral and social implications that would appear to be required by Lord Scarman. This approach to competence sits in stark contrast with the onerous requirements placed on teenagers who have sought to resist life-saving treatment.[191] Second, once the girl had demonstrated capacity to make the decision, the court considered that the choice was hers to make, without the need for an additional assessment of her best interests. By eschewing a paternalistic best interests test in favour of one wholly based on the girl's capacity, the decision appears to give strong support to adolescent reproductive choice. Again, this appears to be a very different approach from the refusal of the courts to treat competent minors as able to make a determinative decision as to whether to accept life-saving treatment.[192] The difference in

---

[181] *R (Axon)* v. *Secretary of State for Health and the Family Planning Association* [2006] EWHC 37 (Admin), [2006] 2 FLR 206, at [90].

[182] Ibid. at [83].   [183] [1986] AC 112.   [184] *R (Axon)*, ibid. at [90]–[91].

[185] *Gillick* v. *West Norfolk and Wisbech Area Health Authority* [1986] AC 112, at 189.

[186] *R (Axon)*, ibid. at [90].   [187] Ibid.   [188] Ibid. at [87] and [90].

[189] [2014] EWHC 1445 (Fam).   [190] K. Moreton (2015).

[191] Considered above; e.g. *Re E (A Minor) (Wardship: Medical Treatment)* [1993] 1 FLR 386.

[192] Sir James Munby cites the decision in this case as one in which the 'decision of a *Gillick* competent child will be determinative': *Re X (A Child) (No. 2)* [2021] EWHC 65 (Fam), [2021] 4 WLR 11, at [30]. The Court of Appeal have stressed that this is not because there is no welfare

approach between the two areas of decision-making appears to reflect a greater sensitivity given to the wishes and feelings of girls on matters of pregnancy, in which there may be no clear 'right' answer to the choice of whether or not to continue that pregnancy.

As discussed above, English law remains uncertain over the circumstances in which a parent may override the decisions of a mature minor. The law is clearest if a girl's parents wish to take legal steps to *oppose* her decision concerning abortion. The parents themselves are not entitled to veto any medical procedure a *Gillick*-competent girl has consented to, although this does not prevent them seeking the assistance of the courts to stop her going ahead with an abortion against their wishes.[193] Depending on her age and maturity, an open disagreement between an adolescent and her parents over whether her pregnancy should be terminated may mean that doctors are reluctant to go ahead without obtaining prior court authorisation. The case law discussed above suggests that the courts are extremely unlikely to be receptive to such a parental application to overrule the girl's competent decision to consent to a lawful abortion.[194] This conclusion is strengthened by the fact that the ECtHR has stated that undue obstacles to obtaining a lawful abortion can constitute a violation of Article 8 and that the personal autonomy of minors is particularly important in the sphere of reproductive rights.[195]

Has a *Gillick*-competent pregnant girl the right to resist the wishes of her parents who *want* her to undergo an abortion? In *Re W (A Minor) (Medical Treatment: Court's Jurisdiction)*,[196] both Lord Donaldson MR and Balcombe LJ admitted that, according to their interpretation of the law, a teenage girl could be forced to undergo an abortion against her wishes, merely on the consent of her parents. Nevertheless, Balcombe LJ thought it difficult to conceive of a court ordering an abortion against the wishes of a competent 16-year-old.[197] Given the growing judicial sympathy for the notion of adolescent autonomy discussed above, it seems inconceivable that parents could have the right to force such an invasive procedure upon a reluctant adolescent without explicit court authorisation. Further, a court today is extremely

---

jurisdiction in relation to abortion decisions, but because the medical team in this case were willing to act on the child's decision provided that she was competent to make the decision and so the court was not asked to determine whether an abortion was in her best interests. The Court of Appeal nonetheless considered that it was 'improbable that the welfare decision would be exercised contrary to the wishes of a young person in an abortion decision': *Re E (Children: Blood Transfusion)* [2021] EWCA Civ 1888, at [67].

[193] I.e. by seeking the court's assistance through its inherent jurisdiction, or by seeking a specific issue order or prohibited steps order under the Children Act (CA) 1989, s. 8.

[194] See also *Re P (A Minor)* [1986] 1 FLR 272: the court authorised a 15-year-old girl in LA care to undergo an abortion, despite her parents' opposition to this procedure.

[195] *P v. Poland* [2013] 1 FCR 476, esp. at [109]: concerning a 14-year-old girl who became pregnant following rape and was placed under considerable pressure not to have an abortion, including being removed from her parents' home and detained in a juvenile shelter.

[196] [1993] Fam 64.   [197] Ibid. at 90.

unlikely to override a pregnant girl's wishes, unless her doctors advise that continuing with her pregnancy is likely to jeopardise her future survival. A challenge enlisting Articles 3,[198] 5 and 8 of the ECHR would almost certainly protect her from undergoing an abortion against her will. Few would quarrel with the proposition that an adolescent has a right to have her choices respected over whether she carries her baby to term or not. The ECtHR has made it clear that the importance of personal autonomy in this sphere means that parents do not have a right to make decisions governing their child's reproductive choices.[199] This right should be translated into clear domestic legal principles to dispel any doubt that remains from the decision in *Re W*.

The situations considered above concern pregnant teenagers who have the competence to make their own decisions. If a girl does not have competence to do so, the court may be asked to make the decision by determining her best interests.[200] Even in such a case, her wishes and feelings will usually be central to the outcome. As Munby P noted in the case of a 13-year-old girl who lacked capacity:

> A child or incapacitated adult may, in strict law, lack autonomy. But the court must surely attach very considerable weight indeed to the albeit qualified autonomy of a mother who in relation to a matter as personal, intimate and sensitive as pregnancy is expressing clear wishes and feelings, whichever way, as to whether or not she wants a termination.[201]

It is surely right to conclude that both forcing a girl to undergo an abortion against her will, or refusing a lawful termination that she wishes to receive, constitute significant violations of her rights that can only be justified by the most compelling circumstances. The psychological and emotional risks of overriding a pregnant girl's wishes and feelings[202] mean that those wishes are likely to be of considerable, often determinative, weight in assessing her best interests. As a result, it will only be in the most extreme cases that overruling the views of the pregnant girl will be justified, even if she is not *Gillick*-competent to make the decision.

---

[198] It is unlikely that the doctors could argue that performing an enforced abortion is a therapeutic necessity and in accordance with accepted medical practice, as required by *Herczegfalvy* v. *Austria* (1992) 15 EHRR 437. See further discussion above.

[199] *P* v. *Poland* [2013] 1 FCR 476, esp. at [109]: in this case, the mother supported her daughter's choice to have an abortion.

[200] An abortion may, of course, only be authorised if it is lawful under the Abortion Act 1967.

[201] *Re X (A Child)* [2014] EWHC 1871 (Fam).

[202] See also *Re AB* [2019] EWCA Civ 1215, in which the wishes and feelings of an adult who lacked capacity were considered as extremely important in assessing her best interests and could be determinative. In this case, her wishes were not clearly expressed, but the judge had erred in placing too little weight upon her evident feelings.

(5) Confidentiality and Medical Treatment

Adults are entitled to assume that their doctors will not divulge their medical secrets[203] – an entitlement which has been reinforced by Strasbourg jurisprudence and domestic case law maintaining that the right to respect for personal privacy[204] embraces the right to medical confidentiality.[205] Young people often place great value on confidentiality too[206] and may be deterred from seeking medical advice and assistance if they fear that they cannot trust that the conversation will remain confidential.[207] The duty of confidentiality owed to young people by medical professionals is recognised under the common law and human rights law. The scope of that duty has come under challenge, both from parents who contend that they have a parental right to access information about their child and from the concern that failure to share information may result in harm to the young person.

The leading case concerning medical confidentiality and young people is *R (Axon)* v. *Secretary of State for Health and the Family Planning Association*.[208] Ms Axon failed in her bid to establish that the Department of Health's guidance was unlawful in asserting that minors under 16 were owed the same duty of confidentiality as that owed to any adult.[209] Silber J acknowledged that their Lordships in *Gillick*[210] had not specifically stated that *Gillick*-competent adolescents were entitled to absolute confidentiality when consulting a medical practitioner over contraception and other sexual matters. Nevertheless, he concluded that such an assumption was implicit in their decision.[211] Consequently, although a doctor should always encourage a *Gillick*-competent patient to confide in her parents, if she refuses to do so, she has a right to medical confidentiality.[212] This duty of confidentiality applies whether it is advice or treatment that is sought and to all forms of advice or

---

[203] But in rare circumstances, disclosure may be justified 'in the public interest' (*W* v. *Egdell* [1990] Ch 359); e.g. where failure to disclose appropriate information would expose a third party to risk of death or serious harm.

[204] I.e. under ECHR, Art. 8.

[205] See: *Z* v. *Finland* (1997) 25 EHRR 371, at [95]; *Campbell* v. *MGN Ltd* [2004] UKHL 22, [2004] 2 AC 457, esp. Baroness Hale of Richmond, at [145]. J. Loughrey (2008) pp. 313–17 assesses the case law developing the right to medical confidentiality.

[206] Inter alia: SEU (1999) para. 7.7: young people had an overriding fear that their doctors would inform their parents of their medical consultations; BMRB International (2004) para. 2.9: 42 per cent of young people aged between 13 and 21 considered 'confidentiality/privacy' to be the most important factor when seeking advice on sex and relationships (a similar finding was obtained in earlier 'waves' carried out by BMRB International); see also similar evidence summarised by Silber J in *R (Axon)* v. *Secretary of State for Health and the Family Planning Association* [2006] EWHC 37 (Admin), [2006] 2 FLR 206, at [67]–[71].

[207] *R (Axon)* v. *Secretary of State for Health and the Family Planning Association* [2006] EWHC 37 (Admin), [2006] 2 FLR 206, at [142]–[143].

[208] *R (Axon)*, ibid.   [209] DH (2004) p. 2.   [210] [1986] AC 112.

[211] *R (Axon)*, ibid. at [55]–[65].

[212] Ibid. at [6]: Ms Axon unsuccessfully argued that doctors should not provide teenagers under the age of 16 with any advice and treatment on contraception, sexually transmitted infections or abortion without their parents' knowledge, *unless* passing on such information would

treatment, including contraception, sexually transmitted infection and abortion.[213] Silber J's decision usefully confirmed that the duty of confidentiality owed at common law was also contained in the HRA 1998 and that the HRA did not require any change to the principles in *Gillick*. Ms Axon had failed to establish that there was a parental right under Article 8 to disclosure of information about her competent daughters. Even if such a right had been established, Silber J found that it would in any case be outweighed by reference to the need, under Article 8(2), to protect her daughters' right to medical confidentiality.[214] Although Ms Axon was primarily concerned with decisions concerning sexual matters, the reasoning in the case was not limited to such cases and has been applied more widely to a range of decisions.[215] Indeed, Ms Axon, like Ms Gillick before her, achieved precisely what she wished to prevent – in this case, that medical practitioners must respect the medical secrets of all *Gillick*-competent adolescents.[216]

Since Ms Axon's daughters were assumed to be *Gillick*-competent, the decision in *Axon* left untouched the official assumption that the *Gillick*-*in*competent adolescent is also entitled to medical confidentiality.[217] The law has been unclear over whether an adolescent not deemed sufficiently mature to understand the contraceptive advice or treatment is also entitled to medical confidentiality. Case law establishes that doctors should not disclose the medical details of very young children to anyone other than their own parents.[218] Case law also shows that children may be protected against invasions of privacy by the press, reinforced by their right to privacy under Article 8 of the ECHR.[219] But can a doctor divulge details of a *Gillick*-*in*competent adolescent's medical consultation to her parents? Some have argued that doctors do not owe a duty of confidentiality to a minor legally incapable of entering into a legal relationship with them.[220] This controversially means that a teenage girl will not know until the end of her consultation whether her doctor considers her to be *Gillick*-competent and cannot be guaranteed secrecy at the outset. It also implicitly links competence for reaching decisions over

---

prejudice their physical or mental health, thereby rendering it against their best interests so to do.

[213] Ibid. at [87].   [214] *R (Axon)*, ibid. at [136]–[150].

[215] E.g. *PD* v. *SD, JD and X County Council* [2015] EWHC 4103 (Fam): the Art. 8 rights of a 16-year-old transgender teenager to keep information concerning his transition and new identity private 'decisively' outweighed any right to information asserted by his parents.

[216] See R. Taylor (2007) for a critique of the *Axon* decision.

[217] Successive health guidance documents have all suggested without qualification that doctors unable to persuade teenagers under 16 to involve their parents in any treatment decisions involving contraception, sexually transmitted infections or abortion must always maintain strict medical confidentiality; e.g. DH (2004).

[218] *Re C (A Minor) (Wardship: Medical Treatment) (No. 2)* [1990] Fam 39.

[219] *Murray* v. *Express Newspapers Plc* [2008] EWCA Civ 446, [2008] HRLR 33, per Sir Arthur Clarke MR, at [16]. But the right to an expectation of privacy is not absolute, ibid. at [58]; discussed by J. Loughrey (2008) pp. 321–3.

[220] I. Kennedy (1992) pp. 111–17.

treatment to competence for expecting medical confidentiality – whereas, as Loughrey points out, children who lack competence for medical decision-making may comprehend the concept of confidentiality.[221] Nevertheless, Ms Axon's claim that a parent's Article 8 rights are infringed by a doctor with-holding information from her about her child's medical needs becomes more sustainable in the case of an adolescent deemed to be *Gillick-in*competent. Loughrey points out that a doctor could certainly justify (under Article 8(2)) divulging the information to a parent who needs it in order to authorise the child's medical treatment.[222] In other circumstances, the child's own right to privacy might trump those of the parents. Whatever the strict state of the law, the younger, more immature adolescent will be deterred from seeking medical advice without guarantees of privacy. It is therefore undoubtedly sensible for the official guidance to encourage doctors to respect the confidentiality of all patients under the age of 16.[223]

Concerns about the scope of medical confidentiality can arise in other contexts. A doctor may fear, for example, that a young person's involvement in sexual activity is not a matter of free choice, but is in fact a sign of exploitation or abuse.[224] In such cases, irrespective of the adolescent's compe-tence, medical confidentiality cannot be absolute. Professional guidance emphasises that medical practitioners must be prepared to pass on medical information, in the public interest, including to assist a child protection investigation into alleged abusive practices. It stresses that a child or young person must always be encouraged to agree to such disclosure before it occurs.[225] Hopefully, aided by an appropriate explanation of such steps, most adolescents will understand why their confidences have to be broken in order to address risks of harm.

(6) Conclusion

The law relating to adolescents' decision-making powers over their health is confusing and arbitrary. On the one hand, the principle of *Gillick* competence recognises their capacity for choice and encourages them to take a responsible attitude to such matters as contraception and other medical procedures that they wish to undergo. But, on the other hand, the law attempts to maintain the right to override their choice to refuse all treatment. While it might be comprehensible for the law to refuse them the right to make life-threatening mistakes, it appears to go much further and enable parents and doctors to correct any decision they consider to be irrational or unreasonable, and not in the patient's best interests. This legal position appears increasingly out of step with a growing professional and judicial respect for the decisions and rights of young people and is ripe for reassessment. As a result, medical professionals

---

[221] J. Loughrey (2008) p. 317.   [222] Ibid. pp. 322–3.   [223] DH (2004).
[224] GMC (2018) paras 57–60.   [225] E.g. ibid. paras 48–49.

are increasingly seeking judicial authorisation in cases of uncertainty or conflict, rather than relying on parental consent to overrule the decisions of mature young people. Judicial decisions will, however, only provide an adequate safeguard for adolescent rights if sufficient weight is placed on their rights to bodily integrity and decision-making. The extent to which courts have been willing to respect these rights has varied, with courts far more willing to place weight on the rights of young people in the context of decisions that do not appear 'unwise'. Overall, the law certainly no longer matches up to the promise implicit in Lord Scarman's judgment in *Gillick* v. *West Norfolk and Wisbech Area Health Authority*[226] that adolescents had gained a degree of autonomy over their own bodies.

Bibliography

NB: Many of these publications can be obtained on the relevant organisation's website.

BMRB International (2004) *Tracking Survey Wave 12 Evaluation of the Teenage Pregnancy Strategy, Report of Results of Twelve Waves of Research*, BMRB International.

Bradshaw, J., Kemp, P., Baldwin, S. and Rowe, A. (2004) *The Drivers of Social Exclusion: A Review of the Literature for the Social Exclusion Unit in the Breaking the Cycle Series*, Social Exclusion Unit.

Brazier, M. and Bridge, C. (1996) 'Coercion or Caring: Analysing Adolescent Autonomy' 16 *Legal Studies* 84.

Bridge, C. (1999) 'Religious Beliefs and Teenage Refusal of Medical Treatment' 62 *Modern Law Review* 585.

British Medical Association (BMA) (2019) *Children and Young People Ethics Tool Kit*, BMA. org.uk.

Bynner, J. and Londra, M. (2004) *The Impact of Government Policy on Social Exclusion Among Young People: A Review of the Literature for the Social Exclusion Unit in the Breaking the Cycle Series*, Social Exclusion Unit.

Cater, S. and Coleman, L. (2006) *'Planned' Teenage Pregnancy: Perspectives of Young Parents from Disadvantaged Backgrounds*, Joseph Rowntree Foundation.

Cave, E. (2014) 'Goodbye *Gillick*? Identifying and Resolving Problems with the Concept of Child Competence' 34 *Legal Studies* 103.

(2021) 'Confirmation of the High Court's Power to Override a Child's Treatment Decision: *A NHS Trust v. X (In the matter of X (A Child) (No 2))* [2021] EWHC 65 (Fam)' 29 *Medical Law Review* 537.

Cave, E. and Purshouse, C. (2020) 'Think of the Children: Liability for Non-Disclosure of Information Post-*Montgomery*' 29 *Medical Law Review* 270.

Cave, E. and Wallbank, J. (2012) 'Minors' Capacity to Refuse Treatment: A Reply to Gilmore and Herring' 20 *Medical Law Review* 423.

Chico, V. and Haggar, L. (2011) 'The Mental Capacity Act 2005 and Mature Minors: A Missed Opportunity?' 33 *Journal of Social Welfare and Family Law* 157.

Department for Children, Schools and Families (DCSF) and Department of Health (DH) (2008) *Teenage Parents: Who Cares?*, DCSF.

Department of Constitutional Affairs (DCA) (2007) *Mental Capacity Act 2005: Code of Practice*, The Stationery Office.

Department of Health (DH) (1986) Circular HC (86) 1, DH.

(2004) *Best Practice Guidance for Doctors and Other Health Professionals on the Provision of Advice and Treatment to Young People under 16 on Contraception, Sexual and Reproductive Health*, Reference No. 3382, DH.

---

[226] [1986] AC 112.

(2009) *Reference Guide to Consent for Examination or Treatment*, 2nd edn, DH.

(2015) *Code of Practice: Mental Health Act 1983*, The Stationery Office.

Douglas, G. (1992) 'The Retreat from *Gillick*' 55 *Modern Law Review* 569.

Downie, A. (1999) 'Consent to Medical Treatment – Whose View of Welfare?' 29 *Family Law* 818.

Eekelaar, J. (1993) 'White Coats or Flak Jackets? Doctors, Children and the Courts – Again' 109 *Law Quarterly Review* 182.

Feldman, D. (2002) *Civil Liberties and Human Rights in England and Wales*, Oxford University Press.

Ferguson, L. (2004) *The End of an Age: Beyond Age Restrictions for Minors' Medical Treatment Decisions*, Law Commission of Canada.

Fortin, J. (2006) 'Accommodating Children's Rights in a Post Human Rights Act Era' 69 *Modern Law Review* 299.

Freeman, M. (2005) 'Rethinking *Gillick*' 13 *International Journal of Children's Rights* 201.

General Medical Council (GMC) (2018) *0–18 Years: Guidance for All Doctors*, GMC.

Gilmore, S. and Herring, J. (2011) '"No" Is the Hardest Word: Consent and Children's Autonomy' 23 *Child and Family Law Quarterly* 3.

Gostin, L. (1992) 'Consent to Treatment: The Incapable Person' in Dyer, C. (ed.) *Doctors, Patients and the Law*, Blackwell Scientific Publications.

Hale, B. and Fortin, J. (2008) 'The Legal Principles Governing the Care and Treatment of Children with Mental Health' in Rutter, M., Bishop, D., Pine, D., Scott, S., Stevenson, J., Taylor, E. and Thapar, A. (eds) *Rutter's Child and Adolescent Psychiatry*, Blackwell Publishing.

Healthcare Commission (2007) HC 97, *State of Healthcare 2007*, The Stationery Office.

Health Development Agency (2004) *Teenage Pregnancy: an Overview of the Research Evidence*, Health Development Agency.

Huxtable, R. (2000) '*Re M (Medical Treatment: Consent)*: Time to Remove the "Flak Jacket"?' 12 *Child and Family Law Quarterly* 83.

Kennedy, I. (1992) *Treat Me Right: Essays in Medical Law and Ethics*, Clarendon Press.

Lansdown, R. (1998) 'Listening to Children: Have We Gone Too Far (or Not Far Enough)?' 91 *Journal of the Royal Society of Medicine* 457.

Lewis, P. (2001) 'The Medical Treatment of Children' in Fionda, J. (ed.) *Legal Concepts of Childhood*, Hart Publishing.

Loughrey, J. (2008) 'Can You Keep a Secret? Children, Human Rights, and the Law of Medical Confidentiality' 20 *Child and Family Law Quarterly* 312.

Lowe, N. and Juss, S. (1993) 'Medical Treatment – Pragmatism and the Search for Principle' 56 *Modern Law Review* 865.

McCafferty, C. (1999) 'Won't Consent? Can't Consent! Refusal of Medical Treatment' 29 *Family Law* 335.

McFarlane, A. (2011) 'Mental Capacity: One Standard for All Ages' 41 *Family Law* 479.

Masson, J. (1993) '*Re W*: Appealing from the Golden Cage' 5 *Journal of Child Law* 37.

Moreton, K. (2015) '*Gillick* Reinstated: Judging Mid-Childhood Competence in Healthcare Law: An NHS Trust v. ABC & A Local Authority' 23 *Medical Law Review* 303.

(2020) 'Reflecting on "Hannah's Choice": Using the Ethics of Care to Justify Child Participation in End of Life Decision-Making' 28 *Medical Law Review* 124.

Office for National Statistics (ONS) (2019) *Conceptions in England and Wales: 2017*, ONS.

Social Exclusion Unit (SEU) (1999) Cm 4342, *Teenage Pregnancy*, Cabinet Office.

Taylor, R. (2007) 'Reversing the Retreat from *Gillick*? R (Axon) v. Secretary of State for Health' 18 *Child and Family Law Quarterly* 81.

Wiggins, M., Oakley, A., Sawtell, M., Austerberry, H., Clemens, F. and Elbourne, D. (2005) *Teenage Parenthood and Social Exclusion: a Multi-method Study*, Summary Report of Findings, Social Science Research Unit Report, Institute of Education.

12

The Child's Right to Participation in Family Proceedings

(1) Introduction

English law allows mature children a remarkable degree of procedural autonomy by allowing them to initiate proceedings themselves, in order to enforce their own substantive rights.[1] They may, for example, apply for an order under the Children Act (CA) 1989 relating to their own healthcare, or gain the right to live with some adult other than their parents.[2] It is clearly important that children should be allowed to challenge any infringements of their substantive rights through the court process. Otherwise, the fact that they are rights-holders may be of little comfort to them. It is, however, relatively unusual for children to initiate their own litigation. Far more are drawn into legal proceedings by parents disagreeing over their upbringing. Indeed, increasing numbers of children find that 'the taken-for-grantedness of family life'[3] is shattered by their parents breaking up. These children may find that the legal system makes it only too easy for their parents not to involve them in any arrangements made for their future upbringing.

A growing body of authors criticise what they see as the outdated view of children as the passive victims of parental and adult quarrels.[4] These writers instead argue that children should be acknowledged as having agency – as autonomous individuals with a right to participation[5] in all aspects of family life, including post-divorce arrangements for their care. The judiciary are increasingly receptive to such arguments concerning children's participation. Lady Hale has spoken of an 'increasing recognition of children as people with a part to play in their own lives, rather than as passive recipients of their parents' decisions'.[6] As Sir James Munby has observed, this has led to a 'sea-change in attitudes' to children's participation in proceedings, a development that 'continues apace'.[7] As a result of this sea-change, the courts have become

---

[1] Discussed in Chapter 10.   [2] By applying for a s. 8 order under the CA 1989.

[3] C. Smart *et al.* (2006) p. 167.

[4] These ideas are summarised by A. Diduck (2003) pp. 80–3 and F. Kaganas and A. Diduck (2004) pp. 961–4.

[5] A. Daly (2018b); A. James (2003) p. 145.

[6] *Re LC (Children) (Reunite International Child Abduction Centre Intervening)* [2014] UKSC 1, [2014] AC 1038, at [87].

[7] *Re F (Children)* [2016] EWCA Civ 546, [2016] 3 FCR 255, at [41].

more willing: to hear children, directly and indirectly; to ensure that they are informed about the process and decision; and to place weight on their views. Nonetheless, despite changing judicial attitudes, the system providing children with procedural rights remains confused and unfair. This is largely due to government reluctance to devote sufficient resources to establishing better support. Financial restraints have ensured that provision remains variable and arbitrary: while some children are enabled to convey their wishes to the courts, others are not, even if they are caught up in similar circumstances to those who are. Depending on the way the litigation started, the courts receive information about some but not all children, with some children being separately represented and others left with no representation at all.

This chapter starts by considering the provisions of international law recognising children's rights to participate in legal proceedings over their future. It then turns to assess the extent to which children participate in family decisions, especially those whose parents separate or divorce. The chapter then considers children's involvement in family proceedings. This section is divided into two parts. The first considers the methods used for ascertaining the views of children involved in private law disputes over their upbringing, including the procedures governing children wishing to instruct their own solicitors and litigate on their own behalf. The second section assesses the system of representation for children involved in public law proceedings.[8] The chapter then concludes by considering the weight given to children's wishes and feelings in assessing their welfare.

(2) International Law and the Child's Right to Participation

(A) UN Convention on the Rights of the Child, Article 12

The right of children to participate in decisions concerning them was established beyond doubt by Article 12 of the UN Convention on the Rights of the Child (CRC).[9] The Article is of fundamental importance: it affirms that children should not be seen as passive individuals, but as fully fledged people with rights to express their own views and be taken seriously on all matters affecting them. The influence of Article 12 extends beyond the substantive right itself. As one of the four general principles of the CRC,[10] it is instrumental in interpreting and implementing all other articles in the Convention. Its guarantees have been widely adopted in other international instruments,[11] establishing it as one of the most important achievements of the CRC.

Article 12(1) requires that states:

---

[8] These issues are all considered in the context of applications brought under the CA 1989, since this is the litigation which most commonly affects children.

[9] For detailed analysis, see L. Lundy *et al.* (2019).   [10] Discussed in Chapter 2.

[11] E.g. Convention on the Rights of Persons with Disabilities (entered into force 3 May 2008), Art. 7(3); Charter of Fundamental Rights of the European Union (30 March 2010), Art. 24(1).

Shall assure to the child who is capable of forming his or her own views the right to express those views freely in all matters affecting the child, the views of the child being given due weight in accordance with the age and maturity of the child.

Article 12(2) further provides that for this purpose:

the child shall in particular be provided with the opportunity to be heard in any judicial and administrative proceedings affecting the child, either directly, or through a representative or an appropriate body, in a manner consistent with the procedural rules of national law.

It should be noted that Article 12 does not promise autonomy to children – neither paragraph promises that children's wishes will be acceded to. The Article guarantees a right to consultation and participation, not self-determination. The Article requires[12] both that children are able to express their views freely and that they are provided with an opportunity to be heard in *any* judicial and administrative proceedings affecting them. Further, the child must not only be heard, but the views they express must be given 'due weight' within the decision-making process. Each of these obligations will be considered in turn.

The right to expression contained Article 12(1) applies to *any* child 'capable of forming his or her own views'. The UN Committee on the Rights of the Child (the 'Committee') has observed that younger children frequently face additional practical and legal barriers to the enjoyment of this right, as do children with disabilities affecting communication. As the Committee notes, the phrasing of Article 12(1) makes clear that specific age barriers to the child's right to express their views are not acceptable.[13] Instead, it recommends that states must start from the presumption that each child has the capacity to form views, even if unable to express them verbally. This means that forms of non-verbal communication, such as play, artwork, facial expressions and body language, should be recognised as expression of views. Further, children should be provided with assistance and equipment to overcome communication difficulties, including those stemming from disability or differences in language. In essence, barriers to communication should not be used to deny children the right to express their views, should they wish to do so; instead, children should be facilitated to express their views in the manner in which they are able.

Article 12(2) grants additional rights in relation to judicial and administrative proceedings, including family proceedings, in which the child must be provided with an opportunity to be heard. Although this appears to guarantee a right to participate in proceedings, how children are to be heard is not clearly

---

[12] The Committee on the Rights of the Child has observed that the obligation to *assure* the right to be heard is of 'special strength' leaving no leeway to state parties as to whether or not to comply: Committee on the Rights of the Child (2009) para. 19.

[13] Ibid. paras 20–21.

specified. The text of Article 12(2) makes no promise that the child will be heard in person, or even by a representative designated to act for that child. It merely refers to the child's views being transmitted either directly or through 'a representative or an appropriate body'. This formula does not specifically rule out the child's own parent claiming to represent the child, despite the obvious conflict of interest in most family proceedings involving both child and parent. The wording of Article 12(2) appears to permit a range of practices, some of which would render the child's right to be heard nugatory.

Despite the rather vague phrasing of Article 12(2), the Committee is in no doubt that it should be interpreted purposefully.[14] In particular, the Committee recommends that '*wherever possible*, the child must be given the opportunity to be directly heard'[15] in an environment that is accessible and child-appropriate.[16] This creates an assumption that children will have the opportunity to be heard directly, but recognises that there will be cases in which the child does not wish to take this opportunity or in which direct participation may not be possible. It is in such cases that the child may be heard through a representative or other appropriate body. The Commission is alive to the risk that there may be a conflict of interests between the child and their representative, particularly if the child is represented by their parents. To address this, the Committee stresses that it is of 'utmost importance that the child's views are transmitted correctly' and that the representative exclusively represents the interests of the child and not those of others.[17] There is an ambiguity as to whether the representative must *only* represent the child's views or may also take a position on the child's best interests that conflicts with the child's views. As discussed further below, the welfare model adopted in English law means that children frequently find that their views are presented to the court by a reporter who advocates a very different solution from that preferred by the child. The Committee does not consider whether this best interests model accords with the requirements of Article 12.[18] Nonetheless, it is clear that the child's own views must be represented to the decision-maker and that there should be an opportunity for the child to be heard directly. As will be seen below, English law frequently fails to provide these opportunities to children embroiled in family proceedings.

It is not sufficient for Article 12 that the child's views are expressed: those views must also be given 'due weight' in the decision-making process, 'in accordance with the age and maturity of the child'. This text of the provision gives very little guidance as to the influence that the child's views should have on the outcome of the decision. The weight that is 'due' will depend on underlying assumptions as to the importance of children's perspectives and their role within the decision-making process. The text of Article 12 is compatible with both a paternalistic approach that prioritises adult perceptions of

---

[14] Committee on the Rights of the Child (2009).   [15] Ibid. para. 35 (emphasis added).
[16] Ibid. paras 33–4.   [17] Ibid. paras 36–7.   [18] Discussed in L. Lundy *et al.* (2019) pp. 428–31.

the child's best interests and one that values the child's autonomy.[19] Some guidance is given by the reference to the child's 'age and maturity', but this provision too is problematic. The implication is that the views of younger and less mature children should be given less weight than those of older or more mature children, but it is not evident that this should necessarily be the case. Article 12 is not concerned with giving children autonomy, but ensuring that decisions are made with an understanding of the child's own perspective. As Article 12(1) recognises, even very young children are capable of forming and expressing views that illuminate their own experience, even if they are not able to appreciate all facets of the case.[20] It is for this reason that some jurisdictions, such as New Zealand, have removed reference to the age and maturity of the child in order to emphasise the importance of considering the perspective of all children involved in family proceedings.[21] The Committee has given little substantive guidance on this aspect of Article 12, although it does require that the views of all children who are capable of forming them are seriously considered.[22] Beyond this, the Committee notes that the concept of maturity is 'difficult to define', but considers that in this context it refers to the child's capacity to express views in a 'reasonable and independent manner'.[23]

Although Article 12 does not grant children a right to self-determination, it might be argued that a child can reach such a state of maturity that the only way to give 'due weight' to their views is to treat them as determinative. If this is the case, Article 12 could be said to give mature children the right to determine the outcome of disputes concerning their upbringing. The Committee does not address this question and arguments can be advanced either way. On the one hand, because Article 12 is to be interpreted in line with Article 3,[24] it might be argued that the child's views can never be used in a way that ousts the decision-maker's own assessment of the child's interests. On the other hand, Article 12 should also be interpreted in the light of Article 5, which recognises children's evolving capacities and the increased level of responsibility that they acquire as their capacity develops.[25] On this view, once a child reaches an equivalent capacity to that expected of adults, there is no basis on which to impose a different view of the child's best interests from that advanced by the child themselves. At this point, it might be argued, the only defensible weight to give to the child's views is to treat them as determinative of the child's interests. For some commentators, even this conclusion does not go far enough in respecting the autonomy of children. Writers such as Kay Tisdall and Aoife Daly note the lack of clarity in the meaning of terms such as 'capacity' and 'maturity'.[26]

---

[19] A. Daly (2018a).   [20] K. Tisdall (2018).

[21] M. Heneghan (2017); as Heneghan explains, this aim has not necessarily been achieved in practice.

[22] Committee on the Rights of the Child (2009) para. 29.

[23] I.e. the requirement that the child's best interests are treated as a 'primary consideration': ibid. para. 30.

[24] Ibid. para. 74.   [25] Ibid. paras 84–5.   [26] K. Tisdall (2018); A. Daly (2018a).

The malleability of these terms means that children who express views that do not accord with adult perceptions of their interests can easily be dismissed as lacking the necessary maturity to be considered seriously. In response, Aoife Daly advocates that the existing Article 12(2) be replaced by an autonomy principle, which would permit children in best interests proceedings to choose both their level of involvement and the outcome, save where those decisions would cause the child significant harm.[27] This proposal would be a significant change from the current position under Article 12, but provides an important challenge to the ease with which children's perspectives are often dismissed in cases concerning their lives and future.

(B) The Council of Europe and European Convention on Human Rights

The European Convention for the Protection of Human Rights and Fundamental Freedoms (1950) (ECHR) contains no equivalent provision to Article 12 of the CRC guaranteeing children the right to be heard and to have their views taken into account. Despite this lacuna, the European Court of Human Rights (ECtHR) has, in recent years, developed an increasingly strong right of participation through the use of the principles protected by Article 12 of the CRC. At first sight, the right to a fair hearing in Article 6 of the ECHR might seem the most fruitful means of improving participation rights for children. Although it encompasses a variety of rights concerning children's participation in litigation, the existing case law is largely confined to the position of children in criminal proceedings.[28] Article 6 also applies to civil proceedings; parents in family proceedings have successfully argued that their own Article 6 rights have been violated by judicial refusal to hear the views of their children.[29] Children who are the subject of parental disputes might similarly claim that Article 6 entitles them to be represented in court or to be present at a hearing. There is, however, only sparse case law to support such an argument. Instead, the procedural rights of Article 8 have provided more fertile ground for developing children's rights to participate in family proceedings.

The developing jurisprudence of the ECtHR is well illustrated by the decision in *M and M* v. *Croatia*,[30] which concerned a custody dispute in the context of allegations that a father had physically and emotionally abused his daughter. The child had had no opportunity to be heard in the domestic custody proceedings, despite the fact that she was articulate, mature and well able to

---

[27] A. Daly (2018b) esp. ch. 1.

[28] *V and T* v. *United Kingdom* (1999) 30 EHRR 121, at [85]–[91].

[29] *Iglesias Casarrubios And Cantalapiedra Iglesias* v. *Spain*, App. No. 23298/12, ECtHR, Judgment of 11 October 2016. The children's own application was found to be inadmissible as they were not parties to the divorce proceedings between their parents. If followed, this could represent a serious limitation on the use of Art. 6 for children, who frequently do not have party status in judicial decisions that affect their future.

[30] (2017) 65 EHRR 9.

form her own views, including her strong desire to live with her mother.[31] The child and her mother complained to the ECtHR on a number of grounds, including that the failure to secure her participation was a violation of her rights under Article 8. The ECtHR considered that Article 8 includes a right to personal autonomy, the scope of which is different for children as compared to adults. The court considered that children:

> lack the full autonomy of adults but are, nevertheless, subjects of rights. This circumscribed autonomy in case of children, which gradually increases with their evolving maturity, is exercised through their right to be consulted and heard. As specified in Art 12 of the Convention on the Rights of the Child, a child who is capable of forming his or her own views has the right to express them and the right to have due weight given to those views, in accordance with his or her age and maturity, and, in particular, has to be provided with the opportunity to be heard in any judicial and administrative proceedings affecting him or her.[32]

In consequence, although Article 8 did not contain any explicit procedural requirements, the court found that the considerations in Article 12 of the CRC applied 'mutatis mutandis' in any proceedings affecting children's rights under Article 8 of the ECHR. In particular, children who were capable of forming their own views could only be said to be sufficiently involved in the decision-making process if they were provided with the opportunity to be heard and express those views.[33] In relation to the weight to be accorded to those views, the court noted that in Croatian law, if both parents were equally fit to care for the child, then the views of a child capable of forming and expressing them would be followed. While this had not been followed in the instant case, the court expressed agreement with this approach, considering that otherwise 'the rule that the views of the child must be given due weight' would be rendered meaningless'.[34] Failure to hear the child and give weight to her views in this case was found to be a violation of her Article 8 rights.

In protecting both the right to be heard and to be taken seriously, *M and M* v. *Croatia* demonstrates the strength of children's procedural rights that are being developed by the ECtHR under Article 8 through the influence of Article 12 of the CRC. There are, however, still significant uncertainties as to the precise requirements and conceptual basis of the court's approach. The development of the right to be heard in *M and M* is closely linked to the right to autonomy and to the child's developing maturity. The content of the right for younger children is far less clear, despite the importance that Article 12 of the CRC places on considering the views of *all* children capable of forming them. The ECtHR has long held that not all young children need to be heard directly[35] and has distinguished between siblings of different ages in assessing

---

[31] The child was aged 9–13 during the lengthy domestic proceedings.   [32] Ibid. at [171].
[33] Ibid. at [181].   [34] Ibid. at [185].
[35] *Sahin* v. *Germany; Sommerfeld v Germany* [2002] 1 FLR 119, [2003] 2 FLR 671, per the Grand Chamber of the ECtHR, at [73]: a domestic court need not always hear a child in court in every

the level of participation required by Article 8.[36] If the child is not heard directly, the court will consider whether an expert opinion is necessary to ensure that the child's views are considered and represented,[37] although there is no absolute requirement to do so.[38] There is further uncertainty as to the weight that should be accorded to children's views once they have been heard. In *M and M* v. *Croatia*, the ECtHR appeared to give decisive weight to the views of the older child (provided that both parents were fit to have custody), but a similar approach was found to be a violation of the father's right in *C* v. *Finland*,[39] and the court has subsequently stressed that the child's views will not necessarily be sufficient to outweigh the parent's interest in having contact.[40] In sum, while the ECtHR has significantly developed the child's right to participation in family proceedings, the precise contours of that right are still being developed.

In clarifying the detailed requirements of the right to participation, the ECtHR has not only drawn on Article 12 of the CRC, but also on the Council of Europe's own work on the matter, including the Guidelines of the Committee of Ministers of the Council of Europe on Child-Friendly Justice[41] and the European Convention on the Exercise of Children's Rights (ECECR).[42] The ECECR goes into some detail regarding the kind of provision children should have.[43] It confines its application to 'family proceedings, in particular those involving the exercise of parental responsibilities such as residence and access to children'.[44] Within this context, it secures for children involved in such proceedings the right to be granted and, indeed, entitles them

---

case. In this case, the child was 5 years old and an expert psychologist had met the child and considered that giving direct evidence in court would be harmful to her.

[36] In *NTS* v. *Georgia* [2017] 1 FLR 898, brothers aged 4 and 8 all had an Art. 8 right to participation in custody proceedings between their father and the maternal family following the death of their mother, but particular attention was drawn to the need to give the 8-year-old the right to be heard directly.

[37] E.g. *Petrov* v. *Russia* (2019) 69 EHRR 10, at [108].

[38] In *Sommerfeld* v. *Germany* [2002] 1 FLR 121, in which a 13-year-old girl was consistent in her opposition to contact with her father, there was no requirement to obtain a psychological assessment to test her reasons.

[39] [2006] 2 FLR 597, at [58]: contrary to earlier decisions in his favour, the Finnish courts denied the father custody of and visiting rights to his children (aged 12 and 14) once the youngest reached 12, on the basis of their wish to remain with their dead mother's partner.

[40] *Zelikha Magomadova* v. *Russia* (2020) 70 EHRR 30, at [115]: the court also drew attention to the need to ensure that the child's views were not unduly influenced by others. See also *AV* v. *Slovenia*, App. No. 878/13.

[41] Council of Europe (2010). See e.g. use in *NTS* v. *Georgia* [2017] 1 FLR 898, at [43] and [78]; *M and M* v. *Croatia* (2017) 65 EHRR 9, at [102].

[42] Adopted by the Council of Europe in 1995, open to signature January 1996 and entered into force on 1 July 2000. The ECECR has been signed by twenty-eight members of the Council of Europe and ratified by twenty. The UK has not signed or ratified the ECECR, but in *NTS* v. *Georgia* [2017] 1 FLR 898, at [44], the ECtHR drew on the ECECR to interpret ECHR, Art. 8 despite the fact that Georgia was also not a party to the Convention.

[43] For a detailed discussion of the Convention's provisions, see C. Sawyer (1999).

[44] Art. 1(3).

to request certain specific rights: to receive all relevant information;[45] to be consulted and express their views;[46] to be informed of the possible consequences of compliance with these views and the possible consequences of any decision;[47] and to apply for the appointment of a special representative,[48] if those with parental responsibilities cannot represent the child due to a conflict of interest.[49]

Although more detailed, in many respects, as Sawyer points out, the ECECR back-pedals on the aims of Article 12 of the CRC. Thus, many of the rights secured only extend to those children who are 'considered by internal law as having sufficient understanding'.[50] This phrase deliberately invites states to specify a qualifying age for children benefiting from the Convention.[51] A state is thereby entitled to adopt an arbitrary and extremely high qualifying age before children can be deemed of 'sufficient understanding', irrespective of their actual competence.[52] Furthermore, since most of the protective provisions apply only to those with 'sufficient understanding', the interests of those excluded are extremely weak, with no rights, inter alia, to information, to be consulted or to express their views.[53] Indeed, the phrase is substantially more restrictive than that used in Article 12(1) of the CRC. Of equal concern is that the child's right to the appointment of a special representative only exists 'where internal law precludes the holders of parental responsibilities from representing the child as a result of a conflict of interest with the latter'.[54] Consequently, children involved in proceedings where a conflict of interest is not formally recognised by internal law cannot demand separate representation. There might, for example, be a conflict of interest if either parent involved in a parental contact dispute attempted to convey their child's views to the court. But unless the ratifying country's internal law formally recognises this, the child is not entitled to demand separate representation under Article 4. Where the internal law does admit a conflict of interest, the ECECR usefully fleshes out the way in which such representation should be provided.[55] Nevertheless, special representatives are given worrying leeway in interpreting their duties. For example, they need not convey to the court the child's views if they consider this to be 'manifestly contrary to the best interests of the child'.[56] As Sawyer points out, there is no indication of what a young child can do if 'represented' by an adult with whom he or she disagrees over the desired outcome of the proceedings.[57] For these reasons, the ECECR is in many ways out of step with the developing law under Article 12 of the CRC and offers only limited scope to meet the current gaps within ECtHR law.

---

[45] Art. 3(a).   [46] Art. 3(b).   [47] Art. 3(c).   [48] Art. 4(1).   [49] Ibid.

[50] I.e. the rights listed in Arts 3, 6(b), 10(1)(a) and (b) contain this qualification. States are also invited to limit the right to a special representative to those children considered by internal law to have sufficient understanding. See Art. 4(1) and (2).

[51] M. Killerby (1995) p. 130.   [52] C. Sawyer (1999) p. 156.   [53] Ibid. pp. 163–4.

[54] Arts 4(1) and 9(1).   [55] The duties of the child's representative are listed in Art. 10.

[56] Art. 10(1).   [57] C. Sawyer (1999) p. 155.

(3) Children's Involvement in Parental Decisions and Disputes: A Right to Consultation?

This chapter is primarily concerned with children's participation in court proceedings. Many significant decisions about children's lives are routinely taken by parents without recourse to court or any third-party assistance. The UN Committee exhorts parents to adopt an approach to parenting that allows children to freely express views and to be taken seriously from the earliest age.[58] States are asked to encourage such parenting styles through legislation, policy and parental education programmes. Whether legislation is an effective means of doing so is perhaps doubtful. Under English law, no child, whatever his or her age, has a legal *right* to be consulted over the arrangements to be made for their future. By way of contrast, Scottish law obliges parents, depending on their children's age and maturity, to consult them over any 'major decision' within their parental responsibility.[59] While this legislation provides a welcome affirmation of the importance of children's involvement in decisions concerning them, it is difficult to enforce and appears to be largely unknown by the parents to whom it applies.[60] A more effective means of fulfilling this obligation may be in the policy measures taken to assist parents who are in dispute over their child's future.

Disputes between parents over aspects of their children's upbringing may arise at any time during their children's lives, but are most likely to occur when their own relationship is breaking down. Some acrimonious disputes polarise existing adult hostilities to such an extent that parents fight over their children as if they were items of property. Certainly, it is at this stage of family life that the conflict between children's rights and parents' rights is very obvious. The law does little, however, to ensure that children are consulted by their parents, or by anyone else, about their parents' future plans for their upbringing. At one time, divorcing parents were obliged to file a 'statement of arrangements'[61] of their plans for their children's upbringing with the court, suggesting that the state had an interest in scrutinising those arrangements. In practice, the operation of this system was severely flawed[62] and did little to provide effective scrutiny[63] or ensure that children were consulted by their parents.[64] Nonetheless, its repeal[65] highlighted the fact that children were effectively denied a voice in divorce arrangements. The repeal formed part of a wider

---

[58] Committee on the Rights of the Child (2009) paras 90–5.
[59] Children (Scotland) Act 1995, s. 6(1).   [60] Tisdall *et al.* (2012) p. 158.
[61] Matrimonial Causes Act 1973, s. 41. The statement of arrangements detailed a divorcing couple's arrangements for their children's future upbringing and welfare. The provision did not apply to unmarried parents. For a summary of the history and purpose of the procedure, see G. Douglas *et al.* (2000) pp. 180–4.
[62] M. Murch *et al.* (1999): research into the working of the s. 41 procedure was carried out in 1997.
[63] G. Douglas *et al.* (2000) p. 189.
[64] M. Murch *et al.* (1999) p. 186: only 34 per cent of parent petitioners in this research study had discussed the arrangements with their children.
[65] By Children and Families Act 2014, s. 17.

withdrawal of the state from involvement in arrangements for children when their parents separate. As considered further below, parents are now strongly encouraged to resolve disputes without court involvement. Even if parents seek to formalise their agreement through a consent order, the court making the order is under no obligation to consider the 'ascertainable wishes and feelings of the child concerned'[66] as it would in a contested case. While there may be good reasons to keep disputes out of court, this shift to private resolution places the onus on parents to consult their children. If they do not do so, there is little that children can do to make their voice heard.

Many writers have criticised the way in which the law seemingly treats children of divorcing and separating parents as passive victims, protecting them from involvement in adult conflict rather than ensuring their participation in arrangements for their future care.[67] As Diduck explains, the proponents of childhood studies[68] seek to understand childhood from children's perspectives.[69] They argue that the legal system itself encourages parents to see divorce and separation as private adult matters[70] and, by defining children as 'non-adults', creates barriers against practitioners treating them as individuals.[71] Thus, James argues that constructions of childhood based on seeing children as the product of parenting, rather than as individuals in their own right, 'effectively deny children a voice' to which they not only have a right, but are quite capable of providing.[72] These writers support their ideas by referring to the research establishing that children are surprisingly self-sufficient and competent,[73] with a 'self-awareness and resourcefulness' in the face of family disruption.[74]

Children's wishes are often disregarded by adults who consider that they know what these wishes will be, without any consultation. A growing body of research consistently supports the view that a damaging aspect of parental separation for children is the considerable shock they suffer on the break-up, often exacerbated by their parents' failure to prepare them adequately for it, or give them any proper explanation. As has been observed: 'Children are amazingly perceptive about what is going on, and not talking to them about the changes in their lives only raises their anxieties.'[75] Few parents are particularly adept at breaking such news sensitively.[76] Furthermore, they often delude themselves over the extent to which their children understand

---

[66] CA 1989, s. 1(3)(a); the obligation to apply this provision as part of the 'welfare checklist' only applies in contested proceedings: CA 1989, s. 1(4)(a).

[67] E.g. S. Day Sclater and C. Piper (2001) pp. 413–22; A. James (2003) pp. 145–6.

[68] Formerly known as the 'new sociology of childhood'; e.g. A. James et al. (1998).

[69] A. Diduck (2003) pp. 80–3. See also: F. Kaganas and A. Diduck (2004) pp. 961–4; J. Pryor and B. Rodgers (2001) ch. 3.

[70] S. Day Sclater and C. Piper (2001) pp. 420–1.   [71] A. James et al. (2004) p. 200.

[72] A. James (2003) p. 145.   [73] C. Smart et al. (2001) pp. 73–4.

[74] A. Wade and C. Smart (2002) p. 22.

[75] I. Gee (1999) p. 50. See also L. Parkinson (2006) p. 484.

[76] I. Butler et al. (2003) p. 42: some children were told about the separation over the phone.

what they are being told regarding an impending separation and how they react to such news.[77] It appears that children are frequently not consulted over arrangements made by their parents for their future care or contact with their parents.[78] In research conducted with adults who had been the subject of parental disputes as children, those who had been closely involved in the arrangements for contact were much more likely to report a positive, continuous relationship with both parents than those who reported that their views had not been considered.[79] It is little surprise that an 'overwhelmingly consistent message' from participants in this research was that parents should consult their children over post-separation arrangements, not merely at the point of separation, but also as the child matured and relationships developed.[80]

Consultation can, however, come with pitfalls if children feel compelled to express a view or to avoid hurting the feelings of one of their parents.[81] But as Diduck and others point out, neither approach need be mutually exclusive; children may neither want complete autonomy nor to be treated as objects.[82] Most children consider that they should have been consulted by their parents, though not necessarily involved in the actual decision-making.[83] Pryor and Rodgers observe:

> It is clear when children are asked, that they want adults to listen to their views and feelings about what is happening in their lives. This does not, though, necessarily mean listening to them in the same way as to adults; there are developmental differences in the ways children make sense of families and family change, and *not* to acknowledge these differences may be to fail to empower them by not communicating and listening in appropriate ways. It does, though, mean according them the respect given to adults by listening to them seriously.[84]

These research findings reinforce the need to consider adult disputes from a child's point of view in order for children to participate effectively. Not only is it imperative for parents and professionals to consult all children early on

---

[77] Ibid. p. 35: although every parent, bar one, stated that they had told their children about their separation, 29 per cent of the children indicated that they had not been told. See also research summarised by L. Parkinson (2006) p. 483.

[78] I. Butler *et al.* (2003) p. 120: 56 per cent of children reported not having been consulted over residence; 52 per cent reported not having been consulted over 'seeing contact'; 58 per cent reported not having been consulted over 'staying contact'. See also A. Smith *et al.* (2003) p. 206: 19 per cent reported being consulted over their initial residence arrangements and 37 per cent reported being consulted over their initial contact arrangements.

[79] J. Fortin *et al.* (2012) ch. 12: 82 per cent of those who said they had been mainly or partly responsible for the contact decisions rated their experience of continuous contact as very or fairly positive, as did 72 per cent of those who said their parents had taken due account of their views. Of those who had had no involvement, none rated contact positively.

[80] Ibid. ch. 13.   [81] Ibid. pp. 225–6.

[82] A. Diduck (2003) p. 101. See also J. Pryor and B. Rodgers (2001) pp. 135–8.

[83] I. Butler *et al.* (2003) pp. 124–5; A. Smith *et al.* (2003) p. 207.

[84] J. Pryor and B. Rodgers (2001) p. 135.

and listen carefully to their views, but also, if a parental dispute is later translated into litigation, to give them a genuine voice through competent representation.

(4) Children's Involvement in Family Proceedings

(A) The Background

The system provided for representing children in family proceedings is extraordinarily complicated and is considered in some detail in the following sections of this chapter. The law draws a fundamental distinction between 'specified proceedings'[85] – essentially public law proceedings – and unspecified proceedings. Children who are the subject of 'specified' proceedings receive significant procedural protection to ensure that they are represented. They have automatic party status and will usually have both a children's guardian and a solicitor to act on their behalf. These protections are certainly warranted, as children involved in public law proceedings have usually suffered serious harm and face the prospect of significant disruption to their family life, including the potential for their removal from the family home. Children involved in unspecified proceedings have no such automatic involvement in the decision concerning them. The extent to which these children are represented depends on the complex web of rules considered further below. Yet, many children involved in such 'private' cases also find themselves in situations in which there are serious allegations of harm and the prospect of orders that will have significant implications for their relationships and family life.[86] Indeed, a substantial minority of children in private law cases have had local authority (LA) involvement during, or prior to, the proceedings.[87] Representing the complex interests and views of children in these circumstances often requires resources and professional involvement. Yet, the methods provided whereby children's wishes are conveyed to the court are still extremely fragmented and arbitrary. The courts receive information from some but not all children, under an archaic set of rules and procedures whose complexity defies simple explanation.

There are, however, reasons to be hopeful: many working within the family justice system are committed to improving children's participation in decisions concerning them. Lady Hale has spoken of an 'increasing recognition of children as people with a part to play in their own lives, rather than as passive

---

[85] Defined by CA 1989, s. 41(6). Under Pt 16 of the Family Procedure Rules 2010 (FPR 2010), children involved in adoption proceedings under FPR 2010, Pt 14 are generally given the same procedural protection as those in 'specified proceedings'.

[86] M. Harding and A. Newnham (2015); R. Hunter *et al.* (2020), discussed further in Chapter 6.

[87] M. Harding and A. Newnham (2017): 28 per cent of the sample cases had LA involvement, in half of these the actions of the LA had initiated the proceedings; e.g. by suggesting that relatives apply for a private order as an alternative to care proceedings. See also A. Bainham (2013).

recipients of their parents' decisions'.[88] Similarly, Sir James Munby has spoken of a 'sea-change in attitudes' to children's participation and emphasised that this 'process of change continues apace'.[89] These sentiments are reflected in an increasing judicial willingness to hear children's evidence,[90] grant them party status[91] and allow competent young people to give direct instructions.[92] There is also a concern to give children the opportunity to be informed about the process, meet the judge deciding the case[93] and understand the final decision.[94] There are also positive signs of improvement in the Children and Family Court Advisory and Support Services ('Cafcass'),[95] the body charged with making provision for children to be represented and supporting children and their families in the court process.[96] In 2018, Cafcass received an 'outstanding' inspection rating from Ofsted, in a report that found that 'listening to children, understanding their world and acting on their views are strongly embedded in practice in both public and private law'.[97] Nonetheless, this greater commitment to hearing children requires significant resource if it is to be implemented in practice. Listening to children, many of whom will have experienced significant conflict and harm, requires care, training and the time to establish trusting relationships. The limited resources available to Cafcass are under considerable strain given the increasing case volumes in the family law courts, extensive cuts to legal aid and limitations on the availability of expert evidence. In consequence, the quality of information available to the court appears to have declined, particularly in private proceedings.[98] Without resources, it is difficult to fulfil the promise implied by the statements of greater commitment to children's participation rights. Sadly, it is perhaps unsurprising that many children still emerge from the court process feeling that they have not been listened to.[99]

---

[88] *Re LC (Children) (Reunite International Child Abduction Centre Intervening)* [2014] UKSC 1, [2014] AC 1038, at [87].

[89] *Re F (Children)* [2016] EWCA Civ 546, [2016] 3 FCR 255.

[90] *Re W (Children) (Family Proceedings: Evidence)* [2010] UKSC 12, [2010] 1 WLR 701.

[91] *Re LC (Children) (Reunite International Child Abduction Centre Intervening)* [2014] UKSC 1, [2014] AC 1038.

[92] *Re W (A Child) (Care Proceedings: Child's Representation)* [2016] EWCA Civ 1051, [2017] 1 WLR 1027.

[93] *Guidelines for Judges Meeting Children Who Are Subject to Family Proceedings* [2010] 2 FLR 1872.

[94] H. Stalford and K. Hollingsworth (2020).

[95] Established on 1 April 2001 by the Criminal Justice and Courts Services Act 2000, Ch. II and Sch. 2. Cafcass simplified children's representation by providing a unified body to replace three former services, i.e.: the Official Solicitor's department, which had formerly acted for children requiring separation representation; the guardian *ad litem* and reporting officer services who represented children in public law proceedings; the court welfare service, which provided in-court conciliation work for parents involved in private disputes over children and carried out the reporting function by preparing 'welfare reports' for the courts if requested to do so under CA 1989, s. 7.

[96] Criminal Justice and Courts Services Act 2000, s. 12. Since Cafcass practitioners often act in various capacities, they are increasingly being referred to as family court advisers (FCAs).

[97] Ofsted (2018) p. 2.   [98] J. Harwood (2019).   [99] E.g. R. Hunter *et al.* (2020) ch. 6.

(B) Private Law Proceedings

(i) An Arbitrary System

If parents are unable to agree over their children's future upbringing, an application may be made to court. The rules governing children's participation in private family disputes are complex and often appear arbitrary in practice. The 'ladder' of these children's involvement appears to have five rungs. On the ladder's bottom rung, there is no court hearing because the parents' dispute is resolved in its early stages through mediation or under the non-court dispute resolution procedures provided by the Child Arrangements Programme (CAP).[100] On the next rung up, the case has proceeded to litigation, but the court relies on the parents' own assessments of what is in the child's best interests. On the third rung of the ladder the child is the subject of a welfare report prepared by the children and family reporter (CFR). This will include an account of the child's own wishes and feelings. On the fourth rung of the ladder are children provided with party status and separate representation. On the top rung, children litigate on their own behalf, possibly even having initiated the proceedings themselves. For children on the bottom rungs of the ladder, there is little, if any, protection for their right to participate in the proceedings that concern their future.

The CA 1989's approach to the participation of children involved in private law proceedings has been a constant subject of criticism. Unlike those who are the subject of public law proceedings, the legislation contains no presumption that these children will be separately represented. The court can ask for a welfare report,[101] which will give it a great deal of background information about the child, including their perspective on the dispute. But courts frequently decide not to call for such a report, either because the case has been settled in its early stages, or because it is concerned about the potential delays involved, or because it considers that there is no need for one. In practice, it appears that welfare reports are only ordered in around a third of private law cases.[102] Without a report, the court has no means of obtaining an independent picture of the child's views regarding the outcome of his or her parents' dispute. In these cases, as Sir James Munby observes, the court proceeds 'on the blithe assumption that the truth – and a proper appraisal of what is in the child's best interests – will in some mysterious way emerge from the adversarial process between the parents'.[103] The UN Committee is surely right to warn of the conflict of interests between children and parents who purport to

---

[100] Practice Direction 12B: Child Arrangements Programme.

[101] CA 1989, s. 7: prepared by a CFR, formerly a child welfare officer (CWO). These 'welfare reports' are sometimes referred to as 'Cafcass reports' or 'court reports'. See J. Doughty (2008) for a historical assessment of the family court welfare service.

[102] R. Hunter *et al.* (2020) p. 69: note that in England in 2018–19, 65,378 children and young people were subject to applications, but reports were only ordered in cases involving around 20,000 children.

[103] Sir James Munby (2015).

represent those interests in family proceedings.[104] Since the parents are unlikely to provide the court with a totally impartial account of the child's wishes, these children are nearly at the bottom of the ladder. But those on the bottom rung are those whose parents are persuaded to settle their dispute. While some children are able to participate in the settlement process, many are not, and their wishes regarding the outcome of their parents' dispute will remain unknown. Article 12(2) of the CRC has almost certainly been infringed in relation to the children on the bottom two rungs of the ladder. A crucial decision has been reached regarding their future without their participation. The developing Strasbourg case law, discussed above, also suggests that children also have procedural rights under Article 8 of the ECHR that require the opportunity to be heard in decisions that significantly affect their family life. For children on the bottom rungs of the ladder, there appears to be no means of protecting these rights.

(ii) Mediation and Non-Court Dispute Resolution

Successive governments have long sought to divert disputing parents from the judicial system towards mediation and alternative forms of dispute resolution. In view of the rising number of litigants in the family justice system, there is an understandable concern to concentrate already stretched resources on those cases where there is a significant welfare or safeguarding concern.[105] In cases where no such risks are present, it is often argued that judicial involvement is likely to exacerbate conflict, which will in turn create a harmful environment for the child concerned.[106] There is, however, a risk that these settlements are arrived at without proper reference to the children's wishes and without their involvement. Despite increasing interest in 'child-friendly' forms of dispute resolution, in practice, the opportunities for children's involvement are often limited by the resources available and the attitudes of the adults involved. In consequence, the push towards facilitating adult agreement often runs counter to the right of children to be involved in decisions concerning them. The right to participation is not limited to judicial proceedings. The UN Committee has made clear that the Article 12(2) right to be 'provided with the opportunity to be heard in any judicial and administrative proceedings affecting the child' extends to alternative dispute mechanisms such as mediation or arbitration.[107] As these methods of dispute resolution are likely to be an enduring aspect of the family justice system, the weak protection currently offered for children's right to involvement has become an increasingly important matter that requires redress.

---

[104] Committee on the Rights of the Child (2009) para. 36.
[105] There was a 23 per cent increase in private law family applications between 2014 and 2019. Of these, Cafcass estimates that around a quarter do not feature child protection or welfare concerns: A. Douglas (2019).
[106] Private Law Working Group (2019) esp. p. 6.
[107] Committee on the Rights of the Child (2009) paras 32 and 51–2.

Current law and policy provide numerous routes to divert parents from court. Some parents make an active choice to seek help in resolving their dispute through methods such as mediation or arbitration.[108] Any parent who instead wishes to apply to court is required by statute to first attend a mediation information and assessment meeting (MIAM)[109] unless they fall under one of the exemptions.[110] The MIAM is intended to assess suitability for mediation and provide information to the parties in the hope of diverting cases to mediation. It was hoped that further incentive would be provided by retaining legal aid for eligible clients who wished to mediate, while largely withdrawing it from private family law litigation.[111] In practice, these measures appear to have been extraordinarily unsuccessful. Prior to the changes to legal aid, the most likely form of referral to a MIAM was through a solicitor. Now that most parties do not have access to funded legal advice, this channel has largely disappeared and court officials do not appear to be consistent in enforcing the requirement to hold one.[112] Far from encouraging mediation, the result of these policies appears to have been a substantial reduction in both MIAMs and publicly funded mediation.[113] These parents now find themselves approaching court, often without the benefit of legal advice and representation – a situation that itself causes great difficulties for courts attempting to ascertain the interests and wishes of children who do not have professional involvement.[114] Attempts to encourage settlement continue once proceedings have been initiated: at each stage of the process, the judge is required to consider non-court dispute resolution.[115] In particular, a Cafcass officer should attend the First Hearing Dispute Resolution Appointment (FHDRA) to work alongside the judge to assess whether further conciliation or non-court dispute resolution can assist the parties in coming to agreement. Again, the immense pressure on court time and resources often means that insufficient time is available to provide a real attempt at conciliation.[116] In conclusion, the current process for diverting parents from court does not appear to be working well. Too many parents who could find solutions are unable to do so as there is insufficient time and resource

---

[108] See the Family Law Arbitration Children Scheme, available at http://ifla.org.uk. The current rules of the scheme (5th edn, effective 11 January 2021) permit either the parties or the arbitrator to appoint an independent social worker to ascertain the child's wishes and feelings and report on welfare, but the arbitrator is prohibited from meeting the child.

[109] Children and Families Act 2014, s. 10. The obligation applies to those family proceedings set out in Family Procedure Rules 2010, r. 3.6 and Practice Direction 3A.

[110] The exemptions include cases in which there is evidence of domestic abuse or there is LA involvement due to child protection concerns: Family Procedure Rules 2010, r. 3.8.

[111] Legal Aid, Sentencing and Punishment of Offenders Act 2012 (LASPO), Sch. 1.

[112] Private Law Working Group (2019).

[113] The number of publicly funded MIAMs dropped from 30,665 in 2012–13 to 10,503 in 2018–19, while the number of publicly funded mediations commenced decreased from 13,983 in 2012–13 to 6,376 in 2018–19. Legal Aid Agency, Legal aid statistics England and Wales tables: January to March 2020 (2020) Tables 7.1 and 7.2.

[114] J. Harwood (2019).

[115] Practice Direction 12B: Child Arrangements Programme (CAP) paras 6.1–6.5.

[116] Private Law Working Group (2019) p. 51.

to work through the issues and consider the child's welfare in depth. At the same time, it appears that many cases that are recognised by the existing rules as entirely unsuitable for non-court resolution, particularly those involving domestic abuse,[117] are still funnelled through the same dispute resolution processes. This not only risks great harm to the victim, but also creates the potential for unsafe arrangements to be agreed without identifying the risks to the child and hearing their views.[118] It is widely recognised that the current system is in need of reform to meet the modern landscape of private family disputes and the diversity of cases before the courts. It is essential that children's participation is a central feature in that reform if Article 12 of the CRC is to be implemented in practice.

There is certainly strong evidence that many children want to be informed and involved in decisions made about their futures, although they do not usually want to be asked to make the final decision.[119] The CAP recognises this, stating that '[c]hildren should be involved, to the extent which is appropriate given their age and level of understanding, in making the arrangements which affect them'[120] whether concluded by the parties themselves, in out-of-court dispute resolution or by the court. Whether this aim is achieved in practice is doubtful. In relation to mediation, Ewing et al. distinguish between child-focused mediation, which emphasises the importance of coming to an agreement based on the child's welfare, and child-inclusive mediation, which gives the child an active part in the process.[121] Although there is certainly a growing interest in child-inclusive mediation among practitioners, many find it easier to adopt a child-focused rather than child-inclusive approach.[122] The Family Mediation Council now requires all of its members to either be trained in child-inclusive mediation or to attend sessions to allow them to understand and promote its principles to parents. Further, the Council's Code of Practice states that all children aged 10 and over will have the opportunity to have their voices heard in mediation if they wish to do so.[123] Nonetheless, mediators express concern as to the lack of appropriate training as to how to include children and in the funding implications of providing additional resources to do so. Further barriers come from the parties themselves. Parents may be reluctant to give consent for their child to be involved, while children are often concerned about confidentiality.[124] Mediators recognise that children who wish to voice their independent perspective on their parents' disputes may need support to do so and that this support requires time and expertise to establish a trusting relationship with the child. Various methods

---

[117] Practice Direction 12J: Child Arrangements and Contact Orders: Domestic Abuse and Harm para. 9 make it clear that in cases where there is evidence of domestic abuse, the parties should not be expected to engage in conciliation or other forms of dispute resolution that are neither suitable nor safe for such circumstances.

[118] R. Hunter et al. (2020) pp. 89–90.   [119] J. Fortin et al. (2012); J. Ewing et al. (2015).

[120] CAP para. 4.4.   [121] J. Ewing et al. (2015).   [122] Ibid.; J. Walker (2014).

[123] L. Parkinson (2019).   [124] J. Walker (2014).

have been adopted to facilitate child involvement. In some cases, the mediator meets with the child directly, although if the child has strong views or does not wish information to be disclosed, this can create difficulties for mediator neutrality. An alternative is for a second mediator, or a specialist such as a child psychologist, to meet with the child separately and relay those views to the parties and the lead mediator.[125] Each of these methods requires additional meetings and time, but there is no additional public funding to support it.[126] Achieving child-inclusive mediation in practice is likely to require substantial additional resource.

Similar problems of resource constraint have also limited the effectiveness of conciliation and other forms of dispute resolution at the FHDRA stage. Little time is often available for working with parents and children to reach sustainable solutions.[127] This pressure exacerbates the existing difficulties of including children effectively. Researchers have long criticised the in-court schemes that do involve children for not doing so more sensitively.[128] In research conducted in the early 2000s, Trinder *et al.* criticised the way in which children were interviewed on court premises, considering such an environment to be too stressful and unfamiliar for them.[129] The very short interview sessions also precluded interviewers from finding an appropriate balance between consulting children and involving them in decision-making themselves. Trinder *et al.* comment:

> The very task-focused approach of conciliation risks placing responsibility for decision making, or resolving the dispute, on children's shoulders. Children are typically seen for a very short interview which inevitably seeks views on the (adult-defined) matters in dispute. Our observations and interviews with professionals confirmed that what children say is often highly influential in determining the outcome, even down to specific details of the contact timetable. It is worth noting that children are not interviewed if the parents are able to reach agreement, suggesting that children's involvement relates to an inability to break an adult impasse rather than a general principle that all children should have their say.[130]

These researchers are not alone in suggesting that placing such obvious weight on children's views may be mistaken, that the onus on wishes expressed in rushed circumstances is too great and many children have no desire to make the final decision.[131] Children should not be rushed into decision-making, especially if there is insufficient time to put them at ease or to explore with them their genuine concerns. Such a view is supported by a number of research projects which have observed the reservations that many children have in talking to someone whom they do not know about their family life, especially

---

[125] Ibid.   [126] L. Parkinson (2019).   [127] Private Law Working Group (2019) esp. p. 51.
[128] HMICA (2006) paras 2.47–2.63: Inspectors observed very variable standards of interviewing techniques.
[129] L. Trinder *et al.* (2006) p. 97.   [130] Ibid. pp. 97–8.   [131] R. Emery *et al.* (2005).

in a formal setting.[132] When there is a member of the family in the room, this problem is greatly exacerbated.[133] Children may feel inhibited from expressing their true views because of their fear of repercussions from one or other parent afterwards.[134]

Given the current crisis in the family justice system, it is likely that non-court dispute resolution will continue to play an important role. In reshaping that role for the new environment, it is essential that effective steps are taken to allow children to exercise their right to involvement in decisions that take place outside of the court room. This involvement is not limited to consulting children during discussions: the reality is that children's needs vary considerably according to their individual circumstances.[135] As Day Sclater and Piper observe, they cannot be 'treated as a homogenous group in relation to whether and how they wish to participate in decision-making'.[136] Rather than direct participation, some children would instead like to have someone in the family justice system whom they can trust and whose job it is to support them and explain the process sympathetically.[137] Others wish to participate, but require the time to build trust and understanding for their voice to be heard accurately. Unfortunately, if the system is to meet these needs, it is likely to require the very resources that are currently in such short supply.

(iii) The Welfare Reporting Process

Those parents who are not able to resolve their dispute through non-court dispute resolution will proceed to a court hearing. When they do, there is no guarantee that the court will receive any evidence concerning the child's wishes and feelings. The most obvious way for such information to be conveyed is through a 'welfare report'[138] – but there is no obligation on the court to request one. Although the proportion of cases in which a report is ordered is increasing,[139] reports are not requested in around two-thirds of cases.[140] Most concerning of all, despite the requirement to consider directing a welfare report in any case involving risk of harm from domestic abuse,[141] many such cases proceed without one.[142] If a report is not requested, it is unlikely that any Cafcass practitioner will carry out an in-depth assessment of the child's background and needs, addressing the factors in the welfare

---

[132] J. Fortin *et al.* (2006) p. 221;   [133] A. Buchanan *et al.* (2001) p. 66.   [134] Ibid.

[135] A. O'Quigley (2000) ch. 3.   [136] S. Day Sclater and C. Piper (2001) p. 427.

[137] J. Fortin *et al.* (2006) p. 221; A. Buchanan *et al.* (2001) p. 67; G. Douglas *et al.* (2006) para. 7.49.

[138] I.e. under CA 1989, s. 7; the circumstances in which a report should be ordered are outlined in Practice Direction 12B: Child Arrangements Programme para. 14.13.

[139] Cafcass (2020) p. 20 note that there has been a 29 per cent increase in requests for s. 7 reports between 2016/17 and 2019/20. The number of private law cases received by Cafcass rose by 13 per cent over the same period.

[140] R. Hunter *et al.* (2020) p. 69.

[141] Unless the court is satisfied that it is not necessary to do so in order to safeguard the child's interests: Practice Direction 12J: Child Arrangements and Contact Orders: Domestic Abuse and Harm para. 21.

[142] R. Hunter *et al.* (2020) p. 69.

checklist, including ascertaining the child's views.[143] In the absence of a report, the court's primary source of information about the children's real wishes and feelings will then be the parents. For children who remain on this second rung of the procedural ladder, there will be no independent evidence regarding their own perspectives available to the court. This problem is exacerbated by the fact that many parents now act as litigants in person with no legal advice to guide them in evaluating and presenting relevant information to the court or alerting the court to circumstances that might justify ordering a welfare report.[144]

If a welfare report is called for, it will usually be prepared by a CFR,[145] who will give a detailed assessment of the child's circumstances and present it to the court. The role of the CFR is not to represent the child, but to report to the court on their welfare, including their wishes and feelings. Children often complain that their views are not accurately reported in welfare reports.[146] Research has long suggested that CFRs dismiss the views of some children by concluding that they are simply too young to be involved,[147] or by filtering out those that are inconsistent with the CFR's own perspective.[148] Some critics argue that the family justice system itself encourages CFRs to place an adult construction on children's wishes and feelings in an effort to produce an 'objective' judgment of the child's capacities, often based on their own perceptions of chronological age.[149] In such cases, it is very difficult for children to ensure that their wishes and feelings are heard by the court.

The case of *Re W (Leave to Remove)*[150] provides a good example of such an approach. There, three children, aged 15, 13 and 11, were caught up in their divorcing parents' battle over whether the mother should be allowed to relocate to Sweden, taking the children with her. The Cafcass officer assigned to the case had considered the possibility of separate representation for the children, but cast this option aside because it would lead to an adjournment of the trial.[151] Instead, she soldiered on with her report, summarising for the court what she considered to be the children's wishes and feelings about the proposed move. She then proceeded to apply her own analysis of the situation, warning the court, to 'exercise a degree of caution in evaluating the children's stated wishes and feelings'.[152] This, as Thorpe LJ pointed out, was unsatisfactory; the children had understood that the Cafcass officer would advance the formulation that they had agreed on with her. She had not returned to explain to them her intention to 'finesse away their stated position by her own analysis'.[153] In particular, the youngest child would have felt that her wishes

---

[143] J. Fortin *et al.* (2006) pp. 226–7.   [144] J. Harwood (2019).

[145] Alternatively, an LA may be asked to produce a s. 7 report; this will usually only apply if the LA has an existing connection to the case.

[146] G. MacDonald (2017); see also J. Fortin *et al.* (2006) pp. 220–1.

[147] Ofsted (2008a) para. 46, (2008b) para. 32.

[148] Inter alia: HMICA (2005) para. 2.29; G. Douglas *et al.* (2006) ch. 3; Ofsted (2008a) para. 74, (2008b) paras 31 and 49–50.

[149] A. James *et al.* (2004) esp. pp. 199–200.   [150] [2008] EWCA Civ 538, [2008] 2 FLR 1170.

[151] Per Thorpe LJ, at [25].   [152] Ibid. at [27].   [153] Ibid. at [28].

and feelings were insufficiently considered by the judge due to their having been 'diminished by the very professional whom she trusted to advance them'.[154] In decisions of this kind, they are effectively denied any voice over their own future, other than through the voice of a Cafcass officer, with whom they may fundamentally disagree.

CFRs should explain to each child what they are including in their report and the outcome that they are recommending, 'in a manner appropriate to the child's age and understanding'.[155] Research suggests that most CFRs do explain very carefully what will go into their report and the recommendations being made.[156] But, as acknowledged by Scottish law,[157] it is arguable that children should receive complete copies of these reports. Indeed, in *Re W (Leave to Remove)*,[158] it was suggested not only that they should be sent a copy of the entire report, but also asked to provide written comments on it before its submission. That case suggests that children should, at the very least, be told in advance *why* the CFR is adopting a particular approach, especially when it is inconsistent with their wishes.

It is, of course, essential that all CFRs are trained to carry out high-quality report-writing work – to interview children skilfully and to obtain detailed assessments of their needs, with plenty of time in which to do so. This does not always happen,[159] particularly given the significant resource constraints under which Cafcass is operating.[160] It appears that the judiciary have sometimes ordered separate representation of children to remedy perceived defects in report writing.[161] While welfare reports can be a useful means by which the child can be heard, the requirements of Article 12 of the CRC will only be met if the report is of sufficient quality and ensures that the 'child's views are transmitted correctly' to the court.[162]

(iv) Separate Representation

(a) The Procedural Context

Welfare reports give children the opportunity to have their wishes and feelings conveyed to the court, but do not give children any direct involvement in the proceedings. Children can, however, become more actively involved in litigation in a number of ways. Most frequently, the court will direct that the child is made a party to the parents under litigation rule 16.2 of the Family Procedure

---

[154] Ibid. at [33].   [155] Practice Direction 16A: Representation of Children para. 9.3.

[156] G. Mantle *et al.* (2007).

[157] Responding to *McMichael* v. *United Kingdom* (1995) 20 EHRR 205, copies of all reports and papers relating to children's hearings are given both to the child and to his parents. See *S* v. *Principal Reporter and Lord Advocate* [2001] UKHRR 514, at [28]–[29].

[158] [2008] EWCA Civ 538, [2008] 2 FLR 1170, per Wilson LJ, at [56].

[159] In *D* v. *E* [2016] EWFC 3, the court refused to give any weight to the poor-quality s. 7 report. This case concerned an LA report and had been produced by a very junior social worker who had been given insufficient training.

[160] J. Harwood (2019).   [161] G. Douglas *et al.* (2006) para. 5.17.

[162] Committee on the Rights of the Child (2009) paras 36–7.

Rules (FPR).[163] If this occurs, the child will usually be given separate representation under rule 16.4 of the FPR and will have a guardian and solicitor (just as in public law proceedings). In such cases, the guardian, not the child, instructs the solicitor.

More rarely, children may instruct their own solicitors, just as an adult would. This can occur in three situations. First, if the court gives the child party status in the parents' litigation and considers the child mature enough to instruct a solicitor without the added assistance of a guardian. Second, where the child initiates the litigation by applying for an order and instructing a solicitor. Third, in public law proceedings, where the child disagrees with the advice of the children's guardian and is deemed sufficiently mature to instruct a solicitor and dispense with the guardian's services.

(b) No Automatic Separate Representation

Before discussing when separate representation might be ordered for children, it is worth considering the reasons for children in private law proceedings being deprived of *automatic* separate representation. Before the CA 1989, although sympathetic to the concept of children receiving separate representation in private proceedings, the Law Commission had provisionally concluded that there was no need for automatic separate representation, as in public proceedings.[164] While children involved in public law proceedings might feel a strong sense of injustice if they were not given some voice,[165] in private law proceedings they considered that a welfare report would normally suffice.[166] Consequently, the procedure rules that accompanied the CA 1989 duly enabled the superior courts to exercise the power to make a child a party, but only on an ad hoc basis. Critics of this position attempted to use the Adoption and Children Act 2002 to amend the CA 1989 to require that *all* children involved in applications for section 8 orders be provided with separate representation in the same way as children in public proceedings. Although they were successful in placing the reform on the statute book, it has not been brought into force and now seems very unlikely to be put into action.[167] In consequence, it remains the case that children are not automatically party to private proceedings concerning them. Instead, the court may make the child a party if it is satisfied that 'it is in the best interests of the child to do so'.[168]

The absence of Strasbourg case law makes it impossible to assert that Article 8 of the ECHR *requires* that all children involved in parental disputes must be separately represented. Nevertheless, the implementation of the HRA 1998

---

[163] FPR 2010, rr. 16.2 and 16.4.   [164] Law Commission (1988) para. 6.26.

[165] Ibid. para. 6.28.   [166] Ibid. para. 6.26.

[167] ACA 2002, s. 122 extended the definition of 'specified proceedings' in CA 1989, s. 41 to include proceedings for the making, varying or discharging of a s. 8 order. The provision requires implementation by the introduction of rules of court detailing the circumstances in which such separate representation would apply. No such action has been taken. See further: N. Wall (2007); J. Fortin (2007).

[168] Now FPR 2010, r. 16.2, replacing the original rule contained in FPR 1991, r. 9.5.

undoubtedly encouraged a growing judicial view that respect for children's rights demands an increasing use of separate representation in parental proceedings.[169] As discussed above, both the UN Committee on the Rights of the Child and the ECtHR have placed increasing importance on the participation rights of children and stressed that the direct involvement of the child may be required in order to give sufficient protection to participation rights on the facts of the case. Judges exercising the discretion to make the child a party to proceedings must pay close attention to this developing law if English law is to keep pace with Strasbourg.

(c) Separate Representation for Some?

Children who are granted party status under rule 16.2 have considerably stronger protection for their participation rights than those on the lower rungs of the ladder. Once a child is granted party status, they will be separately represented and a children's guardian appointed under rule 16.4.[170] The guardian is charged with conducting proceedings on behalf of the child and for the benefit of the child.[171] A Cafcass officer who is appointed as a guardian in a private case has the same duties as a guardian in public proceedings, including the duty to advise on the child's wishes.[172] Together, these duties give much stronger protection to children's right to be involved in proceedings and have their views put to the court than is the case for children who have not been granted party status.

Research reinforces the view that children who do obtain separate representation find the support they receive extremely helpful.[173] In particular, a separate representative may be able to gain children's confidence and support them in long-running intractable disputes.[174] Nevertheless, it appears that, just as they do when writing court reports, CFRs sometimes reinterpret the child's views by reference to their own ideas about what is in their best interests. Again, children report frustration if the CFR appears to misunderstand them or does not convey their strong views to the court in their original form.[175] In some cases, there is a tension between the guardian's role in promoting the child's best interests and their duty to represent the child's views. This is well illustrated by *Re L (A Child)*,[176] a case concerning an application to transfer the

---

[169] *Re A (Contact: Separate Representation)* [2001] 1 FLR 715, per Dame Elizabeth Butler-Sloss P, at [21]–[22] and Hale J, at [31]–[32]. See also *Re L (Family Proceedings Court) (Appeal: Jurisdiction)* [2003] EWHC 1682 (Fam), [2005] 1 FLR 210, at [28].

[170] Unless the child wishes to give independent instructions and is found competent to do so: FPR 2010, r. 16.6, considered further below.

[171] Practice Direction 16A: Representation of Children para. 7.6.

[172] Ibid. paras 6.6 and 7.7. The guardian's duties in public proceedings are considered further below.

[173] G. Douglas *et al.* (2006) para. 7.18.

[174] E.g. *Re H (National Youth Advocacy Service)* [2006] EWCA Civ 896, [2007] 1 FLR 1028. See also R. Davies and S. Mason (2007) pp. 1096–8.

[175] G. Douglas *et al.* (2006) paras 3.30, 3.27–3.28, 3.53–3.54, 3.57 and 3.76.

[176] [2019] EWHC 867 (Fam), [2019] 2 FCR 864.

residence of an 8-year-old boy from the care of his mother, with whom he had lived in London since birth, to that of his father, who lived in Northern Ireland. The guardian was concerned that the boy was unable to speak positively of his father and that he was being manipulated by the mother. In these circumstances, she considered that asking him about his wishes would be emotionally harmful to him and unlikely to elicit a genuine expression of his feelings. The report on his interests was therefore drawn up without discussing the potential move with him. Despite this lack of consultation, the High Court found that there had been no breach of the guardian's duty to report the child's wishes to the court, as that duty was 'tempered by the overarching requirement to afford paramount consideration to the child's welfare'.[177] While the decision may have been justified on the facts of the case, it is nonetheless concerning that a child can be moved from the only home he has known without the opportunity to express his views. Cases in which guardians are appointed will often contain acrimonious disputes and upsetting circumstances. If the potential for emotional distress is readily accepted as a reason for avoiding asking children questions, the duty to advise on the child's wishes will be rendered nugatory.

The court has the discretion to make the child a party to proceedings if it considers that it is in the best interests of the child to do so.[178] Despite the obvious advantages that separate representation can give to children, it is clear from the accompanying practice direction that few children will be granted party status. The practice direction starts from the position that making the child a party 'is a step that will be taken only in cases which involve an issue of significant difficulty and consequently will occur in only a minority of cases'.[179] It further directs that any court considering taking this step should first consider whether an alternative route might be preferable and should also consider that granting party status may cause delay and other detriment to the child's welfare. Given this discouraging start, it is not surprising that only around 7 per cent of children in relevant private proceedings have separate representation under rule 16.4.[180]

It remains unclear exactly what criteria the courts use to determine whether to grant party status. The practice direction guidance, though lengthy, is not particularly specific.[181] In essence, the guidance states that party status will be

---

[177] Ibid. at [65].

[178] As Lord Wilson noted in *Re LC (Children) (Reunite International Child Abduction Centre Intervening)* [2014] UKSC 1, [2014] AC 1038, at [45], the best interests test provides the threshold criterion that opens the door for the court to exercise its discretion, but 'no doubt it is the sort of discretion, occasionally found in procedural rules, which is more theoretical than real: the nature of the threshold conclusion will almost always drive the exercise of the resultant discretion'.

[179] Practice Direction 16A: Representation of Children para. 7.1.

[180] R. Hunter *et al.* (2020) p. 69 calculate that 7 per cent of children have a guardian appointed under r. 16.4. This is an increase from the 3.5 per cent of children in the same position at the time of the Family Justice Review in 2011.

[181] Practice Direction 16A: Representation of Children para. 7.1–7.3.

justified in situations in which separate representation is required, either because of the complexity of the case, or because the child's views cannot be properly presented to the court by the adult parties or a welfare report.[182] The courts are further directed to consider providing children with separate representation in cases involving allegations of domestic abuse.[183] Nevertheless, it is not always clear why one case justifies separate representation and another does not.[184] According to Douglas *et al.*'s research, the case law illustrates the judiciary adopting one of two approaches when deciding whether to direct separate representation for a child. Under the 'welfare approach', the court hopes to achieve a better and more informed outcome for the child, with the guardian often instructing experts to assist the process. Under the 'voice' approach, the court decides that more needs to be known about what the child wants and thinks.[185] The former type of appointment, which often involves relatively young children, reflects the courts' concern to ensure that the parents' own needs and obvious conflict of interest do not obscure the real needs of the child.[186] Despite more use when children implacably oppose contact,[187] there were, in the past, surprisingly few reported examples of the 'voice' approach to separate representation.[188]

The advent of the HRA 1998 seems to have precipitated greater judicial willingness to consider directing separate representation. Almost as soon as the Act came into force, Dame Elizabeth Butler-Sloss P observed that it was likely to lead to an increased use of guardians in private law cases, a change

---

[182] Practice Direction 16A: Representation of Children para. 7.2 lists situations which might justify separate representation, including: '(1) where a Cafcass Officer has notified the court that in his opinion the child should be separately represented (2) where the child has a standpoint or interests which are inconsistent with or incapable of being represented by any of the adult parties (3) where there is an intractable residence or contact dispute, including where all contact has ceased, where there is irrational but implacable hostility to contact or where the child may be suffering harm associated with the contact dispute (4) where the views and wishes of the child cannot be adequately met by a report to the court (5) where an older child is opposing a proposed course of action.'

[183] Practice Direction 12J: Child Arrangements and Contact Orders: Domestic Abuse and Harm para. 24: this consideration is stated to be subject to the 'seriousness of the allegations made and the difficulty of the case'.

[184] J. Whybrow (2004) pp. 507–9; J. Fortin (2007) pp. 505–7.

[185] G. Douglas *et al.* (2006) para. 2.3. This research concerned FPR 1991, r. 9.5., the predecessor to FPR 2010, r. 16.

[186] E.g. *Re A (Contact: Separate Representation)* [2001] 1 FLR 715: a 4.5-year-old girl had made allegations of sexual abuse against her father; *Re K (Replacement of Guardian Ad Litem)* [2001] 1 FLR 663: an 11-year-old child had been the subject of litigation between his parents since his first birthday; *Re F (Contact: Restraint Order)* [1995] 1 FLR 956: two children aged 7 and 6 had been involved in parental contact litigation for many years; it was held that the children should be separately represented, largely to allow them to examined by a child psychiatrist.

[187] J. Hunt and A. Macleod (2008) pp. 199 and 218.

[188] E.g. *L v. L (Minors) (Separate Representation)* [1994] 1 FLR 156: separate representation directed for three children aged just under 14, 12 and 9 to discover their true views, given that their father, who had a dominant personality and who wished to relocate with them in Australia, might be pressurising them to fall in with his wishes.

that, in the right case, she welcomed.[189] The importance of Article 12 of the CRC to this exercise was further emphasised in Thorpe LJ's influential judgment in *Mabon* v. *Mabon*,[190] including his observation that the rights to freedom of expression and participation would often outweigh paternalistic welfare judgments in cases involving articulate teenagers.[191] Many 'articulate teenagers' seek to instruct a solicitor directly rather than doing so with the assistance of a rule 16.4 guardian. In these cases, discussed further below, the focus is on whether they have the maturity to instruct their own solicitor, rather than on whether they should receive separate representation at all. Unusually, the rules do not permit children who are the subject of Hague Convention abduction proceedings to give direct instructions alone: they must do so through a guardian instead.[192] Perhaps for this reason, abduction cases have been the site of the most important developments on appointing rule 16.4 guardians for 'voice' reasons.

(d) Separate Representation in International Abduction Cases?

In the past, children caught up in international child abduction cases seldom obtained separate representation, even in cases in which they had strong opposition to their parent's plans.[193] The domestic courts have always stressed the summary nature of Hague Convention proceedings and the need to ensure a prompt return of all abducted children to the country of their habitual residence.[194] Concern about the practical implications and delays involved in giving children separate representation meant that the judiciary considered it a highly unusual step to take[195] and confined its use to 'exceptional cases'.[196]

---

[189] *Re A (Contact: Separate Representation)* [2001] 1 FLR 715, at [22]. In this case, the Court of Appeal took the unusual step of ordering separate representation for a 4.5-year-old. See also *Re L (Family Proceedings Court) (Appeal: Jurisdiction)* [2003] EWHC 1682 (Fam), [2005] 1 FLR 210, in which Munby J stressed that by making a formal declaration regarding a 15-year-old child's parentage, without giving her notice of the hearing or party status, the court had infringed her procedural rights under Arts 6 and 8 of the ECHR.

[190] [2005] EWCA Civ 634, [2005] 2 FLR 1011; discussed further below.   [191] Ibid. at [28].

[192] In *Re LC (Children) (Reunite International Child Abduction Centre Intervening)* [2014] UKSC 1, [2014] AC 1038, at [44], Lord Wilson could not discern why children in Hague proceedings could not be a party without acting by a guardian. Similarly, in *M (Children) (Abduction: Joinder of Children)* [2021] EWHC 635 (Fam), at [36], it was described as a 'lacuna' with 'no logical reason' behind it. In both cases, it was accepted that the solicitor may also be appointed as guardian, so diminishing the practical consequences of the rule.

[193] Most abduction cases are covered by the Hague Convention on the Civil Aspects of International Child Abduction 1980. Cases occurring within the EU are governed by the Brussels II Revised Regulations: Council Regulation (EC) No. 2201/2003 concerning jurisdiction and the recognition and enforcement of judgments in matrimonial matters and the matters of parental responsibility (2003) OJ L 338/1. These Regulations governed relevant cases prior to the UK's departure from the EU.

[194] *Re P (Abduction: Minor's Views)* [1998] 2 FLR 825, per Butler-Sloss LJ, at 827.

[195] Per Wall J in *Re S (Abduction: Children: Separate Representation)* [1997] 1 FLR 486, at 493; Wall LJ in *Re J (Abduction: Child's Objections to Return)* [2004] EWCA Civ 428, [2004] 2 FLR 64, at [63].

[196] *Re H (Abduction)* [2006] EWCA Civ 1247, [2007] 1 FLR 242, per Thorpe LJ, at [16].

Even the fact that a much older child objected to returning did not, in the past, render the case sufficiently exceptional to justify granting party status.[197] While these points remain of concern, the courts are increasingly alert to the participation rights of children caught up in these fraught battles that often have momentous implications for their future.

The prima facie presumption that underlies the Hague Convention is that a child's welfare is best served by a prompt return to the country of his or her habitual residence, leaving the decision of what should happen to the child to that country's own courts.[198] But the duty to return the child is not absolute and the views of the child will be important to many decisions. In particular, Article 13 authorises the court to refuse to make such an order if 'it finds that the child objects to being returned and has attained an age and degree of maturity at which it is appropriate to take account of its views'.[199] The child's perspective will also be particularly important in cases in which there is a dispute as to where the child is habitually resident. In *Re LC (Children) (Reunite International Child Abduction Centre Intervening)*,[200] the Supreme Court determined that, at least in the case of adolescents,[201] the child's own state of mind would be relevant for determining whether habitual residence was established. In many cases, the child's perspective will be provided through welfare reports and this will be sufficient to satisfy the child's participation rights. But the courts have been increasingly willing to recognise that welfare reports are not always adequate to convey the child's views.[202] Even if a report is able to convey those views accurately, the child may quite reasonably object to this passive role and instead argue that they should be an active participant in decisions that fundamentally change their future.[203]

A greater willingness to accept such arguments in abduction cases can be traced to the decision of Baroness Hale in *Re D (A Child) (Abduction: Rights of Custody)*.[204] Drawing on Article 12 of the CRC, she emphasised that children should be far more frequently heard in *all* types of Hague Convention cases,

---

[197] Ibid. per Wall LJ, at [33]. The Court of Appeal confirmed the trial judge's refusal to provide a 15-year-old abducted girl with separate representation.

[198] *Re P (Abduction: Minor's Views)* [1998] 2 FLR 825, per Butler-Sloss LJ, at 827.

[199] This exception is sometimes described as Art. 13(c) despite its not being specifically given a sub-paragraph. It is sometimes combined with the abducting parent's claim under Art. 13(b) that there is a grave risk that the child's return would 'expose the child to physical or psychological harm or otherwise place the child in an intolerable situation'.

[200] [2014] UKSC 1, [2014] AC 1038.

[201] While Lord Wilson's majority judgment concerned adolescent children (ibid. at [37] and [43]), Lady Hale and Lord Sumption saw no reason why the same questions should not arise in relation to the younger children, aged 8 and 10 in this case (at [57] and [58]).

[202] R. Schuz (2004) p. 727.

[203] *Ciccone v. Ritchie (No. 1)* [2016] EWHC 608, [2017] 1 FLR 795.

[204] [2006] UKHL 51, [2007] 1 All ER 783. See also *Re M and another (Children) (Abduction)* [2007] UKHL 55, [2008] 1 All ER 1157, in which Baroness Hale emphasised that separate representation should be ordered as a matter of 'routine' in those rare cases governed by Art. 12 of the Hague Convention – where the abductor claims that the child has become 'settled' in his or her new environment.

not merely those involving an Article 13 defence.[205] She pointed out that there is now:

> a growing understanding of the importance of listening to the children involved in children's cases. It is the child, more than anyone else, who will have to live with what the court decides. Those who do listen to children understand that they often have a point of view which is quite distinct from that of the persons looking after them.[206]

She stressed that, although it would only be needed in 'a few cases', a child should gain 'full scale legal representation' whenever it is likely that a child's views and interests are not being properly presented or legal arguments are being overlooked by the adult parties.[207] A similar message was sent by the Supreme Court in *Re LC (Children) (Reunite International Child Abduction Centre Intervening)*.[208] The court was concerned to stress that party status should not be 'routine' in objection cases; however, where, as in this case, the child's perspective could not adequately be conveyed by the adult parties, separate representation should be awarded.[209] A good example of such a case can be seen in *M (Children) (Abduction: Joinder of Children)*,[210] in which the children's objections to returning to their father were in part based on their experience of living with him, including their allegations of physical abuse. The older children objected to the welfare reporter's approach to these allegations and were successful in seeking independent representation given that neither the reporter not their mother, who had no first-hand experience of the situation, could adequately represent their perspective.

The cases above all demonstrate that party status may be awarded when it assists the court in obtaining accurate information on the child's perspective. A more controversial question is whether the child's wish to act as an autonomous participant should be sufficient for party status to be awarded. Certainly, as stated in *Re LC*, the mere fact that a child objects to return has not been treated as sufficient in itself for party status to be routinely awarded. Nonetheless, the courts are becoming more sensitive to cases in which older children have strong reasons to participate. In *M (Children) (Abduction: Joinder of Children)*, the fact that the mature, articulate teenagers wanted to convey their strongly held opinions to the court was an important factor, particularly as they would have to live with the consequences.[211] Similarly, in *Ciccone* v. *Ritchie (No. 1)*,[212] the 15.5-year-old's strong wish to play an active part and show a 'moving picture' in developing proceedings, rather than relying on a passive welfare report, was a significant factor in granting him party status. Such considerations were even stronger in *AS* v. *CPW (Inward Return Order)*,[213] in the somewhat different context of an application for an

---

[205] [2006] UKHL 51, [2007] 1 All ER 783, at [58].   [206] Ibid. at [57].   [207] Ibid. at [60].
[208] [2014] UKSC 1, [2014] AC 1038.   [209] Ibid. at [49] and [54].
[210] [2021] EWHC 635 (Fam).   [211] Ibid. at [32].   [212] [2016] EWHC 608, [2017] 1 FLR 795.
[213] [2020] EWHC 1238 (Fam), [2020] Fam Law 1019.

inward return order under the inherent jurisdiction. In that case, a *Gillick*-competent 14.5-year-old was settled in Sierra Leone and strongly objected to return to the UK. In those circumstances, Mostyn J expressed surprise that he had not been joined as a party and that it had been 'thought that the case could be conducted without his case being professionally and forensically put by representatives on his behalf'.[214] Nevertheless, separate representation is far from a foregone conclusion. For example, in *Re P (Abduction: Child's Objections)*,[215] a 13-year-old who was 'wholly negative' about Germany and objected 'very strongly' to being returned there was unsuccessful in seeking party status as his views could be adequately represented by a Cafcass officer. The case law suggests a growing recognition of the importance of autonomy, particularly for older children, but falls far short of establishing a *right* for separate representation.

(v) Independent Participation in Litigation

(a) Independent Instruction under Rule 16.6

Young people who reach the top rung of the participation ladder are able to litigate on their own behalf, possibly even having initiated the proceedings themselves, and to instruct their own solicitor without the need for a guardian or litigation friend. Their ability to do so is set out in the complex provisions provided by rule 16.6 of the FPR. This rule covers two situations. A child who is made a party to a parental dispute, or who wishes to initiate their own proceedings,[216] may seek to act without a guardian through rule 16.6(3). This rule permits the child to do so if either the court gives permission or a solicitor considers the child has sufficient understanding to give instructions independently. Alternatively, a child who is *already* being represented by a guardian, or litigation friend, may object to their continued involvement in the case, particularly if the guardian recommends a course of action with which the child disagrees. The child may then use rule 16.6(5) to seek court permission to remove the guardian or litigation friend, thereby allowing the child to proceed without such assistance. Permission will only be granted if the court considers the child has sufficient understanding to conduct proceedings independently. These procedural methods reflect a remarkable legal acknowledgement of children's capacity to take responsibility for litigation concerning their own upbringing. They certainly promote the aims of Article 12 of the CRC in a radical fashion.

Children deemed to have sufficient understanding to instruct their own solicitor will be assisted by a lawyer whose duties do not encompass those of a children's guardian. A solicitor acting for a child is under no legal duty to provide the child client with any emotional support, or to mediate between the

---

[214] Ibid. at [51].   [215] [2020] EWCA Civ 260.
[216] But they must separately obtain court leave to initiate the proceedings under CA 1989, s. 10(8); discussed further in Chapter 10.

child and their family. Since the child is essentially treated as an adult client, the solicitor need not provide the court with any information about his or her perceptions of the child's best interests. Although this is a remarkable recognition of the autonomy of mature young people, it is evident that there remain judicial concerns that independent participation can sometimes be harmful to children's interests. As discussed below, the courts have retained the final word over whether children are indeed sufficiently competent to instruct a solicitor without the services of a guardian.[217] In establishing the test for competence, a persistent question has emerged as to what role, if any, the child's welfare has in assessing the level of understanding a child requires to undertake such a task.

(b) Competence of Children to Instruct Their Own Solicitors

The test for a court considering a child's application to conduct proceedings independently is whether the child has 'sufficient understanding' to do so.[218] A solicitor approached by a child to provide independent representation may also do so if he or she 'considers that the child is able, having regard to the child's understanding, to give instructions in relation to the proceedings'.[219] Both of these tests are phrased in terms of the child's 'understanding' rather than the child's welfare. Nonetheless, much of the early case law[220] on these provisions interpreted the word 'understanding' in a way designed to prevent children being damaged by involvement in litigation. It reflected judicial anxiety over allowing children to dispense with the services of a guardian who would otherwise be able to shield them from the influence of a domineering parent or provide them with emotional support and advice. In consequence, the rights of young people to participate in litigation concerning their future risked being undermined by a paternalistic approach to their role in proceedings.

The Court of Appeal's seminal decision in *Mabon* v. *Mabon*[221] marked an important turning point in judicial attitudes to young people's participation. The case concerned a residence dispute between the parents of six siblings. The three elder siblings, aged 17, 15 and 13, sought permission to dispense with their guardian and instruct their own solicitor. The solicitor was of the view that there was no doubt as to the sufficiency of the understanding of these

---

[217] *Re T (A Minor) (Child: Representation)* [1993] 4 All ER 518, per Waite LJ, at 530.

[218] FPR 2010, r. 16.6(6): the court *will* grant permission if it considers that the child 'has sufficient understanding to conduct the proceedings concerned or proposed without a litigation friend or children's guardian'. This test applies regardless of whether the child is starting proceedings or seeking to dispense with the services of the guardian in existing proceedings.

[219] FPR 2010, r. 16.6(3)(b).

[220] E.g. *Re S (A Minor) (Independent Representation)* [1993] 3 All ER 36; *Re N (Contact: Minor Seeking Leave to Defend and Removal of Guardian)* [2003] 1 FLR 652. The case law prior to the introduction of FPR, r. 16.6 was decided under the materially identical provisions of Family Proceedings Rules 1991, r. 9.2A.

[221] [2005] EWCA Civ 634, [2005] 2 FLR 1011.

intellectually able, articulate and perceptive older children. Nonetheless, the application was refused by the trial judge, who thought that little benefit would be derived from allowing them to become more directly involved in their parents' dispute and that there numerous disadvantages, including '[d]elay from the prolongation of the proceedings, unquantifiable emotional damage from contact with the material in this case, and exposure to the harshness of the litigation process'.[222] The Court of Appeal declared this approach to be outdated in that it failed to take account of the rights of children to participate in litigation affecting them. The Court of Appeal considered that the test for direct participation was sufficiently widely framed to enable the courts to meet their obligations to comply both with Article 12 of the CRC and with Article 8 of the ECHR. When considering the sufficiency of the child's understanding, the courts should therefore:

> reflect the extent to which, in the twenty-first century, there is a keener appreci-ation of the autonomy of the child and the child's consequential right to participate in decision-making processes that fundamentally affect his family life.[223]

In particular, Thorpe LJ considered that:

> Unless we in this jurisdiction are to fall out of step with similar societies as they safeguard Art 12 rights [UNCRC], we must, in the case of articulate teenagers, accept that the right to freedom of expression and participation outweighs the paternalistic judgment of welfare.[224]

This did not mean that welfare was entirely irrelevant to the exercise. As Thorpe LJ explained, a child who does not appreciate the pitfalls of involve-ment litigation, or the implications of involvement for relationships within the family, is unlikely to be able to demonstrate the level of understanding required to participate in litigation.[225] The test of the child's understanding is not entirely separable from an evaluation of the potential risks to the child's welfare from involvement in litigation.[226] The 'sufficient understanding' test cannot, however, be bypassed by asking whether involvement would be in the child's best interests. A competent young person may appreciate the risks of involvement in litigation, but weigh those risks and assess her interests very differently from the court or professionals involved in the case. Indeed, cases under rule 16.6(5) are likely to arise precisely because the child takes a very different view of her welfare from the guardian whose role she seeks to remove.

The decision in *Mabon* was pivotal in the development of children's partici-pation rights, but, as Black LJ has observed,[227] views within the family justice

---

[222] Ibid. at [18].   [223] Ibid. at [26].   [224] Ibid. at [28].   [225] Ibid. at [29].

[226] For a critical assessment of Thorpe LJ's discussion of the child's welfare and participation rights, see J. Fortin (2007) pp. 507–9.

[227] *Re W (A Child) (Care Proceedings: Child's Representation)* [2016] EWCA Civ 1051, [2017] 1 WLR 1027, at [26]–[27].

system have continued to develop since *Mabon* as the importance of children's participation is increasingly accepted. In consequence, she stressed that:

> The question of whether a child is able, having regard to his or her understanding, to instruct a solicitor must be approached having in mind this acknowledgment of the autonomy of children and of the fact that it can at times be in their interests to play some direct part in the litigation about them.[228]

Similarly, in *Re CS (A Child)*, Williams J considered that:

> there has been a shift away from a paternalistic approach in favour of an approach which gives significantly more weight to the autonomy of the child in the evaluation of whether they have sufficient understanding. Thus the earlier authorities need to be approached with a degree of caution in terms of the level at which they set the 'bar' of understanding. The autonomy issue sounds both in pure 'understanding' terms and in welfare terms.[229]

As these cases recognise, autonomy and welfare can go hand in hand: it can be beneficial for children to be involved in proceedings and therefore afforded the dignity and reassurance that they will be taken seriously. Children's participation in litigation can, however, also pose serious challenges for the child and the family justice system.[230] It can be harmful to expose a child to the same experience of cross-examination and sight of evidence as the adult parties. Children may have to challenge their parents' veracity, or at least criticise them to an outsider and have their own views written down and presented to each parent.[231] Even solicitors who strongly support children's rights express concern about the corrosive effect that such litigation can have on relationships in the family.[232] To some extent, these risks can be managed through judicial discretion in the conduct of proceedings. As Lord Wilson noted in *Re LC (Children) (Reunite International Child Abduction Centre Intervening)*: 'A grant of party status to a child leaves the court with a wide discretion to determine the extent of the role which she should play in the proceedings.'[233]

The cases following *Mabon* have stressed the importance of recognising children's autonomy and participation rights. Translating these broad principles into practice can pose difficulties for solicitors and children themselves. The term 'understanding' remains malleable and care should also be taken not to demand that the child attains a level of understanding of the litigation

---

[228] Ibid. *Re W* itself concerned the child's involvement in public proceedings, considered further below, but these comments address understanding within the context of the wider family justice system.

[229] [2019] EWHC 634 (Fam), [2019] 1 WLR 4286, at [63].

[230] E.g. *Re HB (Abduction: Children's Objections)* [1998] 1 FLR 422, in which an 11-year-old was able to instruct her own solicitor and challenge the order her parent had obtained; she was found to be 'much more burdened and sad about the legal contest, in which her parents, and now she herself, are engaged'. Thorpe LJ (at 427) observed that the 'case illustrates only too vividly the enormous price that is paid when children are permitted to litigate'.

[231] C. Sawyer (1995) p. 155.   [232] Ibid. p. 162.   [233] [2014] UKSC 1, [2014] AC 1038, at [55].

process that exceeds that of many adult litigants.[234] Further, children should not be assumed to lack understanding merely because they express views that appear misguided or influenced by a parent.[235] It appears that there is very little professional guidance to assist a solicitor in assessing the understanding of a child who seeks to give direct instructions.[236] There is also little to guide solicitors as to how their duties to the child client, including the duty to respect the child's right to confidentiality and privacy, interact with the fact that the other parties to the case will usually be the child's parents with parental responsibility for the child. A good example of this problem arose in *S v. S (Relocation)*,[237] in which the father funded the children's representation in an acrimonious dispute concerning the children's possible relocation to live with him in Switzerland. Under this arrangement, the children, aged 12 and 13 at the start of the process, met with their legal team in cafes and at school without the knowledge of the mother, who was their primary carer. These circumstances caused considerable 'unease' to Peter Jackson J, who noted the difficult tension between the mother's need to understand the children's lives in order to care for them, and the children's right to independent and confidential advice. While the case highlights the problems that can arise in acting for child clients, it does little to guide solicitors who encounter similar circumstances. The current system also gives very little help to children who are faced with an extremely complex procedural rule and no specific guidance as to how they should go about using it. Respect for children's involvement requires careful consideration of the practical barriers to children's participation and accessible guidance on how to overcome them.

(C) Public Law Proceedings

(i) 'The Tandem System of Representation'

In contrast to the uncertain ladder of private law, the representation of children involved in public law proceedings is an impressive one which is designed to comply fully with the requirements of international instruments such as the CRC. The child is provided with full party status, automatic public funding and, regardless of age, normally the services of a children's guardian,[238] in addition to those of a legal advocate. The children's guardian,

---

[234] *Re CS (A Child)* [2019] EWHC 634 (Fam), [2019] 1 WLR 4286, at [63].

[235] *Re W (A Child) (Care Proceedings: Child's Representation)* [2016] EWCA Civ 1051, [2017] 1 WLR 1027, at [32]–[33].

[236] Ibid. at [61]; R. Stevens (2020).

[237] [2017] EWHC 2345 (Fam), [2018] 1 FLR 825, esp. at [28]–[32].

[238] CA 1989, s. 41(1) establishes a presumption that the child involved will, regardless of age, receive separate representation in all 'specified proceedings'. These include (see s. 41(6)) most LA interventions to protect children.

who appoints a solicitor[239] to represent the child, provides the court with an assessment of what outcome would be in the child's best interests. Meanwhile, the solicitor acts as the child's legal representative in court and treats the child as the client. The children's guardian, who is qualified in social work, should be experienced in working with children and therefore able to provide the court with a detailed assessment of the needs of even very young children. The solicitor, while unable to assess the needs of the child, particularly if very young, has the legal skills necessary for representing the child in what are sometimes extremely complex legal hearings, involving a number of parties.

The rules of court envisage the children's guardian playing an important part in public law proceedings; he or she must 'safeguard the interests of the child in the manner prescribed by [court] rules'.[240] Working 'in tandem' with the child's solicitor,[241] he or she investigates the child's background in depth,[242] often recommending an expert to assess his or her needs. In this way, the children's guardian is pivotal to representing both the child's best interests and the child's voice to the court.[243] For this reason, the tandem system of representation has consistently received strong support from both judges and practitioners.[244] The greatest challenge to the ability of the guardian to perform this role comes from the immense resource and time pressures under which they are required to work. The resource constraints have in some cases led to a failure to appoint guardians in a timely manner, or indeed at all, a situation that risks breaching the ECHR Articles 6 and 8 rights of children.[245] The time available is further constrained by the tight timetable for completion of proceedings introduced by the Children and Families Act 2014 and further set out in the Public Law Outline (PLO).[246] These constraints appear to have changed the working practices of guardians, reducing the amount of time they spend with children, particularly those of younger ages.[247] Consequently, guardians have little time to establish the trusting relationships necessary to build the confidence of children, many of whom will already have suffered

---

[239] Private solicitors who wish to represent children obtain 'Children Law Accreditation' through the Law Society, having acquired the required training and accreditation to deal with children's cases.

[240] CA 1989, s. 41(2)(b). The duties listed by FPR 2010, r. 16.3 and further expanded upon in Practice Direction 16A: Representation of Children, Pt 3 include advising the court on the child's wishes and giving the child advice as is appropriate to the child's understanding.

[241] This dual system of representation is often called the 'tandem system' of representation.

[242] CA 1989, s. 42: the children's guardian has a right to examine and take copies of all social work records relating to the child and his or her family.

[243] *R and others* v. *Cafcass* [2012] EWCA Civ 853, [2012] 2 FLR 1432, esp. at [24].

[244] A. Summerfield (2018).

[245] In *R and others* v. *Cafcass* [2012] EWCA Civ 853, [2012] 2 FLR 1432, the Court of Appeal found that the failure to immediately appoint a guardian did not in itself amount to a breach of Arts 6 and 8, but may contribute to a breach if the proceedings did not give sufficient protection to the child's rights.

[246] Practice Direction 12A: Care, Supervision and other Part 4 Proceedings: Guide to Case Management.

[247] H. James and D. Lane (2018).

significant trauma in their relationships with adults. Although the tandem system itself has strong support from those working in the system, it is unclear to what extent these constraints have undermined guardians' ability to understand children's perspectives on their situation and to represent children satisfactorily. As discussed below, children who disagree with the guardian's approach to their case may seek to demonstrate that they have the ability to instruct a solicitor without the guardian acting as intermediary. The courts have become increasingly concerned to recognise the participation rights of children who wish to become directly involved in this way, or by giving evidence to the court, although, again, resource constraints have often hampered that participation in practice.

(ii) Children's Involvement in Public Law Proceedings

Children involved in public law proceedings have automatic full party status – quite rightly so, since the outcome of the case will often drastically disrupt their lives. Nevertheless, as Davis points out, party status for a child 'seems to have a different meaning than for everyone else'.[248] For an adult, party status brings with it entitlement to see all the evidence before the court, to put forward evidence, to be represented and to attend court, with a right to give oral evidence and with a presumption that the party will be cross-examined. But this is not the case for children. Indeed, as Davis asserts, 'some parties are more equal than others'.[249] For example, research shows that some, but not all,[250] children strongly favour being present at care or related proceedings.[251] They quite reasonably argue that, even if they cannot give evidence, they should at least be entitled to see and hear the process that determines their future.[252] Children have been automatic parties to public proceedings since 1975 and the rules appear to assume that they will attend.[253] Nevertheless, a decision whether to allow children to attend the hearing of their case is ultimately for the court, and practice has, over the years, been influenced by the senior judiciary's scepticism of the merits of allowing children to attend public law proceedings.[254] Arguably, children who are the focus of public law proceedings know better than anyone what has happened to them and it may be entirely appropriate for them to be present at the final stages of a process which will

---

[248] L. Davis (2007) p. 65.   [249] Ibid.

[250] J. Masson and M. Winn Oakley (1999) pp. 114–15; J. McCausland (2000) pp. 80 and 105: some children strongly oppose the idea of attending the court hearing.

[251] E.g. applications to discharge a care order.

[252] J. Masson and M. Winn Oakley (1999) p. 115; M. Ruegger (2001) pp. 40–1; J. McCausland (2000) pp. 103–4; J. Timms and J. Thoburn (2003) p. 7.

[253] FPR, r. 12.14: the proceedings will take place in the absence of the child party, if considered to be in the child's best interests and he/she is represented by a children's guardian or solicitor. Before deciding, the court should allow the solicitor, children's guardian and the child, if of sufficient understanding, to make representations on this.

[254] Inter alia: *Re C (A Minor) (Care: Child's Wishes)* [1993] 1 FLR 832, per Waite J, at 841; *Re W (Secure Accommodation Order: Attendance at Court)* [1994] 2 FLR 1092, per Ewbank J, at 1097.

affect their lives fundamentally. It is often far too late to protect them from exposure to potentially damaging material.

In theory, there is nothing to prevent the court hearing evidence directly from any child, as long as the court considers that he or she understands the duty to speak the truth and has sufficient understanding to give evidence.[255] In the past, however, the courts have been extremely reluctant to allow a child, however old, to give evidence in care proceedings,[256] preferring to hear the child's account of what occurred to be relayed to them by adults under the relaxed hearsay rules.[257] This reluctance was based on the assumption that for a child to appear in court and provide them with a first-hand account would be a damaging experience.[258] The cautious practice of the family courts appeared over-protective and increasingly out of step with the treatment of child witnesses in the criminal courts. In *Re W (Children) (Family Proceedings: Evidence)*,[259] the Supreme Court rejected this approach, holding that there should be no presumption, or even starting point, against children giving evidence in care proceedings. Instead, in determining whether a child should give direct evidence, the court would 'have to weigh two considerations: the advantages that that will bring to the determination of the truth and the damage it may do to the welfare of this or any other child'.[260] The aim of the balancing test is to ensure a fair process that meets the ECHR Article 6 rights of all participants while taking account of the child's Article 8 rights. The child's welfare is an important component of this test, but is not the paramount consideration, and may be outweighed by the importance of achieving a fair trial and establishing truth. Further, as McFarlane LJ observed in *Re E (A Child) (Family Proceedings: Evidence)*,[261] any immediate adverse impact of giving evidence may well be outweighed by the child's interests in an improved outcome based on accurate findings of fact. For this reason, in the long run, the child may benefit from having given evidence despite any immediate distress caused by doing so. Nonetheless, the Supreme Court in *Re W* was mindful of the potential harm that a child may suffer from the ordeal of giving evidence of abuse. In order to both decrease that risk of harm and to improve the child's ability to give high-quality evidence, careful attention must be given to the conditions in which any evidence would be given. As the UN Committee has observed: 'A child cannot be heard effectively where the environment is

---

[255] CA 1989, s. 96(1) and (2).

[256] E.g. *R v. B County Council, ex p P* [1991] 1 WLR 221; *Re P (Witness Summons)* [1997] 2 FLR 447.

[257] CA 1989, s. 96(3)–(7); Children (Admissibility of Hearsay Evidence) Order 1993 (SI 1993/621).

[258] E.g. *Nottinghamshire County Council v. P* [1993] 1 FLR 514: Ward J (at 519–20) disapproved of the two girls' attendance in court and also of the LA's plan to call the eldest, aged 16, with learning difficulties, to give evidence, rather than relying on the guardian's account of her views.

[259] [2010] UKSC 12, [2010] 1 WLR 701.   [260] Ibid. at [24].

[261] [2016] EWCA Civ 473, [2016] 4 WLR 105, at [53].

intimidating, hostile, insensitive or inappropriate for her or his age.'[262] Achieving an environment conducive to hearing children's evidence requires training, time and resources. In the wake of *Re W*, the Family Justice Council produced guidance as to how children's evidence should be heard,[263] but further progress appears to have stalled. The Vulnerable Witnesses and Children Working Group, established by Sir James Munby, carried out extensive consultation and made detailed recommendations to improve the practice of obtaining children's evidence. A proposed practice direction to implement this reform was drafted, but was ultimately rejected by the government on the basis of its 'resource impact'.[264] Given the reluctance to provide resources for children's involvement, it is perhaps unsurprising that there appears to have been relatively little change in the practice of hearing children's evidence since *Re W*.[265]

If the draft practice direction had been implemented, it would have required courts to consider whether it was necessary to give directions to ensure the child had an opportunity to express views in the proceedings. Such a change would have placed more focus on the child's right to express their views. At present, the approach to children's evidence tends to take a paternalistic and court-focused view, even in relation to older children who wish to give evidence.[266] A good example is the decision in *Re P-S (Children) (Family Proceedings: Evidence)*,[267] which concerned proceedings to determine whether a 15-year-old boy would remain in care or return to his mother. The boy expressed a strong desire to return to his mother and wished to give evidence via video link to make the strength of these feelings clear. The trial judge refused the request on the basis that the child's wish to return to his mother was already before the court and that there was a risk that the mother may engage in extreme emotional outbursts during the evidence. In the Court of Appeal judgment upholding the decision, Sir Alan Ward gave extensive attention to Article 12 of the CRC and the UN Committee's General Comment, but concluded that 'whilst the child must be listened to, there is nothing in the Convention which entitles the child to give evidence to the judge. In my judgment a child has no right to give evidence.'[268] While it is true that neither Article 12 nor the General Comment specifically address the question of oral evidence, this approach overlooks the importance that the UN Committee places on the child's decision as to how they wish to be heard, including the opportunity to be heard directly.[269] As Daly notes, the potential harm that the court raised did not appear particularly acute, especially for an

---

[262] Committee on the Rights of the Child (2009) para. 34.

[263] Guidelines in Relation to Children Giving Evidence in Family Proceedings (2011).

[264] Dame Eleanor King (2017).   [265] [2016] EWCA Civ 473, [2016] 4 WLR 105, at [48].

[266] Although in the converse situation, a child who does not wish to give evidence will rarely, if ever, be required to do so: *Re W (Children) (Family Proceedings: Evidence)* [2010] UKSC 12, [2010] 1 WLR 701, at [26].

[267] [2013] EWCA Civ 223, [2013] 1 WLR 3831.   [268] Ibid. at [43].

[269] Committee on the Rights of the Child (2009) para. 35.

older child who was presumably very familiar with his mother's character. The case appears to downplay both the right of the child to participate and the welfare reasons for giving children the opportunity to participate in fundamental decisions about their future.[270] It is a good example of the way in which paternalistic concerns can be used to limit children's involvement even in cases in which older children have strong and considered reasons to wish to participate.

(iii) Children Instructing Their Own Solicitors in Public Law Proceedings

(a) Competence to Instruct a Solicitor

Under the tandem system, the children's guardian will usually appoint a solicitor and give instructions on the child's behalf.[271] Conflict can arise, particularly in the case of older children, if the child disagrees with the guardian's assessment of his or her interests and seeks to give the solicitor instructions that conflict with those of the guardian. In these circumstances, the FPR require the solicitor to take instructions from the child if satisfied that the child is 'able, having regard to the child's understanding, to give such instructions on the child's own behalf'.[272] Alternatively, the child may seek to terminate the appointment of the solicitor appointed by the guardian and appoint a new solicitor in their place.[273]

The extent to which children are able to give instructions independently will depend on the malleable 'understanding' test, just as it does in private proceedings. As discussed above, in private disputes, the courts have placed increasing weight on the importance of children's autonomy and participation rights in applying this test. The same trend can be seen in public cases; indeed, the leading cases developing these principles have spanned both public and private proceedings. Nonetheless, it cannot be assumed that the test of understanding will be applied in exactly the same way in the two areas, not least because the rules themselves distinguish between the different proceedings. Further, when making an assessment of understanding, close attention must be paid to the particular issues raised by the proceedings[274] and the fact that public proceedings throw up rather different problems from those arising in private disputes. For example, in *Re Z (Interim Care Order)*,[275] a 15-year-old had been found not to have sufficient understanding to give separate instructions in private proceedings concerning contact with his mother. The LA subsequently commenced care proceedings, with the aim of moving Z to foster care and re-establishing the relationship with his mother. The Court of Appeal

---

[270] A. Daly (2018b).   [271] Practice Direction 16A: Representation of Children para. 6.2.

[272] FPR, r. 16.29(2).

[273] FPR, r. 16.29(7): this provision does not set out a separate test as to when the child may make such an application. In *Re W (A Child) (Care Proceedings: Child's Representation)* [2016] EWCA Civ 1051, [2017] 1 WLR 1027, at [21], the Court of Appeal considered that the correct approach was for the court to apply the same matters as in FPR, r. 16.29(2).

[274] *Re H (A Minor) (Care Proceedings: Child's Wishes)* [1993] 1 FLR 440.

[275] [2020] EWCA Civ 1755.

found that the trial judge had been wrong to rely on the assessment of Z's understanding in the private dispute to determine that he was also unable to give instructions in relation to the interim care order four months later. In particular, the public law proceedings raised very different matters from the private proceedings, including the possibility that Z would be removed from his father's care. As the Court of Appeal noted, public proceedings inevitably raise the prospect of state interference with the child's Article 8 rights. As such, particular care is needed in public proceedings to ensure that the child receives the appropriate procedural protections guaranteed by Article 8.[276]

(b) The Child's 'Right' to Instruct a Solicitor

The court rules envisage that children with sufficient understanding, who disagree with their guardian over the desired result of care proceedings, are allowed to instruct their solicitor themselves. The way in which this test is applied appears to have undergone a significant shift away from welfare concerns and towards recognition of children's CRC Article 12 rights. Research into practice in the late 1990s demonstrated that mature children seldom instructed their solicitors directly.[277] There were various reasons for this. In particular, Sawyer found that guardians considered whether separate representation was 'good' for the child, rather than considering it from the viewpoint of the child's legal right.[278] Even in cases where a clear conflict had arisen between child and guardian, either the child's solicitor or guardian might seek to deter the child from seeking to instruct the solicitor directly, for fear of antagonising the court.[279] Some practitioners left a decision over a conflict between child and guardian until the last minute, in the hope that the child would come round to agreeing with the guardian.[280] If children did persist, they may then find themselves faced with a reluctance to change the existing arrangements for fear of losing the fixture for the hearing.[281]

Just as is the case in private proceedings, the courts now appear far more attuned to children's participation rights, especially in the case of older children. The leading case in public proceedings is *Re W (A Child) (Care Proceedings: Child's Representation)*,[282] which concerned a 16-year-old who had absconded from foster care to live with her grandparents. The LA applied for a recovery order[283] to return her to foster care, an application strongly opposed by W herself. The guardian had appointed a solicitor to act for W, but both considered that W was not competent to instruct, in part because they

---

[276] See esp. *M and M* v. *Croatia* (2017) 65 EHRR 9, discussed above.

[277] J. Masson and M. Winn Oakley (1999) p. 77.   [278] C. Sawyer (2000) p. 111.

[279] Ibid.; J. Masson and M. Winn Oakley (1999) p. 78.

[280] E.g. *Re H (A Minor) (Care Proceedings: Child's Wishes)* [1993] 1 FLR 440; *Re M (Minors) (Care Proceedings: Child's Wishes)* [1994] 1 FLR 749.

[281] E.g. *Re P (Representation)* [1996] 1 FLR 486: an appeal was allowed against Douglas Brown J's refusal to allow a teenage girl separate representation from that of her six siblings. He had considered that acting on the application at such a late stage would abort the hearing.

[282] [2016] EWCA Civ 1051, [2017] 1 WLR 1027.   [283] I.e. under CA 1989, s. 50.

considered that her views were strongly influenced by her family. W sought to terminate this appointment and instead instruct the solicitor who had already directly represented her in the original care proceedings and who considered that W remained competent to give instructions. The Court of Appeal overturned the trial judge's refusal to allow W to instruct her own solicitor. In doing so, Black LJ stressed that the test of 'understanding' should be approached with appreciation for the importance of children's autonomy.[284] The test of understanding was not to be confused with the question of whether it was in the child's best interests to be represented, nor with whether the child agreed with professionals about her case. Indeed, the right to separate representation was often of most value to the child when she materially disagreed with the guardian about those interests.[285] Further, it should be recognised that children often benefit from playing a direct part in litigation about important aspects of their lives and that the support of a trusted, independent professional would be of great benefit to her in navigating the difficult situation in which she found herself. In this way, children's interests were relevant to the court, but did not determine the application of the 'understanding' test.

The decision in *Re W* appears to reflect a wider trend towards recognising the importance of autonomy, at least in relation to older children. Older teenagers who wish to give instructions directly appear much more likely to be successful in doing so than in the past. An important point raised by Baker LJ in *Re Z (Interim Care Order)*[286] is that professionals and the court may need to take steps to facilitate the participation of some children, particularly older teenagers with disabilities that place a barrier to participation. This case concerned a 15-year-old with a diagnosis of autistic spectrum disorder, who risked being removed from his home against his will. Observing that most 15-year-olds who wished to do so would now be able to give separate instructions in these circumstances, Baker LJ noted that there was a strong argument that there was an obligation on the court system to work to facilitate the participation of teenagers with disabilities in the same position. This argument is strengthened by Article 13(1) of the UN Convention on the Rights of Persons with Disabilities 2006, which obliges states to make accommodations to ensure that people with disabilities have equal, effective access to justice in the same way as others.[287]

(c) Centring Children in Family Justice

It is evident that many children who are the subject of family proceedings feel that important decisions are taken about their future without sufficient opportunities for their involvement. The involvement of children in family proceedings is not solely concerned with ascertaining their views or providing

---

[284] [2016] EWCA Civ 1051, [2017] 1 WLR 1027, at [26]–[27], discussed further above.

[285] Ibid. at [33]–[35].   [286] [2020] EWCA Civ 1755, at [48], discussed above.

[287] Although it was not cited by the Court of Appeal, the non-discrimination right contained in CRC, Art. 2 would also point to this conclusion.

representation, it is also concerned with ensuring that children have confidence in the process and that they will be at the centre of the decision concerning their future.

One way of providing children with an assurance that their views have been taken seriously is for the judiciary to see and talk to them in private. Case law[288] and research[289] indicates that some children want to see the judge dealing with their case and that they feel extremely frustrated if they are refused such an opportunity. Further, the UN Committee has recommended that 'wherever possible, the child must be given the opportunity to be directly heard' and this might include a direct conversation with the judge.[290] It has always been acknowledged that a judge can decide whether it is appropriate to see a child in private.[291] Whether this practice should become more commonplace has, however, been a controversial question, with members of the judiciary adopting opposing positions.[292] In 2010, the Family Justice Council produced *Guidelines for Judges Meeting Children Who Are Subject to Family Proceedings*,[293] which provides guidance on the procedure to be followed for such meetings. The judge is usually entitled to expect the child's lawyer or Cafcass officer to advise on whether the child wishes to hold a meeting and whether that would be in the child's best interests. The discretion to accede to a request remains that of the judge, although this is not an unconstrained discretion and there is an expectation that judges will consider whether a meeting would be appropriate in line with the *Guidelines*.[294] Although there is no specified time limit on when a request must be made, it is important that it is raised in good time to allow a decision to be made and for the child to be prepared on what to expect from that meeting.[295]

The *Guidelines* state their purpose to be to 'encourage Judges to enable children to feel more involved and connected with proceedings in which important decisions are made in their lives and to give them an opportunity to satisfy themselves that the Judge has understood their wishes and feelings and to understand the nature of the Judge's task'.[296] The purpose of the meeting is thereby conceived of as giving the child the opportunity to feel

---

[288] E.g. *Re JS (Disposal of Body: Prospective Orders)* [2016] EWHC 2859 (Fam), [2017] 4 WLR 1.

[289] M. Ruegger (2001) p. 41; G. Douglas *et al.* (2006) paras 3.7 and 3.56.

[290] Committee on the Rights of the Child (2009) para. 35.

[291] Per Ormrod LJ in *D* v. *D (Custody of Child)* (1981) 2 FLR 74.

[292] E.g. in *Re W (Leave to Remove)* [2008] EWCA Civ 538, [2008] 2 FLR 1170, per Thorpe LJ, at [33], enthusiastically promotes this practice, considering it 'regrettable' that the trial judge had not met the children. Cf. Wilson LJ, at [57], who disagrees, urging that the judiciary should not feel obliged to meet children in private more frequently than hitherto. See also Charles J, at [59], who did not consider that a private meeting between the trial judge and the children would have been appropriate.

[293] [2010] 2 FLR 1872.

[294] *Re J (Abduction: Children's Objections)* [2011] EWCA Civ 1448, [2013] 1 FLR 457.

[295] *London Borough of Brent* v. *D and others (Compliance with Guidelines on Judges Meeting Children)* [2017] EWHC 2452 (Fam), [2017] 4 WLR 193.

[296] [2010] 2 FLR 1872.

involved and reassured as to the way in which decisions about them will be taken. This is firmly distinguished in the *Guidelines* from the process of eliciting evidence and deciding the outcome of the case. The *Guidelines* stress that 'the child's meeting with the judge is not for the purpose of gathering evidence', which remains the role of the Cafcass officer. For example, in *Re KP (A Child) (Abduction: Rights of Custody)*,[297] the judge met the child for an hour, apparently asking eighty-seven questions in that time, a process that the child unsurprisingly found intimidating. The information obtained in that meeting was then used to draw the conclusion that the child's objections were not 'rational' and to reject the recommendation of the Cafcass officer. In taking this active role in questioning the child and placing weight on the information obtained, the judge was found to have departed from the purpose of the meeting and strayed into obtaining evidence. There are good reasons for distinguishing judicial meetings from the process of collecting evidence from the child.[298] The judge cannot promise confidentiality to the child and must pass on any relevant information to each parent.[299] Indeed, it is arguable that the rules of natural justice, and Article 6(1) of the ECHR, require the parents to be given this information and an opportunity to address the judge on it. But even then, there would be an element of unfairness unless the information provided by the child could be tested subsequently in cross-examination.[300] A further concern is that of judicial training. In poorly conducted meetings, children may feel bullied by the judge and the judge may jump to the wrong conclusions.[301] Indeed, as Hunter points out, without extensive and well-structured training, it may be extremely difficult for members of the judiciary to pick up the nuances underlying children's expressed views in a very short interview, however sympathetically carried out.[302] At present, it seems that no such training is available for judges in conducting this delicate task.[303]

The prohibition on using meetings to gather evidence from children is clear in principle, but much more difficult to apply in practice. A child who is given the opportunity to meet the judge deciding the case may understandably hope to use the meeting to explain their views and try to influence the outcome. For example, in *B v. P (Children's Objections)*,[304] the children took the opportunity of a meeting organised under the *Guidelines* to make an emotional plea to the judge not to return them to Hungary as requested by their father. Although the Cafcass report had already recorded these wishes, the meeting with the children added further information that was forensically significant despite the efforts of the judge to divert them from doing so. The extreme distress

---

[297] [2014] EWCA Civ 554, [2014] 1 WLR 4326. See also *Re K (Children) (Contact: Interim Care Order)* [2014] EWCA Civ 1195, [2015] 1 FLR 95.
[298] L. Davis (2007); R. Hunter (2007); N. Wilson (2007).   [299] Guidelines para. 6.
[300] L. Davis (2007) pp. 66–7.   [301] R. Hunter (2007) pp. 290–8.   [302] Ibid. pp. 294–5.
[303] A. MacDonald (2018).
[304] [2017] EWHC 3577 (Fam). The judge hearing this case, MacDonald J, reflected further on this experience in A. MacDonald (2018).

displayed by the children was accompanied by behaviour that had a potential bearing on other evidence in the case. Such an experience puts the judge in an extremely difficult position. The *Guidelines* are clear that this encounter should not be relied upon as evidence, yet it appears artificial and potentially unjust to expect the judge to ignore information and impressions that are directly relevant to the matters to be decided. A child who has gone through the emotional and difficult process of making their perspective known to the judge deciding their case may well feel *more* marginalised to learn that their contribution will have no impact on the decision, an outcome that appears to undermine, rather than promote, the rationale of Article 12 of the CRC. The difficulties that have been encountered in implementing the *Guidelines* demonstrate that further refinement may be needed to design a process that allows children to be informed and involved, but avoids the pitfalls experienced so far.[305]

A further important and undeveloped area of concern relates to the way in which children are informed of the outcome of decisions and how their views have been taken into account in that process. The Council of Europe's Guidelines on Child-Friendly Justice[306] give specific attention to this aspect of the process, stating that:

> Judgments and court rulings affecting children should be duly reasoned and explained to them in language that children can understand, particularly those decisions in which the child's views and opinions have not been followed.[307]

There have been some notable examples of judgments that have been carefully tailored for the child concerned, with a focus on accessible language and the impact the decision will have on the child. Most strikingly, in *Re A (Letter to a Young Person)*,[308] Peter Jackson J presented his decision in the form of a letter to 'Sam', the child concerned, rather than as a formal judgment. The letter addressed the views that Sam had expressed, giving careful reasons for making different orders to those Sam had sought, a decision that Sam received with 'apparent equanimity'. In *Lancashire County Council* v. *M*,[309] the same judge produced a judgment designed to be accessible to the mother and older children through the use of concise, plain language and including the use of emojis. Communicating the decision to children may take other forms. In *Re A (A Child)*,[310] the judge took the unusual step of visiting the child in hospital to explain his decision on her medical treatment, given the significant conflict that had emerged between the child and her medical team and social services. It is unlikely that these methods can be adopted in all cases, particularly given the complexity of the law and evidence that sometimes requires consideration within the decision, as well as the resource pressures on the family justice

---

[305] A. Daly (2018b) pp. 252–61 considers the extensive experience of other jurisdictions in navigating these difficulties.
[306] Council of Europe (2010).   [307] Ibid. para. 49.   [308] [2017] EWFC 48, [2017] 3 FCR 323.
[309] [2016] EWFC 9.   [310] [2014] EWHC 920, at [45].

system.[311] Nonetheless, these examples stand out as thoughtful and innovative means of communicating the decision to the child in an accessible way that furthers child-centred justice.

(5) Giving 'Due Weight' to Children's Views in Family Proceedings

(A) Introduction

Article 12 of the CRC not only protects children's right to be heard, but also the right to have 'due weight' ascribed to their views: there is little point in having a right to express a view if it is not capable of influencing the final outcome. In domestic law, this is primarily reflected in the requirement that when determining a child's welfare,[312] the courts are directed to have regard to 'the ascertainable wishes and feelings of the child concerned (considered in the light of his age and understanding)'.[313] This direction accommodates the fact that children often have a better grasp of their own situation than adults. Indeed, it promotes a diluted form of autonomy by implying that a mature child's best interests may be fulfilled most effectively by the court acceding to his or her own wishes. Furthermore, its inclusion in the welfare checklist reflects a conviction that 'the increasing recognition given both in practice and in law to the child's status as a human being in his own right' should also be matched by the courts, when hearing disputes over children.[314] Whether the direction is realistic depends on children having an effective means of conveying their views to the court – as this chapter has shown, not all are provided with such a facility.

For those children whose views are before the court, there remains a lack of certainty as to exactly what is required by the direction to 'have regard' to the child's wishes and feelings. Mnookin has pointed out that it is often unclear to a judge what questions should be posed when trying to determine the child's best interests. Should this be considered from a short- or long-term viewpoint? Should the court be primarily concerned with the child's happiness?[315] Similar questions could be posed when weighing the impact of a child's wishes and feelings. What precise purpose is the court considering this information for in the circumstances of this case? Is it merely to reinforce the court's own decision or to provide information that may swing a finely balanced case? What risks

---

[311] See further H. Stalford and K. Hollingsworth (2020).

[312] Children Act (CA) 1989, s. 1 requires the courts to reach decisions over children's upbringing, by giving the children's welfare their paramount consideration – a provision often described as the 'paramountcy principle'. For further discussion, see Chapter 3. Not all decisions affecting children are governed by the paramountcy principle. Notably, in abduction cases decided under the Hague Convention, discussed above, the child's welfare is not paramount. Indeed, a prima facie presumption underlies the Convention that a child's welfare is best served by a prompt return to the country of his or her habitual residence, leaving the decision of what should happen to the child to that country's own courts.

[313] CA 1989, s. 1(3)(a).   [314] Law Commission (1988) para. 3.24.

[315] R. Mnookin (1975) p. 260.

are involved in taking account of the child's wishes and of ignoring them? How far are the child's age, understanding and maturity relevant to the way in which their wishes are considered? Many of these questions mirror the uncertainty, discussed above, in the ambit of Article 12 of the CRC itself.

The 'welfare checklist'[316] appears to give children's wishes and feelings particular importance by putting them in the foremost position in the list. Nonetheless, the overtly paternalistic nature of the welfare principle clearly permits a court to discount information about children's views if it considers that an alternative outcome would serve the child's needs better. It can rely on a wealth of other factors in the welfare checklist to substantiate its decision. As Eekelaar observes, the checklist could be applied in such a way as to render the child's viewpoint always irrelevant to the final outcome.[317] This problem is further exacerbated by the malleability of terms such as 'maturity' and 'under-standing', which can be interpreted flexibly to adjust the weight given to the child's views and give courts discretion in how far those views will influence the final outcome.[318] There would, of course, be less scope for criticism if the courts showed greater clarity over the extent to which they should take account of children's wishes. An absence of clarity is hardly surprising, in view of the doubts attending the interpretation of the welfare principle itself. It is univer-sally accepted that in this field of decision-making there are no 'right' answers, but judicial discretion should not be an excuse for an arbitrary approach which suggests to children that the process of seeking their views is a meaningless exercise to be completed and then forgotten.

Consulting children as part of a welfare assessment is very different from delegating the decision-making process to them entirely before they reach adulthood. This distinction may, however, collapse in relation to mature children with strongly felt wishes as to the outcome of their case. For these children, there may be good welfare reasons for deferring to their decision[319] and strong principled arguments for recognising their autonomy. Eekelaar has expressed concern that the judiciary, when subjecting children to coercive paternalism, risk ignoring their interest in making their own choices concern-ing their future.[320] He favours the concept of 'dynamic self-determinism', which introduces a presumption in favour of complying with children's choices as closely as possible without restricting their capacity for fulfilling their future life-goals.[321] This suggestion is useful and, if followed, might ensure that the courts paid more attention to a child's interest in choice and fulfilled the need to treat the individual child with respect. It might also ensure that the judiciary retained a measure of flexibility when confronted by a child whose strong views conflict with their own ideas about the needs of children in

---

[316] The term commonly used to describe the list of factors contained in the CA 1989, s. 1(3).

[317] J. Eekelaar (2006) p. 158.   [318] A. Daly (2018a); K. Tisdall (2018).

[319] C. Sturge and D. Glaser (2000) p. 621.

[320] Eekelaar repeatedly returns to this theme in three papers: J. Eekelaar (1986), (1992) and (1994).

[321] J. Eekelaar (1994) p. 53.

general. Aoife Daly also advocates that the autonomy of children should be highly valued and respected, just as it is for other members of society. She argues that children's autonomy should be restricted by the minimum paternalism necessary. In best interests decisions, this would mean that a child who wished to determine the outcome could do so provided that those wishes were unlikely to cause significant harm and there were no legitimate obstacles to following them.[322] As discussed below, the courts are increasingly attuned to the importance of children's decisions, at least in relation to older children, but domestic law remains a long way from such an 'autonomy principle'.

(B) The Relevance of 'Age and Understanding'

The direction to consider the child's wishes and feelings in the welfare checklist is qualified by the requirement to do so in the light of the child's 'age and understanding'. This qualification is similar to that in Article 12 of the CRC, which directs that the 'due weight' given to children's views must be in accordance with the child's 'age and maturity'. In both contexts, the implication appears to be that the views of younger children should be given less weight than those who are older, but it is not evident that this should necessarily be the case. The direction to consider the child's wishes and feelings is primarily concerned with ensuring that decisions are made with an understanding of the child's perspective. It does not require courts to treat the child's wishes as determinative. Even very young children are capable of forming strong feelings and expressing wishes that illuminate their own experience, even if they are not able to appreciate all facets of the case or express a 'view' as to the outcome.[323] It is difficult to see why the *feelings* of a young child should be given less weight merely on account of their young age.

This does not mean that age should be irrelevant to the way in which courts approach children's wishes and feelings. Those who write critically of legal constructions of childhood strongly criticise what they see as 'a developmentally based model of childhood' rooted in 'Piaget's ideas about the "normal" stages in a child's psychological development'.[324] Nevertheless, it is surely folly to ignore the research on cognitive development indicating that children's cognitive skills develop and differ enormously throughout childhood.[325] These differences may be of crucial importance in understanding the child's perspective and any expressed wishes. Age is one facet of development, but factors such as the child's experiences, upbringing and biology will also affect the child's individual development. For example, child psychiatrists Sturge and Glaser recommend that within the overall context of the child's wishes:

> the older the child the more seriously they should be viewed and the more insulting and discrediting to the child to have them ignored. As a rough rule we

---

[322] A. Daly (2018b).   [323] K. Tisdall (2018); M. Henaghan (2017).
[324] A. James *et al.* (2004) pp. 193–4; see also A. Daly (2018b) pp. 179–89.
[325] Discussed in Chapter 9.

would see these as needing to be taken account of at any age; above 10 we see these as carrying considerable weight with 6–10 as an intermediate stage and at under 6 as often indistinguishable in many ways from the wishes of the main carer (assuming normal development).[326]

These 'rough rules' contrast with the formal age limits adopted by some European countries such as Finland, where children over the age of 12 can veto the enforcement of court decisions concerning their custody and access.[327] Researchers warn that, even at these ages, children's abilities and understanding will vary enormously, depending on a variety of factors, such as peer pressure and family environment.[328] There is also a risk that giving children as young as 12 an absolute legal veto places on their shoulders the responsibility for choice for which they may not be ready. Making *choices* requires very different skills and maturity from those required for taking part in a consultation process.

In the absence of any clear rules related to age, domestic courts have considerable discretion as to how to take into account each child's wishes and feelings. This flexibility is perhaps inevitable given the differences between children and the range of circumstances that come before the court. Much of the judicial unease over taking account of the views of very young children centres on private law disputes and the concern that young children may be more easily subjected to the influence of others,[329] and vulnerable to external factors which may only have a short-term impact.[330] There is, however, considerable criticism of the way in which children's wishes and feelings are often overridden without careful explanation of how they have been assessed and weighed against other factors in the welfare checklist.[331] Malleable terms such as 'understanding', 'maturity' and 'competence' are frequently used to give greater or lesser weight to the child's wishes, but with little clarity on the meaning of these terms or their relevance to the exercise.[332] Many researchers have observed that greater weight appears to be ascribed to children's wishes if they reinforce the court's own view of the best outcome for the child. In particular, children who resist contact with a parent appear much less likely to be taken seriously than those who support contact, even in cases involving domestic abuse allegations.[333] While children do not necessarily wish to determine the outcome of the decision, they often wish to be involved[334] and may feel confused and

---

[326] C. Sturge and D. Glaser (2000) p. 624.

[327] See: *K and T* v. *Finland* [2001] 2 FLR 79, at [88]–[89]; *C* v. *Finland* [2006] 2 FLR 597, at [41].

[328] See Chapter 9.

[329] The risks of young children being indoctrinated by a parent are discussed below.

[330] B. Cantwell and S. Scott (1995) pp. 340–3.   [331] A. Daly (2018a).   [332] K. Tisdall (2018).

[333] G. MacDonald (2017); R. Hunter *et al.* (2020); J. Hunt and A. Macleod (2008) pp. 66 and 200. S. Holt (2018) made similar findings in the context of decisions in Ireland. See e.g. *Re S (Transfer of Residence)* [2011] 1 FLR 1789.

[334] A. Buchanan *et al.* (2001) pp. 64–8; I. Butler *et al.* (2003) ch. 5; A. Daly (2018b) pp. 36–42.

vulnerable if the judiciary appear to ignore their strongly voiced views about the outcome.

A child's age and ability to form views cannot be assessed *in vacuo*, since the context of the dispute and the risk involved in ignoring or acceding to his or her views will always impinge on the decision-making process. An attempt to clarify how the child's views affect the overall decision may lead to a more consistent judicial approach. Whatever the context, a child may not understand why, having expressed strong views one way or the other, the court has apparently ignored them. However young, the courts should consider always including a careful explanation of their decisions in circumstances where they feel unable to comply with a child's own wishes.[335] When older, these children may wish to understand more about the legal process and discover the reasons underlying the present arrangements for their care. This is particularly important in child protection cases as the decision may radically change a child's life. The children involved do not necessarily resent the court for not fulfilling their wishes, as long as an adult, such as their children's guardian, explains to them the terms of the order and reasons for the decision.[336]

(C) Understanding the Child's Views: Influence, Manipulation and Indoctrination

A frequent concern raised by courts is whether the views expressed by a child genuinely reflect their own wishes, or whether those views have been distorted through pressure or indoctrination. This section highlights some of the circumstances which pose particular problems for hearing children's views.

Influence and indoctrination come in many forms and are usually not deliberate, in so far as young children often simply absorb the views of those who care for them. As Eekelaar has observed, it is arguable that children lack competence to make decisions for themselves if their decision is really that of the parent and not their own.[337] On the other hand, few adults could claim that they reach decisions entirely independently of the influence of others:

> If one is to hold a person incompetent because his decision reflects socially tolerated values ingrained in his upbringing, competence could hardly ever be achieved by anyone.[338]

As Black LJ has observed, '[m]ost people's views are influenced by the views of others in one way or another and it can be very difficult to decide reliably

---

[335] N. Wilson (2007) p. 819: children have a right promptly to understand not only the nature of the outcome, but also the main reasons for it; furthermore (p. 817), the judge presiding over private law proceedings should determine prior to their conclusion how the child is to be acquainted with his decision and the reasons for it.

[336] *Re C (A Minor) (Care: Child's Wishes)* [1993] 1 FLR 832: Waite J (at 840) hoped that the court's decision would be conveyed to the 13-year-old girl sympathetically.

[337] J. Eekelaar (1994) p. 56.   [338] Ibid. p. 57.

whether or not someone is simply an agent for another person'.[339] The mere fact that the child and parent have shared views should not in itself be a reason to give less weight to the child's views or treat them as not genuinely those of the child.[340] There are, however, cases in which the family circumstances place such pressure on the child that there are reasons to be cautious about their ability to form and express a considered view of their situation. For example, *L v. L and another (Anticipatory Child Arrangements Order)*[341] concerned N, an 'extremely bright and articulate' 14-year-old who had expressed 'strong feelings' about living with her mother rather than her father. The views of such a young person would often command close to determinative weight. In this case, however, N had borne a 'developmentally inappropriate weight of responsibility' for her mother's complex physical and mental health needs. This onerous sense of responsibility and her mother's emotional dependence on her appeared to be driving N's desire to live with the mother. Her views therefore had to be considered through the 'prism' of this relationship of responsibility and could not be determinative. N was herself very unwell, she had serious anorexia and had been sectioned under the Mental Health Act 1983. In these circumstances, it was crucial to provide a home where her own physical and emotional needs could be prioritised and this imperative out-weighed her expressed wishes.

(i) Religious Indoctrination

Religious indoctrination may be a particularly difficult factor for the courts to deal with in determining how to understand the child's views. To what extent should a court accord freedom of choice to a child it considers has been indoctrinated into the religious tenets of his or her carers? The courts have a tradition of maintaining religious tolerance and abstain from commenting on the views of any particular religious denomination.[342] A decision overrid-ing a child's strong religious views by, for example, removing them from their present home in a religious community[343] might be countered by arguing that the child is entitled to religious freedom under Article 9 of the ECHR. The court might, however, respond by finding that an infringement is necessary under Article 9(2) to preserve the child's best interests. Where adherence to the beliefs of the community causes harm to the child, such an interference is likely to be easily justified.[344] A more difficult issue arises if the child has accepted

---

[339] *Re W (A Child) (Care Proceedings: Child's Representation)* [2016] EWCA Civ 1051, [2017] 1 WLR 1027, at [32].

[340] Ibid.   [341] [2017] EWHC 1212 (Fam), [2018] 1 FLR 108.

[342] E.g. *Re J (Specific Issue Orders: Muslim Upbringing and Circumcision)* [1999] 2 FLR 678.

[343] E.g. *Re R (A Minor) (Residence: Religion)* [1993] 2 FLR 163: despite the vehement wish of a 9.5-year-old boy to remain with members of the Exclusive Brethren sect, with whom he had lived for 4.5 years, his care was transferred to his father.

[344] E.g. *Re S (Parental Alienation: Cult: Transfer of Primary Care)* [2020] EWHC 1940 (Fam), esp. at [62]–[63]: a 9-year-old child had been exposed to harmful practices as a result of her mother's adherence to the teachings of Universal Medicine, which the court described as a cult.

a value system that is very different from that of a parent, particularly if that value system rejects aspects of the parent's life or identity. The child may find it impossible to reconcile life within the community with a relationship with their 'non-believing' parent. In such cases, the courts have demonstrated a commitment to preserving and repairing the relationship with the parent, even if that commitment requires the child to leave the belief system or community in which they have been brought up.[345] There are, however, limits to the court's ability to achieve changed relationships if the child is firmly embedded within the community. For example, in *Re M (Children) (Ultra-Orthodox Judaism: Transgender Parent)*,[346] the father had left the Cheredi Jewish community to live as a transgender woman and in consequence had been ostracised by it. The parents were agreed that the children would remain with their mother in the community, but a dispute arose as to whether the children should have direct contact with the father. The Court of Appeal stressed that the family court should not give up on direct contact without exhausting powers to make that contact work. Nonetheless, it proved impossible to do so without a 'catastrophic' impact on the children's lives within the community. In particular, the older children remained angry and unwilling to meet their father given the chasm between the way in which they lived their lives.[347] In these circumstances, the father reluctantly withdrew the application for contact.

(ii) Parental Hostility and Alienation

Hostility towards a non-resident parent is by no means limited to such cases. Indeed, a not uncommon problem arises when children simply refuse to cooperate with contact arrangements suggested by the non-resident parent. It is clear that some parents deliberately manipulate children emotionally against the other parent. This, of course, makes it very difficult for those children to discover their 'authentic wishes and feelings'.[348] Mantle *et al.* point out that a risk of brainwashing is the wholesale rejection of one parent who is effectively 'written out' of the child's life.[349] Nevertheless, as the judiciary themselves have asserted, some parents find it easier to maintain that their children's hostility to them is attributable to the other parent's behaviour than to accept their own responsibility for this attitude.[350] Research with adults who were the subject of parental disputes as children has also found little

---

[345] E.g. *Re S (Parental Alienation: Cult: Transfer of Primary Care)* [2020] EWHC 1940 (Fam); *Re R (A Minor) (Residence: Religion)* [1993] 2 FLR 163; *Re M (Children) (Ultra-Orthodox Judaism: Transgender Parent)* [2017] EWCA Civ 2164, [2018] 2 FLR 800.

[346] [2017] EWCA Civ 2164, [2018] 2 FLR 800.

[347] *Re A (Children) (Contact: Ultra-Orthodox Judaism: Transgender Parent)* [2020] EWFC 3, [2020] 1 FCR 599.

[348] G. Mantle *et al.* (2007).   [349] Ibid. p. 1.

[350] E.g. *Re C (Prohibition on Further Applications)* [2002] EWCA Civ 292, [2002] 1 FLR 1136, per Dame Elizabeth Butler-Sloss P, at [12]–[13]; *Re O (A Child) (Contact: Withdrawal of Application)* [2003] EWHC 3031 (Fam), [2004] 1 FLR 1258, per Wall J, at [85]; *Re Bradford; Re O'Connell* [2006] EWCA Civ 1199, [2007] 1 FLR 530, per Wall J, at [94].

evidence that parental hostility towards the non-resident parent is a significant cause of contact failure.[351] Possibly spurred on by some of the fathers' pressure groups, some parents counter their children's resistance to contact by arguing that they are suffering from a mental disorder induced by Parental Alienation Syndrome[352] and that they need skilled psychiatric or psychological assessment and therapy.[353] Courts in this jurisdiction show little sign of accepting claims of such a clinical 'syndrome'.[354] Nonetheless, they are increasingly faced with cases in which the child is said to have been alienated from a parent, meaning that their views resisting contact should not be taken at face value.[355] As considered elsewhere in this book,[356] such claims pose real difficulties for the courts, especially when they are raised in response to allegations of abuse against the 'alienated' parent.[357] Careful fact-finding is required to assess whether the child has been manipulated into rejecting a parent or is resisting the continuation of a harmful relationship.[358] Without an evidential basis, the discourse of alienation risks imposing a barrier to hearing the voices of children who are in particular need of court protection.[359]

(iii) Abused Children

Abuse creates additional difficulties in hearing and evaluating children's views. An abused child's right to be consulted may conflict with his or her right to be protected. Indeed, the wishes and feelings of abused children may be so extremely complex that they provide the court with some very mixed messages. As Schofield points out, abused children whose future is being determined by the courts may be so significantly harmed that they are confused about themselves and what has happened to them and therefore present a confusing picture to others:[360]

> Troubled children in crisis … very often and very understandably present entirely conflicting evidence of their wishes and feelings. They may express

[351] J. Fortin *et al.* (2012) p. 246: they instead cited the non-resident parent's failure to maintain contact as the most common reason for contact failure.

[352] The website of the fathers' pressure group, Families Need Fathers (www.fnf.org.uk/), contains a considerable body of information on alienation.

[353] E.g. *Appeal in Re M (A Child)* in *Re L (A Child) (Contact: Domestic Violence) and other appeals* [2000] 4 All ER 609: the psychological expert in PAS had recommended, on the father's behalf, that the child undergo six sessions of therapy; *Re C (Prohibition on Further Applications)* [2002] EWCA Civ 292, [2002] 1 FLR 1136: the father repeatedly applied for a mental health expert or a psychologist, an expert in PAS, to be appointed to assess his daughter's state of mind, given her refusal to have contact with him; *Re Bradford; Re O'Connell* [2006] EWCA Civ 1199, [2007] 1 FLR 530: Mr O'Connell wanted an American expert in PAS to be appointed to assess the children.

[354] J. Doughty *et al.* (2020). There is widespread scepticism as to the evidence base for such claims: C. Bruch (2002) pp. 387–8; R. Emery *et al.* (2005) p. 10; C. Sturge and D. Glaser (2000) pp. 622–3.

[355] E.g. *Re S (Parental Alienation: Cult: Transfer of Primary Care)* [2020] EWHC 1940 (Fam); *Re H (Parental Alienation)* [2019] EWHC 2723 (Fam), [2020] 1 FLR 401.

[356] See Chapter 6.   [357] E.g. *Re J (Children)* [2018] EWCA Civ 115, [2018] 2 FLR 998.

[358] S. Gilmore (2020).   [359] A. Barnett (2020).   [360] G. Schofield (1998) p. 365.

hopes for the future which are incompatible with what professionals and the children themselves know to be reality; for example, the wish to be at home and to be safe, the wish to be with a parent but for that parent to change.[361]

As she explains:

> This does not mean that we should therefore disregard those wishes and feelings but it does mean that the process of ascertaining, understanding and determining the weight to be attached to children's wishes and feelings is more problematic than it may appear from the simple words of the Act.[362]

Children who are allegedly the victims of sexual abuse present special problems, both in private and public law proceedings. A sexually abused child's present views may be grossly distorted by his or her damaging relationship with the abuser.[363] Sexually abused children may not only deny or refuse to acknowledge that abuse has occurred, but also refuse to cooperate with those trying to help them.[364] Those who do disclose the abuse sometimes later deny it due to pressure from the abuser.[365] The courts are well aware that abused children who are the subject of child protection proceedings often strongly desire to stay at home or return home,[366] however illogical this may appear.[367] They understand that a denial of abuse may be attributable to the child's fear of breaking up the home. The courts are obviously fully justified in overriding a child's objections to removal from home if they believe him or her to have been abused; indeed, they are under a duty to consider his or her 'physical, emotional and educational needs'.[368] On the other hand, children should not be disbelieved just because they are denying abuse, as opposed to disclosing it.[369] Children who are suspected to have been the victims of abuse require particular time and care in order to build a relationship of trust in order to be heard.

(D) Are Children's Wishes and Feelings Ever Determinative?

Under the welfare checklist, children's wishes and feelings are merely one factor within a paternalistic assessment of the child's welfare. Nonetheless, in some cases, the courts accept that the child has reached a level of understanding and

---

[361] Ibid. p. 364.   [362] Ibid.   [363] E. Jones and P. Parkinson (1995) pp. 68–75.

[364] H. Westcott (2006) pp. 179–80. E.g. *Nottinghamshire County Council* v. *P; Re P (Minors) (Local Authority: Prohibited Steps Order)* [1993] 3 All ER 815: none of the teenage daughters was prepared to stay away from their sexually abusive father.

[365] E. Jones and P. Parkinson (1995) p. 64.

[366] *Re F (Mental Health Act: Guardianship)* [2000] 1 FLR 192, per Thorpe LJ, at 198.

[367] E.g., inter alia: *Re C (A Minor) (Care: Child's Wishes)* [1993] 1 FLR 832; *Nottinghamshire County Council* v. *P; Re P (Minors) (Local Authority: Prohibited Steps Order)* [1993] 3 All ER 815; *Re F (Mental Health Act: Guardianship)* [2000] 1 FLR 192.

[368] CA 1989, s. 1(3)(b).

[369] *Leeds City Council* v. *YX and ZX (Assessment of Sexual Abuse)* [2008] EWHC 802 (Fam), [2008] 2 FLR 869, per Holman J, at [127].

maturity at which their wishes should determine the outcome despite any misgivings that the court may have as to whether they have reached the right decision. Reasons of pragmatism, welfare and principle are variously cited by courts in order to give decisive weight to the decisions of children, particularly adolescents. This does not, however, amount to a *rule* that the views of mature children will be followed. Although autonomy is increasingly cited by the courts as a reason for giving great weight to the decisions of older children, the courts have not gone so far as to accept the autonomy principle argued for by writers such as Daly.

There are compelling pragmatic reasons for the reluctance to impose outcomes against the firm wishes of adolescents. There may be little point in making court orders against the wishes of children mature enough to have strong views of their own and large enough to vote with their feet if opposed. The CA 1989 recognises this reality for older teenagers, indicating that no orders should be made regarding children over the age of 16, unless the circumstances are exceptional.[370] For young people below this age, the judiciary has long recognised the compelling argument that their wishes should be respected, since to ignore them would be counter-productive. Thus, in the early 1990s, Butler-Sloss LJ made plain the importance of listening to and respecting the views of older children, while not necessarily always doing what they want.[371] But while reflecting a refreshingly liberal approach to the views of a 14-year-old boy, her decision risked little. Allowing him his choice of school – a day school rather than an expensive boarding school – did not endanger his health or restrict his future choices in life. Indeed, in reality, there would have been little point in the court overriding his wishes.

Disputes concerning contact and residence involve greater risks since, in the long term, the child may lose the chance of maintaining a relationship with a parent. While younger children will often be compelled to have contact against their wishes, the courts seem far more prepared to accept the views of older adolescents who oppose contact, particularly if they have obviously thought out their views rationally.[372] This is perhaps a recognition that these adolescents are reaching an age where court orders will not be available and at which a genuine relationship with their parents will only be sustained through choice. A good example of such a case is *S v. S (Relocation)*,[373] in which 13- and 15-year-old brothers expressed the 'most adamant' views in favour of moving to Switzerland to live with their father and were 'in revolt' against their existing life in England with their mother. Peter Jackson J was sympathetic to the mother's argument that these views had been incited by the father, but

---

[370] CA 1989, s. 9(6) and (7).   [371] *Re P (A Minor) (Education)* [1992] 1 FLR 316, at 321.

[372] J. Hunt and A. Macleod (2008) pp. 19 and 241: a notable feature of the research outcomes was the sharp falling-off in direct contact among the children over 13, clearly related to the courts heeding their wishes when expressing opposition to contact.

[373] [2017] EWHC 2345 (Fam), [2018] 1 FLR 825.

ultimately concluded that a court order would not be effective in the light of such strong opposition. He observed that:

> ... these boys are old enough to instruct lawyers to ensure that their wishes and feelings are fully represented. At their age, those wishes and feelings are a very important element in their welfare. That is so even if the wishes and feelings are unwise. There is nothing in the law that says that the wishes and feelings of older children should be wise or reasonable. They may be foolish or immature but respecting children's points of view must, in the case of older children, accept to some extent the risk of them making mistakes. Unless the consequences of mistaken choices are profoundly harmful, the court cannot protect older children from every mistake that they may make. Here, in my view, a move to Switzerland may or may not turn out to have been a good choice but the wishes and feelings of these children have, in my view, made it the <u>only</u> viable choice.[374]

This should not be taken to mean that a court will inevitably capitulate to the likelihood that an older child will refuse to comply with a court order. The Court of Appeal has made it clear that parents may be expected to use 'argument, persuasion, cajolement, blandishments, inducements, sanctions ... or threats falling short of brute force' to secure compliance.[375] But compulsion is likely to be both counter-productive and ineffective, especially if it exacerbates existing hostility. A court may therefore conclude, as it did in *S* v. *S*, that a compelled outcome is likely to be more damaging to future relationships than respecting the child's wishes.[376]

The decision in *S* v. *S* also recognised the welfare benefits that come from respecting the young person's own determination of the best course of action for the future, even if the court would not have made the same decision. A similar approach can be seen in the tragic and unusual case of *Re JS (Disposal of Body: Prospective Orders)*,[377] in which a terminally ill 14-year-old wished to have her remains cryo-preserved after her death in the hope that this may give her a chance of life in the future. The court was clear that it made no judgment on the merits of cryonic preservation or whether JS's wishes were sensible or not. It was, however, clear that JS's acute distress would be somewhat alleviated by the knowledge that her wishes were respected. These emotional benefits were pivotal to the finding that it would be in her best interests to make the orders that allowed those wishes to be carried out. Although these circumstances were highly unusual, the case demonstrates the emotional benefits for young people of being taken seriously and given

---

[374] Ibid. at [23] (emphasis in the original). See also *Re S (Contact: Children's Views)* [2002] EWHC 540 (Fam), [2002] 1 FLR 1156, esp. at 1171.

[375] *Re H-B (Children) (Contact: Prohibition on Further Applications)* [2015] EWCA Civ 389, [2015] 2 FCR 581, at [76].

[376] See e.g. *Re S (Transfer of Residence)* [2011] 1 FLR 1789, in which an attempt to compel a change of residence against the firm wishes of a 12-year-old boy appears to have caused serious harm to the child's mental health and exacerbated the relationship breakdown with the father.

[377] [2016] EWHC 2859 (Fam), [2017] 4 WLR 1.

the opportunity to make fundamental decisions about intimate aspects of their lives.

While these cases illustrate important pragmatic and welfare reasons for giving decisive weight to children's views, they do not amount to principled acceptance of the autonomy of mature children to determine their future. The case that comes closest to doing so is *AS v. CPW (Inward Return Order)*,[378] in which a 14.5-year-old strongly objected to his father's application for an inward return order to return him to the UK, instead wishing to remain in Sierra Leone to complete his education. In refusing the father's application, Mostyn J considered that:

> In my judgment it is not merely a question of giving 'due regard' to the wishes of a *Gillick*-competent child on a particular issue. In my judgment, if the decision of the House of Lords in *Gillick* is not to be hollowed out, the wishes of a *Gillick*-competent child on a particular issue, where they are not objectively foolish or unreasonable, should normally be given effect.

This approach comes close to accepting the 'autonomy principle' for those children who are found to be *Gillick*-competent. It is strikingly similar to the approach of the ECtHR in *M and M v. Croatia*,[379] which emphasised the importance of autonomy and found that failure to respect a mature child's decision on her living arrangements amounted to a violation of her Article 8 rights. Nonetheless, just as is the case at Strasbourg,[380] there is no rule that the decisions of a mature child will *necessarily* be decisive of the outcome. A court considering an application relating to the child's upbringing is required by statute to apply the welfare principle and cannot simply abdicate the decision to the child.[381] A further problem for young people is that *Gillick* competence is itself a malleable test with no clear criteria as to how it should apply within this context.[382] A mature child who has a 'reasonable' view on the outcome can be expected to be taken seriously, but cannot be sure that their decision will be treated as decisive.

There are cases where the courts may decide, for paternalistic reasons, to override adolescents' choices, often on the basis that they are not 'competent' to reach them, or simply in order to avoid harm, or at least to safeguard their future.[383] Judicial decision-making reflects an awareness of the implications of overriding an adolescent's strong views, including the indignity of suffering physical compulsion. Furthermore, the temporal context of the decision is important. Thus, although adolescents are usually assumed to have a good

---

[378] [2020] EWHC 1238 (Fam), [2020] Fam Law 1019.

[379] (2017) 65 EHRR 9, discussed above.   [380] E.g. *AV v. Slovenia*, App. No. 878/13.

[381] See esp. *Re P-S (Children) (Family Proceedings: Evidence)* [2013] EWCA Civ 223, [2013] 1 WLR 3831, at [43], in which the suggestion that there was a presumption in favour of following the wishes of a mature child was rejected.

[382] A. Daly (2018a). For further discussion of assessment of competence, see Chapter 9.

[383] E.g. *L v. L and another (Anticipatory Child Arrangements Order)* [2017] EWHC 1212 (Fam), [2018] 1 FLR 108.

ability to reach decisions about their own future, acceding to some of these may involve extremely high long-term risks, particularly if they are refusing to undergo medical treatment. But, in the short term, maturity may come from being allowed to make mistakes. As considered in other chapters in this book, the courts have a reasonably good record of paying considerable attention to an adolescent's views in cases where the outcome will seriously disrupt his or her life, whether they relate to undergoing medical treatment,[384] or going into LA care.[385] This case law shows the judiciary implicitly adopting a 'risk analysis approach' to information regarding the wishes of older children. If acceding to such a child's wishes risks his or her death or long-term harm, then the court may feel obliged to override them, whatever they think of the individual's competence to form firm and reliable views.[386] In conclusion, while the wishes of older children may well be decisive in particular cases, there is no prima facie right to determine the outcome of an upbringing case. Provided that the court recognises the growing importance of the child's autonomy and ensures that any interference with the child's wishes is proportionate to the welfare risk, it is unlikely that there will be a breach of Article 8.

(6) Conclusion

This chapter assesses the extent to which the legal system protects the rights of children to participate in decisions about their future. The demands of Article 12 of the CRC are relatively simple. Children should be able to participate in decisions reached regarding their future upbringing and their wishes given due weight in the decision that is made. But the extent to which domestic law fulfils this ideal is extremely variable. Although we know that many children whose parents disagree on their upbringing suffer considerable psychological distress, large numbers are left entirely to their own devices. Indeed, the pressure imposed on separating parents to settle their disputes out of court often reinforces their children's isolation, ensuring that outsiders are kept totally unaware of their unhappiness and helplessness, with plans for their upbringing being made over their heads.

Where decisions are made by the courts, there has been a notable shift in judicial attitudes to children's participation. Across a wide range of areas, the courts have shown concern to take children's involvement seriously, particularly in relation to older children. The contrast between judicial attitudes to children involved in public law proceedings and those who are the subject of private parental litigation has started to diminish. Nevertheless, while the first group is served by a system of representation widely considered to be ideal, the second group remain lucky to be represented at all. The limited resources

---

[384] E.g. *Re E (A Minor) (Wardship: Medical Treatment)* [1993] 1 FLR 386.
[385] E.g. *Re H (A Minor) (Care Proceedings: Child's Wishes)* [1993] 1 FLR 440.
[386] E.g. *Re W (A Minor) (Medical Treatment: Courts' Jurisdiction)* [1993] Fam 64.

available to devote to hearing and representing children gives the impression that children's participation is not particularly high on the policy-makers' agenda. The archaic and complex web of rules governing children's participation further impedes any child who hopes to discover how to become involved.

Once children have been heard, the judiciary clearly recognises that children should not be subjected to decision-making which fails to give their wishes and feelings serious weight. It would be difficult to justify such an approach to children who are being brought up in a society which constantly urges them to develop their powers of critical awareness and to act responsibly and independently. Nonetheless, it is difficult to predict how those wishes and feelings will be weighed. In particular, there are significant discrepancies between cases as to when children's autonomy will be valued and when paternalism will operate to override the child's perspective. A more systematic approach to the process of considering a child's wishes in each case might emerge were the courts to show a greater willingness to articulate the basis on which children's views are assessed and weighed.

Bibliography

NB: Many of these publications can be obtained on the relevant organisation's website.

Bainham, A. (2013) 'Public and Private Children Law: An Underexplored Relationship' 25 *Child and Family Law Quarterly* 138.

Barnett, A. (2020) 'A Genealogy of Hostility: Parental Alienation in England and Wales' 42 *Journal of Social Welfare and Family Law* 1.

Bruch, C. (2002) 'Parental Alienation Syndrome and Alienated Children – Getting It Wrong in Child Custody Cases' 14 *Child and Family Law Quarterly* 381.

Buchanan, A., Hunt, J., Bretherton, H. and Bream, V. (2001) *Families in Conflict: Perspectives of Children and Parents on the Family Court Welfare Service*, Policy Press.

Butler, I., Scanlan, L., Robinson, M., Douglas, G. and Murch, M. (2003) *Divorcing Children: Children's Experience of Their Parents' Divorce*, Jessica Kingsley Publishers.

Cantwell, B. and Scott, S. (1995) 'Children's Wishes, Children's Burdens' 17 *Journal of Social Welfare and Family Law* 337.

Children and Family Court Advisory Support Service (Cafcass) (2020) *Annual Report and Accounts 2019–2020*, Cafcass.

Committee on the Rights of the Child (2009) *General Comment No. 12 on the Right of the Child to be Heard*, CRC/C/GC/12, Centre for Human Rights, Geneva.

Council of Europe (2010) *Guidelines of the Committee of Ministers of the Council of Europe on Child-Friendly Justice*, Council of Europe Publishing.

Daly, A. (2018a) 'No Weight for "Due Weight"? A Children's Autonomy Principle in Best Interests Proceedings' 26 *International Journal of Children's Rights* 61.

(2018b) *Children, Autonomy and the Courts: Beyond the Right to Be Heard*, Brill/ Nijhoff.

Davies, R. and Mason, S. (2007) 'NYAS: The Voice and Ears of the Child' 37 *Family Law* 1095.

Davis, L. (2007) 'Children in Court' 37 *Family Law* 65.

Day Sclater, S. and Piper, C. (2001) 'Social Exclusion and the Welfare of the Child' 28 *Journal of Law and Society* 409.

Diduck, A. (2003) *Law's Families*, LexisNexis Butterworths.

Doughty, J. (2008) 'From Court Missionaries to Conflict Resolution: A Century of Family Court Welfare' 20 *Child and Family Law Quarterly* 131.

Doughty, J., Maxwell, N. and Slater, T. (2020) 'Professional Responses to "Parental Alienation": Research-Informed Practice' 42 *Journal of Social Welfare and Family Law* 68.

Douglas, A. (2019) 'The Child Arrangements Programme' 49 *Family Law* 45.

Douglas, G., Murch, M., Miles, C. and Scanlan, L. (2006) *Research into the Operation of Rule 9.5 of the Family Proceedings Rules 1991*, Final Report to the Department of Constitutional Affairs, DCA.

Douglas, G., Murch, M., Scanlan, L. and Perry, A. (2000) 'Safeguarding Children's Welfare in Non-Contentious Divorce: Towards a New Conception of the Legal Process?' 63 *Modern Law Review* 177.

Eekelaar, J. (1986) 'The Emergence of Children's Rights' 6 *Oxford Journal of Legal Studies* 161.

(1992) 'The Importance of Thinking that Children Have Rights' in Alston, P., Parker, S. and Seymour, J. (eds) *Children, Rights and the Law*, Clarendon Press.

(1994) 'The Interests of the Child and the Child's Wishes: The Role of Dynamic Self-Determinism' 8 *International Journal of Law and the Family* 42.

(2006) *Family Law and Personal Life*, Oxford University Press.

Emery, R., Otto, R. and O'Donohue, W. (2005) 'A Critical Assessment of Child Custody Evaluations: Limited Science and a Flawed System' 6 *Psychological Science in the Public Interest* 1.

Ewing, J., Hunter, R., Barlow, A. and Smithson, J. (2015) 'Children's Voices: Centre-Stage or Sidelined in Out-of-Court Dispute Resolution in England and Wales' 27 *Child and Family Law Quarterly* 43.

Fortin, J. (2007) 'Children's Representation through the Looking Glass' 37 *Family Law* 500.

Fortin, J., Hunt, J. and Scanlan, L. (2012) *Taking a Longer View of Contact: The Perspectives of Young Adults Who Experienced Parental Separation in Their Youth*, University of Sussex.

Fortin, J., Ritchie, C. and Buchanan, A. (2006) 'Young Adults' Perceptions of Court-Ordered Contact' 18 *Child and Family Law Quarterly* 211.

Gee, I. (1999) 'Tales of the Unexpected – a Child's Perspective on a Family Breakup' 29 *Family Law* 49.

Gilmore, S. (2020) 'Justice and Implacable Hostility to Contact: Parental Beliefs, Factual Foundation and Justification' 136 *Law Quarterly Review* 99.

Harding, M. and Newnham, A. (2015) *How Do County Courts Share the Care of Children Between Parents? Full Report*, Nuffield Foundation.

(2017) 'Section 8 Orders on the Public–Private Law Divide' 38 *Journal of Social Welfare and Family Law* 83.

Harwood, J. (2019) '"We Don't Know What It Is We Don't Know": How Austerity Has Undermined the Courts' Access to Information in Child Arrangements Cases Involving Domestic Abuse' 31 *Child and Family Law Quarterly* 321.

Henaghan, M. (2017) 'Article 12 of the UN Convention on the Rights of Children' 25 *International Journal of Children's Rights* 537.

HM Inspectorate of Court Administration (HMICA) (2005) *Safeguarding Children in Family Proceedings*, HMICA.

(2006) *An Inspection Undertaken Between October 2005 and March 2006 of the Children and Family Court Advisory and Support Service (CAFCASS) Concerning Private Law Front-Line Practice*, HMICA.

Holt, S. (2018) 'A Voice or a Choice? Children's Views on Participating in Decisions about Post-Separation Contact with Domestically Abusive Fathers' 40 *Journal of Social Welfare and Family Law* 459.

Hunt, J. and Macleod, A. (2008) *Outcomes of Applications to Court for Contact Orders after Parental Separation or Divorce*, MOJ.

Hunter, R. (2007) 'Close Encounters of a Judicial Kind; Hearing Children's "Voices" in Family Law Proceedings' 19 *Child and Family Law Quarterly* 283.

Hunter, R., Burton, M. and Trinder, L. (2020) *Assessing the Risk of Harm to Children and Parents in Private Law Children Cases*, MOJ.

James, A. (2003) 'Squaring the Circle – the Social, Legal and Welfare Organisation of Contact' in Bainham, A., Lindley, B., Richards, M. and Trinder, L. (ed.) *Children and Their Families: Contact, Rights and Welfare*, Hart Publishing.

James, A., James, A. and McNamee, S. (2004) 'Turn Down the Volume? – Not Hearing Children in Family Proceedings' 16 *Child and Family Law Quarterly* 189.

James, A., Jenks, C. and Prout, A. (1998) *Theorizing Childhood*, Polity Press.

James, H. and Lane, D. (2018) 'The Child's Guardian – Listening and Giving Weight to Children's Views' 26 *International Journal of Children's Rights* 117.

Jones, E. and Parkinson, P. (1995) 'Child Sexual Abuse, Access and the Wishes of Children' 9 *International Journal of Law and the Family* 54.

Kaganas, F. and Diduck, A. (2004) 'Incomplete Citizens: Changing Images of Post-Separation Children' 67 *Modern Law Review* 959.

Killerby, M. (1995) 'The Draft European Convention on the Exercise of Children's Rights' 3 *International Journal on Children's Rights* 127.

King, Dame Eleanor (2017) 'Giving Children a Voice in Litigation: Are We There Yet?' 47 *Family Law* 289.

Law Commission (1988) *Review of Child Law, Guardianship and Custody*, Law Com No. 172, HC 594, Her Majesty's Stationery Office.

Lundy, L., Tobin, J. and Parkes, A. (2019) 'Article 12: The Right to Respect for the Views of the Child' in J. Tobin (ed.) *The UN Convention on the Rights of the Child: A Commentary*, Oxford University Press.

MacDonald, A. (2018) 'Hearing the Children's Objections – Some Perspectives from a Judge Hearing Cases in England and Wales' 2 *International Family Law* 113.

MacDonald, G. (2017) 'Hearing Children's Voices? Including Children's Perspectives on Their Experiences of Domestic Violence in Welfare Reports Prepared for the English Courts in Private Family Law Proceedings' 65 *Child Abuse and Neglect* 1.

Mantle, G., Moules, T. and Johnson, K. (2007) 'Whose Wishes and Feelings? Children's Autonomy and Parental Influence in Family Court Enquiries' 37 *British Journal of Social Work* 785.

Masson, J. and Winn Oakley, M. (1999) *Out of Hearing: Representing Children in Care Proceedings*, John Wiley & Sons.

McCausland, J. (2000) *Guarding Children's Interests: The Contribution of Guardians Ad Litem in Court Proceedings*, The Children's Society.

Mnookin, R. (1975) 'Child-Custody Adjudication: Judicial Functions in the Face of Indeterminacy' 39 *Law and Contemporary Problems* 226.

Munby, Sir James (2015) 'Unheard Voices: the Involvement of Children and Vulnerable People in the Family Justice System' 45 *Family Law* 895.

Murch, M., Douglas, G., Scanlan, L., Perry, A., Lisles, C., Bader, K. and Borkowski, M. (1999) *Safeguarding Children's Welfare in Uncontentious Divorce: A Study of s 41 of the Matrimonial Causes Act 1973*, Research Series No 7/99, Lord Chancellor's Department.

Ofsted (2008a) *Ofsted's Inspection of Cafcass South East Region*, Ofsted.

(2008b) *Ofsted's Inspection of Cafcass East Midlands*, Ofsted.

(2018) *Ofsted's Inspection of Cafcass as a National Organisation*, Ofsted.

O'Quigley, A. (2000) *Listening to Children's Views: The Findings and Recommendations of Recent Research*, Joseph Rowntree Foundation.

Parkinson, L. (2006) 'Child-Inclusive Family Mediation' 36 *Family Law* 483.

(2019) 'Mediating in Disputes Concerning Children' 49 *Family Law* 1069.

Private Law Working Group (2019) *A Review of the Child Arrangements Programme [PD12B FPR 2010]*, Report to the President of the Family Division.

Pryor, J. and Rodgers, B. (2001) *Children in Changing Families: Life after Parental Separation*, Blackwell Publishers.

Ruegger, M. (2001) 'Children's Experiences of the Guardian Ad Litem Service and Public Law Proceedings' in Ruegger, M. (ed.) *Hearing the Voice of the Child: the Representation of Children's Interests in Public Law Proceedings*, Russell House Publishing.

Sawyer, C. (1995) *The Rise and Fall of the Third Party: Solicitors' Assessments of the Competence of Children to Participate in Family Proceedings*, Centre for Socio-Legal Studies.

(1999) 'One Step Forward, Two Steps Back – the European Convention on the Exercise of Children's Rights' 11 *Child and Family Law Quarterly* 151.

(2000) 'An Inside Story: Professional Practices in Public Law' 30 *Family Law* 109.

Schofield, G. (1998) 'Making Sense of the Ascertainable Wishes and Feelings of Insecurely Attached Children' 10 *Child and Family Law Quarterly* 363.

Schuz, R. (2004) 'The Hague Child Abduction Convention and the United Nations Convention on the Rights of the Child' in Lødrup, P. and Modvar, E. (eds) *Family Life and Human Rights*, Gyldendal.

Smart, C., Neale, B. and Wade, A. (2001) *The Changing Experience of Childhood: Families and Divorce*, Polity Press.

(2006) 'Children's Narratives of Post-Divorce Family Life: From Individual Experience to an Ethical Disposition' 54 *The Sociological Review* 155.

Smith, A., Taylor, N. and Tapp, P. (2003) 'Rethinking Children's Involvement in Decision-Making after Parental Separation' 10 *Childhood* 201.

Stalford, H. and Hollingsworth, K. (2020) '"This Case Is about You and Your Future": Towards Judgments for Children' 83 *Modern Law Review* 1030.

Stevens, R. (2020) 'Practical Aspects to Assessing Competence in Children' 50 *Family Law* 1068.

Sturge, C. and Glaser, D. (2000) 'Contact and Domestic Violence – the Experts' Court Report' 30 *Family Law* 615.

Summerfield, A. (2018) *The Representation of Children in Public Law Proceedings*, Ministry of Justice.

Tisdall, E. K. M. and Morrison, F. (2012) 'Children's Participation in Court Proceedings When Parents Divorce or Separate: Legal Constructions and Lived Experiences' in Freeman, M. (ed.) *Law and Childhood Studies*, Oxford University Press.

Tisdall, K. (2018) 'Challenging Competency and Capacity? Due Weight to Children's Views in Family Law Proceedings' 26 *International Journal of Children's Rights* 159.

Timms, J. and Thoburn, J. (2003) *Your Shout*, NSPCC.

Trinder, L., Connolly, J., Kellett, J., Notley, C. and Swift, L. (2006) *Making Contact Happen or Making Contact Work? The Process and Outcomes of In-court Conciliation*, DCA Research Series 3/06, DCA.

Wade, A. and Smart, C. (2002) *Facing Family Change: Children's Circumstances, Strategies and Resources*, Joseph Rowntree Foundation.

Walker, J. (2014) 'Hearing the Voices of Children and Young People in Dispute Resolution Processes: Promoting a Child-Inclusive Approach' 44 *Family Law* 1577.

Wall, N. (2007) 'Separate Representation of Children' 37 *Family Law* 124.

Westcott, H. (2006) 'Child Witness Testimony: What Do We Know and Were Are We Going?' 18 *Child and Family Law Quarterly* 175.

Whybrow, J. (2004) 'Children, Guardians and Rule 9.5' 34 *Family Law* 504.

Wilson, N. (2007) 'The Ears of the Child in Family Proceedings' 37 *Family Law* 808.

13

Children's Rights and State Responsibility
Public Authorities and Poverty

(1) Introduction

Children's rights are, first and foremost, secured through obligations on the state. State action is essential to providing the legal, social and economic conditions in which children are protected from violations of their rights and provided with the environment in which they can thrive. Despite its foundational importance, the relationship between children and the state has been underexplored in the theoretical literature on children's rights. This is in part because of the influence of what Archard calls the 'liberal standard' of family life,[1] which situates primary responsibility for children with parents, who have the freedom to raise their children as they see fit within broad limits. On this model, questions about the role of the state in protecting children's rights are primarily concerned with finding the proper limits of state interference in family life.[2] Until recently, far less attention has been given to the protection of children's rights in public law. Many of the children who are most vulnerable to serious violations of their rights are those who need state protection and care precisely because they do not have a safe family environment in which to live, such as unaccompanied child migrants or those who have been removed from abusive families.[3] Providing effective and accountable state responsibility to these children is vital to protection of their rights. Yet, all children, including those who are in the secure care of loving families, need the support of the state to provide services such as education and healthcare and to pursue economic, social and environmental policies which create the conditions in which they can thrive and fulfil their potential. In this way, responsibility for children is a collaboration between families and the state: an understanding that is reflected throughout the UN Convention on the Rights of the Child (CRC).[4] Of course, the need for state services and support is not unique to children, but childhood brings with it distinct needs, such as education, and particular vulnerability to long-term harm if their basic and developmental needs are not met. For example, while poverty can blight the lives of adults and children, it can have a particularly devastating impact on

[1] D. Archard (2014) ch. 12.   [2] See Chapter 4.   [3] See Chapters 15 and 16.
[4] J. Tobin (2013) p. 425. Discussed further in Chapter 4.

children's cognitive development, educational opportunities and physical and mental health, with long-lasting consequences for their future. Children's lack of enfranchisement and their limited opportunity for participation in the political process also leaves their voices and interests in a particularly precarious position in the public sphere.[5] It is easy for the rights and interests of children to be overlooked in a political system run by, and largely for, adults. It is no surprise that it is children who have suffered much of the burden of recent austerity cuts.[6] Children's interests are also easily overlooked in decision-making by public authorities. Decisions that are ostensibly solely concerned with adults, such as deportation decisions or eligibility for benefits, may have a profound and distinct impact on their children. In all of these situations, children's rights have proved to be a tool with great potential to make children's interests visible and to require that they are taken seriously.[7]

It is in the arena of public law that some of the most tangible benefits of children's rights can be seen. Nonetheless, significant challenges remain in securing consistent and practically effective protection for children's rights in public law. First, the privatisation of many public services that affect children can create an accountability gap in which responsibility for children is fragmented. Second, there is the challenge of establishing a firm legal foundation for the rights in question. Many of the rights that are most important to children have a clear basis in the CRC, but more uncertain protection in the European Convention on Human Rights and Fundamental Freedoms (ECHR) and domestic law. This is a particular problem for those socio-economic rights, such as the right to an adequate standard of living,[8] which are often perceived as being aspirational rather than legally enforceable.[9] Finally, consideration of children's interests in public decision-making and legislating is patchy, with no systematic means of reviewing policy or legislation for compatibility with children's rights. This chapter will consider these challenges before looking specifically at the issue of child poverty. Despite some advances in embedding children's rights in public decision-making, recent cases have raised greater hurdles to requiring a child-rights approach across all aspects of government.

(2) Public Authorities and Accountability Gaps

Public authorities owe duties to children, just as they do to adults. In particular, section 6 of the Human Rights Act 1998 (HRA) states that it is unlawful for a public authority to 'act in a way which is incompatible with a Convention right', while section 7 gives 'victims' of such acts the right to bring proceedings against that authority. Child victims have been able to obtain damages[10] for

---

[5] A. Nolan (2014) ch. 2.   [6] JCHR (2015) pp. 28–31. Discussed further below.
[7] E.g. *ZH (Tanzania)* v. *Secretary of State for the Home Department* [2011] UKSC 4, [2011] 2 AC 166. Discussed further below.
[8] CRC, Art. 27.   [9] As discussed in Chapter 2.   [10] HRA 1998, s. 8.

public authority breaches of their human rights just as adults have. Such claims have been particularly important for children whose rights have been breached while in state care or when being removed into that care.[11] These claims have an important role in enforcing human rights duties and compensating children for their breach. Nonetheless, there are barriers to effective accountability which, while not unique to children, have a particularly serious and distinct impact on enforcement of children's human rights. One such barrier is the difficulty and expense of litigation. Children face financial and practical hurdles to bringing claims and further difficulties in ensuring that their voice is heard in court proceedings.[12] A further problem with litigation is that it is reliant on litigants to bring matters to the attention of the court. Litigation brought on behalf of children may fail to capture the interests and views of the children themselves if the adults or groups bringing the claims have their own aims and motivation. Those cases that do come to court are likely to concern particular individuals or groups of children, leaving the rights of others – who may well be more vulnerable – unheard.[13] While judicial claims can be an important way of obtaining redress or enforcing rights, they are insufficient alone. Full implementation of section 6 of the HRA requires public authorities proactively to take effective action to embed children's rights throughout their policies and practices.

While it is clear that public authorities owe duties to act compatibly with the rights of children, the involvement of the private sector creates accountability gaps in ensuring accountability for those rights. Private bodies, from charities to profit-making companies, are increasingly integral to public services involving children, including education, custody and social care. The involvement of the private sector is not necessarily contrary to children's rights principles;[14] it does, however, risk serious gaps in accountability and the potential for tension between obligations to children and to shareholders. The HRA attempts to plug the gap in accountability by including 'hybrid' public authorities within the scope of the duty in section 6. Anybody 'certain of whose functions are functions of a public nature'[15] will be obliged to act compatibly with Convention rights, save where 'the nature of the act is private'.[16] The inclusion of hybrid public authorities in section 6 was clearly designed to ensure that

---

[11] E.g. *Northamptonshire County Council* v. *AS and others* [2015] EWHC 199 (Fam), in which £12,000 was awarded to a child, alongside £4,000 to his mother and £1,000 to his grandparents. The child had been the victim of multiple breaches of his ECHR Arts 6 and 8 rights when removed from his mother as a very young baby and looked after under Children Act 1989, s. 20 for an extended period without proper planning, care proceedings, appointment of a guardian or assessment of his relatives as carers.

[12] Discussed in Chapter 12.

[13] See A. Nolan (2014) ch. 6 for discussion of the use of courts in relation to children's socio-economic rights.

[14] The Committee on the Rights of the Child (2013b) considers the obligations arising from business involvement in services for children. CRC, Art. 3, considered further below, states that it applies to 'private social welfare institutions' as well as public institutions.

[15] HRA 1998, s. 6(3)(b).   [16] HRA 1998, s. 6(5).

private bodies would be subject to the HRA in the delivery of public services. The application of the section has, however, been stymied both by the lack of clarity in the drafting of the provision and by the restrictive reading given to it by the House of Lords in *YL* v. *Birmingham City Council* ('*YL*').[17] In *YL*, a bare majority concluded that a private care home was not performing a 'function of a public nature' in providing care to an older woman with Alzheimer's disease whose care had been arranged and paid for by the local authority (LA) acting under their statutory obligations to her.[18] The majority considered that the fact that the state had committed to meeting an individual's needs, such as care and accommodation, was not sufficient in itself to make provision of that service a public function. Further, the use of public money to pay a fee for that service was also insufficient for the function to be regarded as public.[19] No single test for determining whether a function is 'public' was given in *YL* or the subsequent case law. Instead, courts are required to consider a range of relevant factors, including whether the body is democratically accountable and whether the function: is governmental in nature; requires special statutory power; is subsidised by public funds; and is one for which the UK government would be responsible in international law.[20] The complexity of this test adds an additional layer of difficulty and uncertainty for any child seeking to take legal action for breach of their human rights.[21] Case law has established that some private entities working with children are performing a public function, particularly when exercising a delegated statutory function.[22] It is, however, extremely unclear how this test applies to other bodies, such as private children's homes accommodating looked-after children. Such arrangements may seem analogous to those in *YL*, in that the private home is merely providing care under a contract with the LA; however, the differences in the detailed statutory language leave scope for the argument that the situations should be distinguished.[23] The fact that such a fundamental aspect of the rights

---

[17] [2007] UKHL 27, [2008] 1 AC 95.

[18] Parliament intervened through the Health and Social Care Act 2008, s. 145 and subsequently the Care Act 2014, s. 73, to deem the functions considered in *YL* to be public functions. These statutory provisions only apply to regulated care and support for adults; the majority judgment in *YL* remains the leading authority for determining whether other functions should be regarded as 'public'.

[19] Although if the function were to be subsidised through public funds this would be a relevant factor in determining that the function was 'public' in nature: *R (Weaver)* v. *London and Quadrant Housing Trust* [2009] EWCA Civ 587, [2010] 1 WLR 363.

[20] Summarised in *TH* v. *Chapter of Worcester Cathedral* [2016] EWHC 1117 (Admin), at [64].

[21] S. Choudhry (2013).

[22] *R (Cornerstone)* v. *Ofsted* [2020] EWHC 1679 (Admin): a private adoption and fostering agency was exercising a public function in recruiting potential foster carers as this act was preparatory to placing children with them under a delegated statutory duty. See also *R (C: A Minor)* v. *Secretary of State for Justice* [2008] EWHC 171 (Admin), at [40], in which it was agreed by all parties that Secure Training Centres were public authorities for the purposes of HRA 1998, s. 6.

[23] In particular, while the statutory duty in *YL* merely required the LA to *arrange* accommodation, the duties under the Children Act 1989, ss 20(1) and 22 require that accommodation is *provided* and detail the duties owed to those children.

of children in care is uncertain demonstrates the seriousness of the account-ability gap for this vulnerable group of children. Children have little choice as to whether they are taken into care and where they are accommodated: it is inequitable to impose such uncertainty on the enforceability of human rights for those accommodated by private providers.

To an extent, the difficulty in bringing human rights claims against private bodies should be mitigated by the state fulfilling its own duties to children, including through effective regulation of private providers. Such regulation is, however, not always provided[24] or applied effectively.[25] For example, there is evidence that gaps in regulation for older children in care have been exploited by companies with little or no knowledge of providing for or safeguarding children.[26] There are obvious concerns that the best interests of children can be displaced by businesses competing in a marketplace for profit and that this can further lead to serious systemic failure to provide for the needs of all children. For example, one of the most egregious failings in the current children's social care system is the acute shortage of suitable places for children with the most serious needs.[27] Reliance on private provision means that homes are increasingly located in cheaper areas of the country, rather than planned to meet the best interests of the children likely to need their services.[28] Children frequently find themselves placed far from family, where they become isolated and particularly vulnerable to exploitation and trafficking. Other children are placed in entirely unsuitable accommodation as there is no suitable provision to meet their complex needs. Such systemic failures in planning and resourcing are difficult to remedy through individual legal action: the private provider owes no duty to accommodate particular children and the LA can only work with the resources available to them in placing that child. Legal action to challenge the failures to adequately resource, plan and regulate accommodation for children would face significant hurdles to success.

The failures of planning for children's social care are indicative of a wider problem in legal enforcement of children's rights in the public sphere. As Lady Hale has observed, while the ECHR is mainly about securing freedom *from* state interference, 'children often need a great deal of state interference if they are to survive, let alone thrive'.[29] While people of all ages require some state action to secure the conditions for a healthy, safe and productive life, children are particularly reliant on the state to put in place effective systems and funding

---

[24] See Chapters 10 and 16 for discussion of unregulated accommodation for 16- and 17-year-olds. A challenge to the failure of the government to regulate such placements for this age group failed: *R (Article 39)* v. *Secretary of State for Education* [2022] EWHC 589 (Admin).

[25] See e.g. House of Commons Justice Committee (2021) detailing the failures of oversight of a contract with a private company to run a secure training facility. The Committee found it to be 'a cautionary tale of how badly an arms-length relationship between the Ministry of Justice as a client and MTC as the company hired to deliver on contract can fail to deliver basic standards of care to vulnerable children' (para. 2).

[26] Children's Commissioner (2020) p. 21.   [27] Discussed further in Chapter 16.

[28] Children's Commissioner (2019).   [29] B. Hale (2006) p. 351.

to ensure that their rights are secured in practice. As Aoife Nolan argues, children are *differently* vulnerable to adults, especially in relation to socio-economic rights.[30] Children are unlikely to be able to take action to improve their own resources[31] and are likely to suffer longer-lasting impact from periods of deprivation of resources.[32] Legal redress for state inaction faces a number of significant challenges. The more expansive socio-economic rights found in the CRC have not been incorporated into domestic law, meaning that there is no direct avenue of redress for failure to fulfil them.[33] While the European Court of Human Rights (ECtHR) has made creative use of positive obligations to offset the limited and negative drafting of the ECHR,[34] these are difficult to enforce. There remains scepticism as to the legitimacy of judicial intervention in cases of failure to fulfil those obligations, especially if there are resource implications to doing so. This scepticism has found particular voice in proposals to amend the HRA to prevent recognition of new positive obligations and to require even greater deference to public authority expertise in determining whether existing obligations have been breached.[35] If this proposed change is enacted, it will create even higher hurdles to those seeking to use the courts to challenge failure to fulfil children's rights in practice.

While court proceedings can have an important role to play in enforcing children's rights, there are significant practical and legal obstacles to many children seeking legal redress. Children's rights and interests are more likely to be secured in practice if they are embedded in public decision-making, planning and resource allocation.

(3) Public Decision-Making and Children's Rights

(A) Children and Public Authority Decisions

One of the most significant challenges for children's rights and public decision-making is ensuring that children are visible to decision-makers. Children's interests may be deeply affected by state action or inaction, just as those of adults may be. The decision of an immigration official to deport the child's parents,[36] a new welfare policy that puts the family into significant poverty[37] or refusal of planning permission for the family home[38] all have the potential fundamentally to harm the interests of the child. As it is adults who tend to be the owners of property, recipients of payments and the subjects of decisions, it is

---

[30] A. Nolan (2014) pp. 13–21.   [31] See discussion in Chapter 10.
[32] See discussion of children's rights and poverty below.   [33] Discussed in Chapter 2.
[34] Discussed in Chapter 2. E.g. the state is not only required to refrain from subjecting children to inhuman or degrading treatment, but also to have effective systems for protecting children from abuse or neglect at the hand of others: *Z* v. *United Kingdom* [2001] 2 FLR 612.
[35] Bill of Rights Bill 117, Session 2022–23 cl. 5.
[36] *ZH (Tanzania)* v. *Secretary of State for the Home Department* [2011] UKSC 4, [2011] 2 AC 166.
[37] *R (SG)* v. *Secretary of State for Work and Pensions* [2015] UKSC 16, [2015] 1 WLR 1449.
[38] *Stevens* v. *Secretary of State for Communities and Local Government* [2013] EWHC 792 (Admin).

easy for the impact on children to be overlooked. Further, the ability of children to influence these decisions, or to be represented within the decision-making process, is often extremely limited. Children are also put in a particularly vulnerable position if their interests are adversely affected by a decision, as they have limited ability to take action to change their circumstances and avoid disadvantage. While the interests of many children will be represented by their parents, this is often insufficient. Not all parents have the will or resources to represent their children's interests effectively and, even when they do, the characterisation of those interests by the parent may be misguided, selfish or at odds with the child's own distinct interests. Further, many of the most vulnerable children do not have stable adult care, or have carers whose own position means that they are unable to engage in the decision-making process. In still more cases, the interests of children may be at risk precisely because of the decisions of their parents. For these reasons, careful consideration of the rights and interests of children in public decision-making is vital to protecting children in practice.

While public authorities are under a duty to act compatibly with the rights protected under the HRA,[39] the HRA itself does not directly address the question of how children's interests should be taken into account by public authorities. In contrast, the CRC and the General Comments of the Committee on the Rights of the Child (the 'Committee') give specific and detailed attention to the implementation of children's rights in public decision-making.[40] A particularly important obligation is found in Article 3(1), which requires that:

> In all actions concerning children, whether undertaken by public or private social welfare institutions, courts of law, administrative authorities or legislative bodies, the best interests of the child shall be a primary consideration.[41]

The requirement that children's best interests are treated as an important consideration in all actions concerning them – whether or not they are the subject of the decision – is vital to making children visible in public decision-making. Although Article 3 itself refers only to children's 'best interests', the Committee has been clear that the 'concept of the child's best interests is aimed at ensuring both the full and effective enjoyment of all the rights recognized in the Convention'.[42] If implemented in this way, Article 3 provides a conduit for

---

[39] Human Rights Act 1998 (HRA), s. 6(1). Public authorities are, of course, also subject to specific statutory obligations and private law duties that can protect children's rights in practice, particularly in those areas that are directly concerned with children. E.g. those obligations concerned with children in care are considered in Chapter 16 and education in Chapter 14.

[40] See esp. CRC, Art. 4, which requires states to 'undertake all appropriate legislative, administrative, and other measures' to implement the CRC; and Committee on the Rights of the Child (2016b), concerning children's rights in public budgeting. The requirements for implementation of the CRC in policy-making are considered further by B. Byrne and L. Lundy (2019).

[41] See also Charter of Fundamental Rights of the European Union, Art. 24(2), which imposes a similar obligation to those decisions that fall within its scope.

[42] Committee on the Rights of the Child (2013a) para. 4.

a full children's rights analysis of policy and legislation, as well as ensuring that children are considered in individual decisions that affect them. It is through this innovative use of this obligation that progress has been made in requiring that children's rights and interests are taken more seriously across a wide range of policy areas. That progress has, however, been patchy. While use of Article 3 has substantially increased the attention given to children's interests in some areas, in others that progress has been limited. There are two main challenges to using Article 3 to drive a legal obligation to consider children's interests systematically in administrative decision-making: first, the difficulty in giving rights-based, coherent and practically applicable meaning to the broad obligation contained in Article 3; and, second, the problem of translating the obligation into enforceable domestic law, given that the CRC is an international treaty that has not been incorporated into domestic law. Each of these issues will be addressed in turn.

(B) Interpreting Article 3 of the CRC

Article 3 of the CRC is a wide-ranging right that applies across a diverse range of situations. The wide application of Article 3 is both its strength and its weakness. If applied properly, it can embed children's rights throughout public decision-making and give children's interests a visibility that they often lack. Nonetheless, to accommodate its expansive application, the article is drafted in broad and imprecise terms, which creates uncertainty in determining its precise requirements and application. In response, the Committee has given extensive guidance on the interpretation and application of Article 3, which while not directly binding, carries significant weight.[43] The Committee treats children's best interests as a threefold concept: a substantive right of children to have their best interests assessed and treated as a primary consideration; an interpretive tool to resolve ambiguity in legal provisions; and a procedural rule to ensure that children's interests are fully considered in decisions that concern them.[44]

To understand the requirements of Article 3, three central points on its drafting require further consideration. First, the article applies to all forms of public decision-making, from judicial and administrative decisions concerning an individual child to the creation of generally applicable legislation or policy that will affect disparate groups of children.[45] Article 3(1) is deliberately framed to include *all* actions[46] concerning children; this covers not only

---

[43] Committee on the Rights of the Child (2013a). In *R (AB)* v. *Secretary of State for the Home Department* [2021] UKSC 28, [2021] 3 WLR 494, the Supreme Court adopted a sceptical approach to the use of the General Comment in interpreting the application of Art. 3 in ECHR and UK law, discussed in Chapter 3.

[44] Committee on the Rights of the Child (2013a) para. 6.   [45] Ibid. para. 14(b).

[46] Ibid. paras 17–18; although the term is drafted positively, it is clear that the Committee also uses the term to cover omissions.

actions that directly affect children, but also those that indirectly do so. As such, the principle has force beyond decisions that focus on children. It extends to decisions concerning other family members that indirectly impact children and to wider policies (for example, on housing, the environment and transport).[47] This means that, for the Committee, Article 3(1) applies in principle to all actions and omissions that directly or indirectly affect individual children, groups of children or children in general. On this understanding, almost any administrative or legislative act could be read as falling under Article 3(1).

Second, the term 'a primary consideration' does not equate to the domestic[48] paramountcy principle, which requires that children's interests are the determining factor in judicial decisions concerning their upbringing. The CRC likewise gives children's interests decisive status in relation to decisions that are directly concerned with their upbringing, such as separation from their parents.[49] There is a clear contrast between the role of best interests in these decisions and the lesser standard of best interests as 'a primary consideration' in the more diffuse category of 'actions concerning children' in Article 3. To treat children's interests as a primary consideration does not require those interests to displace all other considerations. Instead, the interests of the child must be treated as a factor of 'substantial importance'[50] with no other consideration to be treated as of greater *intrinsic* importance, even if, on the facts, the interests of children in question are outweighed by those other considerations.[51] The use of the indefinite, rather than definite, article is also significant. As Michael Freeman notes, during the negotiations, the drafting was altered from 'the' to 'a' primary consideration in response to the broadening out of the circumstances in which Article 3(1) applied.[52] This implies that there may be more than one primary consideration in relation to a particular decision. Article 3 does not require a decision that maximises the child's best interests, but it does require that those interests are assessed and considered as a substantially important factor in the decision-making process.

---

[47] Ibid. [19]; P. Alston (1994) p. 14.

[48] Children Act 1989, s. 1; Adoption and Children Act 2002, s. 1. The ECtHR has been rather less careful in distinguishing between the terms 'primary' and 'paramount'. See e.g. *Neulinger and Shuruk* v. *Switzerland* (2012) 54 EHRR 31, at [134]–[135], in which the terms appear to be used interchangeably.

[49] CRC, Art. 9(1). See also: Art. 21, which requires that any system of adoption to recognise the child's rights as paramount; and Art. 9(3), giving the right to parents and children who are separated from one another the right to regular, direct contact except if it is contrary to the child's best interests.

[50] *SS (Nigeria)* v. *Secretary of State for the Home Department* [2013] EWCA Civ 550, [2014] 1 WLR 998, at [44].

[51] *ZH (Tanzania)* v. *Secretary of State for the Home Department* [2011] UKSC 4, [2011] 2 AC 166, at [25] (Baroness Hale); *Zoumbas* v. *Secretary of State for the Home Department* [2013] UKSC 74, [2013] 1 WLR 3690, at [10] (Lord Hodge).

[52] M. Freeman (2007) p. 45; Office of the UN High Commissioner for Human Rights (2007) pp. 345–8.

Finally, the meaning of the term 'best interests' is pivotal to the article. There is a risk that the term is so vague and open to subjective interpretation that decision-makers may frame almost any decision in a way that is said to promote children's interests generally, even if the decision undermines individual children's well-being. This risk is particularly apparent in the case law on child poverty, in which decisions that place individual children into greater poverty have been justified on the basis that children as a class would benefit from a 'long-term shift in welfare culture'.[53] The Committee has been alert to this risk and has emphasised that best interests must be viewed in the light of the wider rights contained in the CRC: 'an adult's judgment of a child's best interests cannot override the obligation to respect all the child's rights under the Convention'.[54] Of particular importance is the child's right to be heard under Article 12 of the CRC, which is regarded by the Committee as inextricably linked to a determination of her best interests,[55] meaning that those children whose interests are affected should be given the opportunity to explain their own understanding of the impact of the decision on their rights and interests. Further, the child's interests should be assessed on an individualised basis with sufficient evidence and information on which a determination of the child's interests can be made.[56] If this approach to 'best interests' is adopted, the result should be an evidence-based approach, which enhances children's rights and includes them within the decision-making process. If it is not followed, the breadth of the term 'best interests' means that it may be reduced to a rhetorical device that displaces serious engagement with children's fundamental rights.

Overall, the Committee's guidance is clear that children's interests must be assessed in accordance with their wider rights and treated as a significant factor in any decision that directly or indirectly affects children. Exactly what this requires in a particular scenario can, as explored below, be more difficult to pinpoint in practice. Nonetheless, if applied in the manner envisaged by the Committee, Article 3 can have a transformative impact on the way in which children's rights and interests are treated by public authorities, in government policy and in legislating. Compliance with Article 3 would make the impact on children visible regardless of whether they are the direct object of the measure. It would ensure that children's interests are taken seriously, despite the weakness of children's position in the democratic process. Article 3 also provides the gateway for assessment of the impact of the full range of children's rights in international law. The Committee has, however, been critical of the UK's failure to ensure that this right is consistently interpreted and applied in all

---

[53] Discussed further below. See esp. *R (SG)* v. *Secretary of State for Work and Pensions* [2015] UKSC 16, [2015] 1 WLR 1449; and contrast Lord Hughes at [153] with Baroness Hale at [226], who describes the government's argument as a misunderstanding of Art. 3(1).

[54] Committee on the Rights of the Child (2013a) para. 4.

[55] Ibid. paras 43–5, (2009) paras 70–4.

[56] *Jeunesse* v. *Netherlands* (2015) 60 EHRR 17, at [120].

areas affecting children.[57] In order to address these criticisms, the obligation requires a secure and consistent basis in domestic law. As demonstrated in the next section, that domestic basis is limited and appears increasingly precarious.

(C) Public Decision-making and Children's Rights: Domestic Law

The CRC is an international treaty that has not been incorporated into domestic law and, as the UK is a dualist system, it is well-established orthodoxy that an unincorporated treaty is not directly applicable in domestic law.[58] To be enforced effectively, it is necessary for the obligations it contains to be incorporated into domestic law. This challenge has been taken up with some enthusiasm in both Wales and Scotland, as both nations have introduced effective obligations to embed children's rights within public decision-making.[59] Attempts to introduce an equivalent measure for England have so far failed.[60] Instead, there are limited statutory obligations applicable in specific contexts. The Children Act 2004 imposes an obligation on specified bodies to 'make arrangements for ensuring that their functions are discharged having regard to the need to safeguard and promote the welfare of children'.[61] The Borders, Citizenship and Immigration Act 2009 puts the same obligation on the Secretary of State in relation to immigration, asylum and nationality.[62] These provisions were both intended to further the UK's obligations under Article 3, although the statutory wording falls some way short of the requirements of that article. First, the provisions only apply to specified agencies, not to the broad range of 'administrative authorities and legislative bodies' covered by Article 3; this significantly curtails the policy areas to which the obligations apply. Second, each obligation only requires the bodies in question to have 'regard to' children's welfare rather than to treat children's interests as

---

[57] Committee on the Rights of the Child (2016a) para. 10. Discussed further in Chapter 3.

[58] In *R (SG)* v. *Secretary of State for Work and Pensions* [2015] UKSC 16, [2015] 1 WLR 1449, at [235]–[257], Lord Kerr advanced an argument that the obligation was directly enforceable in domestic law on the basis of legitimate expectations. While this is an interesting argument, as Lord Kerr himself recognised, it is controversial and unlikely to find favour in the courts of this country, at least at present. The Supreme Court has since reaffirmed the importance of the principle that the dualist nature of the UK constitution means that an unincorporated treaty, such as the CRC, is not directly enforceable in domestic law: *R (SC)* v. *Work and Pensions Secretary* [2021] UKSC 26, [2021] 3 WLR 428, at [76]–[78], discussed further below.

[59] See esp. The Rights of Children and Young Persons (Wales) Measure 2011 and Children and Young People (Scotland) Act 2014, esp. ss 1–2. Discussed further in Chapter 3. A more ambitious attempt to incorporate much of the CRC into Scottish law was found to be outside of the legislative competence of the Scottish Parliament: *Re Attorney-General's Reference, United Nations Convention on the Rights of the Child (Incorporation) (Scotland) Bill* [2021] UKSC 42, [2021] 1 WLR 5106.

[60] Discussed in Chapter 3.

[61] Children Act 2004, s. 11(2): the duty is imposed on the bodies specified in s. 11(1).

[62] Borders, Citizenship and Immigration Act 2009, s. 55.

a 'primary consideration'.[63] Third, the requirement is merely to 'make arrangements', not actually to secure that welfare and safeguarding of the children in question. The duties under the 2004 and 2009 Acts are therefore worded in a way that appears to fall far short of the requirements in Article 3 of the CRC.[64] These duties also differ from those in the Welsh and Scottish legislative obligations, as the focus is on the child's welfare without direct reference to the broad range of rights protected by the CRC. Further, unlike the provisions concerning the devolved administrations in Wales and Scotland, there is no obligation at a ministerial level, save in relation to immigration. Finally, the legislation itself does not lay down requirements for administrative implementation (for example, the detailed reporting and Children's Rights Impact Assessment (CRIA) approach used in the Welsh Measure). Whether or not these duties are able to be effective in improving children's interests and securing compliance with Article 3 depends on judicial interpretation and administrative implementation.

Despite the shortcomings in the drafting of the statutory obligations, there have been notable benefits for children in their application. As the obligations appear to have been enacted in order to meet the UK's international commitments under Article 3, there is a strong argument that it is the intention of Parliament that they be interpreted in line with it.[65] This argument has been influential; the Court of Appeal has observed that although the domestic obligation uses 'different language, it is conventional and convenient to refer to a duty under section 55 as being to have regard, as a primary consideration, to the best interests of the child'.[66] Interpreted in this way, the statutory obligations are a powerful tool for ensuring that children's interests are identified and treated as an important factor in decision-making affecting them. The foundational Supreme Court decision in *ZH (Tanzania) v. Secretary of State for the Home Department*[67] is a good example of the way in which the statutory duty gives children's interests prominence even if they are not directly the subject of the decision. That case concerned a decision to deport a mother following a number of failed applications for asylum. If she were removed, her two children, British citizens aged 12 and 9, would inevitably have to accompany her. The mother's deportation would in effect require them to leave the only home they had ever known and deprive them of their

---

[63] This drafting is also less onerous than the 'due regard' provisions in The Rights of Children and Young Persons (Wales) Measure 2011.

[64] JCHR (2004).

[65] *Nzolameso* v. *Westminster City Council* [2015] UKSC 22, [2015] 2 All ER 942, at [28]–[29]; *R (HC)* v. *Secretary of State for Work and Pensions* [2017] UKSC 73, [2019] AC 845, at [49]. This is particularly clear in relation to Borders, Citizenship and Immigration Act 2009, s. 55, as the obligation was created as a direct consequence of the withdrawal of the UK's immigration reservation to the CRC.

[66] *R (Project for the Registration of British Citizens)* v. *Home Secretary, Speaker Intervening* [2021] EWCA Civ 193, [2021] 1 WLR 3049, at [70].

[67] [2011] UKSC 4, [2011] 2 AC 166.

rights to be educated and brought up within the country of their citizenship. Once these rights were considered and their interests given weight as a 'primary consideration', it was clear that the decision to deport the mother was disproportionate to them. The decision in *ZH (Tanzania)* had a profound impact in making children's interests visible and giving them force in decision-making processes that are usually focused on adults. The impact of the statutory obligations is not limited to individual cases, but also applies to matters of general policy affecting children. For example, *R (Project for the Registration of British Citizens)* v. *Home Secretary*[68] concerned a challenge to the imposition of a high mandatory fee for children applying for citizenship, an amount that was unaffordable for many children and their families, thus rendering their right to apply nugatory. The failure of the Home Secretary to identify and consider the interests of affected children was a breach of the obligation under section 55. As these examples illustrate, the statutory obligations have had a significant role in requiring children's interests to be identified and treated with significant weight in the policy areas to which they apply.

The Supreme Court in *ZH (Tanzania)* did not rely on the statutory obligation alone: at least as much importance was placed on the use of the CRC by the ECtHR in interpreting the ECHR in children's cases.[69] The decision to remove the mother clearly concerned the children's ECHR Article 8 rights, as well as those of the mother. In evaluating those rights, Lady Hale considered that:

> it is clear from the recent jurisprudence that the Strasbourg court will expect national authorities to apply article 3.1 of UNCRC and treat the best interests of a child as 'a primary consideration'.[70]

This line of reasoning was important as it expanded the requirement to treat children's interests as a primary consideration beyond those bodies covered by the statutory obligations, to all public authorities fulfilling their duties under the HRA. This approach has been applied in a series of decisions advancing children's rights in a wide range of areas of public decision-making, including: extradition;[71] planning;[72] welfare benefits;[73] and prisoners' leave.[74] Nevertheless, later Supreme Court cases have adopted a much more restricted approach to exactly how Article 3 should be used in interpreting ECHR rights. While Lady Hale in *ZH (Tanzania)* stated that Strasbourg expected national authorities to *apply* Article 3, in the latter case of *Mathieson*, the court's finding that there had been a breach of Article 3 was merely said to *harmonise* with the conclusion that

---

[68] [2021] EWCA Civ 193, [2021] 1 WLR 3049. This decision was subject to an appeal before the Supreme Court on other grounds.

[69] See Chapter 2.   [70] [2011] UKSC 4, [2011] 2 AC 166, at [25].

[71] *H(H)* v. *Deputy Prosecutor of the Italian Republic* [2012] UKSC 25, [2013] 1 AC 338.

[72] *Stevens* v. *Secretary of State for Communities and Local Government* [2013] EWHC 792 (Admin).

[73] *Mathieson* v. *Secretary of State for Work and Pensions* [2015] UKSC 47, [2015] 1 WLR 3250.

[74] *R (MP)* v. *Secretary of State for Justice* [2012] EWHC 214 (Admin), esp. at [170].

had already been reached without reference to it.[75] Even this more limited role for Article 3 of the CRC was rejected in *R (SC) v. Work and Pensions Secretary*,[76] considered further below. Lord Reed concluded that Strasbourg did not *apply* international treaties as if they were incorporated into the ECHR and did not purport to determine whether states were in breach of those obligations.[77] While Strasbourg jurisprudence had treated children's interests as a relevant factor in applying the ECHR, there was nothing to require domestic courts to assess whether there had been a breach of the CRC itself. This case appears to have been intended to place firm limits on the relevance of Article 3 to HRA duties. This conclusion is reinforced by the Supreme Court's decision in *R (AB) v. Secretary of State for the Home Department*,[78] which decried the previous approach of treating General Comments from the Committee on the Rights of the Child as 'authoritative'.[79] As a result, it has become far more difficult to use the HRA to hold public authorities to account for failure to consider the impact of decisions on children or to give children's interests 'primary' weight. Whether these cases will also limit the use of Article 3 of the CRC where the statutory obligations apply is not yet clear. As the clear intention of Parliament in enacting these provisions was to further the UK's compliance with its international commitments under Article 3 of the CRC, there is a strong argument that those obligations should be interpreted in line with the developing international law.

Article 3 of the CRC is not a panacea for children's rights in public decision-making. Any provision based solely on children's interests risks inviting a paternalistic assessment that can obscure their status as holders of legal and human rights.[80] Unless applied rigorously and with close attention to the requirements of international law, there is a risk that children's 'best interests' can simply become a cover for advancing the aims of adults. This is especially clear in cases in which parents seek to avoid detrimental consequences for themselves by deploying a version of their child's interests that is not grounded in any objective assessment of the child's views, rights and interests.[81] Nonetheless, Article 3 has provided an effective means of making children's interests visible in public decision-making and requiring their interests to be taken seriously. Recent judicial scepticism as to its use will make it more difficult to secure children's rights in practice. The best way to address this weakness would be through the introduction of a general statutory

---

[75] *Mathieson v. Secretary of State for Work and Pensions* [2015] UKSC 47, [2015] 1 WLR 3250. See also *Re McLaughlin* [2018] UKSC 48, [2018] 1 WLR 4250, at [40], in which the conclusion that there had been a breach of ECHR, Art. 14 was 'reinforced' by a number of international measures, including CRC, Art. 3.

[76] [2021] UKSC 26, [2021] 3 WLR 428.   [77] Ibid. at [72]–[86].

[78] [2021] UKSC 28, [2021] 3 WLR 494.   [79] Ibid. at [64]–[67].   [80] J. Fortin (2011).

[81] E.g. in *H v. Lord Advocate* [2012] UKSC 24, [2013] 1 AC 413, a father resisting extradition had a history of child sexual abuse, with victims including one of his children. His argument that his children's best interests would be harmed by his extradition was rather generously described by the Supreme Court as, 'at best, very weak'.

duty to require all ministers and public authorities to have due regard to children's rights and best interests in matters concerning them. At present, it seems very unlikely that there is the political will to extend the existing statutory duties. For decisions that are outside of the current scope of those duties, engagement with children's rights and interests will depend to a significant extent on the approach chosen by the department or public authority involved. As the next section demonstrates, this leaves children vulnerable to majoritarian neglect, especially in decisions that involve economic and social policy or primary legislation.

(4) Child Poverty

(A) The Problem of Poverty

Child poverty[82] is one of the most complex and intractable problems facing children; it is also one of the most serious. Growing up in poverty not only blights children's lives during childhood, but also impacts on children's physical, social and educational development in ways that can inflict significant damage on their future life chances. Although the term 'poverty' does not appear in the CRC, it is now well established that addressing child poverty is a significant children's rights issue, affecting multiple protected rights, and that those rights provide an important framework for responding to child poverty.[83] The text of the CRC includes some tensions that have posed challenges to those seeking to use it to address child poverty. First, the most important rights addressing poverty, such as the right to an adequate standard of living,[84] are drafted in aspirational terms and are expressly dependent on available state resources.[85] This, together with lingering concerns as to the enforceability of socioeconomic rights,[86] can create difficulties in translating these rights into concrete legal obligations. Second, the CRC generally recognises the primary role of parents in raising children and meeting their needs, with the state playing a residual and supporting role.[87] This approach is evident in the primary responsibility that the CRC accords to parents in

---

[82] There are numerous definitions and means measuring poverty: for discussion, cf. A. Minujin and S. Nandy (2012). Fundamentally, poverty is not only concerned with lack of income and resources, but also the inability to participate in society and to enjoy an adequate standard of living. The UN Committee on Economic, Social and Cultural Rights has defined poverty as 'a human condition characterized by the sustained or chronic deprivation of the resources, capabilities, choices, security and power necessary for the enjoyment of an adequate standard of living and other civil, cultural, economic, political and social rights': UN Committee on Economic, Social and Cultural Rights (2001) para. 8. The (now repealed) Child Poverty Act 2010, discussed further below, attempted to capture the different dimensions of poverty by setting targets according to both absolute and relative low income and in relation to experience of material deprivation.

[83] A. Nolan (2020).   [84] CRC, Art. 27, discussed further below.   [85] CRC, Art. 4.
[86] A. Nolan (2014) ch. 1.
[87] See Chapter 4 for broader discussion of the role of parents in the CRC.

providing for their children's living standards.[88] The causes of child poverty are, however, often located deep within the economic and social structure of the state and far beyond the reach of parents to address without extensive state action. It is the obligations that the CRC places on the state that are imperative in meeting the challenge of child poverty.

Considerable work has been done at an international level to develop an effective children's rights framework for addressing child poverty and the obligations of the state within that framework.[89] At a domestic level, there remains the familiar problem that the rights that are most important to child poverty have no direct equivalent within the HRA or other directly enforceable sources of domestic law. It is Article 3 of the CRC, discussed above, that provides perhaps the most promising route to bringing a children's rights response to child poverty into domestic law. Child poverty has, however, been a particular casualty of the patchy response to integrating children's rights and interests in public decision-making. Further, the courts' deferential approach to matters of social and economic policy have led to a disappointing set of defeats for litigants seeking to challenge executive reluctance to engage with children's interests in welfare reform.

The problem of child poverty requires urgent action. Serious engagement with children's rights, while it cannot solve the problem alone, provides a child-focused and robust framework with the potential for effective action. The reluctance of the government and courts to engage with that framework in this area highlights many of the obstacles to recognising and securing children's rights in practice.

(B) Child Poverty and Well-Being

Child poverty in the UK is widespread and growing. Children not only suffer deprivation and disadvantage while poverty persists.[90] A substantial body of research now demonstrates the significant threat that periods spent in poverty pose to children's lifelong well-being and life chances.[91] The impact of poverty is multifaceted, complex and serious. Poverty is associated with poorer physical and mental health throughout childhood, even impacting children before birth. Low-income families have a higher incidence of low-birth-weight babies, premature birth, poor infant growth and child mortality.[92] The impact on physical and mental health persists throughout childhood and into adulthood, when there is a greater risk of early death for those adults who experienced deprivation in childhood.[93] The impact of poverty on children is not limited to health. An inability to access the resources which the vast majority of parents

---

[88] In particular, CRC, Art. 27(2).   [89] A. Nolan (2020).
[90] E.g. A. Knight et al. (2018) consider children's own experiences of poverty and hunger.
[91] Inter alia: S. Wickham *et al.* (2016); T. Ridge (2006) pp. 24–32; HCWPC (2008) ch. 2; P. Attree (2006).
[92] A. Weightman *et al.* (2012).   [93] B. Galobardes *et al.* (2008).

believe to be necessary can lead to social exclusion from peers and harm children's social development and future horizons.[94] Higher levels of truancy, lower self-esteem and greater likelihood of being involved in criminal behaviour can be added to this list.[95] Poverty is also linked to poorer cognitive development and educational outcomes for children. There are already stark differences in the development and school-readiness of children from the lowest and highest income groups as they start school. These differences persist throughout education and are evident in exam attainment for each group.[96] Recent research also suggests that child poverty is associated with structural differences in several areas of brain development and that this may explain at least some of the differences in cognitive development and educational achievement.[97] The research basis that underpins these findings is complex, but a clear picture emerges that growing up in poverty affects all aspects of children's well-being and can have a long-lasting effect that persists beyond childhood and well into adult life.[98]

Poverty is a complex problem that has proved difficult to solve, in part because the means by which these harms are caused is not yet well understood. While the correlation between poverty and these negative outcomes is clear, the extent to which poverty *causes* them has been more difficult to determine. It might be argued that it is not poverty itself that causes these harms to children, but that related factors, such as parental characteristics, are causally related to both poverty and negative outcomes for the children. This is important as, if this is the case, a policy that seeks to raise household income may be ineffective to raise standards for children, as it would fail to address the root cause of the problem. While it is clearly the case that this multifaceted problem will require multifaceted solutions, there is now a substantial body of evidence that raising family income itself has 'significant positive effects' across the range of children's outcomes, including cognitive development and educational achievement, social and behavioural development and children's health, particularly for those in the very poorest households.[99] For these households, additional income is associated with greater available material resources to meet children's basic needs, and a reduction in family stress that itself can cause many negative outcomes for children. While there is no simple solution to this complex problem, the evidence suggests that raising household income and reducing child poverty will have significant, measurable effects on children's development and well-being and is an important aspect of addressing child poverty, alongside other measures, including securing access to high-quality health and education services.

---

[94] C.-A. Hooper *et al.* (2007) pp. 18–20; P. Attree (2006).   [95] HCWPC (2008) ch. 2.

[96] S. Wickham *et al.* (2016) summarise the evidence.   [97] E.g. N. Hair *et al.* (2015).

[98] J. Blanden and S. Gibbons (2006) p. 7; see also chs 5 and 6, for their assessment of the correlation between childhood poverty, lack of employment and low education.

[99] K. Cooper and K. Stewart (2017).

(C) Poverty and International Children's Rights

While there is no specific right to be free from poverty contained in the CRC, or international human rights law, it is clear that poverty impacts on multiple rights held by children. Poverty both arises from, and contributes to, failure to secure children's rights across a wide range of facets of their lives.[100] The consequences of child poverty have clear implications for children's rights to survival and development,[101] enjoyment of the highest attainable standard of health,[102] education[103] and access to recreation and cultural participation.[104] Children in poverty are also at higher risk of maltreatment and neglect[105] and being taken into state care.[106] Poverty also impacts on certain groups disproportionately to others:[107] responses to poverty require careful consideration of the impact on children with particular needs.[108] Other rights, such as the right to benefit from social security, will be relevant to the responses to poverty,[109] while the right to be heard[110] requires that children's own perceptions play an important role in understanding and responding to poverty. Given the range of rights affected by poverty, it is perhaps unsurprising that international and regional organisations, such as the European Union,[111] have increasingly turned to children's rights in forming the framework in which they respond to poverty.

Poverty affects all these facets of children's rights, but it is Article 27 of the CRC, which guarantees a right to an adequate standard of living, that is of particular importance in assessing state obligations to children in poverty. Importantly, in defining the meaning of an 'adequate' standard of living, the article goes beyond the child's basic needs for food, clothing and housing, and instead focuses on the standard of living needed 'for the child's physical, mental, spiritual, moral and social development'.[112] It follows that the right reflects the importance that the CRC places on childhood as a stage of development and also the threat that poverty can pose to all aspects of that development.[113] Despite the strength of this child-focus, the drafting of Article 27 also demonstrates two key difficulties in securing state protection of children's rights: the primacy given to the role of parents; and the imprecision of the obligation on the state.

---

[100] See A. Nolan (2020) for more detailed discussion on this point.   [101] CRC, Art. 6.
[102] CRC, Art. 24.   [103] CRC, Art. 28.   [104] CRC, Art. 31.   [105] CRC, Arts 19 and 39.
[106] CRC, Art. 9.   [107] CRC, Art. 2.
[108] E.g. children with disabilities: UN Convention on the Rights of Persons with Disabilities, esp. Art. 7.
[109] CRC, Art. 26.   [110] CRC, Art. 12.   [111] EU Commission (2013).
[112] CRC, Art. 27(1). Contrast the equivalent right in the International Covenant on Economic, Social and Cultural Rights, Art. 11(1), which instead recognises 'the right of everyone to an adequate standard of living for himself and his family, including adequate food, clothing and housing, and to the continuous improvement of living conditions'. Children are, of course, also protected by this right, an important point as CRC, Art. 27(1) omits the right to 'continuous improvement of living conditions'.
[113] See further A. Nolan (2019).

The CRC reflects the view that responsibility for children is a collaboration between parents and the state, with the state role being one of support for the primary responsibility of parents.[114] In consequence, its provisions are conservative and reflect the way in which childcare is currently organised throughout most of the world. It accepts that children are brought up in family units and that governments should leave them in a degree of privacy, expecting the parents to provide for children out of their own resources. In this way, the CRC limits state intervention in family life, but also limits expectations on the provision granted by the state. The CRC's cautious approach is also reflected in Article 27(2), which sets the expectation that parents have primary responsibility for securing adequate living standards for their children. English law and policy also adopts a conservative approach to parental responsibilities. From 1601,[115] the state expected reimbursement from a father for any public support paid over to a mother for a child who could and should have been maintained by him, and vice versa. In the modern law, this duty applies to parents of either sex: section 1 of the Child Support Act 1991 firmly states that parents are responsible for maintaining their own children. Those caring for children may also incur criminal liability if they ill-treat or neglect them[116] and, more specifically, a parent is deemed to have criminally neglected a child by failing to provide him or her with adequate food, clothing, medical aid or lodging.[117] In recognising parents as having the *primary* responsibility for providing for their children, neither the CRC nor domestic law expects parents to have *sole* responsibility for doing so. Article 27(2) expressly recognises that parents' responsibility will be limited by 'their abilities and financial capacities'. The state is therefore obliged in Article 27(3) to take appropriate measures to support parents in meeting their children's right to an adequate standard of living. In casting the role of the state as one of providing secondary support to the primary responsibility of parents, the CRC risks allowing states to avoid taking responsibility for the economic and social structures in which child poverty proliferates. In reality, the role of the state is vital to providing the conditions in which parents are able to secure adequate living standards for their children.

One important aspect of state responsibility for children's living standards is in ensuring that parents do meet their responsibilities. Ultimately, if parents persistently fail to meet their children's basic needs, the state may intervene to protect children from neglect through the criminal law[118] and by seeking the court's authority to remove them into LA care. Many more children are left in poverty when one parent fails to meet his responsibilities to his child, leaving

---

[114] See esp. CRC, Art. 18. Discussed further in Chapter 4.

[115] The date when the Elizabethan Poor Law was established.

[116] Under Children and Young Persons Act (CYPA) 1933, s. 1(1).

[117] CYPA 1933, s. 1(2)(a) imposes criminal liability on 'a parent or other person legally liable to maintain a child or young person'.

[118] CYPA 1933, s. 1 requires that the neglect is 'wilful': R. Taylor and L. Hoyano (2012).

the other parent struggling to provide alone.[119] Article 27(4) obliges states to take 'all appropriate measures' to recover unpaid maintenance; given the scale of maintenance payments that are uncollected and remain outstanding,[120] it is difficult to conclude that this obligation is being met. An increasing emphasis on children's rights might have led to the state taking a greater interest in the extent to which parents who break up fulfil their obligation to maintain their children. There has, however, been a persistent failure to view payment of maintenance as a matter of children's rights.[121] Instead, the law continues to adopt the view that it is up to individual parents to decide for themselves how to redistribute their resources between them. The current system is based on encouraging even the poorest parents to make their own family-based arrangements, with the focus of the state role on supporting parents to do so.[122] In this way, the maintenance obligation owed by parents to their children is deemed to be part of their private relationship with each other rather than an obligation owed to the child.[123] Parents who 'fail' to make private arrangements may apply to the Child Maintenance Service for help to 'agree, establish and maintain payments',[124] but those parents are charged for this help as an 'incentive' to encourage them to collaborate.[125] Such an approach leaves the millions of children still living in poverty entirely at the mercy of their parents' future arrangements, with the state taking no obvious interest in what is agreed, whether it is paid and whether it either reflects children's actual needs or their parents' financial circumstances.[126]

The fact that parents have the primary responsibility to provide for their children's living standards should not obscure the fact that the economic and social structures of the society in which they live will have a profound impact on their ability to meet those standards in practice. The support of the state is of vital importance to many parents if they are to be able to access the secure housing, income and resources needed to provide for their children. The CRC is not only concerned with state provision of direct support to individual families: the Committee has been increasingly clear that Article 27 is also

---

[119] C. Bryson *et al.* (2012).

[120] In 2017, the Department for Work and Pensions identified £3.7 billion of unpaid maintenance that had accumulated in the decade 1993–2003 under the auspices of the Child Support Agency and proposed that much of this debt be written off: DWP (2017).

[121] The development of the law on maintenance payments and the neglect of children's rights within that development is considered in more detail in ch. 9 of the 3rd edition of this book. See also Baroness Hale of Richmond in *R (on the application of Kehoe)* v. *Secretary of State for Work and Pensions* [2005] UKHL 48, [2005] 4 All ER 905, at [50]–[69], for a brief history of the parental obligation to maintain children from the perspective of the rights of children.

[122] DWP (2012a) p. 1.   [123] N. Wikeley (2006) chs 3–4.   [124] D. Henshaw (2006) para. 7.

[125] DWP (2012a) p. 18.

[126] It is estimated that 44 per cent of separated families have no arrangement for maintenance in place. Of those that do, the majority (38 per cent of separated families) have a family-based arrangement, leaving 18 per cent who use the statutory service. In total, around half of children in separated families receive no maintenance from their non-resident parent: House of Commons Committee of Public Accounts (2022).

concerned with the way in which children's living standards are taken into account in allocating resources and setting policy.[127] It is on this basis that the Committee has criticised the impact of the UK's policies on tax credits, welfare reform and homelessness on child poverty.[128] Nonetheless, it is perhaps inevitable that the right is phrased in a way that appears to give a significant degree of latitude to the state in determining how to apply it. In particular, the obligation to take 'appropriate' measures to assist parents applies in so far as it is 'in accordance with national conditions and within the [state's] means'.[129] This qualification appears to be looser than the general obligation of implementation in Article 4, which requires states to take measures concerning economic, social and cultural rights 'to the maximum extent of their resources', although the Committee has been keen to interpret them in harmony with one another.[130] Further, as Aoife Nolan observes, 'the definition of a standard of living and the measurement of its adequacy are not issues on which agreement can be easily achieved either within or between states'.[131] The reallocation of resources and the relative responsibilities of parents and state are politically contentious issues that are not conducive to bright-line human rights obligations. The CRC does, however, provide an increasingly clear framework and set of minimum standards around which poverty can be addressed.

The rights contained in the CRC are playing an increasingly important role in framing the response to poverty on the international stage. Domestically, the impact has been far more disappointing. Despite escalating numbers of children in poverty and an increasingly clear evidence base demonstrating the harm that this causes, children's rights and interests have rarely received serious consideration in setting the welfare policies of austerity. In the absence of equivalent rights within the HRA, the courts too have offered little by way of protection. This presents a bleak picture for many children in the UK.

(D) Child Poverty in the UK

When the New Labour government came to power in 1997, the child poverty statistics made depressing reading, with a third of all children living in poverty, and staying in poverty for longer than in most other industrialised countries. The New Labour government, rightly concerned by these alarming child poverty statistics, indicated its commitment to tackle this country's dismal record. In 1999, Prime Minister Tony Blair made an ambitious pledge to end child poverty within 20 years,[132] following this with a plethora of policy initiatives designed to meet the target. To oversee progress, a new Child Poverty Unit was established, run by the Department for Work and Pensions

---

[127] Committee on the Rights of the Child (2016b); A. Nolan (2020).
[128] Committee on the Rights of the Child (2016a) paras 69–71, discussed further below.
[129] CRC, Art. 27(3).   [130] A. Nolan (2019) p. 1043.   [131] Ibid. p. 1054.
[132] Tony Blair, the Prime Minister, speech at Toynbee Hall, 18 March 1999.

and the Department for Children, Schools and Families, with a remit to coordinate and develop policy on the ending of child poverty across government. Clear targets for reducing child poverty were backed by new child poverty indicators for measuring poverty and a requirement for annual reports on progress. These four indicators, placed on a statutory footing in the Child Poverty Act 2010, focused on the material circumstances of the child's household and measured absolute,[133] relative[134] and persistent[135] poverty, together with a measure based on combined material deprivation and low income.[136] In a novel approach, the Act created a legal duty to meet these targets[137] and backed that with the requirement that the government produce a child poverty strategy, revised every 3 years, and the creation of a Child Poverty Commission[138] to advise on that strategy. Although not without criticism, particularly on the chosen measures, the approach had the considerable merit of making addressing child poverty a key government objective and creating a cross-governmental approach with clear standards for assessing success or failure. In the 5 years following Tony Blair's initial pledge to eradicate child poverty, the government's efforts made some early and impressive progress.[139] Nevertheless, by then, it was also becoming clear that this progress was slowing and that the government would not achieve its target of halving child poverty by 2010 or eliminating it by 2020.[140] Further, some of the apparent progress made on relative poverty was actually due to a fall in median incomes during the financial crisis, rather than an improvement in the circumstances of those who had apparently moved out of poverty.

The incoming coalition government in 2010 stated that it remained 'firmly committed to the goal of ending child poverty in the UK by 2020'[141] and produced statutory child poverty strategies as required by the 2010 Act.[142] Nonetheless, over the course of that government and those that have followed,

---

[133] Child Poverty Act 2010, s. 5, now repealed, required the proportion of children in households experiencing absolute poverty to be reduced to less than 5 per cent by 2020.

[134] Child Poverty Act 2010, s. 3, now repealed, defined relative poverty as households with less than 60 per cent of median household income and set a target that less than 10 per cent of children would live in such households by 2020.

[135] Child Poverty Act 2010, s. 6, now repealed, measured the proportion of children who had lived in poverty for at least 3 years.

[136] Child Poverty Act 2010, s. 4, now repealed, concerned households with income below 70 per cent of median household income and who experienced material deprivation (defined as lacking the ability to purchase key goods and services) and set a target that by 2020 less than 5 per cent of children fell into this category.

[137] Child Poverty Act 2010, s. 2, now repealed.

[138] Child Poverty Act 2010, ss 8 and 10, now repealed.

[139] DWP (2006) p. 31: between 1998–99 and 2004–05, the number of children in absolute low income fell by 1.6 million, and the proportion of children spending a large number of years in poverty fell from 17 per cent in 1997–2000 to 13 per cent in 2001–04. See also L. Harker (2006) p. 11: 'this sharp fall in child poverty has been a remarkable achievement'.

[140] HCWPC (2008) paras 37–44.   [141] DWP (2014) esp. pp. 11 and 17.

[142] The first of these strategies was the subject of a successful judicial review, on the basis that the government had failed to establish the Child Poverty Commission and that there had therefore been a failure to consult with the Commission in preparing the strategy as required

the structures that had been put in place to address child poverty have been dismantled and the cross-government focus on child poverty has been lost as it has been subsumed within wider aims. A good example of this can be seen in the fate of the Child Poverty Commission envisaged by the 2010 Act. The Commission should have provided an independent expert voice on child poverty to inform government strategy.[143] Following the change in government, the Commission was not established in its intended form; instead a Social Mobility and Child Poverty Commission was created in its place,[144] addressing wider issues of socio-economic disadvantage and social mobility alongside child poverty. It was not long before 'child poverty' disappeared entirely from its remit; the Commission was soon rebranded the Social Mobility Commission, losing all reference to child poverty from its title and terms of reference.[145] At the same time, this loss of cross-departmental oversight for child poverty was compounded by the abolition of the Child Poverty Unit. The dismantling of Labour's child poverty apparatus was concluded by the Welfare Reform and Work Act 2016, which stripped out the legal framework from the Child Poverty Act 2010.[146] The centrepiece of that framework, the exacting legal duty to meet child poverty targets by 2020, was repealed, although by this stage it was abundantly clear that those ambitious targets would not be met within the original time frame. Further, the four indicators of child poverty based on material deprivation and household income that had been core to the 2010 Act were also removed.[147] In their place, new indicators concerned with children in workless households and educational attainment were created;[148] however, these indicators were not backed with targets, but merely a weak duty to report data annually to Parliament. The renaming of what remained of the 'Child Poverty Act' as the 'Life Chances Act' clearly symbolised the downgrading of child poverty in government strategy.[149]

The shift from income-based measures of child poverty to 'life chances' indicators was driven by the government's view that the income measures in the Child Poverty Act did 'not capture the full experience of growing up in

---

by the then Child Poverty Act 2010, s. 10(1): *R (Child Poverty Action Group)* v. *Secretary of State for Work and Pensions* [2012] EWHC 2579 (Admin).

[143] Child Poverty Act 2010 (as enacted), esp. ss 8 and 10(3) and Sch. 1, para. 1(4).

[144] Welfare Reform Act 2012, s. 145 and Sch. 13 amending the Child Poverty Act 2010.

[145] Welfare Reform and Work Act 2016, s. 6, amending the Child Poverty Act 2010, then renamed the Life Chances Act 2010.

[146] In Scotland, the Child Poverty (Scotland) Act 2017 retained the indicators and approach of the Child Poverty Act 2010, creating obligations on Scottish Ministers to meet specified child poverty targets by 2023 and 2030.

[147] Following a government defeat in the House of Lords during the passage of the Bill, a duty to provide annual data on each of the four 2010 measures was included in the Act: Welfare Reform and Work Act 2016, s. 4. The duty to meet these targets and to report on progress was, however, removed from the Child Poverty Act 2010.

[148] Life Chances Act 2010 (previously Child Poverty Act 2010), s. A1A, inserted by Welfare Reform and Work Act 2016, s. 5.

[149] Welfare Reform and Work Act 2016, s. 7(12).

poverty or the barriers to getting out of poverty'.[150] It is certainly true that it is difficult for any measure to capture the multidimensional nature of poverty and its impact on children.[151] It is also true that some of the apparent success in reducing relative child poverty was caused by the drop in median incomes, so lowering the household income required to be above the 'poverty line',[152] rather than by any rise in the living standards of those children who now found themselves in households above that line.[153] While income measures alone cannot fully capture the impact of poverty on a child's well-being and life chances, poverty is at heart concerned with a lack of material resources and there is good evidence that raising family income itself has significant positive effects on child well-being across a wide range of measures.[154] For these reasons, there was almost universal opposition among those working in the area to the downgrading of income-based measures in the government's approach to child poverty.[155] The government's preferred indicators of educational attainment and worklessness, while undoubtedly important, only capture a narrow aspect of children's experience of poverty. This is particularly true of worklessness. The government's own figures show that more than 70 per cent of children in relative poverty are in working households, a figure that is rising.[156] Nonetheless, reinforced by the influential view that work is good for physical and mental well-being and urging a move towards a 'system based on a presumption of robust self-reliance',[157] the government remains convinced that ending child poverty hinges on getting unemployed parents back into work if they can. This view is by no means new. A strong component of New Labour's anti-poverty strategy was also based on increasing the proportion of children with parents in work,[158] backed partly by the ideological 'view that state responsibility should be matched by individual responsibility'.[159] The rising proportion of children living in poverty who are in in-work families demonstrates the need for a shift in the understanding of child poverty in policy-making.[160]

---

[150] HM Government (2012) para. 20.   [151] A. Nolan and K. Pells (2020) esp. p. 119.

[152] Child Poverty Act 2010, s. 3, now repealed, defined relative poverty as households with less than 60 per cent of median household income.

[153] HM Government (2012) p. 5. Although absolute poverty remained relatively static in this period, demonstrating the importance of utilising a number of income-based measures to address these different facets of income-based poverty.

[154] K. Cooper and K. Stewart (2017).

[155] K. Stewart and N. Roberts (2018), noting that only 2 of 251 respondents to the government's consultation supported such removal.

[156] DWP (2021): 73 per cent of children in households with relative low income were in working households. Although most children living in low-income households have working parents, children whose parents are not in work are more likely to be in poverty: 19 per cent of children in working families are in households with relative low-income, while 53 per cent of children whose families do not work are in the same bracket.

[157] D. Freud (2007) pp. 37–8.   [158] DWP (2006) p. 33.   [159] S. Fredman (2006) pp. 509–10.

[160] HCWPC (2021) esp. pp. 27–8.

Child poverty in the UK remains a serious and growing problem, with complex causes that disproportionately affect certain groups of children.[161] The downgrading of child poverty in government strategy has taken place against the backdrop of austerity. Children have borne the brunt of government reforms designed to cut the cost of welfare support.[162] At the same time, budget cuts across government have reduced services for children that would have ameliorated the consequences of that poverty.[163] The subsequent coronavirus pandemic and cost-of-living crisis have further exacerbated the problems facing many families and led to predictions that poverty will rise further.[164] The Committee on the Rights of the Child has expressed 'serious concern' about UK child poverty and the impact of government policies on tax credits, welfare reform and homelessness on children's rights.[165] Despite this, children's rights have so far only played a minimal part in the domestic response to child poverty.

(E) Welfare Reform, Child Poverty and Children's Rights

The decade of welfare reform that followed the election of the coalition government in 2010 demonstrates both the potential and limitations of children's rights in combatting poverty. The attention paid to children's rights by the government in responding to poverty has been minimal and has fallen far short of that envisaged in the CRC. A series of challenges before the Supreme Court have failed to provide a rights-based remedy for children. Instead, that case law demonstrates the increasing barriers to raising children's economic and social rights and interests in the domestic courts. The familiar problems of making children visible, finding a secure domestic legal basis for raising children's rights and judicial deference to policy are well illustrated in this series of cases. The case law also demonstrates clear divergence among the senior judiciary as to how to address these issues. Recent case law reasserting traditional constitutional orthodoxy means that judicial remedy for children's rights in welfare reform looks increasingly remote.

Shortly after entering office in 2010, the coalition government set out its plans to reduce the structural fiscal deficit by making substantial reductions to government spending.[166] A significant portion of these savings were to be achieved by reductions in welfare benefits payable to working age people. This policy was implemented through the Welfare Reform Act 2012, which introduced a benefit cap that imposed a limit on the maximum benefits payable to

---

[161] E.g. children from certain ethnic groups are more than twice as likely to be in poverty than children as a cohort: ibid. esp. p. 46.

[162] JCHR (2015) esp. paras 100–1.

[163] See e.g. the impact on children's services, discussed in Chapter 15.

[164] A. Corlett and L. Try (2022).

[165] Committee on the Rights of the Child (2016a) paras 69–71.

[166] These plans were announced by the Chancellor of the Exchequer in his emergency budget delivered on 22 June 2010.

non-working households. The government's own analysis made clear that many more children than adults would be affected by the cap, given that most of the households affected were those including multiple children.[167] The impact on children was an inevitable consequence of the way in which the cap was calculated: the basic needs of children resulted in increased child benefit and housing benefit, meaning that a household with children was more likely to hit the cap. Indeed, in evidence presented to Parliament, the government predicted that if child-related benefits were to be excluded from the cap, the budget savings would be reduced by 80 to 90 per cent.[168] The reduction in welfare spending was therefore substantially dependent on cutting benefits that were intended to meet the essential needs of children. As the Joint Committee on Human Rights (JCHR) explained, the Bill risked failing to comply with a range of international human rights commitments, including the right to an adequate standard of living in Article 27 of the CRC.[169] Despite the evident impact on resources for children, no children's rights impact assessment was conducted for the cap. The government candidly informed the JCHR that it considered that the proposed legislation did not raise 'any particular issues in respect of these wider obligations such as to merit a detailed analysis'.[170]

The benefit cap was soon challenged before the Supreme Court in *R (SG) v. Secretary of State for Work and Pensions* ('the first benefit cap case').[171] A majority[172] of the Supreme Court found that there had been a clear failure to treat children's interests as a primary consideration as required by Article 3(1) of the CRC. While the government was aware of the effect that the cap was likely to have on children, at no point had children's interests been treated as a primary consideration. Instead, they had been subordinated to other policy considerations without due assessment and weight being given to them.[173] The government had made no attempt to analyse the rights of the children affected and it could not possibly be in their best interests for their families to be deprived of the means to provide them with the core necessities of life. The government's contention that the benefit cap would benefit children generally, by motivating a long-term shift to parental working, was insufficient for Article 3, which required careful consideration of the rights and interests of the children affected by the measure.[174] Such an analysis would require careful identification of the specific CRC obligations, including the child's right to an adequate living standard in Article 27. Although the impact on children had been extensively debated in Parliament, this was insufficient to meet the

---

[167] DWP (2012b) para. 14 estimated that without behavioural change, 75,000 families would be affected, including 90,000 adults and 220,000 children.
[168] *R (SG) v. Secretary of State for Work and Pensions* [2015] UKSC 16, [2015] 1 WLR 1449, at [41]. Evidence suggested that if child benefit and child tax credit were to be excluded from the cap, then there would be a reduction of 80–90 per cent in savings.
[169] JCHR (2015) para. 1.76.   [170] Ibid. para. 1.34.   [171] [2015] UKSC 16, [2015] 1 WLR 1449.
[172] Ibid. Lady Hale at [225], Lord Kerr at [268], Lord Carnwath at [128].
[173] Ibid. at [122]–[128] (Lord Carnwath).   [174] Ibid. at [226] (Lady Hale).

requirements of Article 3, not least because the detailed implementation of the cap had been left to the Secretary of State to achieve through regulations, which were now challenged before the Supreme Court and which had not been the subject of any form of children's rights assessment.[175]

The willingness of the Supreme Court to assess the government's compliance with Article 3 of the CRC appeared to be a significant step forward for children's rights. Nonetheless, the majority found that there was no route by which this failure to comply with international law was a violation of domestic law,[176] and so the challenge failed. As the CRC is not directly enforceable and no statutory obligation required children's interests to be considered in this area of policy, the only route to apply Article 3 of the CRC lay in interpreting the rights in the ECHR. Despite the serious impact on the children concerned, identifying a relevant ECHR right was not straightforward. There is no right to social security payments in the ECHR and the children themselves were not directly losing any payments. These hurdles meant that the case was instead litigated as a sex discrimination case. The burden of the cap was predicted to fall heavily on single-parent households for reasons directly related to the presence of children in those households. As 92 per cent of single-parent households were headed by a woman, the Secretary of State conceded that the consequences of these problems fell disproportionately on women. The question for the Supreme Court was whether such differential treatment could be justified under Article 14 of the ECHR, when taken with the right to property.[177] For the majority, the children's interests were simply not relevant to the questions before the court: the fact that children would be affected by the cap was not capable of bearing on the question of whether the differential impact on women could be justified, particularly as children would be affected in the same way whether that parent were male or female.[178] Further, Article 3 of the CRC could provide no illumination of the meaning of the mother's right not to be discriminated against in the protection of her property.[179] In contrast, for the minority, it was impossible to dissociate the interests of children from those of their mothers as they were intrinsically bound up with the rights of the mothers in question. The women suffered the discriminatory impact by reason of their position as lone mothers and their financial position would inevitably impact on their dependent children.[180] When viewed in this way, the effect on the children was such that the cap could not possibly be a proportionate means of achieving a legitimate aim given the failure of the government to address the impact on the children.[181] In summary, although the first benefit cap case offered some hope to children's rights campaigners

---

[175] Ibid. at [159] (Lady Hale): The Benefit Cap (Housing Benefit) Regulations 2012 (SI 2012/2994).
[176] By a different majority: Lord Carnwath, Lord Reed and Lord Hughes.
[177] ECHR, Protocol 1, Art. 1.   [178] *R (SG)*, at [89] (Lord Reed).
[179] Ibid. at [146] (Lord Hughes).
[180] Ibid. at [220]–[224] (Baroness Hale) and [263]–[269] (Lord Kerr).
[181] Ibid. at [226]–[229].

through the willingness to analyse compliance with Article 3 of the CRC, it also demonstrated the difficulties in making those rights visible through a Convention designed for adult interests and in a welfare system which treats children as the responsibility of adults rather than of direct concern to the state.

In 2015, a new Conservative government came to power, having made a manifesto commitment to further welfare reform. That reform was soon implemented in the Welfare Reform and Work Act 2016, which, among other measures, reduced the benefit cap applicable to non-working families. Once again, the implications for child poverty were given close consideration in Parliament, but children's rights received only scant attention from the government. While the government's impact assessment stated that the obligations under the CRC had been considered, no analysis of the reduction of the cap on affected children's rights was published.[182] Instead, the government again relied on the advantages of having working parents for children as a cohort.[183] Once again, the cap was challenged in the Supreme Court, this time in joined cases involving lone-parent families with children under the ages of 2 and 5 respectively. The breakthrough in *R (DA)* v. *Secretary of State for Work and Pensions*[184] ('the second benefits cap case') was in persuading the Supreme Court that the children's ECHR rights were directly engaged. The imposition of the cap would inevitably affect the children's family life, even if the mother was able to return to work to escape it, and for that reason the legislation fell within the ambit of Article 8.[185] It was then argued that as young children of lone parents, these children had been discriminated against under Article 14, as their mothers faced far greater barriers in returning to work and thus escaping the cap, than those of older children.[186] As children's rights were raised directly, the Supreme Court was persuaded that Article 3 of the CRC was directly relevant to the question of whether interference with those rights was justified, so overcoming the hurdle that had defeated the litigants in the first benefit cap case.[187] As Lord Wilson accepted in his leading judgment, the evidence demonstrated that families subject to the cap would be reduced to an income 'well below the poverty line'.[188] Such a serious impact on this cohort of children might appear especially hard to justify, given the substantial barriers

---

[182] The requirements for effective use of CRIA are considered by L. Payne (2019).

[183] DWP (2016) pp. 7 and 9. Similar points were made in the government's memorandum to the Joint Committee on Human Rights concerning the Bill.

[184] [2019] UKSC 21, [2019] 1 WLR 3289.

[185] Ibid. at [37] (Lord Wilson), [102] (Lord Carnwath) and [137] (Lady Hale).

[186] A similar Art. 14 claim was advanced on behalf of the mothers, on the basis of their status as lone parents of young children.

[187] [2019] UKSC 21, [2019] 1 WLR 3289, at [76]–[78] (Lord Wilson), also accepting that CRC Art. 3 was relevant to the mothers' claim, [102] and [122] (Lord Carnwath), [157] (Lady Hale) and [179]–[183] (Lord Kerr).

[188] Ibid. at [33], using the accepted measure for relative poverty, i.e. households with less than 60 per cent of median household income equivalent to size of households.

to their mothers returning to work. Nonetheless, the claims again failed. In contrast to the first benefit cap case, the challenged provisions were in primary legislation, rather than regulations, so raising a direct challenge to Parliament's assessment. Further, the majority accepted that the test for breach of Article 14 in cases concerning entitlement to welfare benefits was whether the measure was 'manifestly without reasonable foundation'. By a 'narrow margin', Lord Wilson was persuaded that the parliamentary debates were sufficient to show compliance with Article 3 of the CRC and that this high test had not been met. Again, these conclusions were vigorously contested by the minority, who pointed out that evidence of awareness of the impact on children fell far short of the requirement to treat their interests as a primary consideration and to construe those interests in the light of the wider obligations of the CRC.[189] While the case had taken a step forward in finding that children's ECHR rights were directly engaged, it took a substantial step back in the hands-off approach to the requirements of Article 3 of the CRC, at least in cases of primary legislation. Nonetheless, it remained possible to see a future case in which the more searching analysis of Article 3 shown in the first benefit cap case could be combined with the recognition of children's rights in the second in order to provide an effective route for redress in child poverty cases.

Any such hopes of such a development were dashed by the final Supreme Court case in this story of welfare reform and child poverty. The decision in *R (SC)* v. *Work and Pensions Secretary* (hereafter *SC*)[190] also concerned an aspect of the reforms introduced by the Welfare Reform and Work Act 2016: the 'two-child limit' on child tax credit payments.[191] The introduction of this restriction had again been the subject of intense debate in Parliament. The rule prevented parents from claiming additional payments for their third and subsequent children. This was introduced primarily because of the government's view that families in receipt of benefits should make the same financial choices as other families when choosing whether to extend their family. Opponents pointed out that only a minority of pregnancies are believed to be planned and that changes in family circumstances may well mean that families became reliant on benefits having originally expected to be able to meet the costs of the child. Most importantly, the usual increase in benefits for additional children reflected the cost of raising those children. The shortfall between family income and the cost of raising a child would inevitably impact the children within that family who had had no part in the decision on family size. Subsequent research has shown a rapid increase in relative poverty in

---

[189] Ibid. at [154]–[157] (Lady Hale) and [192]–[197] (Lord Kerr).
[190] [2021] UKSC 26, [2021] 3 WLR 428.
[191] The restriction was introduced prospectively and only applied to children born after 6 April 2017; exceptions apply in the case of multiple births, non-consensual conception and adoption from care. The same rules apply to Universal Credit.

larger families, an increase that is expected to continue as more families become subject to the limit.[192]

In *SC*, two families subject to the two-child limit challenged the policy on a number of grounds, including the differential treatment between children in larger households and those in households with two or fewer children. In a single judgment, the panel of seven justices accepted that there was a difference in treatment affecting their family life under Article 8 that required justification under Article 14 of the ECHR.[193] The parties had agreed that the court should consider whether the UK had breached its obligations under Article 3 of the CRC in assessing whether the difference was justified. That agreement was unsurprising given the previous Supreme Court case law. Nonetheless, Lord Reed, giving the judgment of the court, found that it was not only mistaken, but also that it would contradict a fundamental principle of constitutional law for the courts to assess compliance with an unincorporated treaty.[194] Further, he reasoned, Strasbourg did not treat international treaties as if they were incorporated into the ECHR and did not purport to determine whether states were in breach of those obligations.[195] Accordingly, Lord Reed was clear that Strasbourg jurisprudence did not require the courts to assess compliance with the CRC or to treat the Convention as if it formed a part of domestic law. Any domestic authority that appeared to suggest otherwise was either obiter or formed part of a dissenting judgment.[196] This did not mean that the CRC was irrelevant; Strasbourg jurisprudence had treated children's interests as a relevant factor in assessing justification under Article 14. Domestic courts should not, however, assess whether there had been a breach of the CRC itself. This downgrading of the relevance of the CRC was accompanied by higher hurdles for any litigant seeking to challenge Parliament's treatment of children's interests or the balance drawn between those interests and competing considerations. In particular, it was not appropriate to expect Parliament to adopt a judicial model of rationality, or to treat the absence or poverty of debate in Parliament as a reason supporting a finding of incompatibility.[197] In any case, proper application of Parliamentary privilege placed significant constraints on judicial scrutiny of those debates, meaning that the court would have little material on which to assess compatibility with the procedural requirements of Article 3 of the CRC, even it were an appropriate exercise to carry out. Finally, Lord Reed emphasised that Strasbourg had generally given a wide margin of appreciation to general measures of economic or social strategy and that the court should give

---

[192] A. Corlett and L. Try (2022): this analysis found that in 2020–21 50 per cent of households with three plus children were in relative poverty, rising to 70 per cent for those with four or more children. This proportion was expected to rise further as the rule was prospective and as time went on a higher proportion of families would have children born after the commencement date. The government's own analysis shows that 1.3 million children live in households whose benefits are limited by this rule: DWP (2022).

[193] *SC* [2021] UKSC 26, [2021] 3 WLR 428, at [66]–[72].   [194] Ibid. at [74]–[91].

[195] Ibid. at [72]–[86].   [196] Ibid. at [86]–[96].   [197] Ibid. at [163]–[185].

appropriate respect to Parliament's decisions on such matters.[198] On the application of these principles, the court found that it had no legal basis to decide that the measure was disproportionate; instead, it was a matter for Parliament and the democratic process.

The decision in *SC* adopts a much more circumscribed vision of the courts' role in relation to international law and matters of economic and social policy. That vision is expressed in trenchant terms by a unanimous panel of seven justices and will undoubtedly restrict the ability of future litigants to challenge measures that put children further into poverty. Much of the judgment in *SC*, like the second benefit cap case, is concerned with the respect to be accorded to democratic decisions by Parliament. It remains to be seen whether the courts can be persuaded to retain a more searching analysis when contemplating the government's consideration of children's rights in poverty cases. The court's deferential approach to legislative judgments would have been reinforced had the government been successful in passing the Bill of Rights Bill, with its insistence that: 'courts must give the greatest possible weight to the principle that, in a Parliamentary democracy, decisions about the balance between different policy aims ... are properly made by Parliament'.[199] Yet, it is questionable whether the democratic credentials of Parliament should be given such decisive weight in cases involving the rights of children, who are excluded from that democratic process. Indeed, Article 3 of the CRC is necessary, in part, to ensure that decision-makers do not neglect their duties to children who are often unheard in decisions about them. The story of welfare reform and child poverty demonstrates the considerable challenges to upholding children's rights in the public sphere, especially in matters of economic policy. The government's cursory approach to children's rights has been compounded by a legal system that struggles to make children's interests visible or to require that they are taken seriously. Although the complex problem of child poverty cannot be solved by judicial decision alone,[200] the courts offer a forum to hold the government to account for neglect of children's rights and interests. The increasing hurdles to using that forum mean that children are reliant on political will rather than legal requirement to ensure that their rights are heard and taken seriously in welfare policy.

(5) Conclusion

It is easy for the rights and interests of children to be overlooked in a political and administrative system run by, and largely for, adults. Yet, children are frequently affected by public decisions and dependent on the state to secure the conditions in which their rights can be realised in practice. Children's

---

[198] Ibid. at [144]–[162].   [199] Bill of Rights Bill 117, Session 2022–23 cl. 1(2)(c); see also cl. 7.
[200] A. Nolan (2014) pp. 232–41.

rights have the potential to make children's interests visible and ensure that decision-makers recognise their moral worth. That potential has been realised in some cases and given redress to children in a wide range of circumstances. There remain, however, serious barriers to requiring a children's rights approach across public law and in some areas the commitment to children's rights implementation appears to be going backwards. Most obviously, providing effective and accountable responsibility to children in the direct care of the state is vital to protection of their rights. As the subsequent chapters demonstrate, public authorities' duties to these children are well-recognised and have had an important role in shaping policy and practice. Yet, even for these children, there remain significant gaps in accountability. Difficulties in accessing justice and increasing involvement of the private sector in delivering vital public services for children create barriers for children whose rights are neglected when they should be able to rely on the state to take responsibility for them.

There have also been significant strides in ensuring that children are made visible, and their interests given 'primary consideration', in administrative decisions that affect them across a range of policy areas. Yet, these gains look increasingly precarious outside of those policy areas covered by express statutory obligations. The Supreme Court's restrictive approach to using international law, including the CRC, to interpret ECHR rights is likely to curb the development of the use of Article 3 of the CRC in administrative decisions. The same judicial caution appears likely to restrict the use of legal action to require that children's rights and interests are taken seriously in policy-making and legislation. In the light of this judicial caution, political engagement with children's rights has become even more important. The best safeguard for children is through a political and administrative culture that recognises and understands the importance of children's rights. The use of proper CRIA in policy-making and drafting legislation, together with detailed guidance as to how to integrate children's interests in diverse and complex administrative contexts, has greater potential to improve the quality of decision-making for children than judicial decisions after the event. Such developments would have benefits for public authorities too in that proper consideration of children's interests as a primary consideration at the outset will reduce the vulnerability of decisions to subsequent challenge. But without legal force, political engagement is likely to remain patchy. Many of the weaknesses identified in this chapter would be best resolved with the adoption and implementation of a general statutory duty on all ministers and public authorities to have due regard to children's rights and best interests in matters concerning them. At present, it seems unlikely that there will be sufficient political will at Westminster for such a change, despite the greater enthusiasm with which children's interests have been embraced elsewhere in the UK.

Bibliography

NB: Many of these publications can be obtained on the relevant organisation's website.

Alston, P. (1994) 'The Best Interests Principle: Towards a Reconciliation of Culture and Human Rights' 8 *International Journal of Law Policy and the Family* 1.

Archard, D. (2014) *Children: Rights and Childhood*, Routledge.

Attree, P. (2006) 'The Social Costs of Child Poverty: A Systematic Review of the Qualitative Evidence' 20 *Children and Society* 54.

Blanden, J. and Gibbons, S. (2006) *The Persistence of Poverty across Generations: A View from Two British Cohorts*, Joseph Rowntree Foundation.

Bryson, C., Skipp, A., Allbeson, J., Poole, E., Ireland, E. and Marsh, V. (2012) *Kids Aren't Free: The Child Maintenance Arrangements of Single Parents on Benefit in 2012*, Nuffield Foundation.

Byrne, B. and Lundy, L. (2019) 'Children's Rights-Based Childhood Policy: A Six-P Framework' 23 *International Journal of Human Rights* 357.

Children's Commissioner (2019) *Pass the Parcel: Children Posted Around the Care System*, Office of the Children's Commissioner.

    (2020) *Unregulated: Children in Care Living in Semi-Independent Accommodation*, Office of the Children's Commissioner.

Choudhry, S. (2013) 'Children in "Care" after YL – the Ineffectiveness of Contract as a Means of Protecting the Vulnerable' *Public Law* 519.

Committee on the Rights of the Child (2009) *General Comment No. 12 on the Right of the Child to Be Heard*, CRC/C/GC/12, Centre for Human Rights, Geneva.

    (2013a) *General Comment No. 14 on the Right of the Child to Have His or Her Best Interests Taken as a Primary Consideration (Art. 3, Para. 1)*, CRC/C/GC/14, Centre for Human Rights, Geneva.

    (2013b) *General Comment No. 16 on State Obligations Regarding the Impact of the Business Sector on Children's Rights*, CRC/C/GC/16, Centre for Human Rights, Geneva.

    (2016a) *Concluding Observations of the Committee on the Rights of the Child: United Kingdom of Great Britain and Northern Ireland*, CRC/C/GBR/CO/5, Centre for Human Rights, Geneva.

    (2016b) *General Comment No. 19 on Public Budgeting for the Realization of Children's Rights (Art 4)*, CRC/C/GC/19, Centre for Human Rights, Geneva.

Cooper, K. and Stewart, K. (2017) *Does Money Affect Children's Outcomes? An Update*, Centre for Analysis of Social Exclusion, LSE.

Corlett, A. and Try, L. (2022) *The Living Standards Outlook 2022*, Resolution Foundation.

Department for Work and Pensions (DWP) (2006) Cm 6915, *Opportunity for All, Eighth Annual Report 2006, Strategy Document*, The Stationery Office.

    (2012a) Cm 8399, *Supporting Separated Families; Securing Children's Futures*, The Stationery Office.

    (2012b) *Impact assessment for the Household Benefit Cap*, DWP.

    (2014) *Child Poverty Strategy 2014–17*, The Stationery Office.

    (2016) *Welfare Reform and Work Act: Impact Assessment for the Benefit Cap*, DWP.

    (2017) *Child Maintenance: A New Compliance and Arrears Strategy. A Consultation*, DWP.

    (2021) *Households Below Average Income: An Analysis of the Income Distribution FYE 1995 to FYE 2020*, DWP.

    (2022) *Universal Credit and Child Tax Credit Claimants: Statistics Related to the Policy to Provide Support for a Maximum of 2 Children, April 2022*, DWP.

EU Commission (2013) *Investing in Children: Breaking the Cycle of Disadvantage*, Recommendation (2013/112/EU).

Fortin, J. (2011) 'Are Children's Interests Really Best? *ZH (Tanzania) (FC) v. Secretary of State for the Home Department*' 74 *Modern Law Review* 932.

Fredman, S. (2006) 'Human Rights Transformed: Positive Duties and Positive Rights' *AUT Public Law* 498.

Freeman, M. (2007) *Article 3: The Best Interests of the Child*, Martinus Nijhoff.

Freud, D. (2007) *Reducing Dependency, Increasing Opportunity: Options for the Future of Welfare to Work: An Independent Report to the Department for Work and Pensions*, CDS.

Galobardes, B., Lynch, J. W. and Davey Smith, G. (2008) 'Is the Association between Childhood Socioeconomic Circumstances and Cause-Specific Mortality Established? Update of a Systematic Review' 62 *Journal of Epidemiology & Community Health* 387.

Hair, N. L., Hanson, J. L. and Wolfe, B. L and Pollak, S. D. (2015) 'Association of Child Poverty, Brain Development, and Academic Achievement' 169 *JAMA Pediatrics* 822.

Hale, B. (2006) 'Understanding Children's Rights: Theory and Practice' 44 *Family Court Review* 350.

Harker, L. (2006) Cm 6951, *Delivering on Child Poverty: What Would it Take?*, The Stationery Office.

Henshaw, D. (2006) Cm 6894, *Recovering Child Support: Routes to Responsibility*, The Stationery Office.

HM Government (2012) Cm 8483, *Measuring Child Poverty: A Consultation on Better Measures of Child Poverty*, The Stationery Office.

Hooper, C.-A., Gorin, S., Cabral, C. and Dyson, C. (2007) *Living with Hardship 24/7: The Diverse Experiences of Families in Poverty in England*, The Frank Buttle Trust.

House of Commons Committee of Public Accounts (2022) *Child Maintenance, Ninth Report of Session 2022–23*, HC 255, House of Commons.

House of Commons Justice Committee (2021) *Rainsbrook Secure Training Centre, Seventeenth Report of Session 2019–21*, HC 1266, House of Commons.

House of Commons Work and Pensions Committee (HCWPC) (2008) *The Best Start in Life? Alleviating Deprivation, Improving Social Mobility and Eradicating Child Poverty*, Second Report of Session 2007–08, Volume I, HC 42–1, The Stationery Office.

(2021) *Children in Poverty: Measurement and Targets, Third Report of Session 2021–22*, HC 188, House of Commons.

Joint Committee on Human Rights (JCHR) (2004) *Children Bill, 19th Report of Session 2003–04*, HC 537.

(2015) *The UK's Compliance with the UN Convention on the Rights of the Child*, HC 1016.

Knight, A., O'Connell, R. and Brannen, J. (2018) 'Eating with Friends, Family or Not at All: Young People's Experiences of Food Poverty in the UK' 32 *Children & Society* 185.

Minujin, A. and Nandy, S. (2012) *Global Child Poverty and Well-being: Measurements, Concepts, Policy and Action*, Policy Press.

Nolan, A. (2014) *Children's Socio-Economic Rights, Democracy and the Courts*, Hart Publishing.

(2019) 'Article 27. The Right to a Standard of Living Adequate for the Child's Development' in J. Tobin (ed.) *The UN Convention on the Rights of the Child*, Oxford University Press.

(2020) 'Poverty and Child Rights' in Todres, J. and King, S. M. (eds) *Oxford Handbook of Children's Rights*, Oxford University Press.

Nolan, A. and Pells, K. (2020) 'Children's Economic and Social Rights and Child Poverty: The State of Play' 28 *International Journal of Children's Rights* 111.

Office of the UN High Commissioner for Human Rights (2007) *The Legislative History of the Convention on the Rights of the Child*, Vol. 1, United Nations.

Payne, L. (2019) 'Child Rights Impact Assessment as a Policy Improvement Tool' 23 *International Journal of Human Rights* 408.

Ridge, T. (2006) 'Childhood Poverty: A Barrier to Social Participation and Inclusion' in Tisdall, E. K. M., Davis, J., Hill, M. and Prout, A. (eds) *Children, Young People and Social Inclusion*, Policy Press.

Stewart, K. and Roberts, N. (2018) 'Child Poverty Measurement in the UK: Assessing Support for the Downgrading of Income-Based Poverty Measures' 142 *Social Indicators Research* 523.

Taylor, R. and Hoyano, L. (2012) 'Criminal Child Maltreatment: The Case for Reform' *Criminal Law Review* 871.

Tobin, J. (2013) 'Justifying Children's Rights' 21 *International Journal of Children's Rights* 395.

UN Committee on Economic, Social and Cultural Rights (2001) *Statement on Poverty and the International Covenant on Economic, Social and Cultural Rights*, E/C.12/2001/10 (10 May).

Weightman, A., Morgan H., Shepherd M., *et al.* (2012) 'Social Inequality and Infant Health in the UK: Systematic Review and Meta-Analyses' 14 *BMJ Open* 2.

Wickham, S., Anwar, E., Barr, B., Law, C. and Taylor-Robinson, D. (2016) 'Poverty and Child Health in the UK: Using Evidence for Action' 101 *Archives of Disease in Childhood* 759.

Wikeley, N. (2006) *Child Support: Law and Policy*, Hart Publishing.

14

The Right to Education
Participation in School

(1) Introduction

The right to education clearly has a crucial role to play in encouraging pupils to develop a sense of social responsibility and a capacity for planning and achieving their own life goals. As the UN Convention on the Rights of the Child (CRC) recognises, education has a range of important aims, including the development of the child's 'personality, talents and mental and physical abilities to their fullest potential'[1] and their preparation for a 'responsible life in a free society'.[2] The right to education is often regarded as a multiplier of rights: it strengthens the full enjoyment of children's broader rights and freedoms, as well as embedding respect for the rights and freedoms of others within society.

For most children, the right to education will be fulfilled through attendance at school.[3] The importance of schools for children was underlined during the Covid-19 pandemic, in which restrictions and school closures meant that the majority of children were unable to attend school for significant periods. The closure of schools had an obvious impact on children's education, with particularly severe consequences for disadvantaged children and those unable to access online teaching due to digital poverty or their own educational needs or disabilities. Absence from school also had a wider impact on children's health, well-being and safety. In particular, those children living with inadequate housing and nutrition, or at risk of abuse at home, were left in a particularly vulnerable position without the protective role that school can play.[4] In this way, the pandemic highlighted the importance of attendance at school not only to education, but also to children's safety and well-being.

School life may further enable some children to escape from narrow and stultifying home environments and help them assess critically the ideologies with which they have been brought up. But the principles of education law are only slowly adjusting to the maturing pupil's capacity for undertaking responsibilities in school and reaching important decisions over his or her education, without parental interference. Indeed, the efforts of policy-makers to cast

---

[1] CRC, Art. 29(1)(a).   [2] CRC, Art. 29(1)(d).   [3] Home education is considered in Chapter 8.
[4] Children's Commissioner for England (2020).

parents in the role of the consumers of education has produced a system of education law which, more often than not, treats children as adjuncts of their parents, rather than as responsible agents in their own right.[5]

Schools are, however, not only a place in which children's rights are furthered; school regimes can lead to harsh discipline and constraint. The behaviour of teachers and other pupils can further be a source of harm and abuse. Pupils may object to the regime under which they learn or to the values embedded within the school system. At times, pupils' rights movement have made an appearance in British schools.[6] In the late 1960s and early 1970s, student militancy had spread from universities into the schools. Various student bodies[7] started discussing and asserting a range of pupils' rights in schools, including the right to educational democracy through the establishment of school councils, the abolition of school uniform and physical punishment and the right to freedom of expression. On 10 May 1972, up to 1,500 striking children marched to County Hall London[8] and handed in a letter demanding, among other things, the right to publish school magazines without censorship, to organise student meetings during lunch breaks and after school on school premises, to join student unions and to engage in political activity, including strikes.[9] More recently, coordinated global school strikes have been used by pupils to protest against national and international inaction on climate change.[10] Students have also organised online to share testimony of sexual abuse in education and campaign for change.[11]

In the US, the boundaries of children's rights in a school setting have been tested against the provisions of a written constitution. There, Supreme Court decisions like *Tinker* v. *Des Moines Independent Community School District*[12] and *Goss* v. *Lopez*[13] have emphasised the right of schoolchildren to be treated with respect.[14] In *Tinker*, the Supreme Court found that the First Amendment rights of three students had been violated when school authorities suspended them from school for wearing black armbands to protest over the government's policy in Vietnam. The court explained that: 'Students in school as well as out of school are "persons" under our Constitution. They are possessed of

---

[5] See further discussion in Chapter 8.   [6] S. Cunningham and M. Lavalette (2002) pp. 178–82.

[7] The Schools' Action Union (SAU) and the National Union of School Students (NUSS).

[8] The headquarters of the then Greater London Council.

[9] E.g. on 17 May 1972, approximately 2,500 pupils absented themselves from school to attend a 'Schools Demo' in Trafalgar Square mounted by the SAU. Militant action occurred again briefly in 1985; S. Cunningham and M. Lavalette (2002) pp. 182–6.

[10] E.g. BBC, *School Strike for Climate: Protests Staged around the World*, 24 May 2019, www .bbc.co.uk/news/world-48392551.

[11] In particular, through Everyone's Invited: www.everyonesinvited.uk, discussed further below.

[12] 393 US 503 (1969).   [13] 419 US 565 (1975).

[14] But per B. Hafen (1976) p. 646, the decision in *Tinker* protected *parents*' rights to teach and influence their children against state claims that would limit them. The parents of the students involved had encouraged their children to wear the armbands and were obviously instrumental in bringing the litigation that ensued.

fundamental rights which the State must respect.'[15] In *Goss*, the Supreme Court held that students facing disciplinary action by school officials were entitled to due process protection, such as prior notice of the action and a chance to be heard before punishment. In the UK, recognition of rights in school has been more limited.

Education legislation could do far more to promote children's need to be treated as individuals and to reach responsible decisions over their own education, particularly as they reach adolescence. After considering the concept of a right to education per se, this chapter devotes more detailed discussion to four further topics particularly relevant to young people within schools. It first considers the law's response to the problem of school absence; the second discusses the behaviour and discipline in school; the third assesses the extent to which children are involved in school policy and administration; and the fourth relates to the provision of sex education in schools.[16]

(2) The Right to Education

The right to be educated is one of the most important of children's moral and legal rights; without it they may be unable to develop their talents and abilities to 'their fullest potential'.[17] The notion that the right to education is a fundamental human right is embedded in many international documents, notably the International Covenant on Economic, Social and Cultural Rights (ICESCR), which requires all state parties to 'recognize the right of everyone to education',[18] and then expands on the ways in which this should be fulfilled.[19]

Meanwhile, the huge body of English education legislation is oddly perverse in the way it largely ignores those who are the reason for its existence. Indeed, little has changed since 1999 when Tomaševski, UN special reporter, criticised the failure of the educational system here to promote children's human rights in education. She caustically observed of the domestic legislation:

> Statutory enactments relating to education do not use human rights language nor do they mention international human rights law. Where individual rights are mentioned, these relate to parents who have been allowed to challenge school admissions as of 1980.[20]

She considered that while a great deal of jurisprudence had developed on interpreting parental challenges on admissions, conditions in schools, methods of teaching and discipline, this was in the narrow context of

---

[15] 393 US 503 (1969), at 511.
[16] A possible fifth topic, concentrating on the legal principles governing the provision of religious education and collective worship in schools, is discussed in Chapter 8.
[17] Phrasing used in CRC, Art. 29(1)(a).   [18] ICESCR, Art. 13(1).
[19] ICESCR, Art. 13(2)(a)–(d). These provisions are largely mirrored by Art. 28 of the CRC.
[20] K. Tomaševski (1999) para. 29. Under the School Admissions Appeals Code (2012), young people who have ceased to be of compulsory school age now have the right of appeal against a decision to refuse them admission to a sixth form or other school education.

education law, rather than as a means of exploring the human right of education itself. She saw the provision of schooling in the UK being treated as a relationship between school and parents, without children having a legal standing – 'children are thus absent as actors in this process although it is aimed at their learning'.[21] Since then, the government has shown some greater awareness of children 'as actors in this process'. There is, for example, a need for schools to consider their wider role within the community and to promote pupils' well-being.[22] The views of older children now have greater weight if they wish to resist their parents' wish to remove them from sex education.[23] Nonetheless, legislation gives very limited recognition to the importance of pupil participation in other matters concerning them.[24] A more robust requirement for schools to invite and consider pupils' views over 'the conduct of the school'[25] is on the statute book, but has not been brought into force. At present, children's voices are given very limited protection within education law.

Tomaševski is not the only commentator to have criticised the way in which English education law treats parents as the consumers of education, while ignoring children's own educational rights.[26] In an increasingly rights-orientated society, education legislation astonishingly fails to acknowledge openly that children have any 'rights' to education.[27] For example, it refers instead to the duties imposed on every local authority (LA). LAs must secure that there are 'sufficient schools' in their area for providing full-time[28] primary and secondary education,[29] so that all pupils have the opportunity to gain an 'appropriate education'.[30] Despite failing to use 'rights language', one can surmise from these legislative duties that all children do have a legal *right* to free full-time and appropriate education. LAs are also specifically required to promote high standards, a fair access to educational opportunity[31] and the fulfilment by every child's 'learning potential'.[32] Since, in the past, such 'target duties' have not proved easy for individuals to enforce,[33] it seems unlikely that

---

[21] Ibid. para. 31.   [22] Education Act (EA) 2002, s. 21(5)–(9).   [23] Discussed further below.

[24] EA 2002, s. 176(1)(a) and (2) requires LAs to have regard to any guidance about consultation with pupils in connection with decisions affecting them. The guidance issued under this section has been very sparse: N. Harris (2020) p. 9.

[25] EA 2002, s. 29B, to be inserted by Education and Skills Act (ESA) 2008, s. 157. This provision has not been brought into force and there does not appear to be any plan to do so.

[26] Inter alia: P. Meredith (2001) esp. pp. 203–8; D. Monk (2002) esp. pp. 50–6; N. Harris (2020) esp. pp. 7–13.

[27] Ford *et al.* (2016) para. 2.41.   [28] Education Act (EA) 1996, s. 2(1) and (2).

[29] The schools must be sufficient in number, character and equipment: EA 1996, s. 14(2).

[30] EA 1996, s. 14(2). S. 14(3)(a) and (b): education is 'appropriate' if it offers such variety of instruction and training (including practical instruction and training appropriate to their different needs) as may be desirable in view of (a) the pupils' different ages, abilities and aptitudes and (b) the different periods for which pupils may be expected to remain in school.

[31] EA 1996, s. 13A(1)(a)–(b).   [32] Ibid. s. 13A(1)(c).

[33] E.g. *R* v. *Inner London Education Authority, ex p Ali and Murshid* [1990] 2 Admin LR 822: unsuccessful application for judicial review by a parent whose child, along with others, had no school place due to staff shortages. Held: the LA's duty under EA 1944, s. 8 (now EA 1996, s. 14)

such vague aspirational phrases have added significantly to an individual child's ability to obtain a high standard of education.

It seems that the Human Rights Act (HRA) 1998 gives these legislative duties extra teeth – but only up to a point. The inclusion of the right to education within the European Convention for the Protection of Human Rights and Fundamental Freedoms (1950) (ECHR) was derived largely from a concern to protect parents' right to educate their children according to their own beliefs, free from interference by totalitarian regimes.[34] Despite the negative phraseology adopted by Article 2 of Protocol 1 (hereafter A2P1) of the ECHR,[35] it guarantees a right of access to an 'effective' form of education.[36] In effect, this comprises three separate rights: the right of access to such educational establishments as exist; a right to effective (but not the most effective possible) education; and the right to official recognition of academic qualifications. Nevertheless, states are left with complete discretion to determine for themselves issues about resourcing and delivering the educational system.[37] This limitation was apparent in the response to the Covid-19 pandemic, in which school closures and curtailed education provision were imposed on an uncertain legal basis with little detailed attention to the complex balance of rights and interests involved.[38] Further, unless the education available to a pupil is so grossly inadequate that it fails to reach a minimum standard, it offers little succour to those wishing to complain, for example, about the standard of teaching in any particular school.[39] Nor does the Convention entitle a pupil access to, or to remain in, any particular educational institution.[40] Despite these limitations, the HRA has given an individual child wrongfully denied an existing school place a right of action based on A2P1 of the ECHR, with damages or a declaration available against the relevant public authority.[41] Consequently, it seems that the pupil who has not been provided

---

to provide 'sufficient' places is only a 'target' duty, not an absolute duty. A similar conclusion was reached in *R (British Humanist Association)* v. *Richmond LBC* [2012] EWHC 3622 (Admin), [2013] 2 All ER 146. On the difficulty for individuals in enforcing target duties, see also *Morris, Thomas* v. *Rhondda Cynon Taf County Borough Council* [2015] EWHC 1403 (Admin), [2015] ELR 559, esp. at [112], concerning provision of nursery places.

[34] N. Harris (2005) pp. 83–8. Thus, ECHR, A2P1 refers to states' obligation to respect the 'right of parents to ensure such education and teaching in conformity with their own religious and philosophical convictions'. Discussed further in Chapter 8.

[35] 'No one shall be denied the right to education.'

[36] *Belgian Linguistics Case (No. 2)* (1968) 1 EHRR 252, at 280–3, esp. at [4].   [37] Ibid. at [3].

[38] Although the Coronavirus Act 2020, Sch. 16 contained detailed powers to order school closures, the initial decisions were made without recourse to these powers, but were instead announced through press release and policy announcement, obscuring the legal status of those decisions: JCHR (2020) para. 172.

[39] *Ali* v. *Head Teacher and Governors of Lord Grey School* [2006] UKHL 14, [2006] 2 All ER 457, per Lord Bingham, at [24]: the guarantee contained in ECHR, A2P1 is 'a weak one, and deliberately so', providing no Convention guarantee of education of a particular kind or quality. See also *A* v. *Essex County Council* [2010] UKSC 33, [2011] 1 AC 280.

[40] *Simpson* v. *United Kingdom*, App. No. 14688/89, (1989) 64 DR 188.

[41] *R (on the application of E)* v. *Islington LBC* [2017] EWHC 1440 (Admin), [2017] ELR 458.

with any school place at all might also claim that the LA's failure amounts to an infringement of his or her rights under A2P1 of the ECHR.

(3) School Attendance

(A) The Merits of Compulsory School

Children who attend school regularly will spend approximately 2,000 days[42] there between the ages of 5 and 16,[43] a period that will almost certainly have a profound influence on their lives. Regular attendance at school is frequently cited as central to children's ability to fulfil their potential.[44] It is, however, difficult to convince all children that attending school will benefit them when they can think of far better ways to spend their time. Since the right to free state education is wasted on a child who refuses to attend school, the law imposes an absolute duty on parents to see that their children of compulsory school age receive a full-time education.[45] Not all are successful. Truancy in schools has become an intractable problem.[46] Ironically, those children who stay away from school because they consider that it has nothing to offer them may eventually be barred from attending altogether. This is because when disaffected pupils do attend, they often behave so disruptively that they are permanently excluded.

In the face of such problems, should the law attempt to make pupils stay at school if they decide that education is not for them? Children's liberationists such as Holt and Farson urged that children of all ages should have adult freedoms, including the right to decide whether they go to school and what lessons to attend.[47] Today, such attitudes seem extreme. Later children's liberationists acknowledged that allowing young children to choose whether

---

[42]   The Education (School Day and School Year) (England) Regulations 1999 (1999/3181), reg. 3 require LA-maintained schools to be open for at least 380 sessions (190 days) a year. Academies, free schools and independent schools may set their own term dates. Schedule 16 of the Deregulation Act 2015 would have extended this freedom to LA-run schools, but the provision has not been brought into force.

[43]   EA 1996, s. 8: 16-year-olds must wait for the next 'school-leaving date' before they can leave school. As discussed further in Chapter 10, young people aged 16 and 17 are required to continue in education or training.

[44]   E.g. DfE (2020a) p. 5.

[45]   As discussed in Chapter 8, this duty does not require that the child is sent to school; it may be discharged through home education.

[46]   Despite efforts to reduce levels of truancy, the rates of unauthorised absences remain stubbornly high. DfE statistics show that the percentage of half days missed in maintained secondary schools in 2018–19 due to unauthorised absence was 1.4 per cent; this was the same as in 2017–18 and represented the highest figure since consistent data was first recorded in 2006–07. The persistent absence rate (pupils missing at least 10 per cent of sessions) was 10.9 per cent. The impact of the disruption to education during the Covid-19 pandemic is not yet reflected in the official statistics at the time of writing. Statistics in this section are taken from the annual statistical releases available at: www.gov.uk/government/collections/statistics-pupil-absence.

[47]   J. Holt (1974); R. Farson (1978). The ideas of Holt and Farson are discussed in Chapter 1.

they wish to attend school might actually reduce their chances of developing a capacity for autonomy later.[48] Indeed, the international treaties make no attempt to accommodate children's wishes in the matter of school attendance. Thus, the CRC requires states to make primary education 'compulsory and available free to all'[49] and to 'take measures to encourage regular attendance at schools and the reduction of drop-out rates'.[50]

What, however, of those who are too large to frog-march to school? Some argue that compulsion for this older group is not only counterproductive, but also brings education and teaching into disrepute.[51] Since they can take legal responsibility for other decisions, such as seeking contraceptive help, should they not also be allowed to decide whether to attend school, without involving their parents?[52] Despite the plausibility of these arguments, the House of Lords in the *Gillick* decision[53] had not intended to introduce a blanket liberality regarding a fundamental aspect of the lives of all those over a specified age. It introduced the sophisticated and difficult notion of individual children acquiring legal maturity on an incremental and case-by-case basis – a concept which would cause chaos if applied to school attendance. Allowing 13-year-olds to decide for themselves whether to attend school would probably merely swell the numbers of truanting pupils who generally go home or go to friends' houses 'to do nothing in particular'.[54] For many of those who truant, 'doing nothing' involves becoming involved in crime and exploitation.[55] Since an adolescent's ability to reach wise decisions over whether to attend school may be undermined by a variety of factors, ranging from parental illness to peer pressure or bullying, it seems entirely justifiable for the state to insist on their school attendance, at least until they attain the age of 16.

(B) Tackling Absence from School

(i) Criminal Sanctions

The government is strongly committed to tackling truancy and improving school attendance.[56] Despite a plethora of initiatives and policies produced by successive governments, the problem has remained an intractable one. The criminal justice system has played a central role in this response, as ever-more authoritarian sanctions are imposed on parents whose children fail to attend.

---

[48] E.g. R. Lindley (1989) p. 85.   [49] Art. 28(1)(a).   [50] Art. 28(1)(e).
[51] T. Jeffs (2002) esp. p. 56. See also R. Lindley (1989) pp. 88–92, who suggests that those aged between 13 and 16 should be allowed to take full-time employment.
[52] M. Grenville (1988) p. 18.
[53] *Gillick* v. *West Norfolk and Wisbech Area Health Authority* [1986] AC 112.
[54] Audit Commission (1996) p. 68.
[55] Considered further below in the context of children excluded from school. J. Fionda (2005) pp. 220–1: summary of the research linking school non-attendance and crime. See also S. Bhabra *et al.* (2006) p. 101: youthful truants typically commit their first offence at the age of 11 or under.
[56] DfE (2020a).

The possibility of criminal prosecution underlines the importance of the parental duty to ensure that the child receives an effective education. Nonetheless, the criminal law cannot play a particularly constructive part in coercing physically mature young people into school if they are determined not to attend.[57] Further, it does little to address the underlying causes of persistent absence. Even so, an official determination to provide legal sanctions which bite has led to truancy becoming excessively criminalised.

Parents of children who are registered to attend school[58] may be subject to prosecution if the child fails to attend 'regularly'.[59] The meaning of 'regularly' was considered by the Supreme Court in *Isle of Wight Council* v. *Platt*,[60] which concerned the prosecution of a father who had taken his 6-year-old daughter on holiday during term time, having been refused permission to do so by the head teacher.[61] The magistrates hearing the case decided that there was no case to answer. The child had attended 95 per cent of sessions before missing 7 days (14 sessions) for the holiday, taking her to 90.3 per cent attendance. The Divisional Court agreed that this overall attendance rate was sufficiently high to be considered 'regular'. This approach effectively gave parents the discretion to remove their child from some school sessions, provided that the child's overall attendance rate remained sufficiently high. The Supreme Court, however, took a very different view of the term 'regularly' and overturned the lower court's ruling. The Supreme Court determined that 'regularly' meant 'in accordance with the rules prescribed by the school', rather than merely 'at regular intervals' or 'sufficiently frequently'.[62] In consequence, *any* failure to send the child to school in accordance with the school's rules, even for one half-day session, could in theory lead to criminal liability. The decision in *Platt* underlines the expectation that parents who choose to educate their child in school will ensure that they attend unless there are valid reasons for their absence. This considerably limits parental discretion and demonstrates the potential severity of the criminal law in relation to attendance.

---

[57] The legislation requiring 16- and 17-year-olds to engage in education or training also contained extensive enforcement provisions, including parenting contracts and criminal sanctions applicable to parents and young people: ESA 2008, ss 40–58, discussed and criticised in the 3rd edition of this work. These provisions have not been brought into force, perhaps in recognition at the limited effectiveness of such sanctions for this age group.

[58] Since a child can receive suitable full-time education by regular attendance at school 'or otherwise', parents may choose to educate their children at home: EA 1996, s. 7. If an LA is concerned that a child is not receiving a suitable education, they must serve a school attendance notice on the parent requiring him or her to satisfy the LA within a specified time (not less than 15 days) that the child is receiving such an education: EA 1996, s. 437. Failure to do so may result in a school attendance order requiring the child to attend a particular school. A parent who fails to do so may be prosecuted under EA 1996, s. 443, discussed further in Chapter 8.

[59] EA 1996, s. 441(1) and (1A).   [60] [2017] UKSC 28, [2017] 1 WLR 1441.

[61] The law and policy concerning term-time holidays had recently changed, making such permission more difficult to obtain. Harris (2020) pp. 75–6 sets out the background.

[62] [2017] UKSC 28, [2017] 1 WLR 1441, at [40]–[48].

Two separate offences are available to prosecute parents who fail to secure their child's regular attendance at school. The first of these, section 444(1) of the EA 1996, is a strict liability offence that is committed by mere failure to secure the child's regular attendance. The more serious offence,[63] in section 444(1A) of the EA 1996, requires that the parent also had knowledge of the child's failure to attend.[64] The statute specifies a limited number of circumstances in which the child will not be taken to have 'failed to attend regularly' despite being absent from school.[65] These exceptions have been construed narrowly, leaving parents vulnerable to prosecution when struggling with children with long-term difficulties that lead to school refusal.[66] The strict liability offence can have particularly harsh consequences. Parents may be convicted whether or not they knew of their child's absences and irrespective of their attitude to attendance.[67] The law makes no concessions and simply expects them to overcome any reluctance on the child's part. Parents may be convicted even in circumstances in which they have no knowledge of the child's whereabouts,[68] or have been abused by the child and are in fear of them.[69] It is difficult to see how prosecution of these parents is likely to improve attendance or to resolve the problems that underlie absence in such cases.

A number of procedural 'alternatives to prosecution' are used to try to achieve an improvement in pupils' attendance without the need for court proceedings.[70] As discussed below, the governing bodies of schools and LAs

---

[63] Penalties under s. 444(1A) include: a fine up to £2,500 and imprisonment for up to 3 months. Under s. 444(1), the maximum fine is currently £1,000 and imprisonment is not available.

[64] It is a defence to a charge under s. 444(1A) for the parent to show reasonable justification for such failure (s. 444(1B)). E.g. *R (P)* v. *Liverpool City Magistrates* [2006] EWHC 887 (Admin), [2006] ELR 386.

[65] EA 1996, s. 444(2)–(6). The circumstances include that the child is prevented from attending through 'sickness or any unavoidable cause' (s. 444(2A)) or has leave to be absent (s. 444(3)(a)).

[66] See e.g. *Islington LBC* v. *D* [2011] EWHC 990 (Admin), where the child had long-standing behavioural and mental health difficulties that were unresolved. The mother had done all that she could to secure attendance, but this was not relevant to the interpretation of 'unavoidable cause'. There was nothing in the nature of an emergency here and the circumstances did not amount to an unavoidable cause.

[67] *Crump* v. *Gilmore* (1969) 113 Sol Jo 998.

[68] *West Sussex County Council* v. *C* [2013] EWHC 1757 (Admin): the 15-year-old child had a 'chaotic lifestyle' having run away to spend substantial portions of time with the family of her estranged father. The court accepted that the mother had done all that she could to ensure attendance and so had a defence to a charge under s. 444(1A), but this did not amount to an unavoidable cause under s. 444(2A) as there was nothing preventing the child attending. Despite the sympathy of the court, the magistrates were directed to convict the mother of the lesser offence under s. 444(1).

[69] E.g. *Hampshire County Council* v. *E* [2007] EWHC 2584 (Admin), [2008] ELR 260; *Telford and Wrekin Council* v. *Ashley* [2001] CLY 1986. Both of these cases concerned single mothers who had been subject to abuse by their teenage sons. As discussed below, single mothers are disproportionately represented in those prosecuted under s. 444(1).

[70] Many LAs use forms of 'attendance case management' in which intervention to improve children's attendance takes place before the trial, with the prosecution being dropped if matters improve. Around half of prosecutions using this process are discontinued: DfE (2020b) p. 4.

may prefer to avoid resorting to criminal remedies by asking parents of truants to enter into a parenting contract. But these too have an authoritarian flavour. Fixed penalty notices[71] can also be issued in circumstances in which there is reason to believe that an offence under section 444(1) has been committed. A parent who receives such a notice can avoid prosecution through the payment of fines.[72] The use of these notices has soared and the majority are paid within 28 days, allowing the parent to avoid prosecution or an inflated fine; indeed, only 7 per cent of penalty notices end in prosecution.[73] At first glance, these numbers may give the impression that penalty notices have been a great success in diverting cases from court. In reality, the increase appears to be almost entirely driven by parents taking their children on term-time holidays since the decision in *Platt*.[74] Indeed, anecdotal evidence suggests that parents budget for fines when planning holidays.[75] Far from discouraging absence, the presence of fines appears to create the impression that non-attendance can be bought. Some parents consider this policy to be an unwarranted restriction on parental autonomy and the principle that the primary responsibility for determining children's education lies with parents rather than the state. Whatever the merits of the policy, these parents are unlikely to find support from their Article 8 right to family life. As Harris notes, the European Court of Human Rights (ECtHR) has recognised that sending children to school 'necessarily' involves some degree of interference with family life. Interference with parental discretion to organise family holidays or days out is likely to be justified by the child's right to education and the state's interest in running an effective school system.[76]

The criminal justice response to truancy is reinforced by police involvement through the power to issue penalty notices and carry out 'truancy sweeps'. Police officers can collect up children of compulsory school age whom they find in public places during school hours and take them to 'designated premises' or back to their schools.[77] Some police officers also work in schools on a regular basis, offering advice and support over a variety of issues, including

---

[71] EA 1996, ss 444A and 444B. The notices may be issued by LAs, head teachers and police officers.

[72] Parents can avoid prosecution altogether if they pay fixed penalties (£60 if paid within 28 days, rising to £120 if paid after 28 but within 42 days) before/instead of criminal proceedings under EA 1996, s. 444 being brought against them. Education (Penalty Notices) (England) Regulations 2007 (SI 2007/1867).

[73] In 2018–19, 333,400 penalty notices were issued, an increase of 28 per cent on the previous year; this compares to just 25,657 in 2009–10. Fines were paid within 28 days in 76 per cent of cases: DfE (2020b) p. 3; N. Harris (2020) p. 85.

[74] In 2018–19, 86 per cent of notices were issued for an unauthorised term-time holiday: DfE (2020b) p. 3. There appears to have been a sharp increase in the use of penalty notices following the decision in *Isle of Wight Council* v. *Platt* [2017] UKSC 28, [2017] 1 WLR 1441.

[75] E.g. BBC, *School Holiday Fines: Parents Hit by Penalties Rise 93%*, 21 March 2019, www .bbc.co.uk/news/uk-england-47613726.

[76] N. Harris (2020) p. 78, citing *Costello-Roberts* v. *United Kingdom* [1994] 1 FCR 65 and *Wunderlich* v. *Germany* [2019] ELR 435.

[77] Crime and Disorder Act (CDA) 1998, s. 16.

deterring truancy. Researchers found very mixed feelings among LAs and the police over the efficacy of a police presence in schools,[78] and more particularly of truancy sweeps and other similar measures.[79] Nonetheless, children who are absent from school can be at risk of harm and exploitation and police action can have an important role in ensuring their safety.[80]

It is doubtful whether draconian criminal sanctions are effective in dealing with persistent absence. As Jones notes, increasing prosecutions have had no discernible impact on the level of absenteeism.[81] In reality, research indicates that very few parents condone truancy, that most take regular attendance at school very seriously and that they are often unaware of their child's truancy.[82] Few pupils themselves, when asked, admit skipping school with parental consent; pupils of all ages most often identify school-based causes, such as extreme boredom, bullying and problems with teachers.[83] Research with parents suggests that many of these children have unmet special educational needs and disabilities (SEND), mental health difficulties and experience of serious bullying.[84] In such cases, prosecution does nothing to address the underlying causes of school refusal. Mothers, particularly single mothers,[85] are more likely to be prosecuted than fathers.[86] Many of these mothers report great difficulty in forcing unwilling children to go to school.[87] Prosecution often exacerbates existing difficulties in these mothers' lives, including their own experience of mental ill-health and difficulty in maintaining employment alongside meeting their children's needs.[88] Nor is prosecution likely to enhance the children's relationship with their parents, which may be extremely poor already – a factor which may itself underlie their disenchantment with school. While prosecution, or the threat of prosecution,[89] may be successful in persuading parents and children to work with the authorities in some cases, the criminal justice system is unlikely to meet the complex needs that often underlie persistent absence.

(ii) Civil Remedies

The civil law provides less punitive sanctions against parents for their children's failure to attend school. Before prosecuting the parent, the LA must consider the appropriateness of applying to the family courts for an education

---

[78] S. Hallam *et al.* (2005) pp. 110–12.

[79] National Audit Office (2005) paras 3.16–3.19; Action on Rights for Children (2005).

[80] N. Harris (2020) p. 90. The risks to children who are absent from school are discussed further below.

[81] S. Jones (2014): despite a five-fold increase in prosecutions between 2001 and 2011, absenteeism remained virtually constant.

[82] H. Malcolm *et al.* (2003) ch. 4 and p. 63; D. Dalziel and K. Henthorne (2005) ch. 4.

[83] Ibid.   [84] S. Jones (2014) pp. 329–30; R. Epstein *et al.* (2019).   [85] S. Jones (2014).

[86] R. Epstein *et al.* (2019) report that in 2017 women constituted 71 per cent of prosecutions, 74 per cent of convictions, 80 per cent of suspended prison sentences and 90 per cent of custodial sentences.

[87] S. Jones (2014) pp. 327–8.   [88] R. Epstein *et al.* (2019).

[89] Around half of cases progressing through attendance case management are withdrawn before prosecution: DfE (2020b) p. 4.

supervision order (ESO).[90] This order was created by the Children Act (CA) 1989 to replace the old method of applying for a care order regarding persistent truants, the sole ground being that 'the child is of compulsory school age and is not being properly educated'.[91] Since truancy is often attributable to family difficulties, prior consultation with children's services should enable social workers to establish what can be done to support the family and avoid criminal proceedings against the parents for their child's school absences, which may make matters worse. The ESO was intended to help parents who find it difficult to exercise a proper influence over their child, by giving court backing to the efforts of the supervising officer while working with the family and child.[92] The order involves the child being placed under the supervision of the 'designated authority'[93] for its duration[94] and a social worker or education welfare officer being appointed to 'advise, assist and befriend' the child and his or her parents and give them directions intending to achieve the child's proper education.[95] But although its creation indicated a well-intentioned effort to ensure that the individual needs of the non-attending child were considered and addressed, the ESO has proved unpopular with LAs.[96] This is probably because LAs will usually try most strategies authorised by such an order, without going to the trouble and expense of making a court application.[97] The LA will sometimes obtain an ESO in the first instance, but follow it up with criminal sanctions against the parent if the child refuses to cooperate with his or her supervisor.[98]

Parenting contracts and parenting orders were New Labour legislative creations, again of a civil nature.[99] Parenting contracts[100] were designed to ensure that parents of truanting children[101] obtain professional help with attendance problems[102] and to promote a better working relationship between them and the school. A school may 'suggest' to parents of a truanting child that they enter into a parenting contract and, although theoretically voluntary,

---

[90] EA 1996, s. 447(1).

[91] CA 1989, s. 36(3). Such a step should only be contemplated after having consulted children's services.

[92] DH (1991) para. 3.9.   [93] CA 1989, s. 36(7).

[94] CA 1989, Sch. 3, para. 15(1) – in the first place not more than 1 year, although it can be extended for a further 3 years.

[95] CA 1989, Sch. 3, para. 12(1).

[96] Very few orders are made. In 2018–19, only thirty-four were made, a decrease from eighty in 2017–18 and ninety in 2016–17; DfE (2020b) p. 5.

[97] E.g. *Re O (A Minor) (Care Order: Education: Procedure)* [1992] 2 FLR 7.

[98] E.g. *Graves* v. *London Borough of Islington* [2003] EWHC 2817 (Admin), [2004] ELR 1.

[99] Governed by Education (Parenting Contract and Parenting Orders) (England) Regulations 2007 (SI 2007/1869).

[100] Anti-Social Behaviour Act (ASBA) 2003, s. 19(4): a parenting contract is a two-sided formal agreement setting out the parents' undertakings regarding their child's future attendance and the undertakings of the LA or school regarding future support for the parent and child.

[101] ASBA 2003, s. 19(2). NB: parenting contracts and orders may also be used by schools in situations where a pupil is in danger of being excluded due to his or her bad behaviour.

[102] ASBA 2003, s. 19(5) and (6). E.g. parents may be offered parenting skills courses and children provided with mentors.

a parent's refusal to sign such a document must be considered by the court in any future criminal proceedings linked to the child's continuing absence.[103] In those circumstances, parents may feel that the description of a parenting contract as 'voluntary' is misleading.[104] Although it is difficult to assess the effectiveness of parenting contracts, given the various factors which may play a part in any improvement, schools and parents who use them appear to consider them beneficial in improving both children's attendance and parents' relationships with the school.[105]

Parents who are successfully prosecuted for their children's truancy may find that they additionally become the subject of a parenting order[106] requiring compliance with various strategies designed to moderate their own behaviour and that of their children. Although civil in nature, these may have an extensive impact on families. They have two elements: the parents may be required to attend counselling or guidance sessions for up to three months and to fulfil various provisions designed to address the non-attendance.[107] The order may even, in limited circumstances, require parents to attend a residential counselling or guidance course.[108] Breach of a parenting order is a criminal offence.[109] There is a risk that parents will be alienated by schools intervening in ways which result in their being taken to court, particularly if they have been doing their best to make their children attend school regularly. Fionda describes this as 'an anti-partnership approach, which seeks to coerce parents into compliance with their statutory responsibilities' and involves school in policing their behaviour.[110] Parenting orders have not proved popular with LAs and their use is decreasing.[111]

The parental responsibility approach[112] to children's school attendance is of limited efficacy in circumstances in which the parent's attitudes and behaviour are not the primary cause of the child's absence from school. Government policy increasingly recognises that persistent absence from school is often one facet of a more complex set of problems and strongly linked to social and

---

[103] ASBA 2003, s. 21(1)(a) and (b): when deciding whether to make a parenting order, the court must consider: (a) the parent's refusal to enter into a parenting contract; and (b) the parent's breach of any terms of a parenting contract.

[104] DfE (2015) p. 7.

[105] L. Evans *et al.* (2008) chs 6–7. The parents largely found the parenting skills courses helpful. In 2018–19, 18,300 parenting contracts were offered. There is no clear trend in their use: DfE (2020b) p. 4.

[106] Sentencing Act 2020, s. 369, replacing the previous provision in CDA 1998, s. 8(1)(d).

[107] Sentencing Act 2020, s. 365.

[108] Sentencing Act 2020, s. 369(5): a residential requirement may be imposed only if the court considers that: (a) such a course would be more effective than their attendance at a non-residential course in preventing their child from engaging in a repetition of the behaviour which led to the order; and (b) any likely interference with family life is proportionate in all the circumstances.

[109] Sentencing Act 2020, s. 375.   [110] J. Fionda (2005) p. 229.

[111] In 2018–19, 117 parenting orders were made, a decrease of 24 per cent on the previous year and a downward trend from the 439 made in 2010–11.

[112] S. Jones (2014) pp. 331–4.

economic disadvantage.[113] Research also suggests that school refusal is often closely connected to mental health, isolation and anxiety.[114] A holistic approach that addresses these underlying and interconnected problems is more likely to be effective in dealing with intractable cases of persistent absence than one which lays responsibility on parents alone.

(4) Behaviour and Discipline

(A) Schools' Powers and Duties

(i) The Background

The behaviour of some pupils can have a significant impact on the education, well-being and safety of others. Bored children, who cannot see the point of classes, may disrupt the learning of others. Those exhibiting aggressive and anti-social behaviour may intimidate class-mates and teachers alike.[115] Indeed, a couple of violent ill-disciplined pupils in a class can create a highly charged and frightening atmosphere for their peers. Bullying and abusive behaviour can have a devastating impact on the learning and health of victims, with potentially life-long consequences for their education and mental health.

Schools dealing with disruptive, bullying or abusive behaviour must fulfil their obligations to all pupils, whether they are victims, perpetrators or bystanders. The human rights framework provides guidance to schools in meeting this challenge, but also demonstrates the complexities that can be encountered in doing so. All pupils are entitled to the right to education guaranteed by ECHR A2P1: the state must ensure that disruptive and abusive behaviour does not prevent other pupils from receiving an education. It must also ensure that measures taken to deal with that behaviour respect the education rights of the perpetrators. Nonetheless, the right to education in A2P1 does not prevent recourse to disciplinary measures, including exclusion or suspension, provided that those measures are proportionate and fairly administered, and adequate provision is made for the child to receive education.[116] The CRC also recognises that the right to education may entail disciplinary measures and requires states to 'take all appropriate measures to ensure that school discipline is administered in a manner consistent with the

---

[113] Notably through the 'Supporting Families' programme (formerly 'Troubled Families'), which seeks to support families with multiple and complex needs, including persistent absence from school.

[114] M. Kljakovic *et al.* (2021). At the time of writing, these problems had been exacerbated by the Covid-19 pandemic and the response to it.

[115] E.g. In *Leeds City Council and others* v. *Channel 4 Television Corporation* [2007] 1 FLR 678, Munby J, at [5], describes the secretly filmed scenes of poor discipline in three schools, with pupils fighting one another in class, running around the classroom jumping from desk to desk and adopting a 'grossly insubordinate and offensive attitude to their teacher'.

[116] *Ali* v. *United Kingdom*, App. No. 40385/06, [2011] ELR 85, at [54] and [58]; exclusions are discussed further below. See also *Sahin* v. *Turkey* [2006] ELR 73, per Grand Chamber of the European Court of Human Rights (ECtHR), at [156].

child's human dignity'.[117] Such measures are important, as failure to take effective steps to address violent or abusive behaviour may lead to the violation of a range of other rights. Schools must act to protect pupils from behaviour that constitutes inhuman or degrading treatment,[118] violates their physical and psychological integrity[119] or subjects them to discrimination.[120] The ECtHR has recognised that states have a positive obligation to take reasonable steps to protect others from the harmful actions of pupils.[121] Effective action by schools to address such behaviour is an important facet of meeting this obligation.

Domestic law provides the framework in which these obligations should be met. The law clearly requires schools to maintain discipline and to make arrangements to ensure that their functions are 'exercised with a view to safeguarding and promoting the welfare' of pupils,[122] including protecting children from abuse from their peers.[123] Further, the common law imposes a duty of care to pupils on schools and their staff, just as it does on parents. A teacher is required to show the same standard of care as that of 'a reasonably careful parent', taking into account the school context and number of pupils.[124] A failure to do so may be actionable in tort, or under the HRA, by a pupil if it has led to physical or psychological injury.[125] Finally, as considered below, it is increasingly recognised that many forms of bullying and abusive behaviour are directed against pupils on the basis of their sex, race, sexual orientation, disability or other protected characteristics. In responding to such behaviour, schools must have due regard to their obligations under the Equality Act 2010, including the need to eliminate discrimination and harassment and to foster good relations and equality of opportunity within the school community.[126]

---

[117] Art. 28(2).   [118] ECHR, Art. 3.   [119] ECHR, Art. 8.   [120] ECHR, Art. 14.

[121] *Kayak* v. *Turkey*, App. No. 60444/08, 10 July 2012: a pupil with no apparent history of violent behaviour stabbed a former pupil at the school gates using a knife that he had obtained from the school canteen. In these circumstances, the ECtHR found a violation of the state's obligations under ECHR, Art. 2. See also *Kotilainen* v. *Finland* (2021) 72 EHRR 26, in which a violation of Art. 2 was found in relation to a pupil who had killed nine students and a teacher at a school. The failures in this case were concerned with the actions of the police in relation to the perpetrator's possession of firearms.

[122] EA 2002, s. 175: the obligation is placed on LAs and on governing bodies of maintained schools. A similar obligation is placed on proprietors of independent schools under the Education (Independent School Standards) 2014, SI 2014/3283, Sch. 1, para. 7.

[123] The statutory guidance issued under the above provisions sets out the requirements on schools in relation to peer-on-peer abuse: DfE (2021a) esp. pp. 120–1 and 135, discussed further below.

[124] *Van Oppen* v. *Clerk to the Bedford Charity Trustees* [1989] 3 All ER 389, per Balcombe LJ, at 401; *Gower* v. *London Borough of Bromley* [1999] ELR 356, per Auld LJ, at 359.

[125] A number of pupils who have been sexually assaulted in school appear to have obtained settlements from LAs and schools following actions brought in tort and under the HRA for failures to protect the pupil from abuse perpetrated by other pupils. E.g. *The Guardian*, 21 November 2018, reported on the first-known settlement involving sexual abuse at primary school, in a case in which the victim was a 6-year-old girl.

[126] Equality Act 2010, s. 149, setting out the public sector equality duty (PSED).

(ii) Bullying and Peer Abuse in Schools

As the Committee on the Rights of the Child has repeatedly observed,[127] bullying of all kinds has become increasingly common in UK schools. Research and guidance reflect an increasingly complex picture of the kinds of harms that children may be subject to in school. Government guidance requires schools to be aware of, and provide an effective response to, a wide range of peer-on-peer abuse, including bullying, physical abuse, sexual violence and sexual harassment.[128] The widespread availability of technology and access to the internet has made it increasingly easy for students to harass and bully their peers online and to share pornography or explicit images of other pupils.[129] Schools face particular difficulties in identifying and preventing these forms of cyberbullying, especially as the use of personal devices blurs the boundaries between school and home. The Committee's observations also emphasise the particular problem of discrimination- and prejudice-based abuse against students on the basis of their sexual orientation, gender identity, disability and race.[130] Such abusive behaviour is not only especially harmful to the victim, but can also create a hostile environment for all pupils, especially those who share the same characteristics as the victim.

The scale and complexity of the problem facing pupils and schools is well demonstrated by the pervasive problem of sexual harassment and violence. In 2016, an inquiry by the House of Commons' Women and Equalities Committee received substantial evidence demonstrating the normalisation of sexual harassment and violence in schools.[131] The government largely accepted those findings and committed to addressing them, but it took further public pressure for action to be taken. In 2020–21, thousands of pupils and former pupils gave detailed online accounts of their experiences of sexual harassment and abuse in education.[132] Those accounts brought the scale and seriousness of the problem to public attention and under public pressure the government asked Ofsted to conduct a rapid review of the issue.[133] Ofsted's findings supported previous research demonstrating a widespread culture of harmful sexual behaviour in which almost all girls surveyed reported that sexual harassment, circulation of sexual images and sexual assault happened 'a lot' or 'sometimes' within their schools.[134] The perception among the

---

[127] Committee on the Rights of the Child (2016) paras 48–49, (2008) para. 66; (2002) para. 47.

[128] DfE (2021a) esp. paras 46–50.   [129] Ibid. para. 126.

[130] Committee on the Rights of the Child (2016) para. 48.

[131] Women and Equalities Committee (2016).

[132] In particular, on the website Everyone's Invited: www.everyonesinvited.uk.

[133] Ofsted (2021).

[134] The proportion of girls (aged over 13) reporting that the following behaviour happened 'a lot' or 'sometimes' was: sexist name calling (92 per cent); being sent videos or pictures they did not want to see (88 per cent); pressure to send sexual images of themselves (80 per cent); images being circulated without their knowledge or consent (73 per cent); and sexual assault (79 per cent). Boys were much less likely to report that harmful sexual behaviour occurred.

students surveyed was that this harmful behaviour was so ubiquitous and embedded within behaviour at schools that there was no point in challenging or reporting it. New guidance published in the wake of the report is intended to guide colleges and schools – both primary and secondary – in recognising the seriousness of the problem, taking effective action to respond to sexual abuse and to drive cultural change in which such behaviour is not tolerated.[135]

Research into sexual abuse in schools highlights a number of problems that also apply to other forms of bullying and peer abuse. Their prevalence is difficult to estimate. This is partly because of victims' reluctance to tell anyone of its occurrence, and partly because teachers themselves underestimate its frequency.[136] For this reason, the guidance tells schools not to rely on reports of bullying and abuse, but to assume that they are likely to be taking place unreported.[137] Schools are directed to take a 'whole school' approach in which safeguarding underpins all aspects of policies and practices.[138] Ofsted and the Independent Schools Inspectorate, having previously been criticised for failing to give sufficient attention to peer abuse, especially sexual harassment and violence,[139] have strengthened their inspection framework to include closer consideration of the school's approach to peer abuse.[140] Preventing bullying and abuse from taking place requires a culture in which such behaviour is not acceptable. Education can play a key role in creating that culture,[141] as can effective implementation of the school's behaviour policy. Schools must establish written policies designed to 'promote good behaviour and discipline on the part of its pupils'.[142] Head teachers must also determine measures promoting among pupils 'self-discipline and proper regard for authority', encouraging good behaviour and, in particular, 'preventing all forms of bullying among pupils'.[143] The guidance stresses that all forms of bullying, including cyberbullying, should be addressed.[144] The legislation and guidance reflect case law establishing that a school's duty of care towards a pupil does not necessarily

---

[135] DfE (2021b) and the revisions to DfE (2021a), discussed further below.

[136] R. Long *et al.* (2020) pp. 6–9 summarise the available evidence.

[137] DfE (2021a) paras 15, 47, 428 and 447, (2021b) paras 1 and 9.

[138] DfE (2021a) paras 81 and 82, (2021b) paras 31–33.

[139] Women and Equalities Committee (2016) esp. pp. 29–31.

[140] Ofsted (2021). In grading behaviour and attitudes in schools, the current School Inspection Handbook (September 2021) requires inspectors to assess the extent to which the school provides: 'an environment in which pupils feel safe, and in which bullying, discrimination, sexual harassment, sexual abuse and sexual violence – online or offline – are not accepted and are dealt with quickly, consistently and effectively whenever they occur'. The handbook is regularly updated and available at www.gov.uk/government/publications/school-inspection-handbook-eif.

[141] See further the discussion of relationship and sex education below.

[142] Education and Inspections Act (EIA) 2006, s. 88: the governing body of every mainstream school must draw up a written statement on discipline and good behaviour, having consulted the head teacher, relevant school employees, parents and pupils.

[143] EIA 2006, s. 89(1)(a) and (b). EIA 2006, s. 89(6): these measures must, in the form of a written document, be widely publicised within the school.

[144] DfE (2017a) esp. p. 8.

end at the school gate and that, in some circumstances, a school may be liable in tort for failing to take effective steps to prevent bullying outside school – for example, on the bus home.[145] Thus, behaviour policies should also aim to control behaviour off the school premises 'to such extent as is reasonable', even when pupils are not under the control of any member of staff.[146] The guidance is clear that this can include online behaviour, which will often occur when the pupils are not on the school premises.[147]

Legislation and official guidance do not necessarily produce results. As considered below, schools have the power to intervene, investigate and impose sanctions for poor behaviour. Some instances will be too serious to deal with internally and may require the involvement of other agencies, including the police and children's social care services. While there is no specific offence of bullying, many forms of violence, harassment, sexual behaviour and online bullying by pupils will be criminal.[148] Schools are often uncertain as to when to call the police and may be reluctant to do so, particularly as students may be more unwilling to report behaviour if it will lead to police involvement.[149] This has led to wide divergence in practice between schools.[150] The National Police Chiefs' Council now gives detailed advice to schools on how to decide whether to involve the police or to address the matter internally.[151] This advice supplements the statutory guidance, which makes it clear that any report of rape, assault by penetration or sexual assault should be passed to the police.[152] Children should not be expected to suffer from behaviour in school that would not be tolerated elsewhere in society. Recognising that serious offences can be committed by peers, and that police involvement is required in such cases, is an important step in protecting victims. Police involvement does not necessarily mean that there will be a full criminal justice response to the behaviour; the police and Crown Prosecution Service (CPS) may well decide that it is not in the public interest to prosecute even if there is sufficient evidence that a crime has been committed.[153] Criminal behaviour by a child may well indicate that the perpetrator has themselves been the victim of

---

[145] *Bradford-Smart* v. *West Sussex County Council* [2002] EWCA Civ 07, [2002] ELR 139, per Judge LJ, at [34]–[36].

[146] EIA 2006, ss 89(5) and 90(2)(a).   [147] DfE (2017a) p. 15.

[148] Examples of offences that may be relevant include: Voyeurism (Offences) Act 2019 (upskirting); Criminal Justice Act 1988, s. 139A (possession of knife or offensive weapon on school premises); Protection of Children Act 1978, s. 1; and Criminal Justice Act 1988, s. 160 (indecent images of children).

[149] Ofsted (2021).   [150] Women and Equalities Committee (2016) esp. paras 81–85.

[151] This advice is available from www.npcc.police.uk/SysSiteAssets/media/downloads/publications/publications-log/2020/when-to-call-the-police–guidance-for-schools-and-colleges.pdf.

[152] DfE (2021a) p. 108.

[153] There are concerns about the over-policing of children in some settings. E.g. Rod Morgan, the then Chairman of the Youth Justice Board for England and Wales, in *The Times*, 21 August 2006, criticised teachers and children's homes for too often resorting to the police to curb bad behaviour, rather than dealing with it themselves.

abuse.[154] For this reason, the police should still be informed of serious sexual assaults if the perpetrator is under the age of criminal responsibility, as a safeguarding response is likely to be required. Any report to the police will usually be accompanied by a report to children's social care, regardless of the age of those involved, in order to consider the safeguarding needs of the perpetrator and victim.[155] Support and safeguarding for the victim are of particular importance. For a long time, no specific guidance was given to schools as to how they should support victims of serious peer abuse or how to manage circumstances in which victims and alleged perpetrators continue to attend the same school. The guidance has now been revised to make clear that, at least in the case of victims of sexual violence, the alleged perpetrator should be removed from any shared classes and arrangements made to ensure that the victim will not encounter them in school while investigations are ongoing.[156] This is essential to supporting the victim and their ongoing right to education.

(iii) Sanctions, Use of Force and Power to Search

In the event of these preventative measures failing, a teacher may wish to punish a pupil for his or her bad behaviour. The law relating to discipline in schools has become increasingly complex, having been the subject of various reports.[157] The use of sanctions by teachers is now extensively regulated. It has been statutorily confirmed that teachers[158] have a legal power to discipline their pupils.[159] Disciplinary penalties can be imposed for bad behaviour[160] in school,[161] provided that the penalty in question is lawful[162] and reasonable in all the circumstances.[163] However bad a pupil's behaviour, teachers in all schools are prohibited from using physical punishment.[164] Some wrongly assume that this means that teachers can never use force, whatever the circumstances. But as legislation emphasises, forceful measures can be taken by teachers confronted by disruptive and aggressive pupils.[165] Teachers have the power to use 'such force as is reasonable in the circumstances' to prevent

---

[154] DfE (2021b) p. 45.   [155] DfE (2021a) p. 108, (2021b) p. 38.   [156] DfE (2021b) pp. 40–4.

[157] Inter alia: R. Elton (1989); A. Steer (2005).

[158] EIA 2006, s. 91(4): any paid member of staff (unless specifically prohibited by the head teacher) and any other member of staff so authorised by the head teacher.

[159] EIA 2006, ss 90–1, supported by official guidance; DfE (2016).   [160] EIA 2006, s. 90(1).

[161] EIA 2006, s. 91(5)(b): the penalty may also be imposed for bad behaviour out of school if the pupil was under the lawful control or charge of a member of staff. EIA 2006, s.90(2)(a): a penalty may be imposed even if the pupil was neither on the school premises nor under the lawful control or charge of a member of staff, but only to the extent that this is reasonable.

[162] EIA 2006, s. 91(3)(a), i.e. does not infringe any statutory requirement, such as the equality legislation.

[163] EIA 2006, s. 91(3)(b) and (6): the reasonableness must be determined, taking account of whether the penalty is proportionate in the circumstances, and of the pupil's own particular circumstances (e.g. age, special educational needs, disability and religious requirements).

[164] EA 1996, ss 548–9. The prohibition on corporal punishment in schools is further discussed in Chapter 4.

[165] EIA 2006, s. 93, supported by guidance in DfE (2013).

behaviour that would have a serious effect on the school and/or other pupils.[166] The official guidance attempts to address the fact that the ostensibly very broad legislative formula might lead to a disproportionate use of force.[167] It stresses that it must not be used to prevent a pupil committing a trivial misdemeanour, it must only be used as a last resort, and must always be very carefully justified. Above all, force should never be used as a punishment.[168]

Legislation also gives head teachers[169] extensive powers to search pupils without their consent if there are reasonable grounds for suspecting that they have prohibited items within their possession.[170] Reasonable force may be used to search for a range of specified items, including knives, weapons, alcohol, illegal drugs and pornography.[171] The legislation also permits mobiles and other electronic devices to be seized,[172] and data and files examined or erased if the person searching 'thinks there is good reason to do so'.[173] The power to impose a search is subject to a number of statutory safeguards. Any search must be carried out by an authorised person who is the same sex as the pupil being searched. A witness must be present, except in urgent situations in which there is a risk of significant harm if the search is not carried out immediately.[174] No pupil being searched by an authorised member of staff can be required to remove clothing beyond outer clothing.[175] The extensive powers of search and seizure contained in the legislation permit significant

---

[166] EIA 2006, s. 93(1): such force as is reasonable in the circumstances to prevent a pupil from: (a) committing any offence; (b) injuring anyone or damaging anyone's property; (c) prejudicing good order and discipline at the school or among any pupils receiving education at the school, whether during a teaching session or otherwise.

[167] JCHR (2006) para. 52.

[168] DfE (2013) p. 5: the guidance provides a list of clearly described factual examples of situations where force may be justified.

[169] Or other authorised member of staff.

[170] EA 1996, ss 550ZA–550ZD; these powers were extensively amended by the Education Act 2011, Pt 2. Pupils may also be searched for any item with their consent.

[171] EA 1996, s. 550ZB(5); the list of prohibited items for which force may be used is given in s. 550ZA(a)–(f) supplemented by The Schools (Specification and Disposal of Articles) Regulations 2012. The school rules may specify additional items which can be searched for without the pupil's consent, but force may not be used for such searches.

[172] s. 550ZC(6D) provided that the item is either prohibited by the school rules or is reasonably suspected of being, or likely to be, used to commit an offence or cause damage to person or property (s. 550ZA(3)(ea) and (g)).

[173] s. 550ZB(6E) and (6F).

[174] s. 550ZB(6)(b) and (c) and (6A): the conditions are that: (a) the person carrying out the search reasonably believes that there is a risk that serious harm will be caused to a person if the search is not carried out as a matter of urgency; and (b) in the time available it is not reasonably practicable for the search to be carried out by a person of the same sex as the pupil or in the presence of another member of staff (as the case may be).

[175] s. 550ZB (6)(a). The police have more extensive powers to search under the Police and Criminal Evidence Act 1984 and its associated Codes of Practice. The use of these powers in schools, particularly the use of intimate searches, must be tightly constrained if it is to comply with the child's rights and safeguarding standards. For a particularly egregious use of this power, see: J. Gamble and R. McCallum (2022), who concluded that racism was 'likely to have been an influencing factor' in the decision to subject a 15-year-old girl to a 'strip search' following reports that she 'smelt of cannabis'.

interference with pupils' property and personal integrity and clearly engage their rights under Article 8 of the ECHR. That interference will be justified if it is exercised in accordance with law and proportionate to a legitimate aim. As considered above, the protection of other pupils, maintenance of discipline and prevention of harm to others are well-recognised as legitimate aims that may justify such actions. Nonetheless, the legislation is broadly drawn, grants significant discretion to staff and could be used in a manner that is disproportionate to those aims.[176] The accompanying guidance recognises the importance of Article 8, but somewhat complacently assumes that any school acting within the legislation will have 'no difficulty in demonstrating that it has also acted in accordance with Article 8'.[177] Although searches carried out in accordance with the legislation and guidance *may* be in accordance with Article 8, any school using the power to search pupils must give close attention to the proportionality of doing so in the particular circumstances. The powers of search and seizure in school are one of the clearest examples of the difficulties for schools in balancing the rights of pupils with those of their peers and the interest of the wider school community. In carrying out that balance, the school must be alert to the intrusive nature of the search power and the child's right to privacy.

(B) Exclusions

(i) The Background

The most draconian consequence that may be imposed on a pupil is that of exclusion.[178] Teachers cannot pick and choose which children they are prepared to teach and which they are not. Nevertheless, a disruptive child's right to be educated in school may seriously undermine the right of other children to receive instruction in an atmosphere conducive to learning. Further, a school faced with harmful or abusive behaviour by a pupil may conclude that exclusion is necessary for the well-being and safety of affected pupils. In cases of serious infringements of discipline, schools may feel that they have little option but to resort to excluding pupils they are unable to control. Exclusion from school, whether permanent or for a fixed period, constitutes a significant interference with the child's right to education. Although arrangements must be made for the excluded child to continue to receive education, that alternative provision is often poor and exclusion is associated with low future academic attainment, involvement in criminal behaviour and poorer life

---

[176] E.g. the loose wording allowing a member of staff to delete files if he or she 'thinks there is good reason to do so'. The Joint Committee on Human Rights raised a series of concerns during the passage of the Education Bill: JCHR (2011).

[177] DfE (2018a) esp. p. 4, which states that: 'The powers to search in the Education Act 1996 are compatible with Article 8. A school exercising those powers lawfully should have no difficulty in demonstrating that it has also acted in accordance with Article 8.'

[178] The discussion of exclusion in this section applies to state-funded schools. In independent schools, exclusion is primarily governed by contract.

chances.[179] Despite the serious impact of exclusion, there are significant weaknesses in the protection for the excluded pupil's right to education. The law and guidance are characterised by head-teacher discretion, with limited effective accountability for that decision or accessible routes for pupils and parents to challenge it.

After a long period of declining[180] exclusion rates, the period since 2012–13 has seen a significant increase in the use of both fixed-term[181] and permanent exclusion.[182] Most exclusions are for short periods of a few days,[183] but an increasing number of pupils are subject to permanent exclusion. These overall numbers mask substantial variation between schools and between local authorities[184] that cannot be fully explained by demographic differences. Instead, it seems that differences in school and LA culture have a role to play in the exercise of discretion and the likelihood of a pupil being excluded for particular behaviour.[185] Research also suggests that official rates of exclusion are distorted by practices that unlawfully seek to remove children from the classroom without formal exclusion. Despite its official prohibition, there appears to be continued and widespread use of 'unofficial or informal exclusion'[186] through pupils being sent home or put on part timetable without the procedures for formal exclusion being followed.[187] Similar concerns surround the practice of 'off-rolling', through which parents are put under pressure to remove their children rather than facing formal exclusion.[188]

---

[179] Discussed further below. The extent to which exclusion *causes* these consequences is unclear.

[180] From a peak of 12,700 permanent exclusions in 1997. The then Labour government commissioned the Social Exclusion Unit to consider the linked problem of truancy and permanent exclusion; SEU (1998). Measures introduced included official targets for schools to reduce their use of permanent exclusion and new guidance. These measures were initially very successful and by 2001 schools were no longer required to comply with further targets to cut exclusions.

[181] Sometimes referred to as 'suspension'. There were 146,070 fixed-period exclusions in England in 2012–13, a rate of 3.52. In comparison, there were 438,265 fixed-period exclusions in 2018–19, a rate of 5.36. The numbers for 2019–20 and 2020–21 are not comparable due to the disruption to education caused by the response to the Covid-19 pandemic. Statistics in this section are taken from the annual statistical releases available at: www.gov.uk/government/collections/statistics-exclusions. NB: Suspension rates are calculated as the total number of suspensions, divided by the total number of pupils (×100).

[182] Sometimes referred to as 'expulsion'. There were 3,900 permanent exclusions in 2012–13, compared to 7,894 in 2018–19: ibid.

[183] Fixed-period exclusions can last up to a maximum of 45 days in any one school year: School Discipline (Pupil Exclusions and Reviews) (England) Regulations 2012 (SI 2012/1033), reg. 4. In 2018–19, 49 per cent of fixed-period exclusions were for 1 day and 98 per cent were for 5 days or fewer.

[184] The *Timpson Review* found that 85 per cent of mainstream schools issued no permanent exclusions in 2016–17, while forty-seven schools issued at least ten each in the same year. Similarly, 43 per cent issued no fixed-period exclusions, while thirty-eight schools issued over 500: DfE (2019b) p. 9.

[185] L. Ferguson and N. Webber (2015).

[186] See also the use of internal exclusion, which has received some judicial support; *R (L (A Minor))* v. *Governors of J School* [2003] UKHL 9, [2003] 2 AC 633.

[187] DfE (2019b) pp. 99–100.   [188] Ibid. pp. 100–1,

These decisions are taken in the interests of the school, rather than the child, and are often used to avoid their poor academic attainment lowering their school's performance tables and local image.[189] Such practices are prohibited and prevent the student from accessing those protections for their right to education that exist through the formal exclusion process.

As the UN Committee on the Rights of the Child notes with concern, particular groups of pupils remain at much greater risk of permanent exclusion than others.[190] These include boys,[191] pupils of Black Caribbean, Traveller of Irish Heritage and Gypsy/Roma ethnicities,[192] children eligible for free school meals[193] and those with special educational needs (SEN).[194] In relation to pupils with SEN, teachers may not recognise or understand that their poor behaviour may be attributable to their unmet needs.[195] Concern has also been expressed from a variety of sources over the high rates of permanent exclusions among some ethnic groups. Some professionals consider that young Black and ethnic minority pupils are more frequently labelled as troublemakers[196] and many Black young people consider racism or racial stereotyping to play a role in their exclusion from school.[197] Indeed, it is maintained that Black pupils are 'routinely punished more harshly, praised less and told off more often'.[198] Equality legislation should ensure that pupils are not excluded for reasons relating to protected characteristics such as race or disability,[199] but addressing inequality is a complex challenge that requires action beyond eliminating direct discrimination. Many children who are at risk of exclusion face multiple, overlapping disadvantages that all contribute to higher rates of exclusion. As the *Timpson Review* noted, some of these factors, such as poverty and poor mental health, are themselves higher among particular groups and reflect wider inequalities within society.[200] A growing body of research suggests that a variety of factors are associated with behaviour leading to exclusion. These include poor basic skills, limited aspirations, strained or traumatic home circumstances and poor relationships with teachers and other pupils.[201]

[189] Ofsted (2019a).   [190] Committee on the Rights of the Child (2016) para. 71(b).

[191] In 2018–19, boys were more than three times more likely to be the subject of permanent exclusion as girls: 6,000 boys were excluded compared to 1,900 girls. Statistics in this section are taken from the annual statistical releases available at: www.gov.uk/government/collec tions/statistics-exclusions.

[192] Official statistics indicate that in 2018–19, children of Gypsy/Roma ethnicity had a permanent exclusion rate of 0.39, those of Irish Traveller heritage 0.27 and Black Caribbean children 0.25. This compared to an overall rate of 0.1 for all pupils.

[193] In 2019–20, the permanent exclusion rate for children eligible for free school meals was 0.27 compared to 0.06 for those who were not.

[194] In 2019–20, the permanent exclusion rate for children with SEN and an education, health and care plan was 0.15, whereas for those without such a plan it was 0.32. For children without SEN, the rate was 0.06.

[195] F. Taylor (2005) pp. 18–19.   [196] Ibid. p. 20.

[197] Ibid. pp. 10–11; C. Wright *et al.* (2005) pp. 10–14.   [198] P. Wanless (2006) p. 22.

[199] Equality Act 2010.   [200] DfE (2019b) ch. 3.

[201] See D. Berridge *et al.* (2001) pp. 4–6 for a summary of the research, and ch. 3 for the background of the excluded young people interviewed.

The growing rate of exclusion cannot be solved by individual schools alone, but requires wider measures to address these underlying and complex causes.

(ii) Prevention

The guidance is clear that schools should take adequate preventative measures to ensure that permanent exclusion is utilised only as a remedy of last resort.[202] They are directed to put alternatives in place well in advance of turning to exclusion. Schools faced with disruptive behaviour should first consider whether there are any unmet needs or causal factors that can be addressed through early intervention to reduce the need to resort to exclusion.[203] Schools are further advised to consider multi-agency assessments for persistently disruptive pupils, noting that such assessments may help to identify unmet needs or unidentified SEN.[204] The guidance reminds schools of their obligations under the Equality Act 2010, including the need to take steps to advance equality of opportunity, which may involve taking positive steps to address disadvantages affecting particular groups.[205] In fulfilling this duty, schools are reminded that exclusion rates among some groups are significantly higher than those for other pupils and that schools should consider whether any extra support can be given to pupils from these groups to reduce the risk of exclusion.[206] The official guidance also emphasises that permanent exclusion should be exceptional for children who are looked after or who have an education, health and care plan, as such pupils are particularly vulnerable to the impact of exclusion.[207] Overall, the guidance gives schools clear direction that exclusion should be a last resort and that schools should take active preventative steps to support individual children and groups of pupils vulnerable to exclusion.

The increasing use of exclusions and persistent discrepancies between different groups suggest that preventative measures are not working to avoid exclusion in the way envisaged by the guidance. Evidence to the House of Commons Education Committee in 2018 identified lack of expertise and financial resources to implement such measures as a barrier to effective early intervention.[208] Although schools do receive funding for early intervention measures, there is evidence that it is inadequate to provide the right means of support and that exclusion is sometimes seen as a route to accessing more effective resources.[209] The Committee also received evidence that some schools avoid identifying children as having SEND in order to exclude children more easily and to avoid the costs of meeting those needs.[210] Measures of academic attainment used to assess school quality also create incentives for schools to exclude or 'off-roll'

---

[202] DfE (2017c) p. 6.   [203] Ibid. pp. 6 and 10.   [204] Ibid. para. 19.

[205] Ibid. p. 9; i.e. the Public Sector Equality Duty (PSED): Equality Act 2010, s. 149.

[206] Ibid. paras 21–2; the guidance gives the example of engaging with Traveller Education Services to build trust when engaging with families.

[207] Ibid. paras 23–5.   [208] House of Commons Education Committee (2018) paras 19–20.

[209] DfE (2019b) p. 85.   [210] House of Commons Education Committee (2018) para. 21.

pupils who are unlikely to perform well and so penalise schools that develop inclusive practice.[211] For this reason, the *Timpson Review* has recommended holding schools to account for the education outcomes of children that they exclude so as to create incentives for schools to support children rather than to turn to exclusion to avoid that responsibility.

(iii) Grounds for Permanent Exclusion

Preventative measures, however well implemented, cannot remove the need to exclude some children who persist in behaving in a harmful and disruptive manner. A decision to exclude a child permanently is a serious one, but the legislation itself contains surprisingly little detail on the circumstances in which it can be used. The legislation defines the power to exclude as being on 'disciplinary grounds':[212] it is unlawful to exclude a pupil for non-disciplinary reasons.[213] Head teachers are given significant discretion in exercising this power.[214] That discretion must, of course, be exercised fairly, reasonably, rationally and proportionately in accordance with usual principles of public law. The decision must also comply with the school's wider legislative obligations, notably the HRA and Equality Act 2010.[215] But such general statements of the law do little to help head teachers faced with difficult real-life circumstances. Further advice is contained in the statutory guidance to which head teachers must 'have regard' when exercising the power to exclude.[216] That guidance states that a decision to exclude should only be taken: '(a) in response to a serious breach or persistent breaches of the school's behaviour policy; *and* (b) where allowing the pupil to remain in school would seriously harm the education or welfare of the pupil or others in the school'.[217] Previous versions of the guidance gave more detailed advice on the circumstances in which exclusion would be justified, along with specific examples to assist head teachers in their decision. The current guidance has removed these details, a change intended to give greater respect to head-teacher discretion, but which often leaves them unclear as to how best to respond to particular situations.[218] This lack of clarity contributes to inconsistency between schools and the *Timpson Review* has recommended that more accessible and detailed guidance should be given to assist head teachers in navigating the complexities of exclusion decisions.[219] Some commentators consider this insufficient and that it would be preferable to impose greater constraint on discretion through legal reform to ensure that exclusion is only used where necessary.[220]

---

[211] DfE (2019b) ch. 7, notably the Progress 8 framework for assessing pupil performance.

[212] EA 2002 s. 51A(10), inserted by EA 2011. See also School Discipline (Pupil Exclusions and Reviews) (England) Regulations 2012 (SI 2012/1033).

[213] A point reinforced by DfE (2017c) para. 19.   [214] For discussion, see L. Ferguson (2020).

[215] The guidance reminds head teachers of these obligations: DfE (2017c) para. 6.

[216] EA 2002, s. 51A(8)(b). See also School Discipline (Pupil Exclusions and Reviews) (England) Regulations 2012 (SI 2012/1033), reg. 9. The current guidance is DfE (2017c).

[217] DfE (2017c) para. 16 (emphasis added).   [218] DfE (2019b) pp. 59–60.   [219] Ibid.

[220] L. Ferguson (2021).

Some insight into the way in which head teachers use permanent exclusion is given by the reasons they record for those decisions on the school census each year. The rather vague category of 'persistent disruptive behaviour' is consistently the most cited reason for permanent exclusion, with assaults on pupils and staff also frequently recorded as the cause.[221] Despite the prevalence of bullying, racist and sexual abuse in schools, surprisingly few permanent exclusions are specifically recorded as having been made for these reasons.[222] As Lucinda Ferguson notes, the reasons available to head teachers for recording exclusions have a 'soft power' by indicating the forms of behaviour that might justify exclusion.[223] In the absence of detailed statutory guidance, changes to the reasons under which exclusions can be recorded may be influential in guiding the way in which head teachers use their discretion.[224]

Equality legislation protects pupils from being excluded unfairly for reasons relating to protected characteristics, including sex, race and disability. Particularly complex decisions arise if disruptive behaviour displayed by a child is related to a disability. Pupils with disabilities have a right to protection from unjustifiable exclusion for poor behaviour over which they have no control due to that disability.[225] Recent case law has dramatically changed the way in which courts consider such discrimination complaints, increasing the protection available for pupils whose aggressive behaviour is intrinsically connected to their disability. Under previous case law, any 'tendency to physical abuse' connected to the child's condition was 'stripped out' of the definition of disability when applying the Equality Act 2010 to an exclusion decision.[226] This effectively allowed schools to exclude children whose disability left them unable to control their aggressive behaviour, without having to make any reasonable adjustments

---

[221] In 2018–19, of the 7,894 permanent exclusions, 2,781 were for persistent disruptive behaviour, 1,050 for physical assault against a pupil and 817 for physical assault against an adult. These figures were similar to those in the preceding two years. Many head teachers cite 'other' reasons for the exclusion (1,371 in 2018–19), so limiting the utility of this source of information. Statistics in this section are taken from the annual statistical releases available at: www.gov.uk/government/collections/statistics-exclusions.

[222] In 2018–19, of the 7,894 permanent exclusions, 30 were for bullying, 15 for racist abuse and 86 for sexual misconduct. Ibid.

[223] L. Ferguson (2021) p. 106.

[224] As Ferguson notes (ibid.), changes were made in August 2020 to remove the possibility of recording 'other' as a reason for permanent exclusion and adding five new reasons, including 'inappropriate use of social media or online technology', 'abuse against sexual orientation and gender identity' and 'wilful and repeated transgression of protective measures in place to protect public health'. The latter reason was introduced in response to the Covid-19 pandemic, but is not limited to it.

[225] E.g. *R (T)* v. *Independent Appeal Panel for Devon County Council, The Governing Body of X College* [2007] EWHC 763 (Admin), [2007] ELR 499: Walker J quashed on judicial review the IAP's decision to approve the permanent exclusion of a 15-year-old boy with severe Asperger's Syndrome for assaulting a teacher, given its failure to adequately consider the evidence of discrimination, provocation and bullying and its failure to grapple with the requirements of the disability legislation then in place.

[226] E.g. *C* v. *Governing Body of I School (SEN)* [2015] UKUT 217 (AAC). Applying Equality Act 2010 (Disability) Regulations 2010 (SI 2010/2028), reg. 4(1)(c).

or support them in managing that behaviour. In *C & C* v. *the Governing Body of a School and others*,[227] this approach was declared to be unlawful. In that case, an 11-year-old boy with autism, anxiety and pathological demand avoidance had been given a fixed period exclusion for aggressive behaviour to pupils and a teaching assistant. The First Tier Tribunal had found that the behaviour that led to the exclusion resulted from his 'tendency to physical abuse' and so was not protected under the Equality Act 2010. That decision was successfully challenged before the Upper Tribunal, which found it to be in breach of the right to non-discrimination in Article 14 of the ECHR when read with the right to education in A2P1. In particular, excluding children in these circumstances failed to strike a fair balance between the rights of the child and the wider community. The impact on affected children was severe in that they could be more easily excluded for behaviour that they could not control.[228] Granting children in this position the protection of the Equality Act does not mean that other pupils and staff are forced to tolerate violent behaviour whatever the circumstances. Instead, it requires schools to make reasonable adjustments and to put in place support to meet the child's needs.[229] If the violent behaviour persists, the school may still succeed by showing that, having made reasonable adjustments, exclusion is necessary and a proportionate response to a legitimate aim, for example, protecting other pupils in the school.[230]

(iv) Procedural Fairness in Permanent Exclusion

The statutory provisions, regulations and official guidance acknowledge the serious implications of permanent exclusion and provide a carefully regulated procedure which must be followed.[231] A significant body of case law further emphasises that the exclusion procedures must comply with basic notions of fairness.[232] The guidance directs head teachers to 'give the pupil an opportunity to present their case before taking the decision to exclude' and to establish facts on the balance of probabilities.[233] Any permanent exclusion or fixed period exclusion totalling 15 days in a term or affecting an exam period

---

[227] *C & C* v. *the Governing Body of a School, The Secretary of State for Education (First Interested Party) and the National Autistic Society (Second Interested Party) (SEN)* [2018] UKUT 269.

[228] Ibid. at [86]–[89].   [229] Equality Act 2010, s. 20; DfE (2017c) paras 8 and 17.

[230] E.g. *R (T)* v. *Governing Body of OL Primary School* [2005] EWHC 753 (Admin), [2005] ELR 522: exclusion of an 8-year-old girl with global developmental delay and associated behavioural difficulties was justified, the school having taken outside advice and involved outside agencies. The school was obliged to protect other pupils from the girl's violent and disruptive behaviour.

[231] EA 2002, s. 51A(10), inserted by EA 2011, School Discipline (Pupil Exclusions and Reviews) (England) Regulations 2012 (SI 2012/1033); DfE (2017c).

[232] E.g. *R* v. *Headteacher and Independent Appeal Committee of Dunraven School, ex p B* [2000] ELR 156: pupils facing possible expulsion have the right to know the nature of the accusation against them, disclosure of all evidence relied on by the discipline authorities, the opportunity to answer it through their parents, and the right for their parents to appear before the tribunal dealing with the matter.

[233] DfE (2017c) paras 9 and 17. The regulations make clear that the civil standard of proof is to be applied in all decisions during the exclusion process: School Discipline (Pupil Exclusions and Reviews) (England) Regulations 2012 (SI 2012/1033), reg. 10.

must be reviewed by the school's governing board and consideration must be given to reinstating the student.[234] The governing board must itself comply with detailed procedural requirements, including the duty to hear all of the parties and to encourage the child to participate.[235] If the parents object to the decision of the governing board, they may then apply to have the decision reviewed by an independent review panel (IRP). The IRP must also comply with extensive procedural requirements, including the duty to hear the parties and allow representation.[236] In this way, the law and guidance create a framework of accountability with extensive rules to provide for procedural fairness.

Nevertheless, in practice, accountability is often much weaker than it appears from the regulatory framework. The governing board of the school is given a pivotal role in holding the head teacher to account for exclusion decisions. Yet, research suggests that the close relationship between heads and their governors, together with poor training for governors, creates a situation in which decisions are often 'rubber stamped' in a process that does not appear impartial to participants.[237] Parents' right to challenge the decision before an IRP is limited in practice by the fact that few have the resources to access legal advice or to navigate the complex process without that advice.[238] This is likely to contribute to the low uptake of the IRP process, with only around 7 per cent of permanent exclusions challenged in this way.[239] Those parents who successfully challenge a decision are likely to be disappointed by the relative impotence of the IRP. IRPs lack the teeth of their predecessors, the independent appeal panel, and have no power to order the reinstatement of a pupil who has been unlawfully excluded. Instead, they are limited to *recommending* that the governing board reconsiders the decision or, if judicial review grounds are made out, quashing the decision and directing such reconsideration.[240] Only if the decision is challenged under the Equality Act 2010 will parents have recourse to the stronger powers of the First Tier Tribunal and county court, including the power to order reinstatement.[241]

These weaknesses reduce the effectiveness of the system of accountability and mean that relatively few exclusions are successfully challenged. Further, as noted above, schools apparently persist in adopting an 'unofficial or informal

---

[234] School Discipline (Pupil Exclusions and Reviews) (England) Regulations 2012 (SI 2012/1033), reg. 6; DfE (2017c) pp. 18–24.

[235] Ibid.

[236] School Discipline (Pupil Exclusions and Reviews) (England) Regulations 2012 (SI 2012/1033), Sch. 1; DfE (2017c) pp. 27–40.

[237] DfE (2019b) pp. 88–9; Kulz (2015) p. 6.   [238] N. Hodge and C. Wolstenholme (2016).

[239] DfE (2019b) p. 88; L. Ferguson (2020) p. 19.

[240] If the governing board does not reinstate the pupil, the IRP may order a downward revision of up to £4,000 in the school's budget: School Discipline (Pupil Exclusions and Reviews) (England) Regulations 2012 (SI 2012/1033), regs 7(5), 16(5) and 25(5).

[241] Disability discrimination cases can be taken to the First Tier Tribunal and other forms of discrimination to the county court: see Equality Act 2010, Sch. 17, para. 5.

exclusion' process,[242] despite the official guidance emphasising its illegality.[243] There are formidable obstacles to using human rights law to challenge this situation. The Strasbourg authorities' narrow interpretation of the right to a fair hearing under Article 6 of the ECHR undermines its usefulness to a pupil excluded without his or her school following the required formalities.[244] A pupil might have more success by claiming that by being excluded without fair process, his or her right to education under A2P1 of the ECHR has been infringed. Failure to comply with domestic procedure will not in itself constitute a breach of the A2P1, but the process followed will be material to assessing whether the exclusion breached A2P1.[245] In assessing whether a fair balance has been struck between the child's right to education and the justification given for the exclusion, the ECtHR includes consideration of 'the procedural safeguards in place to challenge the exclusion and to avoid arbitrariness'.[246] Failure to follow domestic law is more likely to result in a finding that this balance has not been achieved.

Astonishingly, in spite of the government's concern to ensure that the exclusion process is a fair one, it has doggedly resisted amending the law to give excluded pupils formal party status in any of the exclusion procedures, except in the unlikely situation of their being aged 18 or over. Despite being the focus of the proceedings, a child under 18 is not defined as the 'relevant person' for these purposes, his or her parents being named instead.[247] It is they, not the excluded child, who have a right to challenge a permanent exclusion, attend the proceedings, be represented and offer written or oral submissions. It is particularly unjust where, for example, a teenager lives independently with no contact with his or her parents, or where parents are unwilling to pursue an appeal on their child's behalf. In any event, the excluded pupil is well aware that a parent does not always act as his or her advocate particularly effectively during the appeals process.[248] Unless pupils can persuade the domestic courts to expand the ambit of Article 6 of the ECHR, this gap in the legislation will remain unchallenged.[249] Meanwhile, the official guidance states that the governing board and the IRP should encourage an excluded pupil under the age of

---

[242] I.e. through pupils being sent home informally 'to cool off' or through parents being invited to remove their children.

[243] DfE (2017c) para. 14.

[244] *Simpson* v. *United Kingdom*, App. No. 14688/89, (1989) 64 DR 188: the European Commission on Human Rights (EComHR) rejected a mother's claim that the procedures used to determine her son's special educational needs were in breach of Art. 6 – his right to education was not of a 'civil' nature (as required by Art. 6), falling as it did within the domain of public law. The Court of Appeal has applied the same reasoning: *R (LG)* v. *IAP for Tom Hood School* [2010] EWCA Civ 142.

[245] In *Ali* v. *United Kingdom*, App. No. 40385/06, [2011] ELR 85, the domestic failings were insufficient to succeed in finding a breach of the right.

[246] Ibid. at [58].

[247] School Discipline (Pupil Exclusions and Reviews) (England) Regulations 2012 (SI 2012/1033, reg. 2(1).

[248] F. Taylor (2005) p. 39.   [249] Discussed above.

18 'to attend the hearing and to speak on his or her own behalf, if he or she wishes to do so'.[250] Fortunately, the guidance has now dropped its insistence on parents agreeing to the pupil's involvement. Such a requirement had reinforced the perceptions of many excluded young people that 'the exclusion process was something that happened around them and about them, but did not directly involve them other than incidentally'.[251] The government's position over the child's lack of legal status in the exclusion procedures is in stark contrast to the position elsewhere in the UK.[252] All Welsh children over the age of 11 have, since 2004, had full rights of appeal with or without permission from their parents.[253] Similarly, pupils in Scotland have the same right from the age of 12 provided that they have legal capacity.[254] Nonetheless, the government has remained unmoved by the repeated criticisms of the Committee on the Rights of the Child regarding this aspect of English law.[255]

(v) Alternative Provision and the Impact of Exclusion

The impact on pupils and their families of permanent exclusion is often considerable. Researchers note that most excluded children regret being excluded and worry about its effect on their ability to pass exams and later to obtain jobs.[256] They feel isolated[257] and greatly miss their school friends.[258] The exclusion itself is a traumatic experience and a blow to their self-esteem.[259] The families of excluded pupils also suffer, both in terms of their relationships with one another and with the community at large.[260] Pupils who have been excluded go on to experience poorer outcomes than their peers, including in education, employment, health and criminality.[261] Just 7 per cent of children who have been permanently excluded obtain good passes in English and Maths GCSE.[262] Upon leaving education, these pupils find it more difficult to obtain employment; over a third of pupils who complete their pre-16 education in alternative provision go on to be NEET – not in education, employment or training.[263] Experience of exclusion is also correlated with criminality at all stages of the criminal justice process: over half of UK prisoners experienced a period of exclusion from school.[264] Whether exclusion *causes* these poor outcomes is a more difficult question to assess.

---

[250] DfE (2017c) p. 7 and paras 61, 68 and 113.   [251] F. Taylor (2005) p. 32.

[252] N. Harris (2020) p. 45.

[253] Education (Pupil Exclusions and Appeals) (Maintained Schools) (Wales) Regulations 2003 (SI 2003/3227), reg. 2. Until the age of 16, the pupil's parents also have a right to appeal. From the age of 16, it is exclusively that of the pupil.

[254] Standards in Scotland's Schools Act 2000, s. 41. As is the case in Wales, for pupils under the age of 16, parents also have a right to appeal. From the age of 16, the right to appeal is exclusively that of the pupil.

[255] Committee on the Rights of the Child (1995) paras 14 and 32, (2002) para. 48(b), (2008) para. 66(a), (2016) para 73(c). The UN Committee has given specific guidance on the right to be heard in exclusion decisions: Committee on the Rights of the Child (2009) para. 113.

[256] F. Taylor (2005) pp. 22–3.   [257] C. Wright *et al.* (2005) pp. 47–9.

[258] F. Taylor (2005) pp. 23–4.   [259] C. Wright *et al.* (2005) pp. 16–17.   [260] Ibid. pp. 34–5.

[261] K. Gill *et al.* (2017) ch. 3.   [262] DfE (2019b) pp. 7–8.   [263] Ibid.

[264] Ibid.; K. Gill *et al.* (2017) p. 22.

Students who are excluded are more likely to have existing vulnerabilities and complex needs that are themselves correlated with poorer outcomes and have often contributed to the behaviour that led to exclusion. Nonetheless, exclusion appears to 'compound'[265] the impact of these challenges and to disrupt the support networks that previously surrounded the child. A good example can be seen in the complex relationship between exclusion, knife crime and gang membership. Pupils who report that they are members of a gang are five-and-a-half times more likely than other children to experience exclusion, while those who carry knives are seven times more likely to be excluded.[266] Many of these pupils are already involved in gang activity at the point of exclusion and that involvement is often closely connected to the behaviour that led to exclusion. But exclusion leaves children more vulnerable to being drawn into gangs as they are removed from the safeguarding oversight of school and given more time and freedom to associate with gang members.[267] Indeed, anecdotal evidence suggests that adult gang members encourage children to carry knives into school in order to trigger exclusion, knowing that once children are excluded they will be more vulnerable to criminal exploitation, including involvement in county lines.[268] Effective provision for excluded pupils is not just a matter of ensuring that they receive proper education, but also safeguarding them from exploitation and addressing the underlying causes of the exclusion.

In the past, delays in finding excluded pupils alternative education outside school left many of them free to roam the streets and vulnerable to exploitation. Efforts to prevent this, and to stop exclusion being seen as a reward for bad behaviour,[269] led to legislation and regulations obliging LAs to provide all permanently excluded pupils with full-time education from the sixth day of their exclusion.[270] To reinforce this message, parents may be fined[271] if they fail, without reasonable cause, to ensure that their excluded child is kept away from any public place 'at any time during school hours'[272] during the first five days of his or her exclusion.[273] It is questionable whether such a coercive approach will be beneficial in the long term, given that it may be unrealistic to expect parents to be able to take time off work to ensure that their child remains under what amounts to house arrest.[274] Admittedly, schools'

---

[265] K. Gill *et al.* (2017) p. 21.   [266] Children's Commissioner for England (2019a) p. 24.
[267] Ibid.   [268] Ofsted (2019b) para. 64; APPG on Knife Crime (2019) pp. 11–12.
[269] A. Steer (2005) para. 147.
[270] EA 1996, s. 19(3A); Education (Provision of Full-Time Education for Excluded Pupils) (England) Regulations 2007 (SI 2007/1870). This duty also extends to students who have been subject to multiple fixed-period exclusions that total 5 days or more.
[271] EIA 2006, s. 105: parents may avoid a court appearance by receiving a penalty notice; see Education (Penalty Notices) (England) Regulations 2007 (SI 2007/1867).
[272] EIA 2006, s. 103(2).   [273] EIA 2006, s. 103(3) and (5).
[274] JCHR (2006) para. 57: this provision infringed the parent's rights under ECHR Art. 8 in a disproportionate manner and furthermore would discriminate against single parents or parents in low-paid employment.

obligation to take 'reasonable steps' to set and mark work for the excluded pupil during those five days[275] provides him or her with some opportunity to receive a limited form of education in this period.

LAs are obliged to ensure that permanently excluded pupils continue to receive a full-time education and often use alternative provision to do so.[276] The extent to which pupils receive effective alternative provision varies considerably. Case law indicates that LAs cannot appeal to a lack of resources to justify not providing 'suitable' and 'efficient' education outside mainstream school.[277] Nevertheless, in practice, the expense of 'education otherwise' and the shortage of places in Pupil Referral Units (PRUs) and other facilities results in some excluded pupils being provided with educational provision for only a very few hours each week or put on 'twilight' timetables in which they only attend education after the end of the usual school day.[278] Students in this position have more time on their hands to get into further trouble and are vulnerable to exploitation. On the other hand, there is also considerable evidence of examples of good practice and high-quality alternative provision within the sector.[279] Effective provision can offer tailored programmes that address the multiple challenges that their pupils often face and provide innovative and engaging education that helps pupils to reconnect with education.[280] Nevertheless, many such facilities have experienced considerable problems both in retaining staff and in coping with very inadequate accommodation.[281] As the government has recognised, investment and reform is necessary to address the current shortfalls in the sector and ensure consistent high-quality alternative provision.[282] At present, too many children entering the system are still let down, with insufficient resources to meet their complex needs or to ensure that their right to an education is properly fulfilled.

Although most excluded pupils want to return to mainstream education as soon as possible,[283] at present, some pupils never do so, particularly the older ones.[284] In the past, the difficulty has been to persuade other schools in the area to admit a permanently excluded pupil. But even the worst-behaved pupil has a right to education.[285] There are now very limited circumstances in which a school may refuse to admit a child on the basis of a poor record elsewhere or

---

[275] DfE (2017c) para. 51.

[276] EA 1996, s. 19(3A). Alternative provision includes a wide range of forms of provision outside of mainstream and special schools, including pupil referral units (PRUs), alternative provision academies and free schools, independent providers and home tuition. Not all students in alternative provision have been excluded; others may be unable to attend mainstream provision for other reasons such as medical needs.

[277] R v. *East Sussex County Council, ex p Tandy* [1998] 2 All ER 769.

[278] APPG on Knife Crime (2019) pp. 11–12; Children's Commissioner for England (2019a) p. 24.

[279] DfE (2019b) pp. 74–8.   [280] Children's Commissioner for England (2019a) p. 24, (2019b).

[281] DfE (2019b) pp. 74–8; House of Commons Education Committee (2018) pp. 27–30.

[282] DfE (2018b).   [283] F. Taylor (2005) pp. 22–3.

[284] Ibid. p. 27; House of Commons Education Committee (2018) para. 69.

[285] LAs have the power under SSFA 1998, ss 96–7 to direct a much-excluded pupil's admission by a school (for which the LA is not the admission authority) within a reasonable distance of his

because the child is thought to be potentially disruptive.[286] Nevertheless, admission authorities are entitled to ignore parents' expressed preference for a particular school if their child has, within the last two years, been already excluded from two or more other schools.[287] The government therefore encourages groups of local schools to cooperate over taking their fair share of excluded pupils, thereby avoiding disproportionate numbers being placed in any one school.[288] While these arrangements work well in some areas, there is also evidence of some schools refusing to accept pupils from alternative provision.[289] As the system works on the basis of cooperation, there is little scrutiny of schools' decisions or redress if that cooperation is not forthcoming.

An excluded pupil left with no educational provision at all can mount a challenge under the HRA 1998 arguing a violation of his or her right to education under A2P1 of the ECHR. Pupils wishing to use the same provision to challenge the adequacy of alternative provision are likely to find considerable difficulty in doing so. Both domestic courts and the ECtHR have found the requirements of the right to education under A2P1 to be satisfied in circumstances in which very limited alternative provision has been offered to pupils subject to fixed-term exclusion.[290] These cases establish that there is no requirement in A2P1 that a student who has been temporarily excluded from school must be offered access to the full school curriculum. Instead, it is sufficient that the pupil is provided with effective access to the education that the state provides for pupils in such a situation,[291] even if that education is significantly below the standard offered to other pupils. Pupils who have been permanently excluded are likely to require access to the full curriculum within a reasonable time frame in order to be provided with effective education under A2P1.[292] The article does not protect the right to access a particular school and so is unlikely to assist a pupil unhappy with the new school allocated to

---

or her home. This power's availability is, however, so strictly limited that its usefulness is questionable. See N. Harris (2020) p. 40.

[286] School Admissions Code (2021) paras 3.9–3.13: the statutory Admissions Code of Practice has binding authority. See SSFA 1998, s. 84(3), as amended by EIA 2006, s. 40(4).

[287] School Admissions Code (2021) para. 3.8. NB: SSFA 1998, s. 87.

[288] I.e. through local 'Fair Access Protocols'.

[289] House of Commons Education Committee (2018) paras 67–71.

[290] In *Ali* v. *Head Teacher and Governors of Lord Grey School* [2006] UKHL 14, [2006] 2 All ER 457, a subsequent application to the ECtHR also failed. *Ali* v. *United Kingdom*, App. No. 40385/06, [2011] ELR 85, esp. at [60]: 13–14-year-old pupil excluded for more than the statutory 45-day period. The alternative work to complete at home did not cover all aspects of the national curriculum. Eventually, the pupil was offered a place in a PRU, but this was declined by the parents. It was held that there was no violation of A2P1: the limited provision available was adequate for a temporary suspension. *R (JR 17) (Northern Ireland)* [2010] UKSC 27, [2010] ELR 764: application to the ECtHR declared inadmissible. *CP* v. *United Kingdom*, App. No. 300/11, 6 September 2016: a year 12 pupil was provided with 8 hours of weekly home tuition in limited subjects during a fixed-period exclusion totalling 20 days.

[291] *Ali* v. *Head Teacher and Governors of Lord Grey School* [2006] UKHL 14, [2006] 2 All ER 457, at [24].

[292] *Ali* v. *United Kingdom*, App. No. 40385/06, [2011] ELR 85, at [60].

them.[293] The way in which the courts have interpreted A2P1 to date has rendered it a relatively weak right that is of limited utility for students provided with ineffective alternative provision in all but the most egregious of circumstances.[294]

(5) School Administration

High rates of pupil absence, disruption in the classroom, bullying and high exclusion numbers often combine in failing schools. Were all schools to appeal to the strengths of the pupil population, they might find pupils working with them instead of against them. There is evidence that punitive regimes are associated with worse rather than better standards of behaviour;[295] furthermore, that successfully performing schools adopt systems which reward good work and behaviour rather than focus on negative behaviour and punishments.[296]

Schools which encourage pupils to take responsibility for various aspects of their school life often produce better relationships between staff and pupils and between pupil and pupil.[297] As the Crick Committee recognised, engaging children in the more practical aspects of running their school encourages a sense of responsibility for and pride in the institution. It recommended that schools should consult with pupils over aspects of school life and 'wherever possible to give pupils responsibility and experience in helping to run parts of the school'.[298] Legislation implements this recommendation to a limited extent in that head teachers must not only consult parents before drawing up the school's behaviour policy, but also all registered pupils at the school.[299] The government has been far more ambivalent over consulting pupils more widely over schools' administration.

The most obvious way in which such advice can be followed is for schools to establish school councils. Many schools do so,[300] with some councils proving to be extremely effective, becoming involved in a wide range of school governance, including the appointment of teachers.[301] The way in which school councils are even able to influence particular areas of spending, controlling their own budgets,[302] undoubtedly enhances pupils' own perception of the value of such entities. Some schools link membership of school councils with membership of local youth forums and parliaments,[303] and even, through

---

[293] Ibid. at [54].
[294] Although see N. Harris (2020) p. 61 for an argument that jurisprudence on the application of A2P1 in relation to higher education demonstrates a less restrictive reading of the right.
[295] Inter alia: R. Elton (1989); M. Rutter et al. (1979).
[296] Ofsted (2005) para. 77, (2006a) para. 12.
[297] Ofsted (2006a) para. 12. See also para. 13: some schools provide pupils with training to help others with advice or unofficial support, leading to younger pupils feeling safer.
[298] B. Crick (1998) p. 36.   [299] EIA 2006, s. 88(3)(c) and (d).
[300] G. Whitty and E. Wisby (2007) p. 37.   [301] Ibid. esp. chs 7 and 8.   [302] Ibid. pp. 74–5.
[303] Ibid. p. 49.

associate membership,[304] with the school's governing body.[305] Nonetheless, research suggests that some teachers have reservations about the extent to which pupils could or should become involved in school matters beyond facilities/environment issues.[306] Meanwhile, pupils are bound to assume their school council to be purely tokenistic[307] if confined to dealing only with school facilities, school uniform, food and related matters.[308]

While many schools do have school councils, there is no legal obligation to do so in English schools.[309] Indeed, schools are under no legal obligation to include children in decision-making. The UN Committee on the Rights of the Child has criticised the fact that schoolchildren are 'not *systematically* consulted in matters that affect them'.[310] At one time, it appeared that the law would change and a new duty was placed on the statute book requiring schools to 'invite and consider pupils' views about prescribed matters', having regard to their age and understanding.[311] The duty has not been brought into force and there remains no obligation on schools to ensure that children can participate in decisions affecting them. The position is little better in respect of LA decisions. There is a specific duty on LAs to consult children with special educational and disabilities concerning the provision of education and training in their area.[312] There is, however, no equivalent duty applying to all children beyond a vague requirement that LAs 'have regard to any [statutory] guidance ... about consultation with pupils in connection with the taking of decisions affecting them'.[313] As a result the legal obligation to include children in educational decision-making remains limited and fragmented.

(6) Relationships and Sex Education in Schools

The provision of relationships and sex education (RSE) in schools is one of the most politically sensitive aspects of education law and policy. In a diverse society, with differing social, cultural and religious views on what constitutes appropriate sexual behaviour, the role of schools in educating children on such

---

[304] Education (No. 2) Act 1986, by setting the minimum qualifying age for becoming a school governor at 18, thereby abolishing schools' ability to have pupil governors. Pupils under 18 can be made associate members of the committee of governors, but have no voting rights.
[305] G. Whitty and E. Wisby (2007) pp. 40–1 and 76–8.   [306] Ibid. pp. 78–9.
[307] Ofsted (2006b) para. 42.   [308] G. Whitty and E. Wisby (2007) pp. 46–8.
[309] In Wales, under the School Councils (Wales) Regulations 2005 (SI 2005/3200), reg. 3(2), a head teacher must ensure that school council meetings are held six times per annum; A. Sherlock (2007) pp. 170–2.
[310] Committee on the Rights of the Child (2002) para. 29 (emphasis added); para. 30: further steps should be taken to promote participation more effectively, 'for example though school councils'.
[311] Education Act 2002, s. 29B, as inserted by ESA 2008, s. 157.   [312] CFA 2014, ss 27 and 30.
[313] EA 2002, s. 176(1).

matters has been particularly controversial.[314] Perhaps because of these sensitivities, RSE was a long-neglected aspect of education policy, often poorly taught[315] and occupying an ambivalent place in the curriculum. High quality RSE teaching is, however, important to the realisation of a range of children's rights. Although the text of the CRC does not specify that RSE must be provided as an aspect of education, in its Concluding Observations the Committee has frequently urged states to guarantee access to sex education.[316] Sex education has an important role to play in securing the child's right to health[317] and to seek and receive information and ideas.[318] RSE teaching is also a vital aspect of preparing children for a 'responsible life in a free society' and respecting the rights of others.[319] What it means to behave responsibly in sex and relationships has become increasingly complex in the digital environment and as children are exposed to sexual images and information at increasingly younger ages.[320] The importance of putting in place a more rigorous and updated framework for RSE teaching had long been apparent before the new programme was finally implemented in 2020.

Law and policy on the provision of sex education in schools has, until recently, been curiously ambivalent.[321] For a long time only the narrow biological aspects of reproduction, contraception and sexually transmitted infections were effectively compulsory as aspects of the national curriculum.[322] In addition, sex education formed part of the basic curriculum for secondary school pupils,[323] but children whose parents objected would not be required to receive it and its requirements were not specified in law. Controversially, this meant that education about sexual relationships was only part of the non-statutory Personal, Social and Health Education (PSHE) programme, with schools largely entitled to decide for themselves the content of the classes. Whilst schools were required to have regard to the official guidance, produced in 2000,[324] the guidance was not updated and quickly appeared out of touch with the realities facing children and young people in areas such as online pornography, sexting, sexual exploitation, consent and healthy relationships. Further, gay and lesbian relationships were addressed fleetingly and appeared to be neglected almost entirely in the teaching at some schools.[325] Together with the poor PSHE teaching

---

[314] See e.g. the 2019 protests in Birmingham against the 'No Outsiders' programme, taught in a local primary school, which covered aspects of equality including LGBT relationships: discussed in N. Harris (2020) pp. 4–7.

[315] E.g. Ofsted (2013).   [316] V. Muñoz (2010) pp. 8–9.

[317] CRC, Art. 24 includes the requirement that the state develops 'preventive health care', including 'guidance for parents and family planning education and services': Art. 24(2)(f).

[318] CRC, Art. 13. For further discussion of the rights aspects of sex education, see V. Muñoz (2010).

[319] CRC, Art. 29(1)(d).

[320] See above for discussion of the normalisation of sexual harassment and abuse in schools, including image-based abuse: Ofsted (2021).

[321] N. Harris (2020) pp. 366–71.   [322] I.e. as part of the science curriculum.

[323] EA 2002, s. 80, as originally enacted.   [324] DfEE (2000).   [325] Ibid. paras 1.30–1.32.

found in many schools,[326] there was increasing concern that schools were not adequately equipping children to navigate the increasingly complex world in which they lived.

In September 2020,[327] a new statutory framework[328] and guidance came into force, substantially overhauling the teaching of RSE. There is now a statutory requirement to teach relationships education in all primary schools and RSE in all secondary schools.[329] In addition, health education is required in all state-funded schools.[330] New statutory guidance has now been produced alongside a commitment that it will be reviewed every 3 years.[331] At primary, schoolchildren are to be taught about healthy relationships, including families, friendships and safety in relationships. There is no requirement to include sex education in primary school, beyond the requirements of the science curriculum, although schools may choose to do so. Once a student reaches secondary education, teaching on intimate relationships and sex education becomes compulsory. At secondary school, this should include consideration of harmful relationships, including all aspects of domestic abuse, grooming, sexual exploitation, FGM and forced marriage. Responsible online behaviour and the risks of harm online are also covered in detail. The guidance on including teaching about LGBT relationships remains surprisingly sparse, although schools are directed to comply with the Equality Act 2010 and ensure that LGBT relationships are integrated into teaching and not regarded as a standalone topic.[332] Given the long history of neglecting LGBTQ+ relationships in RSE teaching[333] and widespread reports of homophobic bullying in schools, it is surprising that more detailed guidance is not given on this important aspect of relationships. Schools are free to determine how to implement the guidance and it remains to be seen whether a significant improvement in the quality of RSE will follow from the substantial changes that have taken place in law and policy.

Despite the importance of high-quality RSE teaching to children and to wider society, parents retain the right to request the withdrawal of their

---

[326] Ofsted (2013): PSHE teaching was inadequate or required improvement in 40 per cent of schools; sex and relationships education was found to require improvement in over a third of the surveyed schools.

[327] In view of the substantial disruption caused to schools by the Covid-19 pandemic, schools that were unable to meet this deadline were given a grace period until the summer term of 2021 to fully implement the new requirements.

[328] Children and Social Work Act 2017, ss 34 and 35; The Relationships Education, Relationships and Sex Education, and Health Education (England) Regulations 2019 (SI 2019/924).

[329] Children and Social Work Act 2017, s. 34; EA 2002, s. 80(1)(c) and (d), as amended by The Relationships Education, Relationships and Sex Education, and Health Education (England) Regulations 2019 (SI 2019/924).

[330] Children and Social Work Act 2017, s. 35; EA 2002, s. 80(1)(e).   [331] DfE (2019a).

[332] Ibid. paras 36–7.

[333] Most notoriously, 'clause 28', which prohibited LAs from promoting 'the teaching in any maintained school of the acceptability of homosexuality as a pretended family relationship': Local Government Act 1988, s. 28 (repealed in 2003).

children from sex education. The assumption made by education legislation that the interests of parents and children are identical has been particularly apparent in this area of the law. In 1993, parents were granted an absolute right to withdraw their children from sex education classes,[334] apparently as a means of addressing the needs of those objecting on religious grounds.[335] The revised statutory regime modifies this right. At primary school, parents retain the right to withdraw their child from any sex education that the school chooses to provide, save where that teaching is provided as part of science teaching under the national curriculum.[336] This right does not extend to relationships education. Parents may also *request* that a child is removed from the sex education aspects of relationships and sex education provided at secondary school. If such a request is made, the pupil will be excused, unless the head teacher considers that they should not be.[337] The introduction of head-teacher discretion appears to be primarily concerned with establishing dialogue between the parents and the head teacher, who is advised by the guidance to use the opportunity to inform the parents of the benefits of the education and the detriment that the child may suffer from being withdrawn.[338] If the parents persist in their request, the guidance directs the head teacher to respect the request, except in 'exceptional circumstances' up until three terms before the child turns 16. For teenagers who have reached this age, the school should arrange for sex education to be provided in one of those terms.[339] This change gives greater respect to the rights of 15- and 16-year-olds, but falls some way from the rights-based approach suggested in the initial consultation, which stated that:

> English case law has moved on since the current right to withdraw was put in place and we must now allow young people, once they have reached an age at which they are mature enough to be competent, to make decisions on their education for themselves.[340]

If this approach had been followed, younger teenagers would have had the opportunity to demonstrate their maturity to make their own decisions about their education in this important facet of their personal lives. Such an outcome would have avoided the anomaly whereby these teenagers may well be mature enough to seek contraceptive or abortion advice without their parents' knowledge or consent,[341] but not to receive education on how to do so safely. As discussed above, a teenager of this age might now argue that the parental right to request withdrawal of a pupil from sex education classes infringes his or her

---

[334] EA 1996, s. 405, as originally enacted. This right did not extend to sex education provided as part of the national curriculum.

[335] Baroness Blatch, HL Debs, 1993, vol. 547, col. 140.   [336] EA 1996, s. 405(1), as amended.

[337] Ibid., s. 405(3), as amended.   [338] DfE (2019a) paras 45–6.   [339] Ibid. para. 47.

[340] DfE (2017b) p. 6.

[341] *Gillick* v. *West Norfolk and Wisbech Area Health Authority* [1986] AC 112; *R (Axon)* v. *Secretary of State for Health and the Family Planning Association* [2006] EWHC 37 (Admin), [2006] 2 FLR 206. Discussed further in Chapters 9 and 11.

rights under a variety of international human rights treaties. It not only ignores the right to be consulted,[342] but also the right to freedom of expression.[343] It is astonishing that an area of law involving children whose sexual activity may have long-term implications for themselves and others still gives priority to parental rights for this age group.

At one time, it was argued that the right of parental withdrawal was necessary in order to comply with A2P1 of the ECHR,[344] but such arguments appear to have been misplaced. In *Kjeldsen, Busk and Pedersen* v. *Denmark*,[345] the ECtHR decided that the Danish government had not violated that provision by providing compulsory sex education in schools, since it had been conveyed in a balanced and objective manner, with no element of indoctrination. The fact that the parents had no right to exempt their children from such education did not amount to a breach of A2P1 of the ECHR. So, it seems, the government here could introduce compulsory RSE with no parental right to request withdrawal, as long as it imparts information 'in an objective, critical and pluralistic manner'.[346] The best defence of the current position is perhaps one of pragmatism rather than principle. Very few parents appear to seek to withdraw their children from sex education.[347] Those who do may be more likely to respond to dialogue than confrontation, particularly as they may choose to remove their child from schooling altogether if they are not able to withdraw from sex education.[348] Nonetheless, the current law fails to uphold the rights of a significant group of young people and sends the message that they are treated as appendages of their parents.

(7) Conclusion

Schools must accommodate the rights and interests of all their pupils and often encounter difficult challenges in seeking to do so. These challenges are particularly evident in relation to peer abuse. Recent research demonstrates the

---

[342] CRC, Art. 12.

[343] CRC, Art. 13 and ECHR, Art. 10. See also CRC, Art. 17, which recognises that children need access to information and material from a variety of sources.

[344] Baroness Blatch, HL Debs, 1993, vol. 547, col. 1292.

[345] (1976) 1 EHRR 711. See similarly *Dojan* v. *Germany* [2011] ELR 511. In *AR and LR* v. *Switzerland*, App. No. 22338/15, dec. 19/12/2017, a similar result was achieved under Art. 8 (as Switzerland had not ratified ECHR, Protocol 1) in relation to the provision of sex education to younger children.

[346] A judicial review challenge to the changes to the parental right to withdraw brought about by the 2019 Regulations and 2020 Guidance failed to obtain permission to proceed as it was out of time and did not have any realistic prospect of success: *R (Colchester on Behalf of Let Kids Be Kids Coalition)* v. *Secretary of State for Education* [2020] EWHC 3376 (Admin).

[347] Ofsted (2002) recorded (p. 6) that only about 4 in every 10,000 pupils were withdrawn under the old regime. There do not appear to be more recent reliable statistics. Given the ease with which most young people are able to obtain, possibly dangerous or misleading, information about sexual matters through the internet, the right to withdraw may well seem increasingly futile.

[348] N. Harris (2020) p. 364.

serious harm that pupils inflict on others and the devastating consequences that can have for pupils affected. All schools are faced with the need to protect children from harmful behaviour while also ensuring that all pupils receive their right to education. Rights can have an important role to play in meeting this responsibility,[349] but the right to education in A2P1 is relatively weak and too often children are left without adequate education to meet their needs and little effective recourse available to them or their families to bring about change.

Education legislation has increasingly treated parents as the 'consumers' of education and as their children's proxies or representatives when making educational choices. It progressively increased parental powers over making choices, but without suggesting that children should be involved in the process. Children's participation rights are often conspicuously absent from the education law, a problem most starkly illustrated by the absence of an independent right for teenagers to challenge a decision to permanently exclude them. More recently, the law has become increasingly authoritarian in its approach to parents, attributing to them many problems experienced by schools, such as persistent absence and serious misbehaviour. Indeed, the sanctions made available against parents may have started subtly distorting the balance of power between schools and parents. Furthermore, through their use, the law may exacerbate the pressures experienced by many families already suffering various forms of disadvantage and social exclusion.

Bibliography

NB: Many of these publications can be obtained on the relevant organisation's website.

Action on Rights for Children (2005) *How Effective Are Truancy Sweeps?*, ARCH.
All-Party Parliamentary Group (APPG) on Knife Crime (2019) *Back to School? Breaking the Link between School Exclusions and Knife Crime*, APPG on Knife Crime.
Audit Commission (1996) *Misspent Youth: Young People and Crime*, Audit Commission Publications.
Berridge, D., Brodie, I., Pitts, J., Porteous, D. and Tarling, R. (2001) *The Independent Effects of Permanent Exclusion From School on the Offending Careers of Young People*, RDS Occasional Paper no. 71, Home Office.
Bhabra, S., Dinos, S. and Ghate, D. (2006) *Young People, Risk and Protection: A Major Survey of Secondary Schools in On Track Areas*, DfES Research Report RR 728, Policy Research Bureau.
Children's Commissioner for England (2019a) *Keeping Kids Safe: Improving Safeguarding Responses to Gang Violence and Criminal Exploitation*, Children's Commissioner's Office.
    (2019b) *Exclusions: Children Excluded from Mainstream Schools*, Children's Commissioner's Office.
    (2020) *Childhood in the Time of Covid*, Children's Commissioner's Office.
Committee on the Rights of the Child (1995) *Concluding Observations of the Committee on the Rights of the Child: United Kingdom of Great Britain and Northern Ireland*, CRC/C/15/Add 34, Centre for Human Rights, Geneva.

---

[349] E.g. *C & C* v. *the Governing Body of a School, The Secretary of State for Education (First Interested Party) and the National Autistic Society (Second Interested Party) (SEN)* [2018] UKUT 269.

(2002) *Concluding Observations of the Committee on the Rights of the Child: United Kingdom of Great Britain and Northern Ireland*, CRC/C/15/Add 188, Centre for Human Rights, Geneva.

(2008) *Concluding Observations of the Committee on the Rights of the Child: United Kingdom of Great Britain and Northern Ireland*, CRC/C/GBR/CO/4, Centre for Human Rights, Geneva.

(2009) *General Comment No. 12 on the Right of the Child to be Heard*, CRC/C/GC/12, Centre for Human Rights, Geneva.

(2016) *Concluding Observations of the Committee on the Rights of the Child: United Kingdom of Great Britain and Northern Ireland*, CRC/C/GBR/CO/5, Centre for Human Rights, Geneva.

Crick, B. (Chairman) (1998) *Education for Citizenship and the Teaching of Democracy in Schools*, Final report of the Advisory Group on Citizenship, Qualifications and Curriculum Authority.

Cunningham, S. and Lavalette, M. (2002) 'Children, Politics and Collective Action: School Strikes in Britain' in Goldson, B., Lavalette, M. and McKechnie, J. (eds) *Children, Welfare and the State*, Sage Publications.

Dalziel, D. and Henthorne, K. (2005) *Parents'/Carers' Attitudes Towards School Attendance*, TNS Social Research, DfES Research Report RR 618, DfES.

Department for Education (DfE) (2013) *Use of Reasonable Force*, DfE.

(2015) *School Attendance Parental Responsibility Measures*, DfE.

(2016) *Behaviour and Discipline in School*, DfE.

(2017a) *Preventing and Tackling Bullying*, DfE.

(2017b) *Changes to the Teaching of Sex and Relationships Education and PSHE: A Call for Evidence*, DfE.

(2017c) *Exclusion from Maintained Schools, Academies and Pupil Referral Units in England*, DfE.

(2018a) *Searching Screening and Confiscation*, DfE.

(2018b) *Creating Opportunity for All: Our Vision for Alternative Provision*, DfE.

(2019a) *Relationships Education, Relationships and Sex Education, and Health Education*, DfE.

(2019b) *Timpson Review of School Exclusion* (CP92), DfE.

(2020a) *School Attendance: Guidance for Maintained Schools, Academies, Independent Schools and Local Authorities*, DfE.

(2020b) *Parental Responsibility Measures in England: 2018–19*, DfE.

(2021a) *Keeping Children Safe in Education 2021: Statutory Guidance for Schools and Colleges*, DfE.

(2021b) *Sexual Violence and Sexual Harassment between Children in Schools and Colleges*, DfE.

Department for Education and Employment (DfEE) (2000) *Sex and Relationship Education Guidance*, 0116/2000, DfEE.

Department of Health (DH) (1991) *Guardians Ad Litem and Other Court Related Issues*, Vol. 7: *Children Act 1989 Guidance and Regulations*, Her Majesty's Stationery Office.

Elton, R. (Chairman) (1989) *Discipline in Schools, Report of the Committee of Enquiry into Discipline in Schools*, Her Majesty's Stationery Office.

Epstein, R., Brown, G. and O'Flynn, S. (2019) *Prosecuting Parents for Truancy: Who Pays the Price? Prosecution of Children for Truancy*, Coventry University.

Evans, L., Hall, L. and Wreford, S. (2008) Research Report DCSF-RR030, *Education-Related Parenting Contracts Evaluation*, DCSF.

Farson, R. (1978) *Birthrights*, Penguin.

Ferguson, L. (2020) 'Children at Risk of School Dropout' in Dwyer, J. (ed.) *Oxford Handbook of Children and the Law*, Oxford University Press.

(2021) 'Vulnerable Children's Right to Education, School Exclusion, and Pandemic Law-Making' 26 *Emotional and Behavioural Difficulties* 101.

Ferguson, L. and Webber, N. (2015) *School Exclusion and the Law: A Literature Review and Scoping Survey of Practice*, University of Oxford.

Fionda, J. (2005) *Devils and Angels: Youth Policy and Crime*, Hart Publishing.

Ford, J., Hughes, M., May, K., Shaughnessy, M. and Gill, H. (2016) *Education Law and Practice*, 4th edn, Lexis Nexis.

Gamble, J. and McCallum, R. (2022) *Local Child Safeguarding Practice Review: Child Q*, City of London and Hackney Safeguarding Children Partnership.

Gill, K., Quilter-Pinner, H. and Swift, D. (2017) *Making the Difference: Breaking the Link Between School Exclusion and Social Exclusion*, Institute for Public Policy Research.

Grenville, M. (1988) 'Compulsory School Attendance and the Child's Wishes' 10 *Journal of Social Welfare Law* 4.

Hafen, B. (1976) 'Children's Liberation and the New Egalitarianism: Some Reservations about Abandoning Youth to Their "Rights"' *Brigham Young University Law Review* 605.

Hallam, S., Castle, F. and Rogers, L., with Creech, A., Rhanie, J. and Kokotsaki, D. (2005) *Research and Evaluation of the Behaviour Improvement Programme*, DfES Research Report No. 702, DfES.

Harris, N. (2005) 'Education: Hard or Soft Lessons in Human Rights?' in Harvey, C. (ed.) *Human Rights in the Community*, Hart Publishing.

(2020) *Education, Law and Diversity*, 2nd edn, Hart Publishing.

Hodge, N. and Wolstenholme, C. (2016) '"I Didn't Stand a Chance": How Parents Experience the Exclusions Appeal Tribunal' 20 *International Journal of Inclusive Education* 1297.

Holt, J. (1974) *Escape from Childhood: The Needs and Rights of Childhood*, E. P. Dutton and Co.

House of Commons Education Committee (2018) *HC 342, Forgotten Children: Alternative Provision and the Scandal of Ever Increasing Exclusions, Fifth Report of Session 2017–19*, House of Commons.

Jeffs, T. (2002) 'Schooling, Education and Children's Rights' in Franklin, B. (ed.) *The New Handbook of Children's Rights: Comparative Policy and Practice*, Routledge.

Joint Committee on Human Rights (JCHR) (2006) HL Paper 177/HC 1098, *Legislative Scrutiny: Ninth Progress Report*, The Stationery Office.

(2011) HL Paper 154/HC 1140, *Legislative Scrutiny: Thirteenth Report*, The Stationery Office.

(2020) HL Paper 125/HC 265, *The Government's Response to Covid-19: Human Rights Implications*, House of Commons.

Jones, S. (2014) 'A Last Resort: The Prosecution of Parents for Their Child's Truancy' 26 *Child and Family Law Quarterly* 322.

Kljakovic, M., Kelly, A. and Richardson, A. (2021) 'School Refusal and Isolation: The Perspectives of Five Adolescent School Refusers in London, UK' 26 *Clinical Child Psychology and Psychiatry* 1089.

Kulz, C. (2015) *Mapping the Exclusion Process: Inequality, Justice and the Business of Education*, Communities Empowerment Network.

Lindley, R. (1989) 'Teenagers and Other Children' in Scarre, G. (ed.) *Children, Parents and Politics*, Cambridge University Press.

Long, R., Roberts, N. and Loft, P. (2020) *Bullying in UK Schools: Briefing Paper 8812*, House of Commons Library.

Malcolm, H., Wilson, V., Davidson, J. and Kirk, S. (2003) *Absence from School: A Study of Its Causes and Effects in Seven LEAs*, DfES Research Report No. 424, DfES.

Meredith, P. (2001) 'Children's Rights and Education' in Fionda, J. (ed.) *Legal Concepts of Childhood*, Hart Publishing.

Monk, D. (2002) 'Children's Rights in Education – Making Sense of Contradictions' 14 *Child and Family Law Quarterly* 45.

Muñoz, V. (2010) *Report of the Special Rapporteur on the Right to Education*, A/65/162, 23 July, Centre for Human Rights, Geneva.

National Audit Office (2005) *Improving School Attendance in England*, Report by the Comptroller and Auditor General, HC 212 Session 2004–5, The Stationery Office.

Office for Standards in Education (Ofsted) (2002) *HMI 433, Sex and Relationships: A Report from the Office of Her Majesty's Chief Inspector of Schools*, Ofsted.

(2005) HMI 2363, *Managing Challenging Behaviour*, Ofsted.

(2006a) HMI 2377, *Improving Behaviour*, Ofsted.

(2006b) HMI 2666, *Towards Consensus? Citizenship in Secondary Schools*, Ofsted.

(2013) *Not Yet Good Enough: Personal, Social and Economic Education in Schools*, Ofsted.

(2019a) *Exploring the Issue of Off-Rolling*, Ofsted.

(2019b) *Safeguarding Children and Young People in Education from Knife Crime*, Ofsted.

(2021) *Review of Sexual Abuse in Schools and Colleges*, Ofsted.

Rutter, M., Maughan, B., Mortimore, P. and Ouston, J., with Smith, A. (1979) *Fifteen Thousand Hours: Secondary Schools and Their Effects on Pupils*, Open Book.

Sherlock, A. (2007) 'Listening to Children in the Field of Education: Experience in Wales' 19 *Child Family Law Quarterly* 161.

Social Exclusion Unit (SEU) (1998) Cm 3957, *Truancy and School Exclusion: Report by the Social Exclusion Unit.*

Steer, A. (Chairman) (2005) *Learning Behaviour: The Report of the Practitioners' Group on School Behaviour and Discipline,* DfES.

Taylor, F. (2005) *A Fair Hearing? Researching Young People's Involvement in the School Exclusion Process,* Save the Children.

Tomaševski, K. (1999) *'Special Rapporteur on the Right to Education' Addendum,* Mission to the of Great Britain and Northern Ireland (England) 18–22 October 1999 Report to UN Commission on Human Rights E/CN.4/2000/6/Add 2, Centre for Human Rights, Geneva.

Wanless, P. (2006) *Priority Review: Exclusion of Black Pupils 'Getting It. Getting It Right',* DfES.

Whitty, G. and Wisby, E. (2007) Research Report DCSF-RR001, *Real Decision Making?* School Councils in Action, DCSF.

Women and Equalities Committee (2016) *Sexual Harassment and Sexual Violence in Schools* (HC 91), House of Commons.

Wright, C., Standen, P., John, G., German, G. and Patel, T. (2005) *School Exclusion and Transition into Adulthood in African-Caribbean Communities,* Joseph Rowntree Foundation.

15

The Child's Right to Protection from Harmful Treatment

(1) Introduction

The state assumes that, because parents brought their children into the world, they will care for them and protect them from harm; indeed, it trusts them to do so. The vast majority of parents fulfil these state expectations conscientiously. They not only fulfil their children's right to protection, but bring them up in an atmosphere of love and security. Unfortunately, the children's liberationists' view of childhood as an oppressed state and parents as the chief oppressors, with the freedom to abuse their children in private, is not entirely ill-conceived. Some parents do exploit family privacy and their children's vulnerability, as evidenced by the relentless increase in the number of children who require local authority (LA) protection. The dilemma is that the degree of state surveillance and control necessary to prevent all ill-treatment would involve an unacceptable interference with the upbringing of many thousands of children, the majority of whom are perfectly well cared for by loving parents. This dilemma poses a particularly difficult problem for children's rights. Children have a right to protection from harm, but also have a right not to be removed from their family unless it is necessary to do so. This presents the law with the need to find a satisfactory compromise between an unwanted level of authoritarian state interference and a passive assumption that it is impossible to prevent a minority of children suffering in the privacy of their homes. Indeed, it must ensure that the majority of parents continue to fulfil their parenting role without undermining their willingness or ability to do so by undue intervention.

This chapter considers first the background to this problem, and then proceeds to discuss the lack of clarity over what children need protection *from*. Whether or not the law maintains an acceptable balance between children's rights to family life and protection from abuse and adults' right to parental autonomy is the focus of the remainder of this chapter.

(2) Uncertainty over the State's Role

It is a cardinal feature of western democratic legal systems that parents and families, rather than the state, have the primary right and the primary responsibility to bring up their children: to meet their claims for nurture, care and upbringing and to decide for themselves how this will be done.[1]

Nevertheless, the reports of inquiries into child deaths make overwhelmingly depressing reading.[2] The Beckford Report commenting on society's resistance to acknowledging the existence of child abuse stated:

> Some parents abuse, even kill their children. Throughout history, they always have, and they always will. What is new about child abuse has been the increased and still increasing public awareness of this socially unpalatable, endemic phenomenon. Realisation that the deliberate abuse of children not only occurs but is also by no means a rare occurrence is profoundly shocking both to the individual and to the body politic.[3]

While the early reports into child deaths had focused on physical abuse, or 'non-accidental injuries', as they are euphemistically referred to by practitioners, towards the end of the 1980s, the Cleveland crisis suggested that child sexual abuse might be far more common than most people believed.[4] Information of this kind makes it hard for anyone to deny that children have a basic right to protection from ill-treatment and that the state must ensure that they receive it, even if it means removing them from their parents' care. Governments are unlikely to cavil at the terms of international instruments reminding them of their duties in this respect.[5]

Thus far, there is little scope for disagreement. English criminal law certainly acknowledges children's rights to protection from ill-treatment by setting a line below which parents may not descend, without risking criminal charges. The criminal process is, however, something of a blunt instrument, in so far as it can only punish adults for past abuse which should never have happened. Indeed, criminal proceedings may not improve a child victim's life and may even exacerbate the effects of the abuse if the child is called as a witness at the offender's trial. The principles of civil law attempt to ensure that children are protected from abuse, if possible before it starts, or at least before it becomes very serious. But the fundamental difficulty is that the type of ill-treatment meted out to abused children occurs behind the closed doors of perfectly normal-looking houses.

The law over the last century has reflected an underlying uncertainty experienced by policy-makers over finding an appropriate compromise between obliging the state to find and protect every child who is being abused and maintaining family privacy. Fox Harding's seminal analysis remains helpful.[6] According to her, it is possible to perceive four broad theoretical

---

[1] B. Hale and J. Fortin (2008) p. 99.
[2] DHSS (1982); DH (1991); H. Laming (2003); M. Bichard (2004).
[3] London Borough of Brent (1985) p. 9.   [4] Butler-Sloss (1988).
[5] See esp. CRC, Arts 19 and 37(a), and the European Convention for the Protection of Human Rights and Fundamental Freedoms (1950) (ECHR), Art. 3.
[6] L. Fox Harding (1997) ch. 1.

perspectives underlying the development of childcare policies and all four maintain distinctive positions on the state's duty to protect children from harm. First, there is the 'laissez-faire' and patriarchal approach, typified by case law in the late nineteenth century, which broadly took the view that power in the family should not be disturbed except in very extreme circumstances and the role of the state should be a minimal one. Writers such as Goldstein, Freud and Solnit[7] later adopted a similar position, maintaining that parents fulfil the nurturing role better than anyone else and need family privacy and autonomy in order to bring their children up without undue interference from the state.

The second and third theoretical perspectives both assume state intervention is desirable, but with a differing emphasis placed on the degree of authoritarianism accompanying it. The second perspective considers it justifiable to attribute an essentially paternalistic role to the state, by pointing to the innate vulnerability and dependence of children. The state is thereby obliged to protect them, even if it involves an authoritarian stance which undermines the ties between children and their parents. The third perspective defends the birth family and parents' rights. It legitimises state intervention to protect children, but also sees the dangers of targeting poorer and socially deprived parents who are thereby seen as the victims of heavy-handed state authoritarianism.[8] State intervention should therefore support families and assist them in the difficult task of bringing up children in inadequate home circumstances.

These first three perspectives appear to assume that because the state intervenes on behalf of the child there is no special need to emphasise the child's individual position. Thus, when finding a balance between over-authoritarianism and laissez-faire, the contest is between parents and state. It is assumed that once an appropriate balance is found, the state will automatically adopt the protective role for children. The fourth and last approach is the rights approach maintained by the children's liberationists. This differs fundamentally from the others, in so far as it alone concentrates on the child's own position, seeing the contest as one between children and parents. They consider that children should be treated as independent persons in their own right with a right to adult freedoms, in order to release them from parental domination. The negative aspects of family life are used to substantiate their claim that children should be freed from adult oppression. These are exemplified by parents' ability to exploit their position of power within the family and abuse their children. This last perspective, which focuses almost exclusively on the liberationists' claims regarding children's autonomy, seems to assume that children, once emancipated, will be able to achieve their own physical protection. This emphasis during the 1980s led to the establishment of agencies

---

[7] J. Goldstein *et al.* (1973), (1980).

[8] For an attack couched in these terms on US state interference with parental autonomy, see M. Guggenheim (2005) ch. 6. See also *Soares de Melo* v. *Portugal*, App. No. 72850/14, in which the ECtHR found a violation of Art. 8 following the removal of children due to neglect, which was primarily caused by the parents' poverty.

which set out to 'empower' abused children to help themselves. Childline and the Children's Legal Centre were established and encouraged children to seek help on their own behalf, rather than waiting for the state to assist with their protection. As Fox Harding points out, it is certainly unrealistic to assume that such an approach is sufficient in itself. Very young children who, by reason of their size and dependence, are particularly vulnerable to abuse, are quite unable either to cope with adult freedoms or to protect themselves physically against adult abuse.[9] Older children might be expected to make choices in abusive situations and often do so, but these may be strongly influenced by their past experiences. As in so many other fields of law involving the older child, the difficulty is to find an appropriate balance between the exercise of paternalism to fulfil the child's right to protection and respecting his or her capacity for choice. Arguing that abused children's choices should be respected by the state[10] overlooks the distorted relationships that abused children often have with their abusers. In this context, the need to recognise a child's interest in choice has less obvious relevance than his or her need for protection, bearing in mind that abused children's choices may be strongly influenced by their psychological dependence on parent abusers. The framework of international law, discussed below, recognises this wider network of children's rights involved in child protection cases.

These very different approaches are all discernible in the violent swings in childcare policy during the last 50 years and they are all reflected, to a lesser or greater extent, by provisions of the Children Act (CA) 1989 itself. Indeed, the Act adopts an uneasy compromise between emphasising parents' rights to autonomy and privacy and fulfilling children's rights to protection. It clearly reflects the 'moral panics' arising from the child abuse inquiries of the 1970s and 1980s which led to demands for the government to 'do something about child abuse'. There is a clear commitment to ensuring that LAs have sufficient powers to intervene to protect children when essential. By providing relatively broad grounds for intervention and by strengthening the emergency powers to seek and find a child whose safety is believed to be at risk, LAs gained relatively straightforward methods for protecting children against abusive and uncooperative parents. The 'significant harm' criterion for intervention is intended to flag up the fact that children can only be removed from their parents as a measure of last resort, in order to protect children at severe risk or in potentially dangerous situations.[11] Below this threshold, Part III of the CA 1989 places obligations on LAs to support children 'in need' and their families. The legislation also flirts briefly with the concept of the state respecting the decision-making rights of children.[12]

While the CA 1989 was intent on giving state agencies wide powers to protect children reasonably effectively, one of its other important objectives

---

[9] L. Fox Harding (1997) p. 136.   [10] E.g. F. Olsen (1992) pp. 210–13.   [11] CA 1989, s. 31.
[12] E.g. CA 1989, ss 17(4A), 22(4)–(5), 38(6), 43(8), 44(7), 46(3) and Sch. 3, paras 4(4) and 5(5). Discussed below.

was to respond to the public fears generated by the Cleveland crisis, during which very large numbers of children were taken into state care on a suspicion of being victims of child sexual abuse.[13] This crisis had led, in the late 1980s, to a widely held perception that laws and policies then existed allowing social workers to adopt an over-authoritarian approach to families and a marked lack of respect for parents' own rights. Consequently, the 1989 Act also ensures that parents' own family rights are promoted, with clear boundaries between the family and the state. It stresses that although the state has an important part to play, it is to be residual and supportive – the primary responsibility for bringing up children remains with their parents. In the event of disagreement between parents and LAs over whether the parents are providing appropriate care for the child, state intervention against the parents' wishes is possible, but only with court authority,[14] and then only by establishing clear statutory grounds for intervention.[15] Parents retain their parental responsibilities, even in the event of their child being removed from them on the authority of a care order.[16]

The CA 1989 makes valiant efforts to maintain an appropriate balance between the child's rights and those of his or her parents, but there is now an accumulating body of government-commissioned research[17] which makes one doubt whether an appropriate equilibrium between children's interests and those of their parents can ever be found. Overall, it suggests that matters have not changed greatly since the early 1980s when Dingwall *et al.* described the child protection system as one reflecting 'a liberal compromise'. Now, as then: 'The result is a system which is fully effective neither in preventing mistreatment nor in respecting family privacy but lurches unevenly between these two poles.'[18] This is probably inevitable since no system will ever achieve perfection.

(3) The Rights Dimension

Child protection decisions almost inevitably involve the human rights of parents and children. The potential for both serious harm to the child and excessive state intervention in the family presents a complex network of human rights requirements that can be difficult to resolve. For this reason,

---

[13] Butler-Sloss (1988).

[14] See *R (G)* v. *Nottingham City Council* [2008] EWHC 152 (Admin), [2008] FLR 1660, per Munby J, at [15]: the LA should not have directed hospital staff to separate a mother from her newly born child against her wishes and without judicial authority.

[15] LAs may not accommodate children against their parents' wishes (CA 1989, s. 20(7)) nor avoid applying for a care order (under s. 31) by using the wardship jurisdiction instead, to obtain judicial authority for removing children from their parents (s. 100).

[16] CA 1989, s. 33(3)(b).

[17] See, inter alia, the research summarised in DH (1995), (2001); D. Quinton (2004); J. Beecham and I. Sinclair (2007).

[18] R. Dingwall *et al.* (1983) p. 219. See also N. Parton (2014).

there were fears that the introduction of the Human Rights Act (HRA) 1998 might potentially distort the balance between children's right to protection from abuse and parents' right to family privacy. Nevertheless, the legal framework established by the CA 1989 for protecting children has remained largely unchanged following the introduction of the HRA. In a sense, this is unsurprising; as Lady Hale has made clear, the CA 1989 was 'framed with the developing jurisprudence under article 8 of the European Convention on Human Rights very much in mind'.[19] As a result, the developing human rights law on child protection has been accommodated within the existing framework of the CA 1989. The application of that framework has, however, presented courts and LAs with the difficult task of reconciling competing human rights claims in practice. There are three important aspects of human rights law for child protection. First, the state owes children positive obligations to protect them from harm, including that inflicted by their parents. Second, coercive intervention in the family constitutes an interference with the right to respect for private and family life in Article 8 of the ECHR and can only be justified if the action is proportionate under Article 8(2). Finally, parents and children have important procedural rights both in the processes for LA decision-making and court proceedings. Each of these aspects of rights protection will be considered in turn.

One of the most important aspects of human rights law for children is the recognition that the state has positive obligations to protect them from harm, including harm suffered in the home. The UN Convention on the Rights of the Child (CRC) expressly imposes duties on the state to protect children from intra-familial harm. Article 19 of the CRC[20] requires states to take 'all appropriate legislative, administrative, social and educational measures' to protect children from a comprehensive range of harms that they may suffer at the hands of family members and to take action to prevent such harmful treatment occurring.[21] In contrast, the text of the ECHR makes no specific mention of child protection. Nonetheless, the European Court of Human Rights (ECtHR) has repeatedly emphasised that the ECHR imposes a range of positive

---

[19] *Re B (A Child)* [2013] UKSC 33, at [194].

[20] CRC, Art. 19 states: '(1) States Parties shall take all appropriate legislative, administrative, social and educational measures to protect the child from all forms of physical or mental violence, injury or abuse, neglect or negligent treatment, maltreatment or exploitation, including sexual abuse, while in the care of parent(s), legal guardian(s) or any other person who has the care of the child. (2) Such protective measures should, as appropriate, include effective procedures for the establishment of social programmes to provide necessary support for the child and for those who have the care of the child, as well as for other forms of prevention and for identification, reporting, referral, investigation, treatment and follow-up of instances of child maltreatment described heretofore, and, as appropriate, for judicial involvement.'

[21] Discussed further in: J. Tobin and J. Cashmore (2019); Committee on the Rights of the Child (2011). While CRC, Art. 19 deals explicitly with intra-familial abuse, further provisions of the CRC deal with other aspects of harmful treatment and violence. See particularly CRC, Arts 32–7.

obligations[22] that require states to take action to prevent harmful treatment, particularly in relation to children and other vulnerable people.[23] In particular, Article 3 requires that if the state knows, or ought to have known, that a child is suffering significant abuse or neglect, then it must take reasonable steps to protect the child.[24] A similar obligation arises under Article 2 if the child is at risk of death.[25] These positive obligations are vital in grounding the child protection system in obligations owed to children as an aspect of their fundamental rights, rather than simply treating children as passive victims and recipients of assistance.

The second facet of human rights in child protection is the importance of respect for family life. One of the aims of the CA 1989 was to reassure the public that the traditional privacy and autonomy of parents should not be undermined by over-zealous state intervention. This was very much in tune with the intentions of Article 8 of the ECHR, which reflects the post-war objectives of the Convention's draftsmen, namely to protect private individuals, including parents, from authoritarian regimes.[26] The drafting of the 1989 Act had responded to early decisions reached by the European Commission and Court in favour of parents claiming that their rights to family privacy under Article 8 of the ECHR had been infringed by state intervention to protect their children.[27] But when considering parental complaints over state intervention to protect their children, the ECtHR has repeatedly emphasised the need to maintain an appropriate balance between infringing the parents' rights and protecting those of their child.[28] When considering whether state interference with parents' family life is 'necessary',[29] the fact that a child could be placed in a more beneficial environment for his or her upbringing will not on its own be deemed sufficient to justify compulsory removal from parental care.[30] The reasons for the intervention must be sufficient and the intervention

---

[22] *Osman* v. *United Kingdom* [1999] 1 FLR 193, at [116]: a person's rights under Art. 2 are infringed if the state agency fails to do all that could be reasonably expected of them to avoid a real and immediate risk to life of which they had or ought to have had knowledge; *Z* v. *United Kingdom* [2001] 2 FLR 612, at [73]–[74]: state agencies must take reasonable steps to prevent children being subjected to ill-treatment amounting to torture or inhuman or degrading treatment under Art. 3 in situations where they had or ought to have had knowledge of that ill-treatment; see also *TP and KM* v. *United Kingdom* [2001] 2 FLR 549; *X and Y* v. *The Netherlands* (1985) 8 EHRR 235: Art. 8 protects the child's moral and physical integrity and thereby entitles the child to adequate child protection measures. See also the arguments using Art. 8 presented by the Official Solicitor in *S (by the Official Solicitor)* v. *Rochdale MBC and another* [2008] EWHC 3283 (Fam), [2009] 1 FLR 1090, at [15]–[30].

[23] *Re E (A Child) (Northern Ireland)* [2008] UKHL 66, at [9].

[24] See: *Z* v. *United Kingdom* [2001] 2 FLR 612; *M and M* v. *Croatia* (2017) 65 EHRR 9.

[25] *Osman* v. *United Kingdom* [1999] 1 FLR 193.   [26] J. Fortin (1999) pp. 357–9.

[27] E.g. *W* v. *United Kingdom* (1988) 10 EHRR 29. The success of these parents' applications led to the abolition of the power of LAs to acquire parental responsibility over children by administrative resolution. They also provoked the CA 1989, s. 34 giving parents a right to apply for contact with their children while in state care.

[28] E.g. inter alia: *Johansen* v. *Norway* (1996) 23 EHRR 33; *K and T* v. *Finland* [2001] 2 FLR 707; *Z* v. *United Kingdom* [2001] 2 FLR 612.

[29] I.e. under ECHR, Art. 8(2).   [30] *Kutzner* v. *Germany* (2002) 35 EHRR 25, at [69].

itself proportionate to the aim of protecting the child in question. In assessing this balance, it is important to recognise the complexity of the child's rights in such cases. Children undoubtedly have a right to be protected from harmful treatment, but also have their own right to family life. Both the CRC[31] and the ECtHR[32] recognise *children's* own rights to be brought up by their parents, unless the circumstances are shown to require separation. Nevertheless, when carrying out this balancing act, there is a tendency for evidence to be couched in terms of the adults' rights, with the justification for the infringement of those rights expressed in terms of the child's best interests, rather than their rights.[33]

Due to the wide margin of appreciation allowed states in this context, the ECtHR only rarely criticises the reasons for a child being taken into state care, taking the view that the national authorities had the advantage of seeing the parties concerned.[34] Instead, it often concerns itself with scrutinising the extent to which the decision-making process provided the parents with sufficient protection of their procedural rights. But this may result in the ECtHR considering the state's actions from a particularly adult-orientated viewpoint, that of the parents, again without articulating the child's own rights.[35] Once the child has been removed into state care, the ECtHR is far readier to criticise the state's approach to the child's subsequent management. Thus, it has repeatedly stressed that a child's removal into state care must be seen as a temporary measure only, expecting states to make real efforts to ensure the child's rapid reintegration in his family.[36] This expectation reflects the assumption underlying the phrasing of Article 8 itself that the family is a temporarily disrupted safe haven for the child, to which he or she should be returned as soon as possible.[37] While such an approach certainly strengthens family autonomy and also prevents children being taken away from their parents unnecessarily, it does not so obviously promote an abused child's *own* rights to a happy upbringing free from parental abuse.[38]

---

[31] Esp. CRC, Art. 9(1), which guarantees the right not to be separated from parents, but explicitly recognises that separation may be necessary in cases of abuse or neglect.

[32] The right to family life in Art. 8 is a right to mutual enjoyment.   [33] See Chapter 2.

[34] *Kutzner* v. *Germany* (2002) 35 EHRR 25, at [66]. The examples of state intervention most commonly criticised by the ECtHR are those involving emergency intervention (discussed below). However, the court has shown increasing willingness to find that the right to family life has been violated in circumstances where the state has removed children from families living in poverty and failed to offer sufficient support to keep the family together: *Soares de Melo* v. *Portugal*, App. No. 72850/14.

[35] Discussed further in Chapter 2.

[36] Inter alia: *Olsson* v. *Sweden* (1988) 11 EHRR 259; *Johansen* v. *Norway* (1996) 23 EHRR 33; *Scott* v. *United Kingdom* [2000] 1 FLR 958; *K and T* v. *Finland* [2001] 2 FLR 707; *S and G* v. *Italy* [2000] 2 FLR 771; *EP* v. *Italy* (2001) 31 EHRR 17; *Haase* v. *Germany* [2004] 2 FLR 39.

[37] But see *EP* v. *Italy* (2001) 31 EHRR 17.   [38] J. Fortin (1999) pp. 357–9.

The third important aspect of human rights for child protection is concerned with procedural rights, arising under both Articles 6 and 8. The ECtHR has been clear that:

> whilst Article 8 contains no explicit procedural requirements, the decision-making process involved in measures of interference must be fair and the parents and, as appropriate, the children must have been involved in the process, seen as a whole, to a degree sufficient to provide them with the requisite protection of their interests.[39]

Procedural protection under Article 8 is important in that, unlike Article 6, it is not merely concerned with litigation, but with all aspects of child protection decision-making. As a result, parents have the right to full involvement in decision-making, including notice of judicial applications and significant planning meetings, and disclosure of material information and evidence. While children also have procedural rights, the case law tends to be concerned with those of parents. There are circumstances in which placing too much weight on parents' procedural rights risks infringing children's own rights to protection from harm. In these serious cases, the procedural rights of parents can be outweighed by their child's right to protection.[40]

Thus, the human rights case law presents a complex set of rights and promotes the difficult message that while parents' rights to family life must be respected, children should not be left dangerously unprotected.

(4) Which Children Require Protection? Defining Harm

The question of what forms and level of harm children require protection from is contentious. The uncertainty as to the role of the state, discussed above, has meant that approaches to harm have oscillated in response to crises and to different political conceptions of the role of the state in relation to the family.[41] So, for example, the New Labour period from the late 1990s was characterised by an emphasis on locating child protection within a wider concern for 'safeguarding and promoting children's welfare' and an emphasis on supportive services for families. In contrast, the response to the tragic death of Baby Peter Connolly in 2008 produced a raft of reforms aimed at refocusing attention on child protection and 'rescuing' children at risk.[42] Similarly, the

---

[39] *Dolhamre v. Sweden*, App. No. 67/104 (2010), at [116].

[40] *Re X (Children)* [2018] EWHC 451 (Fam), in which the father's involvement in proceedings concerning his two daughters was significantly curtailed. He had been convicted of seriously sexually abusing them and his involvement in proceedings, including disclosure of information, was likely to be extremely harmful to their recovery and an interference with their Art. 8 rights to privacy. A similar conclusion was reached in *LA* v. *XYZ Authority* [2019] EWHC 2166 (Fam), in which the father had murdered the mother in front of the child and there was a risk that he would use any disclosed information to try to communicate with the child.

[41] N. Parton (2014).   [42] N. Parton (2014).

economic downturn and austerity policies that followed the financial crisis of 2008 appear to have had a significant impact on both demand for children's services and the difficulties for squeezed LAs in responding to that demand.[43] It is often these shifts in society, policy and politics that influence the practical point at which support or intervention occur, rather than the detail of the legislation itself. The CA 1989 provides a broad approach to defining harm, which has accommodated these shifts in practice.

The lawyer might answer the question 'which children need the attentions of a child protection service?' by referring to the formula adopted by the CA 1989. The test used to demarcate the boundary at which compulsory state intervention is permissible is based on identifying those children who are suffering, or at risk of suffering, significant harm.[44] Thus, the legal framework provides the social worker with a metaphorical bottom line below which parental behaviour should not sink without child protection intervention being contemplated. This bottom line may be more apparent than real since there is no specialised definition of 'significant'.[45] Few would countenance the state intervening simply because a child's parents are not particularly adept at parenting. Indeed, as Hedley J has emphasised:

> Basically it is the tradition of the UK, recognised in law, that children are best brought up within natural families . . . It follows inexorably from that, that society must be willing to tolerate very diverse standards of parenting, including the eccentric, the barely adequate and the inconsistent. It follows too that children will inevitably have both very different experiences of parenting and very unequal consequences flowing from it. It means that some children will experience disadvantage and harm, while others flourish in atmospheres of loving security and emotional stability. These are the consequences of our fallible humanity and it is not the provenance of the state to spare children all the consequences of defective parenting. In any event, it simply could not be done.[46]

In this case, as Hedley J's comment makes clear, the parenting was not ideal. Indeed, the children, who were being brought up by parents with very severe learning difficulties, were, he thought being harmed, but he did not consider the harm to be significant.[47] So, in Hedley J's view, they needed state support,[48] but not removal from home. Similarly, dealing with a different aspect of the same case, Ward LJ stressed that it would be impermissible social engineering to remove children from their parents into care because the parents are not sufficiently intelligent.[49] Such an approach is laudable and has been echoed by

---

[43] P. Bywaters *et al.* (2018).

[44] See the 'significant harm' formula used in the CA 1989, ss 31(2) and 47.

[45] *Re B (Care Proceedings: Appeal)* [2013] UKSC 33, [2013] 1 WLR 1911, esp. at [26] and [185]–[186]: the Supreme Court considered it unhelpful to offer a definition of the word 'significant'.

[46] *Re L (Care: Threshold Criteria)* [2007] 1 FLR 2050, at [50].   [47] Ibid. at [52].

[48] They were 'children in need' under CA 1989, s. 17(1), and thus qualified for family support. Discussed below.

[49] *Re L (Children) (Care Proceedings: Significant Harm)* [2006] EWCA Civ 1282, [2007] 1 FLR 1068, at [49].

the ECtHR itself.[50] On the other hand, children are entitled to protection from harmful treatment and the term 'significant' provides little guidance as to where this line is drawn.

The fact that we have no official agreement over the point at which intervention is required makes the social worker's job doubly hard. Regional statistics indicate that social workers are far more likely to intervene in some areas than in others, despite the child's circumstances being similar, thereby suggesting that thresholds for bringing children into care vary considerably.[51] These regional variations may indicate uncertainty over the point at which to intervene or an anxiety over the availability of resources for large numbers of children in care. Nevertheless, when deciding whether abusive behaviour is serious enough to merit protective intervention, practitioners tend to focus on the outcomes of abuse rather than on the severity of the incident in itself. This is predictable given the need to learn from the cases involving children who die or who are very seriously injured or harmed.[52] Social workers are also undoubtedly influenced by the growing body of research evidence clarifying the long-term effects well into adulthood of a variety of types of ill-treatment, such as emotional abuse and neglect and child sexual abuse.[53] Research also shows the damaging impact on children of living in households where domestic violence is commonplace,[54] and with parents who suffer from mental illness or who abuse drugs or alcohol.[55]

The definition of harm in the CA 1989[56] is phrased extremely broadly. It includes ill-treatment, whether physical, sexual and otherwise, and impairment of the child's physical and mental health or physical, intellectual, emotional, social or behavioural development. These wide definitions allow social workers and the courts to respond to changing understandings of harm that

---

[50] *Kutzner* v. *Germany* (2002) 35 EHRR 25, at [69].

[51] M. Narey (2007) chs 3–4; Ofsted (2008) para. 304; H. Laming (2009) para. 3.11; Housing, Government and Local Government Committee (HC) (2019) pp. 35–7.

[52] W. Rose and J. Barnes (2008); M. Brandon *et al.* (2008).

[53] Inter alia: M. Lynch and J. Roberts (1982); D. Cicchetti and V. Carlson (1989); D. Wolfe (1987); P. Mullen *et al.* (1996); D. Jones and P. Ramchandani (1999); D. Glaser (2000), (2002). See also the government-commissioned research projects summarised in: DH (1995), (2001); D. Quinton (2004); J. Beecham and I. Sinclair (2007).

[54] Adoption and Children Act 2002, s. 120 amended the definition of harm in CA 1989, s. 31(9) to make it clear that harm includes 'impairment suffered from seeing or hearing the ill-treatment of another'. The Domestic Abuse Act 2021, s. 3 further recognises the harm that domestic abuse does to children who witness the abuse or its effects. M. Hester *et al.* (2007) ch. 3 summarises the body of international research. See also W. Rose and J. Barnes (2008) ch. 3, research summary; H. Cleaver *et al.* (2007).

[55] H. Cleaver *et al.* (2007).

[56] See CA 1989, s. 31(9), which provides the following definitions which clarify the term 'significant harm': '"harm" means ill-treatment or the impairment of health or development including, for example, impairment suffered from seeing or hearing the ill-treatment of another; "development" means physical, intellectual, emotional, social or behavioural development; "health" means physical or mental health; and "ill-treatment" includes sexual abuse and forms of ill-treatment which are not physical.'

emerge from research and children and from social and technological change. The current statutory guidance, *Working Together*,[57] recognises this developing understanding of harm by adding 'exploitation by criminal gangs and organised crime groups; trafficking; online abuse; sexual exploitation and the influences of extremism leading to radicalisation' to the list of threats to children.[58] The definition of 'harm' in the CA 1989 is flexible enough to accommodate this increasingly complex understanding of risks to children, as demonstrated by a burgeoning case law dealing with issues such as radicalisation,[59] forced marriage[60] and child trafficking.[61] The price of this flexible definition is uncertainty as to the precise boundaries of the term 'harm' and the circumstances in which compulsory child protection measures can be imposed. This uncertainty is particularly apparent as the law expands into new areas. For example, in responding to 'radicalisation', it is readily apparent that a teenager who is involved in violent extremism is at risk of harm; it is far less clear whether children should be seen as at risk if they have a parent who espouses extreme religious or political views.[62] The statute itself gives little guidance to social workers and courts dealing with these complex matters of judgment.

The statutory guidance, *Working Together*,[63] goes to some lengths to try to provide additional guidance through defining the commonly used terms 'physical abuse', 'emotional abuse', 'sexual abuse' and 'neglect', as well as newer forms of harm such as 'extremism' and 'child criminal exploitation'.[64] This guidance is helpful, but, as the case law makes clear, it is the less obviously abusive behaviour that causes disagreement. Indeed, even with the assistance of legal definitions, lawyers, in common with social workers, are often very ambivalent over what amounts to 'normal' and 'abnormal' parental behaviour. This is reflected in the very different approaches of judges to unusual cases. For example, in *Re W*,[65] three sets of judiciary had dramatically different reactions to information from a father that a mother and her new partner walked around nude at home in front of her two children, aged 9 and 6, and may even have bathed with the children.[66] While one of the judges who had dealt with the case clearly considered this information reasonably innocuous, another not only found it alarming, but considered that it raised child protection issues warranting investigation by

---

[57] HM Government (2018a).   [58] Ibid. para. 12.

[59] E.g. *Re K (Children)* [2016] EWHC 1606 (Fam).

[60] *Camden LBC* v. *RZ* [2015] EWHC 3751 (Fam).

[61] *M (Children) (Suspected Trafficking: Competent Authority)* [2017] EWFC 56, although in this case the suspicion of trafficking was found to be false.

[62] Discussed in R. Taylor (2018). E.g. in *Re K (Children)* [2016] EWHC 1606 (Fam), at [13], Hayden J suggested that 'it might be axiomatic that a child brought up by radicalised parents or parent, is by virtue of that fact alone at an unacceptable risk of significant harm'.

[63] HM Government (2018a).   [64] Ibid. Appendix A.

[65] *Re W (Residence Order)* [1999] 1 FLR 869.   [66] Ibid.

the local children's services authority. Butler-Sloss LJ considered the latter reaction to be extreme, but pointed out:

> A balance has to be struck between the behaviour within families which is seen by them as natural and with which that family is comfortable and the sincerely held views of others who are shocked by it. Nudity is an obvious example ... Communal family bathing is another example. This is often entirely innocent. In other families abuse may lie behind it.[67]

Given such differing judicial responses, it is not surprising that social workers display similar uncertainty when confronted with concerns about a child's future well-being.

(5) The Initial Referral: Child Protection or Family Support?

(A) Family Support for Children in Need

A vital element of the state's response to children at risk of harm is the provision of services to children in need and their families. The importance of the right to family life, discussed above, underlines the importance of state action to support families to meet their child's needs within the home. The use of coercive measures, in circumstances in which the family could have met the child's needs with support, may amount to disproportionate interference with those rights to family life.[68] A network of duties requires public authorities to act together to safeguard and promote children's welfare.[69] Of particular importance is section 17 of the 1989 Act, which places a general duty on every LA 'to safeguard and promote the welfare of children within its area' who meet the statutory test of being in need[70] and, 'so far as is consistent with that duty, to promote their upbringing by their own families'. Despite all the exhortations of the government in the guidance accompanying the introduction of the CA 1989,[71] this duty has been inadequately complied with and wide variations are seen in the responses of different LAs.[72]

---

[67] Ibid. at 873.

[68] *Soares de Melo* v. *Portugal*, App. No. 72850/14: violation of Art. 8 following the removal of children without giving sufficient support to address the family's poverty.

[69] CA 2004, s. 11(2) requires a long list of agencies involved in providing children with services to discharge their functions 'having regard to the need to safeguard and promote the welfare of children'. At a local level, LAs, together with the other 'safeguarding partners', i.e. the clinical commissioning group and chief officer of police, are required to work together to safeguard children, promote their welfare and meet children's needs within their area: Children and Social Work Act 2017, s. 16.

[70] CA 1989, s. 17(10): 'a child shall be taken to be in need if – (a) he is unlikely to achieve or maintain, or to have the opportunity of achieving or maintaining, a reasonable standard of health or development without the provision for him of services by a local authority under this Part; (b) his health or development is likely to be significantly impaired, or further impaired without the provision for him of such services; or (c) he is disabled.'

[71] E.g. DH (1991).   [72] P. Bywaters *et al.* (2018).

The statutory guidance, *Working Together*,[73] provides that if an initial referral indicates that the child is 'in need', the LA should then carry out careful assessment work identifying those needs, analysing their extent and producing a detailed children-in-need plan setting out how the services will be delivered.[74] The legislation clearly intends LAs to provide parents caring for children in need with considerable state support if they desire it.[75] Support services are not compulsory forms of intervention, but are provided on the basis that they are 'in partnership'[76] with the parents. A common form of support is the provision of accommodation for a child,[77] with the parents' consent.[78] But an LA cannot remove a child from the parental home and claim that it is lawfully accommodating a child unless a parent consents to its doing so, rather than merely helplessly acquiescing in the LA's plans.[79] These restrictions underline the ethos of Part III of the CA 1989 in providing supportive services for families.

While section 17 imposes a mandatory duty on LAs, there are concerns about its overall effectiveness. Some LAs apparently avoid carrying out 'children-in-need assessments' for fear of their resource implications.[80] A desire to avoid activating any leaving care obligations may certainly explain an LA's failure to assess the needs of an older teenager.[81] While action against the LA may be brought on behalf of any child in the event of the assessment guidance not being followed adequately, such action would require legal assistance and he or she may already have suffered from a lack of adequate support in the interim.[82] There are considerable hurdles to bringing a successful legal challenge to a section 17 assessment or failure to provide one. In *R (G)* v. *Barnet London Borough Council and others*,[83] a majority of the House of Lords held

---

73   HM Government (2018a).   74   Ibid.

75   I.e. under CA 1989, Pt III and Sch. 2 – a wide range of family support services can be provided for families containing children in need, including, inter alia: day care (s. 18); accommodation if the child's parents are prevented from providing it (s. 20); occupational, social, cultural or recreational activities; home help; holiday provision; day centre facilities, etc. See also CA 1989, Sch. 2, para. 7: work should be done to avoid the need to remove the child into care through public law proceedings.

76   B. Hale (2000) p. 464: although the CA 1989 does not specifically express the concept of partnership between state and parents, it is an underlying principle of the Act. This principle has been important in interpreting CA 1989, Pt III: e.g. *Coventry City Council* v. *C, B, CA and CH* [2012] EWHC 2190 (Fam), at [25]–[30].

77   I.e. under CA 1989, s. 20 – a 'section 20 agreement'.

78   CA 1989, s. 20(7): accommodation cannot be provided against the wishes of anyone with parental responsibility who is willing and able to provide or arrange for the child's accommodation. See also s. 20(8): anyone with parental responsibility can remove any child under 16 (s. 20(11)) at any time.

79   *London Borough of Hackney* v. *Williams* [2018] UKSC 37, [2019] AC 421 distinguished such cases of removal from the parental home, which do require voluntary consent, from those cases in which the state is stepping 'into the breach' for a child who is not being looked after by the parents, in which case, no such active consent is required.

80   Ofsted (2008) para. 303; H. Laming (2009) para. 3.11.   81   CA 1989, ss 23A–24A.

82   E.g. *R (LH and MH)* v. *London Borough of Lambeth* [2006] EWHC 1190 (Admin), [2006] 2 FLR 1275; *R (S)* v. *Sutton London Borough Council* [2007] EWHC 1196 (Admin), [2007] 2 FLR 849.

83   [2003] UKHL 57, [2004] 2 AC 208. Lords Nicholls of Birkenhead and Steyn dissenting.

that an LA 's duty under section 17 is a broad and general duty to cater for the needs of *all* children, rather than a duty to meet the specific needs of any child in particular.[84] The Supreme Court in *Poole Borough Council* v. *PN*[85] has further found that section 17 does not in itself create a common law duty of care to protect children from harm caused by its negligent discharge. Although decisions under section 17 may still be challenged under the usual principles of judicial review, the courts have been very reluctant to intervene in assessments of whether a particular child is 'in need'[86] or the appropriate response to a finding of need.[87] Instead, the courts have been willing to grant LAs broad discretion, particularly given the difficulty of managing competing claims on dwindling resources. Collectively, these decisions pose considerable hurdles to a child or parent seeking to challenge a section 17 assessment and risk rendering it a provision with no clear purpose other than to provide the legal basis for the LA's broader approach in setting priorities.[88]

(B) The Section 47 Inquiry

One outcome of a children-in-need assessment is that the LA will find that it must commence inquiries under section 47. The focus of section 47 is very different from that under section 17. Although, unlike some other countries, there is no mandatory duty to report cases of suspected child abuse and neglect to children's services,[89] the law obliges LAs who 'have reasonable cause to suspect' that a child in their area 'is suffering, or is likely to suffer, significant harm' to 'make, or cause to be made, such inquiries as they consider necessary to enable them to decide whether they should take any action to safeguard or promote the child's welfare'.[90] Legally, the threshold of 'suspicion' for intervention through investigation is relatively low.[91] If a 'section 47 inquiry',[92] which should also involve good assessment work, throws up real concerns about the child's safety, a child protection conference will be convened, at which it

---

[84] Ibid., per Lord Millett, at [108].

[85] [2019] UKSC 25, [2020] AC 780. Although it would be possible for a duty to arise in particular circumstances, e.g. if there had been a responsibility to protect the child from harm.

[86] E.g. *R (O)* v. *London Borough of Lambeth* [2016] EWHC 937 (Admin), at [17]–[22].

[87] *R (AE)* v. *London Borough of Brent* [2018] EWHC 2574 (Admin), at [26]–[27].

[88] D. Cowan (2004) p. 334.

[89] A duty to report has been introduced in Wales: Social Services and Well-being (Wales) Act 2014, s. 130. In England, there is a duty to report cases of female genital mutilation (Serious Crime Act 2015, s. 74) and there may be professional duties on particular employees to report abuse, but the government has consulted and does not intend to introduce a general legal duty at present: HM Government (2018b).

[90] CA 1989, s. 47(1).

[91] *Re S (Sexual Abuse Allegations: LA Response)* [2001] EWHC Admin 334, [2001] 2 FLR 776, per Scott Baker J, at [36].

[92] HM Government (2018a) pp. 42–5: involving the child (where appropriate), family members and those professionals most involved in the family. Failure to follow the guidance may render the purported inquiry unlawful: *R (AB)* v. *Haringey LBC* [2013] EWHC 416 (Admin).

will be decided if the child is at continuing risk of significant harm.[93] If so, the child will be recorded as having been abused or neglected under one of the categories of abuse and the child protection plan established.[94] Social workers have, in the past, often concentrated on dangerous incidents of physical abuse, failing to deal adequately with cases involving long-term chronic parental neglect and inadequate parenting.[95] The current guidance emphasises that, whatever the category of abuse, the child protection plan, which should take account of the views of the child and parents so far as they are consistent with the child's welfare,[96] must always clarify what specific action is to be taken and by whom.

Deciding what action to take based on the evidence uncovered by the investigation, confronts child protection practitioners with the dilemmas discussed above. On the one hand, children must be protected from abuse by their own parents, but on the other hand, parents must be protected from unnecessary interference with their family life. The legislative framework gives the LA absolute discretion over whether to act or not; it imposes no duty to take any action, despite evidence that a child is suffering from significant harm and will continue to do so unless removed from home.[97] Nevertheless, the demands of the HRA 1998 must also be addressed. The social worker who stands back and fails to prevent a child from suffering from significant harm which amounts to ill-treatment and neglect so serious that it results in the child's death or amounts to 'torture, or inhuman or degrading treatment', is not only ignoring the protective powers under the CA 1989, but also risks infringing the child's rights under Articles 2, 3 and 8 of the ECHR. But the law also ensures that child protection practitioners can decide whether to intervene or not without their judgment being clouded by knowing that if their views about the abuse proved unfounded, they could be sued in negligence by distressed parents. Thus, even if protective action is taken based on a carelessly formed diagnosis of abuse, by doctors or social workers, the parents cannot sue the practitioners involved.[98]

---

[93] Ibid. pp. 46–7. [94] Ibid. pp. 48–9.

[95] E.g. in *Z* v. *United Kingdom* [2001] 2 FLR 612, despite the LA receiving numerous reports from other agencies that five children were being subjected to appalling abuse and neglect over a period of 5 years, it failed to intervene to protect them. See also D. Quinton (2004) pp. 154–6, M. Brandon *et al.* (2008) pp. 73–7, H. Laming (2009) para. 3.12.

[96] HM Government (2018a) pp. 48–9.

[97] E.g. *Nottinghamshire County Council* v. *P* [1994] Fam 18. But note CA 1989, s. 47(6): if, when carrying out a s. 47 inquiry, the LA is refused access to the child or is denied information about his or her whereabouts, the LA *must* apply for a protective order, unless it is satisfied that the child's welfare is satisfactorily safeguarded without such action.

[98] *D* v. *East Berkshire Community Health NHS Trust and others* [2005] 2 AC 373; *Lawrence* v. *Pembrokeshire County Council* [2007] EWCA Civ 446, [2007] 2 FLR 705; *B* v. *Reading Borough Council and another* [2007] EWCA Civ 1313, [2008] 1 FLR 797. But an action in negligence can probably be brought on behalf of a child in such circumstances.

(C) Section 17 and Section 47: Getting the Balance Right

The balance between supportive services and compulsory intervention has been subject to the tides of political and social opinion discussed above. Following implementation of the CA 1989, research indicated that social services departments were consistently prioritising their child protection work, at the expense of providing long-term family support to families with children in need. The intention of the legislation had been for social workers to intervene early and, wherever possible, to work in partnership with the family on a voluntary basis, thereby avoiding the need for more aggressive intervention. Nevertheless, what often happened was that once cases were labelled 'child protection' cases, the need to investigate incidents of abuse overcame notions of prevention and family support. Such a situation produced a vicious circle. Because other agencies considered social services' supportive work to be inadequate, they would attempt to establish that the family posed substantial risks to the child, thereby increasing the chance of accessing services for the family.[99] But then the response was for social workers to focus almost exclusively on an assessment of risk of harm, without considering the wider needs of the child within the family.[100] Furthermore, with large numbers of section 47 referrals, staff shortages and the deployment of inexperienced and poorly supervised members of staff,[101] social services were often reluctant to undertake section 47 inquiries at all, with 'the downgrading of cases to the status of section 17, and afterwards closure, [was] becoming an attractive option to childcare teams'.[102] When considering the interrelationship of sections 17 and 47, Lord Laming stressed that it was impossible to 'separate the protection of children from wider support to families' and that the best protection for a child was often achieved through the timely intervention of the family support services. In his view, referrals should not be labelled 'child protection' without good reason.[103]

The current *Working Together* guidance does its best to emphasise that measures to safeguard children should not be seen in isolation from the wider range of support and services available to meet the needs of children and their families,[104] and stresses that in many cases, the two processes should march hand in hand. Nonetheless, the media outcry responding to the Baby P tragedy in November 2008 reinforced social workers' fears over not intervening soon enough. Since the risks involved in allowing children to remain with truly dangerous parents are only too obvious, it is perhaps unsurprising that there has been a seemingly relentless rise in both the number of section 47 inquiries and proportions of referrals that result in such inquiries.[105] This rise also appears to have been fuelled by the combination of the pressure on

---

99 DH (2002) para. 6.15.   100 Ibid. para. 6.16.   101 Ibid. para. 6.8.
102 H. Laming (2003) para. 17.102.   103 Ibid. para. 1.30.
104 HM Government (2018a) pp. 12–14.
105 Housing, Government and Local Government Committee (HC) (2019).

families caused by austerity and by the cuts to early intervention services that have followed the tightening of LA budgets.[106] It may be that in consequence, those families who might once have benefitted from early support find themselves left to struggle until the situation deteriorates to the point at which child protection measures must be considered.

(6) Emergency Intervention

(A) Emergency Protection Orders

As Munby J has pointed out, it may be a terrifying experience for a child to be removed summarily from parents with whom he has lived all his life.[107] The Cleveland report also criticised the over-use of place of safety orders to remove children from home with little or no notice.[108] Nevertheless, it is equally terrifying to be subjected to real and immediate danger. Indeed, most children who are the subject of emergency intervention are already known to the LA.[109] If the initial referral indicates that a child's life is at risk of serious harm, or if a section 47 inquiry reveals such dangers, the CA 1989 provides practitioners with a range of powers to take immediate action.[110] An emergency protection order (EPO)[111] is designed to provide immediate authority to safeguard the child by removing him or her from home.[112] An application for an EPO is automatically justified when inquiries being made under section 47 are frustrated by access to the child being unreasonably refused, as long as the applicant has reasonable cause to believe that access to the child is required as a matter of urgency.[113]

The domestic courts are now very aware of the demands of the Strasbourg case law when deciding whether obtaining an EPO is really necessary.[114] The ECtHR has provided a body of trenchant advice over the use of emergency

---

[106] Ibid. pp. 24–7 and 29–30. See also P. Bywaters *et al.* (2018).

[107] *X Council* v. *B (Emergency Protection Orders)* [2004] EWHC 2015 (Fam), [2005] 1 FLR 341, per Munby J, at [34].

[108] Butler-Sloss (1998) ch. 1.   [109] J. Masson (2005) p. 80; J. Masson *et al.* (2008) ch. 3.

[110] EPO under CA 1989, s. 44; an exclusion requirement obtained on application to the court and included in an interim care order or an EPO under ss 38A and 44A – whereunder a perpetrator can be removed from the home instead of the child; police protection powers under CA 1989, s. 46.

[111] CA 1989, s. 44(1)(a): an order can be obtained if there is reasonable cause to believe that the child is likely to suffer significant harm if he is not removed to accommodation provided by the applicant or prevented from being removed from his present accommodation.

[112] CA 1989, s. 44(4)(c): the applicant (an LA, the police or the NSPCC) obtains parental responsibility over the child; s. 44(4)(b): the applicant can remove the child to alternative accommodation or prevent the child's removal from where he is already accommodated, e.g. a hospital; s. 45(1): the order lasts for up to 8 days, unless renewed for up to a further 7 days.

[113] CA 1989, s. 44(1)(b). See also CA 1989, s. 47(4): where inquiries are being made with regard to a child, the LA shall take reasonably practicable steps to obtain access to the child.

[114] E.g. *Langley and others* v. *Liverpool City Council and another* [2005] EWCA Civ 1173, [2006] 2 All ER 202, per Dyson LJ, at [56]–[64]; *X Council* v. *B (Emergency Protection Orders)* [2004] EWHC 2015 (Fam), [2005] 1 FLR 341, per Munby J, at [34]–[35].

intervention,[115] emphasising that it can only be justified[116] if it is a proportionate response to the danger that the child is considered to be in and is therefore a 'necessary' interference with the parents' family life.[117] It has criticised unnecessarily aggressive intervention methods,[118] especially in relation to older children, and if the abuse has already continued for a long period without endangering the child's life.[119] Nevertheless, it acknowledges the need in exceptional cases to obtain an order without notice (ex parte) to the parents, because of the urgency of the situation or because warning a parent who is an immediate threat to the child of such intended action may deprive the measure of its effectiveness.[120]

The senior judiciary have emphasised that LAs must pay great attention to the demands of the HRA 1998 in their use of emergency intervention.[121] Applications for EPOs must be justified by good evidence of a 'genuine emergency'.[122] The applicant LA should also consider whether there are less drastic alternatives to emergency removal,[123] and whether they need an EPO for the full duration of 8 days.[124] In the event of an EPO being granted, the court should explain fully why it is doing so,[125] consider its duration and whether contact with the parents during its operation need be restricted unduly.[126]

---

[115] Inter alia: *K and T* v. *Finland* [2001] 2 FLR 707; *P, C and S* v. *United Kingdom* [2002] 2 FLR 631; *Venema* v. *Netherlands* [2003] 1 FLR 552; *Haase* v. *Germany* [2004] 2 FLR 39. Discussed by J. Masson (2006) pp. 18–20.

[116] I.e. under ECHR, Art. 8(2).

[117] *K and T* v. *Finland* [2001] 2 FLR 707, per Grand Chamber of the ECtHR, at [168].

[118] *Venema* v. *Netherlands* [2003] 1 FLR 552, at [97]–[98].

[119] E.g. in *Haase* v. *Germany* [2004] 2 FLR 39, at [99]–[100]: the childcare authorities' response had not been proportionate in the way six children in one family had been removed from their schools, kindergarten and home, and placed in unidentified foster homes, with contact with their parents forbidden.

[120] Ibid. at [95].

[121] E.g. in *X Council* v. *B (Emergency Protection Orders)* [2004] EWHC 2015 (Fam), [2005] 1 FLR 341, at [77] and [80]: Munby J criticised the LA for applying for an EPO with inadequate supporting evidence and analysis of the case; similarly, in *Re X (Emergency Protection Orders)* [2006] EWHC 510 (Fam), [2006] 2 FLR 701, at [71]: McFarlane J described the LA's decision to apply for the EPO as 'badly flawed'. See also discussed by L. Davis (2007).

[122] *Re X (Emergency Protection Orders)* [2006] EWHC 510 (Fam), [2006] 2 FLR 701, per McFarlane J, at [72].

[123] E.g. a child assessment order (CA 1989, s. 43) or an interim care order (ibid., s. 38). *X Council* v. *B (Emergency Protection Orders)* [2004] EWHC 2015 (Fam), [2005] 1 FLR 341, per Munby J, at [43]–[46].

[124] Ibid., per Munby J, at [49]: many EPOs are made 'unthinkingly' and unnecessarily for the maximum period of 8 days. Per J. Masson (2006) pp. 27–8: practice varies enormously over the length of order sought.

[125] *Re X (Emergency Protection Orders)* [2006] EWHC 510 (Fam), [2006] 2 FLR 701, per McFarlane J, at [56].

[126] *X Council* v. *B (Emergency Protection Orders)* [2004] EWHC 2015 (Fam), [2005] 1 FLR 341, per Munby J, at [57], for a summary of the fourteen points, described by McFarlane J in *Re X (Emergency Protection Orders)*, at [65], as 'required reading' for every magistrate and justices' clerk involved in an EPO application.

The uncritical use of ex parte applications has also been robustly criticised.[127] Despite variations in local practice, growing numbers of courts have, since the implementation of the HRA 1998, been reluctant to allow applications for such orders to be heard, although they may allow an abridged notice period.[128] The statutory guidance also makes it clear that such applications should only be considered if the child's safety would be endangered if the parents were informed of the application or it is not possible to notify them.[129] The ECtHR has pointed out that the absence of a court hearing not only prevents the parents producing evidence opposing the application in court, but may deny the children an opportunity to be heard.[130] The Cleveland report also stressed that it was completely inappropriate for children to be removed from their parents' care at short notice without their own views being listened to.[131] But although children should be represented on applications for EPOs, this seldom happens due to the shortage of Cafcass guardians, particularly if an application is made on abridged notice.[132]

The fact that in this country, many applications for EPOs relate to those under the age of 2[133] suggests that practitioners are anxious about the extreme physical vulnerability of babies. Research indicates that their concerns are well-founded.[134] Very young children have a right to be protected from death, fracture and brain injury – all far more common in babies than in older children and all far more likely in the first 6 months of life.[135] Much of the case law emanating from Strasbourg revolves around intervention to protect very young children. The ECtHR has stressed that removing very young babies from their mothers soon after birth is an extremely harsh measure that can only be justified by extraordinarily compelling reasons.[136] As it has pointed out, the child's removal from his or her mother's care soon after birth will prevent the crucial formation of firm attachments between them and will also prevent the mother breastfeeding,[137] especially if there is no regular contact maintained between them after the removal. But practitioners may have a real dilemma if they doubt a mother's ability to care for her baby.[138] Indeed, they

---

[127] Ibid., per Munby J, at [51]–[55]: EPOs should *normally* be obtained on notice to the parents; ex parte orders can only justified in real emergencies. See also *Re X (Emergency Protection Orders)* [2006] EWHC 510 (Fam), [2006] 2 FLR 701, per McFarlane J, at [95].

[128] J. Masson (2006) pp. 21 and 24–6.   [129] DfE (2014) ch. 4, para. 20.

[130] *Haase* v. *Germany* [2004] 2 FLR 39, at [97].   [131] Butler-Sloss (1998) p. 245.

[132] *X Council* v. *B (Emergency Protection Orders)* [2004] EWHC 2015 (Fam), [2005] 1 FLR 341, per Munby J, at [37]; J. Masson (2006) p. 26.

[133] J. Masson (2004) p. 3.

[134] J. Sibert *et al.* (2002) p. 270: the incidence of severe abuse in babies aged less than 1 year is six times greater than in children aged 1–5 years, and 120 times greater than in children over 5.

[135] Ibid. p. 274.

[136] *K and T* v. *Finland* [2001] 2 FLR 707, at [168]; *Haase* v. *Germany* [2004] 2 FLR 39, at [102].

[137] *P, C and S* v. *United Kingdom* [2002] 2 FLR 631, at [131]; *Haase* v. *Germany* [2004] 2 FLR 39, at [101].

[138] E.g. *K and T* v. *Finland* [2001] 2 FLR 707: the mother was a paranoid schizophrenic with a poor parenting record regarding her older child; *P, C and S* v. *United Kingdom* [2002] 2 FLR 631: the mother's first child had been removed from her by the Californian childcare authorities in

may find the stance of the ECtHR unhelpful, given that they must address the demands of Article 3 which requires vigilance and a preparedness to intervene to prevent serious abuse continuing.[139] While over-aggressive intervention should certainly be discouraged, social workers would be blamed by the public if they failed to avert the child's serious injury or death.[140] Although the ECtHR has acknowledged that a fair balance has to be struck between children's rights and those of their parents,[141] the Strasbourg case law often contains very limited analysis of the child's own Convention rights which might counter-balance those of the parents.[142]

While the domestic courts have taken good note of the Strasbourg case law, it is arguable that Munby J went too far in concluding that parents should have more or less daily contact with their children (supervised by the LA) during the operation of the EPO, and that a breastfeeding mother should have as much contact as she needs to continue her regime.[143] This decision certainly presents challenges to the practicalities of many fostering arrangements.[144] Observing that foster parents might find it very difficult to organise daily contact with parents, particularly at weekends, Bodey J subsequently stated that it is not a principle of law that such generous contact has always to be arranged.[145]

As noted above, it is becoming less common for LAs to seek EPOs without notice, with practitioners apparently having become more aware of the demands of the HRA 1998. Nevertheless, Masson's research suggests less high-minded reasons underlie this reduction. It appears that LAs simply bypass the need for emergency intervention.[146] They either persuade parents to agree to allow their child to be accommodated by foster carers under 'section 20 agreements'[147] or enlist the assistance of the police, who may take the child into police protection. Masson criticises these stratagems. Her research suggests that parents' agreement to their child being fostered may be more apparent than real, since it is often made plain to them that an EPO will be sought in the event of their refusing.[148] More to the point, she considers that a child may be protected better by the LA gaining an EPO than by relying on

---

the belief that he had been the victim of induced illness abuse by his mother. See also *EP* v. *Italy* (2001) 31 EHRR 17: an older child, aged 7, had been removed from her mother in circumstances suggesting that she had been the victim of induced illness abuse (discussed in Chapter 2).

[139] *Z* v. *United Kingdom* [2001] 2 FLR 612.

[140] See the dissenting judges in *K and T* v. *Finland* [2001] 2 FLR 707: Judge Palm, joined by Judge Gaukur Jörundsson (see esp. at 752) and Judge Bonello (see esp. at 755). Judge Bonello complained that those who had wanted to place the baby beyond reach of harm were now themselves 'branded violators of human rights' (at 756).

[141] *Johansen* v. *Norway* (1996) 23 EHRR 33, at [78].   [142] Discussed in Chapter 2.

[143] *Re M (Care Proceedings: Judicial Review)* [2003] EWHC 850 (Admin), [2003] 2 FLR 171, per Munby J, at [44].

[144] In *Kirklees Metropolitan District Council* v. *S (Contact to Newborn Babies)* [2006] 1 FLR 333, per Bodey J, at [34]: this was the second appeal in 2 weeks he had heard on the issue of contact with a young baby on an EPO.

[145] Ibid. at [29]–[37].   [146] J. Masson (2005).

[147] CA 1989, s. 20; discussed further in Chapter 16.   [148] J. Masson (2005) p. 82.

parental agreement. This may be the case, for example, if the child has been placed with a close relative who is unable to prevent intervention from an abusive parent.[149] Nor is police protection preferable to an EPO; indeed, as discussed below, there are concerns about its use.

(B) Police Protection

Section 46 of the CA 1989 grants the police important but limited powers to protect children in an emergency without first seeking judicial approval.[150] The statutory guidance reflects the case law, considered below, that these powers should be used only 'in exceptional circumstances where there is insufficient time to seek an EPO or for reasons relating to the immediate safety of the child'.[151] While these powers can prove vital in a genuine emergency, research has suggested that LAs have sought to avoid ex parte applications for EPOs by requesting police protection instead.[152] Indeed, in some areas, it appears that the police are requested to intervene if social workers consider that they have insufficient evidence to justify applying for an EPO,[153] or if the local court is unwilling to hear cases without notice.[154] Masson et al.'s research on the use of police protection indicates that the interrelationship between social workers and the police over the use of these powers is not always an easy one,[155] with some police officers accusing social workers of opting for police protection 'as an easy way out',[156] in order to avoid going to court themselves, or in the case of teenagers, to sort out family disputes.[157] As Masson et al. point out, the availability of police protection as a kind of backstop for social workers involved in child protection work may not be at all appropriate.[158] Although the legislation envisages that a child will move out of police protection into LA accommodation as soon as possible,[159] police stations have no suitable facilities for children, even for a short time.[160] While the police must explain to the child what action has been taken and why[161] and discover the child's own wishes and feelings about their action,[162] the child is not entitled to any separate representation and there is no external scrutiny of the police intervention in the form of a court hearing.

Case law suggests that the practice of social workers turning to the police for assistance in such circumstances is dubious. In *Langley and others* v. *Liverpool City Council and another*,[163] Dyson LJ emphasised the advantages of an EPO,

---

[149] Ibid. p. 83.
[150] I.e. under CA 1989, s. 46: if he has reasonable cause to believe that the child would otherwise be likely to suffer significant harm, a police officer may remove the child into suitable accommodation (or prevent the child's removal from suitable accommodation, e.g. a hospital) and keep him there for up to 72 hours.
[151] HM Government (2018a) p. 33. See also DfE (2014) ch. 4, para. 30.
[152] J. Masson (2006) p. 23, Table 2.   [153] J. Masson (2005) p. 88.   [154] J. Masson (2006) p. 23.
[155] J. Masson *et al.* (2001) pp. 120–35.   [156] Ibid. p. 54.   [157] Ibid. pp. 67–71.
[158] Ibid. pp. 156–9.   [159] CA 1989, s. 46(3)(a) and (f).   [160] J. Masson *et al.* (2001) ch. 3.
[161] CA 1989, s. 46(3)(c).   [162] CA 1989, s. 46(3)(d).
[163] [2005] EWCA Civ 1173, [2006] 2 All ER 202.

including the fact that while the police officer will be a stranger to the child, the social worker may already be familiar to him or her and certainly able to remove the child from home more skilfully than even the most sensitive police officer.[164] He concluded that a police officer is legally barred from removing a child from an abusive situation if executing an EPO is practicable instead: 'In deciding whether it is practicable to execute the EPO, the police must always have regard to the paramount need to protect children from significant harm.'[165] Dyson LJ further found that where an EPO already exists, the child should be removed from home by social workers or others who have the skills and experience to do so, unless there are compelling reasons for the police to do so.[166] If an EPO is in place and there are no such compelling reasons for removal by the police, resort to section 46 of the CA 1989 is likely to be found not to be 'in accordance with the law',[167] and so will breach the rights of the parents and child to respect for their family life under Article 8 of the ECHR, even if the removal would otherwise be justified. The power to remove a child from home without judicial authority is a draconian one and this judgment underlines the need for it to be reserved for exceptional circumstances. The use of police powers will only be proportionate if, in the circumstances of the case, an application for an EPO is not a practically available means of protecting the child.[168] Police protection provides an important tool to protect children at imminent risk of significant harm,[169] but only if it is used as an exceptional measure, proportionate to that risk.[170]

(7) Compulsory Child Protection Orders: Children's Rights or Justice for Parents?

(A) Child Protection Proceedings

While emergency intervention can be vital in response to a crisis, children at risk of significant harm will often require longer-term intervention. The most serious form of that intervention is a care order, through which a child may be removed from the care of their parents. Such compulsory intervention necessarily involves serious interference with the rights of the child and the parents. The legislative framework and case law interpreting it, discussed below, gives anxious attention to the vital task of protecting children from harmful treatment, while also recognising the importance of family life for both the child and the parents. That legislation cannot, however, be considered in isolation

---

[164] Ibid. at [39].   [165] Ibid. at [40].   [166] Ibid. at [52].   [167] Ibid. at [53].

[168] A v. *East Sussex County Council* [2010] EWCA Civ 743.

[169] K v. *Crown Prosecution Service* [2014] EWHC 1606 (Admin).

[170] A v. *East Sussex County Council* [2010] EWCA Civ 743 suggests that cases of removal under CA 1989, s. 46 should usually be considered at an *inter partes* hearing within 2 days.

from the system in which it operates. That system is widely regarded to be in crisis,[171] struggling to cope in the face of rising demand and diminishing resources. Applications for child protection proceedings have more than doubled within a decade, with a significant increase in the number of looked-after children in the same period.[172] The reasons for this increase are complex and not yet fully understood. One driver appears to be the wider recognition of different forms of harm, discussed above, including those such as radicalisation, child criminal exploitation and child sexual exploitation, which are now better understood and included in the statutory guidance.[173] There is also considerable concern that the increase in child poverty and inequality[174] has placed families under intense stress, particularly when combined with other problems such as parental mental ill health, substance abuse or domestic abuse.[175] This may go some way to explaining research findings that children in the most deprived group are eleven times more likely to be in care than those in the most affluent group.[176] The ability of LAs to respond to these problems has been hampered by falling budgets and a tendency to focus resources on the children who are at most serious risk of harm. To achieve this, many LAs have made deep cuts to the resources allocated to supportive early intervention services, meaning that many problems that could have been addressed with early support are left until the child has suffered significant harm and requires compulsory protection measures.[177] Finally, there is also evidence that social workers have adopted a risk-averse practice, especially in response to high-profile crises. This is seen most clearly in the reaction to the government's direction to all LAs to review their safeguarding arrangements following the death of Baby P,[178] which led to a significant rise both in child protection referrals and care applications.[179] Collectively, these pressures appear to have driven a relentless rise in the number of applications for care proceedings and the complexity of the cases that the system now deals with.

Many children who are the subject of child protection inquiries are never made the subject of legal proceedings of any kind, despite evidence of risk of harm, quite simply because LA protection is provided in cooperation with their parents under section 20 agreements,[180] or the child is able to be accommodated safely with relatives without the need for child protection

---

[171] J. Munby (2016).

[172] Housing, Government and Local Government Committee (HC) (2019); evidence to the Committee demonstrated a 125 per cent increase in child protection proceedings between 2007–08 and 2017–18 and a 27 per cent increase in looked-after children in the same period.

[173] Discussed above.   [174] Discussed in Chapter 13.   [175] B. Featherstone *et al.* (2019).

[176] P. Bywaters *et al.* (2018).   [177] APPGC (2017).

[178] Statement made by Ed Balls, Secretary of State for Children, Schools and Families, on 1 December 2008.

[179] Statistics published in January 2009 showed that Cafcass had handled 693 requests for care cases, a 66 per cent increase on December 2007. Applications had dropped to an all-time low in June 2008, but have increased relentlessly since. A decade later, in January 2019, the equivalent figure was 1,451, more than double that in January 2009.

[180] I.e. under CA 1989, s. 20. Although see below for abuse of this provision.

proceedings.[181] Cases that do proceed to court often involve confrontation and conflict – the battle lines are very readily drawn between the parents and the state.[182] This may be explained by parents' knowledge that a care order risks their losing contact permanently with their children. Furthermore, a considerable stigma attaches 'to having a child being taken into care and being labelled an unfit parent'.[183] Indeed, when battle commences, the parents and their advisers, social workers and even the judiciary themselves take up such formalised positions that the child at the centre is treated very much as a passive pawn.[184] At this stage, the law's role in maintaining a balance between parents' rights to family life and children's welfare and rights to both family life and protection from harm is put to a severe test. As the case law discussed below indicates, there is a danger that the judicial pendulum has at times swung too far towards the rights of parents, resulting in the child's own right to protection being compromised.

The difficulty of balancing these factors is also evident in the process surrounding child protection proceedings. The increasing volume and complexity of cases has put both court and LA resources under considerable pressure as they strive to maintain a system which finds the best solutions for children's future, while also respecting the rights of children and parents. The Public Law Outline seeks to set out the requirements of good practice in doing so. Unless the risk is urgent, an LA considering care proceedings is first expected to engage in pre-proceedings with the family to seek to find a solution that will keep the child safe from harm, without the need to proceed to a court hearing.[185] Research suggests that a substantial minority of cases are diverted from the courts at this stage through parental engagement with the LA, allowing the child to be accommodated at home or under alternative arrangements with parental cooperation.[186] Diversion from court can present the best outcome for children and families. Nevertheless, judicial criticism of the abuse of 'voluntary' accommodation in cases in which parents feel coerced into cooperating[187] have made LAs more cautious about its use. If the case proceeds

---

[181] Bainham (2013) considers the use of private law proceedings with LA involvement as a 'hybrid' of public and private law.

[182] The former President of the Family Division, Sir James Munby, has advocated greater use of courts, such as the Drug and Alcohol Court, that seek to adopt a problem-solving approach rather than an adversarial approach to child protection: J. Munby (2016).

[183] DCA (2006) para. 3.5.   [184] Discussed below.   [185] DfE (2014).

[186] J. Dickens (2014); about a quarter of this sample were diverted from court at the pre-proceedings stage.

[187] In a number of cases, the courts have been highly critical of the use (or abuse) of CA 1989, s. 20 to place pressure on reluctant parents to cooperate with the LA in the removal of the child, rather than issuing care proceedings: *In re W (Parental Agreement with Local Authority)* [2014] EWCA Civ 1065, [2015] 1 FLR 949; *Northamptonshire County Council* v. *AS and others* [2015] EWHC 199 (Fam); *In re A (Application for Care and Placement Order: Local Authority Failings)* [2015] EWFC 11, [2016] 1 FLR 1; *In re N (Children) (Adoption: Jurisdiction)* [2015] EWCA Civ 1112, [2016] 2 WLR 713. In *London Borough of Hackney* v. *Williams* [2018] UKSC 37, [2019] AC 421, the Supreme Court reviewed these cases and

to a court hearing, there is now an expectation that care proceedings will be completed within 26 weeks,[188] cutting the previous average time by around half.[189] Cutting *unnecessary* delay within the system can benefit children, who need settled arrangements within timescales that allow them to develop and experience childhood with security. While the legislation has resulted in considerable reductions in the timing of proceedings, there remains concern that it imposes an arbitrary timescale that inhibits thorough consideration of alternative solutions that may benefit children. The complexity of most child protection litigation requires careful work by social workers and means that no amount of official guidance[190] will ensure the smooth running of every case. There is some evidence that courts are responding to reduced time-scales by making less interventionist orders, rather than risking a care order, particularly if there is a plan for adoption, while doubts remain.[191] There are also a worrying number of cases that identify poor-quality social work assessments and failure to provide proper reasoned and evidenced assessments to the court.[192] Parents and children are entitled to claim damages if their rights under Articles 6 and 8 of the ECHR have been infringed by care proceedings which treated them unfairly.[193] While such awards underline the importance of the human rights at stake in care proceedings, claims after the event are obviously unable to undo the damage caused by poor practice.

(B) The Threshold Criteria

(i) Problems of Proof

The CA 1989 provides that a court may only make a care or supervision order if it is satisfied that the threshold criteria in section 31(2) of the CA 1989 are established and that the order is in the child's best interests.[194] As Baroness

---

emphasised the importance of 'real and voluntary' parental delegation to the LA for the removal to be lawful under CA 1989, s. 20.

[188] Children and Families Act 2014, ss 13–15.

[189] Official data indicated that in 2008, a s. 31 application was taking, on average, 56 weeks in care centres and 45 weeks in family proceedings courts. H. Laming (2009) para. 8.7.

[190] DfE (2014).   [191] Masson *et al.* (2017).

[192] See esp. *In re A (Application for Care and Placement Order: Local Authority Failings)* [2015] EWFC 11, [2016] 1 FLR 1.

[193] E.g.: *Re X; Barnet London Borough Council* v. *Y and X* [2006] 2 FLR 998; *Re C (Breach of Human Rights: Damages)* [2007] EWCA Civ 2, [2007] 1 FLR 1957; *D (Children)* v. *Wakefield MDC* [2016] EWHC 3312 (Fam), [2017] 2 FLR 1353; *Re CZ (Human Rights Claim: Costs)* [2017] EWFC 11, [2017] 1 WLR 2467; *Northamptonshire CC* v. *M* [2017] EWHC 997 (Fam), [2017] 2 FLR 1250.

[194] CA 1989, s. 31(2): a court 'may only make a care order or supervision order if it is satisfied – (a) that the child concerned is suffering, or is likely to suffer, significant harm; and (b) that the harm, or likelihood of harm, is attributable to – (i) the care given to the child, or likely to be given to him if the order were not made, not being what it would be reasonable to expect a parent to give to him; or (ii) the child's being beyond parental control.' An application for a care order under s. 31 must establish: (i) a finding of fact regarding 'significant harm'; (ii) a decision that the 'threshold criteria' under s. 31(2) are satisfied; (iii) a decision that a care order will be in the child's best interests.

Hale observed in *Re J (Children)*,[195] the threshold criteria play an important role in recognising the competing human rights that are an inherent part of compulsory child protection measures:

> In a free society, it is a serious thing indeed for the state compulsorily to remove a child from his family of birth. Interference with the right to respect for family life, protected by article 8 of the European Convention on Human Rights, can only be justified by a pressing social need. Yet it is also a serious thing for the state to fail to safeguard its children from the neglect and ill-treatment which they may suffer in their own homes. This may even amount to a violation of their right not to be subjected to inhuman or degrading treatment, protected by article 3 of the Convention. How then is the law to protect the family from unwarranted intrusion while at the same time protecting children from harm? In England and Wales, the Children Act 1989 tries to balance these two object-ives by setting a threshold which must be crossed before a court can consider what order, if any, should be made to enable the authorities to protect a child.

Whether the threshold criteria manage to achieve this delicate balancing act in practice depends on judicial interpretation of the complex statutory test. At the heart of the threshold criteria is the question of whether the child concerned 'is suffering, or is likely to suffer, significant harm'. The difficulties in interpreting 'significant' and 'harm' have been considered earlier in this chapter. The questions of whether the child 'is suffering' or 'is likely to suffer' that harm have also presented complex questions of interpretation and application, particularly in relation to problems of proof. While the LA will usually have plenty of evidence indicating that a child should be removed from home on the basis of what happened to him or her in the past, some cases present significant evidential problems in determining whether an alleged incident took place or the identity of the perpetrator. Problems of proof raise the tension between the right to family life and the child's right to protection from harm particularly sharply. The alternatives of removing a child from innocent parents or leaving a child at risk of serious harm present an obvious dilemma to a court faced with finely balanced questions of proof. In response, a complex case law has emerged from the House of Lords and later the Supreme Court.[196] These cases demonstrate how difficult it is for the law to maintain an appropriate balance between promoting children's rights to protection and children and parents' right to family life. At times, the law has appeared to favour an exaggerated fairness to parents, thereby allowing children's rights to protection from harm to slip into second place. At other times, although less frequently,

---

[195] *Re J (Children)* [2013] UKSC 9, [2013] 1 AC 680, at [1]–[2].

[196] Notably, *Re H (Minors) (Sexual Abuse: Standard of Proof)* [1996] AC 563; *Re O and N (Children) (Non-Accidental Injury)* [2003] UKHL 18, [2004] 1 AC 523; *Re B (Children) (Sexual Abuse: Standard of Proof)* [2008] UKHL 35, [2009] 1 AC 11; *Re S-B (Children) (Care Proceedings: Standard of Proof)* [2009] UKSC 17, [2010] 1 AC 678; *Re J (Children)* [2013] UKSC 9, [2013] 1 AC 680; *Re B (Care Proceedings: Appeal)* [2013] UKSC 33, [2013] 1 WLR 1911.

the law has adopted a more protective stance. This case law is considered below, addressing three interlinked questions. First, what standard of proof is required to satisfy the court that a child has suffered significant harm in the past? Second, are there any circumstances in which allegations of past incidents concerning one child can be used to establish the likelihood of significant harm in the future for another child? Third, can the threshold be established in circumstances in which it is not possible to prove who caused the harm in question?

(ii) Establishing Significant Harm Has Occurred in the Past

The decision of the House of Lords in *Re H (Minors) (Sexual Abuse: Standard of Proof)*[197] provoked considerable controversy over the correct standard of proof for establishing significant harm. In *Re H*, allegations of child sexual abuse had been made by C, a 15-year-old girl, against her stepfather. She was now in foster care, but the LA wished to obtain care orders over her younger sister and two younger stepsisters, all still living in the family home with the alleged abuser. Although there was no evidence at all of his yet having behaved inappropriately towards any of the three, the LA argued that, given the strength of their older sister's allegations against him, they were 'likely' to suffer significant harm in the future if left in his proximity. The likelihood of future abuse clearly hinged on the truth of C's story. The trial judge addressed the first question identified above – what standard of proof should he use to decide whether the older sister had indeed been sexually abused? He considered 'that there was a real possibility' that the stepfather had sexually abused C, as she claimed. Indeed, in his view, there was a considerable amount of evidence substantiating 'a classic unfolding revelation of progressively worse abuse'. Nevertheless, he could not be satisfied 'on the balance of probabilities' that C had suffered significant harm in the past.

The House of Lords agreed with the trial judge's conclusion in *Re H*; more was required than suspicion, however reasonably based. Lord Nicholls of Birkenhead, who delivered the majority opinion, emphasised that the correct standard of proof for proving that significant harm has occurred in the past is the balance of probabilities. Accordingly, the court should be able to reach a finding that 'on the evidence, the occurrence of the event was more likely than not'.[198] This apparent clarity was, however, fundamentally undermined by his warning that:

> When assessing the probabilities the court will have in mind as a factor ... that the more serious the allegation the less likely it is that the event occurred and, hence, the stronger should be the evidence before the court concludes that the allegation is established on the balance of probability ... Deliberate physical injury is usually less likely than accidental physical injury. A stepfather is usually less likely to have repeatedly raped and had non-consensual oral sex with his

---

[197] [1996] AC 563.   [198] [1996] AC 563, per Lord Nicholls of Birkenhead, at 586.

under age stepdaughter than on some occasion to have lost his temper and slapped her ... The more improbable the event, the stronger must be the evidence that it did occur before, on the balance of probability, its occurrence will be established.[199]

Consternation was provoked by Lord Nicholls' argument that the test remained the balance of probabilities, while at the same time maintaining the need for a degree of increasing scepticism the more serious the alleged behaviour. His view that intrinsically unlikely events should require stronger evidence was particularly strongly attacked, with critics pointing out that LAs only ever bring care proceedings in circumstances which, by their very nature, are unlikely to occur in normal households. The test suggested that in such a case, the courts should always require stronger evidence than they would normally require to establish that the occurrence was more likely than not.[200] As Ryder J pointed out, its effect was that the more serious the offence, the more difficult it was to protect the child.[201] Indeed, *Re H* created an evidential strait-jacket for LAs. Admittedly, if they wished to protect children from the risk of future harm, it would only cause insurmountable problems where no clear evidence existed of any *other* worrying features in the parents' past record of care, which could justify applying for a care order. Fortunately, such cases appear to be unusual. They do, however, occur when the earlier death of a child suggests the likelihood of harm to a surviving child, but there is no evidence of the survivor having yet been ill-treated.[202] More seriously, the 'enhanced standard of proof' obliged LAs to adopt essentially diversionary tactics in cases where there were allegations of serious abuse, such as sexual abuse. Rather than basing their care application on that offence, they would exploit less serious but more certain aspects of the case to substantiate their fears of the children being at risk of abuse in the future.[203] The surer evidence of peripheral abuse would be used merely as a peg on which to hang a finding of significant harm under section 31.[204] Practitioners indicated[205] that since it had become increasingly difficult for allegations of sexual abuse or serious physical abuse to be proved, they were simply not being brought to court to be tested by fact-finding hearings.

There were obvious logical difficulties underlying Lord Nicholls' assertion that although the civil standard of proof was quite unchanged and still governed care proceedings, the judiciary should be sceptical over any event deemed intrinsically unlikely. Indeed, in other branches of law, senior

---

[199] Ibid.   [200] I. Hemingway and C. Williams (1997) pp. 741–2.   [201] Ryder (2008) p. 30.

[202] E.g. *Re P (A Minor) (Care: Evidence)* [1994] 2 FLR 751; *A LA v. S, W and T (by His Guardian)* [2004] EWHC 1270 (Fam), [2004] 2 FLR 129.

[203] E.g. *Re M and R (Minors) (Sexual Abuse: Expert Evidence)* [1996] 4 All ER 239.

[204] E.g. *Re G and R (Child Sexual Abuse: Standard of Proof)* [1995] 2 FLR 867. See also *JFM v. Neath Port Talbot Borough Council, TM, JM and CM (Children) (by Their Guardian)* [2008] EWCA Civ 3, [2008] 1 FCR 97.

[205] K. Maclean and E. Hall (2008) p. 737.

members of the judiciary routinely interpreted his advice as establishing a *higher* standard of proof for cases involving serious allegations. It was maintained that any differences between the standard of proof established in *Re H* and the criminal one were 'largely illusory'.[206] Matters were put on a clearer footing for child protection practitioners by the President of the Family Division, who asserted resolutely that there was still an important difference in the two standards of proof which had to be maintained.[207]

Clarification by the House of Lords was long overdue, particularly when it became clear that members of the judiciary shared critics' concerns about the standard of proof established by *Re H*.[208] *Re B (Children) (Sexual Abuse: Standard of Proof)*[209] provided the much-needed test case to provoke an appeal to the House of Lords. In *Re B*, a not dissimilar situation to *Re H* had occurred, with the LA applying for care orders relating to two children aged 9 and 6, based on allegations made by their older stepsister, R, that their father, Mr B, had sexually abused her. Charles J, the trial judge, had been unable to conclude either that it was more likely than not that R had been sexually abused by Mr B or that she had not. Nevertheless, since he could not conclude that there was no real possibility that Mr B had abused her, he concluded that there was a real possibility that Mr B had abused her. Such a finding failed to comply with the existing standard of proof, but if *Re H* could be overturned, it might be enough to establish the threshold for LA intervention in relation to the two younger children.

Baroness Hale of Richmond[210] rejected outright the view that evidence indicating a *real possibility* that abuse took place is sufficient to establish the likelihood of future harm. If Parliament had intended such a reduced standard of proof,[211] it would have said so.[212] Nor was she convinced that the civil standard of proof was out of step with the case law allowing a broad interpretation of section 31 in cases where it is impossible to identify which of the child's carers was responsible for abuse.[213] In her view, matters are completely different if it has been clearly established that the child has suffered harm in the past. Then the fact that the perpetrator's identity cannot be clarified need not prevent protective intervention.[214]

[206] *B v. Chief Constable of the Avon and Somerset Constabulary* [2001] 1 WLR 340, per Lord Bingham CJ, at [31]. See also *R v. Headteacher and Independent Appeal Committee of Dunraven School, ex p B* [2000] ELR 156, per Brooke LJ, at 204–5; *R (McCann and others) v. Crown Court at Manchester, etc* [2003] 1 AC 787, per Lord Steyn, at [37].

[207] *Re U (Serious Injury: Standard of Proof); Re B* [2004] EWCA Civ 567, [2004] 2 FLR 263, per Dame Elizabeth Butler-Sloss P, at [13], rejecting Bodey J's view in *Re ET (Serious Injuries: Standard of Proof) Note* [2003] 2 FLR 1205, at [2], that there was little difference between the criminal and civil standard of proof in care proceedings.

[208] Ryder (2008).   [209] [2008] UKHL 35, [2009] 1 AC 11.

[210] Majority opinion with which all members of the Appellate Committee agreed.

[211] As urged by Ryder (2008) pp. 34–6.   [212] [2008] UKHL 35, [2009] 1 AC 11, at [54].

[213] *Lancashire County Council v. A (A Child)* [2000] 2 AC 147.

[214] [2008] UKHL 35, [2009] 1 AC 11, at [61].

Re B put beyond doubt that the standard of proof for establishing the occurrence of past abuse remains the balance of probabilities; the LA must show that it is more likely than not that the abuse occurred. Mere suspicions or a 'real possibility' are not enough. This is the case whether or not the LA wants to use the evidence of past harm to show the likelihood of future harm.[215] In most respects, the decision in *Re B* merely affirmed existing law. Subsequent case law has continued to uphold the balance of probabilities as the standard of proof for past abuse.[216] The importance of *Re B*, however, lies in the way in which Lord Hoffmann[217] and Baroness Hale[218] rejected Lord Nicholls' suggestion in *Re H* that the more improbable the event, the stronger the evidence required to establish its occurrence. This approach was consigned to the history books. Both emphasised that neither the seriousness of the allegations nor the seriousness of the consequences should affect the civil standard of proof. As Baroness Hale emphasised, 'there is no logical or necessary connection between seriousness and probability'.[219] This clarification released the law from its erstwhile indefensible position that 'the worse danger a child is in, the less likely the courts are to remove her from it'.[220]

(iii) Establishing the Likelihood of Significant Harm in the Future

The threshold criteria do not only protect children who have already been harmed, but can also be satisfied by a finding that a child is 'likely' to suffer significant harm. While a child protection system that required children to actually suffer harm before they could be protected would be failing in its duty to them, the removal of a child on the basis of speculative harm requires careful scrutiny of the seriousness of the harm and the likelihood of it occurring.[221] In *Re H*, Lord Nicholls considered that 'likely'[222] merely requires the court be satisfied that there is 'a real possibility' of the event occurring in the future, as opposed to being more likely than not.[223] This principle remains unchanged by *Re B* and subsequent case law.[224] By allowing a care order to be made in circumstances in which the child has not been harmed and in which it is more likely than not that the child will not be harmed, this principle appears to move decisively towards child protection, as opposed to family privacy. That permissive interpretation is, however, tempered by the approach to the evidential burden established in *Re H* and *Re B*: the real possibility of harm can only be predicted on the basis of facts that have themselves been proven on the balance of probabilities. For this reason, in *Re H*, the LA was unable to use the evidence relating to C's allegations to show that the three younger girls were not safe

---

[215] Ibid. at [54].
[216] E.g. *Re S-B (Children) (Care Proceedings: Standard of Proof)* [2009] UKSC 17, [2010] 1 AC 678; *Re J (Children)* [2013] UKSC 9, [2013] 1 AC 680.
[217] [2008] UKHL 35, [2009] 1 AC 11, at [13]–[15].   [218] Ibid. at [69]–[73].   [219] Ibid. at [72].
[220] J. Spencer (1994) p. 161.
[221] *Re B (Care Proceedings: Appeal)* [2013] UKSC 33, [2013] 1 WLR 1911, esp. at [187]–[190].
[222] I.e. CA 1989, s. 31(2)(a).   [223] [1996] AC 563, at 585.
[224] Including *Re B (Care Proceedings: Appeal)* [2013] UKSC 33, [2013] 1 WLR 1911.

with him in the future, as the allegations were too weak to show on the balance of probabilities that C had been abused by her stepfather.

The difficulty of protecting children in circumstances of uncertain proof are raised particularly acutely in cases in which there is uncertainty as to the identity of the perpetrator. A court can be satisfied that the child 'is suffering significant harm' under the CA 1989, section 31, simply because he or she is being physically or sexually abused by *somebody*.[225] A generous interpretation of the 'attributable' requirement in section 31(2)(b) allows an order to be made despite there being insufficient evidence to identify the abuser.[226] This means that if the child has already been harmed, a care order may be made despite the fact that a non-parent carer is within the pool of possible perpetrators and it is entirely possible that the parents themselves are entirely innocent. This pro-protection stance towards children who have *already* been harmed is not sustained in assessing the likelihood of harm to children who have not yet suffered that harm.

A finding that a child has suffered serious injuries at the hands of one or both of the carers, but ruling out neither, allows the LA to mount protective measures to protect siblings or future children being cared for by those carers while they are living together.[227] In *Re J (Children)*,[228] the Supreme Court considered the problem of what should happen if the possible perpetrators separate and go on to have subsequent children independently of each another. In that case, the mother's first baby had died when she was a few weeks old, as a result of injuries that had been deliberately inflicted. It was not possible to tell which of the parents had caused the injuries, but both had colluded to hide the truth. The parents had subsequently separated, the mother had gone on to form a new relationship and now lived with her partner in a family unit with three children. The question for the Supreme Court was whether her place in the pool of possible perpetrators for the baby's death could be relied upon to establish the threshold in relation to those children. The Supreme Court found that the 'real possibility' that the mother had harmed her first child was not sufficient to provide a factual basis on which to predict the likelihood of harm

---

[225] Inter alia: *Lancashire County Council v. A (A Child)* [2000] 2 AC 147; *Re O and and N (Children) (Non-Accidental Injury)* [2003] UKHL 18, [2004] 1 AC 523; *North Yorkshire County Council v. SA* [2003] EWCA Civ 839, [2003] 2 FLR 849; *Merton London Borough Council v. K; Re K (Care: Representation: Public Funding)* [2005] EWHC 167 (Fam), [2005] 2 FLR 422.

[226] *Lancashire County Council v. A (A Child)* [2000] 2 AC 147, per Lord Nicholls of Birkenhead, at 165–8: the requirement in s. 31(2) that the harm to the child must be attributable to the care given to him does not mean that the care must be attributable to the parent against whom the order is sought. *Re B (Children: Uncertain Perpetrator)* [2019] EWCA Civ 575: if the perpetrator cannot be determined on the balance of probabilities, the pool of possible perpetrators is determined on the basis of those for whom there is a 'real possibility' that they caused the injury in question.

[227] E.g. *Re K (Care: Threshold Criteria)* [2005] EWCA Civ 1226, [2006] 2 FLR 868. See also *Re S-B (Children) (Care Proceedings: Standard of Proof)* [2009] UKSC 17, [2010] 1 AC 678.

[228] [2013] UKSC 9, [2013] 1 AC 680.

to the current children. As it could not be shown on the balance of probabilities that the mother had caused harm to the baby, there were no established facts upon which a prediction of future harm to these children could be made. The consequence of this decision is that if the possible perpetrators separate and both go on to have further children, neither of those future children can be protected, despite the fact that at least one is living with a child killer. This is another situation in which the burden of uncertainty falls on the child: the risk of the state intervening in an innocent family is prioritised over the risk that a child will remain with a dangerous parent.[229]

(C) Welfare and Proportionality: Getting the Balance Right

The discussion above demonstrates how difficult it is for the law to maintain an appropriate balance between promoting children's rights to protection and the rights of parents and children to family life. Questions of doubt in applying the threshold criteria are often resolved in favour of protecting the family from compulsory state intervention, rather than in protecting the child from an unproven risk of harm. If the threshold criteria are not met, no care or supervision order can be made, even if there is evidence that the child might benefit from that order. Conversely, the fact that the threshold criteria are met in a particular case is not enough in itself to justify the making of a care or supervision order. The court must then go on to consider what form of order, if any, is in the best interests of the child.[230] As any order made will constitute an interference in the Article 8 right to respect for family life, the court must also consider the proportionality of that interference in the particular case in question.[231] The need to consider proportionality before making a compulsory child protection order means that this area of law is particularly responsive to development human rights law. Nonetheless, as the proportionality test is placed at the welfare stage of the decision, rather than at the earlier 'threshold stage', there is a tendency for the balancing act to be couched in terms of the parents' right to protection from state interference in family life and children's best interests, rather than their right to be protected from harm.

A vital aspect of the court's approach to the welfare stage is that the court must make a careful assessment of all of the realistic options for the child, rather than simply assess the LA's preferred solution.[232] In doing so, the court must make a 'global, holistic evaluation'[233] of each of the realistic solutions, assessing the advantages and disadvantages of each for the child's welfare. The

---

[229] M. Hayes (2013); S. Gilmore (2013).

[230] In doing so, the court should take into account the factors contained in the welfare checklist in CA 1989, s. 1(3). E.g. *Re D (Children)* [2018] EWCA Civ 386, [2018] 2 FLR 676.

[231] *Re B (A Child)* [2013] UKSC 33, [2013] 1 AC 680.

[232] *Re G (A Child)* [2013] EWCA Civ 965, [2014] 1 FLR 670.

[233] This approach was first used in the context of cases with a care plan for adoption: *Re B-S (Adoption: Application of s 47(5))* [2013] EWCA Civ 1146; *Re B (A Child)* [2013] UKSC 33, [2013] 1 AC 680. The Court of Appeal has applied the same approach to other cases

aim of this process is to find the least interventionist order which will promote the child's best interests. This process does not create a presumption against the removal of the child from the family,[234] but it does mean that removal of the child will be disproportionate if a less interventionist order would be equally capable of protecting the child's welfare.

(8) The Child's Own Perspectives

The UN Committee on the Rights of the Child has stressed that in protecting children from harm:

> Children's rights to be heard and to have their views given due weight must be respected systematically in all decision-making processes, and their empowerment and participation should be central to child caregiving and protection strategies and programmes.[235]

Children's understanding of the history and relationships within the family can be vital in evaluating those risks and responding to them. Planning for the future is more likely to be successful if the child has had the opportunity to be heard and to participate in the process rather than being alienated from it. More fundamentally, the experience of abuse, maltreatment and neglect is inherently disempowering. Involving, informing and listening to children supports them as agents in their own future, rather than treating them as helpless objects of protection.

While effective participation and empowerment of children are important goals, the realities of the lives of abused children can create significant barriers to achieving effective participation in practice. The harms commonly experienced by abused children can affect their school lives and friendships, with many worrying intensely about various aspects of their own and their parents' lives.[236] Many children who experience abuse often feel alone and confused, either having no one to confide in or feeling very reluctant to do so. This reluctance may stem from a fear of the consequences, or that they will not be believed, combined with a deep distrust of others and of anyone's ability to 'sort things out'.[237] Despite this, the message of child participation has made some progress. The establishment of Childline and initiatives involving teaching young children in schools about acceptable and unacceptable adult familiarity do appear to have encouraged more children to tell adults about ongoing abuse.[238] Statutory guidance stresses that children should be listened to and their views taken seriously by those working with them in the child protection

---

concerning compulsory child protection orders: *Re G (A Child)* [2013] EWCA Civ 965, [2014] 1 FLR 670; *KH v. A County Council, A, EJ, KJ* [2019] EWCA Civ 2300.

[234] *Re H (A Child)* [2015] EWCA Civ 1284, [2016] 2 FLR 1173.

[235] Committee on the Rights of the Child (2011) para. 3(e).   [236] S. Gorin (2004) ch. 3.

[237] Ibid. pp. 49–51.

[238] But see R. Morgan (2007) p. 9: only 19 per cent of children said that they would tell an adult if they had been harmed by someone else.

process.[239] There is, however, considerable evidence that some children are not properly listened to and understood by the professionals around them and that these 'invisible children' are often failed by the system.[240] Lord Laming considered that the consistent failure by a number of practitioners to communicate with Victoria Climbié was partially responsible for concealing her situation.[241] Research suggests that the pressures of day-to-day practice, particularly in an environment of mounting caseloads and time limits, can lead to the failure to listen to and relate to children in practice.[242] Researchers have also found that social workers, when investigating neglect and physical abuse, fail to discuss such matters with teenage family members, thereby missing information about the possible ill-treatment of younger siblings.[243] There is now a legislative duty on those undertaking section 47 inquiries both to ascertain and to give due consideration to children's wishes and feelings, having regard to their age and understanding, over what action should be taken.[244] The qualifying phrase, 'so far as is reasonably practicable and consistent with the child's welfare' should not be taken as a reason for non-compliance.

Sadly, even when they are listened to, abused children may regret disclosing their abuse, feeling ignored and 'walked over' by those who try to protect them.[245] As the Cleveland report found, the victim of abuse is too often treated as 'an object of concern', rather than a person with a right to be involved and consulted.[246] Although child protection practitioners may listen to children in order to discover what happened to them, they may not be so enthusiastic to consult them over the outcome of protective intervention, despite the legislative obligation to do so.[247] Research with children who have experience of the child protection system demonstrates that children place great importance on the ability to build a trusting relationship with the social worker involved in making decisions about them, but that many do not have the opportunity to build that high-quality relationship.[248] A practical reason for the child's own position in child protection work being overlooked is the speed with which decisions to intervene are sometimes taken in the early stages, leaving practitioners feeling that they have no time to provide the child with explanations. An LA may consider it essential to take immediate steps to protect sexually abused children, particularly if a suspected abuser refuses to take responsibility for the abuse and there are fears that the child may come under pressure to

---

[239] HM Government (2018a) para. 14. As the paragraph makes clear, this guidance is partly based on the child's right to freedom of expression and information in CRC, Art. 12.

[240] H. Ferguson (2017).   [241] H. Laming (2003) paras 6.652 and 8.99.

[242] H. Ferguson (2017).   [243] W. Rose and J. Barnes (2008) p. 17.

[244] CA 1989, s. 47(5A). See also s. 17(4A) in relation to providing services for children in need and s. 22(4) in relation to services for looked-after children.

[245] B. Smedley (1999) p. 115.   [246] Butler-Sloss (1998) p. 245.

[247] CA 1989, ss 17(4A), 22(4)–(5), 38(6), 43(8), 44(7), 46(3) and Sch. 3, paras 4(4) and 5(5).

[248] J. Cossar *et al.* (2016).

withdraw his or her allegations if left at home.[249] On the other hand, children who deny that they have been sexually abused should be listened to.[250] Suspicions of serious physical abuse will also normally trigger considerable professional anxiety, particularly if a very young child is concerned, quite simply because of the fear that non-intervention may risk the child's death. But even children old enough to comprehend explanations very often experience a sense of complete bewilderment over the speed with which steps are taken to protect them, without any real effort to involve them in the arrangements being made for their care.[251] Research indicates that 'this uncertainty and loss of control could serve to magnify the sense of powerlessness which was already a central experience for abused children'.[252]

Some feel strongly that abused children's choices over their future care after protective intervention should be respected; otherwise, they will simply retract their allegations of abuse because of their fear of the consequences.[253] But the dilemma is that an abused child's perceptions may be distorted by the abuse and adults therefore need the freedom to override their wishes and protect them. Schofield points out the temptation of assuming that because a child wants to go home or wants more parental contact, the relationship and parenting cannot be as damaging as the otherwise overwhelming evidence would suggest.[254] As she observes, however, one should not ignore the psychological factors underlying the relationship between an abused child and his or her parents:

> Troubled children in crisis, as those subject to care proceedings invariably are, very often and very understandably present entirely conflicting evidence of their wishes and feelings. They may express hopes for the future which are incompatible with what professionals and the children themselves know to be reality; for example, the wish to be at home and to be safe, the wish to be with a parent but for that parent to change.[255]

Schofield's material suggests that an abused child's right to protection by the state can outweigh any right to self-determination. His or her right to make choices should be overridden if those choices will foreclose on a happy and fulfilled maturity. Consistent with this approach, the law maintains the view that the child's need for protection is more important than claims to confidentiality. Practitioners, such as social workers,[256] children's guardians[257] and doctors[258] confided in by a child (or adult) with information indicating that

---

[249] E.g. *JFM v. Neath Port Talbot Borough Council, TM, JM and CM (Children) (by Their Guardian)* [2008] EWCA Civ 3, [2008] 1 FCR 97.

[250] *Leeds City Council v. YX and ZX (Assessment of Sexual Abuse)* [2008] EWHC 802 (Fam), [2008] 2 FLR 869, per Holman J, at [127].

[251] E. Farmer and M. Owen (1995) pp. 73–4.   [252] Ibid. p. 72.

[253] E.g. F. Olsen (1992) pp. 210–13.   [254] G. Schofield (1998) p. 366.   [255] Ibid. p. 364.

[256] *Re M and N (Minors) (Wardship: Freedom of Publication)* [1990] 1 All ER 205.

[257] *Re D (Minors) (Adoption Reports: Confidentiality)* [1996] AC 593.

[258] GMC (2018) para. 49: doctors must disclose information if 'it is necessary to protect the child or young person, or someone else, from risk of death or serious harm . . . Such cases may arise,

a child is being abused should not promise to keep this to themselves. Indeed, they should warn the child that this information will normally be passed on to the relevant authorities and may eventually be used in court in the event of child protection proceedings commencing. Even solicitors consulted by children may feel obliged to infringe their confidentiality in the event of receiving information indicating that a child client is being abused. The child should be warned that such information may eventually have to be disclosed to the court in the event of public law proceedings being brought.[259] The controversial result is that an abused child may feel unable to confide safely in any adult.[260]

Once protective litigation is commenced, children should be given information by their social workers on what is being done on their behalf and what to expect when proceedings are issued. All children who are the subject of care or supervision proceedings will be separately represented in court. Consulting children over protective measures need not involve complying with their stated wishes; indeed, it does not undermine the intervention for practitioners to treat children with respect and sensitivity throughout the process. For some, the children's guardian is the first person available to listen to them and with whom to confide their hopes and fears regarding the outcome of the proceedings. On the whole, the tandem system of representation for children involved in public law proceedings operates extremely well. Although the system is not perfect, many children's guardians develop a very good rapport with children. Some children involved in care proceedings will tell their guardian that the court should allow them to return home. Although the care plan may involve such an arrangement,[261] as Schofield noted above, such wishes may be unreliable, indicating merely that the child's relationship with his or her abuser is a psychologically distorted one. Aware of this, the guardian may feel obliged to recommend that the child leaves home, despite his or her knowledge that the child opposes such a view. If of sufficient understanding, the child may at this point instruct a solicitor and advance his or her own view to the court, regardless of the fact that this conflicts with the guardian's assessment of the child's welfare.[262] Relatively few children involved in care proceedings take this step of becoming actively involved in the decision-making process. Many more simply wish to understand the process better and to speak to the judge who is

---

for example, if (a) a child or young person is at risk of neglect or sexual, physical or emotional abuse'.

[259] The solicitor may be subpoenaed and ordered to disclose documentation or divulge information.

[260] J. Loughrey (2008) discusses whether disclosure of confidential information would be a breach of a child's Art. 8 rights.

[261] A minority of care plan involves the child remaining at home.

[262] Family Procedure Rules, Pt 16. E.g. *W (A Child) (Care Proceedings: Child's Representation)* [2016] EWCA Civ 1051, [2017] 1 WLR 1027: a 16-year-old was of sufficient understanding and able to instruct her own solicitor in accordance with r. 16.29. The test for the court was sufficiency of understanding and the trial judge had been wrong to confuse this with a welfare test. See further discussion in Chapter 12.

making such significant decisions about their future. Although there is no expectation that all children will do so, provision is now made for children to request to meet the judge and ask questions about the process.[263] While too many children still feel alienated from a process that is intended to be a service to them, there are signs of a greater understanding of the importance of centring children within that process.

(9) Conclusion

In his review of the child protection system, Lord Laming considered that the legal framework for the child protection system was 'basically sound'.[264] For the children and their families who are let down by the 'crisis' in the care system, this may be a surprising conclusion. Certainly, the care system faces many challenges in fulfilling the obligation to children to protect them from harmful treatment, particularly in the face of rising workloads and limited resources. The legal framework has been flexible enough to accommodate a broader understanding of the range of harms that children face, but does little to clarify when the state might intervene to protect a child from risks such as 'radicalisation' or gang violence. Nor does it clarify ideas about how bad matters have to become in a child's home before the state must intervene. The balance between early prevention work and state intervention remains difficult to maintain, particularly as LA budgets for early intervention have been cut. Attempts to protect children from abusive parents by removing them from home tend to polarise hostility between parents and state, with the child's own perspectives sometimes being forgotten. When practitioners' efforts are concentrated on an over-technical court process, there are cases of insufficient attention being given to dealing with children's ongoing needs. Many of these problems can be traced to the operation of the child protection system rather than the legal framework itself. Although some judicial decisions have imposed undue hurdles to protecting children from harm,[265] the judiciary is acutely aware of the difficulty of reconciling the competing rights in practice. Overall, the CA 1989 contrives reasonably well to ensure that the state's role in fulfilling children's rights to protection is promoted with some sensitivity. Finding the ideal balance between undue state interference which impinges on parents and children alike and an approach which fails to meet the state's obligations to protect children from harmful treatment is probably as unlikely as finding the Holy Grail.

---

[263] Guidance is given in *Guidelines for Judges Meeting Children Who Are Subject to Family Proceedings* [2010] 2 FLR 1872. For the application of these guidelines, see: *London Borough of Brent* v. *D and others (Compliance with Guidelines on Judges Meeting Children)* [2017] EWHC 2452 (Fam), [2017] 4 WLR 193. The meeting is not intended to form an opportunity for the judge to gather evidence about the case: *Re KP (A Child) (Abduction: Rights of Custody)* [2014] EWCA Civ 554, [2014] 1 WLR 4326. Discussed further in Chapter 12.

[264] H. Laming (2003) para. 1.30, (2009) para. 8.1.   [265] Discussed above.

Bibliography

NB: Many of these publications can be obtained on the relevant organisation's website.

All Party Parliamentary Group for Children (APPGC) (2017) *No Good Options: Report of the Inquiry into Children's Social Care in England*, APPGC.

Bainham, A. (2013) 'Public and Private Law: An Under-Explored Relationship' 25 *Child and Family Law Quarterly* 138.

Beecham, J. and Sinclair, I. (2007) *Costs and Outcomes in Children's Social Care: Messages from Research*, Jessica Kingsley Publishers.

Bichard, M. (Chairman) (2004) *The Bichard Inquiry Report*, HC 653, The Stationery Office.

Brandon, M., Belderson, P., Warren, C., Howe, D., Gardner, R., Dodsworth, J. and Black, J. (2008) *Analysing Child Deaths and Serious Injury through Abuse and Neglect: What Can We Learn? A Biannual Analysis of Serious Case Reviews 2003–2005*, Research Report DCSF – RR023, DCSF.

Butler-Sloss, LJ (Chairman) (1988) Cm 412, *Report of the Inquiry into Child Abuse in Cleveland 1987*, Her Majesty's Stationery Office.

Bywaters, P., Brady, G., Bunting, L., Daniel, B., Featherstone, B., Jones, C., Morris, K., Scourfield, J., Sparks, T. and Webb, C. (2018) 'Inequalities in English Child Protection Practice under Austerity: A Universal Challenge?' 23 *Child and Family Social Work* 53.

Cicchetti, D. and Carlson, V. (eds.) (1989) *Child Maltreatment: Theory and Research on the Causes and Consequences of Child Abuse and Neglect*, Cambridge University Press.

Cleaver, H., Nicholson, D., Tarr, S. and Cleaver, D. (2007) *Child Protection, Domestic Violence and Parental Substance Misuse: Family Experiences and Effective Practice*, Jessica Kingsley Publishers.

Committee on the Rights of the Child (2011) *General Comment No. 13 on the Right of the Child to Freedom from All Forms of Violence*, CRC/C/GC/13, Centre for Human Rights, Geneva.

Cossar, J., Brandon, M. and Jordan, P. (2016) '"You've Got to Trust Her and She's Got to Trust You": Children's Views on Participation in the Child Protection System' 21 *Child & Family Social Work* 103.

Cowan, D. (2004) 'On Need and Gatekeeping – R (G) v. Barnet London Borough Council etc' 16 *Child and Family Law Quarterly* 331.

Davis, L. (2007) 'Protecting Children in an Emergency – Getting the Balance Right' 37 *Family Law* 727.

Department for Constitutional Affairs (DCA) (2006) *Review of the Child Care Proceedings System in England and Wales*, DCA.

Department for Education (DfE) (2014) *Court Orders and Pre-Proceedings for Local Authorities*, DfE.

Department of Health (DH) (1991) *Child Abuse: A Study of Inquiry Reports 1980–1989*, Her Majesty's Stationery Office.

(1995) *Child Protection: Messages from Research*, Her Majesty's Stationery Office.

(2001) *The Children Act Now: Messages from Research*, The Stationery Office.

(2002) *Safeguarding Children: A Joint Chief Inspectors' Report on Arrangements to Safeguard Children*, DH Publications.

Department of Health and Social Security (DHSS) (1982) *Child Abuse: A Study of Inquiry Reports 1973–1981*, Her Majesty's Stationery Office.

Dickens, J. (2014) 'Care Proceedings in 26 Weeks: Justice, Speed and Thoroughness' 44 *Family Law* 650.

Dingwall, R., Eekelaar, J. and Murray, T. (1983) *The Protection of Children: State Intervention and Family Life*, Blackwell.

Farmer, E. and Owen, M. (1995) *Child Protection Practice: Private Risks and Public Remedies*, Her Majesty's Stationery Office.

Featherstone, B., Morris, K., Daniel, B., Bywaters, P., Brady, G., Bunting, L., Mason, W. and Mirza, N. (2019) 'Poverty, Inequality, Child Abuse and Neglect: Changing the Conversation across the UK in Child Protection?' 97 *Children and Youth Services Review* 127.

Ferguson, H. (2017) 'How Children Become Invisible in Child Protection Work: Findings from Research into Day-to-Day Practice' 47 *British Journal of Social Work* 1007.

Fortin, J. (1999) 'Rights Brought Home for Children' 62 *Modern Law Review* 350.

Fox Harding, L. (1997) *Perspectives in Child Care Policy*, Longman.

General Medical Council (GMC) (2018) *0–18 Years: Guidance for All Doctors*, GMC.

Gilmore, S. (2013) 'Re J (Care Proceedings: Past Possible Perpetrators in a New Family Unit) [2013] UKSC 9: Bulwarks and Logic – the Blood which Runs through the Veins of Law – But How Much Will Be Spilled in Future?' 25 *Child and Family Law Quarterly* 215.

Glaser, D. (2000) 'Child Abuse and Neglect and the Brain – A Review' 41 *Journal of Child Psychology and Psychiatry* 97.

(2002) 'Emotional Abuse and Neglect (Psychological Maltreatment): A Conceptual Framework' 26 *Child Abuse and Neglect* 697.

Goldstein, J., Freud, A. and Solnit, A. (1973) *Beyond the Best Interests of the Child*, New York Free Press.

(1980) *Before the Best Interests of the Child*, Burnett Books Ltd.

Gorin, S. (2004) *Understanding What Children Say: Children's Experiences of Domestic Violence, Parental Substance Misuse and Parental Health Problems*, Joseph Rowntree Foundation.

Guggenheim, M. (2005) *What's Wrong with Children's Rights*, Harvard University Press.

Hale, B. (2000) 'In Defence of the Children Act' 83 *Archives of Diseases in Childhood* 463.

Hale, B. and Fortin, J. (2008) 'Legal Issues in the Care and Treatment of Children with Mental Health Problems' in Rutter, M., Bishop, D., Pine, D., Scott, S., Stevenson, J., Taylor, E. and Thapar, A. (eds) *Rutter's Child and Adolescent Psychiatry*, Blackwell Publishing.

Hayes, M. (2013) 'The Supreme Court's Failure to Protect Vulnerable Children: Re J (Children)' 43 *Family Law* 1015.

Hemingway, I. and Williams, C. (1997) 'Re M and R: Re H and R' 27 *Family Law* 740.

Hester, M., Pearson, C. and Harwin, N., with Abrahams, H. (2007) *Making an Impact: Children and Domestic Violence, A Reader*, Jessica Kingsley Publishers.

HM Government (2018a) *Working Together to Safeguard Children: A Guide to Inter-Agency Working to Safeguard and Promote the Welfare of Children*, The Stationery Office.

(2018b) *Reporting and Acting on Child Abuse and Neglect*, The Stationery Office.

Housing, Government and Local Government Committee (House of Commons) (2019) HC 1638, *Funding of Local Authorities' Children's Services*.

Jones, D. and Ramchandani, P. (1999) *Child Sexual Abuse*, Radcliffe Medical Press.

Laming, H. (2003) Cm 5730, *The Victoria Climbié Inquiry: Report on an Inquiry by Lord Laming*, Her Majesty's Stationery Office.

(2009) HC 330, *The Protection of Children in England: A Progress Report*, The Stationery Office.

London Borough of Brent (1985) *'A Child in Trust'. The Report of the Panel of Inquiry into the Circumstances Surrounding the Death of Jasmine Beckford*.

Loughrey, J. (2008) 'Can You Keep a Secret? Children, Human Rights and the Law of Medical Confidentiality' 20 *Child and Family Law Quarterly* 312.

Lynch, M. and Roberts, J. (1982) *Consequences of Child Abuse*, Academic Press.

Maclean, K. and Hall, E. (2008) 'The Standard of Proof in Children Cases: Re B' 38 *Family Law* 737.

Masson, J. (2004) *Emergency Protection Orders: Court Orders for Child Protection Crises*, Executive Summary, Warwick University.

(2005) 'Emergency Intervention to Protect Children: Using and Avoiding Legal Controls' 17 *Child and Family Law Quarterly* 75.

(2006) 'Fair Trials in Child Protection' 28 *Journal of Social Welfare and Family Law* 15.

Masson, J., Dickens, J., Bader, K., Garside, L. and Young, J. (2017) 'Achieving Positive Change for Children? Reducing the Length of Child Protection Proceedings: Lessons from England and Wales' 41 *Adoption & Fostering* 401.

Masson, J., Pearce, J. and Bader, K., with Joyner, O., Marsden, J. and Westlake, D. (2008) Ministry of Justice Research Series 4/08, *Care Profiling Study*, Ministry of Justice.

Masson, J., Winn Oakley, M. and McGovern, D. (2001) *Working in the Dark: The Use of Police Protection*, Warwick University.

Masson, J., Winn Oakley, M. and Pick, K. (2004) *Emergency Protection Orders: Court Orders for Child Protection Crises*, Executive Summary, Warwick University.

Morgan, R. (2007) *Children and Safeguarding: Children's Views for the DfES Priority Review*, CSCI.

Mullen, P., Martin, J., Anderson, J., Roman, S. and Herbison, G. (1996) 'The Long-Term Impact of the Physical, Emotional, and Sexual Abuse of Children: A Community Study' 20 *Child Abuse and Neglect* 7.

Munby, J. (2016) '15th View from the President's Chambers: Care Cases: The Looming Crisis' 46 *Family Law* 1227.

Narey, M. (2007) *Beyond Care Matters: Future of the Care Population*, Working Group Report, DfES.

Ofsted (2008) *Safeguarding Children: The Third Joint Chief Inspectors' Report on Arrangements to Safeguard Children*, Ofsted.

Olsen, F. (1992) 'Children's Rights: Some Feminist Approaches to the United Nations Convention on the Rights of the Child' in Alston, P., Parker, S. and Seymour, J. (eds) *Children, Rights and the Law*, Clarendon Press.

Parton, N. (2014) 'The Changing Politics and Practice of Child Protection and Safeguarding in England' in Wagg, S. and Pilcher, J. (eds) *Thatcher's Grandchildren? Politics and Childhood in the Twenty First Century*, Palgrave Macmillan.

Quinton, D. (2004) *Supporting Parents: Messages from Research*, Jessica Kingsley Publishers.

Rose, W. and Barnes, J. (2008) *Improving Safeguarding Practice, Study of Serious Case Reviews 2001–2003*, Research Report DCSF – RRO22, DCSF.

Ryder, Mr J. (2008) 'The Risk Fallacy: A Tale of Two Thresholds' 38 *Family Law* 29.

Schofield, G. (1998) 'Making Sense of the Ascertainable Wishes and Feelings of Insecurely Attached Children' 10 *Child and Family Law Quarterly* 363.

Sibert, J., Payne, E., Kemp, A., Barber, M., Rolfe, K., Morgan, R., Lyons, R. and Butler, I. (2002) 'The Incidence of Severe Physical Child Abuse in Wales' 26 *Child Abuse and Neglect* 267.

Smedley, B. (1999) 'Child Protection: Facing up to Fear' in Milner, P. and Carolin, B. (eds) *Time to Listen to Children: Personal and Professional Communication*, Routledge.

Spencer, J. (1994) 'Evidence in Child Abuse Cases – Too High a Price for Too High a Standard? Re M (A Minor) (Appeal) (No 2)' 6 *Journal of Child Law* 160.

Taylor, R. (2018) 'Religion as Harm? Radicalisation, Extremism and Child Protection' 30 *Child and Family Law Quarterly* 41.

Tobin, J. and Cashmore, J. (2019) 'Article 19: The Right to Protection against All Forms of Violence' in Tobin, J. (ed.) *The UN Convention on the Rights of the Child*, Oxford University Press.

Wolfe, D. (1987) *Child Abuse: Implications for Child Development and Psychopathology*, Sage Publications.

16

The Child's Right to Protection in State Care and to State Accountability

(1) The Corporate Parent

Society expects parents to fulfil their children's rights to care, protection, optimum health and a good education. Parents should also promote their children's capacity for independence and take an interest in their future. If a child is no longer able to remain in the existing family environment, the UN Convention on the Rights of the Child (CRC) provides that he or she is *entitled* to state care, assistance and alternative care.[1] In this jurisdiction, that right is primarily fulfilled through the obligations owed by local authorities (LAs) to children who are 'looked after'.[2] Theoretically, when an LA obtains a care order for a child, it is deemed to share parental responsibilities with his or her parents.[3] In practice, the sharing is often nominal, since the LA can determine the parents' ability to exercise their parental responsibility, even though they should be consulted over decisions regarding their child's care.[4] Consequently, the state effectively takes over the parenting role and should fulfil the same duties as birth parents. Indeed, the 'no order' principle[5] emphasises that by authorising a care order, the court is expecting the state to do a better job than the parents alone. Similarly, children who are accommodated by an LA with their parents' agreement[6] are owed significant duties by the LA, which must safeguard and promote their welfare.[7] These children also expect their lives to improve when identified as being in need of state assistance and protection.

---

[1] CRC, Art. 20. See also the UN Guidelines for the Alternative Care of Children (A/RES/64/142).
[2] Under CA 1989, s. 22(1) and (2), a 'looked-after child' is either a child who is the subject of a care order or a child being provided with accommodation under s. 20 for a continuous period of more than 24 hours. NB: see *Southwark LBC* v. *D* [2007] EWCA Civ 182, [2007] 1 FLR 2181, per Smith LJ, at [55]: a child becomes a 'looked-after child' as soon as the LA considers that he or she requires accommodation for at least 24 hours, at which point the duty to accommodate him or her arises under s. 20(1) and the child should be provided with such accommodation under s. 23(2) or (6).
[3] Children Act (CA) 1989, s. 33(3) and (5).
[4] CA 1989, ss 33(3)(b) and (4) and 22(4) and (5). The relationship between the parental responsibility of LAs and parents for children accommodated under a care order is discussed further below.
[5] Ibid. s. 1(5).   [6] Ibid. s. 20; discussed below.   [7] Ibid. s. 22(3).

The government agrees that looked-after children should be able to expect the highest standards from state care:

> Looked after children deserve the best experiences in life, from excellent parenting which promotes good health and educational attainment, to a wide range of opportunities to develop their talents and skills in order to have an enjoyable childhood and successful adult life.[8]

But as case law and research indicates, the assumption that intervention to protect children will achieve a real improvement in their lives is all too often over-optimistic. Indeed, as in *Re F; F* v. *Lambeth London Borough Council*,[9] the state sometimes makes matters a great deal worse. In that case, as a result of the LA's long-term neglect of two boys while in care, both suffered 'significant educational, emotional, psychological, social and behavioural harm'.[10] As Munby J observed:

> it is a matter of gravity when the State's failure relates to its duties in relation to children and their families. It becomes a matter of the utmost gravity when the failure, as here, follows the intervention of the State in removing children against their parents' wishes from the parental home.[11]

The state's record as parent has been criticised as being a disastrously poor one for many years. As long ago as 1998, Frank Dobson, the then Secretary of State for Health, acknowledged:

> Too many children taken into care to protect and help them have received neither protection nor help. Instead they have been abused and molested. Many more have been let down, ignored, shifted from place to place, school to school and often simply turned out to fend for themselves when they turned 16.[12]

While legislative and policy reform has improved the situation for looked-after children on some measures, too many children still do not receive the protection and help to which they are entitled. Children experience too many placements,[13] often far from home,[14] and are given too little say about the type of placement to which they are allocated.[15] At every stage of education, looked-after children achieve significantly worse outcomes than children who

---

[8] DfE (2021a) para. 1.1.

[9] [2002] 1 FLR 217: two boys aged 8 and 4, having been removed from home under care orders, were left without adequate care plans for 8 years.

[10] Ibid. at [30(4)].   [11] Ibid. at [42].

[12] Statement in the House of Commons by Frank Dobson, Secretary of State for Health, 5 November 1998.

[13] One in ten children in care experience two or more home moves during a year. Over a three-year period, over half of children in care experience a change in home, with three in ten subject to multiple moves: Children's Commissioner (2019a).

[14] More than 40 per cent of children in care are in placements outside their own LA's boundaries: Children's Commissioner (2019b).

[15] R. Morgan (2006a) p. 11.

are not looked after.[16] Most alarmingly of all, children in care are much more likely to become the victim of child sexual and criminal exploitation than other children, especially if they are placed out of area or in unregulated accommodation.[17]

The state's poor record to date undoubtedly lends some support to the laissez-faire views of Goldstein, Freud and Solnit. They pointed out that the state cannot always offer abused children anything better or indeed compensate them for what they have missed in their own home. 'By its intrusion the state may make a bad situation worse; indeed, it may turn a tolerable or even good situation into a bad one.'[18] Nevertheless, although the statistics paint a bleak picture of the situation for looked-after children, LA care can be a positive outcome when compared with the alternative of staying in a home where there is neglect and abuse. For example, although looked-after children have poor educational outcomes compared to the general population, they achieve more highly than children in need who remain at home.[19] Similarly, there is also research suggesting that children who remain in care have better outcomes in a wide range of areas than those who return home.[20] While the state may have a poor record of parenting, it is sometimes the best alternative for the children for whom it cares.

This chapter assesses the extent to which children's rights to state protection and care are currently being fulfilled for children in LA care. It starts by considering the obligations owed by the state to looked-after children, including the difficult relationship between the responsibility of the state and that of the child's parents. It then proceeds to consider the experiences of children in care. Far more children are placed with foster carers than in residential homes; nevertheless, the latter service has been selected for special consideration due to the many reports highlighting the dangers of children suffering re-abuse while in residential care. The failure to ensure that sufficient high-quality residential placements are available leaves many children vulnerable to exploitation and abuse, despite being under the care of the state. This is particularly a problem for older children in unregulated accommodation and for those who are assessed as needing secure accommodation. The shortage of secure accommodation, often needed by children who are at grave risk of harm, has been described in the Supreme Court as 'a disgraceful and utterly shaming lack of proper provision for children'.[21] For these children, the state has fallen far short of being an adequate corporate parent, and has failed to meet the

---

[16] DfE (2019a): 35 per cent of looked-after children met the expected standard in reading, writing and mathematics by the end of Key Stage 2, compared to 65 per cent of all children.
17.5 per cent of looked-after children received a GCSE pass in English and mathematics, compared to nearly 60 per cent of all children.

[17] APPG (2012), (2019). Unregulated accommodation and the associated risk of exploitation is also discussed in relation to 16- and 17-year-olds in Chapter 10.

[18] J. Goldstein et al. (1980) p. 13.   [19] DfE (2019a); J. Sebba et al. (2015).

[20] N. Biehal et al. (2015).

[21] Re T (A Child) [2021] UKSC 35, [2021] 3 WLR 643, at [166] (per Lord Stephens).

standards of care to which these children are entitled. Finally, this chapter considers the child's own perspectives while in state care and the extent to which abused children can bring the state to account for failing to protect them adequately or at all.

(2) Looked-After Children: State Responsibility and Family Relationships

(A) The Background

'Looked-after children' fall broadly into two groups: those who are considered in sufficient danger to warrant the LA formally assuming their care with the assistance of care orders; and those who are accommodated with foster carers,[22] or in residential homes, under voluntary arrangements with their parents.[23] LAs owe duties to both groups of children looked after by them to: 'safeguard and promote' their welfare';[24] promote educational achievement;[25] and provide accommodation[26] and maintenance.[27] As noted above, the state's track record in fulfilling these duties in a way that enables children to thrive has often been poor. In order to promote the 'excellent parenting' the government recognises that looked-after children deserve, the Children and Social Work Act 2017 sets out seven 'corporate parenting principles'. These principles include the need: to act in the child's best interests; to listen to and take account of children's wishes and feelings; for children to have safety and stability; to have high aspirations for children; and to prepare them for adulthood. The principles themselves were not novel, but largely reflected the existing law and the rights established in the CRC. The 2017 Act requires LAs to 'have regard' to these corporate parenting principles in carrying out their duties for looked-after children,[28] rather than to fulfil them in practice. For these reasons, it seems that they added very little to the pre-existing legal obligations on LAs. The central purpose of the principles lies instead in aiming to foster a corporate parenting 'ethos', in which all LAs and their staff regard themselves as seeking to provide the best possible parenting to children, rather than merely fulfilling discrete legal duties.[29]

The relationship with parents and wider family remains an important aspect of planning and care for looked-after children. Although LAs have corporate parenting responsibilities, parents retain legal parental responsibility for their

---

[22] Family and friends may seek approval as foster carers in order to accommodate a child under CA 1989, s. 20. The Care Planning, Placement and Case Review (England) Regulations 2010 (SI 2010/ 959), reg. 24 allows for temporary approval of 'connected persons' as foster carers, to enable the child to be placed with known carers immediately while full approval as a foster carer is pending.

[23] CA 1989, s. 20(1). NB: s. 20(7): the LA may not accommodate the child against the wishes of anyone with parental responsibility who is able to provide the child with accommodation himself. See *R* v. *Tameside Metropolitan Borough Council, ex p J* [2000] 1 FLR 942.

[24] CA 1989, s. 22(3)(a).   [25] Ibid. s. 22(3A) and (3B).   [26] Ibid. s. 22A.   [27] Ibid. s. 22B.

[28] Children and Social Work Act 2017, s. 1(1).   [29] DfE (2018a).

children. Indeed, for children accommodated under voluntary arrangements, parental responsibility remains solely with the parents and is not acquired by the LA. The LA does obtain parental responsibility for children accommodated under a care order, but, no matter how abusive they may have been, parental responsibility is not removed from the parents of children in care. In theory, this means that LAs and parents will act in partnership[30] to meet their responsibilities to their children. In practice, parents often feel powerless if they wish to oppose the plans of the LA. A series of legal challenges have sought to strengthen the role of parents in decision-making for their looked-after children.[31] The role of parents and the wider family is also important in planning for children's futures. Children have a right to be brought up by their parents unless their safety and best interests require separation;[32] as a result, the state has a duty to seek to return the child to their parents if that can be done safely and while meeting the wider obligations to the child. Children also have a right to respect for their relationships with wider family members, including siblings. The CA 1989 recognises the importance of family relationships by incorporating a presumption that, unless reasonably practicable and consistent with the child's welfare, the child will be accommodated with his or her own parents.[33] Failing such arrangements being appropriate, preference should be given to placements with family or friends.[34] A recurring theme in the law is how state responsibility to looked-after children accommodates their relationship with family and manages the risks that may be involved in those relationships.

(B) Accommodated Children

Many children who become looked after do so through voluntary or 'section 20' accommodation.[35] Children are accommodated under section 20 for a wide variety of reasons. Some children, such as unaccompanied migrants,[36] are

---

[30] B. Hale (2000) p. 464: although the CA 1989 does not specifically express the concept of partnership between state and parents, it is an underlying principle of the Act.

[31] Discussed further below.

[32] Discussed in Chapter 6. See esp. CRC, Art. 9, ECHR, Art. 8, and UN Guidelines for the Alternative Care of Children (A/RES/64/142), paras 49–52.

[33] CA 1989, s. 22C(3)(a); or failing a placement with parents (s. 22C(3)(b) and (c)) with a person with PR for the child or, if the child is already in LA care, a person with a residence order relating to the child.

[34] CA 1989, s. 22C(5), (6)(a) and (7)(a); P. Welbourne (2008) p. 342.

[35] CA 1989, s. 20. Just over half of children entering care in 2017 did so through s. 20. In contrast, the majority of children who are in care are subject to care orders (70 per cent in 2017). The difference between the two figures can be explained by the fact that children with care orders tend to stay in care for longer than those under s. 20 and that children who enter care under s. 20 may later be the subject of a care order: Masson (2018).

[36] *R (Behre)* v. *Hillingdon London Borough Council* [2003] EWHC 2075 (Admin): an LA accommodating unaccompanied asylum-seeking children was not merely providing support under CA 1989, s. 17; instead it was accommodating them under s. 20, and owed them duties as former looked-after children.

accommodated because there is no available parent to care for them. Others are 16- or 17-year-olds who are unable or unwilling to remain in the family home and have turned to the LA for support.[37] For those under 16 with an available parent, section 20 is intended to operate as a partnership between the LA and the parents. Section 20 may not be used to accommodate the child against the objection of a parent who is willing and able to provide or arrange alternative accommodation.[38] Similarly, any person with parental responsibility (PR) may remove the child from LA accommodation at any time.[39] As section 20 does not grant the local authority PR, or remove it from existing holders, the provision is often described as 'voluntary' accommodation. For some parents, such as those dealing with a particular crisis or seeking respite care for a child with disabilities,[40] section 20 can be genuinely voluntary. For families on the edge of care, its use has been more contentious.

LAs have long been said to use section 20 accommodation as an alternative to court proceedings.[41] In other words, despite being concerned about a child's safety, they see applying for a court order, be it a care order or a supervision order, as a last resort, with voluntary accommodation being infinitely preferable. Indeed, there is considerable pressure on LAs to avoid resorting to care proceedings unless other forms of family support have been explored and exhausted. Many parents are persuaded to agree to the child being accommodated away from home, quite often with foster carers.[42] If the parents are genuinely working with the LA to address the reasons for concern, section 20 provides a means of keeping the child safe while not disrupting the relationship with the parents through adversarial care proceedings. But utilising section 20 instead of instigating care proceedings can cause problems, not least when parents feel coerced into agreeing to such arrangements.[43] Parents who agree to section 20 arrangements are not entitled to free legal advice and there is worrying evidence that parents often lack the information and advice necessary to understand the options available to them, especially if the parents have learning difficulties or are themselves very young.[44] Decisions made while a child is accommodated under section 20 may have long-term implications

---

[37] Once a young person reaches 16, they may be accommodated under CA 1989, s. 20 despite the objection of their parents: CA 1989, s. 20(11). Accommodation of this group is discussed further in Chapter 10. *R (G)* v. *Southwark London Borough Council* [2009] UKHL 26, [2009] 1 WLR 1299 held that the duty owed to this group under CA 1989, s. 20 could not be avoided by the LA purporting to use homelessness legislation.

[38] CA 1989, s. 20(7). This applies to any parent or other person who has parental responsibility for the child.

[39] Ibid. s. 20(8).   [40] Ibid. s. 20(4).

[41] J. Masson (2005) pp. 80–4; J. Brophy (2006) pp. 53–4; ibid. p. 12: 50 per cent of children who were the subject of care applications were already living away from their birth parents, most with foster carers under s. 20; J. Masson *et al.* (2008) p. 29: just under 40 per cent of families whose children were later the subject of care proceedings had previously agreed to their children being accommodated under s. 20.

[42] J. Masson (2005) p. 82.   [43] See cases discussed below.

[44] C. Lynch and J. Boddy (2017); C. Lynch (2018).

for the child's future. Particularly concerning is evidence that some very young babies are placed in foster for adoption arrangements under section 20 without their parents receiving legal advice as to the implications of such a placement.[45] If the prospective adopters and child form a close relationship at this stage, it is very difficult for members of the wider family, such as grandparents, to later succeed in arguing that the child should be removed to their care.[46] While foster for adoption may be the best outcome for some children who are not able to be brought up by their parents, a placement with such potentially profound implications for the child's future should not be made without full legal advice to enable the parents to understand the consequences of the decision. Care proceedings offer important safeguards for parents that are not available under section 20: they will be entitled to legal aid; the LA's evidence, allegations and plans for the child will be subject to judicial scrutiny; the parents' rights are safeguarded; and even if the child is taken into care, the court may order contact to continue between parents and child. Care proceedings also offer considerable benefit to the child. As Lady Hale explained in *London Borough of Hackney* v. *Williams*, care proceedings have advantages for a child who is likely to be in long-term state care as:

> They involve a rigorous scrutiny of the risk of harm to her health and development if an order is not made, of the assessment of her needs and of the plans for her future. Her interests are safeguarded by an expert children's guardian. If an order is made, it means that the local authority have parental responsibility for her and can put their plans into effect.[47]

Difficulties may also arise with long-term fostering arrangements under section 20, particularly for children with uncaring parents. The only person able to exercise PR in relation to a child being accommodated voluntarily is the parent, but he or she may have completely lost interest in the child, leaving him or her in a 'legal limbo'.[48] If the LA fails to assume PR, it may feel unable to arrange a stable fostering placement for the child or arrange for appropriate psychiatric support.[49] Meanwhile, it appears that some section 20 cases may receive far less careful planning and monitoring by the LA than those involving children in care on care orders, due to the assumption that they are less serious or complex.[50] The absence of adequate monitoring may, in turn, lead to

---

[45] Ibid.

[46] Adoption and Children Act 2002, s. 1(4)(f), discussed in Chapter 6. See further *Re W (A Child)* [2016] EWCA Civ 793, [2017] 1 WLR 889; R. Taylor (2018).

[47] *London Borough of Hackney* v. *Williams* [2018] UKSC 37, [2019] AC 421, at [51].

[48] See *S (by the Official Solicitor)* v. *Rochdale MBC and another* [2008] EWHC 3283 (Fam), [2009] 1 FLR 1090, Appendix A, esp. at [94]: the Official Solicitor's (OS's) allegations (unproved because the case was compromised) regarding the inadequate care of S (now aged 18) under CA 1989, s. 20, given her mother's refusal to show any interest in her.

[49] Ibid. at [21].

[50] Ibid. Appendix A, at [97] and Appendices B and C: summarising the (unproved) concerns of the OS regarding the use of inexperienced and unqualified social workers without adequate supervision for work on s. 20 cases.

a failure to appreciate the need to assume parental responsibility by instigating care proceedings.[51]

In a series of cases, parents and children have succeeded in human rights claims against LAs for the 'misuse and abuse'[52] of section 20 arrangements. In some of these cases, parents have felt compelled to acquiesce to the child being accommodated,[53] while in others, LAs have failed to respond to parents who expressed a clear wish for the child to be returned.[54] In further cases, there has been a failure to plan for children in voluntary care,[55] or to seek a care order once it has become apparent that the LA requires PR in order to make decisions for the child.[56] It appears that some LAs have become more cautious about relying on section 20 agreements as a result.[57] Nonetheless, section 20 agreements remain a useful means of caring for many looked-after children, particularly in cases in which there is a relationship of trust and cooperation between parents and the LA, which may be disrupted by an application for a care order.[58] The Supreme Court's decision in *London Borough of Hackney* v. *Williams*[59] provides useful guidance to LAs seeking to balance these competing concerns about the use of section 20. As Lady Hale explained, parental responsibility is the starting point for proper use of section 20: the LA cannot remove a child from a parent who wishes to continue caring for them without a court order. Lawful use of section 20 requires a 'real and voluntary' delegation of the exercise of parental responsibility to the LA.[60] As Lady Hale observed, 'helpless submission to asserted power does not amount to a delegation of parental responsibility or its exercise'.[61] As she further observed, there is no statutory requirement for 'informed consent' from parents and delegation of parental responsibility might be voluntary without being fully informed.[62] Nonetheless, the best way to ensure that real and voluntary consent is given is to ensure that parents are fully informed of their rights. Finally, while there are no limits on the duration of section 20 accommodation, LA duties to children it accommodates require long-term

---

[51] Ibid. at [22]. See also P. Welbourne (2008) pp. 338–9.

[52] *In re A (Application for Care and Placement Order: Local Authority Failings)* [2015] EWFC 11, [2016] 1 FLR 1, at [99]–[100]. See also *In re N (Children) (Adoption: Jurisdiction)* [2015] EWCA Civ 1112, [2016] 2 WLR 713, at [171].

[53] E.g. *In re W (Parental Agreement with Local Authority)* [2014] EWCA Civ 1065, [2015] 1 FLR 949.

[54] E.g. *Herefordshire Council* v. *AB and CD* [2018] EWFC 10, [2018] 2 FLR 784.   [55] Ibid.

[56] E.g. *Medway Council* v. *M* [2015] EWFC B164.

[57] The proportion of looked-after children under voluntary agreements dropped from 28 per cent in 2015 to 19 per cent in 2018: DfE (2018b). See also Public Law Working Group (2021) pp. 82–3.

[58] J. Masson (2018).

[59] *London Borough of Hackney* v. *Williams* [2018] UKSC 37, [2019] AC 421.

[60] The court distinguished cases of removal from the parental home, which do require real and voluntary delegation, from those cases in which the state is stepping 'into the breach' for a child who is not being looked after by the parents, in which case no such agreement is required. Ibid. at [40].

[61] Ibid. at [38].   [62] Ibid. at [39] and [56].

planning for the child's future, including, in appropriate cases, consideration of whether the LA should apply for a care order to obtain PR. In appropriate cases, section 20 can provide the best and least intrusive means of providing children with safe accommodation and care. The decision in *Hackney* should give confidence to LAs to use section 20 in these cases, while remaining alert to the risk of overbearing and coercive practices that prevent parents from true voluntary cooperation. As with so many aspects of the care system, improved resources would offer greater protection for the rights of children and families. In particular, funding for legal advice for parents and older children in section 20 cases would do much to ensure that section 20 is not misused.

(C) Children in Care: Family Relationships

Even if a child's need for protection from harm fully justifies removal from home under a care order, the rights of the child and parents to enjoy family life together without undue state interference[63] remain protected in law. The European Court of Human Rights (ECtHR) has consistently stressed that when considering whether state interference with parents' family life is 'necessary',[64] the intervention must be proportionate to the aim of protecting the child in question. Furthermore, removal should be seen as a temporary measure only, with efforts made to reintegrate the child at home as soon as possible.[65] More particularly, totally depriving a child of his or her family life with their parents by taking the child into care and then placing the child for adoption should only be resorted to in exceptional circumstances, in the child's best interests.[66] On the other hand, the state's obligations to children in care include an obligation to plan for a stable and permanent placement without undue delay.[67] Further, the ECtHR has acknowledged that adoption may be the only option in certain circumstances.[68] The boundary between respecting the right to family life between the parents and child, and the child's need for a stable and permanent home, is at the root of many of the most difficult issues in planning for children in care.

An LA granted a care order in respect of a child will thereby obtain parental responsibility for him or her.[69] In theory, this provision creates a partnership

---

[63] Under the European Convention for the Protection of Human Rights and Fundamental Freedoms (1950) (ECHR), Art. 8.

[64] I.e. under ECHR, Art. 8(2). See B. Hale and J. Fortin (2008) p. 101.

[65] Inter alia: *Johansen* v. *Norway* (1996) 23 EHRR 33, esp. at [78]; *EP* v. *Italy* (2001) 31 EHRR 17, esp. at [62]; *Haase* v. *Germany* [2004] 2 FLR 39, esp. at [93]. See also *Olsson* v. *Sweden* (1988) 11 EHRR 259; *K and T* v. *Finland* [2001] 2 FLR 707; *S and G* v. *Italy* [2000] 2 FLR 771. See also the UN Guidelines for the Alternative Care of Children (A/RES/64/142), paras 3 and 14.

[66] *Johansen* v. *Norway* (1996) 23 EHRR 33, at [78]; *Gnahore* v. *France* (2002) 34 EHRR 38, at [59]; discussed by A. Bainham (2003) pp. 81–3; S. Harris-Short (2008) pp. 34–8.

[67] UN Guidelines for the Alternative Care of Children (A/RES/64/142), paras 60–1.

[68] *Johansen* v. *Norway* (1996) 23 EHRR 33, at [80]; *Scott* v. *United Kingdom* [2000] 1 FLR 958, at 970.

[69] CA 1989, s. 33(3)(a).

between the LA and the parents, who retain their existing parental responsibility.[70] In practice, the sharing of responsibility is often illusory, since the LA can determine the parents' ability to exercise their parental responsibility.[71] This gives the LA a 'trump card',[72] which it can deploy in the decision-making process to decide matters such as where the child will live. Nonetheless, the LA is not entitled to simply disregard the parents' role. The LA's power to determine the parents' use of their responsibility is only available if 'they are satisfied that it is necessary to do so in order to safeguard or promote the child's welfare'.[73] Further, the LA may not use this parental responsibility to undermine the child's identity within the family by consenting to the child's adoption, changing the child's surname or causing the child to be brought up according to a different religious persuasion.[74] Finally, if the decision would involve a serious interference with the parents' Article 8 rights, an application to court may be required to ensure that the interference is not disproportionate. For this reason, disagreements between LAs and parents concerning 'grave decisions' require court determination. Such decisions have included disputes over the child's forename[75] and serious matters of medical treatment,[76] but not routine immunisations.[77] Although LAs have the upper hand in relation to day-to-day decisions, the restrictions in place for decisions concerning the child's long-term future and identity recognise that the child does not become the 'child of the state' even if accommodated under a care order.

[70] Ibid. s. 33(3) and (5).   [71] Ibid. s. 33(3)(b) and (4).

[72] Re C (Children) (Child in Care: Choice of Forename) [2016] EWCA Civ 374, [2016] 3 WLR 1557, at [59].

[73] CA 1989, s. 33(4). The parents and child should also be consulted over decisions: CA 1989, s. 22(4) and (5).

[74] Ibid. s. 33(6) and (7). The LA is also restricted from appointing a guardian or removing the child from the UK for more than a month.

[75] Re C (Children) (Child in Care: Choice of Forename) [2016] EWCA Civ 374, [2016] 3 WLR 1557, discussed further in Chapter 5.

[76] Re Jake (A Child) [2015] EWHC 2442 (Fam), [2016] 2 FCR 118; see also Re AB [2018] EWFC 3, in which the application for a care order was withdrawn with the approval of the court, which made it clear that it would usually be inappropriate and ineffective for an LA to apply for a care order for the purpose of consenting to medical treatment against the wishes of parents, esp. at [24].

[77] In Re H (A Child) (Parental Responsibility: Vaccination) [2020] EWCA Civ 664, [2021] Fam 133, the Court of Appeal found that routine vaccinations would usually be in the child's best interests. The court also found that the decision to give routine vaccinations against parental objection for a child in care would not usually be within the category of 'grave' decisions that required court approval. Instead, the LA could give consent under CA 1989, s. 33(3)(b), although the views of the parents should be considered. See also Re C (Looked After Child) (Covid-19 Vaccination) [2021] EWHC 2993 (Fam), which concerned parental objection to Covid-19 vaccination for a child in care. The child was 12 years old and wished to have the vaccine. The court applied the same principles as in Re H and took the view that any vaccination in the national programme would ordinarily be in the child's best interests in the absence of specific concerns related to their individual circumstances.

The right to family life includes the child's right to maintain family relationships while in care, unless it is contrary to the child's best interests to do so. Article 9(3) of the CRC protects the child's right to regular and direct contact with parents whiet separated from them. The ECtHR has similarly recognised that any decision to terminate contact between parents and children in care is a grave interference with Article 8 of the ECHR. Termination of contact will only be justifiable in exceptional circumstances and subject to 'anxious scrutiny' by the court.[78] This right to ongoing contact with parents is reinforced by the UN Guidelines for the Alternative Care of Children, which also emphasise the importance to children of maintaining wider relationships, especially those between siblings.[79] These rights are reflected in the CA 1989, which places a duty on LAs to allow 'reasonable contact' between parents and children in care.[80] While most decisions concerning children in care are for the LA, not the courts, the importance of contact is underlined by the supervisory role given to the courts.[81] Before making a care order, the court is required to consider the proposed arrangements for contact.[82] Further, the court may grant orders requiring defined contact, either on the application of the parent, or other party who obtains leave to do so, or of its own volition.[83] Finally, if the LA wishes to cease contact for a period of more than 7 days, it must obtain a court order terminating contact.[84] Despite the importance placed on contact with parents, it is not always in the child's best interests, not least because contact with abusive parents can be a cause of immense distress to children.[85] Unreliable and low-quality contact can present difficulties for children, especially as the services that are needed to support positive contact are not always available.[86] The legislation reflects the importance of the child's own relationship rights by permitting children in care to bring an application for contact or termination of contact.[87] It appears, however, that these provisions are little used in practice, as children are not given the advice needed to be aware of the possibility of such an application.[88] This is unfortunate, as children could use the provisions in order to apply for contact with any named person, so countering the parent-focused duty in section 34(1). Relationships with their siblings are often one of the highest priorities for children in care,[89] but applications by children for

---

[78] *K and T* v. *Finland* [2001] 2 FLR 707; *S and G* v. *Italy* [2000] 2 FLR 771.

[79] UN Guidelines for the Alternative Care of Children (A/RES/64/142), paras 11, 17, 51 and 81.

[80] CA 1989, s. 34(1).

[81] Although it appears that court orders under these provisions are relatively infrequent, as courts prefer to rely on the LA's discretion under the general duty to allow reasonable contact: A. Bainham (2015); D. Monk and J. Macvarish (2018).

[82] CA 1989, s. 34(11).   [83] Ibid. s. 34(3) and (5).   [84] Ibid. s. 34(4) and (6) and (6A).

[85] E.g. *Re M (A Child)* [2013] EWCA Civ 132, [2013] Fam Law 662: in which parents who had been convicted of criminal offences amounting to inflicting 'torture' on their children, failed in their appeal against an order permitting the LA to terminate contact. The eldest child, aged 16, had initially wanted to have some form of contact, but had changed his mind by the time the appeal was decided.

[86] J. Hunt *et al.* (2010).   [87] CA 1989, s. 34(2) and (4).   [88] D. Monk and J. Macvarish (2018).

[89] DfE (2021a) para. 2.85; D. Monk and J. Macvarish (2018).

contact with their siblings face the additional barrier that they must obtain the leave of the court before making the application.[90] Siblings who are not placed together must instead rely on the much weaker requirement that LAs 'endeavour to promote' contact with family members and to consider the sibling relationship in planning for the child in care.[91] A more child-focused approach to contact would remove this disparity between the duty in relation to sibling relationships and that for parental relationships.

The relationship between children in care and their family members is further important in planning placements for children in care, with preference given to placement with parents,[92] then family and friends.[93] In some cases, social workers may consider that children are in no immediate danger and can therefore be left at home with their parents. Nonetheless, they may apply for a care order in order to obtain parental responsibility, or so that the children can be removed quickly in the event of the home situation deteriorating.[94] The courts may encourage LAs to seek supervision orders instead in such situations,[95] in order to comply with the principle of proportionality.[96] Nonetheless, supervision orders remain unpopular with many practitioners, being seen as 'a complete waste of time' and 'toothless'.[97] They carry less control than care orders;[98] furthermore, LAs have no real sanction when parents or relatives fail to comply with the directions they contain.[99] Indeed, a substantial number of children who are the subject of a supervision order suffer further abuse or neglect and their cases are returned to court through an application for a care order.[100]

---

[90] Under CA 1989, s. 34(3)(b), if the sibling is in care or otherwise, CA 1989, s. 10.

[91] CA 1989, Sch. 2, para. 15(1)(c). See also The Care Planning, Placement and Case Review (England) Regulations 2010 (SI 2010/959), Sch. 1, para. 3(1); DfE (2021a) paras 2.85–2.91.

[92] CA 1989, s. 22C(3)(a); preference is given to a placement with parents (s. 22C(3)(b) and (c)) or with a person with PR for the child or, if the child is already in LA care, a person with a residence order relating to the child.

[93] CA 1989, s. 22C(5), (6)(a) and (7)(a); P. Welbourne (2008) p. 342.

[94] But see *Re DE (A Child)* [2014] EWFC 6, [2014] 3 WLR 1733, discussed further below.

[95] To obtain a supervision order under CA 1989, s. 35, the LA must satisfy the same threshold criteria as those applying to care orders: see s. 31. Masson *et al.* (2017) found a marked increase in the use of supervision orders: 11 per cent of proceedings in their 2010 sample ended in a supervision order, whereas 19 per cent of the 2015 sample did so. Nonetheless, it seems that these orders are rarely sought by LAs and that the growth instead comes from their use to support the growing number of special guardianship orders: Public Law Working Group (2021) p. 77.

[96] *Oxfordshire County Council* v. *L (Care or Supervision Order)* [1998] 1 FLR 70, per Hale J, at 76–8; *Re O (Supervision Order)* [2001] EWCA Civ 16, [2001] 1 FLR 923, at [18]–[28].

[97] J. Hunt and A. Macleod (1999) p. 237. These concerns persist: Public Law Working Group (2021) pp. 75–81.

[98] It is *only* by obtaining a care order that the LA acquires parental responsibility over the child, which it shares with his or her parents. See CA 1989, s. 33(3). NB: A supervision order leaves parental responsibility entirely with the parents.

[99] J. Hunt and A. Macleod (1999) pp. 213, 217–18 and 237.

[100] Public Law Working Group (2021) pp. 75–81: nationally, 10 per cent of supervision order cases return to court within a year and 20 per cent within 5 years. In the case studies considered for the report, 24 per cent of children who were the subject of a supervision order suffered further neglect or abuse while the order was in force.

In some situations, the boot may be on the other foot, so to speak.[101] While the court may agree with the LA's wish to obtain a care order, considering the parents to be extremely dangerous, it may doubt the wisdom of the LA's plan to return the child home once the care order has been made. The LA might argue that such a strategy would promote both the legislation's aim to encourage social workers to work in partnership with parents,[102] even with abusive parents, and with the Strasbourg case law indicating that state care should be viewed as being a short-term measure. Worryingly, there is accumulating research indicating that returning an abused child home can be a high-risk strategy, with some children being re-abused by their parents within a very short period of time.[103] In the light of this, the court may quite justifiably consider that there is insufficient evidence to indicate that the parents have changed sufficiently to make it safe for the child to be returned home.[104] Nevertheless, a court is powerless in such a situation, its role in care proceedings being only 'adjudicative' rather than 'participative'.[105] It can certainly question the format of the LA's care plan if it considers it to be based on inaccurate information.[106] It can insist on making a care order, rather than the supervision order requested by the LA, if it considers that the latter will not offer the child sufficient protection.[107] But where the LA has applied for a care order, all the court can do is decide whether the threshold criteria are made out and, if so, whether or not to make it.[108] It has no power to impose conditions on it or insist that the LA discharge their parental responsibilities in a particular way.[109] The judiciary have expressed a degree of frustration over their inability to influence how the LA provides for the child once in care. For example, they cannot prevent the child being rehabilitated with his or her parents if that is the LA's intention, even if they consider the parents to be inherently dangerous.[110] As discussed below, the absence of any judicial power to supervise the delivery of a care plan, or any reliable procedure whereby LAs can be called to account in cases where they wholly fail to implement such plans, continues to cause frustration.

---

[101]   A metaphor used by Wall J to describe this situation. See Wall J (1998) p. 6.

[102]   B. Hale (2000) p. 464: although the CA 1989 does not specifically express the concept of partnership between state and parents, it is an underlying principle of the Act.

[103]   Inter alia: J. Hunt and A. Macleod (1999) p. 199; M. Brandon *et al.* (2005) pp. 28–9 and 86; B. Ellaway *et al.* (2004); N. Biehal (2006) ch. 8; N. Hindley *et al.* (2006) p. 750: previously maltreated children are approximately six times more likely to be re-abused than children who had never been abused; I. Sinclair *et al.* (2007) p. 107: some LAs seem more prepared to take risks by returning children home than others.

[104]   E.g. *Kent County Council* v. *C* [1993] 1 FLR 308.   [105]   J. Dewar (1995) p. 16.

[106]   E.g. *Re H (Care Plan)* [2008] EWHC 327 (Fam), [2008] 2 FLR 21.

[107]   E.g. *Re D (A Minor) (Care or Supervision Order)* [1993] 2 FLR 423.

[108]   *Re T (A Minor) (Care Order: Conditions)* [1994] 2 FLR 423, per Nourse J, at 429.

[109]   B. Hale and J. Fortin (2008) p. 101. The role of courts in relation to care plans is discussed further below.

[110]   *Re W and B; Re W (Care Plan)* [2001] EWCA Civ 757, [2001] 2 FLR 582, per Thorpe LJ, at [18] (NB: House of Lords' decision is reported sub nom *Re S (Children: Care Plan), Re W (Children: Care Plan)* [2002] UKHL 10, [2002] 2 All ER 192).

(D) Care Planning for Permanence

Too many children experience disruption in care, with multiple home moves that leave them with little sense of security.[111] It is well recognised that children who are unable to return home need permanent alternative care to give them a stable base throughout their childhood and beyond.[112] The child protection system has long been criticised for allowing children to drift in care, without a firm and comprehensive plan for their future upbringing.[113] Research throughout the 1990s and 2000s found LAs failing to plan adequately for the future of children they wished to remove from home. For example, Brandon *et al.* found that over the 7 to 8 years after children had first been identified as suffering or likely to suffer significant harm, some had been:

> languishing on the [child protection] register over long periods, often listed in multiple and changing categories of harm where the ongoing planning was neither promoting their well being, nor keeping them safe.[114]

Long-term planning (including the use of the courts) had taken place in only 40 per cent of the cases considered.[115] In response to such findings, a renewed emphasis on the importance of planning for permanence has been embedded in law and policy. LAs are now required to follow a structured approach to care planning and review,[116] including the requirement that a 'plan for permanence'[117] is in place by the second review of the child's case,[118] within the first 4 months of the child's time in care.[119] Subsequent changes in circumstances, together with the practical challenges of finding stable long-term placements, mean that children still often experience instability in care.[120] Nonetheless, there is a clear expectation that a decision will be made, within a relatively short period of time, as to the plan for the child's long-term home. That plan may involve a return to the birth family, placement with family and friends, long-term foster care, a residential placement or adoption.

---

[111] One in ten children in care experience two or more home moves during a year. Over a three-year period, over half of children in care experience a change in home, with three in ten subject to multiple moves: Children's Commissioner (2019a).

[112] E.g. UN Guidelines for the Alternative Care of Children (A/RES/64/142), paras 2(a), 12 and 60–3.

[113] J. Hunt and A. Macleod (1999) writing on the experience of children in care in the 1990s found that for many, the care experience had done little to ameliorate their problems and, for some, it had even exacerbated them. One-third of the children in their research sample had to cope with the insecurity and/or disappointment of changed or unfulfilled plans.

[114] M. Brandon *et al.* (2005) p. 11 and ch. 3.   [115] Ibid. p. 43.

[116] The Care Planning, Placement and Case Review (England) Regulations 2010 (SI 2010/959); DfE (2021a).

[117] The Care Planning, Placement and Case Review (England) Regulations 2010 (SI 2010/959), reg. 5. See below for discussion of the court's role in reviewing the permanence plan during care proceedings: CA 1989, s. 31(3)(A)–(C).

[118] DfE (2021a) para. 2.3.

[119] The Care Planning, Placement and Case Review (England) Regulations 2010 (SI 2010/959), reg. 33: the first review must take place within 20 working days of the child becoming looked after and the second review must take place within 3 months following the first review.

[120] Children's Commissioner (2019a), (2019b).

The pressure to decide a permanent plan for the child's future can, however, come into tension with the Article 8 obligation, discussed above, to assess whether it is possible to reintegrate the child with the birth family, which may require time-consuming assessment and support. This tension has been particularly acute in relation to adoption.

Successive governments have sought to promote adoption as a solution for the future of children in care. The Adoption and Children Act (ACA) 2002 produced a radical reform of adoption law, which was born largely out of two interlinking resolves. The first was to reduce the delays and ineffective planning undermining adoption practice. The second was to ensure that far more looked-after children were provided with substitute families, rather than being left to 'drift in care', at risk of abuse by unsuitable carers.[121] The government considered that too many looked-after children were waiting far too long for permanent homes and that adoption should be seen as the solution. The government hoped that the introduction of a new highly regulated adoption service, accompanied by adoption targets,[122] guidance and regulations, would transform this situation. These changes were to be combined with the courts gaining the power to dispense with parental consent to adoption on the grounds of the child's welfare.[123] Further, the ACA 2002 introduced an obligation on LAs to apply for adoption placement orders in relation to children they are looking after, if the LA considers that such children *ought to* be adopted and if the threshold criteria for a care order can be made out.[124] Thus, as Lewis observes, adoption became part of the care system.[125] Government policy has continued to favour increasing the number of children adopted from care. Notably, the Children and Families Act 2014 sought to make adoption easier and faster, in particular by encouraging LAs to place children for whom they were contemplating adoption in 'foster for adoption' placements with prospective adopters.[126] This form of 'concurrent planning' allows the LA to continue assessing the possibility of rehabilitation with the birth family, while at the same time allowing the child to form bonds with the prospective adopters and reducing the potential for disruption should the child be adopted. The position of the prospective adopters was strengthened in 2017 by the requirement that an adoption agency or court considering adoption for children in these placements must consider the child's existing relationship

---

[121] PIU (2000); DH (2000) ch. 2.

[122] DH (2000) para. 4.16. See also CSCI (2006a) para. 4.10: in 2000, a target was introduced to increase adoption of looked-after children by 40 per cent in the 5-year period to the end of March 2005. During that period, there was an increase of 38 per cent, with 4,200 more looked-after children adopted than would have been the case had adoption rates remained constant.

[123] The law on adoption is discussed further in Chapter 6.   [124] ACA 2002, s. 22(1)–(2).

[125] J. Lewis (2004) p. 239.

[126] Children and Families Act 2014, s. 2. The Act also introduced further reforms in Pt 1, including removing the explicit requirement that due consideration was given to the ethnicity of the child, with the aim of preventing undue delay in seeking to find a suitable ethnic match with prospective adopters: Children and Families Act 2014, s. 3.

with prospective adopters.[127] Further, it is deliberate statutory policy that applications for care orders are now being accompanied by applications for placement orders or by care plans involving the child being placed for adoption very soon after the care order, if not already in a foster for adoption placement. Arguably, it is kinder to the parent that 'the issue of adoption or no is grasped earlier rather than later, and in the course of a single set of stressful court proceedings, rather than [the parent] having to suffer going through very similar issues in a second set'.[128] Nonetheless, there is a risk that decisions are being made without a full opportunity to assess alternative options within the family.

There are certainly good reasons to support adoption for some children. On balance, research appears to bear out the government's assumption that adoption is more stable than long-term fostering[129] and kinship care,[130] although this depends on the circumstances of the individual child. Clearly, the choice between reunification, adoption and fostering should, in practice, depend on a number of interrelating factors, such as the child's age, views, background, degree of contact with birth parents and extended birth family.[131] The child's age at placement for adoption and the time spent in care are particularly closely related to the likely success of adoption.[132] The dilemma is that if the authorities intervene early, before the child suffers permanent harm, the more likely it will be that an adoption placement can be found for him or her. The later things are left, the more attempts to rehabilitate the child in the family, the more harm suffered and the more difficult it is to repair the damage.[133] The courts are well aware that babies cannot always wait for their mothers to change.[134] On the other hand, as discussed below, early intervention may be difficult to square with the Strasbourg jurisprudence on state intervention if there is still potential for successful reunification.

If the court is concerned about the LA's plans for adoption, considering that there is insufficient evidence showing that the parents are incapable of resuming the child's care, it might direct a parental assessment under an interim care order.[135] It may even direct the LA to undertake a residential assessment of the parents and child,[136] to obtain further evidence regarding their parenting

---

[127] Introduced by Children and Social Work Act 2017, s. 9. The potential for conflict between family members and prospective adopters is considered further in Chapter 6.

[128] *Re T (Placement Order)* [2008] EWCA Civ 248, [2008] 1 FLR 1721, per Hughes LJ, at [16].

[129] D. Quinton (2006) pp. 464–6, who counters the criticisms made by J. Eekelaar (2003) pp. 258–63, of the government's assumption that adoption provides more stable outcomes than long-term fostering.

[130] J. Selwyn *et al.* (2014). Kinship care as an alternative to adoption is considered further in Chapter 6.

[131] N. Lowe and M. Murch (2002) pp. 141–3. See also J. Thoburn (2006).

[132] J. Selwyn *et al.* (2014).   [133] B. Hale and J. Fortin (2008) p. 102.

[134] *A Local Authority* v. *J* [2008] EWHC 1484 (Fam), [2008] 2 FLR 1389, per Hogg J, at [76].

[135] CA 1989, s. 38(1).   [136] Ibid. s. 38(6).

abilities.[137] Such assessment work may not only be immensely expensive,[138] but will also undoubtedly take time, thereby delaying plans for a fast-track adoption. Ultimately, it may ensure that a very young child is left with his or her birth parents rather than being adopted.[139] As Hale and Fortin note:

> The dilemma still remains that adoption is the preferred solution precisely when the harm (or most of it) has yet to be done. This makes the professional task of accurately assessing the future risks all the more important.[140]

When considering LA applications for adoption placement orders, the judiciary are well aware that the public, including parents, may perceive LA adoption practice to be target-driven and motivated by a desire to transfer the cost of raising children in care from the LA to adoptive parents.[141] Older foster children are themselves aware of the pressures on social workers to move them out of foster care into adoption:

> Some [foster children] tell us they think this is to do with targets social workers have to try to meet, rather than what each child wants. Many have told us that they are happy to stay as foster children, and not be adopted – either by their foster parents or by anyone else.[142]

These perceptions are reinforced by government policy that often appears to promote an increase in adoption rates as an end in itself.[143] The courts have therefore stressed that the proper process governing an LA's application for an adoption placement order must be rigorously followed and this includes careful consideration of the important human rights at stake.[144]

Adoption, especially in the absence of parental consent, undoubtedly represents a grave interference with the Article 8 rights of children and parents, requiring 'very exceptional circumstances' in order to be justified under Article

---

[137] That the courts have a power to require such an assessment in the course of interim proceedings under CA 1989, s. 38(6), was confirmed by the House of Lords in *Re C (A Minor) (Interim Care Order: Residential Assessment)* [1997] AC 489. But see *Re G (A Minor) (Interim Care Order; Residential Assessment)* [2005] UKHL 68, [2006] 1 AC 576: s. 38(6) cannot be used to produce services for the child or family, cf. providing the court with information from detailed assessment work. See also *Re Y (A Child): s. 38(6) Assessment* [2018] EWCA Civ 992.

[138] See *A Local Authority* v. *M (Funding of Residential Assessments)* [2008] EWHC 162 (Fam), [2008] 1 FLR 1579, per Bodey J, at [24]–[27]: criticising the funding difficulties experienced by LAs regarding the residential assessments required by the courts.

[139] E.g. as in *Re G* [2005] UKHL 68, [2006] 1 AC 576, discussed by B. Hale and J. Fortin (2008) p. 102.

[140] B. Hale and J. Fortin (2008) p. 102.

[141] *Re F (A Child)* [2008] EWCA Civ 439, [2008] 2 FCR 93, at [14]. See also *Re B (Placement Order)* [2008] EWCA Civ 835, [2008] 2 FLR 1404, per Wall LJ, at [14]; N. Lowe and M. Murch (2002) p. 149.

[142] R. Morgan (2006a) p. 18. The use of targets in adoption is discussed by C. Fenton-Glynn (2016).

[143] E.g. Michael Gove MP, then Education Secretary, in a speech on 23 February 2012, declared that: 'I can assure you that I will not settle for a modest, temporary uplift in adoption numbers . . . Nothing less than a significant and sustained improvement will do.'

[144] *Re B (Placement Order)* [2008] EWCA Civ 835, [2008] 2 FLR 1404, per Wall LJ, at [70]ff.

8(2).[145] In *YC* v. *United Kingdom*, the ECtHR found that the welfare checklist contained in the ACA 2002[146] broadly reflects the 'various elements inherent in assessing the necessity under Article 8 of a measure placing a child for adoption'.[147] While the ECtHR found that the legislative scheme was compliant with Convention rights, that does not mean that any decision reached under it will necessarily be compliant. The court once again stressed that adoption should only be resorted to in exceptional circumstances, once everything had been done to preserve the family's relationships and after an 'in-depth analysis' of the family situation and 'the likely effect on the child of ceasing to be a member of his original family'.[148] In *Re B (Care Proceedings: Appeal)*,[149] the Supreme Court reflected on this case law and emphasised the importance of ensuring that decisions made on adoption complied with ECHR law. Baroness Hale summed up this law as follows:

> ... it is quite clear that the test for severing the relationship between parent and child is very strict: only in exceptional circumstances and where motivated by overriding requirements pertaining to the child's welfare, in short, where nothing else will do.[150]

This message was reiterated by the Court of Appeal in *Re B-S (Adoption: Application of s 47(5))*,[151] in which serious concern was expressed as to the quality of social work practice and judicial decision-making in adoption cases. Building on the ECtHR case law discussed above, the court stressed the need for proper evidence that carefully analysed all of the realistic options for the child's future and the need for properly reasoned judgments that also did so.[152] While these cases were not intended to change the law on adoption,[153] they appear to have come into collision with government policies promoting adoption without increasing LA resources, by stressing that only high-quality social work that gives careful consideration to all realistic options will be sufficient to produce the necessary reasoned evidence required in adoption cases. Certainly, the number of adoptions has fallen sharply, despite increased numbers of looked-after children.[154] The vital question in considering the

---

[145] *YC* v. *United Kingdom* (2012) 55 EHRR 33, at [134].

[146] ACA 2002, s. 1(4). In particular, the checklist requires that consideration is given to 'the likely effect on the child (throughout his life) of having ceased to be a member of the original family and become an adopted person' and to the child's relationships with relatives, including prospective adopters.

[147] *YC* v. *United Kingdom* (2012) 55 EHRR 33, at [135].   [148] Ibid. at [134]–[138].

[149] [2013] UKSC 33, [2013] 1 WLR 1911, discussed further in Chapter 6.

[150] *Re B (Care Proceedings: Appeal)* [2013] UKSC 33, [2013] 1 WLR 1911, at [198]; Baroness Hale dissented on the facts, but not the applicable law.

[151] [2013] EWCA Civ 1146, [2014] 1 WLR 563.

[152] *Re B-S (Adoption: Application of s. 47(5))* [2013] EWCA Civ 1146, [2014] 1 WLR 563, at [34]–[46].

[153] *Re R (A Child) (Adoption: Judicial Approach)* [2014] EWCA Civ 1625, [2015] 1 WLR 3273, esp. at [41]–[44].

[154] DfE (2019b): 3,570 children were adopted from care in the year to 31 March 2019, a drop of 7 per cent on the previous year and down from a peak of 5,360 in 2015.

child's future is which plan provides a proportionate response to meet the child's rights and interests, rather than whether adoption would place the child in a more beneficial environment for his or her upbringing.

An increasingly important alternative to adoption, for children who are not able to return safely to their birth family, is a special guardianship order (SGO).[155] SGOs were introduced to provide a secure, permanent[156] home for children, without removing their legal relationship with the birth family. Special guardians have parental responsibility,[157] including the ability to make decisions relating to a child's upbringing without parental interference.[158] A substantial majority of special guardians are family members or existing family friends, with former foster carers accounting for almost all other orders.[159] In this way, SGOs can give children security within existing caring relationships. Although the numbers of SGOs were initially rather low, there has been a substantial increase, particularly following *Re B-S*,[160] such that more children now leave care through an SGO than through adoption.[161] As SGOs offer children a less intrusive means of securing a long-term home, the increased use of the orders may be welcomed. There are, however, reasons to be cautious as to whether the increase has entirely been to the benefit of children. Whether an SGO is preferable to adoption, or to another placement, will depend on the particular facts of the case, including careful assessment of the placement with the proposed special guardian. The tragic death of 18-month-old Shi-Anne Downer at the hands of her special guardian graphically demonstrated the failures of the assessment process, which, the Serious Case Review found, was 'striking in its superficiality compared to those provided for adoption'.[162] A further concern raised by the Review was that the plan for her care was focused on looking for an extended family member or connected person to become a special guardian, without proper consideration of the merits of adoption.[163] These criticisms demonstrated failings within this case,

---

[155] CA 1989, s. 14A–14G, inserted by ACA 2002. See Chapter 6 for further discussion of the case law on special guardianship within the family, as an alternative to adoption.

[156] While an SGO is intended to offer permanence, it may be discharged (CA 1989, s. 14D) and does not offer the same degree of legal security as adoption: *Re S (Adoption Order or Special Guardianship Order)* [2007] EWCA Civ 54, [2007] 1 FLR 819, at [67]–[68].

[157] CA 1989, s. 14C(1)(a).

[158] Ibid. s. 14C(1)(b). The holder of an SGO is protected by CA 1989, s. 14D(1), (3) and (5) – a birth parent cannot apply to vary or discharge an SGO without obtaining court leave, which can only be granted if the court is satisfied that there has been a significant change of circumstances since the SGO was made; CA 1989, s. 10(7A) – court leave must be obtained before an application can be made for a residence order relating to a child who is the subject of an SGO. But a birth parent can apply without court leave for any s. 8 order challenging any decisions regarding the child's upbringing not involving a change in residence.

[159] DfE (2019b): 90 per cent of SGOs were made to extended family and to friends, 9 per cent to former foster carers.

[160] *Re B-S (Adoption: Application of s 47(5))* [2013] EWCA Civ 1146, [2014] 1 WLR 563.

[161] In 2019, 13 per cent of children leaving care did so through an SGO (3,830 children), compared to 12 per cent through adoption (3,570 children). This represented an 11 per cent increase in SGOs from the previous year and a 7 per cent decrease in adoption: DfE (2019b).

[162] R. Wate (2017) para. 4.36.   [163] Ibid. esp. paras 4.5 and 4.13.

but also highlighted the concern that more widespread unsuitable and risky SGOs were being made without proper assessment of the placement or of the alternatives for the child. In particular, the introduction of the 26-week timetable for care proceedings[164] puts pressure on social workers to complete assessments within a time frame that may be inadequate, especially if family members emerge at a relatively late stage in the process.[165] Research demonstrating that in about a third of cases the child had not lived with the special guardian prior to the order being made, adds to the concerns that orders are being made to secure a placement with *a* family member, rather than to give security to a tested, caring relationship.[166] There also appears to have been a marked increase in the number of SGOs with an attached supervision order, suggesting a lack of confidence in the SGO at the time that the order was made.[167] Although only a small proportion of SGOs return to court for further care proceedings, there has been a significant increase in those that do, suggesting that they may be becoming more fragile.[168] The government have responded to these concerns by strengthening the support offered to special guardians and improving the assessment process to include closer consideration of the special guardian's ability to meet the child's needs over the course of their childhood.[169] With these reforms, it is hoped that plans for SGOs will receive more robust assessment, in keeping with their importance as a permanent option for the child's future.

A stable, permanent home is the foundation of a secure childhood. The right solution for a particular child's future will depend on a difficult assessment of the individual child's needs, relationships, wishes and available options. The pendulum swings caused by government pressure to ensure more children are adopted from care more quickly and court insistence that this should not undermine rights under Article 8 of the ECHR have caused 'widespread uncertainty, misunderstanding and confusion'.[170] The process of planning the child's future must, of course, take place within a framework that respects all of the child's rights. But a focus on the right to family relationships cannot provide a 'hyperlink' to the right outcome[171] or bypass the need for a full and comprehensive evaluation of all of the realistic options for the child's future.

---

[164] Discussed further in Chapter 15.

[165] E.g. *Re P-S (Children)* [2018] EWCA Civ 1407, in which the Court of Appeal emphasised that the timetable may have to be extended to permit proper assessment.

[166] J. Masson *et al.* (2018).   [167] J. Harwin and B. Alrouh (2017).

[168] Ibid.: Compared cohorts of cases between 2012–14 and 2014–16, after the changes to the public law timetable and the response to *Re B-S (Adoption: Application of s 47(5))* [2013] EWCA Civ 1146, [2014] 1 WLR 563. The rate of return to court within 2 years rose from 1.5 to 2.5 per cent for SGOs only and from 3 to 6.5 per cent for children with an SGO and attached supervision order. Of course, these statistics do not capture those SGOs that fail, but do not result in further proceedings, e.g. because the child becomes looked after under CA 1989, s. 20.

[169] Special Guardianship (Amendment) Regulations 2016 (SI 2016/111); Children and Social Work Act 2017, s. 8.

[170] *Re R (A Child)* [2014] EWCA Civ 1625, [2015] 1 WLR 3273, at [41].

[171] *Re W (A Child)* [2016] EWCA Civ 793, [2017] 1 WLR 889, at [68]. Discussed further in Chapter 6.

(3) Protecting Children in Residential Care

(A) Protection from Exploitation and Abuse

The state's intervention to protect children from abusive parents must not lead the children into more danger than before. For the child who can neither return home nor live with anyone in the extended family, residential care is normally rejected in favour of the more natural family life provided by long-term foster carers or adoptive parents.[172] But there are large numbers of children for whom foster care would be quite unsuitable. Some children do not want a family placement, perhaps because they have had repeated bad experiences of foster care; others have complex personal and social difficulties with a need for expert treatment in a residential setting; some are a danger to themselves or others and require secure accommodation; and there are those whose abusive experiences make it undesirable to place them in another family.[173] These are the children who need care in children's homes.

The numerous inquiries into abuse of children that took place in residential care in the late 1980s and 1990s, recording the systematic abuse of children by members of staff, gave the impression that state residential care often subjects abused children to re-abuse.[174] These drew attention to the poor management, recruitment and selection procedures of care staff, which allowed small groups of paedophiles to gain access to vulnerable children. As Utting chillingly pointed out:

> Persistent sexual abusers are a scourge of childhood ... sexual terrorists whose success depends, paradoxically, on their capacity to ingratiate themselves with adults and children. An outstanding characteristic is their ability to establish themselves in roles in which they are trusted to excess as friend, colleague or employee. Their subsequent activities are concealed by suborning, blackmailing and threatening their victims.[175]

These findings are further reinforced by later investigations, including those of the Independent Inquiry into Child Sexual Abuse, which documented the widespread sexual abuse of children in residential homes, from the 1960s to 2000s, primarily by those who were employed to care for them.[176] Despite

---

[172] In March 2019, of the 78,150 looked-after children in England, 58 per cent were in foster homes with a carer who was not a relative/friend, 13 per cent were in a foster home with relatives/friends, 12 per cent were in residential care and 7 per cent were at home with parents.

[173] D. Berridge and I. Brodie (1998) pp. 90ff; I. Sinclair *et al.* (2007) pp. 148–9.

[174] Inter alia: W. Hughes (1985) (the 'Kincora' report) – sexual abuse in Northern Ireland boys' hostels; G. Williams and J. Macreadie (1992) (the 'Ty Mawr' report) – ill-treatment of children in the home leading to incidents of suicide and self-harm; A. Levy and B. Kahan (1991) (.the 'Pindown' report) – regime adopted in some Staffordshire residential homes involving isolation, humiliation and confrontation of the children in their care; R. Waterhouse (2000) – sexual abuse of children in children's homes in North Wales. See also the literature review by B. Gallagher (1999).

[175] W. Utting (1997) paras 9.1–9.2.

[176] E.g. A. Jay *et al.* (2019) concerning abuse in Nottinghamshire; the report also covers the abuse of children placed with foster carers.

persistent reports of abuse over decades, the failure of LAs to respond effect-ively left further generations of children to suffer at the hands of the perpet-rators. As the Inquiry's report into abuse in Nottinghamshire found:

> It was as if anyone could carry out the important work of being a substitute parent to damaged children. In some instances, a sexualised culture existed in residential homes, with staff behaving wholly inappropriately towards children, paving the way for sexual abuse. Whilst set standards of conduct and child protection procedures were put in place, there was little proper training provided to help staff understand their employers' requirements, nor action taken against those who did not comply. Staff ignored these standards and procedures with impunity.[177]

Abuse of children in residential care is not only perpetrated by those who should be caring for them. Reports into child sexual exploitation, most notably the Jay inquiry into abuse in Rotherham, have documented the targeting of children's homes by perpetrators and the failure of LAs to recognise the abuse and safeguard children from it.[178]

The evidence demonstrates that children in care are often at heightened risk of becoming victims of abuse. Detection of abuse may be hampered because the emotional needs of many children in residential homes make them particularly vulnerable 'to the flattering attention of improperly motivated adults'.[179] Children's prior experiences of neglect and abuse can also make it especially difficult to identify inappropriate adult behaviour and perceive that their actions are abusive.[180] Children in residential homes further face considerable barriers to disclosing abuse. Many feel isolated in care and do not have a trusted adult to whom they can turn.[181] Others fear the consequences that disclosure may have, either in reprisals from the perpetrator or in disruption to their placement and relationships.[182] Many children do not have confidence that their disclosure will be believed and are concerned that staff will dismiss their complaints as fantasy or lies. Repeated investigations into abuse have found that too often these fears have been well-founded and that reports which were received were not acted upon by those who should have kept children safe.

The expense of residential child care, combined with the scandals of the 1970s, 1980s and 1990s, led to the closure of many children's homes. Since then, the landscape of children's residential care has changed considerably. Far fewer children in care are now accommodated in children's homes and those who are tend to be in smaller units, with a typical home having places for four children.[183] The regulation of homes has also transformed in response to the safeguarding failings outlined above. The Care Standards Act 2000 sought to impose uniform regulation on a previously fragmented sector. Children's

---

[177] Ibid. p. iii.   [178] A. Jay (2014).
[179] Ibid. para. 8.36. See also R. Waterhouse (2000) para. 29.33.   [180] A. Jay et al. (2019) p. 122.
[181] Discussed further below.   [182] A. Jay et al. (2019) p. 121.
[183] M. Narey (2016) pp. 6–9: in the 1970s, around 40 per cent of children in care were in residential homes; by 2015, the equivalent figure was 12 per cent.

homes are required to be registered[184] and to meet detailed standards,[185] and are subject to regulation by Ofsted. While this is a significant improvement on the previous situation, there remain serious concerns about gaps in the regulatory system for children's homes. Although failure to register a children's home is a criminal offence,[186] a significant minority of homes are unregistered and operating illegally, whether unintentionally or in a deliberate attempt to avoid regulation.[187] Such is the shortage of places, particularly in relation to homes providing secure accommodation, that guidance has been issued to the judiciary as to how to respond to applications to place a child in an unregistered secure children's home.[188] A further gap in the regulatory system is that supported accommodation for older children is not subject to the same system of regulation and inspection as applies to care homes and which is mandatory for placements for children under 16.[189] While LAs are under a duty to ensure that this unregulated accommodation is 'suitable',[190] it is clear that in many cases it is not. Young people placed in these unregulated homes are often housed alongside adults and exposed to significant risks, including drug-taking, sexual exploitation, violence and exploitation by criminal gangs.[191] In these cases, the state is often failing in its role as corporate parent and in its obligations to provide care and assistance according to the child's best interests under the CRC.[192] The government has set out plans to introduce mandatory standards, overseen through Ofsted inspection, for supported accommodation for 16- and 17-year-olds.[193] If implemented, these plans should mean that all forms of residential placement for children in care will be subject to regulation and inspection, a change which, it is hoped, will bring an end to the egregious failures in current unregulated provision.[194]

---

[184] Care Standards Act 2000, ss 11 and 12.

[185] Children's Homes (England) Regulations 2015 (SI 2015/541).

[186] Care Standards Act 2000, s. 11(1).   [187] Ofsted (2020) p. 41.

[188] Practice Guidance: Placements in unregistered children's homes in England or unregistered care home services in Wales, 18 November 2019: while the placement may be authorised, the failure to register should be rectified as soon as possible and the application to do so should be made within 7 days. The shortage of secure accommodation places and judicial response is considered further below.

[189] The Care Planning, Placement and Case Review (England) (Amendment) Regulations 2021 (SI 2021/161) prohibit the placement of children under the age of 16 in unregulated accommodation. It remains open to the High Court to use the inherent jurisdiction to authorise unregulated placements for children under 16 that would otherwise be prohibited by the regulations: *Tameside MBC* v. *AM* [2021] EWHC 2472 (Fam); *A Mother* v. *Derby City Council* [2021] EWCA Civ 1867.

[190] CA 1989, s. 22(6)(d); Care Planning, Placement and Case Review (England) Regulations 2010 (SI 2010/959), reg. 27 and Sch. 6.

[191] Discussed further in Chapter 10. Children's Commissioner (2020a) p. 21 includes reports from the police that some providers of unregulated accommodation are affiliated to major organised crime networks and use the unregulated nature of provision in order to exploit children. See also R. Crellin and I. Pona (2015).

[192] CRC, Arts 20 and 3.   [193] DfE (2021b).

[194] Although some within the sector argue that the government should go further and include all children, of all ages, within the current regulations for provision of care. A challenge to the

A shift in the provision of residential care can be seen in the reduction in the number of homes run directly by LAs; indeed, more than a quarter of LAs no longer run children's homes at all.[195] In place of direct LA care, there has been a significant rise in the number of privately run homes. Around three-quarters of homes are run by private companies, many as part of larger chains of homes.[196] While there is nothing in the CRC to require states to provide care directly, the Committee on the Rights of the Child has made it clear that the involvement of the private sector must be regulated in a way that does not compromise the rights of the children affected.[197] There are obvious concerns that the best interests of children can be displaced by businesses competing in a market place for profit.[198] Private care homes are subject to the same regulations as those run by LAs and it appears from inspection reports that there is little difference in the quality of provision at care homes provided by each sector.[199] Nonetheless, given the increasing importance of larger chains of private homes, it is of concern that Ofsted is confined to inspecting individual homes and has no power to review the overall management structure to ensure that children's safeguarding and best interests are sufficiently protected.[200] The greatest concern, however, is unregulated provision, which is not currently subject to mandatory standards or inspection by Ofsted.[201] Private organisations are currently responsible for providing nearly three-quarters of unregulated placements.[202] There is evidence that the lack of oversight has been exploited by companies with little or no knowledge of children in care.[203] A further concern about the extent of reliance on private provision is that homes are increasingly located in cheaper areas of the country, rather than planned to meet the best interests of the children likely to need their services.[204] Children accommodated in private children's homes are much more likely to be placed out of their home area.[205] While some children will benefit from living away from the source of past harm, children placed out of area are often isolated and particularly vulnerable to exploitation and trafficking.[206] There appears to be little in the way of national planning for provision based on the needs of children; instead, the location and sufficiency of placements depends on the fragmented market place.

---

government's decision not to do so was unsuccessful: *R (Article 39)* v. *Secretary of State for Education* [2022] EWHC 589 (Admin).

[195] APPG (2019) p. 14.   [196] Ofsted (2020) p. 27; Children's Commissioner (2020b).

[197] Committee on the Rights of the Child (2013) esp. paras 33–4.

[198] Children's Commissioner (2020b) highlights the lack of data on how the private market is working.

[199] M. Narey (2016) p. 17; Children's Commissioner (2020b) pp. 22–3.

[200] Ofsted (2020) p. 27. In 2019, there were thirty-five chains running ten or more homes each, together accounting for nearly half of privately run homes.

[201] As noted above, the government intends to introduce a new scheme of standards and inspection for this sector: DfE (2021b).

[202] Children's Commissioner (2020a) p. 21.   [203] Ibid.

[204] Children's Commissioner (2019b).   [205] APPG (2019) pp. 13–14.   [206] APPG (2019).

Children in residential care are among the most vulnerable in society. Over decades, the state has failed many of these children by not only failing to protect them from the most serious harm, but by providing the conditions in which children have been further exploited and abused. Improvements in regulation and a greater awareness of the scale of the problem have provided some reasons for optimism. Yet, too many children remain vulnerable in a system often focused on making the best of the limited resources available, rather than providing the best for the children who need its services.

(B) Secure Accommodation and Deprivation of Liberty

The shortage of appropriate placements has caused particularly acute problems for children who are assessed as needing secure accommodation. The use of secure accommodation is normally seen as a fairly drastic remedy reserved for older children.[207] These children are extremely vulnerable and are usually at risk of causing serious harm to themselves or others. In these circumstances, a secure placement can be the best, or only, means of providing safety and meeting the child's complex needs. Nonetheless, it is clearly a grave matter to deprive any child of their liberty, particularly in circumstances in which they have not been convicted of a crime and do not meet the criteria to be detained under mental health legislation. The power to lock children up 'for their own good' requires the most careful scrutiny to justify the serious interference with the child's right to liberty and to ensure that the conditions respect the child's welfare, dignity and human rights. The statutory means by which such placements can be judicially authorised is through a secure accommodation order (SAO),[208] the use of which is subject to detailed regulations and guidance.[209] There is, however, an extreme shortage of placements that meet the requirements for an SAO and it is frequently not possible to find a place for children assessed as needing one.[210] Courts are increasingly faced with applications by LAs seeking authorisation to deprive children of their liberty outside of the statutory scheme through the use of the inherent jurisdiction.[211] Many of these placements fall far short of meeting the child's needs and some are so inadequate that they risk breaching the child's rights, particularly under Articles 5 and 8 of the ECHR.[212] These cases present courts and LAs with an acute

---

[207] Children (Secure Accommodation) Regulations 1991 (SI 1991/1505), reg. 4: no child under the age of 13 can be made the subject of an SAO without the express permission of the Secretary of State.

[208] CA 1989, s. 25.

[209] Children (Secure Accommodation) Regulations 1991 (SI 1991/1505); DfE (2014), discussed further below.

[210] Whereas in 2003 there were thirty Secure Children's Homes (SCHs) in England and Wales, in 2020 only thirteen exist. Children's Commissioner (2020c) p. 42: in June 2019, thirty children a day were waiting for a place.

[211] E.g. *Lancashire County Council* v. *G* [2020] EWHC 2828 (Fam), [2021] 2 FLR 34.

[212] E.g. *North Yorkshire County Council* v. *C* [2021] EWHC 2171 (Fam).

dilemma between authorising an inadequate placement that may breach the child's rights, or leaving that child in a desperate state knowing that there is a risk of imminent, serious harm. The judiciary have given increasingly stark warnings of the seriousness of the circumstances facing children in this precarious situation.[213]

The law underpinning the use of SAOs was considered in detail by the Court of Appeal in *Re B (A Child) (Secure Accommodation Order)*, in a judgment that stressed the need for careful attention to the child's welfare and rights, as well as the detail of the statutory scheme.[214] The statutory requirements are relatively straightforward. An SAO allows looked-after children[215] to be placed in 'secure accommodation',[216] which should, if it is a secure children's home, be approved by the Secretary of State for such use.[217] It is clear that an SAO can *only* be obtained in two circumstances.[218] First, it may be used to secure 'a child with a history of absconding if he or she is likely to abscond from non-secure accommodation and in the event of doing so is likely to suffer significant harm'. Case law indicates that absconding refers to a young person 'escaping indefinitely from an imposed regime, as opposed to deliberately absenting herself for a limited period'.[219] Second, an SAO may also be made if it appears that if the child is 'kept in any other type of accommodation', they are likely to injure themselves or others. As this ground makes clear, restricting the liberty of a child or young person may simply be to protect the public. This raises the difficult question of whether it is possible to justify imposing such severe restrictions on a child to protect the interests of others rather than those of the child. Although it might be thought that SAOs concern the upbringing of the children subject to them, it

---

[213] E.g. *Re X (A Child)* [2017] EWHC 2036 (Fam), [2018] 1 FLR 1054; *Lancashire County Council v. G* [2020] EWHC 2828 (Fam), [2021] 2 FLR 34; *Re T (A Child)* [2021] UKSC 35, [2021] 3 WLR 643; *An NHS Trust* v. *HT* [2022] EWHC 719 (Fam).

[214] [2019] EWCA Civ 2025, [2020] 2 WLR 568; the 'relevant criteria' for a court hearing an SAO application are summarised at [98].

[215] Or those who fall within the additional categories specified by the Secretary of State: CA 1989, s. 25(1) and (7)(a). Children (Secure Accommodation) Regulations, reg. 7 extends s. 25 to certain children in hospital and care homes.

[216] The meaning of secure accommodation has been the subject of extensive obiter consideration in the Supreme Court. Lady Black considered that secure accommodation is that which is designed for, or has the primary purpose of, restriction of liberty and not to accommodation that is being used to impose a restriction of liberty, but was not for the purpose of doing so: *Re T (A Child)* [2021] UKSC 35, [2021] 3 WLR 643, at [130]–[141]. See also *Re D (A Child)* [2019] UKSC 42, [2019] 1 WLR 5403, at [91]–[115] and [2019] EWCA Civ 2025, [2020] 2 WLR 568, at [46]–[58].

[217] Children (Secure Accommodation) Regulations, reg. 3.

[218] CA 1989, s. 25(1): an SAO may not be made regarding a child who is being looked after by an LA unless it appears that: (a) he has a history of absconding and he is likely to abscond from any other description of accommodation, and if he absconds, he is likely to suffer significant harm; or (b) if he is kept in any other type of accommodation, he is likely to injure himself or other persons. See: M. Parry (2000); J. Fortin (2001) pp. 257–60.

[219] *Re W (A Child) (Secure Accommodation Order)* [2016] EWCA Civ 804, [2016] 4 WLR 159, at [21]–[22].

has long been held that, although relevant, the welfare principle does not govern applications for SAOs.[220] Arguably, this interpretation of the wording of section 25 is unduly restrictive that these are draconian orders and that welfare will normally be paramount in deciding where a child will live. Further, as Lady Black has observed, any deprivation of liberty under the Mental Capacity Act 2005, for those over 16, will only be endorsed if it is in the best interests of the person detained.[221] In these circumstances, she is surely correct to find that it would be surprising if the court's welfare role were to be displaced in SAO cases 'beyond a relatively circumscribed group of children whose circumstances make this unavoidable'.[222] In *Re B (A Child) (Secure Accommodation Order)*, Baker LJ similarly found that welfare was 'plainly of great importance' and that both the LA and the court must 'consider whether the proposed placement would safeguard and promote the child's welfare'.[223] It seems clear that although welfare is not strictly paramount, and may be outweighed by the need to protect others, it will always play an important role in determining an SAO application. In addition to the importance of assessing the child's welfare, the Court of Appeal stressed that the court should expressly consider the child's rights and whether the proposed order was proportionate to the interference with those rights.[224] This exercise throws into doubt official guidance which states that although restricting a child's liberty 'is a serious step which should only be taken where the needs of the child cannot be met by a more suitable placement elsewhere', it should *not* be considered as a 'last resort'.[225] As a number of judges have observed, it is difficult to justify imposing draconian restrictions on a child's liberty if alternative means of meeting the child's needs are available.[226] In this sense, the use of secure accommodation is indeed a 'last resort'. This approach is consistent with the requirements of Article 37 of the CRC, which states that the detention of a child 'shall be used only as a measure of last resort and for the shortest appropriate period of time'. This means that the application for an SAO must[227] be fully justified,

---

[220] *Re M (A Minor) (Secure Accommodation Order)* [1995] 1 FLR 418.

[221] *Re D (A Child)* [2019] UKSC 42, [2019] 1 WLR 5403, at [101].   [222] Ibid.

[223] *Re B (A Child) (Secure Accommodation Order)* [2019] EWCA Civ 2025, [2020] 2 WLR 568, at [72].

[224] Ibid. at [81]–[97]. These rights are further analysed below.

[225] DfE (2014) paras 40–1. This change was first introduced in the 2008 version of the guidance in response to concerns that secure accommodation orders were seen in such a negative light that they were not being used in circumstances in which they would be appropriate and offered the best solution for meeting the child's needs: Jane Held Consulting Ltd (2006) para. 9.3. The current guidance stresses that secure accommodation can be a positive option for some children.

[226] *Re B (A Child) (Secure Accommodation Order)* [2019] EWCA Civ 2025, [2020] 2 WLR 568, at [90]–[91]; *Re D (A Child)* [2019] UKSC 42, [2019] 1 WLR 5403, at [114]; *London Borough of Southwark v. F* [2017] EWHC 2189 (Fam), at [8]–[9].

[227] See s. 25(4): if the court 'determines that any such criteria (the grounds set out by s. 25(3)) are satisfied, it *shall* make an order authorising the child to be kept in secure accommodation and specify the maximum period for which he may be so kept' (emphasis added). Although as these

not only in terms of what the order is seeking to achieve, but also in terms of the duration requested.[228] The child's progress while in secure accommodation must be monitored closely by the LA, since if the grounds for the order having been made are no longer present, the order itself cannot be enforced or relied on and the young person has a right to be released.[229]

There have been persistent doubts as to how far the SAO regime can be reconciled with Article 5 of the ECHR, which only permits deprivation of liberty in limited circumstances. Those considering that children should not be confined at all under civil orders had hoped that section 25 of the Children Act 1989 could itself be challenged under the HRA. These hopes were dashed by the Court of Appeal in *Re K (Secure Accommodation Order: Right to Liberty)*.[230] It controversially rejected the argument that section 25 is too widely drafted to fall within any of the exemptions to Article 5 of the ECHR and is therefore incompatible with its terms.[231] The Court of Appeal ruled that as long as the secure unit to which the particular child is sent provides properly supervised educational provision, the SAO will fall under the Article 5(1)(d) exemption.[232] They clearly considered that by assessing potential infringements of Article 5 on a purely ad hoc basis, they could avoid declaring section 25 incompatible with the ECHR. The Court of Appeal's obvious anxiety to uphold a well-established legislative provision led them to ignore the central question: 'whether section 25 – as drafted – is sufficiently precise to have the quality of law which the ECHR requires.'[233] This is a surprising interpretation. As drafted, the provision plainly fails to prevent the grant of an order falling outside the boundaries of the Article 5(1)(d) exemption, since there is nothing in its wording which refers to an SAO being made for the purposes of educational supervision.[234]

---

criteria include assessment of the child's welfare and the justification for interference with her rights, this section preserves greater judicial discretion than might at first appear to be the case.

[228] Children (Secure Accommodation) Regulations 1991 (SI 1991/1505), regs 11–12: the maximum duration of an SAO is 3 months, extendable by a further 6 months. See *Re W (A Minor) (Secure Accommodation Order)* [1993] 1 FLR 692: Booth J criticised the magistrates for making a secure accommodation order lasting 3 months without clarifying why this was better than a 5-week order, as recommended by the guardian *ad litem*.

[229] *LM* v. *Essex County Council* [1999] 1 FLR 988, per Holman J, at 994–5; *A Borough Council* v. *E* [2021] EWHC 2699 (Fam). See also DfE (2014) [50].

[230] [2001] 1 FLR 526.   [231] J. Masson (2002).

[232] I.e. covering cases where liberty is restrained 'for the purpose of educational supervision'.

[233] AIRE Centre (2001) pp. 4–5.

[234] Ibid. p. 5: according to Strasbourg jurisprudence, e.g. *Huvig* v. *France* (1990) 12 EHRR 528, this is an insufficient delineation of legal discretion. Dame Elizabeth Butler-Sloss P considered that express reference to education was not necessary as there was a statutory obligation to provide education to all children under 16: *Re K (Secure Accommodation Order: Right to Liberty)* [2001] 1 FLR 526, at [36]. This overlooks the fact that Education Act 1996, s. 562 provides that the duties under the Act do not apply to persons detained under an order of the court. The Apprenticeship, Skills, Children and Learning Act 2009, s. 49 would remove children detained under an SAO from this exemption, but the provision has not been brought into force in England.

Despite continued doubts as to its reasoning, *Re K* remains authority for the compatibility of the SAO regime with Article 5 of the ECHR.[235] This does not prevent young people detained under an SAO from challenging the specific order and regime that has been applied to them. An SAO that does not ensure educational provision prima facie infringes the child's rights under Article 5 and can be challenged.[236] Such challenges are made more difficult by the broad definition adopted in *Re K*, which found that educational supervision in Article 5 went beyond classroom teaching and extended to 'the general development of the child's physical, intellectual, emotional, social and behavioural abilities'.[237] While there is some support in ECtHR jurisprudence for this wide definition,[238] later case law requires meaningful educational provision for this exemption to be effective.[239] Further, although Article 5 does not expressly mention proportionality, there is a strong argument that a regime that is disproportionate to the legitimate exemption for the detention would be unlawful.[240] The particular regime proposed under an SAO may also constitute a disproportionate interference with the child's ECHR Article 8 rights, particularly if the child is placed far from family members[241] or is subject to conditions that fail to meet their needs or violate their privacy and dignity.[242] Finding this balance can be difficult in practice, especially if the child is intent on causing themselves harm, so giving rise to positive obligations on the part of the state to protect the child under Article 3, or even 2, of the ECHR.[243] The seriousness of the circumstances of children subject to SAOs requires both LAs and courts to give careful scrutiny to the proportionality of the measures proposed.[244]

The courts are increasingly faced with applications relating to children in desperate circumstances who are not eligible for an SAO either because they fall outside of the criteria or for whom no approved secure place is

---

[235] *Re B (A Child) (Secure Accommodation Order)* [2019] EWCA Civ 2025, [2020] 2 WLR 568, at [80].

[236] *Re K (Secure Accommodation Order: Right to Liberty)* [2001] 1 FLR 526, per Dame Elizabeth Butler-Sloss P, at [42]–[43].

[237] Ibid. at [107].

[238] *Koniarska* v. *United Kingdom*, App. No. 33670/96, 12 October 2000, unreported, an admissibility decision.

[239] *Blokhin* v. *Russia* [2016] ECHR 300 (GC), esp. at [167].

[240] *Re B (A Child) (Secure Accommodation Order)* [2019] EWCA Civ 2025, [2020] 2 WLR 568, at [82].

[241] Children's Commissioner (2019c) p. 28: 91 per cent of children in secure children's homes were placed outside of their county.

[242] *Lancashire County Council* v. *G* [2021] EWHC 244, at [22]–[23]: concerned a placement which not only failed to give the child the therapeutic treatment she needed, but also created further risks for her mental health. See also *North Yorkshire County Council* v. *C* [2021] EWHC 2171 (Fam), esp. at [30]. These cases were decided under the inherent jurisdiction, but the same reasoning would apply to cases under an SAO.

[243] Discussed in *Re T (A Child)* [2021] UKSC 35, [2021] 3 WLR 643, at [175]–[176].

[244] *Re B (A Child) (Secure Accommodation Order)* [2019] EWCA Civ 2025, [2020] 2 WLR 568, at [81]–[90].

available.[245] Given the grave risks that many of these children face, the courts have frequently resorted to the inherent jurisdiction to authorise a deprivation of liberty. Although this practice provides an immediate solution to the severe shortages of secure placements, its use is far from ideal as a substitute for a statutory regime. In many cases, the proposed placement is not approved and regulated for provision of secure accommodation and in others the placement is an unregistered children's home, meaning that the provider of that home is committing an offence.[246] The courts have put in place procedural safeguards and practice guidance on how to deal with such applications,[247] but cannot provide an adequate alternative to a regulatory system with properly designed and inspected secure placements. The Supreme Court has confirmed that the inherent jurisdiction remains available for such applications, despite the existence of the statutory regime.[248] It has also found that the inherent jurisdiction constitutes a 'procedure prescribed by law' through which an Article 5-compliant deprivation of liberty can be approved. Nonetheless, the Supreme Court expressed 'deep anxiety' that it had been put in the position of approving such an 'imperfect stop gap' in the face of the 'enduring well-known scandal of the disgraceful and utterly shaming lack of proper provision for children who require approved secure accommodation'.[249]

The shortage of proper provision for children in desperate circumstances means that courts are being asked to approve placements that not only fail to meet the child's needs, but also impose a regime that is degrading and dangerous. One such example is *An NHS Trust* v. *HT*,[250] in which the application concerned a 14-year-old '*acutely* vulnerable child with *highly* complex needs' who had been detained on a locked paediatric ward solely for her safety and not for the purposes of medical treatment. She was constantly under the supervision of a rotating staff of two security guards and two carers, all provided by a private company. She was frequently subject to chemical and physical restraint by multiple unfamiliar adults and denied any privacy, even while using the toilet. Unsurprisingly, Mr Justice MacDonald concluded that the regime was a breach of her Article 5 rights and that to approve it would 'be to *grossly* pervert the application of best interests principle'.[251] Worryingly, this

---

[245] Children's Commissioner (2020c) p. 37: Cafcass records show that in 2019–20 there were nearly as many inherent jurisdiction applications for deprivation of liberty as applications for SAOs.

[246] *Re T (A Child)* [2021] UKSC 35, [2021] 3 WLR 643, at [143]–[149].

[247] In *A-F (Children)* [2018] EWHC 138 (Fam), [2019] Fam 45, at [46]–[56]: Munby P set out detailed requirements for an ECHR Art. 5-compliant process, including review by a judge at least once every 12 months. See also Practice Guidance: Placements in unregistered children's homes in England or unregistered care home services in Wales, 18 November 2019.

[248] *Re T (A Child)* [2021] UKSC 35, [2021] 3 WLR 643.

[249] Ibid. at [163] and [166]. See also [178] and [185].

[250] [2022] EWHC 719 (Fam), at [2] (emphasis in the original).

[251] Ibid. at [39] (emphasis in the original).

case is far from unique. In a number of recent cases, judges have concluded that they have no choice but to refuse to approve placements despite the absence of a satisfactory alternative for a child who is at grave risk.[252] In *An NHS Trust* v. *HT*, a month had elapsed between the child being detained and the application being made to the court, despite the fact that she had a social worker allocated to her. The Children's Commissioner had highlighted the concern that many more 'invisible children' may be detained without any judicial oversight due to the legal complexity of the current regime and a lack of understanding in LAs as to when authorisation must be sought.[253]

The egregious failings considered in this section demonstrate the obstacles to securing the rights of children who are dependent on the state. Despite the clear commitment of the courts to doing the best for these children and upholding their rights, there is a limit to what they can achieve in the face of a failure to provide the resources that are desperately needed. Although some cases demonstrate failings by LAs, in most cases social workers are doing all that they can to find an adequate place to meet the child's needs. In these circumstances, litigation with LAs responsible for individual children does little to address the root cause of the problem. It is difficult to avoid the conclusion that the state has systemically failed to meet its international obligations to secure the physical and mental health of children within its care, to protect them from abuse or to ensure that children are not deprived of their liberty unlawfully or arbitrarily.[254]

(4) The Child's Own Perspectives

(A) Consulting Children

As Article 12 of the CRC makes clear, children should be consulted on all matters affecting them, and due weight should be given to their views, in accordance with their age and maturity. Most parents recognise the sense of listening to their children and respecting their views. The LA, like any other good parent, should respect the children in their care and consult them over their future upbringing. The CA 1989 acknowledges this and encourages social workers to treat children as individuals and involve them in decision-making about their future.[255] The government has repeatedly emphasised that social workers should take this obligation seriously.[256]

---

[252] In *Wigan MBC* v. *W* [2021] EWHC 1982 (Fam), at [59]–[64], in similar circumstances to *An NHS Trust* v. *HT*, Mr Justice MacDonald found 'it would border on the obscene to use a protective jurisdiction to continue Y's current bleak and dangerous situation simply because those with responsibility for making proper provision for vulnerable children in this jurisdiction have failed to discharge that responsibility'. See also the similar case of *Nottinghamshire County Council* v. *LH* [2021] EWHC 2584 (Fam).

[253] Children's Commissioner (2019c).   [254] See esp. CRC, Arts 24, 25, 27, 37 and 39.

[255] E.g. CA 1989, ss 17(4A), 20(6), 22(4)–(5), 38(6), 43(8), 44(7), 46(3) and Sch. 3, paras 4(4) and 5(5).

[256] E.g. DfE (2021a) paras 1.10–1.14 and 5.31.

Although there have been improvements in the extent to which social workers comply with this duty, many children indicate that they are given no choice at all over foster placements,[257] with others feeling that although they are asked for their views, they are not really being listened to.[258] Legislation imposes on all LAs a duty to provide a range of accommodation sufficient to meet the needs of all looked-after children within their areas.[259] Notably, it does not direct LAs to give looked-after children a veto over what placement is offered to them; instead, the accompanying guidance stresses the importance of ascertaining and considering the views of the child in planning and reviewing the child's placement. While placing looked-after children in placements without any choice may be attributable to shortages in foster care, sudden changes in placement with no warning or consultation is far less excusable, but occurs all too frequently. Research by the Children's Commissioner with young people who had experienced out of area placements and frequent changes in placement found that they 'overwhelmingly felt they had little or no say in decisions made about them, especially where they ended up living'.[260] Unsurprisingly, these young people felt disempowered and mistrustful, often connecting this lack of trust to subsequent deterioration in their mental health.[261]

A common theme of commentaries on the shortcomings of state care is the fact that looked-after children lack the individual attention of an adult committed to them, often due to the shortage of social workers.[262] Children who run into problems with their placements find that the social worker whom they have got to know has left or cancels visits, or is simply unavailable to talk matters over with.[263] They also commonly complain about not being able to speak to their social worker alone without their foster carers being present.[264] It has often been suggested that looked-after children also need a consistent person to act as their 'champion' or mentor, to ensure that their views are heard and that agreed decisions are implemented.[265] Legislation[266] to ensure that looked-after children are visited in their placements and are then seen by an independent visitor, away from their carers, should go some way to meeting this concern. While the legislation does not match the objectives of appointing an individual champion, it is a genuine attempt to improve looked-after

---

[257] R. Morgan (2006a) p. 11: just under half the children and young people had no choice of placement.

[258] Ibid. pp. 6–10; DfES (2006a) para. 4.22. See also *R v. Devon County Council, ex p O (Adoption)* [1997] 2 FLR 388: Scott Baker J (at 396–7) criticised the LA for failing to discover the views of a 9-year-old child about its plans to remove him from his foster carers with whom he had lived for 2.5 years.

[259] CA 1989, s. 22G.   [260] Children's Commissioner (2019b) p. 11; R. Morgan (2006a) p. 6.

[261] Children's Commissioner (2019b) p. 11.

[262] The Children's Commissioner (2019b) found that almost all of the children interviewed had experienced a change of social worker.

[263] J. Timms and J. Thoburn (2003) pp. 16–17; R. Morgan (2006b) pp. 9–16; CSCI (2006b) p. 33.

[264] R. Morgan (2006a) pp. 17–18.   [265] Inter alia: DH (1996) p. 31, (1998) pp. 26–7.

[266] CA 1989, s. 23ZA.

children's feeling of powerlessness when entering the state system of care.[267] Nonetheless, as discussed below, the independent visitor scheme suffers from poor implementation and shortages of available advisors. Similarly, legislation strengthening the role of Independent Reviewing Officers (IROs) should also ensure that looked-after children feel more supported if they are unhappy over decisions being made about their future care, but many children are simply unaware that they exist.[268] In the absence of an advocate who is known and trusted by the child, many children struggle to have their voices heard.

(B) Making Complaints

Despite looked-after children having very clear views about how their lives could be improved, they often find it difficult to complain about any aspect of their care.[269] They should be informed about how to use the statutory complaints procedure,[270] but the assumption that they will feel able to do so underestimates the hurdles that they confront. This is understandable in the case of children in foster placements, because doing so would make it more difficult to continue living with their carers.[271] Many of those in residential care have emotional and/or behavioural difficulties, and a significant proportion may have been sexually abused. Countless inquiry reports find that, when re-abused in a residential setting, few children complain, fearing that complaints will go unheeded and that they may be victimised by members of staff loyal to the abuser.[272] The children in North Wales who did have the courage to complain found that either they or the member of staff involved were moved from the home, but:

> otherwise the complaint would be stifled or lost in the mists of bureaucracy. There was compelling evidence that a number of those in positions of authority did all they could to ensure that complaints did not get out of the system or at least outside the confines of the home.[273]

Research indicates that children still try repeatedly to get social work staff to deal with their concerns, but feel that they are not being given due weight.[274] The current three-tiered complaints system was introduced with the intention of providing children with a more accessible system[275] within clear

---

[267] J. Timms and J. Thoburn (2003) pp. 14–15.   [268] Children's Commissioner (2019b) p. 12.
[269] R. Morgan (2005) p. 6.
[270] CA 1989, ss 26(3) and 24D. Residents in children's homes can also use in-house complaints procedures.
[271] R. Morgan (2005) p. 6.
[272] Staff may be tempted to 'turn a blind eye' to what is happening or to minimise or rationalise it. See W. Utting (1997) para. 18.10; R. Waterhouse (2000) para. 29.50.
[273] E. Ryder (2000) p. 408. See also R. Waterhouse (2000) para. 29.50.
[274] A. Pithouse and C. Crowley (2007) p. 208.
[275] DfES (2006b); the Children Act 1989 Representations Procedure (England) Regulations 2006 (SI 2006/1738).

time-limits.[276] The third (review panel) stage was designed to inject independence from internal LA procedures into the process.[277] Nevertheless, children find the differences between the various stages of the process bewildering,[278] with the various officers involved surely adding extra confusion.[279] As a result, only a small proportion of complaints under the process are made by or on behalf of children. Other complaints are brought by parents, family and friends, meaning that children's own interests can be lost within the bureaucratic process.[280] Complainants are entitled to assistance with making complaints and to independent advocacy services,[281] which may prevent some children from giving up in disgust at the system's complexity. As a last resort, some may find their way to the local government ombudsmen who investigate complaints of maladministration causing injustice. Thus, an ombudsman may assist if the LA has defaulted in the way it carried out one of its functions or in the way it failed to do so. If the complaint is upheld, the ombudsman will recommend a remedy, normally involving returning the complainant to the position he or she should have been in, had the maladministration not occurred. If this is impossible, the ombudsman will normally recommend some financial recompense, which may be placed in trust for the child.

Increasing numbers of LAs have appointed children's rights officers, whose task is to promote good practice among those working with children looked after by the LA. Part of their job is to ensure that children know what rights they have and how to use the statutory complaints procedure, to help them express their views over decisions they object to and to provide formal advocacy if required. Not all children would, however, feel able to trust anyone who is an LA employee with disclosures about members of that LA's staff. The 'independent visitor' scheme provides unpaid volunteers, with no standing within the LA, who are appointed to visit, advise and befriend the child in question. LAs are under a statutory duty to appoint an independent visitor if it would be in the child's best interests to do so.[282] Statutory guidance recommends that this should be done if communication between the child and her parents has become infrequent or the parents have not visited the child for more than 1 year.[283] The LA should also consider the child's needs, including the distance the child is from

---

[276] SI 2006/1738, reg. 9: an applicant must complain within 1 year of the grounds arising, although the LA has discretion to consider the complaint after that period has expired. SI 2006/1738, reg. 17: the time-limit for the LA's response time at stage 2 of the procedure is now 90 working days, including 65 days' extension (an increase on previous time-limits), cf. reg. 18: the period within which a complainant must request a review has reduced from 28 working days to 20 working days with no extension.

[277] The review panel must consist of three independent people – SI 2006/1738, reg. 19.

[278] R. Morgan (2005) p. 6.

[279] At stage 2 of the process, the LA Complaints Manager appoints an Investigating Officer (IO) to investigate and report on the complaint; these findings are considered by an Adjudicating Officer (AO).

[280] LGO (2015).   [281] SI 2006/1738, reg. 11.   [282] CA 1989, s. 23ZB.

[283] Ibid. Sch. 2, para. 17(1) and (2).

home and whether a child in a residential setting would benefit from a more individualised relationship.[284] Demand from children wishing to use the scheme far outstrips supply, with two-thirds of LAs operating a waiting list and some failing to operate the scheme despite the statutory obligation to do so.[285]

(5) State Accountability for Failures in Care

(A) The Background

Hindsight is a wonderful thing. Social workers, police officers, children's guardians and even the courts would all benefit enormously from having a crystal ball when faced with taking decisions over protecting children. Often, such decisions have to be reached rapidly and in harrowing circumstances. Like those of practitioners in any field of work, some are sensible and others turn out to be unwise or plain stupid, but these decisions materially affect a child's future. Children's services authorities are alone obliged by legislation to carry out section 47 investigations and to safeguard and promote the welfare of children within their area who are in need.[286] Ultimately, it is for them to decide whether or not to initiate steps to remove children from their parents and case law makes it plain that sometimes decisions are taken far too late to avert a great deal of suffering.[287]

(B) Children Suing Local Authorities

Some children who have suffered harm as a result of LA action, or inaction, later seek to pursue a private law remedy against the LA. Such actions may offer the best means of obtaining compensation for those who have suffered lasting damage. But monetary compensation is not the only reason for pursuing such claims. Legal action may be viewed as the best means of holding the LA to account and providing a public expression of the wrong done to the claimant.[288] At one time, the prospects for such actions were bleak. The House

---

[284] DfE (2021a) paras 3.261–3.289.   [285] R. Jordan and S. Walker (2019).

[286] I.e. under CA 1989, s. 17(1)(a). See discussion in Chapter 14.

[287] Inter alia: *X (Minors)* v. *Bedfordshire County Council; M (A Minor) and another* v. *Newham London Borough Council and others; E (A Minor)* v. *Dorset County Council; Christmas* v. *Hampshire County Council; Keating* v. *Bromley London Borough Council (X* v. *Bedfordshire County Council)* [1995] 2 AC 633: although fully aware of the appalling abuse and neglect they were suffering, Bedfordshire CC failed for 5 years to intervene to protect five children from further harm at the hands of their parents; *Re E (Care Proceedings: Social Work Practice)* [2000] 2 FLR 254: ineffectual social work intervention spanned 20 years, during which four children were emotionally, physically and sexually abused; *Re F; F* v. *Lambeth London Borough Council* [2002] 1 FLR 217. See also *S (by the Official Solicitor)* v. *Rochdale MBC and another* [2008] EWHC 3283 (Fam), [2009] 1 FLR 1090, at [17]–[22]: unproved allegations made by the OS that the LA had infringed S's rights under ECHR, Arts 3 and 8 by failing to initiate care proceedings.

[288] P. Giliker (2018) explores the use of tort as a response to institutional liability for child sexual abuse.

of Lords' decision in *X* v. *Bedfordshire County Council*[289] indicated that children could not call LAs to account for failing to protect them when they should have done, or for intervening unnecessarily and without sufficient care.[290] Their Lordships had decided that an LA's failure to intervene to protect a child was not a justiciable matter, since it was not just and reasonable for the common law to impose a duty of care in such circumstances. Consequently, authorities could not be sued in negligence by any children they failed to protect, nor could they be sued for breach of their statutory duties. Indeed, the decision gave the unfortunate impression that the whole child protection process had become largely unaccountable.

This gap in LA accountability was eventually partly filled by the combined effect of Strasbourg case law[291] and the HRA 1998.[292] The ECtHR in *Z* v. *United Kingdom*[293] was in no doubt that the neglect and abuse suffered by the children in the *Bedfordshire* case amounted to an infringement of their rights under Article 3.[294] It stressed that state agencies are under a positive obligation to take measures to ensure that children do not suffer abuse of such a severity that it infringes their rights under Article 3 or, indeed, under Article 2.[295] If they fail to do so, as occurred here, the children must be provided with an effective remedy. Because the domestic law of tort excluded liability, the inability of the children to obtain redress against the LA, in the form of an award of compensation, constituted a breach of their right to an effective remedy under Article 13 of the ECHR. It was by then plain that if the suffering was sufficiently serious, a claim could be brought on behalf of a child under the HRA 1998, claiming breach of Article 3.[296] It should, however, be noted that children are not confined to bringing claims under the HRA 1998; rather that the common law has departed from the *Bedfordshire* decision and incorporated the requirements set out in *Z* v. *United Kingdom*. Thus, although the courts have been reluctant to find that a duty of care is owed to parents by those involved in protecting children from abusive behaviour,[297] it seems clear that children are owed a duty of care by all those involved in child protection work,

---

[289] [1995] 2 AC 633.

[290] In the *Newham* case, one of those joined to *X* v. *Bedfordshire*, the LA 's inaccurate identification of the child's sexual abuser as her mother's boyfriend led to their removing the child unnecessarily from home for almost a year.

[291] Inter alia: *TP and KM* v. *United Kingdom* [2001] 2 FLR 549; *Z* v. *United Kingdom* [2001] 2 FLR 612; *Venema* v. *Netherlands* [2003] 1 FLR 552.

[292] I.e. under the HRA 1998, ss 7 and 8.

[293] [2001] 2 FLR 612. These applications, along with those in *TP and KM* v. *United Kingdom* [2001] 2 FLR 549, were made to the ECtHR by the OS, on behalf of the children involved in the *Bedfordshire* case.

[294] This was conceded by the UK government.

[295] *Osman* v. *United Kingdom* [1999] 1 FLR 193.   [296] R. Cornwath (2001) p. 476.

[297] *D* v. *East Berkshire Community Health NHS Trust and others* [2005] 2 AC 373. See also *Lawrence* v. *Pembrokeshire County Council* [2007] EWCA Civ 446, [2007] 2 FLR 705, per Auld LJ, at [27].

be they doctors, social workers, the police, community health workers or those in the education service.[298]

Children may also sue LAs for allowing them to be mistreated once in LA care.[299] This liability is not limited to cases in which the LA itself is at fault. Under the principles of vicarious liability, employers of an abusive care worker may not escape liability by simply arguing that their employee acted in an unauthorised manner when abusing the child in question. An action can be brought on behalf of a child, as long as there was a sufficient connection between the abusive behaviour and the work the employee was employed to do.[300] This principle also extends to the actions of foster carers who are caring for children on behalf of the LA. So, for example, in *Armes* v. *Nottinghamshire County Council*,[301] the LA was vicariously liable for the physical and sexual abuse inflicted by foster carer on a child in care, despite the fact that the LA itself had not been negligent in its choice or supervision of the carers in question. There are, however, limits to the circumstances in which an LA will be liable for the abusive actions of those to whom they have entrusted the child's care. In *SKX* v. *Manchester City Council*,[302] the High Court found that the LA was not vicariously liable for sexual abuse perpetrated by the Chief Executive of a privately run children's home. The claimant had been placed in the home through a contract between the LA and the independent private company that ran the home. This was distinguished from the circumstances in *Armes*, in which the foster carers had been recruited, trained and paid by the LA. Although the company would have been vicariously liable for the actions of the Chief Executive, it had long since gone into liquidation and had not been insured in respect of the claim. In these circumstances, and in the absence of any fault on the part of the LA, there was no redress in tort for the claimant for the extensive abuse that he had suffered while in care. The potential of tort as a source of accountability has been transformed through recognition of the rights of abused children to protection and care. Nonetheless, the increasingly prominent role of private companies in discharging that care means that

---

[298] E.g. *Pierce* v. *Doncaster Metropolitan Borough Council* [2008] EWCA Civ 1416, [2008] All ER (D) 136: the Court of Appeal confirmed the decision of the court below that the claimant, now an adult, had successfully proved the LA's negligence when they returned him to his mother's abusive care without proper assessment and left him with her without adequate monitoring. The LA's appeal succeeded in part, based on a limitation issue.

[299] E.g. *Barrett* v. *Enfield London Borough Council* [1999] 3 All ER 193; *C* v. *Flintshire County Council* [2001] EWCA Civ 302, [2001] 2 FLR 33.

[300] *Lister and others* v. *Hesley Hall Ltd* [2001] UKHL 22, [2002] 2 AC 215: claimants successfully sued the employers of a warden of a boarding school for children with emotional and behavioural difficulties. Per House of Lords: the warden's sexual abuse of his victims had been so closely connected with his employment as warden, that it was fair and just that his employers should be held vicariously liable for his torts.

[301] [2017] UKSC 60, [2018] AC 355.

[302] [2021] EWHC 782 (QB), [2021] 4 WLR 56; the claimant was one of the many victims of the extensive abuse perpetrated in children's homes run by the Bryn Alyn Community: R. Waterhouse (2000).

redress for many abused children will depend on the longevity of that company and the adequacy of its insurance arrangements.[303]

(C) Local Authorities' Accountability for the Implementation of Care Plans

As the discussion above shows, under the combined impact of the ECtHR and the HRA 1998, the principle established by the *Bedfordshire* decision was finally rejected. It had given the impression that the child protection process was a largely unaccountable one; indeed, that children who suffered in the process should not be allowed to sue their LAs because they were undertaking sensitive work as best they could. Such an approach was controversial in itself. When combined with a system which prevents the courts, or any other outside body, from monitoring the way in which LAs care for children, it became even more questionable. The litigation in the *Bedfordshire* case started soon after the implementation of the CA 1989.[304] One wonders whether, had that decision reached the House of Lords before 1989, the draftsmen of the new legislation would have promoted such a strict separation of power between the LAs and the courts. It was their deliberate intention to ensure that LAs should not be accountable to the courts for decisions over the manner they choose to protect children. It is a controversial aspect of the statutory scheme that the courts have very little scope to prompt LA intervention, or to override or circum-scribe the exercise by LAs of their statutory powers.[305] The courts are not only barred from using the inherent jurisdiction to order a child into the care of the LA,[306] but they also have no supervisory powers, similar to those formerly exercised by the courts prior to the CA 1989, over children taken into care under the wardship jurisdiction.

It must be acknowledged that the CA 1989 is not entirely consistent in its attempts to ensure that the courts, when dealing with LA applications for orders to protect children from harm, must always adopt what Dewar described as an 'adjudicative' role rather than a 'participative' one.[307] In particular, case law established the courts' entitlement under section 34 of the CA 1989 to force the LA to reassess the extent of contact it allows a parent to have with a child in care.[308] They also, under section 38(6), have the power to direct an LA to arrange for the child and family to undergo a residential assessment, despite the LA's strong opposition to such a course

---

[303] Ofsted (2021): In England, private companies run 78 per cent of children's homes, a proportion that has been increasing for some years. Independent fostering agencies now provide 41 per cent of foster places. LAs remain liable in tort for their own negligence in the placement of children in these settings.

[304] The applications were made in 1993.

[305] Applying the principle established in *A v. Liverpool City Council* [1982] AC 363.

[306] CA 1989, s. 100(1) and (2).   [307] J. Dewar (1995) p. 16.

[308] *Re B (Minors) (Termination of Contact: Paramount Consideration)* [1993] 3 All ER 524: the courts can make a contact order regarding a child in care, despite the fact that the order will interfere with the long-term plans of the LA.

of action.[309] Furthermore, the courts can force the LA's hand, but only to a very limited extent, by making a section 37 direction,[310] together with an interim care or supervision order, pending the outcome of the LA's investigation.[311] Nonetheless, the decision in *Nottinghamshire County Council* v. *P*[312] demonstrated only too clearly the toothlessness of this power. At both levels, the courts made clear their intense frustration with the LA for merely complying with a section 37 direction to investigate the case, but then refusing to apply for a care order to protect two sexually abused girls from their father.[313]

These exceptions apart, the statutory regime devised by the CA 1989[314] ensures that LAs are essentially free to decide whether to intervene and, if so, to choose the type of protection and care to offer the children they are willing to protect. In other words, the policy aspects of child protection are entirely within the LA's purview, adhering to the view that they are better placed to ascertain how and when to protect children than are the courts. Furthermore: 'Courts neither have the resources nor the expertise to act as substitute parents for children.'[315] Within a short time of the implementation of the CA 1989, the courts conscientiously emphasised the fact that with their former powers in wardship now removed, they had no ability to maintain control over children after making a care order.[316] Nevertheless, a sense of unease had been created by the courts' inability either to persuade LAs to intervene in the first place, or to control how LAs exercised their parental responsibilities over the children, once ordered into their care. A legislative scheme of this nature, with a clear division of powers, can only work well if the courts are satisfied that LAs can invariably improve a child's life. But it radically undermines the courts' ability to satisfy the no order principle[317] if they cannot be confident either that the details of the care plan will remain substantially unchanged or that they will be fully complied with. It can also be a source of frustration to healthcare professionals if their recommendations for treatment are not adopted by the LA looking after the child.[318]

The absence of any system for calling LAs to account for failing to comply with care plans was causing judicial concern[319] well before *Re S (Minors)*

---

[309] *Re C (A Minor) (Interim Care Order: Residential Assessment)* [1996] 4 All ER 871. But see *Re G (A Minor) (Interim Care Order; Residential Assessment)* [2005] UKHL 68, [2006] 1 AC 576: s. 38(6) cannot be used to produce services for the child or family, cf. providing the court with information from detailed assessment work.

[310] CA 1989, s. 37(1).   [311] Ibid., s. 38(1)(a).   [312] [1994] Fam 18.

[313] Ibid., per Sir Simon Brown P, at 43.

[314] But this approach to such a strict separation of powers pre-dated the CA 1989, being established by the House of Lords in *A* v. *Liverpool City Council* [1982] AC 363.

[315] B. Hale and J. Fortin (2008) p. 101.

[316] Inter alia: *Re T (A Minor) (Care Order: Conditions)* [1994] 2 FLR 423: the courts have no power to impose conditions in a care order; *Re J (Minors) (Care: Care Plan)* [1994] 1 FLR 253: interim care orders should not be used to resurrect the supervisory role enjoyed by the wardship court.

[317] I.e. CA 1989, s. 1(5).   [318] E.g. *Re O (Care: Discharge of Care Order)* [1999] 2 FLR 119.

[319] Wall J (1998) esp. p. 8. See also *Re W and B; Re W (Care Plan)* [2001] EWCA Civ 757, [2001] 2 FLR 582, per Thorpe LJ, at [18]–[21].

(Care Order: Implementation of Care Plan), Re W (Minors) (Care Order: Adequacy of Care Plan) (hereafter *Re S and Re W*)[320] reached the House of Lords in 2001. In the years immediately preceding that decision, those involved in the family justice system were familiar with the depressing litany of LA inadequacies which continue to the present day. Then, their greatest frustration was an inability either to monitor what happened to children under care orders or to ensure that LA care plans were complied with.[321] Not only were the care plans of low quality, with a lack of appropriate detail,[322] but, more seriously, there was an apparent inability to deliver the services set out in the plans themselves.[323] Children were understandably upset and bewildered both by the courts' inability to influence placements[324] and by planned placements not materialising and promised contact with relatives not being arranged.[325] Furthermore, compliance with the statutory review process, under which care plans should be regularly reviewed,[326] was patchy in the extreme.[327]

As the judiciary themselves fully appreciate,[328] there may be any number of reasons for LAs failing to comply with care plans, including the difficulty of complying with a child's very complex needs and a lack of resources, particularly the availability of suitable long-term placements.[329] Nevertheless, children suffer greatly when LAs fail to make proper provision for their care. Indeed, to remove a child from his or her home in the first place constitutes an interference with the child's rights to family life, which must be very carefully justified. The Court of Appeal, when hearing *Re S and Re W*,[330] considered that the courts should not simply overlook an LA's failure then to fulfil a child's care plan. Further such failure might constitute a breach of the LA's positive obligations under Article 8 of the ECHR to fulfil the child's rights thereunder, by providing them with a substitute family, or by reuniting them with their birth parents.[331] But the problem confronting the judiciary was the absence of any formal mechanism for bringing care cases back to court – more to the point, there was no systematic procedure available for calling LAs to account

---

[320] [2002] UKHL 10, [2002] AC 291.   [321] J. Hunt and A. Macleod (1999) ch. 9.

[322] E.g. in *Re S and Re W* [2002] UKHL 10, [2002] AC 291, the trial judge described the care plan relating to the second child as being 'inchoate'.

[323] E.g. *Re S and Re W*, ibid.; *Re F; F* v. *Lambeth London Borough Council* [2002] 1 FLR 217.

[324] M. Ruegger (2001) p. 143.

[325] J. Hunt and A. Macleod (1999) chs 7–9; J. Masson and M. Winn Oakley (1999) ch. 8.

[326] Under CA 1989, s. 26(1) and (2) and the Review of Children's Cases Regulations 1991 (SI 1991/895).

[327] SSI (2002) para. 6.8: 'most councils' failed to convene statutory child care reviews within statutory timescales, three councils only met timescales in 50 per cent of cases, and in one of these there were 'weaknesses in completing the tasks laid out in the care plan'.

[328] *Re W and B; Re W (Care Plan)* [2001] EWCA Civ 757, [2001] 2 FLR 582 (CA), per Hale LJ, at [60].

[329] J. Hunt and A. Macleod (1999) pp. 229–36; J. Harwin and M. Owen (2002) p. 71.

[330] [2001] EWCA Civ 757, [2001] 2 FLR 582, reported sub nom *Re W and B; Re W (Care Plan)*.

[331] Ibid., see esp. Hale LJ, at [52]–[59]. See also B. Hale and J. Fortin (2008) p. 102.

for failing to comply with the care plans upon which the courts had relied when making the original care orders.

Theoretically, when care plans are radically changed or left unfulfilled, the parents can apply for a discharge of the care order itself.[332] Although the existence of such a remedy impressed the ECtHR,[333] in practice, it is more apparent than real. Few parents make discharge applications, presumably because they have little faith that the courts will consider them fit to have their children returned to them.[334] Further, legal aid for parents seeking to discharge a care order is subject to strict means test requirements, meaning that parents will often find themselves unable to access legal aid or to afford legal advice to navigate the process.[335] In some cases, the courts may discover the LA's failure to comply with a care plan only when, as in *Re F; F* v. *Lambeth Borough Council*,[336] the parents apply for increased contact,[337] thereby providing the courts with an opportunity to review what has occurred since the initial care orders were made. But parents with a history of involvement with social workers may be reluctant to take such a step. Furthermore, although older children may use the complaints system or, with the help of advocacy services, take their own case back to court,[338] as Thorpe LJ pointed out in *Re S and Re W*, 'the children who are most vulnerable to breakdown and delay are the very young whose healthy future development may depend on forming a sound psychological attachment in time'.[339]

In *Re S and Re W*, the House of Lords, perhaps predictably, rejected the Court of Appeal's radical solution to these problems. This had been simply to read into the CA 1989 a means of supervising the implementation of the fundamental elements of care plans in selected cases.[340] But, as Lord

---

[332] Under CA 1989, s. 39.

[333] *Scott* v. *United Kingdom* [2000] 1 FLR 958: the ECtHR considered that the availability of a discharge application negated the mother's argument that when an LA abandoned the care plan to reunite the child with her, and placed the child for adoption, it had infringed the mother's rights under Art. 8 of the ECHR, leaving her without an effective remedy.

[334] J. Hunt and A. Macleod (1999) p. 197.

[335] *Re D (A Child) (Non-Availability of Legal Aid)* [2014] EWFC 39, [2015] 1 FLR 531 and [2015] EWFC 2, [2015] 1 FLR 1247: this is a particularly egregious example of the injustice caused by the restriction of legal aid in discharge cases. In this case, the parents' modest income was marginally above the means-tested limits, so leaving them without public funding despite the profound implications of the LA's decision to remove the child from a placement at home and to instead seek adoption. The parents faced considerable barriers to navigating the complex legal process without assistance as the father lacked capacity to litigate and the mother had learning difficulties. While the parents were fortunate to receive pro bono advice, the potential for breach of HRA Arts 6 and 8 is manifest in these circumstances.

[336] [2002] 1 FLR 217.   [337] Under CA 1989, s. 34(3).

[338] E.g. by applying for a discharge of the care order under CA 1989, s. 39 or for increased contact with their parents under s. 34(3).

[339] [2001] EWCA Civ 757, [2001] 2 FLR 582, reported sub nom *Re W and B; Re W (Care Plan)*, at [24].

[340] These elements were to be 'starred', with an obligation imposed on the LA to report to the court or to the children's guardian on failure to implement any of them, thereby triggering an application by the children's guardian to apply for a discharge of the care order.

Nicholls of Birkenhead pointed out, reinterpreting the CA 1989 in a way which undermined one of its cardinal principles – the separation of powers between the courts and LAs – went far beyond the scope of section 3 of the HRA 1998.[341] Nevertheless, their Lordships made plain their agreement with the Court of Appeal that a system which allowed LAs to fail children with impunity was quite unsatisfactory and required official review.[342]

Subsequent legislative and policy change has struggled to find the right boundary between the need for LA discretion to respond to changing circumstances, and the desirability of oversight to ensure that plans do not drift or change without careful review. The government's immediate legislative response to the judicial criticism in *Re S and Re W* was to impose a new statutory obligation, requiring LAs to present to courts considering care applications, detailed and properly revised care plans, renamed 'section 31A plans'.[343] The increased judicial scrutiny made more exacting demands on LA planning, but there was also concern that judges were causing delay in proceedings by extensive consideration of matters that were better left to LA discretion. In response, the Children and Families Act 2014 sought to restrict the judicial role by only *requiring* courts to consider the 'permanence provisions' of the care plan, which set out the long-term placement plans for the child, and not the broader aspects of the child's upbringing.[344] The exact boundary between judicial and LA responsibility for care plans remains elusive, as Parliament has continued to adjust exactly what is required of the courts in considering permanence.[345] Nevertheless, as Bainham argues, the legislation reflects a dividing line between the court's responsibility to review the appropriate permanent plan for the child and the LA's responsibility to implement that plan in practice.[346] The legislation is, however, silent as to what the LA should do if the permanence plans approved by the court later prove to be unrealistic or unworkable. This is a particular problem if the revised plan involves a greater interference in the rights of the child and parents than that considered and approved by the court. A good example of this problem can be

---

[341] *Re S and Re W* [2002] UKHL 10, [2002] AC 291, at [34]–[44]; discussed by B. Hale and J. Fortin (2008) p. 102.

[342] Ibid., per Lord Nicholls, at [29]–[30] and [106] and Lord Mackay, at [110].

[343] CA 1989, s. 31A, introduced by the Adoption and Children Act 2002.

[344] CA 1989, s. 31(3)(A)–(C). While the court is only required to consider these aspects of the care plan, there is nothing in the legislation to prohibit the court from considering other aspects of the plan: *Re S-W (Children) (Care Proceedings: Case Management Hearings)* [2015] EWCA Civ 27, [2015] 1 WLR 4099.

[345] The Children and Social Work Act 2017, s. 8, extended the meaning of 'permanence provisions' to include: 'such of the plan's provisions as set out any of the following –
(i) the impact on the child concerned of any harm that he or she suffered or was likely to suffer;
(ii) the current and future needs of the child (including needs arising out of that impact);
(iii) the way in which the long-term plan for the upbringing of the child would meet those current and future needs.'

[346] A. Bainham (2018).

seen in *Re DE (A Child)*,[347] a case concerning a young child born to parents with learning difficulties. The care order had been made with a care plan which would allow the child to remain at home with the parents, who would receive a package of support to assist them in parenting. The LA became increasingly concerned about the child's development and the failure of the parents to recognise risk and predict potential dangers to him. As a result, it decided to remove him from the family home and gave notice to do so. The change in plan clearly represented a significant change in position and a far more intrusive interference with the rights of the parents and child. The court made clear that the LA could not simply rely on the care order to do so. Instead, such a change would only be lawful if done after proper assessment of the evidence and in a way that was proportionate to the interference with the human rights of the child and parents. In *Re DE*, the parents succeeded in an application for an injunction under the HRA. Other cases may come before the court through an application to discharge a care order, or, in rarer cases, through judicial review.[348] As noted above, there are considerable practical barriers for parents who seek to bring such cases, meaning that the way in which care plans are reviewed and implemented by LAs will be crucial for the rights of children and families in practice.

A further important aspect of the government's response to *Re S and Re W* was the introduction of a new system whereunder the care plans of all children received into care should be rigorously reviewed by LA employees in the role of Independent Reviewing Officers (IROs).[349] An IRO must be appointed for every child prior to any statutory review,[350] with the IRO required to monitor the LA's performance in relation to the child. IROs are required to chair statutory reviews for children in care and detect those cases where a child's care plan is not being adequately implemented, in which case they should notify the Children and Family Court Advisory and Support Service (Cafcass). A children's guardian should then be appointed to apply, on the child's behalf, for some further court order, such as a discharge of the care order, or even to institute litigation against the LA. The extensive duties of IROs give them a key role in the scrutiny of changes to care plans and in safeguarding the rights and involvement of children in planning for their future.[351]

The performance of IROs in fulfilling this crucial role has been the subject of long-standing criticism. From the scheme's inception, it was argued that its major weakness lay in the fact that IROs were to be drawn from the LA's

---

[347] [2014] EWFC 6, [2014] 3 WLR 1733, discussed by C. Fenton-Glynn (2015).

[348] *Re T (A Child)* [2018] EWCA Civ 650, [2018] 4 WLR 121, at [42].

[349] CA 1989, s. 26, as extensively amended by ACA 2002, s. 118. See also The Care Planning, Placement and Case Review (England) Regulations 2010, esp. regs 6 and 36.

[350] CA 1989, s. 25A.

[351] The duties of IROs are found in CA 1989, s. 25B(1); The Care Planning, Placement and Case Review (England) Regulations 2010, reg. 45. Statutory guidance on these duties is contained in DfE (2021a) paras 4.7 and 4.38–4.47.

own employees. Sceptics doubted that they would readily identify areas of poor practice among their own colleagues,[352] and cited this weakness as a cause of extreme passivity exhibited by many IROs.[353] The government itself referred to the 'widespread concern that the IRO role is not being carried out effectively across all local authorities' and more specifically to their failure to challenge LAs' decisions 'even in cases where professional practice is obviously poor and not in young people's interests'.[354] A later review by Ofsted similarly found that the role of IROs was underdeveloped in most of the LAs considered, with IROs failing to monitor and challenge LA planning or to take children's views fully into account.[355] IROs reported struggling under heavy caseloads with insufficient support and legal advice on their role. Perhaps of greatest concern was IROs' general failure to use their power to refer cases to Cafcass so that legal proceedings could be brought to achieve a remedy.[356] These weaknesses were vividly illustrated by the case of *A & S* v. *Lancashire County Council*,[357] in which, despite having an IRO, two brothers spent their childhood being moved around the care system (one moving ninety-six times), subject to physical and sexual abuse, and with no stable plan for their future once the initial plan for adoption had failed. As the judgment makes clear, these were not simply individual failings, but linked to the systemic problems in the IRO system. Despite the depressing picture painted by much of this literature, one major research study has found more cause for optimism. Dickens's in-depth research into the practice of IROs found that they were effective in pursuing a collaborative and supportive approach to negotiating better outcomes for children.[358] The research suggests that this 'hidden' constructive work may be more effective than a more confrontational formal challenge.

As the discussion above makes plain, the judicial concerns which led the Court of Appeal to produce its radical solution in *Re S and Re W* still remain a real and serious concern today. The limited role of the court in responding to changing plans for children makes it imperative that LAs have robust means of reviewing plans in practice. Until very effective mechanisms are in place to supervise the manner in which LAs implement and review the care plans they agree to, the lives of at least some looked-after children continue to be damaged even further by their experiences in state care.

---

[352] J. Fortin (2003) p. 513.

[353] See *S (by the Official Solicitor)* v. *Rochdale MBC and another* [2008] EWHC 3283 (Fam), [2009] 1 FLR 1090, at [27]: the OS's allegations (unproved) regarding the IRO's failure to ensure that review meetings were properly conducted or followed up. See also Appendix A [95], describing the IRO as 'largely impotent or supine'.

[354] DfES (2007) para. 7.29.   [355] Ofsted (2013).

[356] It is reported that this power was only used twenty times in the entire period between 2004 and March 2017: L. Davis (2018).

[357] [2012] EWHC 1689 (Fam), [2013] 2 FLR 803.   [358] J. Dickens *et al.* (2015).

(6) Conclusion

The CRC provides that a child who is no longer able to remain in the existing family environment is *entitled* to state care, assistance and alternative care.[359] Child protection work is undoubtedly delicate and difficult, but if LAs set themselves up as being able to carry out the parenting role better than children's own parents, the children have a right to a professional service. It is clear that this is not always delivered. Many of the children coming into state care are already emotionally disturbed and extremely vulnerable. Even making allowances for this, the experience of being looked after by the state is not always a particularly beneficial one. Considerable efforts are now being made to improve the state's record regarding the children it removes from the family home and to improve the legal standards by which state care is provided. The rights of looked-after children are well-recognised and supported in law, although this does not always result in good standards of care in practice, particularly given the acute lack of suitable provision for vulnerable older children. Those children who are failed have a right to hold the state to account and the law must provide ways in which they are able to do so without undue delay or difficulty.

Bibliography

NB: Many of these publications can be obtained on the relevant organisation's website.

AIRE Centre (2001) *Secure Accommodation Orders, Police Protection 'Orders', Curfews from the Convention Perspective*, AIRE Centre Family Law and European Convention on Human Rights Website Materials.

All-Party Parliamentary Group for Runaway and Missing Children (APPG) (2012) *Report from the Joint Inquiry into Children Who Go Missing from Care*, APPG.

(2019) *No Place at Home: Risks Facing Children and Young People Who Go Missing from Out of Area Placements*, APPG.

Bainham, A. (2003) 'Contact as a Right and Obligation' in Bainham, A., Lindley, B., Richards, A. and Trinder, L. (eds) *Children and Their Families: Contact, Rights and Welfare*, Hart Publishing.

(2015) 'Swimming against the Tide: Challenging Contact Arrangements in the Public Law' 45 *Family Law* 1356.

(2018) 'The Forbidden Territories' 48 *Family Law* 1150.

Berridge, D. and Brodie, I. (1998) *Children's Home Revisited*, Jessica Kingsley Publishers.

Biehal, N. (2006) *Reuniting Looked After Children with Their Parents: A Review of the Research*, NCB.

Biehal, N., Sinclair, I. and Wade, J. (2015) 'Reunifying Abused or Neglected Children: Decision-Making and Outcomes' 49 *Child Abuse & Neglect* 107.

Brandon, M., Thoburn, J., Rose, S. and Belderson, P. (2005) *Living with Significant Harm: A Follow Up Study*, NSPCC.

Brophy, J. (2006) *Research Review: Child Care Proceedings under the Children Act 1989*, DCA.

Children's Commissioner (2019a) *Stability Index 2019: Overview Report*, Office of the Children's Commissioner.

(2019b) *Pass the Parcel: Children Posted around the Care System*, Office of the Children's Commissioner.

---

[359] CRC, Art. 20. See also the UN Guidelines for the Alternative Care of Children (A/RES/64/142).

(2019c) *Who Are They? Where Are They? Children Locked Up*, Office of the Children's Commissioner.

(2020a) *Unregulated: Children in Care Living in Semi-Independent Accommodation*, Office of the Children's Commissioner.

(2020b) *Private Provision in Children's Social Care*, Office of the Children's Commissioner.

(2020c) *Who Are They? Where Are They? 2020. Children Locked Up*, Office of the Children's Commissioner.

Commission for Social Care Inspection (CSCI) (2006a) *Adoption: Messages from Inspections of Adoption Agencies*, CSCI.

(2006b) *The Right People for Me: Helping Children do Well in Long-Term Foster Care*, CSCI.

Committee on the Rights of the Child (2013) *General Comment No. 16 on State Obligations Regarding the Impact of the Business Sector on Children's Rights*, CRC/C/GC/16, Centre for Human Rights, Geneva.

Cornwath, R. (2001) 'Welfare Services – Liabilities in Tort after the HRA – Postscript' *Public Law* 475.

Crellin, R. and Pona, I. (2015) *On Your Own Now: The Risks of Unsuitable Accommodation for Older Teenagers*, The Children's Society.

Davis, L. (2018) 'Independent Reviewing Officers: Unloved and under Threat?' *Family Law* 588.

Department for Education (DfE) (2014) *Court Orders and Pre-Proceedings*, DfE.

(2018a) *Applying Corporate Parenting Principles to Looked-After Children and Care-Leavers: Statutory Guidance for Local Authorities*, DfE.

(2018b) *Children Looked After in England (including Adoption), 31 March 2018*, DfE.

(2019a) *Outcomes for Children Looked After by Local Authorities in England, 31 March 2018*, DfE.

(2019b) *Children Looked After in England (Including Adoption), 31 March 2019*, DfE.

(2021a) *The Children Act 1989 Guidance and Regulations, Volume 2, Care Planning, Placement and Care Review*, DfE.

(2021b) *Introducing National Standards for Independent and Semi-Independent Provision for Looked After Children and Care Leavers Aged 16 and 17*, DfE.

Department for Education and Skills (DfES) (2006a) Cm 6932, *Care Matters: Transforming the Lives of Children and Young People in Care*, The Stationery Office.

(2006b) *Getting the Best from Complaints: Social Care Complaints and Representations for Children, Young People and Others*, DfES.

(2007) Cm 7137, *Care Matters: Time for Change*, The Stationery Office.

Department of Health (DH) (1996) *Focus on Teenagers: Research into Practice*, Her Majesty's Stationery Office.

(1998) Cm 4175, *Children Looked After by Local Authorities: Government Response to the Second Report of the Health Committee on Children Looked After by Local Authorities: Session 1997–98*, The Stationery Office.

(2000) White Paper, Cm 5017, *Adoption: a New Approach*, The Stationery Office.

Dewar, J. (1995) 'The Courts and Local Authority Autonomy' 7 *Child and Family Law Quarterly* 15.

Dickens, J., Schofield, G., Beckett, C., Young, J. and Philip, G. (2015) *Care Planning and the Role of the Independent Reviewing Officer*, UEA.

Eekelaar, J. (2003) 'Contact and the Adoption Reform' in Bainham, A., Lindley, B., Richards, A. and Trinder, L. (eds) *Children and Their Families: Contact, Rights and Welfare*, Hart Publishing.

Ellaway, B., Payne, E., Rolfe, K., Dunstan, F., Kemp, A., Butler, I. and Sibert, J. (2004) 'Are Abused Babies Protected from Further Abuse?' 89 *Archive of Diseases of Childhood* 845.

Fenton-Glynn, C. (2015) 'The Rise of Strict Scrutiny: Extending *Re B-S* to Changes in Care Plans' 37 *Journal of Social Welfare and Family Law* 105.

(2016) 'Adoption Targets: The Good, the Bad and the Ugly' 46 *Family Law* 148.

Fortin, J. (2001) 'Children's Rights and the Use of Physical Force' 13 *Child and Family Law Quarterly* 243.

(2003) *Children's Rights and the Developing Law*, LexisNexis Butterworths.

Gallagher, B. (1999) 'The Abuse of Children in Public Care' 8 *Child Abuse Review* 357.

Giliker, P. (2018) 'Analysing Institutional Liability for Child Sexual Abuse in England and Wales and Australia: Vicarious Liability, Non-Delegable Duties and Statutory Intervention' 77 *Cambridge Law Journal* 506.

Goldstein, J., Freud, A. and Solnit, A. (1980) *Before the Best Interests of the Child*, Burnett Books Limited.

Hale, B. (2000) 'In Defence of the Children Act' 83 *Archives of Diseases in Childhood* 463.

Hale, B. and Fortin, J. (2008) 'Legal Issues in the Care and Treatment of Children with Mental Health Problems' in Rutter, M., Bishop, D., Pine, D., Scott, S., Stevenson, J., Taylor, E. and Thapar, A. (eds) *Rutter's Child and Adolescent Psychiatry*, Blackwell Publishing.

Harris-Short, S. (2008) 'Making and Breaking Family Life: Adoption, the State and Human Rights' 35 *Journal of Law and Society* 28.

Harwin, J. and Alrouh, B. (2017) 'Supervision Orders and Special Guardianship: How Risky Are They? Findings from a National Study of Supervision Orders and Special Guardianship' 47 *Family Law* 513.

Harwin, J. and Owen, M. (2002) 'A Study of Care Plans and Their Implementation and Relevance for *Re W and B and Re W (Care Plan)*' in Thorpe LJ and Cowton, C. (eds) *Delight and Dole: The Children Act 10 Years On*, Family Law.

Hindley, N., Rachmandani, P. and Jones, D. (2006) 'Risk Factors for Recurrence of Maltreatment: A Systematic Review' 91 *Archives of Disease in Childhood* 744.

Hughes, W. (Chairman) (1985) *Report of the Committee of Inquiry into Children's Homes and Hostels*, Her Majesty's Stationery Office.

Hunt, J. and Macleod, A. (1999) *The Best-Laid Plans: Outcomes of Judicial Decisions in Child Protection Proceedings*, The Stationery Office.

Hunt, J., Waterhouse, S. and Lutman, E. (2010) 'Parental Contact for Children Placed in Kinship Care through Care Proceedings' 22 *Child and Family Law Quarterly* 71.

Jane Held Consulting Ltd (2006) *Qualitative Study: The Use by Local Authorities of Secure Children's Homes*, Research Report RR 749, DfES.

Jay, A. (2014) *Independent Inquiry into Child Sexual Exploitation in Rotherham 1997–2013*.

Jay, A., Evans, M., Frank, I. and Sharpling, D. (2019) *Children in the Care of Nottinghamshire Councils: Investigation Report*, Independent Inquiry into Child Sexual Abuse.

Jordan, R. and Walker, S. (2019) *The National Independent Visitor Data Report 2019*, Barnardo's.

Levy, A. and Kahan, B. (Chairmen) (1991) *The Pindown Experience and the Protection of Children*, The Report of the Staffordshire Child Care Inquiry, 1990, Staffordshire County Council.

Lewis, J. (2004) 'Adoption: The Nature of Policy Shifts in England and Wales, 1972–2002' 18 *International Journal of Law, Policy and the Family* 235.

Local Government Ombudsman (LGO) (2015) *Are We Getting the Best from Children's Social Care Complaints?*, LGO.

Lowe, N. and Murch, M. (2002) *The Plan for the Child: Adoption or Long-Term Fostering*, BAAF.

Lynch, C. (2018) 'Cooperation or Coercion? Children Coming into the Care System under s 20 Voluntary Arrangements' 48 *Family Law* 191.

Lynch, C. and Boddy, J. (2017) *Cooperation or Coercion? Children Coming into the Care System under Voluntary Arrangements*, Family Rights Group.

Masson, J. (2002) '*Re K (A Child) (Secure Accommodation Order: Right to Liberty)* and *Re C (Secure Accommodation Order: Representation)*' 14 *Child and Family Law Quarterly* 77.

(2005) 'Emergency Intervention to Protect Children: Using and Avoiding Legal Controls' 17 *Child and Family Law Quarterly* 75.

(2018) 'Understanding the Current Use of s 20' 48 *Family Law* 1289.

Masson, J., Dickens, J., Bader, K., Garside, L. and Young, J. (2017) 'Achieving Positive Change for Children? Reducing the Length of Child Protection Proceedings: Lessons from England and Wales' 41 *Adoption and Fostering* 401.

Masson, J., Dickens, J., Garside, L., Bader, K. and Young, J. (2018) *Reforming Care Proceedings 1: Court Outcomes*, University of East Anglia.

Masson, J., Pearce, J. and Bader, K., with Joyner, O., Marsden, J. and Westlake, D. (2008) Ministry of Justice Research Series 4/08, *Care Profiling Study*, Ministry of Justice.

Masson, J. and Winn Oakley, M. (1999) *Out of Hearing: Representing Children in Care Proceedings*, Wiley.

Monk, D. and Macvarish, J. (2018) *Siblings, Contact and the Law: An Overlooked Relationship*, Birkbeck.

Morgan, R. (2005) *'Getting the Best from Complaints': The Children's View*, CSCI.

(2006a) *Placements, Decisions and Reviews: A Children's Views Report*, CSCI.

(2006b) *About Social Workers A Children's Views Report*, CSCI.

Narey, M. (2016) *Residential Care in England: Report of Sir Martin Narey's Independent Review of Children's Residential Care*, DfE.

Ofsted (2013) *Independent Reviewing Officers: Taking up the Challenge*, Ofsted.

(2020) *The Annual Report of Her Majesty's Chief Inspector of Education, Children's Services and Skills 2018/19*, Ofsted.

(2021) *Local Authority and Children's Homes in England Inspections and Outcomes: Autumn 2020*, Ofsted.

Parry, M. (2000) 'Secure Accommodation – the Cinderella of Family Law' 12 *Child and Family Law Quarterly* 101.

Performance and Innovation Unit (PIU) (2000) *The Prime Minister's Review of Adoption*, Cabinet Office.

Pithouse, A. and Crowley, A. (2007) 'Adults Rule? Children, Advocacy and Complaints to Social Services' 21 *Children and Society* 201.

Public Law Working Group (2021) *Recommendations to Achieve Best Practice in the Child Protection and Family Justice Systems: Final Report*, available at: www.judiciary.uk.

Quinton, D. (2006) 'Adoption: Research, Policy and Practice' 18 *Child and Family Law Quarterly* 459.

Ruegger, M. (2001) 'Seen and Heard But How Well Informed? Children's Perceptions of the Guardian Ad Litem Service' 15 *Children and Society* 133.

Ryder, E. (2000) '"Lost and Found" – Looking to the Future after North Wales' 30 *Family Law* 406.

Sebba, J., Berridge, D., Luke, N., Fletcher, J., Bell, K., Strand, S., Thomas, S., Sinclair, I. and O'Higgins, A. (2015) *The Educational Progress of Looked After Children in England: Linking Care and Educational Data*, Rees Centre and University of Bristol.

Selwyn, J., Meakings, S. and Wijedesa, D. (2014) *Beyond the Adoption Order: Challenges, Intervention and Adoption Disruption*, DfE.

Sinclair, I., Baker, C., Lee, J. and Gibbs, I. (2007) *The Pursuit of Permanence: A Study of the English Child Care System*, Jessica Kingsley Publishers.

Social Services Inspectorate (SSI) (2002) *Fostering for the Future: Inspection of Foster Care Services*, DH Publications.

Taylor, R. (2018) 'Grandparents and Grandchildren: Relatedness, Relationships and Responsibility' in Clough, B. and Herring, J. (eds) *Ageing, Gender and Family Law*, Routledge.

Thoburn, J. (2006) 'Planning for Children Who Cannot Return to Their Birth Families: Messages from Research' in Jordan, L. and Lindley, B. (eds) *Special Guardianship: What Does It Offer Children Who Cannot Live with Their Parents?*, Family Rights Group.

Timms, J. and Thoburn, J. (2003) *Your Shout*, NSPCC.

Utting, W. (Chairman) (1997) *People Like Us: The Report of the Review of the Safeguards for Children Living Away from Home*, DH/The Welsh Office, Her Majesty's Stationery Office.

Wall J (1998) 'Care Plans: A Judicial Perspective' in Thorpe LJ and Clarke, E. (eds) *Divided Duties: Care Planning for Children within the Family Justice System*, Family Law.

Wate, R. (2017) *Serious Case Review: Shi-Anne Downer Case Identifier: BSCB 2015-16/2*, Birmingham Safeguarding Children Board.

Waterhouse, R. (Chairman) (2000) *Lost in Care: Report of the Tribunal of Inquiry into the Abuse of Children in Care in the former County Council Areas of Gwynedd and Clwyd since 1974*, The Stationery Office.

Welbourne, P. (2008) 'Safeguarding Children on the Edge of Care: Policy for Keeping Children Safe after the *Review of the Child Care Proceedings System, Care Matters* and the *Carter Review of Legal Aid*' 20 *Child and Family Law Quarterly* 335.

Williams, G. and Macreadie, J. (Chairmen) (1992) *Ty Mawr Community Home Inquiry*, Gwent County Council.

17

Conclusion
Themes and the Way Ahead

(1) Introduction

As the preceding chapters demonstrate, in common with other minority groups, children suffer from being the focus of various specialised branches of law and policy, all with their own distinctive character. We find case law and legislation responding in an ad hoc fashion to various aspects of children's lives in a completely disparate way, which sometimes reflects a rights consciousness, but often ignores such a concept. Underlying this incoherence is the slow pace of the conversion of our legal system to one embodying a rights-based approach. The Human Rights Act (HRA) 1998, by incorporating the European Convention for the Protection of Human Rights and Fundamental Freedoms (1950) (ECHR) into domestic law, undoubtedly enhanced public awareness of the rights enjoyed by all individuals, both against the state and one another. Society is also becoming far more aware of the demands of the Convention on the Rights of the Child (CRC), with most public agencies attempting to comply with its broad aims. Indeed, there have been important developments that demonstrate a willingness to promote children's rights in more realistic and practical ways.[1] Nevertheless, the developing law does not always reflect such a desire and it would be foolish to ignore the scepticism that many retain over the wisdom of utilising the concept of rights to increase children's well-being.[2]

In assessing the extent to which the developing law promotes children's rights, this work has uncovered a variety of approaches which sometimes appear to have little coherence. We must accept, however, that an uncodified legal system such as our own produces legal principles in a peculiarly untidy way. The government introduces draft legislation and the courts' case law, without systematic attention as to how the two sources of law fit together. Lawyers wishing to promote children's rights more effectively are hampered by this haphazard method of producing the legal principles governing children. The courts have to wait for further litigation on the same topic or for the government to be sufficiently motivated to deal with the matter through

---

[1] E.g. the expanding role of the Children's Commissioner, considered in Chapter 3.
[2] See Chapter 1.

special legislation. Case law develops on an incremental basis, with no under-lying policy or cohesion between branches of law and the opportunities for remedying practical gaps and defects uncovered are very limited.[3] Children's rights offer a means of bringing greater coherence and clarity to the law, but require effective engagement throughout judicial and political decision-making. The courts have made significant strides in recognising and developing chil-dren's rights in a range of areas, but practical enjoyment of those rights is often hampered by a failure to provide for them in policy and planning. For example, judicial recognition of children's right to participation in legal proceedings will achieve little in practice if children are not able to access the resources necessary for representation.[4] Similarly, the developing law on children's rights to identity and knowledge of their origins will be difficult to fulfil without reform to the outdated system of birth registration.[5] Careful scrutiny of the right to liberty for children in secure accommodation does little to protect those children if the only placements available are grossly inadequate for their needs.[6] Significant progress has been made in accepting that children have rights, but those rights need to be embedded throughout decision-making and planning if they are to be given practical effect in practice.

This concluding chapter opens by considering the extent to which parents' interests hamper the law's development of children's rights. It proceeds to assess the peculiarly fragmented manner in which children are 'constructed' by law and practice to fulfil adult perceptions of their needs. The difficulties posed by society's negative attitudes towards young people and their exclusion from the political process are also examined. The chapter concludes by arguing that these problems should be addressed by adopting a more vigorous rights-based perspective and assessing the risks that the current climate of rights scepticism pose for the future of children's rights.

(2) The Parental Factor

As the preceding chapters show, some branches of law reflect a good appreci-ation that children have their own rights that must be respected, while in other areas, this appears to be completely lacking. In these latter areas, it is often parents' interests which hold back a fuller legal acknowledgment of children rights. Indeed, many of the principles of child law still reflect an assumption that the state should not interfere in family life, rather that parents should be left alone to bring their children up as they see fit. This may explain the fact that case law and legislation have only slowly and inconsistently adapted to acknowledging that children are independent rights-holders. There is, of course, some irony in the fact that decisions producing the most welcome

---

[3] E.g. the continued uncertainty as to the precise basis, scope and limits of the concept of *Gillick* competence (*Gillick* v. *West Norfolk and Wisbech Area Health Authority* [1986] AC 112), discussed in Chapters 9 and 11.

[4] See Chapter 12.   [5] See Chapter 5.   [6] See Chapter 16.

clarification of children's rights have often been provoked by parents attempting to enforce their own rights to determine decisions about their children's lives. Thus, the group of Christian parents in the *Williamson* case[7] found to their cost that their children had a legal right to protection from the very religious views that they themselves had gone to court to promote. Victoria Gillick[8] and Sue Axon,[9] in attempting to define their own right to control their daughters' medical consultations, also unwittingly provoked a clarification of adolescents' rights to independence and medical privacy.[10] Litigation brought by the parents of the desperately ill baby, Charlie Gard, reinforced the principle that it was his best interests, not their parental rights, that determined his medical treatment.[11]

A prime example of legal inactivity predicated by parental self-interest is the family courts' apparent inability to see the average child arrangements dispute as anything other than a parental quarrel, thinly disguised as an argument about the child's best interests. The notion of children having their own rights in such disputes is barely ever acknowledged.[12] Similarly, the government has left virtually unscathed parents' right to use physical punishment to discipline their children in the privacy of their own homes. Its anxiety not to antagonise those upon whom it relies to bring up the next generation overcomes any notions of promoting children's right to freedom from violent treatment.[13] The state's sensitivity towards parents' rights to family privacy also dictates a reluctance to intervene to protect children from parental abuse and neglect except as a last resort. As a result, there has been a constant difficulty in maintaining an appropriate balance between respecting the right to family life and giving child protection agencies sufficient power and resources with which to intervene.[14]

The willingness of policy-makers to assume that children's interests are united with those of their parents is perhaps most apparent in the large body of legislation governing education. Only by avoiding the jurisdiction of the educational appeal tribunals was Shabina Begum able to reach the House of Lords with her own claim that her school's uniform policy infringed her right to religion under the ECHR. Despite her lack of success, her action demonstrated how important it is for children to be able to test out the boundaries of their own rights.[15] But it is only very occasionally that children emerge from the cloak of parental privacy to bring challenges on their own behalf. Indeed, the fact that children excluded from school still lack party status in the

---

[7] *R (on the application of Williamson and others)* v. *Secretary of State for Education and Employment and others* [2005] UKHL 15, [2005] 2 All ER 1; discussed in Chapter 8.

[8] *Gillick* v. *West Norfolk and Wisbech Area Health Authority* [1986] AC 112.

[9] *R (Axon)* v. *Secretary of State for Health and the Family Planning Association* [2006] EWHC 37 (Admin), [2006] 2 FLR 206.

[10] Discussed in Chapters 9 and 11.   [11] See Chapter 7.   [12] See Chapter 6.

[13] See Chapter 4.   [14] See Chapter 15.

[15] *R (on the application of Begum)* v. *Head Teacher and Governors of Denbigh High School* [2006] UKHL 15, [2007] AC 100, discussed in Chapter 8.

independent review process reflects the official view that education is a service designed for adult consumption.[16] Admittedly, some parents are tenacious enough to challenge inferior educational provision. Their success has produced judicial confirmation that their children have rights to education free from discrimination and that these must be recognised by schools and local authorities (LAs).[17] There must, however, be many more parents who eschew embarking on such potentially stressful litigation, leaving their children's rights unrecognised.

Overall, we see a system of law which fitfully acknowledges the concept of children having rights, with concerns about parents' interests usually far outweighing other considerations. Indeed, as discussed below, the inconsistent development of the law results in various aspects of childhood being singled out for particular attention, with little opportunity to consider children's needs holistically.

(3) The 'Fragmented' Child

Much has been written about the way in which the law constructs children to fulfil adult preconceptions of how they fit into an adult-orientated legal framework. We have discussed, for example, the criticisms levelled at the way in which the family courts deal with private law applications, with their implicit assumption that children are the passive victims of their parents' battles.[18] There are many other ways in which law constructs children, portraying them all with group characteristics often out of tune with reality.[19] The constructed nature of childhood is laid bare by the way in which assumptions about age vary according to context and often appear entirely detached from the underlying research on child development.[20] In many ways, the law's conception of childhood has been extended, through an increase in the ages at which restrictions and protections are imposed on young people.[21] Yet, this increasing perception of 16- and 17-year-olds as requiring protection from the responsibilities of adulthood appears to be abandoned for those who are in the care of the state, who may be placed in unregulated accommodation without the protections offered to younger children.[22] At the same time, children as

---

[16] See Chapter 14.
[17] See e.g. *C & C* v. *the Governing Body of a School, The Secretary of State for Education (First Interested Party) and the National Autistic Society (Second Interested Party) (SEN)* [2018] UKUT 269, discussed in Chapter 14.
[18] See Chapter 12.   [19] C. Piper (2007) pp. 148–52.   [20] See Chapter 9.
[21] Notably in the introduction of the requirement to be in training or education until 18: Education and Skills Act 2008. Other examples include: raising the age at which cigarettes might be purchased from 16 to 18 (Children and Young Persons (Sale of Tobacco etc.) Order 2007); altering the offence concerning indecent images of children to include images of 16- and 17-year-olds (Sexual Offences Act 2003, s. 49(1)(2)); and the increase in the minimum age for entry into marriage or civil partnership from 16 to 18 in the Marriage and Civil Partnership (Minimum Age) Act 2022.
[22] Discussed in Chapters 10 and 16.

young as 10 can still be held criminally responsible for their actions.[23] These differences in perceptions of childhood appear fragmented across different bodies of law and bear little relation to the developing scientific literature.

In more general terms, as far as law and social policy are concerned, there appear to be two main groups of children and their treatment is at complete variance. There are the 'responsible' children, who as they mature, are deemed perfectly able to take responsibility for their own decision-making.[24] Government policies largely leave this group well alone, trusting their parents to bring them up as they think fit. For these children, the civil law has developed the enlightened concept of *Gillick* competence. The House of Lords in *Gillick* v. *West Norfolk and Wisbech Area Health Authority*[25] saw the wisdom of harnessing the goodwill of sensible adolescents by treating them as individuals fast approaching adulthood. This legal approach promotes the idea that children, when sufficiently mature, can act responsibly if given the legal authority and freedom to do so. They may not only understand their own needs better than their parents, but society needs adolescents who know how to act sensibly without their parents' authority, for example, by taking precautions against unwanted pregnancies.

The second group of children are the troubled and the troublesome – those who experience the 'headline' problems: youth crime, truancy and school exclusions, social alienation, unemployment and homelessness. Many of these have the same underlying problems, but the law and policy applied to them depends entirely on the way in which they first attract adults' attention and whose attention they attract. For example, those who are disruptive in school, bully others and truant may end up permanently excluded from mainstream education and in a pupil referral unit. Alternatively, their behaviour may be diagnosed as being attributable to their learning difficulties. Their problems, being defined as an educational issue and dealt with under the umbrella of SEN law and policy, then gain the attention of educational psychologists, special educational needs coordinators and classroom assistants. They may even be sent to a special residential school. On the other hand, their behaviour may suggest mental health problems, with a referral to the CAMHS,[26] with the possibility of ending up as patients in secure children's homes, or psychiatric units, under secure accommodation orders.[27] Some of these children will be identified by LAs as requiring protection from abuse. They may find themselves removed from home and found alternative homes, either through adoption or long-term fostering, or in a children's home.

---

[23] The age of criminal responsibility has been 10 since 1963. See Children and Young Persons Act 1933, s. 50, as amended by Children and Young Persons Act 1963, s. 16. Until the presumption was abolished by s. 34 of the Crime and Disorder Act 1998, children under the age of 14 and above 10 were presumed incapable of knowing that what they had done was wrong and therefore not criminally responsible for whatever offence they might have committed.

[24] C. Piper (2008) pp. 35–50.   [25] [1986] AC 112, discussed in Chapter 9.

[26] Child and Adolescent Mental Health Services.   [27] See Chapter 16.

A fundamental dilemma is posed by the research indicating that children who have faced these challenges are more likely to become involved in troublesome behaviour themselves. Their treatment will depend on whether the law's response is punitive or recognises the vulnerabilities of those who are drawn into criminal activity. Increasing awareness of the vulnerability of some children to criminal exploitation means that they are now more likely to be seen as victims in need of protection than perpetrators requiring punishment.[28]

The extent to which a child or young person will be able to oppose any interventions with the help of separate representation depends entirely on the law relating to the process. If, for example, legal proceedings are mounted to ensure that a young person enters secure accommodation on a welfare placement,[29] he or she will be represented by a children's guardian and a solicitor. Equally, if the same young person is required to answer charges in a youth court, he or she gains legal representation. If, however, he or she is excluded from school, the parents alone are entitled to speak on behalf of their offspring, but only if they appeal. If health problems force a child under the age of 16 to seek medical attention, he or she may be treated in a way that requires deprivation of liberty on the authority only of the parents.[30] In each situation, a different set of practitioners with their own specialised training and expertise will see the child's problems and background from an entirely different and sometimes opposing viewpoint. This fragmented approach to childhood problems encourages practitioners to categorise children according to sets of rigidly defined symptoms, rather than to view them as individuals. It promotes a simplistic approach to diagnosis, undermines an efficient coordination of services and prevents problems being picked up early in children's lives.

(4) Negative Perceptions of 'Youth' and Exclusion from Public Life

Alongside this fragmented approach to childhood, children and young people are being portrayed in various negative ways and in return feel excluded from public life. They are often seen as irresponsible – unwilling to adopt a responsible attitude to community affairs. More dangerously, it is society's own attitudes towards young people which risks alienating them against an adult society which appears to view them as 'problematic' or even 'a threat'.[31] In its unconcerned use of dispersal orders, mosquito devices and surveillance, we see symptoms of a society unwilling to tolerate young people in public spaces.[32] As the Committee on the Rights of the Child observes, young people in the UK are growing up in 'a general climate of intolerance and negative

---

[28] See Chapter 10.   [29] See Chapter 16.   [30] See Chapter 9.

[31] C. Piper (2007) p. 149; Children's Commissioner (2020) p. 8.

[32] Children's Commissioner (2020) p. 9; Committee on the Rights of the Child (2016a) para. 37. 'Mosquito devices' emit a high-pitched sound at frequencies that only children can hear and are used with the aim of dispersing children.

public attitudes towards children, especially adolescents'.[33] Young people are themselves keenly aware of their reputation in the community for being anti-social. Raz's comment in a general context has particular resonance:

> The existence within a political society of estranged groups, who do not identify with the state, or the nation, and regard the government as an alien, potentially hostile, government, is destabilizing. Beyond that is the fact that human beings are political animals. That means more than that they can only thrive in political societies which provide the opportunities for the activities which make their lives. It also means that feeling part of a larger community, and being able to identify oneself as a member of such communities is an essential ingredient in people's well-being. Those who are second class citizens are marked by this experience which forces a flawed life on them.[34]

A fundamental problem is that, currently, many young people do not consider that their views are valued by decision-makers.[35] This is particularly evident in the political process, which excludes mature young people from voting[36] and gives only limited and haphazard attention to children's participation, interests and rights.[37] It is unsurprising if children and young people feel that they are not sufficiently considered in the political process. Policies such as austerity and the response to the Covid-19 pandemic have placed a disproportionate burden on children and young people for relatively little benefit to them.[38] The perception that their rights and interests are neglected in the public sphere is magnified for certain groups of children, as is evident from the higher inci-dence of poverty and exclusion from school for children and young people from particular racial groups or with particular disabilities.[39] Similarly, young people in the care system have suffered from an appalling failure to plan for and provide sufficient safe accommodation to meet their basic needs, let alone provide a healthy environment in which they can thrive.[40] It is no surprise that many young people feel alienated from, and disempowered by, the very systems that are supposed to provide for them.[41]

Many of these problems could be alleviated through more systematic and thorough engagement with children's rights, and with children themselves, in public decision-making.[42] The work of the Committee on the Rights of the Child (the 'Committee') has set international standards for integrating

---

[33] Committee on the Rights of the Child (2008) para. 24, (2016a) para. 23.

[34] J. Raz (1996) p. 125.

[35] Unpublished research by MORI/Office for the Children's Commissioner (2006): a survey of over 2,000 11–16-year-olds revealed that 50 per cent did not consider that they had enough say in decisions affecting them.

[36] Chapter 10 discusses the case for extending the right to vote to 16- and 17-year-olds.

[37] Children's Commissioner (2020) p. 4.   [38] Chapter 13.

[39] Chapters 13 and 14. See also Children's Commissioner (2020) p. 9.

[40] Chapters 10 and 16. See esp. discussion of unregulated placements and of deprivation of liberty.

[41] See discussion of children in court proceedings (Chapter 12), child protection proceedings (Chapter 15), in care (Chapter 16) and in education (Chapter 14).

[42] Chapter 13.

children's rights into public decision-making and budgeting.[43] In particular, the Committee has called for a statutory obligation to carry out a thorough children's rights impact assessment before adopting laws and policy that affect children.[44] It has also emphasised the importance of ensuring meaningful participation of children in the development of those laws and policies, as well as in decisions that are directed at them as individuals.[45] Despite progress in the devolved administrations in Scotland and Wales, the commitment to such measures in Westminster remains patchy and limited.[46] A deeper commitment to children's rights, which took children's perspectives seriously, could address the feelings of alienation that many children evidently feel, as well as result in decisions and policy that better reflect the needs of children.

(5) Strengthening Rights for Children

The problems noted above remain despite the decades that have passed since the ratification by the UK of the CRC in 1991 and the coming into force of the HRA in 2000. Does this mean that the rights-based approach has been a failure for children? Certainly, the recognition of enforceable human rights for children did not have the dramatic impact predicted by some. The legal principles most closely affecting children have remained largely intact, only gradually absorbing the requirements of a rights-based system. This is well illustrated by the fact that the framework of the Children Act 1989 and the centrality of the welfare principle have remained in place, relatively unscathed by the interaction with children's rights.[47] Further, the introduction of rights has not been a panacea for the problems that children face in law and society. There is a danger that the language of rights can be used to mask claims made by adults on behalf of children, which might not otherwise escape critical analysis. This concern can be seen particularly clearly in cases in which the courts pay lip-service to children's rights when reaching decisions which appear to be disguised claims for the rights of their parents.[48] It can also be seen in the way in which children often express their feeling of alienation from the processes that are ostensibly designed for them. There is also a criticism that the language of rights will achieve little if it is not backed by the resources and political will required to make those rights a practical reality.

Nonetheless, the rights-based approach has had notable advantages for children. The courts are now much more aware of the potential for their decisions to affect the rights of children. Any decision which risks breaching

---

[43] Esp. Committee on the Rights of the Child (2013), (2016b). The requirements for implementation of the CRC in policy-making are considered further by B. Byrne and L. Lundy (2019).

[44] Committee on the Rights of the Child (2016a) para. 10.   [45] Ibid. para. 31.   [46] Chapter 3.

[47] As argued in Chapter 3, the notion that a rights-based approach is necessarily incompatible with a welfare-based approach misconstrues the concept of rights and does not reflect the practice of the domestic courts or the ECtHR.

[48] E.g. applications for DNA tests, discussed in Chapter 5, and the approach to child arrangements orders, discussed in Chapter 6.

those rights – for example, by removing the child from home, seriously impeding a relationship with a parent or constraining the child's liberty – will be subject to a rights-based analysis.[49] The courts are also increasingly sensitive to the participation of children in cases concerning them and to the importance of the child's views.[50] In public law, too, the statutory obligations on specified public bodies to act to 'safeguard and promote the welfare of children' have been interpreted to require those bodies to act compatibly with children's rights.[51] Although the integration of children's rights into public decision-making remains haphazard and sometimes superficial, the status of children's rights has been enhanced, notably with the strengthened role of the Children's Commissioner.[52]

Many of the weaknesses for children's rights in the current law stem from the fact that the ECHR was drafted in an adult-focused manner at a time when distinct children's rights were not recognised in international law.[53] Although the European Court of Human Rights (ECtHR) has increasingly turned to international law, including the CRC, to interpret the ECHR for children, it remains unable to address many of the wider rights recognised by the CRC. The HRA, in turn, remains limited in its ability to remedy the full range of children's rights recognised in international law today. Reform of the HRA to include specific consideration of children's rights would be the most effective way of addressing the limitations of the current domestic law. The CRC would be the best starting point for such an approach, its scope being far wider than that of the ECHR, which focuses on civil and political rights. As Newell observes:

> The particular task of the Convention is to emphasise that children too are holders of human rights. They are not possessions of their parents or of the state. They are not simply objects of concern. They are not people-in-the-making. They are individuals *now* with views, feelings and rights.[54]

Attempts to persuade the government to promote children's rights more vigorously are substantially undermined by the fact that the CRC is not part of English law and so is not directly legally enforceable.[55] Incorporation of the CRC into domestic law would address the particular vulnerabilities and circumstances of children. Further, a general statutory duty on all ministers and public authorities to have due regard to children's rights and best interests in matters concerning them would provide a more effective basis for redressing the current neglect of children in many facets of the public sphere.[56] Only a dramatic change of this kind will provoke a change in attitude in the various government departments which still retain traditional and hidebound assumptions about children and young people. Such an approach would go some way towards achieving the goal set out by the UN General Assembly in 2002:

[49] Discussed in Chapter 3. See also Chapters 6, 9 and 15.   [50] Chapter 12.   [51] Chapter 13.
[52] Discussed in Chapter 3.   [53] Discussed in Chapter 2.
[54] P. Newell (2000) p. 18 (emphasis in the original).   [55] See Chapter 3.   [56] Chapter 13.

together we will build a world in which all girls and boys can enjoy childhood – a time of play and learning, in which they are loved, respected and cherished, their rights are promoted and protected, without discrimination of any kind, in which their safety and well-being are paramount and in which they can develop in health, peace and dignity.[57]

(6) Rights Scepticism and Reform

The strength of the case for incorporation of the CRC has been accepted with enthusiasm in the devolved nations.[58] Unfortunately, the current direction of reform of rights in England, and the UK as a whole, seems more likely to lead to a curtailment of children's rights rather than an expansion. The current government's scepticism of the HRA reached its height with the proposal to repeal the HRA and replace it with a UK Bill of Rights.[59] Although the Bill has now been withdrawn, the proposals demonstrate the precariousness of children's rights in the face of political opposition to the HRA. The proposed change would not have extended the range of rights protected in this domestic Bill of Rights; instead, the intention was to retain the current rights derived from the ECHR, but to replace the framework by which those rights are protected. This proposed reform represented a double blow for children: not only was the opportunity to incorporate specific rights for children missed, but the reforms to the mode of protection were likely to have a disproportionate impact on children. The government acknowledged that likely disproportionate impact, but made no attempt at detailed analysis of the effect on children or how it might be mitigated.[60]

There are many reasons why the proposed reforms were likely to be particularly detrimental to children. Although the reforms were not specifically directed at children or their rights, they demonstrate scepticism about developments in human rights law that have had particular benefit for children. This underlying scepticism remains politically salient, leaving children's rights vulnerable to further attempts to curtail the operation of the HRA. A key purpose behind the proposed reform was to strengthen the deference that courts exhibit in human rights cases to the decisions of Parliament and to the

---

[57] UN General Assembly (2002) para. 9.

[58] Discussed in Chapter 3. An attempt to incorporate much of the CRC into Scottish law was contained in the UN Convention on the Rights of the Child (Incorporation) (Scotland) Bill. This Bill was found to be outside of the legislative competence of the Scottish Parliament, although the judgment did not preclude legislation to incorporate the CRC into Scottish law in a different form: *Re Attorney-General's Reference, United Nations Convention on the Rights of the Child (Incorporation) (Scotland) Bill* [2021] UKSC 42, [2021] 1 WLR 5106.

[59] MoJ (2021).

[60] MoJ (2021) Appendix 3, para. 16. The impact assessment accompanying the draft Bill also gives no detailed consideration, but does note that 45 per cent of claimants with legal aid certificates for human rights claims are children under 16, while they make up just 20 per cent of the population: MoJ (2022) paras 275 and 284.

expertise of public authorities.[61] While the broader debate on the separation of powers and human rights is outside the scope of this book, any such rebalancing is likely to have a detrimental effect on children and particularly on the most vulnerable children. As discussed above, the barriers to children's participation in legislation and public decision-making are such that it is easy for their interests to be neglected, particularly if there is no group championing those interests in the political process.[62] That danger is particularly clear in relation to socio-economic rights given their precarious place in domestic law and the deferential approach adopted by the courts to matters of social and economic policy.[63] A further aim of the reform was to reduce the influence of developments in the Strasbourg court by emphasising that the Supreme Court is the ultimate arbiter of the meaning of rights in domestic law.[64] The freedom of the Supreme Court would, however, be curtailed by the requirement to have particular regard to the text of the right and the proposed prohibition on adopting any interpretation that expands the protection given by a right.[65] These limitations are driven by criticism of the ECtHR's 'living instrument' approach to interpretation. Strasbourg's willingness to interpret the ECHR purposefully and with regard to international law has been especially important in ensuring that the Convention is relevant for children,[66] who were given limited consideration in its drafting. Any retrenchment to the text of the rights is likely to stunt their utility for children.

The proposals to restrict recognition of positive obligations in the Bill of Rights are perhaps the most concerning aspect of the intended reform and demonstrate well the dangers of this rights-scepticism for children. By requiring the state to take action to secure rights, positive obligations[67] have been of particular benefit to children, who are likely to find themselves reliant on the state for protection from harm and for the provision of services that enable them to realise rights in practice.[68] The examples of positive obligations given by the Ministry of Justice are a good illustration of this. It cites the well-established principle that reasonable steps must be taken to protect children from abusive parents if state agencies are aware, or ought to be aware, that they are being subjected to serious neglect or ill-treatment.[69] The importance of this principle is demonstrated by the seminal case of *Z v. United Kingdom*,[70] in

---

[61] MoJ (2021) paras 151–81.   [62] See discussion above and Chapter 3.

[63] See: Chapter 13; A. Nolan (2014).

[64] Bill of Rights Bill 117, Session 2022–23 cl. 1(2)(a) and (3) and cl. 3. See also MoJ (2021) paras 189–201.

[65] Bill of Rights Bill 117, Session 2022–23 cl. 3(3)(a): the restriction would apply 'unless the court has no reasonable doubt that' Strasbourg would adopt the same interpretation if the case were before it.

[66] Discussed in Chapter 2.   [67] Discussed in Chapter 3.

[68] See Chapter 13 for further discussion of why children are especially likely to benefit from positive obligations.

[69] MoJ (2021) para. 108. Discussed in Chapter 15.

[70] [2001] 2 FLR 612, at [73]–[74]: state agencies must take reasonable steps to prevent children being subjected to ill-treatment amounting to torture or inhuman or degrading treatment

which four children suffered 'horrific' experiences and 'appalling neglect' that amounted to treatment that met the threshold for Article 3 of the ECHR. The state had failed to intervene for 4.5 years after it was first made aware of the children's plight, during which time the children suffered physical and psychiatric injury. Although the ECtHR noted the difficult and sensitive decisions facing social services, it found that this case represented a serious failure of the system to protect the children from serious long-term neglect and abuse, of which the state was well aware, and so amounted to a violation of Article 3 of the ECHR. This positive obligation is vital to children in establishing that they have a fundamental right to protection from abuse and are not merely to be treated as passive victims of their parents' cruelty and the state's apathy. The Ministry of Justice also cites the case law that established the principle that the right to family life remains important for children in care and that steps must be taken to assess whether it is possible to maintain contact and safely reintegrate the child back into the family.[71] This is also an important obligation, ensuring that children do not unnecessarily lose relationships with their families.[72] These examples demonstrate the vital importance of positive obligations to children's fundamental rights and it is surprising to see them cited in support of the need to *curtail* positive obligations.[73] The government's reasoning appears to be that these are 'judicial extensions of human rights' that 'have enabled the Strasbourg Court to prescribe domestic principles and rules'.[74] In fact, these principles were essentially in place prior to the enactment of the HRA. Further, the ECtHR has been careful to recognise the sensitivity of the decisions made in this area and so grants a very wide margin of appreciation, only criticising decisions as to whether to take children into care in egregious circumstances such as those in *Z* v. *United Kingdom*.[75] Rather than prescribing domestic principles and rules, the case law places wide outer limits on the duties of the state, without which children would have no *right* to protection from abusive families. Nevertheless, the proposed Bill of Rights sought to prohibit recognition of new positive obligations and to give even greater weight to the discretion and expertise of public authorities in deciding how to fulfil current obligations.[76] Given the wide margin of appreciation already

---

under Art. 3 in situations where they had or ought to have had knowledge of that ill-treatment. The case is cited in MoJ (2021) para. 108 in favour of a different proposition (custody arrangements of international families living in the UK), but this appears to be an error.

[71] MoJ (2021) para. 108 cites *W* v. *United Kingdom* (1988) 10 EHRR 29. The success of these parents' applications led to the abolition of the power of LAs to acquire parental responsibility over children by administrative resolution. They also provoked CA 1989, s. 34, giving parents a right to apply for contact with their children while in state care.

[72] Although, as discussed in Chapter 15, there has been a tendency for the ECtHR to reason primarily in terms of the rights of the parents to maintain family relationships, rather than the independent rights of the child.

[73] See discussion in Chapter 15 on the balance to be drawn between these two obligations.

[74] MoJ (2021) para. 109.   [75] See discussion in Chapter 15.

[76] Bill of Rights Bill 117, Session 2022–23 cl. 5, esp. 5(2): 'In deciding whether to apply a pre-commencement interpretation of a Convention right that would require a public authority to

applied in these cases, raising that bar still further is likely to render such obligations nugatory. Curtailing positive obligations in this way would hollow out much of the work done to provide accountability for securing children's rights in practice.

Reforms such as those proposed in the Bill of Rights Bill are unlikely to undo all of the progress that has been made on children's rights to date. They do, however, have the potential to pose significant obstacles to interpreting the Convention rights in a manner that is relevant and practically useful for children. These obstacles are likely to be highest in relation to public decision-making and areas of economic and social policy. If reforms of this nature are implemented, it will be especially important for there to be rapid and substantial improvement in the way in which public authorities and legislators engage with children's rights. Unfortunately, there appears to be little will to do so at present. Whether or not these proposals become law, it is clear that the current trend in rights-scepticism is a real risk for the future of children's rights in this country.

(7) Conclusion

Despite the current dangers of rights-scepticism, it is clear that much progress has been made in developing children's rights in law and in policy since the enactment of the HRA. It is not, however, enough for lawyers and policy-makers simply to resolve to adopt a rights-based framework for their work, without being clear what children really require to enhance their well-being. Children's rights are not promoted if adults merely deliver a rough approximation of what children need, based on their own prejudices. As this work shows, law and policy can usefully draw on a growing body of research which considers children's needs from a variety of perspectives. Practitioners who are sympathetic to the concept of fulfilling children's rights should bear in mind that to ignore this information produces principles and policies which are devoid of practical utility and which may do more harm than good. Above all else, the concept of children's rights should be utilised honestly and not as a politically correct tool which only thinly disguises adult caution and narrow-mindedness.

Bibliography

NB: Many of these publications can be obtained on the relevant organisation's website.

Byrne, B. and Lundy, L. (2019) 'Children's Rights-Based Childhood Policy: A Six-P Framework' 23 *International Journal of Human Rights* 357.

comply with a positive obligation, the court must give great weight to the need to avoid applying an interpretation that would – (a) have an impact on the ability of the public authority or of any other public authority to perform its functions; (b) conflict with or otherwise undermine the public interest in allowing public authorities to use their own expertise when deciding how to allocate the financial and other resources available to them, including in particular the professional judgment of those involved in operational matters; . . . '

Children's Commissioner (2020) *Report of the Children's Commissioners of the United Kingdom of Great Britain and Northern Ireland to the United Nations Committee on the Rights of the Child*, Children's Commissioners.

Committee on the Rights of the Child (2008) *Concluding Observations of the Committee on the Rights of the Child: United Kingdom of Great Britain and Northern Ireland*, CRC/C/GBR/CO/4, Centre for Human Rights, Geneva.

(2013) *General Comment No. 14 on the Right of the Child to Have His or Her Best Interests Taken as a Primary Consideration (Art. 3, Para. 1)*, CRC/C/GC/14, Centre for Human Rights, Geneva.

(2016a) *Concluding Observations of the Committee on the Rights of the Child: United Kingdom of Great Britain and Northern Ireland*, CRC/C/GBR/CO/5, Centre for Human Rights, Geneva.

(2016b) *General Comment No. 19 on Public Budgeting for the Realization of Children's Rights (Art. 4)*, CRC/C/GC/19, Centre for Human Rights, Geneva.

Ministry of Justice (MoJ) (2021) *Human Rights Act Reform: A Modern Bill of Rights, CP 588*, Her Majesty's Stationery Office.

(2022) *Impact Assessment: Draft Bill of Rights*, MOJ19/2021, MoJ.

Newell, P. (2000) *Taking Children Seriously: A Proposal for a Children's Rights Commissioner*, Calouste Gulbenkian Foundation.

Nolan, A. (2014) *Children's Socio-Economic Rights, Democracy and the Courts*, Hart Publishing.

Piper, C. (2007) 'Will Law Think about Children? Reflections on Youth Matters' in Invernizzi, A. and Williams, J. (eds) *Children and Citizenship*, Sage Publications.

(2008) *Investing in Children: Policy, Law and Practice in Context*, Willan Publishing.

Raz, J. (1996) 'Liberty and Trust' in George, R. (ed.) *Natural Law, Liberalism and Morality*, Oxford University Press.

UN General Assembly (2002) A/RES/S-27/2, *A World Fit for Children, Resolution Adopted by the General Assembly*, Geneva.

Appendix I

UN Convention on the Rights of the Child

The Convention on the Rights of the Child was adopted and opened for signature, ratification and accession by General Assembly resolution 44/25 of 20 November 1989. It entered into force 2 September 1990, in accordance with article 49.

Preamble

The States Parties to the present Convention,

Considering that, in accordance with the principles proclaimed in the Charter of the United Nations, recognition of the inherent dignity and of the equal and inalienable rights of all members of the human family is the foundation of freedom, justice and peace in the world,

Bearing in mind that the peoples of the United Nations have, in the Charter, reaffirmed their faith in fundamental human rights and in the dignity and worth of the human person and have determined to promote social progress and better standards of life in larger freedom,

Recognizing that the United Nations has, in the Universal Declaration of Human Rights and in the International Covenants on Human Rights, proclaimed and agreed that everyone is entitled to all the rights and freedoms set forth therein, without distinction of any kind, such as race, colour, sex, language, religion, political or other opinion, national or social origin, property, birth or other status,

Recalling that, in the Universal Declaration of Human Rights, the United Nations has proclaimed that childhood is entitled to special care and assistance,

Convinced that the family, as the fundamental group of society and the natural environment for the growth and well-being of all its members and particularly children, should be afforded the necessary protection and assistance so that it can fully assume its responsibilities within the community,

Recognizing that the child, for the full and harmonious development of his or her personality, should grow up in a family environment, in an atmosphere of happiness, love and understanding,

Considering that the child should be fully prepared to live an individual life in society and brought up in the spirit of the ideals proclaimed in the Charter of the United Nations and in particular in the spirit of peace, dignity, tolerance, freedom, equality and solidarity,

Bearing in mind that the need to extend particular care to the child has been stated in the Geneva Declaration of the Rights of the Child of 1924 and in the Declaration of the Rights of the Child adopted by the General Assembly on 20 November 1959 and recognized in the Universal Declaration of Human Rights, in the International Covenant on Civil and Political Rights (in particular in articles 23 and 24), in the International Covenant on Economic, Social and Cultural Rights (in particular in article 10) and in the statutes and relevant instruments of specialized agencies and international organizations concerned with the welfare of children,

Bearing in mind that, as indicated in the Declaration of the Rights of the Child, "the child, by reason of his physical and mental immaturity, needs special safeguards and care, including appropriate legal protection, before as well as after birth",

Recalling the provisions of the Declaration on Social and Legal Principles relating to the Protection and Welfare of Children, with Special Reference to Foster Placement and Adoption Nationally and Internationally; the United Nations Standard Minimum Rules for the Administration of Juvenile Justice (The Beijing Rules); and the Declaration on the Protection of Women and Children in Emergency and Armed Conflict,

Recognizing that, in all countries in the world, there are children living in exceptionally difficult conditions and that such children need special consideration,

Taking due account of the importance of the traditions and cultural values of each people for the protection and harmonious development of the child,

Recognizing the importance of international co-operation for improving the living conditions of children in every country, in particular in the developing countries,

Have agreed as follows:

Part I

Article 1

For the purposes of the present Convention, a child means every human being below the age of eighteen years unless under the law applicable to the child, majority is attained earlier.

Article 2

1. States Parties shall respect and ensure the rights set forth in the present Convention to each child within their jurisdiction without discrimination of any kind, irrespective of the child's or his or her parent's or legal guardian's race, colour, sex, language, religion, political or other opinion, national, ethnic or social origin, property, disability, birth or other status.

2. States Parties shall take all appropriate measures to ensure that the child is protected against all forms of discrimination or punishment on the basis of the status, activities, expressed opinions, or beliefs of the child's parents, legal guardians, or family members.

Article 3

1. In all actions concerning children, whether undertaken by public or private social welfare institutions, courts of law, administrative authorities or legislative bodies, the best interests of the child shall be a primary consideration.
2. States Parties undertake to ensure the child such protection and care as is necessary for his or her well-being, taking into account the rights and duties of his or her parents, legal guardians, or other individuals legally responsible for him or her, and, to this end, shall take all appropriate legislative and administrative measures.
3. States Parties shall ensure that the institutions, services and facilities responsible for the care or protection of children shall conform with the standards established by competent authorities, particularly in the areas of safety, health, in the number and suitability of their staff, as well as competent supervision.

Article 4

States Parties shall undertake all appropriate legislative, administrative and other measures for the implementation of the rights recognized in the present Convention. With regard to economic, social and cultural rights, States Parties shall undertake such measures to the maximum extent of their available resources and, where needed, within the framework of international co-operation.

Article 5

States Parties shall respect the responsibilities, rights and duties of parents or, where applicable, the members of the extended family or community as provided for by local custom, legal guardians or other persons legally responsible for the child, to provide, in a manner consistent with the evolving capacities of the child, appropriate direction and guidance in the exercise by the child of the rights recognized in the present Convention.

Article 6

1. States Parties recognize that every child has the inherent right to life.
2. States Parties shall ensure to the maximum extent possible the survival and development of the child.

Article 7

1. The child shall be registered immediately after birth and shall have the right from birth to a name, the right to acquire a nationality and, as far as possible, the right to know and be cared for by his or her parents.
2. States Parties shall ensure the implementation of these rights in accordance with their national law and their obligations under the relevant international instruments in this field, in particular where the child would otherwise be stateless.

Article 8

1. States Parties undertake to respect the right of the child to preserve his or her identity, including nationality, name and family relations as recognized by law without unlawful interference.
2. Where a child is illegally deprived of some or all of the elements of his or her identity, States Parties shall provide appropriate assistance and protection, with a view to re-establishing speedily his or her identity.

Article 9

1. States Parties shall ensure that a child shall not be separated from his or her parents against their will, except when competent authorities subject to judicial review determine, in accordance with applicable law and procedures, that such separation is necessary for the best interests of the child. Such determination may be necessary in a particular case such as one involving abuse or neglect of the child by the parents, or one where the parents are living separately and a decision must be made as to the child's place of residence.
2. In any proceedings pursuant to paragraph 1 of the present article, all interested parties shall be given an opportunity to participate in the proceedings and make their views known.
3. States Parties shall respect the right of the child who is separated from one or both parents to maintain personal relations and direct contact with both parents on a regular basis, except if it is contrary to the child's best interests.
4. Where such separation results from any action initiated by a State Party, such as the detention, imprisonment, exile, deportation or death (including death arising from any cause while the person is in the custody of the State) of one or both parents or of the child, that State Party shall, upon request, provide the parents, the child or, if appropriate, another member of the family with the essential information concerning the whereabouts of the absent member(s) of the family unless the provision of the information would be detrimental to the well-being of the child. States Parties shall further ensure that the submission of such a request shall of itself entail no adverse consequences for the person(s) concerned.

Article 10

1. In accordance with the obligation of States Parties under article 9, paragraph 1, applications by a child or his or her parents to enter or leave a State Party for the purpose of family reunification shall be dealt with by States Parties in a positive, humane and expeditious manner. States Parties shall further ensure that the submission of such a request shall entail no adverse consequences for the applicants and for the members of their family.
2. A child whose parents reside in different States shall have the right to maintain on a regular basis, save in exceptional circumstances personal relations and direct contacts with both parents. Towards that end and in accordance with the obligation of States Parties under article 9, paragraph 1, States Parties shall respect the right of the child and his or her parents to leave any country, including their own and to enter their own country. The right to leave any country shall be subject only to such restrictions as are prescribed by law and which are necessary to protect the national security, public order (ordre public), public health or morals or the rights and freedoms of others and are consistent with the other rights recognized in the present Convention.

Article 11

1. States Parties shall take measures to combat the illicit transfer and non-return of children abroad.
2. To this end, States Parties shall promote the conclusion of bilateral or multilateral agreements or accession to existing agreements.

Article 12

1. States Parties shall assure to the child who is capable of forming his or her own views the right to express those views freely in all matters affecting the child, the views of the child being given due weight in accordance with the age and maturity of the child.
2. For this purpose, the child shall in particular be provided the opportunity to be heard in any judicial and administrative proceedings affecting the child, either directly, or through a representative or an appropriate body, in a manner consistent with the procedural rules of national law.

Article 13

1. The child shall have the right to freedom of expression; this right shall include freedom to seek, receive and impart information and ideas of all kinds, regardless of frontiers, either orally, in writing or in print, in the form of art, or through any other media of the child's choice.

2. The exercise of this right may be subject to certain restrictions, but these shall only be such as are provided by law and are necessary:

(a) For respect of the rights or reputations of others; or
(b) For the protection of national security or of public order (ordre public), or of public health or morals.

Article 14

1. States Parties shall respect the right of the child to freedom of thought, conscience and religion.
2. States Parties shall respect the rights and duties of the parents and, when applicable, legal guardians, to provide direction to the child in the exercise of his or her right in a manner consistent with the evolving capacities of the child.
3. Freedom to manifest one's religion or beliefs may be subject only to such limitations as are prescribed by law and are necessary to protect public safety, order, health or morals, or the fundamental rights and freedoms of others.

Article 15

1. States Parties recognize the rights of the child to freedom of association and to freedom of peaceful assembly.
2. No restrictions may be placed on the exercise of these rights other than those imposed in conformity with the law and which are necessary in a democratic society in the interests of national security or public safety, public order (ordre public), the protection of public health or morals or the protection of the rights and freedoms of others.

Article 16

1. No child shall be subjected to arbitrary or unlawful interference with his or her privacy, family, home or correspondence, nor to unlawful attacks on his or her honour and reputation.
2. The child has the right to the protection of the law against such interference or attacks.

Article 17

States Parties recognize the important function performed by the mass media and shall ensure that the child has access to information and material from a diversity of national and international sources, especially those aimed at the promotion of his or her social, spiritual and moral well-being and physical and mental health. To this end, States Parties shall:

(a) Encourage the mass media to disseminate information and material of social and cultural benefit to the child and in accordance with the spirit of article 29;

(b) Encourage international co-operation in the production, exchange and dissemination of such information and material from a diversity of cultural, national and international sources;

(c) Encourage the production and dissemination of children's books;

(d) Encourage the mass media to have particular regard to the linguistic needs of the child who belongs to a minority group or who is indigenous;

(e) Encourage the development of appropriate guidelines for the protection of the child from information and material injurious to his or her well-being, bearing in mind the provisions of articles 13 and 18.

Article 18

1. States Parties shall use their best efforts to ensure recognition of the principle that both parents have common responsibilities for the upbringing and development of the child. Parents or, as the case may be, legal guardians, have the primary responsibility for the upbringing and development of the child. The best interests of the child will be their basic concern.

2. For the purpose of guaranteeing and promoting the rights set forth in the present Convention, States Parties shall render appropriate assistance to parents and legal guardians in the performance of their child-rearing responsibilities and shall ensure the development of institutions, facilities and services for the care of children.

3. States Parties shall take all appropriate measures to ensure that children of working parents have the right to benefit from child-care services and facilities for which they are eligible.

Article 19

1. States Parties shall take all appropriate legislative, administrative, social and educational measures to protect the child from all forms of physical or mental violence, injury or abuse, neglect or negligent treatment, maltreatment or exploitation, including sexual abuse, while in the care of parent(s), legal guardian(s) or any other person who has the care of the child.

2. Such protective measures should, as appropriate, include effective procedures for the establishment of social programmes to provide necessary support for the child and for those who have the care of the child, as well as for other forms of prevention and for identification, reporting, referral, investigation, treatment and follow-up of instances of child maltreatment described heretofore, and, as appropriate, for judicial involvement.

Article 20

1. A child temporarily or permanently deprived of his or her family environment, or in whose own best interests cannot be allowed to remain in that environment, shall be entitled to special protection and assistance provided by the State.
2. States Parties shall in accordance with their national laws ensure alternative care for such a child.
3. Such care could include, inter alia, foster placement, kafalah of Islamic law, adoption or if necessary placement in suitable institutions for the care of children. When considering solutions, due regard shall be paid to the desirability of continuity in a child's upbringing and to the child's ethnic, religious, cultural and linguistic background.

Article 21

States Parties that recognize and/or permit the system of adoption shall ensure that the best interests of the child shall be the paramount consideration and they shall:

(a) Ensure that the adoption of a child is authorized only by competent authorities who determine, in accordance with applicable law and procedures and on the basis of all pertinent and reliable information, that the adoption is permissible in view of the child's status concerning parents, relatives and legal guardians and that, if required, the persons concerned have given their informed consent to the adoption on the basis of such counselling as may be necessary;

(b) Recognize that inter-country adoption may be considered as an alternative means of child's care, if the child cannot be placed in a foster or an adoptive family or cannot in any suitable manner be cared for in the child's country of origin;

(c) Ensure that the child concerned by inter-country adoption enjoys safeguards and standards equivalent to those existing in the case of national adoption;

(d) Take all appropriate measures to ensure that, in inter-country adoption, the placement does not result in improper financial gain for those involved in it;

(e) Promote, where appropriate, the objectives of the present article by concluding bilateral or multilateral arrangements or agreements and endeavour, within this framework, to ensure that the placement of the child in another country is carried out by competent authorities or organs.

Article 22

1. States Parties shall take appropriate measures to ensure that a child who is seeking refugee status or who is considered a refugee in accordance with applicable international or domestic law and procedures shall, whether

unaccompanied or accompanied by his or her parents or by any other person, receive appropriate protection and humanitarian assistance in the enjoyment of applicable rights set forth in the present Convention and in other international human rights or humanitarian instruments to which the said States are Parties.

2. For this purpose, States Parties shall provide, as they consider appropriate, co-operation in any efforts by the United Nations and other competent intergovernmental organizations or non-governmental organizations cooperating with the United Nations to protect and assist such a child and to trace the parents or other members of the family of any refugee child in order to obtain information necessary for reunification with his or her family. In cases where no parents or other members of the family can be found, the child shall be accorded the same protection as any other child permanently or temporarily deprived of his or her family environment for any reason, as set forth in the present Convention.

Article 23

1. States Parties recognize that a mentally or physically disabled child should enjoy a full and decent life, in conditions which ensure dignity, promote selfreliance and facilitate the child's active participation in the community.

2. States Parties recognize the right of the disabled child to special care and shall encourage and ensure the extension, subject to available resources, to the eligible child and those responsible for his or her care, of assistance for which application is made and which is appropriate to the child's condition and to the circumstances of the parents or others caring for the child.

3. Recognizing the special needs of a disabled child, assistance extended in accordance with paragraph 2 of the present article shall be provided free of charge, whenever possible, taking into account the financial resources of the parents or others caring for the child and shall be designed to ensure that the disabled child has effective access to and receives education, training, health care services, rehabilitation services, preparation for employment and recreation opportunities in a manner conducive to the child's achieving the fullest possible social integration and individual development, including his or her cultural and spiritual development.

4. States Parties shall promote, in the spirit of international cooperation, the exchange of appropriate information in the field of preventive health care and of medical, psychological and functional treatment of disabled children, including dissemination of and access to information concerning methods of rehabilitation, education and vocational services, with the aim of enabling States Parties to improve their capabilities and skills and to widen their experience in these areas. In this regard, particular account shall be taken of the needs of developing countries.

Article 24

1. States Parties recognize the right of the child to the enjoyment of the highest attainable standard of health and to facilities for the treatment of illness and rehabilitation of health. States Parties shall strive to ensure that no child is deprived of his or her right of access to such health care services.
2. States Parties shall pursue full implementation of this right and, in particular, shall take appropriate measures:
   (a) To diminish infant and child mortality;
   (b) To ensure the provision of necessary medical assistance and health care to all children with emphasis on the development of primary health care;
   (c) To combat disease and malnutrition, including within the framework of primary health care, through, inter alia, the application of readily available technology and through the provision of adequate nutritious foods and clean drinking-water, taking into consideration the dangers and risks of environmental pollution;
   (d) To ensure appropriate pre-natal and post-natal health care for mothers;
   (e) To ensure that all segments of society, in particular parents and children, are informed, have access to education and are supported in the use of basic knowledge of child health and nutrition, the advantages of breastfeeding, hygiene and environmental sanitation and the prevention of accidents;
   (f) To develop preventive health care, guidance for parents and family planning education and services.
3. States Parties shall take all effective and appropriate measures with a view to abolishing traditional practices prejudicial to the health of children.
4. States Parties undertake to promote and encourage international cooperation with a view to achieving progressively the full realization of the right recognized in the present article. In this regard, particular account shall be taken of the needs of developing countries.

Article 25

States Parties recognize the right of a child who has been placed by the competent authorities for the purposes of care, protection or treatment of his or her physical or mental health, to a periodic review of the treatment provided to the child and all other circumstances relevant to his or her placement.

Article 26

1. States Parties shall recognize for every child the right to benefit from social security, including social insurance and shall take the necessary measures to achieve the full realization of this right in accordance with their national law.

2. The benefits should, where appropriate, be granted, taking into account the resources and the circumstances of the child and persons having responsibility for the maintenance of the child, as well as any other consideration relevant to an application for benefits made by or on behalf of the child.

Article 27

1. States Parties recognize the right of every child to a standard of living adequate for the child's physical, mental, spiritual, moral and social development.
2. The parent(s) or others responsible for the child have the primary responsibility to secure, within their abilities and financial capacities, the conditions of living necessary for the child's development.
3. States Parties, in accordance with national conditions and within their means, shall take appropriate measures to assist parents and others responsible for the child to implement this right and shall in case of need provide material assistance and support programmes, particularly with regard to nutrition, clothing and housing.
4. States Parties shall take all appropriate measures to secure the recovery of maintenance for the child from the parents or other persons having financial responsibility for the child, both within the State Party and from abroad. In particular, where the person having financial responsibility for the child lives in a State different from that of the child, States Parties shall promote the accession to international agreements or the conclusion of such agreements, as well as the making of other appropriate arrangements.

Article 28

1. States Parties recognize the right of the child to education and with a view to achieving this right progressively and on the basis of equal opportunity, they shall, in particular:
   (a) Make primary education compulsory and available free to all;
   (b) Encourage the development of different forms of secondary education, including general and vocational education, make them available and accessible to every child and take appropriate measures such as the introduction of free education and offering financial assistance in case of need;
   (c) Make higher education accessible to all on the basis of capacity by every appropriate means;
   (d) Make educational and vocational information and guidance available and accessible to all children;
   (e) Take measures to encourage regular attendance at schools and the reduction of drop-out rates.

2. States Parties shall take all appropriate measures to ensure that school discipline is administered in a manner consistent with the child's human dignity and in conformity with the present Convention.

3. States Parties shall promote and encourage international cooperation in matters relating to education, in particular with a view to contributing to the elimination of ignorance and illiteracy throughout the world and facilitating access to scientific and technical knowledge and modern teaching methods. In this regard, particular account shall be taken of the needs of developing countries.

Article 29

1. States Parties agree that the education of the child shall be directed to:
    (a) The development of the child's personality, talents and mental and physical abilities to their fullest potential;
    (b) The development of respect for human rights and fundamental freedoms, and for the principles enshrined in the Charter of the United Nations;
    (c) The development of respect for the child's parents, his or her own cultural identity, language and values, for the national values of the country in which the child is living, the country from which he or she may originate, and for civilizations different from his or her own;
    (d) The preparation of the child for responsible life in a free society, in the spirit of understanding, peace, tolerance, equality of sexes, and friendship among all peoples, ethnic, national and religious groups and persons of indigenous origin;
    (e) The development of respect for the natural environment.

2. No part of the present article or article 28 shall be construed so as to interfere with the liberty of individuals and bodies to establish and direct educational institutions, subject always to the observance of the principle set forth in paragraph 1 of the present article and to the requirements that the education given in such institutions shall conform to such minimum standards as may be laid down by the State.

Article 30

In those States in which ethnic, religious or linguistic minorities or persons of indigenous origin exist, a child belonging to such a minority or who is indigenous shall not be denied the right, in community with other members of his or her group, to enjoy his or her own culture, to profess and practise his or her own religion, or to use his or her own language.

Article 31

1. States Parties recognize the right of the child to rest and leisure, to engage in play and recreational activities appropriate to the age of the child and to participate freely in cultural life and the arts.
2. States Parties shall respect and promote the right of the child to participate fully in cultural and artistic life and shall encourage the provision of appropriate and equal opportunities for cultural, artistic, recreational and leisure activity.

Article 32

1. States Parties recognize the right of the child to be protected from economic exploitation and from performing any work that is likely to be hazardous or to interfere with the child's education, or to be harmful to the child's health or physical, mental, spiritual, moral or social development.
2. States Parties shall take legislative, administrative, social and educational measures to ensure the implementation of the present article. To this end and having regard to the relevant provisions of other international instruments, States Parties shall in particular:

   (a) Provide for a minimum age or minimum ages for admission to employment;
   (b) Provide for appropriate regulation of the hours and conditions of employment;
   (c) Provide for appropriate penalties or other sanctions to ensure the effective enforcement of the present article.

Article 33

States Parties shall take all appropriate measures, including legislative, administrative, social and educational measures, to protect children from the illicit use of narcotic drugs and psychotropic substances as defined in the relevant international treaties and to prevent the use of children in the illicit production and trafficking of such substances.

Article 34

States Parties undertake to protect the child from all forms of sexual exploitation and sexual abuse. For these purposes, States Parties shall in particular take all appropriate national, bilateral and multilateral measures to prevent:

(a) The inducement or coercion of a child to engage in any unlawful sexual activity;
(b) The exploitative use of children in prostitution or other unlawful sexual practices;

(c) The exploitative use of children in pornographic performances and materials.

Article 35

States Parties shall take all appropriate national, bilateral and multilateral measures to prevent the abduction of, the sale of or traffic in children for any purpose or in any form.

Article 36

States Parties shall protect the child against all other forms of exploitation prejudicial to any aspects of the child's welfare.

Article 37

States Parties shall ensure that:

(a) No child shall be subjected to torture or other cruel, inhuman or degrading treatment or punishment. Neither capital punishment nor life imprisonment without possibility of release shall be imposed for offences committed by persons below eighteen years of age;

(b) No child shall be deprived of his or her liberty unlawfully or arbitrarily. The arrest, detention or imprisonment of a child shall be in conformity with the law and shall be used only as a measure of last resort and for the shortest appropriate period of time;

(c) Every child deprived of liberty shall be treated with humanity and respect for the inherent dignity of the human person and in a manner which takes into account the needs of persons of his or her age. In particular, every child deprived of liberty shall be separated from adults unless it is considered in the child's best interest not to do so and shall have the right to maintain contact with his or her family through correspondence and visits, save in exceptional circumstances;

(d) Every child deprived of his or her liberty shall have the right to prompt access to legal and other appropriate assistance, as well as the right to challenge the legality of the deprivation of his or her liberty before a court or other competent, independent and impartial authority and to a prompt decision on any such action.

Article 38

1. States Parties undertake to respect and to ensure respect for rules of international humanitarian law applicable to them in armed conflicts which are relevant to the child.

2. States Parties shall take all feasible measures to ensure that persons who have not attained the age of fifteen years do not take a direct part in hostilities.

3. States Parties shall refrain from recruiting any person who has not attained the age of fifteen years into their armed forces. In recruiting among those persons who have attained the age of fifteen years but who have not attained the age of eighteen years, States Parties shall endeavour to give priority to those who are oldest.

4. In accordance with their obligations under international humanitarian law to protect the civilian population in armed conflicts, States Parties shall take all feasible measures to ensure protection and care of children who are affected by an armed conflict.

Article 39

States Parties shall take all appropriate measures to promote physical and psychological recovery and social reintegration of a child victim of: any form of neglect, exploitation, or abuse; torture or any other form of cruel, inhuman or degrading treatment or punishment; or armed conflicts. Such recovery and reintegration shall take place in an environment which fosters the health, selfrespect and dignity of the child.

Article 40

1. States Parties recognize the right of every child alleged as, accused of, or recognized as having infringed the penal law to be treated in a manner consistent with the promotion of the child's sense of dignity and worth, which reinforces the child's respect for the human rights and fundamental freedoms of others and which takes into account the child's age and the desirability of promoting the child's reintegration and the child's assuming a constructive role in society.

2. To this end and having regard to the relevant provisions of international instruments, States Parties shall, in particular, ensure that:

   (a) No child shall be alleged as, be accused of, or recognized as having infringed the penal law by reason of acts or omissions that were not prohibited by national or international law at the time they were committed;

   (b) Every child alleged as or accused of having infringed the penal law has at least the following guarantees:

      (i) To be presumed innocent until proven guilty according to law;

      (ii) To be informed promptly and directly of the charges against him or her, and, if appropriate, through his or her parents or legal guardians and to have legal or other appropriate assistance in the preparation and presentation of his or her defence;

(iii) To have the matter determined without delay by a competent, independent and impartial authority or judicial body in a fair hearing according to law, in the presence of legal or other appropriate assistance and, unless it is considered not to be in the best interest of the child, in particular, taking into account his or her age or situation, his or her parents or legal guardians;

(iv) Not to be compelled to give testimony or to confess guilt; to examine or have examined adverse witnesses and to obtain the participation and examination of witnesses on his or her behalf under conditions of equality;

(v) If considered to have infringed the penal law, to have this decision and any measures imposed in consequence thereof reviewed by a higher competent, independent and impartial authority or judicial body according to law;

(vi) To have the free assistance of an interpreter if the child cannot understand or speak the language used;

(vii) To have his or her privacy fully respected at all stages of the proceedings.

3. States Parties shall seek to promote the establishment of laws, procedures, authorities and institutions specifically applicable to children alleged as, accused of, or recognized as having infringed the penal law, and, in particular:

(a) The establishment of a minimum age below which children shall be presumed not to have the capacity to infringe the penal law;

(b) Whenever appropriate and desirable, measures for dealing with such children without resorting to judicial proceedings, providing that human rights and legal safeguards are fully respected.

4. A variety of dispositions, such as care, guidance and supervision orders; counselling; probation; foster care; education and vocational training programmes and other alternatives to institutional care shall be available to ensure that children are dealt with in a manner appropriate to their well-being and proportionate both to their circumstances and the offence.

Article 41

Nothing in the present Convention shall affect any provisions which are more conducive to the realization of the rights of the child and which may be contained in:

(a) The law of a State party; or

(b) International law in force for that State.

Part II

Article 42

States Parties undertake to make the principles and provisions of the Convention widely known, by appropriate and active means, to adults and children alike.

Article 43

1. For the purpose of examining the progress made by States Parties in achieving the realization of the obligations undertaken in the present Convention, there shall be established a Committee on the Rights of the Child, which shall carry out the functions hereinafter provided.
2. The Committee shall consist of ten experts of high moral standing and recognized competence in the field covered by this Convention. The members of the Committee shall be elected by States Parties from among their nationals and shall serve in their personal capacity, consideration being given to equitable geographical distribution, as well as to the principal legal systems.
3. The members of the Committee shall be elected by secret ballot from a list of persons nominated by States Parties. Each State Party may nominate one person from among its own nationals.
4. The initial election to the Committee shall be held no later than six months after the date of the entry into force of the present Convention and thereafter every second year. At least four months before the date of each election, the Secretary-General of the United Nations shall address a letter to States Parties inviting them to submit their nominations within two months. The Secretary-General shall subsequently prepare a list in alphabetical order of all persons thus nominated, indicating States Parties which have nominated them and shall submit it to the States Parties to the present Convention.
5. The elections shall be held at meetings of States Parties convened by the Secretary-General at United Nations Headquarters. At those meetings, for which two thirds of States Parties shall constitute a quorum, the persons elected to the Committee shall be those who obtain the largest number of votes and an absolute majority of the votes of the representatives of States Parties present and voting.
6. The members of the Committee shall be elected for a term of four years. They shall be eligible for re-election if renominated. The term of five of the members elected at the first election shall expire at the end of two years; immediately after the first election, the names of these five members shall be chosen by lot by the Chairman of the meeting.
7. If a member of the Committee dies or resigns or declares that for any other cause he or she can no longer perform the duties of the Committee, the

State Party which nominated the member shall appoint another expert from among its nationals to serve for the remainder of the term, subject to the approval of the Committee.

8. The Committee shall establish its own rules of procedure.

9. The Committee shall elect its officers for a period of two years.

10. The meetings of the Committee shall normally be held at United Nations Headquarters or at any other convenient place as determined by the Committee. The Committee shall normally meet annually. The duration of the meetings of the Committee shall be determined and reviewed, if necessary, by a meeting of the States Parties to the present Convention, subject to the approval of the General Assembly.

11. The Secretary-General of the United Nations shall provide the necessary staff and facilities for the effective performance of the functions of the Committee under the present Convention.

12. With the approval of the General Assembly, the members of the Committee established under the present Convention shall receive emoluments from United Nations resources on such terms and conditions as the Assembly may decide.

Article 44

1. States Parties undertake to submit to the Committee, through the Secretary-General of the United Nations, reports on the measures they have adopted which give effect to the rights recognized herein and on the progress made on the enjoyment of those rights:

   (a) Within two years of the entry into force of the Convention for the State Party concerned;

   (b) Thereafter every five years.

2. Reports made under the present article shall indicate factors and difficulties, if any, affecting the degree of fulfilment of the obligations under the present Convention. Reports shall also contain sufficient information to provide the Committee with a comprehensive understanding of the implementation of the Convention in the country concerned.

3. A State Party which has submitted a comprehensive initial report to the Committee need not, in its subsequent reports submitted in accordance with paragraph 1 (b) of the present article, repeat basic information previously provided.

4. The Committee may request from States Parties further information relevant to the implementation of the Convention.

5. The Committee shall submit to the General Assembly, through the Economic and Social Council, every two years, reports on its activities.

6. States Parties shall make their reports widely available to the public in their own countries.

Article 45

In order to foster the effective implementation of the Convention and to encourage international co-operation in the field covered by the Convention:

(a) The specialized agencies, the United Nations Children's Fund and other United Nations organs shall be entitled to be represented at the consideration of the implementation of such provisions of the present Convention as fall within the scope of their mandate. The Committee may invite the specialized agencies, the United Nations Children's Fund and other competent bodies as it may consider appropriate to provide expert advice on the implementation of the Convention in areas falling within the scope of their respective mandates. The Committee may invite the specialized agencies, the United Nations Children's Fund and other United Nations organs to submit reports on the implementation of the Convention in areas falling within the scope of their activities;

(b) The Committee shall transmit, as it may consider appropriate, to the specialized agencies, the United Nations Children's Fund and other competent bodies, any reports from States Parties that contain a request, or indicate a need, for technical advice or assistance, along with the Committee's observations and suggestions, if any, on these requests or indications;

(c) The Committee may recommend to the General Assembly to request the Secretary-General to undertake on its behalf studies on specific issues relating to the rights of the child;

(d) The Committee may make suggestions and general recommendations based on information received pursuant to articles 44 and 45 of the present Convention. Such suggestions and general recommendations shall be transmitted to any State Party concerned and reported to the General Assembly, together with comments, if any, from States Parties.

Appendix II

Human Rights Act 1998

1998 Chapter 42

An Act to give further effect to rights and freedoms guaranteed under the European Convention on Human Rights; to make provision with respect to holders of certain judicial offices who become judges of the European Court of Human Rights; and for connected purposes.

9th November 1998

BE IT ENACTED by the Queen's most Excellent Majesty, by and with the advice and consent of the Lords Spiritual and Temporal, and Commons, in this present Parliament assembled, and by the authority of the same, as follows: –

Introduction

1 **The Convention Rights**

(1) In this Act 'the Convention rights' means the rights and fundamental freedoms set out in –

    (a) Articles 2 to 12 and 14 of the Convention,

    (b) Articles 1 to 3 of the First Protocol, and

    (c) Articles 1 and 2 of the Sixth Protocol, as read with Articles 16 to 18 of the Convention.

(2) Those Articles are to have effect for the purposes of this Act subject to any designated derogation or reservation (as to which see sections 14 and 15).

(3) The Articles are set out in Schedule 1.

(4) The Lord Chancellor may by order make such amendments to this Act as he considers appropriate to reflect the effect, in relation to the United Kingdom, of a protocol.

(5) In subsection (4) 'protocol' means a protocol to the Convention –

    (a) which the United Kingdom has ratified; or

    (b) which the United Kingdom has signed with a view to ratification.

(6) No amendment may be made by an order under subsection (4) so as to come into force before the protocol concerned is in force in relation to the United Kingdom.

2 Interpretation of Convention rights

(1) A court or tribunal determining a question which has arisen in connection with a Convention right must take into account any –

    (a) judgment, decision, declaration or advisory opinion of the European Court of Human Rights,

    (b) opinion of the Commission given in a report adopted under Article 31 of the Convention,

    (c) decision of the Commission in connection with Article 26 or 27(2) of the Convention, or

    (d) decision of the Committee of Ministers taken under Article 46 of the Convention, whenever made or given, so far as, in the opinion of the court or tribunal, it is relevant to the proceedings in which that question has arisen.

(2) Evidence of any judgment, decision, declaration or opinion of which account may have to be taken under this section is to be given in proceedings before any court or tribunal in such manner as may be provided by rules.

(3) In this section 'rules' means rules of court or, in the case of proceedings before a tribunal, rules made for the purposes of this section –

    (a) by the Lord Chancellor or the Secretary of State, in relation to any proceedings outside Scotland;

    (b) by the Secretary of State, in relation to proceedings in Scotland; or

    (c) by a Northern Ireland department, in relation to proceedings before a tribunal in Northern Ireland –

        (i) which deals with transferred matters; and

        (ii) for which no rules made under paragraph (a) are in force.

Legislation

3 Interpretation of legislation

(1) So far as it is possible to do so, primary legislation and subordinate legislation must be read and given effect in a way which is compatible with the Convention rights.

(2) This section –

    (a) applies to primary legislation and subordinate legislation whenever enacted;

    (b) does not affect the validity, continuing operation or enforcement of any incompatible primary legislation; and

    (c) does not affect the validity, continuing operation or enforcement of any incompatible subordinate legislation if (disregarding any possibility of revocation) primary legislation prevents removal of the incompatibility.

4 **Declaration of incompatibility**

(1) Subsection (2) applies in any proceedings in which a court determines whether a provision of primary legislation is compatible with a Convention right.

(2) If the court is satisfied that the provision is incompatible with a Convention right, it may make a declaration of that incompatibility.

(3) Subsection (4) applies in any proceedings in which a court determines whether a provision of subordinate legislation, made in the exercise of a power conferred by primary legislation, is compatible with a Convention right.

(4) If the court is satisfied –

(a) that the provision is incompatible with a Convention right, and

(b) that (disregarding any possibility of revocation) the primary legislation concerned prevents removal of the incompatibility, it may make a declaration of that incompatibility.

(5) In this section 'court' means –

(a) the House of Lords;

(b) the Judicial Committee of the Privy Council;

(c) the Courts-Martial Appeal Court;

(d) in Scotland, the High Court of Justiciary sitting otherwise than as a trial court or the Court of Session;

(e) in England and Wales or Northern Ireland, the High Court or the Court of Appeal.

(6) A declaration under this section ('a declaration of incompatibility') –

(a) does not affect the validity, continuing operation or enforcement of the provision in respect of which it is given; and

(b) is not binding on the parties to the proceedings in which it is made.

5 **Right of Crown to intervene**

(1) Where a court is considering whether to make a declaration of incompatibility, the Crown is entitled to notice in accordance with rules of court.

(2) In any case to which subsection (1) applies –

(a) a Minister of the Crown (or a person nominated by him),

(b) a member of the Scottish Executive,

(c) a Northern Ireland Minister,

(d) a Northern Ireland department, is entitled, on giving notice in accordance with rules of court, to be joined as a party to the proceedings.

(3) Notice under subsection (2) may be given at any time during the proceedings.

(4) A person who has been made a party to criminal proceedings (other than in Scotland) as the result of a notice under subsection (2) may, with leave, appeal to the House of Lords against any declaration of incompatibility made in the proceedings.

(5) In subsection (4) –

'criminal proceedings' includes all proceedings before the Courts-Martial Appeal Court; and
'leave' means leave granted by the court making the declaration of incompatibility or by the House of Lords.

Public authorities

6 **Acts of public authorities**
   (1) It is unlawful for a public authority to act in a way which is incompatible with a Convention right.
   (2) Subsection (1) does not apply to an act if –
       (a) as the result of one or more provisions of primary legislation, the authority could not have acted differently; or
       (b) in the case of one or more provisions of, or made under, primary legislation which cannot be read or given effect in a way which is compatible with the Convention rights, the authority was acting so as to give effect to or enforce those provisions.
   (3) In this section 'public authority' includes –
       (a) a court or tribunal, and
       (b) any person certain of whose functions are functions of a public nature, but does not include either House of Parliament or a person exercising functions in connection with proceedings in Parliament.
   (4) In subsection (3) 'Parliament' does not include the House of Lords in its judicial capacity.
   (5) In relation to a particular act, a person is not a public authority by virtue only of subsection (3)(b) if the nature of the act is private.
   (6) 'An act' includes a failure to act but does not include a failure to –
       (a) introduce in, or lay before, Parliament a proposal for legislation; or
       (b) make any primary legislation or remedial order.

7 **Proceedings**
   (1) A person who claims that a public authority has acted (or proposes to act) in a way which is made unlawful by section 6(1) may –
       (a) bring proceedings against the authority under this Act in the appropriate court or tribunal, or
       (b) rely on the Convention right or rights concerned in any legal proceedings, but only if he is (or would be) a victim of the unlawful act.
   (2) In subsection (1)(a) 'appropriate court or tribunal' means such court or tribunal as may be determined in accordance with rules; and proceedings against an authority include a counterclaim or similar proceeding.

(3) If the proceedings are brought on an application for judicial review, the applicant is to be taken to have a sufficient interest in relation to the unlawful act only if he is, or would be, a victim of that act.

(4) If the proceedings are made by way of a petition for judicial review in Scotland, the applicant shall be taken to have title and interest to sue in relation to the unlawful act only if he is, or would be, a victim of that act.

(5) Proceedings under subsection (1)(a) must be brought before the end of –

(a) the period of one year beginning with the date on which the act complained of took place; or

(b) such longer period as the court or tribunal considers equitable having regard to all the circumstances, but that is subject to any rule imposing a stricter time limit in relation to the procedure in question.

(6) In subsection (1)(b) 'legal proceedings' includes –

(a) proceedings brought by or at the instigation of a public authority; and

(b) an appeal against the decision of a court or tribunal.

(7) For the purposes of this section, a person is a victim of an unlawful act only if he would be a victim for the purposes of Article 34 of the Convention if proceedings were brought in the European Court of Human Rights in respect of that act.

(8) Nothing in this Act creates a criminal offence.

(9) In this section 'rules' means –

(a) in relation to proceedings before a court or tribunal outside Scotland, rules made by the Lord Chancellor or the Secretary of State for the purposes of this section or rules of court,

(b) in relation to proceedings before a court or tribunal in Scotland, rules made by the Secretary of State for those purposes,

(c) in relation to proceedings before a tribunal in Northern Ireland –

(i) which deals with transferred matters; and

(ii) for which no rules made under paragraph (a) are in force, rules made by a Northern Ireland department for those purposes, and includes provision made by order under section 1 of the Courts and Legal Services Act 1990.

(10) In making rules, regard must be had to section 9.

(11) The Minister who has power to make rules in relation to a particular tribunal may, to the extent he considers it necessary to ensure that the tribunal can provide an appropriate remedy in relation to an act (or proposed act) of a public authority which is (or would be) unlawful as a result of section 6(1), by order add to –

(a) the relief or remedies which the tribunal may grant; or

(b) the grounds on which it may grant any of them.

(12) An order made under subsection (11) may contain such incidental, supplemental, consequential or transitional provision as the Minister making it considers appropriate.

(13) 'The Minister' includes the Northern Ireland department concerned.

8 **Judicial remedies**

(1) In relation to any act (or proposed act) of a public authority which the court finds is (or would be) unlawful, it may grant such relief or remedy, or make such order, within its powers as it considers just and appropriate.

(2) But damages may be awarded only by a court which has power to award damages, or to order the payment of compensation, in civil proceedings.

(3) No award of damages is to be made unless, taking account of all the circumstances of the case, including –

   (a) any other relief or remedy granted, or order made, in relation to the act in question (by that or any other court), and

   (b) the consequences of any decision (of that or any other court) in respect of that act, the court is satisfied that the award is necessary to afford just satisfaction to the person in whose favour it is made.

(4) In determining –

   (a) whether to award damages, or

   (b) the amount of an award, the court must take into account the principles applied by the European Court of Human Rights in relation to the award of compensation under Article 41 of the Convention.

(5) A public authority against which damages are awarded is to be treated –

   (a) in Scotland, for the purposes of section 3 of the Law Reform (Miscellaneous Provisions) (Scotland) Act 1940 as if the award were made in an action of damages in which the authority has been found liable in respect of loss or damage to the person to whom the award is made;

   (b) for the purposes of the Civil Liability (Contribution) Act 1978 as liable in respect of damage suffered by the person to whom the award is made.

(6) In this section –

   'court' includes a tribunal;

   'damages' means damages for an unlawful act of a public authority; and

   'unlawful' means unlawful under section 6(1).

9 **Judicial acts**

(1) Proceedings under section 7(1)(a) in respect of a judicial act may be brought only –

   (a) by exercising a right of appeal;

   (b) on an application (in Scotland a petition) for judicial review; or

   (c) in such other forum as may be prescribed by rules.

(2) That does not affect any rule of law which prevents a court from being the subject of judicial review.

(3) In proceedings under this Act in respect of a judicial act done in good faith, damages may not be awarded otherwise than to compensate a person to the extent required by Article 5(5) of the Convention.

(4) An award of damages permitted by subsection (3) is to be made against the Crown; but no award may be made unless the appropriate person, if not a party to the proceedings, is joined.

(5) In this section –

'appropriate person' means the Minister responsible for the court concerned, or a person or government department nominated by him;
'court' includes a tribunal;
'judge' includes a member of a tribunal, a justice of the peace and a clerk or other officer entitled to exercise the jurisdiction of a court;
'judicial act' means a judicial act of a court and includes an act done on the instructions, or on behalf, of a judge; and
'rules' has the same meaning as in section 7(9).

Remedial action

10 Power to take remedial action

(1) This section applies if –

(a) a provision of legislation has been declared under section 4 to be incompatible with a Convention right and, if an appeal lies –

(i) all persons who may appeal have stated in writing that they do not intend to do so;

(ii) the time for bringing an appeal has expired and no appeal has been brought within that time; or

(iii) an appeal brought within that time has been determined or abandoned; or

(b) it appears to a Minister of the Crown or Her Majesty in Council that, having regard to a finding of the European Court of Human Rights made after the coming into force of this section in proceedings against the United Kingdom, a provision of legislation is incompatible with an obligation of the United Kingdom arising from the Convention.

(2) If a Minister of the Crown considers that there are compelling reasons for proceeding under this section, he may by order make such amendments to the legislation as he considers necessary to remove the incompatibility.

(3) If, in the case of subordinate legislation, a Minister of the Crown considers –

(a) that it is necessary to amend the primary legislation under which the subordinate legislation in question was made, in order to enable the incompatibility to be removed, and

(b) that there are compelling reasons for proceeding under this section, he may by order make such amendments to the primary legislation as he considers necessary.

(4) This section also applies where the provision in question is in subordinate legislation and has been quashed, or declared invalid, by reason of incompatibility with a Convention right and the Minister proposes to proceed under paragraph 2(b) of Schedule 2.

(5) If the legislation is an Order in Council, the power conferred by subsection (2) or (3) is exercisable by Her Majesty in Council.

(6) In this section 'legislation' does not include a Measure of the Church Assembly or of the General Synod of the Church of England.

(7) Schedule 2 makes further provision about remedial orders.

Other rights and proceedings

11 **Safeguard for existing human rights**

A person's reliance on a Convention right does not restrict –

(a) any other right or freedom conferred on him by or under any law having effect in any part of the United Kingdom; or

(b) his right to make any claim or bring any proceedings which he could make or bring apart from sections 7 to 9.

12 **Freedom of expression**

(1) This section applies if a court is considering whether to grant any relief which, if granted, might affect the exercise of the Convention right to freedom of expression.

(2) If the person against whom the application for relief is made ('the respondent') is neither present nor represented, no such relief is to be granted unless the court is satisfied –

(a) that the applicant has taken all practicable steps to notify the respondent; or

(b) that there are compelling reasons why the respondent should not be notified.

(3) No such relief is to be granted so as to restrain publication before trial unless the court is satisfied that the applicant is likely to establish that publication should not be allowed.

(4) The court must have particular regard to the importance of the Convention right to freedom of expression and, where the proceedings relate to material which the respondent claims, or which appears to the court, to be journalistic, literary or artistic material (or to conduct connected with such material), to –

(a) the extent to which –

(i) the material has, or is about to, become available to the public; or

(ii) it is, or would be, in the public interest for the material to be published;

(b) any relevant privacy code.

(5) In this section –

'court' includes a tribunal; and

'relief' includes any remedy or order (other than in criminal proceedings).

13 Freedom of thought, conscience and religion

(1) If a court's determination of any question arising under this Act might affect the exercise by a religious organisation (itself or its members collectively) of the Convention right to freedom of thought, conscience and religion, itmust have particular regard to the importance of that right.

(2) In this section 'court' includes a tribunal.

Derogations and reservations

14 Derogations

(1) In this Act 'designated derogation' means –

. . .

any derogation by the United Kingdom from an Article of the Convention, or of any protocol to the Convention, which is designated for the purposes of this Act in an order made by the Lord Chancellor.

(2) . . .

(3) If a designated derogation is amended or replaced it ceases to be a designated derogation.

(4) But subsection (3) does not prevent the Lord Chancellor from exercising his power under subsection (1) . . . to make a fresh designation order in respect of the Article concerned.

(5) The Lord Chancellor must by order make such amendments to Schedule 3 as he considers appropriate to reflect –

(a) any designation order; or

(b) the effect of subsection (3).

(6) A designation order may be made in anticipation of the making by the United Kingdom of a proposed derogation.

15 Reservations

(1) In this Act 'designated reservation' means –

(a) the United Kingdom's reservation to Article 2 of the First Protocol to the Convention; and

(b) any other reservation by the United Kingdom to an Article of the Convention, or of any protocol to the Convention, which is designated for the purposes of this Act in an order made by the Lord Chancellor.

(2) The text of the reservation referred to in subsection (1)(a) is set out in Part II of Schedule 3.

(3) If a designated reservation is withdrawn wholly or in part it ceases to be a designated reservation.

(4) But subsection (3) does not prevent the Lord Chancellor from exercising his power under subsection (1)(b) to make a fresh designation order in respect of the Article concerned.

(5) The Lord Chancellor must by order make such amendments to this Act as he considers appropriate to reflect –

(a) any designation order; or

(b) the effect of subsection (3).

16 Period for which designated derogations have effect

(1) If it has not already been withdrawn by the United Kingdom, a designated derogation ceases to have effect for the purposes of this Act –

...

at the end of the period of five years beginning with the date on which the order designating it was made.

(2) At any time before the period –

(a) fixed by subsection (1) . . ., or

(b) extended by an order under this subsection, comes to an end, the Lord Chancellor may by order extend it by a further period of five years.

(3) An order under section 14(1) . . . ceases to have effect at the end of the period for consideration, unless a resolution has been passed by each House approving the order.

(4) Subsection (3) does not affect –

(a) anything done in reliance on the order; or

(b) the power to make a fresh order under section 14(1) . . .

(5) In subsection (3) 'period for consideration' means the period of forty days beginning with the day on which the order was made.

(6) In calculating the period for consideration, no account is to be taken of any time during which –

(a) Parliament is dissolved or prorogued; or

(b) both Houses are adjourned for more than four days.

(7) If a designated derogation is withdrawn by the United Kingdom, the Lord Chancellor must by order make such amendments to this Act as he considers are required to reflect that withdrawal.

17 Periodic review of designated reservations

(1) The appropriate Minister must review the designated reservation referred to in section 15(1)(a) –

(a) before the end of the period of five years beginning with the date on which section 1(2) came into force; and

(b) if that designation is still in force, before the end of the period of five years beginning with the date on which the last report relating to it was laid under subsection (3).

(2) The appropriate Minister must review each of the other designated reservations (if any) –

(a) before the end of the period of five years beginning with the date on which the order designating the reservation first came into force; and

(b) if the designation is still in force, before the end of the period of five years beginning with the date on which the last report relating to it was laid under subsection (3).

(3) The Minister conducting a review under this section must prepare a report on the result of the review and lay a copy of it before each House of Parliament.

Schedule 1 The Articles

Section 1(3)

Part I The Convention

Rights and Freedoms

Article 2 Right to life

1 Everyone's right to life shall be protected by law. No one shall be deprived of his life intentionally save in the execution of a sentence of a court following his conviction of a crime for which this penalty is provided by law.

2 Deprivation of life shall not be regarded as inflicted in contravention of this Article when it results from the use of force which is no more than absolutely necessary:

(a) in defence of any person from unlawful violence;

(b) in order to effect a lawful arrest or to prevent the escape of a person lawfully detained;

(c) in action lawfully taken for the purpose of quelling a riot or insurrection.

Article 3 Prohibition of torture

No one shall be subjected to torture or to inhuman or degrading treatment or punishment.

Article 4 Prohibition of slavery and forced labour

1 No one shall be held in slavery or servitude.

2 No one shall be required to perform forced or compulsory labour.

3 For the purpose of this Article the term 'forced or compulsory labour' shall not include:

(a) any work required to be done in the ordinary course of detention imposed according to the provisions of Article 5 of this Convention or during conditional release from such detention;

(b) any service of a military character or, in case of conscientious objectors in countries where they are recognised, service exacted instead of compulsory military service;

(c) any service exacted in case of an emergency or calamity threatening the life or well-being of the community;

(d) any work or service which forms part of normal civic obligations.

Article 5 Right to liberty and security

1 Everyone has the right to liberty and security of person. No one shall be deprived of his liberty save in the following cases and in accordance with a procedure prescribed by law:

(a) the lawful detention of a person after conviction by a competent court;

(b) the lawful arrest or detention of a person for non-compliance with the lawful order of a court or in order to secure the fulfilment of any obligation prescribed by law;

(c) the lawful arrest or detention of a person effected for the purpose of bringing him before the competent legal authority on reasonable suspicion of having committed an offence or when it is reasonably considered necessary to prevent his committing an offence or fleeing after having done so;

(d) the detention of a minor by lawful order for the purpose of educational supervision or his lawful detention for the purpose of bringing him before the competent legal authority;

(e) the lawful detention of persons for the prevention of the spreading of infectious diseases, of persons of unsound mind, alcoholics or drug addicts or vagrants;

(f) the lawful arrest or detention of a person to prevent his effecting an unauthorised entry into the country or of a person against whom action is being taken with a view to deportation or extradition.

2 Everyone who is arrested shall be informed promptly, in a language which he understands, of the reasons for his arrest and of any charge against him.

3 Everyone arrested or detained in accordance with the provisions of paragraph 1(c) of this Article shall be brought promptly before a judge or other officer authorised by law to exercise judicial power and shall be entitled to trial within a reasonable time or to release pending trial. Release may be conditioned by guarantees to appear for trial.

4 Everyone who is deprived of his liberty by arrest or detention shall be entitled to take proceedings by which the lawfulness of his detention shall

be decided speedily by a court and his release ordered if the detention is not lawful.

5 Everyone who has been the victim of arrest or detention in contravention of the provisions of this Article shall have an enforceable right to compensation.

Article 6 Right to a fair trial

1 In the determination of his civil rights and obligations or of any criminal charge against him, everyone is entitled to a fair and public hearing within a reasonable time by an independent and impartial tribunal established by law. Judgment shall be pronounced publicly but the press and public may be excluded from all or part of the trial in the interest of morals, public order or national security in a democratic society, where the interests of juveniles or the protection of the private life of the parties so require, or to the extent strictly necessary in the opinion of the court in special circumstances where publicity would prejudice the interests of justice.

2 Everyone charged with a criminal offence shall be presumed innocent until proved guilty according to law.

3 Everyone charged with a criminal offence has the following minimum rights:
   (a) to be informed promptly, in a language which he understands and in detail, of the nature and cause of the accusation against him;
   (b) to have adequate time and facilities for the preparation of his defence;
   (c) to defend himself in person or through legal assistance of his own choosing or, if he has not sufficient means to pay for legal assistance, to be given it free when the interests of justice so require;
   (d) to examine or have examined witnesses against him and to obtain the attendance and examination of witnesses on his behalf under the same conditions as witnesses against him;
   (e) to have the free assistance of an interpreter if he cannot understand or speak the language used in court.

Article 7 No punishment without law

1 No one shall be held guilty of any criminal offence on account of any act or omission which did not constitute a criminal offence under national or international law at the time when it was committed. Nor shall a heavier penalty be imposed than the one that was applicable at the time the criminal offence was committed.

2 This Article shall not prejudice the trial and punishment of any person for any act or omission which, at the time when it was committed, was criminal according to the general principles of law recognised by civilised nations.

Article 8 Right to respect for private and family life

1 Everyone has the right to respect for his private and family life, his home and his correspondence.
2 There shall be no interference by a public authority with the exercise of this right except such as is in accordance with the law and is necessary in a democratic society in the interests of national security, public safety or the economic wellbeing of the country, for the prevention of disorder or crime, for the protection of health or morals, or for the protection of the rights and freedoms of others.

Article 9 Freedom of thought, conscience and religion

1 Everyone has the right to freedom of thought, conscience and religion; this right includes freedom to change his religion or belief and freedom, either alone or in community with others and in public or private, to manifest his religion or belief, in worship, teaching, practice and observance.
2 Freedom to manifest one's religion or beliefs shall be subject only to such limitations as are prescribed by law and are necessary in a democratic society in the interests of public safety, for the protection of public order, health or morals, or for the protection of the rights and freedoms of others.

Article 10 Freedom of expression

1 Everyone has the right to freedom of expression. This right shall include freedom to hold opinions and to receive and impart information and ideas without interference by public authority and regardless of frontiers. This Article shall not prevent States from requiring the licensing of broadcasting, television or cinema enterprises.
2 The exercise of these freedoms, since it carries with it duties and responsibilities, may be subject to such formalities, conditions, restrictions or penalties as are prescribed by law and are necessary in a democratic society, in the interests of national security, territorial integrity or public safety, for the prevention of disorder or crime, for the protection of health or morals, for the protection of the reputation or rights of others, for preventing the disclosure of information received in confidence, or for maintaining the authority and impartiality of the judiciary.

Article 11 Freedom of assembly and association

1 Everyone has the right to freedom of peaceful assembly and to freedom of association with others, including the right to form and to join trade unions for the protection of his interests.

2 No restrictions shall be placed on the exercise of these rights other than such as are prescribed by law and are necessary in a democratic society in the interests of national security or public safety, for the prevention of disorder or crime, for the protection of health or morals or for the protection of the rights and freedoms of others. This Article shall not prevent the imposition of lawful restrictions on the exercise of these rights by members of the armed forces, of the police or of the administration of the State.

Article 12 Right to marry

Men and women of marriageable age have the right to marry and to found a family, according to the national laws governing the exercise of this right.

Article 14 Prohibition of discrimination

The enjoyment of the rights and freedoms set forth in this Convention shall be secured without discrimination on any ground such as sex, race, colour, language, religion, political or other opinion, national or social origin, association with a national minority, property, birth or other status.

Article 16 Restrictions on political activity of aliens

Nothing in Articles 10, 11 and 14 shall be regarded as preventing the High Contracting Parties from imposing restrictions on the political activity of aliens.

Article 17 Prohibition of abuse of rights

Nothing in this Convention may be interpreted as implying for any State, group or person any right to engage in any activity or perform any act aimed at the destruction of any of the rights and freedoms set forth herein or at their limitation to a greater extent than is provided for in the Convention.

Article 18 Limitation on use of restrictions on rights

The restrictions permitted under this Convention to the said rights and freedoms shall not be applied for any purpose other than those for which they have been prescribed.

Part II The First Protocol

Article 1 Protection of property

Every natural or legal person is entitled to the peaceful enjoyment of his possessions. No one shall be deprived of his possessions except in the public interest and subject to the conditions provided for by law and by the general principles of international law.

The preceding provisions shall not, however, in any way impair the right of a State to enforce such laws as it deems necessary to control the use of property in accordance with the general interest or to secure the payment of taxes or other contributions or penalties.

Article 2 Right to education

No person shall be denied the right to education. In the exercise of any functions which it assumes in relation to education and to teaching, the State shall respect the right of parents to ensure such education and teaching in conformity with their own religious and philosophical convictions.

Article 3 Right to free elections

The High Contracting Parties undertake to hold free elections at reasonable intervals by secret ballot, under conditions which will ensure the free expression of the opinion of the people in the choice of the legislature.

Part III The Sixth Protocol

Article 1 Abolition of the death penalty

The death penalty shall be abolished. No one shall be condemned to such penalty or executed.

Article 2 Death penalty in time of war

A State may make provision in its law for the death penalty in respect of acts committed in time of war or of imminent threat of war; such penalty shall be applied only in the instances laid down in the law and in accordance with its provisions. The State shall communicate to the Secretary General of the Council of Europe the relevant provisions of that law.

Index